TORTS *in* NEW ZEALAND

Cases and Materials

THIRD EDITION

Bill Atkin

Katrine Evans

Geoff McLay

Sandra Petersson

with the assistance of David Carter

OXFORD
UNIVERSITY PRESS

OXFORD

UNIVERSITY PRESS

253 Normanby Road, South Melbourne, Victoria 3205, Australia

Oxford University Press is a department of the University of Oxford.
It furthers the University's objective of excellence in research, scholarship,
and education by publishing worldwide in

Oxford New York

Auckland Bangkok Buenos Aires Cape Town Chennai
Dar es Salaam Delhi Hong Kong Istanbul Karachi Kolkata
Kuala Lumpur Madrid Melbourne Mexico City Mumbai Nairobi
São Paulo Shanghai Singapore Taipei Tokyo Toronto

with an associated company in Berlin

OXFORD is a trade mark of Oxford University Press
in the UK and in certain other countries

National Library of New Zealand Cataloguing-in-Publication Data
Cataloguing-in-Publication data:

Torts in New Zealand: cases and materials/Bill Atkin ... [et al.]. 3rd ed.
Previous ed.: 1997.
Includes bibliographical references and index.
ISBN 0-19-558452-X
1. Torts—New Zealand—Cases. I. Atkin, W. R.
346.93030264—dc 21

Edited by Tim Fullerton
Cover designed by Racheal Stines
Typeset by Desktop Concepts P/L, Melbourne
Printed through Bookpac Production Services, Singapore

Contents

Table of Legislation

Table of Cases

Acknowledgments

We would like to acknowledge Bill Hodge of the University of Auckland and Bruce Pardy of Queens University, Canada, for their contributions to the previous edition. This third edition would not have been possible without their earlier work, and we hope that they might be able to contribute, either formally or informally, to the development of future editions.

We gratefully acknowledge the judges, authors, and publishers whose material we have used in this casebook, in particular: Justice Linden and Butterworths Canada for *Canadian Tort Law* (4th edn); Professor Richard Gaskins for 'Recalling the Future of ACC' (2000) 31 VUWLR 215; and *University of Chicago Law Review* for Henderson 'The New Zealand Accident Compensation Reform' (1981) 48 U Chic LR 781.

The project owes a great deal to the enormous contribution of David Carter, our research assistant. He worked tirelessly, searching out information, editing extracts, and assisting with proofing.

Thanks are due to the Victoria University of Wellington Law Faculty, which made research money available for this project, and to Oxford University Press and its staff for enabling the publication of this third edition. We are also grateful to Joan Johnson and Jan Backhouse for their secretarial assistance on this book.

Chapter 1

Introduction

The law of torts is part of the law of civil obligations. It is one of the classic creations of the common law. Its lifeblood is the vast body of decisions handed down by the courts. It typically deals with situations where harm has occurred but there is no liability in contract. At times there will be overlap with other branches of the law but not in the majority of situations.

While case law still provides the core of the law of torts, legislation has sometimes been passed to alter the ground rules. The Contributory Negligence Act 1947 is a prime example. In New Zealand, however, there has been much more radical statutory intervention where the harm is personal injury. To better achieve social policy goals of assisting the victims of accidents, New Zealand introduced its accident compensation scheme first in 1974. This established a state mechanism to provide comprehensive coverage for people who suffered personal injury by accident and, as a quid pro quo, removed the right to sue for damages at common law.

Some people thought that the accident compensation scheme might be the death knell of the law of torts. But tort has proven to be resilient and continues to flourish. Tort law's inherent flexibility has allowed its continual development. It is able to encompass new concepts and situations. One of the most recent developments has pushed out the limits of vicarious liability. Negligence continues to extend and question the limits of the 'neighbourhood' principle—who owes a duty of care to whom? This has been especially relevant in the context of government and public liability. In the true common law spirit, tort law remains flexible and fluid, and is capable of interesting and unique developments.

So, what is the purpose of the law of torts? What social and economic objects does it serve? One of the finest modern discussions of these questions is by Linden, the Canadian jurist. After reading the extract from his work, consider the two controversial Canadian judgments that follow. These cases involve clashing values, in particular the clash between women's rights and children's rights. Where does the protective role of the state fit in? How well did the Canadian judges deal with these issues? How do the cases fit in with the various aims of the law of torts discussed by Linden? To what extent should the common law around the world be similar? Is it important that New Zealand follow suit?

A.M. Linden, *Canadian Tort Law* (5th edn, Butterworths, 1993, Toronto)
Reprinted with the permission of Butterworths Canada Ltd © 1997

Introduction: the functions of tort law
The law of torts hovers over virtually every activity of modern society. The driver of every automobile on our highways, the pilot of every aeroplane in the sky, and the captain of every ship plying our waters must abide by the standards of tort law. The producers, distributors and repairers of every product, from bread to computers, must conform to tort law's counsel of caution. No profession is beyond its reach: a doctor cannot raise a scalpel, a lawyer cannot advise a client, nor can an architect design a building without being subject to potential tort liability. In the same way, teachers, government officials, police, and even jailers may be required to pay damages if some-one is hurt as a result of their conduct. Those who engage in sports, such as golfers, hockey-players, and snowmobilers, may end up as parties to a tort action. The terri-tory of tort law encompasses losses resulting from fires, floods, explosions, electricity, gas, and many other catastrophes that may occur in this increasingly complex world. A person who punches another person in the nose may have to answer for it in a tort case as well as in the criminal courts. A person who says nasty things about another may be sued for defamation. Hence, any one of us may become a plaintiff or a defend-ant in a tort action at any moment. Tort law, therefore, is a subject of abiding concern not only to the judges and lawyers who must administer it, but also to the public at large, whose every move is regulated by it.

Although it is relatively easy to point to the activities within the compass of tort law, it is not so simple to offer a satisfactory definition of tort. The term itself is a deri-vation of the Latin word, *tortus*, which means twisted or crooked. The expression found its way into the early English language as a synonym for the word 'wrong'. It is no longer used in everyday language, but it has survived as a technical legal term to this day.

...

Tort law is not one-dimensional: it serves several functions. The purpose of this chapter is to identify in a preliminary and tentative way the main aims of modern tort law. Not all of its goals are harmonious, indeed some may be in conflict with others. Not all the purposes of tort law are expressed openly in the case law. On the contrary, some of them are unrecognised or dimly perceived, or even vehemently denied. Some are achieved only indirectly and some not at all. Thus tort law services a potpourri of objectives, some conscious and some unconscious.

...

A Compensation
First and foremost, tort law is a compensator. A successful action puts money into the pocket of the claimant. This payment is supposed to reimburse the claimant for the economic and psychic damages suffered at the hands of the defendant.

The reparation function of modern tort law is so fundamental that some commentators have asserted that it is tort law's *only* legitimate task. The late Dean CA Wright, for example, contended simply that the 'purpose of the law of torts is to adjust [the] losses [arising out of modern living] and to afford compensation for injuries sustained by one person as the result of the conduct of another'. Another scholar has argued that justice requires, most of all, the reparation of wrongs. Indeed, he thought that penal sanctions might well be replaced by civil ones, once the latter 'acquired a sufficient efficacy'.

This view is inaccurate. If the sole role of tort law were universal compensation, it would have become extinct long ago. The truth is that only certain victims, 'the deserving', win damages in tort. The 'undeserving' are denied recovery. In other words, those who are able to prove that they were injured through another's fault or negligence receive reparation, and those who cannot go without. 'A loss must lie where it falls', asserted Oliver Wendell Holmes, unless there is a good reason to shift it. That good reason was fault. Holmes argued that the state's 'cumbrous and expensive machinery ought not to be set in motion unless some clear benefit is to be derived from disturbing the status quo. State interference is an evil, where it cannot be shown to be a good.' Such a benefit was derived when a loss was shifted from an innocent plaintiff to a wrong-doing defendant.

This theory had its heyday prior to the advent of the welfare state and widespread liability insurance. The interaction of these two factors changed the face of tort law. Increased social awareness coupled with liability insurance led to an increase in the incidence of tort liability ...

A new rationale for tort law—loss distribution—was devised to reflect these developments and to spur further growth along these lines. According to this theory, accident losses are no longer shifted from one individual to another. Rather, the costs are transferred to industrial enterprises and insured activities which generate most accidence. These activities do not bear these costs themselves but spread them throughout the community *via* price increases or insurance premiums. Thus, the expense is borne by the segment of society participating in the activity. Consequently, a massive loss which might bankrupt a defendant, if shifted to that individual, can be divided into infinitesimal portions to be exacted from many people without undue hardship to any of them. Pursuant to this reasoning, if tort law fails to compensate everyone, it is not performing its loss distribution task adequately. It is somewhat unsporting, however, to criticise tort law for not doing something it was never designed to do: the new criterion of loss-spreading was never taken into account by the architects of tort law.

When one begins to advocate that *all* accidental losses should be recompensed, one departs from the territory of tort law and enters the regime of social welfare. The logical extension of loss-distribution is social security. It is a mere 'palliative,' a temporary stopping-place on the way to a complete social insurance system. For tort law could not perform the role of social welfare adequately, even if its basis were strict liability rather than fault. Tort recovery certainly helps to cushion the financial blow of accidental injury. It is welcome enough if there is nothing else available, but if full and swift compensation is the only task of tort law, it should be replaced by something else less costly and less dilatory.

...

B Deterrence

The second historic function of tort law is deterrence or the prevention of accidents. Such legal luminaries as Bentham, Austin, and Salmond believed that the purpose of tort law was not much different from that of the criminal law. Lord Mansfield once wrote that damages acted 'as a punishment to the guilty, to deter from any such proceedings in the future ... '. This should surprise no one in view of the common roots of tort and criminal law. Judges often express their desire to deter future torts in holding defendants liable, especially when an award of punitive damages in *Norberg v Wynrib* [[1992] 2 SCR 226, at p 268] declared that 'the exchange of drugs for sex by a doctor in a position of power is conduct that cries out for deterrence'.

The admonitory function of tort law operates in two ways. Firstly, individuals who are required to pay damages for losses caused by their substandard conduct will try to avoid a recurrence. Secondly, tort judgments against transgressors are meant to warn others. The threat of tort liability is supposed to deter wrongful conduct and to stimulate caution on the part of those who wish to avoid civil liability for their conduct. In other words, the lesson being taught to society is that tort, like crime, does not pay.

Deterrence has been one of the fundamental assumptions of tort law, but assumptions do not necessarily correspond with reality. On the empirical evidence so far collected, it is hard to tell whether the civil sanction has any sting left in it. Some scholars contend that tort law's deterrent role is a myth, while more charitable authors suggest that the possibility of deterrence is 'of a low order'.

Certainly, there are impediments in the way of successful deterrence through tort law. Firstly, some individuals are unwilling to conform to the behaviour patterns prescribed by tort law. Some motorists, for example, persist in driving too fast or with their ability impaired, in spite of legal prohibitions ...

Secondly, certain persons may be willing to conform to the standard of care expected of them, but they may be unable to live up to it. The awkward, the accident-prone, and those of limited intelligence are sometimes incapable of performing reasonably, however hard they may try. Fortunately, most people are not inadequate to the demands of modern living and will act cautiously in order to avoid mishaps.

Thirdly, someone willing and able to live up to the standards of tort law may be totally ignorant of them. People cannot change their conduct to comply with directions of which they are not apprised. Fortunately most everyday activity can be performed in a right way or in a wrong way. In most instances one can tell the difference between responsible and risky conduct. Juries have had to pass judgment upon these acts for centuries and they have not met with any major difficulties. In an event, the rules of the road are in statutory form and are known to drivers. Speed limits must be posted. Professional people and entrepreneurs learn the customs of their trades, which are relied upon as important indicators of due care. Of course there are borderline cases, but those individuals should realise that their conduct is at least questionable in these circumstances. People may sometimes investigate the risks inherent in a particular course of conduct and may even hire experts to advise them how to proceed. Another point to consider is that there are a substantial number of people who know more about tort law than the average person. Because of this, the behaviour of certain people, such as doctors, lawyers, law students, police officers, insurance people, adjusters, court officials, and service station employees may be affected more by tort law than that of the general public. In addition, there are many citizens who have been involved in tort litigation as parties, witnesses or jurors and have learned something about the operation of tort law.

Fourthly, an every graver deficiency plagues tort law. The advent of liability insurance has removed some of its prophylactic power because the civil sanction is rarely applied against the tortfeasors themselves. When a judgment against an individual is paid by the individual's insurer, whatever preventive force tort law retains is further enfeebled. Some scholars have argued, therefore, that there is no sting left in tort law in the motor vehicle accident area because liability insurance coverage for motorists is almost universal. This position is too simplistic. Despite compulsory insurance laws, a tiny percentage of Canadian motorist are still uninsured ... There are, moreover, many motorists who carry out the minimum limits of liability insurance required by law. These people are personally responsible if a damage award against them exceeds this figure. Furthermore, the loss in question may not be covered by the terms of the insurance policy at all. For example, the person injured by the driver may be some person excluded by the provisions of the policy. Another possibility is that the motorist may have forfeited the right to be indemnified by violating one of the conditions of the policy. For instance, if driving while drunk, the motorist is not covered by the policy, even though the insurer is initially responsible by statute to any third person who has suffered loss. Lastly, even if the insurer stands behind the motorist, the motorist must still undergo the inconvenience of being involved in a civil suit, something no one enjoys. Despite all these potentially unpleasant repercussions, one survey revealed that 58 per cent of the respondents felt that civil liability did not affect careful driving, whereas only 14 per cent thought that it did. It is hard to assess the reliability of this study, but it does seem to reveal the public's perception of the problem.

In addition to imposing civil liability for negligence, the common law courts withhold or reduce the recovery of anyone who is contributorily negligent with regard to their own safety. Contributory negligence is still being used to encourage care by plaintiffs ... The application of the seat belt defence is an example of the use of contributory negligence law as a deterrent to dangerous conduct.

...

C Education

Tort law is an educator. Along with criminal prosecutions, coroners' inquests, royal commissions and the like, a tort trial is a teacher. Indeed, Glanville Williams has suggested that making someone pay compensation may be 'educationally superior to a fine' in that 'it teaches a moral lesson'. The communications explosion has magnified the importance of this didactic role of tort law. Malpractice, libel and product liability cases in particular attract the attention of the press. Doctors, journalists, and manufacturers closely observe the outcomes of these disputes which concern them so vitally. Their trade journals often report the results of litigation involving fellow professionals. Each annual report of the Canadian Medical Protective Association, for example, contains a summary of the medical malpractice suits which go to trial each year in Canada. Advice may be given. Conferences may be convened to discuss the problems dealt with in the litigation. To be sure, this is not the most efficient way of curtailing sub-standard practices; other forms of regulations would undoubtedly be preferable. The sad fact is, however, that professional groups are reluctant to police their own profes-sions strenuously, and manufacturers are often largely immune from government supervision. Until our society is prepared to use more effective weapons, the educa-tional force of tort law may be all there is.

Tort law is also a reinforcer of values. Like the criminal law, tort law enshrines many of the traditional moral principles of Anglo-American society. This is a mixed blessing for many of these values are in need of reassessment. Tort law may well impede the birth of new moral principles through its conservation of the older values. If, however, any new moral ideals catch hold, they will infiltrate the principles of tort law. At worst, tort law slows down their acceptance and permits some sober second thoughts.

...

One value at the heart of tort law is the notion of individual responsibility, some-thing that is central to Western civilisation. If people act responsibly, they should be rewarded; if they act irresponsibly, they should be punished. There is no need to dis-guise the fact that this is the underlying morality of the fault system. No one denies that the fault system is riddled with imperfections; it is costly, difficulty to administer, denies compensation to many injured people, and is replete with delays. Nevertheless, it is also a mark of nobility when a society directs its members to conduct themselves reasonably in their relations with their fellow citizens or pay for the consequences. A concomitant of this is that people must also look after themselves, or be denied com-pensation if they are hurt. There are some exceptions made for children and the men-tally disabled, but none for the dull-witted or the awkward. Many people seem to feel that it is 'just and fair' to make the 'guilty' pay, not the 'innocent', and that the 'inno-cent' *should* receive compensation, but not the 'guilty'. Philosophers call this corrective justice. The philosophy of the age of reason, not determinism, still permeates tort law. The fundamental goal is individual restraint and respect for one's fellow creatures, something which is required more than ever in mass urban societies.

Tort law also demonstrates abiding respect for the dignity of the individual. It treats every claimant as unique, special, and different to everyone else in the world. In assessing damages under tort theory, each person is supposed to recover what each *per-sonally* has lost. Not only does the person with a large salary or heavy medical costs receive full compensation, but the non-pecuniary or psychic losses are also recom-pensed ... Only tort law is tailored to deal with each person as an individual entity. This is unquestionably one of its weaknesses, but it is also one of its greatest strengths.

Tort law is, therefore, performing some of the functions of the school and, to an extent, the church. The moral principles upon which tort law is based are constantly being reiterated for the benefit of those who are involved and those who observe. This is a healthy thing, for these principles are useful guidelines for individuals to follow in ordering their relations with their fellow human beings.

D Psychological function

Tort law may perform certain psychological functions. For example, the tort action, like the criminal law, may provide some appeasement to those injured by wrongful conduct.

Lord Diplock has contended that no one would suggest using tort law for the purpose of vengeance. Nevertheless, though it is distasteful to most of us, this has always been one of the unexpressed uses of tort law and criminal law. Too many human beings still seem to have need for such an outlet for their desire for revenge. The sad fact is that there is in many of us something primitive which tort law may satisfy.

This questionable service that tort law performs can be put in a more positive and acceptable form. It can be said that tort law helps to keep the peace by providing a legal method of quenching the thirst for revenge. It will be recalled that this was the historical rationale for the creation of tort law. Money damages were paid to the victims of tortious conduct in the hope of curtailing blood feuds. If these legal avenues to revenge were closed today, some victims of wrongful conduct might once against take up clubs and tomahawks to 'get even' with their aggressors. It is better to pursue a wrongdoer with a writ than a rifle.

...

Tort law may counteract the feeling of alienation and despair which pervades our society. Governments, corporations, unions, and universities have grown too large and impersonal. A feeling of helplessness and personal insignificance grips too many of our people. Many individuals feel that they have lost control over their lives. No one seems to care about them anymore. A protest march, a sit-in or some other dramatic act can change all this. For a time, people *do* seem to care about the protestors. The media takes notice of them. They seem to matter more. They become 'relevant'. There seems to be a psychological need for personal recognition, which may contribute something to the popularity of this type of activity. A tort suit may likewise provide some psychological satisfaction ...

...

Tort trials enrich our society with ritual and symbolism. The solemnity, the formality, and the languages of tort litigation contribute to a sense of mystery. This is something all societies seem to require. As agnosticism supplants religion in the modern world, rituals such as court proceedings are gaining in importance. More and more of us, suffering from 'future shock', are searching for bridges with the past, points of stability, to comfort us as the world races by. Traditions of litigation may supply some medicine for this ailment.

...

E Market deterrence

The law of tort may reduce accidents through market deterrence. This must be distinguished from the type of deterrence discussed above, whereby tort law *directly* attacks the specific occasions of danger. Market or general deterrence functions *indirectly*. It lowers accident costs by making those activities which are accident-prone more expensive by requiring them to bear the full costs of the mishaps they produce. This renders safer substances more attractive, because they cost less.

There are certainly more effective ways of reducing accidents. The criminal law and administration regulation are widely used to cut accidents. We prohibit certain activities altogether if they are too dangerous, even if they could pay their way in the market. For example, we forbid dynamite blasting or the firing of guns in the centre of the city. Further, we regulate the way in which certain activities are conducted.

Automobiles, although they are allowed on the highways, may not exceed the speed limit and must comply with the rules of the road.

There are, however, many types of activities we do not wish to prohibit altogether nor to supervise too closely. Market deterrence can function here as a useful adjunct to criminal and administrative law. We permit these activities to be carried on with only the minimum of control—tort law's general guideline of reasonable care. Thus businesspeople may carry on business as long as they do not negligently injure anyone. If they do hurt someone, they are required to pay the costs incurred by the victim. As the total of damage costs rises, the price of products or activities will increase accordingly. Eventually, businesspeople would have to institute safer practices or be driven out of business as their customers switch to less costly substitutes. This is accomplished automatically through the ordinary forces of the market, without any help from politicians and bureaucrats.

...

The foundation of this doctrine is simply economics, the theory that individuals know what is best for themselves. Because of this, we should permit them to make their own decisions about how to spend their money. In other words, the way a society allocates its resources should be a reflection of the individual choices made by all its members. If people want automobiles rather than schools, they should have automobiles rather than schools. As long as the prices of the various goods and services available reflect the full cost of providing them, the buyers will be able to make informed decisions.

...

This market or general deterrence approach reduces accident costs in two ways. Firstly, it creates a financial incentive for people who are engaged in dangerous activities to switch to safer activities. If the participants in a risky activity have to pay for its full cost, some of them may transfer to a safer activity which is cheaper. Whenever someone decides to substitute a less hazardous activity for a more dangerous one, society benefits. Of course, any such decision would take into account not only the cost differential, but also the quality of the substitute activity.

...

The second way in which general deterrence diminishes the expenses of accidents is to encourage people to alter the *way* in which they conduct their activities, rather than changing the *type* of activities altogether. Perhaps another example will be of assistance. Let us assume that a motorist spends an average amount of $200 per year on accident costs. Further, suppose that the motorist were to adopt a different kind of braking system on the car, the accident expenses would total only $100. The safer brakes are available at a cost of $50. The motorist might well decide to spend the $50 for the new brakes, cut the accident costs to $100, and thereby save $50 annually in accident costs. If the $200 accident costs were paid by the state, there would be no cost incentive to switch to the new brakes.

The market deterrence theory has not yet been empirically tested. We do not know how efficiently it operates, or indeed if it functions at all. It may work only with some activities, but not with others. Its effectiveness will partially depend upon the elasticity of the demand for the product or activity ...

Another serious shortcoming of the market deterrence approach is that it discriminates heavily against the poor. By placing the full costs of accidents on the activities which generate them, we are permitting the rich to engage in dangerous activities which the poor cannot afford. In short this 'works like a regressive tax' ...

...

F Ombudsman

Tort law is an ombudsman. It can be used to apply pressure upon those who wield political, economic or intellectual power. This is rarely the expressed aim of a tort suit, but it can be an important side-effect.

The burgeoning regulatory activities of modern government have been much discussed in recent years. Some people complain about excessive governmental intrusion into their affairs. Others advocate the complete regulation of nearly every aspect of our daily lives. By and large we have adopted a middle course; we regulate only certain activities and to varying degrees. Some governmental agencies are zealous in the enforcement of their mandates, whereas others are rather somnolent. The history of some agencies has revealed that instead of diligently pursuing their legislative mandate, administrators often try to win the approval and support of those they must regulate. To some extent this may be necessary, since conflict and antagonism should be held to a minimum. But without some conflict and antagonism, the job cannot be done effectively. Too often personnel are exchanged between a regulated industry and the board supposed to supervise it. In such circumstances the public interest may be sacrificed.

Tort law can be of service here. Individuals victimised by conduct violating legislative provisions may initiate civil proceedings. The civil courts will utilise the statutory directives in evaluating the offending conduct. The illegal activity may be penalised by civil sanctions, even where the administrative or criminal ones are not applied. The legislative policy can be advanced by tort law even where those responsible for promoting the policy fail to do so. The damages sought in such a case may not be of primary concern to the plaintiff; the main goal may be to stimulate administrative action.

Through the actions of false imprisonment, assault, battery, and negligence, tort law spurs police forces to act more responsibly in their dealings with citizens. The law reports contain several cases in which undue police interference with liberty has yielded a tort judgment ...

...

Perhaps the most spectacular success of tort law as a weapon of social reform has been in the products liability area. The captains of industry have at last been made accountable to ordinary people. Irate consumers have deployed the tort action in their battle against the manufacturers of shoddy goods. The producers of thalidomide have been required to pay millions of dollars in damages to the children deformed by that drug. The manufacturers of automobiles have had to pay a fortune to motorists injured by their substandard products ...

This capacity of tort law to challenge industrial decision-making opens up exciting possibilities for consumer democracy. Although Professor Fleming has questioned the capacity of negligence trials to second-guess experts, this watch-dog function, especially if performed by a jury, is vital in a world increasingly run by distant bureaucrats ...

The struggle for the environment provides new opportunities for tort law. Professor Joseph Sax contends that tort litigation provides an 'additional source of leverage in making environmental decision-making operate rationally, thoughtfully, and with a sense of responsiveness to the entire range of citizen concerns'. Although he agrees that courts alone cannot do an adequate job, he says they can help to 'open the doors to a far more limber governmental process', since the 'more leverage citizens have, the more responsive and responsible their officials and fellow citizens will be'.

...

The various professional groups in society are not immune to attack by negligence action. A medical malpractice action has repercussions not only for the doctor involved but for the entire medical profession whose procedures can be challenged thereby. Medical decisions in treatment and in experimentation are increasingly under judicial eyes for approbation or condemnation. Although this may strike terror into the hearts of some doctors, a healthy and vibrant profession must constantly justify its stewardship. So too the conduct of lawyers, architects, accountants and other skilled groups may be subject to examination in courts at the behest of any unsatisfied customer who has suffered loss at their hands.

1 Publicity

Tort law provides a wronged individual with a weapon to direct unfavourable publicity against a tortfeasor. Because of the communications revolution this publicity sanction can be a powerful force for social reform ...

The media have focussed considerable attention on civil suits against auto manufacturers, drug producers, polluters, and over-enthusiastic police officers. Consequently, by commencing a tort action a claimant may be able to cast a spotlight upon the defendant. This may act as a deterrent to the defendant and to other potential transgressors in three ways. Adverse publicity can cost the defendant money ... When a number of tort actions were launched in the early 1960s against the Richardson-Merrell Company, the North American producers of thalidomide and Mer/29, their stock, which had been selling at 25–35 times the earnings, plunged to 15–20 times the earnings. This was a massive paper loss to the stock-holder, one that was not justified by the actual threat to the company's financial health.

Secondly, the defendant can suffer a loss of prestige. Although this too may result in monetary loss, it is important for its own sake. Everyone, even corporate managers and bureaucrats, is anxious to be held in public esteem. Businesses spend millions on public relations campaigns to polish their corporate images. This may all be squandered by civil suits which tarnish their reputation for quality goods and services.

Thirdly, negative publicity may induce government intervention. Public officials may become apprised of dangerous or improper activities. Criminal prosecutions or administrative sanctions may follow. Where legislative jurisdiction is lacking, public opinion may be aroused to such an extent that the politicians respond with new legislation to control the perceived abuse.

...

Another advantage of the publicity sanction is that it is both triggered and imposed by ordinary citizens. Any individual who is injured by another's wrongful conduct may institute civil proceedings. One does not have to wait until a prosecutor or civil servant decides to act ...

2 Institutional limitations

There are institutional limitations on the effectiveness of tort law as a tool for social reform. Firstly, the substantive law may be incapable of producing an acceptable decision. For example, present negligence law may dictate a dismissal of a defective product claim, nuisance law may be unavailable against certain polluters, and an erroneous police arrest may be held to have been reasonable in the circumstances. Our judges are understandably reluctant to reformulate the law. As a consequence, the content of the law may lag behind the popular will ...

A second fetter on the effective use of tort law as an ombudsman stems from the economics of litigation. Lawyers usually work for fees, not for principles; litigants usually sue for money, not for ideals. Investigation of accidents is expensive. Expert witnesses must be paid for their work. In short, tort trials cost money. Lots of it. Unless there is a good chance of winning, litigants are unwise to sue, for losers must pay not only their own legal costs but also those of the winning parties. The allure of a quick settlement dulls the crusading ardour of many a claimant. Because of this, law suits which test the frontiers of tort law are difficult to finance. Only the rare case, the rare litigant and the rare lawyer become involved in such litigation.

...

The third restraint on bold intrusions into the conduct of government, business, and the professions stems from the nature of the judicial process itself. Judges cannot decide cases the way they, personally, would prefer. *Stare decisis* forbids this. The only paths upon which judges may travel are well-worn ruts. They cannot take wing on flights of fancy. That is not the judicial way. There is also some question about the capacity of judges to make expert decisions for which they may be ill-equipped ...

...

G The future of tort law

These are some of the functions of modern tort law which any cost–benefit analysis of the system will have to consider. The compensation aim of tort law is still significant, even though its importance is waning, because it recompenses in full the losses of victims, including general damages. The deterrence element may still be helpful, though its therapeutic power has been eroded, because individual defendants remain responsible, in theory at least, for their conduct. Market deterrence may influence accident cost, although we cannot be sure of this until it has been empirically tested. These matters can and should be measured over the next few years.

The other functions of tort law are more difficult to analyse because they cannot be quantified. They lie more in the ephemeral realm of values. They are directed at the tone and the quality of life. It is hard to tell whether the educational function of tort law has any impact on our citizenry. We do not know whether the moral beacon which emanates from tort principles enlightens anyone. We cannot know whether the psychological impact of tort law draws people closer together or whether it alienates them further from their society. The use of tort law is as an ombudsman and as a weapon of social reform may turn out to be its most promising function in the decades ahead. It may well become its primary *raison d'être* in the future …

Winnipeg Child and Family Services (Northwest Area) v G (DF)
[1997] 3 SCR 925 (SC)
McLachlin J [joined by a majority]:
1 In August 1996, a judge of the Manitoba Court of Queen's Bench ordered that the respondent, five months pregnant with her fourth child, be placed in the custody of the Director of Child and Family Services and detained at the Health Sciences Centre until the birth of her child, there to follow a course of treatment prescribed by the Director. The purpose of the order was to protect the respondent's unborn child. The respondent was addicted to glue sniffing which may damage the nervous system of the developing fetus.

A *Does the law of tort permit an order for the detention and treatment of a pregnant woman for the purpose of preventing harm to the unborn child?*
1 Does the existing law of tort support the order?
… 15 The position is clear. Neither the common law nor the civil law of Quebec recognizes the unborn child as a legal person possessing rights. This principle applies generally, whether the case falls under the rubric of family law, succession law or tort. Any right or interest the fetus may have remains inchoate and incomplete until the birth of the child.

16 It follows that under the law as it presently stands, the fetus on whose behalf the agency purported to act in seeking the order for the respondent's detention was not a legal person and possessed no legal rights. If it was not a legal person and possessed no legal rights at the time of the application, then there was no legal person in whose interests the agency could act or in whose interests a court order could be made.

17 Putting the matter in terms of tort, there was no right to sue, whether for an injunction or damages, until the child was born alive and viable. The law of tort as it presently stands might permit an action for injury to the fetus to be brought in the child's name after its birth. But there is no power in the courts to entertain such an action before the child's birth. The action at issue was commenced and the injunctive relief sought before the child's birth. It follows that under the law as it presently stands, it must fail.

2 Should the law of tort be extended to permit the order?
18 It is necessary at the outset to consider the principles that govern judicial extension of common law principles. As a general rule, judicial change is confined to incremental change 'based largely on the mechanism of extending an existing principle to new circumstances'; courts will not extend the common law 'where the revision is major and its ramifications complex'.

19 The changes which the agency asks this Court to make to the law of tort may be summarized as follows:

　　1　Overturn the rule that rights accrue to a person only at birth (the 'live-birth' rule);

2   Recognize a fetal right to sue the mother carrying the fetus;

3   Recognize a cause of action for lifestyle choices which may adversely affect others;

4   Recognize an injunctive remedy which deprives a defendant of important liberties, including her involuntary confinement.

20 The proposed changes to the law of tort are major, affecting the rights and remedies available in many other areas of tort law. They involve moral choices and would create conflicts between fundamental interests and rights. They would have an immediate and drastic impact on the lives of women as well as men who might find themselves incarcerated and treated against their will for conduct alleged to harm others. And, they possess complex ramifications impossible for this Court to fully assess, giving rise to the danger that the proposed order might impede the goal of healthy infants more than it would promote it. In short, these are not the sorts of changes which common law courts can or should make. These are the sorts of changes which should be left to the legislature.

(a) Overturning the rule that rights accrue only at birth

21 A child may sue in tort for injury caused before birth. However, only when the child is born does it have the legal status to sue and damages are assessed only as of the date of birth …

22 The rule that a fetus does not have a cause of action for prenatal injuries until 'born alive' also governs in other common law countries such as England and Australia. In England, the Congenital Disabilities (Civil Liability) Act 1976 (UK), c 28, s 1, creates the basis of civil liability where a child is born disabled in consequence of tortious action of some person before the child's birth.

23 To permit intervention prior to birth in recognition of a duty of care owed to the fetus *in utero* would constitute a major departure from the common law as it has stood for decades. It would reverse the long-standing principle of tort law that remedies for negligent behaviour cannot be pursued until a cause of action is brought by a juridical person.

24 This change to the law of tort is fraught with complexities and ramifications, the consequences of which cannot be precisely foretold. At what stage would a fetus acquire rights? Could women who choose to terminate a pregnancy face injunctive relief prohibiting termination, relief which this Court rejected in *Tremblay v Daigle* [1989] 2 SCR 530? Alternatively, could they face an action for damages brought on behalf of the fetus for its lost life? If a pregnant woman is killed as a consequence of negligence on the highway, may a family sue not only for her death, but for that of the unborn child? If it is established that a fetus can feel discomfort, can it sue its mother (or perhaps her doctor) and claim damages for the discomfort? If the unborn child is a legal person with legal rights, arguments can be made in favour of all these propositions. Some might endorse such changes, others deplore them. The point is that they are major changes attracting an array of consequences that would place the courts at the heart of a web of thorny moral and social issues which are better dealt with by elected legislators than by the courts. Having broken the time-honoured rule that legal rights accrue only upon live birth, the courts would find it difficult to limit

application of the new principle to particular cases. By contrast, the legislature, should it choose to introduce a law permitting action to protect unborn children against substance abuse, could limit the law to that precise case …

(b) Recognizing a fetal right to sue the mother carrying the fetus
27 Before birth the mother and unborn child are one in the sense that '[t]he life of the foetus is intimately connected with, and cannot be regarded in isolation from, the life of the pregnant woman': *Paton v United Kingdom* (1980) 3 EHRR 408 (Comm), at p 415, applied in *Re F (in utero)*, *supra*. It is only after birth that the fetus assumes a separate personality. Accordingly, the law has always treated the mother and unborn child as one. To sue a pregnant woman on behalf of her unborn fetus therefore posits the anomaly of one part of a legal and physical entity suing itself …

(c) Recognizing a cause of action for lifestyle choices which may adversely affect others
30 If the problem of permitting an unborn child to sue its future mother could be surmounted, a further difficulty presents itself: could the unborn child sue her for lifestyle choices? The difficulty of this question may be discerned from the cases considering the right of born children to sue their mothers for prenatal injuries. To date, courts and legislatures have confined the right to the child suing its mother for prenatal injuries to injuries due to motor vehicle accidents.
…
33 Behind the refusal of the courts and at least one legislature to permit a child to sue its mother for prenatal injuries related to her lifestyle, lies the fear that such suits would take the courts into the difficult policy issue of the extent to which a mother's lifestyle is actionable. Leaving the special relationship between mother and unborn child aside for the moment, there is little precedent for suing any defendant in tort for damages one has suffered as a consequence of his or her lifestyle. While it is not inconceivable that the courts, proceeding properly in their incremental law-making capacity, may one day recognize such claims, the appellant agency faces the difficulty that on this point too it is asking this Court to break new ground in a controversial area. Once again, the consequences for the law of tort generally might be great. Are children to be permitted to sue their parents for second-hand smoke inhaled around the family dinner table? Could any cohabitant bring such an action? Are children to be permitted to sue their parents for spanking causing psychological trauma or poor grades due to alcoholism or a parent's undue fondness for the office or the golf course? If we permit lifestyle actions, where do we draw the line?
34 The difficulties multiply when the lifestyle in question is that of a pregnant woman whose liberty is intimately and inescapably bound to her unborn child …
…
37 … The potential for intrusions on a woman's right to make choices concerning herself is considerable. The fetus' complete physical existence is dependent on the body of the woman. As a result, any intervention to further the fetus' interests will necessarily implicate, and possibly conflict with the mother's interests. Similarly, each choice made by the woman in relation to her body will affect the fetus and potentially attract tort liability …

...

40 These difficulties would be complicated by the fact that determining what will cause grave and irreparable harm to a fetus—the threshold for injunctive relief—is a difficult endeavour with which medical researchers continually struggle. The difference between confinement and freedom, between damages and non-liability, may depend on a grasp of the latest research and its implications. The pregnant women most likely to be affected by such a 'knowledge' requirement would be those in lower socio-economic groups. Minority women, illiterate women, and women of limited education will be the most likely to fall afoul of the law and the new duty it imposes and to suffer the consequences of injunctive relief and potential damage awards.

...

43 If it could be predicted with some certainty that all these negative effects of extending tort liability to the lifestyle choices of pregnant women would in fact diminish the problem of injured infants, the change might nevertheless arguably be justified. But the evidence before this Court fails to establish this. It is far from clear that the proposed tort duty will decrease the incidence of substance-injured children. Indeed, the evidence suggests that such a duty might have negative effects on the health of infants. No clear consensus emerges from the debate on the question of whether ordering women into 'places of safety' and mandating medical treatment provide the best solution or, on the contrary, create additional problems.

44 Indeed, changing tort law to make a pregnant mother liable for lifestyle-related fetal damage may be counterproductive in at least two ways. First, it may tend to drive the problems underground. Pregnant women suffering from alcohol or substance abuse addictions may not seek prenatal care for fear that their problems would be detected and they would be confined involuntarily and/or ordered to undergo mandatory treatment. As a result, there is a real possibility that those women most in need of proper prenatal care may be the ones who will go without and a judicial intervention designed to improve the health of the fetus and the mother may actually put both at serious health risk. Second, changing the law of tort as advocated by the agency might persuade women who would otherwise choose to continue their pregnancies to undergo an abortion. Women under the control of a substance addiction may be unable to face the prospect of being without their addicting substance and may find terminating the pregnancy a preferable alternative. In the end, orders made to protect a fetus' health could ultimately result in its destruction ...

Major J (dissenting) [joined by **Sopinka J**]:

109 Present medical technology renders the 'born alive' rule outdated and indefensible. We no longer need to cling to an evidentiary presumption to the contrary when technologies like real time ultrasound, fetal heart monitors and fetoscopy can clearly show us that a foetus is alive and has been or will be injured by conduct of another. We can gauge fetal development with much more certainty than the common law presumed. How can the sophisticated micro-surgery that is now being performed on foetuses in utero be compatible with the 'born alive' rule?

110 However, there is the temptation to assume that the courts of the past that treated the 'born alive' rule as one of substantive law knew as much as is known today about fetal development. Since medical technology has improved to the point of eliminating nearly all

of the evidentiary problems from which the 'born alive' rule sprang, it no longer makes sense to retain the rule where its application would be perverse. The blind application of the 'born alive' rule in this context clearly runs afoul of Holmes' dictum that:

> It is revolting to have no better reason for a rule of law than that so it was laid down in the time of Henry IV. It is still more revolting if the grounds upon which it was laid down have vanished long since, and the rule simply persists from blind imitation of the past.

(Oliver Wendell Holmes 'The Path of the Law' (1897)
10 Harv L Rev 457, 469.)

F Conclusion

138 I do not believe our system, whether legislative or judicial, has become so paralysed that it will ignore a situation where the imposition required in order to prevent terrible harm is so slight. It may be preferable that the legislature act but its failure to do so is not an excuse for the judiciary to follow the same course of inaction. Failure of the court to act should occur where there is no jurisdiction for the court to proceed. Outdated medical assumptions should not provide any licence to permit the damage to continue. Where the harm is so great and the temporary remedy so slight, the law is compelled to act.

Dobson (Litigation Guardian of) v Dobson
[1999] 2 SCR 753 (SC)
[**FACTS**: While pregnant, Dobson had a car accident, which resulted in her child being born with severe disabilities. The child brought an action for damages against the mother and another, alleging that the collision was caused by her negligent driving. The mother was covered by insurance.]
Cory J:
...

1 *Privacy and autonomy rights of women*
23 First and foremost, for reasons of public policy, the Court should not impose a duty of care upon a pregnant woman towards her foetus or subsequently born child. To do so would result in very extensive and unacceptable intrusions into the bodily integrity, privacy and autonomy rights of women. It is true that Canadian tort law presently allows a child born alive and viable to sue a third-party for injuries which were negligently inflicted while in utero ... However, of fundamental importance to the public policy analysis is the particularly unique relationship that exists between a pregnant woman and the foetus she carries.

(a) Overview
...

25 The unique and special relationship between a mother-to-be and her foetus determines the outcome of this appeal. There is no other relationship in the realm of human existence which can serve as a basis for comparison. It is for this reason that

there can be no analogy between a child's action for prenatal negligence brought against some third-party tortfeasor, on the one hand, and against his or her mother, on the other. The inseparable unity between an expectant woman and her foetus distinguishes the situation of the mother-to-be from that of a negligent third-party. The biological reality is that a pregnant woman and her foetus are bonded in a union. This was recognized in the majority reasons of McLachlin J in *Winnipeg* …

…

31 On behalf of the infant respondent, it was argued that the reasoning in *Winnipeg* is not determinative because it dealt with the standing of the foetus to sue while still in utero. In *Winnipeg*, the foetus which sought the detention of its mother-to-be was not a legal person and possessed no legal rights. By contrast, the present action is brought on behalf of an infant born alive whose legal rights and interests vested at the moment of birth. In other words, the sole issue in this appeal is whether a child born alive—as opposed to a foetus—should be able to recover damages for prenatal negligence from every person except his or her mother. Despite the important legal distinction between a foetus and a child born alive, as a matter of social policy and pragmatic reality, both situations involve the imposition of a duty of care upon a pregnant woman towards either her foetus or her subsequently born child. To impose either duty of care would require judicial scrutiny into every aspect of that woman's behaviour during pregnancy. Irrespective of whether the duty of care is imposed upon a pregnant woman towards her foetus or her subsequently born child, both would involve severe intrusions into the bodily integrity, privacy and autonomous decision-making of that woman …

(d) Consequences of recognizing this cause of action
…

46 Moreover, the imposition of tort liability in this context would carry psychological and emotional repercussions for a mother who is sued in tort by her newborn child. To impose tort liability on a mother for an unreasonable lapse of prenatal care could have devastating consequences for the future relationship between the mother and her born alive child. In essence, the judicial recognition of a cause of action for maternal prenatal negligence is an inappropriate response to the pressing social issue of caring for children with special needs. Putting a mother through the trauma of a public trial to determine whether she was at fault for the injury suffered by her child can only add emotional and psychological trauma to an already tragic situation.

47 Such litigation would, in all probability, have detrimental consequences, not only for the relationship between mother and child, but also for the relationship between the child and his or her family. Yet, family harmony will be particularly important for the creation of a caring and nurturing environment for the injured child, who will undoubtedly require much loving attention. It seems clear that the well-being of such a child cannot be readily severed from the interests of his or her family. In short, neither the best interests of the injured child, nor those of the remainder of the family, would be served by the judicial recognition of the suggested cause of action.

48 The primary purposes of tort law are to provide compensation to the injured and deterrence to the tortfeasor. In the ordinary course of events, the imposition of tort

liability on a mother for prenatal negligence would provide neither compensation nor deterrence. The pressing societal issue at the heart of this appeal is the lack of financial support currently available for the care of children with special needs. The imposition of a legal duty of care on a pregnant woman towards her foetus or subsequently born child will not solve this problem. If anything, attempting to address this social problem in a litigious setting would merely exacerbate the pain and trauma of a tragic situation. It may well be that carefully considered legislation could create a fund to compensate children with prenatally inflicted injuries. Alternatively, amendments to the motor vehicle insurance laws could achieve the same result in a more limited context. If, as a society, Canadians believe that children who sustain damages as a result of maternal prenatal negligence should be financially compensated, then the solution should be formulated, after careful study and debate, by the legislature ...

(d) Insurance-dependent rationale
71 Clearly, the judicial creation of a motor vehicle exception would be predicated, in large part, on the existence of a mandatory insurance regime for automobile negligence. This underlying rationale was accepted by the Australian High Court in *Lynch* [(1991) 25 NSWLR 411], *supra*. In that case, the facts were strikingly similar to those presented in this appeal. The court strictly limited maternal tort liability for prenatal injuries to cases of motor vehicle negligence on the basis that insurance was compulsory in that context. In arriving at this conclusion, Clarke JA considered the policy concerns that all those injured in road accidents should be compensated and that all owners of motor vehicles should contribute to the cost of injury through insurance. By adopting an insurance-dependent rationale, it was not necessary for the court to consider whether a pregnant woman owed a duty of care to her foetus or subsequently born child.

72 It must be recognized that, although the appellant mother is in the legal position of defending this action, an award of damages in favour of the respondent would greatly assist the appellant and her husband with the financial requirements of caring for their severely disabled child. It is true that, in this particular case, the material interests of the mother and child are aligned, notwithstanding the fact that their legal relationship is adversarial. As one author notes, '[i]f there is automobile insurance, allowing such suits does not make the mother and fetus—or, rather, subsequently born child—genuine adversaries, since the whole family benefits by allowing the child to recover': Steinbock, *supra*, at p 100.

73 An insurance-driven judicial solution to the issue raised in this appeal imposes liability on a mother on the basis of her ability to satisfy a judgment by means of her insurance coverage. However, tort law is not, and should not be, result-oriented in this manner ...

McLachlin J [joined by **L'Heureux-Dubé J**]:
84 In my view, to apply common law liability for negligence generally to pregnant women in relation to the unborn is to trench unacceptably on the liberty and equality interests of pregnant women. The common law must reflect the values enshrined in the Canadian Charter of Rights and Freedoms. Liability for foetal injury by pregnant

women would run contrary to two of the most fundamental of these values—liberty and equality.

85 I turn first to liberty. Virtually every action of a pregnant woman—down to how much sleep she gets, what she eats and drinks, how much she works and where she works—is capable of affecting the health and well-being of her unborn child, and hence carries the potential for legal action against the pregnant woman. Such legal action in turn carries the potential to bring the whole of the pregnant woman's conduct under the scrutiny of the law. This in turn has the potential to jeopardize the pregnant woman's fundamental right to control her body and make decisions in her own interest: *R v Morgentaler* [1988] 1 SCR 30, per Wilson J.

86 The intrusion upon the pregnant woman's autonomy worked by the proposed common law rule would also violate her right to equal treatment. Canadians generally enjoy the full right to decide what they will eat or drink, where they will work and other personal matters. Pregnant women, however, would not enjoy that right. In addition to the usual duties of prudent conduct imposed on all who engage in life's various activities, pregnant women would be subject to a host of additional restrictions. Any other individual can avoid being a tortfeasor by isolating himself or herself from other members of society. The pregnant woman has no such choice. She carries her foetus 24 hours a day, seven days a week.

87 To say women choose pregnancy is no answer. Pregnancy is essentially related to womanhood. It is an inexorable and essential fact of human history that women and only women become pregnant. Women should not be penalized because it is their sex that bears children: To say that broad legal constraints on the conduct of pregnant women do not constitute unequal treatment because women choose to become pregnant is to reinforce inequality by the fiction of deemed consent and the denial of what it is to be a woman.

88 Those who urge intrusion of common law tort liability into the lives of pregnant women do not, in the main, contest the impermissibility of broad interference with the rights of women to make decisions about their bodies and lives. They seek rather to reduce the intrusion on the autonomy of the pregnant woman to the point where the infringement on her liberty and equality interests is acceptable.

89 My difficulty is that the common law is unable to achieve this restrained result without distortion of the very methodology by which it operates and the introduction of new difficulties. The first proposal—the rule that only children 'born alive' can sue—eliminates liability for abortion but leaves vast scope for curtailment of the pregnant woman's autonomy. The second proposal—a rule that liability follows only where the mother has an insurance policy to cover the damage—flies in the face of the maxim that tort liability cannot be predicated on the means of the defendant. A third proposal, adopted by the Court of Appeal—that liability be restricted to situations where the pregnant woman already owes a duty to other people 'generally' (in this case, a general duty to 'drive carefully')—violates the precept that a common law duty of care arises from the relationship of the parties before the court, not from the relationship between the defendant and a hypothetical plaintiff. Finally, the variant on the Court of Appeal's theory adopted by Major J—that the additional duty must be owed to an actual third party—still violates the principle that the duty of care in tort must be

founded on the relationship between the actual parties to the dispute before the court, and makes recovery conditional on the serendipitous coincidence that another person stood to be injured by the pregnant woman's act or omission. I am not persuaded that the common law can be narrowed to achieve the result here sought while staying true to its principles.

[**Note**: **Major J**, joined by **Bastarache J**, dissented by reasserting his arguments from *Winnipeg Child and Family Services*.]

Chapter 2
Intentional Torts

Introduction

Modern tort law provides two main avenues of recovery for personal injury—trespass to the person and negligence. Briefly stated, the distinction between actions in trespass and those in negligence is one of intention. Actions in trespass require the plaintiff to prove that the defendant acted intentionally. For this reason, the torts of trespass are often referred to as intentional torts. In contrast, actions in negligence do not require the plaintiff to prove that the defendant acted intentionally but rather that the plaintiff was harmed by the defendant's negligent conduct. This chapter introduces the intentional torts while negligence is the subject of Chapter 4.

It is appropriate to mention that the distinction between the intentional torts and negligence is not always clear; throughout their historical evolution, developments in trespass have prompted developments in negligence and vice versa. Originally, the distinction between the two was whether the plaintiff's injury was the direct or merely indirect result of the defendant's behaviour. Where the plaintiff's injury was the direct result of the defendant's behaviour, as where A is struck by a stone thrown by B, the action was begun with a writ of trespass, precursor to modern trespass. In contrast, where the plaintiff's injury was merely the indirect result of the defendant's behaviour, as where A trips over a stone B had thrown onto the path, the action was begun by a writ of trespass on the case, precursor to modern negligence. Statutory reform of the writ system in the nineteenth century and subsequent decisions have rendered the direct/indirect distinction largely obsolete. However, occasionally reference to the historic distinction is made in modern cases, as in *Letang v Cooper* below.

The torts of trespass also have a close historical connection to the criminal law. It is not in the interests of society at large to allow people to go around throwing stones. Not only might someone be injured, as in the example given above, but the injured party and others might be provoked to retaliate leading to a breach of the peace. Thus, in the situation where A is struck by a stone thrown by B, it is a wrong not only against A but also potentially against society. Therefore, our understanding of trespass to the person is sometimes clarified by reference to the parallel provisions of criminal law.

This chapter introduces five torts of trespass to the person—battery, assault, false imprisonment, intentional infliction of emotional distress, and invasion of privacy. (Trespass to land is dealt with in Chapter 5 along with other land-based torts.) Each tort consists of several elements that the plaintiff must establish on the civil standard of the balance of probabilities. Once the plaintiff has established that it is more likely than not that a tort has been committed, the burden of proof shifts to the defendant. The defendant may avoid liability if the circumstances indicate a valid defence or statutory bar to the plaintiff's claim. This chapter also introduces the defences of consent, lawful authority, self-defence, defence of others, defence of property, and necessity, as well as the concepts of sovereign immunity and limitation periods. Finally, this chapter considers the concept of vicarious liability whereby a person or organisation may be held liable for a tort committed by another.

As a final point, it should be noted that the cases in this and the following chapters cover a significant timeframe, several dating as far back as the fifteenth century. These older cases reflect the political and social circumstances of their time. Just as it would be impossible to understand modern tort law without these foundational cases, so would it be impossible to study them ignoring the attitudes and prejudices of earlier times.

Battery

Cole v Turner
(1704) 6 Mod 149, 90 ER 958 (KB)
Holt CJ:
At *Nisi Prius*, upon evidence in trespass for assault and battery, Holt CJ declared:
1 That the least touching of another in anger is a battery. 2 If two or more meet in a narrow passage, and without any violence or design of harm, the one touches the other gently, it is no battery. 3 If any of them use violence against the other, to force his way in a rude inordinate manner, it is a battery; or any struggle about the passage, to that degree as may do hurt, is a battery.

Forde v Skinner and Others
(1830) 4 Car & P 239, 172 ER 687 (Circuit)
[**FACTS**: The defendants were parish officers. The plaintiff was a young woman, who was a pauper in the parish poor-house. By force, and against her consent, the defendants cut off her hair. In the struggle, one of her arms was bruised. The plaintiff had long hair, and kept it in a clean and neat state. The plaintiff sued in trespass. There was also evidence given that one of the defendants said to the magistrates that he would soon do something to the plaintiff and her sister 'to take their pride down'. The sister's hair was cut off in a similar way.]
Bayley J: [instructing the jury]
However desirable such a regulation as that of cutting off the hair of persons in a poor-house may be with regard to health and cleanliness, yet it is altogether unauthorised by law, and is a wrongful act, if done without the consent of the party. If, in this case, it was done violently and with force, and with the malicious intent imputed, namely, of 'taking down their pride', and not with a view to cleanliness, that will be

an aggravation, and ought to increase the damages. You will therefore decide on the motives which actuated the defendants, and according to that decision you will estimate the amount of damages.

Verdict for the plaintiff—Damages £60.

Crimes Act 1961

2(1) Interpretation

'Assault' means the act of intentionally applying or attempting to apply force to the person of another, directly or indirectly, or threatening by any act or gesture to apply such force to the person of another, if the person making the threat has, or causes the other to believe on reasonable grounds that he has, present ability to effect his purpose; and 'to assault' has a corresponding meaning.

Moir v Police

Unreported, 10 November 1986, AP 220/86 (HC)

[**Note**: *Moir v Police* is a criminal case. Moir was charged with assault under the Crimes Act 1961. The definition of criminal assault, set out above, includes the civil concepts of battery and assault.]

Jeffries J:

… The facts have been found by the learned Judge in the lower court, and must be accepted by this court, and are not in dispute. Appellant, in circumstances already described, spat at Constable Wylde with saliva striking his uniform at his shoulder. There is no suggestion he was in any way whatsoever physically injured by the act … The verb 'to spit' is the act of ejecting saliva from the mouth, but in appropriate circumstances spitting can include ejecting small objects such as peas, or food. It also has a figurative meaning in the sense one can be described as spitting when quickly uttering oaths or threats. Intentionally spitting saliva at another person is, apart from any strict act of assault, universally regarded as a gesture of contempt and defiance. It is unquestionably a highly provocative insult more often than not presaging violence.

… I turn now to the next point, and it is whether the charge does reveal that spitting in the circumstances described is in law an act of assault … The question is whether saliva ejected from the mouth of appellant landing on the Constable's body, albeit on his clothing and not on his skin, is in law an assault. The physical act of spitting was, in my view, clearly intentional and malevolent. It is sound law … and part of the definition that a threat which is completely devoid of any physical transference could be an assault. That emphasises another legal principle that the degree of force used is not an ingredient necessary to be proved. In this court's view the act of intentionally spitting by one person at another whereby the saliva ejected from the mouth lands on the body or clothing of the object person, is an assault. The court adopts and applies to the circumstances of this case the ancient case of *Cotesworth* (1704) 6 Mod 172.

Letang v Cooper

[1965] 1 QB 282 (CA)

[**FACTS**: The plaintiff was sunbathing on a lawn used for parking cars. The defendant did not see her and drove his car over her legs causing injury. The plaintiff did not sue within the 3-year statutory limitation period for negligence. She tried, instead, to bring her action within trespass using the older distinction of direct injury. Trespass allowed a longer 6-year limitation period. (Limitation periods are discussed further in this chapter in the section on statutory bars).]

Lord Denning MR:

... The argument, as it was developed before us, became a direct invitation to this court to go back to the old forms of action and to decide this case by reference to them. The statute bars an action on the case, it is said, after three years, whereas trespass to the person is not barred for six years. The argument was supported by reference to text-writers, such as *Salmond on Torts*, 18th edn (1961), p 700. I must say that if we are, at this distance of time, to revive the distinction between trespass and case, we should get into the most utter confusion. The old common lawyers tied themselves in knots over it, and we should do the same. Let me tell you some of their contortions. Under the old law, whenever one man injured another by the direct and immediate application of force, the plaintiff could sue the defendant in trespass to the person, without alleging negligence (see *Leame v Bray* [(1803) 3 East 593]), whereas if the injury was only consequential, he had to sue in case. You will remember the illustration given by Fortescue J in *Reynolds v Clarke* [(1725) 2 Ld Raymond 1399]: 'If a man throws a log into the highway, and in that act it hits me, I may maintain trespass because it is an immediate wrong; but if as it lies there I tumble over it, and receive an injury, I must bring an action upon the case; because it is only prejudicial in consequence'. Nowadays, if a man carelessly throws a piece of wood from a house into a roadway, then whether it hits the plaintiff or he tumbles over it the next moment, the action would not be trespass or case, but simply negligence.

If we were to bring back these subtleties into the law of limitation, we should produce the most absurd anomalies; and all the more so when you bear in mind that under the Fatal Accidents Act the period of limitation is three years from the death. The decision of Elwes J if correct would produce these results: it would mean that if a motorist ran down two people, killing one and injuring another, the widow would have to bring her action within three years, but the injured person would have six years. It would mean also that if a lorry driver was in a collision at a cross-roads with an owner-driver, an injured passenger would have to bring his action against the employer of the lorry driver within three years, but he would have six years in which to sue the owner-driver. Not least of all the absurdities is a case like the present. It would mean that the plaintiff could get out of the three-year limitation by suing in trespass instead of in negligence.

I must decline, therefore, to go back to the old forms of action in order to construe this statute. I know that in the last century Maitland said 'the forms of action we have buried, but they still rule us from their graves' (see Maitland, *Forms of Action* (1909), p 296), but we have in this century shaken off their trammels. These forms of action have served their day. They did at one time form a guide to substantive rights; but they do so no longer. Lord Atkin, in *United Australia Ltd v Barclays Bank Ltd* [[1941] AC 129], told us what to do about them: 'When these ghosts of the past stand in the path of justice clanking their mediaeval chains the proper course for the judge is to pass through them undeterred'.

The truth is that the distinction between trespass and case is obsolete. We have a different sub-division altogether. Instead of dividing actions for personal injuries into trespass (direct damage) or case (consequential damage), we divide the causes of action now according as the defendant did the injury intentionally or unintentionally. If one man intentionally applies force directly to another, the plaintiff has a cause of action in assault and battery, or, if you so please to describe it, in trespass to the person. 'The least touching of another in anger is a battery', per Holt CJ in *Cole v Turner*. If he does not inflict injury intentionally, but only unintentionally, the plaintiff has no cause of action today in trespass. His only cause of action is in negligence, and then only on proof of want of reasonable care. If the plaintiff cannot prove want of reasonable care, he may have no cause of action at all. Thus, it is not enough nowadays for the plaintiff to plead that 'the defendant shot the plaintiff'. He must also allege that he did it intentionally or negligently. If intentionally, it is the tort of assault and battery. If negligent and causing damage, it is the tort of negligence.

The modern law on this subject was well expounded by Diplock J in *Fowler v Lanning* [[1959] 1 QB 426], with which I fully agree. But I would go this one step further: when the injury is not inflicted intentionally, but negligently, I would say that the only cause of action is negligence and not trespass. If it were trespass, it would be actionable without proof of damage; and that is not the law today.

Fagan v Commissioner of Metropolitan Police
[1969] 1 QB 439
Lord Parker CJ:
I will ask James J to read the judgment which he has prepared, and with which I entirely agree.
James J:
The sole question is whether the prosecution proved facts which in law amounted to an assault.

On August 31, 1967, the appellant was reversing a motor car in Fortunegate Road, London, NW 10, when Police Constable Morris directed him to drive the car forwards to the kerbside and standing in front of the car pointed out a suitable place in which to park. At first the appellant stopped the car too far from the kerb for the officer's liking. Morris asked him to park closer and indicated a precise spot. The appellant drove forward towards him and stopped it with the offside wheel on Morris's left foot. 'Get off, you are on my foot', said the officer. 'Fuck you, you can wait', said the appellant. The engine of the car stopped running. Morris repeated several times 'Get off my foot'. The appellant said reluctantly 'Okay man, okay', and then slowly turned on the ignition of the vehicle and reversed it off the officer's foot. The appellant had either turned the ignition off to stop the engine or turned it off after the engine had stopped running.

...

In our judgment the question arising, which has been argued on general principles, falls to be decided on the facts of the particular case. An assault is any act which intentionally—or possibly recklessly—causes another person to apprehend immediate and unlawful personal violence. Although 'assault' is an independent crime and is to be treated as such, for practical purposes today 'assault' is generally synonymous with the term 'battery' and is a term used to mean the actual intended use of unlawful force to another person without his consent. On the facts of the present case the 'assault' alleged involved a 'battery'. Where an assault involves a battery, it matters not, in our judgment, whether the battery is inflicted directly by the body of the offender or through the medium of some weapon or instrument controlled by the action of the offender. An assault may be committed by the laying of a hand upon another, and the action does not cease to be an assault if it is a stick held in the hand and not the hand itself which is laid on the person of the victim. So for our part we see no difference in principle between the action of stepping on to a person's toe and maintaining that position and the action of driving a car on to a person's foot and sitting in the car whilst its position on the foot is maintained.

To constitute the offence of assault some intentional act must have been performed: a mere omission to act cannot amount to an assault. Without going into the question whether words alone can constitute an assault, it is clear that the words spoken by the appellant could not alone amount to an assault: they can only shed a light on the appellant's action. For our part we think the crucial question is whether in this case the act of the appellant can be said to be complete and spent at the moment of time when the car wheel came to rest on the foot or whether his act is to be regarded as a continuing act operating until the wheel was removed. In our judgment a distinction is to be drawn between acts which are complete—though results may continue to flow—and those acts which are continuing. Once the act is complete it cannot thereafter be said to be a threat to inflict unlawful force upon the victim. If the act, as distinct from the result thereof, is a continuing act there is a continuing threat to inflict unlawful force. If the assault involves a battery and that battery continues there is a continuing act of assault.

… On the facts found the action of the appellant may have been initially unintentional, but the time came when knowing that the wheel was on the officer's foot the appellant (1) remained seated in the car so that his body through the medium of the car was in contact with the officer, (2) switched off the ignition of the car, (3) maintained the wheel of the car on the foot and (4) used words indicating the intention of keeping the wheel in that position. For our part we cannot regard such conduct as mere omission or inactivity.

There was an act constituting a battery …

We would dismiss this appeal.

Bridge J:

… I have no sympathy at all for the appellant who behaved disgracefully. But I have been unable to find any way of regarding the facts which satisfies me that they amounted to the crime of assault. This has not been for want of trying. But at every attempt I have encountered the inescapable question: after the wheel of the appellant's car had accidentally come to rest on the constable's foot, what was it that the appellant did which constituted the act of assault? However the question is approached, the answer I feel obliged to give is: precisely nothing. The car rested on the foot by its own weight and remained stationary by its own inertia. The appellant's fault was that he omitted to manipulate the controls to set it in motion again.

Neither the fact that the appellant was in the driver's seat nor that he switched off the ignition seem to me to be of any relevance. The constable's plight would have been no better, but might well have been worse, if the appellant had alighted from the car leaving the ignition switched on. Similarly I can get no help from the suggested analogies. If one man accidentally treads on another's toe or touches him with a stick, but deliberately maintains pressure with foot or stick after the victim protests, there is clearly an assault. But there is no true parallel between such cases and the present case. It is not, to my mind, a legitimate use of language to speak of the appellant 'holding' or 'maintaining' the car wheel on the constable's foot. The expression which corresponds to the reality is that used by the justices in the case stated. They say, quite rightly, that he 'allowed' the wheel to remain.

With a reluctantly dissenting voice I would allow this appeal and quash the appellant's conviction.

Wilson v Pringle
[1987] QB 237; [1986] 2 All ER 440 (CA)

[**FACTS**: The plaintiff Wilson and defendant Pringle were both 13-year-old schoolboys. The defendant pulled a sports bag off the plaintiff's shoulder. As a result, the plaintiff fell to the ground and injured his hip. The defendant pleaded that his act was simply horseplay between fellow students. He also asserted that the plaintiff was breaking a school rule by carrying the bag over his shoulder, and so he was entitled to pull it off. The plaintiff was granted summary judgment. The defendant appealed the order. As a result of his success here, the matter was referred back for retrial. We do not know what the final result was.]

Croom-Johnson J:

... A convenient starting point is *Weaver v Ward* (1616) Hob 134, 80 ER 284. The plaintiff and defendant were exercising in the trained band with live ammunition. The defendant shot the plaintiff. The plaintiff sued the defendant in trespass. The defendant confessed and avoided. He pleaded that he had not shot the plaintiff intentionally. That plea was held to be demurrable. The defendant could not be excused of trespass 'except it be judged utterly without his fault'. In other words the defendant would be liable in trespass if he acted negligently, even though he had no intention to shoot the plaintiff. Nowadays an action such as that could only be brought in trespass on the case, in negligence.

Tuberville v Savage (1669) 1 Mod Rep 3, 86 ER 684 was an action for assault. The defendant clapped his hand on his sword and said to the plaintiff, 'If it were not assize time, I would not take such language'. The court ruled that there was no threat, and accordingly no assault. This case is authority that there must be not only a deliberate threat (in an assault) or a deliberate touching (in battery) but also hostile behaviour. If the intention is obviously hostile, that will suffice, but it was recognised that there are many circumstances in life where contact with one's fellow men is not only unavoidable but even if deliberate may also be innocent. It was said, 'If one strike another upon the hand, the arm, or breast in discourse, it is no assault, there being no intention to assault; but if one, intending to assault, strike at another and miss him, this is an assault'.

Cole v Turner (1704) Holt KB 108, 90 ER 958 was an action in trespass for assault and battery. Holt CJ ruled that the least touching is a battery if it is done in anger, but that touching without violence or design of harm is no battery, and that violence in a rude and inordinate manner is a battery. Again, the case is authority for the proposition that for a battery there must be either an intention to harm or overt hostility.

...

In the action for negligence the physical contact (where it takes place at all) is normally though by no means always unintended. In the action for trespass, to constitute battery, it is deliberate. Even so, it is not every intended contact which is tortious. Apart from special justifications (such as acting in self-defence) there are many examples in everyday life where an intended contact or touch is not actionable as a trespass. These are not necessarily those (such as shaking hands) where consent is actual or to be implied. They may amount to one of the instances had in mind in *Tuberville v Savage* which take place in innocence. A modern instance is the batsman walking up the pavilion steps at Lords after making a century. He receives hearty slaps of congratulation on his back. He may not want them. Some of them may be too heavy for comfort. No one seeks his permission, or can assume he would give it if it were asked. But would an action for trespass to the person lie?

Another ingredient in the tort of trespass to the person is that of hostility. The references to anger sufficing to turn a touch into a battery (*Cole v Turner*) and the lack of an intention to assault which prevents a gesture from being an assault are instances of this. If there is hostile intent, that will by itself be cogent evidence of hostility. But the hostility may be demonstrated in other ways.

The defendant in the present case has sought to add to the list of necessary ingredients. He has submitted that before trespass to the person will lie it is not only the touching that must be deliberate, but the infliction of injury. The plaintiff's counsel, on the other hand, contends that it is not the injury to the person which must be intentional, but the act of touching or battery which precedes it; as he put it, 'what must be intentional is the application of force and not the injury' ...

[**Note**: The Court discussed *Fowler v Lanning* [1959] 1 QB 426 and *Letang v Cooper* [1965] 1 QB 382.]

In our view, the submission made by counsel for the plaintiff is correct. It is the act and not the injury which must be intentional. An intention to injure is not essential to an action for trespass to the person. It is the mere trespass by itself which is the offence.

That does not answer the question, what does entitle an injured plaintiff to sue for the tort of trespass to the person? Reference must be made to one further case: *Williams v Humphrey* (12 February 1975, unreported), decided by Talbot J. There the defendant, a boy just under 16, pushed the plaintiff into a swimming pool and caused him physical injury. The judge found the defendant acted negligently and awarded damages. But there was another claim of trespass. Talbot J rejected the submission that the action would not lie unless there was an intent to injure. He held that it was sufficient, if the act was intentional, that there was no justification for it. In the present proceedings the judge relied on that decision.

The reasoning in *Williams v Humphrey* is all right as far as it goes, but it does not go far enough. It did not give effect to the reasoning of the older authorities, such as *Tuberville v Savage*, *Cole v Turner*, and *Williams v Jones* that for there to be either an assault or a battery there must be something in the nature of hostility. It may be evinced by anger, by words or gesture. Sometimes the very act of battery will speak for itself, as where somebody uses a weapon on another.

What, then, turns a friendly touching (which is not actionable) into an unfriendly one (which is)?

[**Note**: The Court discussed *Collins v Wilcock* [1984] 3 All ER 374, [1984] 1 WLR 1172—see the case report below in the section entitled 'Lawful authority'.]

In our view, the authorities lead one to the conclusion that in a battery there must be an intentional touching or contact in one form or another of the plaintiff by the defendant. That touching must be proved to be hostile touching. That still leaves unanswered the question, when is a touching to be called hostile? Hostility cannot be equated with ill-will or malevolence. It cannot be governed by the obvious intention shown in acts like punching, stabbing or shooting. It cannot be solely governed by an expressed intention, although that may be strong evidence. But the element of hostility, in the sense in which it is now to be considered, must be a question of fact for the tribunal of fact. It may be imported from the circumstances. Take the example of the police officer in *Collins v Wilcock*. She touched the woman deliberately, but without an intention to do more than restrain her temporarily. Nevertheless, she was acting unlawfully and in that way was acting with hostility. She was acting contrary to the woman's legal right not to be physically restrained. We see no more difficulty in establishing what she intended by means of question and answer, or by inference from the surrounding circumstances, than there is in establishing whether an apparently playful blow was struck in anger. The rules of law governing the legality of arrest may require strict application to the facts of appropriate cases, but in the ordinary give and take of everyday life the tribunal of fact should find no difficulty in answering the question, 'was this, or was it not, a battery?' Where the immediate act of touching does not itself demonstrate hostility, the plaintiff should plead the facts which are said to do so. Although we are all entitled to protection from physical molestation, we live in [a] crowded world in which people must be considered as taking on themselves some risk of injury (where it occurs) from the acts of others which are not in themselves unlawful. If negligence cannot be proved, it may be that an injured plaintiff who is also unable to prove a battery, will be without redress.

Defences like self-defence, and exercising the right of arrest, are relevant here. Similarly, it may be that allowances must be made, where appropriate, for the idiosyncrasies of individuals or (as was demonstrated in *Walmsley v Humenick* [1954] 2 DLR 232) the irresponsibility of childhood and the degree of care and awareness which is to be expected of children.

In our judgment the judge who tried the proceedings took too narrow a view of what has to be proved in order to make out a case of trespass to the person. It will be apparent that here are a number of questions which must be investigated in evidence. Accordingly we would allow this appeal, and give unconditional leave to defend. The court will invite submissions as to what directions are required for the further conduct of the action.

Lambertson v United States

(1976) 528 F 2d 441 (2nd Cir)

Van Graafeiland J:

This is an appeal from an order of Judge Edmund Port of the United States District Court from the Northern District of New York dismissing plaintiff's action against the United States as barred by 28 USC § 2680(h). We affirm.

Appellant, an employee of Armour & Co, sustained serious injuries to his mouth as a result of the actions of one William Boslet, a meat inspector for the United States Department of Agriculture. For the most part, the circumstances of the incident are not in dispute. What variations do exist are not significant for purposes of this appeal.

On August 30, 1972, a truck shipment of beef arrived at the receiving dock of Armour's Syracuse plant. Plaintiff was one of the employees assigned to unload this truck. While he was so engaged, he was suddenly and without warning jumped by Boslet (Boslet was on duty at the time) who, screaming 'boo', pulled the plaintiff's wool stocking hat over his eyes and, climbing on his back, began to ride him piggy-back. As a result of this action, plaintiff fell forward and struck his face on some meat hooks located on the receiving dock (these meat hooks were no more than six inches away from plaintiff's head when Boslet jumped on his back), suffering severe injuries to his mouth and teeth.

It is apparently agreed by all witnesses that the mishap was the result of one-sided horseplay with no intention on Boslet's part to injure the plaintiff. Indeed, immediately after the incident Boslet apologised to the plaintiff, telling him that he was only playing around and meant no harm.

Seeking redress for his injuries, plaintiff commenced the instant action against the United States pursuant to the Federal Tort Claims Act, 28 USC § 1346(b).

Traditionally, the sovereign has always been immune from suit. To alleviate the harshness of this rule, Congress enacted the Federal Tort Claims Act which permits civil actions against the United States for personal injury and property damage caused by the 'negligent or wrongful act or omission of any employee of the Government while acting within the scope of his office or employment': 28 USC § 1346(b). 28 USC § 2680, however, lists several claims expressly excepted from the purview of the Act, among which are any claims arising out of an assault or battery. Since the United States has not consented to be sued for these torts, federal courts are without jurisdiction to entertain a suit based on them.

Although his order contains no express statement to that effect, the parties agree that the sole basis for Judge Port's dismissal was his conclusion that Boslet's actions constituted a battery. Appellant contests this conclusion and steadfastly maintains that his complaint sounds in negligence.

...

It is hornbook law in New York, as in most other jurisdictions, that the intent which is an essential element of the action for battery is the intent to make contact, not to do injury. *Masters v Becker*, 22 AD 2d 118, 254 NYS 2d 633 (2d Dept 1964); W. Prosser, *Law of Torts* §8, at 31 (4th edn 1971); 1 Harper and James, *The Law of Torts* 216 (1956). As the court stated in *Masters, supra*, 22 AD 2d 120, 254 NYS 2d 635: 'A plaintiff in an action to recover damages for an assault founded on bodily contact, must prove only that there was bodily contact; that such contact was offensive; and that the defendant intended to make the contact. The plaintiff is not required to prove that defendant intended physically to injure him. Certainly he is not required to prove an intention to cause the specific injuries resulting from the contact'.

Harper and James put it that 'it is a battery for a man ... to play a joke upon another which involves a harmful or offensive act'. Prosser says that 'a defendant may be liable where he has intended only a joke': Accord *Restatement (Second) of Torts* §13, comment c [1995]. Since there is not the remotest suggestion that Boslet's leap onto plaintiff's back, his piggyback ride and his use of plaintiff's hat as a blindfold might have been accidental, there was no error in the District Court's determination that it was a battery.

To say the plaintiff's claim was not one 'arising out of' a battery would be to blink at the exclusionary provisions of § 2680. This has not been done in other cases in which plaintiffs have sought to avoid the intentional tort exclusions of § 2680 by claims of negligence.

...

We would find it much more pleasant to reach a decision based on what we wish Congress had said, rather than what it did say. However, to permit plaintiff to recover by 'dressing up the substance of battery in the garments of negligence would be to judicially admit at the back door that which has been legislatively turned away at the front door'. *Laird v Nelms*, 406 US 797, 802, 32 L Ed 2d 499 (1972). Affirmed.

Bettel v Yim
(1978) 88 DLR 3d 543 (Ont Co Ct)
[**FACTS**: Bettel was shaken by Yim, receiving a broken nose and suffering complications necessitating multiple surgeries. Yim had not meant to cause severe injuries. However, Judge Borins found Yim liable for all damages.]
Borins J:

In the law of intentional torts, it is the dignitary interest, the right of the plaintiff to insist that the defendant keep his hands to himself, that the law has for centuries sought to protect. In doing so, the morality of the defendant's conduct, characterised as 'unlawful', has predominated the thinking of the Courts and is reflected in academic discussions. The logical test is whether the defendant was guilty of deliberate, intentional and unlawful violence or threats of violence. If he was, and a more serious harm befalls the plaintiff than was intended by the defendant, the defendant, and not the innocent plaintiff, must bear the responsibility for the unintended result.

If physical contact was intended, the fact that its magnitude exceeded all reasonable or intended expectations should make no difference. To hold otherwise, in my opinion, would unduly narrow recovery where one deliberately invades the bodily interests of another with the result that the totally innocent plaintiff would be deprived of full recovery for the totality of the injuries suffered as a result of the deliberate invasion of his bodily interests. To import negligence concepts into the field of intentional torts would be to ignore the essential difference between the intentional infliction of harm and the unintentional infliction of harm resulting from a failure to adhere to a reasonable standard of care, and would result in bonusing the deliberate wrongdoer who strikes the plaintiff more forcefully than intended. For example, in the case of a deliberate blow to the eye, liability should cover not only the black eye and the bloody nose but also the resultant brain damage caused when the plaintiff falls to the ground and strikes his head, even though the latter was never intended. Thus, the intentional wrongdoer should bear the responsibility for the injuries caused by his conduct and the negligence test of 'foreseeability' to limit, or eliminate, liability should not be imported into the field of intentional torts.

Defences to intentional torts

Once the plaintiff has established that a tort has likely been committed, it is open to the defendant to argue that liability should not be imposed by invoking a defence to the plaintiff's claim. The defences are presented here within a series of cases, mostly in response to the tort of battery. However, these defences are also generally available under the other intentional torts, including, where appropriate, the tort of trespass to land, which appears in the later chapter on land-based torts. Note that *Collins v Wilcock* (below, under 'Lawful authority', establishes what Goff LJ terms a 'general exception' to battery—that is, touching that comes within 'the exigencies of everyday life'. He further supported this view in *F v West Berkshire Health Authority* (below, under 'Necessity'). Occasionally, casual touching, which is not generally seen as offensive, is also seen as covered by implied consent, though Lord Goff disputes this in *F v West Berkshire Health Authority*. It is necessary to be aware, therefore, that the defence cases overlap to some extent.

Consent

Mulloy v Hop Sang
[1935] 1 WWR 714 (Alta DC)

Jackson DCJ:

The plaintiff's claim is for professional fees for an operation involving the amputation of the defendant's hand which was badly injured in a motor-car accident. The accident took place near the town of Cardston and the defendant was taken to the hospital there. The plaintiff, a physician and surgeon duly qualified to practice, was called to the hospital and the defendant, being a stranger and unacquainted with the plaintiff, asked him to fix up his hand but not to cut it off as he wanted to have it looked after in Lethbridge, his home city. Later on in the operating room the defendant repeated his request that he did not want his hand cut off. The doctor, being more concerned in relieving the suffering of the patient, replied that he would be governed by the conditions found when the anaesthetic had been administered. The defendant said nothing. As the hand was covered by an old piece of cloth and it was necessary to administer an anaesthetic before doing anything, the doctor was not in a position to advise what should be done. On examination he decided an operation was necessary and the hand was amputated. Dr Mulloy said the wounds indicated an operation as the condition of the hand was such that delay would mean blood poisoning with no possibility of saving it. In this he was supported by the two other attending physicians. I am, however, not satisfied that the defendant could not have been rushed to Lethbridge where he evidently wished to consult with a physician whom he knew and relied on. Dr Mulloy took it for granted when the defendant, a Chinaman without much education in English and probably not of any more than average mentality, did not reply or make any objection to his statement that he would be governed by conditions as he found them, that he had full power to go ahead and perform an operation if found necessary. On the other hand, the defendant did not, in my opinion, understand what the doctor meant, and he would most likely have refused to allow the operation if he did. Further, he did not consider it necessary to reply as he had already given explicit instructions.

Under these circumstances I think the plaintiff should have made full explanation and should have endeavoured to get the defendant to consent to an operation, if necessary. It might have been different if the defendant had submitted himself generally to the doctor and had pleaded with him not to perform an operation and the doctor found it necessary to do so afterwards. The defendant's instructions were precedent and went to the root of the employment. The plaintiff did not do the work he was hired to do and must, in my opinion, fail in his action.

The defendant has counterclaimed for damages in the sum of $400, being $150 for an artificial hand and the balance for loss of wages due to the operation and possibly general damages.

In my opinion the operation was necessary and performed in a highly satisfactory manner. Indeed, there was no suggestion otherwise. The damage and loss and the cost of an artificial hand are the results of the accident and not the unauthorised operation. The defendant, however, is, in my opinion, entitled to damages because of the trespass to the person, which at the same time became trespass *ab initio*, having in mind the old case of *The Six Carpenters* (1610) 8 Co Rep 146a, 77 ER 695. The damages are *per se* and should be more than nominal. Personally, I in a similar position might have been able to satisfy myself that the operation was necessary, and that I should be glad to pay the reasonable fee charged, but it was not my hand and the defendant will always no doubt feel that he might have saved the hand if he had consulted with a doctor he knew. While I might have been able to forego my rights, I cannot ask the defendant to do so and he is entitled to rely on his rights. There also must have been some shock to him when he found out his hand had been taken off in the manner in which it was, over and above the ordinary shock from an operation. His damages, should, therefore, be substantial but only sufficient to make them substantial rather than nominal. I place the amount at $50.

McNamara v Duncan

(1971) 26 ALR 584 (SC ACT)

Fox J:

In this case the plaintiff sues for damages for injuries he suffered while playing a game of Australian Rules Football. The defendant was a member of the opposing team. The cause of action relied upon is trespass to the person, the principal contention being that the defendant struck the plaintiff intentionally.

The plaintiff's skull was fractured at a point just behind the top of the right ear. Complications followed which were for a time very serious and the plaintiff has been left with a degree of permanent disability. There is no doubt that the injury was caused by contact with some portion of the defendant's body.

As perhaps is only to be expected when a number of people try to give their accounts of one incident in a football match which took place two and a half years ago, there is a considerable diversity of evidence as to exactly what happened. In general I do not doubt that the witnesses have endeavoured to give an honest recollection of what they saw, but the evidence of some at least of them is obviously unreliable …

It is, I think, a reasonable inference that the fracture of the plaintiff's skull was caused by a fairly sharp and fairly forceful blow. It is certainly more likely that it was caused by a fist or an elbow than by an open hand, the lower or upper part of an arm or the side of the defendant's body. The field umpire, who was only some 10 or 15 yards away, and in a good position to observe, said that he took particular notice of what was happening. He says that after the ball was kicked the defendant continued to run towards the plaintiff and, as he came upon him, he raised his left elbow and struck the plaintiff on the right side of his head. The umpire says that he immediately blew his whistle, took the defendant's number and told him that he would be reported ...

... I feel comfortably satisfied that the account given by the umpire is substantially correct.

Counsel for the defendant says, however, that even if the defendant struck the plaintiff with his elbow in the way mentioned, it was accidental or, in any event, it was the sort of blow which a person playing Australian Rules must expect. The injury, it was said, was part of the game.

... It is agreed on both sides that an intentional striking of the head of a player (ie any part above the shoulders) is an infringement of the laws [of the game]. For such an act a free kick should be awarded to the opposing team (laws 17(j), 17(k)) and the player concerned should be reported to the controlling body (laws 28(a)(xii), 28(a)(xiii)). Whether an unintentional blow to the head is an infringement is not so clear. Perhaps, in practice, the umpire ignores such acts when obviously accidental, and treats all others as infringements. Interfering with a player who is not in possession of the ball is an infringement (laws 17(e), 17(o)), but there is some disagreement by the experts who gave evidence before me as to the relevant laws a lawyer could venture the view that the tackling or interference must be deliberate.

I have come to the conclusion that the striking of the plaintiff by the defendant was intentional; he meant to do it. I do not suggest that he meant to incapacitate the plaintiff or indeed to cause him any serious injury ... I suspect that his purpose was to get the plaintiff out of his way, or discourage him from getting in the way. There is no suggestion that he had to raise his arm to fend off any movement of the plaintiff. The elbow was raised high and, as I see the position, it was sharply bent. The evidence is to the effect that such a posture is not part of any movement or manoeuvre which at the time and in the circumstances was appropriate. What he did can hardly be understood as an act in the ordinary, legitimate, course of a game of football.

The striking was an infringement, a serious infringement, of the rules. The risk of being injured by such an act is not part of the game, if the game is being played according to the rules. But counsel [for the defendant] says that this sort of thing, even if not within the rules, is bound to happen from time to time, and the plaintiff must be treated as having accepted the risk that it would happen. The thesis is that a little bit of foul play is a common, if not invariable, concomitant of a game of football (or at least of Australian Rules Football) and no legal right arises in a player who is injured thereby.

...

I do not think it can be reasonably held that the plaintiff consented to receiving a blow such as he received in the present case. It was contrary to the rules and was deliberate. Forcible bodily contact is of course part of Australian Rules Football, as it is with some other codes of football, but such contact finds justification in the rules and usages of the game. *Winfield* ... says (at p 748) in relation to a non–prize fight, 'a boxer may consent to accidental fouls, but not to deliberate ones'. *Street on Torts* (4th edn, p 75) deals with the presumed ambit of consent in cases of accidental injury: 'A footballer consents to those tackles which the rules permit, and, it is thought, to those tackles contravening the rules where the rule infringed is framed to maintain the skill of the game; but otherwise if his opponent gouges out an eye or perhaps even tackles against the rules and dangerously'. Prosser, *Law of Torts* (3rd edn, p 103) says: 'One who enters into a sport, game or contest may be taken to consent to physical contacts consistent with the understood rules of the game'.

...

The *American Restatement of the Laws of Torts*, 2nd edn (1965), which deals at length with consent in relation to battery, states the following proposition (at p 86):

> (b) *Taking part in a game*: Taking part in a game manifests a willingness to submit to such bodily contacts or restrictions of liberty as are permitted by its rules or usages. Participating in such a game does not manifest consent to contacts which are prohibited by rules or usages of the game if such rules or usages are designed to protect the participants and not merely to secure the better playing of the game as a test of skill. This is true, although the player knows that those with or against whom he is playing are habitual violators of such rules.

Sports and games differ in their objects and in what is expected of the actors. In the game of Australian Rules Football, deliberate injury, in the sense of something done solely or principally with a view to causing sensible hurt, is not justified by the rules and usages of the game. Sensible hurt, produced as a result of intentional acts, is on the other hand an inevitable concomitant of ordinary play.

It will have been seen that in the view of the *Restatement* a player is not to be taken as having consented to prohibited acts, even although it is known that they may, and probably will occur. As the present case is concerned with deliberate injury, it is not necessary to inquire whether there are any qualifications to this proposition when the injury is not deliberate. In my view, there is none when the injury was deliberately inflicted, in the sense that I have mentioned ...

I am therefore of the opinion that the plaintiff is entitled to succeed. It remains to consider the question of damages.

The plaintiff was 23 at the time of the injury. He was operated on the night on which it occurred (15 September 1968) and a large extradural clot, which would soon have proved fatal, was drained from around his brain. As the operation was not completely successful, he again underwent surgery on the following afternoon when an extensive area of bone was removed from the side of his head. He remained unconscious for about 10 days, but thereafter improved rapidly. About 12 days later he was discharged from hospital. He was at home a further three weeks before returning to his employment as a public servant with the Treasury. In March 1969 he returned to hospital to have a protective plate inserted in his skull. Although his head was sore after this operation he returned to work almost immediately. His employment in the public service has not been adversely affected by the injury, although, because of the permanent effects I have mentioned, some forms of employment may be denied to him. He was a keen sport and his activities in that direction have had to be limited because of the effects of the injury. The main sequelae have been as follows:

(a) headaches, which were very frequent, but which now occur every two or three weeks;

(b) difficulty in focusing the right eye because of damage to the nerve behind it; this was bad for about two months but has now virtually disappeared;

(c) discomfort in the left leg ('a tired' feeling) which is described by Dr Robson as spacticity; this condition is due to nerve damage and is now static and permanent.

The plate in the plaintiff's skull does not of itself cause any trouble, although, because of it, special care must always be taken to avoid further injury in that area and contact sports have to be avoided. The leg condition leads to lack of balance and loss of agility but Dr Robson thinks that, to some extent, the plaintiff will learn to adapt. The out-of-pocket expenses, and loss of wages to date, amount to $1279.42. In my opinion the appropriate award of damages is $6000 and I order that judgment be entered for the plaintiff for that amount with costs.

H v R
[1996] 1 NZLR 299 (HC)

[**FACTS**: P was seven years old when he first met D in 1967. Between 1967 and 1975, D sexually assaulted P with acts of anal and oral sex. P had a troubled adolescence. He attempted to confront D in an altercation in 1976. P later married in 1989. In the course of relationship counselling in 1991–92, P recognised that he had been sexually abused as a child and adolescent. P filed a criminal complaint against D in 1993. The prosecution did not proceed as P did not want to involve friends who might corroborate the instances of abuse. P filed the current proceedings in 1994.]

Hammond J:
The plaintiff claims compensatory and exemplary damages for sexual abuse alleged to have been inflicted on him by the defendant over 20 years ago. The plaintiff was then in his early teens. The causes of action alleged are tortious battery; and breach of fiduciary duty. The defences are a denial of the abuse; limitation defences are pleaded; and the damages sought (if the claim is made out) are said to be excessive. Counsel suggest this is the first judgment, on the merits, in a claim of this kind to be handed down in New Zealand.

...

In sexual abuse cases, a conceptual difficulty with the tort has been as to whether an absence of consent is an element of the tort, or a defence. It seems to me that to the extent that it has always been necessary for the plaintiff to prove a hostile intent to ground this tort, the burden of demonstrating a lack of consent must be surmounted by the plaintiff, of course on the civil standard. If this is so, lack of consent has always been, *strictu sensu*, an element of the offence. In any event, whatever doubts there might have been on this issue, in this Court it seems to me that the point is resolved by the decision of the Court of Appeal in *S v G* [1995] 3 NZLR 681. Gault J there said at p 687:

With reference to the cause of action for assault and battery in which damage is not an element, Blanchard J applied the reasonable discoverability approach to the recognition of the lack of true consent to the conduct (which is an element of the cause of action). On appeal no argument was directed to that point—it seems on the basis that if reasonable discoverability is to be applied in cases such as this, it can be invoked in this manner also. We accept that as a correct view.

As to 'consent', that word has its ordinary everyday meaning: such must be a rational decision by a person who is in a position to make an informed decision. Generally, under-aged children cannot make such decisions. It is precisely for that reason that there are extensive protection provisions against sexual activities in our Crimes Act 1961.

[**Note**: Hammond J went on to find that the tort of battery was made out and, further, that it was not statute barred under the Limitation Act 1950.]

… [D's counsel] candidly said that the amended claim for exemplary damages (in the sum of $250 000) was set at that figure to bring the claim within the jurisdiction of the High Court rather than another Court.

As to the factors bearing on a claim for exemplary damages in this case, P was grossly abused. The effect on his life has already been set out. But I doubt if every adverse effect that occurred during his life can be laid at D's door …

There is this too to consider. As P told me, what he seeks in this case is 'justice'. What he meant by that, as he specifically told me, is less 'money' than recognition of what had occurred to him at the hands of D. He has not had that recognition in a Court of law. That is important to him, for all sorts of complex psychosocial reasons; socially; and for his future. Perhaps I might note in passing that I made the observation to counsel in the course of argument that the Court wondered whether, even if the actions were time-barred, it might not be open to a Court to make a declaration under the Declaratory Judgments Act 1908 in a case like this declaring the wrong and perhaps awarding a successful plaintiff full costs. The Limitation Act merely bars the remedy; it does not destroy the underlying cause of action. And our legal system does have such things as paternity orders, which are essentially declaratory in nature. Too often common lawyers undervalue the therapeutic and restorative value of declaratory orders. That is one of the weak features of our present body of jurisprudence. But I need not finally pass on that matter here, and I do not do so.

Other factors in this case are the financial position of the defendant. He is not legally aided. He is funding his defence himself.

Doing the best I can with it, I award the plaintiff $20 000 in exemplary damages.

Non-Marine Underwriters, Lloyd's of London v Scalera

[2000] 1 SCR SS 1; (2000) SCC 24 (SC)

[**FACTS**: Scalera was sued for several acts of sexual battery against a young girl ('the "plaintiff"'). The acts took place over several years, when the plaintiff was between the ages of 12 and 16. Scalera had an insurance policy with Non-Marine Underwriters to indemnify against certain lawsuits. The policy excluded claims arising from bodily injury caused by intentional or criminal acts or omissions. Whether there was a viable defence of consent was relevant to Scalera's ability to claim.]

McLachlin J:

I have read the reasons of Iacobucci J and agree with the result he reaches and with much of his reasoning. I would respectfully disagree, however, from the view that in the tort of sexual battery, the onus rests on the plaintiff to prove that the defendant either knew that she was not consenting or that a reasonable person in the defendant's position would have known that she was not consenting.

As Goff LJ (as he then was) stated in *Collins v Wilcock* [1984] 3 All ER 374 (QB) at p 378, '[t]he fundamental principle, plain and incontestable, is that every person's body is inviolate'. The law of battery protects this inviolability, and it is for those who violate the physical integrity of others to justify their actions. Accordingly, in my respectful view, the plaintiff who alleges sexual battery makes her case by tendering evidence of force applied directly to her. 'Force', in the context of an allegation of sexual battery, simply refers to physical contact of a sexual nature, and is neutral in the sense of not necessarily connoting a lack of consent. If the defendant does not dispute that the contact took place, he bears the burden of proving that the plaintiff consented or that a reasonable person in his position would have thought that she consented. My reasons for so concluding are the following.

... In *Reibl v Hughes* [1980] 2 SCR 880 at p 890, dealing with medical battery, Laskin CJ stated for the Court that:

> The tort [of battery] is an intentional one, consisting of an unprivileged and unconsented to invasion of one's bodily security. True enough, it has some advantages for a plaintiff over an action of negligence since it does not require proof of causation and it casts upon the defendant the burden of proving consent to what was done.

And in *Norberg v Wynrib* [1992] 2 SCR 226, dealing with sexual battery, La Forest J, for the plurality, stated, at p 246, that '[a] battery is the intentional infliction of unlawful force on another person. Consent, express or implied is a defence to battery'. None of the members of the Court participating in the decision dissented from the view that the burden lies on the defendant to prove consent.

The question, then, is whether we should in this case depart from the settled rule that requires the plaintiff in a battery case to show only contact through a direct, intentional act of the defendant and places the onus on the defendant of showing consent or lawful excuse, including actual or constructive consent. For the reasons that follow, I am not convinced that we should alter the established rule.

...

The proposition that the law should require a plaintiff in an action for sexual battery to prove that she did not consent, is supported, it is suggested, by a requirement that the contact involved in battery must be harmful or offensive. The argument may be summarised as follows. The plaintiff must prove all the essential elements of the tort of battery. One of these is that the contact complained of was inherently harmful or offensive on an objective standard. Consensual sexual contact is neither harmful nor offensive. Therefore the plaintiff, in order to make out her case, must prove that she did not consent or that a reasonable person in the defendant's position would not have thought she consented.

I do not dispute that a plaintiff generally must prove all elements of the tort she alleges. Nor do I dispute that contact must be 'harmful or offensive' to constitute battery. However, I am not persuaded that plaintiffs in cases of sexual battery must prove that contact was 'non-consensual' in order to prove that it was 'harmful or offensive'. If one accepts that the foundation of the tort of battery is a violation of personal autonomy, it follows that all contact outside the exceptional category of contact that is generally accepted or expected in the course of ordinary life, is *prima facie* offensive. Sexual contact does not fall into the category of contact generally accepted or expected in the course of ordinary activities. Hence the plaintiff may establish an action for sexual battery without negativing actual or constructive consent.

The idea that battery is confined to conduct that is 'harmful or offensive' finds root in the old cases involving trivial contacts. While the law of battery traditionally has held that the defendant, not the plaintiff, bears the onus of proving consent, it has also held that not every trivial contact suffices to establish battery. The classic example is being jostled in a crowd. A person who enters a crowd cannot sue for being jostled; such contact is not 'offensive'. Two theories have been put forward to explain this wrinkle on the general rule that all a plaintiff in a battery action must prove is direct contact. The first is implied consent: *Salmond and Heuston on the Law of Torts* (21st edn 1996) at p 121. The second sees these cases as 'a general exception embracing all physical contact which is generally acceptable in the ordinary conduct of everyday life': *In re F* [1990] 2 AC 1 (HL) at p 73 per Lord Goff.

Both these theories are consistent with the settled rule in Canadian law that a plaintiff in a battery action need not prove the absence of consent. On the implied consent theory, even if the plaintiff proves contact, the burden never shifts to the defendant to prove consent because consent is implied by law. On the 'exception' theory, the plaintiff cannot succeed merely by proving contact if such contact falls within the exceptional category of conduct generally acceptable in ordinary life. It is not necessary in this appeal to choose between these approaches, but in my view both refer to the sort of everyday physical contact which one must be expected to tolerate, even if one does not actually consent to it.

The question then becomes whether sexual battery falls into the extraordinary category of cases where proving contact will not suffice to establish the plaintiff's case. Is sexual activity the sort of activity where consent is implied? Clearly it is not. Alternatively, is it the sort of activity, like being jostled in a crowd, that is generally accepted and expected as a normal part of life? Again, I think not. The sort of conduct the cases envision is the inevitable contact that goes with ordinary human activity, like brushing someone's hand in the course of exchanging a gift, a gratuitous handshake, or being jostled in a crowd. Sexual contact does not fall into this category. It is not the casual, accidental or inevitable consequence of general human activity and interaction. It involves singling out another person's body in a deliberate, targeted act.

The assertion in some of the authorities that the contact must be harmful or offensive to constitute battery (see, eg La Forest J in *M (K) v M (H)* [1992] 3 SCR 6 at p 25), reflects the need to exclude from battery the casual contacts inevitable in ordinary life. It does not, however, require the conclusion that to make out a case of battery, a plaintiff must prove that the contact was physically or psychologically injurious or morally offensive. The law of battery protects the inviolability of the person. It starts from the presumption that apart from the usual and inevitable contacts of ordinary life, each person is entitled not to be touched, and not to have her person violated. The sexual touching itself, absent the defendant showing lawful excuse, constitutes the violation and is 'offensive'. Sex is not an ordinary casual contact which must be accepted in everyday life, nor is it the sort of contact to which consent can be implied. To require a plaintiff in an action for sexual battery to prove that she did not consent or that a reasonable person in the defendant's position would not have thought she consented, would be to deny the protection the law has traditionally afforded to the inviolability of the body in the situation where it is perhaps most needed and appropriate.

Only two cases, one in England concerning therapeutic administration of drugs and one in New Zealand concerning sexual assault, are cited in favour of the proposition that the plaintiff must show harm by proving a lack of consent as an element of the tort of battery: see *Freeman v Home Office* [1983] 3 All ER 589 (QB), aff'd [1984] 1 All ER 1036 (CA), *H v R* [1996] 1 NZLR 299 (HC). The proposition that the plaintiff must prove a lack of consent, on the basis that she must prove that the impugned contact was harmful, is not supported by the law of battery, which has traditionally not been confined to acts which are inherently harmful, like hitting, shooting or stabbing someone. Rather, its focus is on the protection of one's bodily integrity from any unwanted contact. Many of the older cases concern contacts devoid of any real harm apart from the violation of bodily integrity: *Pursell v Horn* (1838) 8 AD & E 602, 112 ER 966 (pouring water on a person); *Green v Goddard* (1704) 2 Salkeld 641, 91 ER 540 (forcibly taking an object held by another); *Humphries v Connor* (1864) 17 Ir Com L Rep 1 (QB) (taking [off a] flower worn by plaintiff), and *Forde v Skinner* (1830) 4 Car & P 239, 172 ER 687 (cutting a person's hair). In more modern times, the same is true of medical battery cases. Like sexual acts, medical interventions may incidentally produce physical and psychological harm which may go to damages, but the basic 'offence' or 'harm' upon which the tort rests is the violation of the plaintiff's bodily integrity. As I discuss below, Canadian courts do not require plaintiffs alleging medical battery to prove that the defendant medical practitioner knew or ought to have known that the plaintiff did not consent to the medical contact.

The practical counterpart of the argument that battery must involve inherently harmful or offensive conduct in some larger sense is the suggestion that absent such a requirement, plaintiffs will be able to unfairly drag defendants into court as a result of consensual sex, putting them to the trouble and risk of proving that the plaintiff consented or that a reasonable person would have concluded she consented. This point was not strongly argued, and with reason. Few plaintiffs to consensual sex or in situations where consent is a reasonable inference from the circumstances, are likely to sue if they are virtually certain to lose when the facts come out. Moreover, the rules of court provide sanctions for vexatious litigants. There is no need to change the law of battery to avoid vexatious claims.

Moreover, the prospect of plaintiffs suing and saying nothing about consent is more theoretical than real. In fact, plaintiffs suing for sexual battery usually testify that they did not consent to the sexual contact. Failure to do so, absent an explanation, makes it more likely the defendant could win when he calls evidence of consent or reasonable appearance of consent. Even if a plaintiff were to bring an action in sexual battery against the estate of a deceased defendant, many provincial and territorial evidence acts would not allow the plaintiff to obtain a judgment against the estate unless her evidence were corroborated by other material evidence ...

I conclude that the fact that the law of battery excludes trivial contact and requires contact that is 'harmful or offensive' does not require us to conclude that the plaintiff bears the burden of proving that the defendant actually or constructively knew she did not consent to sexual contact.

...

To require plaintiffs in actions for sexual battery to prove that they did not consent and that a reasonable person in the circumstances of the defendant would not have believed they consented, is to place a burden on plaintiffs in actions for sexual battery that plaintiffs in other types of battery do not bear. It is to do so, moreover, in the absence of any compelling reason. Indeed, there are powerful reasons for applying the usual rules that require a plaintiff to prove only direct contact in cases of sexual battery.

...

Requiring the plaintiff to disprove constructive consent seems all the more unfair because the relevant facts lie first and foremost within the defendant's sphere of knowledge. He alone knows whether he actually believed the plaintiff was consenting, and if he believed she was consenting, he is in the best position to give evidence on the facts that led him to believe that. The plaintiff, by contrast, is not in a position to produce evidence of what was in the defendant's mind nor in as good a position to say what factors led him to that state of mind and whether he acted reasonably. While the defendant's particular knowledge about his state of mind regarding consent is not determinative of who bears the burden of proof regarding consent, it is one of the principles of fairness and policy that are said to influence the allocation of this burden: see J. Sopinka, S.N. Lederman, and A.W. Bryant, *The Law of Evidence in Canada* (2nd edn 1999) at § 337.

I conclude that there is nothing about sexual battery that requires that the traditional rules of onus governing battery actions be changed. On the contrary, placing the onus on the plaintiff of disproving consent and constructive consent seems unfairly to impose special obligations on plaintiffs who sue for sexual assault ...

Iacobucci J:

This appeal raises the novel question of whether an insurance company has a duty to defend the holder of a homeowner's insurance policy against a civil sexual assault suit. In answering this question, we must also address the role of consent in an action for sexual assault.

...

There is no dispute in this case that the plaintiff's allegations fall within the general coverage provisions of the policy. All that is at stake is whether the exclusion clause applies. That clause states that the appellant is 'not insured for claims arising from ... bodily injury or property damage caused by any intentional or criminal act or failure to act' by the insured.

At the outset, the wording of this clause presents a threshold issue. The respondent argues that the clause requires only an intentional act, not an intent to injure. The majority below agreed with this interpretation. However, I agree with Finch JA's dissent on this point. If the respondent were correct, almost any act of negligence could be excluded under this clause. After all, most every act of negligence can be traced back to an 'intentional ... act or failure to act'. As this Court made clear in *Canadian Indemnity Co v Walkem Machinery & Equipment Ltd* [1976] 1 SCR 309, 'negligence is by far the most frequent source of exceptional liability which [an insured] has to contend with. Therefore a policy which would not cover liability due to negligence could not properly be called 'comprehensive' (pp 316–17). Consistent with this decision, the purpose of insurance, and the doctrines of reasonable expectations and *contra proferentem* referred to above, I believe the exclusion clause must be read to require that the injuries be intentionally caused, in that they are the product of an intentional tort and not of negligence.

...

What is necessary, therefore, is to decide what role consent plays in an action for sexual battery. It is clear that for traditional batteries, consent is conceived of as an affirmative defence that must be raised by the defendant. As Cartwright J said in *Cook v Lewis* [1951] SCR 830 at p 839, 'where a plaintiff is injured by force applied directly to him by the defendant his case is made by proving this fact and the onus falls upon the defendant to prove that such trespass was utterly without his fault'. Obviously, one way to make this showing, is by establishing that the plaintiff consented to the touching. Therefore in *Norberg v Wynrib* [1992] 2 SCR 226, La Forest J stated in *obiter dictum* that '[c]onsent, express or implied, is a defence to battery'.

...

If consent is merely a defence to battery, then presumably the plaintiff could establish battery without showing lack of consent. To paraphrase Cartwright J in *Cook*, the plaintiff's case would be made by showing the mere application of force by the defendant. As I understand it, this is the position taken by McLachlin J. However, I have trouble concluding on these terms that the appellant necessarily intended injury. Without a fault requirement of any kind, I cannot agree that the exclusion clause would necessarily apply, and the respondent would therefore have a duty to defend.

... [N]ot all intentional touchings are presumptively instances of battery. There are any number of contacts that are usually consensual. For example, in *Mandel v The Permanent* (1985) 7 OAC 365 (Div Ct) at p 370, Henry J noted that a man's placing his hand on the plaintiff's arm to guide her to the door was 'merely a polite gesture and an accepted usage in daily life in a civilised society, whether or not she was in fact consenting to it'. A more obvious example is certain sports, where physical contact is expected and even encouraged. What these examples show is that, in all cases, one must look to the context to understand the role of consent.

While, for reasons already given, consent is not a well-developed concept in battery cases, it is closely related to the more familiar requirement in tort law that a given contact be 'harmful or offensive' if it is to generate liability: see *M (K)*, *supra*, at p 25. Unlike more traditional batteries, sexual activity by itself is not inherently harmful. Without denying the seriousness and frequency of sexual assault, the simple fact is that sexual activity—unlike being punched, stabbed, or shot—is usually consensual. It generally becomes harmful only if it is non-consensual, in the wider meaning of that word.

…

In England, courts have concluded that '[t]he absence of consent is so inherent in the notion of a tortious invasion of interests in the person that the absence of consent must be established by the plaintiff': *Street on Torts* (10th edn 1999) at p 32. This issue was decided by *Freeman v Home Office* [1983] 3 All ER 589 (QB), aff'd [1984] 1 All ER 1036 (CA), where the court held that a prisoner suing for battery because of therapeutic drug injections had the burden of proving non-consent. While it is not necessary in this appeal to decide whether the burden of proving non-consent will always rest on the plaintiff, I believe that it should for sexual battery. To repeat, sexual contact is only 'harmful or offensive' when it is non-consensual. To succeed in an action for intentional battery, one must prove both that (a) the defendant intended to do the action; and (b) the reasonable person would have perceived that action as being harmful or offensive. For sexual activity an action is harmful or offensive if it is non-consensual. Therefore in sexual battery, the trier of fact must be satisfied that the defendant intended to engage in sexual activity which a reasonable person would have perceived to be non-consensual.

The New Zealand High Court came to the same conclusion in *H v R* [1996] 1 NZLR 299 … In short, the appellant's attempt to convert an intentional tort into negligence because of the possibility that he lacked a subjective intent to injure must fail. Consent, in so far as it is concerned with whether something is harmful or offensive, is an objective standard. If the plaintiff can prove that the appellant failed to meet this standard, the latter is liable for intentional sexual battery, not negligence.

In summary, I would advise the following basic propositions. For there to be a duty to defend, there must be the possibility of a duty to indemnify. In the context of the pleadings in this case raising in substance a sexual assault through a sexual battery, the issue of consent produces two possible results for the purposes of the duty to defend, both of which are unfavourable to the appellant. If the consent of the plaintiff was present, then no claim of sexual battery is made out since the conduct of the appellant would not be regarded objectively as being harmful or offensive, and therefore the duty to indemnify would not arise because the plaintiff's claim has no possibility of success. See *State Farm Fire and Casualty Co v Williams* 355 NW 2d 241 (Minn 1984) at p 424. On the other hand, if consent of the plaintiff is absent, the conduct of the appellant would be actionable as an intentional tort of sexual battery. As I will discuss, *infra*, in such a case an intent to harm is inferred, the exclusion clause would apply, and there would be no duty to indemnify. There being no state of affairs in which there could be a duty to indemnify, the duty to defend does not apply.

I wish to emphasise that the foregoing should not be taken to endorse in any way the inappropriate stereotype that women are to be presumed willing partners to sexual activity. See *R v Mills* [1999] 3 SCR 668 at para 90; *R v Osolin* [1993] 4 SCR 595 at p 670; *R v Seaboyer* [1991] 2 SCR 577 at p 604; Federal/Provincial/Territorial Working Group of Attorneys General Officials on Gender Equality in the Canadian Justice System, *Gender Equality in the Canadian Justice System: Summary Document and Proposals for*

Action (1992). Nothing in these reasons should be read to the contrary. Putting the onus of proving lack of consent on the plaintiff simply recognises that in the sexual assault context, 'non-consensual' is equivalent to 'harmful or offensive'; and the latter has always been an element of the plaintiff's case ...

Lawful authority
Collins v Wilcock
[1984] 3 All ER 374

Goff LJ:

There is before the court an appeal by way of a case stated by a metropolitan stipendiary magistrate sitting at Marylebone, under which the appellant, Alexis Collins, appeals against her conviction on 20 January 1983, of assaulting the respondent, Tracey Wilcock, a constable of the Metropolitan Police Force, in the execution of her duty at Craven Road, London W2, on 22 July 1982, contrary to s 51(1) of the Police Act 1964.

The magistrate found the following facts. On 22 July 1982 the respondent and Police Sgt Benjamen were on duty in a police vehicle and saw two women walking along the street; one of the two was a known prostitute, the other was the appellant. The officers observed the two women, both of whom appeared to them to be soliciting men in the street. The officers, without alighting from their vehicle, asked the two women to get into the police car so that they could have a word with them. One woman got into the car, the appellant refused to do so. The officers repeated their request to the appellant, who again refused and walked away, followed by the police car which then pulled up alongside her. She again walked away. The respondent got out of the car and followed the appellant on foot, asking her why she didn't want to talk to the police, and also for her name and address. The appellant again started to walk away. The respondent told her that she had not finished talking to her and the appellant replied, 'Fuck off', and started to walk away yet again. The respondent took hold of the appellant by the left arm to restrain her and the appellant shouted, 'Just fuck off, Copper' and scratched the respondent's right forearm with her fingernails. The appellant was then arrested for assaulting a police officer in the execution of her duty.

Before the magistrate, the contentions of the parties were as follows. For the appellant, it was contended that the respondent was not acting in the execution of her duty at the time when the assault (if any) took place, had gone beyond the scope of her duty in detaining the appellant in circumstances short of arresting her. It was contended by the respondent, on the other hand, that there was on the evidence good ground for her to make inquiries and administer a caution under the Street Offences Act 1959, and that she was therefore acting in the execution of her duty at the time when the assault took place.

[**Note**: Goff LJ set out the provisions of the 1959 Act, s 1(1) of which made it an offence for 'common prostitutes' to loiter or solicit in public places. He also set out the details of a police system for cautioning suspected prostitutes.]

The system, which has been encouraged by the Home Office as a way of discouraging young women from becoming prostitutes, is extra-statutory. It has nevertheless received statutory recognition in that s 2 of the 1959 Act provides a procedure for applying to a court for an order that no entry be made in respect of a caution and that any entry already made be expunged. This procedure enables a respectable woman, who has been mistakenly identified by the police as a common prostitute, to have the records corrected. We were told that, in practice, the system of cautioning is carried into effect as follows. A police officer who observes a woman in a street or public place, whom he believes to be a common prostitute loitering or soliciting there for the purpose of prostitution, will approach her and ask her for her name and address. Having been given it, he will check by radio with the police station to ascertain whether there are any cautions on her record. If there are none, he will caution her; if there is one, he will administer a second caution; and if there are two, he will arrest her on suspicion of committing an offence under s 1(1) ... The system also requires the co-operation of the woman in question in providing her name and address; and, since the system is designed to discourage women from embarking on a career of prostitution, it is understandable that police officers may think it right to persist in an attempt to give the caution, despite initial non-co-operation, rather than proceed without more ado to exercise the power of arrest under s 1(3) of the Act.

...

We are here concerned primarily with battery. The fundamental principle, plain and incontestable, is that every person's body is inviolate. It has long been established that any touching of another person, however slight, may amount to a battery. So Holt CJ held in 1704 that 'the least touching of another in anger is a battery': see *Cole v Turner* (1704) 6 Mod Rep 149, 90 ER 958. The breadth of the principle reflects the fundamental nature of the interest so protected; as Blackstone wrote in his Commentaries, 'the law cannot draw the line between different degrees of violence, and therefore totally prohibits the first and lowest stage of it; every man's person being sacred, and no other having a right to meddle with it, in any the slightest manner' (see 3 Bl Com 120). The effect is that everybody is protected not only against physical injury but against any form of physical molestation.

But so widely drawn a principle must inevitably be subject to exceptions. For example, children may be subjected to reasonable punishment; people may be subjected to the lawful exercise of the power of arrest; and reasonable force may be used in self-defence or for the prevention of crime. But, apart from these special instances where the control or constraint is lawful, a broader exception has been created to allow for the exigencies of everyday life. Generally speaking, consent is a defence to battery; and most of the physical contacts of ordinary life are not actionable because they are impliedly consented to by all who move in society and so expose themselves to the risk of bodily contact. So nobody can complain of the jostling which is inevitable from his presence in, for example, a supermarket, an underground station or a busy street; nor can a person who attends a party complain if his hand is seized in friendship, or even if his back is (within reason) slapped (see *Tuberville v Savage* (1669) 1 Mod Rep 3, 86 ER 684). Although such cases are regarded as examples of implied consent, it is more common nowadays to treat them as falling within a general exception embracing all physical contact which is generally acceptable in the ordinary conduct of daily life. We observe that, although in the past it has sometimes been stated that a battery is only committed where the action is 'angry, or revengeful, or rude, or insolent' (see 1

Hawk PC c 62, s 2), we think that nowadays it is more realistic, and indeed more accurate, to state the broad underlying principle, subject to the broad exception.

Among such forms of conduct, long held to be acceptable, is touching a person for the purpose of engaging his attention, though of course using no greater degree of physical contact than is reasonably necessary in the circumstances for that purpose. So, for example, it was held by the Court of Common Pleas in 1807 that a touch by a constable's staff on the shoulder of a man who had climbed on a gentleman's railing to gain a better view of a mad ox, the touch being only to engage the man's attention, did not amount to a battery (see *Wiffin v Kincard* (1807) 2 Bos & PNR 471, 127 ER 713; for another example, see *Coward v Baddeley* (1859) 4 H & N 478, 157 ER 927). But a distinction is drawn between a touch to draw a man's attention, which is generally acceptable, and a physical restraint, which is not. So we find Parke B observing in *Rawlings v Till* (1837) 3 M & W 28 at 29, 150 ER 1042, with reference to *Wiffin v Kincard*, that 'There the touch was merely to engage a man's attention, not to put a restraint on his person'. Furthermore, persistent touching to gain attention in the face of obvious disregard may transcend the norms of acceptable behaviour, and so be outside the exception. We do not say that more than one touch is never permitted; for example, the lost or distressed may surely be permitted a second touch, or possibly even more, on a reluctant or impervious sleeve or shoulder, as may a person who is acting reasonably in the exercise of a duty. In each case, the test must be whether the physical contact so persisted in has in the circumstances gone beyond generally acceptable standards of conduct; and the answer to that question will depend on the facts of the particular case.

The distinction drawn by Parke B in *Rawlings v Till* is of importance in the case of police officers. Of course, a police officer may subject another to restraint when he lawfully exercises his power of arrest; and he has other statutory powers, for example, his power to stop, search and detain persons under s 66 of the Metropolitan Police Act 1839, with which we are not concerned. But, putting such cases aside, police officers have for present purposes no greater rights than ordinary citizens. It follows that, subject to such cases, physical contact by a police officer with another person may be unlawful as a battery, just as it might be if he was an ordinary member of the public. But a police officer has his rights as a citizen, as well as his duties as a policeman. A police officer may wish to engage a man's attention, for example if he wishes to question him. If he lays his hand on the man's sleeve or taps his shoulder for that purpose, he commits no wrong. He may even do so more than once; for he is under a duty to prevent and investigate crime, and so his seeking further, in the exercise of that duty, to engage a man's attention in order to speak to him may in the circumstances be regarded as acceptable (see *Donnelly v Jackman* [1970] 1 All ER 987, [1970] 1 WLR 562). But if, taking into account the nature of his duty, his use of physical contact in the face of non-co-operation persists beyond generally acceptable standards of conduct, his action will become unlawful; and if a police officer restrains a man, for example by gripping his arm or his shoulder, then his action will also be unlawful, unless he is lawfully exercising his power of arrest. A police officer has no power to require a man to answer him, though he has the advantage of authority, enhanced as it is by the uniform which the state provides and requires him to wear, in seeking a response to his inquiry. What is not permitted, however, is the unlawful use of force or the unlawful threat (actual or implicit) to use force; and, excepting the lawful exercise of his power of arrest, the lawfulness of a police officer's conduct is judged by the same criteria as are applied to the conduct of any ordinary citizen of this country.

We have been referred by counsel to certain cases directly concerned with charges of assaulting a police officer in the execution of his duty, the crucial question in each case being whether the police officer, by using physical force on the accused in response to which the accused assaulted the police officer, was acting unlawfully and so not acting in the execution of his duty. In *Kenlin v Gardiner* [1966] 3 All ER 931, [1967] 2 QB 510 it was held that action by police officers in catching hold of two schoolboys was performed not in the course of arresting them but for the purpose of detaining them for questioning and so was unlawful (see [1966] 3 All ER 931 at 934, [1967] 2 QB 510 at 519 per Winn LJ). Similarly, in *Ludlow v Burgess* (1971) 75 Cr App R 227 at 228 per Lord Parker CK it was held that 'this was not a mere case of putting a hand on [the defendant's] shoulder, but it resulted in the detention of [the defendant] against his will', so that the police officer's act was 'unlawful and a serious interference with the citizen's liberty' and could not be an act performed by him in the execution of his duty.

In *Donnelly v Jackman* the police officer wished to question the defendant about an offence which he had cause to believe that the defendant had committed. Repeated requests by the police officer to the defendant to stop and speak to him were ignored. The officer tapped him on the shoulder; he made it plain that he had no intention of stopping to speak to him. The officer persisted and again tapped the defendant on the shoulder, whereupon the defendant turned and struck him with some force. The justices convicted the defendant of assaulting the officer in the execution of his duty, and this court dismissed an appeal from that conviction by way of case stated. The court was satisfied that the officer had not detained the defendant, distinguishing *Kenlin v Gardiner* as a case where the officers had in fact detained the boys (see [1970] 1 All ER 987 at 989, [1970] 1 WLR 562 at 565). It appears that they must have considered that the justices were entitled to conclude that the action of the officer, in persistently tapping the defendant on the shoulder, did not in the circumstances of the case exceed the bounds of acceptable conduct, despite the fact that the defendant had made it clear that he did not intend to respond to the officer's request to stop and speak to him; we cannot help feeling that this is an extreme case.

Finally, in *Bentley v Brudzinski* (1982) 75 Cr App R 217 it was found by the justices that the police officer, having caught up with the defendant, said, 'Just a minute'; then, not in any hostile way, but merely to attract attention, he placed his right hand on the defendant's left shoulder. The defendant then swore at the police officer and punched him in the face; and a struggle ensued. The justices considered that the act of the police officer amounted to an unlawful attempt to stop and detain the defendant, and so dismissed an information against the defendant alleging that he assaulted the police officer in the execution of his duty. This court dismissed the prosecutor's appeal by way of case stated; it appears that they considered that, having regard to all the facts of the case as found by the justices, they were entitled to hold that the police officer's act was performed not merely to engage the attention of the defendant, but as part of a course of conduct in which the officer was attempting unlawfully to detain the defendant.

We now return to the facts of the present case. Before us, counsel for the respondent police officer sought to justify her conduct, first by submitting that, since the practice of cautioning women found loitering or soliciting in public places for the purposes of prostitution is recognised by s 2 of the 1959 Act, therefore it is implicit in the statute that the police officers have a power to caution, and for that purpose they must have the power to stop and detain women in order to find out their names and addresses and, if appropriate, caution them. This submission, which accords with the opinion expressed by the magistrate, we are unable to accept. The fact that the statute recognises the practice of cautioning by providing a review procedure does not, in our judgment, carry with it an implication that police officers have the power to stop and detain women for the purpose of implementing the system of cautioning. If it had been intended to confer any such power on police officers that power could and should, in our judgment, have been expressly conferred by the statute.

Next, counsel for the respondent submitted that the purpose of the police officer was simply to carry out the cautioning procedure and that, having regard to her purpose, her action could not be regarded as unlawful. Again, we cannot accept that submission. If the physical contact went beyond what is allowed by law, the mere fact that the police officer has the laudable intention of carrying out the cautioning procedure in accordance with established practice cannot, we think, have the effect of rendering her action lawful. Finally, counsel for the respondent submitted that the question whether the respondent was or was not acting in the execution of her duty was a question of fact for the magistrate to decide; and that he was entitled, on the facts found by him, to conclude that the respondent had been acting lawfully. We cannot agree. The fact is that the respondent took hold of the appellant by the left arm to restrain her. In so acting, she was not proceeding to arrest the appellant; and since her action went beyond the generally acceptable conduct of touching a person to engage his or her attention, it must follow, in our judgment, that her action constituted a battery on the appellant, and was therefore unlawful. It follows that the appellant's appeal must be allowed, and her conviction quashed.

We turn finally to the question posed by the magistrate for our consideration. As we have already observed, this question is in wide general terms. Furthermore, the word 'detaining' can be used in more than one sense. For example, it is a commonplace of ordinary life that one person may request another to stop and speak to him; if the latter complies with the request, he may be said to do so willingly or unwillingly, and in either event the first person may be said to be 'stopping and detaining' the latter. There is nothing unlawful in such an act. If a police officer so 'stops and detains' another person, he in our opinion commits no unlawful act, despite the fact that his uniform may give his request a certain authority and so render it more likely to be complied with. But if a police officer, not exercising his power of arrest, nevertheless reinforces his request with the actual use of force, or with the threat (actual or implicit) to use force if the other person does not comply, then his act in thereby detaining the other person will be unlawful. In the former event, his action will constitute a battery; in the latter event, detention of the other person will amount to false imprisonment. Whether the action of a police officer in any particular case is to be regarded as lawful or unlawful must be a question to be decided on the facts of the case.

Self-defence and defence of others

Cockcroft v Smith
(1705) 11 Mod 43, 2 Salk 642, 88 ER 872

Cockcroft in a scuffle ran his finger towards Smith's eyes, who bit a joint off from the plaintiff's finger.

The question was, whether this was a proper defence for the defendant to justify in an action of mayhem?

Holt CJ, said, if a man strike another, who does not immediately after resent it, but takes his opportunity, and then some time after falls upon him and beats him, in the case, *son assault* is a good plea; neither ought a man, in case of a small assault, give a violent or an unsuitable return: but in such case pleas what is necessary for a man's defence, and not who struck first, though this, he said, has been the common practice, but this he wished was altered: for hitting a man a little blow with a little stick on the shoulder, it is not a reason for him to draw a sword and cut and hew the other, & c.

[**Note**: The scuffle happened in court. Cockcroft was a court clerk and Smith was a lawyer. Smith's defence succeeded because Cockcroft's action threatened the sight in his eye.]

Crimes Act 1961
48. Self-defence and defence of another—

Everyone is justified in using, in the defence of himself or another, such force as, in the circumstances as he believes them to be, it is reasonable to use.

Defence of property

Katko v Briney
(1971) 183 NW 2d 657

Moore CJ:

The primary issue presented here is whether an owner may protect personal property in an unoccupied boarded-up farm house against trespassers and thieves by a spring gun capable of inflicting death or serious injury.

We are not here concerned with a man's right to protect his home and members of his family. Defendant's home was several miles from the scene of the incident to which we refer *infra*.

At defendants request plaintiff's action was tried to a jury consisting of residents of the community where defendants property was located. The jury returned a verdict for plaintiff and against defendants for $20 000 actual and $10 000 punitive damages.

Most of the facts are not disputed. In 1957 defendant Bertha L Briney inherited her parents' farm land in Mahaska and Monroe Counties. Included was an 80-acre tract in southwest Mahaska County where her grandparents and parents had lived. No one occupied the house thereafter. Her husband, Edward, attempted to care for the land. He kept no farm machinery thereon. The outbuildings became dilapidated.

For about 10 years, 1957 to 1967, there occurred a series of trespassing and house-breaking events with loss of some household items, the breaking of windows and 'messing up of the property in general'. The latest occurred June 8, 1967, prior to the event on July 16, 1967 herein involved.

Defendants through the years boarded up the windows and doors in an attempt to stop the intrusions. They had posted 'no trespass' signs on the land several years before 1967. The nearest one was 35 feet from the house. On June 11, 1967 defendant set 'a shotgun trap' in the north bedroom. After Mr Briney cleared and oiled his 20-gauge shotgun, the power of which he was well aware, defendants took it to the old house where they secured it to an iron bed with the barrel pointed at the bedroom door. It was rigged with wire from the doorknob to the gun's trigger so it would fire when the door was opened. Briney first pointed the gun so an intruder would be hit in the stomach but at Mrs Briney's suggestion it was lowered to hit the legs. He admitted he did so 'because I was mad and tired of being tormented' but 'he did not intend to injure anyone'. He gave no explanation of why he used a loaded shell and set it to hit a person already in the house. Tin was nailed over the bedroom window. The spring gun could not be seen from the outside. No warning of its presence was posted.

Plaintiff lived with his wife and worked regularly as a gasoline station attendant in Eddyville, seven miles from the old house. He had observed it for several years while hunting in the area and considered it as being abandoned. He knew it had long been uninhabited. In 1967 the area around the house was covered with high weeds. Prior to July 16, 1967 plaintiff and McDonough had been to the premises and found several old bottles and fruit jars which they took and added to their collection of antiques. On the latter date about 9.30 pm they made a second trip to the Briney property. They entered the old house by removing a board from a porch window which was without glass. While McDonough was looking around the kitchen area plaintiff went to another part of the house. As he started to open the north bedroom door the shotgun went off striking him in the right leg above the ankle bone. Much of his leg, including part of the tibia, was blown away. Only by McDonough's assistance was plaintiff able to get out of the house and after crawling some distance was put in his vehicle and rushed to a doctor and then to a hospital. He remained in the hospital 40 days.

Plaintiff's doctor testified he seriously considered amputation but eventually the healing process was successful. Some weeks after his release from the hospital plaintiff returned to work on crutches. He was required to keep the injured leg in a cast for approximately a year and wear a special brace for another year. He continued to suffer pain during this period.

...

The main thrust of defendants' defence in the trial court and on this appeal is that 'the law permits use of a spring gun in a dwelling or warehouse for the purpose of preventing the unlawful entry of a burglar or thief' ... In the statement of issues the trial court stated plaintiff and his companion committed a felony when they broke and entered defendants' house. In instruction 2 the court referred to the early case history of the use of spring guns and stated under the law their use was prohibited except to prevent the commission of felonies of violence and where human life is in danger. The instruction included a statement that breaking and entering is not a felony of violence.

Instruction 5 stated: 'You are hereby instructed that one may use reasonable force in the protection of his property, but such right is subject to the qualification that one may not use such means of force as will take human life or inflict great bodily injury. Such is the rule even though the injured party is a trespasser and is in violation of the law himself'.

Instruction 6 stated: 'An owner of premises is prohibited from wilfully or intentionally injuring a trespasser by means of force that either takes life or inflicts great bodily injury; and therefore a person owning a premise is prohibited from setting out 'spring guns' and like dangerous devices which will likely take life or inflict great bodily injury, for the purpose of harming trespassers. The fact that the trespasser may be acting in violation of the law does not change the rule. The only time when such conduct of setting a spring gun or a like dangerous device is justified would be when the trespasser was committing a felony of violence or a felony punishable by death, or where the trespasser was endangering human life by his act'.

... The overwhelming weight of authority, both textbook and case law, supports the trial court's statement of the applicable principles of law.

Prosser on Torts, 3rd edn, pages 116–18, states:

> ... the law has always placed a higher value upon human safety than upon mere rights in property, it is the accepted rule that there is no privilege to use any force calculated to cause death or serious bodily injury to repel the threat to land or chattels, unless there is also such a threat to the defendants personal safety as to justify a self-defence ... [S]pring guns and other man-killing devices are not justifiable against a mere trespasser, or even a petty thief. They are privileged only against those upon whom the landowner, if he were present in person would be free to inflict injury of the same kind.

Restatement of Torts, section 85, page 180, states:

> The value of human life and limb, not only to the individual concerned but also to society, so outweighs the interest of a possessor of land in excluding from it those whom he is not willing to admit thereto that a possessor of land has, as is stated in [section] 79, no privilege to use force intended or likely to cause death or serious harm against another whom the possessor sees about to enter his premises or meddle with his chattel, unless the intrusion threatens death or serious bodily harm to the occupiers or users of the premises ... A possessor of land cannot do indirectly and by a mechanical device that which, were he present, he could not do immediately and in person. Therefore, he cannot gain a privilege to install, for the purpose of protecting his land from intrusions harmless to the lives and limbs of the occupiers or users of it, a mechanical device whose only purpose is to inflict death or serious harm upon such as may intrude, by giving notice of his intention to inflict, by mechanical means and indirectly, harm which he could not, even after request, inflict directly were he present.

[**Note**: Moore CJ noted several American cases where property owners were held civilly liable for spring gun injuries.]

... In addition to civil liability many jurisdictions hold a land owner criminally liable for serious injuries or homicide caused by spring guns or other set devices. See *State v Childers*, 133 Ohio 508, 14 NE 2d 767 (melon thief shot by spring gun); *Pierce v Commonwealth*, 135 Va 635, 115 SE 686 (policeman killed by spring gun when he opened unlocked front door of defendants shoe repair shop); *State v Marfaudille*, 48 Wash 117, 92 P 939 (murder conviction for death from spring gun set in a trunk); *State v Beckham*, 306 Mo 566, 267 SW 817 (boy killed by spring gun attached to window of defendants chill stand); *State v Green*, 118 SC 279, 110 SE 145, 19 ALR 1431 (intruder shot by spring gun when he broke and entered vacant house. Manslaughter conviction of owner—affirmed); *State v Barr* 11 Wash 481, 39 P 1080 (murder conviction affirmed for death of an intruder into a boarded up cabin in which the owners had set a spring gun).

… The legal principles stated by the trial court in instructions 2, 5 and 6 are well established and supported by the authorities cited and quoted *supra*. There is no merit in defendants objections and exceptions thereto. Defendants various motions based on the same reasons stated in exceptions to instructions were properly overruled.

[**Note**: Judgment of $30 000 for the defendant was upheld. Ed and Bertha Briney had to sell 80 acres of their 120-acre farm in order to pay the judgment of $30 000. Neighbours bought the 80 acres, and then leased it back to the Brineys. Eventually, however, the land was sold at a profit. Briney and Katko then became joint plaintiffs in an action against the neighbour to establish a constructive trust on the profits. A settlement was reached, and Briney was able to pay off the still partially unpaid judgment to Katko.]

Crimes Act 1961

52. Defence of movable property against trespasser—

(1) Every one in peaceable possession of any movable thing, and every one lawfully assisting him, is justified in using reasonable force to resist the taking of the thing by any trespasser or to retake it from any trespasser, if in either case he does not strike or do bodily harm to the trespasser.

55. Defence of dwellinghouse—

Every one in peaceable possession of a dwellinghouse, and every one lawfully assisting him or acting by his authority, is justified in using such force as is necessary to prevent the forcible breaking and entering of the dwellinghouse by any person if he believes, on reasonable and probably grounds, that there is no lawful justification for the breaking and entering.

56. Defence of land or building—

(1) Every one in peaceable possession of any land or building, and every one lawfully assisting him or acting by his authority, is justified in using reasonable force to prevent any person from trespassing on the land or building or to remove him therefrom, if he does not strike or do bodily harm to that person.

202. Setting traps, etc—

(1) Every one is liable to imprisonment for a term not exceeding 5 years who, with intent to injure, or with reckless disregard for the safety of others, sets or places or causes to be set or placed any trap or device that is likely to injure any person.

Necessity

Southwark London Borough Council v Williams

[1971] 1 Ch 734 (CA)

[**FACTS**: Two families, in dire need of housing, were 'put into' empty housing by the Family Squatting Association. The houses were owned by the local body, and were being prepared for redevelopment to provide more housing. The local body had some

9000 persons on a waiting list and resented the defendant 'jumping the queue'. Southwark London Borough Council sought an order for possession against the defendants as trespassers to land. The lower court granted the order. The defendants appealed.]

Lord Denning MR:

I will next consider the defence of 'necessity'. There is authority for saying that in case of great and imminent danger, in order to preserve life, the law will permit of an encroachment on private property. That is shown by *Mouse's Case* (1609) 12 Co Rep 63, where the ferryman at Gravesend took 47 passengers into his barge to carry them to London. A great tempest arose and all were in danger. Mouse was one of the passengers. The defendant threw a casket belonging to the plaintiff (Mouse) overboard so as to lighten the ship. Other passengers threw other things. It was proved that, if they had not done so, the passengers would have drowned. It was held by the whole court 'that in case of necessity, for the saving of lives of the passengers it was lawful for the defendant, being a passenger, to cast the casket of the plaintiff out of the barges ... '. The courts said it was like the pulling down of a house, in time of fire, to stop it spreading; which has always been held justified *pro bono publico*.

The doctrine so enunciated must, however, be carefully circumscribed. Else necessity would open the door to many an excuse. It was for this reason that it was not admitted in *Reg v Dudley and Stephens* (1884) 14 QBD 273, where the three shipwrecked sailors, in extreme despair, killed the cabin boy and ate him to save their own lives. They were held guilty of murder. The killing was not justified by necessity. Similarly, when a man, who is starving, enters a house and takes food in order to keep himself alive. Our English law does not admit the defence of necessity. It holds him guilty of larceny. Lord Hale said that 'if a person, being under necessity for want of victuals, or clothes, shall upon that account clandestinely, and *animo furandi*, steal another man's food, it is felony ... '. Hale, *Pleas of Crown* i 54. The reason is because, if hunger were once admitted as a defence to trespass, no one's house could be safe. Necessity would open a door which no man could shut. It would not only be those in extreme need who would enter. There would be others who would imagine that they were in need, or would invent a need, so as to gain entry. Each man would say his need was greater than the next man's. The plea would be an excuse for all sorts of wrongdoing. So the courts must for the sake of law and order, take a firm stand. They must refuse to admit the plea of necessity to the hungry and the homeless: and trust that their distress will be relieved by the charitable and the good.

Applying these principles, it seems to me the circumstances of these squatters are not such as to afford any justification or excuse in law for their entry into these houses. We can sympathise with the plight in which they find themselves. We can recognise the orderly way in which they made their entry. But we can go no further. They must make their appeal for help to others, not to us. They must appeal to the council, who will, I am sure, do all they can. They can go to the Minister, if need be. But, so far as these courts are concerned, we must, in the interest of law and order itself, uphold the title to these properties. We cannot allow any individuals, however great their despair, to take the law into their own hands and enter upon these premises. The court must exercise its summary jurisdiction and order these people to go out.

Edmund Davies LJ:

Nobody of even ordinary sensitivity could have read the affidavit evidence presented in this case without experiencing a feeling of deep depression. It serves to illustrate afresh the extent of the grave social problem presented by the dire shortage of adequate housing accommodation. But in fairness it has to be remembered that the circumstances present great difficulties to the local authorities concerned as well as to the benighted who are living in deplorable conditions or who may even be lacking a roof over their heads ...

... But when and how far is the plea of necessity available to one who is *prima facie* guilty of tort? Well, one thing emerges with clarity from the decisions, and that is that the law regards with the deepest suspicion any remedies of self-help, and permits those remedies to be resorted to only in very special circumstances. The reason for such circumspection is clear—necessity can very easily become simply a mask for anarchy. As far as my reading goes, it appears that all the cases where a plea of necessity has succeeded are cases which deal with an urgent situation of imminent peril: for example, the forcible feeding of an obdurate suffragette, as in *Leigh v Gladstone* (1909) 26 TLR 139, 142, where Lord Alverstone CJ spoke of preserving the health and lives of the prisoners who were in the custody of the Crown; or performing an abortion to avert a grave threat to the life, or, at least, to the health of a pregnant young girl who had been ravished in circumstances of great brutality, as in *Rex v Bourne* [1939] 1 KB 687; or as in the case tried in 1500 where it was said in argument that a person may escape from a burning gaol notwithstanding a statute making prison-breach a felony, 'for he is not to be hanged because he would not stay to be burnt'. Such cases illustrate the very narrow limits with which the plea of necessity may be invoked. Sad though the circumstances disclosed by these appeals undoubtedly are, they do not in my judgment constitute the sort of emergency to which the plea applies.

... Finally, even if necessity could be invoked in such circumstances as the present it could surely at most justify merely an initial entry into premises in such circumstances as those to which I have referred. I do not see how it could possibly be permitted to extend to and authorise continuing in occupation for an indefinite period of time, which was the understandable aim of the appellants when entering these premises. I therefore have to concur with Lord Denning MR in holding that the public weal demands that these appeals be dismissed.

F v West Berkshire Health Authority
(1990) 2 AC 1 (HL)
Lord Goff of Chieveley:

My Lords, the question in this case is concerned with the lawfulness of a proposed operation of sterilisation on the plaintiff, F, a woman of 36 years of age, who by reason of her mental incapacity is disabled from giving her consent to the operation. It is well established that, as a general rule, the performance of a medical operation on a person without his or her consent is unlawful, as constituting both the crime of battery and the tort of trespass to the person. Furthermore, before Scott Baker J and the Court of Appeal, it was common ground between the parties that there was no power in the court to give consent on behalf of F to the proposed operation of sterilisation, or to dispense with the need for such consent. This was because it was common ground that the *parens patriae* jurisdiction in respect of persons suffering from mental incapacity, formerly vested in the courts by royal warrant under the sign manual, had ceased to be so vested by revocation of the last warrant on 1 November 1960, and further that there was no statutory provision which could be invoked in its place ...

It follows that, as was recognised in the courts below, if the operation on F is to be justified, it can only be justified on the applicable principles of common law. The argument of counsel revealed the startling fact that there is no English authority on the question whether as a matter of common law (and if so in what circumstances) medical treatment can lawfully be given to a person who is disabled by mental incapacity from consenting to it. Indeed, the matter goes further, for a comparable problem can arise in relation to persons of sound mind who are, for example, rendered unconscious in an accident or rendered speechless by a catastrophic stroke. All such persons may require medical treatment and, in some cases, surgical operations. All may require nursing care. In the case of mentally disordered persons, they may require care of a more basic kind, dressing, feeding and so on, to assist them in their daily life, as well as routine treatment by doctors and dentists. It follows that, in my opinion, it is not possible to consider in isolation the lawfulness of the proposed operation of sterilisation in the present case. It is necessary first to ascertain the applicable common law principles and then to consider the question of sterilisation against the background of those principles.

Counsel for the Official Solicitor advanced the extreme argument that, in the absence of a *parens patriae* or statutory jurisdiction, no such treatment or care of the kind I have described can lawfully be given to a mentally disordered person who is unable to consent to it. This is indeed a startling proposition, which must also exclude treatment or care to persons rendered unconscious or unable to speak by accident or illness. For centuries, treatment and care must have been given to such persons, without any suggestion that it was unlawful to do so. I find it very difficult to believe that the common law is so deficient as to be incapable of providing for so obvious a need. Even so, it is necessary to examine the point as a matter of principle.

I start with the fundamental principle, now long established, that every person's body is inviolate. As to this, I do not wish to depart from what I myself said in the judgment of the Divisional Court in *Collins v Wilcock* [1984] 3 All ER 374, [1984] 1 WLR 1172, and in particular from the statement that the effect of this principle is that everybody is protected not only against physical injury but against any form of physical molestation (see [1984] 3 All ER 374 at 378) ...

Of course, as a general rule physical interference with another person's body is lawful if he consents to it; though in certain limited circumstances the public interest may require that his consent is not capable of rendering the act lawful. There are also specific cases where physical interference without consent may not be unlawful: chastisement of children, lawful arrest, self-defence, the prevention of crime and so on. As I pointed out in *Collins v Wilcock* [1984] 3 All ER 374 at 378 ... a broader exception has been created to allow for the exigencies of everyday life: jostling in a street or some other crowded place, social contact at parties and such like. This exception has been said to be founded on implied consent, since those who go about in public places, or go to parties, may be taken to have impliedly consented to bodily contact of this kind. Today this rationalisation can be regarded as artificial; and, in particular, it is difficult to impute consent to those who, by reason of their youth or mental disorder, are unable to give their consent. For this reason, I consider it more appropriate to regard such cases as falling within a general exception embracing all physical contact which is generally acceptable in the ordinary conduct of everyday life.

In the old days it used to be said that, for a touching of another's person to amount to a battery, it had to be a touching 'in anger' (see *Cole v Turner* (1704) Holt KB 108, 90 ER 958 per Holt CJ); and it has recently been said that the touching must be 'hostile' to have that effect (see *Wilson v Pringle* [1986] 2 All ER 440 at 447, [1987] QB 237 at 253). I respectfully doubt whether that is correct. A prank that gets out of hand, an over-friendly slap on the back, surgical treatments by a surgeon who mistakenly thinks that the patient has consented to it, all these things may transcend the bounds of lawfulness, without being characterised as hostile. Indeed, the suggested qualification is difficult to reconcile with the principle that any touching of another's body is, in the absence of lawful excuse, capable of amounting to a battery and a trespass. Furthermore, in the case of medical treatment, we have to bear well in mind the libertarian principle of self-determination which, to adopt the words of Cardozo J (in *Schloendorff v Society of New York Hospital* (1914) 211 NY 125 at 126), recognises that—

> Every human being of adult years and sound mind has a right to determine what shall be done with his own body; and a surgeon who performs an operation without his patient's consent, commits an assault ...

This principle has been reiterated in more recent years by Lord Reid in *S v S, W v Official Solicitor* [1970] 3 All ER 107 at 111, [1972] AC 24 at 43.

It is against this background that I turn to consider the question whether, and if so when, medical treatment or care of a mentally disordered person who is, by reason of his incapacity, incapable of giving his consent can be regarded as lawful. As is recognised in Cardozo J's statement of principle, and elsewhere (see eg *Sidaway v Bethlem Royal Hospital Governors* [1985] 1 All ER 643 at 649, [1985] AC 871 at 882 per Lord Scarman), some relaxation of the law is required to accommodate persons of unsound mind. In *Wilson v Pringle* the Court of Appeal considered that treatment or care of such persons may be regarded as lawful, as falling within the exception relating to physical contact which is generally acceptable in the ordinary conduct of everyday life. Again, I am with respect unable to agree. That exception is concerned with the ordinary events of everyday life, jostling in public places and such like, and affects all persons, whether or not they are capable of giving their consent. Medical treatment, even treatment for minor ailments, does not fall within that category of events. The general rule is that consent is necessary to render such treatment lawful. If such treatment administered without consent is not to be unlawful, it has to be justified on some other principle.

On what principle can medical treatment be justified when given without consent? We are searching for a principle on which, in limited circumstances, recognition may be given to a need, in the interests of the patient, that treatment should be given to him in circumstances where he is (temporarily or permanently) disabled from consenting to it. It is this criterion of a need which points to the principle of necessity as providing justification.

That there exists in the common law a principle of necessity which may justify action which would otherwise be unlawful is not in doubt. But historically the principle has been seen to be restricted to two groups of cases, which have been called cases of public necessity and cases of private necessity. The former occurred when a man interfered with another man's property in the public interest, for example (in the days before we could dial 999 for the fire brigade) the destruction of another's property to save his own person or property from imminent danger, for example when he entered on his neighbour's land without his consent in order to prevent the spread of fire onto his own land.

There is, however, a third group of cases, which is also properly described as founded on the principle of necessity and which is more pertinent to the resolution of the problem in the present case. These cases are concerned with action taken as a matter of necessity to assist another person without his consent. To give a simple example, a man who seizes another and forcibly drags him from the path of an oncoming vehicle, thereby saving him from injury or even death, commits no wrong. But there are many emanations of this principle, to be found scattered through the books. These are concerned not only with the preservation of the life or health of the assisted person, but also with the preservation of his property (sometimes an animal, sometimes an ordinary chattel) and even to certain conduct on his behalf in the administration of his affairs. Where there is a pre-exiting relationship between the parties, the intervener is usually said to act as an agent of necessity on behalf of the principal in whose interests he acts, and his action can often, with not too much artificiality, be referred to the pre-existing relationship between them. Whether the intervener may be entitled either to reimbursement or to remuneration raises separate questions which are not relevant to the present case.

We are concerned here with action taken to preserve the life, health or well-being of another who is unable to consent to it. Such action is sometimes said to be justified as arising from an emergency; in Prosser and Keeton *Torts* (5th edn, 1984) p 117 the action is said to be privileged by the emergency. Doubtless, in the case of a person of sound mind, there will ordinarily have to be an emergency before such action taken without consent can be lawful; for otherwise there would be an opportunity to communicate with the assisted person and to seek his consent. But this is not always so; and indeed the historical origins of the principle of necessity do not point to emergency as such as providing the criterion of lawful intervention without consent. The old Roman doctrine of *negotiorum gestio* presupposed not so much an emergency as a prolonged absence of the *dominus* from home as justifying intervention by the *gestor* to administer his affairs. The most ancient group of cases in the common law, concerned with the action taken by the master of a ship in distant parts in the interests of the shipowner, likewise found its origin in the difficulty of communication with the owner over a prolonged period of time, a difficulty overcome today by modern means of communication. In those cases, it was said that there had to be an emergency before the master could act as agent of necessity; though the emergency could well be of some duration. But, when a person is rendered incapable of communication either permanently or over a considerable period of time (through illness or accident or mental disorder), it would be an unusual use of language to describe the case as one of 'permanent emergency', if indeed such a state of affairs can properly be said to exist. In truth, the relevance of an emergency is that it may give rise to a necessity to act in the interests of the assisted person without first obtaining his consent. Emergency is however not the criterion or even a prerequisite; it is simply a frequent origin of the necessity which impels intervention. The principle is one of necessity, not of emergency.

We can derive some guidance as to the nature of the principle of necessity from the cases on agency of necessity in mercantile law …

… From them can be derived the basic requirements, applicable in these cases of necessity, that, to fall within the principle, not only must there be a necessity to act when it is not practicable to communicate with the assisted person, but also the action taken must be such as a reasonable person would in all the circumstances take, acting in the best interests of the assisted person.

On this statement of principle, I wish to observe that officious intervention cannot be justified by the principle of necessity. So intervention cannot be justified when another more appropriate person is available and willing to act; nor can it be justified when it is contrary to the known wishes of the assisted person, to the extent that he is capable of rationally forming such a wish. On the second limb of the principle, the introduction of the standard of a reasonable man should not in the present context be regarded as materially different from that of Sir Montague Smith's 'wise and prudent man' [in *Australasian Steam Navigation Co v Morse*], because a reasonable man would, in the time available to him proceed with wisdom and prudence before taking action in relation to another man's person or property without his consent. I shall have more to say on this point later. Subject to that, I hesitate at present to indulge in any greater refinement of the principle, being well aware of many problems which may arise in its application, problems which it is not necessary, for present purposes, to examine. But as a general rule, if the above criteria are fulfilled, interference with the assisted person's person or property (as the case may be) will not be unlawful. Take the example of a railway accident, in which injured passengers are trapped in the wreckage. It is this principle which may render lawful the actions of other citizens, railway staff, passengers or outsiders, who rush to give aid and comfort to the victims: the surgeon who amputates the limb of an unconscious passenger to free him from the wreckage; the ambulance man who conveys him to hospital; the doctors and nurses who treat him and care for him while he is still unconscious. Take the example of an elderly person who suffers a stroke which renders him incapable of speech or movement. It is by virtue of this principle that the doctor who treats him, the nurse who cares for him, even the relative or friend or neighbour who comes in to look after him will commit no wrong when he or she touches his body.

The two examples I have given illustrate, in the one case, an emergency and, in the other, a permanent or semi-permanent state of affairs. Another example of the latter kind is that of a mentally disordered person who is disabled from giving consent. I can see no good reason why the principle of necessity should not be applicable in his case as it is in the case of the victim of a stroke. Furthermore, in the case of a mentally disordered person, as in the case of a stroke victim, the permanent state of affairs calls for a wider range of care than may be requisite in an emergency which arises from accidental injury. When the state of affairs is permanent, or semi-permanent, action properly taken to preserve the life, health or well-being of the assisted person may well transcend such measures as surgical operation or substantial medical treatment and may extend to include such humdrum matters as routine medical or dental treatment, even simple care such as dressing and undressing and putting to bed.

The distinction I have drawn between cases of emergency and cases where the state of affairs is (more or less) permanent is relevant in another respect. We are here concerned with medical treatment, and I limit myself to cases of that kind. Where, for example a surgeon performs an operation without his consent on a patient temporally rendered unconscious in an accident, he should do no more than is reasonably required, in the best interests of the patient, before he recovers consciousness. I can see no practical difficulty arising from this requirement, which derives from the fact that the patient is expected before long to regain consciousness and can then be consulted about longer term measures. The point has however arisen in a more acute form where a surgeon, in the course of an operation, discovers some other condition which, in his opinion, requires operative treatment for which he has not received the patient's consent. In what circumstances he should operate forthwith, and in what circumstances he should postpone the further treatment until he has received the patient's consent, is a difficult matter which has troubled the Canadian courts (see *Marshall v Curry* [1933] 3 DLR 260 and *Murray v McMurchy* [1949] 2 DLR 442), but which it is not necessary for your Lordships to consider in the present case.

But where the state of affairs is permanent or semi-permanent, as may be so in the case of a mentally disordered person, there is no point in waiting to obtain the patient's consent. The need to care for him is obvious; and the doctor must then act in the best interests of his patient, just as if he had received his patient's consent so to do. Were this not so, much useful treatment and care could, in theory at least, be denied to the unfortunate. It follows that, on this point, I am unable to accept the view expressed by Neil LJ in the Court of Appeal, that the treatment must be shown to have been necessary. Moreover, in such a case, as my noble and learned friend Lord Brandon has pointed out, a doctor who has assumed responsibility for the care of a patient may not only be treated as having the patient's consent to act, but also be under a duty so to act. I find myself to be respectfully in agreement with Lord Donaldson MR when he said:

> I see nothing incongruous in doctors and others who have a caring responsibility being required, when acting in relation to an adult who is incompetent, to exercise a right of choice in exactly the same way as would the court or reasonable parents in relation to a child, making due allowance, of course, for the fact that the patient is not a child, and I am satisfied that that is what the law does in fact require.

In these circumstances, it is natural to treat the deemed authority and the duty as inter-related. But I feel bound to express my opinion that, in principle, the lawfulness of the doctor's action is, at least in its origin, to be found in the principle of necessity. This can perhaps be seen most clearly in cases where there is no continuing relationship between doctor and patient. The 'doctor in the house' who volunteers to assist a lady in the audience who, overcome by the drama or by the heat in the theatre, has fainted away is impelled to act by no greater duty than that imposed by his own Hippocratic oath. Furthermore, intervention can be justified in the case of a non-professional, as well as a professional, man or woman who has no pre-existing relationship with the assisted person, as in the case of a stranger who rushes to assist an injured man after an accident. In my opinion, it is the necessity itself which provides the justification for the intervention.

I have said that the doctor has to act in the best interests of the assisted person. In the case of routine treatment of mentally disordered persons, there should be little difficulty in applying this principle. In the case of more serious treatment, I recognise that its application may create problems for the medical profession; however, in making decisions about treatment, the doctor must act in accordance with a responsible and competent body of relevant professional opinion, on the principles set down in *Bolam v Friern Hospital Management Committee* [1957] 2 All ER 118, [1957] 1 WLR 582. No doubt, in practice, a decision may involve others besides the doctor. It must surely be good practice to consult relatives and others who are concerned with the care of the patient. Sometimes, of course, consultation with a specialist or specialists will be required; and in others, especially where the decision involves more than a purely medical opinion, an inter-disciplinary team will in practice participate in the decision. It is very difficult, and would be unwise, for a court to do more than to stress that, for those who are involved in these important and sometimes difficult decisions, the overriding consideration is that they should act in the best interests of the person who suffers from the misfortune of being prevented by incapacity from deciding for himself what should be done to his own body in his own best interests.

[**Note**: Lord Goff then considered whether the present case fell within the defence of necessity. He considered that as regards sterilisation of adults lacking capacity, it was in the best interests of the person concerned to require a court hearing to determine whether the operation was lawful. A court hearing would allow an independent and authoritative assessment of whether the operation was necessary in the circumstances. He concluded that, in the present case, it was appropriate to issue a declaration that F's sterilisation would be lawful and that the court had jurisdiction to issue such an injunction.]

Lord Jauncey of Tullichettle:

My Lords, the difficult questions raised in this appeal have been fully examined in the speeches of my noble and learned friends Lord Brandon and Lord Goff and I entirely agree with their conclusions as to the manner in which this appeal should be disposed of and with their reasons for such disposal.

My Lords, I should like only to reiterate the importance of not erecting such legal barriers against the provision of medical treatment for incompetents that they are deprived of treatment which competent persons could reasonably expect to receive in similar circumstances. The law must not convert incompetents into second class citizens for the purposes of health care.

There are four stages in the treatment of a patient, whether competent or incompetent. The first is to diagnose the relevant condition. The second is to determine whether the condition merits treatment. The third is to determine what the merited treatment should be. The fourth is to carry out the chosen form of merited treatment. In the case of a long-term incompetent, convenience to those charged with his care should never be a justification for the decision to treat. However, if such persons take the decision in relation to the second and third stages (*supra*) solely in his best interests and if their approach to and execution of all four stages is such as would be adopted by a responsible body of medical opinion skilled in the particular field of diagnosis and treatment concerned, they will have done all that is required of them and their actions will not be subject to challenge as being unlawful.

[**Result**: Appeal dismissed.]

Note: the New Zealand position

The position in New Zealand in regards to the *F v West Berkshire Health Authority* (above) situation is different. New Zealand has specific statutory provisions that attempt to deal with consent issues. Therefore, there is not the same gap as regards consent in New Zealand that necessitated the difficult decision by the House of Lords. The relevant statutory provisions are provided below.

Mental Health (Compulsory Assessment and Treatment) Act 1992

57. No compulsory treatment except as provided in this Part or in section 110A—

A proposed patient or patient may refuse consent to any form of treatment for mental disorder, except as provided in this Part or in section 110A …

59. Treatment while subject to compulsory treatment order—

(1) Every patient who is subject to a compulsory treatment order shall, during the first month of the currency of the order, be required to accept such treatment for mental disorder as the responsible clinician shall direct.

(2) Except during the period of 1 month referred to in subsection (1) of this section, no patient shall be required to accept any treatment unless—

(a) The patient, having had the treatment explained to him or her in accordance with section 67 of this Act consents in writing to the treatment; or

(b) The treatment is considered to be in the interests of the patient by a psychiatrist (not being the responsible clinician) who has been appointed for the purposes of this section by the Review Tribunal.

…

(4) The responsible clinician shall, wherever practicable, seek to obtain the consent of the patient to any treatment even though that treatment may be authorised by or under this Act without the patient's consent.

62. Urgent treatment—

Nothing in section 59(2) of this Act shall apply to any treatment that is immediately necessary—

(a) To save the patient's life; or

(b) To prevent serious damage to the health of the patient; or

(c) To prevent the patient from causing serious injury to himself or herself or others.

Statutory bars

Sovereign immunity

In *Lambertson v United States* (above) the plaintiff was not able to sue the state for an intentional tort committed by its employee. New Zealand also operates on a principle of sovereign immunity. However, in New Zealand the Crown has waived immunity in tort, at least in part.

Crown Proceedings Act 1950

2. Interpretation—

(1) In this Act, unless the context otherwise requires—

'Agent', in relation to the Crown, includes an independent contractor employed by the Crown:

'Servant', in relation to the Crown, means any servant of Her Majesty, and accordingly (but without prejudice to the generality of the foregoing provision) includes a Minister of the Crown, and a member of the New Zealand armed forces; but does not include the Governor-General, or any Judge, District Court Judge, Justice of the Peace, Community Magistrate, or other judicial officer:

6. Liability of the Crown in tort—

(1) Subject to the provisions of this Act and any other Act, the Crown shall be subject to all those liabilities in tort to which, if it were a private person of full age and capacity, it would be subject—

   (a) In respect of torts committed by its servants or agents;

   (b) In respect of any breach of those duties which a person owes to his servants or agents at common law by reason of being their employer; and

   (c) In respect of any breach of the duties attaching at common law to the ownership, occupation, possession, or control of property:

Provided that no proceedings shall lie against the Crown by virtue of paragraph (a) of this subsection in respect of any act or omission of a servant or agent of the Crown unless the act or omission would apart from the provisions of this Act have given rise to a cause of action in tort against that servant or agent or his estate.

...

(4) Any enactment which negatives or limits the amount of the liability of any Government Department or officer of the Crown in respect of any tort committed by that Department or officer shall, in the case of proceedings against the Crown under this section in respect of a tort committed by that Department or officer, apply in relation to the Crown as it would have applied in relation to that Department or officer if the proceedings against the Crown had been proceedings against that Department or officer.

(5) No proceedings shall lie against the Crown by virtue of this section in respect of anything done or omitted to be done by any person while discharging or purporting to discharge any responsibilities of a judicial nature vested in him, or any responsibilities which he has in connection with the execution of judicial process.

Limitation of actions

Limitation Act 1950

4. Limitation of actions of contract and tort, and certain other actions—

(1) Except as otherwise provided in this Act, the following actions shall not be brought after the expiration of 6 years from the date on which the cause of action accrued, that is to say—

   (a) Actions founded on simple contract or on tort:

...

(7) An action in respect of the bodily injury to any person shall not be brought after the expiration of 2 years from the date on which the cause of action accrued unless the action is brought with the consent of the intended defendant before the expiration of 6 years from that date:

Provided that if the intended defendant does not consent, application may be made to the Court, after notice to the intended defendant, for leave to bring such an action at any time within 6 years from the date on which the cause of action accrued; and the Court may, if it thinks it is just to do so, grant leave accordingly, subject to such conditions (if any) as it thinks it is just to impose, where it considers that the delay in bringing the action was occasioned by mistake of fact or mistake of any matter of law other than the provisions of this subsection or by any other reasonable cause or that the intended defendant was not materially prejudiced in his defence or otherwise by the delay.

24. Extension of limitation period in case of disability—

If, on the date when any right of action accrued for which a period of limitation is prescribed by or may be prescribed under this Act the person to whom it accrued was under a disability—

(a) In the case of any action ... in respect of the death of or bodily injury to any person, or of any action to recover a penalty or forfeiture or sum by way thereof by virtue of any enactment where the action is brought by an aggrieved party, the right of action shall be deemed to have accrued on the date when the person ceased to be under a disability or died, whichever event first occurred; or

(b) In any other case the action may be brought before the expiration of 6 years from the date when the person ceased to be under a disability or died, whichever event first occurred—

notwithstanding that, in any case to which either of the foregoing paragraphs of this section applies, the period of limitation has expired ...

28. Postponement of limitation period in case of fraud or mistake—

Where, in the case of any action for which a period of limitation is prescribed by this Act, either—

(a) The action is based upon the fraud of the defendant or his agent or of any person through whom he claims or his agent; or

(b) The right of action is concealed by the fraud of any such person as aforesaid; or

(c) The action is for relief from the consequences of a mistake—

the period of limitation shall not begin to run until the plaintiff has discovered the fraud or the mistake, as the case may be, or could with reasonable diligence have discovered it:

32. Application to the Crown—

Save as in this Act otherwise expressly provided and without prejudice to the provisions of section 33 thereof, this Act shall apply to proceedings by or against the Crown in like manner as it applies to proceedings between subjects.

33. Savings for other limitation enactments—

(1) This Act shall not apply to any action or arbitration for which a period of limitation is prescribed by any other enactment, or to any action or arbitration to which the

Crown is a party and for which, if it were between subjects, a period of limitation would be prescribed by any other enactment.

(2) Any reference in any enactment to any of the enactments specified in the First Schedule to this Act or to any provision of any such enactment shall be construed as a reference to the corresponding provision of this Act.

T v H
[1995] 3 NZLR 37 (CA)

[**FACTS:** M sexually abused T as a child between 1959 and 1970. T lived in fear of M until M's death in 1992. T sued M's estate in 1993. Her action was dismissed as statute barred. Section 33 of the Limitations Act 1950 provides that the Act does not apply where a limitation period is prescribed in another Act. Section 3 of the Law Reform Act 1936 provides that a cause of action survives the tortfeasor's death if the tort action was pending at the time of death or had accrued within two years of death, or, with leave of the Court, if the tort arose within six years of death.]

Cooke P:

This is an application, removed into this Court by an order under R 264(4) of the High Court Rules, for review of an interlocutory decision given by Master Kennedy-Grant on 24 January 1994. Our decision has been delayed by the need to request and consider written submissions for the parties on points not adverted to by counsel at our hearing. Having had the advantage of reading in draft the judgments of Hardie Boys and Tipping JJ, with their analyses of the issues, I can state my opinion quite shortly.

...

Until this Court made the request already mentioned, the arguments of counsel had proceeded without apparent regard to s 33(1) of the Limitation Act 1950; but that sub-section provides that the Act shall not apply to any action for which a period of limitation is prescribed by another enactment. The Law Reform Act 1936 does prescribe periods of limitation if a tortfeasor has died. The action here is founded in tort ... The limitation issue turns on, first, defining when the alleged cause of action arises at common law; secondly, applying s 3 of the Law Reform Act 1936 ...

...

If the causes of action are identified simply as assaults or batteries, the proceeding against the personal representative must be barred by the 1936 Act; leave could not be granted under s 3(3A) because such causes of action must have arisen more than six years before the death of the tortfeasor. The only way whereby the applicant could overcome that difficulty would be resort to or analogy with the reasonable discoverability principle for which the leading Commonwealth authority in relation to the closely comparable subject of incest is *KM v HM* (1992) 96 DLR (4th) 289. The powerful judgment in that case of La Forest J, concurred in on this point by six of his colleagues in the Supreme Court of Canada, is summarised in his proposition at p 305: 'It is at the moment when the incest victim discovers the connection between the harm she has suffered and her childhood history that her cause of action crystallises'. Essentially the judgment recognises the medically-established fact that victims of child sexual abuse may not realise at the time the gravity of what has been done to them; or may understand only much later, as the result of psychiatric or psychological advice, that problems in adult life are attributable to what was done to them in their childhood. Further, in relation to policy considerations, the judgment lays weight on the following, at p 302:

> While there are instances where the public interest is served by granting repose to certain classes of defendants, for example, the cost of professional services if practitioners are exposed to unlimited liability, there is absolutely no corresponding public benefit in protecting individuals who perpetrate incest from the consequences of their wrongful actions. The patent inequity of allowing these individuals to go on with their life without liability, while the victim continues to suffer the consequences, clearly militates against any guarantee of repose.

...

Of course the Canadian reasoning can quite readily be distinguished on the ground that in a case such as the present the claimant knows, either at the time of the offending or at least quite soon after she becomes an adult, that what was done to her was wrong and damaging.

The question, however, is whether that distinction is not superficial. If the wrongdoer is still alive, there may be perfectly genuine inhibitions preventing her from raising allegations against him. If he is dead, that may have operated as a release to her: it is true that he is no longer able to answer her allegations, but in other fields (such as testamentary promises) the Courts cope with that handicap. Like inability to associate abuse with its consequences, inability to complain is a product of the abuse itself. Is inability to reveal the abuse essentially different from inability to perceive its results? Here, it seems, is the issue which we must now confront. The Supreme Court of Canada were not required to confront it, but their approach in this field can hardly be dismissed on that account.

In *KM v HM* at p 299, La Forest J said 'Assault and battery can only serve as a crude legal description of incest ...'. The same may be said of other cases of sexual abuse of children inflicting, not merely unlawful physical contact extending sometimes to real bodily injury, but serious continuing psychological damage. The Canadian Supreme Court, building on discoveries of psychiatric research and to some extent on United States jurisprudence, have pointed the way to a realistic analysis of when a cause of action in tort for this kind of continuing psychological injury arises. Such injury is in a sense 'bodily' but it is also of a special nature justifying a distinct legal classification or approach. As noted by Sir Nicholas Browne-Wilkinson V-C in *Stubbings v Webb* [1992] QB 197, 212, in a passage of which the factual accuracy is unaffected by the reversal of the Court of Appeal decision on further appeal, civil actions against child abusers have been virtually unknown until recently. There is no body of case law directly in point to draw upon. The subject is *sui generis*. Since there is no clearly applicable precedent, the decision of the particular question arising in the present case inevitably entails judicial 'legislation' in one direction or another, as has always been the case with new questions at common law. The Court cannot avoid the responsibility of making new law when there is no existing law. Of course, analogy with existing law and incrementalism are legitimate considerations; and here the closest case is *KM v HM*.

In these circumstances, in my opinion, no insuperable obstacle arises or need be conjured up to prevent the Courts from holding that a cause of action accrues when the victim has been relieved from the continuing psychological injury sufficient to enable her to understand the effect that it has had on her life or to feel safe and free to pursue a complaint. That is to say, actionable damage should be treated as not having been suffered until the victim has emerged from the effects of the abuse so far as to be able to sue on all the damage that has occurred previously, as in cases of delayed discoverability.

In *Hawkins v Clayton* (1988) 164 CLR 539, 590, Deane J said, with the concurrence on this point of Mason CJ and Wilson J (see at p 543), that reference in the Limitation Act there under consideration to the cause of action first accruing should be construed as excluding any period during which the wrongful act itself effectively precluded the institution of proceedings. That produces much the same result as the approach just suggested, with the difference that in relation to childhood sexual abuse (which was not the subject-matter of *Hawkins v Clayton*) I would prefer to speak in terms of the accrual at common law of a cause of action for psychological or psychiatric harm.

In a case like the present the cause of action would not accrue until after the abuser's death, when the victim obtains release from fear by learning of the death. Under the old common law that would have been too late, because of the rule that a cause of action for personal injury did not survive death, *actio personalis moritur cum persona*. But that rule has been done away with the 1936 Act.

...

Of course everything will turn on whether at trial the complainant will be able to establish not only the childhood abuse but also the continuing damage and the disabling fear. The evidence would have to be capable of withstanding close scrutiny. It would be viewed with great caution. But the affidavits now before the Court provide a sufficient factual foundation to justify the granting of leave to proceed under s 3(3A) if, as I think, such a claim is tenable in law. Nor is there anything to suggest that the personal representative has been prejudiced on his defence or otherwise by such delay as has occurred in bringing proceedings after the death of the deceased.

[**Note**: Casey and Gault JJ agreed with the reasons of Hardie Boys and Tipping JJ.]

Hardie Boys J:
Primacy of the Law Reform Act
It seems that s 33(1) of the Limitation Act was not referred to in the High Court; and it was given attention in this Court only in written submissions the Court called for after the hearing had been completed.

In her written submissions, Ms Hughes accepted that s 33(1) means that 'the Law Reform Act takes precedence over the Limitation Act', but she submitted that it does so only at the death of the tortfeasor. This means, she argued, that if T came within the terms of s 24 of the Limitation Act during M's lifetime, his death did not deprive her of the benefit of that section, but merely resulted in her no longer being under a disability, and the cause of action thereupon accruing for the purposes of s 3(3) of the

Law Reform Act. Thus the argument before the Master, although advanced without reference to s 33(1), remains substantially the same.

For the reasons I give later, I cannot accept this argument. But because the point may be of importance in other cases, I turn next to the meaning of the expression 'under a disability'. I will return to s 33(1) in due course.

'Under a disability'

Calling in aid the example of the Supreme Court of Canada in *KM v HM* (1992) 96 DLR (4th) 289, which too I will discuss later, Ms Hughes urged the Court to construe these words in a way that recognises the present state of medical and other specialist knowledge of the problem of child abuse. I agree that we should do so as far as we properly can; and I have no difficulty in accepting that a person who for clearly established psychological reasons is disabled from instructing a solicitor and commencing proceedings is under a disability for the purposes of the Limitation Act. I see from the judgment of La Forest J in *KM v HM* at p 311 that Courts in Michigan have taken a similar view in cases of memory repression by incest victims.

The expression 'under a disability' has a particular although not precise meaning in law, well conveyed by the second of the meanings of 'disability' in *The Oxford English Dictionary* (2nd edn, 1989) '2. Incapacity in the eye of the law, or created by the law; a restriction framed to prevent any person or class of persons from sharing in duties or privileges which would otherwise be open to them; legal disqualification'. See *Re Carew* [1896] 2 Ch 311, where Lindley LJ gave as examples under the law of that time bankruptcy, conviction for felony, attainder for treason and lunacy. At times, statutes have contained their own definition, such as that in the Naturalisation Act 1870 (UK): 'the status of being an infant, lunatic, idiot or married woman'. But times change, and today the only complete disabilities imposed by law are infancy and unsoundness of mind. To a limited extent, as undischarged bankrupts and certain inmates of penal institutions may be said to be under a disability, but not one that could affect their ability to sue for damages for personal injury.

Thus while subss (2) and (3) of s 2 of the Limitation Act do not purport to give an exhaustive definition of 'under a disability', it is unlikely that in the context of that Act the expression now goes beyond the two deemed circumstances, infancy and unsoundness of mind. In *Matai Industries Ltd v Jensen* [1989] 1 NZLR 525 Tipping J held that it does not include a company in receivership 'legally capable of suing but unlikely to be able to do so' (p 541). It certainly does not extend to physical disability, or a mental inability or incapacity short of unsoundness of mind. Consideration must therefore focus on what is meant by the words 'of unsound mind'.

...

Whether or not a person is of unsound mind must depend on the purpose of the inquiry, and must in all cases be a matter of fact and degree. In the present context, the question must be determined in the light of the purpose of s 24 of the Limitation Act. Read against the definition in s 2, that purpose is plainly to ensure that a person who is incapable of, or disabled in the more general sense from instituting proceedings does not lose the right to do so while the incapacity or disablement continues. In the light of that purpose, I have no doubt that one who from established psychiatric or psychological causes is unable to bring him or herself to initiate proceedings is to that extent of unsound mind and so under a disability while that condition lasts.

When did the cause of action arise?

This is the primary question to be answered under s 3(3) of the Law Reform Act. Ms Hughes put forward alternative answers. The first, as already mentioned, was that the cause of action arose upon M's death, because until then T had been under a disability. The second was that the cause of action continued until his death and even for a time after it; this was in essence the second argument put to the Master.

Assuming T is able to establish that she was indeed under a disability in the sense I have discussed, Mr Williams submitted that on the evidence that disability came to an end not when M died, but when T learnt of his death. He argued that this situation does not readily fit into the scheme of s 3(3), which contemplates a cause of action already subsisting at the date of death, which would at common law have been extinguished by death but which was survived by virtue of the section. Subsection (4) would not assist, for it deals only with the damage component of a cause of action. The section simply does not contemplate the situation where a person is under a disability prior to death and subsequently ceases to be under that disability. However this argument confuses disability with the substance of a cause of action. Where a person is under a disability, the cause of action is deemed not to have accrued. But as I have said that does not prevent proceedings being commenced on behalf of the person concerned. The cause of action exists, and is subsisting, even though for limitation purposes it is deemed not to have accrued. This may explain the use of the word 'subsisting' in s 3(1) rather than the word 'accrued'. The real point to be taken from s 3 is not that which counsel argued, but that by making no provision for disability it emphasises the full scope of s 33(1).

...

From the first of the limitation statutes, it has generally been recognised that time should not run where an action could not, or could not conveniently, be brought: see Preston and Newsom's *Limitation of Actions* (3rd edn, 1953) p 219. Thus s 24 of our Act of 1950 is an essential feature of, and inseparable from the statute as a whole. And so when s 33(1) excludes the application of the Act it excludes s 24, with the result that for the purposes of s 3 of the Law Reform Act the time when a cause of action arises is to be ascertained without reference to any disability. This is the conclusion reached by Anderson J in *Petersen v Shearer* (Rotorua, A/92/95, judgment 8 June 1989) in a judgment with which I largely agree. I would however qualify one observation he made: while it is true that in the general run of cases the effect of s 3 may be overcome by the ability to bring proceedings on behalf of a person under disability, that would not be so in a case such as the present is said to be. But this kind of case would not have been in anyone's mind in 1936. The law as it stands may be thought inadequate to deal with a case such as this. If that is so, it is an inadequacy that must be addressed by the legislature. The Court cannot rewrite the statute ...

Tipping J:

... The first question in terms of s 3(3)(b) of the 1936 Act is whether T can show that her cause of action against H arose not earlier than two years before H's death. The question concerns when her cause of action arose. It is to be noted that the 1936 Act does not speak of when the cause of action accrued to T but rather of when it arose. I doubt there is any difference but T cannot suggest the possibility that the concept of accrual is more favourable to her. Section 24 of the Limitation Act 1950 is drafted on the premise that a cause of action does accrue to a person under a disability. The section starts by saying that if, on the date when any right of action accrued, the person to whom it accrued was under a disability, then in certain types of case the right of action shall be deemed to have accrued on the date when the person ceased to be under a disability and in all other cases the action may be brought before the expiration of six years from the date when the person ceased to be under a disability.

The point is that the structure and composition of s 24 presupposes that the cause of action has accrued to the person under a disability and, but for the extension of time granted by the section, it would have become statute-barred. This leads me to the view that when in s 3(3)(b) of the 1936 Act Parliament used the expression 'the cause of action arose' that expression was being used on the basis a cause of action arises when the necessary ingredients are complete, irrespective of whether the person is then under a disability. The same constructional issue arises in s 3(3A). Clearly T's cause of action was complete and accrued or arose at the latest in 1970 when the last alleged abuse occurred.

I recognise, of course, that the Limitation Act 1950 was passed 14 years after the 1936 Act but it is clear that historically even when some ground for extension of time existed (eg disability, mistake or fraud) the cause of action was nevertheless regarded as having accrued. The disability of the plaintiff did not mean that the cause of action had not accrued. The plaintiff could always sue to enforce the cause of action by guardian *ad litem* or other appropriate procedure. What the disability did was to extend the limitation period by suspending the running of time while it continued: see *Franks on Limitation of Actions* (1959) at pp 174, 207 and 212 and *Josling on Periods of Limitation* (6th edn, 1986) at p 21 ...

S v G
[1995] 3 NZLR 681 (CA)
Gault J:
The respondent applied for and obtained leave under s 4(7) of the Limitation Act 1950 to bring a proceeding for remedies in respect of bodily injury allegedly sustained more than two years but less than six years after the date on which the alleged causes of action accrued.

...

It has long been accepted that a cause of action accrues when all of its elements are subsisting. It is postponed in certain cases while the plaintiff is under a disability (s 24 of the Limitation Act), when there has been fraudulent concealment of the cause of action (s 28) or where the plaintiff reasonably has not discovered all of the elements (*Invercargill City Council v Hamlin* [1994] 3 NZLR 513).

Upon the pleadings as outlined, subject to disability during her minority so far as s 24 of the Limitation Act applies, the respondent's respective causes of action would appear on their face to have arisen at the time of the alleged conduct. Injury or damage is a necessary element of the cause of action in negligence but in the absence of any other allegation that element perhaps can be assumed from the nature of the alleged conduct to have existed in the form of the injuries resulting at the time. It follows that the limitation period under the Act commenced to run when the respondent ceased to be under a disability upon reaching the age of majority in 1984 and that cause of action became finally statute-barred by s 4(7) in 1990, well before the present application was made.

...

We therefore proceed to consider whether, as a matter of law, for the purpose of the Limitation Act, it can be said that where a victim of sexual abuse suffers psychological and emotional harm resulting from that abuse, the cause of action against the abuser accrues only when the victim discovers the link between the abuse and the harm. The Supreme Court of Canada held that to be the case under the Ontario Limitations Statute in *KM v HM* (1992) 96 DLR (4th) 289.

In that case it was held at p 312, even with reference to the cause of action for assault and battery of which injury or damage is not an essential element, that:

> ... the issue properly turns on the question of when the victim becomes fully cognisant of who bears the responsibility for her childhood abuse, for it is then that she realises the nature of the wrong done to her.

We accept that where damage is an element of the cause of action, as in negligence, the reasonable discoverability of the link between psychological and emotional harm and past sexual abuse may be employed to determine the accrual of the cause of action. We have more difficulty with that approach to causes of action of which damage is not an element and all other elements are known, unless ss 24 or 28 of the Limitation Act can be invoked. Even in cases of negligence, where some recognised damage flows immediately from the alleged conduct, the limitation period commences to run, subject only to postponement under the Act by reason of disability (s 24) or fraudulent concealment (s 28). In the present case the alleged physical abuse such as the infecting of the respondent with anal and vaginal venereal warts and the physical assaults can hardly be regarded as wholly latent such that no cause of action should arise until later therapy linked the consequential psychological damage to the abuse.

...

Of course the Limitation Act itself does not define when a cause of action accrues. It is not a matter of statutory construction. It is a question of when as a matter of law the cause of action accrues for the purpose of the Limitation Act. In the *Hamlin* case the majority view was that the cause of action in negligence in causing defective foundations accrued when the house owner discovered the defect or acting reasonably would have done so. That he had earlier seen cracks around the house was not sufficient since those observations did not lead to discovery of the defective foundations nor would they have led a reasonable house owner to that discovery. By analogy it can be said that the sexual abuse victim who reasonably has not linked serious psychological and emotional damage to the abuse does not have the limitation period run merely because of awareness of the symptoms of that damage. It is only when the psychological damage is or reasonably should have been identified and linked to the abuse that it can be said that the elements of the negligence cause of action are known and thus the cause of action has accrued. That approach was followed by Gallen J in *G v G D Searle and Co* [1955] 1 NZLR 341.

...

With reference to the cause of action for assault and battery in which damage is not an element, Blanchard J applied the reasonable discoverability approach to the recognition of the lack of true consent to the conduct (which is an element of the cause of action). On appeal no argument was directed to that point—it seems on the basis that if reasonable discoverability is to be applied in cases such as this, it can be invoked in this manner also. We accept that as a correct view.

On the evidence available to us it may be that recognition of the absence of true consent emerged at a different and earlier time than the discovery of the link between the psychological damage and the abuse and it will be necessary to bear that in mind.

Section 28 of the Limitation Act also can have application in cases of the kind under consideration. It provides that where the right of action is concealed by the fraud of the intended defendant the limitation period does not begin to run until the plaintiff discovers the fraud or could with reasonable diligence have discovered it.

As it well documented, sexual abuse of children frequently is accompanied by deceit as to the nature of the acts and leads to victims constructing psychological blocks or denials and underlying psychological and emotional damage may be neither recognised nor linked to the abuse. Where it is established that the very conduct of the defendant and accompanying deceit had the effect of preventing the victim from recognising the true nature of the abuse and the damage caused by it, it does not strain interpretation to hold that there has been fraudulent concealment of the right of action.

...

For the purpose of considering the present application we will proceed on the basis that although the proposed defendant's conduct occurred some 13 to 15 years before the application was made, the applicant did not discover all of the elements of the causes of action until much more recently. The latest date seems accepted as being on the occasion of the third counselling session with Ms Goodison on 1 October 1990.

...

It was not until the beginning of 1992 that the applicant received legal advice that she could bring civil proceedings but that is not the point at which time began to run. It was when she discovered, or reasonably ought to have discovered, all facts making up her causes of action. However even after receiving advice the necessary letter before proceedings required by s 4(7) was not sent to the intended defendant until 29 July 1993, and the present application was filed on 6 October 1993. We do not overlook the evidence that even after recognising the conduct as abuse and having advice that civil proceedings might be brought, the applicant continued to suffer from the inhibiting effects of the alleged and other abuse. That of course is relevant to the discretion to be exercised under s 4(7) where leave is sought after two years but within six years of the accrual of the cause of action. But it is not relevant to when the cause of action accrued.

...

We commence with the proposition that where the matters giving rise to the proceeding are old in relation to what the legislature has indicated by the statutory limitation periods are reasonable benchmarks, and the intended plaintiff is seeking to rely upon delayed discovery of the cause of action or the exclusion in s 4(9) from the Act, he or she reasonably should be expected to act promptly once the right of action is recognised. With reference to this case, if it is shown to have been reasonable that the applicant did not discover the causes of action for a period of ten years she should then reasonably be expected to proceed within the two-year limitation period thereafter. To obtain further benefit in the Court's discretion for what was at least another year should require good grounds bearing in mind the competing interest of the intended defendant to be sued some 15 years after the events. It is not a strong argument at this preliminary stage to contend that child abusers who cause such devastating damage to the lives of their victims deserve no protection. At this stage the allegations are unproved—though it is clear some sexual misconduct will not be denied.

...

We are satisfied on the affidavit evidence that there was good reason for the respondent's delay in proceeding. The alleged conduct in respect of which she wishes to bring the proceeding must be assumed to have contributed in part to that.

...

On balance we consider that in the unusual circumstances of this case there should not be leave to proceed. The prejudice to the appellant outweighs the desirability of permitting the respondent to bring her intended proceeding.

Owen v Residual Health Management Unit
[2000] 3 NZLR 475 (CA)
Blanchard J:
This is an appeal against a decision of Smellie J in the High Court to strike out a claim by the parents of a severely disabled child for compensatory and exemplary damages for what they have called nervous shock.

Background
The appellants' child was born on 14 April 1993. During the birth he suffered brain damage and is now seriously impaired. Almost six years later, on 9 April 1999, the appellants filed a claim against the respondents in the High Court. The appellants allege that the three respondents (the hospital where the child was born, and the doctors involved in the prenatal care and birth of the child) failed to ensure that proper advice, services, knowledge and skill to enable a safe delivery of their child was available. They claim they suffered 'nervous shock' as a result of the respondents' negligence. They have not at any time sought leave under s 4(7) of the Limitation Act 1950 for the bringing of the proceeding more than two years after the cause of action accrued.

In a reserved judgment delivered on 12 October 1999 (High Court, Auckland, CP 144-SD/99), Smellie J struck out the appellants' claim on the following grounds:

(a) That because the appellants claimed only 'nervous shock' and not 'a recognisable psychiatric disorder or illness', the pleadings disclosed no reasonable cause of action; and

(b) That the claim was in any case barred by s 4(7) of the Limitation Act 1950, because it was brought more than two years after the cause of action accrued.

The appellants appeal both grounds.

...

'Bodily injury'?

It is plain that, as the appellants submit, their claim is not for the injury to their child but is brought in respect of their own mental injuries ... Consequently, in the absence of any application under s 4(7), their claim is statute-barred if it is one within that provision for 'bodily injury'.

The question can be restated as being whether an injury to the mind is a bodily injury. Although Ms Davenport was able to point to authority which spoke of bodily injury as something involving physical or physiological injury (*Deeble v Nott* (1941) 65 CLR 104), there is now a considerable body of case law which regards a recognisable psychiatric disorder or illness inflicted as a result of sudden shock as a 'bodily injury' or 'personal injury', terms which Williams J in *Deeble v Nott* at p 113 regarded as expressions used indiscriminately to mean the same thing. Ms Davenport herself accepted that 'bodily injury', 'bodily harm' and 'personal injury' have the same meaning in this context.

...

We consider that the matter is put beyond doubt by two English decisions and two recent decisions of this Court. The first in time was *R v Chan-Fook* [1994] 2 All ER 552, a decision of the Court of Appeal, Criminal Division. In a judgment delivered on behalf of the Court by Hobhouse LJ it was held that the phrase 'actual bodily harm' in the Offences Against the Person Act 1861 (UK) was capable of including psychiatric injury but did not include mere emotions such as fear, distress, panic or a hysterical or nervous condition, nor did it include states of mind that were not themselves evidence of some identifiable clinical condition. The Court commented that the body of a victim includes all parts of the body, including organs, nervous system and brain.

'Bodily injury therefore may include injury to any of those parts of his body responsible for his mental and other faculties.' The judgment contains a quotation from Lord Wilberforce in *McLoughlin v O'Brian* [1983] 1 AC 410 at p 418:

> Whatever is unknown about the mind-body relationship (and the area of ignorance seems to expand with that of knowledge), it is now accepted by medical science that recognisable and severe physical damage to the human body and system may be caused by the impact, through the senses, of external events on the mind.

In *R v Mwai* [1995] 3 NZLR 149, after referring to *McCraw* and *Chan-Fook*, this Court, speaking through Hardie Boys J, said at pp 154–5 that:

> ... one must acknowledge the artificiality of separating the mind from the physical body, and treating them as distinct entities. Mind and body are inseparable. Both go to make the whole being. Any part of the whole is susceptible to harm. For there to be 'bodily harm' there must be a hurt or injury (other than of a transient or trifling kind): *R v Donovan* [1934] 2 KB 498, 509. A discernible intrusion upon or interference with the normal functioning of the physical or the mental process is required. It must be apparent, and identifiable as such. That is the only certain way of determining what is enough to

constitute the offence and what is not. Therefore we would respectfully adopt the approach taken in *R v Chan-Fook* and, applying it to a charge under s 188(2) [of the Crimes Act 1961], hold that grievous bodily harm includes really serious psychiatric injury identified as such by appropriate specialist evidence.

…

Finally, we refer to *R v Kneale* [1998] 2 NZLR 169 in which, having reviewed most of these authorities, this Court concluded that it was artificial and out of tune with current thinking to limit bodily harm to physical harm since every person consisted of mind and body. This was in the context of whether it might constitute self-defence if the accused had used force in the genuine belief that it was necessary to protect a third party from mental harm. These authorities lead, we think, inevitably to the conclusion that the term 'bodily injury' in s 4(7) includes a recognisable psychiatric disorder or ill-ness of the kind described in *van Soest* [[2000] 1 NZLR 179 (CA)]. Nor do we see this as creating any anomaly of the kind mentioned by Ms Davenport. She was obliged to concede that, if there were no accident compensation legislation, an application would be necessary under s 4(7) if it were desired to bring a claim for a physical injury after two years notwithstanding that it might be accompanied by another claim in tort of a kind falling outside s 4(7), such as assault or false imprisonment.

Accordingly, sympathetic though any Judge would be to the misfortune which has befallen the appellants, we are unable to regard their pleaded mental injuries as other than bodily injury. Thus an application under s 4(7) was required as a prerequisite to bringing their proceeding.

…

Consequence of non-compliance with s 4(7)
As it is now too late to bring an application under s 4(7) for an extension, six years having long since expired, the appellants' claim is plainly statute-barred. We agree with the conclusion of Tipping J in *A v D* (1996) 10 PRNZ 68 that the proviso in s 4(7) does not authorise an application for leave outside the six-year period merely because a sub-stantive proceeding may have been filed, without leave, during that period.

Smellie J was therefore correct in concluding that the proceeding must be struck out. It is bound to fail because of the limitation defence, which has been pleaded.

The appeal is dismissed with costs of $2500 to the Residual Health Management Unit and the same amount to the other respondents jointly. Each of the respondents is also to have their reasonable disbursements, including travel and accommodation costs of one counsel.

[**Result**: Appeal dismissed.]

Assault

Tuberville v Savage
(1669) 1 Mod 3, 86 ER 684 (KB)
[**FACTS**: Savage made a statement to which Tuberville took offence. Tuberville placed his hand on his sword, warning Savage that 'If it were not assize-time, I would not take such language from you'. Savage, in turn, took offence, his actions towards

Tuberville being the basis of the action in assault, battery, and wounding brought against him here. However, Savage alleged his actions were provoked, Tuberville's words amounting to an assault.]

[The Court found] The evidence to prove a provocation was, that the plaintiff put his hand upon his sword and said, 'If it were not assize-time, I would not take such language from you'. The question was, If that were an assault? The Court agreed that it was not; for the declaration of the plaintiff was, that he would not assault him, the judges being in town; and the intention as well as the act makes an assault. Therefore if one strike another upon the hand, or arm, or breast in discourse, it is no assault, there being no intention to assault; but if one, intending to assault, strike at another and miss him, this is an assault: so if he hold up his hand against another in a threatening manner and say nothing, it is an assault. In the principal case the plaintiff had judgment.

Stephens v Myers
(1830) 4 C & P 349, 172 ER 735 (CP)
[**FACTS**: Stephens was chairing a parish meeting at which Myers became angry and vociferous. The meeting voted to turn Myers out of the room. His reaction to this was to say that he would pull Stephens out of the chair instead. Myers immediately advanced with clenched fists towards Stephens who was seated at the head of the table. Six or seven people were between them, one of whom stopped Myers before he was close enough to hit Stephens. It appeared, however, that he intended to strike Stephens.]

Tindal CJ: [instructing the jury]
It is not every threat, when there is no actual personal violence, that constitutes an assault[;] there must, in all cases, be the means of carrying the threat into effect. The question I shall leave to you will be, whether the defendant was advancing at the time, in a threatening attitude, to strike the chairman, so that his blow would almost immediately have reached the chairman, if he had not been stopt; then, though he was not near enough at the time to have struck him, yet if he was advancing with that intent, I think it amounts to an assault in law. If he was so advancing, that, within a second or two of time, he would have reached the plaintiff, it seems to me it is an assault in law. If you think he was not advancing to strike the plaintiff, then only can you find your verdict for the defendant; otherwise you must find it for the plaintiff, and give him such damages as you think the nature of the case requires. Verdict for the plaintiff—Damages 1s.

Richardson v Rix
(1989) 12 MVR 522 (NSW SC)
[**FACTS**: On 10 April 1985, there was a motor vehicle collision between Rix and Richardson. Rix provided Richardson with some personal particulars and then returned to his car. Richardson was not satisfied that he had all the necessary particulars. He followed Rix to the car, reached in and grabbed the keys from the ignition to stop Rix from leaving. A scuffle followed, with Rix trying to recover his keys; his hand was slightly cut.

At trial, the magistrate held that removing the keys from the ignition constituted an assault. Richardson appealed.]

Allen J:

For the appellant the only matters which have been argued are that the magistrate erred in law in determining that the mere removal of the keys from the ignition lock constituted an assault and that she erred also in law in regarding it as material to the determination of whether that conduct constituted an assault, that the purpose for the removal of the keys was to prevent the respondent departing from the scene.

In modern usage 'assault' is used to comprehend both 'assault' in the strict sense and also trespass to the person (battery). The distinction between assault in the sense of 'battery' and assault in its former limited and strict connotation is, so far as relevant, as follows. Assault in the sense of battery is committed by any intentional physical force applied to the body of the victim which is offensive to a reasonable sense of honour and dignity. No physical harm need be intended or need result. Thus, going up to a woman whom one does not know and kissing her would be, except in unusual circumstances, battery ... The slightest intentional physical contact suffices but there is no battery unless the defendant does some positive and affirmative act. For example, not stepping aside and thereby preventing a person passing is not a battery—nor, indeed, is stepping in front of the person so that he cannot pass. Assault in its former limited and strict sense is committed intentionally creating in the victim a reasonable apprehension of imminent harmful or offensive bodily contact by the aggressor. The apprehension of such contact is all that is called for. It is not necessary that the victim actually be afraid. The assault is complete upon the causing of the apprehension whether or not the perceived threat ensues (so that there is an assault in the sense of battery).

In the present case if, when the appellant reached into the car, as it turned out, to grab the keys, the respondent reasonably apprehended that the appellant was about to make physical contact with his body, there was an assault by the appellant upon him at that point—for the contact, if made, undoubtedly would have been harmful or offensive. Further, if in the process of getting the keys out of the ignition lock there was any intentional bodily contact by the appellant upon the respondent, no matter how slight, there would have been [a battery]—for undeniably the contact would have been, in the circumstances, offensive to a reasonable sense of honour and dignity.

Thus intentional holding, pushing away, or pulling of any part of the plaintiff's body, no matter how slight, would have been [a battery] in the circumstances. So too, in the events immediately following the physical separation of the keys from the ignition lock, the 'tussle' as the magistrate described it, any intentional holding, pushing or pulling away by the appellant of any part of the respondent's body, no matter how slight, would have been [a battery]. However, the mere separation by the appellant of the keys of the respondent from the ignition lock was not an assault upon the respondent in the absence of any reasonable apprehension by the respondent that he was about to be subjected to harmful or offensive physical contact with him by the appellant or any actual holding, pushing, pulling or other intentional physical contact by the appellant upon him before or after that actual separation of the keys from the lock. In the absence of any such apprehension or of the occurrence of physical contact by the appellant upon the respondent all that the physical separation of the keys from the lock constituted was trespass to goods—not trespass to the person.

In these circumstances the proper course is to remit the matter to the magistrate with the opinion of the court in order that she may continue with the proceedings and give judgment according to law. The court so orders. The costs of the appeal will be costs in the cause in the proceedings before the magistrate.

I add this. The damages in these proceedings awarded by the magistrate were $200. There must be some limit to human folly and pig headedness and I strongly urge the parties to consider the realities of the final consequence of not settling the matter.

Brady v Schatzel; Ex parte Brady

[1911] St R Qd 206 (NC)

[**FACTS**: Schatzel, with two other men, went to Brady's house to talk to a boy who was living there. Brady became abusive. She sent the boy inside, fetched a rifle, appeared to load it and pointed it at Schatzel, who was standing within range. Brady threatened the men, saying 'If the lot of you don't clear out of this I will put something in your bloody arses'. Schatzel sued for assault but testified that he was not at all afraid. Brady stated that the rifle was not loaded. The lower court found Brady guilty of assault. Brady appealed.]

Chubb J:

… To point a loaded firearm at any one is an assault. *Reg v James*, per Tindal CJ (1844) 1 C & K 530. In *R v St George* (1840) 9 C & P 483, Parke B was of opinion that it is an assault to present a pistol at all, whether loaded or not, if the person pointed at believes the weapon to be loaded, and is thereby put in fear and alarm. In *Osborne v Veitch* (1858) 1 F & F 317, Willes J said, 'Pointing a loaded gun at a person is in law an assault', and did not qualify this by saying the person pointed at must be thereby put in fear. See also East, *Pleas of the Crown*, p 406. In *Blake v Barnard* (1840) 9 NSWSCR 75, part of the cause of action was 'presenting a pistol at the plaintiff, and threatening to shoot him', and Lord Abinger CB, in summing up, said that if the pistol was not loaded, it would be no assault and it was the plaintiff to prove that it was. In *The Queen v Cleary* (1870) 9 NSWSCR 75, where the prisoner presented a pistol, which was not loaded, at the prosecutor, who was within two or three yards, saying at the same time, 'It's loaded; I'll blow your brains out', the Full Court held there was no assault, because the weapon was powerless to injure by being discharged, and the threat was harmless. This case was questioned in *R v Hamilton* (1891) 12 NSWLR (L) 111, where the pistol presented was loaded …

As to the element of intention, every person is presumed to intend the consequences of his acts … Here the presenting of the rifle was accompanied by a threat to fire it, which was certainly inferential, if not positive, evidence that it was loaded. In my opinion, it is not material that the person assaulted should be put in fear, as observed by Parke B in *R v St George* (1840) 9 C & P 483. If that were so, it would make an assault not dependent upon the intention of the assailant, but upon the question whether the party assaulted was a courageous or a timid person. Possibly, the learned Baron, by the term 'bodily fear', only meant to imply apprehension or expectation, and not a physical fear, of assault. I am of opinion, therefore, that there was evidence on which the Justices, disbelieving the appellant's evidence, could reasonably find that the rifle was loaded, in which case, of course, the appellant having the actual 'present ability' to effect her purpose, was guilty of assault. And I think—if, in fact, the rifle was not loaded—the Justices, on the evidence, could find that she pretended that it was, and so had 'apparently' a present ability to effect her purpose, and in that case was also guilty of assault. The rule must therefore be discharged, with costs.

Holcombe v Whitaker

(1975) 318 So 2d 289 (Alabama SC)

[**FACTS**: The plaintiff, Joan Whitaker, and the defendant, Dr M C Holcombe Jr, met and began seeing each other socially. Some months later they married. However, the defendant began seeing a woman he had been dating prior to his marriage to the plaintiff. When the plaintiff objected, the defendant told her that he was still married to his first wife. She then asked him to either divorce his first wife and marry her legally or have the marriage with her annulled. The defendant refused both options.]

Shores J:

To say the least, the relationship between Miss Whitaker and Dr Holcombe began to disintegrate from this point forward. He moved out of the apartment, but came back from time to time, staying for as long as a week on at least one occasion. The plaintiff continued to ask him to get an annulment or to get a divorce from his wife and legally marry her. She went to the apartment occupied by the woman the defendant was then seeing again and found him there. Again, she had a conversation with him about getting an annulment. On that occasion he said 'If you take me to court, I will kill you'.

From that point on, the plaintiff testified that she began receiving telephone calls from Dr Holcombe and from his lady friend all hours of the night. She also received anonymous calls.

There was other evidence to the effect that, after Dr Holcombe threatened the plaintiff the first time, she moved to another apartment and got an unlisted telephone number. For a period of time the calls from Dr Holcombe and his friend stopped. Then her apartment was broken into and some of her clothes were soaked with what later appeared to be iodine. Thereafter, the calls resumed. After the break-in, she had new locks put on the door and the windows were nailed closed. She also had friends spend the night with her thereafter.

The plaintiff filed the instant suit in September, 1971. In October of that year, Dr Holcombe went to her apartment. When she refused to let him in, he began to beat on the door, tried to get in, and again said 'If you take me to court, I will kill you'.

...

... The plaintiff claimed that the defendant committed an assault when in June of 1971, she went to see him and tried to get him to get an annulment, he said 'If you take me to court, I will kill you'; and again in October, 1971, after she had filed the instant suit on September 29, 1971, when he went to her apartment and beat on the door, tried to pry it open, and said again, 'If you take me to court, I will kill you' ... The defendant claims this in no way can constitute an assault, because it was merely a conditional threat of violence and because no overt act was involved. In order to safeguard freedom from apprehension of harm or offensive conduct, the law provides an individual with a remedy at law. See Prosser, *Law of Torts*, p 37 (4th edn 1971).

An assault consists of '... an intentional, unlawful, offer to touch the person of another in a rude or angry manner under such circumstances as to create in the mind of the party alleging the assault a well-founded fear of an imminent battery, coupled with the apparent present ability to effectuate the attempt, if not prevented'. *Western Union Telegraph Co v Hill*, 25 Ala App 540, 542, 150 So 709, 710 (1933).

While the words standing alone cannot constitute an assault, they may give meaning to an act and both, taken together, may constitute an assault. Prosser, *supra*, (2nd edn 1955). In addition, words may negative an act in a manner that apprehension in such a case would be unreasonable. 'On the other hand, a show of force accompanied by an unlawful or unjustifiable demand, compliance with which will avert the threatened battery, is an assault'. 1 Harper & James, *The Law of Torts*, page 223 (1956). '... the defendant is not free to compel the plaintiff to buy his safety by compliance with a condition which there is no legal right to impose'. Prosser, *supra*, page 40 (4th edn 1971). It is obvious that the defendant in the instant case had no right to impose the condition he did on the plaintiff; and we cannot say that this condition explained away his threat to harm her.

The defendant says his conduct cannot constitute an assault because there was no overt action taken by him. The evidence from the plaintiff was that the defendant was pounding on her door making every effort to get into the apartment, and threatening to kill her if she persisted in 'taking him to court'. We cannot say, as a matter of law, that this was not sufficient to arouse an apprehension of harm or offensive conduct. We think it was a jury question, as was the question of whether the defendant had the apparent ability to effectuate the threatened act.

The defendant next complains that the trial court erred in allowing evidence of various events from the time of the break between the plaintiff and defendant.

...

According to the testimony offered on behalf of the plaintiff, the doctor succeeded in his efforts to frighten the plaintiff. She was fearful enough to ask friends to stay with her at night; never left the apartment alone after the threats on her life; had her brother-in-law nail the windows closed after the break-in of her apartment; and told one of her friends that she was afraid there might be poison in her coffee. We believe this testimony was relevant under the circumstances of this case. The defendant threatened to kill the plaintiff if she did something she had a legal right to do. We think the evidence of what occurred subsequent to his threats and emanating from them was relevant to the issues being tried.

[**Result**: Judgment affirmed.]

Police v Greaves

[1964] NZLR 295 (CA)

[**FACTS**: The police received a complaint that Greaves had attacked a neighbour. The police went to Greaves's house to investigate. Greaves met them at the door with a knife. He pointed the knife at one officer and said, 'Don't you bloody move. You come a step closer and you will get this straight through your *** guts'. The officer advanced. Greaves said 'Get off this *** property before you get this in your guts'. The officer withdrew. Greaves was charged with assault and convicted.]

North P:

In the Magistrate's Court, counsel for the respondent submitted that no *prima facie* case had been made out for the reason that the threat was a conditional one, and that the constable was in no peril unless he took a step forward. The learned Magistrate over-ruled this submission and convicted the respondent, saying, 'I find that Constable Ravelich had cause to believe the defendant had ability to carry out his threat'. The respondent then appealed to the Supreme Court when his appeal was allowed by Hutchison J, who expressed the opinion that as the threat was a conditional one, the police officer had no reasonable ground to believe that an assault was imminent ...

An assault is defined by s 2 of the Crimes Act 1961 to mean:

> The act of intentionally applying or attempting to apply force to the person of another, directly or indirectly, or threatening by any act or gesture to apply such force to the person of another, if the person making the threat has, or causes the other to believe on reasonable grounds that he had, present ability to effect his purpose.

In our opinion, if the other conditions of the definition were met—as they undoubt-edly were—there is no reason why a conditional threat should not constitute an assault. A threat in its very nature usually provides the person threatened with an alter-native, unpleasant though it may often be. It is only necessary to recall the oft repeated threat of the highwayman, 'Your money or your life' to see that if a pistol be pointed at the victim it would be idle to say that there was not a threat to apply force to the person of another in circumstances in which the person making the threat had, or at least caused the other to believe on reasonable grounds that he had, present ability to effect his purpose, and therefore that an assault had been committed. On the facts of the present case it was enough that the menacing attitude of the respondent caused the police officers to retire. As Lush J said in *Wood v Bowron* (1866) LR 2 QB 21, in speaking of the kind of threat we are here concerned with: 'It is the very essence of a threat that it should be made for the purpose of intimidating or overcoming the will of the person to whom it is addressed' (*ibid*, 30). The present case is to be distinguished from such cases as *Tuberville v Savage* (1669) 1 Mod 3, 86 ER 684, where the person from whom the threat came made it clear that he had no present intention of carrying out his threat. In that case the words used were, 'Were it not assize time' he would tell more of his mind.

With all respect for the view of the learned Judge, we do not think that *Read v Coker* (1853) 13 CB 850; 138 ER 1437 which was relied on by the prosecution is distinguishable from the present case. There the plaintiff, being in the defendant's workshop and refusing to quit when desired, was surrounded by the defendant's serv-ants, who tucked up their sleeves and aprons and threatened to break his neck if he did not go out. It was argued that this did not constitute an assault, but the Court was clearly of opinion that it did, Jervis CJ saying, 'If anything short of actual striking will in law constitute an assault, the facts here clearly show that the defendant was guilty of an assault. There was a threat of violence exhibiting an intention to assault and a present ability to carry the threat into execution' (*ibid*, 860; 1441). There is not the slightest suggestion in the argument or in the judgment that the fact that the plaintiff was offered an alternative prevented the threat from constituting an assault. Again, in *Blake v Barnard* (1840) 9 Car & P 626; 173 ER 985, the report of Lord Abinger's sum-ming up to the jury makes no point of the fact that the cocked pistol presented at the defendant's head was accompanied by the statement that 'if Blake was not quiet he would blow his brains out'. We can see no difference in principle between a demand that the person threatened should retire and a demand that he should not proceed further on his lawful occasions. The policemen were present here on their lawful occasions and their entry was barred; that in our opinion was sufficient. But in any event—though nothing was made of this either in the Court below or before us—it would appear that in fact both kinds of threats were made.

Accordingly, we are of opinion that the appeal must be allowed and the conviction and sentence entered by the Magistrate restored.

R v Kerr

(1987) 2 CRNZ 407 (CA)

[**FACTS**: The complainant was sunbathing in a bikini in her back garden. To stop her hat from blowing away, she had placed a handy axe across the brim. She fell asleep. Her next-door neighbour, Mr Kerr, entered the garden, allegedly with indecency on his mind. At one point, the Crown said, he picked up the axe and held it over the sleeping woman. Her daughter saw this and thought he was going to strike her mother. She shouted and woke her mother up, by which time Kerr had put the axe down, so the complainant never saw it in his hands. He was charged with assault. The trial judge, Jeffries J, directed the jury that as 'a matter of law, it is possible to threaten a person even though the object of the threat may not have been aware and that would be the case in a sleeping person'. His Honour said that the essential matter is whether the person has the present ability to effect his purpose of threatening.]

McMullin J: [Delivering the judgment of the Court]

… In differentiating between assault and battery Dr Glanville Williams in his *Textbook of Criminal Law*, (2nd edn), 173, describes a battery, involving as it does bodily contact, as a physical assault and the threat creating the apprehension of immediate force as a psychic assault. It follows from the difference in the meaning of the terms that under the common law there can be no assault where a person does not know that he is being threatened as would be the case where he is asleep or has his back to the person threatening him—*Russell* [on Crime (12th edn, 1964) vol 1, p 655]. It is otherwise with a battery because in that case there is the actual application of unlawful force by the aggressor to the victim …

[**Note**: The Court of Appeal found, however, that the Judge's directions were correct, because the language of the statute ('threatening by any act or gesture' to apply force) could cover situations where the complainant was unaware of the threat at the time it was made.]

False imprisonment

Bird v Jones

(1845) 7 QB 742, 115 ER 668 (QB)

Coleridge J:

In this case, in which we have unfortunately been unable to agree in our judgment, I am now to pronounce the opinion which I have formed: and I shall be able to do so very briefly, because, having had the opportunity of reading a judgment prepared by my brother Patteson, and entirely agreeing with it, I may content myself with referring to the statement he has made in detail of those preliminary points in which we all, I believe, agree, and which bring the case up to that point upon which its decision must certainly turn, and with regard to which our differences exist.

...

These are the facts: and, setting aside those which do not properly bear on the question now at issue, there will remain these: that the plaintiff, being in a public highway and desirous of passing along it, in a particular direction, is prevented from doing so by the orders of the defendant, and that the defendant's agents for the purpose are policemen, from whom, indeed, no unnecessary violence was to be anticipated, or such as they believed unlawful, yet who might be expected to execute such commands as they deemed lawful, with all necessary force, however resisted. But, although thus obstructed, the plaintiff was at liberty to move his person and go in any other direction, at his free will and pleasure: and no actual force or restraint on his person was used, unless the obstruction before mentioned amounts to so much.

I lay out of consideration the question of right or wrong between these parties. The acts will amount to imprisonment neither more nor less from their being wrongful or capable of justification.

And I am of opinion that there was no imprisonment. To call it so appears to me to confound partial obstruction and disturbance with total obstruction and detention. A prison may have its boundary large or narrow, visible and tangible, or, though real, still in the conception only; it may itself be moveable or fixed: but a boundary it must have; and that boundary the party imprisoned must be prevented from passing; he must be prevented from leaving that place, within the ambit of which the party imprisoning would confine him, except by prison-breach. Some confusion seems to me to arise from confounding imprisonment of the body with mere loss of freedom: it is one part of the definition of freedom to be able to go whithersoever one pleases; but imprisonment is something more than the mere loss of this power; it includes the notion of restraint within some limits defined by a will or power exterior to our own.

...

If it be said that to hold the present case to amount to an imprisonment would turn every obstruction of the exercise of a right of way into an imprisonment, the answer is, that there must be something like personal menace or force accompanying the act of obstruction, and that, with this, it will amount to imprisonment. I apprehend that is not so. If, in the course of a night, both ends of a street were walled up, and there was no egress from the house but into the street, I should have no difficulty in saying that the inhabitants were thereby imprisoned; but, if only one end were walled up, and an armed force stationed outside to prevent any scaling of the wall or passage that way, I should feel equally clear that there was no imprisonment. If there were, the street would obviously be the prison; and yet, as obviously, none would be confined to it.

Patteson J:

... Now the facts of this case appear to be as follows. A part of Hammersmith Bridge which is ordinarily used as a public footway was appropriated for seats to view a regatta on the river, and separated for that purpose from the carriage way by a temporary fence. The plaintiff insisted on passing along the part so appropriated, and attempted to climb over the fence. The defendant, being clerk of the Bridge Company, seized his coat, and tried to pull him back: the plaintiff, however, succeeded in climbing over the fence. The defendant then stationed two policemen to prevent and, they did prevent, the plaintiff from proceeding forwards along the footway; but he was told that he might go back into the carriage way, and proceed to the other side of the bridge, if he pleased. The plaintiff would not do so, but remained where he was above half an hour: and then, on the defendant still refusing to suffer him to go forwards along the footway, he endeavoured to force his way, and, in so doing, assaulted the defendant: whereupon he was taken into custody.

...

I have no doubt that, in general, if one man compels another to stay in any given place against his will, he imprisons that other just as much as if he locked him up in a room: and I agree that it is not necessary, in order to constitute an imprisonment, that a man's person should be touched. I agree, also, that the compelling of a man to go in a given direction against his will may amount to imprisonment. But I cannot bring my mind to the conclusion that, if one man merely obstructs the passage of another in a particular direction, whether by threat of personal violence or otherwise, leaving him at liberty to stay where he is or to go in any other direction if he pleases, he can be said thereby to imprison him. He does him wrong, undoubtedly, if there was a right to pass in that direction, and would be liable to an action on the case for obstructing the passage, or of assault, if, on the party persisting in going in that direction, he touched his person, or so threatened him as to amount to an assault. But imprisonment is, as I apprehend, a total restraint of the liberty of the person, for however short a time, and not a partial obstruction of his will, whatever inconvenience it may bring on him. If it be an imprisonment to prevent a man passing along the public highway, it must be equally so to prevent him passing further along a field into which he has broken by a clear act of trespass.

Lord Denman CJ:

I have not drawn up a formal judgment in this case, because I hoped to the last that the arguments which my learned brothers would produce in support of their opinion might alter mine. We have freely discussed the matter both orally and in written communications; but, after hearing what they have advanced, I am compelled to say that my first impression remains. If, as I must believe, it is a wrong one, it may be in some measure accounted for by the circumstances attending the case. A company unlawfully obstructed a public way for their own profit, extorting money from passengers, and hiring policemen to effect this purpose. The plaintiff, wishing to exercise his right of way, is stopped by force, and ordered to move in a direction which he wished not to take. He is told at the same time that a force is at hand ready to compel his submission. That proceeding appears to me equivalent to being pulled by the collar out of the one line and into the other.

...

I had no idea that any person in these times supposed any particular boundary to be necessary to constitute imprisonment, or that the restraint of a man's person from doing what he desires ceases to be an imprisonment because he may find some means of escape.

It is said that the party here was at liberty to go in another direction. I am not sure that in fact he was, because the same unlawful power which prevented him from taking one course might, in case of acquiescence, have refused him any other. But this liberty to do something else does not appear to me to affect the question of imprisonment. As long as I am prevented from doing what I have a right to do, of what importance is it that I am permitted to do something else? How does the imposition of an unlawful condition shew that I am not restrained? If I am locked in a room, am I not imprisoned because I might effect my own escape through a window, or because I might find an exit dangerous or inconvenient to myself, as by wading through water or by taking a route so circuitous that my necessary affairs would suffer by delay?

It appears to me that this is a total deprivation of liberty with reference to the purpose for which he lawfully wished to employ his liberty and, being effected by force, it is not the mere obstruction of a way, but a restraint of the person ...

Whittaker v Sandford

(1912) 110 Me 77, 85 A 399 (Supreme Judicial Court of Maine)

Savage J:

Action for false imprisonment. The plaintiff recovered a verdict for $1100. The case comes up on defendant's exceptions and motion for a new trial.

The case shows that for several years prior to 1910, at a locality called Shiloh, in Durham, in this state, there had been gathered together a religious sect, of which the defendant was at least the religious leader. They dwelt in a so-called colony. There was a similar colony under the same religious leadership at Jaffa, in Syria. The plaintiff was a member of this sect, and her husband was one of its ministers. For the promotion of the work of the 'movement', as it is called, a Yacht Club was incorporated, of which the defendant was president. The Yacht Club owned two sailing yachts, the *Kingdom* and the *Coronet*. So far as this case is concerned, these yachts were employed in transporting members of the movement, back and forth, between the coast of Maine and Jaffa.

[**Note**: The plaintiff, with her four children, sailed on the *Coronet* to Jaffa in 1905. In 1909, she decided to leave the sect and return to America by steamer. The defendant insisted she travel on the yacht *Kingdom*.]

The plaintiff fearing, as she says, that if she came on board the defendant's yacht she would not be let off until she was 'won to the movement' again, discussed that subject with the defendant, and he assured her repeatedly that under no circumstances would she be detained on board the vessel after they got into port, and that she should be free to do what she wanted to the moment they reached shore. Relying upon this promise, she boarded the *Kingdom* on December 28th and sailed for America. She was treated as a guest, and with all respect. She had her four children with her. The defendant was also on board.

The *Kingdom* arrived in Portland Harbour on the afternoon of Sunday, May 8, 1910. The plaintiff's husband, who was at Shiloh, was telephoned to by some one, and went at once to Portland Harbour, reaching the yacht about midnight of the same day ... From this time until June 6th following the plaintiff claims that she was prevented from leaving the *Kingdom*, by the defendant, in such manner as to constitute false imprisonment.

...

The case shows that on June 4, 1910, application was made to a justice of this court for a writ of *habeas corpus* to take, and bring to the court, the plaintiff and her four minor children, who it was alleged were restrained of their liberty on a certain yacht named *Kingdom* by the defendant, or by the captain or commanding officer of said *Kingdom,* or by the person or persons in charge of said *Kingdom.*

[**Note**: The plaintiff and her children were released when the writ was presented.]

…

The court instructed the jury that the plaintiff to recover must show that the restraint was physical, and not merely a moral influence; that it must have been actual physical restraint, in the sense that one intentionally locked into a room would be physically restrained but not necessarily involving physical force upon the person; that it was not necessary that the defendant, or any person by his direction, should lay his hand upon the plaintiff: that if the plaintiff was restrained so that she could not leave the yacht *Kingdom* by the intentional refusal to furnish transportation as agreed, she not having it in her power to escape otherwise, it would be a physical restraint and unlawful imprisonment. We think the instructions were apt and sufficient. If one should, without right, turn the key in a door, and thereby prevent a person in the room from leaving, it would be the simplest form of unlawful imprisonment. The restraint is physical. The four walls and the locked door are physical impediments to escape. Now is it different when one who is in control of a vessel at anchor, within practical rowing distance from the shore, who has agreed that a guest on board shall be free to leave, there being no means to leave except by rowboats, wrongfully refuses the guest the use of a boat? The boat is the key. By refusing the boat he turns the key. The guest is effectually locked up as if there were walls along the sides of the vessel. The restraint is physical. The impassable sea is the physical barrier.

…

A careful study of the evidence leads us to conclude that the jury were warranted in finding that the defendant was guilty of unlawful imprisonment. This, to be sure, is not an action based upon the defendant's failure to keep his agreement to permit the plaintiff to leave the yacht as soon as it should reach shore. But his duty under the circumstances is an important consideration. It cannot be believed that either party to the agreement understood that it was his duty merely to bring her to an American harbour. The agreement implied that she was to go ashore. There was no practical way for her to go ashore except in the yacht's boats. The agreement must be understood to mean that he would bring her to land, or to allow her to get to land, by the only available means. The evidence is that he refused her a boat. His refusal was wrongful. The case leaves not the slightest doubt that he had the power to control the boats, if he chose to exercise it. It was not enough for him to leave it to the husband to say whether she might go ashore or not. She had a personal right to go on shore. If the defendant personally denied her the privilege, as the jury might find he did, it was a wrongful denial.

…

But the damages awarded seem to us manifestly excessive. The plaintiff, if imprisoned, was by no means in close confinement. She was afforded all the liberties of the yacht. She was taken on shore by her husband to do shopping and transact business at a bank. She visited neighbouring islands with her husband and children, on one of which they enjoyed a family picnic. The case lacks the elements of humiliation and disgrace that frequently attend false imprisonment. She was respectfully treated as a guest in every way, except that she was restrained from quitting the yacht for good and all.

[**Result**: The plaintiff's damages were reduced to $500.]

Meering v Grahame-White Aviation Co Ltd
(1919) 122 LT 44 (CA)

[**FACTS**: The plaintiff Meering was 18, then a minor. He worked at the defendant aviation works and was building his own plane. The defendant's shopkeeper assisted Meering to obtain parts and tools for constructing his plane. However, the aviation works had suffered extensive thefts and Meering fell under suspicion. Under warrant, police searched his residence and found items that could be traced to the aviation works.

Meanwhile, Meering was told that he was wanted at the defendant's office. At the office he asked why he was wanted, stating he would leave if not answered. In fact, people were stationed outside to stop him from leaving, but he was unaware of this. He was told he was wanted to give evidence about some thefts. Though later charged with theft, Meering accounted for all items found in his residence. He sued for false imprisonment for the hour he spent in the defendant's office.]

Atkin LJ:

I think that we are obliged to take it that the issue as to false imprisonment raised on the pleadings was extended by the assent of both parties to an allegation that the plaintiff had in fact been falsely imprisoned at the works of the defendants before he was formally arrested by the detective sergeant. In respect of that it is said that that, after all, cannot be true because the plaintiff himself never supposed that he was imprisoned at the time. He used language which indicated that he was intending to go away if the persons who were proposing to see him and to take his evidence did not come soon. Therefore it is said that inasmuch as the plaintiff did not know that he was being imprisoned it is not possible that there could be evidence that he was imprisoned. I think that the case is important when that contention is to be dealt with, because it seems to me upon a review of the possibilities of what is meant by imprisonment, that it is perfectly possible for a person to be imprisoned in law without his knowing the fact and appreciating that he is imprisoned.

I do not think that it is necessary at this stage of the case and with the time at our disposal to go through the authorities dealing with the question of imprisonment. I am disposed to think that the definition of 'imprisonment' read by my brother Duke from 'Termes de la Ley' is an adequate and sufficient statement of what is meant by that expression. I think that one might add to that a reference to the case of *Bird v Jones* (7 QB 742), where Coleridge J indicated that to the definition of imprisonment and restraint of liberty, there has got to be added restraint within a particular space. A further discussion of the question of imprisonment and whether there can be imprisonment without the fact laying hands upon the person of the party imprisoned, is to be found in the case of *Warner v Burford* (4 CB NS 204), in a discussion by a very learned judge Wills J.

It appears to me that a person could be imprisoned without his knowing it. I think a person can be imprisoned while he is asleep, while he is in a state of drunkenness, while he is unconscious, and while he is a lunatic. Those are cases where it seems to me that the person might properly complain if he were imprisoned, though the imprisonment began and ceased while he was in that state. Of course, the damages might be diminished and would be affected by the question whether he was conscious of it or not.

So a man might in fact, to my mind, be imprisoned by having the key of a door turned against him so that he is imprisoned in a room in fact although he does not know that the key has been turned. It may be that he is being detained in that room by persons who are anxious to make him believe that he is not in fact being imprisoned, and at the same time his captors outside that room may be boasting to persons that he is imprisoned, and it seems to me that if we were to take this case as an instance supposing it could be proved that Prudence had said while the plaintiff was waiting: 'I have got him detained there waiting for the detective to come in and take him to prison'—it appears to me that that would be evidence of imprisonment. It is quite unnecessary to go on to show that in fact the man knew that he was imprisoned.

If a man can be imprisoned by having the key turned upon him without his knowledge, so he can be imprisoned if, instead of a lock and key or bolts and bars, he is prevented from, in fact, exercising his liberty by guards and warders or policemen. They serve the same purpose. Therefore it appears to me to be a question of fact. It is true that in all cases of imprisonment so far as the law of civil liability is concerned that 'stone walls do not a prison make', in the sense that they are not the only form of imprisonment, but any restraint within defined bounds which is a restraint in fact may be an imprisonment.

Under those circumstances, it appears to me that the sole issue in this case is whether there is evidence upon which the jury could find, quite apart from the plaintiff's knowledge of what the real fact was—that he was in fact imprisoned in the sense which I have mentioned, so that his liberty was in fact restrained; so that he was substantially in the same position as if the key had been turned in the door of the waiting-room where he was in fact waiting.

I think that there is evidence. We have to consider the whole of the facts, because we have to remember that, after all, this was a young man who was under suspicion at that time of stealing, and in respect of whom it would appear that the defendants had been taking some steps to ascertain what the true facts were for at least a week if not more. A search warrant had been executed and his room had been searched, and there can be no question, I think, but that at the time the police—both the works police represented by Hickie and the detective police—were suspicious of the plaintiff, and having this suspicion they had determined to see him and to interrogate him when they found him at nine o'clock.

Robinson v Balmain New Ferry Ltd
[1910] AC 295 (PC)
[**FACTS**: Archibald Robinson, a barrister, purchased a one-penny ferry ticket to travel from Sydney to Balmain. Upon learning that the next ferry would not go for 20 minutes, he decided to leave the wharf. As he was leaving the wharf, he was asked to pay another penny. The Balmain New Ferry Ltd's practice was to collect all fares on

the Sydney side of the harbour. Anyone entering or leaving the wharf in Sydney was charged one penny. Balmain Ferry had posted signs on either side of its turnstiles stating 'Notice. A fare of one penny must be paid upon entering or leaving the wharf. No exemption will be made to this rule, whether the passenger has travelled by the ferry or not'. Robinson refused to pay another penny. He tried to force his way past two of Balmain's employees. He was briefly prevented but managed to get past them and through the turnstile.

Robinson sued for false imprisonment. He succeeded at trial on the basis that he had not seen the signs. This verdict was set aside by rule *nisi*. The rule *nisi* was then discharged by the Supreme Court of New South Wales; two judges finding Robinson had no notice of the signs and a third finding that Balmain Ferry had given reasonable public notice of the conditions for entering the wharf. The matter went to the High Court of Australia where Robinson was found to have had notice. Robinson appealed to the Privy Council.]

Lord Loreburn LC:

In this case their Lordships entirely agree with the conclusion of the High Court. There has been considerable difficulty because of the way in which the case seems to have been presented in the Courts in Australia, and particularly in the Supreme Court of New South Wales. There is no note of the summing up of the learned judge who tried the case, and some of the arguments which have been advanced by the learned counsel for the respondents are not consistent with the arguments that were advanced on their behalf in the Australian Courts. But their Lordships think that the relevant facts are all quite beyond dispute, and that some of the facts disputed are quite immaterial.

The plaintiff paid a penny on entering the wharf to stay there till the boat should start and then be taken by the boat to the other side. The defendants were admittedly always ready and willing to carry out their part of this contract. Then the plaintiff changed his mind and wished to go back. The rules as to the exit from the wharf by the turnstile required a penny for any person who went through. Thus the plaintiff refused to pay, and he was by force prevented from going through the turnstile. He then claimed damages for assault and false imprisonment.

There was no complaint, at all events there was no question left to the jury by the plaintiff's request, of any excessive violence, and in the circumstances admitted it is clear to their Lordships that there was no false imprisonment at all. The plaintiff was merely called upon to leave the wharf in the way in which he contracted to leave it. There is no law requiring the defendants to make the exit from their premises gratuitous to people who come there upon a definite contract which involves their leaving the wharf by another way; and the defendants were entitled to resist a forcible passage through their turnstile.

The question whether the notice which was affixed to these premises was brought home to the knowledge of the plaintiff is immaterial, because the notice itself is immaterial.

When the plaintiff entered the defendants' premises there was nothing agreed as to the terms on which he might go back, because neither party contemplated his going back. When he desired to do so the defendants were entitled to impose a reasonable condition before allowing him to pass through their turnstile from a place to which he had gone of his own free will. The payment of a penny was a quite fair condition, and if he did not choose to comply with it the defendants were not bound to let him through. He could proceed on the journey he had contracted for.

Under these circumstances their Lordships consider that, when the defendants at the end of the case submitted that there ought to be a nonsuit, the learned judge ought to have nonsuited the plaintiff. Their Lordships are glad that they can thus arrive, in accordance with law, at this decision, because they regard the plaintiff's conduct as thoroughly unreasonable in this case.

...

Their Lordships will humbly advise His Majesty that this appeal should be dismissed with costs.

Herd v Weardale Steel, Coal and Coke Co
[1915] AC 67 (HL)
[**FACTS**: Herd worked as a hewer for Weardale Steel. On 30 May 1911 he went down the mine at 9.30 am to work a shift until 4 pm. He and two others were ordered to do some work, but they refused apparently on safety grounds. At 11 am, these three men with 29 others acting in sympathy with them requested to be taken to the surface in the cage lift, which was the only way out of the mine. The lift was available for the carriage of men at 1.10 pm. Some of the protesters (not including Herd) occupied the cage, but the employers refused to take them up until 1.30 pm. Weardale Steel sued Herd for breach of contract and was awarded 5 shillings damages and costs. Herd sued for false imprisonment. He succeeded at first instance and was awarded 20 shillings plus costs. The Court of Appeal reversed this by a majority, and found for the company.]
Viscount Haldane LC:
My Lords, by the law of this country no man can be restrained of his liberty without authority in law. That is a proposition the maintenance of which is of great importance; but at the same time it is a proposition which must be read in relation to other propositions which are equally important. If a man chooses to go into a dangerous place at the bottom of a quarry or the bottom of a mine, from which by the nature of physical circumstances he cannot escape, it does not follow from the proposition I have enunciated about liberty that he can compel the owner to bring him up out of it. The owner may or may not be under a duty arising from circumstances, on broad grounds the neglect of which may possibly involve him in a criminal charge or a civil liability. It is unnecessary to discuss the conditions and circumstances which might bring about such a result, because they have, in the view I take, nothing to do with false imprisonment.

My Lords, there is another proposition which has to be borne in mind, that is the application of the maxim *volenti non fit injuria*. If a man gets into an express train and the doors are locked pending its arrival at its destination, he is not entitled, merely because the train has stopped by signal, to call for the doors to be opened to let him out. He has entered the train on the terms that he is to be conveyed to a certain station without the opportunity of getting out before that, and he must abide by the terms on which he has entered the train. So when a man goes down a mine, from which access to the surface does not exist in the absence of special facilities given on the part of the owner of the mine, he is only entitled to the use of these facilities (subject possibly to the exceptional circumstances to which I have alluded) on the terms on which he has entered. I think it results from what was laid down by the Judicial Committee of the Privy Council in *Robinson v Balmain New Ferry Co* [[1910] AC 295] that that is so. There was a pier, and by the regulations a penny was to be paid by those who entered and a penny on getting out. The manager of the exit gate refused to allow a man who had gone in, having paid his penny, but having changed his mind about embarking on a steamer, and wishing to return, to come out without paying his penny. It was held that that was not false imprisonment; *volenti non fit injuria*. The man had gone in upon the pier knowing that those were the terms and conditions as to exit, and it was not false imprisonment to hold him to conditions which he had accepted. So, my Lords, it is not false imprisonment to hold a man to the conditions he has accepted when he goes down a mine ...

Now, my Lords, in the present case what happened was this. The usage of the mine—a usage which I think must be taken to have been notified—was that the workman was to be brought up at the end of his shift. In this case the workman refused to work; it may have been for good reasons or it may have been for bad—I do not think that question concerns us. He said that the work he had been ordered to do was a kind that was dangerous, and he threw down his tools and claimed to come up to the surface. The manager, or at any rate the person responsible for the control of the cage, said: 'No, you have chosen to come at a time which is not your proper time, and although there is the cage standing empty we will not bring you up in it', and the workman was in consequence under the necessity of remaining at the bottom of the shaft for about twenty minutes. There was no refusal to bring him up at the ordinary time which was in his bargain; but there was a refusal—and I am quite ready to assume that the motive of it was to punish him, I will assume it for the sake of argument, for having refused to go on with his work—by refusing to bring him up at the moment when he claimed to come. Did that amount to false imprisonment? In my opinion it did not.

Kuchenmeister v Home Office
[1958] 1 QB 496
[**FACTS**: Carl Kuchenmeister was a German citizen. He had been interned in England for some years and was effectively deported in 1948. He moved to Ireland and was still living there in 1955 when he made a trip to Amsterdam. The flight to Amsterdam was direct from Dublin. However, the return flight required him to transfer planes in London. His connecting flight left from a different terminal located a mile away and accessed via an open road. Although he told immigration officials that he was in transit and had no intention to remain in the United Kingdom, he was refused entry and told to wait. He was detained in the arrival terminal from 6 pm till 8.20 pm during which time various phone calls were made to find out what should happen to him. At 8.20 pm, an immigration officer escorted him to the departure terminal. However, they arrived too late for Kuchenmeister to catch his 8.40 pm flight to Dublin. He had to spend the night at the airport and was escorted to a flight the next morning. Kuchenmeister sued the immigration officials and the Home Office for false imprisonment. The defendants claim that the plaintiff, as an 'alien' under the Aliens Order 1953, had no right to enter the United Kingdom without permission.]

Barry J:

This is a claim for damages for wrongful imprisonment. Despite the fact that the plaintiff sustained no pecuniary damage, this case should certainly not be regarded, in my judgment, as anything in the nature of a storm in a teacup. Apart from the inconvenience, annoyance and humiliation which the plaintiff must undoubtedly have suffered, the right of individual liberty is here in issue. Anyone lawfully on British soil is entitled to the protection of the law, and if he is illegally deprived of his freedom, he has every right to seek the protection of the courts. The defendants do not otherwise contend. Their case is that the immigration officers who caused his detention were properly performing the duties imposed upon them by the Aliens Order, 1953, and they, too, regret the inconvenience (which they say was unavoidable) which the plaintiff suffered as a result.

The situation on April 27, 1955, was this: The plaintiff had left Ireland a few days before; he was returning to Dublin at the time of his detention; he was person acceptable to the Irish authorities, but he was one to whom the immigration authorities in this country were instructed to refuse leave to land [under the Aliens Order].

…

The gist of the problem is this: The defendants' contention is that it is within the sole discretion of the immigration authorities to lay down the prescribed limits or premises in which an alien landing under the provisions of article 2(1)(b) may remain. For various reasons, some of which are obvious, the senior immigration officer considered that aliens landing at the north section of the airport should be confined to the transit hall and certain other buildings in that section of the airport. His view was, and both the defendants' view is today, that if aliens were allowed to stray beyond those very narrow limits and wander off unescorted towards the central buildings, all effective control over their movements would be lost, because, unless a policemen was sent to accompany them, it was perfectly open to them never to proceed to the central buildings at all but to walk out of the airport and so travel to any part of England.

In those circumstances the defendants contend that they were entitled to say that, having landed lawfully under article 2(1)(b), the plaintiff was bound to remain in the transit lounge, or in some part of the buildings of the north section of the airport. All they did was to confine him within that perimeter, and in the circumstances it cannot possibly be alleged that they were guilty of any unlawful or enforced imprisonment. The plaintiff's rights were limited. He could only pray in aid article 2(1)(b) of the Order so long as he remained for the whole period between his landing and embarkation within such premises or limits as may be approved for the purpose by an immigration officer, and the fact that remaining within those limits caused him to lose his flight to Dublin is an unfortunate fact but one which was quite unavoidable, and about which the plaintiff had no legal ground for complaint. According to the defendants' view, if the plaintiff was to proceed outside the narrow confines of the north buildings, or such parts of the north buildings as were approved by the immigration authorities, he would be required leave to land. He never obtained leave to land, and in those circumstances no wrong has been done to him in insisting that he remain in the north buildings until about 8.20 in the evening.

…

The question therefore arises whether or not the plaintiff can maintain an action for wrongful imprisonment. As I have already indicated, if the immigration authorities were entitled to confine the approved area to the narrow limits to which they did in fact confine it, then the plaintiff could not say that he had been wrongfully imprisoned. If, however, they were not entitled so to confine the permitted area as to prevent him from obtaining access to the aeroplane for the purpose of catching which he had landed at the airfield, then I think that he is entitled to regard that as an unlawful imprisonment. His liberty was restricted to a greater degree than the immigration authorities were entitled to restrict it under article 2(1)(b). The fact that they might have restricted his liberty by employing the powers conferred upon them by other articles of the Order seems to me to be immaterial. It is no answer, when a man says 'I have been unlawfully arrested without a warrant', to say 'Well, had I (the person making the arrest) taken the trouble to go and ask for a warrant, I would undoubtedly have got it'. That would be no answer to a claim for unlawful arrest. Similarly here, although the second defendant and his colleagues could have detained the plaintiff by refusing him leave to land, that does not entitle them to detain him on the grounds on which they did.

No express powers of detention are conferred under article 2(1)(b). Mr Scarman has rightly conceded that immigration officials would be entitled to a reasonable time in which to satisfy themselves that the alien who arrived at the approved port really did intend to embark in an aircraft at the same port. If the immigration authorities' inquiries had been confined to that question and they had been completed within a reasonable time, the plaintiff would have raised no complaint: certainly Mr Scarman disclaims any suggestion that he would raise any such complaint on the plaintiff's behalf. Similarly, I think, without deciding the point, that they would be entitled to a reasonable time to consider whether or not to refuse the alien leave to land. Here the point does not appear ever to have been considered at all, and, if it were considered, it would not give rise to the type of inquiry which formed the subject-matter of the various telephone messages and conversations which took place between shortly after 6 o'clock and approximately 8.30 on the night of April 27.

Whatever view one takes of this case, on the interpretation of the law which I now adopt, I cannot see that his delay of nearly two and a half hours could possibly be regarded as reasonable. If I am wrong as to my view of the law, then no question as to reasonable time arises, because the plaintiff has never been unlawfully detained, but on the law as I understand it the plaintiff is entitled to recover damages.

He does not ask for an extravagant figure, but, on the other hand, it would be quite wrong for the court to award a contemptuous figure. No pecuniary damage has been suffered, but the very precious right of liberty—which is a right available to everyone who can for the time being be regarded as a subject by local allegiance to Her Majesty—is one which must be protected. I think that a fair figure which will vindicate the plaintiff's rights without amounting to a vindictive award would be £150. I should have felt fully entitled to increase that amount to a very great extent if there had been any suggestion here that the plaintiff was being ill treated by any of the immigration officials, but I am quite satisfied that they all genuinely considered that they were doing the best possible thing in difficult circumstances, and in my judgment no blame of any kind rests upon them. In these circumstances there must be judgment for the plaintiff for £150.

Murray v Ministry of Defence
[1988] 2 All ER 521 (HL)

[**FACTS**: Lance Cpl Davies and five armed soldiers were ordered to go to the plaintiff Margaret Murray's house at 7 am one morning to arrest her. Two of the plaintiff's brothers had earlier been convicted of arms offences in the United States connected with the purchase of weapons for the IRA.

Between 7 and 7.30 am, Cpl Davies remained with the plaintiff while she got dressed to leave. Other members of the family were kept in the living room during that time. At 7.30 am Cpl Davies formally arrested the plaintiff and, when asked by the plaintiff, Davies stated that the arrest was being made under s 14(a) of the Northern Ireland (Emergency Provisions) Act 1978, which provided for members of the armed forces on duty to arrest people without a warrant and detain for up to four hours a person suspected of committing an offence.

Her action was dismissed. She appealed.

The Court of Appeal found that the plaintiff was under restraint from 7 am but that she was not aware of it until she was told she was arrested at 7.30. As the plaintiff was not aware of restraint, the Court of Appeal found she was not falsely imprisoned, stating:

> Knowledge of the fact of restraint by the suspect is an essential element of an arrest. There was some indication to the contrary in *Meering v Grahame-White Aviation Co Ltd* (1919) 122 LT 44. In that case the Court of Appeal divided on the question. Atkin LJ expressly stated that awareness of the fact of detention was unnecessary. In the first place it is plainly inconsistent with the decision of the Court of Exchequer in *Herring v Boyle* (1834) [1 Cr M & R 377; 149 ER 1126]. I consider that the conclusion in *Herring v Boyle* is to be preferred to the dictum of Atkin LJ which was not part of the ratio of the decision, and, therefore, that the plaintiff was not subject to imprisonment until formally arrested.]

Lord Griffiths:
Counsel for the plaintiff attacked the finding of the Court of Appeal that the plaintiff did not know that she was under restraint until she was told she was arrested. He submitted that it is an irresistible inference that once the armed soldiers had entered the house and the plaintiff had identified herself and had been told to get dressed, she must have realised that she was under restraint. It is true she says she asked if she was under arrest whilst dressing, but this is to be interpreted as a challenge to authority rather than as indicating any doubt in her mind about the fact of restraint. It is pointed out that Cpl Davies was actually with her as she was getting dressed which was when she said she asked the question. Counsel for the Ministry of Defence felt constrained to accept this part of the plaintiff's submission and, in my view, he was right to do so. The plaintiff was in fact under restraint in her house from the moment she was identified. Cpl Davies stayed with her throughout the time it took her to dress and prepare to leave, and the plaintiff must have realised that she was under restraint and was not free to leave the house.

The next step in the plaintiff's argument is the submission that during the time that she was under restraint, between 7 and 7.30 am, she was not under arrest, and her arrest only commenced when she was told she was arrested at 7.30 am. Therefore, the plaintiff submits, the period of detention before arrest was unlawful and the Ministry of Defence liable for the tort of unlawful imprisonment during that period of half an hour whilst the plaintiff was getting dressed. If the plaintiff had been told she was under arrest the moment she identified herself, it would not have made the slightest difference to the sequence of events before she left the house. It would have been wholly unreasonable to take her off, half clad, to the army centre, and the same half hour would have elapsed while she gathered herself together and completed her toilet and dressing. It would seem a strange result that in these circumstances, whether or not she has an action for false imprisonment should depend on whether the words of arrest are spoken on entering or leaving the house, when the practical effect of the difference on the plaintiff is non-existent.

I do not accept the distinction drawn by the plaintiff's counsel between detention to the knowledge of the detainee and arrest. In *Shaaban bin Hussien v Chong Fook Kam* [1969] 3 All ER 1626 at 1629, [1970] AC 942 at 947 Lord Devlin said:

> An arrest occurs when a police officer states in terms that he is arresting or when he uses force to restrain the individual concerned. It occurs also when, by words or conduct, he makes it clear that he will, if necessary, use force to prevent the individual from going where he may want to go.

In *Spicer v Holt* [1976] 3 All ER 71 at 79, [1977] AC 987 at 1000 Viscount Dilhorne said:

> 'Arrest' is an ordinary English word ... Whether or not a person has been arrested depends not on the legality of the arrest but on whether he has been deprived of his liberty to go where he pleases.

In *Holgate-Mohammed v Duke* [1984] 1 All ER 1054 at 1056, [1984] AC 437 at 441 Lord Diplock said:

> First, it should be noted that arrest is a continuing act: it starts with the arrester taking a person into his custody (so by action or words restraining him from moving anywhere beyond the arrester's control), and it continues until the person so restrained is either released from custody or, having been brought before a magistrate, is remanded in custody by the magistrate's judicial act.

In the light of these authorities I can entertain no doubt that the plaintiff was under arrest from the moment that Cpl Davies identified her on entering the house at 7 am.

The question remains, however, whether the failure to tell the plaintiff that she was being arrested until the soldiers were about to leave the house renders the arrest unlawful. It has been well-settled law, at least since *Christie v Leachinsky* [1947] 1 All ER 567, [1947] AC 573, that a person must be informed of the reason for his arrest at or within a reasonable time of the arrest. There can be no doubt that in ordinary circumstances the police should tell a person the reason for his arrest at the time they make the arrest. If a person's liberty is being restrained, he is entitled to know the reason. If the police fail to inform him, the arrest will be held to be unlawful, with the consequence that if the police are assaulted as the suspect resists arrest, he commits no offence, and if he is taken into custody, he will have an action for wrongful imprisonment. However, it is made plain in the speeches in *Christie v Leachinsky* that there are exceptions to this general rule.

It is a feature of the very limited power of arrest contained in s 14 that a member of the armed forces does not have to tell the arrested person the offence of which he is suspected, for it is specifically provided by s 14(2) that it is sufficient if he states that he is effecting the arrest as a member of Her Majesty's forces. Cpl Davies was carrying out this arrest in accordance with the procedures in which she had been instructed to make a house arrest pursuant to s 14. This procedure appears to me to be designed to make the arrest with the least risk of injury to those involved including both the soldiers and the occupants of the house. When arrests are made on suspicion of involvement with the IRA, it would be to close one's eyes to the obvious not to appreciate the risk that the arrest may be forcibly resisted.

The drill the army follow is to enter the house and search every room for occupants. The occupants are all directed to assemble in one room and when the person the soldiers have come to arrest has been identified and is ready to leave, the formal words of arrest are spoken just before they leave the house. The army do not carry out a search for property in the house and, in my view, they would not be justified in doing so. The power of search is given 'for the purpose of arresting a person', not for a search for incriminating evidence. It is however a proper exercise of the power of search for the purpose of effecting the arrest to search every room for other occupants of the house in case there may be those there who are disposed to resist the arrest. The search cannot be limited solely to looking for the person to be arrested and must also embrace a search whose object is to secure that the arrest should be peaceable. I also regard it as an entirely reasonable precaution that all the occupants of the house should be asked to assemble in one room. As Cpl Davies explained in evidence, this procedure is followed because the soldiers may be distracted by other occupants in the house rushing from one room to another, perhaps in a state of alarm, perhaps for the purpose of raising the alarm and to resist the arrest. In such circumstances a tragic shooting accident might all too easily happen with young, and often relatively inexperienced, armed soldiers operating under conditions of extreme tension. Your Lordships were told that the husband and children either had commenced, or were contemplating commencing, actions for false imprisonment arising out of the fact that they were asked to assemble in the living room for a short period before the plaintiff was taken from the house. That very short period of restraint when they were asked to assemble in the living room was a proper and necessary part of the procedure for effecting the peaceable arrest of the plaintiff. It was a temporary restraint of very short duration imposed not only for the benefit of those effecting the arrest but also for the protection of the occupants of the house and would be wholly insufficient to found an action for unlawful imprisonment.

It was in my opinion entirely reasonable to delay speaking the words of arrest until the party was about to leave the house. If words of arrest are spoken as soon as the house is entered before any precautions have been taken to search the house and find the other occupants, it seems to me that there is a real risk that the alarm may be raised and an attempt made to resist, not only by those within the house but also by summoning assistance from those in the immediate neighbourhood. When soldiers are employed on the difficult and potentially dangerous task of carrying out a house arrest of a person inspected of an offence in connection with the IRA, it is I think essential that they should have been trained in the drill they are to follow. It would be impracticable and I think dangerous to leave it to the individual discretion of the particular soldier making the arrest to devise his own procedures for carrying out this unfamiliar military function. It is in everyone's best interest that the arrest is peaceably effected and I am satisfied that the procedures adopted by the army are sensible, reasonable and designed to bring about the arrest with the minimum of danger and distress to all concerned. I would, however, add this rider: that if the suspect, for any reason, refuses to accept the fact of restraint in the house he should be informed forthwith that he is under arrest.

In the circumstances in this case it was, in my opinion, reasonable to speak the words of arrest as they were leaving the house and the failure to do so at an earlier time did not render the plaintiff's arrest unlawful. I therefore agree with the conclusion of the Court of Appeal that the plaintiff was not unlawfully imprisoned between 7 and 7.30 am albeit my reasons for doing so are different from those of the Court of Appeal.

Although on facts of this case I am sure that the plaintiff was aware of the restraint on her liberty from 7.00 am, I cannot agree with the Court of Appeal that it is an essential element of the tort of false imprisonment that the victim should be aware of the fact of denial of liberty. The Court of Appeal relied on *Herring v Boyle* (1834) 1 Cr M & R 377; 149 ER 1126 for this proposition which they preferred to the view of Aktin LJ to the opposite effect in *Meering v Grahame-White Aviation Co Ltd* (1919) 122 LT 44. *Herring v Boyle* is an extraordinary decision of the Court of Exchequer: a mother went to fetch her 10-year-old son from school on 24 December 1833 to take him home for the Christmas holidays. The headmaster refused to allow her to take her son home because she had not paid the last term's fees, and he kept the boy at school over the holidays. An action for false imprisonment brought on behalf of the boy failed. In giving judgment Bolland B said (1 Cr M & R 377 at 381, 149 ER 1126 at 1127):

> … as far as we know, the boy may have been willing to stay; he does not appear to have been cognisant of any restraint, and there was no evidence of any act whatsoever done by the defendant in his presence. I think that we cannot construe the refusal to the mother in the boy's absence, and without his being cognisant of any restraint, to be an imprisonment of him against his will
> …

I suppose it is possible that there are schoolboys who prefer to stay at school rather than go home for the holidays but it is not an inference that I would draw, and I cannot believe that on the same facts the case would be similarly decided today.

[**Note**: The Court discussed *Meering v Grahame-White Aviation* approving Aktin LJ's ruling.]

[I]t is not difficult to envisage cases in which harm may result from unlawful imprisonment even though the victim is unaware of it. Dean William L. Prosser gave two examples in 'False Imprisonment: Consciousness of Confinement' (1955) 55 Col LR 847, in which he attacked §42 of the American Law Institute's *Restatement of the Law of Torts*, which at that time stated the rule that 'there is no liability for intentionally confining another unless the person physically restrained knows of the confinement'. Dean Prosser wrote (at 849):

> Let us consider several illustrations. A locks B, a child two days old, in the vault of a bank. B is, of course, unconscious of the confinement, but the bank vault cannot be opened for two days. In the meantime, B suffers from hunger and thirst, and his health is seriously impaired; or it may be that he even dies. Is this no tort? Or suppose that A abducts B, a wealthy lunatic, and holds him for ransom for a week. B is unaware of his confinement, but vaguely understands that he is in unfamiliar surroundings, and that something is wrong. He undergoes mental suffering affecting his health. At the end of the week, he is discovered by the police and released without ever having known that he has been imprisoned. Has he no action against A? ... If a child of two is kidnapped, confined, and deprived of the care of its mother for a month, is the kidnapping and the confinement in itself so minor a matter as to call for no redress in tort at all?

The *Restatement of the Law of Torts* has now been changed and requires that the person confined 'is conscious of the confinement or is harmed by it' (see *Restatement of the Law*, Second, Torts 2d (1965) §35, p 52).

If a person is unaware that he has been falsely imprisoned and has suffered no harm, he can normally expect to recover no more than nominal damages, and it is tempting to define the tort in the terms of the present rule in the American Law Institute's *Restatement of the Law of Torts*. On reflection, however, I would not do so. The law attaches supreme importance to the liberty of the individual and if he suffers a wrongful interference with that liberty it should remain actionable even without proof of special damage.

[**Result**: Appeal dismissed.]

Crimes Act 1961

32. Arrest by constable of person believed to have committed offence—Where under any enactment any constable has power to arrest without warrant any person who has committed an offence, the constable is justified in arresting without warrant any person whom he believes, on reasonable and probable grounds, to have committed that offence, whether or not the offence has in fact been committed, and whether or not the arrested person committed it.

35. Arrest of persons found committing certain crimes—

Every one is justified in arresting without warrant—

    (a) Any person whom he finds committing any offence against this Act that is punishable by death or for which the maximum punishment is not less than 3 years' imprisonment:

    (b) Any person whom he finds by night committing any offence against this Act.

New Zealand Bill of Rights Act 1990

21. Unreasonable search and seizure—

Everyone has the right to be secure against unreasonable search or seizure, whether of the person, property, or correspondence or otherwise.

22. Liberty of the person—

Everyone has the right not to be arbitrarily arrested or detained.

23. Rights of persons arrested or detained—

(1) Everyone who is arrested or who is detained under any enactment—

    (a) Shall be informed at the time of the arrest or detention of the reason for it; and

    (b) Shall have the right to consult and instruct a lawyer without delay and to be informed of that right; and

    (c) Shall have the right to have the validity of the arrest or detention determined without delay by way of *habeas corpus* and to be released if the arrest or detention is not lawful.

(2) Everyone who is arrested for an offence has the right to be charged promptly or to be released.

(3) Everyone who is arrested for an offence and is not released shall be brought as soon as possible before a court or competent tribunal ...

Whithair v Attorney-General

[1996] 2 NZLR 45 (HC)

Eichelbaum CJ:

The agreed facts are as follows:

1   The plaintiff was arrested and charged with being a male assaulting a female on Friday 23 July 1993.

2   He was arrested at Paraparaumu and on being denied police bail was detained at the Porirua Police Station until Monday 26 July 1993 when he was brought before Justices and released on bail, subject to conditions. There is no evidence of the plaintiff being told that the District Court at Wellington was sitting [on Saturday] nor that the District Court at Porirua could be requested to sit. These questions of law may be determined on the basis that no such advice was given.

3   The refusal to grant police bail was founded on a policy applicable to cases of domestic violence. The particular policy is known as the Kapiti Abuse Intervention Programme.

4   There was no regular sitting of the District Court at Porirua on Saturday 24 July 1993 but the District Court at Wellington sat on the morning of that day ...

The plaintiff has issued proceedings against the Attorney-General (sued in respect of the New Zealand Police) claiming $75 000 general damages and $75 000 exemplary damages.

...

4 *Can the failure of the police to bring a person arrested in accordance with law before a Court as soon as practicable after the arrest, in itself constitute the tort of wrongful imprisonment?*

The tort of false imprisonment has two ingredients: the fact of imprisonment and the absence of lawful authority to justify it ... The present question relates to the second.

[In] the recent decision of the High Court of Australia of *Michaels v R* (1995) 130 ALR 581 ... the appellant was convicted of escape from lawful custody, and the issue was whether the appellant was in lawful custody at the time of the escape. The lawfulness of the arrest was not challenged but the appellant put his argument that he was not in lawful custody in two ways; first that there had been undue delay in taking him before a Justice, and secondly, whether that was so or not, the detention was unlawful because he was being detained for questioning. It is clear that the majority of the Court accepted that the lawfulness of a detention may fluctuate with the circumstances. (See also *Lewis v Chief Constable of the South Wales Constabulary* [1991] 1 All ER 206.) In fact the appellant's conviction was upheld on the basis that any unlawfulness in detaining him for questioning had passed and that he was again in lawful custody. It is equally clear that the Court accepted that a detention, though originally lawful, may be rendered unlawful by unauthorised police questioning.

Mr Pike argued that in *Michaels* it appeared to be accepted that where the police had delayed in bringing a person before a Court, this would be regarded as unlawful detention only where the purpose for which he was held was not lawful. I do not agree. The appellant's separate argument on delay failed on the facts, see p 584. There is nothing in the judgment to suggest that if the appellant could have established 'undue delay' (the relevant statutory expression) in bringing him before a Justice, the detention would not have been held unlawful. There is no difficulty with the concept that if a person is detained for an excessive period without being brought before a Court, the detention becomes unlawful. Whether at any given moment the status of the detention had changed from lawful to unlawful must be a question of fact and degree. It follows that I do not accept Mr Pike's submission that the plaintiff's rights did not ascend to a point beyond that of a chance to apply for bail. The further submission that the plaintiff could not lawfully have used reasonable force to escape, notwithstanding that the hour of 10 am on the Saturday had passed, begs the question. A charge of escaping custody would have raised the issue whether the detention was lawful.

The principal argument for the defendant was based on the historical analysis of wrongful imprisonment as a form of trespass, requiring an intentional act by the defendant. On this footing, citing *Herd v Weardale Steele, Coal & Coke Co Ltd* [1915] AC 67 Todd, Burrows, Chambers, Mulgan & Vennell, *The Law of Torts in New Zealand* (1991) (Todd) argue (at p 94) that a mere omission to release a person from confinement may not be actionable in false imprisonment, the harm suffered being not direct but consequential. With respect I think counsel's contention is based on a misapprehension as to the proposition being advanced in Todd. The learned authors are not saying that an initially lawful arrest which has become unlawful because of undue delay cannot ground an action for unlawful imprisonment. If that were the case the proposition would run counter to authorities such as *Wright v Court* (1825) 4 B & C 596, *Davis v Capper* (1829) 10 B & C 28, *Drymalik v Feldman* [1966] SASR 227 (Full Court) and indeed the decision of the House of Lords in *John Lewis & Co Ltd v Tims* [1952] AC 676. It would also be contrary to what the authors of Todd say themselves (at p 105) to the effect that where undue delay can be established the detention is unlawful from the time the person should have been produced before a Court. Accordingly the answer to question (4) is Yes.

R v Governor of Brockhill Prison (ex parte Evans) (No. 2)

[2000] 3 WLR 843 (HL)

Lord Slynn of Hadley:

My Lords, this appeal raised an important question on which the judges in the courts below were divided. Many issues have been ventilated in argument before your Lordships and many cases cited: in the event it seems to me that the principles to be followed have been clearly established and the matter can be dealt with shortly since on the view I have reached on the first point other difficult questions do not arise.

On 12 January 1996 the respondent was sentenced *inter alia* to two years in prison. Because of the period she had spent in prison before trial she was entitled to a reduction in the actual period to be served pursuant to section 67 of the Criminal Justice Act 1967. It was for the governor of the prison where she was detained, not the sentencing judge, to work out the reduction and hence her release date. She was entitled to release on the date properly calculated and any detention after that date was unlawful unless some justification can be found.

The governor calculated the release date in accordance with earlier decisions of the Divisional Court in other cases which the Home Office and the governor thought that they were bound to follow ... Accordingly the governor said that her release date was to be 18 November 1996. The applicant contended that the governor, and therefore the Divisional Court in the earlier cases, were wrong and that her release date should be 17 September 1996. On 6 September she applied for a writ of *habeas corpus* to procure her release and on 16 October she sought leave for judicial review of the decision fixing her release date together with damages for false imprisonment. On 15 November 1996 the Divisional Court [1997] AB 443 held that her release date properly calculated was 17 September 1996 and ordered that she be released immediately. On 10 June 1997 Collins J dismissed her application for damages for false imprisonment: the Court of Appeal [1999] QB 1043 by a majority allowed her appeal on liability and increased the judge's assessment of damages from £2000 to £5000.

It is accepted that false imprisonment is a tort of strict liability; equally clearly deprivation of liberty may be shown to be lawful or justified. It may be so for example where it is pursuant to an order of a court or pursuant to the exercise of statutory powers. Here the court order did not specify the release date and the sentence of two years' imprisonment had to be read subject to the governor's duty to calculate the release date. The governor cannot therefore rely on the court's sentence alone. He has to rely on compliance with the statutory provisions. He thought that he was complying with those provisions because what he did was in compliance with what the law was thought to be. The Divisional Court has since held that that is not the law; the statutory provisions have never had the meaning he thought they had.

Is it a defence to a claim for false imprisonment that he complied with the law as the court then said it was? The Solicitor-General has adduced forceful arguments to the effect that the governor had no choice. He was bound to obey the law as expounded by the court not just once but several times. Not to do so would be to ignore the separation of powers between the judiciary and the executive.

Whatever the answer the governor cannot be criticised for what he did and I do not consider that the doubt raised in *Reg v Secretary of State for the Home Department, Ex parte Naughton* [1997] 1 WLR 118 as to the correctness of the earlier decisions meant that he was obliged to depart from those decisions.

If the claim is looked at from the governor's point of view liability seems unreasonable; what more could he have done? If looked at from the applicant's point of view she was, it is accepted, kept in prison unlawfully for 59 days and she should be compensated. Which is to prevail?

Despite sympathy for the governor's position it seems to me that the result is clear. She never was lawfully detained after 17 September 1996. She was merely thought to be lawfully detained. That is not a sufficient justification for the tort of false imprisonment even if based on rulings of the court. Although in form it is the governor, it is in reality the State which must compensate her for her unlawful detention ...

Lord Hope of Craighead:

... The Solicitor-General accepted that the question whether there was a lawful justification for the imprisonment had to be determined at the time of the imprisonment. He accepted that as a general rule it was false imprisonment for a person to be detained after his term of imprisonment had expired: *Mee v Cruikshank* (1902) 20 Cox CC 210; *Halsbury's Laws of England*, 4th edn reissue, vol 11(1) (1990), para 492; *Archbold Criminal Pleading, Evidence and Practice* (2000), para 19-331. But he submitted that the question whether the imprisonment was justified was a separate question from the question whether the imprisonment was lawful. He made it clear that his argument assumed, according to the concession which I have already mentioned, that the continued imprisonment of the applicant after 17 September 1996 was unlawful. What he sought to do was to show that, as the detention was thought at the time to be lawful as the calculation of the conditional release date had been made according to the existing state of the authorities, there was a justification for that imprisonment.

My Lords, I would be inclined to reject this argument on the ground that the defence of justification lacks a secure foundation on the facts. The judgment in *Reg v Secretary of State for the Home Department, Ex parte Naughton* [1997] 1 WLR 118, in which doubt was cast on the existing state of the authorities, was given on 4 September 1996. Two days later, on 6 September 1996, the applicant applied for *habeas corpus* on the ground that she was entitled to be released on 17 September 1996 and that her proposed release date of 18 November 1996, calculated according to the existing Home Office guidelines, was unlawful. On 15 November 1996 the Divisional Court granted her application and made a declaration that her detention was unlawful as from 17 September 1996. I do not think that the situation which arose in this case can be compared with those where the defence of justification is advanced on the ground that the alleged tortfeasor was acting within the four corners of a warrant issued which had been issued to him by the court. The order for imprisonment which was made by the Crown Court in this case recorded simply that on 12 January 1996 'it was ordered that the defendant be sentenced to two years imprisonment'. This was a sufficient authority to the governor to accept the applicant upon her arrival at the prison for which he was responsible as a person who had been lawfully commuted to his custody. But it did not give him any instructions about her conditional release date. Under the system laid down by section 67 of the Criminal Justice Act 1967 as amended it was for the governor, not the sentencing judge, to calculate the length of the period of discount. Furthermore the soundness of the existing guidelines had already been put in doubt by the observations in *Naughton*'s case by 6 September 1996 when, prior to the date which she maintained was her release date, the applicant applied to the court for *habeas corpus* and for judicial review of the decision which has been made by the governor. From the moment when her application was served on him the governor was on notice that he was at risk of it being held that his calculation was erroneous.

...

The Solicitor-General developed his argument along these lines. He said that the defence of justification was available to the governor because he was the addressee of a valid order of the Crown Court for the applicant's imprisonment and he had been instructed by the decisions of the court in similar cases as to how the conditional release date should be calculated. This argument was presented in a variety of ways. There was the justification point: the governor's method of calculation was based on what at the time was generally understood to be a clear line of authority. There was the obedience point: the governor had to construe the order of the court which imposed the sentence of imprisonment according to the law at the time when he was required to act upon it. He had to do, in obedience to that order, what the court through its decisions had told him to do. There was the constitutional point: it was unseemly for the governor, as a member of the executive, to do otherwise than comply with the law as laid down by the court. The executive's relationship with the courts did not depend on coercion. It depended on the executive's respect for the principle that an order of a court had to be obeyed until it was set aside. And there was the byelaw point: the position of the governor was analogous to that of a constable enforcing a byelaw which he had reasonable grounds to think was being breached but was later held to be *ultra vires*.

   The justification, obedience and constitutional points all depended on the Solicitor-General's basic proposition that the governor was complying with an order made by the court at all times during the period of the applicant's detention in custody until the Divisional Court issued its judgment as to the correct method of calculating her release date ...

   On further reflection I have reached the view that neither of these lines of authority can be applied by analogy to the position of the governor. The order which was issued by the Crown Court did no more than set out the date when the sentence of imprisonment was imposed and the length of that sentence. It did not identify the applicant's conditional release date. This was because the calculation of a prisoner's release date is a matter which has been committed by the statute to the governor. His obligation is to release the prisoner on a date which he has calculated in the manner laid down by the statute. It is for him to make the calculation, so the responsibility for any error in the calculation lies with him and not with the court which imposed the sentence of imprisonment. In practice he will no doubt rely on the relevant Home Office guidelines, and such guidance as is available from decisions of the courts in similar cases will no doubt be taken into account in the course of their preparation by the Home Office. But relying upon guidance of that kind is not the same thing as complying with the terms of a court order. It is no answer to a claim based on a tort of strict liability to say that the governor took reasonable care or that he acted in good faith when he made the calculation. Nor can he say, as in the case of the constables who were seeking to enforce the byelaws in the reasonable belief that a byelaw offence was being committed, that he had a lawful justification for doing what he did. His position would have been different if he had been able to show that he was acting throughout within the four corners of an order which had been made by the court for the applicant's detention. The justification for the continued detention would have been that he was doing what the court had ordered him to do. As it is, the court order when construed in the light of the provisions of the statute left it to the governor to calculate the release date according to the statute laid down. The justification had to be found in the terms of the statute.

I respectfully agree with Judge LJ's observation in the Court of Appeal [1999] QB 1043, 1078E-F, that for the governor to escape liability for any extended period of detention on the basis that he was acting honestly or on reasonable grounds analogous to those which apply to arresting police officers would reduce the protection currently provided by the tort of false imprisonment. I can see no justification for limiting the application of the tort in this way. The authorities are at one in treating it as a tort of strict liability. That strikes the right balance between the liberty of the subject and the public interest in the detection and punishment of crime. The defence of justification must be based upon a rigorous application of the principle that the liberty of the subject can be interfered with only upon grounds which a court will uphold as lawful. The Solicitor-General was unable to demonstrate that the applicant's detention was authorised or permitted by law after the date which was held by the Divisional Court to be her release date. I would hold that she is entitled to damages.

Damages

Collins J was confronted by the fact that there was almost no authority to which he could turn for guidance as to the right amount to award as damages in a case of this kind. He said that he would have awarded the sum of £2000 as general damages. There was no claim for special damages, and the applicant accepted that this was not a case for aggravated or exemplary damages. The Court of Appeal increased his figure to £5000. The Solicitor-General submitted that they should not have interfered with the decision of the judge at first instance. For the applicant Mr Emmerson said that the figure which has been fixed by Collins J was out of line with awards which had been made by the Strasbourg Court as compensation for contraventions of article 5 of the Convention. But he accepted that the question in this case related to the position in domestic law.

It is clear from the reasons which Lord Woolf MR has given [1999] QB 1043, 1060F-G, that the decision of the Court of Appeal to increase the amount of the award can be explained in part by the fact that the sum fixed by Collins J resulted in an amount per day which, when spread over the 59 extra days of imprisonment, was less than the daily figure which had been contended for by the governor. But these reasons indicate that the Court of Appeal were also taking the opportunity to provide guidance, in an area where guidance was almost entirely lacking, as to which approach should be taken into account in the assessment and as to the general level of award which should be made in similar cases. I consider that in each of these respects they were performing a legitimate function. I do not think that their decision as to the appropriate sum to be awarded is one with which your Lordships should interfere.

Conclusion

For the reasons which I have given I too would dismiss the appeal.

Intentional infliction of emotional distress

Victorian Railways Commissioners v Coultas
(1888) 13 AC 222 (PC)
Sir Richard Couch:

The respondents brought a suit against the appellants in the Supreme Court of the colony of Victoria to recover damages for injuries sustained by the respondent Mary Coultas, through the negligence of a servant of the appellants, and expenses incurred by the respondent James Coultas, her husband, through her illness. The statement of claim stated that, through the negligence of the servant of the defendants in charge of a railway gate at a level crossing, the plaintiffs, while driving over the level crossing, were placed in imminent peril of being killed by a train; and, by reason of the premises, the plaintiff, Mary Coultas, received a severe shock, and suffered personal injuries, and still suffered from delicate health and impaired memory and eye-sight. The defendants, by their defence, denied the allegations in the statement of claim, and further said they would contend that no cause of action was disclosed by it, as it was not stated that either the plaintiffs or their property were struck or touched by the train of the defendants; and, further, that the alleged damage arising from shock or fright, without impact, was too remote to sustain the action.

...

According to the evidence of the female plaintiff her fright was caused by seeing the train approaching, and thinking they were going to be killed. Damages arising from mere sudden terror unaccompanied by any actual physical injury, but occasioning a nervous or mental shock, cannot under such circumstances, their Lordships think, be considered a consequence which, in the ordinary course of things, would flow from the negligence of the gate-keeper. If it were held that they can, it appears to their Lordships that it would be extending the liability for negligence much beyond what that liability has hitherto been held to be. Not only in such a case as the present, but in every case where an accident caused by negligence had given a person a serious nervous shock, there might be a claim for damages on account of mental injury. The difficulty which now often exists in cases of alleged physical injuries of determining whether they were caused by the negligent act would be greatly increased, and a wide field opened for imaginary claims. The learned counsel for the respondents was unable to produce any decision of the English Courts in which, upon such facts as were proved in this case, damages were recovered.

Wilkinson v Downton
(1897) 2 QB 57
Wright J:

In this case the defendant, in the execution of what he seems to have regarded as a practical joke, represented to the plaintiff that he was charged by her husband with a message to her to the effect that her husband was smashed up in an accident, and was lying at The Elms at Leytonstone with both legs broken, and that she was to go at once in a cab with two pillows to fetch him home. All this was false. The effect of the statement on the plaintiff was a violent shock to her nervous system, producing vomiting and other more serious and permanent physical consequences at one time threatening her reason, and entailing weeks of suffering and incapacity to her as well as expense to her husband for medical attendance. These consequences were not in any way the result of previous ill-health or weakness of constitution; nor was there any evidence of predisposition to nervous shock or any other idiosyncrasy.

...

The defendant has, as I assume for the moment, wilfully done an act calculated to cause physical harm to the plaintiff—that is to say, to infringe her legal right to personal safety, and has in fact thereby caused physical harm to her. That proposition without more appears to me to state a good cause of action, there being no justification alleged for the act. This wilful *injuria* is in law malicious, although no malicious purpose to cause the harm which was caused nor any motive of spite is imputed to the defendant.

It remains to consider whether the assumptions involved in the proposition are made out. One question is whether the defendant's act was so plainly calculated to produce some effect of the kind which was produced that an intention to produce it ought to be imputed to the defendant, regard being had to the fact that the effect was produced on a person proved to be in an ordinary state of health and mind. I think that it was. It is difficult to imagine that such a statement, made suddenly and with apparent seriousness, could fail to produce grave effects under the circumstances upon any but an exceptionally indifferent person, and therefore an intention to produce such an effect must be imputed, and it is no answer in law to say that more harm was done than was anticipated, for that is commonly the case with all wrongs. The other question is whether the effect was, to use the ordinary phrase, too remote to be in law regarded as a consequence for which the defendant is answerable. Apart from authority, I should give the same answer and on the same ground as the last question, and say that it was not too remote ... It is, however, necessary to consider two authorities which are supposed to have laid down that illness through mental shock is a too remote or unnatural consequence of an *injuria* to entitle the plaintiff to recover in a case where damage is a necessary part of the cause of action. One is the case of *Victorian Railways Commissioners v Coultas* 13 App Cas 222, where it was held in the Privy Council that illness which was the effect of shock caused by fright was too remote a consequence of a negligent act which caused that fright, there being no physical harm immediately caused. That decision was treated in the Court of Appeal in *Pugh v London, Brighton and South Coast Ry Co* [1896] 2 QB 248 as open to a question. It is inconsistent with a decision in the Court of Appeal in Ireland: see *Bell v Great Northern Ry Co of Ireland* (1890) 26 LR Ir 428, where the Irish Exchequer Division refused to follow it; and it has been disapproved in the Supreme Court of New York: see *Pollock on Torts*, 4th edn p 47. Nor is it altogether in point, for there was not in that case any element of wilful wrong; nor perhaps was the illness so direct and natural a consequence of the defendant's conduct as in this case. On these grounds it seems to me that the case of *Victorian Railways Commissioners v Coultas* is not an authority on which this case ought to be decided.

A more serious difficulty is the decision in *Allsop v Allsop* 5 H & N 534, which was approved by the House of Lords in *Lynch v Knight* 9 HLC 577. In that case it was held by Pollock CB, Martin, Bramwell, and Wilde BB, that illness caused by a slanderous imputation of unchastity in the case of a married woman did not constitute such special damage as would sustain an action for such a slander. That case, however, appears to have been decided on the ground that in all the innumerable actions for slander there were no precedents for alleging illness to be sufficient special damage, and that it would be of evil consequence to treat it as sufficient, because such a rule might lead to an infinity of trumpery or groundless actions. Neither of these reasons is applicable to the present case. Nor could such a rule be adopted as of general applications without results which it would be difficult or impossible to defend. Suppose that a person is in a precarious and dangerous condition, and another person tells him that his physician has said that he has but a day to live. In such a case, if death ensued from the shock caused by the false statement, I cannot doubt that at this day the case might be one of criminal homicide, or that if a serious aggravation of illness ensued damages might be recovered. I think, however, that it must be admitted that the present case is without precedent. Some English decisions—such as *Jones v Boyce* (1816) 1 Stark 493; *Wilkins v Day* (1883) 12 QBD 110; *Harris v Mobbs* (1873) 3 Ex D 268—are cited in *Beven on Negligence* as inconsistent with the decision in *Victorian Railways Commissioners v Coultas*. But I think that those cases are to be explained on a different ground, namely, that the damage which immediately resulted from the act of the passenger or of the horse was really the result, not of that act, but of a fright which rendered that act involuntary, and which therefore ought to be regarded as itself the direct and immediate cause of the damage. In *Smith v Johnson & Co* unreported, decided in January last, Bruce J and I held that where a man was killed in the sight of the plaintiff by the defendant's negligence, and the plaintiff became ill, not from the shock from fear of harm to himself, but from the shock of seeing another person killed, this harm was too remote a consequence of the negligence. But that was a very different case from the present.

There must be judgment for the plaintiff for £100 1s 10½ d.

Stevenson v Basham

[1922] NZLR 225 (SC)

Herdman J:

This appeal raises a question of interest. In proceedings commenced in the Magistrate's Court the respondent Frances Caroline Basham, who is the wife of the respondent Claude Basham, claimed from the defendant the sum of £50 as general damages, and the respondent Claude Basham claimed the sum of £22 4s 6d as special damages, for loss sustained and injury caused by reason, it is alleged, of the wrongful conduct of the appellant.

The facts upon which the respondents relied in the Court below are simple. During the evening of the 3rd December, 1920, about 8.15, the appellant visited a dwellinghouse which was occupied by respondents and demanded that possession of the premises be given to him. There is evidence which justifies a finding that in the course of an appeal which appellant made for the surrender of the premises he said to Mr Basham, 'I'll have you out within twenty-four hours. If I can't get you out I'll burn you out'. When this statement was made Mrs Basham was in bed. She had not been feeling well and had retired to her room, presumably because she felt indisposed. At this time she was pregnant, having been in that condition for about three months. There is evidence which goes to prove that, although the threat to burn down the house was not made in Mrs Basham's presence, she nevertheless heard the appellant make the threat, and in consequence became seriously upset.

Mr Basham said that when he saw his wife after his interview with appellant she was sitting on her bed and was hysterical. It would appear that she was genuinely afraid that appellant would carry his threat into execution. That Mrs Basham was in a state of distress bordering on hysteria about something that had happened is made plain by the evidence of Mr Carr, who was in the house that night, and by Mrs Hepburn, a neighbour who was called in to look after Mrs Basham. On the following day Mrs Basham was unwell and had a temperature, so Dr Pettitt was called in. The doctor found that she was threatened with a miscarriage, and ordered her removal to a hospital, where, in due course, a miscarriage took place. It is contended that the appellant's conduct was responsible for this misadventure, and the learned Magistrate found that the miscarriage was caused by the fright which appellant's threat to destroy the house had given her.

In the light of the statement made by the doctor who was called in that 'undoubtedly the fright did prejudice her chances to a serious extent', and of the other facts proved, I am not prepared to hold there was not sufficient evidence to justify the Magistrate in coming to the conclusion that appellant's conduct was responsible for the mischief.

It is true that she had not been feeling well before appellant's conduct disturbed her, but I have not been able to discover any evidence which proves that she had gone to bed because symptoms of a miscarriage had appeared, or because she had any reason before Stevenson made his threat to suspect that a miscarriage was imminent. But even if a miscarriage was threatened before Stevenson frightened her, there is, I think, evidence which would entitle a jury to infer, if they thought fit, that Stevenson's conduct accelerated the trouble.

A consideration of the evidence satisfies me that the Magistrate, after hearing the witnesses, was entitled to hold that a threat to burn down the house was in fact made by appellant; that Mrs Basham, although not actually present, heard the threat, and that, because of the threat and appellant's noisy behaviour, she suffered a violent nervous shock which, in her then delicate state, produced serious physical consequences.

The only other matter that may be relevant to the question which the Magistrate had to determine is the extent of appellant's knowledge about Mrs Basham's presence in the house, and about the state of her health. It is clear that Stevenson knew that Mrs Basham was in the house. He says, 'I heard her talking. She was in the room'. But there is no proof that he knew that she was pregnant. Although ignorant of the state of her health, he must have known, or should have known, that his boisterous and threatening behaviour was calculated to frighten any person who at the time might be an inmate of the house.

The defendant represented [in *Wilkinson v Downton*] that the plaintiff's husband had met with a serious accident intending that the statement should be believed. In the present case Mr Stevenson may or may not have intended in his reckless mood that his threat to burn down the house would be believed. Whatever his intention was,

Mrs Basham heard what he said and did in fact believe that his threat was serious. The inference is that she feared for her own safety and for the safety of her children. If on all other grounds appellant is liable, he cannot escape because Mrs Basham erroneously interpreted his words. From the reported decisions, as I understand them, it appears to be settled law in England that if a physical injury follows fright or shock caused either wilfully or negligently, and the injury is the natural and direct consequence of the fright or shock and arises from a reasonable fear of personal injury, a defendant is liable in damages.

…

In the present case it cannot be said that appellant exercised the care which a prudent man should have exercised in the circumstances. Not only did he act with a lack of care, but when he angrily declared that he would burn the house down he accepted the risk that those who heard him would take his words seriously and would believe that he intended to carry out his threat. He went to the house in a fit of temper. He became abusive, he talked in a loud voice, and, although he knew that Mrs Basham could hear him, he was quite careless about the consequences which his unjustifiable conduct might have upon the nervous organisations of persons who at the time were living on the premises.

The one serious difficulty about the case is created by a decision of the Privy Council in *Victorian Railway Commissioners v Coultas*, a decision which, in the course of the last thirty-three years, has been criticised adversely in several judgments of great weight …

[**Note**: Herdman J set out the facts of *Coultas*.]

[T]heir Lordships decided that 'damages arising from mere sudden terror, unaccompanied by any physical injury but occasioning a nervous or mental shock, cannot under such circumstances be considered a consequence which, in the ordinary course of things, would flow from the negligence of the gatekeeper'.

It is difficult to understand this pronouncement, because, from the statement of facts given in *Mayne on Damages*, it appears that not only was there a mental shock caused by fright, but it also appears that the mental shock produced delicate health and impaired memory and eyesight.

Their Lordships refused to decide that impact was necessary, but held upon the facts proved that the damage which Mrs Coultas suffered was too remote to be recovered. In other words, the Privy Council appears to have decided that, because physical injury was not contemporaneous with the shock which Mrs Coultas received, she was not entitled to any relief. As I have already stated, this opinion has been unfavourably reviewed.

…

Although modern opinion in Great Britain seems to be unanimous in holding that the statement of the law in the Victorian case is either erroneous or obsolete, we in New Zealand are no doubt bound to follow their Lordships' judgment unless the facts of the present case can be distinguished from the facts of the case which the Privy Council decided.

The Privy Council judgment is founded on the assumption that the sudden terror which Mrs Coultas experienced was unaccompanied by actual physical injury. To what extent that finding was justified by the evidence I am unable to say, because it is not clear when any physical injury manifested itself. In the present case I think that there is evidence from which it can be inferred that a physical disturbance of some kind accompanied the shock which Mrs Basham received. Mrs Hepburn, who was called in to look after Mrs Basham on the evening when she was alarmed by appellant's behaviour, states that she was frightened and hysterical, and that next morning she was unwell and had a temperature. It is, no doubt, impossible to determine the precise moment at which the physical change which means the beginning of the process of miscarriage arises. It may accompany a shock immediately, or one day, or two days, or a long period, may elapse before evidence of the physical injury caused by the shock becomes apparent. About this kind of thing I have no knowledge, but, looking at all the circumstances of the case, I think that if a jury found that Stevenson was responsible for the shock which Mrs Basham got, they would also be entitled to hold that the premature expulsion of the contents of the uterus commenced immediately, and that therefore shock to the system was accompanied by actual physical injury.

Then again, in the Victorian case the element of wilfulness was not present, but in the case under consideration there is evidence from which a jury could draw an inference that Stevenson intended to terrify the occupants of the house. He knew that Mrs Basham was in the house, for he says that he heard her talking. If he did not intend to frighten Basham and those in the house, why did he make the threat? No matter how foolish he was, no matter how empty he intended his threat to be, I am not prepared to hold that Mrs Basham should have treated his words as meaningless.

The case against appellant, therefore, can be placed upon either of two grounds: either he was negligent when he uttered the threat which did the harm, or he wilfully intended to do harm. But, whether he acted negligently or wilfully, I think that the evidence proves that physical harm was so closely bound up with the shock which Mrs Basham suffered that it may be said that shock was accompanied by actual physical injury.

For these reasons I hold that the case is distinguishable from *Victorian Railway Commissioners v Coultas*, and that the Magistrate's judgment was right.

The appeal will accordingly be dismissed, with costs £7 7s.

McLoughlin v O'Brian
[1983] AC 410 (HL)
[**Note**: This case is based in negligence and not in intentional infliction of emotional distress and is discussed more fully in Chapter 4. These brief extracts are included here to illustrate the types of distress for which the law has allowed or refused compensation under principles of negligence. Consider whether the law should provide compensation for similar distress caused by intentional acts.]
Lord Wilberforce:
... Although we continue to use the hallowed expression 'nervous shock', English law, and common understanding, have moved some distance since recognition was given to this symptom as a basis for liability. Whatever is unknown about the mind-body relationship (and the area of ignorance seems to expand with that of knowledge), it is now accepted by medical science that recognisable and severe physical damage to

the human body and system may be caused by the impact, through the senses, of external events on the mind. There may thus be produced what is as identifiable an illness as any that may be caused by direct physical impact. It is safe to say that this, in general terms, is understood by the ordinary man or woman who is hypothesised by the courts in situations where claims for negligence are made.

[**Note**: Lord Wilberforce then set out five categories where the law had allowed recovery for nervous shock. These are set out in Chapter 4, under the heading 'Nervous shock'.]

Lord Bridge of Harwich:

The basic difficulty of the subject arises from the fact that the crucial answers to the questions which it raises lie in the difficult field of psychiatric medicine. The common law gives no damages for the emotional distress which any normal person experiences when someone he loves is killed or injured. Anxiety and depression are normal human emotions. Yet an anxiety neurosis or a reactive depression may be recognisable psychiatric illnesses, with or without psychosomatic symptoms. So, the first hurdle which a plaintiff claiming damages of the kind in question must surmount is to establish that he is suffering, not merely grief, distress or any other normal emotion, but a positive psychiatric illness. That is here not in issue. A plaintiff must then establish the necessary chain of causation in fact between his psychiatric illness and the death or injury of one or more third parties negligently caused by the defendant. Here again, this is not in dispute in the instant case. But when causation in fact is in issue, it must no doubt be determined by the judge on the basis of the evidence of psychiatrists.

Khorasandjian v Bush

[1993] QB 727 (CA)

[**Note**: This case is predominantly famous for the majority finding that Khorasandjian could claim in private nuisance for the harassment of her home. This was controversial, as she had no proprietary interest in the house. This finding was overruled in the House of Lords in *Hunter* (below in Chapter 5). The statements on intentional infliction of emotional distress are still good authority however.]

Dillon LJ:

In the present case the plaintiff and the defendant first met in the spring of 1990 at a snooker club in North Finchley which they and other young people of their acquaintance frequented ... They became friends. But the friendship then broke down. As the defendant put it in one of his affidavits, 'the [plaintiff] and I were friends but she told me that she wanted no more to do with me'. That she wanted no more to do with him is something which the defendant had, plainly, been unable to accept.

Among the earlier complaints of the plaintiff are complaints that the defendant assaulted her over Christmas 1991 and in the early months of 1992. There were also threats of violence, he behaved aggressively when he saw her, and he followed her around shouting abuse. Also he pestered her with telephone calls to her parents' home and at her grandmother's, to such an extent that the telephone number had to be changed. Also in January 1992 he stole her handbag from the snooker club and told her that he would keep it as a memento of her. As a result of threats and abusive behaviour to the plaintiff he was arrested by the police on 7 March and kept in custody over the weekend until 9 March when the magistrates gave him a 12 months' conditional discharge. Notwithstanding that, the defendant made further threats against the plaintiff, and on 13 May 1992 he was sent to prison by the Hendon magistrates for threatening to kill the plaintiff.

...

The injury for which damages were claimed in *Wilkinson v Downton* and *Janvier v Sweeney* [[1919] 2 KB 316] was in both those cases described as 'nervous shock'. On modern authorities in the law of negligence, that term is understood as referring to recognisable psychiatric illness with or without psychosomatic symptoms (see *per* Lord Bridge in *McLoughlin v O'Brian* [1983] 1 AC 410, 431H) or, as put by Lord Wilberforce in the same case, at p 418B, recognisable and severe physical damage to the human body and system caused by the impact, through the senses, of external events on the mind. It is distinguished from mere emotional distress. From the judgment of Bankes LJ in *Janvier v Sweeney*, it seems that he had much the same concept in mind, in that he refers in various citations to physical damage inflicted through the medium of the mind.

In the present case, the plaintiff in her evidence referred to the defendant's conduct as putting her under an enormous weight of stress. This is amply borne out by much else that she says. On the facts in evidence that is the predictable and, so far as the defendant is concerned, intended effect of the defendant's conduct. There is no medical evidence, and it could not as yet be said, that the plaintiff is suffering from any physical or psychiatric illness. But there is, in my judgment, an obvious risk that the cumulative effect of continued and unrestrained further harassment such as she has undergone would cause such an illness. The law expects the ordinary person to bear the mishaps of life with fortitude and, as was put in a case cited by Lord Bridge in *McLoughlin v O'Brian*, customary phlegm; but it does not expect ordinary young women to bear indefinitely such a campaign of persecution as that to which the defendant has subjected the plaintiff. Therefore, in my judgment, on the facts of this case and in line with the law as laid down in *Janvier v Sweeney*, the court is entitled to look at the defendant's conduct as a whole and restrain those aspects on a *quia timet* basis also of his campaign of harassment which cannot strictly be classified as threats.

Privacy

Tucker v News Media Ownership Ltd
[1986] 2 NZLR 716 (HC)
McGechan J:
Previous procedures and course of hearing
These proceedings necessarily have been conducted under conditions of considerable urgency and some secrecy. It is time that what has happened be placed on record. Proceedings by Mr Tucker commenced on 20 October 1986. An initial application was made to the District Court at Wellington seeking orders pursuant to s 140 of the Criminal Justice Act 1985 prohibiting publication of Mr Tucker's name and particulars in respect of certain past offences. The District Court decided it had no particulars in respect of certain past offences. The District Court decided it had no jurisdiction and an appeal, without additional paperwork, was taken to the High Court that same day.

News Media Ownership Ltd was not a party to that application. It was refused. The result was an immediate written application by Mr Tucker in the first instance on an ex parte basis for an interim injunction against News Media Ownership made and heard also on 20 October 1986 ... At a special hearing Jeffries J granted the interim injunction sought against News Media Ownership. The factual basis then known and reasons for that interim injunction are outlined later in this judgment. An urgent appeal was taken to the Court of Appeal by News Media Ownership on 23 October 1986 and was heard and dismissed that day. Again the factual situation then known and reasons for dismissal are discussed later in this judgment. The injunction of 20 October 1986 against News Media Ownership was followed by further ex parte injunctions sought by and granted to Mr Tucker against the Broadcasting Corporation of New Zealand and Auckland Star Ltd.

...

The first cause of action is based upon the tort of intentional infliction of distress, based on the principle set out in *Wilkinson v Downton* [1897] 2 QB 57 and *Stevenson v Basham* [1922] NZLR 225. The second cause of action alleges a tort of invasion of privacy seemingly along the lines of *Melvin v Reid* 297 P 91 (1931) and *Briscoe v Readers' Digest Association* 483 P 2d 34 (1971).

The statement of claim against New Media Ownership was accompanied by an ex parte notice of application for an interlocutory injunction restraining News Media Ownership 'from printing or publishing any newspaper article or other publication referring in any way to convictions entered, or alleged to be entered, against the plaintiff' until further order of the Court. A similar ex parte application against the Broadcasting Corporation referred to 'broadcasting or publishing any information' of that character. The application against the Star was in terms similar to that relating to News Media Ownership.

Facts
... Mr Tucker in past years was convicted of certain offences, including offences of indecency. I have no details of those convictions or penalties imposed. I wish it to be very clear that I do not confirm by this judgment the accuracy of various details of those convictions which sections of the media, notably Radio Windy, have seen fit to publish. Mr Tucker in the past has had at least one episode of suicidal tendencies, and in times past has sought psychiatric assistance. He may have a psychiatric or medical problem constituting a background to these convictions. I do not know, but I accept the possibility and the need for a sympathetic approach accordingly.

Mr Tucker has also suffered from serious heart disease for at least seven years. It has been at least exacerbated by viral infections. His condition is now described as a dilated cardiomyopathy. At some point prior to October 1986 a highly experienced cardiologist at Wellington Hospital, Dr Richard Thompson, with the benefit of seven years knowledge of Mr Tucker as a patient, reached as a matter of professional opinion a conclusion that he required a heart transplant operation.

It is obvious that the better the mental and physical shape of a patient facing major cardiac surgery, the better his prospects of success. It is also clear that stress can cause adverse effects both mentally and physically upon persons with cardiac problems, and in severe cases can be lethal. Such stress is to be avoided so far as practicable. Consistently, medical thinking is that transplant patients facing the major surgery involved should be kept stress-free so far as possible, and must be brought to an emotional condition where their attitude to the pending surgery and doubtless its recovery phase is positive. Accordingly, Dr Thompson was most anxious to see that his patient Mr Tucker built up to the proposed transplant operation in a stress-free and positive way. Mr Tucker had no greater resistance to stress than the average person.

Heart transplants were not then and as at the date of this judgment still are not carried out in New Zealand. This is a consequence of Government policy. I make no comment upon that policy. Such matters are for the Government of the day and its electorate, and are not for this Court. Where a transplant operation was required, the practice was for the patient to travel abroad, often involving huge expense. The Government made only partial grants towards that expense. Mr Tucker had only minimal funds ... A public fund raising drive was necessary if that which was believed to be a life-saving operation was to be arranged. That fund raising drive was undertaken. As a consequence, Mr Tucker found himself propelled reluctantly into the limelight. This fund raising drive over the period 10 to 21 October 1986 included at least one television appearance, radio interviews, and certain emotively couched newspaper advertisements supported in some cases by commercial sponsors. Those advertisements include a profile of Mr Tucker's nine-year-old daughter. The drive met with some success. The climax came when the Belinda Trainor Trust pledged up to $30 000 which together with Government assistance and other private donations provided sufficient funding. In fact it was anticipated that only some $20 000 would be needed from the Trainor Trust.

Meantime however a whispering campaign was gaining momentum. By at the latest 17 October 1986 *Truth* (owned by News Media Ownership) had received information to the effect that Mr Tucker previously had been convicted of criminal offences. The *Truth* reporter visited Mr Tucker and made this known. In the absence of evidence I do not suggest the visit was malicious in any way. It may have been a simple and proper inquiry in an endeavour to verify facts. Its results unfortunately were adverse. Dr Thompson describes Mr Tucker's state afterwards as approaching the hysterical requiring some 30 minutes conversation to restore calm. The reporter also spoke to Dr Thompson. Concerned, on 17 October 1986 Dr Thompson spoke to the editor of *Truth* and pleaded for editorial restraint. He was left, however, with the impression that *Truth* intended to publish ... Given the nature of the information, the controversy which has surrounded the matter, and the style of the newspaper concerned, I infer without difficulty that there is a very real possibility of such publication in the event of freedom given ...

In the belief that funds were arranged, and despite knowledge that *Truth* was on the trail of his previous convictions, Mr Tucker travelled to Sydney as arranged. He was assessed for his suitability for transplant at St Vincent's Hospital, and moved into accommodation to await further assessment and the availability of a donor heart. I infer from his settling down to wait in this fashion that there was nothing in the preliminary assessment made which indicated he would not be accepted as suitable.

A number of events then took place which must have led to accumulating and undesirable stress factors ...

[**Note**: The Trainor Trust withdrew its financial support and details of Mr Tucker's convictions were published on Radio Windy in Wellington, Radio Pacific in the

Auckland area, and in a Sydney newspaper. The hospital also decided to refuse the transplant operation apparently on medical grounds.]

Mr Tucker is a person at risk. He has coped so far with some considerable stresses. That does not mean his system can continue to cope if stresses continue to mount indefinitely. Everyone has a breaking point, and the breaking point for a cardiac patient can be unpredictable. There is no doubt that from a medical viewpoint it is highly desirable Mr Tucker be insulated from further stresses. Mr Tucker has a nine-year-old daughter. I accept that part of his concern will be for her as well as for himself. There must also be community concern for her if his convictions are disclosed. Children can be terribly cruel to children.

...

Interim injunction principles

I adopt of course the basic approach required by *American Cyanamid Co v Ethicon Ltd* [1975] AC 396, read in this case with *NWL Ltd v Woods* [1979] 3 All ER 614. I must first determine whether there is a serious question to be tried. If such exists, I must determine the balance of convenience. In relation to the latter, I must ask myself whether Mr Tucker could be adequately compensated by damages if an interim injunction is refused. If not, I must ask myself whether the defendants can be adequately compensated by damages if an interlocutory injunction is granted wrongly. If not, I must then look to other factors including the relative degrees of noncompensability, and the status quo. I must bear in mind in this case the approach stated in *NWL Ltd v Woods* as encapsulated by Lord Diplock at p 626:

> Where, however, the grant of refusal of the interlocutory injunction will have the practical effect of putting an end to the action because the harm that will have been already caused to the losing party by its grant or its refusal is complete and of a kind for which money cannot constitute any worthwhile recompense, the degree of likelihood that the plaintiff would have succeeded in establishing his right to an injunction if the action had gone to trial is a factor to be brought into the balance by the judge in weighing the reasons that injustice may result from his deciding the application one way rather than the other.

This is such a case. If the interim injunctions are discharged pursuit of the substantive proceeding by Mr Tucker, damages questions aside, will be pointless ...

Serious question to be tried

... Jeffries J accepted the possible applicability of the tort of intentional infliction of emotional distress or physical damage. Further, the learned Judge did not withdraw from finding for the first time in New Zealand the existence of a tort of invasion of privacy. He regarded the latter as a natural progression from the former. On appeal, the Court of Appeal did not hesitate to regard this case as raising a serious question to be tried ...

[**Note**: The Judge quoted the relevant passages from the judgments.]

Nothing has changed since those rulings which would persuade me that I can or should differ. Given the similarity of the three cases, the rulings as above in the *News*

Media Ownership case apply with equal force to the other two. There is a serious question to be tried.

Indeed, albeit with caution and hesitation in the absence of considered argument on the point and the warnings as to difficulty sounded by the Court of Appeal, particularly as regards the truth of the information is relevant. I go further. I support the introduction into the New Zealand common law of a tort covering invasion of personal privacy at least by public disclosure of private facts. The legislature has recognised a need for protection in the privacy field. I refer for example to s 67 of the Human Rights Commission Act 1977; s 22(1) of the Wanganui Computer Centre Act 1976; the heading to Part IXA of the Crimes Act 1961; and in a broadcasting context ss 24(1)(g) and 95(1)(g) of the Broadcasting Act 1976. The tort is well known in the United States of America. I refer for example to the general discussion albeit now somewhat dated in *Prosser on Torts* (4th edn, 1971) pp 809–12. The particular aspect of the general right to privacy relevant is that which has come to be known as protection from 'public disclosure of private facts'. The approach in such cases is well illustrated by *Melvin v Reid* 297 P 91 (1931) and *Briscoe v Readers' Digest Association* 483 P 2d 34 (1971) the former a decision of the District Court, Fourth District, California and the second a decision of the Supreme Court of California. It is a notable feature of the tort of invasion of personal privacy in that jurisdiction that truth is not a defence: *Prosser* at p 809. While the American authorities have a degree of foundation upon constitutional provisions not available in New Zealand, the good sense and social desirability of the protective principles enunciated are compelling. I do not think it beyond the common law to adapt the *Wilkinson v Downton* principles to significantly develop the same field and meet the same needs. Beyond these expressions of support for the concept I will not presently go, although I observe that the need for protection whether through the law of tort or by statute in a day of increasing population pressures and computerised information retrieval systems is becoming more and more pressing. If the tort is accepted as established, its boundaries and exceptions will need much more working out on a case by case basis so as to suit the conditions of this country. If the legislature intervenes during the process, so much the better.

…

Overall justice

In the end, the present case is very much to be decided by standing back and looking at the 'overall justice' of the situation. In stepping backwards to do so I remind myself however of the dangers of the Chancellor's foot and also that hard cases can make bad law. There are a number of factors to be weighed and balanced.

Great care must be exercised where the Court is aware that life potentially is at risk. The Courts are familiar enough with the exercise of jurisdiction where health and mental well-being are in issue. There is a clear duty to protect so far as practicable. Where life itself is at risk, that duty is even higher. However once again is it duty to protect only so far as practicable, and with regard and appropriate weight to other compelling requirements.[*sic*] In this case, Mr Tucker's life and health definitely are at risk to a degree. On the evidence, given his resilience to bad news over recent weeks, and his possible improvement even if it is only temporary (the latter to the point where at least one school of medical thought thinks a transplant operation is no longer immediately necessary) point to some margin of safety in that risk. The same can be said of medical evidence that reading or seeing an adverse media item has not traditionally been known to result in immediately lethal consequences. Some risk can be run, as long as it is borne in mind that a serious risk area exists.

Great care must be taken to preserve freedom of speech and its associated freedom of information ... I regard freedom of speech as important in the present case, but by no means the decisive element which the news media seeks to demand.

The protection of personal privacy is entitled to weight. Whether or not it is an independent right capable of protection by tort action, it is certainly a factor which can be taken into account where appropriate by a Court exercising such a judicial duty as determination of overall justice. Stated merely to that point, considerations of personal privacy favour maintaining the injunctions granted. However, in this case there is more to be considered. It may well be that a person loses a right to privacy by presenting himself to the public eye for evaluation. This concept is well recognised in American privacy law, and is not unknown to our own law in the somewhat cognate field of breach of confidence ... No doubt the Court of Appeal had this in mind when it referred to the plaintiff who makes an appeal to the public for funds. In this case Mr Tucker undoubtedly did put himself and his character forward to the public when appealing for funds through the media. By doing that he invited some degree of examination of his personal background and 'worth' in the eyes of persons considering requests for assistance. However, on the facts of this case I do not place undue weight on this qualification to privacy. Mr Tucker was a reluctant debutante so far as public exposure was concerned. It gave him no pleasure, and was forced upon him by a desperate need for funds for what then was perceived to be a life saving operation. There is some element of unfairness in holding that inevitable situation against him.

The Court must also have some regard to the interests of third parties. Third party interests traditionally are not regarded as carrying any great weight. The topic is conveniently discussed in Spry, *Equitable Remedies* (3rd edn, 1984) pp 385–6. The third party interests which I here perceive are those of the public, desiring information on topics in which it is interested, and Mr Tucker's nine-year-old daughter. I have discussed the former aspect already in relation to freedom of speech. The latter consideration deserves some weight. The Court must have some regard to the interests of an innocent infant. However, this is not a custody case in which the interests of a child are the first and paramount consideration, and a sense of proportion must be kept. I regard the protection of this child's interests very much in the same way as I would give it regard in an application under s 140 of the Criminal Justice Act 1985.

The Court should not engage in a futility. The principle is conveniently discussed in Spry, *Equitable Remedies* (3rd edn, 1984) pp 389–90, repeating a passage unchanged from the words of the first edition which were approved as 'a good general summary' by Cooke J in *Grocott v Ayson* [1975] 2 NZLR 586, 589. Put at its shortest, the general principle is:

> ... relief will not ordinarily be refused on the ground of futility *unless that futility is quite clear* or unless, at least, there is an additional circumstance, such as disproportionate hardship to the defendant, that renders damages more appropriate. (Emphasis added)

I consider here the italicised exception applies. Taking events to the close of hearing as at 5 pm on 4 November 1986, and adhering strictly to the evidence presented in the case and available reasonable inferences based on that evidence, certain things are very clear. Alleged convictions (correct or otherwise) had been broadcast over the Wellington area twice by Radio Windy and in Auckland and elsewhere in New Zealand by Radio Pacific and other independent radio stations at least once. Such convictions had been revealed in at least one newspaper in Sydney. At that date it was entirely predictable that news of such convictions would spread given the topicality of the affair. In New Zealand once the proverbial cat is out of the bag her progeny spread like lightning. While I do not take events subsequent to the close of hearing into account for the purposes of this judgment I note with no surprise at all that such is exactly what happened. This predictable situation raises points which have been concerning me. First, the Courts look somewhat ridiculous when attempting to bar publication by certain components of the news media while others, against whom no application has been made for injunctive relief, are running riot. The Courts are achieving nothing and the limited relief granted is seen as achieving nothing. Justice, as in the famous statue, certainly should appear blind, but should not appear stupid. It is all very well to contend that a Court should not allow the resumption of a wrong simply because other such wrongs have occurred meantime. That point has force, but the realities of the current situation must also be looked at. First, it is clear from the evidence that at the close of hearing the injunctions issued had been subverted by other publications to the point where their continuation was futile. While I do not take subsequent additional publications into account, the point has become even plainer since. Second, there is an element of unfairness in a situation where three elements of the media are restrained, but competitors are not. Such an obviously pointless frustration creates a justifiable sense of injustice. While I accept that point, I would remind the Broadcasting Corporation in passing of s 24(1)(g) of the Broadcasting Act 1976 [now s 4(c) of the Broadcasting Act 1989] requiring the Corporation to have regard to 'The privacy of the individual'. (A similar obligation rests upon Radio Windy and other private radio stations under s 95(1)(g).) It may be said that the statutory restraints imposed create some greater level of obligation than that which exists in relation to private newspapers. However, even in a situation of added duty if such exists, the position of all three does call for equalisation vis-à-vis their unrestrained competitors.

I am far from convinced that in the end it will be in the best interests of Mr Tucker to allow this matter to drag on. Even allowing for his state of health, the consequences socially must be faced at some point. In many ways it is better to 'get things over with' rather than to postpone the inevitable. It would not surprise me and I would sincerely hope, that he will find the greater part of the community is sympathetic to his unfortunate plight. There are always those who are not. They are best ignored.

Exercise of discretion
Weighing up these factors, in the end I am driven to the conclusion that Mr Tucker's private interests, even despite precarious health, must give way to the public interest in the situation which has developed. While taking all factors into account, I am particularly moved towards that decision by the clear futility of continuing the existing

injunctions. With respect, they were correct when granted, but they have been subverted by subsequent events.

...

Reform

This whole affair, in which all have been losers, points to the need for certain reforms.
I say nothing as to current Governmental policy on transplant procedures. That is a
political matter to be resolved elsewhere. However, on the legal front, something must
be done with urgency as to the following:

...

(3) Legislative action on some comprehensive basis determining the extent of
the right to privacy and the relationship of that right to freedom of speech. As
this case shows, the Courts are being forced into a position where they must
soon create new law as they see appropriate. This process which will be painful
and expensive to the litigants involved, might not be thought the ideal
approach. It will however be necessary if nothing is done.

Bradley v Wingnut Films Ltd
[1993] 1 NZLR 415 (HC)
Gallen J:
The film [*Brain Dead*] was shot on various locations in and around Wellington city,
including the Karori Cemetery and this was done with the permission of the Wellington City Council, to which body a fee was paid although a reduced fee. It is contended that the Wellington city authorities were not made fully aware of the nature of
the film or what was intended. After the filming had been completed but before the
film itself had reached final form, it received some publicity in *The Dominion* newspaper which included a photograph of the filming at Karori Cemetery.

The plaintiff is the holder of an exclusive right of burial in perpetuity to a burial
plot at the Karori Cemetery, Wellington. This right was originally acquired by the
plaintiff's grandfather who acquired it in 1911 when an uncle of the plaintiff died tragically at the age of 20 years. The plaintiff's grandfather imported a large marble tombstone which consists of a substantial plinth with a cross on top. The plot has a marble
wall around it and is reached by marble steps which led [*sic*] up from the adjacent path.
The bottom step which is on the path is concrete. The family name of 'Bradley'
appears in large letters at the base of the plinth. The tombstone is said to be something
of a landmark in the cemetery and the sexton, Mr McKee, indicated that it is sufficiently prominent to be used as a direction point when persons are being given directions as to finding their way around the cemetery.

The article in *The Dominion* included a photograph of night filming in the Karori
Cemetery and to the right of the photograph, the Bradley tombstone can be seen. It is
not possible to read the name, although the letters 'BRA' are visible behind a person
who is sitting on the wall at the side of the plot. The plaintiff did not initially see this
material but was telephoned by a member of his family, as a result of which he
acquired the newspaper and immediately recognised the family tombstone. The plain-

tiff and his wife were, in there own words, shocked and upset that the family tombstone appeared to be associated with what was described as a 'splatter movie'.

…

[**Note**: The first cause of action alleged intentional infliction of emotional distress.]

It is the plaintiff's case here that the action of the defendant was plainly calculated to produce some effect of the kind which was produced so that an intention to produce it ought to be imputed, in the words of Wright J in *Wilkinson v Downton*. The plaintiff says that bearing in mind that attitude of a considerable number of members of the public towards the sacredness of a burial plot, to deliberately associate that plot with a film of this kind and in particular with the behaviour which was depicted as having occurred in the cemetery, was plainly calculated to produce the distress which the plaintiff and his family have undoubtedly suffered.

…

Mr Allen for the defendant submitted that the nature of the reaction of which the plaintiff and his family gave evidence, was not such as to bring the situation within that contemplated by those cases where the tort has been considered and defined. He drew attention to the fact that in *Stevenson v Basham* the shock required was a violent nervous shock which produced serious physical consequences. He referred to a comment in *Tucker v News Media Ownership Ltd* [1986] 2 NZLR 716 where McGechan J referred to 'severe emotional distress provided that bodily harm results from it' and also he referred to certain English cases where he contended it is clear 'something more than mere shock is a requirement in establishing the tort' and also he referred to certain English cases where he contended it is clear 'something more than mere shock is a requirement in establishing the tort'. In particular he referred to the discussion in *Ravenscroft v Rederiaktiebolaget Transatlantic* [1991] 3 All ER 73 at p 76 where Ward J said that the word 'shock' describing the immediate response to the unpleasant stimulus, short in duration and subjective in duration, was not the kind of emotional distress for which the law gives damages. What it is necessary for the plaintiff to prove is a secondary longer-lasting reaction to the tragedy. Mr Allen submitted that there was no evidence of actual bodily harm being sustained by the plaintiff, Mr Bradley.

I accept that on the authorities to which I was referred, it is necessary for the plaintiff to establish something more than a transient reaction, however initially severe. This must translate itself into something physical and having a duration which is more than merely transient. Mr Allen submits that there is no evidence in this case which would satisfy those requirements.

I should say that I am satisfied on the evidence that Mr Bradley did receive a shock which is at least analogous to those discussed in the authorities and that it has had continuing consequences on his mental state, outlook and general well-being. There is no medical evidence before me to support any such conclusion and the only material I have to go on is the account given by Mr Bradley himself, supported as it is by his wife. If the case is to be taken further, then this is an aspect of the matter which may need to be explored. For the purposes of the present application, that is to the issue or non-issue of a perpetual injunction, I propose to assume that the plaintiff's condition is sufficient to satisfy the requirements of the cause of action provided the other requirements are also met. It therefore becomes necessary to consider what those other requirements are.

Wright J referred to proof that the defendant had wilfully done an act calculated to cause physical harm to the plaintiff. No doubt the defendant photographed those sequences of the film in which the plaintiff's tombstone appears, deliberately. The question arises as to whether that action or actions was calculated to cause physical harm to the plaintiff. In *Stevenson v Basham*, Herdman J accepted a formulation in Pollock, *The Law of Torts* (11th edn, 1920) to the effect that the question was whether the shock and the illness were natural consequences of the wrongful act or default. Pollock drew attention in the quotation to which reference has been made, to the two separate bases of action arising from negligence and wilful false statements. In both cases the terms used give rise to questions of foreseeability and foreseeability, in respect of nervous shock induced by negligence, has been considered in detail by the House of Lords in *McLoughlin v O'Brian* [1983] 1 AC 410. Herdman J in *Stevenson v Basham* accepted on the facts as found by the Magistrate that the person shouting the threats must have known in the circumstances that Mrs Basham to whom his comments were not directly addressed but was known to be in the house could have heard them. Foreseeability in the cases discussed has depended upon some kind of immediate relationship whether in the literal sense as between for example a mother and child or the more figurative sense which arises in the rescue cases. In considering that the nature of the action complained of will obviously be of relevance and I have already expressed the view that the extent to which the tombstone could be said to have been associated with the actions in the film and of which the plaintiff complains, was minimal.

In those circumstances I do not think that it could reasonably be said that it was foreseeable that the plaintiff would sustain physical damage arising out of mental shock by the extent to which the family tombstone appeared in the sequence concerned. I note too that the tort depends upon the actions concerned being intentional. I note too that the tort depends upon the actions based on negligence but it also has certain elements of direction in it. Intention may be imputed and in this context also, foreseeability is important. There is no evidence in this case to suggest that the defendant intended, in the ordinary sense of that word, to cause any distress to the plaintiff or his family in filming the sequence under consideration and in context I do not think that the consequences were so foreseeable in terms of the plaintiff's distress bearing in mind the position occupied by the tombstone in the film and its lack of relation to the action, that the damage even if proven could be said to have been intentional.

It is therefore my view that in two respects at least the requirements of the cause of action cannot be met. That is, I would not be prepared to find in the circumstances of this case, that the harm was foreseeable or that the action was directed against the plaintiff.

For those reasons I conclude that the plaintiff is unable to make out a case for relief under the first cause of action as pleaded ...

[**Note**: The second cause of action was breach of privacy.]

The present situation in New Zealand then is that there are three strong statements in the High Court in favour of the acceptance of the existence of such a tort in this country and an acceptance by the Court of Appeal that the concept is at least arguable. I too am prepared to accept that such a cause of action forms part of the law of this country but I also accept at this stage of its development its extent should be regarded with caution … So far in this country the only two detailed discussions of the nature and extent of the tort appear in *Tucker*'s case in the decisions of Jeffries and McGechan JJ. Jeffries J refers to the private aspects of a person's life and to 'unwarranted' publicity or public disclosure. Further on in his decision he suggests that the two adjectives protect against disclosure of intimate details which are outside the realm of legitimate public concern or curiosity. It is not unimportant to notice, however, that he regards the tort as being a natural progression from the tort of intentional infliction of emotional distress. That may well add aspects of motivation or imputed motivation. McGechan J did not attempt to define the matter in any greater depth, although he did refer to a basis of the tort being the good sense and social desirability of the protective principles enunciated in the American authorities referred to in Prosser, *The Law of Torts* (4th edn, 1971).

Ms Cull also referred to *Prosser and Keeton on The Law of Torts*, in her case the fifth edition (1984) at p 851. She relied in particular on two separate formulations which in that publication are referred to as in fact amounting to distinct torts: [t]he cases involving public disclosure of private facts, which is highly offensive and objectionable to a reasonable person of ordinary sensibilities[; and] secondly at p 863: '… publicity which places the plaintiff in a false light in the public eye'. Ms Cull indicated that three requirements have to be satisfied. First, that the disclosure of the private facts must be a public disclosure and not a private one.

Clearly enough in this case any disclosure will be public. Secondly, the facts disclosed to the public must be private facts and not public ones. It is here that I think an immediate difficulty arises. As Neazor J said in his decision in respect of an application for an interim injunction in this case, there could scarcely be anything less private than a tombstone in a public cemetery. I agree with that comment. The whole purpose of the stone is as a memorial and a publication to all those who choose to read it of the facts which the inscription is designed to preserve.

Reference can also be made to those cases where photographs were taken on public property of private land; see *Bathurst City Council v Saban* (1985) 2 NSWLR 704 and such cases as *Sports and General Press Agency Ltd v 'Our Dogs' Publishing Co Ltd* [1917] 2 KB 125 and there are dicta to the effect that there is no right to prevent one person photographing another. I do not see on the authorities that the plaintiff could possibly object to a photograph being taken of the tombstone and in fact what the plaintiff really objects to here is not that the tombstone was shown in the film, but that the tombstone is claimed to have been associated with activities which the plaintiff and his family find upsetting. When the matter is formulated in that way, it becomes clear that the situation is much more analogous with an action for defamation than one for breach of privacy.

The third requirement is that the matter made public must be one which would be highly offensive and objectionable to a reasonable person of ordinary sensibilities. Here too I think the plaintiff has difficulties. There is nothing in the film which reflects directly on the tombstone or persons associated with it, assuming that the plaintiff can properly be so described. No part of the action relates to the tombstone or indeed the burial plot or reflects upon it, other than the fact that one of the actors is shown for a very short period, sitting on one of the steps leading up to it, but there is nothing in the sequence or in this particular shot to suggest anything sinister or unpleasant in relation to the tombstone or the plot. The actions and incidents which the plaintiff and his family find unsavoury and unpleasant take place on or in relation to graves and vaults which were fabricated for the purpose. There is no suggestion that there is any connection with the plaintiff's tombstone or burial plot. The actor sits on the steps because they are there, not because they form any significant part of the sequence or do other than provide part of the general background of the cemetery.

…

If the matter were looked at in terms of the formulations by Jeffries J, I do not think that a tombstone in a public cemetery containing information which appears to be directed at the public, can be said to be a private aspect of the plaintiff's life, nor do I think that it is subjected to in the film to unwarranted publicity or public disclosure bearing in mind the limited extent to which it appears and the limited significance attached to it.

I do not think that the second cause of action has been made out and it seems to me that in the circumstances of this case, to accept that the tort was satisfied would be to extend the boundaries of an emerging tort far beyond what is safe and would impose restrictions on the freedom of expression which would alter the balance against such freedom more than could be justified.

P v D
[2000] 2 NZLR 591 (HC)
Nicholson J:
Circumstances
Because of P's occupation activities and publicity relating to those activities, P is a public figure. D is a journalist employed by the second defendant Independent News Auckland Ltd (Independent News) which publishes the *Sunday Star-Times* weekly newspaper.

About mid-March 1999 D was asked by Donna Chisholm of Independent News to prepare a profile article on P. As background material for the profile, D had a copy of a magazine article on P. D was also generally aware of the high profile P had from work activities and P's comments in the media on work matters. D made a call to P's office requesting an interview. The telephonist said that P would require written questions, names of other parties D would be talking to and a guarantee that P would see a draft of the article before it was published and could then make any deletions or alterations P wanted. D reported this to Ms Chisholm who said to press on with inquiries for the article and to interview other people who knew P personally and workwise. D did and obtained comments from a number of people. In his affidavit D said that it soon became evident that few would go on record with what they had to say.

D said that as part of his general knowledge of P he was aware of a suggestion that P had suffered some psychological or psychiatric problem. He said that he understood this suggestion was known by a number of people, including some police and people in P's occupation in P's district but it had never been made specific or had been the subject of comment in any profile on P. D deposed that it had occurred to him that if the topic could be properly verified and P was willing to comment on it, it would provide an interesting aspect to P's profile—someone who has experienced personal difficulties but has overcome them to become successful. D said that at that stage his thoughts on the topic were quite preliminary and it was, and could be, only one topic in any profile that might ultimately be considered for publication. He said that he recognised he needed to be very discreet about making an inquiry about such a topic. He made one inquiry of 'one trusted source'. That source was able to be no more specific than to confirm that D was not the only person to understand P had experienced some psychiatric problem. D said that the source indicated P had been treated at H, a psychiatric hospital, and that a local policeman had come to P's aid in an emergency situation. He said the source had no direct knowledge of the circumstances and was unable to give him verification. The source was only able to tell him the name of the policeman who, the source believed, had come to P's aid. D deposed that the source has had no contractual or [occupational] relationship with P.

D contacted the police officer, C, who D understood had attended an incident involving P. D said that C would not discuss it, or even confirm it. C was more interested in knowing how D knew to contact him. D said that he couched the first and only question to C along the lines that he believed C had been involved in a medical situation and may even have saved P's life.

D deposed that during an interview with one of the 'unnamed' members of P's [occupation group], D also asked if that person knew anything about whether P had any upheavals in P's life. That person responded by saying that he was aware of where D was going but he would not go anywhere down that path. D commented that whether that person was referring to the circumstances into which he was inquiring or something else was not clear. D said that he did not say anything more specific than 'upheavals'.

D then rang P's office and asked the receptionist for a box number as he intended to post P a letter containing some questions relating to 'that topic'. D said that he did not mention to the receptionist why he wanted the box number. He said the receptionist had a brief discussion with someone else and then said to him 'I have recorded you have made this call Mr [D]. Good bye' and hung up. D then obtained the box number and posted P a letter dated 24 March 1999 stating:

> Dear [P]
>
> You are probably aware from a telephone call I made to your office last week that the *Sunday Star-Times* is preparing an article on yourself.
>
> Your secretary said for you to participate in the article you would require written questions, a list of names of people whom we would also be talking to, and an assurance that you could read the article before publication and omit material.
>
> Unfortunately, we cannot agree to the conditions.
>
> However, I think it is important I put the following questions to you for a response:
>
> I am aware that a [named town] police officer (who I can inform you has refused to talk to us, or even confirm our information) once came to your aid over an emergency medical situation, and that you have been treated at [H].

I would like to talk to you about these matters, particularly in respect to how you have apparently overcome these matters to be the … of the high standing that you are.

There is also a number of other things I want to talk to you about like your background, [occupation activities,] you[r] future and so on, but of course that is information which I can glean from other interviews you have given.

I would appreciate you calling me on [telephone number] before Saturday to give me an indication or answer as to whether you are prepared to discuss the above.

Regards

[D]

D marked the envelope confidential so that none of P's staff would open it.

D was unable to advance the matter further then as he was due to take a month's holiday starting on 30 March 1999. He said that apart from reporting to Ms Chisholm and the editor, he had spoken only to his source and the policeman on the topic. He decided that if he was to follow up that issue before he went on holiday he could do so only by approaching P directly. D prepared a draft profile on P which he did not consider to be in publishable form. He said that as far as he is concerned, there is no currency in a profile of P and that the draft he prepared is not in a form he would contemplate submitting for publication.

On Thursday 25 March 1999, solicitors acting for P faxed the editor of the *Sunday Star-Times* stating '… [D] has provided written advice that the article is to contain matters that, if correct, would amount to a gross breach of confidentiality and a serious damage of [P's] privacy'. The solicitors said that unless they received confirmation forthwith that no such information was to be published, then an interim injunction preventing publication would be sought the next day.

On Friday 26 March 1999, solicitors for P filed an ex parte application for interim injunction. There followed communication between lawyers acting for P and the defendants. Upon the defendants undertaking not to publish without giving notice, the proceedings were adjourned with restricted file access orders.

…

[**Note**: The judge dismissed the claim in breach of confidence; there was no evidence that the information had come to D's attention as a result of a breach of an obligation of confidence. The information could easily have come from someone who was not under such an obligation.]

Privacy

Mr Tizard submitted that it is far from settled whether there is a tort of privacy in New Zealand law. Mr Miles submitted that the number of judgments in New Zealand now supporting a right of action for invasion of privacy are such that it is clear that such a tort is recognised and the only remaining issues are to the tort's ambit.

In *Bradley v Wingnut Films Ltd* [1993] 1 NZLR 415 Gallen J decided a direct contest on whether a tort of privacy existed in New Zealand. In that case the plaintiff sought an injunction restraining the defendant film producer from publishing film which showed the plaintiff's family tombstone. Having canvassed the submissions of counsel and pertinent decisions and articles, Gallen J said at p 423:

> The present situation in New Zealand then is that there are three strong statements in the High Court in favour of the acceptance of the existence of such a tort in this country and an acceptance by the Court of Appeal that the concept is at least arguable. I too am prepared to accept that such a cause of action forms part of the law of this country but I also accept at this stage of its development its extent should be regarded with caution ...

Two of the High Court statements referred to by Gallen J were those of Jeffries J in *Tucker v News Media Ownership Ltd* (High Court, Wellington, CP 477/86, 22 October 1986) and McGechan J in *Tucker v News Media Ownership Ltd* [1986] 2 NZLR 716 (the *News Media Ownership* case). Jeffries J granted interim injunctions stopping newspaper proprietors from publishing Mr Tucker's criminal convictions in circumstances where Mr Tucker was seeking public donations for his overseas heart transplant. The Court of Appeal upheld the injunctions in *New Media Ownership Ltd v Tucker* (Court of Appeal, Wellington, CA 172/86, 23 October 1986). McGechan J later rescinded the injunctions because the convictions had been revealed to the public by organisations other than the defendant.

[**Note**: The judge quoted from the three judgments in the *Tucker* decision.]

I take into account the decision of the Court of Appeal in England in *Kaye v Robertson* [1991] FSR 62 that there is no right of action for a breach of personal privacy in England and the provisions of s 14 of the New Zealand Bill of Rights Act 1990:

> 14. Freedom of expression—Everyone has the right to freedom of expression, including the freedom to seek, receive, and impart information and opinions of any kind in any form.

However, the right of freedom of expression is not an unlimited and unqualified right and in my view is subject to limitations of privacy as well as other limitations such as indecency and defamation. I adopt the statements of Jeffries J, the Court of Appeal and McGechan J in the *News Media Ownership* case and I join with Gallen J in accepting that the tort of breach of privacy forms part of the law of New Zealand.

In the *Bradley* case Gallen J recognised the constant need to bear in mind that the rights and concerns of the individual must be balanced against the significance in a free country of freedom of expression and he noted the difficulty in formulating bounds which would ensure that both concerns are appropriately recognised.

In the *News Media Ownership* case Jeffries J referred at p 6 to 'unwarranted publication of intimate details of a plaintiff's private life which are outside the realm of legitimate public concern, or curiosity'.

In the *Bradley* case at pp 423–4 Gallen J applied three factors propounded by the American jurist William L. Prosser as reported in *Prosser and Keeton on Torts* (5th edn, 1984) at p 856. They applied to public disclosure of private facts. First, that the disclosure of the private facts must be a public disclosure and not a private one. Second, facts disclosed to the public must be private facts and not public ones. Third, the matter made public must be one which would be highly offensive and objectionable to a reasonable person of ordinary sensibilities. The authors of the fifth edition of *Prosser and Keeton on Torts* also referred to a fourth factor 'that the public must not have a legitimate interest in having the information made available' (p 857).

In *TV3 Network Services Ltd v Broadcasting Standards Authority* [1995] 2 NZLR 720, Eichelbaum CJ decided an appeal against the decision of the Broadcasting Standards Authority that TV3 had failed to comply with its responsibility under the Broadcasting Act 1989 to maintain standards consistent with the privacy of the individual. The acts complained of were surreptitiously filming a woman on her own property and revealing that she had been an incest victim. Eichelbaum CJ emphasised that he was not considering whether the publication complained of constituted a tort but whether it was one fit for the imposition of a standard by the authority which was charged with maintaining standards consistent with the privacy of the individual (p 728).

In considering the privacy principles enunciated by the authority, he said at p 727:

> Essentially the first branch of the appellant's argument was an attack on the authority's adoption of USA case law. As noted the authority went to this source because of the perceived paucity of reported cases and absence of a clear definition of privacy in New Zealand. At the time of issue of the advisory opinion, so far as I am aware the only New Zealand reported cases on the topic were the judgments of McGechan J in *Tucker v News Media Ownership Ltd* [1986] 2 NZLR 716 and Neazor J in *Bradley v Wingnut Films Ltd* (1992) 24 IPR 205. I am sure the authority's reference to the absence of clear definition was not intended as criticism of the terms of those judgments, the point being rather that by contrast with North America, in New Zealand this field of law was still in its infancy and the scope of any tort of privacy and the principles applicable had not yet been fully developed.

It is to be noted that the judgment of Gallen J in Bradley was delivered after the authority issued its advisory opinion.

The privacy principles enunciated by the authority were:

(i) The protection of privacy includes legal protection against the public disclosure of private facts where the facts disclosed are highly offensive and objectionable to a reasonable person of ordinary sensibilities.

(ii) The protection of privacy also protects against the public disclosure of some kinds of public facts. The 'public' facts contemplated concern events (such as criminal behaviour) which have, in effect, become private again, for example through the passage of time. Nevertheless, the public disclosure of public facts will have to be highly offensive to the reasonable person.

(iii) There is a separate ground for a complaint, in addition to a complaint for the public disclosure of private and public facts, in factual situations involving the intentional interference (in the nature of prying) with an individual's interest in solitude or seclusion. The intrusion must be offensive to the ordinary person but an individual's interest in solitude or seclusion does not provide the basis for a privacy action for an individual to complain about being observed or followed or photographed in a public place.

(iv) Discussing the matter in the 'public interest', defined as a legitimate concern to the public, is a defence to an individual's claim for privacy.

(v) An individual who consents to the invasion of his or her privacy cannot later succeed in a claim for breach of privacy.

Eichelbaum CJ did not regard the privacy principles as incorrect or inappropriate and concluded that the Authority was justified in holding that principle (i) had been breached. Therefore, although his decision did not relate to tort it did endorse the principle that the protection of privacy includes protection against the publication of private facts where the facts disclosed are highly offensive and objectionable to a reasonable person of ordinary sensibilities.

I consider that the tort of privacy in New Zealand encompasses public disclosure of private facts and in that regard breach should be determined by consideration of the three factors propounded by *Prosser and Keeton* and adopted by Gallen J in the *Bradley* case plus a fourth factor of the nature and extent of legitimate public interest in having the information disclosed. The nature and extent of legitimate public interest can vary considerably and ranges from idle curiosity and amusement to assessment of character, credibility and competence.

The four factors are:

(i) That the disclosure of the private facts must be a public disclosure and not a private one.

(ii) Facts disclosed to the public must be private facts and not public ones.

(iii) The matter made public must be one which would be highly offensive and objectionable to a reasonable person of ordinary sensibilities.

(iv) The nature and extent of legitimate public interest in having the information disclosed.

I believe these four factors provide an appropriate balance for deciding between the right of freedom of expression and the right of privacy in cases of public disclosure of private facts.

Applying those factors to the facts presently before the Court, I consider that information that a person had been treated at a psychiatric hospital is in the category of private fact and that disclosure of that information by publication in a newspaper or other news media would be public disclosure. Decision on the third and fourth factors is not as clear-cut.

With the increasingly enlightened public attitude that disabilities such as mental illness are not cause for exclusion, scorn or embarrassment, it can be argued that a person who has been treated at a psychiatric hospital should not be embarrassed or upset by public disclosure of that information. However, that is an idealistic point of view which does not take into account actual human emotion and the value which people place on having intimate personal information such as their medical treatment kept private.

In P's affidavit, P said:

... I will be devastated if the *Sunday Star-Times* or any other publication were allowed to print material such as that referred to in [D's] letter ... were information or rumour such as that contained in the attached exhibit 'C' published I believe my [family] will be caused serious stress and harm ... Such is the value I put upon my privacy and my [family] that I would be prepared to cease [occupation] if I felt that my continued [occupation] would expose the most private and sensitive parts of my life to media exposure ... I also believe that publication would have a serious affect on my own confidence and my ability to free myself from rumour, speculation and innuendo ...

The factor that the matter must be one which would be highly offensive and objectionable to a reasonable person of ordinary sensibilities prescribes an objective test. But this is on the basis of what a reasonable person of ordinary sensibilities would feel if they were in the same position, that is, in the context of the particular circumstances. I accept that P has the stated feelings and consider that a reasonable person of ordinary sensibilities would in the circumstances also find publication of information that they had been a patient in a psychiatric hospital highly offensive and objectionable.

I do not consider, however, that a reasonable person of ordinary sensibilities would in the circumstances find publication of the information that police had come to their aid over an emergency medical situation highly offensive and objectionable unless it was linked with the information that the person had been treated at a psychiatric hospital. On its own the statement could relate to a wide range of situations including the frequent giving of emergency medical aid to hapless road accident victims.

On the material before me there is no basis for concern that P's past or present mental health renders P unfit to carry out P's occupation to an appropriate standard and that the disclosure of the information is in the public interest in so far as assessment of P's character, credibility or competence is concerned I accordingly consider that legitimate public interest in having the information disclosed is minimal.

I therefore find that publication by either defendant of the information that P had been treated at a psychiatric hospital or information to that effect would be a breach of the tort of privacy with relation to P.

Mr Tizard submitted that P needed to prove that the defendants were in possession of specific information concerning P. The defendants have been informed that P was in a psychiatric hospital. That is sufficient. Whether or not that information is true or false and whether the defendants are able to verify it does not rob it of the quality of being information.

Mr Tizard submitted that P also needed to prove that the defendants were likely to publish the information if not restrained by the Court. He referred to the affidavit of Ms Chetwin, the editor of the *Sunday Star-Times* in which she deposed that the newspaper had not even reached a point where serious consideration was being given to publishing any specific article on P and that the newspaper 'does not presently propose to publish any article on P although it cannot rule out that possibility in the future'.

This point is linked with Mr Tizard's further submission that a permanent injunction would preclude any future publication by the defendants of whatever information it was that P wished to prevent whatever the circumstances ...

I am satisfied that there is sufficient risk that the defendants will publish the information if and when they receive verification that it is correct. The tenacity with which the defendants pursued verification is testament to the attractiveness to them of publishing the information and their wish to do so. I accept that publication is likely to have the gravity of result that P deposed to and that the harm of publication could not be adequately compensated by damages.

Although the principle of freedom of expression is a very important principle which the defendants strive to uphold, I consider that there will not be any substantial degree of hardship caused to them by an order prohibiting publication if that order grants leave to them to apply for its revocation or amendment if there is a significant change in circumstances. This meets Mr Tizard's point that injunction would preclude any future publication by the defendants. However, in fairness to the plaintiff, such an application should be on notice to the plaintiff giving suitable opportunity to be heard. The order which I propose to make does not amount to a ban on legitimate inquiry but solely on publication.

For the reasons stated, I consider that this is an appropriate case to make an injunction order. I do not consider a declaration appropriate. I order that an injunction issue and apply until further Order of the Court prohibiting the defendants, their servants or agents from printing, publishing or distributing any information that the plaintiff had been treated at a psychiatric hospital or information to that effect. A defendant may apply to revoke or amend this order with seven days' notice of the application to the plaintiff before it is considered.

I further order that the identity of the plaintiff, the first defendant and the contents of the Court file be not disclosed without further Order of the Court. To preserve anonymity I have referred to the plaintiff, the first defendant, the police constable and the psychiatric hospital by the letters stated and have generalised references to the plaintiff's occupation. Such restricted reference is to continue until further Order of the Court.

Any party who seeks costs is to apply within 21 days. Documents in opposition are to be filed and served within 21 days of service of the application. The applicant can file and serve documents dealing with points raised in the opposition documents within 21 days of service of those documents.

The Broadcasting Standards Authority Privacy Principles (September 1999)

[**Note**: Principles (i), (ii) and (iii) remain as Nicholson J quoted them in *P v D*. The remaining principles are as follows:]

(iv) The protection of privacy also protects against the disclosure of private facts to abuse, denigrate or ridicule personally an identifiable person. This principle is of particular relevance should a broadcaster use the airwaves to deal with a private dispute. However, the existence of a prior relationship between the broadcaster and the named individual is not an essential criterion.

(v) The protection of privacy includes the protection against the disclosure by the broadcaster, without consent, of the name and/or address and/or telephone number of an identifiable person. This principle does not apply to details which are public information, or to news and current affairs reporting, and is subject to the 'public interest' defence in principle (vi).

(vi) Discussing the matter in the 'public interest'. Defined as of legitimate concern or interest to the public, is a defence to an individual's claim for privacy.

(vii) An individual who consents to the invasion of his or her privacy cannot later succeed in a claim for a breach of privacy. Children's vulnerability must be a prime concern to broadcasters. When consent is given by the child, or by a parent or someone in *loco parentis*, broadcasters shall satisfy themselves that the broadcast is in the best interest of the child.

Vicarious liability

Bazley v Curry
[1999] 2 SCR 534 (SCC)
McLachlin J:
I *Introduction*

1 It is tragic but true that people working with the vulnerable sometimes abuse their positions and commit wrongs against the very people they are engaged to help. The abused person may later seek to recover damages for the wrong. But judgment against the wrongdoer may prove a hollow remedy. This raises the question of whether the organization that employed the offender should be held liable for the wrong. The law refers to such liability as 'vicarious' liability. It is also known as 'strict' or 'no-fault' liability, because it is imposed in the absence of fault of the employer. The issue in this case is whether such liability lies for an employee's sexual abuse of children in his care.

II *Facts*

2 The appellant, the Children's Foundation, is a non-profit organization. It operated two residential care facilities for the treatment of emotionally troubled children between the ages of six and twelve. As substitute parent, it practised 'total intervention' in all aspects of the lives of the children it cared for. The Foundation authorized its employees to act as parent figures for the children. It charged them to care for the children physically, mentally and emotionally. The employees were to do everything a parent would do, from general supervision to intimate duties like bathing and tucking in at bedtime.

3 The Foundation hired Mr Curry, a pedophile, to work in its Vancouver home. The Foundation did not know he was a pedophile. It checked and was told he was a suitable employee. Into this environment, too, came the child Patrick Bazley, young and emotionally vulnerable. Curry began a seduction. Over the months, step by subtle step, bathing became sexual exploration: tucking in in a darkened room became sexual abuse.

4 ... In 1992, Curry was convicted of 19 counts of sexual abuse, two of which related to Bazley. Curry has since died.

5 Bazley sued the Foundation for compensation for the injury he suffered while in its care. The Foundation took the position that since it had committed no fault in hiring or supervising Curry, it was not legally responsible for what he had done ...

V *Analysis*

A May employers be held vicariously liable for their employees' sexual assaults on clients or persons within their care?

10 Both parties agree that the answer to this question is governed by the *Salmond* test, which posits that employers are vicariously liable for (1) employee acts authorized by the employer; or (2) unauthorized acts so connected with authorized acts that they may be regarded as modes (albeit improper modes) of doing an authorized act. Both parties also agree that we are here concerned with the second branch of the test. They diverge, however, on what the second branch of the test means. The Foundation says that its employee's sexual assaults of Bazley were not 'modes' of doing an authorized act. Bazley, on the other hand, submits that the assaults were a mode of performing authorized tasks, and that courts have often found employers vicariously liable for intentional wrongs of employees comparable to sexual assault.

11 The problem is that it is often difficult to distinguish between an unauthorized 'mode' of performing an authorized act that attracts liability, and an entirely independent 'act' that does not. Unfortunately, the test provides no criterion on which to make this distinction. In many cases, like the present one, it is possible to characterize the tortious act either as a mode of doing an authorized act (as the respondent would have us do), or as an independent act altogether (as the appellants would suggest). In such cases, how is the judge to decide between the two alternatives?

12 One answer is to look at decided cases on similar facts. As Salmond and Heuston, *supra*, put it, 'the principle is easy to state but difficult to apply. All that can be done is to provide illustrations on either side of the line' (p 522). The problem is that only very close cases may be useful. Fleming observes that '[n]o statistical measurement is possible [of when such torts are properly said to be within the "scope of employment"], and precedents are helpful only when they present a suggestive uniformity on parallel facts' (J.G. Fleming, *The Law of Torts* (9th edn 1998), at p 421).

13 Where decided cases do not help, Salmond and Heuston, *supra*, at p 522, suggest the impasse may be resolved by the devices of a *prima facie* case and shifting evidentiary burden. If the plaintiff establishes that the employee's act was done on the employer's premises, during working hours, and that it bears a close connection with the work that the employee was authorized to do, then the responsibility shifts to the employer to show that the act is one for which it was not responsible. But this is not so much a test as a default position, and it remains unclear exactly what the employer would need to show to escape responsibility.

14 Increasingly, courts confronted by issues of vicarious liability where no clear precedent exists are turning to policy for guidance, examining the purposes that vicarious liability serves and asking whether imposition of liability in the new case before them would serve those purposes: see Fleming, *supra*, at p 410; *London Drugs Ltd v Kuehne & Nagel International Ltd* [1992] 3 SCR 299, per La Forest J.

15 This review suggests that the second branch of the *Salmond* test may usefully be approached in two steps. First, a court should determine whether there are precedents which unambiguously determine on which side of the line between vicarious liability and no liability the case falls. If prior cases do not clearly suggest a solution, the next step is to determine whether vicarious liability should be imposed in light of the

broader policy rationales behind strict liability. This Court has an additional duty: to provide guidance for lower tribunals. Accordingly, I will try to proceed from these first two steps to articulate a rule consistent with both the existing cases and the policy reasons for vicarious liability.

1 Previous cases

16 This is one of those difficult cases where there is little helpful precedent to guide the Court in determining whether the employee's tortious act should be viewed as an unauthorized mode of an authorized act, or as an altogether independent act. Apart from one recent case in the United Kingdom, the issue before us appears not to have been previously considered in depth by higher tribunals. Nevertheless, it may be useful to review the situations where courts have held employers vicariously liable for the unauthorized torts of employees. At very least, they may suggest recurring concepts and policy considerations that shed light on how the issue should be resolved.

17 The relevant cases may usefully be grouped into three general categories: (1) cases based on the rationale of 'furtherance of the employer's aims'; (2) cases based on the employer's creation of a situation of friction; and (3) the dishonest employee cases. If we can find a common thread among these three categories of cases, it may suggest how the test should be interpreted.

18 The cases confirming vicarious liability on the basis that the employee was acting in furtherance of the employer's aims rely on the agency rationale implicit in the *Salmond* test: see, eg, *Kay v ITW Ltd* [1968] 1 QB 140 (CA). Because the employee was acting in furtherance of the employer's aims, he or she is said to have 'ostensible' or 'implied' authority to do the unauthorized act. This rationale works well enough for torts of negligent accident. It does not suffice for intentional torts, however. It is difficult to maintain the fiction that an employee who commits an assault or theft was authorized to do so, even 'ostensibly': see H.J. Laski, 'The Basis of Vicarious Liability' (1916), 26 Yale LJ 105. I would put the line of cases addressing the distinction between a 'frolic' and a 'detour' in this group.

19 The cases based on the employer's creation of a situation of friction rest on the idea that if the employer's aims or enterprise incidentally create a situation of friction that may give rise to employees committing tortious acts, an employee's intentional misconduct can be viewed as falling within the scope of the employment and the employer is vicariously liable for ensuing harm. This rationale was used to extend vicarious liability to intentional torts like a provoked bartender's assault on an obnoxious customer. While it does not rest on ostensible or implied authority, it builds on the logic of risk and accident inherent in the cases imposing vicarious liability on the basis that the employee was acting to further the employer's aims. Intentional torts arising from situations of friction are like accidents in that they stem from a risk attendant on carrying out the employer's aims. Like accidents, they occur in circumstances where such incidents can be expected to arise because of the nature of the business, and hence their ramifications appropriately form part of the cost of doing business. See, eg, *Ryan v Fildes* [1938] 3 All ER 517 (KBD) (schoolteachers' discipline); *Daniels v Whetstone Entertainments, Ltd* [1962] 2 Lloyd's Rep 1 (CA) (dance hall 'bouncer'); *Dyer v Munday* [1895] 1 QB 742 (CA) (furniture repossessor); *Lakatosh v*

Ross (1974), 48 DLR (3d) 694 (Man QB) (bouncer); *Cole v California Entertainment Ltd* [1989] BCJ No 2162 (QL) (CA) (bouncer).

20 Neither furtherance of the employer's aims nor creation of situations of friction, however, suffice to justify vicarious liability for employee theft or fraud, according to cases like *Lloyd v Grace, Smith & Co* [1912] AC 716 (HL), and *The Queen v Levy Brothers Co* [1961] SCR 189. The language of authority, whether actual or ostensible, is inappropriate for intentional, fraudulent conduct like the theft of a client's property. A bank employee stealing a client's money cannot be said to be furthering the bank's aims. Nor does the logic of a situation of friction apply, unless one believes that any money-handling operation generates an inexorable temptation to steal. Nevertheless, courts considering this type of case have increasingly held employers vicariously liable, even when the employee's conduct is antithetical to the employer's business: see, eg, *Boothman v Canada* [1993] 3 FC 381 (TD) (unauthorized intentional infliction of nervous shock by supervisory employee on his subordinate found to invoke vicarious liability for the employer, albeit it based on statutory, as opposed to common law, principles).

21 At the heart of the dishonest employee decisions is consideration of fairness and policy: see Laski, *supra*, at p 121. As P. S. Atiyah, *Vicarious Liability in the Law of Torts* (1967), at p 263, puts it, 'certain types of wilful acts, and in particular frauds and thefts, are only too common, and the fact that liability is generally imposed for torts of this kind shows that the courts are not unmindful of considerations of policy'. The same logic dictates that where the employee's wrongdoing was a random act wholly unconnected to the nature of the enterprise and the employee's responsibilities, the employer is not vicariously liable. Thus an employer has been held not liable for a vengeful assault by its store clerk: *Warren v Henlys, Ltd* [1948] 2 All ER 935 (KBD).

22 Looking at these three general classes of cases in which employers have been held vicariously liable for employees' unauthorized torts, one sees a progression from accidents, to accident-like intentional torts, to torts that bear no relationship to either agency-like conduct or accident. In search of a unifying principle, one asks what the three classes of cases have in common. At first glance, it may seem little. Yet with the benefit of hindsight it is possible to posit one common feature: in each case it can be said that the employer's enterprise had created the risk that produced the tortious act. The language of 'furtherance of the employer's aims' and the employer's creation of 'a situation of friction' may be seen as limited formulations of the concept of enterprise risk that underlies the dishonest employee cases. The common theme resides in the idea that where the employee's conduct is closely tied to a risk that the employer's enterprise has placed in the community, the employer may justly be held vicariously liable for the employee's wrong. If employers are vicariously liable for acts like employee theft, why not for sexual abuse? That was the question before the English Court of Appeal in *ST v North Yorkshire County Council* [1999] IRLR 98, where the court applied the *Salmond* test to reverse a finding of vicarious liability against a school council for a teacher who sexually accosted a mentally handicapped student during a school field trip to the continent. It held that the sexual tort was not an unauthorized mode of performing an authorized act; it was an independent act, outside the scope of the teacher's authority. The court recognized the difficulty of saying that some

intentional acts, like a store clerk's assault, do not attract vicarious liability, while other intentional acts, like theft, do. In the end, however, it did not confront the underlying policy of vicarious liability, preferring to reason that sexual abuse was closer to the store clerk's assault than to a solicitor's clerk's theft. It interpreted the stolen property cases of *Levy Brothers* and *Lloyd*, thought by many to be developing law, as a minor off-shoot of a line of cases concerning entrustment of goods—a departure from the 'general' rule.

24 The *ST* decision thus fails to successfully integrate the dishonest employee cases. It also rests on the questionable conclusion that sexual torts by caretakers against children are closer to a shop assault than a bank employee's conversion. (While a molestation is a physical attack, it is equally arguable that the trust-abusing character of child abuse fits more in the dishonesty genre.) Furthermore, the opinion's reasoning depends on the level of generality with which the sexual act is described. Instead of describing the act in terms of the employee's duties of supervising and caring for vulnerable students during a study trip abroad, the Court of Appeal cast it in terms unrelated to those duties. Important legal decisions should not turn on such semantics. As Atiyah points out (*supra*, at p 263): 'conduct can be correctly described at varying levels of generality, and no one description of the "act" on which the servant was engaged is necessarily more correct than any other'. Finally, the reasoning in *ST* leads to anomalies. Lowry J's question in the chambers decision appealed from (at p 223) remains unanswered: 'If a postal clerk's theft and a solicitor's clerk's fraud can be said to have been committed in the course of their employment, I can see no sound basis in principle on which it can be concluded that Curry's criminal conduct should not attract vicarious liability'. Or, as Wilkinson J expressed more bluntly in the companion appeal (*GJ v Griffiths* [1995] BCJ No 2370 (QL) (SC), at para 76), '[s]urely a distinction is not to be drawn attributing a higher standard to the way society looks after its jewellery than its children'.

[**Note**: The *ST* case is named *Trotman* in other reports. The case was subsequently overruled by the House of Lords in *Lister and Others v Hesley Hall Ltd* [2001] UKHL 22. This case is discussed later.]

25 To return to the approach suggested earlier, precedent does not resolve the issue before us. We must therefore proceed to the second stage of the inquiry—a consideration of the policy reasons for vicarious liability, in the hope of discerning a principle to guide courts in future cases.

2 Policy considerations

26 Vicarious liability has always been concerned with policy: Fleming, *supra*, at pp 409 *et seq*. The view of early English law that a master was responsible for all the wrongs of his servants (as well as his wife's and his children's) represented a policy choice, however inarticulate, as to who should bear the loss of wrongdoing and how best to deter it. The narrowing of vicarious responsibility with the expansion of commerce and trade and the rise of industrialism also represented a policy choice. Indeed, it represented a compromise between two policies—the social interest in furnishing an innocent tort victim with recourse against a financially responsible defendant, and a concern not to foist undue burdens on business enterprises: Fleming, *ibid*. The expan-

sion of vicarious liability in the twentieth century from authorization-based liability to broader classes of ascription is doubtless driven by yet other policy concerns. '[V]icarious liability cannot parade as a deduction from legalistic premises, but should be frankly recognised as having its basis in a combination of policy considerations' (Fleming, at p 410).

27 A focus on policy is not to diminish the importance of legal principle. It is vital that the courts attempt to articulate general legal principles to lend certainty to the law and guide future applications. However, in areas of jurisprudence where changes have been occurring in response to policy considerations, the best route to enduring principle may well lie through policy. The law of vicarious liability is just such a domain.

28 Recognizing the policy-driven perspective of the law of vicarious liability, La Forest J in *London Drugs*, *supra*, opined that vicarious liability was traditionally considered to rest on one of two logical bases: (1) that the employee's acts are regarded in law as being authorized by the employer and hence as being the employer's acts (the 'master's tort theory' or 'direct liability theory'); or (2) that the employer was the employee's superior in charge or command of the employee (the 'servant's tort theory') (at pp 335–6, citing G.H.L. Fridman, *The Law of Torts in Canada* (1990), vol 2, at pp 314–15; Atiyah, *supra*, at pp 6–7; G. Williams, 'Vicarious Liability: Tort of the Master or of the Servant?' (1956), 72 LQ Rev 522). La Forest J, quoting Fridman (at p 315), went on to note, however, that 'neither of the logical bases for vicarious liability succeeds completely in explaining the operation of the doctrine ... "express[ing] not so much the true rationale of vicarious liability but an attempt by the law to give some formal, technical explanation of why the law imposes vicarious liability"' (p 336). Faced with the absence in the existing law of a coherent principle to explain vicarious liability, La Forest J found its basis in policy (at p 336): 'the vicarious liability regime is best seen as a response to a number of policy concerns. In its traditional domain, these are primarily linked to compensation, deterrence and loss internalization'.

...

34 The policy grounds supporting the imposition of vicarious liability—fair compensation and deterrence—are related. The policy consideration of deterrence is linked to the policy consideration of fair compensation based on the employer's introduction or enhancement of a risk. The introduction of the enterprise into the community with its attendant risk, in turn, implies the possibility of managing the risk to minimize the costs of the harm that may flow from it.

...

3 From precedent and policy to principle

37 Underlying the cases holding employers vicariously liable for the unauthorized acts of employees is the idea that employers may justly be held liable where the act falls within the ambit of the risk that the employer's enterprise creates or exacerbates. Similarly, the policy purposes underlying the imposition of vicarious liability on employers are served only where the wrong is so connected with the employment that it can be said that the employer has introduced the risk of the wrong (and is thereby fairly and usefully charged with its management and minimization). The question in each case is

whether there is a connection or nexus between the employment enterprise and that wrong that justifies imposition of vicarious liability on the employer for the wrong, in terms of fair allocation of the consequences of the risk and/or deterrence.

...

41 Reviewing the jurisprudence, and considering the policy issues involved, I conclude that in determining whether an employer is vicariously liable for an employee's unauthorized, intentional wrong in cases where precedent is inconclusive, courts should be guided by the following principles:

(1) They should openly confront the question of whether liability should lie against the employer, rather than obscuring the decision beneath semantic discussions of 'scope of employment' and 'mode of conduct'.

(2) The fundamental question is whether the wrongful act is *sufficiently related* to conduct authorized by the employer to justify the imposition of vicarious liability. Vicarious liability is generally appropriate where there is a significant connection between the *creation or enhancement of a risk* and the wrong that accrues therefrom, even if unrelated to the employer's desires. Where this is so, vicarious liability will serve the policy considerations of provision of an adequate and just remedy and deterrence. Incidental connections to the employment enterprise, like time and place (without more), will not suffice. Once engaged in a particular business, it is fair that an employer be made to pay the generally foreseeable costs of that business. In contrast, to impose liability for costs unrelated to the risk would effectively make the employer an involuntary insurer.

(3) In determining the sufficiency of the connection between *the employer's creation or enhancement of the risk* and the wrong complained of, subsidiary factors may be considered. These may vary with the nature of the case. When related to intentional torts, the relevant factors may include, but are not limited to, the following:

  (a) the opportunity that the enterprise afforded the employee to abuse his or her power;

  (b) the extent to which the wrongful act may have furthered the employer's aims (and hence be more likely to have been committed by the employee);

  (c) the extent to which the wrongful act was related to friction, confrontation or intimacy inherent in the employer's enterprise;

  (d) the extent of power conferred on the employee in relation to the victim;

  (e) the vulnerability of potential victims to wrongful exercise of the employee's power.

42 Applying these general considerations to sexual abuse by employees, there must be a strong connection between what the employer was asking the employee to do (the risk created by the employer's enterprise) and the wrongful act. It must be possible to say that the employer significantly increased the risk of the harm by putting the employee in his or her position and requiring him to perform the assigned tasks. The policy considerations that justify imposition of vicarious liability for an employee's sexual misconduct are unlikely to be satisfied by incidental considerations of time and place. For example, an incidental or random attack by an employee that merely

happens to take place on the employer's premises during working hours will scarcely justify holding the employer liable. Such an attack is unlikely to be related to the business the employer is conducting or what the employee was asked to do and, hence, to any risk that was created. Nor is the imposition of liability likely to have a significant deterrent effect; short of closing the premises or discharging all employees, little can be done to avoid the random wrong. Nor is foreseeability of harm used in negligence law the test. What is required is a material increase in the risk as a consequence of the employer's enterprise and the duties he entrusted to the employee, mindful of the policies behind vicarious liability.

43 What factors are relevant to whether an employer's enterprise has introduced or significantly exacerbated a risk of sexual abuse by an employee? (Again, I speak generally, supplementing the factors suggested above.) It is obvious that the risk of an employee sexually abusing a child may be materially enhanced by giving the employee an opportunity to commit the abuse. There are many kinds of opportunity and the nature of the opportunity in a particular case must be carefully evaluated in determining whether it has, in fact, materially increased the risk of the harm that ensued. If an employee is permitted or required to be with children for brief periods of time, there may be a small risk of such harm—perhaps not much greater than if the employee were a stranger. If an employee is permitted or required to be alone with a child for extended periods of time, the opportunity for abuse may be greater. If in addition to being permitted to be alone with a child for extended periods, the employee is expected to supervise the child in intimate activities like bathing or toiletting, the opportunity for abuse becomes greater still. As the opportunity for abuse becomes greater, so the risk of harm increases.

44 The risk of harm may also be enhanced by the nature of the relationship the employment establishes between the employee and the child. Employment that puts the employee in a position of intimacy and power over the child (ie, a parent-like, role-model relationship) may enhance the risk of the employee feeling that he or she is able to take advantage of the child and the child submitting without effective complaint. The more the employer encourages the employee to stand in a position of respect and suggests that the child should emulate and obey the employee, the more the risk may be enhanced. In other words, the more an enterprise requires the exercise of power or authority for its successful operation, the more materially likely it is that an abuse of that power relationship can be fairly ascribed to the employer. See *Boothman v Canada*, *supra*.

45 Other factors may be important too, depending on the nature of the case. To require or permit an employee to touch the client in intimate body zones may enhance the risk of sexual touching, just as permitting an employee to handle large sums of money may enhance the risk of embezzlement or conversion. This is the common sense core of the 'mode of conduct' argument accepted by the trial judge in this case. (The same factor might of course be analyzed in terms of enhanced opportunity.) Time and place arguments may also be relevant in particular cases. The mere fact that the wrong occurred during working hours or on the jobsite may not, standing alone, be of much importance; the assessment of material increase in risk cannot be resolved by the mechanical application of spatial and temporal factors. This said, spatial

and temporal factors may tend to negate the suggestion of materially enhanced risk of harm, insofar as they suggest that the conduct was essentially unrelated to the employment and any enhanced risk it may have created (for example, the employee's tort occurred offsite and after hours). The policy considerations of fair compensation and deterrence upon which vicarious liability is premised may be attenuated or completely eliminated in such circumstances.

46 In summary, the test for vicarious liability for an employee's sexual abuse of a client should focus on whether the employer's enterprise and empowerment of the employee materially increased the risk of the sexual assault and hence the harm. The test must not be applied mechanically, but with a sensitive view to the policy considerations that justify the imposition of vicarious liability—fair and efficient compensation for wrong and deterrence. This requires trial judges to investigate the employee's specific duties and determine whether they gave rise to special opportunities for wrongdoing. Because of the peculiar exercises of power and trust that pervade cases such as child abuse, special attention should be paid to the existence of a power or dependency relationship, which on its own often creates a considerable risk of wrongdoing.

[**Note**: McLachlin then rejected the Foundation's suggestion that there should be a special 'not for exception' to liability. The appeal was dismissed and the case remitted to trial.]

Lister and Others v Hesley Hall Limited
[2001] UKHL 22 (HL)
[**FACTS**: Axeholme House, a boarding annex to Wilsic Hall School was opened in 1979 to provide residence, generally, for children with emotional and behavioural difficulties. Mr and Mrs Grain were employed as warden and housekeeper, and were responsible for the day to day running of the House. On most days, these two were the only staff on the premises. The employers accept that the boarding school environment provided opportunities for sexual abuse and they accept, unbeknown to them, that the warden systematically sexually abused the appellants. There were no complaints at the time. In the early 1990s a police investigation led to Mr Grain being criminally charged for multiple offences involving sexual abuse. Upon conviction, Mr Grain received seven years' imprisonment. In 1997, the appellants brought claims for personal injury against the employers of Mr Grain.]
Lord Steyn:

I *The question*
1 The central question before the House is whether as a matter of legal principle the employers of the warden of a school boarding house, who sexually abused boys in his care, may depending on the particular circumstances be vicariously liable for the torts of their employee …

V *The issues before the House*
10 Since the decision in the Court of Appeal the law reports of two landmark decisions in the Canadian Supreme Court, which deal with vicarious liability of employers

for sexual abuse of children, have become available: *Bazley v Curry* (1999) 174 DLR (4th) 45; *Jacobi v Griffiths* (1999) 174 DLR (4th) 71. Enunciating a principle of 'close connection' the Supreme Court unanimously held liability established in *Bazley*'s case and by a 4 to 3 majority came to the opposite conclusion in *Jacobi*'s case. The Supreme Court judgments examine in detail the circumstances in which, though an employer is not 'at fault,' it may still be 'fair' that it should bear responsibility for the tortious conduct of its employees. These decisions have been described as 'a genuine advance on the unauthorised conduct/unauthorised mode distinction': Peter Cane, 'Vicarious Liability for Sexual Abuse' (2000) 116 LQR 21, 24. Counsel for the appellants invited your Lordships to apply the test developed in *Bazley*'s case and in *Jacobi*'s case and to conclude that the employers are vicariously liable for the sexual torts of their employee.

11 In another sense the approach to the appeals before the House differs from that adopted in the Court of Appeal. The House is not bound to follow the decision in *Trotman v North Yorkshire County Council* [1999] LGR 584. On the contrary, quite apart from the high persuasive value of the two Canadian decisions, the first task of the House is to consider whether the decision in *Trotman v North Yorkshire County Council*, when examined from a perspective of legal principle, correctly states the position ...

VI *The perspective of principle*

13 It is right to acknowledge at once that *Trotman v North Yorkshire County Council* is a carefully considered and reasoned decision. The leading judgment was given by Butler-Sloss LJ whose views are entitled to great weight. Nevertheless, our allegiance must be to legal principle. That is the subject to which I now turn.

...

15 For nearly a century English judges have adopted Salmond's statement of the applicable test as correct. Salmond said that a wrongful act is deemed to be done by a 'servant' in the course of his employment if 'it is either (a) a wrongful act authorised by the master, or (b) a wrongful and unauthorised mode of doing some act authorised by the master': *Salmond on Torts*, 1st edn (1907), p 83; and *Salmond and Heuston on Torts*, 21st edn (1996), p 443. Situation (a) causes no problems. The difficulty arises in respect of cases under (b). Salmond did, however, offer an explanation which has sometimes been overlooked. He said (*Salmond on Torts*, 1st edn, pp 83–4) that 'a master ... is liable even for acts which he has not authorised, provided they are so connected with acts which he has authorised, that they may rightly be regarded as modes—although improper modes—of doing them' ... Salmond's explanation is the germ of the close connection test adumbrated by the Canadian Supreme Court in *Bazley* ... and *Jacobi* ...

...

20 Our law no longer struggles with the concept of vicarious liability for intentional wrongdoing. Thus the decision of the House of Lords in *Racz v Home Office* [1994] 2 AC 45 is authority for the proposition that the Home Office may be vicariously liable for acts of police officers which amounted to misfeasance in public office—and hence for liability in tort involving bad faith. It remains, however, to consider how vicarious liability for intentional wrongdoing fits in with Salmond's formulation. The answer is that it does not cope ideally with such cases. It must, however, be

remembered that the great tort writer did not attempt to enunciate precise propositions of law on vicarious liability. At most he propounded a broad test which deems as within the course of employment 'a wrongful and unauthorised mode of doing some act authorised by the master'. And he emphasised the connection between the authorised acts and the 'improper modes' of doing them. In reality it is simply a practical test serving as a dividing line between cases where it is or is not just to impose vicarious liability. The usefulness of the Salmond formulation is, however, crucially dependent on focussing on the right act of the employee. This point was explored in *Rose v Plenty* [1976] 1 WLR 141. The Court of Appeal held that a milkman who deliberately disobeyed his employers' order not to allow children to help on his rounds did not go beyond his course of employment in allowing a child to help him. The analysis in this decision shows how the pitfalls of terminology must be avoided. Scarman LJ said, at pp 147–8:

> The servant was, of course, employed at the time of the accident to do a whole number of operations. He was certainly not employed to give the boy a lift, and if one confines one's analysis of the facts to the incident of injury to the plaintiff, then no doubt one would say that carrying the boy on the float— giving him a lift—was not in the course of the servant's employment. But in *Ilkiw v Samuels* [1983] 1 WLR 991 Diplock LJ indicated that the proper approach to the nature of the servant's employment is a broad one … I think it is clear from the evidence that he was employed as a roundsman to drive his float round his round and to deliver milk, to collect empties and to obtain payment. That was his job … He chose to disregard the prohibition and to enlist the assistance of the plaintiff. As a matter of common sense, that does seem to me to be a mode, albeit a prohibited mode, of doing the job with which he was entrusted. Why was the plaintiff being carried on the float when the accident occurred? Because it was necessary to take him from point to point so that he could assist in delivering milk, collecting empties and, on occasions obtaining payment.

If this approach to the nature of employment is adopted, it is not necessary to ask the simplistic question whether in the cases under consideration the acts of sexual abuse were modes of doing authorised acts. It becomes possible to consider the question of vicarious liability on the basis that the employer undertook to care for the boys through the services of the warden and that there is a very close connection between the torts of the warden and his employment. After all, they were committed in the time and on the premises of the employers while the warden was also busy caring for the children.

VII The correctness of *Trotman v North Yorkshire County Council*

[**Note**: The essential facts of *Trotman* include that the defendants operated a school for mentally handicapped children. The school took a holiday to Spain, totally within the control and care of the defendants' staff at the school. The plaintiff shared a bedroom with the deputy headmaster who indecently assaulted the plaintiff on several nights.]
…

23 But at the root of the reasoning of the Court of Appeal lay a terminological difficulty. Butler-Sloss LJ thought, at p 591, that the sexual assaults were 'far removed

from an unauthorised mode of carrying out a teacher's duties on behalf of his employer' ... In giving the unanimous judgment of the Canadian Supreme Court in *Bazley* ... McLachlin J criticised the decision in *Trotman* ... in the following terms, at p 57, para 24:

> the opinion's reasoning depends on the level of generality with which the sexual act is described. Instead of describing the act in terms of the employee's duties of supervising and caring for vulnerable students during a study trip abroad, the Court of Appeal cast it in terms unrelated to those duties. Important legal decisions should not turn on such semantics. As Atiyah points out (*Vicarious Liability in the Law of Torts*, p 263): 'conduct can be correctly described at varying levels of generality, and no one description of the "act" on which the servant was engaged is necessarily more correct than any other'.

I am in respectful agreement with this comment.

24 It is useful to consider an employer's potential liability for non-sexual assaults. If such assaults arise directly out of circumstances connected with the employment, vicarious liability may arise: see Rose, 'Liability for an employee's assaults' (1977), 40 MLR 420, 432–3. Butler-Sloss LJ considered this analogy. In the critical paragraph of her judgment, which I have already quoted in full, she stated, at p 591:

> Acts of physical assault may not be so easy to categorise, since they may range, for instance, from a brutal and unprovoked assault by a teacher to forceful attempts to defend another pupil or the teacher himself. But in the field of serious sexual misconduct, I find it difficult to visualise circumstances in which an act of the teacher can be an unauthorised mode of carrying out an authorised act, although I would not wish to close the door on the possibility.

If I correctly understand this passage, it appears to be indicating that there could not be vicarious liability by an employer for a brutal assault, or serious sexual misconduct, whatever the circumstances. That appears to be a case of saying 'The greater the fault of the servant, the less the liability of the master': *Morris v C W Martin & Sons Ltd* [1966] 1 QB 716, 733, per Diplock LJ. A better approach is to concentrate on the relative closeness of the connection between the nature of the employment and the particular tort.

25 In my view the approach of the Court of Appeal in *Trotman* ... was wrong. It resulted in the case being treated as one of the employment furnishing a mere opportunity to commit the sexual abuse. The reality was that the county council were responsible for the care of the vulnerable children and employed the deputy headmaster to carry out that duty on its behalf. And the sexual abuse took place while the employee was engaged in duties at the very time and place demanded by his employment. The connection between the employment and the torts was very close. I would overrule *Trotman* ...

VII *The application of the correct test*

27 My Lords, I have been greatly assisted by the luminous and illuminating judgments of the Canadian Supreme Court in *Bazley* ... and *Jacobi* ... Wherever such problems are considered in future in the common law world these judgments will be the starting point ...

28 Employing the traditional methodology of English law, I am satisfied that in the case of the appeals under consideration the evidence showed that the employers entrusted the care of the children in Axeholme House to the warden. The question is whether the warden's torts were so closely connected with his employment that it would be fair and just to hold the employers vicariously liable. On the facts of the case the answer is yes. After all, the sexual abuse was inextricably interwoven with the carrying out by the warden of his duties in Axeholme House. Matters of degree arise. But the present cases clearly fall on the side of vicarious liability.

IX *The outcome*

30 I would allow the appeal and order that judgment on liability be entered in favour of the appellants.

Chapter 3
Accident Compensation

Introduction

New Zealand has a revolutionary way of handling compensation for personal injury caused by accidents. A radical scheme first introduced by the Accident Compensation Act 1972 swept away the previous mixed bag of remedies: common law actions usually in negligence, workers' compensation legislation, criminal injuries legislation, third party insurance for motor vehicle accidents, social security benefits for some residual categories of accident, and no compensation at all for some victims. The new grand scheme placed New Zealand on the international map as a leader in the development of social policy, as it had been in the 1890s and the 1930s.

The vision came from the Royal Commission on Compensation for Personal Injury in New Zealand, which reported in December 1967 and owed much to its chairperson, Sir Owen Woodhouse. The principles of the Woodhouse Report are beguiling in their simplicity, cutting through the morass of concepts and procedures that previously existed. Many would say that when the scheme finally came into force on 1 April 1974, New Zealand had the most impressive compensation system in the world. Victims who were income earners received payments relative to their income. Earners and non-earners could receive lump sums for various losses they incurred. All victims had medical expenses paid.

A model scheme does not, however, appear novel and enlightened for too long. It has been criticised by both sides of the political spectrum. On the left, it was pointed out that there is a major anomaly in the way in which accident and sickness sufferers are treated. Why not extend the principles to sickness as well as accident? On the right, employers claimed that the levies they had to pay as part of the scheme's funding rules were financing their workers' recreational injuries and were too high (although they would almost certainly have paid much higher insurance premiums under an insurance-dominated system). The scheme, some have argued, needs to be opened up to competition and market forces. The emergence in New Zealand politics of New Right thinking partially won the day for the right. The Accident Rehabilitation and Compensation Insurance Act 1992 abolished lump sum payments, narrowed the scope of coverage, and reduced the levels of compensation. Then, a further revision of the law in the Accident Insurance Act 1998 saw the opening up of employment-related accidents to private insurance companies. The newly elected Labour/Alliance Government reversed this early in 2000. The Injury Prevention, Rehabilitation, and Compensation Act 2001 partly reverses the abolition of lump sum payments. Part 3 of Schedule 1 provides for payment of lump sum compensation for permanent impairment. Initially, the maximum amount is $100 000 but this will increase, as it is indexed to inflation.

One of the hallmarks of the New Zealand law is the removal of the right to sue at common law for personal injury. Some of the extracts below will explore the reasons for this. Much of the interest for tort lawyers lies in discerning the boundary line between cases where a common law action is barred and those where such proceedings are still possible. We shall look at the principal statutory provisions that impinge on this and at the expanding case law. The following two developments are worth noting.

(1) Parliament is aware that in removing the right to sue it has removed an important device for setting standards in the workplace, in product safety, in professions such as medicine, and in other areas. Legislation such as the Health and Safety in Employment Act 1992 and the Consumer Guarantees Act 1993 in part make up for the loss. A further move by Parliament enables the whole or part of a fine to be paid to a victim of an unprovoked crime if the victim has suffered physical or emotional harm (s 28 of the Criminal Justice Act 1985 as amended in 1987). Thus, for example, in *Department of Labour v FAI Metropolitan Life Assurance* [1995] 1 ERNZ 317, half of the fines imposed under the Health and Safety in Employment Act 1992 for failure to take all practicable steps to ensure employee safety was ordered to be paid to an occupational overuse syndrome ('OOS') sufferer.

(2) As the level of statutory compensation becomes less attractive, lawyers and their clients are searching for ways around the Act in order to be able to sue. They are meeting with varying success. In addition, doctors face a higher level of professional disciplinary claims, which remain available despite the accident compensation scheme.

Overall, we might conclude that as in pre-accident compensation days when there was a conglomeration of different mechanisms to deal with safety and accidents, the same is true again today. Only the goal posts have changed.

Policy development

The Woodhouse Report

[The accident compensation scheme is based on the Woodhouse Report: the Report of the Royal Commission of Inquiry *Compensation for Personal Injury in New Zealand* (1967). The extract set out here deals with the objectives of a compensation scheme.]

55. In the final analysis any change in present methods must depend upon whether it can be afforded; and whether the need for it is clear. The first severely practical question is dealt with in Part 8 of this Report. The other involves an analysis of the system in operation. To make an effective analysis it is desirable at this point to decide what should be the role of any modern system of compensation for injured persons. Unless the target is identified it is unlikely that present achievements will be evaluated on any

rational basis or the key be found to something better. It is possible to lay down five guiding principles for such a system.

First, in the national interest, and as a matter of national obligation, the community must protect all citizens (including the self employed) and the housewives who sustain them from the burden of sudden individual losses when their ability to contribute to the general welfare by their work has been interrupted by physical incapacity.

Second, all injured persons should receive compensation from any community financed scheme on the same uniform method of assessment, regardless of the causes which gave rise to their injuries.

Third, the scheme must be deliberately organised to urge forward the physical and vocational recovery of these citizens while at the same time providing a real measure of money compensation for their losses.

Fourth, real compensation demands for the whole period of incapacity the provision of income-related benefits for lost income and recognition of the plain fact that any permanent bodily impairment is a loss in itself regardless of its effect on earning capacity.

Fifth, the achievement of the system will be eroded to the extent that its benefits are delayed, or are inconsistently assessed, or the system itself is administered by methods that are economically wasteful.

These principles can be summarised as:

- Community responsibility
- Comprehensive entitlement
- Complete rehabilitation
- Real compensation
- Administrative efficiency.

We proceed to examine them in turn.

COMMUNITY RESPONSIBILITY

56. This first principle is fundamental. It rests on a double argument. Just as a modern society benefits from the productive work of its citizens, so should society accept responsibility for those willing to work but prevented from doing so by physical incapacity. And, since we all persist in following community activities, which year by year exact a predictable and inevitable price in bodily injury, so should we all share in sustaining those who become the random but statistically necessary victims. The inherent cost of these community purposes should be borne on a basis of equity by the community.

COMPREHENSIVE ENTITLEMENT

57. The second principle involves an acceptance of the argument advanced in paragraphs 42 to 46. It cannot be regarded as just that workmen sustaining equal losses should be treated unequally by society. The productive section of the community must sustain the elderly and the young, and the latter groups cannot reasonably expect to be provided with a form of social insurance on the same level. But subject to this consideration there can be no justification for providing from community funds for the same class of worker entirely inconsistent awards for precisely similar incapacities

merely because fortuitously the causes which gave rise to them have at different stages of our social development been the subject of conflicting responses.

COMPLETE REHABILITATION

58. The third principle would seem to state the obvious. Nevertheless, although it is always remembered that injury losses must be quantified in money terms, it is often overlooked that the rehabilitation of incapacitated workers cannot be achieved by money payments except to the extent of money losses. The consideration of overriding importance must be to encourage every injured worker to recover the maximum degree of bodily health and vocational utility in a minimum of time. Any impediment to this should be regarded as a serious failure to safeguard the real interests of the man himself and the interest which the community has in his restored productive capacity.

REAL COMPENSATION

59. Clearly if compensation is to meet real losses it must provide adequate recompense, unrestricted by earlier philosophies which put forward tests related merely to need. Such an approach may have been appropriate when poverty was a widespread evil demanding considerable mobilisation of the country's financial resources. But average modern households, geared to the regular injection of incomes undreamed of at the turn of the century, have corresponding commitments which do not disappear conveniently if one of the hazards of modern life suddenly produces physical misfortune. Increasing affluence has brought with it additional social hazards for every citizen; but fortunately, at the same time, it has left society better able to afford their real cost.

60. To the individual concerned, the cost will include any permanent physical deprivation which he might have to endure following an accident. Such disabilities can have damaging effects upon the ordinary activities of both young and old, regardless of their influence upon a capacity to work in any given occupation.

61. Accordingly, we are in no doubt that in modern conditions a compensation system of the type under discussion should rest upon a realistic assessment of actual loss, both physical and economic, followed by a shifting of that loss on a suitably generous basis. If there might seem to be an issue as to whether the compensation due to injured workers should be restricted to meet their current needs or be assessed on a uniform flat rate basis, then these are propositions which we reject as entirely unacceptable. These are the considerations which support the fourth principle.

ADMINISTRATIVE EFFICIENCY

62. This final principle needs no elaboration. It speaks for itself in terms which are clear enough. It looks to evenness and method in every aspect of assessment, adjudication, and administration. The collection of funds and their distribution as benefits should be handled speedily, consistently, economically, and without contention.

CONCLUSION

63. Against the background of these principles it is convenient to bring forward the general conclusion we have reached concerning the present processes. For all the

reasons which follow we are satisfied that no useful, logical, or economic purpose remains in this categorised system; that it gives rise to injustice; that it perpetuates anomalies; and that the time has clearly arrived for its replacement.

Accident Compensation 1995

[In 1994, the Government began a review of accident compensation: one of several that have taken place over the last decade. It established a so-called 'eminent persons group', convened by the then Minister, the Hon B Cliffe. The report is simply entitled *Accident Compensation 1995*. The following extracts are from that report.]

The right to sue

3.1 Based on the Woodhouse Principle of community responsibility the accident compensation scheme is a compact under which the common law right to sue for damages was withdrawn in return for the comprehensive availability and cover of the scheme. Although the scheme's benefits may be less than damages awarded under some successful actions at common law, this is balanced by the universal availability of the scheme's benefits without having to prove fault.

3.2 The 1967 Woodhouse Report gave several reasons why common law action was an inadequate way to deal with personal injury in our community. These were:

- the failure of the common law to compensate large numbers of accident victims. In 1967 it was estimated that no more than eight tenths of 1% of persons injured in industrial accidents were successful in common law actions through the court system
- the waste involved in a system where much of the money was eaten up in legal and administrative expenses
- the long delays in delivering benefits to those few accident victims who managed to win their actions through the courts
- personal blameworthiness was not the rationale of the law, as negligence law required individuals to meet an average community standard of care
- compulsory liability insurance had blunted or removed the deterrent of court action
- the assessment of damages in one lump sum involved guesswork and speculation, and tended to over-compensate less serious injuries
- the process of adjudication was a lottery and impeded rehabilitation of injured people
- there were strong incentives to maximise misery
- accident prevention did not form part of the system.

3.3 There are gaps in the scheme's cover in respect of which, implicitly, the right to sue remains. However, perhaps because the boundaries are blurred, no cases have been pursued in these areas, though some potential cases have received media attention.

3.4 However, there is evidence of mounting pressure to establish the right to sue. The possibilities include actions for employer liability where negligence can be established; actions in respect of medical misadventure; and actions by persons who, while they may suffer no personal injury, do experience severe trauma as, for instance, in the case of workers who witness a colleague suffering an horrific accident, or bank staff who experience an armed hold-up.

3.5 Insurance companies are already offering cover to employers in areas they identify as being outside ACC coverage. This raises the prospect, not only of damages actions being taken, but of insurance companies standing behind the employer's liability. It is only a matter of time before individuals will be encouraged to take comprehensive public liability cover.

3.6 Several issues arise:

- is there a need to address the gaps in the scheme where cover is not provided?
- should the right to sue be acknowledged?
- should steps be taken to fill these gaps either by providing cover, even where entitlements are limited, or by excluding the right to sue, even though cover is not available under the scheme?

3.7 To succeed in an action for damages at common law the claimant (plaintiff) had to prove that his or her injuries were caused by a breach of a legal duty of care owed by another person (the defendant). The damages would be reduced if it was shown that the plaintiff was guilty of negligence which contributed to the injuries.

3.8 When we examine the experience of common law countries like the United States, and project that experience onto our own situation, it can be safely concluded that the reintroduction of the right to sue for damages in New Zealand would not result in any significant benefit, either for the great majority of accident victims, or for the New Zealand community and economy as a whole. Nothing in this review to date has, in any way, supported a case for reintroducing the right to sue, even on a limited basis.

3.9 Criticisms of the scheme's coverage principally arise in areas of non-economic loss, including pain and suffering, mental or sexual abuse, and secondary trauma. It is important to consider the consequences of not providing cover in these areas.

3.10 The options to preclude the re-establishment of the right to sue are:

- close the gaps in the scheme's coverage by establishing entitlements appropriate to the cover, and consistent with the compact on which the scheme is based; or
- simply preclude the right of common law action even where gaps exist.

Accident compensation for women

3.11 The Woodhouse Commission Report reflects the era in which it was produced—a time of full employment, the forty hour week, and fewer women in fulltime employment. Not surprisingly, the report has come under increasing scrutiny regarding the situation of women today. Practical issues relate to the scheme's entitlements, particularly as regards home help and attendant care, where women are earners, solo parents, and perhaps also care givers. Those caring for dependants are concerned there is no provision for anything other than medical costs. These are matters which should be under constant review.

3.12 The dramatic increase in the number of women in the workforce and the growing recognition that their labour, even when unpaid, has value, raises a number of issues of importance within the scheme. Should women, or men, who temporarily withdraw from the labour force to care for others, and who suffer serious injury during that time, be entitled to full vocational rehabilitation? This question has not been fully addressed in the ACC context, although the provision of help under the scheme does give some recognition of the needs of unpaid workers in the home. Nevertheless there is a clear differentiation to be made between the needs of this group and of those in the paid labour force.

Maori and other ethnic groups

3.13 The Regulations Review Panel commented as follows:

> We raise one further but, in our view, very important point about the development of regulations, guidelines, codes of practice and forms. On meeting with representatives of Maori and Pacific Island communities, we were surprised and disappointed to learn that, up to the present, neither has been consulted about ACC. This must change. Both groups have much to offer in advising on how ACC can best meet the particular needs of their people.

3.14 This advice has already been accepted by the Government, and forms part of the brief of the Inter-Departmental Committee which is advising the Government on ways to implement the outcomes of this review. It is important that the needs of Maori are addressed. Separate provision should be made for other minority group representations.

...

What should be covered
Pain and suffering and loss of function

6.9 Given the common view that compensation should be available for serious physical incapacity, the question remains whether or not it is correct to extend cover for pain and suffering and loss of bodily function. While these are areas in which there is constant pressure to push out the boundaries of cover, the issue can be seen in two examples:

Case History, scarring—a person involved in a motor accident where the vehicle catches fire is rehabilitated to the point of being able to return unimpaired to the work force, but suffers permanent scarring for which no compensation is available.

Case History, loss of function—a woman is diagnosed as having cancer of the uterus, which is removed. Subsequently the diagnosis is found to have been incorrect. She is able to return to the work force without any impairment in a work sense, but no compensation is available for the loss of the ability to bear children.

6.10 In these cases it may be said that from a claimant's standpoint, as regards entitlement to compensation, there is little difference between the loss of a limb and the (accidental) loss of the ability to bear children as a result of medical misdiagnosis; or between the loss of a limb and permanent disfigurement.

6.11 If cover for pain and suffering and loss of function were to be re-instituted under the scheme, however, the appropriate form and extent of compensation would need to be carefully determined.

Secondary trauma

6.12 Secondary trauma occurs where a person suffers trauma as a consequence of witnessing injury to others. Compensation became available under the 1982 Act as a consequence of a series of Court decisions, but was excluded under the 1992 Act.

6.13 It is extremely doubtful that the architects of the ACC scheme ever envisaged secondary trauma being included, and it is difficult to make the case:

- the trauma that results from being a witness to life's calamities is one of life's calamities, and the fact of the trauma being more intense when someone close is involved, or when the injury witnessed is particularly horrific, does not alter this reality
- there is no reason why trauma resulting from the witness of, say, a gang beating, should be regarded differently from the trauma experienced by participants in an earthquake or flood.

6.14 Nonetheless, at common law, prior to the introduction of the scheme, and in overseas jurisdictions, damages would have been available for secondary trauma where negligence on the part of one or another party could be established. Indeed, in the United States there is seemingly no limit to the ingenuity of claimants and their lawyers in finding opportunities to mount such claims. Action was taken recently on behalf of others who claimed to be traumatised from watching an accident on a television news broadcast.

6.15 While it could be argued that the compensation of secondary trauma has no place in the scheme, the possibility of common law rights being reactivated if it is not covered suggests that it ought to be acknowledged as part of the scheme. Compensation however should fall within the existing provisions of the scheme, for example, counselling.

Sexual abuse

6.16 ACC cover for sexual abuse remains available under the 1992 Act, but lump sum compensation is no longer available. Annual claims are as follows:

Financial year	Number of claims lodged
1992/93	13 000
1993/94	11 000
1-7-94/31-12-94	5 951

The following amounts have been paid by ACC for counselling services, including assessment to determine the acceptability of a claim:

1992/93 *Financial year*	$6 744 390
1993/94 *Financial year*	$7 723 153

6.17 Regarding the extent of trauma suffered as a result of abuse, there is often an understandable degree of subjectivity involved which has repercussions with regard to standards of proof. In these highly sensitive areas the Corporation is heavily dependent on the counselling professions. Recent high-profile court cases based on recovered memories underline the sensitivity and complexity of the issues and suggest that increased standards of professional care are required.

6.18 As long as alternative procedures, such as well-structured victim support schemes, are unavailable, cover under the scheme should remain. However it may be inappropriate for society to treat the victims of sexual abuse under processes which have been developed primarily for those who suffer injury in the work place or in motor vehicle accidents.

Mental abuse

6.19 There is an apparent inconsistency in that the scheme covers sexual abuse but not mental abuse. While it is difficult to put strict boundaries around a definition of mental abuse, it may be appropriate to look at whether mental abuse, like sexual abuse, should be covered by ACC.

Lump sums or periodic payments

6.20 While there has been general acceptance that periodic payments are more appropriate than lump sums for the compensation of non-economic loss, two further issues need consideration:

- is the current allowance appropriate and adequate?
- should periodic payments be able to be capitalised?

6.21 Recent cases indicate that the independence allowance rates for certain disabilities are quite inadequate, and may suggest that a single and final lump sum or capitalised payment may be a more appropriate option, especially where the claimant can then be discharged from the scheme.

6.22 In the context of the review and assessment processes outlined earlier, an option arises to substitute a disability allowance for the current independence allowance, and to relate it more specifically to degrees of permanent impairment or, if agreed, enduring non-economic loss.

6.23 Although the rationale for periodic payments is widely endorsed, there is still the option of allowing claimants, as a matter of personal choice, to capitalise all or part of their periodic entitlements; something which they can do in any case through financial institutions. Such an option would need to be limited to cases where it can be established that claimants will make no subsequent demands on the scheme, and that the capitalisation is appropriate to their rehabilitation.

Perspective and options

6.24 There is a clear need to reconcile these conflicting requirements:

- to maintain the integrity of the scheme by not undermining its comprehensive cover for non-economic loss and thereby reopening the opportunity for common law actions based on negligence
- to contain pressures to push out the boundaries and costs of the scheme which the provision of cover for non-economic loss invites

- to avoid the re-introduction to New Zealand of a view that society owes compensation to those who suffer anguish, no matter how tenuous the suffering.

6.25 The following appear to be the valuable options:

- to widen the cover for non-economic loss under the scheme to include all matters in respect of which common law actions may lie
- to establish compensation entitlements which are appropriate and affordable (and which, in certain cases, would not involve monetary payments of any kind)
- to prohibit specifically any common law actions in the fields of non-economic loss, regardless of whether cover is explicitly or implicitly available under the scheme
- to leave the scheme as it is and to deal with the possibility of common law actions undermining the scheme if and when an issue arises
- in any event, to limit compensation to periodic payments (except, perhaps for minor injuries), but to allow capitalisation of the periodic payments in certain circumstances.

Further perspectives on accident compensation

[New Zealand's accident compensation scheme is unique in that it was the first of its kind. It has attracted much academic and practical attention, with some in favour and others against, and also makes for some interesting reading. Below is one such evaluation of the New Zealand accident compensation model. It critiques Sir Geoffrey Palmer's book *Compensation for Incapacity* (OUP, 1979, Wellington) concerning the merits of the old tort system and the role of the accident compensation system. A second extract, from an article written by Professor Richard Gaskins before the latest reforms initiated by the Labour/Alliance Government, presents a positive picture of the New Zealand scheme. It focuses on the underlying causes of accidents and the difficult question of accident prevention.]

James A. Henderson, 'The New Zealand Accident Compensation Reform'

(1981) 48 U Chic L Rev 781

… The primary problem with Palmer's rationale is accepting his first premise, namely, that the failure of the New Zealand common law tort system to compensate everyone who suffered injury was an 'important social problem'. The common law never was intended as a means of accomplishing such a compensation objective. Even if one accepts the premise that every injured victim would be compensated, the insistence of the New Zealand system that in order to be compensable the injuries must be suffered 'accidentally' is clearly inconsistent with that premise. Furthermore, the system's potential negative effects on allocative efficiency, rather than having been exaggerated, have been underestimated. In the paragraphs that follow, I shall consider each of these points in turn.

A *The failure to compensate some accident victims was not a significant social problem*

One who believes that accident victims who recover little or nothing through the tort system present a significant social problem probably is thinking of the relatively few instances in which serious and permanent injuries cause great financial hardship for the victims and their families. Such cases do occur, and some are tragic. But there was no strong correlation in New Zealand between suffering accidental injury and experiencing financial hardship. Only a small percentage of accident victims encountered significant financial hardships, because of the availability of free medical care and, for many accident victims, of other benefits, including public welfare and personal savings. To the unfortunate few who fell into the hardship category, of course, the problems were significant. But it would seem more realistic to view this minority as part of the problem of poverty than as part of the problem of uncompensated accident victims. Given New Zealand's traditional commitment to ambitious welfare programs aimed at helping the poor and the disadvantaged, it may not even have been a significant poverty problem ...

This is, in essence, a social welfare system for the middle and upper-middle classes ...

B *The common law tort system never purported to address all unexpected financial hardships of individuals*

The book implies that the tort system failed in its efforts to compensate accident victims and therefore deserved to be replaced with a more efficient means of providing compensation. Palmer recognises that the first part of this statement is wrong—tort law never set out to compensate victims of misfortune. But the impression conveyed by the book is to the contrary.

A mistaken interpretation of the actual objectives of tort law pervades Palmer's thesis, as it did the analysis of the reformers who supported the Act. The reformers understood that the expanded no-fault compensation system could become a reality only if it replaced the tort system, because otherwise the need for new funding would be so great as to render unattractive any expanded commitment to compensation. Thus, there had to be an 'utterly devastating' attack on the common law. If the reformers had focused on the true objectives of tort law—the enhancement of social utility and the promotion of shared notions of fairness—the attack would have fallen short. The reformers possessed no empirical data to support conclusions that the tort system had failed to achieve either of these objectives, so the focus of attention had to be shifted to the compensation objective for the attack to succeed. Indeed, once the compensation objective is considered paramount, it is self-evident that a system promising 'integrated and comprehensive ... compensation that is usually swift and sure' is preferable to one that offers only '[u]ncertain, uncoordinated, and capricious remedies' ...

C *The New Zealand system is an inadequate solution to the problem of financial disruptions*

... My criticism of the New Zealand system in this context is that there is no reason why victims of misfortunes other than accidents should not have equally valid claims to compensation as accident victims. Why, for example, should the working person whose leg must be amputated because of cancer be denied benefits because he lost his leg through disease rather than by accident? Diseases such as cancer may often cause more significant disruptions in people's lives than accidents.

One answer offered by some proponents of the New Zealand reform seems truly remarkable: they extended the compensation system to include only accident victims because that is as far as the common law tort system extended. The statement must be considered in connection with another argument advanced earlier by these same reformers in a different context: 'The tort system deserves to be replaced because it fails to extend accident compensation far enough'. It appears that the tort system's benefits policy is either to be condemned as short-sighted or relied upon for support, depending on whether it suits the reformers' purposes.

The real reasons for limiting the New Zealand system to accident victims have little to do with basic principles. An important point in favour of the reforms of 1972 and 1983 was the promise that the total cost of the new system would not exceed the cost of the old; the savings generated by dismantling the tort system were to cover the additional costs of extending benefits to all accident victims. There also may have been a few vague promises of actually reducing total costs; similar promises, rather than an appeal to basic principles, generated much of the support for motor vehicle no-fault legislation in the United States in the early 1970s. No such promises of holding costs constant, or reducing them, would have been possible if harm associated with diseases were included along with electrical injuries, so the line was drawn at accidents. To the stirring reformist rhetoric of 'community responsibility' and 'comprehensive entitlement' was added the unspoken contradictory phrase, 'so long as it does not add to our costs' ...

D *The New Zealand system is likely to have negative effects on allocative efficiency and fairness*

The tort system's objectives include the enhancement of allocative efficiency and the promotion of shared notions of fairness. The former objective is accomplished by deterring unacceptably risky conduct, the latter by providing private remedies against those who commit wrongs. The tort system does fail to compensate some accident victims who have suffered loss, but it must neglect the compensation objective if it is to accomplish the others. Replacing the tort system with a compensation system may well generate benefits only at the cost of detracting from efficiency and fairness ...

Generally, if actors are not required to pay a fair share of the costs of their activities, including the accident costs, they will tend to overengage in those activities whose costs they can most successfully escape from paying. Thus, if everyone were required to pay into a universal accident compensation fund on a flat-rate, per capita basis, those who engaged in comparatively safe activities would pay more than their share of the total accident costs generated by all activities, and those who engaged in relatively risky activities would pay less. The resulting wealth transfers would encourage actors at the margin (those indifferent to which sort of activities to engage in) to switch from safe to risky activities. Not everyone would switch, but enough would to cause the overall accident costs in the society to increase over what they would have been if those engaging in relatively safe activities had not been required to subsidise their risk-preferring fellow citizens. Resources would be misallocated to relatively risky activities; the increase in accident costs would constitute social waste.

The solution to this problem of waste, one that to a limited extent was incorporated in the New Zealand scheme, is to require contribution to the compensation fund in proportion to the risk of accidents created by the actor. If the amount contributed is appropriate, the proper balance between safe and risky activities will be achieved. The tort system consciously aims at attaching the appropriate price tags to risky conduct, but there is no reason in theory why a system providing universal compensation could not do the same thing ...

In addition to considering the potential negative effects on allocative efficiency of moving to a compensation system such as the one adopted in New Zealand, such a move must be assessed from the standpoint of shared notions of fairness. A New Zealand-type system can be criticised on several fairness grounds. First, citizens would no longer have some of the traditional methods of vindicating individual rights in our legal system. A person intentionally struck by another, for example, would no longer be entitled to a legal judgment that his right to personal integrity had been violated. Second, the anomalies created by the Act are open to attack. For example, distinctions drawn between illness and accidental injury under the system cause persons similarly disadvantaged to be treated differently. Third, the measures of recovery include a number of arbitrary limits that cause persons dissimilarly disadvantaged to receive essentially the same benefits. Finally, the procedures under the compensation system reflect a willingness to sacrifice the interests of the individual to the greater good.

These criticisms of the New Zealand system do not suggest that the common law tort system achieves nearly perfect fairness. In areas of tort law that have come to be dominated by vague rules and excessive reliance on supposed experts and lay juries, fairness can sometimes be difficult to detect. But the tort system creates the appearance, at least, of trying to reach individualised results that are fair to all concerned. If the necessary reforms of the rules and processes of decision in the tort system were achieved, the appearance might begin to conform more closely to reality. Moving from a properly functioning common law tort system to a system like that in New Zealand might cause many citizens to feel that traditional commitments to fairness had been compromised or even abandoned. Although more victims of misfortune would be receiving benefits under the new regime and in a democracy it may be presumed that the appropriate balance of interests had been struck, I would not be surprised to discover a general feeling in the community that fairness to the individual had been sacrificed in the name of the greatest good for the greatest number.

R. Gaskins, 'Recalling the Future of ACC'
(2000) 31 VUWLR 215

... Time permits only a brief explanation of this last but most central part of the Woodhouse message, which defines 'accidents' in a new way. Let me paraphrase it as follows. Accidents are complex human events, involving multiple lines of responsibility. All events—including accidental events—are overdetermined by multiple causes, guided by multiple agents. This message is not some descent into chaos theory, but a dose of sociological realism supported by a long tradition of progressive social analysis. Strictly personal choices are not the ultimate building blocks of the universe, but are always socially embedded. Collective action is more than the sum of its parts. It follows that responsibility for accidents is not completely reduced to private individuals and their discrete choices, but assumes parallel lines of responsibility for groups, networks, organisations, corporations and government agencies. These agents, in turn, act upon each other through a matrix of structures, forces and systems; some of which they only dimly understand. Human beings can control their environment, but not entirely. Their success depends on social co-ordination, not just assertions of personal choices.

People have begun to recognise that the accidents regularly befalling large numbers of their fellow citizens are due not so much to human error as to the complicated and uneasy environment which everybody tolerates for its apparent advantages. The risks are the risks of social progress, and if there are instinctive feelings at work today in this general area they are not concerned with the greater or lesser faults of individuals, but with the wider responsibility of the whole community.

Just because Woodhouse says it does not mean it is true, of course. In 1967 there was possibly little recognition of where this rather dense concept might lead. Community responsibility was a malleable phrase within the Woodhouse Report. For some readers, it meant simply that the accident scheme should be funded by a wide range of contributors. At times it seemed to play with metaphysical abstractions, projecting some brooding societal agent as vicariously responsible for all the accidents that happen, no matter how private or personal they may seem. Thirty years later, however, I think we can explain this concept better as an ecological perspective on accidents. Human ecology was a young discipline at mid-century and by the 1960s it was applied to environmental degradation in books like Rachel Carson's *Silent Spring*. Epidemiological science and its universe of risk factors matured during the 1960s as a corollary of these trends. I am not saying that the environmental movement influenced Woodhouse directly, the way Terry Ison's book obviously did. I think rather that Woodhouse discovered for himself the equivalent ecological relations at work in modern industrial accidents, much as Durkheim found them by studying social relations at the turn of the last century. Finally, please note that this perspective applies equally to chronic disease and traumatic injury. Indeed, it absorbs personal injuries into a public health framework.

This is not the occasion to push this interpretation much further. Instead let me apply it to one highly contentious issue in the current New Zealand debate: the problem of accident prevention. If the Woodhouse philosophy of social welfare strikes you as dated, his ecological theory of accidents may seem rather far ahead of its time. By comparison with the welfare-economic theory of accident deterrence, which still dominates the writings of most legal academics and policy analysts, the Woodhouse principle is closer in spirit to different injury prevention methods that are now in the ascendancy. And finally, at the end of the day, the ecological theory of accidents provides entirely new reasons to revisit the Woodhouse welfare philosophy, which should not be counted as entirely dead.

Briefly, then, let me return through history and take you back to the 1970s, after the Woodhouse Report had been transformed into the early ACC. Despite their concurrence on the limits of common law as a compensation system, up-and-coming tort theorists around 1970 were poised to diverge from the Woodhouse approach. They found a new social function for common law in the field of accident prevention. It soon became fashionable among international (as well as New Zealand) commentators to dismiss the Woodhouse project as naïve and unlettered for failing to acknowledge this trend toward deterrence-based prevention. The New Zealand Business Roundtable (NZBRT) considers this omission in Woodhouse a massive 'non sequitur,' although the NZBRT's own vision prefers private contracts to tort in pursuit of deterrence. I must admit, for my part, that I share the quite different view expressed in 1980 by the Israeli legal scholar Izhak Englard, who described this whole shift to deterrence theory in torts scholarship as '... a desperate scholarly rearguard action to preserve a traditional system of individualism in a changing world ...'

My time permits me only to assert, without any real defence, that the Calabresi–Posner turn to accident deterrence was a costly diversion from the richer possibilities contained in the Woodhouse Report. Calabresi made a brilliant contribution to analytic theory by applying new formal concepts in welfare economics to a small, time-bound question within tort law: the choice between doctrines of strict liability and negligence in the new field of product liability. Posner answered him in 1972 on this limited topic, importing still further neo-classical assumptions about human behaviour from his Chicago School colleagues. The full-blown theory of accident deterrence then emerged the way many academic fashions develop, as a scholastic exercise in formal modelling, exploiting all the intellectual rigor of economic theory-building. In historical terms, this academic trend soon dovetailed with a major ideological shift in public policy in the 1980s, away from state-building policies and toward market systems as the new guardians of public welfare. What neo-liberal policy analysts liked about the Calabresi–Posner movement was the theory of deterrence through market-style signals. Indeed, tort law became a baroque afterthought, and in America most deterrence theorists want to trim tort doctrines severely to match their deeper image of ideal markets. Tort law as an independent force, let alone its sense of justice, drops out of the equation, to the extent it is not instrumental toward achieving market goals.

New Zealand, of course, is the one place on earth where personal injury law has already dropped out entirely, although for reasons quite different from those advocated by the NZBRT and others. When Woodhouse recommended an end to personal injury lawsuits, he did not envision a world without deterrence. His scheme left clear space for a comprehensive accident prevention strategy that is still waiting to be discovered and implemented. Rather than calling it 'deterrence', which preserves a musty Benthamite vocabulary, I believe we should follow Woodhouse and imagine a broader public policy of injury 'prevention'.

Prevention is broader than deterrence because it includes a range of strategies beyond manipulation of personal motives through monetary rewards. It also requires careful attention to environmental design, public education, group interaction, organisational cultures and political coordination. Any modern policy of accident prevention that does not consider these strategies will miss the important health and safety challenges of the coming century. During the years that legal scholars have perfected their models of optimal deterrence, a very different literature has developed using ecological models of injury prevention, resting on established public health principles. That literature speaks to the challenge laid down by the Woodhouse Report when it made accident prevention its top priority, calling for a comprehensive and coordinated response to health and safety risks. This coordinated response is certainly one of the key meanings of 'community responsibility'.

The current ACC policy debate in New Zealand highlights these two competing approaches to accident prevention. On the one hand, the National Party's 1998 Accident Insurance Act advances the market-deterrence strategy, relying on insurance premiums set by private contracts. On the other hand, the Labour Party's proposed model borrows more from the ecological perspective, which subordinates market incentives to risk-reduction practices. Assuming that competition is always a good thing, it is time these two visions were encouraged to compete head-on in the academic literature, as well as in the policy arena.

Cover

[The concept of 'cover' is crucial for determining whether a person has a claim under the Injury Prevention, Rehabilitation, and Compensation Act 2001 or whether there is a claim at common law.]

Injury Prevention, Rehabilitation, and Compensation Act 2001

Section 20 Cover for personal injury suffered in New Zealand (except mental injury caused by certain criminal acts)

(1) A person has cover for a personal injury if—

(a) he or she suffers the personal injury in New Zealand on or after 1 April 2002; and

(b) the personal injury is any of the kinds of injuries described in section 26(1)(a) or (b), (c) or (e); and

(c) the personal injury is described in any of the paragraphs in subsection (2).

(2) Subsection (1)(c) applies to—

(a) personal injury caused by an accident to the person:

(b) personal injury caused by medical misadventure suffered by the person:

(c) personal injury caused by medical misadventure in circumstances described in section 32(6):

(d) personal injury caused by treatment given to the person for personal injury for which the person has cover:

(e) personal injury caused by a work-related gradual process, disease, or infection suffered by the person:

(f) personal injury caused by a gradual process, disease, or infection that is personal injury caused by medical misadventure suffered by the person:

(g) personal injury caused by a gradual process, disease, or infection consequential on personal injury suffered by the person for which the person has cover:

(h) personal injury caused by a gradual process, disease, or infection consequential on treatment given to the person for personal injury for which the person has cover:

(i) personal injury that is a cardio-vascular or cerebro-vascular episode that is personal injury caused by medical misadventure suffered by the person:

(j) personal injury that is a cardio-vascular or cerebro-vascular episode that is a personal injury suffered by the person to which section 28(3) applies.

(3) Subsections (1) and (2) are subject to the following qualifications:

(a) section 23 denies cover to some persons otherwise potentially within the scope of subsection (1):

(b) section 24 denies cover to some persons otherwise potentially within the scope of subsections (1) and (2)(d).

(4) A person who suffers personal injury that is mental injury in circumstances described in section 21 has cover under section 21, but not under this section.

Section 21 Cover for mental injury caused by certain criminal acts

(1) A person has cover for a personal injury that is a mental injury if—

(a) he or she suffers the mental injury inside or outside New Zealand on or after 1 April 2002; and

(b) the mental injury is caused by an act performed by another person; and

(c) the act is of a kind described in subsection (2).

(2) Subsection (1)(c) applies to an act that—

(a) is performed on, with, or in relation to the person; and

(b) is performed—

(i) in New Zealand; or

(ii) outside New Zealand on, with, or in relation to a person who is ordinarily resident in New Zealand when the act is performed; and

(c) is within the description of an offence listed in Schedule 3.

(3) For the purposes of this section, it is irrelevant whether or not the person is ordinarily resident in New Zealand on the date on which he or she suffers the mental injury.

(4) Section 36 describes how the date referred to in subsection (3) is determined.

(5) For the purposes of this section, it is irrelevant that—

(a) no person can be, or has been, charged with or convicted of the offence; or

(b) the alleged offender is incapable of forming criminal intent.

[**Note**: The offences listed in Schedule 3 are all found in the Crimes Act 1961 and relate to sexual crimes and crimes of indecency.]

Personal injury

['Personal injury' is defined in s 26.]

Section 26 Personal injury

(1) 'Personal injury' means—

(a) the death of a person; or

(b) physical injuries suffered by a person, including, for example, a strain or a sprain; or

(c) mental injury suffered by a person because of physical injuries suffered by the person; or

(d) mental injury suffered by a person in the circumstances described in section 21; or

(e) damage (other than wear and tear) to dentures or prostheses that replace a part of the human body.

(2) 'Personal injury' does not include personal injury caused wholly or substantially by a gradual process, disease, or infection unless it is personal injury of a kind described in section 20(2)(e) to (h).

(3) 'Personal injury' does not include a cardiovascular or cerebrovascular episode unless it is personal injury of a kind described in section 20(2)(i) or (j).

(4) 'Personal injury' does not include—

(a) personal injury caused wholly or substantially by the ageing process; or

(b) personal injury to teeth caused by the natural use of those teeth.

(5) For the purposes of subsection (1)(e) and to avoid doubt, prostheses does not include hearing aids, spectacles, or contact lenses.

[The next sections are also relevant to a full understanding of the concept of 'personal injury'.]

Section 27 Mental injury

'Mental injury' means a clinically significant behavioural, cognitive, or psychological dysfunction.

Section 28 Work-related personal injury

(1) A 'work-related personal injury' is a personal injury that a person suffers—

(a) while he or she is at any place for the purposes of his or her employment, including, for example, a place that itself moves or a place to or through which the claimant moves; or

(b) while he or she is having a break from work for a meal or rest or refreshment at his or her place of employment; or

(c) while he or she is travelling to or from his or her place of employment at the start or finish of his or her day's work, if he or she is an employee and if the transport—

(i) is provided by the employer; and

(ii) is provided for the purpose of transporting employees; and

(iii) is driven by the employer or, at the direction of the employer, by another employee of the employer or of a related or associated employer; or

(d) while he or she is travelling, by the most direct practicable route, between his or her place of employment and another place for the purposes of getting treatment for a work-related personal injury, if the treatment—

(i) is necessary for the injury; and

(ii) is treatment of a type that the claimant is entitled to under Part 1 of Schedule 1.

(2) In subsection (1)(d), most direct practicable route does not include those parts of a route that deviate unreasonably from, or interrupt, a journey for purposes unrelated to the employment or the treatment.

(3) 'Work-related personal injury' includes a cardio-vascular or cerebro-vascular episode suffered by a person, if the episode is caused by physical effort or physical strain, in performing his or her employment, that is abnormal in application or excessive in intensity for the person.

(4) 'Work-related personal injury' includes personal injury caused by a work-related gradual process, disease, or infection.

(5) 'Work-related personal injury' includes personal injury suffered by a person resulting from treatment for a work-related personal injury as defined in subsections (1), (3), or (4), whether or not the injury is a personal injury caused by medical misadventure.

(6) 'Work-related personal injury' does not include personal injury suffered by a person when all the following conditions exist:

(a) the personal injury is suffered in any of the circumstances described in subsection (1); and

(b) the personal injury is suffered in the circumstances described in section 21; and

(c) the person elects to have the personal injury regarded as a non-work injury, in which case that personal injury is a non-work injury.

(7) It is irrelevant to the decision whether the person suffered a work-related personal injury that, when the event causing the injury occurred, he or she—

(a) may have been acting in contravention of any Act or regulations applicable to the employment, or in contravention of any instructions, or in the absence of instructions; or

(b) may have been working under an illegal contract; or

(c) may have been indulging in, or may have been the victim of, misconduct, skylarking, or negligence; or

(d) may have been the victim of a force of nature.

(8) [Omitted.]

Section 30 Personal injury caused by a work-related gradual process, disease, or infection

(1) 'Personal injury caused by a work-related gradual process, disease, or infection' means personal injury—

(a) suffered by a person; and

(b) caused by a gradual process, disease, or infection; and

(c) caused in the circumstances described in subsection (2).

(2) The circumstances are—

(a) the person—

(i) performs an employment task that has a particular property or characteristic; or

(ii) is employed in an environment that has a particular property or characteristic; and

(b) the particular property or characteristic—

(i) causes, or contributes to the cause of, the personal injury; and

(ii) is not found to any material extent in the non-employment activities or environment of the person; and

(iii) may or may not be present throughout the whole of the person's employment; and

(c) the risk of suffering the personal injury—

(i) is significantly greater for persons who perform the employment task than for persons who do not perform it; or

(ii) is significantly greater for persons who work in that environment than for persons who do not work in it.

[The remaining subsections are omitted.]

[The case *Accident Compensation Corporation v E* was decided under pre-1992 legislation. Under the 1982 Act, 'personal injury by accident' included '[t]he physical and mental consequences of any such injury or of the accident' (s 2). As you read it, consider how it would have been dealt with under the 2001 Act. Consider also other situations such as personal grievance claims. In *Northern Distribution Union v Sherildee Holdings* [1991] 2 ERNZ 675, 681, where a supermarket employee lost part of her hand in a mincing machine, it was said that 'the accident to Ms Prince's hand and its effects caused her distress, embarrassment, humiliation, loss of dignity and injured feelings. Such consequences are, of course, exclusively compensatible under the Accident Compensation Act 1982'. In *Jennings v University of Otago* [1995] 1 ERNZ 229, 266, which concerned a cashier who developed occupational overuse injury, it was said 'I hold Ms Jennings' claims in a personal grievance setting are prohibited by s 14(3)(c) of the Accident Rehabilitation and Compensation Insurance Act. In my view there will be personal grievance claims where this particular consequence does not follow but I conclude the present case is not such a case'. Still in the employment context, an English social worker successfully sued his employer for stress and a nervous breakdown brought on by excessive workloads: *Walker v Northumberland County Council* [1995] 1 All ER 737. In *Brickell v AG* (2000) 5 NZELC 96,077, the Court followed *Walker* and awarded a former police video producer nearly a quarter of a million dollars. The plaintiff had videoed and edited a considerable amount of horrific material, as a result of which he was subjected to undue stress, resulting in disabling post-traumatic stress disorder. The claim was based on common law negligence and the Health and Safety in Employment Act 1992.]

Accident Compensation Corporation v E
[1992] 2 NZLR 426 (CA)
[**FACTS**: The claimant was a 49-year-old woman holding a position of responsibility in a large organisation. She was sent on a management course but after four days on the course she suffered a psychiatric breakdown and was admitted to hospital. She subsequently left her employment for health reasons. She had exhibited no mental illness symptoms prior to going on the course.]
Gault J:
… The questions for determination are:
(a) Whether the particular injury suffered by the claimant in the present case properly arises within the meaning of the words 'personal injury by accident' in the Accident Compensation Act 1982.
(b) Whether the incident alleged to have caused the personal injury must be unexpected and undesigned for such injury to come within the description of 'personal injury by accident'.
(c) Whether when injury occurs and the specific causative incident of the injury is not identifiable, or identifiable as occurring at a particular time, the injury can be personal injury by accident within the scheme of the Act.
(d) Whether mental consequences or disturbance not accompanied by physical injury to the claimant can come within the meaning of the words 'personal injury by accident'.
… To construe injury by accident so as to require the identification of a separate causative unexpected event from which injury results would be to enter the 'Serbonian bog' negotiated by Hardie Boys J in *Groves v AMP Fire & General Insurance Co (NZ) Ltd* [1990] 2 NZLR 408 when construing the expression 'bodily injury caused by

accidental means' in a policy of insurance. The expression in the Act is 'personal injury by accident' not 'personal injury by an accident' and is well capable of construction in a popular sense without the need to distinguish between accidental means and accidental results.

Further, to interpret the expression narrowly would be to exclude injuries in respect of which compensation has been paid as a matter of course in the past, such as back injuries sustained in the course of normal lifting work or muscle injuries sustained in sport. Cover for such injuries has been commonplace under the workers' compensation Acts and has been commonplace under the Accident Compensation Act at least since the decision of Davison CJ in *Wallbutton v Accident Compensation Commission* [1983] NZACR 629 ... .

The findings of fact set out in the case stated include that the management course was an instrumental factor in the respondent's mental breakdown and although there were possibly other predisposing factors it was the course which working on the vulnerability of the respondent caused the consequential depression and later results.

The argument for the appellant was that the respondent's mental disorder caused by the stresses of the confrontational style management course should be likened to incapacity produced as a result of a continuous process rather than by an accident or series of accidents. Mr McKenzie relied on the industrial disease case of *Roberts v Dorothea Slate Quarries Co Ltd* and two decisions of the Accident Compensation Appeal Authority, *Re Rivers* (1982) 3 NZAR 204 involving a disease of the foot developed from constant pounding from long distance running and *Owen v ACC* [1991] NZAR 122 involving a physical condition caused by strenuous exercise programmes and not attributable to any particular mishap or untoward event.

The finding of fact that the mental disorder of the respondent was caused by the management course virtually decides this third question. We do not consider that because the breakdown manifested itself on the fourth day of the course and at a time when there apparently was no particular stressful event, the case is carried into the class analogous with industrial disease resulting from a process extending over a sustained period of which it can be said there has been no accident or series of accidents. There are, of course, statutory provisions for compensation in respect of industrial diseases but they are not relevant here.

We agree with Greig J when he said ... : '... although there may be no single identifiable incident it is quite clear what the triggering incident was and its occurrence which was accidental.' ...

We return to the first question. In light of the answers to the other three questions already given it can be said that in this case the respondent suffered personal injury by accident.

The argument for the appellant was that just as in *Willis v Attorney-General* [1989] 3 NZLR 574, by a decision of policy, cover under the Act was excluded for certain mental consequences of false imprisonment, so should the mental consequences to the respondent in the circumstances of this case be held to be outside the Act on policy grounds. It was argued that if the respondent is covered in this case then no distinguishing line can be drawn to exclude a whole range of dramatic experiences where the emotional distress has significant mental consequences eg trauma experienced through sitting examinations, through receiving disturbing news or through suffering bereavement.

In this area it is not possible to define accurately the borderlines. However, we are satisfied that the particular facts of this case are such that cover under the Act is appropriate and that this conclusion will not necessarily open floodgates. Each case will require consideration in light of established principles and if that exercise is to be constrained on policy grounds that is a matter for the legislature.

Lukken v Accident Compensation Corporation
(26 June 2000) District Court, Wellington, DCA 427/98

[**FACTS**: This case concerns occupational overuse syndrome (OOS) or, more specifically, a claim relating to fibromyalgia. The appellant maintains that she developed OOS while employed at Telecom as a Customer Services Representative with their 123 service. The date of injury was recorded as 18 July 1996. Her role required constant typing in a seated position. The original injury concern was noticed in her right hand, thumb, and up the right arm. She was first diagnosed with OOS on 29 July 1996, with further confirmation soon after. Two and a half years later the symptoms had become dramatically worse including a chronic thoracic sprain. Following a referral to a psychiatrist, Dr Marks noted the recurrence of panic attacks since the OOS diagnosis. In November 1997, the appellant was moved to an alternative position with less keyboard work, and more varied duties. ACC initially provided cover for the OOS, but the subsequent findings of the Review Officer denied the appellant's claim. At issue in the case was the appellant's entitlement to cover under s 7 of the Accident Rehabilitation and Compensation Insurance Act 1992, now s 30, Injury Prevention, Rehabilitation, and Compensation Act 2001.]

Barber DCJ:

…

Reasons for the decision
27 The essential submission for the first respondent is that for the appellant to be entitled to cover under section 7 of the Act, she must establish that she has suffered personal injury by gradual process and that the three requirements of section 7(1) have been met. These are:

    (a) that her employment task, or the environment in which it was performed, had a particular property or characteristic which caused or contributed to her personal injury by gradual process; and

    (b) the property or characteristic identified in (a) is not found to any material extent in the appellant's non-employment activities or environment; and

    (c) the risk of suffering that personal injury is significantly greater for persons performing the appellant's employment task in that environment than for persons who do not perform the task in that environment.

28 I agree with counsel for the first respondent that the two primary issues are whether the appellant suffered a personal injury and whether the appellant's employment with the second respondent causally contributed to her chronic pain syndrome/fibromyalgia.

29 By meticulous reference to some of the medical reports, counsel for the Corporation spent some time endeavouring to show that the appellant had not suffered personal injury. Despite the conflicting medical evidence, when I stand back and look at the evidence overall, there can be no doubt that the appellant has suffered personal injury. By 18 July 1996 she developed OOS at her said work and that condition has not healed. Its physical manifestation may not be apparent but its pain and consequential stress has never cleared.

30 It was submitted for the second respondent that the weight of the medical evidence available does not support a finding that the appellant's chronic pain syndrome or fibromyalgia was caused by her employment with the second respondent. Counsel refers to Dr Chiu being the only Specialist who considers that the appellant's chronic pain syndrome resulted from her employment with the second respondent, and he proceeded to criticise Dr Chiu's reasoning. Again, when I stand back and look at the evidence overall, I am readily able to find, on the balance of probability, that the appellant's said condition was caused by her employment with the second respondent.

31 I find that the appellant did suffer a personal injury as described above. This included tenderness and pain to thumbs, fingers, wrists, and right arm and neck, and spine sprain. There is clear evidence of physical injury and/or physical stress. I accept that pain is not an injury; but, here, the pain flowed from the said injury as has mental stress, anxiety and some panic. Whether or not the appellant has a chronic pain syndrome, or whatever the medical parlance, it is substantial and flows from her said work injury. I find it puzzling that medical opinion could suggest that ergonomic factors cannot cause chronic pain syndrome in the workplace; but I find many of the medical propositions put to me in this case to be somewhat unreal.

32 I note the submissions for the respondents that the relationship between psychological/emotional factors and pain syndromes have been well documented by many medical authors and that, in the present case, both Dr Bremner and Professor Gorman consider that the appellant's chronic pain syndrome is caused by psychological factors and that she has a history of anxiety and panic disorder as far back as 1995.

33 For all that, I can only assess the evidence adduced to me as showing, on the balance of probabilities, that the appellant's employment with the second respondent causally contributed to her chronic pain syndrome to a substantial extent. I do not accept that the weight of the medical evidence suggests that her condition was caused by psychosocial and emotional factors so that cover for that condition is precluded by section 7(4) of the Act. I disagree with the findings of the Review Officer. I am well satisfied from the evidence, overall, that the appellant's condition has been caused by her said work injury and all her stress and concerns and pain flow from that.

34 I am, of course, sensitive to the onus of proof being on the claimant ...

35 I take into account the requirement expressed by Panckhurst J in *JBBD v ACC*, High Court Dunedin M 121/98, that gradual process injury be compensated only in 'clear cases' and that the essential focus of s 7 is on causation ...

36 In terms of the application of the criteria of section 7, I simply find that the particular property or characteristic which caused or contributed to the injury by gradual process is that of prolonged computer use under stress. There was appropriate evidence to that effect at the recent hearing. Also the appellant's workstation did not suit her.

There is no convincing evidence that any non-work activities of the appellant had any influence on her injury. I think it is self-evident that there is a very high risk of injury for someone performing computer tasks in the environment in which the appellant worked. There is a clear risk of contracting OOS after extensive computer work than for persons who do little or no computer work at all ...

37 I agree with Ms Drayton-Glesti that Judge Middleton's words at page 13 of *Teen v ARCIC* and *Telecom* (No. 335/99 19 November 1999) are entirely appropriate to this case, namely 'It appears to me that by virtue of her work and the physical stress it caused, her body has reacted by revolting against its natural purpose which has brought about the onset of pain and restrictions in movement. That must surely be an injury, hurt or damage to the body. If the body is restricted in its normal movements by reason of the problems created by the nature of her work, then it seems to me that constitutes an injury.' Indeed, most of Judge Middleton's reasoning on page 13 of *Teen* could relate to this case also. The appellant in the *Teen* decision had been a Credit Service Representative for the second respondent and her duties had consisted of making outbound calls and receiving inbound calls (from customers) by using her computer. Her duties were somewhat similar to the appellant in the present case.

38 I find that the appellant suffered an initial injury, as described above, in the form of body tenderness and thoracic spine sprain, as described above, which either led to a chronic pain syndrome or included a chronic pain syndrome from the outset. All this arose from the appellant's said working environment. Accordingly, she is entitled to ongoing cover and this appeal succeeds. I think it is curious to suggest, in this particular case, that the appellant's chronic pain syndrome was not caused by anything at her said workplace. The medical theories put to me are simply not credible to me in relation to the facts of this case. I find on the facts of this case that there is a clear nexus between the ongoing injury/pain of the appellant and her work injury of July 1996.

ZXE v Accident Compensation Corporation

(6 October 2000) District Court, Auckland, AI 271/98

[**FACTS**: ZXE was an undercover police officer involved in one particular deployment between 3 September 1990 and 4 September 1991, with a focus on drug enforcement in the city where he was deployed. His role included the use of cannabis. Following his deployment, he returned to normal policing duties, but he struggled to adjust to the requirements. Thus, on 18 October 1994, the appellant applied to disengage from the force. The appellant then applied for cover from ACC citing 'prolonged exposure to hazardous work environment (intoxicating chemicals)' as causing the injury. He was referred to Dr G. Cliff, a consultant psychiatrist, who concluded that the appellant suffered from cannabis dependency and chronic post-traumatic stress disorder (PTSD). ACC acknowledged the appellant's entitlement to cover under s 7(1) of the Accident Rehabilitation and Compensation Insurance Act 1992 (now s 30, Injury Prevention, Rehabilitation, and Compensation Act 2001) as he had suffered the addiction as a result of his employment. However, ACC also stated that his incapacity for work was the result of the PTSD, which was not compensatible under the Act, as no physical injury was suffered. The appellant applied for a review. The Review Officer concluded that due to the diagnosis of the dependency some time after the undercover role, and the recreational use in the appellant's non-employment activities, the appellant had not satisfied the requirements of s 7(1)(b). Similarly, the PTSD had not arisen from physical stress, and could not, then, be accepted as a personal injury. Therefore, the appellant was not entitled to any form of cover. The appellant's appeal concerns this decision.]

Middleton DCJ:

... The facts of this case are very similar to the facts which confronted Judge Beattie in *CBA v ARCIC* 25/98. In that case CBA had been introduced to cannabis use in training for undercover work, and consumed cannabis during deployment, and continued to use it when he returned to regular Police work in June 1990. He obtained a discharge from the Police in June 1995, but no relevant medical examination had been made regarding his consumption of cannabis. Judge Beattie then had to assess whether CBA had become cannabis dependent by the end of his undercover activities in order to qualify for cover under the Act. In the circumstances Judge Beattie concluded that as the only evidence of cannabis dependency was that provided by CBA himself, the Court could not be satisfied on the balance of probabilities that CBA had suffered cannabis dependency before his non-employment cannabis use. CBA had contended that he had become cannabis dependent in about November 1994, although medical evidence suggested that it may have been somewhat earlier, but in any event it was at least two years after he had ceased the undercover deployment, and he had continued to use cannabis from personal choice.

Judge Beattie's findings in *CBA* were confirmed by Panckhurst J when the matter went to appeal in the High Court. In a decision issued on 18 March 1999 from the Dunedin Registry of the High Court Panckhurst J stated:

> To my mind a dominating feature of this case is the policy which plainly underlies s 7(1) of the Act. Personal injury is defined elsewhere in the Act. The purpose of s 7 is to prescribe when a particular type of personal injury, namely that caused by gradual process, disease or infection in the course of employment, is established: The essential focus of the section is upon causation. Hence it begins: 'Personal injury shall be regarded as being caused by gradual process ... only if—'. Then follow the three cumulative statutory preconditions which must be satisfied. First that the employment task had a particular causative property or characteristic. Next that such property or characteristic is not materially found in the person's non-employment activities. Third, that persons performing the particular employment task are known to be at significantly greater risk of suffering the injury in question It follows that the onus upon a claimant is a particularly heavy one. No doubt the intention of Parliament was to ensure that personal injury, said to be caused by employment-related gradual process, disease or infection would only be compensated in clear cases. Where injury may be attributable to work place effects, but also to other non-work activities, causation would not be established. Likewise, unless there was a known significant risk to persons performing the employment task, the case will not be recognised.
>
> Given the strictures of the section, it was hardly surprising that the appellant encountered difficulties. Two matters in particular clouded the issue of causation. First, on the appellant's own evidence, voluntary and prolonged use

of cannabis on a recreational basis, was established. This, it seems to me, would almost inevitably produce an adverse finding in terms of s 7(1)(b), unless there was cogent evidence to establish that the appellant's cannabis dependency pre-dated his extensive social use of the drug. Second, was the problem that assessment of the appellant's cannabis dependency was not attempted until 1996. Indeed the appellant did not think he was dependent until about November 1994. No doubt dependency and recognition of that fact are different things and accordingly the condition may have been of long standing before the appellant appreciated it. Regardless, where there had been a pattern of prolonged recreational drug use, and there was no timely medical assessment, the onus of disproving pre-condition 1(b) was indeed a heavy one.

In order to qualify for cover the appellant must satisfy the three elements of s 7(1).

In relation to s 7(1)(a) the Court has to be satisfied that the appellant's involvement in the undercover assignment required him to undertake a task in an environment which had a particular property or characteristic which *caused* or *contributed* to that personal injury by gradual process, disease or infection. The appellant claims that the injury was cannabis dependency. While the appellant's evidence at review and before this Court sets out in great detail the manner in which he considered it was necessary for him to preserve his undercover status by indulging in the consumption of cannabis to a heavy extent, he said that he was encouraged by his supervisor to adopt the stance of a heavy user in order to infiltrate the criminal fraternity from whom it was hoped to obtain evidence. While he was engaged in that deployment for a period of one year, it appears that he maintained to the official Police specialists that he had no difficulty in handling the job, including the requirement to make some use of cannabis. While the induction course clearly indicated that the use of cannabis should be minimal if it was not possible to simulate its use, the appellant said that in his case that was not possible. On completion of the deployment he was examined by a number of specialists by way of debriefing.

My concern is that while I consider that the purpose of the debriefing and the referral to specialists was to ascertain that the appellant's health had not been compromised in any way through his deployment, the specialists reported no difficulties based on the appellant's own evidence, and statements to them that he had no problem with cannabis. Had he been open with them at that time and given them details which he now puts before the Court, the situation may well have been different. Certainly he was diagnosed by Dr Cliff in 1997 as suffering from cannabis dependency, but he was the first specialist to make that diagnosis. In the meantime he had been undertaking normal Police duties from September 1991 until December 1994 during which time he acknowledged a serious use of cannabis when off duty.

While he now states that he was having difficulty in carrying out his work, and with the benefit of hindsight attributes the difficulty to his cannabis dependency, his superiors did not report any similar problems. He had at his own request, taken Sick Leave for stress-related problems from 18 August 1994, but there was no suggestion at that time of a cannabis problem. Then in October 1994 when he made an application to disengage from the Police Force no mention was made in his application or in the relevant medical and other examinations of his complaints of cannabis problems.

While it would appear that his work as an undercover agent did provide an environment in which there was a particular characteristic which could have caused cannabis dependency, there is no evidence that at the time he ceased the deployment he was suffering cannabis dependency. It was not until he was examined by Dr Cliff in November 1997 that the question of cannabis dependency was raised. In making this assessment Dr Cliff has to rely on the appellant's recollection of events.

In her decision the Review Officer concluded that the undercover work involved cannabis smoking which had the particular property or characteristic that could cause or contribute to cannabis dependency. I agree with her finding on that issue. However, I am placed in the same position as Judge Beattie in *CBA* that on the balance of probabilities I do not consider that the evidence establishes that the appellant suffered from cannabis dependency at the time he ceased the undercover deployment. Accordingly the appellant cannot satisfy the requirements of s 7(1)(a).

While the Review Officer did not address the requirements of s 7(1)(c), the first respondent concedes that the cannabis smoking in the course of undercover deployment can satisfy the requirements of that section.

The appellant's evidence, however, is that while he was deployed he also smoked cannabis when off duty, and that the consumption got heavier. However, when he returned to normal Police duties after the one-year deployment, he said that he gradually increased the consumption of cannabis. While he applied to disengage from the Force in October 1994, no reference was made to what must then have been his serious intake of cannabis in his off-duty periods. This was clearly recreational use. My concern again, is that at no time did he mention those problems to the specialists who examined him in relation to his application for disengagement. The appellant' [sic] answer to that, of course, is that he has only realised the problem since he has had the opportunity to discuss his case with Dr Cliff. However, it seems to me that it would have been extremely pertinent to the questions put to him by the specialists at the time he applied for disengagement to have mentioned that the problems had gradually increased since his return to normal Police duties following the year of undercover work. However, in line with the findings of both Judge Beattie in *CBA* and Panckhurst J, I consider that the appellant cannot satisfy the requirements of s 7(1)(b) of the Act.

The other issue before the Court is whether or not the appellant suffers Post Traumatic Stress Disorder (PTSD). Section 7(4) provides:

> Notwithstanding anything in subsection (1) of this section, personal injury that is related to *non-physical* stress shall be deemed not to have been caused by gradual process, disease, or infection arising out of and in the course of employment.

In the decision in *E v ARCIC* [2000] NZAR 446, the High Court had to consider an appeal against the decision of Judge Beattie who had dismissed an appeal by an undercover Police Officer for cover for PTSD under s 7(1) of the Act. In its decision the High Court stated:

> 24 Contrary to the submissions for the appellant, we find nothing strange in such a result. Section 7(4) is dealing with a quite different situation from that envisaged in the definition of 'accident'. Paragraph (a) of the latter definition makes plain that the concepts of 'accident' and 'gradual process' are distinct and different. 'Gradual process' is dealt with under s 7. It deals with a different situation from 'accident' and both definitions contain policy factors.

25 Here the District Court Judge had before him clear medical evidence as to the chain of events which led to the physical injury arising out of the post-traumatic stress disorder. The appellant seeks to argue, in effect, that the Judge was not entitled to look at the whole chain of those events commencing with the triggering situation which led to the appellant's fear which gave rise to the physical sequellae. The appellant's submission is, in effect, that the Judge had to look solely at the situation after the physical sequellae had occurred. However, in every case where s 7(4) is relevant there has to be personal injury, and in every case the personal injury will be the physical sequellae of stress. If, however, it is related to non-physical stress, cover is excluded. Here it is clear the triggering stimuli to which the physical consequences were related were non-physical. Thus the decision under appeal was justified.

26 In taking the approach that the Judge did to the construction of s 7(4) of the Act, we can see no error of law. It is difficult to see that any other approach was open to him. The provision only makes sense if there has to be an external physical factor which is related to the stress which gives rise to the physical sequellae. It is not suggested that there was any such factor in the present case. The Legislature cannot have intended that the physical sequellae of non-physical stress which are ultimately related to the personal injury suffered are themselves physical stress excluding the application of s 7(4). To find otherwise would, as is submitted for the respondent and the previous employer, result in s 7(4) having no meaning or application. That could not be right.

27 We therefore cannot see any substantive error of law in the Judge's approach to the construction of s 7(4) of the Act. He may have been wise to have referred not to 'cause' but to the words of the section itself 'related to' or a synonym such as 'connected to'. However, that is not to criticise his conclusion, because the essence of it is that, whenever the triggering stimuli that give rise to the stress are non-physical, as in the present case, the consequences would have to be excluded under s 7(4) for that provision to have application.

While Dr Cliff urges adoption of his view that it is impossible to attribute the appellant's disability to cannabis dependence on the one hand, and PTSD on the other and that, the interactive processes involved should be viewed as a whole that unfortunately does not conform to the wording of the Act. The appellant must suffer an identifiable injury, but in order to qualify for cover the appellant must establish that his PTSD was caused by a *physical* stressor. In the appellant's own evidence, he suffered mental stress brought about by the fear that his cover would be 'blown' and the thought that thereafter he might be subjected to physical stress. However, that does not amount to physical stress as contemplated by s 7(4) as Judge Beattie noted in *ETN*:

> The thought of, or fear of, physical injury does not make that thought or feeling of fear a physical stressor.

Accordingly it follows for the reasons I have given that the appellant is unable to establish that he suffered a personal injury by gradual process arising out of and in the course of his employment with the New Zealand Police. The evidence does not establish that the appellant's cannabis dependency arose out of and in the course of his employment. Furthermore, it was accepted when he disengaged from the Force that it was not because of cannabis dependency that he was incapacitated from work, but PTSD. The appellant's evidence satisfies me that the PTSD with which he has now been diagnosed did not arise out of his employment because that is not evidence that during his employment he suffered physical stress as contemplated by s 7(4) …

Accident

[Like the definition of 'personal injury', the definition of 'accident' is fundamental to the operation of the Injury Prevention, Rehabilitation, and Compensation Act 2001.]

Section 25 Accident

(1) 'Accident' means any of the following kinds of occurrences:

  (a) a specific event, or a series of events, that—

   (i) involves the application of a force (including gravity) or resistance external to the human body, or involves the sudden movement of the body to avoid such a force or resistance external to the human body; and

   (ii) is not a gradual process:

  (b) the inhalation or oral ingestion of any solid, liquid, gas, or foreign object on a specific occasion, which kind of occurrence does not include the inhalation or ingestion of a virus, bacterium, protozoa, or fungi, unless that inhalation or ingestion is the result of the criminal act of a person other than the injured person:

  (c) a burn, or exposure to radiation or rays of any kind, on a specific occasion, which kind of occurrence does not include a burn or exposure caused by exposure to the elements:

  (d) the absorption of any chemical through the skin within a defined period of time not exceeding 1 month:

  (e) any exposure to the elements, or to extremes of temperature or environment, within a defined period of time not exceeding 1 month, that—

   (i) for a continuous period exceeding 1 month, results in any restriction or lack of ability that prevents the person from performing an activity in the manner or within the range considered normal for the person; or

   (ii) causes death.

(2) However, 'accident' does not include—

  (a) any of those kinds of occurrences if the occurrence is treatment given—

   (i) in New Zealand, by or at the direction of a registered health professional; or

   (ii) outside New Zealand, by or at the direction of a person who has qualifications that are the same as or equivalent to those of a registered health professional; or

  (b) any ecto-parasitic infestation (such as scabies), unless it is work-related; or

  (c) the contraction of any disease carried by an arthropod as an active vector (such as malaria that results from a mosquito bite), unless it is work-related.

(3) The fact that a person has suffered a personal injury is not of itself to be construed as an indication or presumption that it was caused by an accident.

G v Auckland Hospital Board

[1976] 1 NZLR 638 (SC)

[**FACTS**: The plaintiff, while a patient in hospital, was raped by an employee of the hospital. She sued at common law because of the consequent deterioration in her mental and physical health. One day before the rape, the Accident Compensation Act 1972 came into force. The key question in determining whether someone had cover under the Act turned on the meaning of the phrase 'personal injury by accident'.]

Henry J:

… The short question is whether plaintiff is a person who suffered personal injury by accident. If she is, then it is conceded that this action is a proceeding for damages arising out of the said injury. The inquiry must be whether, on the true construction of the statute, the personal injury to plaintiff was suffered by her in such a state of circumstances that it was 'by accident'. The use of the word 'suffer' clearly indicates that it is from the viewpoint of the person who undergoes or sustains the injury that the term 'injury by accident' must be construed. What is important is the question: what was the quality of the event (which caused the injury) when viewed as a happening to the person injured? Thus the actor may intend the injury whereas, from the point of view of the injured person [it] may be quite unintended, unexpected or even merely fortuitous. As will be seen later, the injured person may be author of his (or her) own misfortune and yet still be able to claim compensation.

In *Trim Joint District School Board of Management v Kelly* [1914] AC 667, Earl Loreburn said:

> A good deal was said about the word 'accident'. Etymologically, the word means something which happens—a rendering which is not very helpful. We are to construe it in the popular sense, as plain people would understand it, but we are also to construe it in its setting, in the context, and in the light of the purpose which appears from the Act itself (ibid, 680–1).

Later his Lordship said:

> In short, the common meaning of this word is ruled neither by logic nor by etymology, but by custom, and no formula will precisely express its usage for all cases (ibid, 681).

His Lordship was there dealing with the Workmen's Compensation Act 1906 (UK). Lord Shaw of Dunfermline said:

> When, over and over again, it is announced that the words of the Workmen's Compensation Act must be construed according to their ordinary and popular signification, I entirely agree; but I think it is surely part of that popular and ordinary signification that for seventy years in England the word 'accident' has been publicly and descriptively used as inclusive of occurrences intentionally caused (ibid, 708).

And later his Lordship said:

> 'Injury by accident' cannot be treated apart from the fact that it is such injury by accident which is caused to a workman arising out of, and in the course of,

his employment that is the subject of the legislation. Every part of this cumulative expression may bear upon every other. And an easy instance of the value of such collocation arises to assist the solution of the problem of whether a designed occurrence falls within the term accident. For the point of view of the Legislature is seen from the composite expression to be the workman's point of view. And it is to be observed that what occurs to the workman may from his point of view be plainly an accident although some mischievous person may have designedly caused the occurrence (ibid).

His Lordship further said:

But in the case of *Nisbet v Rayne* [1910] 2 KB 689 the same view, namely, that 'accident' to an employee may include what was an occurrence designed by someone else, is taken. That was the case of a cashier who, while travelling by rail to a colliery with a large sum of money for the payment of workmen, was robbed and murdered, and the Master of the Rolls says, 'I think it was an accident from the point of view of Nisbet', that is, the servant. And Farwell LJ says this: 'It is argued, first, that there was no 'accident' at all, because death resulted from the intentional act of the murderer, and intention excludes any idea of accident. But the intention of the murderer is immaterial; so far as any intention on the part of the victim was concerned his death was accidental'. I am humbly of opinion that both [*Anderson v Balfour*] [1910] 2 IR 497 and *Nisbet* were rightly decided (ibid, 709).

In the *Trim* case there was a preconceived plan of attack and the victim was killed. Four of their Lordships held that the death was by accident. Three were of the contrary view. All the relevant cases up till this time were reviewed, so it is unnecessary to refer to previous authority. This case has since been treated as authoritative on the language of the Worker's Compensation Acts.

In my respectful view the reasoning of the majority in the *Trim* case ought to be applied to the words in the Accident Compensation Act 1972. I do not overlook the fact that the matter of construction is *res integra* and must be considered in the context of the present legislation, but looking at the Act as a whole, as I have set it out earlier, it is designed to provide compensation for those who suffer injury (or death). The injury (or death) is qualified by the term 'by accident' which seems to me to preclude the test from being an inquiry into whether or not the person who caused the injury was an intentional wrongdoer, reckless wrongdoer, negligent wrongdoer or merely the innocent cause of injury. That is the description of the actor and not a description of what the victim suffered. Indeed, an accident may happen without the intervention of a second party but result from something done solely by the injured person. The legislation must be construed from the point of view of the person who suffers the injury and in the light of the wide language used, including the incorporation of the Workers' Compensation Act and the Deaths by Accident Act and the very limited classes of persons whose claims are excluded.

In *Jones v Secretary of State for Social Services* [1972] AC 945, 1009, [1972] 1 All ER 145, 184, Lord Diplock, when dealing with an accident causing personal injury, in not dissimilar legislation, drew attention to what Lord Macnaghten said in *Fenton v*

J Thorley & Co Ltd [1903] AC 443. It was stated in that case and approved by Lord Diplock that the events which the term covered were:

(1) An event which was not intended by the person who suffers the misfortune, and

(2) An event which, although intended by the person who caused it to occur, resulted in a misfortune to him which he did not intend.

In either event, if personal injury results, it is within the term 'personal injury by accident'.

The event, qua the plaintiff, in the present case was unintended, unexpected, unlooked for and was in every way an untoward event which befell her and caused her injury. The fact that the acts alleged are also a breach of the criminal law is irrelevant. The criminal law has in general to do with *mens rea* (per Lord Dunedin in the *Trim* case ... A civil claim of the kind under consideration is concerned with trespass to the person when that results in injury and the fact that the causative act of the person responsible was criminal is irrelevant. The one exception is, of course, s 138 to which reference was earlier made. In my judgment the present claim comes within the provisions of s 5 of the Accident Compensation Act 1972 in that the plaintiff is a person who has suffered personal injury by accident.

Accident Compensation Corporation v Booth
[1990] NZAR 529 (HC)

[**FACTS**: The respondent ate some saveloys while serving as a seaman on board a ship. He became violently ill. When he did not recover speedily, he went into hospital and was diagnosed with lung clots and a renal disease. The Accident Compensation Appeal Authority held that he had suffered personal injury by accident and was covered under the Act. This was reversed by the High Court.]

Holland J:

... Food poisoning to the respondent in this case was undoubtedly an unlooked-for mishap or an untoward event which was neither expected nor designed. It must be remembered however that the definition taken from *Fenton v Thorley & Co Ltd* [1903] AC443 is to be no more than a 'traditional starting point'. The question is one of statutory construction of a unique statutory provision providing for compensation for injuries sustained by accident and without being in any way dependent on negligence. It was likewise a statutory provision intended not to provide for compensation for those suffering solely from illness by disease, infection or ageing processes.

The problems were recognised and carefully considered in a lengthy decision given by another Appeal Authority, Mr BH Blackwood, subsequent to the delivery of the present decision under appeal delivered by Judge Middleton. In Decision No 219/90, *McMillan v Accident Compensation Corporation*, 20th August 1990, Mr Blackwood declined to follow the decision of Judge Middleton in this case. Mr McMillan had consumed infected food in a coffee house which was claimed to have triggered off a condition known as Guillain Barré Syndrome. The Appeal Authority considered the claim as if it were one for medical misadventure ... .

However, I do not see the present as a case of medical misadventure at all. It is simply an allegation that the respondent suffered bodily injury by food poisoning leading to more serious and permanent injury and that the food poisoning was caused by accident … . It is common ground that if there were an 'accident' it was an infection obtained from consuming poisoned food. I am unable to see any logical or legal distinction justifying a conclusion that an infection obtained by consuming food is any more or less of an accident than an infection obtained by contact with a person carrying an infection unknown to the donee or even obtaining an infection 'inhaled or absorbed into the system' as was stated by the Appeal Authority in the present case. Mr Somers recognised the difficulties in this regard and submitted that in most such cases the actual manner in which the infection was obtained could not be ascertained. That may well be so in many cases but there will be many cases where the source of the infection can be established. In all cases the infection will be an unlooked-for mishap neither expected nor designed as far as the patient is concerned.

Accident Rehabilitation and Compensation Insurance Corporation v Stephens

(7 September 1998) District Court, Auckland, DCA 45/98

[**FACTS**: On 28 June 1997 the respondent while climbing the stairs suffered a lower back strain when he turned round suddenly to respond to his grandson calling out to him. Clear medical evidence outlined that incapacity was the consequence of the twisting movement at his home. The Corporation determined, in light of the medical evidence and the respondent's explanation, that no accident caused the injury and declined to grant cover. The subsequent review overturned the earlier decision, finding both an accident and a personal injury consequent to the accident. However, the Review Officer provided no reasoning. ACC appealed from this decision, and the principal issues in the case concerned the meaning of accident and the role of gravity within that definition, as well as the requirement for the application of external force or resistance.]

Beattie DCJ:

…

Decision

The definition of *accident* in the Act requires that there be the application of a force or resistance external to the human body. It matters not that that force or resistance is natural or artificial. Being struck by a bolt of lightening would be considered no differently than electrocution from contact with a live wire. Furthermore that external force or resistance can be applied by the injured person himself or through some external agency, animate or inanimate. The common thread that must exist is that the *source* of the force must come from without and not within the human body of the injured person.

With the greatest of respect to His Honour Judge Imrie, I do not entirely agree with his analysis of the role of gravity in the accident which occurred to the worker in the *Auckland City Council* [*v ARCIC* (46/95] case. Gravity was not the external force which caused the injury, rather it was the human body heeding the law of gravity which caused it to strike the external force of the pavement and it was that hard pavement which was the cause of the injury, not the force of gravity.

Thus I find that gravity per se is unlikely to ever be the actual force or resistance which causes the injury. It would require another force or resistance external to the body to physically cause the injury in an accident involving the body complying with the law of gravity. Equally of course, an injury could occur during an instance where the human body is defying the law of gravity. Thus gravity alone is unlikely to ever be the sole cause or source of the accident.

In this present case the law of gravity is entirely neutral. The evidence is clear that the act of twisting caused disc herniation and the compression of the right L5 nerve root. The injury did not occur during the application of any external force or resistance such as lifting a heavy object, or falling and striking a hard surface. There was no impact between the respondent's body and any other force or source of force or resistance whatsoever. It is probably true from a medical perspective that there was the interaction of two or more body parts in the respondent's back which interacted one on the other causing the compression but as previously noted, such interaction was internal only and not from any external force.

Accordingly, I find that in the circumstances of the twisting movement which the respondent carried out and which caused the disc herniation, such did not constitute an accident as defined in s 3 of the Act [now s 25]. For this reason the respondent cannot have cover under s 8 of the Act [now s 20] and the Review Officer's decision is hereby revoked.

[**Note**: The reference to 'gravity' in the definition of 'accident' appeared for the first time in the Injury Prevention, Rehabilitation, and Compensation Act 2001. Do the words 'or involves the sudden movement of the body to avoid such a force or resistance external to the human body' in s 25(1)(a)(i), also added by the 2001 Act, make any difference to the result in *Stephens*?]

Medical misadventure

[One of the special categories of injury for which a person may be covered under the Injury Prevention, Rehabilitation, and Compensation Act 2001 is personal injury by 'medical misadventure'. This concept is defined somewhat narrowly in sections 32–34 of the Act.]

Section 32 Personal injury caused by medical misadventure

(1) 'Personal injury caused by medical misadventure' means personal injury that—
   (a) is suffered by the person seeking or receiving treatment given by or at the direction of a registered health professional (except when subsection (6) applies); and
   (b) is caused by medical error or medical mishap.

(2) 'Personal injury caused by medical misadventure' does not include the following kinds of personal injury unless the medical error or medical mishap occurs at the time of the treatment:
   (a) personal injury caused by a person's abnormal reaction to treatment given to him or her;
   (b) personal injury caused by a complication the person suffers later because of the treatment given to him or her.

(3) 'Personal injury caused by medical misadventure' includes personal injury a person suffers as a result of medical error or medical mishap in anything done or omitted as

part of a clinical trial, in the circumstances described in subsection (4) or subsection (5).

(4) One of the circumstances referred to in subsection (3) is where the claimant did not agree, in writing, to participate in the trial.

(5) The other circumstance referred to in subsection (3) is where—

   (a) an ethics committee—

   (i) approved the trial; and

   (ii) certified that it was satisfied that the trial was not to be conducted principally for the benefit of the manufacturer or distributor of the medicine or item being trailed; and

   (b) the ethics committee was approved by the Health Research Council or the Director-General of Health at the time it gave its approval and certificate.

(6) 'Personal injury caused by medical misadventure' includes personal injury that is an infection suffered by the spouse, child, or any other third party if—

   (a) the person suffered a personal injury caused by medical misadventure and the injury is an infection; and

   (b) the person passed the infection on to his or her spouse, child, or that other third party directly or through his or her spouse.

Section 33 Medical error

(1) 'Medical error' means the failure of a registered health professional to observe a standard of care and skill reasonably to be expected in the circumstances.

(2) If the treatment in question is being provided at the direction or under the management of an organisation (other than the Corporation) and the error cannot readily be attributed to a particular registered health professional involved in the provision of the treatment, 'medical error' includes the failure of the organisation to observe a standard of care and skill reasonably to be expected in the circumstances.

(3) 'Medical error' can arise in any of the following circumstances:

   (a) the giving of treatment:

   (b) deciding whether or not to give treatment:

   (c) deciding what treatment to provide:

   (d) obtaining consent to treatment from—

   (i) the person to whom the treatment is to be given; or

   (ii) the person's parent, legal guardian, or welfare guardian, as appropriate, if the person does not have legal capacity; or

   (e) diagnosis of a person's medical condition.

(4) 'Medical error' does not exist solely because—

   (a) desired results are not achieved; or

   (b) subsequent events show that different decisions might have produced better results; or

   (c) the failure in question consists of a delay or failure attributable to the resource allocation decisions of the organisation.

Section 34 Medical mishap

(1) 'Medical mishap' means an adverse consequence of treatment, when—

   (a) the treatment is given to a person, is given properly, and is given by or at the direction of a registered health professional; and

   (b) the adverse consequence is suffered by the person; and

(c) the adverse consequence is severe (as defined in subsection (2)); and

(d) the likelihood that treatment of the kind that was given would have the adverse consequence is rare (as defined in subsections (3) and (4)).

(2) The adverse consequence is severe only if it results in the person—

(a) dying; or

(b) being hospitalised as an inpatient for more than 14 days; or

(c) suffering a restriction or lack of ability that—

(i) is significant; and

(ii) prevents the person from performing an activity in the manner or within the range considered normal for the person; and

(iii) lasts more than 28 days in total.

(3) The likelihood that treatment of the kind that was given would have the adverse consequence is rare only if the probability is that the adverse consequence would not occur in more than 1% of cases in which that treatment is given.

(4) However, regulations ... may specify a different rarity level (being the percentage of cases in which the treatment is given) in relation to any particular kind or kinds of treatment specified in the regulations, and in that case the percentage rarity level in the regulations applies in place of that in subsection (3).

(5) If the likelihood that treatment of the kind that was given would have the adverse consequence is rare in the ordinary course, but is not rare having regard to the circumstances of the person, medical mishap does not exist if the greater risk to the person—

(a) was known to the person before the treatment; or

(b) was known to the person's parent, legal guardian, or welfare guardian, as appropriate, before the treatment, if the claimant does not have legal capacity.

Bridgeman v Accident Compensation Corporation
[1993] NZAR 199 (HC)

[**FACTS**: The appellant underwent surgery for an occlusion of a coronary artery. During surgery, he suffered damage to the nerves of his leg. The Appeal Authority had held that this was not 'medical misadventure' because, although the damage was a very unusual outcome, there was nothing to show that it should not have happened during the course of the treatment. There was no claim that the surgeons were negligent or in error. Thorp J allowed the appeal and examined many of the previous decisions on 'medical misadventure'. Consider whether what was said is affected by the more recent definition of 'medical misadventure' set out above.]

Thorp J:

... Previous judicial interpretation

(a) *Court of Appeal*

The term was considered by the Court of Appeal in *Green v Matheson* [1989] 3 NZLR 564. The principal issue before the Court was whether claims for damages for trespass, breach of fiduciary duty and negligence were barred by s 27 of the Accident Compensation Act 1982. Its first finding was that all the matters for which the plaintiff sued would come within the ordinary meaning of 'personal injury by accident' without reference to medical mishap. Its second finding was that the plaintiff's claim was 'in respect of "medical misadventure"'. On that point Cooke P said at p 572:

These words are entirely apt to describe from the plaintiff's point of view everything culpable on the part of the defendants that she alleges to have occurred. The description applies naturally whether the cause of action be trespass to the person, breach of fiduciary duty or negligence, and whether the failure alleged be in insufficient or wrong treatment, failure to inform, misdiagnosis, misrepresentation (innocent or fraudulent) or administrative shortcomings. It all arose from the way in which she was dealt with as a medical case. If her case was mishandled, it was her misfortune or ill luck; this falls squarely within the idea of misadventure. To the extent that she may be able to establish that she suffered in any actionable way from any acts or omissions of the defendants, we think that inevitably she must establish 'medical misadventure'.

It is not clear whether those comments were coloured by the fact that the kind of misadventure the Court was considering involved 'culpable' acts by the defendants. Whether or not that be the case neither counsel saw *Green v Matheson* as having intended to define the general ambit of medical misadventure. My own view is similar, particularly as the judgment itself so suggests in its statement at p 573:

> We were referred to a number of decisions of the Accident Compensation Appeal Authority on the meaning of 'medical misadventure'. None either deals with facts close to the present case or leads us to try to limit the scope of the expression in a way that could affect the outcome of the present case.

...

(b) *High Court*

The first attempt in this Court to define 'medical misadventure' was in *ACC v Auckland Hospital Board* [1980] 2 NZLR 748, which considered the consequences of an unsuccessful operation for sterilisation by tubal ligation, the failure arising from a mechanical defect in the device used to divide the fallopian tubes ... .

Speight J gave his own exegesis of 'medical misadventure' at p 751.

> The word 'misadventure' is defined in some dictionaries as being 'ill luck' or 'bad fortune'. It would seem that this wording has been introduced into the Act to cover a wider variety of accidental occurrences than merely the consequence of medical negligence. It is in the nature of medical and surgical treatment that unexpected and abnormal consequences may follow to a greater or less degree depending upon the simplicity or sophistication of the treatment being undertaken. Where there is an unsatisfactory outcome of treatment, which can be classified as merely within the normal range of medical or surgical failure attendant upon even the most felicitous treatment, it could not be held to be a misadventure.

Finally, at p 753, he stated his conclusions:

> The question here is whether or not the failure of the operation on Mrs M is merely due to it falling within an accepted failure rate or whether it has been shown as attributable to operational negligence or difficulties of an unexpected and undesigned variety. If it was the first of these, then in my view it

is not a medical misadventure. If it is the second of these then it is a medical misadventure ...

The next decision in this Court was *MacDonald v ACC* (1985) 5 NZAR 276. There Bisson J analysed the words 'medical misadventure' by considering their derivation and natural grammatical meaning ... . In examining the ordinary meaning of the term he noted (at p 278) that:

[T]he derivation of the word misadventure is from the French, *mesavenir*, 'to turn out badly'. I find that phrase particularly apt for the meaning of misadventure in the context of the Act.

The same theme is developed at p 280, where he stated:

In my view the key word in the two passages cited and approved by Speight J is 'mischance' because it conveys the meaning of misadventure. 'Mischance' in the *Shorter Oxford English Dictionary* (3rd edn) means '1. Ill-luck, ill success. 2. A piece of bad luck, a mishap'. The words stressed by Speight J 'in the nature of medical error or medical mishap' are two ways in which personal injury may result from medical treatment turning out badly and both fall within the meaning of misadventure. But they are not exclusive and were not meant to be.

That theme was further developed at p 281:

For example, if the risk of an adverse consequence is considered slight but nevertheless the patient suffers that adverse consequence, it can be said that such an unlikely occurrence is injury by misadventure as having the factor of mischance or bad fortune. Similarly, if the risk of some minor adverse consequence is likely but in the event the consequence proves to be grave, it can be said that such a grave consequence is injury by misadventure for the same reason. An adverse consequence not foreseen at all would clearly be injury by misadventure. An adverse consequence from a known risk which might well have been avoided, had certain damage been detected (without negligence or medical error) could also be injury by misadventure, as the patient is either the worse for some mishap or has been the victim of 'a piece of bad fortune'.

All three passages identify the essential element of 'medical misadventure' as 'mischance, bad fortune, or mishap', the unexpected nature, from the patient's point of view, of the result. Although the judgment makes no direct comment upon the appropriateness of *Auckland Hospital Board*'s support for the objective test of the 'normal rate of medical or surgical failure', a test necessarily depending on medical or surgical opinion rather than patient analysis, the two judgments clearly proceed from different basic concepts, and cannot lie together. It is also reasonably clear that Bisson J considered the tests proposed in *Auckland Hospital Board* and earlier cases to be too restrictive ...

In *Polansky v ACC* [[1990] NZAR 481] the appellant had been diagnosed as having carcinoma of the stomach. The surgeon removed her entire stomach and adjacent organs in the belief that he was removing a malignant tumour. A subsequent report showed no malignancy, and the surgeon acknowledged that in its absence the condition might have been successfully treated medically. The appellant recovered from the surgery, but with significant permanent injury. She did not suggest that the diagnosis of carcinoma had been otherwise than in accordance with proper medical practice, and neither she nor any other witness criticised the decision of the surgeon to remove the stomach without seeking further evidence of its contents. Holland J found she had suffered medical misadventure, the central passages in his judgment (appearing at p 488) being:

> In my view the word misadventure in its context connotes the concept of something which should not have happened in the course of the medical or surgical treatment and not merely an unfortunate result.
>
> Hence there is some difficulty in accepting the submission that a diagnosis which later turned out to be wrong can be a misadventure when the medical evidence is that the diagnosis was 'what any prudent surgeon would have done'. On the other hand, a misdiagnosis is something which is not expected to occur, and, even although there is no element of fault, should not occur ...
>
> Both the misdiagnosis and the removal of the stomach and organs in the mistaken belief that they were affected by a malignant tumour were non routine events and were events in the course of medical or surgical treatment which should not have happened leading to unexpected and unfortunate results.

Review and conclusions

(1) Previous judicial attempts to identify the critical characteristics of medical misadventure have produced three different bases, ie:

(a) Whether the unsatisfactory outcome is within or without the normal range of medical or surgical failure attendant upon the treatment: *Auckland Hospital Board and Viggars* [(1986) 6 NZAR 235];

(b) Whether the consequence was the result of 'mischance, bad fortune, or mishap': *MacDonald*; and

(c) Whether the consequence was something 'which should not have happened in the course of the medical or surgical treatment and was not merely an unfortunate result': *Polansky*.

(2) Academic commentators have suggested other alternatives, the most attractive being that suggested by Hughes which would exclude 'predictable failure to respond to treatment' but include the consequences of 'medical treatment which has itself injured the plaintiff in a way in which he would not otherwise have been injured'.

(3) This diversity of opinion results principally from the circumstances that the phrase 'medical misadventure' is not self-explanatory, and that the normal aids to interpretation of statutory terms do not in this instance produce sufficient additional enlightenment to make any of the alternative meanings which have been proposed clearly more appropriate than the others.

(4) I am myself unable to devise a formula which could justifiably claim preference over those already proposed; and am sure it would not assist to add a further contender to the list absent clear grounds for preference.

(5) At this time, in view of the limited effect of any judicial redefinition of the term, the desirability of achieving even-handedness between those whose claims have been determined and those whose claims remain for determination must be a significant factor; and see as to 'consistency' Gault J in *ACC v E* at 431:

> To interpret the expression (personal injury by accident) narrowly would be to exclude injuries in respect of which compensation has been paid as a matter of course in the past.

(6) While the *MacDonald* approach has an attractive directness in its basic principle, like Holland J I find it undesirably broad in application. By contrast the *Polansky* alternative seems to me to be difficult to apply in practice for the quite different reasons previously discussed. Both alternatives seem to me to involve in those respects at least as many problems as the tests proposed in *Auckland Hospital Board*, as those tests have been reformulated in the four-part analysis made in *Hazel* [[1991] NZAR 362] and *Child* [[1991] NZAR 397]. As that analysis has had the most extensive acceptance to this date its retention for the determination of the remaining (pre-September 1992) cases would accordingly most promote even-handedness and in my view should be supported for that reason.

I accordingly conclude that the Appeal Authority misdirected itself by preferring the *Polansky* formulation to that recognised in *Auckland Hospital Board* as restated in *Hazel* and *Child*, which I adopt as the appropriate interpretation of medical misadventure for the purposes of the legislation I am asked to interpret.

I accordingly allow the appeal and hold that the injuries suffered by the appellant constituted a medical misadventure and for that reason a personal injury by accident entitling him to cover under the Act.

Common law actions and accident compensation

[The corollary of a comprehensive compensation scheme is the removal of the common law right to sue. The Injury Prevention, Rehabilitation, and Compensation Act 2001 contains the bar on proceedings for damages for personal injury. Whether this applied to exemplary as well as compensatory damages was a matter of some controversy in the courts until finally resolved in the negative by the Court of Appeal in *Donselaar*. Other issues such as the effect of the scheme on false imprisonment and claims for nervous shock have occupied the attention of the courts.]

Section 317: Proceedings for personal injury
(1) No person may bring proceedings independently of this Act, whether under any rule of law or any enactment, in any court in New Zealand, for damages arising directly or indirectly out of—
  (a) personal injury covered by this Act; or
  (b) personal injury covered by the former Acts.

(2) Subsection (1) does not prevent any person bringing proceedings relating to, or arising from—

(a) any damage to property; or

(b) any express term of any contract or agreement (other than an accident insurance contract under the Accident Insurance Act 1998); or

(c) the unjustifiable dismissal of any person or any other personal grievance arising out of a contract of service.

(3) However, no court, tribunal, or other body may award compensation in any proceedings referred to in subsection (2) for personal injury of the kinds described in subsection (1).

[Subsections (4)–(7) omitted.]

(a) 'Exemplary' or 'punitive' damages

Donselaar v Donselaar

[1982] 1 NZLR 97 (CA)

[**FACTS**: The facts for the purposes of the appeal showed something of a family feud. Whereas John was referred to as 'the principal irritant', Andrew attacked John about the head and upper body with a hammer. John was knocked unconscious, badly concussed, and hospitalised for a short period.

The Court set out several provisions of the 1972 Act, including, in part, section 5: '*Act to be a code*— ... where any person suffers personal injury by accident in New Zealand ... no proceedings for damages arising directly or indirectly out of the injury ... shall be brought in any Court in New Zealand'.]

Cooke J:

In the litigation between the brothers John and Andrew Donselaar there is one issue of general importance ... .

In short the issue is whether actions for exemplary damages following assault or battery can still be brought in New Zealand notwithstanding the provisions of the Accident Compensation Act 1972. Quilliam J held that the Act did not permit physical injury and a hurt to dignity and the like, if caused by the same conduct, to be separated so as to enable an action for damages to be brought for the second kind of consequences. The Judge accordingly struck out a prayer in John's re-amended statement of claim whereby he sought such damages from Andrew for what was there described as an assault ... John appeals from that decision ... .

Cases and arguments

As to whether such an action can be brought since the Act, opinion among High Court Judges has varied. In the present case Quilliam J pointed out that the means of punishing assaults was maintained by the right of prosecution and the power of the Courts to direct that part of a pecuniary penalty be paid to the person assaulted. The relevant statutory provision is s 45A of the Criminal Justice Act 1954, enacted in place of some old provisions in 1975. It gives the Court power to award half of a fine as compensation to the victim of an unprovoked assault which has caused bodily injury

...

Quilliam J went on to hold that, in referring to damages arising directly or indirectly out of personal injury by accident, s 5(1) of the Accident Compensation Act was intended to relate to both branches of damages, compensatory and exemplary. As he put it, 'The foundation of the right to claim exemplary damages is still assault which has caused injury'. White J took a similar view of *Koolman v Attorney-General* (Wellington, A 519/76, judgment 3 October 1977).

But in *Howse v Attorney-General* (Palmerston North, A 132/75, judgment 22 December 1977) O'Regan J, while accepting that the Act prevented claims for aggravated damages, held that punitive damages could still be awarded, on the ground that they arise 'from the acts done contrary to law and not from the harm caused to the plaintiff by such acts. The harm done him is met by the award of aggravated compensatory damages. It is the act contrary to law which is punished by punitive damages and it is recurrences of such which are deterred by such damages'.

Then in *Betteridge v McKenzie* (Wellington, A 103/77, judgment 7 December 1978) Jeffries J felt forced to disagree with *Howse*, preferring the approach in the two earlier cases and adding 'I am tolerably certain the legislature did not wish to leave to injured persons the right to impose private fines on wrongdoers when there are ample avenues available elsewhere, if the circumstances call for it'. And in *Stowers v Auckland City Council* (Auckland, A 1064/77, judgment 2 May 1979) McMullin J undertook an extensive review of the competing considerations and previous cases, as a result of which he agreed with Quilliam J's conclusions in the present case. But he adverted to the distinction between battery and assault and saw the theoretical possibility of an action for assault (intentionally creating in another person an apprehension of imminent harmful or offensive conduct) where there had been, as he put it 'no personal injury, physical or mental'. Such a case would not be, he thought, one of 'personal injury by accident' within the meaning of the Act, so proceedings for damages would still lie.

Next came the judgment of Prichard J in *Lucas v Auckland Regional Authority* (Auckland, A 1003/79, judgment 24 March 1980), a case of pursuit of a motorist's car by a traffic officer. Collisions occurred but there was no allegation or evidence of physical injury to the plaintiff. The Judge awarded 'aggravated or exemplary damages' of $1000 for high-handed conduct on the part of the officer. He did not treat these as arising out of any injury to the plaintiff's feelings, but did say:

> Aggravated and exemplary damages, although treated as a separate head in assessing damages, are essentially an augmentation—for special reasons—of compensatory damages recoverable by the plaintiff on a substantive cause of action. A claim for aggravated or exemplary damages can, therefore, never survive, independently, on its own roots. To exist, successfully, it has to be grafted on to some cause of action entitling the plaintiff to compensatory damages. From the nature of the case, the root-stock on to which is grafted the claim for aggravated or exemplary damages—the substantive cause of action to which the claim for aggravated or exemplary damages has to be related—is almost invariably a cause of action in tort and very commonly a tort involving personal injury to the plaintiff ...

In the argument of the present case in this Court, Mr Barton's position was that 'exemplary damages' is a misnomer, as they represent in truth not damages, at least not to the plaintiff, but a means of marking the Court's disapproval of contumacious and insolent conduct … .

On the other hand Mr Inglis submitted that there are not three separate remedies—compensatory, aggravated and exemplary damages—but only one remedy, damages, the level of which may be raised in some cases on the ground of aggravation and in a few cases higher still to mark the Court's disapproval of conduct and to discourage its commission. No award of damages based solely on exemplary or punitive factors can be made, he said, unless the plaintiff's cause of action entitles him to compensatory damages 'even if his loss which would justify compensatory damages is only nominal'. Accordingly Mr Inglis argued that, no matter how John's claim was framed, it must amount to seeking damages arising directly or indirectly out of personal injury by accident.

[**Note**: The Court discussed the availability of punitive damages in New Zealand, and concluded that New Zealand courts were not bound by *Rookes v Barnard* [1964] AC 1129. The issue is reviewed more extensively in *Taylor v Beere* [1982] 1 NZLR 81, a decision of the Court of Appeal released on the same day as *Donselaar*.]

On turning to the Accident Compensation Act the first matter that must be mentioned is that it is common ground that the plaintiff's allegations, set out in his reamended statement of claim and supported by his evidence, amount to or at the very least include allegations that he suffered personal injury by accident in New Zealand, within the meaning of the Act. It is immaterial that there may have been a deliberate attack by the defendant. It is from the viewpoint of the person who suffers the injury that the matter has to be seen for the purposes of the Act. Henry J so held in *G v Auckland Hospital Board* [1976] 1 NZLR 638, a rape case, and no one doubts that this is right.

It is obvious from the long title, s 4 and the provisions of Part VI of the Act (which is headed 'Compensation') that it does not have any punitive purpose. Whether it nevertheless excludes exemplary damages is not an easy question. There is attraction in the view that in the public interest the Courts are left free to recognise and develop exemplary damages as an independent remedy.

The 'mischief' which the Accident Compensation Act set out to remedy must have been primarily the uneven and inadequate scope of common law negligence actions as a means of securing compensation for personal injury in modern society. There is no reason to suppose that any suggested deficiency in the common law remedies for intentional wrongs was a real source of concern … .

In the first place, when personal injury has been inflicted on a person by what is commonly called an assault, and in legal language is often a combination of assault and battery, it is obviously arguable that in the natural and ordinary use of words a claim for exemplary damages against the assailant does arise 'indirectly out of the injury'. It is true that such damages are not given for the injury to his or her body or feelings; but it is just because the plaintiff has been the victim of the conduct regarded by the Court as reprehensible that such damages are claimed. The Judge or jury would have no right to award the plaintiff damages as a punishment to the defendant unless a link between the defendant's conduct and the plaintiff were established. When the link is bodily injury to the plaintiff, or mental distress suffered by the plaintiff, it may seem a little unreal to say that the damages do not arise indirectly out of 'the physical and mental consequences of … the accident'. However, the point is a purely semantic one on which two views are open; and it need not be treated as decisive if one thinks, as I do, that Parliament did not have the problem of exemplary damages in mind.

In the second place there is a practical problem. If one point more than any other emerged from the examination of exemplary damages made in *Rookes v Barnard* and *Broome v Cassell*, it was that the questions of compensatory damages and exemplary damages are overlapping and cannot be considered in isolation.

… An award of exemplary damages alone, unaccompanied by even nominal damages on any other head, might itself look something of an oddity. It would seem from *Prosser on Torts* (4th edn, 1971) s 2 that this is so even in the United States, where among the various jurisdictions some authority may be found for most theses concerning tort law. Indeed Prosser records as to punitive damages that 'The greater number of courts have said that they are limited to cases in which actual compensatory damages are found by the jury'. But the difficulty arising from the House of Lords analysis goes deeper for us. To set about assessing exemplary damages without the possibility of saying that aggravated damages are enough punishment would be to travel into terra incognita on a course never contemplated by their Lordships.

But whatever novelty is involved has to be balanced against other considerations. Adapting some of the words of Lord Wilberforce ([1972] AC at pp 1119–20 …) I think that there is a need to have effective sanctions against the irresponsible, malicious or oppressive use of power; and also to maintain a punitive remedy for the commonplace types of trespass or assault, if accompanied by insult or contumely, which touch the life of ordinary men and women.

The sphere is one of those recognised by the Privy Council in the *Australian Consolidated Press* case, in that a decision has to be made as to the policy of the law and the needs of the particular country have to be judicially assessed.

It is a matter of everyday observation that New Zealand society has become more vocal, factional and discordant. There is a scepticism about established institutions. Allegations of misuse of power by the police and other authorities seem quite common. Individuals and groups are readier to pursue their goals by protests and similar action, sometimes on or beyond the fringes of the law, no doubt because rightly or wrongly they feel driven to such courses.

Perhaps not all of this is unhealthy. And perhaps the appearance of a rather restive and abrasive surface gives partly a false impression, leading one to underestimate the extent of broad social unity underneath. But at all events this is no time for the law to be withholding constitutional remedies for high-handed and illegal conduct, public or private, if it is reasonably possible to provide them. It would be absurd to suggest that such isolated awards of exemplary damages as may occur will be a panacea for the country's social ills. On the other hand a useful weapon in the legal armoury should not be sacrificed without compelling reason.

All in all, in a situation where the right course for this Court is far from self-evident I think that we should try to meet a problem occasioned by the Accident

Compensation Act by consciously moulding the law of damages to meet social needs. The only feasible way of doing so, without intruding into the field of compensation which the Act has taken over, appears to be to allow actions for damages for purely punitive purposes; and to accept that, as compensatory damages (aggravated or otherwise) can no longer be awarded, exemplary damages will have to take over part of the latter's former role. In other words, as benefits under the Act are in no sense punitive, exemplary damages will have to do not only the work assigned to them by *Broome v Cassell* but also some of the work previously done by the other heads of damages.

The Courts will have to keep a tight rein on actions, with a view to countering any temptation, conscious or unconscious, to give exemplary damages merely because the statutory benefits may be felt to be inadequate. Immoderate awards will have to be discouraged. Trial Judges will have to be clearly satisfied that the case is a proper one for considering exemplary damages, bearing in mind the kind of conduct which such damages are designed for, and not lightly to allow a claim to go to a jury. Cases of this kind are apt to raise difficult questions of mixed law and fact for which trial with a jury may not be appropriate; the present case is an example. Whether a case is one which may reasonably be considered fit for an award, and the level of damages, are matters which at times may have to be scrutinised carefully on appeal also.

If, such precautions notwithstanding, unmeritorious claims are successfully brought in any numbers, the remedy of abolishing exemplary damages for certain classes of case is in the hands of Parliament.

The present case is also an example, in my opinion, of a claim for exemplary damages that should not be entertained … .

Richardson J:

… It is well settled that ordinary damages (including aggravated damages) and exemplary damages serve essentially different purposes: the former are compensatory; the object of the latter is to punish and deter (see the discussion in our contemporaneous judgments in *Taylor v Beere* [1982] 1 NZLR 81). Accordingly, it cannot in my view be said that exemplary damages in battery arise out of injury sustained by the plaintiff. The damages are not compensatory at all. They are not directed to the loss sustained by the plaintiff. They are awarded against the defendant because of the outrageous manner in which he has conducted himself in the course of committing the tort. In a strict sense such damages do not 'arise' at all. In a looser sense it may be said that they arise out of the acts of the defendant. It does not follow that their source is the personal injury sustained by the plaintiff. In determining liability for exemplary damages, it is the quality of the defendant's conduct which is in question not whether the plaintiff has suffered a particular type of harm … .

Somers J:

… Thus far I have said nothing of the words 'directly or indirectly'. It is hardly conceivable that Parliament was addressing its attention to the distinction between trespass and case. Nor are the words apt to describe recoverable damages in defined ranges of remoteness … . The inclusion of those words seems likely to have been *ex abundanti cautela*—as to include for example recovery of funeral expenses when death has occurred and which would otherwise be recoverable … . The most that can be asserted with confidence is that Parliament's attention was not directed to exemplary damages.

That leads to the final consideration. Exemplary damages though payable to the victim are in proper cases a salutary punishment of and a deterrent to high-handed contumelious activity. Parliament may upon reflection conclude that in the case of personal injury they ought to be done away with. But where continued existence does not in any way strike at the apparent objects of the enactment—the substitution of compensation under statute for actions for damages—and the words used are at best doubtful the proper course for the Court to take is to leave the issue to Parliament which may readily enough put the matter aright if its true intent were other than that which I conceive it to be.

Ellison v L
[1998] 1 NZLR 416 (CA)
[**FACTS**: On 27 July 1992, Mrs Ellison had a tooth extracted, and the dentist packed the site of the extraction. One week later, the dentist checked her mouth but over-looked the packing. On 20 August 1992, Mrs Ellison returned to the dentist com-plaining of swelling, but the dentist failed to discover the packing. It was not until 8 February 1993, when visiting another oral surgeon, that the offending packing was found and removed. Meanwhile, Mrs Ellison had suffered a number of distressing symptoms attributable to an infection caused by the failure to remove the packing. Mrs Ellison was able to obtain accident compensation for the second oral surgeon, but received nothing for the original incident. Upon seeking legal advice, her solicitors advised the respondent of the claim for exemplary damages. Elias J refused leave pursu-ant to s 4(7) of the Limitation Act 1950. Section 4(7) prohibits actions in respect of bodily injury after the expiration of two years from the date on which the cause of action accrued. However, it empowers the Court to grant leave to bring the proceed-ings upon an application made within six years of the accrual of the cause of action 'if it thinks it is just to do so'.]
Blanchard J:
...

Elias J concluded that the applicant's ignorance of her ability to claim exemplary dam-ages was capable of constituting a mistake of law for the purposes of the subsection and that it was understandable for Mrs Ellison not to have sought legal advice until her application under the accident compensation legislation had been dealt with. The Judge also accepted that the respondent had not suffered prejudice as a result of the delay. Therefore the conditions upon which the Court's exercise of discretion under s 4(7) are predicated had been made out.

However, turning to the question of whether it was just to grant the application for leave Elias J was of the view that it was not. She was influenced by the delay itself, pointing out that it is the policy of the Limitation Act that there be an end to litigation and stale demands. In the case of claims for exemplary damages whose basis depends upon outrageous conduct, 'the policy of finality of exposure applies not simply to financial risk but also to the upset of allegations which are serious enough to justify exemplary damages'.

More importantly, however, the Judge said that the proposed claim as pleaded and as described in the evidence was 'well short of the conduct which would justify an award of exemplary damages'. She said that in circumstances where personal injury was caused by negligence, such claims will be available only where the conduct giving rise to the negligence is outrageous and merits condemnation, citing the decision of Tipping J in the High Court in *McLaren Transport Limited v Somerville* [1996] 3 NZLR 424. She referred also to this Court's observation in *Cable v Robertson* (CA 125/95, 19 May 1996) that exemplary damages should not be trivialised. Nor, said Elias J, are they to be invoked in circumstances which would undermine the policy of the Accident Rehabilitation and Compensation Insurance Act 1992. That legislation does not bar a claim for exemplary damages but the policy of the Act would be undermined if the standard of the conduct of the defendant was not maintained. The actions of the present respondent, in the view of the Judge, fell far short of such standard. There was no prospect that exemplary damages would be available.

Notwithstanding everything that Mr Koya has been able to say in his written submissions and orally this morning, we find ourselves in entire agreement with the views expressed by Elias J. We are prepared to accept for the sake of argument, though leaving the matter to be decided on another occasion, that in some cases of negligence exemplary damages may be awarded. But because the negligence is an unintentional tort those cases are likely to be rare indeed. Exemplary damages are awarded to punish a defendant for high-handed disregard of the rights of a plaintiff or for acting in bad faith or for abusing a public position or behaving in some other outrageous manner which infringes the rights of the defendant. Negligence *simpliciter* will never suffice. We said in *Cable v Robertson*:

> New Zealand Courts are conservative in their approach to exemplary damages, reserving them for cases of truly outrageous conduct which cannot be adequately punished in any other way. They are awarded only in serious and exceptional cases.

Although there may be no doubting that the appellant has suffered considerably because of the respondent's alleged breach of a duty of care owed to her, the proposed statement of claim does not allege that he acted in bad faith and there cannot be any serious suggestion that his omission to remove the packing was deliberate or his conduct high-handed or even in flagrant disregard for the safety of his patient. Exemplary damages are quite out of the question in this case which in the days before the accident compensation scheme would have been a fairly routine proceeding for negligence. Mr Koya sought an opportunity to amend the proposed pleadings in order to clarify or expand the factual allegations but we can see no matter that could be re-pleaded so as to bring the case within the sphere of exemplary damages.

Before leaving the matter we desire to make an observation about the level of damages claimed. Mrs Ellison has sought leave to bring a claim for $250 000. Even if the conduct of the respondent had been outrageous and deserved to be marked by an award of exemplary damages, a claim of this size would be quite unrealistic. As far as we are aware, Judges in this country have restricted such awards to a mere fraction of the sum claimed here (for example, in *McLaren Transport*, where apparently gross negligence in the inflating of a tyre caused serious injury, $15 000 was awarded). They have been right to do so. The marking out and punishment of outrageous behaviour can be adequately achieved by a relatively modest penalty. It is to be remembered that such awards are not intended as compensation.

Legal advisors should be careful not to be associated with claims for amounts of damages which on any objective view are unattainable and give the appearance of being brought *in terrorem*. It is accepted, however, that in the present case the claim has been genuinely, if misguidedly, put forward.

The appeal is dismissed ...

Bottrill v A
[2001] 3 NZLR 622
[**FACTS**: Dr Bottrill was a pathologist who misread and misreported the results of cervical smears taken from Mrs A between 1990 and 1994. Mrs A sued Bottrill in negligence claiming exemplary damages but Young J dismissed the claim in March 1999. Later, as part of a highly publicised public inquiry into the testing of a number of women's smears from the Gisborne area, new evidence about the level of errors came from laboratories in Sydney, Australia. In March 2000, Young J, on the basis of the new evidence, which implied that Dr Bottrill might have been 'grossly negligent', ordered a new trial. Dr Bottrill appealed to the Court of Appeal.]
Richardson P, Gault and Blanchard JJ (delivered by **Richardson P**):
...

[41] Now that the point is clearly before us it is appropriate to confirm that in those necessarily rare cases where the stringent requirements of the remedy are satisfied exemplary damages may be awarded where the cause of action is in negligence. The crucial question is whether such damages may be awarded only where the negligent conduct is deliberate or reckless and not merely inadvertent. As to that, we are satisfied that the considerations of principle and legal policy underlying exemplary damages in this country weigh heavily in favour of confining the remedy to those cases where the defendant is subjectively aware of the risk to which his or her conduct exposes the plaintiff and acts deliberately or recklessly taking that risk.

[42] There are six immediate points. First, the purpose of exemplary damages is conventionally described as being to punish and to deter ... It is, we consider, both too late and inconsistent with the evolution of exemplary damages in New Zealand ... to change the focus and emphasise a general deterrence rationale. If, then, the primary purpose is to punish, it should be directed to advertent wrongdoing, that is, where the defendant is consciously aware that the conduct is wrong.

[43] Second, it is the quality of the defendant's conduct, not the cause of action pleaded, which is the focus of the inquiry. Exemplary damages are awarded because of the manner in which the defendant has conducted herself or himself in the course of committing the tort. Where there is no intention to harm, the quality of the defendant's conduct must so closely approach that involved in an intentional harming that civil punishment is an appropriate response. It is where there is conscious risk taking. That will be so where the defendant appreciated the risk to which he or she was putting the plaintiff and, though hoping no harm would ensue, went ahead and took that risk. It will also be so where viewed objectively the defendant must be taken to have appreciated the risk and to have gone ahead indifferent to the consequences. In

such cases the claims will be brought in negligence because of the lack of an intention to harm but the quality of the defendant's conduct so closely approaches that involved in an intentional harming that civil punishment is an appropriate response.

[44] Third, exemplary damages are available only in respect of the wrong done to the plaintiff ... But there should be no element of compensation in an award of exemplary damages. They are not directed to the loss suffered by the plaintiff. The exemplary or punitive element is the amount, in addition to the amount referable to compensation for the wrong suffered, which the plaintiff is awarded because the defendant's conduct requires that censure.

[45] Fourth, the replacement of a tort remedy for compensatory damages by the accident compensation scheme should not lead the courts to extend the role of exemplary damages to reflect any assumed inadequacies in that legislative scheme. To do so would be to subvert the social and economic policies underlying that scheme and require people to carry insurance cover or self-cover themselves against compensation liability intended to be paid for by ACC premiums.

[46] Fifth, while the judicial epithets often used to describe conduct qualifying for an award of exemplary damages are not determinative of the scope of the remedy, they do give the flavour of the misconduct that is required ...

[47] In this country we have used the ... language 'contumelious disregard of the plaintiff's rights' ... and have also spoken of 'high-handed disregard' of the rights of the plaintiff or behaving in an 'outrageous' manner or 'oppressively' or 'flagrantly'. These are not epithets which are fittingly applied to inadvertent wrongdoing, no matter how carelessly the defendant has acted. They apply much more naturally to acts or omissions which are deliberate. So is the concept of disregarding something, which connotes a conscious lack of regard—a putting to one side of regard.

[48] Sixth, a test of subjective recklessness is in harmony with the requirement of subjective recklessness for murder involving conscious risk taking (*R v Harney* [1987] 2 NZLR 576, 579) and with the requirement of reckless indifference to the consequences for misfeasance in public office (*Garrett v Attorney-General* [1997] 2 NZLR 332 and *Rawlinson v Rice* [1997] 2 NZLR 651 ... And in misfeasance cases it would be odd if the threshold for exemplary damages was lower than for compensatory damages.

[49] There are, too, three powerful legal policy considerations which in our view point strongly against removing the need for conscious appreciation on the defendant's part of risk to the plaintiff and relying on a wholly objective test of qualifying misconduct.

[50] The first is the difficulty of drawing any line between that need for advertence of risk and simple negligence by invoking an epithet such as 'gross', 'wanton', 'extreme' or 'exceptional'. The indeterminacy would necessarily create uncertainty as to the reach of exemplary damages.

[51] Second, wherever the line is drawn, the consequences for the public interest would be unacceptably expansive. The class of potential claimants would still be so wide and the circumstances for consideration so variable that the practical limits of the potential liability for punishment would be very difficult to predict. An example which illustrates the potential for a massive increase in the scope for liability is furnished by the case of a car driver who drives through a residential area in excess of the speed limit and causes personal injury. There are probably thousands of such incidents

every year. And Young J went so far as to suggest ... that drivers who drive through an intersection when the traffic lights have turned orange are *objectively reckless* as opposed to merely *grossly negligent*.

[52] Third, there are the economic and social policy implications of the expansion of the scope of exemplary damages including the responses of those then at risk of suit and, in particular, the impact of the cost of the services, if any, they supply or of the non-remunerated activity in which they engage and the insurance ramifications.

[53] For these reasons, in our opinion, considerations of principle and legal policy require that the remedy of exemplary damages in negligence cases be available only where the defendant is subjectively aware of the risk to which his or her conduct exposes the plaintiff ...

[62] For these reasons we have concluded, as foreshadowed at para [41] that exemplary damages may be awarded for negligence only in those cases where the defendant is subjectively aware of the risk to which his or her conduct exposes the plaintiff and acts deliberately or recklessly taking that risk. That inquiry involves an objective assessment of whether the defendant's conduct amounted to deliberate or reckless risk taking and so whether in that latter situation he or she was subjectively reckless. That test of conscious risk taking will be satisfied where on an objective assessment the defendant had an actual appreciation of the risk or was recklessly indifferent to the consequences and must be taken to have been content for the consequences to happen as they did. And where the particular risk was obvious but there is an absence of evidence as to the defendant's actual state of mind, the circumstances may justify the inference that she or he was aware of it and accepted the risk that it could well happen.

Exemplary damages: new trial order

[63] It follows from these conclusions that in our judgment Young J erred in law in concluding that the fundamental issue was whether Dr Bottrill's errors could be regarded as grossly negligent ... and that recklessness, in the sense of a subjective consciousness on the part of Dr Bottrill that he was exposing women to an unacceptable risk of harm, is not an essential element in a claim for exemplary damages for negligence ...

[67] The difficulty for the plaintiff in the new trial application is that ... the Sydney evidence does not address or bear on issues of Dr Bottrill's awareness at the times he read and reported on the plaintiff's smears. There is nothing in that retrospective post-trial analysis of his error rate in reading slides to support an argument that at the relevant time, when he was reading and reporting on the plaintiff's smears, he was aware of his deficiencies in that regard, or of failings in instituting and maintaining systems and procedures ...

[68] We would therefore allow the appeal and dismiss the application for a new trial.

Class action

[69] In the result it is unnecessary to rule on Mr Hodson's challenge to the reasoning and conclusions of Young J on the class action argument and to the Judge's discussion of costs. On the first point, and without expressing a final view, an obvious consideration is that ... this is not a case of a single act or omission causing damage to a multi-

plicity of persons. The plaintiff here seeks exemplary damages for Dr Bottrill's acts and omissions associated with the reading and reporting of her smears. She seeks to have Dr Bottrill punished in respect of his conduct towards her and, if satisfying an award in her favour depletes his resources with the result that in subsequent proceedings another plaintiff is unable to recover substantial exemplary damages, then that reflects the 'first in first served' standard. It seems difficult to argue from principle that a plaintiff should be prevented from claiming and receiving exemplary damages on the ground that some others may have their own claims against the defendant ...

Thomas J (dissenting):

...

[80] The main respects in which I will differ from the majority in the course of developing this judgment may be listed as follows:

- I adhere to the general principle that exemplary damages may be awarded in exceptional cases where the defendant's conduct is so flagrant as to deserve condemnation and punishment.
- I would not therefore impose a legal bar on exemplary damages so as to preclude an award unless the defendant acts intentionally or is subjectively aware of the risk to which his or her conduct exposes the plaintiff and acts deliberately or recklessly in taking the risk.
- In rare cases there may be some feature or features associated with the defendant's negligent conduct which are so flagrant as to warrant an award of exemplary damages, notwithstanding that the defendant is not subjectively aware of the risk created and deliberately takes that risk.
- The question whether the negligent conduct in issue, or some feature or features of that negligent conduct, is so flagrant as to warrant an award of exemplary damages is a question which should be left to the trier of fact to be determined in accordance with the function of exemplary damages.
- While punishment can be said to be the primary function of exemplary damages, such damages also serve other functions of the law of torts, and adhering to the general principle of exemplary damages assists to achieve those functions.
- Adhering to the general principle is not to 'extend' the role of exemplary damages or to seek to reflect any inadequacies in the accident compensation legislation.
- Having regard to basic principle, and the policy considerations which bear upon it, no such restriction as the majority propose is justified ...

...

4) An exemption for those who are obtuse!

[149] The majority's formulation provides an unacceptable exemption for those persons who are simply obtuse. Take two persons. The first is grossly incompetent, but not so incompetent that he or she does not realise the risk which their incompetent conduct exposes others to, and deliberately carries on. The second person is also grossly incompetent, but so much so that he or she does not realise the risk that his or her incompetent conduct exposes others to, and so also carries on. Under the

majority's formulation the first is consciously aware of the risk he or she is creating and deliberately takes that risk. Due to his or her greater incompetence, the second person has no such conscious awareness and is legally exempt from any award of exemplary damages! Clearly, in so far as exemplary damages are concerned, it is better to be more incompetent rather than less incompetent. In such circumstances, it is only by being obtuse that the person is unaware that his or her conduct is a risk to others. To exempt a wrongdoer's shortcomings or limitations when they reach the point that he or she is no longer subjectively aware of the risk they are creating cannot be a sound prescription for this area of the law ...

Tipping J (concurring with the majority):

[163] I agree that this appeal should be allowed for the reasons and with the consequences stated in the judgment prepared by Richardson P. The crucial first question concerns exemplary damages in negligence cases involving personal injury. More specifically it concerns whether, before exemplary damages can be awarded, the person guilty of negligence must be shown to have consciously appreciated the risk to the plaintiff's safety which his or her conduct was creating.

[164] In *McLaren Transport Limited v Somerville* [1996] 3 NZLR 424, 434 I adopted a test in these terms:

> Exemplary damages for negligence causing personal injury may be awarded if, but only if, the level of negligence is so high that it amounts to an outrageous and flagrant disregard for the plaintiff's safety, meriting condemnation and punishment.

I had earlier said that I would be inclined to keep recklessness out of the test because:

> it is, at best, a difficult concept, capable of varying from the wholly subjective to the wholly objective with various points in between.

I added that the concept of gross negligence had a seductive simplicity but that:

> I would prefer not to put the test solely on that basis because I do not consider it sufficiently incorporates the various ingredients which go to make up the totality of the criteria ...

[166] Gross negligence is apt to convey the idea of very bad but still inadvertent negligence—objective recklessness might be another way of putting it. Thus the expression 'gross negligence' would not of itself convey what I then considered, and still consider, to be an essential prerequisite for an award of exemplary damages in this field. That ingredient can be called the subjective element, namely the deliberate running of a known risk of causing physical harm to another person. That will usually, if not always, be more deserving of punishment than causing the same harm, albeit as a result of gross negligence, but without appreciating the risk involved. The difference is between advertence and inadvertence; between subjective and objective recklessness if you like.

[167] Although in *McLaren's* case I preferred not to use the word 'reckless' for the reasons given, I was not intending to signal that objective recklessness at a sufficiently high level would be enough. I considered the conjunction of the words 'outrageous

and flagrant disregard' would sufficiently flag the need for the person concerned to have appreciated the risk his conduct posed for the physical safety of the plaintiff.

[168] I acknowledge however that my application of the test to the facts of the case was not a model of clarity. I held at 435 that Mr Stumbles, the person who was guilty of grossly inflating the tyre, 'must have been conscious of the risk', yet in the next paragraph I said that there was no evidence that Mr Stumbles 'was consciously considering' either his own safety or that of the plaintiff. What I should have said was that there was no direct evidence, but I was prepared to infer that Mr Stumbles must have appreciated the risk inherent in what he was doing ...

[174] In order to reflect the foregoing with clarity and with the benefit of having given further thought to the issue since I wrote the *McLaren* judgment, I would take this opportunity of amending the test I then adopted in this way. Exemplary damages for negligence causing personal injury may be awarded if, but only if, the negligence is at such a level and is of such a kind that it amounts to a conscious, outrageous and flagrant disregard for the plaintiff's safety, meriting condemnation and punishment. The concept of conscious disregard means that the defendant consciously appreciated the risk to the plaintiff's safety caused by his or her conduct but nevertheless deliberately chose to run that risk ...

[**Note**: The Court of Appeal refers to *McLaren Transport v Somerville* [1996] 3 NZLR 424. Somerville took a wheel rim from his hay-conditioning machine to the defendant's garage to have a new tyre fitted. The garage foreman with the apt Dickensian name of Mr Stumbles read a warning sign on the tyre but inflated the tyre to twice the maximum pressure. The tyre exploded, causing serious injury to Somerville, who was standing nearby. The trial judge found that Stumbles' conduct had been 'grossly negligent and reckless' and awarded Somerville $15 000 in exemplary damages. Tipping J upheld this on appeal. What would be the result of this case using the *Bottrill* test?]

(b) Potential claims for compensatory damages

Green v Matheson

[1989] 3 NZLR 564 (CA)

[**FACTS**: The plaintiff was a patient at the National Women's Hospital in Auckland from 1964 to 1979 and the defendant was her gynaecologist. As part of a research experiment, the defendant decided to treat the plaintiff with lesser procedures than usual. The plaintiff did not know about or consent to the experiment. She subsequently developed invasive cancer, requiring surgery and radiation treatment. She sued in trespass to the person, breach of fiduciary duty, and negligence.]

Cooke P:

... [W]e do not think that the issues arising at this stage in this case present any great difficulty. They may be covered in two basic propositions, with some explanation.

First, as is common ground, none of the plaintiff's claims for exemplary damages are barred by the Accident Compensation Act ... .

The second basic proposition, in our opinion, is that all the plaintiff's other claims under the various causes of action are proceedings for damages arising directly or indirectly out of personal injury by accident. Accordingly, if the alleged accident occurred on or after 1 April 1974, the claims are barred by the Act. If the alleged injury resulted from an accident which occurred before that date, the claim is not barred ... .

... In the context of an Act dealing with compensation for personal injuries, it is obvious that 'personal injury by accident' refers to a mishap causing harm to the person. It cannot include harm to financial or property interests or reputation, even though the damages recoverable for that kind of harm may include in some cases redress for injured feelings or disappointed expectations. For instance the Act can have no bearing on actions for damages for breach of ordinary commercial contracts or for defamation. No one would normally describe such events or their consequences as personal injuries by accident and the purpose of the Act clearly does not warrant a strained interpretation bringing them within that description. In *Willis v Attorney-General* [1989] 3 NZLR 574, which is being decided contemporaneously, we have to say more on the theme of interpreting 'personal injury by accident' as an integrated phrase and in accordance with the natural and ordinary use of language. The judgments in the two cases should be read together.

On the other hand, having heard the point fully argued we adopt definitely the opinion indicated provisionally in *Blundell* at pp 738–9 that, once there is a personal injury by accident within the scope of the Act, all the emotional or psychological effects fall within the statutory words 'The physical and mental consequences of any such injury or of the accident'. Those words are not limited to mental consequences identifiable by some particular medical or psychiatric description, nor to what is often called shock or trauma. Parliament cannot have intended fine distinctions in this area ... .

Here the consequences pleaded for the plaintiff include 'interference with her bodily integrity', 'diminished life expectancy' and 'being made the subject of research and experimentation without her knowledge or consent'. If there was a personal injury by accident or a number of personal injuries by accident within the meaning of the Act, we think that any of those pleaded consequences must be within the words 'The physical and mental consequences of any such injury or of the accident', giving those words their natural and ordinary meaning in their context. The words are all-embracing as regards effects on the person.

Willis v Attorney-General
[1989] 3 NZLR 574 (CA)
[**FACTS**: The plaintiffs were detained by customs officers in connection with the importation of certain cars. Charges, which were subsequently laid against them, were dismissed. Claims were then lodged alleging malicious prosecution, negligence, and false imprisonment.]
Cooke P:
... ['Personal injury by accident'] is a total and non-technical phrase. As is well known, the Act is designed fundamentally to supplant the vagaries of actions for damages for negligence at common law. It is not coincident with the field of such actions, but interpretations taking the bar in the Act beyond that field have to be carefully scrutinised. It has been settled for some time that physical and mental injuries caused by intentional assaults or batteries (including rape) are personal injuries by accident from the point of view of the victim, so actions for damages of that kind are within

the statutory bar … . But that does not mean that the bar extends to other tort actions where a suggested link with the subject-matter of the Act is more tenuous. It has been authoritatively recognised that the integrity of the accident compensation system will not be significantly threatened by holding some grey-area claims to be outside the bar: see the passage from Mr Geoffrey Palmer's *Compensation for Incapacity* (1979) quoted in *Donselaar v Donselaar* [1982] 1 NZLR 97, 104–5.

'Personal injury by accident' is an integrated phrase, to be seen and applied as a whole and without an unnatural breaking down which would rob it of the impact it makes as a whole. Perhaps it can be called holistic, in that the sum is more than the parts. But we are concerned with the ordinary use of language, not philosophical concepts. It is not an expression that would naturally be used in ordinary speech to describe malicious prosecution or breach of a duty of care to safeguard the plaintiff's proprietary or economic interests or reputation. The fact that damages for distress and the like may be claimed, and in some cases recovered, on these causes of action does not in the natural and ordinary use of language convert the incident complained of and its consequences into personal injury by accident. In *Auckland City Council v Blundell* [1986] 1 NZLR 732, 738, counsel rightly conceded that claims for damages for malicious prosecution are unaffected by the Accident Compensation Act. Having regard to the scope of the Act and the natural and ordinary use of language, we think that the same applies where the duty of care alleged to have been broken is not one imposed for the protection of the plaintiff's personal safety.

On these views it follows as a matter of law that the second and third causes of action here cannot be barred by the Act and that there is accordingly no real question under those heads to be referred to the Corporation.

The position regarding false imprisonment is less clear. The point was expressly left open in … *Blundell* at p 738. It must now be decided.

… False imprisonment is the unlawful total restraint of the liberty of a person. It may be but is not necessarily brought about by force or the threat of force … Applying again the tests of the purposes of the Accident Compensation legislation and the natural and ordinary use of language, we have come to the conclusion that false imprisonment as such is outside the purview of the Act. In ordinary speech we do not think that it would be said of anyone who had been detained as the plaintiffs claim to have been that he or she had suffered personal injury by accident.

Accordingly we hold that claims for damages for false imprisonment or abuse of rights amounting to false imprisonment (which appears to add nothing) are not barred by the Act. If a plaintiff were to claim damages (other than exemplary) for assault or battery, the position would be different. Such claims are barred, but they are not made by the plaintiffs here. If the detention of a plaintiff has been accompanied by physical injuries, damages cannot be claimed for those or for the pain and suffering they have caused.

No doubt there is a grey area in which it can be argued that distress or humiliation or fear for which a plaintiff alleging false imprisonment seeks damages amounts to or overlaps with personal injury by accident. But to make the Act work as Parliament must have intended … we think that the clear rule must be adopted that any claims for any kind of damages for false imprisonment alone and for any distress, humiliation or fear caused thereby are outside the scope of the accident compensation system and unaffected by the Act. If such mental consequences have been caused by both false imprisonment and assault or battery, a plaintiff can still claim damages for them. It is enough if the false imprisonment has been a substantial cause.

Innes v Wong
[1996] 3 NZLR 238 (HC)
[**FACTS**: The plaintiffs were the administrators of the estate of Matthew Innes, who died during a violent struggle while being transported to a psychiatric hospital for mental health assessment. Actions were brought in false imprisonment, breach of the New Zealand Bill of Rights Act 1990 (pursuant to *Simpson v Attorney-General* [*Baigent's Case*] [1994] 3 NZLR 667), and negligence. There was some evidence that Innes suffered cardiac arrest. Under s 4(2) of the Accident Rehabilitation and Compensation Insurance Act 1992, no cardiovascular episode was personal injury unless it was the result of medical misadventure or was a work injury (see now s 27(3) of the Injury Prevention, Rehabilitation, and Compensation Act 2001 to similar effect).]
Cartwright J:
… As Matthew was being transported to Kingseat Hospital for the purposes of an assessment and prospectively treatment, his situation does not fall within the meaning of 'medical mishap'. It is arguable whether the incident can fall within the meaning of 'medical error' given that he was transported by the police at the request of a registered health professional, but (and without in any way intending to indicate a view) the circumstances which led to Matthew's transportation by the police would seem to place an undue strain on the meaning of 'medical error' as defined in s 5 of the Act … .

In the present instance, Associate Professor Koelmeyer's conclusion (which must at this stage be described as tentative) that there was a cardiovascular incident in the chain of medical events which led to Matthew's death, and that cardiovascular incident at first sight could not be described as arising from a medical misadventure, then there is at least room to argue that Matthew's death arose in circumstances other than as the result of personal injury by accident.

[**Note**: Cartwright J gave the plaintiffs the opportunity to amend their pleadings to incorporate the expert witness's evidence. Her Honour then refused to strike out the false imprisonment claim and then considered the Bill of Rights claim.]

Parts of this cause of action overlap with those set out in the first cause already determined by me and are in any event expressed to be in the alternative. Public law compensation for breach of the Bill of Rights is a new remedy in New Zealand, first awarded by the Court of Appeal in [*Baigent's Case*] … Cooke P said at p 678 that public law compensation is distinct from common law damages, and he held that such compensation is not 'pecuniary damages' within the meaning of s 19A of the Judicature Act 1908. This finding makes it clear that public law damages must be approached as an entirely new form of remedy, whose precise nature and relationship with other areas of the law will need to be worked out incrementally. What is apparent is that the object of public law damages is 'to affirm the right [infringed]' (per Hardie Boys J at p 703) and that 'In the assessment of the compensation, the emphasis must be on the compensatory and not the punitive element'.

I am not aware of any case which has considered the relationship between the Accident Rehabilitation and Compensation Insurance Act and public law compensation for breach of the Bill of Rights. It appears to be at least arguable in this case that public law compensation would not arise directly or indirectly out of personal injury covered by the Act. Leaving aside the question of cover, it also appears arguable that the public law compensation arises from the breach of the Bill of Rights Act, not from personal injury.

[**Note**: One of the most interesting aspects of recent accident compensation law has been in respect of exemplary damages for injuries sustained from alleged or convicted criminals or an acquitted defendant. In *Daniels v Thompson* [1998] 3 NZLR 22, the Court of Appeal held that there was an absolute bar on civil proceedings claiming exemplary damages where the acts relied on as the basis for an award have been the subject of a conviction in the criminal Courts. A subsequent appeal was dismissed by the Privy Council, for it would not substitute its own views for those of the Court of Appeal (*W v W* [1999] 2 NZLR 1).

However, the Accident Insurance Act 1998 was passed receiving the Royal assent on 18 December 1998. Of importance was the introduction of s 396 (set out in the case below), which effectively overruled the decision in *Daniels v Thompson*. Section 396 is repeated in s 319 of the Injury Prevention, Rehabilitation, and Compensation Act 2001. The case below considers how the courts approach this provision.]

W v W
[2000] 14 PRNZ 157 (CA)

[**FACTS**: The appellant's proceedings against the respondent psychologist considered exemplary damages for sexual abuse on three grounds including assault and battery, breach of the duty of care, and breach of fiduciary duty. The major issue was the application of s 396, as this was a strike-out application.]

Richardson P:

...

[2] The decision of this Court of 12 February 1998, reported as *Daniels v Thompson* ... considered a number of test cases as to the availability of relief by way of award of exemplary damages. The majority (Richardson P, Gault J, Henry J, Keith J; Thomas J dissenting) concluded that there should be an absolute bar on civil proceedings claiming exemplary damages where the acts relied on as the basis for an award had been the subject of a conviction in the criminal Courts; that a claim for exemplary damages should be struck out as an abuse of process if the defendant has been acquitted and essentially the same acts which constituted the criminal offending are relied on; and that similarly, to prevent abuse of process, it would be appropriate to stay a civil proceeding if it appeared a criminal prosecution was likely in respect of the subject-matter of the claim for exemplary damages.

[3] Two of the test cases were taken on appeal to the Privy Council, that of the present appellant, in which the respondent had been acquitted in the criminal proceedings, and another in which a respondent had been convicted. In their judgment of 19 January 1999 reported as *W v W* [1999] 2 NZLR 1; (1999) 16 CRNZ 336, their Lordships held that in these cases, on a matter of the policy of the law in a particular

country, the Board would not substitute its own views (if different) from those of the Court of Appeal. The appeal was dismissed.

[4] Meanwhile, the Accident Insurance Act 1998 was enacted and received the Royal assent on 18 December 1998 ...

[5] At a later stage in the parliamentary consideration of the Bill a supplementary order paper introduced what became s 396 of the Act. The section reads:

(1) Nothing in this Act, and no rule of law, prevents any person from bringing proceedings in any court in New Zealand for exemplary damages for conduct by the defendant that has resulted in—

   (a) Personal injury covered by this Act; or

   (b) Personal injury covered by the former Acts.

(2) The court may make an award of exemplary damages for conduct of the kind described in subsection (1) even though—

   (a) The defendant has been charged with, and acquitted or convicted of, an offence involving the conduct concerned in the claim for exemplary damages; or

   (b) The defendant has been charged with such an offence, and has been discharged without conviction under section 19 of the Criminal Justice Act 1985 or convicted and discharged under section 20 of that Act; or

   (c) The defendant has been charged with such an offence and, at the time at which the court is making its decision on the claim for exemplary damages, the charge has not been dealt with; or

   (d) The defendant has not, at the time at which the court is making its decision on the claim for exemplary damages, been charged with such an offence, or

   (e) The limitation period for bringing a charge for such an offence has expired.

(3) In determining whether to award exemplary damages and, if they are to be awarded, the amount of them, the court may have regard to—

   (a) Whether a penalty has been imposed on the defendant for an offence involving the conduct concerned in the claim for exemplary damages; and

   (b) If so, the nature of the penalty.

...

[7] The appeal has been heard in the Privy Council before the enactment of the Accident Insurance Act 1998. Their Lordships' attention was drawn to it and referring to s 396 in their judgment they said:

The appellants have submitted in writing that the section, when it comes into force, will retrospectively confer upon the appellants a cause of action. Their Lordships express no view on this point, which may be a matter of decision in the Courts of New Zealand after the section has come into force. They can dispose of this appeal only in accordance with the law as it now stands.

...

[10] In respect of each cause of action the statement of claim averred that the defendant's acts set out ... constituted a trespass to the person ... and breach of duty ... and that the actions were high-handed, contumacious, a deliberate abuse by the defendant of his position of trust, and a deliberate invasion of the plaintiff's rights, and accordingly deserved punishment by means of an award of exemplary damages ...

...

[17] Mr Turkington's [counsel for the respondent] first argument was that the section enables proceedings to be commenced after 1 July 1999 but not before. We are satisfied that 'bringing' is not to read in that narrow sense. As reference to the *Oxford English Dictionary* confirms, 'bring' may be used in a variety of senses including 'advance' or 'conduct' as well, of course, as 'institute' or 'commence'. The subsection speaks in the present and in our view 'bringing' means conducting any proceedings whether existing or not. Differing from the majority of this Court on policy conclusions, the Legislature decided that the public interest required that relief should be available by way of an award for exemplary damages in this class of case. The clear intent of s 396 is to declare that position. The language, 'no rule of law prevents' is not time limited, and the references to former Acts and to the disregarding of time limits for bringing charges shows that the Legislature contemplated proceedings in relation to well past misconduct. Clearly, Parliament had in mind all those affected and seeking relief. It would be artificial and inconsistent with the broad thrust of the section to read in a limitation of the kind suggested ...

[18] Finally, this immediately comprehensive legislative response on policy grounds is clearly intended to have retrospective effect applying to past as well as future conduct.

[19] The next question concerns the scope of the expression 'no rule of law' in the statutory context. The subject-matter is exemplary damages. In context it is necessarily directed to any rule of law in relation to exemplary damages. It is not concerned with procedural or substantive rules of general application. It could never have been intended that a plaintiff in this class of case should be free from the rules applying in all other litigation such as limitation of actions, abuse of process, and the myriad of provisions which govern the fair and orderly conduct of litigation. Thus any limitation arguments will remain for consideration if the proceeding otherwise remains able to continue and is continued.

[20] On this aspect of the case there are two further matters for consideration. The first is Mr Turkington's argument that, at least so far as the first cause of action is concerned, the respondent is entitled to rely on the determination of the issue of law in his favour by this Court and the Privy Council. That, he says, is *res judicata*, and the legislation should not be read as depriving him of that existing right.

[21] That would ordinarily be a formidable argument ... But here, unusually, the Legislature responded before the appeal had been determined by the Privy Council and without expressly acknowledging the respondent's position under this Court's order; it did so with an unusually long but necessary lead time ... and the Privy Council left open for decision in the Courts of New Zealand, and after the section had come into force, whether s 396 protected the present appellant's cause of action ... In this perhaps unique situation we are, we consider, driven back to the section and to the conclusion that the Legislature reversed the effect of this Court's ruling and intended that

those affected, including these parties, should come within its provisions. As a matter of construction the Legislature must be taken as intending this conclusion …

[24] The appeal is allowed, the orders in the High Court are quashed and the strike-out application is dismissed …

(c) Compensatory damages for pure nervous shock

[Up until the passage of the Accident Rehabilitation and Compensation Insurance Act 1992, claims for pure nervous shock were caught by the bar on common law proceedings. This was because of the wider definition of 'personal injury' in earlier versions of the accident compensation legislation. From 1992, mental injury not consequential upon physical injury or not associated with certain specified criminal offences was no longer covered. The question of whether common law claims for pure nervous shock could now be made in New Zealand was addressed in the following decision of the Court of Appeal.]

Queenstown Lakes District Council v Palmer
[1999] 1 NZLR 549 (CA)

[**FACTS**: Mr and Mrs Palmer, visitors from the United States, decided to undertake a rafting trip down the Shotover River. During the trip, the raft veered to the left and was swept down a rapid called the 'toaster'. The raft capsized and Mrs Palmer was subsequently drowned. Mr Palmer suffered serious mental injuries from this episode, and consequently commenced a negligence proceeding claiming $150 000 for general and special damages, and $50 000 for exemplary damages. The exemplary damages issue was not questioned as it was clearly capable of proceeding to trial. However, the critical issue in this case concerned whether the bar on common law actions then contained in s 14(1) of the Accident Rehabilitation and Compensation Act 1992 (now s 317, as set out above) precluded Mr Palmer bringing this proceeding and seeking to recover compensatory damages at common law in respect of mental injuries suffered in witnessing his wife's death in an accident. Panckhurst J, in his High Court judgment, held that s 14(1) did not extend to a secondary victim of an accident. The defendant appealed.]

Thomas J:

…

The correct interpretation
We have no hesitation in rejecting the appellant's contention. Counsels' arguments represent a stilted approach to the interpretation of s 14(1). The subsection must be interpreted as a whole, having regard not only to the language that is used but also to the context of the subsection, to the scheme and purpose of the Act, with reference, if that is necessary, to the history and policy of the legislation and to the consequences of the interpretation which is under consideration. When that is done Parliament's intention becomes clear. The reasons or considerations which lead to this view may be shortly stated.

(1) The plain meaning?
We do not agree that the appellants' construction represents the ordinary and natural meaning of the subsection, particularly when it is read as a whole and in context. In

the first place, s 14(1) must be read in conjunction with subsections (1) and (2) of s 8, which defines the cover for personal injury occurring in New Zealand. Subsection (1) provides that the Act is to apply in respect of personal injury 'in respect of which there is *cover under this Act*'. (Emphasis added). Subsection (2) provides that cover under the Act is to extend to personal injury which '... is caused by an accident *to the person concerned*'. (Emphasis added). The scope of the Act, in other words, is coterminous with cover provided under the Act. This defining section has an obvious import for s 14(1), which necessarily relates back to s 8, when referring to proceedings for damages arising out of personal injury 'covered by this Act'.

This construction is supported, in the second place, by the wording of the Long Title to the Act. The stated object of the Act is 'to establish an insurance-based scheme to rehabilitate and compensate ... those persons who suffer personal injury'. Section 14(1) is necessarily complementary and correlated to that object. The notion of an insurance-based scheme implies that the persons who are entitled to rehabilitation and compensation are those persons who suffer a personal injury covered by the scheme.

In the third place, once the subsection is placed in context, the structure of subsection (1) is more readily discernible. The substantive part of the subsection is that part which precludes proceedings for damages for personal injury covered by the Act which are suffered by any person being brought in any Court in New Zealand independently of the Act. The following words, 'whether by that person or any other person', can be seen to be added *ex abundanti cautela* to ensure that other persons, such as an injured person's legal representatives, are also unable to bring an action. The abundance of the draftsperson's caution is illustrated by reference to the final phase, 'whether under any rule of law or any enactment'. It is difficult to see what those words add to the foregoing part of the subsection stipulating that no proceeding can be brought independently of the Act.

We therefore agree with Panckhurst J. The critical words in s 14(1) are the words 'personal injury covered by this Act'. It is the impact of these words on the scope of the subsection which the appellants have neglected in pressing for the interpretation which they claim represents the plain meaning of the subsection.

(2) The correct analysis

The appellants' interpretation is based on an analysis which we consider flawed. They contend that the proceedings arise (indirectly) out of Mrs Palmer's death. This is not an appropriate analysis. Mr Palmer is not seeking damages for his wife's death. The relevant injuries for which he seeks damages are the mental injuries which he himself suffered as a result of the alleged breach of a duty of care owed to him by the defendants. Mrs Palmer's death was part of the sequence of events which provides the factual basis for Mr Palmer's claim that the defendants owed him a ... duty, that they acted in breach of that duty and that he suffered an injury resulting from that breach. To make the point in another way, if Mrs Palmer had survived and not suffered any personal injury, Mr Palmer's cause of action, had he still suffered nervous shock at the sight of his wife being thrown into the turbulent water, would remain intact.

In our view, therefore, the relevant personal injury for the purposes of s 14(1) must be that personal injury for which damages are sought. Such a view accords with common sense. It may also be observed that it accords with this Court's reasoning in

Donselaar v Donselaar [1982] 1 NZLR 87. In that case the Court accepted that claims for exemplary damages arise, not from the personal injury as such, but from the conduct of the wrong-doer.

(3) The legislative history and policy of the Act

We are also satisfied that the legislative history and the policy behind that legislation support this conclusion. There is no need to go into this aspect in great detail. Following the Report of the Royal Commission of Inquiry Compensation for Personal Injury in New Zealand (1967) (The 'Woodhouse Report'), a White Paper entitled *Personal Injury—A commentary on the Report of the Royal Commission of Inquiry into Compensation for Personal Injury in New Zealand* (1969), and the Report of the Select Committee on Compensation for Personal Injury in New Zealand (1970), the Accident Compensation Act 1972 was passed, with amendments, in 1973. The legislation was initially restricted to 'earners' who suffered personal injury and persons who suffered personal injury by a motor vehicle accident. It was substantially amended so as to provide a comprehensive scheme for the rehabilitation and compensation of those persons who suffer personal injuries for which they have cover under the Act and for the dependants of those persons where death resulted from the injury. It abolished actions for damages arising directly or indirectly out of a personal injury by accident as defined in the Act. The legislation was consolidated in 1982. It was amended by the current Act in 1992 to provide a more restrictive definition of what injuries constituted 'personal injury by accident' in place of the more open concept which allowed the courts to adopt a 'generous unniggardly interpretation' (see *Accident Compensation v Mitchell* [1992] 2 NZLR 436, per Richardson J at 438), a more limited approach to the responsibility of employees for work-related injuries, the abolition of lump sum compensation, and added emphasis to vocational rehabilitation.

Essentially, the accident compensation legislation in both its original and amended forms denied those persons covered under the Act access to the courts at common law in return for the perceived advantages of the statutory scheme. The legislation reflected this policy from the outset. The exchange has frequently been spoken of as a social contract or social compact.

...

There have not been any developments in the subsequent legislation, whether consolidation or otherwise, which indicate any change in the basic structure of the legislation. Indeed, the contrary is indicated. Compensation for mental injury was available under the 1972 Act and the 1982 consolidation. See *Accident Compensation Corporation v E* [1992] 2 NZLR 426, esp. Gault J at 434; *Accident Compensation Corporation v Cochrane* [1994] NZAR 6; and *Accident Compensation Corporation v F* [1991] 1 NZLR 234. The express restriction in s 4(1) of the present Act providing cover for mental injury only where that mental injury is the outcome of physical injuries to any person must, in the absence of an express provision abolishing such claims, be taken as showing an intention that the corresponding right at common law would be revived where the mental injury is not an outcome of physical injuries suffered by the plaintiff.

The legislation therefore falls short of supporting the appellants' contention that the purpose of the accident compensation legislation in New Zealand was not only to produce a statutory compensation scheme, but also to proscribe common law claims arising out of accidents. Rather, as Mr Oxnevad who appeared for Mr Palmer argued, the purpose of the provision barring common law claims is to prevent persons who suffer personal injury being compensated twice over, once under the statute and then at common law. The bar is not designed to prevent them recovering compensation at all.

Such a view is in accordance with the traditional principle, which enjoys fundamental constitutional status in our free and democratic society, that citizens are not to be denied access to the courts, save in rare and appropriate circumstances, and then only pursuant to explicit statutory language. The right to seek damages at common law for personal injury suffered because of the fault or negligence of another was removed by the legislation, but the *quid pro quo* was the right to compensation under the statutory scheme. (See Stephen Todd, 'Accident Compensation and the Common Law', in S. Todd (gen ed) *The Law of Torts in New Zealand* (2nd edn, 1997), at p 63.) The design of restricting the right of access to the courts by, as it were, a sidewind; that is, by simply withdrawing or curtailing the scope of the cover under the Act without at the same time addressing the fundamental principle of access to the Courts, should not be imputed to Parliament. Indeed, the policy document accompanying the 1991 Budget, while stipulating that there would be no return to the right to sue, explained that because the boundaries of coverage would be more clearly drawn under the new legislation, 'it may be possible that [in cases not covered by the scheme] there will be more court action than in the past'. (See Rt Hon Sir Geoffrey Palmer, 'New Zealand's Accident Compensation Scheme: Twenty Years On' (1994) 44 UTLJ 223, at 240.)

It follows from what has been said that the application of the Act and the corresponding scope for common law proceedings automatically adjust as and when the scope of the cover provided by the Act is extended or contracted. To the extent that the statutory cover is extended, the right to sue at common law is removed; to the extent that the cover is withdrawn or contracted, the right to sue at common law is revived. So it is in this case.

(4) *An injustice, and anomalies*
The principal injustice which would result if the interpretation contended for by the appellants were to be accepted would be that persons who suffer a mental injury witnessing the personal injury or death of another person would not be entitled to either compensation under the Act or damages at common law. They would have lost the right to sue for damages without obtaining the corresponding right to recover compensation under the statutory scheme.

Apart from this basic injustice, critical anomalies arise from the interpretation preferred by the appellants. First, as already indicated, it would be undoubtedly odd if a person in Mr Palmer's position were to be precluded from commencing proceedings for damages for the mental injury which he suffered because his wife dies but would not be barred from bringing such proceedings if she had not been injured. In the latter case, the person would be entitled to sue for damages for nervous shock, including the shock due to the mistaken belief that his wife had drowned. As Mr Oxnevad observed, the distinction is illogical.

Secondly, a person like Mr Palmer would be able to bring a common law claim for nervous shock if that injury was caused by the trauma of a personal experience. If the appellants' argument is correct, however, he would not have a claim if the shock resulted from witnessing the personal injury or death of a third person. In this case, Mr Palmer would be able to bring a claim for his mental injury if that injury was caused by the personal ordeal of being swept down the 'Toaster', but he would not have a claim if the shock resulted from seeing his wife swept down the 'Toaster'. Again, there is little if any logic in such a distinction. Moreover, in many if not most cases the mental injury may be attributable to both the act of witnessing the other person's personal injury or death and the trauma of his own personal experience. The causative effects of the two events are likely to be inseparable.

It cannot be lightly thought that Parliament intended this fundamental injustice or to create anomalies of this kind, both of which are an affront to common sense. A construction which would avoid these consequences must be preferred.

It is true that, while acknowledging that some unfairness or injustice could result from a legislative bar, other than when the injuries are consequential upon a physical injury or suffered where the person is the victim of a sexual offence, Mr Maling contended that, allowing a secondary victim to bring a claim where the primary victim cannot, may create an unjust result with the secondary victim recovering substantially more by way of common law damages than the primary victim could obtain by way of compensation under the Act. This is particularly so, he claimed, as lump sum compensation has been abandoned in New Zealand and when virtually no compensation is available in practice in the case of overseas victims. Mr Maling also argued that an anomaly would be created if a person in Mrs Palmer's position had not died but instead had suffered some permanent disability and as a result of the accident would have been entitled, because she was an overseas visitor, to receive minimal compensation.

We consider, however, that injustices or anomalies of this kind, if they are to be perceived as such, are inherent in the scheme of the Act under which the quantum of compensation is limited relative to the quantum of common law damages which would have been available but for the Act. The two were never intended to correspond. Uncertainty of recovery at common law was exchanged for a no-fault scheme which included provision for the rehabilitation of the injured person as well as ongoing earnings-related compensation. Disparity between the compensation which is payable under the Act and the amount of damages which might have been recoverable at common law will therefore always exist. So, too, will difficulties which may be perceived to be anomalies necessarily arise when a line is drawn between injuries arising from accidents and other injuries and conditions which are not attributable to accidents.

Conclusion

We have therefore concluded that s 14(1) does not preclude Mr Palmer bringing a common law proceeding to recover compensatory damages in respect of the mental injuries which he suffered after witnessing his wife's death in the rafting accident. The critical phrase in that subsection is 'personal injury covered by the Act'. Unless the personal injury for which damages are sought is covered by the Act, the right to bring proceedings at common law remains.

The particular phrases on which the appellants' counsel have focused in order to arrive at the plain meaning they contend for must give way to a construction which is based on a reading of the section as a whole and in context, and which has regard to the scheme and purpose of the Act and, in this case, the history and policy of the legis-lation and the consequences of the alternative view. On a proper approach, therefore, Mr Palmer's mental injury cannot be said to arise indirectly out of his wife's death for the purposes of the subsection. Moreover, in this Court, Somers J has already held that the words 'directly or indirectly' have been included *ex abundanti cautela* so as to include, for example, the recovery of funeral expenses. See *Donselaar v Donselaar, supra*, at 115. In the same way, the words 'any other person' have also been included out of an abundance of caution to remove any possible argument that a proceeding can be brought by persons, such as personal representatives, on behalf of the person who is injured by accident and covered by the Act.

For the above reasons the appeal is dismissed.

Chapter 4
Negligence

Introduction

Negligence is at the heart of the modern law of torts. Indeed, sometimes it looks as if it will take over the whole subject.

Like the other torts, negligence has its elements: there must be a duty of care, that duty must be breached, and the plaintiff must suffer loss as a result. And like the other torts, merely stating these elements begs the question of what they actually mean. For that we look to the case law.

Negligence is not like the intentional torts, defamation, and nuisance in the way it has developed. The other chapters in this book show the development of the law by the classic common law process, slowly developing as new cases bring new facts, which are at once similar and different from the facts of established cases. Take, for example, the notion of consent in battery or the concept of 'non-natural' use in *Rylands v Fletcher*. Many of the following negligence cases, when compared to cases in the other chapters, may appear confusing on the first read. Rather than looking for the ratios of particular cases, subsequent cases look for a general principle that lies behind imposing liability in the earlier cases.

It is this search for a general principle that has excited and bedevilled negligence law since Lord Atkin's speech in *Donoghue v Stevenson*. Sometimes formulae like Atkin's neighbour principle, or the current 'voluntary assumption of responsibility' are talked about as ways of explaining previous cases, and applied as tests in seemingly completely different cases. Often on first reading the following cases it will seem that the general principle that unifies negligence is just out of reach. It may sometimes be difficult to agree with the judgments that follow; the inability of judges to agree on the 'correct' approach may be somewhat frustrating. However, the intellectual challenge of trying to put the cases into one's own order is anything but frustrating: resolving seemingly conflicting opinions and deciding which of them accord with one's own way of thinking about the world.

The cases ask the question whether there is a general principle, and try to find what that general principle looks like, and how it varies over a range of facts. They ask the more practical questions: who should compensate whom, for what, and why?

There are three parts to this chapter. In Part 1, the cases are grouped around the established elements of negligence. The first section asks what a duty of care is and how it is determined. The second section asks what it means to say that someone has breached that duty, the third asks what it means to say that the defendant has caused the plaintiff loss, and the fourth looks at the defences of contributory negligence and limitations.

Part 2 deals with questions that have caused judges and lawyers immense difficulties over the last thirty years. First, does it make any sense to distinguish between physical loss and economic loss, and, if it does, how does that difference affect liability? Second, it deals with the much vexed question of whether local councils should be liable for negligent building inspections.

Part 3 asks what the limits of negligence are. It looks at how negligence interacts with public law, other torts like defamation, and the law of contract.

Part 1: Basic negligence

To succeed in a negligence action, a plaintiff must establish that the defendant owed the plaintiff a duty of care, that that duty was breached, and that the breach of the duty caused the plaintiff loss. If the plaintiff fails to establish one of these elements then there is simply no liability. Sometimes this is self-evident—we all know that we owe a duty of care to others when we are driving, and that for instance running a red light is negligent, but we also know that unless we actually cause harm to someone else while driving we cannot be sued in a civil court. Sometimes it is not so simple and the cases in this section naturally focus on the situations were there is some issue as to whether one of these three elements has been satisfied.

Duty of care

General approaches

The cases in this section ask the question 'what is a duty of care?'—what it means to say that someone is legally responsible to someone else for the harm than he or she has caused. It may be helpful to think of the cases in this section as decided on two levels. The first level is the judge's determination of the actual case. The second level is the judge's search for a general principle: in a sense the judge's history of what the law has been and the judge's sense of what the law should become. Each case raises complicated issues that will recur throughout the cases in this chapter. The *Dorset Yacht* case will be considered again in both the Damage and Limits of negligence (government liability) sections. The 'Anns test' will become a familiar friend, and the actual decision in the case will be talked about throughout Parts 2 and 3. Lord Atkin's attempt to find a moral principle behind liability is at the root of all the cases in this book.

McAlister (or Donoghue) (Pauper) v Stevenson
[1932] AC 562 (HL)

Lord Buckmaster (dissenting):

My Lords, the facts of this case are simple. On August 26, 1928, the appellant drank a bottle of ginger-beer, manufactured by the respondent, which a friend had bought from a retailer and given to her. The bottle contained the decomposed remains of a snail which were not, and could not be, detected until the greater part of the contents of the bottle had been consumed. As a result she alleged, and at this stage her allegations must be accepted as true, that she suffered from shock and severe gastro-enteritis. She accordingly instituted the proceedings against the manufacturer which have given rise to this appeal.

The foundation of her case is that the respondent, as the manufacturer of an article intended for consumption and contained in a receptacle which prevented inspection, owed a duty to her as consumer of the article to take care that there was no noxious element in the goods, that he neglected such duty and is consequently liable for any damage caused by such neglect ... .

Before examining the merits two comments are desirable: (1) That the appellant's case rests solely on the ground of a tort based not on fraud but on negligence; and (2) that throughout the appeal the case has been argued on the basis, undisputed by the Second Division and never questioned by counsel for the appellant or by any of your Lordships that the English and the Scots law on the subject are identical.

It is therefore upon the English law alone that I have considered the matter, and in my opinion it is on the English law alone that in the circumstances we ought to proceed. The law applicable is the common law, and, though its principles are capable of application to meet new conditions not contemplated when the law was laid down, these principles cannot be changed nor can additions be made to them because any particular meritorious case seems outside their ambit.

Now the common law must be sought in law books of writers of authority and in judgments of the judges entrusted with its administration. The law books give no assistance because the work of living authors, however deservedly eminent, cannot be used as authority, though the opinions they express may demand attention; and the ancient books do not assist. I turn, therefore, to the decided cases to see if they can be construed so as to support the appellant's case. One of the earliest is the case of *Langridge v Levy* (2 M & W 519; 4 M & W 376). It is a case often quoted and variously explained. There a man sold a gun which he knew was dangerous for the use of the purchaser's son. The gun exploded in the son's hands and he was held to have a right of action in tort against the gunmaker. How far it is from the present case can be seen from the judgment of Park B, who, in delivering the judgment of the Court, used these words: 'We should pause before we made a precedent by our decision which would be an authority for an action against the vendors, even of such instruments and articles as are dangerous in themselves, at the suit of any person whomsoever into whose hands they might happen to pass, and who should be injured thereby'; and in *Longmeid v Holliday* (6 Ex 761) the same eminent judge points out that the earlier case was based on a fraudulent misstatement, and he expressly repudiates the view that it has any wider application. The case of *Langridge v Levy*, therefore, can be dismissed from consideration with the comment that it is rather surprising it has so often been cited for a proposition it cannot support ... .

The general principle of these cases is stated by Lord Sumner in the case of *Blacker v Lake & Elliot Ltd* in these terms: 'The breach of the defendant's contract with A to use care and skill in and about the manufacture or repair of an article does not of itself give any cause of action to B when he is injured by reason of the article proving to be defective.'

From this general rule there are two well-known exceptions: (1) in the case of an article dangerous in itself; and (2) where the article not in itself dangerous is in fact dangerous, by reason of some defect or for any other reason, and this is known to the manufacturer ... .

In my view, therefore, the authorities are against the appellant's contention, and, apart from authority, it is difficult to see how any common law proposition can be formulated to support her claim.

The principle contended for must be this: that the manufacturer, or indeed the repairer, of any article, apart entirely from contract, owes a duty to any person by whom the article is lawfully used to see that it has been carefully constructed. All rights in contract must be excluded from consideration of this principle; such contractual rights as may exist in successive steps from the original manufacturer down to the ultimate purchaser are ex hypothesis immaterial. Nor can the doctrine be confined to cases where inspection is difficult or impossible to introduce. This conception is simply to misapply the tort doctrine applicable to sale and purchase.

The principle of tort lies completely outside the region where such considerations apply, and the duty, if it exists, must extend to every person who, in lawful circumstances, uses the article made. There can be no special duty attaching to the manufacturer of food apart from that implied by contract or imposed by statute. If such a duty exists, it seems to me it must cover the construction of every article, and I cannot see any reason why it should not apply to the construction of a house. If one step, why not fifty? Yet if a house be, as it sometimes is, negligently built, and in consequence of that negligence the ceiling falls and injures the occupier or any one else, no action against the builder exists according to the English law, although I believe such a right did exist according to the laws of Babylon. Were such a principle known and recognized, it seems to me impossible, having regard to the numerous cases that must have arisen to persons injured by its disregard, that, with the exception of *George v Skivington* (LR 5 Ex 1) no case directly involving the principle has ever succeeded in the Courts, and, were it well known and accepted, much of the discussion of the earlier cases would have been waste of time, and the distinction as to articles dangerous in themselves or known to be dangerous to the vendor would be meaningless.

In *Mullen v Barr & Co* (1920 SC 461, 470) a case indistinguishable from the present excepting upon the ground that a mouse is not a snail, and necessarily adopted by the Second Division in their judgment, Lord Anderson says this: 'In a case like the present, where the goods of the defenders are widely distributed throughout Scotland, it would seem little short of outrageous to make them responsible to members of the public for the condition of the contents of every bottle which issues from their works. It is obvious that, if such responsibility attached to the defenders, they might be called on to meet claims of damages which they could not possibly investigate or answer.'

In agreeing, as I do, with the judgment of Lord Anderson, I desire to add that I find it hard to dissent from the emphatic nature of the language with which his judgment is clothed. I am of opinion that this appeal should be dismissed, and I beg to move your Lordships accordingly.

[**Lord Tomlin** also dissented.]

...

Lord Atkin:

My Lords, the sole question for determination in this case is legal: Do the averments made by the pursuer in her pleading, if true, disclose a cause of action? ... The question is whether the manufacturer of an article of drink sold by him to a distributor, in circumstances which prevent the distributor or the ultimate purchaser or consumer from discovering by inspection any defect, is under any legal duty to the ultimate purchaser or consumer to take reasonable care that the article is free from defect likely to cause injury to health. I do not think a more important problem has occupied your Lordships in your judicial capacity ... .

It is remarkable how difficult it is to find in the English authorities statements of general application defining the relations between parties that give rise to the duty. The Courts are concerned with the particular relations which come before them in actual litigation, and it is sufficient to say whether the duty exists in those circumstances. The result is that the Courts have been engaged upon an elaborate classification of duties as they exist in respect of property, whether real or personal, with further divisions as to ownership, occupation or control, and distinctions based on the particular relations of the one side or the other, whether manufacturer, salesman or landlord, customer, tenant, stranger, and so on. In this way it can be ascertained at any time whether the law recognizes a duty, but only where the case can be referred to some particular species which has been examined and classified. And yet the duty which is common to all the cases where liability is established must logically be based upon some element common to the cases where it is found to exist. To seek a complete logical definition of the general principle is probably to go beyond the function of the judge, for the more general the definition the more likely it is to omit essentials or to introduce non-essentials. The attempt was made by Brett MR in *Heaven v Pender* [11 QBD 503, 509], in a definition to which I will later refer. As framed, it was demonstrably too wide, though it appears to me, if properly limited, to be capable of affording a valuable practical guide.

At present I content myself with pointing out that in English law there must be, and is, some general conception of relations giving rise to a duty of care, of which the particular cases found in the books are but instances. The liability for negligence, whether you style it such or treat it as in other systems as a species of 'culpa', is no doubt based upon a general public sentiment of moral wrongdoing for which the offender must pay. But acts or omissions which any moral code would censure cannot in a practical world be treated so as to give a right to every person injured by them to demand relief. In this way rules of law arise which limit the range of complainants and the extent of their remedy. The rule that you are to love your neighbour becomes in law, you must not injure your neighbour; and the lawyer's question, Who is my neighbour? receives a restricted reply. You must take reasonable care to avoid acts or omissions which you can reasonably foresee would be likely to injure your neighbour. Who, then, in law is my neighbour? The answer seems to be—persons who are so closely and directly affected by my act that I ought reasonably to have them in contemplation as being so affected when I am directing my mind to the acts or omissions which are called in question. This appears to me to be the doctrine of *Heaven v Pender* [*supra*], as laid down by Lord Esher (then Brett MR) when it is limited by the notion of proximity introduced by Lord Esher himself and A.L. Smith LJ in *Le Lievre v Gould* [1893] 1 QB 491, 497, 504. Lord Esher says: 'That case established that, under certain circumstances, one man may owe a duty to another, even though there is no contract between them. If one man is near to another, or is near to the property of another, a duty lies upon him not to do that which may cause a personal injury to that other, or may injure his property.' So A.L. Smith LJ: 'The decision of *Heaven v Pender* was founded upon the principle, that a duty to take due care did arise when the person or property of one was in such proximity to the person or property of another that, if due care was not taken, damage might be done by the one to the other.' I think that this sufficiently states the truth if proximity be not confined to mere physical proximity, but be used, as I think it was intended, to extend to such close and direct relations that the act complained of directly affects a person whom the person alleged to be bound to take care would know would be directly affected by his careless act. That this is the sense in which nearness of 'proximity' was intended by Lord Esher is obvious from his own illustration in *Heaven v Pender* of the application of his doctrine to the sale of goods. 'This' (ie, the rule he has just formulated) 'includes the case of goods, etc, supplied to be used immediately by a particular person or persons, or one of a class of persons, where it would be obvious to the person supplying, if he thought, that the goods would in all probability be used at once by such persons before a reasonable opportunity for discovering any defect which might exist, and where the thing supplied would be of such a nature that a neglect of ordinary care or skill as to its condition or the manner of supplying it would probably cause danger to the person or property of the person for whose use it was supplied, and who was about to use it. It would exclude a case in which the goods are supplied under circumstances in which it would be a chance by whom they would be used or whether they would be used or not, or whether they would be used before there would probably be means of observing any defect, or where the goods would be of such a nature that a want of care or skill as to their condition or the manner of supplying them would not probably produce danger of injury to person or property.' I draw particular attention to the fact that Lord Esher emphasizes the necessity of goods having to be 'used immediately' and 'used at once before a reasonable opportunity of inspection.' This is obviously to exclude the possibility of goods having their condition altered by lapse of time, and to call attention to the proximate relationship, which may be too remote where inspection even of the person using, certainly of an intermediate person, may reasonably be interposed.

With this necessary qualification of proximate relationship as explained in *Le Lievre v Gould*, I think the judgment of Lord Esher expresses the law of England; without the qualification, I think the majority of the Court in *Heaven v Pender* were justified in thinking the principle was expressed in too general terms. There will no doubt arise cases where it will be difficult to determine whether the contemplated relationship is so close that the duty arises. But in the class of case now before the Court I cannot conceive any difficulty to arise. A manufacturer puts up an article of food in a container which he knows will be opened by the actual consumer. There can be no inspection by any purchaser and no reasonable preliminary inspection by the consumer. Negligently, in the course of preparation, he allows the contents to be mixed with poison. It is said that the law of England and Scotland is that the poisoned consumer has no remedy against the negligent manufacturer. If this were the result of the authorities, I should consider the result a grave defect in the law, and so contrary to principle that I should hesitate long before following any decision to that effect which had not the authority of this House ... . There are other instances than of articles of food and drink where goods are sold intended to be used immediately by the consumer, such as many forms of goods sold for cleaning purposes, where the same liability must exist. The doctrine supported by the decision below would not only deny a remedy to the consumer who was injured by consuming bottled beer or chocolates poisoned by the negligence of the manufacturer, but also to the user of what should be a harmless proprietary medicine, an ointment, a soap, a cleaning fluid or cleaning powder. I confine myself to articles of common household use, where every one, including the manufacturer, knows that the articles will be used by other persons than the actual ultimate purchaser—namely, by members of his family and his servants, and in some cases his guests. I do not think so ill of our jurisprudence as to suppose that its principles are so remote from the ordinary needs of civilized society and the ordinary claims it makes upon its members as to deny a legal remedy where there is so obviously a social wrong ... .

My Lords, if your Lordships accept the view that this pleading discloses a relevant cause of action you will be affirming the proposition that by Scots and English law alike a manufacturer of products, which he sells in such a form as to show that he intends them to reach the ultimate consumer in the form in which they left him with no reasonable possibility of intermediate examination, and with the knowledge that the absence of reasonable care in the preparation or putting up of the products will result in an injury to the consumer's life or property, owes a duty of care to the consumer to take reasonable care.

It is a proposition which I venture to say no one in Scotland or England who was not a lawyer would for one moment doubt. It will be an advantage to make it clear that the law in this matter, as in most others, is in accordance with sound common sense. I think this appeal should be allowed.

> [**Result**: **Lords Thankerton** and **Macmillan** gave separate
> speeches in agreement with **Lord Atkin**.]

Palsgraf v Long Island Railway Co
(1928) 162 NE 99 (9th Circuit)
Cardozo CJ:
Plaintiff was standing on a platform of defendant's railroad after buying a ticket to go to Rockaway Beach. A train stopped at the station, bound for another place. Two

men ran forward to catch it. One of the men reached the platform of the car without mishap, though the train was already moving. The other man, carrying a package, jumped aboard the car, but seemed unsteady as if about to fall. A guard on the car, who had held the door open, reached forward to help him in, and another guard on the platform pushed him from behind. In this act, the package was dislodged, and fell upon the rails. It was a package of small size, about fifteen inches long, and was covered by a newspaper. In fact it contained fireworks, but there was nothing in its appearance to give notice of its contents. The fireworks when they fell exploded. The shock of the explosion threw down some scales at the other end of the platform many feet away. The scales struck the plaintiff, causing injuries for which she sues.

The conduct of the defendant's guard, if a wrong in its relation to the holder of the package, was not a wrong in its relation to the plaintiff, standing far away. Relatively to her it was not negligence at all. Nothing in the situation gave notice that the falling package had in it the potency of peril to persons thus removed. Negligence is not actionable unless it involves the invasion of a legally protected interest, the violation of a right. 'Proof of negligence in the air, so to speak, will not do.' ... Salmond, *Torts* (6th edn) ... 'Negligence is the absence of care, according to the circumstances.' ... The plaintiff as she stood upon the platform of the station, might claim to be protected against intentional invasion of her bodily security. Such invasion is not charged. She might claim to be protected against unintentional invasion by conduct involving in the thought of reasonable men an unreasonable hazard that such invasion would ensue. These, from the point of view of the law, were the bounds of her immunity, with perhaps some rare exceptions, survivals for the most part of ancient forms of liability, where conduct is held to be at the peril of the actor ... If no hazard was apparent to the eye of ordinary vigilance, an act innocent and harmless, at least to outward seeming, with reference to her, did not take to itself the quality of a tort because it happened to be a wrong, though apparently not one involving the risk of bodily insecurity, with reference to someone else ... . The plaintiff sues in her own right for a wrong personal to her, and not as the vicarious beneficiary of a breach of duty to another.

A different conclusion will involve us, and swiftly too, in a maze of contradictions. A guard stumbles over a package which has been left upon a platform. It seems to be a bundle of newspapers. It turns out to be a can of dynamite. To the eye of ordinary vigilance, the bundle is abandoned waste, which may be kicked or trod on with impunity. Is a passenger at the other end of the platform protected by the law against the unsuspected hazard concealed beneath the waste? If not, is the result to be any different, so far as the distant passenger is concerned, when the guard stumbles over a valise which a truckman or a porter has left upon the walk? The passenger far away, if the victim of a wrong at all, has a cause of action, not derivative, but original and primary. His claim to be protected against invasion of his bodily security is neither greater nor less because the act resulting in the invasion is a wrong to another far removed. In this case, the rights that are said to have been violated, the interests said to have been invaded, are not even of the same order. The man was not injured in his person nor even put in danger. The purpose of the act, as well as its effect, was to make his person safe. If there was a wrong to him at all, which may very well be doubted it was a wrong to a property interest only, the safety of his package. Out of this wrong to property, which threatened injury to nothing else, there has passed, we are told, to the plaintiff by derivation or succession a right of action for the invasion of an interest of another order, the right to bodily security. The diversity of interests emphasizes the futility of the effort to build the plaintiff's right upon the basis of a wrong to some one else. The gain is one of emphasis, for a like result would follow if the interests were the same. Even then, the orbit of the danger as disclosed to the eye of reasonable vigilance would be the orbit of the duty. One who jostles one's neighbor in a crowd does not invade the rights of others standing at the outer fringe when the unintended contact casts a bomb upon the ground. The wrong-doer as to them is the man who carries the bomb, not the one who explodes it without suspicion of the danger. Life will have to be made over, and human nature transformed, before prevision so extravagant can be accepted as the norm of contact, the customary standard to which behavior must conform.

The argument for the plaintiff is built upon the shifting meanings of such words as 'wrong' and 'wrongful,' and shares their instability. What the plaintiff must show is 'a wrong' to herself; ie, a violation of her own right, and not merely a wrong to someone else, nor conduct 'wrongful' because unsocial, but not 'a wrong' to anyone. We are told that one who drives at reckless speed through a crowded city street is guilty of a negligent act and therefore of a wrongful one, irrespective of the consequences. Negligent the act is, and wrongful in the sense that it is unsocial, but wrongful and unsocial in relation to other travelers, only because the eye of vigilance perceives the risk of damage. If the same act were to be committed on a speedway or a race course, it would lose its wrongful quality. The risk reasonably to be perceived defines the duty to be obeyed, and risk imports relation; it is risk to another or to others within the range of apprehension ... . This does not mean, of course, that one who launches a destructive force is always relieved of liability, if the force, though known to be destructive, pursues an unexpected path ... . Some acts, such as shooting, are so imminently dangerous to anyone who may come within reach of the missile, however unexpectedly, as to impose a duty of prevision not far from that of an insurer ... .

Negligence, like risk, is thus a term of relation. Negligence in the abstract, apart from things related, is surely not a tort, if indeed it is understandable at all ... . Negligence is not a tort unless it results in the commission of a wrong, and the commission of a wrong imports the violation of a right, in this case, we are told, the right to be protected against interference with one's bodily security. But bodily security is protected, not against all forms of interference or aggression, but only against some. One who seeks redress at law does not make out a cause of action by showing without more that there has been damage to his person. If the harm was not wilful, he must show that the act as to him had possibilities of danger so many and apparent as to entitle him to be protected against the doing of it though the harm was unintended. Affront to personality is still the keynote of the wrong. Confirmation of this view will be found in the history and development of the action on the case. Negligence as a basis of civil liability was unknown to mediaeval law ... . For damage to the person, the sole remedy was trespass, and trespass did not lie in the absence of aggression, and that direct and personal ... . Liability for other damage, as where a servant without orders from the master does or omits something to the damage of another, is a plant of later growth ... . When it emerged out of the legal soil, it was thought of as a variant of trespass, an offshoot of the parent stock. This appears in the form of action, which was known as trespass on the case ... . The victim does not sue derivatively, or by right of subrogation, to vindicate an interest invaded in the person of another. Thus to view his cause of action is to ignore the fundamental difference between tort and crime. Holland, *Jurisprudence* (12th edn) ... He sues for breach of a duty owing to himself.

The law of causation, remote or approximate, is thus foreign to the case before us. The question of liability is always anterior to the question of the measure of the consequences that go with liability. If there is no tort to be redressed, there is no occasion to consider what damage might be recovered if there were a finding of a tort. We may assume, without deciding, that negligence, not at large or in the abstract, but in relation to the plaintiff, would entail liability for any and all consequences, however novel or extraordinary ... . There is room for argument that a distinction is to be drawn according to the diversity of interests invaded by the act, as where conduct negligent in that it threatens an insignificant invasion of an interest in property results in an unforeseeable invasion of an interest of another order, as, eg, one of bodily security. Perhaps other distinctions may be necessary. We do not go into the question now. The consequences to be followed must first be rooted in a wrong.

Home Office v Dorset Yacht Co Ltd
[1970] AC 1004 (HL)
Lord Reid:
My Lords, on September 21, 1962, a party of Borstal trainees were working on Brownsea Island in Poole Harbour under the supervision and control of three Borstal officers. During that night seven of them escaped and went aboard a yacht which they found nearby. They set this yacht in motion and collided with the respondents' yacht which was moored in the vicinity. Then they boarded the respondents' yacht. Much damage was done to this yacht by the collision and some by the subsequent conduct of these trainees. The respondents sue the appellants, the Home Office, for the amount of this damage.

The case comes before your Lordships on a preliminary issue whether the Home Office or these Borstal officers owed any duty of care to the respondents capable of giving rise to a liability in damages ... . It is admitted that the Home Office would be vicariously liable if an action would lie against any of these Borstal officers.

The facts which I think we must assume are that this party of trainees were in the lawful custody of the governor of the Portland Borstal institution and were sent by him to Brownsea Island on a training exercise in the custody and under the control of the three officers with instructions to keep them in custody and under control. But in breach of their instructions these officers simply went to bed leaving the trainees to their own devices. If they had obeyed their instructions they could and would have prevented these trainees from escaping ... . All the escaping trainees had criminal records and five of them had a record of previous escapes from Borstal institutions. The three officers knew or ought to have known that these trainees would probably try to escape during the night, would take some vessel to make good their escape and would probably cause damage to it or some other vessel. There were numerous vessels moored in the harbour and the trainees could readily board one of them. So it was a likely consequence of their neglect of duty that the respondents' yacht would suffer damage.

The case for the Home Office is that under no circumstances can Borstal officers owe any duty to any member of the public to take care to prevent trainees under their control or supervision from injuring him or his property ... . That case is based on three main arguments. First it is said that there is virtually no authority for imposing a duty of this kind. Secondly it is said that no person can be liable for a wrong done by another who is of full age and capacity and who is not the servant or acting on behalf of that person. And thirdly it is said that public policy (or the policy of the relevant legislation) requires that these officers should be immune from any such liability.

The first would at one time have been a strong argument. About the beginning of this century most eminent lawyers thought that there were a number of separate torts involving negligence, each with its own rules, and they were most unwilling to add more ... . In later years there has been a steady trend towards regarding the law of negligence as depending on principle so that, when a new point emerges, one should ask not whether it is covered by authority but whether recognised principles apply to it. *Donoghue v Stevenson* ... may be regarded as a milestone, and the well-known passage in Lord Atkin's speech should I think be regarded as a statement of principle. It is not to be treated as if it were a statutory definition. It will require qualification in new circumstances. But I think that the time has come when we can and should say that it ought to apply unless there is some justification or valid explanation for its exclusion ... .

Even so, it is said that the respondents must fail because there is a general principle that no person can be responsible for the acts of another who is not his servant or acting on his behalf. But here the ground of liability is not responsibility for the acts of the escaping trainees; it is liability for damage caused by the carelessness of these officers in the knowledge that their carelessness would probably result in the trainees causing damage of this kind. So the question is really one of remoteness of damage ... .

These cases show that where human action forms one of the links between the original wrongdoing of the defendant and the loss suffered by the plaintiff, that action must at least have been something very likely to happen if it is not to be regarded as *novus actus interveniens* breaking the chain of causation. I do not think that a mere foreseeable possibility is or should be sufficient, for then the intervening human action can more properly be regarded as a new cause than as a consequence of the original wrongdoing. But if the intervening action was likely to happen I do not think that it can matter whether that action was innocent or tortious or criminal. Unfortunately, tortious or criminal action by a third party is often the 'very kind of thing' which is likely to happen as a result of the wrongful or careless act of the defendant. And in the present case, on the facts which we must assume at this stage, I think that the taking of a boat by the escaping trainees and their unskilful navigation leading to damage to another vessel were the very kind of thing that these Borstal officers ought to have seen to be likely.

... I would therefore hold that damage to have been caused by the Borstal officers' negligence.

If the carelessness of the Borstal officers was the cause of the plaintiffs' loss, what justification is there for holding that they had no duty to take care? The first argument was that their right and power to control the trainees was purely statutory and that any duty to exercise that right and power was only a statutory duty owed to the Crown. I would agree, but ... Parliament cannot reasonably be supposed to have licensed those who do such things to act negligently in disregard of the interests of others so as to cause them needless damage.

Where Parliament confers a discretion the position is not the same. Then there may, and almost certainly will, be errors of judgment in exercising such a discretion and Parliament cannot have intended that members of the public should be entitled to sue in respect of such errors. But there must come a stage when the discretion is exercised so carelessly or unreasonably that there has been no real exercise of the discretion which Parliament has conferred. The person purporting to exercise his discretion has acted in abuse or excess of his power. Parliament cannot be supposed to have granted immunity to persons who do that. The present case does not raise this issue because no discretion was given to these Borstal officers. They were given orders which they negligently failed to carry out ... .

Governors of these institutions and other responsible authorities have a difficult and delicate task ... . This system is based on the belief that it assists the rehabilitation of trainees to give them as much freedom and responsibility as possible. So the responsible authorities must weigh on the one hand the public interest of protecting neighbours and their property from the depredations of escaping trainees and on the other hand the public interest of promoting rehabilitation. Obviously there is much room here for differences of opinion and errors of judgment. In my view there can be no liability if the discretion is exercised with due care. There could only be liability if the person entrusted with discretion either unreasonably failed to carry out his duty to consider the matter or reached a conclusion so unreasonable as again to show failure to do his duty.

It was suggested that these trainees might have been deliberately released at the time when they escaped and that then there could have been no liability. I do not agree. Presumably when trainees are released either temporarily or permanently some care is taken to see that there is no need for them to resort to crime to get food or transport. I could not imagine any more unreasonable exercise of discretion than to release trainees on an island in the middle of the night without making any provision for their future welfare.

... It was suggested that a decision against the Home Office would have very far-reaching effects; it was indeed, suggested in the Court of Appeal that it would make the Home Office liable for the loss occasioned by a burglary committed by a trainee on parole or a prisoner permitted to go out to attend a funeral. But there are two reasons why in the vast majority of cases that would not be so. In the first place it would have to be shown that the decision to allow any such release was so unreasonable that it could not be regarded as a real exercise of discretion by the responsible officer who authorised the release. And secondly it would have to be shown that the commission of the offence was the natural and probable, as distinct from merely a foreseeable, result of the release—that there was no *novus actus interveniens* ... . I think that the fears of the appellants are unfounded: I cannot believe that negligence or dereliction of duty is widespread among prison or Borstal officers.

Finally I must deal with public policy. It is argued that it would be contrary to public policy to hold the Home Office or its officers liable to a member of the public for this carelessness—or, indeed, any failure of duty on their part. The basic question is: who shall bear the loss caused by that carelessness—the innocent respondents or the Home Office, who are vicariously liable for the conduct of their careless officers? I do not think that the argument for the Home Office can be put better than it was put by the Court of Appeals of New York in *Williams v State of New York* (1955) 127 NE 2d 545, 550:

> ... public policy also requires that the State be not held liable. To hold otherwise would impose a heavy responsibility upon the State, or dissuade the wardens and principal keepers of our prison system from continued experimentation with 'minimum security' work details—which provide a means for encouraging better-risk prisoners to exercise their senses of responsibility and honor and so prepare themselves for their eventual return to society. Since 1917, the legislature has expressly provided for out-of-prison work. Correction Law, s. 182, and its intention should be respected without fostering the reluctance of prison officials to assign eligible men to minimum security work, lest they thereby give rise to costly claims against the State, or indeed inducing the State itself to terminate this 'salutary procedure' looking toward rehabilitation.

It may be that public servants of the State of New York are so apprehensive, easily dissuaded from doing their duty and intent on preserving public funds from costly claims that they could be influenced in this way. But my experience leads me to believe that Her Majesty's servants are made of sterner stuff. So I have no hesitation in rejecting this argument. I can see no good ground in public policy for giving this immunity to a government department. I would dismiss this appeal.

Problems

1   The oil light came on in Algernon's new BMW car. He did not stop at a garage to have the oil checked, thinking that the light was a minor electrical fault. The engine was eventually badly damaged. The oil plug had been negligently manufactured and allowed oil to escape. Is the manufacturer liable for the damage to the engine? Algernon had been on his way to visit his friend, Perpetua. When he got there, he parked the BMW on the newly laid cobblestone driveway. Can Perpetua sue the manufacturer for the ugly oil slick that appeared on her driveway?

2   Brahms was a patron sitting in the Paisley pub. When he heard the sound of Strauss's accident only 50 metres away from the pub, his hand jerked and he spilt a drink over his new $1000 suit, which was ruined. Can Brahms sue anyone?

Anns v Merton London Borough Council
[1978] AC 728 (HL)
Lord Wilberforce:
... Through the trilogy of cases in this House—*Donoghue v Stevenson* [1932] AC 562, *Hedley Byrne & Co Ltd v Heller & Partners Ltd* [1964] AC 465, and *Dorset Yacht Co Ltd*

v Home Office [1970] AC 1004—the position has now been reached that in order to establish that a duty of care arises in a particular situation, it is not necessary to bring the facts of that situation within those of previous situations in which a duty of care has been held to exist. Rather the question has to be approached in two stages. First one has to ask whether, as between the alleged wrongdoer and the person who has suffered damage there is a sufficient relationship of proximity or neighbourhood such that, in the reasonable contemplation of the former, carelessness on his part may be likely to cause damage to the latter—in which case a *prima facie* duty of care arises. Secondly, if the first question is answered affirmatively, it is necessary to consider whether there are any considerations which ought to negative, or to reduce or limit the scope of the duty or the class of person to whom it is owed or the damages to which a breach of it may give rise.

Hill v Chief Constable of West Yorkshire
[1989] AC 53; [1988] 2 All ER 238 (HL)
Lord Keith:
My Lords, in 1975 a man named Peter Sutcliffe embarked on a terrifying career of violent crime, centred in the metropolitan police area of West Yorkshire. All his victims were young or fairly young women. Between July 1975 and November 1980 he committed 13 murders and 8 attempted murders on such women, the modus operandi in each case being similar. Sutcliffe's last victim was a 20-year-old student called Jacqueline Hill, whom he murdered in Leeds on 17 November 1980. By chance, Sutcliffe was arrested in suspicious circumstances in Sheffield on 2 January 1981 and he confessed to the series of murders and attempted murders following interrogation. On 22 May 1981, in the Central Criminal Court, Sutcliffe was convicted of, *inter alia*, the murder of Miss Hill … .

The question of law which is opened up by the case is whether the individual members of a police force, in the course of carrying out their functions of controlling and keeping down the incidence of crime, owe a duty of care to individual members of the public who may suffer injury to person or property through the activities of criminals, such as to result in liability in damages, on the ground of negligence, to anyone who suffers such injury by reason of breach of that duty.

By common law police officers owe to the general public a duty to enforce the criminal law … . That duty may be enforced by mandamus, at the instance of one having title to sue. But as that case shows, a chief officer of police has a wide discretion as to the manner in which the duty is discharged. It is for him to decide how available resources should be deployed, whether particular lines of inquiry should or should not be followed and even whether or not certain crimes should be prosecuted. It is only if his decision on such matters is such as no reasonable chief officer of police would arrive at that someone with an interest to do so may be in a position to have recourse to judicial review. So the common law, while laying on chief officers of police an obligation to enforce the law, makes no specific requirements as to the manner in which the obligation is to be discharged. That is not a situation where there can readily be inferred an intention of the common law to create a duty towards individual members of the public … .

It has been said almost too frequently to require repetition that foreseeability of likely harm is not in itself a sufficient test of liability in negligence. Some further ingredient is invariably needed to establish the requisite proximity of relationship between the plaintiff and defendant, and all the circumstances of the case must be carefully considered and analysed in order to ascertain whether such an ingredient is present. The nature of the ingredient will be found to vary in a number of different categories of decided cases. In the *Anns* case there was held to be sufficient proximity of relationship between the borough and future owners and occupiers of a particular building the foundations of which it was decided to inspect, and there was also a close relationship between the borough and the builder who had constructed the foundations.

The *Dorset Yacht* case was concerned with the special characteristics or ingredients beyond reasonable foreseeability of likely harm which may result in civil liability for failure to control another man to prevent his doing harm to a third. The present case falls broadly into the same category. It is plain that vital characteristics which were present in the *Dorset Yacht* case and which led to the imposition of liability are here lacking. Sutcliffe was never in the custody of the police force. Miss Hill was one of a vast number of the female general public who might be at risk from his activities but was at no special distinctive risk in relation to them, unlike the owners of the yacht moored off Brownsea Island in relation to the foreseeable conduct of the borstal boys. It appears from the passage quoted from the speech of Lord Diplock in the *Dorset Yacht* case that in his view no liability would rest on a prison authority, which carelessly allowed the escape of an habitual criminal, for damage which he subsequently caused, not in the course of attempting to make good his getaway to persons at special risk, but in further pursuance of his general criminal career to the person or property of members of the general public. The same rule must apply as regards failure to recapture the criminal before he had time to resume his career. In the case of an escaped criminal his identity and description are known. In the instant case the identity of the wanted criminal was at the material time unknown and it is not averred that any full or clear description of him was ever available. The alleged negligence of the police consists in a failure to discover his identity. But, if there is no general duty of care owed to individual members of the public by the responsible authorities to prevent the escape of a known criminal or to recapture him, there cannot reasonably be imposed on any police force a duty of care similarly owed to identify and apprehend an unknown one. Miss Hill cannot for this purpose be regarded as a person at special risk simply because she was young and female. Where the class of potential victims of a particular habitual criminal is a large one the precise size of it cannot in principle affect the issue. All householders are potential victims of an habitual burglar, and all females those of an habitual rapist. The conclusion must be that although there existed reasonable foreseeability of likely harm to such as Miss Hill if Sutcliffe were not identified and apprehended, there is absent from the case any such ingredient or characteristic as led to the liability of the Home Office in the *Dorset Yacht* case. Nor is there present any additional characteristic such as might make up the deficiency. The circumstances of the case are therefore not capable of establishing a duty of care owed towards Miss Hill by the West Yorkshire police.

That is sufficient for the disposal of the appeal. But in my opinion there is another reason why an action for damages in negligence should not lie against the police in circumstances such as those of the present case, and that is public policy ... I expressed the view that the category of cases where the second stage of Lord Wilberforce's two-stage test in *Anns* might fail to be applied was a limited one, one example of that category being *Rondel v Worsley* [1969] 1 AC 191. Application of that second stage is, however, capable of constituting a separate and independent ground for holding that the existence of liability in negligence should not be entertained. Potential existence of such liability may in many instances be in the general public interest, as tending towards the observance of a higher standard of care in the carrying on of various different types of activity. I do not, however, consider that this can be said of police activities. The general sense of public duty which motivates police forces is unlikely to be appreciably reinforced by the imposition of such liability so far as concerns their function in the investigation and suppression of crime. From time to time they make mistakes in the exercise of that function, but it is not to be doubted that they apply their best endeavours to the performance of it. In some instances the imposition of liability may lead to the exercise of a function being carried on in a detrimentally defensive frame of mind. The possibility of this happening in relation to the investigative operations of the police cannot be excluded. Further, it would be reasonable to expect that if potential liability were to be imposed it would be not uncommon for actions to be raised against police forces on the ground that they had failed to catch some criminal as soon as they might have done, with the result that he went on to commit further crimes. While some such actions might involve allegations of a simple and straightforward type of failure, for example that a police officer negligently tripped and fell while pursuing a burglar, others would be likely to enter deeply into the general nature of a police investigation, as indeed the present action would seek to do. The manner of conduct of such an investigation must necessarily involve a variety of decisions to be made on matters of policy and discretion, for example as to which particular line of inquiry is most advantageously to be pursued and what is the most advantageous way to deploy the available resources. Many such decisions would not be regarded by the courts as appropriate to be called in question, yet elaborate investigation of the facts might be necessary to ascertain whether or not this was so. A great deal of police time, trouble and expense might be expected to have to be put into the preparation of the defence to the action and the attendance of witnesses at the trial. The result would be a significant diversion of police manpower and attention from their most important function, that of the suppression of crime. Closed investigations would require to be reopened and retraversed, not with the object of bringing any criminal to justice but to ascertain whether or not they had been competently conducted. I therefore consider that Glidewell LJ ... was right to take the view that the police were immune from an action of this kind on grounds similar to those which in *Rondel v Worsley* [see Note below] were held to render a barrister immune from actions for negligence in his conduct of proceedings in court ([1988] QB 60, 76).

My Lords, for these reasons I would dismiss the appeal.

[**Note**: *Rondel v Worsley* was overruled by the House of Lords in *Arthur J S Hall & Co v Simons* [2000] 3 WLR 543; [2000] 3 All ER 673.]

Case of Osman v The United Kingdom

[1999] 1 FLR 193; EHRR 245 (European Court of Human Rights)

[**FACTS**: Mr Ali Osman was shot dead by Mr Paul Paget-Lewis on 7 March 1988. Paget-Lewis, a former teacher of Mr Osman's son, Ahmet Osman, had become obsessed with Ahmet Osman and had been sacked from Ahmet's school because of inappropriate behaviour towards Ahmet and his friends. After Paget-Lewis' dismissal, the Osman property was subjected to various minor criminal nuisances including bricks thrown through windows, and tyres being slashed. No police records could be found in relation to these attacks. The police denied being informed by the school of Paget-Lewis' obsession. The criminal damage to the Osman property escalated. The police decided to arrest Paget-Lewis on suspicion of criminal damage. However, Paget-Lewis' whereabouts could not be traced. On 7 March 1988, Paget-Lewis shot and killed Ali Osman, as well as wounding and killing three other people. He was prosecuted but pled diminished responsibility. The Osman family then sued the police. The English Courts (*Osman v Fargesun* [1993] 4 AII ER 344 (CA)) while accepting that there was 'proximity' between the police and the Osmans, struck out the claim on the basis of public policy regarding police. The claim to the European Court of Human Rights concerned a failure to protect the life of Ali Osman and to prevent harassment, and that they had no access to an effective remedy in respect of that failure.]

Judgment delivered by a Grand Chamber

...

Article 2 of the European Convention on Human Rights reads:

> Everyone's right to life shall be protected by law. No one shall be deprived of his life intentionally save in the execution of a sentence of a court following his conviction of a crime for which this penalty is provided by law ...

2 *As to the alleged failure of the authorities to protect the rights to life of Ali and Ahmet Osman*

115 The Court notes that the first sentence of Article 2 § 1 enjoins the State not only to refrain from the intentional and unlawful taking of life, but also to take appropriate steps to safeguard the lives of those within its jurisdiction ... It is common ground that the State's obligation in this respect extends beyond its primary duty to secure the right to life by putting in place effective criminal-law provisions to deter the commission of offences against the person backed up by law-enforcement machinery for the prevention, suppression and sanctioning of breaches of such provisions. It is thus accepted by those appearing before the Court that Article 2 of the Convention may also imply in certain well-defined circumstances a positive obligation on the authorities to take preventive operational measures to protect an individual whose life is at risk from the criminal acts of another individual. The scope of this obligation is a matter of dispute between the parties.

116 For the Court, and bearing in mind the difficulties involved in policing modern societies, the unpredictability of human conduct and the operational choices which must be made in terms of priorities and resources, such an obligation must be interpreted in a way which does not impose an impossible or disproportionate burden

on the authorities. Accordingly, not every claimed risk to life can entail for the authorities a Convention requirement to take operational measures to prevent that risk from materialising. Another relevant consideration is the need to ensure that the police exercise their powers to control and prevent crime in a manner which fully respects the due process and other guarantees which legitimately place restraints on the scope of their action to investigate crime and bring offenders to justice, including the guarantees contained in Articles 5 and 8 of the Convention.

In the opinion of the Court where there is an allegation that the authorities have violated their positive obligation to protect the right to life in the context of their above-mentioned duty to prevent and suppress offences against the person (see paragraph 115 above), it must be established to its satisfaction that the authorities knew or ought to have known at the time of the existence of a real and immediate risk to the life of an identified individual or individuals from the criminal acts of a third party and that they failed to take measures within the scope of their powers which, judged reasonably, might have been expected to avoid that risk. The Court does not accept the Government's view that the failure to perceive the risk to life in the circumstances known at the time or to take preventive measures to avoid that risk must be tantamount to gross negligence or wilful disregard of the duty to protect life ... Such a rigid standard must be considered to be incompatible with the requirements of Article 1 of the Convention and the obligations of Contracting States under that Article to secure the practical and effective protection of the rights and freedoms laid down therein, including Article 2 ... For the Court, and having regard to the nature of the right protected by Article 2, a right fundamental in the scheme of the Convention, it is sufficient for an applicant to show that the authorities did not do all that could be reasonably expected of them to avoid a real and immediate risk to life of which they have or ought to have knowledge. This is a question which can only be answered in the light of all the circumstances of any particular case.

On the above understanding the Court will examine the particular circumstances of this case.

117 The Court observes, like the Commission, that the concerns of the school about Paget-Lewis' disturbing attachment to Ahmet Osman can be reasonably considered to have been communicated to the police over the course of the five meetings which took place between 3 March and 4 May 1987 ... having regard to the fact that Mr Prince's decision to call in the police in the first place was motivated by the allegations which Mrs Green had made against Paget-Lewis and the school's follow-up to those allegations. It may for the same reason be reasonably accepted that the police were informed of all relevant connected matters which had come to light by 4 May 1987 including the graffiti incident, the theft of the school files and Paget-Lewis' change of name.

It is the applicants' contention that by that stage the police should have been alert to the need to investigate further Paget-Lewis' alleged involvement in the graffiti incident and the theft of the school files or to keep a closer watch on him given their awareness of the obsessive nature of his behaviour towards Ahmet Osman and how that behaviour manifested itself. The Court for its part is not persuaded that the police's failure to do so at this stage can be impugned from the standpoint of Article 2 having regard to the state of their knowledge at that time. While

Paget-Lewis' attachment to Ahmet Osman could be judged by the police officers who visited the school to be most reprehensible from a professional point of view, there was never any suggestion that Ahmet Osman was at risk sexually from him, less so that his life was in danger. Furthermore, Mr Perkins, the deputy headmaster, alone had reached the conclusion that Paget-Lewis had been responsible for the graffiti in the neighbourhood of the school and the theft of the files. However Paget-Lewis had denied all involvement when interviewed by Mr Perkins and there was nothing to link him with either incident. Accordingly, at that juncture, the police's appreciation of the situation and their decision to treat it as a matter internal to the school cannot be considered unreasonable ...

118 The applicants have attached particular weight to Paget-Lewis' mental condition and in particular to his potential to turn violent and to direct that violence at Ahmet Osman. However, it is to be noted that Paget-Lewis continued to teach at the school up until June 1987. Dr Ferguson examined him on three occasions and was satisfied that he was not mentally ill. On 7 August 1987 he was allowed to resume teaching, although not at Homerton House ... It is most improbable that the decision to lift his suspension from teaching duties would have been made if it had been believed at the time that there was the slightest risk that he constituted a danger to the safety of young people in his charge. The applicants are especially critical of Dr Ferguson's psychiatric assessment of Paget-Lewis. However, that assessment was made on the basis of three separate interviews with Paget-Lewis and if it appeared to a professional psychiatrist that he did not at the time display any signs of mental illness or a propensity to violence it would be unreasonable to have expected the police to have construed the actions of Paget-Lewis as they were reported to them by the school as those of a mentally disturbed and highly dangerous individual.

119 In assessing the level of knowledge which can be imputed to the police at the relevant time, the Court has also had close regard to the series of acts of vandalism against the. Osmans' home and property between May and November 1987 ... It observes firstly that none of these incidents could be described as life-threatening and secondly that there was no evidence pointing to the involvement of Paget-Lewis ... The Court notes in this regard that when the decision was finally taken to arrest Paget-Lewis it was not based on any perceived risk to the lives of the Osman family but on his suspected involvement in acts of minor criminal damage ...

120 The Court has also examined carefully the strength of the applicants' arguments that Paget-Lewis on three occasions communicated to the police, either directly or indirectly, his murderous intentions ... However, in its view these statements cannot be reasonably considered to imply that the Osman family were the target of his threats and to put the police on notice of such ...

121 In the view of the Court the applicants have failed to point to any decisive stage in the sequence of the events leading up to the tragic shooting when it could be said that the police knew or ought to have known that the lives of the Osman family were at real and immediate risk from Paget-Lewis. While the applicants have pointed to a series of missed opportunities which would have enabled the police to neutralise the threat posed by Paget-Lewis, for example by searching his home for evidence to link him with the graffiti incident or by having him detained under the Mental Health

Act 1983 or by taking more active investigative steps following his disappearance, it cannot be said that these measures, judged reasonably, would in fact have produced that result or that a domestic court would have convicted him or ordered his detention in a psychiatric hospital on the basis of the evidence adduced before it. As noted earlier … the police must discharge their duties in a manner which is compatible with the rights and freedoms of individuals. In the circumstances of the present case, they cannot be criticised for attaching weight to the presumption of innocence or failing to use powers of arrest, search and seizure having regard to their reasonably held view that they lacked at relevant times the required standard of suspicion to use those powers or that any action taken would in fact have produced concrete results.

122 For the above reasons, the Court concludes that there has been no violation of Article 2 of the Convention in this case.

…

III *Alleged violation of Article 6 § 1 of the Convention*

131 The applicants alleged that the dismissal by the Court of Appeal of their negligence action against the police on grounds of public policy amounted to a restriction on their right of access to a court in breach of Article 6 § 1 of the Convention, which provides to the extent relevant:

> In the determination of his civil rights and obligations … , everyone is entitled to a … hearing … by [a] … tribunal …

132 The Commission agreed with the applicants' arguments in this respect. The Government however contended that the applicants could not rely on Article 6 § 1, maintaining in the alternative that there had been no breach of that provision in the circumstances of the case.

…

B *Compliance with Article 6 § 1*

…

147 The Court recalls that Article 6 § 1 embodies the 'right to a court', of which the right of access, that is, the right to institute proceedings before a court in civil matters, constitutes one aspect.

However, this right is not absolute, but may be subject to limitations; these are permitted by implication since the right of access by its very nature calls for regulation by the State. In this respect, the Contracting States enjoy a certain margin of appreciation, although the final decision as to the observance of the Convention's requirements rests with the Court. It must be satisfied that the limitations applied do not restrict or reduce the access left to the individual in such a way or to such an extent that the very essence of the right is impaired. Furthermore, a limitation will not be compatible with Article 6 § 1 if it does not pursue a legitimate aim and if there is not a reasonable relationship of proportionality between the means employed and the aim sought to be achieved …

148 Against that background the Court notes that the applicants' claim never fully proceeded to trial in that there was never any determination on its merits or on

the facts on which it was based. The decision of the Court of Appeal striking out their statement of claim was given in the context of interlocutory proceedings initiated by the Metropolitan Police Commissioner and that court assumed for the purposes of those proceedings that the facts as pleaded in the applicants' statement of claim were true. The applicants' claim was rejected since it was found to fall squarely within the scope of the exclusionary rule formulated by the House of Lords in the *Hill* case.

149 The reasons which led the House of Lords in the *Hill* case to lay down an exclusionary rule to protect the police from negligence actions in the context at issue are based on the view that the interests of the community as a whole are best served by a police service whose efficiency and effectiveness in the battle against crime are not jeopardised by the constant risk of exposure to tortious liability for policy and operational decisions.

150 Although the aim of such a rule may be accepted as legitimate in terms of the Convention, as being directed to the maintenance of the effectiveness of the police service and hence to the prevention of disorder or crime, the Court must nevertheless, in turning to the issue of proportionality, have particular regard to its scope and especially its application in the case at issue. While the Government have contended that the exclusionary rule of liability is not of an absolute nature ... and that its application may yield to other public-policy considerations, it would appear to the Court that in the instant case the Court of Appeal proceeded on the basis that the rule provided a watertight defence to the police and that it was impossible to prise open an immunity which the police enjoy from civil suit in respect of their acts and omissions in the investigation and suppression of crime.

151 The Court would observe that the application of the rule in this manner without further enquiry into the existence of competing public-interest considerations only serves to confer a blanket immunity on the police for their acts and omissions during the investigation and suppression of crime and amounts to an unjustifiable restriction on an applicant's right to have a determination on the merits of his or her claim against the police in deserving cases.

In its view, it must be open to a domestic court to have regard to the presence of other public-interest considerations which pull in the opposite direction to the application of the rule. Failing this, there will be no distinction made between degrees of negligence or of harm suffered or any consideration of the justice of a particular case. It is to be noted that in the instant case McCowan LJ ... appeared to be satisfied that the applicants, unlike the plaintiff Hill, had complied with the proximity test, a threshold requirement which is in itself sufficiently rigid to narrow considerably the number of negligence cases against the police which can proceed to trial. Furthermore, the applicants' case involved the alleged failure to protect the life of a child and their view that that failure was the result of a catalogue of acts and omissions which amounted to grave negligence as opposed to minor acts of incompetence. The applicants also claimed that the police had assumed responsibility for their safety. Finally, the harm sustained was of the most serious nature.

152 For the Court, these are considerations which must be examined on the merits and not automatically excluded by the application of a rule which amounts to the grant of an immunity to the police. In the instant case, the Court is not persuaded by

the Government's argument that the rule as interpreted by the domestic court did not provide an automatic immunity to the police.

153 The Court is not persuaded either by the Government's plea that the applicants had available to them alternative routes for securing compensation (see paragraph 145 above). In its opinion the pursuit of these remedies could not be said to mitigate the loss of their right to take legal proceedings against the police in negligence and to argue the justice of their case. Neither an action against Paget-Lewis nor against Dr Ferguson, the ILEA psychiatrist, would have enabled them to secure answers to the basic question which underpinned their civil action, namely why did the police not take action sooner to prevent Paget-Lewis from exacting a deadly retribution against Ali and Ahmet Osman. They may or may not have failed to convince the domestic court that the police were negligent in the circumstances. However, they were entitled to have the police account for their actions and omissions in adversarial proceedings.

[**Note**: In *Z v United Kingdom* [2001] 2 FLR 245, the ECHR accepted that it had erred in applying Article 6 (1), but the United Kingdom government accepted that it might be liable under Article 13.]

IV *Alleged violation of Article 13 of the Convention*

155 The applicants complained that they had no effective remedy enabling them to have an adjudication on their claim that the authorities had not done all that was required of them under Article 2 to protect the lives of Ali and Ahmet Osman. They relied on Article 13 of the Convention, which provides:

> Everyone whose rights and freedoms as set forth in [the] Convention are violated shall have an effective remedy before a national authority notwithstanding that the violation has been committed by persons acting in an official capacity.

156 The applicants submitted that the only effective mechanism in the circumstances for holding the authorities accountable for their failure in the instant case to comply with their positive obligation under Article 2 of the Convention would have been a civil action in negligence against the police. However the pursuit of that remedy was blocked when the Court of Appeal accepted the Metropolitan Police Commissioner's plea of police immunity and struck out their statement of claim.

157 The Commission considered that no separate issue arose under Article 13 in view of its finding of a violation of Article 6 § 1 of the Convention. The Government invited the Court to follow this view should it be minded to find a breach of Article 6 § 1 ...

Problems

1 After consuming 12 cans of beer at the Wig & Pen Pub, Strauss drove to Paisley Pub. Wagner, who owns the Paisley Pub, refused to serve Strauss as he was obviously drunk, but Wagner made no effort to stop him from driving away. Strauss crashed his car 50 metres from the Paisley Pub, causing extensive damage to Mahler's Jaguar car. Can Mahler sue Wagner, Strauss, or Bruckner (who is the owner of the Wig & Pen Pub) in negligence? Sigfried is an on-duty policeman who observed Strauss stagger back to his car. When asked why he did not stop Strauss from driving, Sigfried claimed that

he had 'more important things to do'. In particular, he said that he had to follow up on reports that stolen property was being sold at the Paisley Pub, and that in any case, Wagner was not staggering 'that much'. Can Mahler sue the police?

Nervous shock

This section contains a series of cases about whether someone who causes an accident can owe a duty of care to prevent not only the physical consequences to their immediate victims but also the psychological consequences of those not actually in the accident. Together with *Page v Smith*, which will be studied in the Damage section, the cases will show how various judges have gone about applying the general principles discussed in the previous cases to a particular area. The judges struggle with Lord Atkin's foreseeability and proximity requirements and their decisions show how foreseeability and proximity can be used to limit liability in one particular type of case. What problem do the judges see with imposing liability for nervous shock? How do they use the concepts of foreseeability and proximity to deal with it?

Hay (or Bourhill) v Young

[1943] AC 92 (HL)

[**FACTS:** John Young lost control of his motorbike, and was killed when he struck an oncoming car. His estate was sued.]

Lord Russell of Killowen:

My Lords, the foundation of the appellant's claim is fault or negligence alleged against John Young, an allegation which postulates a breach by him of some duty owed by him to her. Therefore, the first essential for the appellant to establish is the existence of a duty owed to her by John Young of which he committed a breach. As between John Young and the driver of the motor-car, John Young was admittedly negligent, in that he was in breach of the duty which he owed to him of not driving, while passing the stationary tramcar, at such a speed as would prevent him from pulling up in time to avoid a collision with any vehicle which might come across the front of the tramcar from Colinton Road into Glenlockhart Road, but it by no means follows that John Young owed any duty to the appellant. The facts relevant to this question seem to me to be these: The appellant was not in any way physically involved in the collision. She had been a passenger in the tramcar which had come from the direction of the city and had stopped some fifteen or sixteen yards short of the point of collision. She was standing in the road on the off-side of the tramcar (which was at rest), with her back to the driver's platform. The front part of the tramcar was between her and the colliding vehicles. She was frightened by the noise of the collision, but she had no reasonable fear of immediate bodily injury to herself.

Can it be said that John Young could reasonably have anticipated that a person, situated as was the appellant, would be affected by his proceeding towards Colinton at the speed at which he was travelling? I think not. His road was clear of pedestrians. The appellant was not within his vision, but was standing behind the solid barrier of the tramcar. His speed in no way endangered her. In these circumstances I am unable to see how he could reasonably anticipate that, if he came into collision with a vehicle coming across the tramcar into Glenlockhart Road, the resultant noise would cause physical injury by shock to a person standing behind the tramcar. In my opinion, he owed no duty to the appellant, and was, therefore, not guilty of any negligence in relation to her.

Lord Wright:

… There may indeed be no one injured in a particular case by actual impact, but still a wrong may be committed to anyone who suffers nervous shock or is injured in an act of rescue. The man who negligently allows a horse to bolt, or a car to run at large down a steep street, or a savage beast to escape is committing a breach of duty towards every person who comes within the range of foreseeable danger, whether by impact or shock, but, if there is no negligence or other default, there can be no liability for either direct impact or for nervous shock. Thus, if, owing to a latent defect or some mischance for which no one is liable, a terrifying collision occurs between vehicles on the road, and the occupants are killed or suffer horrible injuries, a bystander who suffers shock, whether through personal fear or merely horror, would have no action. On somewhat similar principles may be solved the problem of the old lady at Charing Cross, who suffers shock because she narrowly escapes being run over. She cannot claim damages if the driver is driving carefully, whether he hits her or not.

The present case, like many others of this type, may, however, raise the different question whether the appellant's illness was not due to her peculiar susceptibility. She was eight months gone in pregnancy. Can it be said, apart from everything else, that it was likely that a person of normal nervous strength would have been affected in the circumstances by illness as the appellant was? … What is now being considered is the question of liability, and this, I think, in a question whether there is duty owing to members of the public who come within the ambit of the act, must generally depend on a normal standard of susceptibility. This, it may be said, is somewhat vague. That is true, but definition involves limitation which it is desirable to avoid further than is necessary in a principle of law like negligence which is widely ranging and is still in the stage of development. It is here, as elsewhere, a question of what the hypothetical reasonable man, viewing the position, I suppose *ex post facto*, would say it was proper to foresee. What danger of particular infirmity that would include must depend on all the circumstances, but generally, I think, a reasonably normal condition, if medical evidence is capable of defining it, would be the standard. The test of the plaintiff's extraordinary susceptibility, if unknown to the defendant, would in effect make him an insurer. The lawyer likes to draw fixed and definite lines and is apt to ask where the thing is to stop. I should reply it should stop where in the particular case the good sense of the jury or of the judge decides.

McLoughlin v O'Brian

[1983] 1 AC 410 (HL)

[**FACTS**: Mrs McLouglin suffered severe mental distress with physical consequences as a result of seeing her husband and children in a hospital almost immediately after they had been involved in a car accident.]

Lord Wilberforce:

… Although in the only case which has reached this House (*Bourhill v Young*) a claim for damages in respect of 'nervous shock' was rejected on its facts, the House gave clear recognition to the legitimacy, in principle, of claims of that character. As the result of that and other cases, assuming that they are accepted as correct, the following position has been reached:

1 While damages cannot, at common law, be awarded for grief and sorrow, a claim for damages for 'nervous shock' caused by negligence can be made without the necessity of showing direct impact or fear of immediate personal injuries for oneself … .

2 A plaintiff may recover damages for 'nervous shock' brought on by injury caused not to him- or herself but to a near relative, or by the fear of such injury. So far (subject to 5 below), the cases do not extend beyond the spouse or children of the plaintiff … .

3 Subject to the next paragraph, there is no English case in which a plaintiff has been able to recover nervous shock damages where the injury to the near relative occurred out of sight and earshot of the plaintiff. In *Hambrook v Stokes Brothers* an express distinction was made between shock caused by what the mother saw with her own eyes and what she might have been told by bystanders, liability being excluded in the latter case.

4 An exception from, or I would prefer to call it an extension of, the latter case, has been made where the plaintiff does not see or hear the incident but comes upon its immediate aftermath … .

5 A remedy on account of nervous shock has been given to a man who came upon a serious accident involving numerous people immediately thereafter and acted as a rescuer of those involved (*Chadwick v British Railways Board* [1967] 1 WLR 912). 'Shock' was caused neither by fear for himself nor by fear or horror on account of a near relative. The principle of 'rescuer' cases was not challenged by the respondents and ought, in my opinion, to be accepted. But we have to consider whether, and how far, it can be applied to such cases as the present.

Throughout these developments, as can be seen, the courts have proceeded in the traditional manner of the common law from case to case, upon a basis of logical necessity. If a mother, with or without accompanying children, could recover on account of fear for herself, how can she be denied recovery on account of fear for her accompanying children? If a father could recover had he seen his child run over by a backing car, how can he be denied recovery if he is in the immediate vicinity and runs to the child's assistance? If a wife and mother could recover if she had witnessed a serious accident to her husband and children, does she fail because she was a short distance away and immediately rushes to the scene (cf *Benson v Lee*)? I think that unless the law is to draw an arbitrary line at the point of direct sight and sound, these arguments require acceptance of the extension mentioned above under 4 in the interests of justice.

If one continues to follow the process of logical progression, it is hard to see why the present plaintiff also should not succeed. She was not present at the accident, but she came very soon after upon its aftermath. If, from a distance of some 100 yards … she had found her family by the roadside, she would have come within principle 4 above. Can it make any difference that she comes upon them in an ambulance, or, as here, in a nearby hospital, when, as the evidence shows, they were in the same condition, covered with oil and mud, and distraught with pain? If Mr Chadwick can recover when, acting in accordance with normal and irresistible human instinct, and indeed moral compulsion, he goes to the scene of an accident, may not a mother recover if, acting under the same motives, she goes to where her family can be found? …

To allow her claim may be, I think it is, upon the margin of what the process of logical progression would allow. But where the facts are strong and exceptional, and, as I think, fairly analogous, her case ought, *prima facie*, to be assimilated to those which have passed the test.

To argue from one factual situation to another and to decide by analogy is a natural tendency of the human and the legal mind. But the lawyer still has to inquire whether, in so doing, he has crossed some critical line behind which he ought to stop. That is said to be the present case.

… Though differing in expression, in the end, in my opinion, the two presentations [in the Court of Appeal] rest upon a common principle, namely that, at the margin, the boundaries of a man's responsibility for acts of negligence have to be fixed as a matter of policy. Whatever is the correct jurisprudential analysis, it does not make any essential difference whether one says, with Stephenson LJ, that there is a duty but, as a matter of policy, the consequences of breach of it ought to be limited at a certain point, or whether, with Griffiths LJ, one says that the fact that consequences may be foreseeable does not automatically impose a duty of care, does not do so in fact where policy indicates the contrary. This is an approach which one can see very clearly from the way in which Lord Atkin stated the neighbour principle in *Donoghue v Stevenson* … 'persons who are so closely and directly affected by my act that I ought reasonably to have them in contemplation as being so affected … '. This is saying that foreseeability must be accompanied and limited by the law's judgment as to persons who ought, according to its standards of value or justice, to have been in contemplation. Foreseeability, which involves a hypothetical person, looking with hindsight at an event which has occurred, is a formula adopted by English law, not merely for defining, but also for limiting, the persons to whom duty may be owed, and the consequences for which an actor may be held responsible. It is not merely an issue of fact to be left to be found as such. When it is said to result in a duty of care being owed to a person or a class, the statement that there is a 'duty of care' denotes a conclusion into the forming of which considerations of policy have entered. That foreseeability does not of itself, and automatically, lead to a duty of care is, I think, clear.

We must then consider the policy arguments. In doing so we must bear in mind that cases of 'nervous shock,' and the possibility of claiming damages for it, are not necessarily confined to those arising out of accidents on public roads. To state, therefore, a rule that recoverable damages must be confined to persons on or near the highway is to state not a principle in itself, but only an example of a more general rule that recoverable damages must be confined to those within sight and sound of an event caused by negligence or, at least, to those in close, or very close, proximity to such a situation.

The policy arguments against a wider extension can be stated under four heads.

First, it may be said that such extension may lead to a proliferation of claims, and possibly fraudulent claims, to the establishment of an industry of lawyers and psychiatrists who will formulate a claim for nervous shock damages, including what in America is called the customary miscarriage, for all, or many, road accidents and industrial accidents.

Secondly, it may be claimed that an extension of liability would be unfair to defendants, as imposing damages out of proportion to the negligent conduct complained of. In so far as such defendants are insured, a large additional burden will be placed on insurers, and ultimately upon the class of persons insured—road users or employers.

Thirdly, to extend liability beyond the most direct and plain cases would greatly increase evidentiary difficulties and tend to lengthen litigation.

Fourthly, it may be said—and the Court of Appeal agreed with this—that an extension of the scope of liability ought only to be made by the legislature, after careful research. This is the course which has been taken in New South Wales and the Australian Capital Territory ... .

... It is necessary to consider three elements inherent in any claim: the class of persons whose claims should be recognised; the proximity of such persons to the accident; and the means by which the shock is caused. As regards the class of persons, the possible range is between the closest of family ties—of parent and child, or husband and wife—and the ordinary bystander. Existing law recognises the claims of the first: it denies that of the second, either on the basis that such persons must be assumed to be possessed of fortitude sufficient to enable them to endure the calamities of modern life, or that defendants cannot be expected to compensate the world at large. In my opinion, these positions are justifiable, and since the present case falls within the first class, it is strictly unnecessary to say more. I think, however, that it should follow that other cases involving less close relationships must be very carefully scrutinised. I cannot say that they should never be admitted. The closer the tie (not merely in relationship, but in care) the greater the claim for consideration. The claim, in any case, has to be judged in the light of the other factors, such as proximity to the scene in time and place, and the nature of the accident.

As regards proximity to the accident, it is obvious that this must be close in both time and space. It is, after all, the fact and consequence of the defendant's negligence that must be proved to have caused the 'nervous shock'. Experience has shown that to insist on direct and immediate sight or hearing would be impractical and unjust and that under what may be called the 'aftermath' doctrine one who, from close proximity, comes very soon upon the scene should not be excluded ... .

My Lords, I believe that these indications, imperfectly sketched, and certainly to be applied with common sense to individual situations in their entirety, represent either the existing law, or the existing law with only such circumstantial extension as the common law process may legitimately make. They do not introduce a new principle. Nor do I see any reason why the law should retreat behind the lines already drawn. I find on this appeal that the appellant's case falls within the boundaries of the law so drawn. I would allow her appeal.

Alcock v Chief Constable of South Yorkshire
[1992] 1 AC 310 (HL)
Lord Ackner:
My Lords, if sympathy alone were to be the determining factor in these claims, then they would never have been contested. It has been stressed throughout the judgments in the courts below and I would emphasise it yet again in your Lordships' House that the human tragedy which occurred on the afternoon of 15 April 1989 at the Hillsborough Stadium, when 95 people were killed and more than 400 others received injuries from being crushed necessitating hospital treatment, remains an utterly appalling one.

It is, however, trite law that the defendant, the Chief Constable of South York-shire, is not an insurer against psychiatric illness occasioned by the shock sustained by the relatives or friends of those who died or were injured, or were believed to have died or to have been injured. This is, of course, fully recognised by the appellants, the plaintiffs in these actions, whose claims for damages to compensate them for their psy-chiatric illnesses are based upon the allegation that it was the defendant's negligence, that is to say his breach of his duty of care owed to them as well as to those who died or were injured in controlling the crowds at the stadium, which caused them to suffer their illnesses. The defendant, for the purposes of these actions, has admitted that he owed a duty of care only to those who died or were injured and that he was in breach of only that duty. He has further accepted that each of the plaintiffs has suffered some psychiatric illness. Moreover for the purpose of deciding whether the defendant is liable to pay damages to the plaintiffs in respect of their illnesses, the trial judge, Hidden J, made the assumption that the illnesses were caused by the shocks sustained by the plaintiffs by reason of their awareness of the events at Hillsborough. The defendant has throughout contested liability on the ground that, in all the circum-stances, he was not in breach of any duty of care owed to the plaintiffs.

The three elements
Because 'shock' in its nature is capable of affecting such a wide range of persons, Lord Wilberforce in *McLoughlin v O'Brian* ... , concluded that there was a real need for the law to place some limitation upon the extent of admissible claims and in this context he considered that there were three elements inherent in any claim. It is common ground that such elements do exist and are required to be considered in connection with all these claims. The fundamental difference in approach is that on behalf of the plaintiffs it is contended that the consideration of these three elements is merely part of the process of deciding whether, as a matter of fact, the reasonable foreseeability test has been satisfied. On behalf of the defendant it is contended that these elements oper-ate as a control or limitation on the mere application of the reasonable foreseeability test. They introduce the requirement of 'proximity' as conditioning the duty of care.

The three elements are (1) the class of persons whose claims should be recognised; (2) the proximity of such persons to the accident—in time and space; (3) the means by which the shock has been caused.

I will deal with those three elements *seriatim*.

(1) The class of persons whose claim should be recognised
When dealing with the possible range of the class of persons who might sue, Lord Wilberforce in *McLoughlin v O'Brian* ... contrasted the closest of family ties—parent and child and husband and wife—with that of the ordinary bystander ... .

As regards claims by those in the close family relationships referred to by Lord Wilberforce, the justification for admitting such claims is the presumption, which I would accept as being rebuttable, that the love and affection normally associated with persons in those relationships is such that a defendant ought reasonably to contemplate that they may be so closely and directly affected by his conduct as to suffer shock resulting in psychiatric illness. While as a generalisation more remote relatives and, *a fortiori*, friends, can reasonably be expected not to suffer illness from the shock, there can well be relatives and friends whose relationship is so close and intimate that their love and affection for the victim is comparable to that of the normal parent, spouse or child of the victim and should for the purpose of this cause of action be so treated.

Whether the degree of love and affection in any given relationship, be it that of relative or friend, is such that the defendant, in the light of the plaintiff's proximity to the scene of the accident in time and space and its nature, should reasonably have foreseen the shock-induced psychiatric illness, has to be decided on a case by case basis.

(2) The proximity of the plaintiff to the accident

It is accepted that the proximity to the accident must be close both in time and space. Direct and immediate sight or hearing of the accident is not required. It is reasonably foreseeable that injury by shock can be caused to a plaintiff, not only through the sight or hearing of the event, but of its immediate aftermath.

Only two of the plaintiffs before us were at the ground. However, it is clear from *McLoughlin v O'Brian* ... that there may be liability where subsequent identification can be regarded as part of the 'immediate aftermath' of the accident. Mr Alcock identified his brother-in-law in a bad condition in the mortuary at about midnight, that is some eight hours after the accident. This was the earliest of the identification cases. Even if this identification could be described as part of the 'aftermath', it could not in my judgment be described as part of the *immediate* aftermath. *McLoughlin*'s case was described by Lord Wilberforce as being upon the margin of what the process of logical progression from case to case would allow. Mrs McLoughlin had arrived at the hospital within an hour or so after the accident. Accordingly in the post-accident identification cases before your Lordships there was not sufficient proximity in time and space to the accident.

(3) The means by which the shock is caused

Lord Wilberforce concluded that the shock must come through sight or hearing of the event or its immediate aftermath but specifically left for later consideration whether some equivalent of sight or hearing, eg through simultaneous television, would suffice ... Of course it is common ground that it was clearly foreseeable by the defendant that those who would be watching would be parents and spouses and other relatives and friends of those in the pens behind the goal at the Leppings Lane end. However he would also know of the code of ethics which the television authorities televising this event could be expected to follow, namely that they would not show pictures of suffering by recognisable individuals. Had they done so, Mr Hytner accepted that this would have been a '*novus actus*' breaking the chain of causation between the defendant's alleged breach of duty and the psychiatric illness. As the defendant was reasonably entitled to expect to be the case, there were no such pictures. Although the television pictures certainly gave rise to feelings of the deepest anxiety and distress, in the circumstances of this case the simultaneous television broadcasts of what occurred cannot be equated with the 'sight or hearing of the event or its immediate aftermath.' Accordingly shocks sustained by reason of these broadcasts cannot found a claim. I agree, however, with Nolan LJ that simultaneous broadcasts of a disaster cannot in all cases by ruled out as providing the equivalent of the actual sight or hearing of the event or its immediate aftermath. Nolan LJ gave, *ante*, pp 386G–387A, an example of a situation where it was reasonable to anticipate that the television cameras, whilst filming and transmitting pictures of a special event of children travelling in a balloon, in which there was media interest, particularly amongst the parents, showed the balloon suddenly bursting into flames. Many other such situations could be imagined where the impact of the simultaneous television pictures would be as great, if not greater, than the actual sight of the accident.

Conclusion

Only one of the plaintiffs, who succeeded before Hidden J, namely Brian Harrison, was at the ground. His relatives who died were his two brothers. The quality of brotherly love is well known to differ widely—from Cain and Abel to David and Jonathan. I assume that Mr Harrison's relationship with his brothers was not an abnormal one. His claim was not presented upon the basis that there was such a close and intimate relationship between them, as gave rise to that very special bond of affection which would make his shock-induced psychiatric illness reasonably foreseeable by the defendant. Accordingly, the judge did not carry out the requisite close scrutiny of their relationship. Thus there was no evidence to establish the necessary proximity which would make his claim reasonably foreseeable and, subject to the other factors, to which I have referred, a valid one. The other plaintiff who was present at the ground, Robert Alcock, lost a brother-in-law. He was not, in my judgment, reasonably foreseeable as a potential sufferer from shock-induced psychiatric illness, in default of very special facts and none was established. Accordingly their claims must fail, as must those of the other plaintiffs who only learned of the disaster by watching simultaneous television. I, too, would therefore dismiss these appeals.

Lord Oliver:

... I would only add that I cannot, for my part, regard the present state of the law as either entirely satisfactory or as logically defensible. If there exists a sufficient degree of proximity to sustain a claim for damages for nervous shock, why, it may justifiably be asked, does not that proximity also support that perhaps more easily foreseeable loss which the plaintiff may suffer as a direct result of the death or injury from which the shock arises. That it does not is, I think, clear from *Hinz v Berry* [1970] 2 QB 40 ... But the reason why it does not has, I think, to be found not in logic but in policy. Whilst not dissenting from the case-by-case approach advocated by Lord Bridge in *McLoughlin's* case, the ultimate boundaries within which claims for damages in such cases can be entertained must I think depend in the end upon considerations of policy. For example, in his illuminating judgment in *Jaensch v Coffey* 155 CLR 549, Deane J expressed the view that no claim could be entertained as a matter of law where the primary victim is the negligent defendant himself and the shock to the plaintiff arises from witnessing the victim's self-inflicted injury. The question does not, fortunately, fall to be determined in the instant case, but I suspect that an English court would be likely to take a similar view. But if that be so, the limitation must be based upon policy rather than upon logic for the suffering and shock of a wife or mother at witnessing the death of her husband or son is just as immediate, just as great and just as foreseeable whether the accident be due to the victim's own or to another's negligence and if the claim is based, as it must be, on the combination of proximity and foreseeability, there is certainly no logical reason why a remedy should be denied in such a case. Indeed, Mr Hytner, for the plaintiffs, has boldly claimed that it should not be. Take, for instance, the case of a mother who suffers shock and psychiatric injury through witnessing the death of her son when he negligently walks in front of an oncoming motor car. If liability is to be denied in such a case such denial can only be because the policy of the law forbids such a claim, for it is difficult to visualise a greater proximity or a greater degree of foreseeability. Moreover, I can visualise great difficulty arising, if this be the law, where the accident, though not solely caused by the primary victim has been materially contributed to by his negligence. If, for instance, the primary victim is himself 75 per cent responsible for the accident, it would be a curious and wholly unfair situation if the plaintiff were enabled to recover damages for his or her traumatic injury from the person responsible only in a minor degree whilst he in turn remained unable to recover any contribution from the person primarily responsible since the latter's negligence vis-à-vis the plaintiff would not even have been tortious.

White v Chief Constable of South Yorkshire Police
(alt cit: Frost)
[1999] 2 AC 455; [1999] 1 All ER 1 (HL)
[**FACTS**: A number of policemen who were working during the Hillsborough disaster sued alleging that they had suffered as a result of their roles in the disaster. A majority of the Court of Appeal had distinguished policemen from other 'secondary' victims on two bases. Some had been involved as rescuers; all were owed a duty to be kept safe, including from psychological harm, as police employees.]
Lord Goff of Chieveley:
…
[After expressing strong disapproval of *Page v Smith*, his Lordship continued.]
…

Employees and rescuers
(1) Employees
An employee (I will for present purposes include in this category a 'quasi-employee' such as a police officer who, although he holds an office and is not therefore strictly an employee, is owed the same duty by his 'employer'—here the Chief Constable of the South Yorkshire Police) may recover damages from his employer in respect of psychiatric injury suffered by him by reason of his employer's breach of duty to him. The basic obligation of the employer arises from the relationship between him and his employee, under which the employer is under a duty to take reasonable care for the safety of his employee at work … and in particular not to expose his employees to unnecessary or unreasonable risk …

However all the employer's duties 'are connected in some sense to what happens to the employee while at work' … ; and it is with cases arising in this context that we are concerned. I put on one side those cases in which an employee is seeking damages from his employer in respect of stress at work … But in the authorities relating to the recovery by an employee from his employer of damages for psychiatric injury, arising from the death or physical injury of another, we find a distinction being drawn between those cases in which the employee has in the course of his employment been involved in the event which resulted in the other's physical injury or death, to which I would add involvement in the aftermath of that event, and other cases in which he had, while at work, incidentally witnessed that event and its outcome ...

The importance of this conclusion is that it avoids what otherwise might be regarded as an unacceptable distinction between employees on the one hand, and relatives on the other ... The difference between the two categories arises not from the applicability of special rules in the case of secondary victims (which, in my opinion, apply to both categories) but from the fact that, whereas police officers who became involved on the ground in the aftermath of the disaster can claim against the chief constable as 'employees', strangers who intervened will have to justify their intervention, for example by bringing themselves within the broad category of 'rescuers', to which I will turn in a moment. In this connection I wish to record that the claims of the plaintiffs in *Alcock*'s case were not advanced on the basis that they were rescuers, a fact which must be borne in mind when comparisons are drawn between those plaintiffs and the plaintiffs in the present case ...

(2) Rescuers

I turn next to the category of rescuers. This category is of particular importance for outsiders who intervene in a situation created by a wrongdoer. The fact that an outsider may intervene in such a situation to rescue a victim of the wrongdoing is reasonably foreseeable by a person in the position of the wrongdoer. The intervention is justified by the necessity of the moment, and so is not unlawful. It does not break the chain of causation between the wrongful act of the defendant and injury suffered by the intervener by reason of his act of rescue, whether the rescue is successful or not. Compensation for such an injury may be recovered by the intervener from the wrongdoer, whether the injury is physical as in the classic rescue cases such as *Ward v T E Hopkins & Son Ltd*, *Baker v T E Hopkins & Son Ltd* [1959] 3 All ER 225 ... , or psychiatric as in *Chadwick v British Transport Commission* [1067] 2 All ER 945, [1967] 1 WLR 912.

Chadwick's case is important in another respect. It shows that we must not be prisoners of our concepts, here the concept of rescue. Mr Chadwick was not attempting to rescue anybody. He was a small and agile man, who lived close to the railway line in Lewisham, on which two trains collided with catastrophic results. Many passengers were killed or injured; and many of the injured were trapped in the wreckage for a long time during the night before they could be rescued. Mr Chadwick worked for many hours during the night, crawling under the wreckage of the train and bringing aid and comfort to the victims, some of them severely injured, who were trapped in the wreckage. He was exposed to some physical danger, but the trial judge (Waller J) treated that as irrelevant. It was, he held, the whole horror of the situation which affected Mr Chadwick, who as a result suffered psychiatric injury in a form which would nowadays probably be classified as PTSD. When we contemplate the full horror of the disaster—the terrible injuries suffered by some of the victims, dead and alive, and the cries of the living for help; the long hours of darkness; the claustrophobic conditions in which Mr Chadwick worked—it is scarcely surprising that the judge treated the physical danger as irrelevant; and it is scarcely surprising too that, in *McLoughlin v O'Brian* ... at 438, Lord Bridge of Harwich stated that, as far as he knew, no one had ever doubted that the case was rightly decided. But it is also plain that the circumstances were wholly exceptional. It must be very rare that a person bringing aid and comfort to a victim or victims will be held to have suffered foreseeable psychiatric injury as a result ...

I wish also to add that, obviously, a rescuer will normally come on the scene after the disastrous event has occurred. It is most unlikely that he will be involved in that event himself. He is involved in the aftermath of that event, and is concerned with its consequences. That involvement is, however, sufficient to bring him within the category of primary victims, so far as liability for psychiatric injury is concerned ...

(3) Employees and rescuers
It is of course perfectly possible for an employee of the tortfeasor to be a rescuer. If so, the basis on which he may claim damages from his employer in respect of any psychiatric injury which he may suffer by reason of his involvement will depend on the circumstances of the case. Where he becomes involved in the course of his employment (see *Priestley v Fowler* (1837) 3 M & W 1 ... Lord Abinger CB ...) he may be able to claim damages simply on the basis of breach by his employer of his duty of care. If not, however, he can rely on his intervention in the character of a rescuer as a stranger may do ...

In some cases, however, the circumstances may be such that an employee is involved in the aftermath of the relevant event when acting in the course of his employment with the tortfeasor, and that a part of his involvement may fall within the description of rescue and the remainder not. If as a result of his involvement the employee suffers psychiatric injury, it will be necessary to have regard to his involvement as a whole, including his actions of rescue, when deciding whether or not such psychiatric injury is a reasonably foreseeable consequence of a breach by his employer of his duty to him. That is, in my opinion, the position in the present case. It follows that if, as in the present case, there is a group of employees who were involved in the aftermath of the event, and only some of them were involved in acts of rescue, it does not follow that the latter only will be entitled to recover. It is the involvement of each as a whole which has to be considered; and if the involvement is such that the acts of rescue were no more than incidental parts of a wider involvement which caused the psychiatric injury, there is no reason why those employees who were involved in acts of rescue should be singled out as those who alone are entitled to recover. This is because, in such a case, as in *Chadwick*'s case, it is the whole horror of the situation which is the cause of the psychiatric injury suffered by all of the employees so involved.

A new control mechanism?
As I have already recorded, it was submitted by Mr Collender on behalf of the appellants, relying on certain passages in the opinion of Lord Lloyd in *Page v Smith* ... that it was a prerequisite of the right of recovery by primary victims in respect of psychiatric injury suffered by them that they should have been within the range of foreseeable physical injury. I have already expressed the opinion that no such conclusion can be drawn from Lord Lloyd's opinion in *Page v Smith*. I understand however that, even if

my view on that point is accepted as correct, some of your Lordships nevertheless consider that a new control mechanism to the same effect should now be introduced and imposed by this House as a matter of policy.

I am compelled to say that I am unable to accept this suggestion because in my opinion (1) the proposal is contrary to well-established authority; (2) the proposed control mechanism would erect an artificial barrier against recovery in respect of foreseeable psychiatric injury and as such is undesirable; and (3) the underlying concern is misconceived. I will consider each of these objections in turn.

(1) The proposal is contrary to well-established authority
I have here in mind the cases to which I have previously referred, concerned (a) with rescuers, and (b) with those who have, as a result of another's negligence, been put in the position of being, or of thinking that they are, the involuntary cause of another's death or injury ... In this connection it is important that the decision in *Chadwick*'s case was approved, without qualification, in your Lordships' House in *McLoughlin* ... and again in *Alcock*'s case ... As to the second category, the most relevant case is *Dooley v Cammell Laird & Co Ltd* [1951] 1 Lloyd's Rep 271 in which, as in other cases of this kind, the plaintiff was never in any personal danger. Furthermore, both categories of case were stated by Lord Oliver in *Alcock*'s case ... to be examples of primary victims, in the case of which he plainly did not consider that there was any applicable control mechanism, for example any requirement that the plaintiff should have been within the range of foreseeable physical injury. Having regard in particular to the prominence now given to Lord Oliver's opinion in *Alcock*'s case in segregating cases of secondary victims as those cases to which special control mechanisms apply, it would be a remarkable departure from existing authority now to create a new control mechanism, *viz* that the plaintiff must have been exposed to the risk of physical injury, and to hold that this mechanism is applicable in the case of primary victims. What is here at issue therefore is not whether we should *extend* liability for psychiatric injury to primary victims who do not come within the range of foreseeable physical injury. The question is whether, having regard to existing authority, we should *restrict* liability for psychiatric injury to primary victims who are within the range of such injury.

(2) The proposed control mechanism would erect an artificial barrier against recovery in respect of foreseeable psychiatric injury and as such is undesirable
The control mechanisms now in force are those established in *Alcock*'s case to be applicable in the case of secondary victims, *viz* (a) a close tie of love and affection to the immediate victim, (b) proximity in time and space to the incident or its aftermath, and (c) perception by sight or hearing, or its equivalent, of the event or its aftermath. These rules being arbitrary in nature, are widely perceived to create unjust and unacceptable distinctions ... To introduce the control mechanism now proposed in the case of primary victims would in the same way create distinctions regarded as unjust and unacceptable.

To illustrate the point, let me take the always useful extreme example. Suppose that there was a terrible train crash and that there were two Chadwick brothers living nearby, both of them small and agile window cleaners distinguished by their courage and humanity. Mr A Chadwick worked on the front half of the train, and

Mr B Chadwick on the rear half. It so happened that, although there was some physical danger present in the front half of the train, there was none in the rear. Both worked for 12 hours or so bringing aid and comfort to the victims. Both suffered PTSD in consequence of the general horror of the situation. On the new control mechanism now proposed, Mr A would recover but Mr B would not. This is surely unacceptable. May I stress that, although I have taken an extreme example, the contrast I have drawn could well arise in real life; and the new control mechanism now proposed could provoke criticisms of the same kind as those which have been made of the mechanisms recognized in *Alcock*'s case.

(3) The underlying concern is misconceived
I sense that the underlying concern, which has prompted a desire to introduce this new control mechanism, is that it is thought that, without it, the policemen who are plaintiffs in the present case would be 'better off' than the relatives in *Alcock*'s case who failed in their claims, and that such a result would be undesirable. To this, there are at least three answers. First, the control mechanisms which excluded recovery by the relatives in *Alcock*'s case would, in my opinion, have been equally applicable to the policemen in the present case if on the facts they had (like the relatives) been no more than witnesses of the consequences of the tragedy. Second, the question whether any of the relatives might be able to recover because he fell within the broad category of rescuer is still undecided; and strangely, the control mechanism now proposed to exclude the claims of the policemen in the present case would likewise exclude the claims of relatives if advanced on the basis that they were rescuers. Third, however, it is in any event misleading to think in terms of one class of plaintiffs being 'better off' than another. Tort liability is concerned not only with compensating plaintiffs, but with awarding such compensation against a defendant who is responsible in law for the plaintiff's injury. It may well be that one plaintiff will succeed on the basis that he can establish such responsibility, whereas another plaintiff who has suffered the same injury will not succeed because he is unable to do so. In such a case, the first plaintiff will be 'better off' than the second, but it does not follow that the result is unjust or that an artificial barrier should be erected to prevent those in the position of the first plaintiff from succeeding in their claims. The true requirement is that the claim of each plaintiff should be judged by reference to the same legal principles.
Lord Steyn:
Policy considerations and psychiatric harm
Policy considerations have undoubtedly played a role in shaping the law governing recovery for pure psychiatric harm. The common law imposes different rules for the recovery of compensation for physical injury and psychiatric harm. Thus it is settled law that bystanders at tragic events, even if they suffer foreseeable psychiatric harm, are not entitled to recover damages: *Alcock* ... The courts have regarded the policy reasons against admitting such claims as compelling ...

I do not doubt that public perception has played a substantial role in the development of this branch of the law. But nowadays we must accept the medical reality that psychiatric harm may be more serious than physical harm. It is therefore necessary to consider whether there are other objective policy considerations which may justify different rules for the recovery of compensation for physical injury and psychiatric harm.

And in my view it would be insufficient to proceed on the basis that there are unspec-ified policy considerations at stake. If, as I believe, there are such policy considerations it is necessary to explain what the policy considerations are so that the validity of my assumptions can be critically examined by others.

My impression is that there are at least four distinctive features of claims for psychi-atric harm which in combination may account for the differential treatment. Firstly, there is the complexity of drawing the line between acute grief and psychiatric harm … The symptoms may be the same. But there is greater diagnostic uncertainty in psy-chiatric injury cases than in physical injury cases. The classification of emotional injury is often controversial. In order to establish psychiatric harm expert evidence is required. That involves the calling of consultant psychiatrists on both sides. It is a costly and time-consuming exercise. If claims for psychiatric harm were to be treated as generally on a par with physical injury it would have implications for the adminis-tration of justice. On its own this factor may not be entitled to great weight and may not outweigh the considerations of justice supporting genuine claims in respect of pure psychiatric injury. Secondly, there is the effect of the expansion of the availability of compensation on potential claimants who have witnessed gruesome events. I do not have in mind fraudulent or bogus claims. In general it ought to be possible for the administration of justice to expose such claims. But I do have in mind the *unconscious* effect of the prospect of compensation on potential claimants. Where there is generally no prospect of recovery, such as in the case of injuries sustained in sport, psychiatric harm appears not to obtrude often. On the other hand, in the case of industrial acci-dents, where there is often a prospect of recovery of compensation, psychiatric harm is repeatedly encountered and often endures until the process of claiming compensation comes to an end … The litigation is sometimes an unconscious disincentive to rehabil-itation. It is true that this factor is already present in cases of physical injuries with con-comitant mental suffering. But it may play a larger role in cases of pure psychiatric harm, particularly if the categories of potential recovery are enlarged. For my part this factor cannot be dismissed.

The third factor is important. The abolition or a relaxation of the special rules gov-erning the recovery of damages for psychiatric harm would greatly increase the class of persons who can recover damages in tort. It is true that compensation is routinely awarded for psychiatric harm where the plaintiff has suffered some physical harm. It is also well established that psychiatric harm resulting from the apprehension of physical harm is enough: *Page v Smith* … These two principles are not surprising. Inbuilt in such situations are restrictions on the classes of plaintiff who can sue: the requirement of the infliction of some physical injury or apprehension of it introduces an element of immediacy which restricts the category of potential plaintiffs. But in cases of pure psy-chiatric harm there is potentially a wide class of plaintiffs involved. Fourthly, the imposition of liability for pure psychiatric harm in a wide range of situations may result in a burden of liability on defendants which may be disproportionate to tortious con-duct involving perhaps momentary lapses of concentration, eg in a motor car accident.

The wide scope of potential liability for pure psychiatric harm is not only illus-trated by the rather unique events of Hillsborough but also by accidents involving trains, coaches and buses, and the everyday occurrence of serious collisions of vehicles all of which may result in gruesome scenes. In such cases there may be many claims for psychiatric harm by those who have witnessed and in some ways assisted at the scenes of the tragic events. Moreover, protagonists of very wide theories of liability for pure psychiatric loss have suggested that 'workplace claims loom large as the next growth area of psychiatric injury law', the paradigm case being no doubt a workman who has witnessed a tragic accident to an employee ...

The police officers' claims
In the present case, the police officers were more than mere bystanders. They were all on duty at the stadium. They were all involved in assisting in the course of their duties in the aftermath of the terrible events. And they have suffered debilitating psychiatric harm. The police officers therefore argue, and are entitled to argue, that the law ought to provide compensation for the wrong which caused them harm. This argument cannot be lightly dismissed. But I am persuaded that a recognition of their claims would substantially expand the existing categories in which compensation can be recovered for pure psychiatric harm. Moreover, as the majority in the Court of Appeal was uncomfortably aware, the awarding of damages to these police officers sits uneasily with the denial of the claims of bereaved relatives by the decision of the House of Lords in *Alcock* ... The decision of the Court of Appeal has introduced an imbalance in the law of tort which might perplex the man on the Underground. Since the answer may be that there should be compensation in all these categories I must pursue the matter further.

The case law
In order to understand the law as it stands it is necessary to trace in outline its development ...

The decision of the House of Lords in *Page v Smith* ... was the next important development in this branch of the law. The plaintiff was directly involved in a motor car accident. He was within the range of potential physical injury. As a result of the accident he suffered from chronic fatigue syndrome. In this context Lord Lloyd ... adopted a distinction between primary and secondary victims: Lord Ackner and Lord Browne-Wilkinson agreed. Lord Lloyd said that a plaintiff who had been within the range of foreseeable injury was a primary victim. Mr Page fulfilled this requirement and could in principle recover compensation for psychiatric loss. In my view it follows that all other victims, who suffer pure psychiatric harm, are secondary victims and must satisfy the control mechanisms laid down in *Alcock*'s case. There has been criticism of this classification ... But, if the narrow formulation by Lord Lloyd ... of who may be a primary victim is kept in mind, this classification ought not to produce inconsistent results. In any event, the decision of the House of Lords in *Page v Smith* was plainly intended, in the context of pure psychiatric harm, to narrow the range of potential secondary victims. The reasoning of Lord Lloyd and the Law Lords who agreed with him was based on concerns about an ever-widening circle of plaintiffs ...

The employment argument
The majority in the Court of Appeal upheld the argument of counsel for two police officers that they fall into a special category. That argument was again deployed on

appeal to the House. The argument was that the present case can be decided on conventional employer's liability principles. And counsel relies on the undoubted duty of an employer to protect employees from harm through work. It is true that there is no contract between police officers and a chief constable. But it would be artificial to rest a judgment on this point: the relationship between the police officers and the chief constable is closely analogous to a contract of employment. And I am content to approach the problem as if there was an ordinary contract of employment between the parties. Approaching the matter in this way it became obvious that there were two separate themes to the argument. The first rested on the duty of an employer to care for the safety of his employees and to take reasonable steps to safeguard them from harm. When analysed this argument breaks down. It is a non sequitur to say that because an employer is under a duty to an employee not to cause him physical injury, the employer should as a necessary consequence of that duty (of which there is no breach) be under a duty not to cause the employee psychiatric injury ... The rules to be applied when an employee brings an action against his employer for harm suffered at his workplace are the rules of tort. One is therefore thrown back to the ordinary rules of the law of tort which contain restrictions on the recovery of compensation for psychiatric harm. This way of putting the case does not therefore advance the case of the police officers. The duty of an employer to safeguard his employees from harm could also be formulated in contract. In that event, and absent relevant express provisions, a term is implied by law into the contract as an incident of a standardised contract ... But such a term could not be wider in scope than the duty imposed by the law of tort. Again one is thrown back to the ordinary rules of the law of tort. The first way of formulating the argument based on the duty of an employer does not therefore assist the police officers.

The second theme is, on analysis, an argument as to where the justice lay on this occasion. One is considering the claims of police officers who sustained serious psychiatric harm in the course of performing their duties and assisting in harrowing circumstances. That is a weighty moral argument: the police perform their duties for the benefit of us all. The difficulty is, however, twofold. First, the pragmatic rules governing the recovery of damages for pure psychiatric harm do not at present include police officers who sustain such injuries while on duty. If such a category were to be created by judicial decision, the new principle would be available in many different situations, eg doctors and hospital workers who are exposed to the sight of grievous injuries and suffering. Secondly, it is common ground that police officers who are traumatised by something they encounter in their work have the benefit of statutory schemes which permit them to retire on pension. In this sense they are already better off than bereaved relatives who were not allowed to recover in *Alcock*'s case. The claim of the police officers on our sympathy, and the justice of the case, is great but not as great as that of others to whom the law denies redress.

The rescue argument
... The law has long recognised the moral imperative of encouraging citizens to rescue persons in peril. Those who altruistically expose themselves to danger in an emergency to save others are favoured at law. A rescue attempt to save someone from danger will

be regarded as foreseeable. A duty of care to a rescuer may arise even if the defendant owed no duty to the primary victim, for example, because the latter was a trespasser. If a rescuer is injured in a rescue attempt, a plea of *volenti non fit injuria* will not avail a wrongdoer. A plea of contributory negligence will usually receive short shrift. A rescuer's act in endangering himself will not be treated as *novus actus interveniens*. The meaning given to the concept of a rescuer in these situations is of no assistance in solving the concrete case before the House. Here the question is: who may recover in respect of pure psychiatric harm sustained as a rescuer?

Counsel for the appellant is invoking the concept of a rescuer as an exception to the limitations recognised by the House of Lords in *Alcock*'s case and *Page v Smith*. The restrictive rules, and the underlying policy considerations, of the decisions of the House are germane. The specific difficulty counsel faces is that it is common ground that none of the four police officers were at any time exposed to personal danger and none thought that they were so exposed. Counsel submitted that this is not a requirement. He sought comfort in the general observations in *Alcock*'s case of Lord Oliver about the category of 'participants' ... None of the other Law Lords in *Alcock*'s case discussed this category. Moreover, the issue of rescuers' entitlement to recover for psychiatric harm was not before the House on the occasion and Lord Oliver was not considering the competing arguments presently before the House. The explanation of Lord Oliver's observations has been the subject of much debate. It was also vigorously contested at the bar. In my view counsel for the appellant has tried to extract too much from general observations not directed to the issue now before the House ... Counsel was only able to cite one English decision in support of his argument namely the first instance judgment in *Chadwick* ... Mr Chadwick had entered a wrecked railway carriage to help and work among the injured. There was clearly a risk that the carriage might collapse. Waller J ... said ... 'although there was clearly an element of personal danger in what Mr Chadwick was doing, I think I must deal with this case on the basis that it was the horror of the whole experience which caused his reaction.'

On the judge's findings the rescuer had passed the threshold of being in personal danger but his psychiatric injury was caused by 'the full horror of his experience' when he was presumably not always in personal danger. This decision has been cited with approval ... I too would accept that *Chadwick*'s case was correctly decided. But it is not authority for the proposition that a person who never exposed himself to any personal danger and never thought that he was in personal danger can recover pure psychiatric injury as a rescuer. In order to recover compensation for pure psychiatric harm as a rescuer it is not necessary to establish that his psychiatric condition was *caused* by the perception of personal danger. And Waller J rightly so held. But in order to contain the concept of rescuer in reasonable bounds for the purposes of the recovery of compensation for pure psychiatric harm the plaintiff must at least satisfy the threshold requirement that he objectively exposed himself to danger or reasonably believed that he was doing so. Without such limitation one would have the unedifying spectacle that, while bereaved relatives are not allowed to recover as in *Alcock*'s case, ghoulishly curious spectators, who assisted in some peripheral way in the aftermath of a disaster, might recover. For my part the limitation of the actual or apprehended dangers is what proximity in this special situation means. In my judgment it would be an unwarranted extension of the law to uphold the claims of the police officers. I would dismiss the argument under this heading.

Thus far and no further

My Lords, the law on the recovery of compensation for pure psychiatric harm is a patchwork quilt of distinctions which are difficult to justify. There are two theoretical solutions. The first is to wipe out recovery in tort for pure psychiatric injury ... But that would be contrary to precedent and, in any event, highly controversial. Only Parliament could take such a step. The second solution is to abolish all the special limiting rules applicable to psychiatric harm ... Mullany and Handford ... would allow claims for pure psychiatric damage by mere bystanders ... Precedent rules out this course and, in any event, there are cogent policy considerations against such a bold innovation. In my view the only sensible general strategy for the courts is to say thus far and no further. The only prudent course is to treat the pragmatic categories as reflected in authoritative decisions such as *Alcock*'s case and *Page v Smith* as settled for the time being but by and large to leave any expansion or development in this corner of the law to Parliament. In reality there are no refined analytical tools which will enable the courts to draw lines by way of compromise solution in a way which is coherent and morally defensible. It must be left to Parliament to undertake the task of radical law reform ...

> [**Result**: Three Law Lords agreed with **Lord Steyn** as to the employment point; two Law Lords agreed with him on the rescuer point.]

Van Soest v Residual Health Management

[2000] 1 NZLR 179 (CA)

[**FACTS**: The relatives of a number of patients who had died, allegedly as the result of the negligence of the defendant's surgeon, sued the management. The surgeon was Keith Ramstead.]

Blanchard J:

...

[26] We now move to consider whether the next of kin plaintiffs can maintain a common law claim against the defendants. High authority establishes that it is not enough for a plaintiff to show that his or her mental suffering as a secondary victim is a reasonably foreseeable consequence of the defendant's negligence towards the primary victim. Three further matters need to be considered:

(a) The nature of the secondary victim's mental suffering;
(b) The physical proximity of the secondary victim to the primary victim's accident or misadventure; and
(c) The relational proximity (the closeness of the relationship) of the primary and secondary victims.

...

Australia

[45] In Australia the Courts have indicated a willingness to take a more relaxed approach to questions of proximity. However, proof of a psychiatric disorder or illness as a result of a sudden shock has been required.

[46] The leading case is *Jaensch v Coffey* (1984) 155 CLR 549, a decision of the High Court of Australia which was referred to with approval in *Alcock*. A motorcyclist had suffered serious injury in a collision with a vehicle which was being driven negligently.

His wife, who was not at the accident scene, saw him in hospital shortly afterwards and understood that her husband's condition was 'pretty bad'. She was informed by telephone at 5.30 am the next morning that her husband was in intensive care and at 8.30 am that he had had 'a change for the worse' and was requested to come to the hospital as quickly as possible. She stayed at the hospital for much of the day not knowing whether her husband would survive. His condition did, however, gradually improve over the following weeks and he made a full recovery. Some six days after the accident Mrs Coffey began to experience the first symptoms of an anxiety depressant state. Serious psychiatric illness followed. An award of damages to Mrs Coffey was upheld in the High Court. The Court found that she had perceived the aftermath of the accident when at the hospital. Brennan J remarked that a psychiatric illness induced by mere knowledge of a distressing fact is not compensable; perception by the plaintiff of a distressing phenomenon is essential ... But the Judge did not find it desirable as a matter of policy or permissible as a technique of judicial development of the law to create new criteria of limitation upon the scope of the cause of action in negligence causing psychiatric illness.

[47] Deane J said that it was settled law in Australia that there is a distinction, for the purposes of the law of negligence, between mere grief or sorrow which does not sound in damages, and forms of psychoneurosis and mental illness (which lawyers have imprecisely termed 'nervous shock') which may ...

[49] The Judge found it 'somewhat difficult' to discern an acceptable reason why a rule based on public policy should preclude recovery for psychiatric injuries sustained by a wife and mother who was so devastated by being told on the telephone that her husband and children had all just been killed that she was unable to attend at the scene, while permitting recovery for the reasonably, but perhaps less readily, foreseeable psychiatric injury sustained by a wife who attended at the scene of the accident or its aftermath at the hospital when her husband had suffered serious but not fatal injuries ...

[50] In *Spence v Percy* [1992] 2 Qd R 299, the plaintiff was the mother of a woman who was very severely injured in a motor vehicle accident caused by the negligence of the defendants. The daughter was left comatose after the accident and died without any recovery about four years later. The plaintiff suffered shock, anxiety, anguish and general stress through being told of the accident and her daughter's condition and likely death, through first seeing her daughter after the accident in a pitiable state, through tending her daughter during her hospitalisation, through a series of sudden shocks when the daughter had fits in her presence or required emergency medical procedures during her hospitalisation, and finally when the daughter died unexpectedly. After the daughter's death the plaintiff developed a depressive neurotic condition. It was held that the plaintiff was not entitled to recover damages as there was not sufficient causal proximity between the onset of her psychiatric illness and the events of the accident. The plaintiff's injuries were not a result of perceiving the aftermath of the accident.

[51] *Coates v Government Insurance Office of NSW* (1995) 36 NSWLR 1 involved a claim by children of a man killed in a motor accident caused by the negligence of a driver for whom the defendant was legally responsible. They had not seen the accident nor been anywhere near to it at any relevant times. They had not seen the body of their father. Each claimed to have suffered nervous shock as a consequence of being

informed of the father's death. The case turned on a New South Wales statute creating statutory liability for mental or nervous shock, but Kirby P made certain observations which are of general application. The other members of the Court (Gleeson CJ and Clarke JA) were of the opinion that neither appellant was shown to have suffered a recognisable psychiatric illness or injury. Kirby P dissented from that view on the particular facts of the case. He was of the opinion that, provided the requisite factors of foreseeability and proximity were demonstrated, the logic which traditionally prohibits recovery where a plaintiff has been told of the incident and its effects, as opposed to directly perceiving the incident, was unsustainable.

[52] He suggested that it was clearly foreseeable that the young loving children, at least, of a particular person seriously injured or killed would shortly be informed of the injuries or death and might, in certain cases, then suffer such a serious instance of 'nervous shock' as to warrant holding the tortfeasor liable.

[53] Kirby P added that hearing by telephone, or by later oral message, could, in today's world, be just as foreseeable and just as directly related to the wrong sued upon as if the vulnerable observer had received the shocking perception by his or her own eyes and ears at the moment of the relevant wrong. The suggested rule was 'hopelessly out of contact with the modern world of telecommunications.' He said that the law should now recognise that, at least from a medical understanding of the outdated legal denomination of 'nervous shock', it is as much the direct emotional involvement of a plaintiff in an accident or perilous situation, as his or her physical presence at the scene or directly at its aftermath that is pertinent to the level and nature of the injury suffered, and the consequent psychological damage.

[54] Kirby P was also critical of the 'scarcely delineated distinction made between grief and suffering following tragic news and psychological or psychiatric injury.' Even more open to criticism, he said, must be the suggestion that illness resulting from grief, as opposed to shock caused by sight or sound, is not compensable:

> If Courts are to maintain that the requirement for damages is proof of a recognisable psychiatric illness, the existence of that condition is what should matter and not the classification of the initial reaction or catalyst as one either of extreme grief, shock or horror ...

[55] The judgment continues:

> Nineteenth century notions of psychological illness and an abiding suspicion of such claims (not so susceptible to objective scrutiny and determination) lurk in the cases to forbid recovery where prolonged grief is shown, extending beyond the norm deemed acceptable to our society. The changing composition of the Australian community, and different cultural attitudes to the demonstration of profound grief, afford yet another reason for reconsidering this area of the law. To adhere to stereotypes expressed in terms of 'abnormal grief' derived from England, may work an injustice upon Australian litigants for whom the norms are different and grief reaction more variable than was hitherto expressed to be the case.

[56] For his part, Clarke JA found little assistance to be gained from the use of expressions such as 'normal grief' or 'abnormal grief' and said that a Court is concerned to

determine whether on the evidence presented the grief or suffering of a particular plaintiff constituted, or formed part of, a psychological or psychiatric injury (p 19) …

Next of kin claims—conclusions

[65] We are not persuaded that the Courts of this country should depart from the position established in England and also, with isolated dissents, in Australia and Canada, namely that a claim by a secondary victim for mental suffering caused by awareness of death or injury to a primary victim through the negligence of the defendant will not lie unless the effect on the mind of the secondary victim has manifested itself in a recognisable psychiatric disorder or illness. The English Law Commission saw it as a point of significance that psychiatry does draw a distinction between mere mental distress and psychiatric illness, even though the distinction is a matter of degree rather than kind and may change as medical knowledge advances (para 3.33 (1)). Todd (ed) *The Law of Torts in New Zealand* … refers to the psychiatric profession's two diagnostic classification systems which are internationally recognised—the American Diagnostic and Statistical Manual of Mental Disorders and the International Classification of Diseases and Related Health Problems.

[66] We would, like the Law Commission, use the expression 'recognisable' rather than 'recognised'. These expressions seem to mean the same thing, but 'recognisable' perhaps will indicate an awareness by the Court that over time medical experts' views about the nature of particular mental conditions are bound to be subject to some alteration, just as they are with respect to physical ailments. Certainly the law, whilst recognising post traumatic stress disorder, pathological grief syndrome and the like, should not become tied to present day classifications or terminology when in the future our knowledge of the workings of the human mind under conditions of stress becomes greater. If the medical profession as a body is prepared to recognise a particular condition of the mind the Court should be willing to give credence to it as it does to a new virus or physical condition, such as occupational overuse syndrome.

[67] If the Courts are prepared, as they should be, to adopt a receptive attitude to medical evidence about what constitutes a recognisable psychiatric disorder or illness, the law will have a means of determining what kind of mental suffering can properly be the basis for a claim by a secondary victim. But the present plaintiffs have disclaimed any psychiatric injury and, although readily accepting that damages should not be available for every instance of mental suffering caused to a secondary victim, have been quite unable to assist the Court by delineating what degree of distress may or may not be the subject of a claim. Everyone who suffers the sudden loss of a relative with whom he or she has a loving relationship will experience grief, and probably intense grief, either continuously or intermittently over a period weeks and months. Often that grief will never completely fade away. The loss of a child, for example, is always with us. If grief per se is not to be the subject of a claim for damages, and no one seems to suggest that it should be, how can it be determined what degree of grief and its accompanying anger should sound in damages? It is all very well to argue, as Mullany does, that because technically a small cut on the finger caused by the negligence of some person would sustain a claim for damages, albeit nominal only, the Courts should take a similar attitude to the negligent infliction of grief. People do not bother to sue for very minor injuries. Therefore, he says, they will not bother to sue

for minor amounts of grief. With respect, it is naïve to believe that this is how a prospective plaintiff suffering from grief would see the situation. Minor flesh wounds will heal before grief fades. It will be easier to forgive someone who negligently causes us a slight physical injury than to forgive someone who has negligently killed or maimed our loved one.

[68] Whilst a 'floodgates' argument is often to be treated suspiciously, there seems to be good reason to believe that, unless the ability to claim is restricted to situations in which the damage to the secondary victim's mind has been so severe as to produce psychiatric disorder, there will be a flood of claims and that emotionally distressed plaintiffs may not be deterred by the likelihood that damages awards will be modest. It is to be remembered that Lord Bridge's criticism ([in] *McLoughlin*) that the argument has always been 'greatly exaggerated', was made in a case in which the issue was not whether a claim could be made for mental suffering per se. Mrs McLoughlin had undoubtedly suffered a psychiatric injury. The case was about her proximity, not the nature of her condition. And, notwithstanding Lord Bridge's comments, the House of Lords has continued to concern itself with limiting the scope of potential liability in this area ...

[69] It does not seem in the best interests of society either to throw the Courts open to everyone caused distress by the negligent injuring of a loved one or to create the great uncertainty which would result from attempting to limit claims for emotional distress falling short of psychiatric injury by resort to vague epithets such as 'abnormal grief' or 'severe emotional suffering.' Although the shifting boundaries of psychiatric knowledge and the nature of any diagnosis of the workings of the human mind may leave room for uncertainty in an individual case, as of course exists quite often in a diagnosis of physical illness or injury, the Court should in our view deny a damages claim of a secondary victim unless there is proof of a recognisable psychiatric disorder or illness.

[70] The 1992 [Accident Compensation and Rehabilitation] Act uses the term 'mental injury' which it defines (in s 3), in relation to a person, as 'a clinically significant behavioural, psychological, or cognitive dysfunction.' Any such injury is covered under the Act if it is an outcome of physical injuries to that person. It seems to us that this is another way of describing a recognisable psychiatric disorder or illness. There is accordingly a measure of consistency between the cover generally provided under the Act for primary victims and what may be claimed at common law. (Section 8(3), which applies to criminal injuries, uses the term 'mental or nervous shock' which also appears to equate the expression often used in case law.)

[71] As the first, second and fourth plaintiffs do not allege that they experienced any such condition, it must follow that their claims fail and that the Master's decision was correct.

[72] Relational proximity was not a live issue, the plaintiffs being in a very close and loving relationship with the deceased parents (of the first and second plaintiffs) and spouse (of the fourth plaintiff). It seems to us that the position on this question taken by the House of Lords in *Alcock*, and followed in theory if not in practice in the English Courts, can preserve sufficient flexibility. Provided the particular relationship, whether family (*de jure* or *de facto*) or friend, is proven to be close and loving, there will be sufficient relational proximity.

[73] In the circumstances of this case it is unnecessary to express any view on whether a secondary victim may bring a claim for psychiatric injury which is not consequential upon a shocking incident involving actual or threatened injury to a primary victim.

[74] As for physical proximity, we would reserve the position. It may well be that, as the English Law Commission recommends, the restrictions based on physical and temporal proximity to the accident or misadventure and the means by which the plaintiff learnt of it should be removed or relaxed, and that *Alcock* and subsequent English cases will be seen to be unnecessarily restrictive. On this point the criticisms in Kirby P's judgment in *Coates* cannot lightly be dismissed. All that presently needs to be said is that the plaintiffs' next of kin claims are not being struck out for want of physical proximity to the relevant operation and its aftermath ...

Thomas J (concurring in result):
The law is indefensible

[83] For my part ... I would ... abandon the rules dependent on the geographical, temporal and relational proximity of the plaintiff to the accident and accept reasonable foreseeability as the sole test of liability for nervous shock.

...

The fear of 'opening the floodgates'

[89] In my view, the fear that the floodgates will open and flood the Courts is an exaggerated fear. And it is certainly over-used. Any experienced counsel has both advanced and been required to respond to the floodgates argument many times over in the course of his or her career. Judges have had to sit through such arguments on an equal number of occasions. Many Judges have tired of the point. Time and time again it has proved unfounded. The law has advanced and yet the floodgates have not opened. With centuries of development to its credit the law has not yielded one ascertained example of the Courts being inundated with the predicted flood of litigation. It may, of course, be claimed that this outcome is due to the suitably circumspect and cautious approach which the Courts have adopted. To the contrary, however, the absence of actual instances where the floodgates have opened and the dearth of empirical evidence that the Courts have been flooded with litigation following a change in the law would suggest that the judiciary has been cautious to a fault ...

[93] It should not be thought that the jettisoning of the restrictive approach would mean that there was no limitation at all on recovery. A limitation exists in the concept of reasonable foreseeability itself. The harm must be reasonably foreseeable. A negligent wrongdoer is not liable for a consequence which is not foreseeable. The fundamental principle itself provides a safeguard against unrestricted liability.

[94] But, even if the fear that there will be a significant increase in litigation were correct, it would not follow that recovery should be denied for harm which is reasonably foreseeable. The question arises of doing justice by providing a remedy for a wrong. Holt CJ said in *Ashby v White* (1703) 2 Ld Raym 938; 92 ER 126, at 137:

> [I]t is no objection to say, that it will occasion multiplicity of actions; for if men will multiply injuries, actions must be multiplied too; for every man that is injured ought to have his recompense.

...

[117] For myself, however, I would also abandon the requirement that a relational proximity must exist between the trauma victim and a primary victim of the accident. This question can also be best answered in the context of reasonable foreseeability, the relationship of the primary victim to the plaintiff being essentially a matter to be considered and taken into account when determining whether the plaintiff's mental suffering was reasonably foreseeable. Nor should the Courts be side-tracked into deciding whether the plaintiff's relationship with the primary victim is comparable to some other imprecisely delineated relationship when they should be asking the more direct question; was the plaintiff's harm a reasonably foreseeable result of the defendant's negligence?

[118] Further, although adding some flexibility to the law, I cannot accept that the rebuttable presumptions introduced in *Alcock* are helpful. It is presumed that the necessary ties will exist in the case of parents, spouses, and for Lord Keith and Lord Oliver, engaged couples, whilst a negative rebuttable presumption is adopted in respect of siblings, more remote relatives, and friends. Such a categorisation, of course, may be entirely unrealistic in any given circumstances. As Professor Stapleton asks: 'Is it not a disreputable sight to see brothers of Hillsborough victims turned away because they had no more than brotherly love towards the victim?' Recovery, of course, may be possible for a mere bystander who witnesses an exceptionally horrific event. It has been pointed out that the benefits of this modest flexibility must be weighed against the harrowing evidential consequences as plaintiffs try to prove that their love for the victim was strong enough, or the circumstances sufficiently horrific, to justify liability while the defendants attempt to undermine such arguments. Will it not be a grotesque sight to see relatives scrabbling to prove their especial love for the deceased in order to win money damages and for the defendant to have to attack that argument?

Conclusion

[119] As is so often the case, the law relating to nervous shock would become so much more coherent and just if the Courts were prepared to abandon inhibitions born of a past era and revert to fundamental principle. The nineteenth century attitude that non-physical harm was always irrecoverable has been substantially modified over the past century. But full recognition that there is no sound reason why psychiatric injury should not be as compensatible as physical injury, and that mental and emotional harm can be reliably established by psychiatric evidence has not yet informed the law. The consequential fear of a proliferation of claims and an instinctive desire to restrict the scope of recovery has resulted in a law which is in disarray. Such are these inhibitions that the Courts seem to have virtually adjusted to the idea that the law as it stands is the best that can be achieved. Although often recognised, some sort of immunity seems to attach to the arbitrary, illogical and unjust distinctions and requirements which persist. In the result, it is doubtful whether the law in this area will ever be rationalised without the attention of the Law Commission and an Act of Parliament.

[120] Be that as it may, the law could be significantly improved if the Courts were to hold that the sole test for recovery for mental and emotional harm in this area of the law, as in others, is the reasonable foreseeability of that harm. The requirements of geographical, temporal and relational proximity can be safely abandoned. And within

that framework the rule requiring the plaintiff to be suffering from a recognisable psychiatric illness can be relaxed so as to become a general principle, but one which does not preclude plaintiffs from recovering if they are able to demonstrate that, notwithstanding that their mental suffering is not or cannot be identified as a psychiatric illness, their suffering is plainly outside the range of ordinary human experience. Recovery in such cases will not depend on the existence or non-existence of a psychiatric label, and the critical question in issue will not be diverted from the plaintiff's real suffering into a clash of opinion as to whether or not his or her mental and emotional harm constitutes a recognisable psychiatric illness. Eventually, even that requirement may give way to the implementation of the fundamental principle of reasonable foreseeability so that the plaintiff will recover damages if the mental or emotional injury is simply out of the ordinary.

Breach of the duty of care

If a plaintiff owes a duty of care, it is necessary to establish that the defendant has breached that duty. What does this mean? As a practical matter how is this done? Commonwealth lawyers have remained largely convinced that there should not be strict liability; that liability should depend on something more than just causing harm to the plaintiff. This contrasts with much American thinking that strict liability has many advantages over 'negligence' liability, especially in road accident cases or product liability cases. American theorists argue that much of the cost of litigating cases is removed by not requiring a plaintiff to prove negligence or allowing defendants to prove that the defendant did not act negligently. Some also argue that strict liability means that those who undertake activities like supplying water to a city must absorb the costs of the inevitable accidents that result. These costs would then be reflected in the cost of the water supplied and be borne by those who benefit from the supply. See, as a famous example, Calabresi and Hirschoff, 'Toward a Test for Strict Liability' (1971) 81 Yale Law Journal 1055.

As you read the following cases, ask why the judges think that fault is so important and look at how they define fault. What kind of factors do Learned Hand J or Lord Reid think go into determining whether a defendant is at fault? Are those factors the same when people are being injured, as opposed to property? And how does res ipsa loquitur fit into the picture?

The reasonable person standard
Blyth v The Company of Proprietors of the Birmingham Waterworks
(1856) 11 Ex 781 (Ex Ch)
[FACTS: An unprecedented frost caused the fire plug in the defendant's water pipe to come out and as a result a large amount of water flooded into the plaintiff's house.]
Alderson B:
… The case turns upon the question whether the facts proved shew that the defendants were guilty of negligence. Negligence is the omission to do something which a reasonable man, guided upon those considerations which ordinarily regulate the conduct of human affairs, would do, or doing something which a prudent and reasonable

man would not do. The defendants might have been liable for negligence, if unintentionally, they omitted to do that which a reasonable person would have done, or did that which a person taking reasonable precautions would not have done. A reasonable man would act with reference to the average circumstances of the temperature in ordinary years. The defendants had provided against such frosts as experience would have led men, acting prudently, to provide against; and they are not guilty of negligence, because their precautions proved insufficient against the effects of the extreme severity of the frost of 1855, which penetrated to a greater depth than any which ordinarily occurs south of the polar regions. Such a state of circumstances constitutes a contingency against which no reasonable man can provide. The result was an accident, for which the defendants cannot be held liable.

Bramwell B:

The Act of Parliament directed the defendants to lay down pipes, with plugs in them, as safety-valves, to prevent the bursting of the pipes. The plugs were properly made, and of proper material; but there was an accumulation of ice about this plug, which prevented it from acting properly. The defendants were not bound to keep the plugs clear. It appears to me that the plaintiff was under quite as much obligation to remove the ice and snow which had accumulated, as the defendants. However that may be, it appears to me that it would be monstrous to hold the defendants responsible because they did not foresee and prevent an accident, the cause of which was so obscure, that it was not discovered until many months after the accident had happened.

United States v Carroll Towing Co Inc

(1947) 159 F 2d 162 (2nd Circuit)

[**FACTS**: The *Anna C* sunk after a collision resulting from the defendants' failure to retie the unattended barge after they had moved it. Having found the defendants negligent, Judge Learned Hand considered whether the 'bargee' left in charge of the moored barge had been also negligent in leaving the barge unattended and hence guilty of contributory negligence.]

Learned Hand J:

… It appears from the foregoing review that there is no general rule to determine when the absence of a bargee or other attendant will make the owner of the barge liable for injuries to other vessels if she breaks away from her moorings. However, in any cases where he would be so liable for injuries to others, obviously he must reduce his damages proportionately, if the injury is to his own barge. It becomes apparent why there can be no such general rule, when we consider the grounds for such a liability. Since there are occasions when every vessel will break from her moorings, and since, if she does, she becomes a menace to those about her; the owner's duty, as in other similar situations, to provide against resulting injuries is a function of three variables: (1) the probability that she will break away; (2) the gravity of the resulting injury, if she does; (3) the burden of adequate precautions. Possibly it serves to bring this notion into relief to state it in algebraic terms: if the probability be called P; the injury, L; and the burden, B; liability depends upon whether B is less than L multiplied by P: ie, whether $B < PL$. Applied to the situation at bar, the likelihood that a barge will break from her fasts and the damage she will do, vary with the place and time; for example, if a storm threatens, the danger is greater; so it is, if she is in a crowded harbor where moored barges are constantly being shifted about. On the other hand, the barge must not be the bargee's prison, even though he lives aboard; he must go ashore at times. We need not say whether, even in such crowded waters as New York Harbor a bargee must be aboard at night at all; it may be that the custom is otherwise ... and that, if so, the situation is one where custom should control. We leave that question open; but we hold that it is not in all cases a sufficient answer to a bargee's absence without excuse, during working hours, that he has properly made fast his barge to a pier, when he leaves her. In the case at bar the bargee left at five o'clock in the afternoon of January 3rd, and the flotilla broke away at about two o'clock in the afternoon of the following day, twenty-one hours afterwards. The bargee had been away all the time, and we hold that his fabricated story was affirmative evidence that he had no excuse for his absence. At the *locus in quo*—especially during the short January days and in the full tide of war activity—barges were being constantly 'drilled' in and out. Certainly it was not beyond reasonable expectation that, with the inevitable haste and bustle, the work might not be done with adequate care. In such circumstances we hold—and it is all that we do hold—that it was a fair requirement that the Conners Company should have a bargee aboard (unless he had some excuse for his absence), during the working hours of daylight.

Watt v Hertfordshire County Council
[1954] 1 WLR 835 (CA)
[**FACTS**: The plaintiff was employed as a firefighter by the defendants and was on duty when an emergency call was received that a woman was trapped under a heavy vehicle 200 or 300 yards away. The officer in charge instructed the plaintiff's team to transport in a Fordson lorry a jack weighing about two or three hundredweight. The jack was loaded into the back of the lorry and was accompanied by the plaintiff and two other firemen who steadied the jack. The lorry had nothing to which the jack could have been lashed. Shortly after the lorry had left the fire station the driver had to apply the brakes suddenly; all three men were thrown off their balance, the men steadying the jack were unable to hold it, and it harmed the plaintiff.

Three vehicles were in regular use at the fire station. Two were unsuitable for the carriage of the jack, but an Austin tender was properly equipped for the carriage of the jack. The Austin tender was put to other uses and was out of the station and not available for the carriage of the jack during about thirty hours in the week; at the time that the emergency call was received it was not in the station. Emergency calls other than fire calls were fairly frequent at the fire station, but it was rare for the heavy jack to be required, and in the normal course, if the jack was required when the Austin tender was not available to carry it, another station would be notified and would answer the call.]

Singleton LJ:

It is not alleged that there was negligence on the part of any particular individual ... .
The case put forward in this court is that as the defendants had a jack, it was their duty to have a vehicle fitted in all respects to carry that jack, from which it follows, I suppose, that it is said that there must be a vehicle kept at the station at all times, or

that if there is not one the lifting jack must not be taken out; indeed Mr Baker claimed that in the case of a happening such as this, if there was not a vehicle fitted to carry the jack the sub-officer ought to have telephoned to the fire station at St Albans and arranged that they should attend to the emergency. St Albans is some seven miles away, and it was said that an extra ten minutes or so would have elapsed if that had been done. I cannot think that that is the right way to approach the matter.

There was a real emergency; the woman was under a heavy vehicle; these men in the fire service thought that they ought to go promptly and to take a lifting jack, and they did so. Most unfortunately this accident happened.

... Would the reasonably careful head of the station have done anything other than that which the sub-officer did? I think not. Can it be said, then, that there is a duty on the employers here to have a vehicle built and fitted to carry this jack at all times, or if they have not, not to use the jack for a short journey of 200 or 300 yards? I do not think that that will do.

Denning LJ:

It is well settled that in measuring due care you must balance the risk against the measures necessary to eliminate the risk. To that proposition there ought to be added this: you must balance the risk against the end to be achieved. If this accident had occurred in a commercial enterprise without any emergency there could be no doubt that the servant would succeed. But the ... saving of life or limb justifies taking considerable risk ... .

In this case the risk involved in sending out the lorry was not so great as to prohibit the attempt to save life. I quite agree that fire engines, ambulances and doctors' cars should not shoot past the traffic lights when they show a red light. That is because the risk is too great to warrant the incurring of the danger. It is always a question of balancing the risk against the end.

Bolton v Stone
[1951] AC 850 (HL)
Lord Reid:

My Lords, it was readily foreseeable that an accident such as befell the respondent might possibly occur during one of the appellants' cricket matches. Balls had been driven into the public road from time to time and it was obvious that, if a person happened to be where a ball fell, that person would receive injuries which might or might not be serious. On the other hand it was plain that the chance of that happening was small. The exact number of times a ball has been driven into the road is not known, but it is not proved that this has happened more than about six times in about thirty years. If I assume that it has happened on the average once in three seasons I shall be doing no injustice to the respondent's case. Then there has to be considered the chance of a person being hit by a ball falling in the road. The road appears to be an ordinary side road giving access to a number of private houses, and there is no evidence to suggest that the traffic on this road is other than what one might expect on such a road. On the whole of that part of the road where a ball could fall there would often be nobody and seldom any great number of people. It follows that the chance of a person ever being struck even in a long period of years was very small.

This case therefore raises sharply the question what is the nature and extent of the duty of a person who promotes on his land operations which may cause damage to persons on an adjoining highway? Is it that he must not carry out or permit an operation which he knows or ought to know clearly can cause such damage, however improbable that result may be, or is it that he is only bound to take into account the possibility of such damage if such damage is a likely or probable consequence of what he does or permits, or if the risk of damage is such that a reasonable man, careful of the safety of his neighbour, would regard that risk as material?

... I think that reasonable men do in fact take into account the degree of risk and do not act on a bare possibility as they would if the risk were more substantial ... .

Counsel for the respondent in this case had to put his case so high as to say that, at least as soon as one ball had been driven into the road in the ordinary course of a match, the appellants could and should have realized that that might happen again and that, if it did, someone might be injured; and that that was enough to put on the appellants a duty to take steps to prevent such an occurrence. If the true test is foreseeability alone I think that it must be so. Once a ball has been driven on to a road without there being anything extraordinary to account for the fact, there is clearly a risk that another will follow, and if it does there is clearly a chance, small though it may be, that someone may be injured. On the theory that it is foreseeability alone that matters it would be irrelevant to consider how often a ball might be expected to land in the road and it would not matter whether the road was the busiest street, or the quietest country lane; the only difference between these cases is in the degree of risk.

It would take a good deal to make me believe that the law has departed so far from the standards which guide ordinary careful people in ordinary life. In the crowded conditions of modern life even the most careful person cannot avoid creating some risks and accepting others. What a man must not do, and what I think a careful man tries not to do, is to create a risk which is substantial ... . In my judgment the test to be applied here is whether the risk of damage to a person on the road was so small that a reasonable man in the position of the appellants, considering the matter from the point of view of safety, would have thought it right to refrain from taking steps to prevent the danger.

In considering that matter I think that it would be right to take into account not only how remote is the chance that a person might be struck but also how serious the consequences are likely to be if a person is struck; but I do not think that it would be right to take into account the difficulty of remedial measures. If cricket cannot be played on a ground without creating a substantial risk, then it should not be played there at all ... . Oliver J ... considered whether the appellants' ground was large enough to be safe for all practical purposes and held that it was. This is a question not of law but of fact and degree. It is not an easy question and it is one on which opinions may well differ. I can only say that having given the whole matter repeated and anxious consideration I find myself unable to decide this question in favour of the respondent. But I think that this case is not far from the borderline. If this appeal is allowed that does not in my judgment mean that in every case where cricket has been played on a ground for a number of years without accident or complaint those who organize matches there are safe to go on in reliance on past immunity. I would have reached a different conclusion if I had thought that the risk here had been other than extremely small, because I do not think that a reasonable man considering the matter from the point of view of safety would or should disregard any risk unless it is extremely small.

Overseas Tankship (UK) Ltd v The Miller Steamship Co Pty (The Wagon Mound) (No. 2)
[1967] 1 AC 617 (PC)
Lord Reid:

... The appellant was charterer by demise of a vessel, the *Wagon Mound*, which in the early hours of October 30, 1951, had been taking in bunkering oil from Caltex Wharf not far from Sheerlegs Wharf. By reason of carelessness of the *Wagon Mound* engineers a large quantity of this oil overflowed from the *Wagon Mound* onto the surface of the water. Some hours later much of the oil had drifted to and accumulated round Sheerlegs Wharf and the respondents' vessels. About 2 pm on November 1 this oil was set alight: the fire spread rapidly and caused extensive damage to the wharf and to the respondents' vessels ... .

In the course of repairing the respondents' vessel the Morts Dock Co, the owners of Sheerlegs Wharf, were carrying out oxy-acetylene welding and cutting. This work was apt to cause pieces or drops of hot metal to fly off and fall in the sea. So when their manager arrived on the morning of October 30 and saw the thick scum of oil round the wharf he was apprehensive of fire danger and he stopped the work while he took advice. He consulted the manager of Caltex Wharf and after some further consultation he was assured that he was safe to proceed: so he did so, and the repair work was carried on normally until the fire broke out on November 1. Oil of this character with a flash point of 170°F is extremely difficult to ignite in the open. But we now know that that is not impossible. There is no certainty about how this oil was set alight, but the most probable explanation, accepted by Walsh J, is that there was floating in the oil-covered water some object supporting a piece of inflammable material, and that a hot piece of metal fell on it when it burned for a sufficient time to ignite the surrounding oil.

... It is now necessary to turn to the respondents' submissions that the trial judge was wrong in holding that damage from fire was not reasonably foreseeable. In *The Wagon Mound (No. 1)* [[1961] AC 388] the finding on which the Board proceeded was that of the trial judge: 'the defendant did not know and could not reasonably be expected to have known that [the oil] was capable of being set afire when spread on water.' In the present case the evidence led was substantially different from the evidence led in *The Wagon Mound (No. 1)* ... . That is not due to there having been any failure by the plaintiffs in *The Wagon Mound (No. 1)* in preparing and presenting their case. The plaintiffs there were no doubt embarrassed by a difficulty which does not affect the present plaintiffs. The outbreak of the fire was consequent on the act of the manager of the plaintiffs in *The Wagon Mound (No. 1)* in resuming oxy-acetylene welding and cutting while the wharf was surrounded by this oil. So if the plaintiffs in the former case had set out to prove that it was foreseeable by the engineers of the *Wagon Mound* that this oil could be set alight, they might have had difficulty in parrying the reply that this must also have been foreseeable by their manager. Then there would have been contributory negligence and at that time contributory negligence was a complete defence in New South Wales.

Before *Bolton v Stone* the cases had fallen into two classes: (1) those where, before the event, the risk of its happening would have been regarded as unreal either because the event would have been thought to be physically impossible or because the possibility of its happening would have been regarded as so fantastic or far-fetched that no reasonable man would have paid any attention to it—'a mere possibility which would never occur to the mind of a reasonable man' (per Lord Dunedin in *Fardon v Harcourt-Rivington*)—or (2) those where there was a real and substantial risk or chance that something like the event which happens might occur, and then the reasonable man would have taken the steps necessary to eliminate the risk.

Bolton v Stone posed a new problem. There a member of a visiting team drove a cricket ball out of the ground onto an unfrequented adjacent public road and it struck and severely injured a lady who happened to be standing in the road. That it might happen that a ball would be driven onto this road could not have been said to be a fantastic or far-fetched possibility: according to the evidence it had happened about six times in 28 years. And it could not have been said to be a far-fetched or fantastic possibility that such a ball would strike someone in the road: people did pass along the road from time to time. So it could not have been said that, on any ordinary meaning of the words, the fact that a ball might strike a person in the road was not foreseeable or reasonably foreseeable—it was plainly foreseeable. But the chance of its happening in the foreseeable future was infinitesimal. A mathematician given the data could have worked out that it was only likely to happen once in so many thousand years. The House of Lords held that the risk was so small that in the circumstances a reasonable man would have been justified in disregarding it and taking no steps to eliminate it.

But it does not follow that, no matter what the circumstances may be, it is justifiable to neglect a risk of such a small magnitude. A reasonable man would only neglect such a risk if he had some valid reason for doing so, eg, that it would involve considerable expense to eliminate the risk. He would weigh the risk against the difficulty of eliminating it. If the activity which caused the injury to Miss Stone had been an unlawful activity, there can be little doubt but that *Bolton v Stone* would have been decided differently. In their Lordships' judgment *Bolton v Stone* did not alter the general principle that a person must be regarded as negligent if he does not take steps to eliminate a risk which he knows or ought to know is a real risk and not a mere possibility which would never influence the mind of a reasonable man. What that decision did was to recognise and give effect to the qualification that it is justifiable not to take steps to eliminate a real risk if it is small and if the circumstances are such that a reasonable man, careful of the safety of his neighbour, would think it right to neglect it.

In the present case there was no justification whatever for discharging the oil into Sydney Harbour. Not only was it an offence to do so, but it involved considerable loss financially. If the ship's engineer had thought about the matter, there could have been no question of balancing the advantages and disadvantages. From every point of view it was both his duty and his interest to stop the discharge immediately.

It follows that in their Lordships' view the only question is whether a reasonable man having the knowledge and experience to be expected of the chief engineer of the *Wagon Mound* would have known that there was a real risk of the oil on the water catching fire in some way: if it did, serious damage to ships or other property was not only foreseeable but very likely. Their Lordships do not dissent from the view of the trial judge that the possibilities of damage 'must be significant enough in a practical sense to require a reasonable man to guard against them.' ... In this difficult chapter of the law decisions are not infrequently taken to apply to circumstances far removed from the facts which gave rise to them and it would seem that here too much reliance has been placed on some observations in *Bolton v Stone* and similar observations in other cases.

In their Lordships' view a properly qualified and alert chief engineer would have realised there was a real risk here and they do not understand Walsh J to deny that. But he appears to have held that if a real risk can properly be described as remote it must then be held to be not reasonably foreseeable ... . [T]heir Lordships cannot accept this view. If a real risk is one which would occur to the mind of a reasonable man in the position of the defendant's servant and which he would not brush aside as far-fetched, and if the criterion is to be what that reasonable man would have done in the circumstances, then surely he would not neglect such a risk if action to eliminate it presented no difficulty, involved no disadvantage, and required no expense.

In the present case the evidence shows that the discharge of so much oil onto the water must have taken a considerable time, and a vigilant ship's engineer would have noticed the discharge at an early stage. The findings show that he ought to have known that it is possible to ignite this kind of oil on water, and that the ship's engineer probably ought to have known that this had in fact happened before. The most that can be said to justify inaction is that he would have known that this could only happen in very exceptional circumstances. But that does not mean that a reasonable man would dismiss such a risk from his mind and do nothing when it was so easy to prevent it. If it is clear that the reasonable man would have realised or foreseen and prevented the risk, then it must follow that the appellant is liable in damages.

Problems

I   The Erewhon Golf Course backs on to a road. The course is organised so that only an extremely incompetent golfer could slice the ball so that it hits a passing car. This happens, say, once a year. The cost of building a fence that would completely remove the risk is, say, $50 000, which the golf club cannot afford. Similarly, redesigning the course would cost over $100 000. The inevitable happens: a member's guest slices the ball, which smashes into a passing BMW, breaking the windscreen, causing a crash that makes the car a write-off. Can the motorist sue either the golfer or the Erewhon golf club?

Goldman v Hargrave
[1967] 1 AC 645 (PC)

[**FACTS**: There was an electrical storm on 25 February 1961, and a tall redgum tree was struck by lightning and caught fire. It was impossible to deal with the blaze while the tree was standing so the appellant telephoned the district fire control officer and asked for a tree feller to be sent. Pending his arrival the appellant cleared combustible material away from the tree and sprayed the surrounding area with water. The tree feller arrived at midday on Sunday, 26 February, at which time the tree was burning fiercely; he cut down the tree. If the appellant had taken reasonable care he could have put out the fire with the use of water that evening (26 February) or the next morning. The appellant instead decided to let the fire burn itself out. On Wednesday, 1 March, there was a change in the weather. The fire revived and spread onto the respondents' properties.]

Lord Wilberforce:

... The result of the evidence, in their Lordships' opinions, is that the appellant both up to February 26 and thereafter was endeavouring to extinguish the fire; that initially he acted with prudence, but that there came a point, about the evening of February 26 or the morning of February 27, when, the prudent and reasonable course being to put the fire out by water, he chose to adopt the method of burning it out. That method was, according to the finding of the trial judge, unreasonable, or negligent in the circumstances: it brought a fresh risk into operation, namely, the risk of a revival of the fire, under the influence of changing wind and weather, if not carefully watched, and it was from this negligence that the damage arose. That a risk of this character was foreseeable by someone in the appellant's position was not really disputed ...

This ... case is not one where a person has brought a source of danger onto his land, nor one where an occupier has so used his property as to cause a danger to his neighbour. It is one where an occupier, faced with a hazard accidentally arising on his land, fails to act with reasonable prudence so as to remove the hazard ... . What is the standard of the effort required? What is the position as regards expenditure? It is not enough to say merely that these must be 'reasonable,' since what is reasonable to one man may be very unreasonable, and indeed ruinous, to another: the law must take account of the fact that the occupier on whom the duty is cast has, *ex hypothesi*, had this hazard thrust upon him through no seeking or fault of his own. His interest, and his resources, whether physical or material, may be of a very modest character either in relation to the magnitude of the hazard, or as compared with those of his threatened neighbour. A rule which required of him in such unsought circumstances in his neighbour's interest a physical effort of which he is not capable, or an excessive expenditure of money, would be unenforceable or unjust. One may say in general terms that the existence of a duty must be based upon knowledge of the hazard, ability to foresee the consequences of not checking or removing it, and the ability to abate it. And in many cases ... where the hazard could have been removed with little effort and no expenditure, no problem arises. But other cases may not be so simple. In such situations the standard ought to be to require of the occupier what it is reasonable to expect of him in his individual circumstances. Thus, less must be expected of the infirm than of the able-bodied: the owner of a small property where a hazard arises which threatens a neighbour with substantial interests should not have to do so much as one with larger interests of his own at stake and greater resources to protect them: if the small owner does what he can and promptly calls on his neighbour to provide additional resources, he may be held to have done his duty: he should not be liable unless it is clearly proved that he could, and reasonably in his individual circumstance should, have done more ... . In the present case it has not been argued that the action necessary to put the fire out on February 26–27 was not well within the capacity and resources of the appellant. Their Lordships therefore reach the conclusion that the respondents' claim for damages, on the basis of negligence, was fully made out.

Nettleship v Weston
[1971] 3 All ER 581 (CA)
Lord Denning MR

...

[**Note**: Lord Denning MR considered the liability of Mrs Weston who had lost control of her car, injuring her instructor.]

...

The responsibility of the learner-driver towards persons on or near the highway

Mrs Weston is clearly liable for the damage to the lamp-post. In the civil law if a driver goes off the road on to the pavement and injures a pedestrian, or damages property, he is *prima facie* liable. Likewise if he goes on to the wrong side of the road. It is no answer for him to say: 'I was a learner-driver under instruction. I was doing my best and could not help it.' The civil law permits no such excuse. It requires of him the same standard of care as any other driver. 'It eliminates the personal equation and is independent of the idiosyncrasies of the particular person whose conduct is in question': see *Glasgow Corpn v Muir* [1943] 2 All ER 44, 48 per Lord Macmillan. The learner-driver may be doing his best, but his incompetent best is not good enough. He must drive in as good a manner as a driver of skill, experience and care, who is sound in wind and limb, who makes no errors of judgment, has good eyesight and hearing, and is free from any infirmity ...

The high standard thus imposed by the judges is, I believe, largely the result of the policy of the Road Traffic Acts. Parliament requires every driver to be insured against third-party risks. The reason is so that a person injured by a motor-car should not be left to bear the loss on his own, but should be compensated out of the insurance fund. The fund is better able to bear it than he can. But the injured person is only able to recover if the driver is liable in law. So the judges see to it that he is liable, unless he can prove care and skill of a high standard ... Thus we are, in this branch of the law, moving away from the concept: 'No liability without fault'. We are beginning to apply the test: 'On whom should the risk fall?' Morally the learner-driver is not at fault; but legally she is liable to be because she is insured and the risk should fall on her.

Bolam v Friern Hospital Management Committee
[1957] 1 WLR 582 (QB)
[**FACTS**: During ECT shock treatment for depression, Bolam suffered a fracture as result of a muscle convulsion. He sued the hospital, claiming that as well as not having been properly informed of the risks he should have been given a muscle relaxant and/or been more fully restrained.]

McNair J:

Members of the jury, it is now my task to try to help you to reach a true verdict, bearing in mind that you take the law from me and that the facts are entirely a matter for your consideration. You will only give damages if you are satisfied that the defendants have been proved to be guilty of negligence … .

Before I turn to that, I must tell you what in law we mean by 'negligence.' In the ordinary case which does not involve any special skill, negligence in law means a failure to do some act which a reasonable man in the circumstances would do, or the doing of some act which a reasonable man in the circumstances would not do; and if that failure or the doing of that act results in injury, then there is a cause of action. How do you test whether this act or failure is negligent? In an ordinary case it is generally said you judge it by the action of the man in the street. He is the ordinary man. In one case it has been said you judge it by the conduct of the man on the top of a Clapham omnibus. He is the ordinary man. But where you get a situation which involves the use of some special skill or competence, then the test as to whether there has been negligence or not is not the test of the man on the top of a Clapham omnibus, because he has not got this special skill. The test is the standard of the ordinary skilled man exercising and professing to have that special skill. A man need not possess the highest expert skill; it is well-established law that it is sufficient if he exercises the ordinary skill of an ordinary competent man exercising that particular art. I do not think that I quarrel much with any of the submissions in law which have been put before you by counsel. Mr Fox-Andrews put it in this way, that in the case of a medical man, negligence means failure to act in accordance with the standards of reasonably competent medical men at the time. That is a perfectly accurate statement, as long as it is remembered that there may be one or more perfectly proper standards: and if he conforms with one of those proper standards, then he is not negligent. Mr Fox-Andrews also was quite right, in my judgment, in saying that a mere personal belief that a particular technique is best is no defence unless that belief is based on reasonable grounds. That again is unexceptionable. But the emphasis which is laid by the defence is on this aspect of negligence, that the real question you have to make up your minds about on each of the three major topics is whether the defendants, in acting in the way they did, were acting in accordance with a practice of competent respected professional opinion.

… I myself would prefer to put it in this way, that he is not guilty of negligence if he has acted in accordance with a practice accepted as proper by a responsible body of medical men skilled in that particular art. I do not think there is much difference in sense. It is just a different way of expressing the same thought. Putting it the other way round, a man is not negligent, if he is acting in accordance with such a practice, merely because there is a body of opinion who would take a contrary view. At the same time, that does not mean that a medical man can obstinately and pig-headedly carry on with the same old technique if it has been proved to be contrary to what is really substantially the whole of informed medical opinion. Otherwise you might get men today saying: 'I do not believe in anaesthetics. I do not believe in antiseptics. I am going to continue to do my surgery in the way it was done in the eighteenth century.' That clearly would be wrong.

Before I get to the details of the case, it is right to say this, that it is not essential for you to decide which of two practices is the better practice, as long as you accept that what the defendants did was in accordance with a practice accepted by responsible persons; if the result of the evidence is that you are satisfied that his practice is better than the practice spoken of on the other side, then it is really a stronger case. Finally, bear this in mind, that you are now considering whether it was negligent for certain action to be taken in August, 1954, not in February, 1957; and in one of the well-known cases on this topic it has been said you must not look with 1957 spectacles at what happened in 1954 ... .

I now pass to what I venture to believe is the real point which you have to consider, or the two real points you have to consider: Was it negligent, in the sense which I have indicated not to use relaxants? It is really a double point: Was it negligent not to use relaxants and, if no relaxants were used, was it negligent to fail to use manual control? But it is easier to take them separately. On the plaintiff's side, the argument is put this way, that if relaxants had been used, it is common ground that the risk of fracture in the operation would, to all intents and purposes, be excluded; therefore it ought to be excluded. On the other hand, the defendants say: 'It is really not as simple as that.' They say: 'The risk of fracture without relaxants is really minimal, although if it does occur, of course, to the individual patient it may be very serious, but the actual risk is minimal. But there is also, in the use of relaxants with an anaesthetic, another risk which has got to be balanced against it, and that is the mortality risk.' They say: 'forming a judgment as best we can as medical men, balancing what we believe to be a remote risk of fracture on the one hand with what we believe to be a remote risk of mortality on the other hand, we, as a matter of professional skill, have decided not to use relaxants except in cases where there is something special in the man's condition which indicates that a relaxant should be used.' For instance, if a man has had a recent fracture or is suffering from some arthritic condition, or hernia, they say: 'We would use relaxants merely to avoid the greater risk of straight ECT in those particular cases, but we select the cases for relaxants by the exercise of our clinical judgment.'

[**Note**: His Honour reviewed the evidence on this issue summarised above and continued.]

... On that body of evidence, is it open to you to say that mere failure to give relaxants is itself any evidence of negligence in the case of a medical man? There is a firm body of opinion against using relaxants as a routine, and there is agreement from all the witnesses that there is this body of opinion, although one (Dr Randall) prefers to take the risk of relaxants and thus eliminate the risk of fractures. That is all I will say to you on that.

Now we come to the question of manual control. It is urged by the plaintiff: 'If you do not use relaxants, which you know will eliminate all risk of fracture, the least you can do is to exercise some form of manual control. You did not use any manual control, and this disaster happened.' Here again the defendants say you are in the realm of two schools of thought. They say: 'There is a school of thought, to which we adhere, which believes honestly, on reasonable grounds, that if you definitely hold a man down firm, either with a restraining sheet or by a nurse lying over his body or holding him down firmly, you do in fact increase the risk of fracture.' They hold that view; and, holding that view, they, since the end of 1951, have adopted a new technique of leaving the limbs free to move, except that the man is held down at the shoulders and a nurse stands on either side of the couch ready to catch the man if he shows any sign of falling off.

Dr Randall, called on behalf of the plaintiff, was quite definitely of the opinion, a personal opinion which he said was shared by others, that some manual control was necessary. Indeed, it is not disputed by the defendants, that some people think that manual control is desirable. But Dr Randall was asked: 'In your view, would a practitioner in this art of ordinary competence in 1954 have administered this treatment without any precaution?' said 'It is the opinion of some people that restraint is not indicated; but I would not have given the treatment without some form of restraint. (Q) There is a school of thought who would take a different view? (A) Yes. (McNair J): And who would give ECT without any restraint? (A) Yes, my Lord.'

[**Note**: His Honour referred to the evidence of Dr Randall and continued.]

That is the view of a skilled person whose evidence you have heard, and you have to form your judgment as to how far he was merely expressing a personal view in favour of the practice which he preferred, or to what extent (if at all) he was condemning the practice advocated by the defendants. But, as against that, you have got to weigh the whole body of opinion represented by the witnesses called by the defendants. Dr Bastarrechea was quite definite in his view that since he changed over to the use of no manual control after 1951, a decision which he took as a matter of clinical judgment, he got the impression that the fracture risk at any rate had not increased. He had got the impression that it had diminished. He had not at that time got out the figures, merely basing that judgment upon his clinical experience and on discussions with colleagues.

[**Note**: His Honour reviewed the evidence on this issue and continued.]

... Dr Allfrey dealt with this matter. I have not said anything about Dr Allfrey in detail, though he is primarily the man under attack, for it was during his operation that the disaster occurred. You have got to form your judgment of Dr Allfrey, and make up your minds whether you think that he was a careful practitioner interested in his art, giving thought to the different problems, or whether he was a man who was quite content just to follow the swim. You may recall that on quite a number of occasions in the course of his evidence he gave instances where he had really applied his inquiring mind to the problem and come to a conclusion. On the use of restraint, he told you that during his training he knew that there was a school of thought that favoured restraint, but that he got the impression that the general view was against it. He recalls how he was taught by the man responsible for his training that there was a greater danger of fracture if two ends of a rigid member like a stick were held firm than if one was left swinging or both were left swinging, and that rather persuaded him that there was something in the view that restraint should not be used. At Knole Hospital he adopted under tuition (and, as he got older, on his own responsibility) the practice of leaving the limbs free to move, merely holding down the shoulders. When he got to Friern he found the same practice was being carried out by his chief there, Dr Bastarrechea. Having had his technique shown to him, he followed it. The question you have got to make up your minds about is whether he is, in following that practice, doing something which no competent medical practitioner using due care would do, or whether, on the other hand, he is acting in accordance with a perfectly well-recognized school of thought. Dr Marshall of Netherne adopts the same practice. Dr Baker at Banstead adopts the same practice. It is true, and in fact interesting as showing the diversity of practice, that Dr Page at the Three Counties mental institution adopts a modification of that, inasmuch as he prefers to carry out the treatment in bed, with the patient controlled to some extent by the blanket, sheets and counterpane. That may be of interest to you as showing the diversity of practice; but it would not be right, would it, to take that as a condemnation of the practice adopted by the defendants?

Res ipsa loquitur

Scott v London & St Katherine Docks Co
[1861–1873] All ER Rep 246; (1865) 3 H & C 596 (Ex Ch)
Erle CJ:
There must be reasonable evidence of negligence. But where the thing is shown to be under the management of the defendant or his servants, and the accident is such as in the ordinary course of things does not happen if those who have the management use proper care, it affords reasonable evidence, in the absence of explanation by the defendants, that the accident arose from want of care.

Hawke's Bay Motor Co Ltd v Russell
[1972] NZLR 542 (SC)
[**FACTS**: The appellant's motor coach was proceeding around a bend and was struck by a car driven by the respondent. The appellant's vehicle was completely on the correct side of the road. The respondent failed to negotiate the bend and proceeded on his incorrect side where the collision occurred. The appellant sued for its uninsured losses of $849.60.]
Beattie J:
The respondent's defence before the Magistrate was that he had or may have had a 'turn' or 'blackout' immediately before the collision and that this condition was the reason for his vehicle proceeding directly ahead towards the motor coach instead of taking the left-hand bend. The Magistrate has found that this medical condition derives support from the evidence of Dr Bergin, neurologist … .

The appellant invoked the doctrine of *res ipsa loquitur* and, further, alleged failure to keep properly to the left and failing to keep a proper look out.

Looking a little more closely at the evidence, as counsel invited me to, the evidence of the coach driver was that he had reached the brow of the hill when he saw a vehicle coming straight up the road, up the hill, and it was travelling pretty fast. He said this vehicle which was in the middle of the road, made no attempt whatsoever to negotiate the corner and went straight into him. Later he said, as he saw it, it was correct that the car was simply following a straight course without taking the bend at all. Such evidence immediately raised the doctrine and the respondent, indeed, conceded it was a proper case for invoking the doctrine but claimed that the cause of the collision was a blackout attributable to an aneurysm and that the respondent could not have reasonably been aware of such a condition before the accident ... .

Dr Bergin ... considered that one of the 'turns' would be a very adequate explanation for the accident. Under cross-examination he agreed the fact that the respondent did nothing to prevent the accident could be equally consistent with inattentiveness as with his having a 'turn', but he said he was impressed (when he heard of it) by the failure to react ... . When pressed further, Dr Bergin said 'the aneurysm is just in the right place for the particular variety of turn which the respondent has'.

With this background, the Magistrate found there was in fact a failure to keep left, but that this head of negligence, as well as failing to keep a proper look out, would be destroyed if the respondent's physical condition were such if, at the relevant moment, his mental faculties were through no fault of his own not operative and that a similar fate could befall the *res ipsa loquitur* plea. On the evidence, it seemed to the Magistrate that he must accept the reasonable possibility that the respondent was in the act of suffering a 'turn' and, to use his words, 'it can be no more than a reasonable possibility and something less than a reasonable probability'.

The important question before the Magistrate concerned the extent of the *res ipsa loquitur* rule ... . I quote his judgment ... .

> It must frequently happen that in such circumstances without evidence from a defendant, the inference of negligence would be irresistible. But if evidence is adduced, as in the present case, whether by the defendant or otherwise, which weakens the inference from the *res* then it seems to me to be a matter for the Court to consider on the probabilities, whether negligence has been, in fact, on the whole of the evidence established. The burden of proof may often shift, or appear to shift in any evidentiary way, during the course of a hearing but nevertheless the onus does not as a matter of law shift to the defendant. If, therefore, the applicability or otherwise of the rule does not require affirmative disproof on the probabilities then, while the plaintiff has shown beyond any shadow of any doubt that the defendant's vehicle went on to its incorrect side of the highway and struck the coach, nevertheless, ... I cannot say on the probabilities that the plaintiff has shown the defendant to be negligent.

In claiming the Magistrate was wrong in law the appellant ... argued that he who avers must prove, so that the respondent should have proved as a fact on the balance of probabilities his mental faculties failed him and that this standard was not achieved ... .

Undoubtedly there is a conflict of judicial opinion as to the extent of the *res ipsa* rule ... .

Although the tide of authority has ebbed and flowed in various parts of the Commonwealth I am of the same view as the Magistrate that the legal burden of proof does not shift to a defendant where the maxim applies. Is it not really a question of the effect certain pieces of evidence may have on the Court during the course of hearing, rather than a shifting of the final burden of proof?

Salmond on Torts 15th edn suggests the burden remains with the plaintiff but at p 310 refers to the contrary view, which in a footnote is claimed to be the prevailing view in New Zealand. The author says:

But if this latter view were adopted, it would mean that a plaintiff who establishes a prima facie case by invoking the maxim would be in a stronger position than one who made out a prima facie case in another way.

Fleming on Torts 4th edn 259 refers to the 'persuasion' concept where in negligence litigation the legal or ultimate burden ordinarily lies on the plaintiff and remains with him to persuade the trier of fact that on all the evidence the balance of probability preponderates in his favour. The plaintiff having established a prima facie case, he crosses the threshold, being no longer vulnerable to a non-suit, and at that point the 'provisional', 'evidential' or 'burden of going forward with the evidence' shifts to the defendant in the sense he stands the risk of a verdict against him. As the author says, accordingly as the trial proceeds, the balance may tilt to and fro so that, at any given point, one or the other party faces the risk of a probably, but not necessarily, adverse verdict until eventually the trier of fact will have to conclude whether the balance preponderates in favour of the plaintiff. Then so far as the effect of this proposition on the maxim is concerned *Fleming* at p 267 says that if there are two hypotheses that might account for the accident, one consistent, the other inconsistent with the defendant's negligence, and both are evenly poised, the plaintiff has not discharged the onus incumbent on him of proving the issue on a preponderating balance.

Clerk and Lindsell on Torts 13th edn para 372 takes the opposite view to *Salmond*. It is true that apart from Gresson J in *Voice*'s and *Heywood*'s cases, support for the shifting onus principle may be found in *F Maeder Pty Ltd v Wellington City Corporation* [1969] NZLR 222. However, in my respectful opinion, Roper J had really no alternative possibility to the inference of negligence and apparently was not referred to the decision of Henry J in *Watson v Davidson* or the decisions of the Australian High Court where judgments in four cases all reach the same conclusion as occurs in the preponderance of New Zealand cases, namely, that the burden does not shift … .

Being of the opinion that the Magistrate correctly decided that the legal burden of proof in the sense I have endeavoured to explain remained with the respondent, I turn to consider whether on the facts it was proper to find that the plaintiff had not discharged that onus.

The basic fact proved by the appellant was the respondent's failure to keep to the left but there was no direct evidence as to the cause of that failure. The plaintiff by adducing that evidence took the case to the point where the Court could infer negligence and while the appellant could not be non-suited it had by no means then achieved an entrenched position. The Magistrate dealt with the matter step by step, giving the 'res' its proper place. He considered the defence and related evidence of the respondent's turn, describing it as a 'reasonable possibility'. I take that to mean in the context of this case as acceptable or adequate evidence to displace the prima facie inference of negligence. I cannot agree with the contention that if one explanation is described as a possibility then some competing contention must be a probable one, because the fallacy in that argument to my mind is there may be several reasons, possibly none of which tips the scales in its own favour to become a probability. That was the Magistrate's conclusion here that on the totality of the evidence he was left undecided on the probabilities. Put another way, at the end of the case, he was left in doubt because neither of the two possibilities, *viz* negligence or the suffering of a 'turn' appealed to him as a greater probability than the other. It was therefore in this sense he used the word 'possibility'.

The damage requirement

What does it mean to say that the defendant has caused harm to the defendant? This section deals with three different aspects of the question. The first, raised by the *Barnett* case, is how we go about determining whether in fact the defendant caused the plaintiff's loss. If that is established, the next issue, raised by *The Wagon Mound (No. 1)*, is whether that defendant should recover all loss resulting from the plaintiff's negligence or whether some damage is not recoverable, because as lawyers might say, it is too remote. The third question, dealt with by *Lamb* and *Littlewoods*, is that raised by *Dorset Yacht*, of when can a defendant be liable for harm caused by others? Consider how each judge uses the notion of 'cause' and how it alters from case to case.

Cause-in-fact
Barnett v Chelsea and Kensington Hospital Management Committee
[1969] 1 QB 428
[**FACTS**: At a hospital casualty department, provided and run by the defendants, three men arrived and complained to a nurse on duty that they had been vomiting for three hours after drinking tea. The nurse reported their complaints by telephone to the duty medical casualty officer, who thereupon instructed her to tell the men to go home to bed and call in their own doctors. That she did. The men then left, and about five hours later, one of them died from poisoning by arsenic in the tea. His widow claimed that the death resulted from the defendants' negligence in not diagnosing or treating his condition when he presented himself at the casualty department.]
Nield J:

… It remains to consider whether it is shown that the deceased's death was caused by that negligence or whether, as the defendants have said, the deceased must have died in any event … . If the principal condition is one of enzyme disturbance—as I am of the view it was here—then the only method of treatment which is likely to succeed is the use of the specific antidote which is commonly called BAL. Dr Goulding said in the course of his evidence:

> The only way to deal with this is to use the specific BAL. I see no reasonable prospect of the deceased being given BAL before the time at which he died.

… I find that the plaintiff has failed to establish, on the balance of probabilities, that the defendants' negligence caused the death of the deceased.

'Remoteness'
Overseas Tankship (UK) Ltd v Morts Dock & Engineering Co Ltd (The Wagon Mound) (No. 1)
[1961] AC 388 (PC)

[**FACTS**: While a vessel, of which the appellants were the charterers, was taking in bunkering oil in Sydney Harbour, a large quantity of the oil was, through the carelessness of the appellants' servants, allowed to spill into the harbour. The oil caught fire and seriously damaged the respondents' nearby wharf.

In an action by the respondents to recover compensation for the damage it was found by the trial judge that the appellants 'did not know and could not reasonably be expected to have known that it [the furnace oil] was capable of being set afire when spread on water'; and that apart from the damage by fire, the respondents had suffered some damage in that oil had congealed upon and interfered with the use of their slipways, 'damage which beyond question was a direct result of the escape of the oil'.]

Viscount Simonds:

... It is inevitable that first consideration should be given to the case of *In re Polemis and Furness Withy & Co Ltd* which will henceforward be referred to as *Polemis* ... .

[T]he Court of Appeal held that the charterers were responsible for all the consequences of their negligent act even though those consequences could not reasonably have been anticipated. The negligent act was nothing more than the carelessness of stevedores (for whom the charterers were assumed to be responsible) in allowing a sling or rope by which it was hoisted to come into contact with certain boards, causing one of them to fall into the hold. The falling board hit some substances in the hold and caused a spark: the spark ignited petrol vapour in the hold: there was a rush of flames, and the ship was destroyed. The special case submitted by the arbitrators found that the causing of the spark could not reasonably have been anticipated from the falling of the board, though some damage to the ship might reasonably have been anticipated. They did not indicate what damage might have been so anticipated.

There can be no doubt that the decision of the Court of Appeal in *Polemis* plainly asserts that, if the defendant is guilty of negligence, he is responsible for all the consequences whether reasonably foreseeable or not. The generality of the proposition is perhaps qualified by the fact that each of the Lords Justices refers to the outbreak of fire as the direct result of the negligent act. There is thus introduced the conception that the negligent actor is not responsible for consequences which are not 'direct' whatever that may mean.

... Enough has been said to show that the authority of *Polemis* has been severely shaken though lip-service has from time to time been paid to it. In their Lordships' opinion it should no longer be regarded as good law. It is not probable that many cases will for that reason have a different result, though it is hoped that the law will be thereby simplified, and that in some cases, at least, palpable injustice will be avoided. For it does not seem consonant with current ideas of justice or morality that for an act of negligence, however slight or venial, which results in some trivial foreseeable damage the actor should be liable for all consequences however unforeseeable and however grave, so long as they can be said to be 'direct'. It is a principle of civil liability, subject only to qualifications which have no present relevance, that a man must be considered to be responsible for the probable consequences of his act. To demand more of him is too harsh a rule; to demand less is to ignore that civilised order requires the observance of a minimum standard of behaviour.

This concept applied to the slowly developing law of negligence has led to a great variety of expressions which can, as it appears to their Lordships, be harmonised with little difficulty with the single exception of the so-called rule in *Polemis*. For, if it is asked why a man should be responsible for the natural or necessary or probable consequences of his act (or any other similar description of them) the answer is that it is not because they are natural or necessary or probable, but because, since they have this quality, it is judged by the standard of the reasonable man that he ought to have foreseen them. Thus it is that over and over again it has happened that in different judgments in the same case, and sometimes in a single judgment, liability for a consequence has been imposed on the ground that it was reasonably foreseeable or, alternatively, on the ground that it was natural or necessary or probable. The two grounds have been treated as coterminous, and so they largely are. But, where they are not, the question arises to which the wrong answer was given in *Polemis*. For, if some limitation must be imposed upon the consequences for which the negligent actor is to be held responsible—and all are agreed that some limitation there must be—why should that test (reasonable foreseeability) be rejected which, since he is judged by what the reasonable man ought to foresee, corresponds with the common conscience of mankind, and a test (the 'direct' consequence) be substituted which leads to nowhere but the never-ending and insoluble problems of causation.

Hughes v Lord Advocate
[1963] AC 837 (HL)
Lord Guest:
The Lord Ordinary, after a very careful analysis of the evidence, has found that the cause of the explosion was as a result of the lamp which the appellant knocked into the hole being so disturbed that paraffin escaped from the tank, formed vapour and was ignited by the flame. The lamp was recovered from the manhole after the accident; the tank of the lamp was half out and the wick-holder was completely out of the lamp. This explanation of the accident was rated by the experts as a low order of probability. But as there was no other feasible explanation, it was accepted by the Lord Ordinary, and this House must take it as the established cause.

The Lord Ordinary has held that the presence of children in the shelter and in the manhole ought reasonably to have been anticipated by the Post Office employees. His ground for so holding was that the lighted lamps in the public street adjacent to a tented shelter in which there was an open manhole provided an allurement which would have been an attraction to children passing along the street.

I pause here to observe that the respondent submitted an argument before the Division and repeated in this House that, having regard to the evidence, the presence of children in Russell Road on that day, which was a Saturday, could not reasonably have been anticipated ... . Having regard to the fact that this was a public street in the heart of the city there was no necessity, in my view, for the appellant to prove the likelihood of children being present. If the respondent had to establish the unlikelihood of the presence of children, his evidence fell far short of any such situation. It was entirely dependent on the experience of the Post Office employees during the preceding five days of the week. They had no previous experience of traffic at any other time. The Lord Ordinary, in my view, was well entitled to reach the conclusion which he did.

The next step in the Lord Ordinary's reasoning was that it was reasonable to anticipate that danger would be likely to result from the children's interference with the red lamps and their entrance to the shelter. He has further held that in these circumstances 'the normal dangers of such children falling into the manhole or being in some way injured by a lamp, particularly if it fell or broke, were such that a reasonable man would not have ignored them.' This view of the evidence was not, as I read the judgments, dissented from in the Inner House. Reference may be particularly made to Lord Guthrie's remarks, where he says: 'The Lord Ordinary had held that it should have been anticipated that a boy might in the circumstances fall into the manhole and sustain injuries by burning from the paraffin lamp.' It seems to have been accepted by both parties in the hearing before the Division that burning injuries might reasonably have been foreseen. But whether this be the position, there was ample evidence upon which the conclusion could be drawn that there was a reasonable probability of burning injuries if the children were allowed into the shelter with the lamp.

The Solicitor-General endeavoured to limit the extent of foreseeability in this connection by reference to certain passages in the evidence regarding the safety of the red paraffin lamps. It might very well be that paraffin lamps by themselves, if left in the open, are not potentially dangerous even to children. But different considerations apply when they are found in connection with a shelter tent and a manhole, all of which are allurements to the inquisitive child. It is the combination of these factors which renders the situation one of potential danger.

In dismissing the appellant's claim the Lord Ordinary and the majority of the judges of the First Division reached the conclusion that the accident which happened was not reasonably foreseeable. In order to establish a coherent chain of causation it is not necessary that the precise details leading up to the accident should have been reasonably foreseeable: it is sufficient if the accident which occurred is of a type which should have been foreseeable by a reasonably careful person ... or as Lord Mackintosh expressed it in the *Harvey* case ... [[1960] SC 135, 172] the precise concatenation of circumstances need not be envisaged. Concentration has been placed in the courts below on the explosion which, it was said, could not have been foreseen because it was caused in a unique fashion by the paraffin forming into vapour and being ignited by the naked flame of the wick. But this, in my opinion, is to concentrate on what is really a non-essential element in the dangerous situation created by the allurement. The test might better be put thus: Was the igniting of paraffin outside the lamp by the flame a foreseeable consequence of the breach of duty? In the circumstances, there was a combination of potentially dangerous circumstances against which the Post Office had to protect the appellant. If these formed an allurement to children it might have been foreseen that they would play with the lamp, that it might tip over, that it might be broken, and that when broken the paraffin might spill and be ignited by the flame. All these steps in the chain of causation seem to have been accepted by all the judges in the courts below as foreseeable. But because the explosion was the agent which caused the burning and was unforeseeable, therefore the accident, according to them, was not reasonably foreseeable. In my opinion, this reasoning is fallacious. An explosion is only one way in which burning can be caused. Burning can also be caused by the contact between liquid paraffin and a naked flame. In the one case paraffin vapour and in the other case liquid paraffin is ignited by fire. I cannot see that these are two different types of accident. They are both burning accidents and in both cases the injuries would be burning injuries. Upon this view the explosion was an immaterial event in the chain of causation. It was simply one way in which burning might be caused by the potentially dangerous paraffin lamp. I adopt, with respect, Lord Carmont's observation in the present case ... 'The defender cannot, I think, escape liability by contending that he did not foresee all the possibilities of the manner in which allurements—the manhole and the lantern—would act upon the childish mind.'

The respondent relied upon the case of *Muir v Glasgow Corporation* [1943] AC 448, 467 and particularly on certain observations by Lords Thankerton and Macmillan. There are, in my view, essential differences between the two cases. The tea urn was, in that case, not like the paraffin lamp in the present circumstance, a potentially dangerous object. Moreover, the precise way in which the tea came to be spilled was never established, and, as Lord Romer said: 'It being thus unknown what was the particular risk that materialised, it is impossible to decide whether it was or was not one that should have been within the reasonable contemplation of Mrs Alexander or of some other agent or employee of the appellants, and it is, accordingly, also impossible to fix the appellants with liability for the damage that the respondents sustained.'

I have therefore reached the conclusion that the accident which occurred and which caused burning injuries to the appellant was one which ought reasonably to have been foreseen by the Post Office employees and that they were at fault in failing to provide a protection against the appellant entering the shelter and going down the manhole.

I would allow the appeal.

Problems

1   Some railway workers were repairing a railway line. They had a little camp kitchen where they brewed up their tea and coffee. One day, the fire from their old 1940s billy suddenly got out of control. This had never happened before and there was no immediate explanation for it. Fanned by the wind, sparks set light to some nearby cut hay in Farmer Brown's paddock. The fire spread quickly across Farmer Brown's farm to Farmer O'Reilley's farm. O'Reilley had some highly inflammable chemicals stored in a barn and these exploded, causing massive damage to all the adjacent farm buildings, including a special quail coop. The quails were being reared for the Christmas market and their loss meant a loss in profits for Farmer O'Reilley of $100 000 as well as $15 000 for the actual cost of the birds. The local volunteer fire brigade had been called out as soon as the fire spread from the railway line, but they had been exceedingly slow in taking the call and when they reached O'Reilley's farm they failed to follow their usual drill. They also decided to check the farmhouse in case anyone was caught inside, rather than dealing with the quail coop, which otherwise might have been saved. Farmers O'Reilley and Brown want to know whether they can sue anyone in negligence.

Stephenson v Waite Tileman Ltd

[1973] 1 NZLR 152 (CA)

[**FACTS**: The plaintiff was employed by the defendant and was working with a rusty and frayed wire rope, which cut his hand. He washed the cut and covered it with a plaster, but he became progressively more ill and debilitated. He is now unable to concentrate, suffers from headaches and loss of balance, and is scarcely able to look after himself. He walks with the aid of a stick. He sued the defendant for negligence.]

Richmond J:

The central issue in this appeal is the correct application of the decision of the Privy Council in ... *The Wagon Mound* (*No. 1*) ... to actions for damages for bodily injury.

... [T]he initial injury suffered by the appellant, namely a cut on the hand from the sprags on the rope, was an injury of a kind which was reasonably foreseeable by the respondent.

... [I]t is now quite clear that the rule of foreseeability of damage is concerned only with foreseeability of a real risk of injury of a kind (or class or character) which embraces the actual damage in suit. Although the broad basis of the rule is that it would be unjust to hold a wrongdoer liable for damage of a *kind* which he could not reasonably foresee, nevertheless the rule accepts the position that there are many matters of detail which nobody could predict but for which the wrongdoer nevertheless remains liable. These details may occur either in an unforeseeable concatenation of circumstances which lead up to the occurrence of damage of the foreseeable kind or they may consist of unpredictable details going to the extent or severity of the damage. To this extent then the general language used in the judgment in *The Wagon Mound* (*No. 1*) is clearly to be read with some qualification.

... Their Lordships regarded damage by fire as a kind of damage (in contrast no doubt to what seems to have been the obvious kind of damage which was foreseeable, namely damage by pollution). In another part of the judgment they clearly treated damage by shock as a 'kind' of damage but that is really as far as the matter went and in particular their Lordships did not advert in any way to the question as to what would be a 'kind' of damage in relation to actions for damages for bodily injury.

In these circumstances it is no wonder that the minds of both practising lawyers and academicians turned immediately to consider the effect of the decision on the most common form of all actions for negligence. One of the obvious questions to ask was, 'What would become of the 'eggshell skull' cases?' So far as I have been able to ascertain, nobody seriously felt that the long-standing principle that a wrongdoer should take his victim as he found him should be altered ... .

Smith v Leech Brain & Co Ltd [[1962] 2 QB 405] was the first case in which the matter arose in England. In that case a galvaniser employed by the defendants was exposed in the ordinary course of his work to a foreseeable risk of receiving a burn from molten metal unless adequately protected. As a result of the failure of the defendants to provide such protection he was struck on the lower lip by a piece of molten metal, causing a burn. The burn was the promoting agent of cancer which developed at the site of the burn, and from which he died some three years later. The cancer developed in tissues which already had a pre-malignant condition. Lord Parker ...

expressed himself as satisfied that the Judicial Committee in *The Wagon Mound* case did not have the thin skull cases in mind ... .

It is of importance to note that Lord Parker regarded the *kind* of damage which had to be foreseeable as a burn from molten metal. He regarded the effects of that burn on the latent susceptibility of the deceased workman to cancer as going only to the *extent* of the damage and regarded it as irrelevant that those effects might be unforeseeable ... . The latter case of *Tremain v Pike* [1969] 1 WLR 1556 ... is in no way inconsistent ... . In that case the plaintiff had contracted a rare disease known as Weil's disease. This disease is contracted by human beings through contact with water or other substances contaminated by the urine of rats. Payne J took the view that the *kind* of injury which would have to be foreseeable would be the contraction of disease through such contact as opposed to the ordinary possibility of disease contracted through food contaminated by rats or through ratbites ... .

The decisions in England, Scotland, Ireland and Canada are of importance because in all of them the Courts have limited the test of foreseeability to the initial kind of injury. The consequences, often unforeseeable, of the initial injury have been treated as falling within the field of *extent* of the injury ... . In my opinion this Court should adopt a similar attitude. It may be difficult to decide upon an adequate theoretical reconciliation of the continued existence of this rule and *The Wagon Mound* principle, but for practical purposes it does not matter whether it be regarded as an exception to the general rule or whether the unforeseeable consequences are regarded simply as going to the extent of the injury rather than to the kind of the injury ... .

Page v Smith
[1996] 1 AC 155 (HL)
[**FACTS**: The plaintiff claimed that a low-speed car accident caused by the defendant, in which he had suffered no physical injury, had aggravated the Chronic Fatigue Syndrome condition from which he suffered, leaving him unable to work.]
Lord Jauncey:
... The appellant argued that if foreseeability of nervous shock was required to be proved by a participant, the assumption of reasonable fortitude, which applied in the case of a bystander, did not apply to him but rather that the respondent tortfeasor must take his victim as he found him. The rule that a tortfeasor is entitled to assume that his victim is of normal fortitude is designed to limit the class of bystanders to whom a duty is owed and is neither relevant nor necessary in the case of participants. Taking your victim as you find him however is relevant, not to the existence of a duty owed to him but rather to a question of damages payable in respect of breach of a duty otherwise established. So far as the fortitude rule is concerned it is necessary to look at a number of authorities.

None of these cases [including *Bourhill v Young*, *McLoughlin v O'Brian*, *Alcock* and *Jaensch v Coffey* (1984) 155 CLR 549] involved participants but the observations of Lord Wright and Brennan J were stated in fairly broad terms and were not specifically confined by bystander cases. That there appear to have been no similar expressions of opinion in relation to participants is, perhaps, hardly surprising since cases such as the present where a participant sustains no immediate physical injuries must be rare. However there do not appear to be reasons in principle or logic for drawing a distinction between the two classes of person. To take a simple example, suppose A while slowly reversing his car into a tight parking space inadvertently bumps the car of B which is stationary. B, who is a woman prone to hysteria, promptly develops that condition with consequential physical injury. The circumstances are such that no normal person would have been in any way mentally or physically affected by the bump. Is B to be compensated because A should have foreseen that a hysterical woman might be in the car and thereby sustain a shock from a minor bump? Common sense would loudly say No and in my view the law should and does likewise. I am satisfied that in determining whether a tortfeasor should have foreseen that either a participant or a bystander would suffer nervous shock as a result of his negligent act the proper test is to assume that the victim is of reasonable fortitude and susceptibility unless, of course, the tortfeasor has special knowledge of the victim's unusual condition.

In applying this test in the present appeal consideration must be given to the precise circumstances in which foresight is to be exercised. The appellant maintained that the respondent should have applied his mind to the position immediately before the impact without regard to the consequences thereof while the respondent submitted that what had actually occurred must be taken into account.

The appellant's argument was that if the respondent had considered the matter immediately before impact he should have foreseen that a serious accident was likely to occur. The difficulty about this argument is that it appears to ignore reality. The question ceases to be whether it is foreseeable that a reasonably robust person would have suffered psychiatric illness as a result of what actually happened and becomes instead whether it is foreseeable that such a person would have suffered psychiatric illness as a result of what might have happened but did not in fact do so ... .

My Lords I have no hesitation in adopting the approach of Lord Wilberforce in *McLoughlin v O'Brian* ... and in concluding that foreseeability whether of danger or of injury likely to be suffered necessarily involves consideration of events as they have actually occurred.

Against this background I now turn to consider whether it was foreseeable that the appellant would have suffered some nervous shock with consequential physical injury as a result of this accident. In all the reported cases in which a plaintiff has recovered damages for nervous shock the causative event has been of a dramatic and horrifying nature.

On no view could it here be suggested that the appellant suffered an acute emotional trauma. Otton J found that the collision was one of moderate severity. However neither the plaintiff nor the occupants of the other car were injured. The appellant suffered no bruises from his seat belt and did not suggest that he was at any time in fear for his own safety or that of the occupants of the other car. He was able to write down the name and address of the respondent, to telephone his wife quite normally and then drive home. His car sustained damage which resulted in it being written off by his insurers but it appears that it was on the ground of economics due to its age and small value rather than because of the severity of the damage. This case is accordingly far removed from those cases in which foreseeability of nervous shock has been established. A motor car collision in which the only damage is to the vehicles involved neither of which even leave the road is not an event which could normally be expected to produce nervous shock with consequential psychiatric illness to one or more of the occupants …

Lord Lloyd:

… If … the plaintiff had suffered a head injury or a broken leg, or significant bruising, with consequential psychiatric illness, it is very doubtful whether the case would ever have reached the Court of Appeal at all. It would be like many other personal injury cases which are tried or settled every day in the High Court and the county courts. Of course, it would have been necessary to prove that the psychiatric illness was genuine, and that it was caused by the accident. But nobody would have stopped to consider the foreseeability of nervous shock. Nobody would have referred to *Bourhill v Young* … We now know that the plaintiff escaped without external injury. Can it be the law that this makes all the difference? Can it be the law that the fortuitous absence of foreseeable physical injury means that a different test has to be applied? Is it to become necessary, in ordinary personal injury claims, where the plaintiff is the primary victim, for the court to concern itself with different 'kinds' of injury?

Suppose, in the present case, the plaintiff had been accompanied by his wife, just recovering from a depressive illness, and that she had suffered a cracked rib, followed by an onset of psychiatric illness. Clearly, she would have recovered damages, including damages for her illness, since it is conceded that the defendant owed the occupants of the car a duty not to cause physical harm. Why should it be necessary to ask a different question, or apply a different test, in the case of the plaintiff? Why should it make any difference that the physical illness that the plaintiff undoubtedly suffered as a result of the accident operated through the medium of the mind, or of the nervous system, without physical injury? If he had suffered a heart attack, it cannot be doubted that he would have recovered damages for pain and suffering, even though he suffered no broken bones. It would have been no answer that he had a weak heart.

… Foreseeability of psychiatric injury remains a crucial ingredient when the plaintiff is the secondary victim, for the very reason that the secondary victim is almost always outside the area of physical impact, and therefore outside the range of foreseeable physical injury. But where the plaintiff is the primary victim of the defendant's negligence, the nervous shock cases, by which I mean the cases following on from *Bourhill v Young*, are not in point. Since the defendant was admittedly under a duty of care not to cause the plaintiff foreseeable physical injury, it was unnecessary to ask whether he was under a separate duty of care not to cause foreseeable psychiatric injury.

Apart from its simplicity, Otton J's approach has other attractions. As medical science advances, it is important that the law should not be seen to limp too far behind … . As long ago as 1901 the courts were already beginning to become aware that there may be no hard and fast line between physical and psychiatric injury, such as had hitherto been supposed … . In an age when medical knowledge is expanding fast, and psychiatric knowledge with it, it would not be sensible to commit the law to a distinction between physical and psychiatric injury, which may already seem somewhat artificial, and may soon be altogether outmoded. Nothing will be gained by treating them as different 'kinds' of personal injury, so as to require the application of different tests in law … .

Are there any advantages in taking the simple approach adopted by Otton J? It may be said that it would open the door too wide, and encourage bogus claims. As for opening the door, this is a very important consideration in claims by secondary victims. It is for this reason that the courts have, as a matter of policy, rightly insisted on a number of control mechanisms. Otherwise, a negligent defendant might find himself being made liable to all the world. Thus in the case of secondary victims, foreseeability of injury by shock is not enough. The law also requires a degree of proximity ... . This means not only proximity to the event in time and space, but also proximity of relationship between the primary victim and the secondary victim. A further control mechanism is that the secondary victim will only recover damages for nervous shock if the defendant should have foreseen injury by shock to a person of normal fortitude or 'ordinary phlegm.'

None of these mechanisms are required in the case of a primary victim. Since liability depends on foreseeability of physical injury, there could be no question of the defendant finding himself liable to all the world. Proximity of relationship cannot arise, and proximity in time and space goes without saying.

Nor in the case of a primary victim is it appropriate to ask whether he is a person of 'ordinary phlegm.' In the case of physical injury there is no such requirement. The negligent defendant, or more usually his insurer, takes his victim as he finds him. The same should apply in the case of psychiatric injury. There is no difference in principle, as Geoffrey Lane J pointed out in *Malcolm v Broadhurst* ... between an eggshell skull and an eggshell personality. Since the number of potential claimants is limited by the nature of the case, there is no need to impose any further limit by reference to a person of ordinary phlegm. Nor can I see any justification for doing so.

As for bogus claims, it is sometimes said that if the law were such as I believe it to be, the plaintiff would be able to recover damages for a fright. This is not so. Shock by itself is not the subject of compensation, any more than fear or grief or any other human emotion occasioned by the defendant's negligent conduct. It is only when shock is followed by recognisable psychiatric illness that the defendant may be held liable.

There is another limiting factor. Before a defendant can be held liable for psychiatric injury suffered by a primary victim, he must at least have foreseen the risk of physical injury. So that if, to take the example given by my noble and learned friend, Lord Jauncey of Tullichettle, the defendant bumped his neighbour's car while parking in the street, in circumstances in which he could not reasonably foresee that the occupant would suffer any physical injury at all, or suffer injury so trivial as not to found an action in tort, there could be no question of his being held liable for the onset of hysteria. Since he could not reasonably foresee any injury, physical or psychiatric, he would owe the plaintiff no duty of care. That example, is, however, very far removed from the present.

So I do not foresee any great increase in unmeritorious claims. The court will, as ever, have to be vigilant to discern genuine shock resulting in recognised psychiatric illness. But there is nothing new in that. The floodgates argument has made regular appearances in this field, ever since it first appeared in *Victorian Railways Commissioners v Coultas* (1888) 13 App Cas 222. I do not regard it as a serious obstacle here.

My provisional conclusion, therefore, is that Otton J's approach was correct. The test in every case ought to be whether the defendant can reasonably foresee that his conduct will expose the plaintiff to risk of personal injury. If so, then he comes under a duty of care to that plaintiff.

[**Result**: **Lord Keith** agreed with **Lord Jauncey**; **Lords Ackner** and **Browne-Wilkinson** agreed with **Lord Lloyd**.]

Third party intervention

Lamb v London Borough of Camden

[1981] QB 625 (CA)

[**FACTS**: In 1972 the plaintiff let her house while she was away in the United States. In 1973, while replacing a sewer pipe in the road outside the plaintiff's house, contractors employed by the local council breached a water main, causing the foundations of the house to be undermined and the house to subside. The house became unsafe, the tenant moved out, and the plaintiff moved her furniture into storage. The house was then left unoccupied to await repair. In 1974 squatters moved in but were evicted. The house was boarded up and the plaintiff returned to the United States. In 1975 squatters again moved in and caused substantial damage to the interior of the house before being evicted.]

Lord Denning MR:

Lord Reid's test

On those facts this point of law arises: can Mrs Lamb recover from the council the £30 000 due to the squatters' damage? The official referee found that it was too remote and was not recoverable. He cited the speech of Lord Reid in *Home Office v Dorset Yacht Co Ltd* [1970] 2 All ER 294 at 30 ... .

> These cases show that, where human action forms one of the links between the original wrongdoing of the defendant and the loss suffered by the plaintiff, that action must at least have been something very likely to happen if it is not to be regarded as *novus actus interveniens* breaking the chain of causation. I do not think that a mere foreseeable possibility is or should be sufficient, for then the intervening human action can more properly be regarded as a new cause than as a consequence of the original wrongdoing. But if the intervening action was likely to happen I do not think that it can matter whether that action was innocent or tortious or criminal. Unfortunately, tortious or criminal action by a third party is often the 'very kind of thing' which is likely to happen as a result of the wrongful or careless act of the defendant. And in the present case, on the facts which we must assume at this stage, I think that the taking of a boat by the escaping trainees and their unskilful navigation leading to damage to another vessel were the very kind of thing that these borstal officers ought to have seen to be likely.

... Now I would test the rulings of the Law Lords by asking: suppose that by some negligence of the staff, a borstal boy, or an adult prisoner, escapes over the wall, or from a working party. It is not only reasonably foreseeable, it is, as we all know, *very likely*, that he will steal a car in the immediate vicinity. He will then drive many miles, abandon the car, break into a house and steal clothes, get a lift in a lorry, and continue his depredations. On Lord Diplock's test, and I fancy on that of Lord Morris and Lord Pearson also, the Home Office would owe a duty of care to the owner of the stolen car but to none of the others who suffered damage. So the owner of the car could sue, but the others could not.

But on Lord Reid's test of 'very likely' to happen, the Home Office would be liable not only to the owner of the stolen car but also to all others who suffered damage: because it was very likely to happen.

That illustration convinces me that Lord Reid's test was wrong. If it were adopted, it would extend the liability of the Home Office beyond all reason. The Home Office should not be liable for the depredations of escaped convicts. The householders should recover for the damage not against the Home Office but on their insurance policies. The insurers should not by subrogation be able to pass it on to the Home Office … .

The alternative test

If Lord Reid's test is wrong, what is the alternative test? Logically, I suppose that liability and compensation should go hand in hand. If reasonable foresight is the criterion in negligence, so also it should be in remoteness of damage … .

To my mind that alternative test is also not acceptable. It would extend the range of compensation far too widely … .

The truth

The truth is that … duty, remoteness and causation, are all devices by which the courts limit the range of liability for negligence or nuisance … .

Sometimes it is done by limiting the range of the persons to whom duty is owed. Sometimes it is done by saying that there is a break in the chain of causation. At other times it is done by saying that the consequence is too remote to be a head of damage. All these devices are useful in their way. But ultimately it is a question of policy for the judges to decide … .

A question of policy—return to the present case

Looking at the question as one of policy, I ask myself: whose job was it to do something to keep out the squatters? And, if they got in, to evict them? … It was the job of the owner of the house, Mrs Lamb, through her agents. That is how everyone in the case regarded it. It has never been suggested in the pleadings or elsewhere that it was the job of the council. No one ever wrote to the council asking them to do it … .

On broader grounds of policy, I would add this: the criminal acts here, malicious damage and theft, are usually covered by insurance. By this means the risk of loss is spread throughout the community. It does not fall too heavily on one pair of shoulders alone. The insurers take the premium to cover just this sort of risk and should not be allowed, by subrogation, to pass it on to others … .

So here, it seems to me, that, if Mrs Lamb was insured against damage to the house and theft, the insurers should pay the loss. If she was not insured, that is her misfortune … .

Oliver LJ:

... As it seems to me, all that Lord Reid was saying [in *Dorset Yacht*] was this, that, where as a matter of fact the consequence which the court is considering is one which results from, or would not have occurred but for, the intervention of some independent human agency over which the tortfeasor has no control it has to approach the problem of what could be reasonably foreseen by the tortfeasor, and thus of the damage for which he is responsible, with particular care.

... It cannot be said that you cannot foresee the possibility that people will do stupid or criminal acts, because people are constantly doing stupid or criminal acts. But ... all that Lord Reid seems to me to be saying is that the hypothetical reasonable man in the position of the tortfeasor cannot be said to foresee the behaviour of another person unless that behaviour is such as would, viewed objectively, be very likely to occur. Thus, for instance, if by my negligent driving I damage another motorist's car, I suppose that theoretically I *could* foresee that, whilst he leaves it by the roadside to go and telephone his garage, some ill-intentioned passer-by may jack it up and remove the wheels. But I cannot think that it could be said that, merely because I have created the circumstances in which such a theft might become possible, I ought reasonably to foresee that it would happen.

... The test of remoteness is said to be the same as the test of duty in negligence (see *The Wagon Mound* (*No. 1*)) ... If the instant case is approached as a case of negligence and one asks the question, did the defendants owe a duty not to break a water pipe so as to cause the plaintiff's house to be invaded by squatters a year later, the tenuousness of the linkage between act and result becomes apparent. I confess that I find it inconceivable that the reasonable man, wielding his pick in the road in 1973, could be said reasonably to foresee that his puncturing of a water main would fill the plaintiff's house with uninvited guests in 1974.

... [W]hether or not it is right to regard questions of remoteness according to some flexible test of the policy of the law from time to time (on which I prefer at the moment to express no view) I concur with Lord Denning MR in regarding the straight test of foreseeability, at least in cases where the acts of independent third parties are concerned, as one which can, unless subjected to some further limitation, produce results which extend the ambit of liability beyond all reason. Speaking for myself, I would respectfully regard Lord Reid's test as a workable and sensible one, subject only to this, that I think that he may perhaps have understated the *degree* of likelihood required before the law can or should attribute the free act of a responsible third person to the tortfeasor ... . There may, for instance, be circumstances in which the court would require a degree of likelihood amounting almost to inevitability before it fixes a defendant with responsibility for the act of a third party over whom he has and can have no control ... .

Watkins LJ:

... It seems to me that if the sole and exclusive test of remoteness is whether the fresh damage has arisen from an event or act which is reasonably foreseeable, or reasonably foreseeable as a possibility, or likely or quite likely to occur, absurd, even bizarre, results might ensue in actions for damages for negligence ... .

I do not think that words such as, among others, 'possibility', 'likely' or 'quite likely' assist in the application of the test of reasonable foreseeability ... .

In my view the *Wagon Mound* (*No. 2*) test should always be applied without any of the gloss which is from time to time being applied to it.

But when so applied it cannot in all circumstances in which it arises conclude consideration of the question of remoteness, although in the vast majority of cases it will be adequate for this purpose. In other cases, the present one being an example of these in my opinion, further consideration is necessary, always providing, of course, a plaintiff survives the test of reasonable foreseeability.

This is because the very features of an event or act for which damages are claimed themselves suggest that the event or act is not on any practical view of it remotely in any way connected with the original act of negligence. These features will include such matters as the nature of the event or act, the time it occurred, the place where it occurred, the identity of the perpetrator and his intentions, and responsibility, if any, for taking measures to avoid the occurrence and matters of public policy.

A robust and sensible approach to this very important area of the study of remoteness will more often than not produce, I think, an instinctive feeling that the event or act being weighed in the balance is too remote to sound in damages for the plaintiff. I do not pretend that in all cases the answer will come easily to the inquirer. But that the question must be asked and answered in all these cases I have no doubt.

To return to the present case, I have the instinctive feeling that the squatters' damage is too remote. I could not possibly come to any other conclusion, although on the primary facts I, too, would regard that damage or something like it as reasonably foreseeable in these times.

We are here dealing with unreasonable conduct of an outrageous kind … . In my opinion this kind of antisocial and criminal behaviour provides a glaring example of an act which inevitably, or almost so, is too remote to cause a defendant to pay damages for the consequences of it.

Smith and Others v Littlewoods Org Ltd
[1987] AC 241 (HL)
[**FACTS**: Youths set fire to the defendant's disused cinema, which was awaiting demolition. The resulting fire damaged surrounding businesses.]
Lord Mackay of Clashfern:
… While no doubt in this case, as the judges in the courts below have found, it was probable that children and young persons might attempt to break into the vacated cinema, this by no means establishes that it was a probable consequence of its being vacated with no steps being taken to maintain it lockfast that it would be set on fire with consequent risk of damage to neighbouring properties. A telling point in favour of Littlewoods is that, although Littlewoods' particulars were shown on a board prominently displayed at the front of the premises, no one made any protest to them about the state of the premises, or indicated to them any concern that, unless they took some action, neighbouring premises were at risk. If, in the light of the common knowledge in the neighbourhood, it had been anticipated that the cinema might be set on fire, with consequent risk to adjoining properties, I should have thought the persons concerned with the safety of adjoining properties, who were certainly among those acquainted with the situation, would have communicated their anxieties to Littlewoods. Neither is there evidence that the police were ever informed of the situation

with regard to the cinema, and this I would take as further confirmation that, in the circumstances, no one anticipated any adverse consequences arising from it. It is true that Mr Scott, the beadle, spoke of anxiety for the safety of children, and also made some reference, in that connection, to the possibility of fire, but any concern he had was not apparently sufficiently substantial to prompt him to take any action whatever in the way of seeking to have the situation remedied by the owners or the police.

This is sufficient for the disposal of this appeal but in view of the general importance of some of the matters raised in the parties' submissions it is right that I should add some observations on these.

First, counsel for the appellants urged us to say that the ordinary principle to be deduced from Lord Atkin's speech in *Donoghue v Stevenson* should apply to cases where the damage in question was caused by human agency. It is plain from the authorities that the fact that the damage, on which a claim is founded, was caused by a human agent quite independent of the person against whom a claim in negligence is made does not, of itself, preclude success of the claim, since breach of duty on the part of the person against whom the claim is made may also have played a part in causing the damage.

… It is true, as has been pointed out by Oliver LJ in *Lamb v Camden London Borough* … that human conduct is particularly unpredictable and that every society will have a sprinkling of people who behave most abnormally. The result of this consideration, in my opinion, is that, where the only possible source of the type of damage or injury which is in question is agency of a human being for whom the person against whom the claim is made has no responsibility, it may not be easy to find that as a reasonable person he was bound to anticipate that type of damage as a consequence of his act or omission. The more unpredictable the conduct in question, the less easy to affirm that any particular result from it is probable and in many circumstances the only way in which a judge could properly be persuaded to come to the conclusion that the result was not only possible but reasonably foreseeable as probable would be to convince him that, in the circumstances, it was highly likely. In this type of case a finding that the reasonable man should have anticipated the consequence of human action as just probable may not be a very frequent option. Unless the judge can be satisfied that the result of the human action is highly probable or very likely he may have to conclude that all that the reasonable man could say was that it was a mere possibility. Unless the needle that measures the probability of a particular result flowing from the conduct of a human agent is near the top of the scale it may be hard to conclude that it has risen sufficiently from the bottom to create the duty reasonably to foresee it.

In summary I conclude, in agreement with both counsel, that what the reasonable man is bound to foresee in a case involving injury or damage by independent human agency, just as in cases where such agency plays no part, is the probable consequences of his own act or omission, but that, in such a case, a clear basis will be required on which to assert that the injury or damage is more than a mere possibility. To illustrate, it is not necessary to go further than the decision of this House in *Home Office v Dorset Yacht Co Ltd*, where I consider that all the members of the majority found such a possible basis in the facts that the respondents' yacht was situated very close to the island on which the borstal boys escaped from their custodians, that the only effective means of avoiding recapture was to escape by the use of some nearby vessel and that the only means of providing themselves with the means to continue their journey was likely to be theft from such nearby vessels. These considerations so limited the options open to the escaping boys that it became highly probable that the boys would use, damage or steal from one or more of the vessels moored near the island.

... The next case referred to was *P Perl (Exporters) Ltd v Camden London BC* ... [1984] QB 342, in which the plaintiffs were tenants of the defendants who used the basement of the demised premises in accordance with the terms of the lease for the storage of garments. The defendants were also the owners of the adjoining premises. These premises had a broken lock on the front door. Unauthorised persons were often seen on those premises and burglaries had also taken place there, but the defendants had done nothing about complaints regarding lack of security. During a weekend, intruders entered the basement of the premises adjoining the plaintiff's premises, knocked a hole through the wall separating that basement from the plaintiffs' basement, and stole some knitwear belonging to the plaintiffs from their basement. The plaintiffs brought an action against the defendants claiming damages for negligence. The Court of Appeal held that the claim failed. Waller and Oliver LJJ held that, although it was a foreseeable possibility that thieves might gain access through the defendants' property to the plaintiffs' property, the defendants were not reasonably bound to foresee as the natural and probable consequence of their omission to secure their premises that persons over whom they had no control would steal the plaintiffs' goods. My noble and learned friend Lord Goff, as Robert Goff LJ, gave the third judgment ... He quoted from Dixon J in *Smith v Leurs* (1945) 70 CLR 256 at 262 ... The full passage, cited in the *Dorset Yacht Co Ltd* ... at 307 ... is:

> But, apart from vicarious responsibility, one man may be responsible to another for the harm done to the latter by a third person; he may be responsible on the ground that the act of the third person could not have taken place but for his own fault or breach of duty. There is more than one description of duty the breach of which may produce this consequence. For instance, it may be a duty of care in reference to things involving special danger. It may even be a duty of care with reference to the control of actions or conduct of the third person. It is, however, exceptional to find in the law a duty to control another's actions to prevent harm to strangers. The general rule is that one man is under no duty of controlling another man to prevent his doing damage to a third. There are, however, special relations which are the source of a duty of this nature.

Robert Goff LJ continued:

> It is of course true that in the present case [the plaintiffs] do not allege that [the defendants] should have controlled the thieves who broke into their storeroom. But they do allege that [the defendants] should have exercised reasonable care to prevent them from gaining access through their own premises; and in my judgment the statement of principle by Dixon J is equally apposite in such a case. I know of no case where it has been held, in the absence of a

special relationship, that the defendant was liable in negligence for having failed to prevent a third party from wrongfully causing damage to the plaintiff.

Earlier he had made reference to *Stansbie v Troman* ... [1948] 2 KB 48, in which a decorator who had contracted to carry out work in the plaintiff's home went out for a time when no one else was in the house, leaving the door unsecured. In consequence, a thief entered and removed some of the plaintiff's property from the house and the plaintiff succeeded in recovering damages against the decorator. There was in that case no special relationship between the decorator and the thief although there was a contract between the decorator and the plaintiff. I should have thought that, on the same facts, a guest of the plaintiff's [*sic*] who had left property in the house, if it had been stolen, might also have succeeded in recovering damages in respect of that theft from the decorator. That case proceeded on the basis that the decorator was liable because it was as 'a direct result of his negligence that the thief got in through this door which was left unlocked' ... I think it could be said that the purpose of the security arrangements at the door of the house was to prevent unlawful intrusion, that a reasonable man, in the decorator's position, would have secured the door, and that, on analysis, his reason for doing so would be to prevent the consequence which he ought reasonably to foresee of unauthorised intrusion and theft from the house whose door it was. On the other hand, if the thief, instead of confining his attention to the house whose door it was, bored a hole through the wall into the house next door, and stole items from the adjoining proprietor, assuming the first house was in a terrace or semi-detached, I consider that the decorator would not be liable in respect of the adjoining proprietor's loss, in the absence of circumstances from which this was shown to be reasonably foreseeable.

If the proprietor of the first house returned in time to find the thief boring a hole in the wall with the intention of effecting entry to the adjoining house, in the light of the decision in *Sedleigh-Denfield v O'Callaghan* ... I consider the first proprietor would be under a duty of care to the second proprietor to take what reasonable steps were open to him to cause the boring to cease. In some sense a thief who goes through one proprietor's property in order to reach the adjoining property of his neighbour creates a special relationship between himself and the first proprietor as a user of the first proprietor's land. In my opinion, therefore, the reason that in the circumstances of *P Perl (Exporters) Ltd* ... no duty was owed by the defendants to Perl was that the defendants were not bound as reasonable occupiers to foresee that, if they took no steps to improve the security of their property, a probable consequence of that was that thieves would first unlawfully enter their property and then, by making an opening in the dividing wall or otherwise, use the defendants' property to make an entry into the property of Perl for the purpose of stealing goods belonging to Perl. Although a duty to prevent a person from unlawfully entering my property may, in a sense, be described as a duty to control that person, I would not consider this a very natural use of the word 'control'. Control signifies, to my mind, a more extended relationship than would be involved in simply keeping another off my property. If this be right, the duty alleged by Perl to be incumbent on Camden was a duty falling under the earlier part of Dixon J's dictum, as giving rise to responsibility on the ground that the act of the thief could not have taken place but for the fault or breach of duty of the defendant but not to a duty of care with reference to the control of actions or conduct of the thief. Like Oliver LJ in the *Perl* case, I would regard the mode of entry in question in that case to the plaintiffs' premises as a foreseeable possibility and no more, and in my view, that reasoning amply supports the decision of the Court of Appeal in the *Perl* case ... .

Cases of theft where the thief uses a neighbour's premises to gain access to the premises of the owner of the stolen goods are, in my opinion, in an important respect different from cases of fire such as that with which your Lordships are concerned in the present appeal. In the case of fire, a hazard is created on the first occupier's premises and it is that hazard which operating from the first occupier's premises creates danger to the neighbouring properties. As I have said, even though that hazard is created by the act of a trespasser on the first premises the occupier of these premises, once he knows of the physical facts giving rise to the hazard, has a duty to take reasonable care to prevent the hazard causing damage to neighbouring properties. In the ordinary case of theft where the thief uses the first proprietor's property only as an access to the property of the person from whom the stolen property is taken there is no similar hazard on the first proprietor's land which causes the damage to the neighbouring property. Success of the theft depends very much on its mode and occasion being unexpected. The only danger consists in the thief or thieves who, having passed from trespassing on the first proprietor's property, go on to trespass on his neighbour's. There is also a sense in which neighbouring proprietors can, independently, take action to protect themselves against theft in a way that is not possible with fire. Once the fire had taken hold on Littlewoods' building, St Paul's proprietors could not be expected to take effective steps to prevent sparks being showered over on their property.

My Lords, I think it is well to remember as Lord Radcliffe pointed out in *Bolton v Stone* ...

> ... a breach of duty has taken place if [the facts] show the appellants guilty of a failure to take reasonable care to prevent the accident. One may phrase it a 'reasonable care' or 'ordinary care' or 'proper care'—all these phrases are to be found in decisions of authority—but the fact remains that, unless there has been something which a reasonable man would blame as falling beneath the standard of conduct that he would set for himself and require of his neighbour, there has been no breach of legal duty ...

This is the fundamental principle and in my opinion various factors will be taken into account by the reasonable man in considering cases involving fire on the one hand and theft on the other, but since this is the principle the precise weight to be given to these factors in any particular case will depend on the circumstances and rigid distinctions cannot be made between one type of hazard and another. I consider that much must depend on what the evidence shows is done by ordinary people in like circumstances to those in which the claim of breach of duty arises.

In my view, if the test of the standard of the reasonable man is applied to the steps an occupier of property must take to protect neighbouring properties from the hazard of fire arising on his property no further consideration of policy arises that should lessen the responsibility of the occupier in a case such as this ... .

Lord Goff of Chieveley:

My Lords, the Lord President (Lord Emslie) founded his judgment on the proposition that the defenders, who were both owners and occupiers of the cinema, were under a general duty to take reasonable care for the safety of premises in the neighbourhood.

Now if this proposition is understood as relating to a general duty to take reasonable care *not to cause damage* to premises in the neighbourhood (as I believe that the Lord President intended it to be understood) then it is unexceptionable. But it must not be overlooked that a problem arises when the pursuer is seeking to hold the defender responsible for having failed to *prevent* a third party from causing damage to the pursuer or his property by the third party's own deliberate wrongdoing. In such a case, it is not possible to invoke a general duty of care; for it is well recognised that there is no *general* duty of care to prevent third parties from causing such damage.

I wish to add that no such general duty exists even between those who are neighbours in the sense of being occupiers of adjoining premises. There is no general duty on a householder that he should act as a watchdog, or that his house should act as a bastion, to protect his neighbour's house.

Why does the law not recognise a general duty of care to prevent others from suffering loss or damage caused by the deliberate wrongdoing of third parties? The fundamental reason is that the common law does not impose liability for what are called pure omissions. If authority is needed for this proposition, it is to be found in the speech of Lord Diplock in *Home Office v Dorset Yacht Co Ltd* ...

> The very parable of the good Samaritan (Luke 10:30) which was evoked by Lord Atkin in *Donoghue v Stevenson* ... illustrates, in the conduct of the priest and of the Levite who passed by on the other side, an omission which was likely to have as its reasonable and probable consequence damage to the health of the victim of the thieves, but for which the priest and Levite would have incurred no civil liability in English law.

... In one recent French decision, the condition was imposed that the danger to the claimant must be 'grave, imminent, constant ... nécessitant une intervention immédiate', and that such an intervention must not involve any 'risque pour le prévenu ou pour un tiers': see Lawson and Markesinis, *Tortious Liability for Unintentional Harm in the Common Law and the Civil Law* (1982) vol 1, pp 74–5. The latter requirement is consistent with our own law which likewise imposes limits on steps required to be taken by a person who is under an affirmative duty to prevent harm being caused by a source of danger which has arisen without his fault (see *Goldman v Hargrave* ...), a point to which I shall return later. But the former requirement indicates that any affirmative duty to prevent deliberate wrongdoing by third parties, if recognised in English law, is likely to be strictly limited. I mention this because I think it important that we should realise that problems like that in the present case are unlikely to be solved by a simple abandonment of the common law's present strict approach to liability for pure omission.

Another statement of principle, which has been much quoted, is the observation of Lord Sumner in *Weld-Blundell v Stephens* [1920] AC 956 at 986 ... 'In general ... even though A is in fault, he is not responsible for injury to C which B, a stranger to him, deliberately chooses to do.'

This dictum may be read as expressing the general idea that the voluntary act of another, independent of the defender's fault, is regarded as a *novus actus interveniens* which, to use the old metaphor, 'breaks the chain of causation'. But it also expresses a general perception that we ought not to be held responsible in law for the deliberate wrongdoing of others. Of course, if a duty of care is imposed to guard against deliberate wrongdoing by others, it can hardly be said that the harmful effects of such wrongdoing are not caused by such breach of duty. We are therefore thrown back to the duty of care. But one thing is clear, and that is that liability in negligence for harm caused by the deliberate wrongdoing of others cannot be founded simply on foreseeability that the pursuer will suffer loss or damage by reason of such wrongdoing. There is no such general principle. We have therefore to identify the circumstances in which such liability may be imposed.

That there are special circumstances in which a defender may be held responsible in law for injuries suffered by the pursuer through a third party's deliberate wrongdoing is not in doubt … . But there is a more general circumstance in which a defender may be held liable in negligence to the pursuer, although the immediate cause of the damage suffered by the pursuer is the deliberate wrongdoing of another. This may occur where the defender negligently causes or permits to be created a source of danger, and it is reasonably foreseeable that third parties may interfere with it and, sparking off the danger, thereby cause damage to persons in the position of the pursuer. The classic example of such a case is, perhaps, *Haynes v Harwood* [1935] 1 KB 146 … where the defendant's carter left a horse-drawn van unattended in a crowded street and the horses bolted when a boy threw a stone at them. A police officer who suffered injury in stopping the horses before they injured a woman and children was held to be entitled to recover damages from the defendant. There, of course, the defendant's servant had created a source of danger by leaving his horses unattended in a busy street. Many different things might have caused them to bolt, a sudden noise or movement, for example, or, as happened, the deliberate action of a mischievous boy. But all such events were examples of the very sort of thing which the defendant's servant ought reasonably to have foreseen and to have guarded against by taking appropriate precautions. In such a case, Lord Sumner's dictum in *Weld-Blundell v Stephens* … can have no application to exclude liability.

… It is, in my opinion, consistent with the existence of such liability that an occupier who negligently causes or permits a source of danger to be created on his land, and can reasonably foresee that third parties may trespass on his land and, interfering with the source of danger, may spark it off, thereby causing damage to the person or property of those in the vicinity, should be held liable to such a person for damage so caused to him. It is useful to take the example of a fire hazard, not only because that is the relevant hazard which is alleged to have existed in the present case, but also because of the intrinsically dangerous nature of fire hazards as regards neighbouring property. Let me give an example of circumstances in which an occupier of land might be held liable for damage so caused. Suppose that a person is deputed to buy a substantial quantity of fireworks for a village fireworks display on Guy Fawkes night. He stores them, as usual, in an unlocked garden shed abutting onto a neighbouring house. It is well known that he does this. Mischievous boys from the village enter as trespassers and, playing with the fireworks, cause a serious fire which spreads to and burns down the neighbouring house. Liability might well be imposed in such a case; for, having regard to the dangerous and tempting nature of fireworks, interference by naughty children was the very thing which, in the circumstances, the purchaser of the fireworks ought to have guarded against.

But liability should only be imposed under this principle in cases where the defender has negligently caused or permitted the creation of a source of danger on his land, and where it is foreseeable that third parties may trespass on his land and spark it off, thereby damaging the pursuer or his property. Moreover, it is not to be forgotten that, in ordinary households in this country, there are nowadays many things which might be described as possible sources of fire if interfered with by third parties, ranging from matches and firelighters to electric irons and gas cookers and even oil-fired central heating systems. These are commonplaces of modern life; and it would be quite wrong if householders were to be held liable in negligence for acting in a socially acceptable manner. No doubt the question whether liability should be imposed on defenders in a case where a source of danger on his land has been sparked off by the deliberate wrongdoing of a third party is a question to be decided on the facts of each case, and it would, I think, be wrong for your Lordships' House to anticipate the manner in which the law may develop; but I cannot help thinking that cases where liability will be so imposed are likely to be very rare.

There is another basis on which a defender may be held liable for damage to neighbouring property caused by a fire started on his (the defender's) property by the deliberate wrongdoing of a third party. This arises where he has knowledge or means of knowledge that a third party has created or is creating a risk of fire, or indeed has started a fire, on his premises, and then fails to take such steps as are reasonably open to him (in the limited sense explained by Lord Wilberforce in *Goldman v Hargrave* ... to prevent any such fire from damaging neighbouring property. If, for example, an occupier of property has knowledge, or means of knowledge, that intruders are in the habit of trespassing on his property and starting fires there, thereby creating a risk that fire may spread to and damage neighbouring property, a duty to take reasonable steps to prevent such damage may be held to fall on him. He could, for example, take reasonable steps to keep the intruders out. He could also inform the police; or he could warn his neighbours and invite their assistance. If the defender is a person of substantial means, for example a large public company, he might even be expected to employ some agency to keep a watch on the premises. What is reasonably required would, of course, depend on the particular facts of the case. I observe that in *Goldman v Hargrave* such liability was held to sound in nuisance; but it is difficult to believe that, in this respect, there can be any material distinction between liability in nuisance and liability in negligence.

Turning to the facts of the present case, I cannot see that the defenders should be held liable under either of these two possible heads of liability. First, I do not consider that the empty cinema could properly be described as an unusual danger in the nature of a fire hazard.

... It is not difficult to multiply the homely examples of cases where a thief may gain access to a house or flat which is not lockfast: for example, where an old lady goes out to spend the day with her married daughter and leaves a ground floor window open for her cat; or where a stone-deaf asthmatic habitually sleeps with his bedroom window wide open at night; or where an elderly gentleman leaves his French windows open when he is weeding at the bottom of his garden, so that he can hear the telephone. For my part, I do not think that liability can be imposed on an occupier of property in negligence simply because it can be said that it is reasonably foreseeable, or even (having regard, for example, to some particular temptation to thieves in adjacent premises) that it is highly likely, that if he fails to keep his property lockfast a thief may gain access to his property and thence to the adjacent premises. So to hold must presuppose that the occupier of property is under a general duty to *prevent* thieves from entering his property to gain access to neighbouring property, where there is a sufficient degree of foresight that this may occur. But there is no general duty to *prevent* third parties from causing damage to others, even though there is a high degree of foresight that they may do so. The practical effect is that everybody has to take such steps as he thinks fit to protect his own property, whether house or flat or shop, against thieves. He is able to take his own precautions; and, in deciding what precautions to take, he can and should take into account the fact that, in the ordinary course of life, adjacent property is likely to be from time to time unoccupied (often obviously so, and sometimes for a considerable period of time) and is also likely from time to time not to be lockfast. He has to form his own judgment as to the precautions which he should take, having regard to all the circumstances of the case, including (if it be the case) the fact that his premises are a jeweller's shop which offers a special temptation to thieves. I must confess that I do not find this practical result objectionable … .

The present case is, of course, concerned with entry not by thieves but by vandals. Here the point can be made that, whereas an occupier of property can take precautions against thieves, he cannot (apart from insuring his property and its contents) take effective precautions against physical damage caused to his property by a vandal who has gained access to adjacent property and has there created a source of danger which has resulted in damage to his property by, for example, fire or escaping water. Even so, the same difficulty arises. Suppose, taking the example I have given of the family going away on holiday and leaving their front door unlocked, it was not a thief but a vandal who took advantage of that fact; and that the vandal, in wrecking the flat, caused damage to the plumbing which resulted in a water leak and consequent damage to the shop below. Are the occupiers of the flat to be held liable in negligence for such damage? I do not think so, even though it may be well known that vandalism is prevalent in the neighbourhood. The reason is the same, that there is no general duty to *prevent* third parties from causing damage to others, even though there is a high degree of foresight that this may occur. In the example I have given, it cannot be said that the occupiers of the flat have caused or permitted the creation of a source of danger (as in *Haynes v Harwood* … or in the example of the fireworks which I gave earlier) which they ought to have guarded against; nor of course were there any special circumstances giving rise to a duty of care. The practical effect is that it is the owner of the damaged premises (or, in the vast majority of cases, his insurers) who is left with a worthless claim against the vandal, rather than the occupier of the property which the vandal entered (or his insurers), a conclusion which I find less objectionable than one which may throw an unreasonable burden on ordinary householders.

I wish to emphasise that I do not think that the problem in these cases can be solved simply through the mechanism of foreseeability. When a duty *is* cast on a person to take precautions against the wrongdoing of third parties, the ordinary standard of foreseeability applies; and so the possibility of such wrongdoing does not have to be very great before liability is imposed. I do not myself subscribe to the opinion that liability for the wrongdoing of others is limited because of the unpredictability of human conduct.

... *Per contra*, there is at present no general duty at common law to prevent persons from harming others by their deliberate wrongdoing, however foreseeable such harm may be if the defender does not take steps to prevent it.

Of course, if persons trespass on the defender's property and the defender either knows or has the means of knowing that they are doing so and that in doing so they constitute a danger to neighbouring property, then the defender may be under an affirmative duty to take reasonable steps to exclude them, in the limited sense explained by Lord Wilberforce in *Goldman v Hargrave* ... but that is another matter. I incline to the opinion that this duty arises from the fact that the defender, as occupier, is in exclusive control of the premises on which the danger has arisen.

In preparing this opinion, I have given careful consideration to the question whether *P Perl (Exporters) Ltd* ... in which I myself was a member of the Court of Appeal, was correctly decided. I have come to the conclusion that it was, though on rereading it I do not think that my own judgment was very well expressed. But I remain of the opinion that to impose a general duty on occupiers to take reasonable care to prevent others from entering their property would impose an unreasonable burden on ordinary householders and an unreasonable curb on the ordinary enjoyment of their property; and I am also of the opinion that to do so would be contrary to principle. It is very tempting to try to solve all problems of negligence by reference to an all-embracing criterion of foreseeability, thereby effectively reducing all decisions in this field to questions of fact. But this comfortable solution is, alas, not open to us. The law has to accommodate all the untidy complexity of life; and there are circumstances where considerations of practical justice impel us to reject a general imposition of liability for foreseeable damage.

Problems

1 For various reasons of convenience, the Wellington Quarry Company has for many years kept detonation caps on site with its other equipment. Of course, the company itself removes the explosives for safe keeping. Because of the very low risk of anyone being able to accidentally detonate the caps, it has always been felt that any safety concerns were satisfied by keeping the detonation caps in a safe. One Sunday, Joe and James, both 14 years old, were exploring the quarry (in the company's words they were trespassers and had ignored many signs warning of the quarry's dangers). The boys soon came across the safe. They opened it with a nearby crowbar. Sensing that the detonation caps were valuable, but without realising exactly what they were, Joe and James took a box of caps and returned to James' house where they hid them under James' bed. The caps were discovered there by Sarah, James' ten-year-old sister, who without telling her brother took the caps to school where she traded them for some marbles. Unfortunately, Jill, the marbles' owner, had a cap gun with her into which she loaded a detonation cap. The cap gun remarkably replicated the conditions needed for detonation to occur and the resulting flash burnt her hand and sparked a fire in a pile of old newspapers, which destroyed the girls' classroom. Who might be liable in negligence on the facts above?

2 Angus is watching a film at a private cinema when he negligently throws his cigarette butt onto the floor, meaning to stub it out with his foot. However, owing to the

negligence of the manufacturers, the carpet has been impregnated with a dangerously inflammable dye. Part of the cinema is destroyed. Consider the liability of (a) the manufacturers to the cinema owner; and (b) Angus to the cinema owner.

The defendant's case

This section looks at the defences of contributory negligence and limitations.

Contributory negligence

Before the Contributory Negligence Act 1947, contributory negligence was an absolute defence to a negligence action. Much of New Zealand's Act derives from the United Kingdom's Law Reform (Contributory Negligence) Act 1945. The New Zealand Act (and the United Kingdom equivalent) enables the cost of the accident to be shared by the defendant and the plaintiff according to their respective responsibility for the accident. *Reeves* considers the contributory negligence attributable to the police under the United Kingdom Act. *Nettleship* and *March* show how the Act has changed the law and how it interrelates with common law doctrines such as consent and causation. Section 6 of the Law Reform Act 1936 gives a defendant the ability to seek contribution from others who might have also been responsible for the loss suffered.

Contributory Negligence Act 1947
2. Interpretation—In this Act, unless the context otherwise requires— ...
'Fault' means negligence, breach of statutory duty, or other act of omission which gives rise to a liability in tort, or would, apart from this Act, give rise to a defence of contributory negligence.
3. Apportionment of liability in case of contributory negligence—
(1) Where any person suffers damage as the result partly of his own fault and partly of the fault of any other person or persons, a claim in respect of that damage shall not be defeated by reason of the fault of the person suffering the damage, but the damages recoverable in respect thereof shall be reduced to such extent as the Court thinks just and equitable having regard to the claimant's share in the responsibility for the damage:
   Provided that—
   (a) This subsection shall not operate to defeat any defence arising under a contract:
   (b) Where any contract or enactment providing for the limitation of liability is applicable to the claim, the amount of damages recoverable by the claimant by virtue of this subsection shall not exceed the maximum limit so applicable.

Reeves v Commissioner of Police of the Metropolis
[2000] 1 AC 360; [1999] 3 WLR 363 (HL)
[**FACTS**: The police admitted that they failed to take normal precautions by failing to close a door hatch, which enabled Mr Lynch to hang himself.]
Lord Hoffmann:
… The Commissioner appeals to your Lordships' House. Mr Pannick argued two points on his behalf. The first was the question of causation: was the breach of duty by the police a cause of Mr Lynch's death?

... The other point argued by Mr Pannick was contributory negligence. The question of public policy or *ex turpi causa non oritur actio* [a suit cannot be based on the plaintiff's own wrongdoing], which had not found favour with any member of the Court of Appeal, was not pursued.

On the first question, Mr Pannick relied upon the general principle stated in Hart and Honoré, *Causation in the Law*, (2nd edn, 1985) ... 'the free, deliberate and informed act or omission of a human being, intended to exploit the situation created by a defendant, negatives causal connection.' However, as Hart and Honoré also point out, at pp 194–204, there is an exception to this undoubted rule in the case in which the law imposes a duty to guard against loss caused by the free, deliberate and informed act of a human being. It would make nonsense of the existence of such a duty if the law were to hold that the occurrence of the very act which ought to have been prevented negatived causal connection between the breach of duty and the loss. This principle has been recently considered by your Lordships' House in *Environment Agency (formerly National Rivers Authority) v Empress Car Co (Abertillery) Ltd* [1998] 2 WLR 350. In that case, examples are given in which liability has been imposed for causing events which were the immediate consequence of the deliberate acts of third parties but which the defendant had a duty to prevent or take reasonable care to prevent.

Mr Pannick accepted this principle when the deliberate act was that of a third party. But he said that it was different when it was the act of the plaintiff himself. Deliberately inflicting damage on oneself had to be an act which negatived causal connection with anything which had gone before.

This argument is based upon the sound intuition that there is a difference between protecting people against harm caused to them by third parties and protecting them against harm which they inflict upon themselves. It reflects the individualist philosophy of the common law. People of full age and sound understanding must look after themselves and take responsibility for their actions. This philosophy expresses itself in the fact that duties to safeguard from harm deliberately caused by others are unusual and a duty to protect a person of full understanding from causing harm to himself is very rare indeed. But, once it is admitted that this is the rare case in which such a duty is owed, it seems to me self-contradictory to say that the breach could not have been a cause of the harm because the victim caused it to himself.

Morritt LJ drew a distinction between a prisoner who was of sound mind and one who was not. He said that when a prisoner was of sound mind, 'I find it hard to see how there is any material increase in the risk in any causative sense.' In *Kirkham v Chief Constable of the Greater Manchester Police* [1990] 2 QB 28, 289–90 Lloyd LJ said much the same. It seems to me, however, they were really saying that the police should not owe a person of sound mind a duty to take reasonable care to prevent him from committing suicide. If he wants to take his life, that is his business. He is a responsible human being and should accept the intended consequences of his acts without blaming anyone else.

... The police might owe a general moral duty not to provide any prisoner with the means of committing suicide, whether he is [of] sound mind or not. Such a duty might even be enforceable by disciplinary measures. But the police did not owe Mr

Lynch, a person of sound mind, a duty of care so as to enable him or his widow to bring an action in damages for its breach.

My Lords, I can understand this argument, although I do not agree with it. It is not, however, the position taken by the commissioner. He accepts that he owed a duty of care to Mr Lynch to take reasonable care to prevent him from committing suicide. Mr Lynch could not rely on a duty owed to some hypothetical prisoner who was of unsound mind. The commissioner does not seek to withdraw this concession on the ground that Mr Lynch has been found to have been of sound mind. For my part, I think that the commissioner is right not to make this distinction. The difference between being of sound and unsound mind, while appealing to lawyers who like clear-cut rules, seems to me inadequate to deal with the complexities of human psychology in the context of the stresses caused by imprisonment. The duty, as I have said, is a very unusual one, arising from the complete control which the police or prison authorities have over the prisoner, combined with the special danger of people in prison taking their own lives.

Mr Pannick also suggested that the principle of human autonomy might be infringed by holding the commissioner liable. Autonomy means that every individual is sovereign over himself and cannot be denied the right to certain kinds of behaviour, even if intended to cause his own death. On this principle, if Mr Lynch had decided to go on hunger strike, the police would not have been entitled to administer forcible feeding. But autonomy does not mean that he would have been entitled to demand to be given poison, or that the police would not have been entitled to control his environment in non-invasive ways calculated to make suicide more difficult. If this would not infringe the principle of autonomy, it cannot be infringed by the police being under a duty to take such steps. In any case, this argument really goes to the existence of the duty which the commissioner admits rather than to the question of causation ...

This brings me to the question of contributory negligence ...

Plainly Mr Lynch's act in committing suicide would not have given rise to liability in tort. That part of the definition is concerned with fault on the part of the defendant. The question is whether, apart from the Act, it would have given rise to a defence of contributory negligence. I recognise, of course, that it is odd to describe Mr Lynch as having been negligent. He acted intentionally and intention is a different state of mind from negligence. On the other hand, the 'defence of contributory negligence' at common law was based upon the view that a plaintiff whose failure to take care for his own safety was cause of his injury could not sue. One would therefore have thought that the defence applied *a fortiori* to a plaintiff who intended to injure himself. The late Professor Glanville Williams, in his book *Joint Torts and Contributory Negligence* (1951) ... expressed the view that 'contributory *intention* should be a defence.' It is not surprising that there is little authority on the point, because the plaintiff's act in deliberately causing injury to himself is almost invariably regarded as negativing causal connection between any prior breach of duty by the defendant and the damage suffered by the plaintiff. The question can arise only in the rare case, such as the present, in which someone owes a duty to prevent, or take reasonable care to prevent, the plaintiff from deliberately causing injury to himself. Logically, it seems to me that Professor Glanville Williams is right.

Buxton LJ took a different view and I must examine the reasons which he gave. First, he said, at p 182, that there was no authority that the intentional act of the plaintiff could be 'fault' within the meaning of section 4 of the Act of 1945. This, as I have said, is true but, logically, I think it can be.

Secondly, he said that the conclusion that Mr Lynch's act did not prevent the negligence of the police from being a cause of his death meant that his death could not have been partly as a result of his own fault and partly as a result of the fault of the police ...

This reasoning seems to me fallacious. It is saying that because Mr Lynch's own act did not negative the causal connection between the negligence of the police and his death, it would be inconsistent to say that he caused his own death at all. Neither logic nor common sense requires such a conclusion. Mr Lynch's suicide did not prevent the breach of duty by the police from being a cause of his death but that does not mean that his suicide was not also a cause of his death. As I said in ... *Empress Car Co* ... 358: 'one cannot give a common-sense answer to a question of causation for the purposes of attributing responsibility under some rule without knowing the purpose and scope of the rule.' Because the police were under a duty to take reasonable care not to give Mr Lynch the opportunity to kill himself, the common sense answer to the question whether their carelessness caused his own death is 'Yes.' Because Mr Lynch also had responsibility for his own life, the common-sense answer to the question whether he caused his own death is 'Yes.' Therefore both causes contributed to his death and the Act of 1945 provides the means of reflecting this division of responsibility in the award of damages ...

Thirdly, Buxton LJ referred to cases under the Factories Acts, in which appellate judges have warned against allowing the legislative policy in imposing an absolute duty on the employer to be undermined by too readily allowing a defence of contributory negligence ...

It is not surprising that judges, faced with an all or nothing decision between the policy of the Factories Acts and the common law rule which made contributory negligence a complete defence, should have given priority to the legislative policy even if in practice it often meant overriding the common law rule ...

... It is commonly the case that people are held liable in negligence for not taking precautions against the possibility that someone may do something careless and hurt themselves, like diving into a shallow swimming pool, but I do not think it has been suggested that in such cases damages can never be reduced on account of the plaintiff's contributory negligence.

Fourthly, Buxton LJ referred ... to cases in which a defence of contributory negligence failed against child plaintiffs who had injured themselves by taking opportunities to play with dangerous things which the defendant had carelessly given or left unguarded. He treated these as cases in which the defence failed because the child had done the very thing which it was the defendant's duty to take reasonable care to prevent. In my opinion, however, they have a different explanation. It is because the plaintiffs were children, without full understanding of the dangers they were running, that it would not have been just and equitable to attribute responsibility to them. This may be equally true in the case of a prisoner of unsound mind who commits suicide. In *Kirkham v Chief Constable of the Greater Manchester Police* [1989] 3 All ER 882, where a prisoner suffering from clinical depression committed suicide in his cell, Tudor Evans J decided that no share of responsibility should be attributed to him under the Act ... But it does not follow that no prisoner committing suicide in consequence of a breach of duty by the police or prison officers can ever be treated as sharing the responsibility for his own death.

In my view it would therefore have been right to apportion responsibility between the commissioner and Mr Lynch in accordance with the Act of 1945. The judge and Morritt LJ would have apportioned 100 per cent to Mr Lynch. But I think that this conclusion was heavily influenced by their view, expressed in connection with the question of causation, that Mr Lynch, as a person of sound mind, bore full responsibility for taking his own life. This is of course a tenable moral view ... But whatever views one may have about suicide in general, a 100 per cent apportionment of responsibility to Mr Lynch gives no weight at all to the policy of the law in imposing a duty of care upon the police. It is another different way of saying that the police should not have owed Mr Lynch a duty of care. The law of torts is not just a matter of simple morality but contains many strands of policy, not all of them consistent with each other, which reflect the complexity of life. An apportionment of responsibility 'as the court thinks just and equitable' will sometimes require a balancing of different goals. It is at this point that I think that Buxton LJ's reference to the cases on the Factories Acts is very pertinent. The apportionment must recognise that a purpose of the duty accepted by the commissioner in this case is to demonstrate publicly that the police do have a responsibility for taking reasonable care to prevent prisoners from committing suicide. On the other hand, respect must be paid to the finding of fact that Mr Lynch was 'of sound mind.' I confess to my unease about this finding, based on a seven-minute interview with a doctor of unstated qualifications, but there was no other evidence and the judge was entitled to come to the conclusion which he did. I therefore think it would be wrong to attribute no responsibility to Mr Lynch and compensate the plaintiff as if the police had simply killed him. In these circumstances, I think the right answer is that which was favoured by Lord Bingham of Cornhill CJ, namely to apportion responsibility equally ...

Lord Hobhouse: (dissenting)

...

My Lords ... let me take two hypothetical situations, neither unduly fanciful. Suppose that the detainee is a political agitator whose primary motivation is to further a political cause. Such persons are liable to see self-destruction, in circumstances which they hope will attract as much publicity and media attention as possible, as an appropriate means of advancing their political cause. Can such a person, having taken advantage of a careless oversight by the police and carried out his purpose, vicariously bring an action against the police and recover damages from them? Or suppose a detainee who and whose family are in serious financial difficulties and who, knowing what the Court of Appeal decided in the present case, says to himself 'the best way for me to help those I love is to commit suicide' and then carries out that purpose by taking advantage of the careless oversight. As Mr Pannick said in argument, he might even leave a suicide note for his wife telling her this. In cases such as these it would be surprising if the courts were to say that, notwithstanding the determinative, rational and deliberate choice of the deceased, that choice had not become the only legally relevant cause of the death. It would also in my judgment be contrary to principle. It certainly would be contrary to principle to resort to the fiction of saying that he was guilty of 100 per cent contributory negligence: if the responsibility of his death was his alone, the principled answer is to say that the sole legal cause was his own voluntary choice. Yet, if such a case were hereafter to come before a court, that court, on the basis of the majority decision of the Court of Appeal, would be bound to award the plaintiff damages.

I give these examples to illustrate the need to identify a dividing line unless one is to say that even in such cases the deliberate voluntary choice of the deceased, the quasi-plaintiff, can never break the chain of causation. The view accepted by the majority of the Court of Appeal reduces all such questions to an examination of the scope of the duty of care or remoteness (which in the context of the law of negligence is effectively the same thing: ... [*The Wagon Mound (No. 1)*] ... The reason why this is contrary to principle is that it is a basic rule of English law that a plaintiff cannot complain of the consequences of *his own* fully voluntary conduct—his own 'free, deliberate and informed' act: see Hart and Honoré, *Causation in the Law*, p 136. This principle, overlooked by the plaintiff, is to be found in a variety of guises in most branches of the law. In the law of tort it overlaps with other principles and invites recourse to expressions (usually Latin maxims) not all of which have consistent usage ...

[**Result**: **Lords Mackay** and **Hope** agreed with **Lord Hoffmann** while **Lord Jauncey**, who would otherwise have apportioned responsibility at one-third to the police and two-thirds to Mr Lynch, compromised by accepting **Lord Hoffmann's** apportionment. **Lord Hobhouse** was the sole dissenting judge.]

Nettleship v Weston
[1970] 2 QB 691 (CA)
[**FACTS**: Mrs W's friend, N, was teaching her how to drive. N was not a professional instructor. He checked to see if there was insurance in the event of an accident. Mr and Mrs W assured him there was comprehensive insurance cover and showed him the policy. Mrs W negligently caused an accident in which N was injured. N sued and Mrs W pleaded *volenti non fit injuria*.]
Lord Denning MR:
... In former times this defence was used almost as an alternative defence to contributory negligence. Either defence defeated the action. Now that contributory negligence is not a complete defence, but only a ground for reducing the damages, the defence of *volenti non fit injuria* has been closely considered, and, in consequence, it has been severely limited. Knowledge of the risk of injury is not enough. Nor is a willingness to take the risk of injury. Nothing will suffice short of an agreement to waive any claim for negligence. The plaintiff must agree, expressly or impliedly to waive any claim for any injury that may befall him due to the lack of reasonable care by the defendant ...

Applying the doctrine in this case, it is clear that Mr Nettleship did not agree to waive any claim for injury that might befall him. Quite the contrary. He enquired about the insurance policy so as to make sure that he was covered. If and insofar as Mrs Weston fell short of the standard of care which the law required of her, he has a cause of action. But his claim may be reduced insofar as he was at fault himself—as in letting her take control too soon or in not being quick enough to correct her error.

I do not say that the professional instructor—who agrees to teach for reward—can likewise sue. There may well be implied in the contract an agreement by him to waive any claim for injury. He ought to insure himself, and may do so, for aught I know. But the instructor who is just a friend helping to teach never does insure himself. He should, therefore, be allowed to sue.

March v Stramore
(1990–91) 171 CLR 506 (HCA)
[**FACTS**: The plaintiff, while driving intoxicated, crashed into the defendant's truck, which had been parked straddling the centre line of a six-lane road. The defendant claimed that the plaintiff had caused his own accident and therefore he should not be liable.]
Mason CJ:
Causation in the context of legal responsibility
It has often been said that the legal concept of causation differs from philosophical and scientific notions of causation. That is because 'questions of cause and consequence are not the same for law as for philosophy and science' … In philosophy and science, the concept of causation has been developed in the context of explaining phenomena by reference to the relationship between conditions and occurrences. In law, on the other hand, problems of causation arise in the context of ascertaining or apportioning legal responsibility for a given occurrence. The law does not accept John Stuart Mill's definition of cause as the sum of the conditions which are jointly sufficient to produce it. Thus, as law, a person may be responsible for damage when his or her wrongful conduct is one of a number of conditions sufficient to produce that damage …

The defence of contributory negligence
Another fertile source of confusion in the development of a coherent legal concept of causation has been the common law defence of contributory negligence. The existence of the defence, as well as the absence of any mechanism for apportionment of liability as between a plaintiff guilty of contributory negligence and a defendant and as between co-defendants who were concurrent tortfeasors, was a potent factor in inducing courts to embrace a view of causation which assigned occurrences to a single cause. So long as contributory negligence remained a defence, the adoption of this approach was more likely to produce just results. The approach was reflected in the question: what was the 'effective cause' of the injury, being 'the one to which may be variously ascribed the qualities of reality, predominance, efficiency' in the words of Lord Shaw of Dunfermline: *Leyland Shipping Co*. Although his Lordship was speaking in the context of a claim under a policy of marine insurance, this notion of effective cause came to be applied in cases of contributory negligence by means of the 'last opportunity' or 'last clear chance' rule. In ordinary circumstances, the plaintiff was defeated by the defence of contributory negligence when his or her negligence was an effective cause of his or her injury, notwithstanding that the defendant's negligence was also an effective cause of that injury …

According to the 'last opportunity' or 'last clear chance' rule, the plaintiff was entitled to recover, despite his or her own negligence, if the defendant had the last opportunity of avoiding the accident but failed to do so due to negligence ... Then the
defendant's negligence was the effective cause of the plaintiff's injury. The result
achieved by the application of the rule was explained in the language of causation; the
defendant's later negligence broke the chain of causation so that the defendant's negligence was left as the effective cause of the plaintiff's injury. And it is in that sense that,
in the present case, Prior J described the appellant's negligence as the 'real cause' of his
injuries ... .

The last opportunity rule served only to confuse even further the legal concept of
causation because it did not apply as between co-defendants, so that a failure by one
defendant to avail himself or herself of a last opportunity to avoid the accident did not
prevent the negligence of the other defendant from being the effective cause of the
plaintiff's injury.

The effect of the legislation providing for apportionment of liability
The elimination of the defence of contributory negligence and the introduction by
legislation (s. 27a(3) of the Wrongs Act 1936) [equivalent to the Contributory Negligence Act 1947] providing for the apportionment between tortfeasors of damages in
accordance with the degree of responsibility of the parties for the damage have meant
that issues of causation could be approached afresh. True it is that there are to be
found, since the enactment of the legislation, statements which indicate that the courts
will still identify, in some situations, one of two preconditions to a consequence resulting in injury as the effective (and sole) cause of that injury, treating the other precon-
dition as a *causa sine qua non* having merely the status of an incident preceding the
critical occurrence and, hence, irrelevant ... .

Notwithstanding these statements, the courts are no longer as constrained as they
were to find a single cause for a consequence and to adopt the 'effective cause' formula. These days courts readily recognize that there are concurrent and successive
causes of damage on the footing that liability will be apportioned as between the
wrongdoers ... .

This Court severely criticized the last opportunity rule in *Alford v Magee*. In so
doing, the Court noted (1952) 85 CLR 452, with apparent approval, Professor Glanville Williams' comment (*Joint Torts and Contributory Negligence* (1951) 223) that the
rule was introduced to mitigate the hardship caused by the existence of the defence of
contributory negligence and went on to point out that the effect of the rule was to
preclude negligence of the plaintiff found to be a cause of the damage from affording a
good defence ...

This conclusion was fatal to the argument that the last opportunity rule survived
the enactment of s. 27a(3) of the Wrongs Act which requires an apportionment of
damages where a person has suffered damage as the result partly of his or her fault
and partly of the fault of any other person or persons. That argument depended
upon the proposition that the rule was devised as a test of causation so that, when
applied, its effect was to brand the defendant's negligence as the sole cause of the
plaintiff's injuries ... In England also, the view has been taken that the rule did not

survive the enactment of the apportionment legislation. In *Davies v Swan Motor Co (Swansea) Ltd; James, Third Party* [1949] 2 KB 291, 322, Denning LJ offered a different reason for the conclusion:

> [T]he practical effect of the Act is wider than its legal effect. Previously ... the courts in practice sought to select, from a number of competing causes, which was the cause—the effective or predominant cause—of the damage and to reject the rest. Now the courts have regard to all the causes and apportion the damages accordingly.

So the end result of the apportionment legislation was to abolish not only the defence of contributory negligence but also the last opportunity rule.

Although the rule did not in reality go to the issue of causal connexion, its operation was often described in the language of causation. Hence the abolition of the rule enabled the courts to apportion liability as between a plaintiff whose contributory negligence and a defendant whose negligence both were concurrent causes of the plaintiff's injuries, in the same way that the courts can now apportion liability between concurrent tortfeasors whose negligence materially contributes to a plaintiff's injuries. In this respect some of the obstacles which precluded the adoption of a legal approach to causation similar to that taken by philosophy and science have disappeared. But, because legal questions of causation are asked and answered with a view to allocating legal responsibility, very often on the basis of fault, an identity of approach is not possible.

Nonetheless, the law's recognition that concurrent or successive tortious acts may each amount to a cause of the injuries sustained by a plaintiff is reflected in the proposition that it is for the plaintiff to establish that his or her injuries are 'caused or materially contributed to' by the defendant's wrongful conduct ... .

Causation as a question of fact

The common law tradition is that what was the cause of a particular occurrence is a question of fact which 'must be determined by applying common sense to the facts of each particular case', in the words of Lord Reid [in] *Stapley* ...

It is beyond question that in many situations the question whether Y is a consequence of X is a question of fact. And, prior to the introduction of the legislation providing for apportionment of liability, the need to identify what was the 'effective cause' of the relevant damage reinforced the notion that a question of causation was one of fact and, as such, to be resolved by the application of common sense.

Commentators subdivide the issue of causation in a given case into two questions: the question of causation in fact—to be determined by the application of the 'but for' test—and the further question whether a defendant is in law responsible for damage which his or her negligence has played some part in producing: see, eg, Fleming, *Law of Torts*, 7th edn (1987) 172–3; Hart and Honoré, *Causation in the Law*, 2nd edn (1985) 110. It is said that, in determining this second question considerations of policy have a prominent part to play, as do accepted value judgments: see Fleming, 173. However, the approach to the issue of causation (a) places rather too much weight on the 'but for' test to the exclusion of the 'common sense' approach which the common law has always favoured; and (b) implies, or seems to imply, that value judgment has, or should have, no part to play in resolving causation as an issue of fact. As Dixon CJ, Fullagar and Kitto JJ remarked in *Fitzgerald v Penn* 'it is all ultimately a matter of common sense' and '[i]n truth the conception in question [ie, causation] is not susceptible of reduction to a satisfactory formula' (1954) 91 CLR 277, 278.

That said, the 'but for' test, applied as a negative criterion of causation, has an important role to play in the resolution of the question … .

The commentators acknowledge that the 'but for' test must be applied subject to certain qualifications. Thus, a factor which secures the presence of the plaintiff at the place where and at the time when he or she is injured is not causally connected with the injury, unless the risk of the accident occurring at that time was greater: see Hart and Honoré, 122.

The 'but for' test gives rise to a well-known difficulty in cases where there are two or more acts or events which would each be sufficient to bring about the plaintiff's injury. The application of the test 'gives the result, contrary to common sense, that neither is a cause': *Winfield and Jolowicz on Tort*, 13th edn (1989) 134. In truth, the application of the test proves to be either inadequate or troublesome in various situations in which there are multiple acts or events leading to the plaintiff's injury … . The cases demonstrate the lesson of experience, namely, that the test, applied as an exclusive criterion of causation, yields unacceptable results and that the results which it yields must be tempered by the making of value judgments and the infusion of policy considerations … .

Much the same approach was adopted by this Court in *Caterson* where Gibbs J (with whom Barwick CJ, Menzies and Stephen JJ agreed) pointed out that, if the plaintiff's action in jumping from the train was, in the ordinary course of things, the very kind of thing likely to happen as a result of the defendant's negligence and was not unreasonable, the jury was entitled to find that the plaintiff's injuries were caused by the defendant's negligence. The finding that the plaintiff's action was not unreasonable was then essential to that conclusion because contributory negligence was a defence in New South Wales at the relevant time … .

As a matter of both logic and common sense, it makes no sense to regard the negligence of the plaintiff or a third party as a superseding cause or *novus actus interveniens* when the defendant's wrongful conduct has generated the very risk of injury resulting from the negligence of the plaintiff or a third party and that injury occurs in the ordinary course of things. In such a situation, the defendant's negligence satisfies the 'but for' test and is properly to be regarded as a cause of the consequence because there is no reason in common sense, logic or policy for refusing to so regard it.

Conclusion

Viewed in this light, the respondents' negligence was a cause of the accident and of the appellant's injuries. The second respondent's wrongful act in parking the truck in the middle of the road created a situation of danger, the risk being that a careless driver would act in the way that the appellant acted. The purpose of imposing the common law duty on the second respondent was to protect motorists from the very risk of injury that befell the appellant. In these circumstances, the respondents' negligence was a continuing cause of the accident. The chain of causation was not broken by a *novus actus*. Nor was it terminated because the risk of injury was not foreseeable; on the contrary, it was plainly foreseeable.

In the result I would allow the appeal.

Law Reform Act 1936

17. Proceedings against, and contribution between, joint and several tortfeasors—

(1) Where damage is suffered by any person as a result of a tort (whether a crime or not)—

- (a) Judgment recovered against any tortfeasor liable in respect of that damage shall not be a bar to an action against any other person who would, if sued, have been liable as a joint tortfeasor in respect of the same damage:
- (b) If more than one action is brought in respect of that damage by or on behalf of the person by whom it was suffered, or for the benefit of the estate, or of the wife, husband, parent, or child of that person, against tortfeasors liable in respect of the damage (whether as joint tortfeasors or otherwise), the sums recoverable under the judgments given in those actions by way of damages shall not in the aggregate exceed the amount of the damages awarded by the judgment first given; and in any of those actions, other than that in which judgment is first given, the plaintiff shall not be entitled to costs unless the Court is of opinion that there was reasonable ground for bringing the action:
- (c) Any tortfeasor liable in respect of that damage may recover contribution from any other tortfeasor who is, or would if sued [in time] have been, liable in respect of the same damage, whether as a joint tortfeasor or otherwise, so, however, that no person shall be entitled to recover contribution under this section from any person entitled to be indemnified by him in respect of the liability in respect of which the contribution is sought.

(2) In any proceedings for contribution under this section the amount of the contribution recoverable from any person shall be such as may be found by the Court to be just and equitable having regard to the extent of that person's responsibility for the damage; and the Court shall have power to exempt any person from liability to make contribution, or to direct that the contribution to be recovered from any person shall amount to a complete indemnity.

Limitation periods—the problem of latent defects

The policy behind statutory limitation periods is clear. There should be a time when the book is closed on past events to enable people to get on to plan for the future. In modern times the insurance industry has lobbied hard for definite limitation periods, arguing that uncertainty is costly (see the Law Commission's Report on Limitations, to which Cooke P refers in *Hamlin*). There is always a practical consideration that the passage of time makes justice harder: evidence is destroyed, witnesses' memories fade, and witnesses may even die; it becomes increasingly difficult to separate out present-day expectations of what is reasonable from what could have been reasonably expected in the past. Limitation periods provide incentives for plaintiffs to bring their claims. But there is often a tension between this public policy and the justice of a particular case before the courts where it has seemed wrong to judges to prevent an otherwise successful claim. This tension is exhibited in the cases presented here dealing with latent defects, which are often not apparent until after the limitation period has expired.

Limitation Act 1950

Sect 4. Limitation Of Actions Of Contract and Tort, And Certain Other Actions—
(1) Except as otherwise provided in this Act, the following actions shall not be brought after the expiration of 6 years from the date on which the cause of action accrued, that is to say,—

    (a) Actions founded on simple contract or on tort.

[**Note**: A cause of action arises when all the elements are satisfied. An action in contract is complete when the service is negligently performed. The cases that follow explore when a negligence action arises.]

Mount Albert Borough Council v Johnson

[1979] 2 NZLR 234 (CA)
[**FACTS**: Due to the negligence of the developer and the Council, flats were built with inadequate foundations. In 1966 flat No. 3 was sold. In 1967 cracks appeared. Remedial work of a comparatively minor nature was done. The Council was not notified of the 1967 cracking. In 1968 the purchaser resold to Harris, who in 1970 sold to Johnson. At that time Johnson knew nothing of the remedial work carried out in 1967 and on inspection the flat appeared to be in immaculate condition. Towards the end of 1970 slight cracks began to appear, becoming worse in the following years. An engineer consulted by Johnson gave evidence that a progressive subsidence of the flat was occurring because the foundations were not adequate. The cracking that appeared during Johnson's occupancy corresponded to some extent to the 1967 cracking but the later cracks were significantly worse and more extensive.]
Cooke J:
...

Limitation Act

Since the judgment under appeal the House of Lords have decided *Anns v Merton London Borough Council* ... . Being of the opinion that an essentially pragmatic approach is currently appropriate in the field of negligence and related subjects, we will state our conclusions in the present case quite shortly.

As there was here no assignment of any right of action, Miss Johnson can only succeed on a cause of action arising during her ownership. That ownership began in 1970 and her writ was issued in 1973. So if she has a cause of action no question of limitation can arise. Whether she has a cause of action turns on the effect of the intermediate events in 1967 ... . Lord Wilberforce said that the [cause of action accrued] when the state of the building was such that there was present or imminent danger to the health or safety of persons occupying it ... He did not deal explicitly with whether it may be relevant that the plaintiff did not know of the danger or could not reasonably be expected to have known of it ... .

But the speeches in *Anns* were influenced by the emphasis in the background legislation there on the health and safety of persons ... In *Bowen* all three members of this Court held that a purchaser in Miss Johnson's position can recover in tort for economic loss caused by negligence, at least when the loss is associated with physical damage. That is the current law in New Zealand. Even apart from the effect of *Bowen* as a precedent we are attracted to that view. Such a cause of action must arise, we think, either when the damage occurs or when the defect becomes apparent or manifest. The latter appears to be the more reasonable solution.

... [W]e need add only that, if (contrary to the view that we prefer) imminent danger to personal safety were essential, the separation of the outside steps from the house and the sloping of the floor would no doubt satisfy such a test ... . What the appellants have contended is ... that ... this action is ruled out by what happened in 1967 ... .

The events of 1967

... A somewhat more difficult question is whether the damage which occurred in 1967 should be classified as the same damage as occurred in 1970 and later. It was suggested in *Bowen* at pp 424–5 that in such a context one has to consider questions of causation and intermediate examination, and that it is a question of fact and degree whether damage is sufficiently distinct to result in a separate cause of action ... .

Applying the approach outlined above, we think that Mr Woodhouse was right in accepting that a cause of action arose in 1967. The damage then was not trivial. But it was remedied, although without eradicating the underlying cause. The filling of the cracks and the underpinning may have arrested the problem temporarily, or subsidence may have abated naturally for a few years. Whatever the explanation it is reasonable to accept that there was no further damage of any significance until Miss Johnson's ownership. On these facts we think the case is in that respect similar to *Bowen*. Between the slight damage during the ownership of the original purchasers and the considerable damage after Miss Johnson bought there was a difference and an interval marked enough to justify treating the later damage as distinct. On this view the question of continuous damage need not be discussed. Moreover, as the radical problem was not suspected in 1967, there is no difficulty in the way of treating the later damage as caused by the 1965 negligence. An adequate intermediate examination had not occurred. There was no new or different cause of the damage. The events of 1967 do not insulate the defendants from liability to the plaintiff.

Pirelli General Cable Works Ltd v Oscar Faber & Partners
[1983] 2 AC 1 (HL)

[**FACTS**: The defendant negligently designed a 160-foot chimney and cracks occurred in it. The plaintiffs discovered the damage in November 1977 and issued a writ in October 1978. The judge held that the cracks occurred by April 1970, but the plaintiffs could not reasonably have discovered the cracks before October 1972.]

Lord Fraser:

... My Lords, it was decided by this House in *Cartledge v E Jopling & Sons Ltd* [1963] 1 All ER 341 at 343 ... that ... : '... a cause of action accrues as soon as a wrongful act has caused personal injury beyond what can be regarded as negligible, even when that

injury is unknown to and cannot be discovered by the sufferer; and that further injury arising from the same act at a later date does not give rise to a further cause of action.'
Lord Reid went on, however, to say:

... If this were a matter governed by the common law I would hold that a cause of action ought not to be held to accrue until either the injured person has discovered the injury or it would be possible for him to discover it if he took such steps as were reasonable in the circumstances ... . But the present question depends on statute, the Limitation Act 1939, and s 26 of that Act appears to me to make it impossible to reach the result which I have indicated. That section makes special provisions where fraud or mistake is involved: it provides that time shall not begin to run until the fraud has been or could with reasonable diligence have been discovered ... . The necessary implication from that section is that, where fraud or mistake is not involved, time begins to run whether or not the damage could be discovered ... .

... Parliament passed the Limitation Act 1963, ... evidently ... to deal with the mischief disclosed by *Cartledge v Jopling*. It extended the time limit for raising of actions for damages where material facts of a decisive character were outside the knowledge of the plaintiff until after the action would normally have been time-barred, but it applied only to actions for damages consisting of or including personal injuries. It must, therefore, be taken that Parliament deliberately left the law unchanged so far as actions for damages of other sorts was [*sic*] concerned. It is, therefore, not surprising that until the decision in *Sparham-Souter* such authority as exists is to the effect that in cases of latent defects to a building, the cause of action accrues and the damage occurs when the defective work is done, even if that was before the date of discoverability ... .

I think that there is an element of confusion between damage to the plaintiff's body and latent *defect* in the foundations of a building. Unless the defect is very gross, it may never lead to any damage to all [*sic*] to the building. It would be analogous to a predisposition or natural weakness in the human body which may never develop into disease or injury. The plaintiff's cause of action will not accrue until *damage* occurs, which will commonly consist of cracks coming into existence as a result of the defect even though the cracks or the defect may be undiscovered and undiscoverable. There may perhaps be cases where the defect is so gross that the building is doomed from the start, and where the owners' cause of action will accrue as soon as it is built, but it seems unlikely that such a defect would not be discovered within the limitation period. Such cases, if they exist, would be exceptional.

... Counsel for the plaintiffs argued that in *Anns v Merton London Borough* Lord Wilberforce, and the other members of this House who agreed with his speech, had approved of the observations in *Sparham-Souter* to the effect that the discoverability date was the date when the cause of action accrued ... . He simply narrated the conflict between the cases of *Dutton* and *Sparham-Souter* without indicating any preference ... . His Lordship did not say, nor in my opinion did he imply, that the date of discoverability was the date when the cause of action accrued. The date which he regarded as material (when there is 'present or imminent danger ... [to] health or safety') was, of course, related to the particular duty resting on the defendants as the local authority, which was different from the duty resting on the builders or architects, but I see nothing to indicate that Lord Wilberforce regarded the date of discoverability of the damage as having any relevance … .

There is one other matter on which I am, with the utmost respect, unable to agree with the reasoning in *Sparham-Souter*. Both Roskill and Geoffrey Lane LJJ held that the earliest moment at which time could begin to run against each successive owner of the defective property was when he bought, or agreed to buy, it … . If that is right, it would mean that if the property happened to be owned by several owners in quick succession, each owning it for less than six years, the date when action would be time-barred might be postponed indefinitely.

… I cannot agree … . I think the true view is that the duty of the builder and of the local authority is owed to owners of the property as a class, and that if time runs against one owner, it also runs against all his successors in title. No owner in the chain can have a better claim than his predecessor in title.

… It seems to me that, except perhaps where the advice of an architect or consulting engineer leads to the erection of a building which is so defective as to be doomed from the start, the cause of action accrues only when physical damage occurs to the building. In the present case that was April 1970 when, as found by the judge, cracks must have occurred at the top of the chimney, even though that was before the date of discoverability. I am respectfully in agreement with Lord Reid's view expressed in *Cartledge v Jopling* that such a result appears to be unreasonable and contrary to principle, but I think the law is now so firmly established that only Parliament can alter it. The action is, therefore, time-barred.

Invercargill City Council v Hamlin
[1996] 1 All ER 756; [1996] 1 NZLR 513 (PC)

[**FACTS**: Hamlin sued the Invercargill City Council for having negligently inspected his house when it was built in 1972 and therefore failing to notice that the house's foundations were negligently constructed. The Council argued that the action filed in 1990 was time-barred as significant if unnoticed damage must have occurred before 1984. The High Court and the majority of the Court of Appeal held that while there had been some cracking throughout the life of the building, a reasonable home owner, as opposed to a builder, would not have realised the seriousness of the harm until told of it by a building inspector.]

Lord Lloyd:

Limitation

The negligent act or omission of the building inspector in approving the foundations occurred on 1 June 1972. The first cracks in the masonry veneer, and in the north wall of the kitchen, appeared in 1974. By 1979 a crack in the eastern wall had developed to such an extent that a brick was loose. In the early 1980's the plaintiff noticed some cracks in the foundation wall. Yet proceedings were not issued until November 1990.

The facts as found by the judge thus raise in an acute form the question when the plaintiff's cause of action accrued. If the cause of action arose at the time of the negligent act or omission, or when the first cracks appeared, then it is obvious that the plaintiff's claim in tort against the council would be time-barred. But if the cause of action did not accrue until the plaintiff was advised in 1989 that the foundations were defective, and if, as the judge found, a reasonably prudent homeowner would not have discovered the cause of the cracks any earlier, then the proceedings were in time. Which view is correct?

This is an important question of principle which has been much debated in recent years in different common law jurisdictions, in a number of different contexts. Their Lordships propose to confine their advice to the particular context of latent defects in buildings.

In New Zealand the law has been relatively clear and straightforward since at least the decision of the Court of Appeal in *Mount Albert BC v Johnson* [1979] 2 NZLR 234.

Once it is appreciated that the loss in respect of which the plaintiff in the present case is suing is loss to his pocket, and not for physical damage to the house or foundations, then most, if not all the difficulties surrounding the limitation question fall away. The plaintiff's loss occurs when the market value of the house is depreciated by reason of the defective foundations, and not before. If he resells the house at full value before the defect is discovered, he has suffered no loss. Thus in the common case the occurrence of the loss and the discovery of the loss will coincide.

But the plaintiff cannot postpone the start of the limitation period by shutting his eyes to the obvious ... .

In other words, the cause of action accrues when the cracks become so bad, or the defects so obvious, that any reasonable homeowner would call in an expert. Since the defects would then be obvious to a potential buyer, or his expert, that marks the moment when the market value of the building is depreciated, and therefore the moment when the economic loss occurs. Their Lordships do not think it is possible to define the moment more accurately. The measure of the loss will then be the cost of repairs, if it is reasonable to repair, or the depreciation in the market value if it is not: see *Ruxley Electronics and Construction Ltd v Forsyth* [1994] 3 All ER 801, [1995] 3 WLR 118.

This approach avoids almost all the practical and theoretical difficulties to which the academic commentators have drawn attention, and which led to the rejection of *Pirelli* by the Supreme Court of Canada in the *Kamloops* case. The approach is consistent with the underlying principle that a cause of action accrues when, but not before, all the elements necessary to support the plaintiff's claim are in existence. For in the case of a latent defect in a building the element of loss or damage which is necessary to support a claim for economic loss in tort does not exist so long as the market value of the house is unaffected. Whether or not it is right to describe an undiscoverable crack as damage, it clearly cannot affect the value of the building on the market. The existence of such a crack is thus irrelevant to the cause of action. It follows that the judge applied the right test in law.

Their Lordships repeat that their advice on the limitation point is confined to the problem created by latent defects in buildings. They abstain, as did Cooke P, from considering whether the 'reasonable discoverability' test should be of more general application in the law of tort.

It is regrettable that there should be any divergence between English and New Zealand law on a point of fundamental principle. Whether *Pirelli* should still be regarded as good law in England is not for their Lordships to say. What is clear is that it is not good law in New Zealand.

Building Act 1991

The following is the new limitation period for actions relating to building construction.

Section 91. Limitation Defences—

(1) ... the provisions of the Limitation Act 1950 apply to civil proceedings against any person where those proceedings arise from—

(a) Any building work associated with the design, construction, alteration, demolition, or removal of any building; or

(b) The exercise of any function under this Act or any previous enactment relating to the construction, alteration, demolition, or removal of that building.

(2) Civil proceedings relating to any building work may not be brought against any person 10 years or more after the date of the act or omission on which the proceedings are based.

...

(5) ... subsection (2) applies to any proceedings ... except proceedings commenced before the 1st day of July 1993.

Limitation Act 1950

Another increasingly important section is s 24 of the Limitation Act 1950:

24. Extension of limitation period in case of disability—If, on the date when any right of action accrued for which a period of limitation is prescribed by or may be prescribed under this Act the person to whom it accrued was under a disability—

(a) In the case of any action ... in respect of the death of or bodily injury to any person, or of any action to recover a penalty or forfeiture or sum by way thereof by virtue of any enactment where the action is brought by an aggrieved party, the right of action shall be deemed to have accrued on the date when the person ceased to be under a disability or died, whichever event first occurred; or

(b) In any other case the action may be brought before the expiration of 6 years from the date when the person ceased to be under a disability or died, whichever event first occurred ...

Part 2: Advanced negligence

South Pacific Manufacturing Co Ltd v New Zealand Security Consultants and Investigations Ltd
Mortensen v Laing

[1992] 2 NZLR 282 (CA)

[**FACTS**: In both *South Pacific* and *Laing* the plaintiffs, having lost their businesses to fire, alleged that investigators employed by their insurance companies had been negligent in concluding that the fires had been started by the plaintiffs. In the following extract, Cooke P outlined how New Zealand courts had approached the application of negligence to 'novel' cases.]

Cooke P:

... I will follow our established approach ... adding, so far as generalities are concerned, a series of points. These may be numbered, not because they are meant to be seen as carved in stone but in the hope of making my meaning more understandable. It may be as well to do so, because experience suggests that the huge volume of published discussion in the field makes it unrealistic to expect that any one view will be understood unless presented fairly simply and systematically:

(i) A broad two-stage approach or any other approach is only a framework, a more or less methodical way of tackling a problem. How it is formulated should not matter in the end. Ultimately the exercise can only be a balancing one and the important object is that all relevant factors be weighed. There is no escape from the truth that, whatever formula be used, the outcome in a grey area case has to be determined by judicial judgment. Formulae can help to organise thinking but they cannot provide answers.

(ii) Sometimes it is suggested that a certain formula, for instance that of Lord Wilberforce in *Anns*, creates a prima facie presumption of a duty based on reasonable foresight. I am of the school of thought that has never subscribed to that view, largely because of Lord Wilberforce's reference to a sufficient relationship or proximity or neighbourhood. It would be naïve, and I believe absurd and dangerous, to assert that a duty of care prima facie arises whenever harm is reasonably foreseeable. Even quite unlikely consequences may be reasonably foreseeable ... Naturally the degree of likelihood and the seriousness of the foreseeable consequences can be important factors in the balancing exercise.

(iii) It would appear that the English Courts are coming to speak of reasonable foresight in a deliberately artificial sense. It is exemplified by the judgments in the English Court of Appeal in the cases about 'nervous shock' arising from the loss of loved ones in a disaster ...

(iv) In my respectful opinion the judgments in [*Alcock*] read as a whole, do clearly acknowledge that policy decisions are being made. The duty of care is not extended to those suffering psychiatric illness as a result of seeing a live television broadcast of the disaster, nor normally to those outside the categories of spouse or parent. Such limitations may be reasonable as a matter of policy, but they are by no means commensurate with reasonable foresight in fact. They are limitations thought to be dictated by considerations of fairness to defendants or, to put the same idea in other words, the floodgates argument. The decision in [*Alcock*] can be called judicial legislation and so it is— but not in any pejorative or dyslogistic sense. After all, the whole of the common law is judicial legislation.

(v) Some Australian and English Judges speak in terms of an 'incremental' approach. I fully and respectfully agree that in deciding whether or not there is a duty of care in a new situation the Courts should decide gradually, step by step and by analogy with previous cases. That has invariably been done in New Zealand ...

(vi) But it seems to me that the label 'incremental' solves few problems. Taken in *Murphy v Brentwood District Council*, the House of Lords reaffirmed unanimously that a careless builder is liable in damages to a subsequent purchaser who suffers personal injury from a latent defect. Lord Bridge of Harwich ... expressed the opinion that the building owner ought to be able to recover in tort from the negligent builder the cost of obviating a danger, by repair or demolition, to persons or property on neighbouring land or the highway. Subject to that qualification or possible qualification, their Lordships held remedial expenditure irrecoverable. To others ... this seemed an impossible distinction. In their view the defendant is liable in either case. That view treats the liability as almost self-evidently incremental. I am not here intruding an opinion about which view is correct, but merely making the point that the problem is not answered by saying that the approach should be incremental ...

(vii) As already noted, the fact that economic loss rather than personal physical injury has been suffered may weigh against a duty of care, but is certainly not decisive per se.

(viii) The reasons for treating prevention of pecuniary loss as within the scope of a duty of care, if the relationship of the parties is sufficiently close and there are insufficient countervailing factors, are strengthened when it is borne in mind that in *Murphy* the House of Lords treated the risk of harm to the plaintiff's person and the risk of harm to other property of the plaintiff as in the same category, each carrying a duty to take reasonable care to avoid creating latent defects. The first concern of the law is naturally personal safety. Injury to the person is a kind of damage in a class of its own. Or at least most people would, I think, say so. On the other hand a plaintiff awarded damages for harm to property is being compensated essentially for economic loss. It would be a crude system of law that drew a vital distinction for this purpose between tangible and intangible property interests ...

(ix) In New Zealand, duties of care for personal safety are no longer the concern of the common law (except for old cases) as actions for damages for personal injuries caused by accident are barred by the Accident Compensation Act 1982. Disaster claims such as *Jones v Wright* could not succeed here in any event. In the personal injuries area we are relieved of the spectre of the floodgates which has so haunted present-day English and Australian Judges. That in itself is of course no reason for extending the bounds of negligence liability for economic harm. Nevertheless it may help a more rational and less distracted approach to the evolution of what is now the economic tort of negligence.

... In 'pure' economic loss cases it seems that in the United Kingdom the dictates of justice may be being met, where possible, by expanding the extent of implied contractual duties on the one hand, while reducing the scope of tortious duties on the other. If so, the constraints leading to that approach have not been seen to be the same in New Zealand. Indeed if the strong trend in question were adopted here and carried remorselessly to its logical conclusion, the law of torts as to negligence could virtually cease to exist in New Zealand because of the Accident Compensation Act. What may be demonstrated by this contrast is that the tort–contract dichotomy can be used as a legal technique in varying ways. Perhaps that is not surprising. When the question is whether a defendant should be held to have assumed a certain responsibility, the dividing line between tort and contract is necessarily somewhat arbitrary. Whichever rubric is used, in the end it seems to me inescapable that the criterion being employed by the Courts is in the words of Lord Keith of Kinkel in *Governors of the Peabody Donation Fund v Sir Lindsay Parkinson & Co Ltd* [1985] AC 210, 241, whether it is just and reasonable to uphold a duty of particular scope.

... Moreover in *Brown v Heathcote County Council* ... the Privy Council decided that specific reliance is not essential:

But in circumstances such as these reliance cannot be required from the ignorant and the Council on behalf of the Browns relied upon the practice followed by the Drainage Board.

Thus the prospect of indirect reliance on the carefulness of a general practice may be
enough, at least if the factors point otherwise to a duty of care. Generalisation is hazardous, but the true view seems to be that the extent to which the plaintiff may fairly
be said to have relied foreseeably on the carefulness of the defendant is one, and sometimes an important one, of the factors to be weighed in the balancing exercise.

(xii) Where a statute has a bearing on whether a duty of care should be recognised,
the position is relatively straightforward if the true interpretation of the statute is either
that it covers the field to the exclusion of the common law or that it gives rise to a
statutory cause of action on the principles considered in *Cutler v Wandsworth Stadium
Ltd* [1949] AC 398. The position is more complex if, as in the present case (s 73 of the
Private Investigators and Security Guards Act 1974) and *Murphy* ... (s 6(2) of the
Defective Premises Act 1972), the statute expressly leaves the common law to operate
as well. Clearly enough, however, such provisions show that the statute is not
intended to inhibit the Courts in developing the common law; and I think that they
can be a real help in deciding whether there is a common law duty. For example they
may encourage the Court to hold that certain interests warrant protection. This point
is taken further in the next two paragraphs.

(xiii) The analogy of a statute may properly influence the development of the
common law.

(xiv) The acceptance by the New Zealand Parliament in 1974 that third parties
affected by the activities of licensed private investigators should have the right to file a
disciplinary complaint based on negligence is, in my opinion, one of the strongest
points in favour of recognising in this country a corresponding common law duty of
care. The statute is hardly a controversial or party political one. Rather it aims at regulating in the public interest the activities of a type of business closely affecting members
of the public. To be investigated is an intrusion into one's life, in return for submitting
to which it is not unreasonable to ask for reasonable care.

(xv) Conversely, a point telling against recognising a new common law duty of
care arises when such a duty would cut across established patterns of law in special
fields wherein experience has shown that certain defences, not dependent on absence
of negligence, are needed; or wherein an adequate remedy is already available to a
party who takes the necessary steps. A leading instance of the latter situation is to be
found in the speech of Lord Brandon of Oakbrook in *Leigh and Sillavan Ltd v Aliakmon
Shipping Co Ltd* [1986] AC 785, 819: his Lordship indicated that the ordinary law of
contract and assignability of rights, in an intricate area of commercial law, would have
sufficiently protected the buyers if they had been properly advised. As to the former
situation, in *Bell-Booth Group Ltd v Attorney-General* [1989] 3 NZLR 148 this Court
declined to extend negligence law to a claim that the reputation of the plaintiffs had
been damaged by a television broadcast. In the field of injury to reputation the
defences of justification, privilege and fair comment, and the balance of competing
interests represented thereby, would have been undermined by superimposing a right

to sue in negligence. The approach was taken a degree further in this Court in *Balfour v Attorney-General* [1991] 1 NZLR 519, 529, where it was said that the cause of action unsuccessfully alleged came 'perilously close to defamation' and that any attempt to merge defamation and negligence is to be resisted.

Economic loss

Negligent misstatement

Cases studied so far involved injury to either people or property. The classic negligence case is a car accident in which one driver damages the car of another. Can the same rules of foreseeability and proximity, of reasonableness and of causation, apply when an investor, having relied on negligently prepared accounts when he invested in a company, loses money on the company's collapse? If there is a difference, why? How is the relationship between the accountant and the investor different from the relationship between drivers on the road? How does the type of loss differ between an unfortunate investor and an unfortunate car owner? How can the accountant be said to cause the investor's loss, and is that the same way in which a negligent driver causes harm to another car owner?

These are some of the questions that judges had to deal with in the cases in the following section. They are not easy questions and it will be seen that there has been much judicial conflict about whether and when it is appropriate to impose liability for negligent misstatements.

As well as conflict over substance, there is also conflict about the style of judging. Denning LJ's dissent in *Candler Crane* and Lord Devlin's speech in *Hedley Byrne* are often seen as common law classics. What marks them out as special?

Denning LJ in *Candler Crane* drew a distinction between bold spirits and timid souls. This is a contrast that has often been drawn between the New Zealand Court of Appeal in cases such as *Scott Group* and the House of Lords in *Caparo*. Is such a distinction useful or fair? Is the better approach, following *Boyd Knight*, to focus on causation rather than on duty?

The most important lesson from these cases may be not just the rules relating to misstatement, but that they make us think about why one person should be responsible for the loss of another.

Candler v Crane, Christmas & Co
[1951] 2 KB 164 (CA)
[**FACTS**: The plaintiff invested in a company in reliance on accounts produced by the defendant, who had been told that he would use them as the basis for his investment. The accounts, however, had overstated the value of the company and after its collapse the plaintiff sued to recover both his original investment and a subsequent investment.]

Denning LJ (dissenting):
This case raises a point of law of much importance; because Mr Lawson on behalf of the plaintiff submitted that, although there was no contract between the plaintiff and the accountants, nevertheless the relationship between them was so close and direct that the accountants did owe a duty of care to him within the principles stated in *Donoghue v Stevenson*; whereas Mr Foster on behalf of the accountants submitted that

the duty owed by the accountants was purely a contractual duty owed by them to the company, and therefore they were not liable for negligence to a person to whom they were under no contractual duty ... .

Now I come to the great question in the case: did the accountants owe a duty of care to the plaintiff? If the matter were free from authority, I should have said that they clearly did owe a duty of care to him. They were professional accountants who prepared and put before him these accounts, knowing that he was going to be guided by them in making an investment in the company. On the faith of those accounts he did make the investment, whereas if the accounts had been carefully prepared he would not have made the investment at all. The result is that he has lost his money. In the circumstances, had he not every right to rely on the accounts being prepared with proper care; and is he not entitled to redress from the accountants on whom he relied? I say that he is, and I would apply to this case the words of Knight Bruce, LJ, in an analogous case ninety years ago: 'A country whose administration of justice did not afford redress in a case of the present description would not be in a state of civilization': *Slim v Croucher* (1860) 1 De GF & J 518, 527.

... Before I consider the decision in *Le Lievre v Gould* [1893] 1 QB 491 itself, I wish to say that, in my opinion, at the time it was decided current legal thought was infected by two cardinal errors. The first error was one which appears time and time again in nineteenth century thought, namely, that no one who is not a party to a contract can sue on it or on anything arising out of it. This error has had unfortunate consequences both in the law of contract and in the law of tort ... . So far as tort is concerned, it led the lawyers of that day to suppose that, if one of the parties to a contract was negligent in carrying it out, no third person who was injured by that negligence could sue for damages on account of it ... except in the case of things dangerous in themselves, like guns ... . This error lies at the root of the reasoning of Bowen, LJ, in *Le Lievre v Gould* [at page 502], when he said that the law of England 'does not consider that what a man writes on paper is like a gun or other dangerous instrument', meaning thereby that, unless it was a thing which was dangerous in itself, no action lay. This error was exploded by the great case of *Donoghue v Stevenson*, which decided that the presence of a contract did not defeat an action for negligence by a third person, provided that the circumstances disclosed a duty by the contracting party to him.

The second error was an error as to the effect of *Derry v Peek* (1889) 14 App Cas 337, an error which persisted for thirty-five years at least after the decision, namely, that no action ever lies for a negligent statement even though it is intended to be acted on by the plaintiff and is in fact acted on by him to his loss.

In my opinion these decisions of the House of Lords in *Donoghue v Stevenson* and *Nocton v Ashburton* [1914] AC 932 are sufficient to entitle this court to examine afresh the law as to negligent statements, and that is what I propose to do.

Let me first be destructive and destroy the submissions put forward by Mr Foster. His first submission was that a duty to be careful in making statements arose only out of a contractual duty to the plaintiff or a fiduciary relationship to him. Apart from such cases, no action, he said, had ever been allowed for negligent statements, and he urged that this want of authority was a reason against it being allowed now. This argument about the novelty of the action does not appeal to me in the least. It has been put forward in all the great cases which have been milestones of progress in our law, and it has always, or nearly always, been rejected. If you read the great cases of *Ashby v White* (1703) 2 Ld Raym 938, *Pasley v Freeman* (1789) 3 Term Rep 51 and *Donoghue v Stevenson* you will find that in each of them the judges were divided in opinion. On the one side there were the timorous souls who were fearful of allowing a new cause of action. On the other side there were the bold spirits who were ready to allow it if justice so required. It was fortunate for the common law that the progressive view prevailed. Whenever this argument of novelty is put forward I call to mind the emphatic answer given by Pratt, CJ, nearly two hundred years ago in *Chapman v Pickersgill* (1762) 2 Wilson 145, 146 when he said: 'I wish never to hear this objection again. This action is for a tort: torts are infinitely various; not limited or confined, for there is nothing in nature but may be an instrument of mischief'. The same answer was given by Lord Macmillan in *Donoghue v Stevenson* ... when he said: 'The criterion of judgment must adjust and adapt itself to the changing circumstances of life. The categories of negligence are never closed'. I beg leave to quote those cases and those passages against those who would emphasize the paramount importance of certainty at the expense of justice. It needs only a little imagination to see how much the common law would have suffered if those decisions had gone the other way.

The second submission of Mr Foster was that a duty to take care only arose where the result of a failure to take care will cause physical damage to persons or property. It was for this reason that he did not dispute two illustrations of negligent statements which I put in the course of the argument, the case of an analyst who negligently certifies to a manufacturer of food that a particular ingredient is harmless, whereas it is in fact poisonous, or the case of an inspector of lifts who negligently reports that a particular lift is safe, whereas it is in fact dangerous. The analyst and the lift inspector would, I should have thought, be liable to any person who was injured by consuming the food, or using the lift, at any rate if there was no likelihood of intermediate inspection: see *Donoghue v Stevenson*. Mr Foster said that that might well be so because the negligence here caused physical damage, but that the same would not apply to negligence which caused financial loss.

I must say, however, that I cannot accept this as a valid distinction. I can understand that in some cases of financial loss there may not be a sufficiently proximate relationship to give rise to a duty of care, but, if once the duty exists, I cannot think that liability depends on the nature of the damage.

The third submission of Mr Foster was that the duty owed by the accountants was purely a contractual duty and therefore they were not liable for negligence to a person to whom they were under no contractual obligation. This seems to me to be simply a repetition of the nineteenth century fallacy which was stated in *Alton v Midland Ry* and exploded in *Donoghue v Stevenson*.

Let me now be constructive and suggest the circumstances in which I say that a duty to use care in statement does exist apart from a contract in that behalf. First, what persons are under such duty? My answer is that persons such as accountants, surveyors, valuers, and analysts, whose profession and occupation it is to examine books, accounts, and other things, and to make reports on which other people—other than their clients—rely in the ordinary course of business. Their duty is not merely a duty to use care in their reports. They have also a duty to use care in their work which results in their reports. Herein lies the difference between these professional men and other persons who have been held to be under no duty to use care in their statements, such as promoters who issue a prospectus: *Derry v Peek* (now altered by statute), and trustees who answer inquiries about the trust funds: *Low v Bouverie* [1891] 3 Ch 82. Those persons do not bring, and are not expected to bring, any professional knowledge or skill into the preparation of their statements: they can only be made responsible by the law affecting persons generally, such as contract, estoppel, innocent misrepresentation or fraud. But it is very different with persons who engage in a calling which requires special knowledge and skill. From very early times it has been held that they owe a duty of care to those who are closely and directly affected by their work, apart altogether from any contract or undertaking in that behalf.

... Secondly, to whom do these professional people owe this duty? I will take accountants, but the same reasoning applies to the others. They owe the duty, of course, to their employer or client; and also I think to any third person to whom they themselves show the accounts, or to whom they know their employer is going to show the accounts, so as to induce him to invest money or take some other action on them. But I do not think the duty can be extended still further so as to include strangers of whom they have heard nothing and to whom their employer without their knowledge may choose to show their accounts. Once the accountants have handed their accounts to their employer they are not, as a rule, responsible for what he does with them without their knowledge or consent.

A good illustration is afforded by the decision in *Le Lievre v Gould* itself, which I certainly would not wish to call in question. The facts are somewhat differently stated in the various reports, but collecting them together they come to this: A surveyor there surveyed work for a building owner and handed certificates to him so that he could know the amounts which he had to pay the builder. The building owner then chose to show the certificates to his own mortgagees who advanced money on them instead of on the certificates of their own surveyor. The mortgagees then said that the owner's surveyor owed a duty of care to them. That was obviously untenable, because they should have had the work surveyed by their own surveyor. Indeed they had actually stipulated for it. The relationship was therefore one in which the inspection of an intermediate person might reasonably be interposed, and was consequently too remote to raise a duty of care: see per Lord Atkin in *Donoghue v Stevenson*. But excluding such cases as those, there are some cases—of which the present is one—where the accountants know all the time, even before they present their accounts, that their employer requires the accounts to show to a third person so as to induce him to act on them: and then they themselves, or their employers, present the accounts to him for the purpose. In such cases I am of opinion that the accountants owe a duty of care to the third person.

The text of proximity in these cases is: did the accountants know that the accounts were required for submission to the plaintiff and use by him?

Thirdly, to what transactions does the duty of care extend? It extends, I think, only to those transactions for which the accountants knew their accounts were required. For instance, in the present case it extends to the original investment of £2000 which the plaintiff made in reliance on the accounts, because the accountants knew that the accounts were required for his guidance in making that investment; but it does not extend to the subsequent £200 which he made after he had been two months with the company ... .

It will be noticed that I have confined the duty to cases where the accountant prepares his accounts and makes his report for the guidance of the very person in the very transaction in question. That is sufficient for the decision of this case. I can well understand that it would be going too far to make an accountant liable to any person in the land who chooses to rely on the accounts in matters of business, for that would expose him to 'liability in an indeterminate amount for an indeterminate time to an indeterminate class': see *Ultramares Corporation v Touche* (1931) 174 NE 441, 444 per Cardozo, CJ. Whether he would be liable if he prepared his accounts for the guidance of a specific class of persons in a specific class of transactions, I do not say. I should have thought he might be, just as the analyst and lift inspector would be liable in the instances I have given earlier ... .

My conclusion is that a duty to use care in statement is recognized by English law, and that its recognition does not create any dangerous precedent when it is remembered that it is limited in respect of the persons by whom and to whom it is owed and the transactions to which it applies.

One final word: I think that the law would fail to serve the best interests of the community if it should hold that accountants and auditors owe a duty to no one but their client. Its influence would be most marked in cases where their client is a company or firm controlled by one man. It would encourage accountants to accept the information which the one man gives them, without verifying it; and to prepare and present the accounts rather as a lawyer prepares and presents a case, putting the best appearance on the accounts they can, without expressing their personal opinion of them ... .

I would therefore be in favour of allowing the appeal and entering judgment for the plaintiff for damages in the sum of £2000.

Asquith LJ:

On two points I entirely agree with the judgment delivered by Denning LJ. I agree that the cause of action based on an alleged breach of duty occurring after the plaintiff became a shareholder cannot be made out if only because the damage relied on preceded the breach. I also agree, for the reasons he has given, that Fraser was clearly acting within the scope of his employment by the defendant firm in showing the draft accounts and giving certain other information to the plaintiff.

But I have the misfortune to differ from my brother on the more important point raised in this case. The point may be put in this way: assume that Fraser's negligent misrepresentations had been made by his employers, the partners in the defendant firm ... . Their proposition is that, under the conditions assumed in this case, the defendants were under no duty, sounding in tort, to the plaintiff to take care that their representations of fact should be true. They rule in support of this contention on *Le Lievre v Gould*, a decision binding on this court. I agree with the trial judge in considering that authority to be conclusive in their favour, unless it can be shown to have been overruled or to be distinguishable.

The plaintiff's case is that whatever may have been the position before *Donoghue v Stevenson*, the rule applied by the majority of the House of Lords in that case necessarily involves the consequence that (even where fraud, contract and fiduciary relationship are absent) A will be liable to B for any negligent misrepresentations on which B acts to his detriment, provided always that there exists between A and B the necessary degree of so-called 'proximity'.

Apart, however, from any limitation which should be read into Lord Atkin's language by reference to the facts of the case before him—the *'subjecta materies'*—it seems to me incredible that if he thought his formula was inconsistent with *Gould*'s case he would not have said so. This case, now nearly sixty years old, had at that time stood for nearly forty years. He must have considered it closely. Yet his only reference to it is as annexing a valid and essential qualification to Lord Esher's formula in *Heaven v Pender*. Not a word of disapproval of the decision on its merits. The inference seems to me to be that Lord Atkin continued to accept the distinction between liability in tort for careless (but non-fraudulent) misstatements and liability in tort for some other forms of carelessness, and that his formula defining 'who is my neighbour' must be read subject to his acceptance of this overriding distinction ... .

... Lord Atkin, in affirming the *Donoghue* type of liability, and annexing to it the condition of proximity, did not say: 'There is no proximity unless the defendant can identify the ultimate victim of his carelessness in advance'. The manufacturers of the peccant bottle of ginger beer had no idea who would in the end consume it. All they knew was that someone would. You may adapt the formula *'Certum est quod certum reddi potest'* and say *'certus est qui certus reddi potest'*. The unidentifiability in advance of the ultimate consumer and victim did not, by displacing the notion of proximity or in any other way, protect the aggressors from liability. I am therefore of opinion that this argument fails.

... The case has been instanced by Professor Winfield and referred to by my brother Denning of a marine hydrographer who carelessly omits to indicate on his map the existence of a reef. The captain of the *Queen Mary*, in reliance on the map and having no opportunity of checking it by reference to any other map, steers her on the unsuspected rocks, and she becomes a total loss. Is the unfortunate cartographer to be liable to her owners in negligence for some millions of pounds damages? If so, people will, in future, think twice before making maps. Cartography would become an ultra-hazardous occupation. Yet what line can be drawn between the map-maker and the defendants in the present case? If it be said that there is no proximity between the cartographer and those for whose use his map is designed, the reply surely is that there is just as much 'proximity' as there was between the manufacturer of the peccant ginger beer bottle and its ultimate consumer.

In the present state of our law different rules still seem to apply to the negligent misstatement on the one hand and to the negligent circulation or repair of chattels on the other; and *Donoghue*'s case does not seem to me to have abolished these differences. I am not concerned with defending the existing state of the law or contending that it is strictly logical—it clearly is not. I am merely recording what I think it is.

If this relegates me to the company of 'timorous souls', I must face that consequence with such fortitude as I can command. I am of opinion that the appeal should be dismissed.

[**Result: Cohen LJ** agreed with **Asquith LJ**.]

Hedley Byrne & Co Ltd v Heller & Partners Ltd
[1964] AC 465 (HL)

[**FACTS**: The appellants (Hedley Byrne & Co) were advertising agents who would be personally liable for advertising orders placed on behalf of a company. The appellants asked their bank (National Provincial Bank) to make inquiries about the company's financial stability from the company's bankers, the respondents. The appellants inquired 'in confidence and without responsibility on [the respondents'] part'. The respondents gave favourable credit references in which they stated that they would incur 'no responsibility' for the references. The references were misleading, the company could not pay for the advertising, and the appellants lost over £17 000. They sought to recover from the respondents on the basis that the replies were given negligently and in breach of the respondents' duty of care to the appellants.]

Lord Reid:

… Before coming to the main question of law, it may be well to dispose of an argument that there was no sufficiently close relationship between these parties to give rise to any duty. It is said that the respondents did not know the precise purpose of the inquiries and did not even know whether the National Provincial Bank wanted the information for its own use or for the use of a customer: they knew nothing of the appellants. I would reject that argument. They knew that the inquiry was in connection with an advertising contract, and it was at least probable that the information was wanted by the advertising contractors. It seems to me quite immaterial that they did not know who these contractors were: there is no suggestion of any speciality which could have influenced them in deciding whether to give information or in what form to give it. I shall therefore treat this as if it were a case where a negligent misrepresentation is made directly to the person seeking information, opinion or advice, and I shall not attempt to decide what kind or degree of proximity is necessary before there can be a duty owed by the defendant to the plaintiff …

The appellants' first argument was based on *Donoghue v Stevenson*. That is a very important decision, but I do not think that it has any direct bearing on this case. That decision may encourage us to develop existing lines of authority, but it cannot entitle us to disregard them. Apart altogether from authority, I would think that the law must treat negligent words differently from negligent acts. The law ought so far as possible to reflect the standards of the reasonable man, and that is what *Donoghue v Stevenson* sets out to do. The most obvious difference between negligent words and negligent acts is this. Quite careful people often express definite opinions on social or informal occasions even when they see that others are likely to be influenced by them; and they often do that without taking that care which they would take if asked for their opinion professionally or in a business connection … . But it is at least unusual casually to put into circulation negligently made articles which are dangerous … .

Another obvious difference is that a negligently made article will only cause one accident, and so it is not very difficult to find the necessary degree of proximity or neighbourhood between the negligent manufacturer and the person injured. But words can be broadcast with or without the consent or the foresight of the speaker or writer. It would be one thing to say that the speaker owes a duty to a limited class, but it would be going very far to say that he owes a duty to every ultimate 'consumer' who acts on those words to his detriment. It would be no use to say that a speaker or

writer owes a duty but can disclaim responsibility if he wants to. He, like the manufacturer, could make it part of a contract that he is not to be liable for his negligence: but
that contract would not protect him in a question with a third party, at least if the
third party was unaware of it.

So it seems to me that there is good sense behind our present law that in general
an innocent but negligent misrepresentation gives no cause of action. There must be
something more than the mere misstatement. I therefore turn to the authorities to
see what more is required. The most natural requirement would be that expressly or
by implication from the circumstances the speaker or writer has undertaken some
responsibility ... .

... In *Robinson v National Bank of Scotland Ltd* [1916] SC 154, 157 Lord Haldane
did not think that a duty to take care must be limited to cases of fiduciary relationship
in the narrow sense of relationships which had been recognised by the Court of Chancery as being of a fiduciary character. He speaks of other special relationships, and I
can see no logical stopping place short of all those relationships where it is plain that
the party seeking information or advice was trusting the other to exercise such a
degree of care as the circumstances required, where it was reasonable for him to do
that, and where the other gave the information or advice when he knew or ought to
have known that the inquirer was relying on him. I say 'ought to have known'
because in questions of negligence we now apply the objective standard of what the
reasonable man would have done.

A reasonable man, knowing that he was being trusted or that his skill and judgment were being relied on, would, I think, have three courses open to him. He could
keep silent or decline to give the information or advice sought: or he could give an
answer with a clear qualification that he accepted no responsibility for it or that it was
given without that reflection or inquiry which a careful answer would require: or he
could simply answer without any such qualification. If he chooses to adopt the last
course he must, I think, be held to have accepted some responsibility for his answer
being given carefully, or to have accepted a relationship with the inquirer which
requires him to exercise such care as the circumstances require.

If that is right, then it must follow that *Candler v Crane, Christmas & Co* was
wrongly decided. This seems to me to be a typical case of agreeing to assume a
responsibility: they knew why the plaintiff wanted to see the accounts and why their
employers, the company, wanted them to be shown to him, and agreed to show them
to him without even a suggestion that he should not rely on them.

... But here the appellants' bank, who were their agents in making the inquiry,
began by saying that 'they wanted to know in confidence and without responsibility
on our part,' that is, on the part of the respondents. So I cannot see how the appellants
can now be entitled to disregard that and maintain that the respondents did incur a
responsibility to them.

... I am therefore of opinion that it is clear that the respondents never undertook
any duty to exercise care in giving their replies ... .

Lord Morris:
... My Lords, I consider that if ... someone possessed of a special skill undertakes,
quite irrespective of contract, to apply that skill for the assistance of another person
who relies upon such skill, a duty of care will arise. The fact that the service is to be

given by means of or by the instrumentality of words can make no difference. Furthermore, if in a sphere in which a person is so placed that others could reasonably rely upon his judgment or his skill or upon his ability to make careful inquiry, a person takes it upon himself to give information or advice to, or allows his information or advice to be passed on to, another person who, as he knows or should know, will place reliance upon it, then a duty of care will arise.

... [I]n my judgment, the bank in the present case, by the words which they employed, effectively disclaimed any assumption of a duty of care. They stated that they only responded to the inquiry on the basis that their reply was without responsibility.

Lord Devlin:

A simple distinction between negligence in word and negligence in deed might leave the law defective but at least it would be intelligible. This is not, however, the distinction that is drawn in Mr Foster's argument and it is one which would be unworkable. A defendant who is given a car to overhaul and repair if necessary is liable to the injured driver (a) if he overhauls it and repairs it negligently and tells the driver it is safe when it is not; (b) if he overhauls it and negligently finds it not to be in need of repair and tells the driver it is safe when it is not; and (c) if he negligently omits to overhaul it at all and tells the driver that it is safe when it is not. It would be absurd in any of these cases to argue that the proximate cause of the driver's injury was not what the defendant did or failed to do but his negligent statement on the faith of which the driver drove the car and for which he could not recover. In this type of case, where if there were a contract there would undoubtedly be a duty of service, it is not practicable to distinguish between the inspection or examination, the acts done or omitted to be done, and the advice or information given. So neither in this case nor in *Candler v Crane, Christmas & Co* (Denning LJ noted the point where he gave the example of the analyst who negligently certifies food to be harmless) has Mr Foster argued that the distinction lies there ... .

This is why the distinction is now said to depend on whether financial loss is caused through physical injury or whether it is caused directly. The interposition of the physical injury is said to make a difference of principle. I can find neither logic nor common sense in this. If irrespective of contract, a doctor negligently advises a patient that he can safely pursue his occupation and he cannot and the patient's health suffers and he loses his livelihood, the patient has a remedy. But if the doctor negligently advises him that he cannot safely pursue his occupation when in fact he can and he loses his livelihood, there is said to be no remedy. Unless, of course, the patient was a private patient and the doctor accepted half a guinea for his trouble: then the patient can recover all. I am bound to say, My Lords, that I think this to be nonsense. It is not the sort of nonsense that can arise even in the best system of law out of the need to draw nice distinctions between borderline cases. It arises, if it is the law, simply out of a refusal to make sense. The line is not drawn on any intelligible principle. It just happens to be the line which those who have been driven from the extreme assertion that negligent statements in the absence of contractual or fiduciary duty give no cause of action have in the course of their retreat so far reached ... .

In my opinion, the appellants in their argument tried to press *Donoghue v Stevenson* too hard. They asked whether the principle of proximity should not apply as well to words as to deeds. I think it should, but as it is only a general conception it does not get them very far. Then they take the specific proposition laid down by *Donoghue v Stevenson* and try to apply it literally to a certificate or a banker's reference. That will not do, for a general conception cannot be applied to pieces of paper in the same way as to articles of commerce or to writers in the same way as to manufacturers. An inquiry into the possibilities of intermediate examination of a certificate will not be fruitful. The real value of *Donoghue v Stevenson* to the argument in this case is that it shows how the law can be developed to solve particular problems. Is the relationship between the parties in this case such that it can be brought within a category giving rise to a special duty? As always in English law, the first step in such an inquiry is to see how far the authorities have gone, for new categories in the law do not spring into existence overnight.

It would be surprising if the sort of problem that is created by the facts of this case had never until recently arisen in English law. As a problem it is a by-product of the doctrine of consideration. If the respondents had made a nominal charge for the reference, the problem would not exist. If it were possible in English law to construct a contract without consideration, the problem would move at once out of the first and general phase into the particular; and the question would be, not whether on the facts of the case there was a special relationship, but whether on the facts of the case there was a contract.

The respondents in this case cannot deny that they were performing a service. Their sheet anchor is that they were performing it gratuitously and therefore no liability for its performance can arise. My Lords, in my opinion this is not the law. A promise given without consideration to perform a service cannot be enforced as a contract by the promisee; but if the service is in fact performed and done negligently, the promisee can recover in an action in tort. This is the foundation of the liability of a gratuitous bailee … .

My Lords, it is true that this principle of law has not yet been clearly applied to a case where the service which the defendant undertakes to perform is or includes the obtaining and imparting of information. But I cannot see why it should not be: and if it had not been thought erroneously that *Derry v Peek* negatived any liability for negligent statements, I think that by now it probably would have been. It cannot matter whether the information consists of fact or of opinion or is a mixture of both, nor whether it was obtained as a result of special inquiries or comes direct from facts already in the defendant's possession or from his general store of professional knowledge. One cannot, as I have already endeavoured to show, distinguish in this respect between a duty to inquire and a duty to state.

I think, therefore, that there is ample authority to justify your Lordships in saying now that the categories of special relationships which may give rise to a duty to take care in word as well as in deed are not limited to contractual relationships or to relationships of fiduciary duty, but include also relationships which in the words of Lord Shaw in *Nocton v Lord Ashburton* are 'equivalent to contract,' that is, where there is an assumption of responsibility in circumstances in which, but for the absence of consideration, there would be a contract. Where there is an express undertaking, an express warranty as distinct from mere representation, there can be little difficulty. The difficulty arises in discerning those cases in which the undertaking is to be implied. In this respect the absence of consideration is not irrelevant. Payment for information or advice is very good evidence that it is being relied upon and that the informer or adviser knows that it is. Where there is no consideration, it will be necessary to exercise greater care in distinguishing between social and professional relationships and between those which are of a contractual character and those which are not. It may often be material to consider whether the adviser is acting purely out of good nature or whether he is getting his reward in some indirect form. The service that a bank performs in giving a reference is not done simply out of a desire to assist commerce. It would discourage the customers of the bank if their deals fell through because the bank had refused to testify to their credit when it was good … .

I shall therefore content myself with the proposition that wherever there is a relationship equivalent to contract, there is a duty of care. Such a relationship may be either general or particular. Examples of a general relationship are those of solicitor and client and of banker and customer. For the former *Nocton v Lord Ashburton* has long stood as the authority and for the latter there is the decision of Salmon J in *Woods v Martins Bank Ltd* [1959] 1 QB 55 which I respectfully approve. There may well be others yet to be established. Where there is a general relationship of this sort, it is unnecessary to do more than prove its existence and the duty follows. Where, as in the present case, what is relied on is a particular relationship created ad hoc, it will be necessary to examine the particular facts to see whether there is an express or implied undertaking of responsibility.

I regard this proposition as an application of the general conception of proximity. Cases may arise in the future in which a new and wider proposition, quite independent of any notion of contract, will be needed … .

I have another reason for caution. Since the essence of the matter in the present case and in others of the same type is the acceptance of responsibility, I should like to guard against the imposition of restrictive terms notwithstanding that the essential condition is fulfilled. If a defendant says to a plaintiff: 'Let me do this for you; do not waste your money in employing a professional, I will do it for nothing and you can rely on me', I do not think he could escape liability simply because he belonged to no profession or calling, had no qualifications or special skill and did not hold himself out as having any. The relevance of these factors is to show the unlikelihood of a defendant in such circumstances assuming a legal responsibility, and as such they may often be decisive. But they are not theoretically conclusive and so cannot be the subject of definition. It would be unfortunate if they were. For it would mean that plaintiffs would seek to avoid the rigidity of the definition by bringing the action in contract … and setting up something that would do for consideration. That, to my mind, would be an undesirable development in the law; and the best way of avoiding it is to settle the law so that the presence or absence of consideration makes no difference … .

I am satisfied, for the reasons I have given, that a person for whose use a banker's reference is furnished is not, simply because no consideration has passed, prevented from contending that the banker is responsible to him for what he has said. The question is whether the appellants can set up a claim equivalent to contract and rely on an implied undertaking to accept responsibility.

… I agree entirely with the reasoning and conclusion on this [disclaimer] point of my noble and learned friend, Lord Reid. A man cannot be said voluntarily to be undertaking a responsibility if at the very moment when he is said to be accepting it he declares that in fact he is not. The problem of reconciling words of exemption with the existence of a duty arises only when a party is claiming exemption from a responsibility which he has already undertaken or which he is contracting to undertake. For this reason alone, I would dismiss the appeal.

Problems

I Jean went to Surfers Paradise on a package tour purchased from Sunshine Tours. The price included return airfares and hotel accommodation. As a bonus, she also received free round-trip vouchers for bus transportation. In Brisbane, Jean boarded the bus and received a free ticket from Surfers Paradise back to the airport. Later at the hotel, Jean looked at the bus ticket. No departure time was written on the ticket. The bus office was two miles from where Jean was staying. She found a bus schedule, which indicated the buses left hourly for the airport. The schedule was slightly out of date so she rang the bus company. Jean stated her name and that she had to catch a flight and wanted to confirm that buses left hourly for the airport. An unidentified woman confirmed the schedule.

On her departure date, Jean arrived early at the bus stop. No bus arrived. She rang the bus company and was told the bus schedule had been altered long ago and that buses left every two hours. Jean rang a taxi but missed her flight. She wants to sue the bus company in tort for the $500 it cost her for another flight to New Zealand. Does she have a chance of recovering the amount?

2 Alpha is a client of Beta, a stockbroker. Alpha heard through colleagues in the business world that there has been an oil find off Banks Peninsula. Alpha tells Beta about this. Beta puts a notice in his 'confidential' newsletter sent to clients that there has been an oil discovery, that the information is generally known to the public and that shares in the oil company were already being bought up. Xeta buys shares in the company on the strength of the newsletter. Gamma does the same after speaking directly to Beta, and Zeta does so after a chance meeting with Alpha (who said that all he knew was that there had been an oil find). It turns out that the amount of oil found is extremely small, of no commercial use and the oil company was on the verge of going into receivership. Xeta, Gamma and Zeta have all suffered losses. Can anyone sue Alpha or Beta?

3 Bill Sutch is an analyst in one of the large stock broking firms, which means he usually does not advise clients but rather is the number cruncher who tells the brokers what to advise their clients. On 1 June, however, he made two exceptions. He finally gave in to his wife's request that he advise her parents (Steve and Sandra) as to where they should invest the $400 000 from the recent sale of their family home, pending the purchase of their retirement home on the Kapiti Coast and investing the remainder for their long-awaited retirement. Bill knows that this money is their only real savings. He advised them to put all the proceeds into Xerxes, a company whose shares on the latest set of accounts he has, was extremely undervalued and ripe for takeover and hence likely to appreciate rapidly in the immediate future. That afternoon they put the whole proceeds into Xerxes shares. Bill gave the same advice to James Stele, the managing director of a large potential client who subsequently invested $50 000 of his own money.

That night Bill attended a family gathering with his parents-in-law where he told his sister-in-law, June, the same news and told her she should think about investing. Meanwhile his parents-in-law told their third daughter, Jane, to invest in 'Bill's hot tip'. Both put $20 000 into the Xerxes shares.

Situation A. A serious error in the Xerxes' accounts was discovered by one of Bill's co-analysts and that has led not only to Xerxes suffering a loss, but after a stock exchange investigation, to the discovery of a major fraud by the managing director. The company has been delisted and shares have lost all value. Bill has acknowledged that he should have picked up the error but was so excited by the idea of impressing James that his normal judgment deserted him.

Situation B. There was a serious error in the accounts but it has meant only that potential acquirers have lost interest in Xerxes. The value of the shares has not increased as much as Bill predicted. All the investors would have been better off if they had simply put their money in the bank.

a   To whom does Bill owe a duty of care? Can we simply apply *Donoghue v Stevenson*? If not, why not?

b   Did Bill breach his duties of care and if so, exactly how?

c   In what sense did Bill cause the losses suffered? Can Bill claim that the others caused their own loss?

d   What is the difference between the types of losses that occurred in Situation A and in Situation B?

4   Consider whether Hugh has a cause of action against Dennis or the Home Mortgage Company surveyor, and what damages, if any, he might recover from either.

Hugh is a 35-year-old investor with a young family and an interest in restoring old houses. Last year he saw a beautiful old, but run-down, villa for sale in Mount Victoria for $250 000. He believed that the house was incredibly undervalued and that with a bit of repair work it could be worth upwards of $500 000 in a couple of years. His plan was to buy the house, move in his family downstairs (saving on the rent he was already paying), work for the first six months on the upstairs part of the house, then divide the house into flats and rent out the upstairs to cover costs while he continued to work on the downstairs. Not knowing anything about house foundations, he asked his friend Dennis, who has just built his own house in Karori, to look over the house. Dennis is a foreign exchange dealer who likes to boast of his building ability and has often said at parties that he feels like a real builder and knows more than most of them. Having spent half an hour at Hugh's house, he concluded, 'Look's great to me'.

Hugh then convinced the Home Mortgage Company, a building society that only lends money for family homes, to lend him the $50 000 that he needed to purchase the house and another $50 000 for repairs. Afraid of falling outside their criteria, he never told them about renting out part of the house or his plans to sell the house for a profit. The Home Mortgage Company, because the house was extremely old, sent its own surveyor to the house (they charged Hugh for this) and after a two-hour inspection, agreed the house was fine.

In May of this year, after he had moved in his family and had spent another $50 000 on the repairs to the upstairs part of the house, Hugh approached the Council for a building permit for the division of the house into two flats, only to be told by its inspectors, after a very detailed check of the foundations, that the house was unsafe and would require $100 000 to make it habitable, money that Hugh simply does not have. While he is considering his options, he has had to move his family into a motel. Without the planned income from the upstairs flat he is about to default on the mortgage.

5   Karl Dewes bought farm land from Joan Lawrence, intending to build a fertiliser factory on it. He paid $300 000 for the land. During the construction, his builder discov-
ered that part of the block contained a 'soft spot' of some 20 metres in diameter.
The 'soft spot' turned out to be an old 'borehole' dug during the nineteenth century
when the property was being mined, as part of the creation of a mine shaft, which in
the end had never been finished. The borehole had been filled during the 1930s and
hence the surface looked exactly like the rest of the block. However, the loose dirt
and clay (as well as other junk in the borehole including old car bodies) meant that
building could not proceed until the borehole had been properly filled in and the fill
made stable, by constant pounding with a battering ram for a month. Even with all of
this work, a valuer has said that the land will be worth only $250 000 because of the
presence of the borehole.

When Karl bought the property from Joan Lawrence, he realised that the property
was in an area of old mines. However, he was relieved to find at the local council that
attached to the documents relating to the property, there was a 1995 engineer's report
from Arthur Clark, which said that while part of Joan's property has been mined and
should not be built on, the part that Karl planned to build on had not been mined.

Arthur, when first employed by Joan, was told that the property would be divided
into 'Block A' and 'Block B'. Block A is the area on which Karl wanted to build his factory.

Arthur told Joan that he would investigate the property in two stages. First, he
would look at old mining plans held by the local council to see if there were any old
mines on the property, and second, he would drill some holes to find how far the
mines stretched. He discovered from the plans that all the recorded mines had been
dug only on Block B. The borehole was not recorded because it was not part of a
completed mine shaft. The plans claimed to be 'a record of all the mines dug in the
region'. Joan then abandoned plans to build on Block B and began to consider offers
for Block A. She registered Arthur's report, as required by local by-laws, with the
local council. In his report, Arthur simply noted that Block B should not be built on
without further tests but that Block A was 'free of mines'. Joan paid Arthur $500 for
his work. Joan did not see any point in investigating things further, especially as the
drilling test would have cost $10 000. Arthur admits that he would have preferred to
do the drill tests; however, he claims that there was nothing in the old mining plans
or his long experience to indicate that there would be unfinished mine shafts or
boreholes on Block A. Karl has since discovered that aerial photographs available at
the local office of Land Information New Zealand clearly show a depression in the
property where he discovered the borehole.

When Karl had asked Joan about the report she told him that she had commis-
sioned the report when she planned to subdivide her property into two lifestyle blocks
and that the local council would not let her do so until she had a report. Because of the
report, Karl did not investigate the possibility of mine shafts or any other unpleasant
leftovers from the mining era in planning his factory.

Joan has disappeared and Karl wants to recover from Arthur. Can he successfully
sue Arthur in negligence for the following losses?

a $20 000, being the cost of extra work he needs done to make the land stable enough for his factory.

b $50 000, being the difference between what was paid for the land and what it will be worth after he has finished the stabilisation project.

Scott Group Ltd v McFarlane and Others
[1978] 1 NZLR 553 (CA)
Richmond P:

The case raises an important question as to the extent of the liability of the auditors of a public company for negligence in conducting their audit and giving their auditor's report in relation to the annual accounts. The central question concerns the extent of that liability as regards persons other than the company or its members who rely on the accuracy of the accounts when entering into some business transaction either with the company or with its members. In the present case Scott Group Ltd relied on the 1970 accounts of a company called John Duthie Holdings Ltd for the purposes of making a takeover bid which was eventually accepted by all the shareholders of John Duthie Holdings Ltd. Those accounts had been audited by the respondents who at that time were practising in partnership together as chartered accountants. The ... [plaintiff McFarlane] was the partner who, in practice, attended to the audit of the accounts of John Duthie Holdings Ltd.

The 1970 consolidated group accounts contained an error. The bank overdraft was understated by $38 000 and the revenue reserves and undistributed profits were overstated by the same amount. This meant that the total value of the shareholders funds was overstated by $38 000 so that, in acquiring all the shares of John Duthie Holdings Ltd, Scott Group Ltd acquired shares which did not have as much asset backing as appeared from the balance sheet. The error was discovered at a time when the takeover was virtually complete. It had arisen from the fact that the subsidiary companies of John Duthie Holdings Ltd all balanced as at 30 June, whereas the holding company balanced as at 30 September. Dividends from the subsidiary companies had been included in the holding company's accounts as well as the profits of the subsidiaries from which those dividends had come. In other words the profits of the subsidiary companies were reflected twice in the same set of accounts ... .

All the speeches in *Hedley Byrne* seem to me to recognise the need for a 'special' relationship: a relationship which can properly be treated as giving rise to a special duty to use care in statement. The question in any given case is whether the nature of the relationship is such that one party can fairly be held to have assumed a responsibility to the other as regards the reliability of the advice or information. I do not think that such a relationship should be found to exist unless, at least, the maker of the statement was, or ought to have been, aware that his advice or information would in fact be made available to and be relied on by a particular person or class of persons for the purposes of a particular transaction or type of transaction. I would especially emphasise that to my mind it does not seem reasonable to attribute an assumption of responsibility unless the maker of the statement ought in all the circumstances, both in preparing himself for what he said and in saying it, to have directed his mind, and to have been able to direct his mind, to some particular and specific purpose for which he was aware that his advice or information would be relied on. In many situations that purpose will be obvious. But the annual accounts of a company can be relied on in all sorts of ways and for many purposes. It would be going too far to treat accountants as assuming a responsibility towards all persons dealing with the company or its members, in reliance to some greater or lesser degree on the accuracy of the accounts, merely because it was reasonably foreseeable, in a general way, that a transaction of the kind in which the plaintiff happened to become involved might indeed take place. The relationship between the parties would, I think, be too general and not sufficiently 'special' to come within the principles underlying the decision in *Hedley Byrne*. As I have said, I believe it to be essential to the existence of a 'special relationship' that the maker of the statement was or should have been aware that his advice was required for use in a specific type of contemplated transaction. This requirement has not always required emphasis in the course of judicial discussion as to the nature of a special relationship.

Probably this is because in most cases the purpose for which the information was required was, on the facts, quite obvious. But certainly this particular point was made very clear indeed in Lord Denning's judgment in *Candler v Crane, Christmas & Co*. I would think that it must almost inevitably follow, once the maker of the statement is aware of a specific purpose for which his information will be used, that he will also have in direct contemplation a specific person or class of persons, even though unidentified by name.

In the present case the evidence failed to disclose circumstances which either made the auditors aware, or ought to have made them aware, that the 1970 accounts were indeed required as a basis for a takeover offer. It is true that at that time John Duthie Holdings Ltd was a company with a very strong asset backing but a poor trading record. For the latter reason the shares in the company were available at a low price on the Stock Exchange. It may be that in these circumstances the general possibility of a takeover bid being made by someone at some time or other was a reasonably foreseeable possibility. However, like Quilliam J, I have come to the conclusion that a mere general possibility of that kind is not sufficient to give rise to a special relationship. I particularly note in this context that no suggestion was made to Mr MacMorran (or elsewhere in the evidence), to the effect that the strong asset backing and poor trading record of John Duthie Holdings Ltd made the prospects of a takeover bid so strong as to remove them from the area of mere reasonable foreseeability into a realm bordering on inevitability … .

I have taken the view that the effect of *Hedley Byrne* was to establish a limited exception to the general rule of the common law whereby a person who negligently but honestly supplied incorrect information could not be held liable in damages in tort. That exception was held to exist in the case of a 'special relationship' arising from a voluntary assumption of responsibility by one person towards another. The metes and bounds of such a relationship were left for further definition as individual cases came before the courts. Against that background I have felt that the facts of the present case call for such a further definition by this court rather than for a departure from the concept of a special relationship into the realms of a general duty of care based on the reasonable foreseeability of harm. I confess that I have found the task most difficult, and not the least so in deciding what effect I should give to Lord Wilberforce's statement of principle in *Anns v Merton London Borough Council* which after all, was not a case involving the supply of inaccurate information. But in the end, and for the reasons which I have given, I would dismiss the appeal.

Woodhouse J:

… I return to the present case and the first stage of the inquiry suggested by Lord Wilberforce in the *Anns* case. Was there a relationship between the parties sufficient to give rise to a prima facie duty of care? In my opinion there are four broad reasons which require the court to answer that question, 'Yes'. They are:

(1) The auditors are professionals. They were in the business of providing expert advice for reward. Their work was undertaken voluntarily and their advice was then given in a considered and deliberate way by certifying in effect that the accounts could safely be relied on. It would be a fruitless exercise if they did not intend that the audited accounts could and would be relied on. So their audit report gave an added quality to the accounts and that was its purpose. Certainly there was nothing casual about any aspect of their professional function: cf the *MLC* case.

(2) Although an audit is undertaken on behalf of the members of a public company it must be within the reasonable contemplation of any auditor that confidence in its ability to handle its commercial arrangements would depend upon the authenticity of its accounts—a confidence that would disappear if reliance could not be put upon the audit report. So I think that when auditors deliberately undertake to provide their formal report upon the accounts of a public company they must be taken to have accepted not merely a direct responsibility to the shareholders but a further duty to those persons whom they can reasonably foresee will need to use and rely upon them when dealing with the company or its members in significant matters affecting the company assets and business. An example, no doubt, would be the banker asked to make substantial advances on the security of the company undertaking. On the other hand, there would seem to be formidable difficulties for a plaintiff who attempted to prove that an auditor should have foreseen the plaintiff's likely reliance upon some newspaper or a stock exchange reference to a company's accounts. However, it is sufficient for present purposes to restrict consideration to a takeover offer related, as so frequently is the position, to the value of shareholders' funds. In such a situation the need to rely upon audited accounts is, I think, quite obvious. As a matter of commercial reality I think the auditor and offeror are in a relationship of close proximity.

(3) There is no opportunity in the ordinary case for any intermediate examination of the underlying authenticity of a company's accounts. Nor would it be practicable for numbers of persons to make independent examinations on an individual basis. All this an auditor must be taken to realise when he accepts his delegated function for the shareholders.

(4) The auditors had no direct knowledge of Scott Group Ltd or that a takeover from any quarter was contemplated. That lack of knowledge distinguishes the case from *Hedley Byrne* for example. But they undertook the audit knowing that the accounts, together with their report, would become a matter of public record in the Companies Office by reason of s 133 of the Companies Act 1955. That fact cannot involve them in some statutory responsibility to members of the public but it does mean that anybody sufficiently concerned will have direct access to the authenticated accounts when making decisions concerning the company. In my opinion that last matter is an important reason for the statutory requirement that the audited

accounts should be filed annually with the registrar. It enables significant information to become available to those who need it and at the same time, I think, that process complements the administrative oversight of those who have regulation responsibility in terms of the Act.

The second stage of the inquiry is to consider whether there are factors in the case which ought to negative or limit the scope of the duty of care. In my opinion there are not. For reasons touched on earlier I do not think that the imposition of responsibility for negligent advice would lead to an intolerable burden upon auditor defendants. There is the initial need to establish a duty of care situation in terms of the critical requirement of reasonable foresight; and then there is the need to provide evidence in terms of causation. I am satisfied that these matters alone would prevent any risk of an open-ended type of duty. In the area of foresight I have referred to the difficulties likely to face a plaintiff who attempted to show that it could fairly be anticipated that he would act upon some casual reference to a company's accounts. And in the area of causation there would be the further need to show that the plaintiff actually had relied on the information (whether obtained informally or even in a formal way from the Companies Office or the company itself) to the point that it had become a real and effective cause of the loss. At least in the present case it is clear that Scott Group Ltd obtained the accounts directly from John Duthie Holdings Ltd.

... I would allow the appeal with an award of damages to the appellant in the sum of $24 500.

Cooke J:

... As to the duty of care, the essential facts of this case have no parallel in any of the cases cited in argument. That is to say, this is a case of a *takeover offer* for the shares of a *public company*—a company which accordingly, by s 133 of the Act of 1955, is required to annex to its annual return a copy of the report of the auditors on the balance sheet. To that particular combination of features may be added a third: there was *no disclaimer* of liability to members of the public who might rely on the published accounts.

This third point must go far to dispel any suggestion that undue hardship would flow from imposing liability on auditors in such a case. No one would suggest that a duty of care exists simply because it could have been disclaimed. But in deciding whether it is just to recognise a duty of care, or whether on the other hand this would be to impose too severe a burden on potential defendants, it seems to me that the possibility of a disclaimer is one relevant factor. By s 204 of the Act provisions for exempting an auditor from any liability which by virtue of any rule of law would otherwise attach to him in respect of any negligence of which he may be guilty in relation to the company shall be void. The section would prevent an auditor from contracting out of liability to the company and possibly its members. In relation to members of the public proposing to rely on the published accounts, however, a disclaimer would operate, not as an exemption from liability attaching by virtue of any rule of law, but as negating any assumption of a duty of care: see per Lord Reid in *Hedley Byrne*. I do not think that s 204 is aimed at such a case. Nor would there be any difficulty in appending a disclaimer of *general* liability to the auditors' certificate, so one reason given by Lord Reid in that case for limiting rights of action for negligent words does not apply. Perhaps some auditors, naturally jealous of their professional reputation, would hesitate to announce such a disclaimer, nor do we know what the attitude of the stock exchange might be. But if there were any reservations of that kind, they would only serve to underline that reason—people thought that liability for negligence should be accepted.

... The statutory requirements regarding the filing of financial information stem, I think, from the view that those *dealing with* or *investing in* a limited liability company have a legitimate interest in being afforded reasonable access to relevant information; and that this interest has to be balanced against the wish for confidentiality naturally entertained by family companies and the like which do not appeal to the public for funds ... . I would agree, though, that the provisions are probably not aimed, or at least not primarily, at protecting purchasers of shares in the market.

... The relevance of the public availability of the certified accounts, as I see it, is simply that the certifying auditors know that the accounts and their certificate will indeed be made public. As the President says, in itself this only means that the auditor knows that the accounts and report may be relied on by one or more members of the public, to some greater or lesser degree, as the basis of some business transaction. I do not say that this alone is enough to give rise to a duty. But then one comes to the second feature of the present case—that it was a takeover transaction, and moreover a reasonably foreseeable one. The evidence shows that John Duthie Holdings Ltd was rich in assets but somewhat unimpressive in earnings ... . It was a classic case for a takeover or merger ... . And it was no less obvious that, as the company was a public one, any takeover would be preceded by a study of the published accounts. It is hardly conceivable that they would be ignored. The careful bargaining between the two boards of directors which in fact occurred here, against the background of the mutually exchanged accounts, is exactly the sort of dealing and use of the accounts that must reasonably have been foreseen as virtually inevitable if a takeover proposal did eventuate.

The authorities show that the degree and magnitude of the risk are among the factors to be weighed in deciding whether liability for negligence should be imposed ... . They are factors relevant both to whether a duty exists and to what a reasonable man would do to discharge a duty. Here we are concerned with the first question, there being no dispute about the second. I think the evidence discloses a plain risk of a takeover and the virtual certainty that in such an event the accounts would be relied on by an offeror. Another important factor, as *Mutual Life and Citizens' Assurance Co Ltd v Evatt* (1970) 122 CLR 628 establishes, is whether the defendants have held themselves out as having professional skill; no problem arises here under that head. Then there is the pervasive fear of imposing indeterminate liability to indeterminate numbers. Again this need not cause anxiety. A company purchasing all or the majority of the shares is more directly and closely affected than, for instance, an ordinary purchaser of shares on the stock market. And in all ordinary circumstances there will in fact be only one offeror who makes a successful takeover offer on the basis of the carelessly certified accounts. There is no need to express an opinion on the perhaps unusual case of an ordinary market purchaser who first makes a careful study of the audited accounts or even on the case of a quite unforeseeable takeover.

... With regard to *Hedley Byrne*, while there are various passages in the speeches that can be prayed in aid of one side or the other in the present appeal, the facts were so different that I think it would be straining that case to try to make it yield an answer to this one. Both *Hedley Byrne* and *MLC* were concerned with specific requests for advice, and in both the reasoning of their Lordships naturally centred on that sort of situation. Neither was concerned with an elementary factual error in the certifying of accounts which were to be made public, or with a complete purchase of a company. For the reasons already given, I think that on the facts of this case as between the alleged wrongdoer and the person who has allegedly suffered damage there is a sufficient relationship of proximity or neighbourhood such that, in the reasonable contemplation of the former, carelessness on his part may be likely to cause damage to the latter. So a prima facie duty of care arises. Then Lord Wilberforce says in *Anns*, it is necessary to consider whether there are any considerations which ought to negative, or to reduce or limit the scope of the duty or the class of person to whom it is owed or the damages to which a breach of it may give rise. The class here is most narrowly limited. In my view, even that limited class could have been excluded by disclaimer. The damages are also necessarily limited by the principle to be discussed shortly. Seeing no sufficient negativing considerations, I would hold, agreeing in this conclusion with Woodhouse J, that a duty of care was owed.

... [I]n the Supreme Court I had to consider the approach to cases in the field of negligence law not clearly covered by existing authority in *Rutherford v Attorney-General* [1976] 1 NZLR 403, 411, which was about the negligent issue of a certificate of fitness for a heavy motor vehicle ... . I mention it only because the authorities there cited led me to think that the proper approach was to look at all the material facts in combination, in order to decide as a question of mixed law and fact whether or not liability should be imposed. Ultimately it might be simply what Lord Morris called in the *Dorset Yacht* case ... a decision as to whether it was fair and reasonable that a duty of care should arise; or it might be described as a question of the policy of the common law ... . Lord Pearson had said in the *Dorset Yacht* case that to some extent the decision in that case 'must be a matter of impression and instinctive justice as to what is fair and just' ... In *Rutherford's* case I ventured to suggest that it is more than Chancellor's-foot justice. The courts have evolved signposts or guidelines or relevant considerations—involving such notions as neighbours, control, proximity, opportunity for intermediate examination, deeds or words, the degree and kind of risk to be guarded against—and these are all available as aids to the end result. I also thought, and still think, that it was very important to have regard to Lord Pearson's observations in the *Dorset Yacht* case that, while negligence is often conveniently analysed into components, it is only an analysis and should not eliminate consideration of the tort of negligence as a whole; and that it may be artificial and unhelpful to consider the question as to the existence of a duty of care in isolation from the other elements needed to make up a complete cause of action.

... The statements of general principle in *Anns* can be seen as an important simplification of the law, embodying an indication of emphasis but qualified sufficiently to prevent development from getting out of hand; and I would unhesitatingly apply them ... . But, whatever the general formulations current from time to time, an essentially pragmatic approach has been characteristic of the leading English tort cases in modern times, and the New Zealand ones also (for example *Heard v New Zealand Forest Products Ltd* [1960] NZLR 329 and *Dimond Manufacturing Co Ltd v Hamilton* [1969] NZLR

609) ... . Approaching the case as in the end an issue of practical justice, it is difficult
to see that any question of relativity of standard arises. Provided that, as Lord Pearson's
observations stress, the kind of damage for which tort gives a remedy can be shown to
have been caused to the appellant by the mistake, it seems to me fair and reasonable
that the professional auditors should accept the consequences.

Damages

On the question of damages, however, I am against the appellant. It is essential to
remember that we are in the sphere of damages for tort—that is to say, reparation for
harm done. It is not a case in contract, where the damages broadly represent the benefit which the plaintiff was promised. In an action in tort for deceit leading to a contract
of purchase, the normal measure of damages is the difference between the price paid
and the fair value at the time of purchase ... .

To make out its case, therefore, the plaintiff had to show on the balance of probabilities that the true value of the Duthie shares was less than the true value of the Scott
shares issued as consideration. The takeover was of shares controlling assets recognised
by the parties at the time to be worth well over $1 million but incapable of exact
assessment. In that setting it is apparent that a diminution of $38 000 in the amount of
a part of the Duthie assets would not necessarily make the agreed consideration inadequate. There was evidence that, on the two-to-one ratio ultimately offered, the Scott
company provisionally calculated that the Duthie assets would exceed the value of the
shares to be allotted by $263 885. This calculation was based on the assumption,
accepted by Mr Scott in evidence as conservative, that the Duthie land was worth only
$75 000 more than book value. It is true that it was also based on the assumption that
the Scott shares were worth $1 each, whereas the subsequent takeover documents
showed $1.10 as the latest available sale price before notice of the scheme; but, if that
or the even higher figure of $1.15 be taken, there is still an ample margin ... .

Further as to the true test: the distinction between inducement and damages is crucial. Suing in tort, the plaintiff must prove not only that it acted on the defendants'
statement but that it sustained damage by so doing. Authority is not really needed for
this elementary proposition, but see for instance *Edgington v Fitzmaurice* (1885) 29 Ch
D 459, 481–2, per Bowen LJ. There is evidence that if aware of the mistake the plaintiff would have offered less. I doubt whether there is any substantial evidence that the
Duthie directors would have accepted or recommended acceptance of less, but if that
question were important I would concur in Quilliam J's view that an inquiry into
damages would have been appropriate ... .

In principle it must be so, because the tort measure is the plaintiff's loss, which
cannot be ascertained without taking into account the benefit that the transaction has
in fact brought him.

When this takeover is looked at from that point of view it becomes clear, I think,
from the Scott company's own evidence that it did not make any loss. All that happened was that its profit was not as great as it would have been if the accounts had
been correct.

In summary: what has to be compared, in my opinion, is on the one hand, the
value of the Scott shares issued as consideration and, on the other, the value to the
Scott company of the Duthie shares (representing the control of assets) immediately

after the takeover. In the light of the evidence just quoted and quoted earlier, I do not see any basis for finding a loss.

The case is epitomised in a question put by Quilliam J to Mr MacMorran and the latter's answer:

> Q. Do I understand you to say that what has happened is that rather than talk-
> ing in terms of a figure of $38 000 you say that this plaintiff received a very
> good bargain for what it paid but as it turns out a fractionally less good bargain
> than at first sight it appeared? A. I think you have summarised my view very
> well.

On the ground that, when there is no contract between the parties and the plaintiff has to fall back on a duty of care arising from the circumstances, the law is not designed to assure to the plaintiff the profit which he had hoped to make, I would dismiss this appeal.

Caparo Industries v Dickman
[1990] 2 AC 605 (HL)
Lord Oliver:
My Lords, this appeal, having come to this House on a preliminary point, involves the making of a number of assumptions of fact which might or might not be substantiated at the trial of the action. To begin with, it is to be assumed against the appellants that they showed a lack of reasonable care in certifying that the accounts of Fidelity for the year ended 31 March 1984 gave a true and fair view of Fidelity's position. It is also to be assumed that, when they certified the accounts, the appellants knew or would, if they had thought about it, have known that Fidelity was vulnerable to take-over bids, that a potential bidder would be likely to rely upon the accuracy of the accounts in making his bid and that investors in the market generally, whether or not already members of Fidelity, would also be likely to or might well rely upon the accounts in deciding to purchase shares in that company.
[**Note:** The plaintiff in fact purchased Fidelity shares in reliance on the accounts.]
Your Lordships are not, however, either required or entitled to make any assumption that the purpose of the certification was anything other than that of fulfilling the statutory duty of carrying out the annual audit with a view to the circulation of the accounts to persons who were either registered shareholders or debenture-holders of Fidelity and the subsequent laying of the accounts before the annual general meeting of that company ... .

... It is argued on behalf of the respondent that there is to be discerned in the legislation an additional or wider commercial purpose, namely that of enabling those to whom the accounts are addressed and circulated, to make informed investment decisions, for instance, by determining whether to dispose of their shares in the market or whether to apply any funds which they are individually able to command in seeking to purchase the shares of other shareholders. Of course, the provision of any information about the business and affairs of a trading company, whether it be contained in annual accounts or obtained from other sources, is capable of serving such a purpose just as it is capable of serving as the basis for the giving of financial advice to others, for arriving at a market price, for determining whether to extend credit to the company, or for the writing of financial articles in the press. Indeed, it is readily foreseeable by anyone who gives the matter any thought that it might well be relied on to a greater or less extent for all or any of such purposes. It is, of course, equally foreseeable that potential investors having no proprietary interest in the company might well avail themselves of the information contained in a company's accounts published in the newspapers or culled from an inspection of the documents to be filed annually with the Registrar of Companies (which includes the audited accounts) in determining whether or not to acquire shares in the company. I find it difficult to believe, however, that the legislature, in enacting provisions clearly aimed primarily at the protection of the company and its informed control by the body of its proprietors, can have been inspired also by consideration for the public at large and investors in the market in particular ... .

The extension of the concept of negligence since the decision of this House in *Hedley Byrne & Co Ltd v Heller & Partners Ltd* ... . to cover cases of pure economic loss not resulting from physical damage has given rise to a considerable and as yet unsolved difficulty of definition ... . But although the cases in which the courts have imposed or withheld liability are capable of an approximate categorisation, one looks in vain for some common denominator by which the existence of the essential relationship can be tested. Indeed it is difficult to resist a conclusion that what have been treated as three separate requirements are, at least in most cases, in fact merely facets of the same thing, for in some cases the degree of foreseeability is such that it is from that alone that the requisite proximity can be deduced, whilst in others the absence of that essential relationship can most rationally be attributed simply to the court's view that it would not be fair and reasonable to hold the defendant responsible. 'Proximity' is, no doubt, a convenient expression so long as it is realised that it is no more than a label which embraces not a definable concept but merely a description of circumstances from which, pragmatically, the courts include that a duty of care exists.

... The fact is that once one discards, as it is now clear that one must, the concept of foreseeability of harm as the single exclusive test—even a prima facie test—of the existence of the duty of care, the attempt to state some general principle which will determine liability in an infinite variety of circumstances serves not to clarify the law but merely to bedevil its development in a way which corresponds with practicality and common sense ... .

The damage which may be occasioned by the spoken or written word is not inherent. It lies always in the reliance by somebody upon the accuracy of that which the word communicates and the loss or damage consequential upon that person having adopted a course of action upon the faith of it. In general, it may be said that when any serious statement, whether it takes the form of a statement of fact or of advice, is published or communicated, it is foreseeable that the person who reads or receives it is likely to accept it as accurate and to act accordingly. It is equally foreseeable that if it is inaccurate in a material particular the recipient who acts upon it may suffer a detriment which, if the statement had been accurate, he would not have undergone. But it is now clear that mere foreseeability is not of itself sufficient to ground liability unless by reason of the circumstances it itself constitutes also the element of proximity (as in the case of direct physical damage) or unless it is accompanied by other circumstances from which that element may be deduced. One must, however, be careful about seeking to find any general principle which will serve as a touchstone for all cases, for even within the limited category of what, for the sake of convenience, I may refer to as 'the negligent statement cases', circumstances may differ infinitely and, in a swiftly developing field of law, there can be no necessary assumption that those features which have served in one case to create the relationship between the plaintiff and the defendant on which liability depends will necessarily be determinative of liability in the different circumstances of another case. There are, for instance, at least four and possibly more situations in which damage or loss may arise from reliance upon the spoken or written word and it must not be assumed that because they display common features of reliance and foreseeability they are necessarily in all respects analogous. To begin with, reliance upon a careless statement may give rise to direct physical injury which may be caused either to the person who acts on the faith of the statement or to a third person. One has only to consider, for instance, the chemist's assistant who mislabels a dangerous medicine or a medical man who gives negligent telephonic advice to a parent with regard to the treatment of a sick child, or an architect who negligently instructs a bricklayer to remove the keystone of an archway (as in *Clayton v Woodman & Sons (Builders) Ltd* [1962] 2 QB 533). In such cases it is not easy to divorce foreseeability simpliciter and the proximity which flows from the virtual inevitability of damage if the advice is followed. Again, economic loss may be inflicted upon a third party as a result of the act of the recipient of the advice or information carried out in reliance upon it (as, for instance, the testator [who has instructed a solicitor to prepare a will] in *Ross v Caunters* [1980] Ch 297 or the purchaser [of a property who has checked official records] in *Ministry of Housing and Local Government v Sharp* [1970] 2 QB 223, both cases which give rise to certain difficulties of analysis). For present purposes, however, it is necessary to consider only those cases of economic damage suffered directly by a recipient of the statement or advice as a result of him personally having acted in reliance upon it.

In his dissenting judgment in *Candler v Crane, Christmas & Co*, Denning LJ suggested three conditions for the creation of a duty of care in tort in such cases … .

It is plain, however, from other passages in his judgment, that Denning LJ did not consider these conditions as necessarily exhaustive criteria of the existence of a duty and the speeches in this House in the *Hedley Byrne* case, where his judgment was approved indicate a number of directions in which such criteria are to be extended.

The point that is, as it seems to me, significant in the present context, is the unanimous approval in this House of the judgment of Denning LJ in *Candler's* case in which he expressed the test of proximity in these words: 'did the accountants know that the accounts were required for submission to the plaintiff and use by him?' In so far as this might be said to imply that the plaintiff must be specifically identified as the ultimate recipient and that the precise purpose for which the accounts were required must be known to the defendant before the necessary relationship can be created, Denning LJ's formulation was expanded in the *Hedley Byrne* case, where it is clear that, but for an effective disclaimer, liability would have attached. The respondents there were not aware of the actual identity of the advertising firm for which the credit reference was required nor of its precise purpose, save that it was required in anticipation of the placing of advertising contracts. Furthermore, it is clear that 'knowledge' on the part of the respondents embraced not only actual knowledge but such knowledge as would be attributed to a reasonable person placed as the respondents were placed. What can be deduced from the *Hedley Byrne* case, therefore, is that the necessary relationship between the maker of a statement or giver of advice ('the adviser') and the recipient who acts in reliance upon it ('the advisee') may typically be held to exist where (1) the advice is required for a purpose, whether particularly specified or generally described, which is made known, either actually or inferentially, to the adviser at the time when the advice is given; (2) the adviser knows, either actually or inferentially, that his advice will be communicated to the advisee, either specifically or as a member of an ascertainable class, in order that it should be used by the advisee for that purpose; (3) it is known either actually or inferentially, that the advice so communicated is likely to be acted upon by the advisee for that purpose without independent inquiry; and (4) it is so acted upon by the advisee to his detriment. That is not, of course, to suggest that these conditions are either conclusive or exclusive, but merely that the actual decision in the case does not warrant any broader propositions.

... As I have already mentioned, it is almost always foreseeable that someone, somewhere and in some circumstances, may choose to alter his position upon the faith of the accuracy of a statement or report which comes to his attention and it is always foreseeable that a report—even a confidential report—may come to be communicated to persons other than the original or intended recipient. To apply as a test of liability only the foreseeability of possible damage without some further control would be to create a liability wholly indefinite in area, duration and amount and would open up a limitless vista of uninsurable risk for the professional man.

In *Scott Group Ltd v McFarlane*, the defendants were the auditors of a company which had been successfully taken over in reliance upon certified consolidated accounts in which, as a result of double-counting, the assets were overstated. It was admitted that the failure of the defendants to discover the discrepancy was due to negligence. In the Supreme Court of New Zealand, Quilliam J dismissed the plaintiffs' claim on the ground that the appellants, though careless, owed them no duty of care. An appeal to the Court of Appeal failed but the court was divided as to the reasons. Richmond P held that the appeal failed for the same reason as that stated by the trial judge. Woodhouse J would have allowed the appeal. Cooke J, on the other hand, whilst concurring with Woodhouse J that the respondents did in fact owe a duty of care to the appellants, held that the appeal failed because they had failed to show any recoverable loss.

Both Woodhouse and Cooke JJ, who favoured a wider view of responsibility, based themselves upon an interpretation of the speech of Lord Wilberforce in the *Anns* case which required, as the first stage of the two-stage inquiry to which he there referred, no more than a consideration of whether harm was foreseeable, thus equating the 'proximate relationship' as comprehending foresight and nothing more.

... [Cooke J] adopted, as the first step of Lord Wilberforce's two-stage approach, the formulation which equates the relationship of proximity with foreseeability, although at an earlier stage of his judgment he seemed to be disposed to regard the essential relationship as arising not simply from the foreseeability that a member of the public might rely on the accounts as a basis of some transaction but, for a reason which I confess I do not fully understand, from the foreseeability that some member of the public might rely on the accounts for the making of a takeover bid … . Thus the majority of the Court of Appeal favoured a more extensive view of the circumstances from which the essential relationship between plaintiff and defendant may be inferred in a negligent statement case than had yet emerged from any decision in the United Kingdom.

Now, of course, any decision of the Court of Appeal of New Zealand is entitled to the very greatest respect, but it has to be observed that the majority view was based upon an interpretation of Lord Wilberforce's observations in the *Anns* case which has since been severely qualified by subsequent decisions of this House.

This case, therefore, falls into the same category as the other two cases. All three were based upon the view of Lord Wilberforce's exposition in the *Anns* case which would result in foreseeability and proximity being treated as synonymous—a view which this House (and, indeed, Lord Wilberforce himself in *McLoughlin v O'Brian*) has now decisively rejected. That, of course, does not conclude the question for it would still be open to your Lordships to find in the circumstances of this case that a special relationship existed between the auditor conducting an annual audit in pursuance of his statutory duty and every potential investor in the market or, indeed, any other person who might do business with the company without relying solely upon the foreseeability of potential damage to such person. Just as, for instance, in *Smith v Eric S Bush* [1990] 1 AC 831, one of the factors giving rise to the relationship in that case was the circumstance that the plaintiff was the person who paid for the report upon which the reliance was placed, so here it might be said that a special relationship was to be found in the nature and extent of the statutory duties which the auditor is called upon to fulfil.

… For my part, however, I can see nothing in the statutory duties of a company's auditor to suggest that they were intended by Parliament to protect the interests of investors in the market and I see no reason in policy or in principle why it should be either desirable or appropriate that the ambit of the special relationship required to give rise to liability in cases such as the present should be extended beyond those limits which are deducible from the cases of *Hedley Byrne* and *Smith v Eric S Bush*. Those limits appear to me to be correctly and admirably stated in the passages from the judgment of Richmond P in the *Scott Group* case to which I have already referred. In particular, I see no reason why any special relationship should be held to arise simply from the circumstance that the affairs of the company are such as to render it susceptible to the attention of predators in the market who may be interested in acquiring all or the majority of the shares rather than merely a parcel of shares by way of addition to a portfolio. It follows that I would dismiss the respondents' cross-appeal.

I turn, therefore, to the question raised by the appellants' appeal. The Court of Appeal, whilst rejecting unanimously the respondents' contention that the appellants owed them a duty of care simply as potential investors in the market, nevertheless by a majority allowed their claim that a similar duty was owed to them in their capacity as shareholders from the date when they first became registered in respect of shares which they had purchased. Now it cannot be nor is it claimed that this event created for the appellants any new or greater risk of harm in relation to a certification which had already taken place; nor can it be claimed that it brought about some change in the quality or extent of the respondents' reliance upon the (*ex hypothesi*) inaccurate information which they had previously received and digested. The only difference in their position before registration and their position afterwards was that, as registered shareholders, they now had the statutory right to receive the accounts on which they had already relied in acquiring their original shares and to receive notice of and attend the annual general meeting of Fidelity at which the accounts were to be read and, if thought fit, approved and passed. This change of position seems, on the face of it, less than momentous and in fact they did not trouble to appoint a representative to attend the meeting on their behalf. If a distinction is to be found at all, therefore, it can only be that the nature and purpose of the statutory provisions governing the appointment and duties of auditors and the certification and publication to shareholders and others of the accounts have the effect of creating, between the auditors and individual share-holders, as potential investors in that capacity, that special relationship of proximity which is required to give rise to the duty of care and which does not exist between the auditors and the investing public generally.

Now if it be right, as, for my part, I believe that it is and as the Court of Appeal has held, that no relationship of proximity and thus no duty of care exists between auditors and the investing public generally in relation to the statutory audit—I say nothing, of course, about a case where accounts are audited specifically for the purpose of submission to a potential investor—the attribution of such a duty arising from the receipt of exactly the same information by a person who happens to be the registered holder of a share in the company whose accounts are in question produces entirely capricious results. For example, a shareholder who, having purchased further shares at an overvalue on the basis of the accounts, shows the accounts to a friend who has no existing shareholding but proceeds to make a similar purchase. Each receives exactly the same information; each relies upon it in exactly the same way and for the same purpose; and the loss sustained in both cases is identical and is equally foreseeable. Yet liability is said to exist in the one case but not in the other. One has indeed only to consider the circumstances of the instant case which must ultimately result in drawing a distinction between the loss sustained as a result of the initial purchase of shares (irre-coverable) and that sustained as a result of purchase made after the first registration (recoverable) although all purchases were made in reliance upon exactly the same information.

So unreasonable a distinction must call in question the analysis which leads to it. The majority in the Court of Appeal deduced the relationship from what Bingham LJ described, as 'the degree of closeness between the parties.' It was pointed out that although the auditors are appointed and paid by the company that is the result of the vote of the shareholders in general meeting and that remuneration is paid out of funds which might otherwise be available for distribution to shareholders by way of divi-dend. Their duty is to report to the shareholders whether the accounts give a true and fair view of the company's financial position and their report is sent to each share-holder as an identifiable individual. Thus, it was said, the relationship, although not a contractual one, was very close to being contractual and was moreover one in which a lack of care would be likely directly to affect the very person whose interest the audi-tor is engaged to protect, should that person choose to rely upon the accounts for the purpose of making or disposing of an investment. My Lords, of course I see the force of this, but, as I have already suggested, 'proximity' in cases such as this is an expression used not necessarily as indicating literally 'closeness' in a physical or metaphorical sense but merely as a convenient label to describe circumstances from which the law will attribute a duty of care … .

In seeking to ascertain whether there should be imposed on the adviser a duty to avoid the occurrence of the kind of damage which the advisee claims to have suffered it is not, I think, sufficient to ask simply whether there existed a 'closeness' between them in the sense that the advisee had a legal entitlement to receive the information upon the basis of which he has acted or in the sense that the information was intended to serve his interest or to protect him. One must, I think, go further and ask, in what capacity was his interest to be served and from what was he intended to be protected? A company's annual accounts are capable of being utilised for a number of purposes and if one thinks about it it is entirely foreseeable that they may be so employed. But many of such purposes have absolutely no connection with the recipient's status or capacity, whether as a shareholder, voting or non-voting, or as a debenture-holder. Before it can be concluded that the duty is imposed to protect the recipient against harm which he suffers by reason of the particular use that he chooses to make of the information which he receives, one must, I think, first ascertain the purpose for which the information is required to be given. Indeed the paradigmatic *Donoghue v Stevenson* case of a manufactured article requires, as an essential ingredient of liability, that the article has been used by the consumer in the manner in which it was intended to be used … I entirely follow that if the conclusion is reached that the very purpose of providing the information is to serve as the basis for making investment decisions or giving investment advice, it is not difficult then to conclude also that the duty imposed upon the adviser extends to protecting the recipient against loss occasioned by an unfortunate investment decision which is based on carelessly inaccurate information … .

In my judgment, accordingly, the purpose for which the auditors' certificate is made and published is that of providing those entitled to receive the report with information to enable them to exercise in conjunction those powers which their respective proprietary interests confer upon them and not for the purposes of individual speculation with a view to profit. The same considerations as limit the existence of a duty of care also, in my judgment, limit the scope of the duty and I agree with O'Connor LJ that the duty of care is one owed to the shareholders as a body and not to individual shareholders … .

I, too, would allow the appeal and dismiss the cross-appeal.

Williams v Natural Life Health Foods Ltd
[1998] 1 WLR 830; [1998] 2 All ER 577 (HL)
Lord Steyn:
My Lords, [t]he principal question on this appeal is whether a director of a franchisor company is personally liable to franchisees for loss which they suffered as a result of negligent advice given to them by the franchisor company. At first instance the judge

answered that question in the affirmative ... By a majority the Court of Appeal upheld this conclusion and dismissed an appeal ...

The franchising transaction

The underlying dispute arose in the context of a marketing system sometimes described as business format franchising. It involves a contractual licence under which the franchisor permits a franchisee to carry on business under a trade name belonging to the franchisor. The franchisor provides advice and assistance to the franchisee about the manner in which the franchisee does business and exercises some control over it. In return the franchisee pays stipulated fees to the franchisor.

In about 1980 Mr Richard Mistlin, the appellant, started to work in the health food trade. In 1983 he opened a health food shop in Salisbury. In 1986, he formed Natural Life Health Foods Limited, a company incorporated with limited liability, in order to franchise the concept of retail health food shops under the 'Natural Life Health Foods'. Mr Mistlin was the managing director and principal shareholder of the company. Mr Mistlin's wife was a nominal shareholder and she was also employed by the company. Mr Ron Padwick and Miss Sara Shepherd were the only other employees of the company. Both had some experience in the franchising business.

In 1987, Mr David Williams and Mrs Christine Reid, the respondents, approached the new company with a view to obtaining a franchise for a health shop in Rugby. The respondents asked for a brochure and Mr Padwick gave them one. The brochure described the company's system as 'a proven concept.' The flavour of the brochure is conveyed by the following:

YOUR VERY OWN HEALTH FOOD STORE UNDER THE
NATURAL LIFE BANNER
offers you
Independence and Security
Substantial Income
Freedom to run your own business
Full support from an experienced company
bulk buying power
new product knowledge
on-going training

It described the company's team in glowing terms. Dealing with Mr Mistlin the brochure stated:

In 1983, he opened Salisbury Health Foods, a store that has been a leader in the trade ever since and was awarded 'Retailer of the Year' in 1983. It is still a regular winner of awards and competitions within the industry and is the pilot unit for the NATURAL LIFE franchise network.

The company sent detailed financial projections to the respondents. The projections demonstrated the likely future profitability of the shop. Mr Mistlin had played a prominent part in the production of the projections. All the material pre-contractual documents were on the company's notepaper. The respondents dealt with Mr Padwick.

They did not know Mr Mistlin and they had no material pre-contractual dealings with him.

Encouraged by the brochure and the prospectus, the respondents entered into a franchise agreement with the company dated 1 May 1987. The respondents took a lease of the shop premises in Rugby and set up business there. The shop opened in October 1987. The turnover proved substantially less than predicted by the company. The business traded at a loss over the next 18 months and then ceased trading ...

The theory of the extended Hedley Byrne principle

... It is clear, and accepted by counsel on both sides, that the governing principles are stated in the leading speech of Lord Goff of Chieveley in *Henderson v Merrett Syndicates Ltd* ... First, in *Henderson* it was well settled that the assumption of responsibility principle enunciated in *Hedley Byrne & Co Ltd* ... is not confined to statements but may apply to any technique adopted by English law to provide a remedy for the recovery of damages in respect of economic loss caused by the negligent performance of services. Secondly, it was established that once a case is identified as falling within the extended *Hedley Byrne* principle, there is no need to embark on any further inquiry whether it is 'fair, just and reasonable' to impose liability for economic loss. Thirdly, and applying *Hedley Byrne*, it was made clear that 'reliance upon [the assumption of responsibility] by the other party will be necessary to establish a cause of action (because otherwise the negligence will have no causative effect).' Fourthly, it was held that the existence of a contractual duty of care between the parties does not preclude the concurrence of a tort duty in the same respect.

... Waite LJ took the view that in the context of directors of companies the general principle must not 'set at naught' the protection of limited liability. In *Trevor Ivory Ltd v Anderson* [1992] 2 NZLR 517, 524, Cooke P ... expressed a very similar view. It is clear what they meant. What matters is not that the liability of the shareholders of a company is limited but that a company is a separate entity, distinct from its directors, servants or other agents. The trader who incorporates a company to which he transfers his business creates a legal person on whose behalf he may afterwards act as director. For present purposes, his position is the same as if he had sold his business to another individual and agreed to act on his behalf. Thus the issue in this case is not peculiar to companies. Whether the principal is a company or a natural person, someone acting on his behalf may incur personal liability in tort as well as imposing vicarious or attributed liability upon his principal. But in order to establish personal liability under the principle of *Hedley Byrne*, which requires the existence of a special relationship between the plaintiff and tortfeasor, it is not sufficient that there should have been a special relationship with the principal. There must have been an assumption of responsibility such as to create a special relationship with the director or employee himself.

The practical application of the extended Hedley Byrne principle

Not surprisingly, opposing counsel approached the application of the principle of assumption of risk from different perspectives. Counsel for the respondents (the plaintiffs) concentrated in his argument on the pivotal role of Mr Mistlin in the affairs of the company. Counsel for Mr Mistlin (the defendant) concentrated on the absence of direct dealings between the respondents and Mr Mistlin. The practical application of the extended *Hedley Byrne* principle was not agreed. Before I turn to the facts of the present case it is therefore necessary to explore this aspect. Two matters require consideration. First, there is the approach to be adopted as to what may in law amount to an assumption of risk. This point was elucidated in *Henderson* by Lord Goff of Chieveley. He observed ...

> ... especially in a context concerned with a liability which may arise under a contract or in a situation 'equivalent to contract,' it must be expected that an objective test will be applied when asking the question whether, in a particular case, responsibility should be held to have been assumed by the defendant to the plaintiff.

The touchstone of liability is not the state of mind of the defendant. An objective test means that the primary focus must be on things said or done by the defendant or on its behalf in dealings with the plaintiff. Obviously, the impact of what a defendant says or does must be judged in the light of the relevant contextual scene. Subject to this qualification the primary focus must be on exchanges (in which term I include statements and conduct) which cross the line between the defendant and the plaintiff. Sometimes such an issue arises in a simple bilateral relationship. In the present case a triangular position is under consideration: the prospective franchisees, the franchisor company, and the director. In such a case where the personal liability of the director is in question the internal arrangements between a director and his company cannot be the foundation of a director's personal liability in tort. The enquiry must be whether the director, or anybody on his behalf, conveyed directly or indirectly to the prospective franchisees that the director assumed personal responsibility towards the prospective franchisees. An example of such a case being established is *Fairline Shipping Corp v Adamson* [1975] QB 180. The plaintiffs sued the defendant, a director of a warehousing company, for the negligent storage of perishable goods. The contract was between the plaintiff and the company. But Kerr J ... held that the director was personally liable. That conclusion was possible because the director wrote to the customer, and rendered an invoice, creating the clear impression that he was personally answerable for the services. If he had chosen to write on company notepaper, and rendered the invoice on behalf of the company, the necessary factual foundation for finding an assumption of risk would have been absent. A case on the other side of the line is *Trevor Ivory Ltd v Anderson*. This case concerned negligent advice given by a one-man company to a commercial fruit grower. Despite proper application of the spray it killed the grower's fruit crop. The company was found liable in contract and tort. The question was whether the beneficial owner and director of the company was personally liable. The plaintiff had undoubtedly relied on the expertise of the director in contracting with the company. New Zealand Court of Appeal unanimously concluded that the defendant was not personally liable. McGechan J, who analysed the evidence in detail said ... that there was merely 'routine involvement' by a director for and through his company. He said that there 'was no singular feature which would justify belief that Mr Ivory was accepting a personal commitment, as opposed to the known company obligation.' That was the basis of the decision in the Court of Appeal. In his

1997 Hamlyn Lecture Lord Cooke of Thorndon commented that if the plaintiff in *Trevor Ivory Ltd v Anderson* 'had reasonably thought that it was dealing with an individual, the result might have been different:' see *Taking Salomon Further, Turning Points of the Common Law*, p 18, note 50. Such a finding would have required evidence of statements or conduct crossing the line which conveyed to the plaintiff that the defendant was assuming personal liability.

That brings me to reliance by the plaintiff upon the assumption of personal responsibility. If reliance is not proved, it is not established that the assumption of personal responsibility had causative effect. In his Hamlyn Lecture Lord Cooke of Thorndon referred two judgments of La Forest J in the Canadian Supreme Court on the element of reliance. In *London Drugs Ltd v Kuehne & Nagel International Limited* 97 DLR (4th) 261, La Forest J emphasized in the context of an issue of personal liability of a company's employee the distinction between 'mere reliance in fact and *reasonable* reliance on the employee's pocket book.' The second case is *Edgeworth Construction Ltd v M D Lea & Associates Ltd* [1993] 3 SCR 206. The plaintiff company made a successful bid for a road building contract with a province. The plaintiffs allegedly lost money as a result of errors in the specifications and drawings prepared for the province by an engineering company. The Supreme Court held that the plaintiffs had a prima facie cause of action against the engineering company for negligent misrepresentation. I do not pause to consider that part of the decision. But the Supreme Court unanimously held that by affixing their seals to the drawing the individual engineers did not assume personal responsibility to the plaintiffs. La Forest J said, at p 212:

> The situation of the individual engineers is quite different. While they may, in one sense, have expected that persons in the position of the appellant would rely on their work, they would expect that the appellant would place reliance on their firm's pocketbook and not theirs for indemnification ... Looked at the other way, the appellant could not reasonably rely for indemnification on the individual engineers. It would have to show that it was relying on the particular expertise of an individual engineer without regard to the corporate character of the engineering firm. It would seem quite unrealistic, as my colleague observes, to hold that the mere presence of an individual engineer's seal was sufficient indication of personal reliance (or for that matter voluntary assumption of risk).

This reasoning is instructive. The test is not simply reliance in fact. The test is whether the plaintiff could *reasonably* rely on an assumption of personal responsibility by the individual who performed the services on behalf of the company. To that extent I regard what La Forest J said in *Edgeworth* as consistent with English law.

Academic criticism of the principle of assumption of risk
Distinguished academic writers have criticised the principle of assumption of responsibility as often resting on a fiction used to justify a conclusion that a duty of care exists ... In my view the general criticism is overstated. Coherence must sometimes yield to practical justice. In any event, the restricted conception of contract in English law, resulting from the combined effect of the principles of consideration and privity of contract, was the backcloth against which *Hedley Byrne* was decided and the principle

developed in *Henderson*. In *The Pioneer Container* [1994] 2 AC 324, 335, Lord Goff of Chieveley (... a Hong Kong appeal) said it was open to question how long the principles of consideration and privity of contract will continue to be maintained. It may become necessary for the House of Lords to re-examine the principles of consideration and privity of contract. But while the present structure of English contract law remains intact the law of tort, as the general law, has to fulfil an essential gap-filling role. In these circumstances there was, and is, no better rationalization for the relevant head of tort liability than assumption of responsibility. Returning to the particular question before the House it is important to make clear that a director of a contracting company may only be held liable where it is established by evidence that he assumed personal liability and that there was the necessary reliance. There is nothing fictional about this species of liability in tort.

Applying the principle to the facts

Mr Mistlin owned and controlled the company. The company held itself out as having the expertise to provide reliable advice to franchisees. The brochure made clear that this expertise derived from Mr Mistlin's experience in the operation of the Salisbury shop. In my view these circumstances were insufficient to make Mr Mistlin personally liable to the respondents. Stripped to essentials the reasons of Langley J; the reasons of the majority in the Court of Appeal and the arguments of counsel for the respondents can be considered under two headings. First, it is said that the terms of the brochure, and in particular its description of the role of Mr Mistlin, are sufficient to amount to an assumption of responsibility by Mr Mistlin. In his dissenting judgment Sir Patrick Russell rightly pointed out that in a small one-man company 'the managing director will almost inevitably be the one possessed of qualities essential to the functioning of the company' ... By itself this factor does not convey that the managing director is willing to be personally answerable to the customers of the company. Secondly, great emphasis was placed on the fact that it was made clear to the franchisees that Mr Mistlin's expertise derived from his experience in running the Salisbury shop for his own account. Hirst LJ summarized the point by saying that 'the relevant knowledge and experience was entirely his *qua* Mr Mistlin, and not his *qua* director' ... The point will not simply bear the weight put on it. Postulate a food expert who over ten years gains experience in advising customers on his own account. Then he incorporates his business as a company and he so advises his customers. Surely, it cannot be right to say that in the new situation his earlier experience on his own account is indicative of an assumption of personal responsibility towards his customers. In the present case there were no personal dealings between Mr Mistlin and the respondents. There were no exchanges or conduct crossing the line which could have conveyed to the respondents that Mr Mistlin was willing to assume personal responsibility to them. Contrary to the submissions of counsel for the respondents, I am also satisfied that there was not even evidence that the respondents believed that Mr Mistlin was undertaking personal responsibility to them. Certainly, there was nothing in the circumstances to show that the respondents could reasonably have looked to Mr Mistlin for indemnification of any loss. For these reasons I would reject the principal argument of counsel for the respondents ...

Boyd Knight v Purdue
[1999] 2 NZLR 278 (CA)
Blanchard J:
Introduction
The appellant firm, Boyd Knight, the auditor of a failed finance company, Burbery Mortgage Finance & Savings Ltd (Burbery), appeals against a judgment ordering it to pay damages to a class of persons, represented by the respondents Mr Purdue and Mr Matthew, who invested new funds with Burbery on secured debentures between 1 July 1988 and 10 August 1988 in response to an offer made in a prospectus issued by Burbery. The prospectus contained an audit report signed by the appellant. The respondents claim that Boyd Knight was in breach of a duty of care owed to them and to those they represent when making the report and allowing it to be used in the prospectus. The essential question on this appeal is the extent, if any, to which it was necessary to prove reliance on Burbery's financial statements to which the audit report was directed.

Facts
Burbery's business consisted of the borrowing of money from the public and on-lending it at a margin. As required by the Securities Act 1978 and the Securities Regulations 1983, for time to time it issued prospectuses. The one with which this case is concerned is Prospectus No. 11, which operated from 1 July 1988. The Perpetual Trustees Estate & Agency Co of NZ Limited (the trustee) was acting as trustee for depositors under a trust deed dated 1 October 1983. A crucial ratio set by that deed was that Burbery's total liabilities were not to exceed nine times its adjusted shareholders' funds.

... Nearly 40% of its lending was to six borrowers. There had been significant defaults—arrears in excess of three months existed for more than 10% of Burbery's monetary assets. Worse still, however, and undetected by the auditors, Mr Burbery had committed frauds, creating fictitious loan accounts, as a result of which the shareholders' funds (shown as $1.6 million in the consolidated balance sheet to 31 March 1988 which appeared in Prospectus No. 11) were overstated by $1.15 million and total liabilities actually exceeded the limit imposed by the trust deed by about $15 million. (Although it did not know of the fictitious loan accounts, the trustee was aware of what it called a 'technical breach' of this ratio. It was mentioned in a letter from the trustee to the directors, a copy of which appeared in the prospectus, the trustee expressing itself as being 'satisfied with the steps taken to rectify the position.')

As required by clause 36(1) of the Second Schedule to the Securities Regulations, Boyd Knight's audit report, addressed to the directors of Burbery and included in the prospectus, read [that the accounts were]:

> ... [a] true and fair view of the state of affairs of the Group as at the 31 March 1988 ...
> ... [and] that the amounts stated ... have been correctly taken from audited financial statements.

Boyd Knight has made two important admissions, namely, (a) that reasonable care on its part would have led to the discovery of Mr Burbery's frauds before that date; and

(b) that if they had been discovered the audit report would not have been given and the prospectus would accordingly not have been issued. It is clear from the evidence that, such was the magnitude of the company's problems, no borrowing from the public could have occurred after the discovery of the frauds because the Act and the Regulations could not have been complied with. The frauds were in fact detected only after the trustee appointed receivers on 10 August 1988.

The persons represented by Mr Purdue and Mr Matthew all invested with Burbery for the first time during the currency of Prospectus No. 11. They managed to recover, on average, two-thirds of their principal and sued for the balance and interest. The claims of unsecured creditors, who recovered nothing from the company, failed in the High Court and they have not appealed. It was held that they had not shown, through their representation, sufficient reliance upon the information contained in the audit report ...

The duty of care

...

In *Deloitte Haskins & Sells v National Mutual Life Nominees Ltd* [1993] 3 NZLR 1 the Privy Council placed a narrow construction, some might say a surprisingly narrow one, on the auditor's duty towards the trustee under s 50(2) of the Securities Act, saying that the effect of the decisions in the courts below, which were reversed, 'was to impose upon the auditor a common law duty more extensive than that imposed by the Act'. There is a need, therefore, to give close consideration to the form of the report required by the regulations in order to determine the extent of the responsibility assumed by the auditors in signing and delivering it for incorporation in a prospectus.

The philosophy of the Securities Act is that investment decisions in relation to offers to the public should be made only upon a basis of adequate information about the issuer. To be adequate it obviously must be up to date, sufficiently comprehensive and, of course, accurate in the sense of expressing a true and fair view. To this end the Act and the Regulations made under it prevent the issue by a fundraiser of equity, debt and participatory securities to the public, or any member of the public, without registration and use of a prospectus incorporating audited accounts drawn up as at a recent date. The Act also requires appointment of a trustee or statutory supervisor whose task is to provide certain safeguards for would-be investors. The *Deloitte* case concerned an alleged duty of auditors towards the trustee, said by their Lordships to have a 'primary responsibility' towards depositors.

For a debt security, clause 36(1) requires a prospectus to contain a copy of a report by a qualified auditor stating whether or not the prescribed audited financial statements comply with the regulations and in accordance with the regulations give a true and fair view of the state of affairs of the 'group' (the issuer and guaranteeing subsidiaries) as at the date thereof and of the results and changes in the financial position of the group for the period to which those statements relate.

An auditor giving such a report must know full well that in order to raise funds from the public the company is obligated to give the document in which it appears to investors and will do so as part of a process to encourage them to invest. The audit report will obviously give comfort in relation to the financial statements. I have no doubt that these factors give rise to the necessary closeness of relationship between the auditor and those who invest on the strength of the prospectus, so that the auditor owes them a duty to be careful in the giving of the certificate. He or she knows what sum is being raised by the issuer. I agree with Chisholm J that there is no indeterminate liability. The harder question is as to the nature of the duty, when and to whom it is owed. On this question the common law background which I have been discussing and the respective roles of the auditor and trustee are of importance ...

When auditors furnish a report for inclusion in a prospectus they express an opinion about the financial statements of the company which they have audited: they confirm the accuracy of those statements, in the sense of that word used above. However, they are not called upon to make any comment on the state of the company's affairs. They undertake no duty to assess for would-be investors whether it is creditworthy. Their duty is to inform, not to give advice. The true and fair view may be one of prosperity or poverty. The report therefore has no context for anyone who has not read the accounts. Without such a reading the report tells the reader nothing except that the company has a set of accounts which comply with the regulations and present a true and fair view. In so far as such a report refers to a true and fair view, it is almost meaningless unless read in conjunction with the figures in the accounts. It must follow, it seems to me, that in so certifying the accounts the auditors cannot be taken to have accepted an obligation to an investor who has not read and relied upon them. Reliance, and a consequential duty of care, cannot be asserted, as it were, in a vacuum. There must first have been a specific influence of the financial statements on the mind of the investor. It is not enough for the investor to say that, without troubling to look at the accounts, he or she relied in a general way upon the statutory scheme, making an assumption that an investment is sound or the issuer creditworthy because there was a trustee playing a supervisory role in connection with the prospectus and an auditor had furnished the report required by the Regulations.

It would be casting upon an auditor a burden going even beyond anything suggested for the unsuccessful plaintiff in *Caparo* if this Court were to hold careless auditors liable for the accuracy of figures which were not directly relied upon by plaintiff investors. Since the purpose of the legislation is to ensure information is available to investors, so that they can make their own assessment of the prospects of the issuer, it would be exceeding the statutory scheme if the Court were to find auditors responsible for inaccuracies in information which was not utilised by an investor. There is no room in this context for an indirect reliance which Cooke P adverted to in a rather different case (*South Pacific Manufacturing Co Ltd* ...). And, like the British Columbia Court of Appeal in *Kripps v Touche Ross & Co* (1992) 94 DLR (4th) 284, I find no attraction in the doctrine of reliance on the integrity of the market which has been developed in some jurisdictions in the United States. It is quite contrary to the position taken in *Caparo*.

In circumstances in which, if the true position had been revealed, the accounts could have been corrected and a prospectus would probably still have issued seeking the investment a plaintiff investor must, I think, show reliance on a particular item or items in the financial statements which were inaccurate. It must be proved that, if the true and fair view in that regard had been known to the plaintiff, the investment decision would have been different. For, if the inaccurate material was not an influence on the investor, how can it be alleged that the investor would not have gone ahead with the investment? The loss suffered on the investment would not then be attributable to the uncorrected inaccuracy of the report. The plaintiff therefore cannot say that he or she was worse off because the information was wrong. 'A duty of care which imposes upon the informant responsibility for losses which would have occurred even if the information which he gave had been correct is not in my view fair and reasonable as between the parties' (*Banque Bruxelles Lambert SA v Eagle Star Insurance Co Ltd* [1997] AC 191 at 214, per Lord Hoffmann).

A broader approach is permissible where it is proved or, as here, admitted that if the accounts had been accurate no prospectus would have been issued and no investment could then have been made—in other words, that 'but for' the inaccuracy there could have been no loss to a new investor. But even in such circumstances the limited scope of the duty of care must be remembered. In such a case there must at least be a reliance on the basic features of the financial statements—the results they show (profit level, balance of shareholders' funds and, perhaps, the current assets/liability ratio). There must be evidence that these features were considered by the plaintiff and, taken as a whole, relied upon. The investor must prove that he or she paid attention to the content of the financial statements and noted these basic features—that it was not simply a case of glancing at the accounts, but in reality failing to consider them and, instead, relying in a general way on the fact that the investment offer was being made pursuant to a prospectus and that the Regulations put some safeguards in place.

Absence of reliance on accounts in this case

Earlier in this judgment ... I described the evidence given on behalf of the class of plaintiffs by Mr Purdue. The trial Judge set out in the judgment a small portion of the testimony and said that he accepted it as proof of actual reliance *on the financial statements*. He did not say how he arrived at this conclusion other than mentioning that Mr Purdue is by occupation a financial planner and that it was 'not surprising that he paid particular attention to the information contained *in the audit report* and that the satisfactory audit report persuaded him that Burbery was a suitable company in which to invest.'

Having carefully considered the evidence in question, I must respectfully disagree with the view taken by the Judge. Mr Purdue claimed to have relied upon the audit report, but, except in relation to the matters to which he was referred in cross-examination, he did not assert that he had read, let alone relied upon, the accounts or any particular features of them. He did not even say that he had made himself aware of matters such as profitability and shareholders' funds. He made no reference to any financial ratios. It is clear from the cross-examination that, to the extent that Mr Purdue may have looked at the accounts, he was blind to matters which might have caused alarm to a careful investor. In fact, so plain were the warning signs that I find it difficult to credit that someone who styles himself a financial planner would have overlooked them if he had considered and relied upon the financial statements. It is my reading of Mr Purdue's evidence that he was asserting only an indirect or general reliance, having taken comfort from the role of the trustee, the fact that an auditor was a part of the process and certain inquiries which he had made. He did not actually rely on the financial statements.

I am of course hesitant to differ from the views of the trial Judge but as Mr Purdue has expressly claimed reliance upon the existence of the audit report rather than upon a perusal of the financial statements backed up by the comfort of such a report, this is a matter of interpreting what the witness actually said rather than differing from the Judge on the credibility of the witness. In view of the evidence given by Mr Purdue actual reliance on the accounts is not to be inferred, as was done in the *Kripps* case in British Columbia ...

'Pure' economic loss

Traditionally, tort law focused on compensating physical loss and excluded economic loss that was not the result of physical injury. Indeed, cases such as *Cattle v Stockton Waterworks Co* (1875) LR 10 QB 453 were often considered as having created an exclusionary rule preventing the recovery for purely economic loss. *Hedley Byrne* opened up the prospect that tort could allow the recovery of economic loss in the sense that it involved the recovery of lost money without physical loss.

After *Hedley Byrne*, the courts have been faced with other cases in which plaintiffs have sought to recover similar 'pure economic loss'. The cases that follow explore which kinds of loss should be recoverable. Once again this is not such an easy question and is one that has divided the Commonwealth courts. Labels such as 'conservative' have been used to describe courts like the House of Lords during the later 1980s and early 1990s, which seemed reluctant to allow the recovery of economic loss. Labels such as 'liberal' have been used to describe courts like those in Canada or New Zealand, which seem to have been more prepared to allow recovery. In reading the following cases, however, try to look beyond these labels, or even 'pure economic loss' itself. Try to determine what factors motivate the judges to allow recovery or to deny recovery. How does the judge go about categorising the type of loss suffered and how does that categorisation affect whether recovery will be allowed?

Spartan Steel & Alloys v Martin & Co (Contractors) Ltd
[1973] QB 27 (CA)

[**FACTS**: The plaintiffs obtained electricity by a direct cable from the electricity board. The defendant contractors were digging up a road about a quarter of a mile from the plaintiff's factory. The defendants knew the location of the power cable but negligently damaged it. The electricity board shut down the power while the cable was being repaired. At the time, the plaintiffs were melting metal, for which electricity was essential. When the power failed, there was a danger that the metal might solidify in the furnace and damage its lining, so the plaintiffs used oxygen to melt the material. The resulting melted material was of much less value; the physical damage to the melt was £368 and the loss of profits on that melt was £400. While the power was off, the plaintiffs were prevented from completing four other melts, with a loss of profit of £1767.]

Lord Denning MR:

... At bottom I think the question of recovering economic loss is one of policy. Whenever the courts draw a line to mark out the bounds of *duty*, they do it as matter of policy so as to limit the responsibility of the defendant. Whenever the courts set bounds to the *damages* recoverable—saying that they are, or are not, too remote—they do it as matter of policy so as to limit the liability of the defendant.

In many of the cases where economic loss has been held not to be recoverable, it has been put on the ground that the defendant was under no *duty* to the plaintiff. Thus … when property is damaged by the negligence of another, the negligent tortfeasor owes a duty to the owner or possessor of the chattel, but not to one who suffers loss only because he had a contract entitling him to use the chattel or giving him a right to receive it at some later date …

In other cases, however, the defendant seems clearly to have been under a duty to the plaintiff, but the economic loss has not been recovered because it is *too remote*. Take the illustration given by Blackburn J in *Cattle v Stockton Waterworks Co* (1875) LR 10 QB 453, 457, when water escapes from a reservoir and floods a coal mine where many men are working. Those who had their tools or clothes destroyed could recover: but those who only lost their wages could not. Similarly, when the defendants' ship negligently sank a ship which was being towed by a tug, the owner of the tug lost his remuneration, but he could not recover it from the negligent ship: though the same duty (of navigation with reasonable care) was owed to both tug and tow: see *Société Anonyme de Remorquage à Hélice v Bennetts* [1911] 1 KB 243, 248. In such cases if the plaintiff or his property had been physically injured, he would have recovered: but, as he only suffered economic loss, he is held not entitled to recover. This is, I should think, because the loss is regarded by the law as too remote: see *King v Phillips* [1953] 1 QB 429, 439–40.

On the other hand, in the cases where economic loss by itself has been held to be recoverable, it is plain that there was a duty to the plaintiff and the loss was not too remote. Such as when one ship negligently runs down another ship, and damages it, with the result that the cargo has to be discharged and reloaded. The negligent ship was already under a duty to the cargo owners: and they can recover the cost of discharging and reloading it, as it is not too remote: see *Morrison Steamship Co Ltd v Greystoke Castle (Cargo Owners)* [1947] AC 265. Likewise, when a banker negligently gives a reference to one who acts on it, the duty is plain and the damage is not too remote: see *Hedley Byrne* …

The more I think about these cases, the more difficult I find it to put each into its proper pigeon-hole. Sometimes I say: 'There was no duty.' In others I say: 'The damage was too remote.' So much so that I think the time has come to discard those tests which have proved so elusive. It seems to me better to consider the particular relationship in hand, and see whether or not, as a matter of policy, economic loss should be recoverable, or not … .

The first consideration is the position of the statutory undertakers … . If the electricity boards are not liable for economic loss due to negligence which results in the cutting off of the supply, nor should a contractor be liable.

The second consideration is the nature of the hazard, namely, the cutting of the supply of electricity. This is a hazard which we all run … when the supply is cut off. [People] who have been cut off do not go running round to their solicitor. They do not try to find out whether it was anyone's fault. They just put up with it. They try to make up the economic loss by doing more work next day. This is a healthy attitude which the law should encourage.

The third consideration is this: if claims for economic loss were permitted for this particular hazard, there would be no end of claims. Some might be genuine, but many might be inflated, or even false … .

The fourth consideration is that, in such a hazard as this, the risk of economic loss should be suffered by the whole community who suffer the losses—usually many but comparatively small losses—rather than on the one pair of shoulders, that is, on the contractor on whom the total of them, all added together, might be very heavy.

The fifth consideration is that the law provides for deserving cases. If the defendant is guilty of negligence which cuts off the electricity supply and causes actual physical damage to person or property, that physical damage can be recovered … .

These considerations lead me to the conclusion that the plaintiffs should recover for the physical damage to the one melt (£368), and the loss of profit on that melt consequent thereon (£400): but not for the loss of profit on the four melts (£1767), because that was economic loss independent of the physical damage. I would, therefore, allow the appeal and reduce the damages to £768.

Edmund Davies LJ:

… In my respectful judgment, however it may formerly have been regarded, the law is today otherwise. I am conscious of the boldness involved in expressing this view, particularly after studying such learned dissertations as that of Professor Atiyah on 'Negligence and Economic Loss' (1967) 83 LQR 248, where the relevant cases are cited. I recognise that proof of the necessary linkage between negligent acts and purely economic consequences may be hard to forge. I accept, too, that if economic loss of itself confers a right of action this may spell disaster for the negligent party. But this may equally be the outcome where physical damage alone is sustained, or where physical damage leads directly to economic loss. Nevertheless, when this occurs it was accepted in *SCM (United Kingdom) Ltd v W J Whittall & Son Ltd* [1971] 1 QB 337 that compensation is recoverable for both types of damage. It follows that this must be regardless of whether the injury (physical or economic, or a mixture of both) is immense or puny, diffused over a wide area or narrowly localised, provided only that the requirements as to foreseeability and directness are fulfilled. I therefore find myself unable to accept as factors determinant of legal principle those considerations of policy canvassed in the concluding passages of the judgment just delivered by Lord Denning MR.

… For my part, I cannot see why the £400 loss of profit here sustained should be recoverable and not the £1767. It is common ground that both types of loss were equally foreseeable and equally direct consequences of the defendants' admitted negligence, and the only distinction drawn is that the former figure represents the profit lost as a result of the physical damage done to the material in the furnace at the time when power was cut off. But what has that purely fortuitous fact to do with legal principle?

I should perhaps again stress that we are here dealing with economic loss which was both reasonably foreseeable and a direct consequence of the defendants' negligent act. What the position should or would be were the latter feature lacking … is not our present concern. By stressing this point one is not reviving the distinction between direct and indirect consequences which is generally thought to have been laid at rest by *The Wagon Mound (No. 1)* [1961] AC 388, for, in the words of Professor Atiyah 'Negligence and Economic Loss', 83 LQR 263, that case

> was solely concerned with the question whether the directness of the damage is a *sufficient* test of liability ... . In other words, *The Wagon Mound* merely decides that a plaintiff cannot recover for unforeseeable consequences even if they are direct; it does not decide that a plaintiff can always recover for fore-seeable consequences even if they are indirect.

Both directness and foreseeability being here established, it follows that I regard Faulks J as having rightly awarded the sum of £2535.

Having regard to the route which has led me to this conclusion, it is not necessary for me to express any concluded view regarding the topic of 'parasitic damages.' I content myself with saying that, whatever be the scope of such a concept in other and wholly different branches of the law, I am at present not satisfied that it can be invoked in cases of the type now under consideration.

I would be for dismissing the appeal.

[**Result**: **Lawton LJ** agreed with **Lord Denning MR**.]

Bowen and Another v Paramount Builders (Hamilton) Ltd and Another

[1977] 1 NZLR 394 (CA)

[**FACTS**: In 1968 the trustees of a family trust (Pemberton Trust) were subdividing land owned by the trust. The land was in peat country. There had been little experience in Hamilton with the use of peat land for building purposes. The McKays entered into an agreement with the Pemberton Trust to purchase one of the sections. The agreement contained a clause that the vendors would provide subfoundations adequate for normal house foundations. Mr McKay (the second respondent) entered into a contract with Paramount Builders (Paramount, the first respondent) to build a two-flat dwelling. Paramount drew up the plans and specifications.

In 1968 the managing director of Paramount at Hamilton was a Mr Robinson. Mr Bunting, who was the building manager, and Mr McKenzie were employed by Paramount. McKay's original discussions were with McKenzie, who already had some knowledge of the Pemberton subdivision. He had been told earlier by Pemberton not to be concerned about the depth of the peat in the sections 'as the foundations would be brought up to a standard whereby normal foundations could be built on this land'. When McKenzie mentioned the fact that the land was peat, McKay said, 'Don't worry about that, just price as on normal foundation'. McKenzie, rightly or wrongly, was content to rely on the fact that the Pemberton Trust was to bring the section up to a standard whereby normal foundations could be provided. Paramount and McKay entered into a contract for the dwelling to be built with normal foundations (or footings). Robinson included the following clause in the contract: 'The owner agrees that any extra to footings as specified under footings, due to unstable ground on peat, shall be charged as an extra'. A building permit was obtained and Pemberton installed the sand pad. Bunting dug down about a foot in the sand pad, but no further. He estimated the pad to be about eighteen inches and thought that should be adequate for foundation purposes.

When the foundation was installed to a certain point, a building inspector, Mr Prinn, stopped the work because the foundation used was not adequate for peat. Paramount changed the plans for the foundation to another type of normal foundation that would spread the load better. The council records do not show whether any approval of this change was communicated to Paramount, but the work recommenced. Mr McKay was unaware of the change until he visited the site and saw the change. Prinn inspected the foundations again but was not satisfied. He did not stop the work but wrote a memorandum expressing his concern to the chief building inspector. The council records contain no record of any further action being taken and Paramount was not aware of Prinn's concern.

When construction was nearing completion, McKay noticed that some bricks had cracked in an exterior wall. At McKay's insistence, Bunting took levels and found a half-inch fall. Later Bunting took levels again and found a 2.5-inch fall. There is no evidence that McKay was told of the 2.5-inch fall as opposed to the 0.5-inch fall.

McKay was not pleased and Paramount built a carport, free of charge, to disguise the line of bricks. Nevertheless, McKay decided to sell the units. A real estate agent took the Bowens (appellants) to see the property. The ground was muddy and the Bowens were there for about half an hour. They knew nothing of any trouble with the flats and bought them from McKay.

The Bowens took possession in June 1969. Mr Bowen's mother-in-law moved into the rear flat, paying a nominal rent. Tenants occupied the other flat. By the end of 1970 Mr Bowen realised something was seriously wrong and proceedings were commenced. When levels were taken in December 1971 the fall was 8.5 inches, with further subsidence evident in 1973. The exterior brick veneer walls showed signs of cracking, the internal partition wall was cracked, the doors and windows were jamming and the floor was obviously out of level.

The sand pad had not provided an adequate base and the foundations were not adequate. Early in 1971 the council adopted a practice of requiring engineers' certificates in relation to new buildings to be erected on peat. Although it was not normal practice in 1968 to consult experts about building on peat, such experts were available in the area.]

Richmond P:

… The first question is whether in the circumstances Paramount owed a legal duty of care to the Bowens and if so what was the nature of that duty. The first point to note is that the present case is not one of an owner-builder selling a house, after completion, which he has erected for sale on his own land. It is, therefore, not necessary to decide whether *Bottomley v Bannister* [1932] 1 KB 458 still represents the law … . I think that in this developing field of the law it is preferable for this court to move with some caution [and this issue is] likely to be considered by the House of Lords early next year … in *Anns* … . So I shall confine myself to the position of a builder who erects a building under a building contract for the owner of the land on which it is erected.

Quite clearly English law has now developed to the point where contractors, architects and engineers are all subject to a duty to use reasonable care to prevent damage to persons whom they should reasonably expect to be affected by their work

... . In the present case Speight J accepted the position that the principles laid down in *Donoghue v Stevenson* would apply in the case of negligence by a builder causing damage to property as well as to negligence causing personal injury. He said, and I respectfully agree:

> It seems to me not to matter whether the collapsing wall injures a visitor to premises or merely destroys the chattel he is carrying with him.

It may be that this liability extends to damage caused by *patent* defects in certain circumstances ... . [B]ut for the purposes of the present case I go no further than to recognise that a builder is liable for the negligent creation of a hidden defect which is a source of danger to third persons whom he ought reasonably to foresee as likely to suffer damage either in the form of personal injury or injury to their property. I shall say something later as to the extent of this class of persons.

Although Speight J accepted the legal position as I have just stated it, he thought that the facts of the present case did not bring the claim made by the Bowens against Paramount within those principles. He did not regard the present case as a claim for damage to property suffered by a third person as a result of the dangerous defect. He said:

> It is a claim for the diminished value of the article, as for example, if the lady in *Donoghue v Stevenson* had sued for damages for inferior quality ginger beer. The claim for such a defect in the quality of an article purchased is an action in contract not in tort and privity of contract still remains an essential part of that concept.

Later, after citing a lengthy passage from the judgment of Stamp LJ in *Dutton v Bognor Regis Urban District Council* [1972] 1 QB 373, 414–15 ... the judge expressed the view:

> ... that there can be a cause of action for physical damage against a builder but an action to repair the fabric of the building which [has] collapsed lies only against the vendor.

I shall return to this particular point later but it is necessary at this stage to consider whether or not Paramount was in fact negligent ... .

It is clear that a builder or architect cannot defend a claim in negligence made against him by a third person by saying that he was working under a contract for the owner of the land. He cannot say that the only duty which he owed was his contractual duty to the owner. Likewise he cannot say that the nature of his contractual duties to the owner sets a limit to the duty of care which he owes to third parties. As regards this latter point it is, for example, obvious that a builder who agreed to build a house in a manner which he knows or ought to know will prove a source of danger to third parties cannot say, in answer to a claim by third parties, that he did all that the owner of the land required him to do. Nevertheless the nature of the contractual duties may have considerable relevance in deciding whether or not the builder was negligent. In relation to a claim made against an architect, Windeyer J in *Voli v Inglewood Shire Council* (1963) 110 CLR 74 put the matter in the following way (at 85):

> ... neither the terms of the architect's engagement, nor the terms of the building contract, can operate to discharge the architect from a duty of care to

persons who are strangers to those contracts. Nor can they directly determine what he must do to satisfy his duty to such persons. That duty is cast upon him by law, not because he made a contract, but because he entered upon the work. Nevertheless his contract with the building owner is not an irrelevant circumstance. It determines what was the task upon which he entered. If, for example, it was to design a stage to bear only some specified weight, he would not be liable for the consequences of someone thereafter negligently permitting a greater weight to be put upon it.

One interesting feature of the facts in *Voli v Inglewood Shire Council* was that before the building was erected the plans prepared by the architect had to be submitted for approval by the Government Public Works Department. It was argued that this resulted in an 'intermediate examination' of the kind referred to by Lord Atkin in *Donoghue v Stevenson*. Windeyer J pointed out that in the light of later cases no hard and fast rule could be laid down as to the effect of an intermediate examination. The real problem was one of causation, namely, whether the proximate cause of the harm was the negligence of the person who made the faulty thing, or the negligence of the person who was to examine, test, or treat it, or the combined negligence of both persons. At the same time, however, it seems to me that the fact that plans have to be approved by persons with a degree of expert knowledge is obviously relevant to the question whether a builder is negligent if he goes ahead and constructs the building. The position is somewhat analogous to that of an employer who purchases equipment from a reputable supplier. Up to some reasonable point such an employer is entitled to rely on the supplier providing him with safe equipment: *Davie v New Merton Board Mills Ltd* [1959] AC 604.

... [The] real question seems to me to be whether Paramount ought to have insisted on Mr McKay obtaining expert advice and assistance rather than have allowed him to rely on his contract with the Pemberton Trust ... .

[**Note**: The Trust was financially sound and had developed 15 or 16 sections of the land.]

... So that the fact that the trust had given a contractual undertaking as to suitable subfoundations was a very important consideration. Moreover, Paramount knew that a building permit was required and were evidently aware of the interest which the local authority was likely to take in the adequacy of the foundations, as is indicated by Mr Robinson's evidence as to the alteration made to the specification regarding footings. So far as one can judge from the evidence given by Mr Thomas it was not the ordinary practice of builders at that time to refer such problems to consulting engineers, and the city council had not then introduced the requirement of an engineer's certificate for buildings on peat. All in all, I cannot feel affirmatively satisfied that Paramount acted in a way which no ordinary reasonably prudent and skilful builder would have acted at that time when they proceeded to design and commence work on the building without obtaining expert advice. There was no such obvious danger, in a field where Paramount was not being asked to take responsibility, as should have resulted in their refusing to act on Mr McKay's instructions in the interest of future purchasers.

... I think it is a borderline case, and, indeed, the other members of the court take a different view from my own and consider that the evidence does establish negligence on the part of Paramount. Accordingly, it becomes necessary for me to say something further as to the legal questions which arise consequent upon that finding of negligence ... .

Does damage to the house itself give rise to a cause of action?

As I have already said, I agree with Speight J that the principles laid down in *Donoghue v Stevenson* apply to a builder erecting a house under a contract with the owner. He is under a duty of care not to create latent sources of physical danger to the person or property of third persons whom he ought reasonably to foresee as likely to be affected thereby. If the latent defect causes actual physical damage to the structure of the house then I can see no reason in principle why such damage should not give rise to a cause of action, at any rate if that damage occurs after the house has been purchased from the original owner ... . For the purposes of the present case it is not necessary to deal with the question of 'pure' economic loss, that is to say economic loss which is not associated with a latent defect which causes or threatens physical harm to the structure itself.

What is the correct measure of damages in the present case?

... [I]t has not been feasible in the present case to raise the building in such a way as to get rid of the sag which has occurred in the structure, and at the same time to strengthen the subfoundations. The proposed alterations are designed:

(a) to reduce the risk of further subsidence by getting rid of the weight of the concrete block wall dividing the two units;
(b) to restore the appearance of the house as far as possible; and
(c) to put doors and windows into proper working condition.

As to (a), when a defect has actually caused structural damage to a building it must be proper for the owner not only to repair the damage but also to take reasonable steps to prevent further damage, rather than wait for that damage to occur. In some cases this may give rise to the question whether some credit ought not to be given to the builder for betterment but no such question arises in the present case. As to (b), I can see no reason why the Bowens should not be able to claim for the cost of alterations carried out to improve the appearance of the building in circumstances where it is not feasible to raise the building in such a way as to eliminate the sag in the structure. Finally, there can, I think, be no question as to (c). These repairs are obviously necessary ... .

Apart from the actual cost of the alterations, there is a sum of $2000 claimed as depreciation or diminution in value. This sum represents the difference between the market value of the property after all repairs are done and the market value had there been no subsidence. This claim, in my opinion, should be allowed. In one sense it can be described as economic loss, but it is economic loss directly and immediately connected with the structural damage to the building and as such is properly recoverable ... .

Does any question of intermediate examination arise in the present case?

Speight J thought that the claim must fail in any event because Mr McKay had actual knowledge of the nature of the foundations and of the suspect nature of the ground and also because the Bowens could have acquired that knowledge ...

There are, I think, two ways in which the question of intermediate examination may be relevant. The first relates to the question whether a plaintiff is in sufficient proximity to the negligent act of the defendant to bring him within the ambit of the defendant's duty of care. In *Jull v Wilson and Horton* [1968] NZLR 88, after a somewhat extensive consideration of the authorities, I ventured the opinion that a person who creates a dangerous situation '... cannot shelter behind a reasonable expectation of intermediate inspection unless the expectation was strong enough to justify him in regarding the contemplated inspection as an adequate safeguard to persons who might otherwise suffer harm'. I was there emphasising the strength of the expectation required on the part of a negligent defendant. The nature of the anticipated examination is obviously also of great importance, as is emphasised by the way the matter is put in *Salmond on Torts* (16th edn) 314: '... the proper question is whether he [the defendant] should reasonably have expected that the plaintiff would use the opportunity for inspection in such a way as to give him warning of the risk'.

In like manner, if the contemplated inspection is to be carried out by a person other than the plaintiff then the test must be whether the defendant should reasonably have expected that the intermediate examination would be an adequate protection for the plaintiff.

In the present case it must have been quite clear to Paramount that the knowledge of the foundations and subfoundations which Mr McKay possessed had not in fact given him warning of the risk. Nor could Paramount have had any sufficient expectation that Mr McKay would use any knowledge of the risk which he might subsequently acquire in a way which would be an adequate safeguard to protect anyone to whom he might sell the house while the existence of the defect was not reasonably apparent. Indeed, when Mr McKay in fact became most apprehensive about the foundations Paramount obviously regarded it as a sensible and natural thing for him to do when he informed them that he proposed to get rid of the house by selling it. In like manner, I cannot see how Paramount could have any reasonable expectation that anyone who purchased the house while still in the process of completion by the builder, as the Bowens did, would use their opportunity of inspection in such a way as to obtain warning of a risk which was not then reasonably apparent.

The second way in which the question of intermediate examination may become relevant is in relation to causation. In the present case I do not think it can be said that the act of Mr McKay in selling the house to the Bowens, after he had knowledge of some subsidence and because he was apprehensive about the stability of the building, amounted to a *novus actus interveniens*. As I have already said, it was the very type of conduct which ought to have been foreseen by Paramount as a likely consequence of a discovery by Mr McKay of the source of danger which Paramount had created. Likewise, and in the same context of causation, it cannot be said that in the circumstances of this case the Bowens acted with such disregard to their own interests as to make their own conduct the sole cause of the damage which they subsequently suffered. Indeed, it was not even contended that they had been guilty of contributory negligence.

... I now propose to draw attention to certain problems which could arise in other cases as a result of our recognising the existence of a duty of care of the kind now in issue.

(1) To whom is a builder's duty of care owed?
Mr Webb urged upon us that if the court were to acknowledge the existence of such a duty it would not be possible to control the class of purchasers to whom that duty is owed. I accept the position that it is not possible for the court to lay down some period of time after which purchasers will no longer be in sufficient proximity to the builder. In this field the builder's only protection will be the Limitation Act 1950, and there are some difficulties in that connection as appears from *Sparham-Souter v Town and Country Developments (Essex) Ltd* [1976] QB 858 ... . It would also seem to me impossible to limit the class of purchasers to the first purchaser or any particular subsequent purchaser. At present I think that the ambit of the duty can be effectively controlled only by a strict insistence on the proximity principle to which I have earlier made reference in this judgment. In other words, I take the view that the duty of the builder is not owed to anyone who purchases a building with actual knowledge of the defect or in circumstances where he ought to have used his opportunity of inspection in a way which would have given him warning of that defect. Subject to that qualification, and to the provisions of the Limitation Act, I see no reason why the loss caused by damage to a building resulting from a latent defect should fall on an innocent purchaser rather than on the builder who negligently created it.

(2) Does the builder's duty extend beyond negligence causing a source of physical damage?
As at present advised I do not think that the courts would be justified in imposing a duty of care on builders tantamount to the full warranties normally implied in a building contract. Any such extension of the present law seems to me to be more properly a matter for legislation. It is coincidental in this connection that a bill designed to take some important steps in that direction, the Building Performance Guarantee Corporation Bill, has recently been introduced into Parliament ...

(4) Problems of the builder in obtaining release from liability
A builder who negligently and in breach of contract creates a source of danger is liable to be sued for breach of contract at once by the owner for whom he has built the house. The owner does not have to wait for actual damage to occur nor is he obliged to apply money received by him as damages or on a compromise in remedying the builder's defective work. The question may arise whether the builder can be sued a second time in tort by an innocent purchaser to whom the property has been sold without disclosure of the defect. This is a difficult question. Certainly a builder in such a situation would be wise to take all practical steps to see that the defect is actually remedied. Also I would hope that the time has not arrived when the courts can recognise a duty in tort on the part of a vendor who has actual knowledge of a dangerous but latent defect to warn his purchaser of the existence of that defect. If such a duty is recognised then a vendor who failed to give such a warning could be brought in as a joint tortfeasor with the negligent builder. The court could order indemnity or contribution. I mention this possible situation because I have considered it, along with the various other problems to which I have adverted, in an endeavour to weigh up the overall wisdom of recognising the existence of a builder's duty of care towards subsequent purchasers. On balance I think it should be recognised.

Having regard, however, to my own view as to the facts of this case I would dismiss the appeal.

Cooke J:

The first question is whether, in designing and constructing the foundations, the building company owed a duty of care to the person who later bought the property from the company's client. At the present day no one is likely to doubt that if those persons were injured in consequence of a hidden defect in the foundations an action would lie on proof of causative carelessness on the part of the company ... . The issue is whether it does make a difference that the damage has been limited to the structure of the building itself. As a simple matter of fairness there seems to be no reason why that should be so ... Further, no authority was cited in argument which would bind us to deny a cause of action to the appellants ... .

The arguments against allowing a cause of action in a case like the present tend to be largely either *in terrorem* or doctrinaire. The floodgates argument seems to me specious. If many meritorious claims follow, the desirability of the development is proved; who would now retreat from *Donoghue v Stevenson*? And the courts should be able to ensure that unmeritorious claims do not succeed ... .

An objection of a more doctrinal nature is that the loss is economic and that only contract should give a remedy. As to the first branch of this objection, the loss in the instant case is not purely economic. The building has undergone some damage and deterioration, the damages claimed being merely the measure. In any event it is clear from *Hedley Byrne* ... that negligent advice in breach of a duty of care may be actionable though the loss be purely economic; and more generally the House of Lords has at least left open the door to recovery in negligence for purely economic loss: see the speeches in *Moorgate Mercantile Co Ltd v Twitchings* [1976] 3 WLR 66 ... . In the present class of case, however, Speight J ... classified this kind of claim as being for diminished value or for a defect in the quality of the property purchased, and he held that privity of contract is essential for such a claim. The idea is put in another way by Stamp LJ in *Dutton v Bognor Regis Urban District Council* ... 415 ... 'I have a duty not carelessly to put out a dangerous thing which may cause damage to one who may purchase it; but the duty does not extend to putting out carelessly a defective or useless or valueless thing'. In view of the origin of contractual liability in the old action on the case in tort, any tendency to exclude tort because the field is already covered by contract would perhaps be ironical. In principle, ... I do not see why the law of tort should necessarily stop short of recognising a duty not to put out carelessly a defective thing, nor any reason compelling the courts to withhold relief in tort from a plaintiff misled by the appearance of the thing into paying too much for it. But for the purposes of disposing of the present case it is enough to say that the damage is basically physical.

One of the submissions of Mr Webb for the builder was that the principles of the law of negligence could not be applied in this case in a way enabling the court satisfactorily to circumscribe the effects in other situations of a decision in favour of these purchasers. As to that, the particular facts of this case do not require decisions of some far-reaching questions. The proximity or propinquity between the plaintiffs and the builder, though not contractual, is close. The plaintiffs bought the property before the flats were quite finished. An early sale by the builder's client, Mr McKay, who (with his wife) was having the flats built largely for investment purposes, could readily have been foreseen … . An owner in the first year or so of the life of such a building in peat country would be likely to be especially closely and directly affected by any careless-ness on the part of the builder in respect of the foundations. The damage which occurred and became manifest towards the end of 1969 can reasonably be described, I think, as a direct and proximate consequence of the work done in 1968. It seems pos-sible that the House of Lords may shortly throw light on builders' liability in the appeal from *Anns* … . Subject to that reservation, I agree with the President and Woodhouse J that the mere fact that a purchaser was later in the chain than the present plaintiffs, or that a much longer time went by before damage occurred, should not automatically rule out a cause of action against the builder. Causation would always have to be proved, and a reasonable expectation of adequate intermediate examination would always be a defence … .

It seems to me that reasonably prudent builders in Paramount's position would at least have told Mr McKay of the council's stop-work order and the building inspec-tor's concern about the foundations; and would have made it clear to Mr McKay that they were not qualified to judge the adequacy of the normal concrete floor they had in mind, and that expert advice should be obtained. Building on peat land was quite a new departure in Hamilton; even the council's engineers and inspectors were probably in no position to be authoritative on the subject on the basis of experience. Instead of recommending that advice be sought, Paramount were content to rely on what they regarded as their own freedom of responsibility for assessing the subfoundation in any way, and to a lesser extent on the attitude of the council. Precisely what was the coun-cil's final attitude is not clear on the evidence. Certainly no final consent or approval was recorded.

[**Result**: **Woodhouse J** reached the same result as **Cooke J**.]

Canadian National Railway Co v Norsk Pacific Steamship Co Ltd
(1992) 91 DLR (4th) 289 (SC)
[**FACTS**: Norsk's tugboat damaged a bridge owned by Canada and used under con-tract by railway companies, including Canadian National Railways (CN). Canadian National sought to recover damages caused by having to reroute trains bound for Van-couver. The contract between Canada and Canadian National explicitly excluded any liability to Canadian National.]
La Forest J:
… [C]ontractual relational economic loss cases typically involve accidents. This distin-guishes them from both products liability economic loss cases like *Rivtow Marine Ltd v Washington Ironworks* (1973) 40 DLR (3d) 530, in which by definition there is no acci-dent, and negligent misrepresentation cases like *Hedley Byrne* …

Policy
Cases of contractual relational loss have a number of specific characteristics that differ-entiate them from other economic loss cases, and certainly from other non-relational loss cases. The first is that in such cases, the right of action of the property owner

already puts pressure on the defendants to act with care. The deterrent effect of tort law, to the extent that it survives the advent of widespread insurance, is already present. In this case PWC [Canada] collected substantial damages. Consequently, Norsk was already under a substantial incentive to take care with respect to the bridge since its liability to the bridge owner would and did require the payment of substantial damages. In most cases of this type, imposing further liability cannot reasonably be justified on the grounds of deterrence (unless a policy of full internalization of all losses resulting from accidents to the party who could have avoided the accident is to be pursued at all costs).

... [Secondly, a] firm exclusionary rule in this area does not have the effect of necessarily excluding compensation to the plaintiff for his or her loss. Rather, it simply channels to the property owner both potential liability to the plaintiff and the right of recovery against the tortfeasor. The property owner is both entitled to recover from the tortfeasor and potentially liable under contract to the plaintiff. Here, the licence explicitly rejected any liability, so the plaintiff cannot recover under it against [Canada]. In contracts between sophisticated parties such as those in the case at bar, who are well advised by counsel, such exclusions of liability often result from determinations regarding who is in the best position to insure the risk at the lowest cost.

A third distinction is that perfect compensation of all contractual relational economic loss is almost always impossible because of the ripple effects which are of the very essence of contractual relational economic loss. This aspect has been recognized as critical from the very beginning. It is in this sense that the solution to cases of this type is necessarily pragmatic and involves drawing a line that will exclude at least some people who have been undeniably injured owing to the tortfeasor's admitted failure to meet the requisite standard of care.

[In] consequential economic loss [cases], the plaintiff claims for economic loss in addition to his claims for property damage or personal injury. Focusing on the issue of remoteness of damage, the courts have established guidelines regarding the availability of damages for economic loss in these cases.

[In non-relational economic loss cases,] the plaintiff claims for pure economic loss unrelated to any personal injury or property damage suffered by either the plaintiff or any third party. The law in this area is developing. In view of my analysis of the issues in this case, it is not necessary for me to say much about these cases. I doubt, however, that this group can be analyzed in terms of a single rule ... . It is sufficient to say that I fully support this court's rejection of the broad bar on recovery of pure economic loss in *Rivtow* and [*City of Kamloops v Nielson* (1984) 10 DLR (4th) 641]. I would stress again the need to take into account the specific characteristics of each case. I agree with McLachlin J that *Murphy v Brentwood District Council* does not represent the law in Canada.

The present case, however, is of a third type. It involves a claim for contractual relational economic loss by the plaintiff as a result of damage caused to someone else's property.

English precedent

... A new stage in the development of the law on economic loss opened with the great case of *Hedley Byrne* ... The speeches of the Law Lords were principally concerned with the problem of liability for negligent words, rather than with the issue of economic loss itself. As Atiyah notes, the problems of liability for negligent misstatements and the problem of economic loss had become entangled before *Hedley Byrne* and with both problems arising again in that case, it is perhaps not surprising that in subsequent cases, the two issues have not always been completely distinguished … .

Many recent cases on economic loss have approached the problem at a very high level of generality. They have addressed the question of whether we should abandon the broad rule altogether … .

The result of this broad approach is that cases on relational economic loss are bound up with other types of economic loss cases which raise different policy concerns. This leads to all types of economic loss cases being canvassed in order to resolve the case at hand … .

… [C]ases decided on the narrow facts of contractual relational economic loss had been interpreted very broadly to exclude liability for all pure economic loss. Now, it was argued, the rejection of the broad rule in cases like *Hedley Byrne* and *Rivtow* should eliminate the specificities of economic loss in all cases. Today CN urges us to extend this approach to include contractual relational economic loss cases.

The decisions in this court

… The respondent argues that these cases refute the existence of a broad exclusionary rule. I agree but, in my view, both these cases … [are] claims for pure economic loss where the defendant has not caused damage to a third party's property … .

An examination of *Rivtow* reveals that the concern over indeterminate liability is only one among several policy issues that arise in economic loss cases. What is particularly instructive about *Rivtow*, rather than any wide dicta about proximity in economic loss cases, is the manner in which both judgments analyzed the policy considerations underlying the exclusionary rule. Of these, indeterminate liability was only of secondary importance. The broad rule was qualified and recovery for economic loss upheld only after a searching examination of the functions the rule served in the type of case there in question.

In *Rivtow*, the plaintiff (appellant) chartered by demise a log barge, the *Rivtow Carrier*, fitted with two cranes designed and manufactured by the first defendant and for which the second defendant was the sole representative and distributor in British Columbia. Neither defendant was in a contractual relationship with Rivtow. The manufacturer and distributor had become aware of structural defects in this type of crane as early as 1963, and certainly by late 1965 they were aware of many cracks in the legs of the cranes. They also knew that the plaintiff was using the cranes for the logging work but did not warn it of the potential danger.

On September 16, 1966, the aft crane of the *Straits Logger*, another barge fitted with the same type of crane, collapsed owing to a failure in the rear legs. It tore itself free of the front legs, fell to the deck and bounced into the ocean, killing the crane operator. The same day, the *Rivtow Carrier* was about to begin loading logs at Kitimat. Word was received of the *Straits Logger* accident, and the *Rivtow Carrier* was ordered to return empty to Vancouver. As a result, the barge had to be taken out of service for repairs in the busiest part of the logging season.

Rivtow sued for loss of the use of the barge during the repair period and for the cost of repairs to the cranes. Ritchie J, for the seven judges in the majority, held that the lower courts were right in disallowing the claim for repairs and for such economic loss as it would in any event have sustained even if proper warning had been given. The full court concurred with the part of Ritchie J's judgment that recognized a manufacturer's duty to warn of known dangerous defects and held the manufacturer liable for loss of extra profit caused by the failure to warn promptly in a slack period.

Two judges, dissenting in part, would have included in the allowable loss the cost of repair of the cranes on the ground that threatened physical harm should be treated in the same way as actual physical harm. Laskin J (Hall J concurring) specifically excluded general contractual relational loss.

... [T]he *Rivtow* case involves significant policy considerations. The incursion into the broad rule is carefully justified on policy grounds. As Laskin J notes, at p 552, '[t]he case is not one where a manufactured product proves to be merely defective (in short, where it has not met promised expectations) but rather one where by reason of the defect there is a foreseeable risk of physical harm from its use and where the alert avoidance of such harm gives rise to economic loss'. In Laskin J's view, the courts must be careful to avoid giving redress in tort for 'safe but shoddy' products. Where the products are unsafe, however, tort may have a role: prevention of threatened harm resulting directly in economic loss should not be treated differently from post-injury treatment. The narrow rule barring contractual relational economic loss is explicitly left intact.

The majority's examination of the policy issues lead to a lesser incursion on the broad exclusionary rule. Ritchie J, at p 546, expressly considered whether the tort duty he imposed would have the effect of disrupting contractual relations:

> ... In the present case ... I am of opinion that the failure to warn was 'an independent tort' unconnected with the performance of any contract either express or implied.

However, because in Ritchie J's view the failure to warn was an independent tort, he considered that the plaintiffs should recover for the economic loss resulting from the inactivity of the barge for the period after the respondent became seized with the defects.

The respondent CN submitted that, in Ritchie J's judgment in *Rivtow*, proximity was based on the defendants' knowledge of the use of the cranes by Rivtow and on their potential danger, and that similar knowledge by Norsk should also give rise to proximity here. This argument fails to recognize that the defendants' knowledge in *Rivtow* was pertinent with respect to a particular duty: the duty to warn. Because they knew about Rivtow as a specific user, they could have warned Rivtow. In the case at bar, Norsk had no opportunity to warn CN in any meaningful sense.

Transferred loss

... True transferred loss cases involve a claim which is in essence a claim for property damage which the owner himself would have recovered, had the loss not fallen on the plaintiff because of their contract. A true transferred loss case requires that the risk of property damage have passed, as in the case of goods damaged in transit after the risk (but not the property) has passed to the buyer. In such a case, unless the buyer is given a right of action, the carrier will be liable to neither party; not to the seller because he has suffered no loss, nor to the buyer who has no protected interest: see John G. Fleming, *The Law of Torts*, 7th edn (Sydney: Law Book Co, 1987) ... 164–5.

Even in that type of case, recovery was denied in the recent House of Lords decision in *Leigh and Sillavan v Aliakmon* [1986] 1 AC 785 (HL), essentially on the ground that contract law provided a sufficient protection in the circumstances of that case. It was only the particular variation of the contract to which the buyers agreed that deprived them of their usual right of action.

The present is not a true transferred loss case. [Canada] has collected for the property damage it has sustained. The transferred loss claimed in this case is thus not with respect to the property damage claim. Rather, it is a claim for the transferred loss of use, or transferred economic loss.

In these circumstances, I fail to see how the respondent suffered a transferred loss such as to create an alternative protected interest to its contractual interest.

Common adventure or joint ventures

... I do not find the respondent's arguments to the effect that it had more than a mere contractual interest convincing. CN's entitlement to use the bridge finds its sole source in the contract. The contract sets out the full extent of CN's rights: without the contract, CN would be trespassing. It has wisely not argued the existence of any possessory interest. Its transferred loss is merely the transfer of a loss of use and is a less compelling case for recovery than the loss incurred by a time charterer. This case does not involve a common adventure ... . As a result, I cannot accept the rationale for recovery set forth by McLachlin J ... .

Part III: The proposed tests

... A good test should distinguish on a rational basis between potential plaintiffs, all of whom were injured by the defendants' negligence. The plaintiff's proposed rule should offer a convincing and practical rationale for distinguishing its claim from those other claims, contractual or otherwise, which are to be rejected. Victims whose claims are to be denied must perceive a minimum of justice in the result. In my view, none of the theories that involve the acceptance of CN's claim but which would lead to the rejection of the claims of the other railways can be accepted as just from this perspective.

... A good rule should thus place some incentive on both parties to act in an economically rational manner to reduce total accident costs.

The rule must, of course, also confront the problem of indeterminacy. It is often suggested that this is the only problem the rule must confront. This was perhaps natural in light of the importance of potential indeterminate liability in negligent misrepresentation cases and the fact that the breakthrough in allowing recovery for economic loss came in *Hedley Byrne*. However, this confusion between the two issues tended to obscure the variety of issues raised in different kinds of economic loss cases. If the principal reason lying behind the broad exclusionary rule for pure economic loss is the concern over indeterminate liability, then the exclusionary rule can be easily discarded in favour of a more direct test of whether liability would be indeterminate. The plaintiff's case here is essentially built on this proposition and they offer this court a wide variety of factual distinctions which they contend respond to the concern about indeterminate liability ... . I do not agree with that approach; a rule in this area should serve to do more than simply exclude indeterminate liability. However, in contractual economic loss cases, the proposed rule must certainly confront this issue.

... A company like CN should be able to consult legal counsel and receive reasonably clear advice with respect to potential recovery in the case of an accident that is as common as a ship hitting a bridge ... . Even more importantly, when the shoe is on the other foot, CN should also be able to get some reasonably clear guidance from counsel with respect to its potential liabilities in a case where a train derails and damages a factory. Estimating such liability is, of course, a key aspect to the pricing of insurance for potential tortfeasors. Under the exclusionary rule, liability is determinate *before* the accident; unless the contract is such as to create a joint venture or a possessory interest, all parties are aware that no recovery will lie for damage to those contractual interests.

The second important point is that the objection is not simply to a large number of claims since an accident may injure a large number of people or cause extensive property damage ... .

A third important consideration is *the indeterminacy of each claim*. Recovery for contractual expectancies requires analysis of who bore the loss. What would happen if CN effectively passed on any increased costs incurred owing to the unavailability of the bridge to its customers? Refusing to address this question could result in a very expensive tort case leading to compensation for a party who suffered no loss. In a multi-stage chain of contracts, it becomes very difficult to analyze the economic effects of an accident on a particular link in the chain. A related concern is with false or inflated claims: see *Spartan Steel*.

... The fact that Norsk was fortunate enough to hit a bridge with few users does not make its potential liability for contractual relational economic loss any less indeterminate. Its liability after the accident is, of course, determinate; but beforehand, when potential tortfeasors are looking for insurance, they and their insurance company do not know which bridge will be hit. It seems odd to establish one set of rules for negligent tortfeasors who hit busy bridges—liability for economic loss is excused because of indeterminacy—and a different set for those who hit bridges used by few users.

I turn to an examination of the proposed tests. The principal authority in the Commonwealth allowing recovery for contractual relational economic loss is *Caltex Oil (Australia) Pty Ltd v The Dredge 'Willemstad'* (1976) 136 CLR 5. *Caltex* involved an oil refinery and pipeline owned by the Australian Oil Refinery ('AOR') that carried oil to a terminal owned by the plaintiff Caltex. While oil was moving through the pipeline between the refinery and the Caltex terminal a dredge negligently damaged the pipeline. AOR was compensated for its loss as property owner.

Under the terms of the Caltex–AOR contract, the oil in the pipeline was owned by Caltex but was at the risk of AOR. Caltex claimed against the dredge and its owners for its economic loss resulting from the damage, specifically the expense to which it was put in arranging for continued supply of its terminal either by ship or road. One of the questions before the court was whether the plaintiff could recover damages for economic loss sustained as a result of damage negligently caused to the property of a third party. Although all five judges held that the right to economic loss must rest on something more than mere foreseeability they all agreed that the plaintiff must succeed. Each, however, suggested different approaches for the appropriate test to be applied. I shall examine the various proposed rules under the headings set out below.

Foreseeability of the individual plaintiff or of an ascertained class of plaintiffs

CN heavily stressed the defendants' undoubtedly high level of subjective and objective knowledge that CN as a particular company would suffer loss. My colleague Stevenson J relies on this factor as his principal ground for finding liability in this case. There is no question that Norsk knew and ought to have known that CN would suffer loss. Indeed, the facts reveal that the tug captain thought CN would suffer even more than it did, since he erroneously thought the bridge belonged to it. I am unable to see the importance of this 'excess of foresight' in policy terms, however.

First, the subjective view of the defendants with respect to the ownership of the bridge is obviously not sufficient to ground a claim. Such an error does not, of course, negate the defendants' duty with respect to the actual owner of the property. Why should it have the effect of creating new duties in the absence of a protected interest? It remains true, however, that Norsk could reasonably foresee that a specific plaintiff, CN, would suffer loss as a contractual claimant. Should this factor distinguish CN from other contractual claimants?

Two judges in *Caltex* suggested versions of an individual plaintiff test, at least one that would allow recovery in this case. At the level of a general test for all cases of pure economic loss, Mason J adopted what can be termed the specific individual test ... . Gibbs J also incorporated the known plaintiff test into his analysis as a necessary but not sufficient condition for liability. As he saw it, the existence of a common adventure or physical propinquity may have supporting roles, but are neither necessary nor sufficient. The ascertained class test would allow recovery where the defendant knows or has the means of knowing that the persons likely to be affected by his or her negligence consist of a definite number of persons.

In my view, problems also exist at the level of principle. In the absence of any malicious intent on the part of the defendant, of what significance is the fact that the defendant knew that the individual plaintiff would suffer? In my view, its only role is to limit liability. The individual plaintiff or class of plaintiff or special relationship test serves a very different and more focused policy function in the context of the negligent misrepresentation cases where it has been employed: see *Hedley Byrne*; *Candler v Crane, Christmas & Co.*

... Those cases involve the defendant's making a representation voluntarily. It makes sense to impose upon the defendant a requirement that he or she put his or her mind to the question of who might be affected, since the defendant has the opportunity to reflect on this issue before making the representation ... .

Here we are dealing with an *accident*. There is no intention to affect the plaintiff; rather the effect on the plaintiff is merely a result of the accident. Norsk cannot be said to contemplate a particular act of negligence, a particular plaintiff or a particular loss in the same sense as a bank manager who provides financial information. Knowledge of the individual plaintiff serves solely to eliminate 'indeterminate liability'; it operates arbitrarily both in terms of singling out defendants and in terms of singling out plaintiffs.

In the context of an accident, this criterion has thus no link with fault or with a lack of care; surely no one is suggesting tort law should strive to protect bridges with high profile users more than bridges used by anonymous users, or that defendants who damage bridges with high profile users are more guilty than others. Its sole function is to distinguish one plaintiff from another and thus 'solve' the indeterminacy problem, a function that could be as effectively performed by a rule based on the colour of CN's trains.

Allowing CN's claim to be distinct from the other contractual victims by virtue of its particular foreseeability as an individual victim would in my view give rise to an unjust rule owing to its sheer arbitrariness. It serves neither to distinguish particularly meritorious victims, nor to single out particularly careless tortfeasors. Its sole function is to reduce the class of claimants to a small group, a function that could be equally well performed by any other factual distinction. Further, the test would have the effect of singling out the wrong parties for relief. It would offer a premium to notoriety, a premium for which I can find no legal or social justification, particularly since such persons are most likely to advert to the matter and to contract out or insure against any harm.

The defendant's foresight with respect to the specific nature of the loss incurred by the plaintiff

... It is thus incorrect to say that, because Norsk knew that CN's use of the bridge would be interrupted, it knew the 'precise nature of the loss' CN would incur. The precise nature of the loss, and in fact whether any loss is incurred at all, would be a result of the contractual allocation of risk, of which Norsk would normally be unaware. In many cases of contractual relational loss, the variety of contractual entitlements will be much greater and more complex.

Physical propinquity

The third factor that is said to found proximity is the physical proximity of CN's property to the accident. CN's property is closely joined to the bridge on both sides of the river and the bridge forms an integral part of its railway network. CN relies here primarily on the judgment of Jacobs J in *Caltex*. Jacobs J there recognized that where the plaintiff's loss arises solely from a contractual relationship with a third party, recovery will be denied. However, he held that if the damage arose owing to 'physical effect on the person or property of the plaintiff, it will not be irrecoverable simply because it is economic loss'. The judge defined physical effect short of physical injury as an act or omission that prevents physical movement of a person or physical movement or operation of property. In that case, the physical effect was the immobilization or the flow of crude oil through the pipeline.

CN does not, in my view, meet this physical effect test, even if such a test were adopted. Its trains have certainly not been immobilized. Its land has not been damaged and it makes no sense to speak of it being immobilized. In the absence of such a 'physical effect', physical propinquity of property cannot constitute an alternative potential interest. As the appellants rightly point out, the other railways suffered identical damages despite not owning any property in physical propinquity to the accident ... .

Part IV: A refined proximity analysis in contractual relational economic loss cases

... In my view, it is legitimate ... to consider explicitly the ability of the plaintiff to bear the risk of loss in this type of case.

Turning then to an application of these criteria to this case, a determination of which party is the better loss bearer is relatively straightforward. CN is undoubtedly in a better position to bear the loss than Norsk. First, in light of the significant information available regarding bridge failure and CN's long use of the bridge, CN was probably at least equally competent in terms of *estimating the potential risks* of bridge failure. This aspect seems to me to be clear in light of the facts.

Second, CN would clearly be in a better position than [Canada] to *estimate the potential costs of bridge failure to CN's operations*. CN knows exactly how much use it gets out of the various bridges crossed by its trains. It also knows what the alternatives are in cases of bridge failure. Norsk, of course, is very poorly placed to estimate the value of the use that various people and companies get out of the bridges that cross the rivers its tugs sail on. It is also poorly placed to estimate the potential costs to those users of an interruption in bridge service. Unlike the first factor, which depends to a large degree on the facts of each case, this factor tends to weigh heavily in favour of the defendant in almost every case of this type.

Third, CN was better placed to *protect itself from the consequences of those losses* ... . It is hard to imagine a more sophisticated group of plaintiffs than the users of railway bridges. These parties have access to the full range of protective options: first party commercial insurance or self-insurance, contracts with both the bridge owner and with the railway's customers.

McLachlin J:

...

3 *The approach which should be adopted to recovery of pure economic loss*

... The matter may be put thus: before the law will impose liability there must be a connection between the defendant's conduct and plaintiff's loss which makes it just for the defendant to indemnify the plaintiff. In contract, the contractual relationship provides this link. In trust, it is the fiduciary obligation which establishes the necessary connection. In tort, the equivalent notion is proximity. Proximity may consist of various forms of closeness—physical, circumstantial, causal or assumed—which serve to identify the categories of cases in which liability lies.

Viewed thus, the concept of proximity may be seen as an umbrella, covering a number of disparate circumstances in which the relationship between the parties is so close that it is just and reasonable to permit recovery in tort. The complexity and diversity of the circumstances in which tort liability may arise defy identification of a single criterion capable of serving as the universal hallmark of liability. The meaning of 'proximity' is to be found rather in viewing the circumstances in which it has been found to exist and determining whether the case at issue is similar enough to justify a similar finding.

In summary, it is my view that the authorities suggest that pure economic loss is *prima facie* recoverable where, in addition to negligence and foreseeable loss, there is sufficient proximity between the negligent act and the loss. Proximity is the controlling concept which avoids the spectre of unlimited liability. Proximity may be established by a variety of factors, depending on the nature of the case. To date, sufficient proximity has been found in the case of negligent misstatements where there is an undertaking and correlative reliance (*Hedley Byrne*), where there is a duty to warn (*Rivtow*), and where a statute imposes a responsibility on a municipality toward the owners and occupiers of land (*Kamloops*). But the categories are not closed. As more cases are decided, we can expect further definition on what factors give rise to liability for pure economic loss in particular categories of cases. In determining whether liability should be extended to a new situation, courts will have regard to the factors traditionally relevant to proximity such as the relationship between the parties, physical propinquity, assumed or imposed obligations and close causal connection. And they will insist on sufficient special factors to avoid the imposition of indeterminate and unreasonable liability. The result will be a principled, yet flexible, approach to tort liability for pure economic loss. It will allow recovery where recovery is justified, while excluding indeterminate and inappropriate liability, and it will permit the coherent development of the law in accordance with the approach initiated in England by *Hedley Byrne* and followed in Canada in *Rivtow* [and] *Kamloops* ... .

I add the following observations on proximity. The absolute exclusionary rule adopted in *Cattle v Stockton* and affirmed in *Murphy* (subject to *Hedley Byrne*) can itself be seen as an indicator of proximity. Where there is physical injury or damage, one posits proximity on the ground that if one is close enough to someone or something to do physical damage to it, one is close enough to be held legally responsible for the consequences. Physical injury has the advantage of being a clear and simple indicator of proximity. The problem arises when it is taken as the only indicator of proximity. As the cases amply demonstrate, the necessary proximity to found legal liability fairly in tort may well arise in circumstances where there is no physical damage.

Viewed in this way, proximity may be seen as paralleling the requirement in civil law that damages be direct and certain. Proximity, like the requirement of directness, posits a close link between the negligent act and the resultant loss. Distant losses which arise from collateral relationships do not qualify for recovery.

In many of the cases discussed above, the judiciary has focused upon the relationship between the tortfeasor and the plaintiff as an indication of proximity, a focus closely related to the foreseeability analysis inherent to all negligence actions. In the classic case of *Hedley Byrne*, the reliance analysis focuses upon the connection between the party who made the negligent misstatement and the injured party, ie, is that plaintiff a party that the tortfeasor ought reasonably to have foreseen would rely on his or her statement? The judgments below focused on the relationship between the tortfeasor Norsk and the plaintiff CN both within and outside their discussion of proximity. A more comprehensive, and I submit objective, consideration of proximity requires that the court review all of the factors connecting the negligent act with the loss; this includes not only the relationship between the parties but all forms of proximity—physical, circumstantial, causal or assumed indicators of closeness. While it is impossible to define comprehensively what will satisfy the requirements of proximity or directness, precision may be found as types of relationships or situations are defined in which the necessary closeness between negligence and loss exists.

While proximity is critical to establishing the right to recover pure economic loss in tort, it does not always indicate liability. It is a necessary but not necessarily sufficient condition of liability. Recognizing that proximity is itself concerned with policy, the approach adopted in *Kamloops* (paralleled by the second branch of *Anns*), requires the court to consider the purposes served by permitting recovery as well as whether there are any residual policy considerations which call for a limitation on liability. This permits courts to reject liability for pure economic loss where indicated by policy reasons not taken into account in the proximity analysis.

I conclude that, from a doctrinal point of view, this court should continue on the course charted in *Kamloops* rather than reverting to the narrow exclusionary rule as the House of Lords did in *Murphy*.

Economic theory

… A third argument focuses on the liability of persons who stand to suffer economic loss due to damage to the property of another, to allocate the risk within their contracts effectively with property owners. The law of negligence has no business compensating such persons, it is argued, because it makes better economic sense for them to provide for the possibility of damage to the bridge by negotiating a term that in the event of failure, the owner of the bridge would compensate them. The argument, applied to the facts of this case, proceeds as follows: the lessee (CN) would negotiate for indemnification in the event of damage to the bridge; any increase in the lease payments, should they result, would be based on estimates derived from information obtained directly from the parties who will suffer the loss; in the event of damage to the bridge by the negligence of a third party, the lessee (CN) would claim under its contract with the lessor [(Canada)] for indemnification in the amount negotiated; the lessor could, as the party suffering physical damage, turn around the claim against the tortfeasor (Norsk) for the consequent economic losses including the amount it had to pay out under its contract to the lessee CN. Such a loss is reasonably foreseeable and falls within the established exception for recovery of economic loss where physical damage is suffered as well. In this way, relational economic losses are 'channelled' rather than denied.

The proponents of this position argue that judicial affirmation of a rule that recovery of economic loss is confined to cases where the plaintiff has sustained physical damage to its person or property or has relied in the sense of *Hedley Byrne*, will send a clear message to the business community to plan its affairs accordingly. Following this argument, the court can presume that if CN failed to contract for this indemnification: (a) CN paid less for its lease; (b) CN did not consider the risk of unavailability to be significant enough to negotiate for such indemnification (or, alternatively, to insure itself); or (c) CN did not act reasonably and was itself negligent in organizing its business affairs. As such, the preclusion of CN from recovery is justified.

The 'contractual allocation or risk' argument rests on a number of important, but questionable assumptions. First, the argument assumes that all persons or business entities organize their affairs in accordance with the laws of economic efficiency, assigning liability to the 'least-cost risk avoider'. Second, it assumes that all parties to a transaction share an equality of bargaining power which will result in the effective allocation of risk. It is not considered that certain parties who control the situation (eg, the owners of an indispensable bridge) may refuse to indemnify against the negligence of those over whom they have no control, or may demand such an exorbitant premium for this indemnification that it would be more cost-effective for the innocent victim to insure itself. Third, it overlooks the historical centrality of personal fault to our concept of negligence or 'delict' and the role this may have in curbing negligent conduct and thus limiting the harm done to innocent parties, not all of whom are large enterprises capable of maximizing their economic situation. Given the uncertainty of these premises, it is far from clear that the court should deny recovery of pure economic loss on the basis of arguments based on allocation of risk.

… MacGuigan JA summarized the trial judge's findings on proximity as follows, at p 361:

> In effect, the trial judge found that the CNR was so closely assimilated to the position of [Canada] that it was very much within the reasonable ambit of risk of the appellants at the time of the accident. That, it seems to me, is sufficient proximity: in Deane J's language, it is both physical and circumstantial closeness.

Such a characterization brings the situation into the 'joint' or 'common venture' category under which recovery for purely economic loss has heretofore been recognized in maritime law … . The reasoning, as I apprehend it, is that where the plaintiff's operations are so closely allied to the operations of the party suffering physical damage and to its property (which—as damaged—causes the plaintiff's loss) that it can be considered a joint venturer with the owner of the property, the plaintiff can recover its economic loss even though the plaintiff has suffered no physical damage to its own property. To deny recovery in such circumstances would be to deny it to a person who for practical purposes is in the same position as if he or she owned the property physically damaged.

The second question is whether extension of recovery to this type of loss is desirable from a practical point of view. Recovery serves the purpose of permitting a plaintiff whose position for practical purposes, vis-à-vis the tortfeasor, is indistinguishable from that of the owner of the damaged property, to recover what the actual owner could have recovered. This is fair and avoids an anomalous result. Nor does the recovery of economic loss in this case open the floodgates to unlimited liability. The category is a limited one. It has been applied in England and the United States without apparent difficulty. It does not embrace casual users of the property or those secondarily and incidentally affected by the damage done to the property. Potential tortfeasors can gauge in advance the scope of their liability … .

In deference to the learned judgments of my colleagues, I add the following comments. With respect to the reasons of my colleague Stevenson J, I, like La Forest J, would not accept, by itself, the 'known plaintiff' test or the 'ascertained class' test, which, to borrow La Forest J's phrase, places a premium on notoriety. With respect to the reasons of La Forest J, we are in agreement that the broad and flexible approach set out in *Anns* governs the right to recover for economic loss in tort. We also agree that the law of tort does not permit recovery for all economic loss. We further agree that where the plaintiff establishes a joint venture with the owner of the damaged property, it should be able to recover economic loss. Where we differ, in the final analysis, is on the test for determining joint venture.

[In contrast to La Forest J,] I do not read the authorities which have considered the implications of a joint venture between the plaintiff and the owner of the damaged property as confining themselves to the formal terms of the contract. I prefer a more flexible test which permits the trial judge to consider all factors relevant to their relationship. The terms of the contract are an important consideration in determining whether economic loss is recoverable. But the contract may tell only part of the story between the parties. If the evidence establishes that having regard to the entire relationship between the owner of the damaged property and the plaintiff, the plaintiff must be regarded as standing in the relation of joint or common venturer (or a concept akin thereto) with the property owner with the result that in justice his rights against third parties should be the same as the owner's, then I would not interfere. Here, as elsewhere in the law of tort, the question is where the balance between certainty and flexibility should be struck. It is my conviction, based on the development of the law relating to recovery of economic loss thus far, that the balance must be struck.

In the end, I conclude that a test for recovery of economic loss outside situations akin to *Hedley Byrne*—whether 'contractual relational' economic loss or otherwise—should be flexible enough to meet the complexities of commercial reality and to permit the recognition of new situations in which liability ought, in justice, to lie as such situations arise. With the greatest respect, it seems to me that a test which is confined to the terms of the formal contract between the owner of the property damaged and the person who suffers economic loss as a consequence of that damage, may not fill these objectives.

[**Result**: Two judges agreed with **La Forest J**, two with **McLachlin J**, while **Stevenson J** held Canada liable for the reasons discussed in the judgment.]

Bow Valley Husky (Bermuda) Ltd v Saint John Shipbuilding Ltd
[1997] 3 SCR 1210; [1998] 153 DLR (4th) 385 (SC)

McLachlin J: (dissenting on other issues)

I *Introduction*
1 On April 21, 1987, a fire broke out on the Bow Drill III, which was drilling for oil on the Grand Banks of Newfoundland. The Bow Drill III suffered major damage. Extensive repairs were required and the companies which had contracted for the lease of the rig suffered financial loss while it was out of commission. At issue in this appeal is the legal responsibility for the damages and the extent of the damages recoverable …

II Facts
2 In the early 1980s, Husky Oil Operations Ltd ('HOOL') and Bow Valley Industries Ltd ('BVI') decided to take advantage of a drilling opportunity off the east coast of

Canada. They purchased one oil rig and made arrangements to have two others constructed. To this end, a subsidiary of BVI contracted with Saint John Shipbuilding Limited ('SJSL') for the construction of the drilling rig Bow Drill III.

3 In order to take advantage of Export Development Corporation financing, HOOL and BVI incorporated an offshore company, Bow Valley Husky (Bermuda) Ltd ('BVHB'). Before construction of Bow Drill III began, ownership of the rig was transferred to BVHB, and the contract with SJSL for the construction of the rig was assigned to BVHB. HOOL and BVI entered into contracts with BVHB for the hire of Bow Drill III to conduct drilling operations at sites chosen by HOOL and BVI. These contracts were for four years (with an optional extension for a further year), and provided that HOOL and BVI would continue to pay day rates to BVHB in the event that the rig was out of service.

4 A heat trace system was required in order to prepare the rig for winter operation. The purpose of a heat trace system is to prevent the rig's pipes or 'mud lines' from freezing …

[**Note**: The defendant shipyard installed this system without warning the plaintiffs of the fire danger that it posed].

(1) The Law

…

42 The plaintiffs HOOL and BVI had contracts with BVHB for the use of the rig owned by BVHB. They seek damages for economic loss incurred as a result of the shutdown of the drilling rig during the period it was being repaired. In other words, the plaintiffs HOOL and BVI seek to recover the economic loss they suffered as a result of damage to the property of a third party. This sort of loss is often called 'contractual relational economic loss'. The issue is whether the loss suffered by HOOL and BVI is recoverable …

[**Note**: Her Honour reviewed the conflicting approaches to relational economic loss and continued.]

46 The differences between the reasons of La Forest J and myself in *Norsk* are of two orders: difference in result and difference in methodology. The difference in result, taken at its narrowest, is a difference in the definition of what constitutes a 'joint venture' for the purposes of determining whether recovery for contractual relational economic loss should be allowed. We both agreed that if the plaintiff is in a joint venture with the person whose property is damaged, the plaintiff may claim consequential economic loss related to that property. We parted company because La Forest J took a stricter view of what constituted a joint venture than I did.

47 The difference in methodology is not, on close analysis, as great as might be supposed. Broadly put, La Forest J started from a general exclusionary rule and proceeded to articulate exceptions to that rule where recovery would be permitted. I, by contrast, stressed the two-step test for when recovery would be available, based on the general principles of recovery in tort as set out in *Anns* … and *Kamloops* …

48 Despite this difference in approach, La Forest J and I agreed on several important propositions: (1) relational economic loss is recoverable only in special circumstances where the appropriate conditions are met; (2) these circumstances can be defined by

reference to categories, which will make the law generally predictable; (3) the categories are not closed. La Forest J identified the categories of recovery of relational economic loss defined to date as: (1) cases where the claimant has a possessory or proprietary interest in the damaged property; (2) general average cases; and (3) cases where the relationship between the claimant and property owner constitutes a joint venture.

49 The case at bar does not fall into any of the above three categories. The plaintiffs here had no possessory or proprietary interest in the rig and the case is not one of general averaging. While related contractually, the Court of Appeal correctly held that the plaintiff and the property owner cannot, on any view of the term, be viewed as joint venturers.

50 However, that is not the end of the matter. The categories of recoverable contractual relational economic loss in tort are not closed. Where a case does not fall within a recognized category the court may go on to consider whether the situation is one where the right to recover contractual relational economic loss should nevertheless be recognized ...

More particularly, La Forest J suggested that the general rule against recovery for policy-based reasons might be relaxed where the deterrent effect of potential liability to the property owner is low, or, despite a degree of indeterminate liability, where the claimant's opportunity to allocate the risk by contract is slight, either because of the type of transaction or an inequality of bargaining power. I agreed with La Forest J that policy considerations relating to increased costs of processing claims and contractual allocation of the risk are important ... I concluded that the test for recovery 'should be flexible enough to meet the complexities of commercial reality and to permit the recognition of new situations in which liability ought, in justice, to lie as such situations arise' ... It thus appears that new categories of recoverable contractual relational economic loss may be recognized where justified by policy considerations and required by justice. At the same time, courts should not assiduously seek new categories; what is required is a clear rule predicting when recovery is available.

51 More recently, in *Hercules Managements Ltd* ... this Court described the general approach that should be followed in determining when tort recovery for economic loss is appropriate. The plaintiffs in that case were shareholders in a company, Hercules Managements Ltd. The auditors for the company allegedly failed to disclose in their annual audits matters detrimental to the company. The company failed and the plaintiffs suffered financial loss. The plaintiff shareholders sued the auditors. The first issue was whether the plaintiffs' action against the auditors could be maintained in law. Although styled as an action for negligent misrepresentation, the plaintiffs' claim was treated as a case of relational economic loss owing to the fact that the services were performed pursuant to a contract with the company. The primary loser was the company, which had contracted with the auditors. The plaintiffs' loss was derivative of, or relational to, the company's loss. The defendant auditors asserted that their only duty was to the company with which they had contracted. They argued that no relational tort duty to third parties lay in the circumstances. To affirm such a duty, they maintained, would be contrary to the policy considerations that had led courts in the past to deny recovery for relational economic loss.

The Court, per La Forest J, unanimously held that the shareholders had no cause of action against the auditors ...

56 ... The first step is to inquire whether the relationship of neighbourhood or proximity necessary to found a *prima facie* duty of care is present. If so, one moves to the second step of inquiring whether the policy concerns that usually preclude recovery of contractual relational economic loss, such as indeterminacy, are overridden.

(2) Application of the law

57 Before applying the law set out above to the facts of this case, a preliminary point arises: is the loss claimed by the plaintiff's contractual relational economic loss at all? The plaintiffs argue that the loss they claim against the defendants is really loss transferred from BVHB, the rig owner. The plaintiffs argue that they were in a 'common venture' (as distinguished from a joint venture) with BVHB, which resulted in BVHB's losses being transferred to them. Therefore, they argue, they should be able to claim the losses as though they stand in the shoes of BVHB. BVHB could have claimed consequential losses for loss of use of the drilling rig; so then, on this theory, can HOOL and BVI.

58 This argument suffers from a number of difficulties. First, insofar as courts have recognized transferred loss, it has been confined to physical damage: *Norsk* ... Applied to relational economic loss, it would need to meet the criteria for recovery of that category of loss, and hence would seem not to advance the plaintiffs' case. Second, the plaintiffs claim not only for loss of use of the drilling rig, but for losses related to unavoidable expenses they incurred for other supplies, including food, drilling mud and additional equipment. It is more difficult to see how these losses, based entirely on contracts between the plaintiffs and others, independent of BVHB, can be said to be transferred from BVHB. Third, there is nothing to show that the day rates paid by HOOL and BVI while the rig was idle are identical to what BVHB's consequential losses would have been. Finally, what does one do about the contributory negligence of BVHB? Given that BVHB is 60 per cent at fault, under the transferred loss theory would the plaintiffs be able to recover only 40 per cent of their claim? These difficulties suggest that the plaintiffs' loss is not the transferred loss of BVHB, the owner of the damaged rig. It is contractual relational economic loss, and should be treated as such ...

60 ... The decision as to whether a *prima facie* duty of care exists requires an investigation into whether the defendant and the plaintiff can be said to be in a relationship of proximity or neighbourhood. Proximity exists on a given set of facts if the defendant may be said to be under an obligation to be mindful of the plaintiff's legitimate interests in conducting his or her affairs ... On the facts of this case, I agree with the Court of Appeal that a *prima facie* duty of care arises. Indeed, the duty to warn raised against the defendants is the correlative of the duty to disclose financial facts raised against the auditors in *Hercules*.

61 Where a duty to warn is alleged, the issue is not reliance (there being nothing to rely upon), but whether the defendants ought reasonably to have foreseen that the plaintiffs might suffer loss as a result of use of the product about which the warning should have been made. I have already found that the duty to warn extended to

BVHB. The question is, however, whether it extended as far as HOOL and BVI. The facts establish that this was the case. The defendants knew of the existence of the plaintiffs and others like them and knew or ought to have known that they stood to lose money if the drilling rig was shut down.

62 The next question is whether this *prima facie* duty of care is negatived by policy considerations. In my view, it is. The most serious problem is … the problem of indeterminate liability. If the defendants owed a duty to warn the plaintiffs, it is difficult to see why they would not owe a similar duty to a host of other persons who would foreseeably lose money if the rig was shut down as a result of being damaged. Other investors in the project are the most obvious persons who would also be owed a duty, although the list could arguably be extended to additional classes of persons. What has been referred to as the ripple effect is present in this case. A number of investment companies which contracted with HOOL are making claims against it, as has BVI.

63 No sound reason to permit the plaintiffs to recover while denying recovery to these other persons emerges. To hold otherwise would pose problems for defendants, who would face liability in an indeterminate amount for an indeterminate time to an indeterminate class. It also would pose problems for potential plaintiffs. Which of all the potential plaintiffs can expect and anticipate they will succeed? Why should one type of contractual relationship, that of HOOL, be treated as more worthy than another, eg, that of the employees on the rig? In this state, what contractual and insurance arrangements should potential plaintiffs make against future loss?

64 The plaintiffs propose a number of solutions to the problem of indeterminacy. None of them succeeds, in my respectful view. The first proposal is to confine liability to persons whose identity was known to the defendants. This is a reversion to the 'known plaintiff' test, rejected by a majority of this Court in *Norsk* … As commentators have pointed out, the fact that the defendant knew the identity of the plaintiff should not in logic or justice determine recovery. On such a test, the notorious would recover, the private would lose: *Norsk*. The problem of indeterminate liability cannot be avoided by arbitrary distinctions for which there is no legal or social justification: *Norsk* … There must be something which, for policy reasons, permits the court to say this category of person can recover and that category cannot, something which justifies the line being drawn at one point rather than another.

65 Second, and in a similar vein, the plaintiffs argue that determinacy can be achieved by restricting recovery to the users of the rig, a class which they say is analogous in time and extent to the owners and occupiers of the building in *Winnipeg Condominium* [1995] 1 SCR 85. This argument fails for the same reasons as the known plaintiff test. There is no logical reason for drawing the line at users rather than somewhere else.

66 Third, the plaintiffs attempt to distinguish themselves from other potential claimants through the concept of reliance. The defendants correctly answer this argument by pointing out that any person who is contractually dependent on a product or a structure owned by another 'relies' on the manufacturer or builder to supply a safe product.

67 Finally, the plaintiffs argue that a finding of a duty to warn negates the spectre of indeterminate liability as the duty to warn does not extend to everyone in any way connected to the manufactured product. This argument begs the question. The duty to warn found to this point is only a *prima facie* duty to warn in accordance with the

first requirement of *Anns*, *supra*, that there be sufficient proximity or neighbourhood to found a duty of care. It is not circumscribed and imports no limits on liability. Considerations of indeterminate liability arise in the second step of the *Anns* analysis. Hence the *prima facie* duty of care, by itself, cannot resolve the problem of indeterminate liability.

68 The problem of indeterminate liability constitutes a policy consideration tending to negative a duty of care for contractual relational economic loss. However, the courts have recognized positive policy considerations tending to support the imposition of such a duty of care. One of these, discussed by La Forest J in *Norsk*, is the need to provide additional deterrence against negligence. The potential liability to the owner of the damaged property usually satisfies the goal of encouraging persons to exercise due care not to damage the property. However, situations may arise where this is not the case. In such a case, the additional deterrent of liability to others might be justified. The facts in the case at bar do not support liability to the plaintiffs on this basis. BVHB, the owner of the drilling rig, suffered property damage in excess of five million dollars. This is a significant sum. It is not apparent that increasing the defendants' potential liability would have led to different behaviour and avoidance of the loss.

69 Another situation which may support imposition of liability for contractual relational economic loss, recognized by La Forest J in *Norsk*, is the case where the plaintiff's ability to allocate the risk to the property owner by contract is slight, either because of the type of the transaction or inequality of bargaining power. Again, this does not assist the plaintiffs in this case. BVI and HOOL not only had the ability to allocate their risks; they did just that. It cannot be said that BVI and HOOL suffered from inequality of bargaining power with BVHB, the very company they created. Moreover, the record shows they exercised that power. The risk of loss caused by down-time of the rig was specifically allocated under the Drilling Contracts between BVI, HOOL and BVHB. The contracts provided for day rate payments to BVHB and/or termination rights in the event of lost or diminished use of the rig. The parties also set out in the contracts their liability to each other and made provision for third party claims arising out of rig operations. Finally, the contracts contained provisions related to the purchase and maintenance of insurance.

70 I conclude that the policy considerations relevant to the case at bar negative the *prima facie* duty of care to BVI and HOOL ...

Iacobucci J:

112 ... I have had the advantage of reading the lucid reasons of my colleague, Justice McLachlin. At the outset, I wish to commend my colleague for her treatment of the approaches taken by her and La Forest J ... in *Norsk* ... In that respect, I simply wish to add one comment regarding the issue of contractual relational economic loss.

113 I understand my colleague's discussion of this matter to mean that she has adopted the general exclusionary rule and categorical exceptions approach set forth by La Forest J in *Norsk*. My colleague has found that the circumstances of the present case do not fall within any of the three exceptions identified in that case. She points out that both her reasons and those of La Forest J in *Norsk* recognize that the categories of recoverable contractual relational economic loss are not closed and that whether or not a new category ought to be created is determined on a case-by-case basis. In that

connection, I approve of her analysis of the facts of this case and applaud the approach she has taken to meld her reasoning in *Norsk* with that of La Forest J in this very difficult area of the law.

Problems

I   Consider the following facts of *Mainguard Packing Ltd v Hilton Haulage* [1990] I NZLR 360. Apply the reasoning of Lord Denning MR and Edmund Davis LJ from *Spartan Steel* and that of the three judges from *Norsk* and then the combined approach in *Bow Valley Husky*. What would the various judges allow to be recovered? How do the approaches differ? Do the fact variations make any difference?

HH Ltd had delivered supplies many times to MP Ltd's packing factory. On one delivery trip, the driver drove past the factory and had to back up the factory's driveway. It was the driver's first delivery to the factory and unfortunately he hit a power cable on the street just outside the factory. This did not cut the power to the factory (which had a different power cable), but it set in train a series of events that caused a power surge, which in turn started a fire that destroyed the factory's telephone switching equipment (the PABX). The factory had to shut while the power was restored.

Consider these following variations:

a   The power line was owned by MP Ltd.

b   The power line was owned by the local power company.

c   The PABX, owned by MP Ltd, took three weeks to repair. This meant that many potential customers were unable to place phone orders, which as a result decreased by 20%.

d   The PABX was leased from Ring North—a very unusual arrangement by industry standards.

The government inspection or building cases

In the previous section the cases involved a variety of claims for economic loss. In this section the cases deal with negligent government inspection, mostly of buildings. It is in these cases that judicial debate has been at its fiercest: the English courts, having started the move towards liability, then retreated from and ultimately reversed *Anns*; whereas the New Zealand and Canadian courts have seemingly embraced *Anns*. In *Hamlin* this debate ends with statements by both the Court of Appeal and the Privy Council that New Zealand must be free to develop its own common law. The cases combine two problems: whether to allow economic loss of the sort talked about in *Bowen*, and an attempt to articulate why a local council should be liable for what essentially is a builder's error in construction.

Anns v Merton London Borough Council
[1978] AC 728 (HL)
Lord Wilberforce:
… The present actions were begun on February 21, 1972. The plaintiffs are lessees under long leases of seven flats or maisonettes in a two-storey block at 91, Devonshire Road, Wimbledon. The owners of the block and also the builders were the first defendants, Walcroft Property Co Ltd: after its completion in 1962 they granted long

leases of the maisonettes: the fifth and sixth plaintiffs (O'Shea) are original lessees, having acquired their lease in 1962; the other plaintiffs acquired their leases by assignment at dates in 1967 and 1968.

The local authority at the time of construction was the Mitcham Borough Council: on February 9, 1962, they passed building plans for the block, which were deposited under the byelaws. Later this council was superseded by the London Borough of Merton, the second defendants, which took over their duties and liabilities.

In February 1970 structural movements began to occur resulting in cracks in the walls, sloping of floors, etc. The plaintiffs' case is that these were due to the block being built on inadequate foundations, there being a depth of 2 feet 6 inches only instead of 3 feet or deeper as shown on the deposited plans … .

In these circumstances I take the questions in this appeal to be:

1 Whether the defendant council was under: (*a*) a duty of care to the plaintiffs to carry out an inspection of the foundations … (*b*) a duty, if any inspection was made, to take reasonable care to see that the byelaws were complied with … (*c*) any other duty including a duty to ensure that the building was constructed in accordance with the plans, or not to allow the builder to construct the dwelling house upon foundations which were only 2 feet 6 inches deep instead of 3 feet or deeper (as pleaded) … .

Through the trilogy of cases in this House—*Donoghue v Stevenson, Hedley Byrne* … and *Dorset Yacht* … [—] the position has now been reached that in order to establish that a duty of care arises in a particular situation, it is not necessary to bring the facts of that situation within those of previous situations in which a duty of care has been held to exist. Rather the question has to be approached in two stages. First one has to ask whether, as between the alleged wrongdoer and the person who has suffered damage there is a sufficient relationship of proximity or neighbourhood such that, in the reasonable contemplation of the former, carelessness on his part may be likely to cause damage to the latter—in which case a prima facie duty of care arises. Secondly, if the first question is answered affirmatively, it is necessary to consider whether there are any considerations which ought to negative, or to reduce or limit the scope of the duty or the class of person to whom it is owed or the damages to which a breach of it may give rise.

The factual relationship between the council and owners and occupiers of new dwellings constructed in their area must be considered in the relevant statutory setting—under which the council acts. That was the Public Health Act 1936 …

To summarise the statutory position. The Public Health Act 1936, in particular Part II, was enacted in order to provide for the health and safety of owners and occupiers of buildings, including dwelling houses, by inter alia setting standards to be complied with in construction and by enabling local authorities, through building byelaws, to supervise and control the operations of builders. One of the particular matters within the area of local authority supervision is the foundations of buildings—clearly a matter of vital importance, particularly because this part of the building comes to be covered up as building proceeds. Thus any weakness or inadequacy will create a hidden defect which whoever acquires the building has no means of discovering: in legal parlance there is no opportunity for intermediate inspection. So, by the byelaws, a definite standard is set for foundation work … the builder is under a statutory (sc byelaw) duty to notify the local authority before covering up the foundations: the local authority has at this stage the right to inspect and to insist on any correction necessary to bring the work into conformity with the byelaws. It must be in the reasonable contemplation not only of the builder but also of the local authority that failure to comply with the byelaws' requirement as to foundations may give rise to a hidden defect which in the future may cause damage to the building affecting the safety and health of owners and occupiers. And as the building is intended to last, the class of owners and occupiers likely to be affected cannot be limited to those who go in immediately after construction.

What then is the extent of the local authority's duty towards these persons? Although, as I have suggested, a situation of 'proximity' existed between the council and owners and occupiers of the houses, I do not think that a description of the council's duty can be based upon the 'neighbourhood' principle alone or upon merely any such factual relationship as 'control' as suggested by the Court of Appeal. So to base it would be to neglect an essential factor which is that the local authority is a public body, discharging functions under statute: its powers and duties are definable in terms of public not private law. The problem which this type of action creates, is to define the circumstances in which the law should impose, over and above, or perhaps alongside, these public law powers and duties, a duty in private law towards individuals such that they may sue for damages in a civil court. It is in this context that the distinction sought to be drawn between duties and mere powers has to be examined.

Most, indeed probably all, statutes relating to public authorities or public bodies, contain in them a large area of policy. The courts call this 'discretion' meaning that the decision is one for the authority or body to make, and not for the courts. Many statutes also prescribe or at least presuppose the practical execution of policy decisions: a convenient description of this is to say that in addition to the area of policy or discretion, there is an operational area. Although this distinction between the policy area and the operational area is convenient, and illuminating, it is probably a distinction of degree; many 'operational' powers or duties have in them some element of 'discretion'. It can safely be said that the more 'operational' a power or duty may be, the easier it is to superimpose upon it a common law duty of care … .

Let us examine the Public Health Act 1936 in the light of this. Undoubtedly it lays out a wide area of policy. It is for the local authority, a public and elected body, to decide upon the scale of resources which it can make available in order to carry out its functions under Part II of the Act—how many inspectors, with what expert qualifications, it should recruit, how often inspections are to be made, what tests are to be carried out, must be for its decision. It is no accident that the Act is drafted in terms of functions and powers rather than in terms of positive duty. As was well said, public authorities have to strike a balance between the claims of efficiency and thrift (du Parcq LJ in *Kent v East Suffolk Rivers Catchment Board* [1940] 1 KB 319, 338): whether they get the balance right can only be decided through the ballot box, not in the courts. It is said there are reflections of this in the judgments in *Dutton v Bognor Regis Urban District Council* [1972] 1 QB 373—that the local authority is under no duty to inspect, and this is used as the foundation for an argument, also found in some of the cases, that if it need not inspect at all, it cannot be liable for negligent inspection: if it were to be held so liable, so it is said, councils would simply decide against inspection.

I think that this is too crude an argument. It overlooks the fact that local authorities are public bodies operating under statute with a clear responsibility for public health in their area. They must, and in fact do, make their discretionary decisions responsibly and for reasons which accord with the statutory purpose ... If they do not exercise their discretion in this way they can be challenged in the courts. Thus, to say that councils are under no duty to inspect, is not a sufficient statement of the position. They are under a duty to give proper consideration to the question whether they should inspect or not. Their immunity from attack, in the event of failure to inspect, in other words, though great is not absolute. And because it is not absolute, the necessary premise for the proposition 'if no duty to inspect, then no duty to take care in inspection' vanishes.

Passing then to the duty as regards inspection, if made. On principle there must surely be a duty to exercise reasonable care. The standard of care must be related to the duty to be performed—namely to ensure compliance with the byelaws. It must be related to the fact that the person responsible for construction in accordance with the byelaws is the builder, and that the inspector's function is supervisory. It must be related to the fact that once the inspector has passed the foundations they will be covered up, with no subsequent opportunity for inspection. But this duty, heavily operational though it may be, is still a duty arising under the statute. There may be a discretionary element in its exercise—discretionary as to the time and manner of inspection, and the techniques to be used. A plaintiff complaining of negligence must prove, the burden being on him, that action taken was not within the limits of a discretion bona fide exercised, before he can begin to rely upon a common law duty of care. But if he can do this, he should, in principle, be able to sue.

Is there, then, authority against the existence of any such duty and any reason to restrict it? It is said that there is an absolute distinction in the law between statutory duty and statutory power—the former giving rise to possible liability, the latter not, or at least not doing so unless the exercise of the power involves some positive act creating some freak or additional damage.

My Lords, I do not believe that any such absolute rule exists: or perhaps, more accurately, that such rules as exist in relation to powers and duties existing under particular statutes, provide sufficient definition of the rights of individuals affected by their exercise, or indeed their non-exercise, unless they take account of the possibility that, parallel with public law duties, there may co-exist those duties which persons—private or public—are under at common law to avoid causing damage to others in sufficient proximity to them ... .

It is irrelevant to the existence of this duty of care whether what is created by the statute is a duty or a power: the duty of care may exist in either case. The difference between the two lies in this, that, in the case of a power, liability cannot exist unless the act complained of lies outside the ambit of the power. In *Dorset Yacht* ... officers may (on the assumed facts) have acted outside any discretion delegated to them and having disregarded their instructions as to the precautions which they should take to prevent the trainees from escaping. So in the present case, the allegations made are consistent with the council or its inspector having acted outside any delegated discretion either as to the making of an inspection, or as to the manner in which an inspection was made. Whether they did so must be determined at the trial. In the event of a positive determination, and only so, can a duty of care arise ... .

To whom the duty is owed. There is, in my opinion, no difficulty about this. A reasonable man in the position of the inspector must realise that if the foundations are covered in without adequate depth or strength as required by the byelaws, injury to safety or health may be suffered by owners or occupiers of the house. The duty is owed to them—not of course to a negligent building owner, the source of his own loss. I would leave open the case of users, who might themselves have a remedy against the occupier under the Occupiers' Liability Act 1957. A right of action can only be conferred upon an owner or occupier, who is such when the damage occurs. This disposes of the possible objection that an endless, indeterminate class of potential plaintiffs may be called into existence.

The nature of the duty. This must be related closely to the purpose for which powers of inspection are granted, namely, to secure compliance with the byelaws. The duty is to take reasonable care, no more, no less, to secure that the builder does not cover in foundations which do not comply with byelaw requirements. The allegations in the statements of claim, in so far as they are based upon non-compliance with the plans, are misconceived.

The position of the builder. I agree with the majority in the Court of Appeal in thinking that it would be unreasonable to impose liability in respect of defective foundations upon the council, if the builder, whose primary fault it was, should be immune from liability. So it is necessary to consider this point, although it does not directly arise in the present appeal. If there was at one time a supposed rule that the doctrine of *Donoghue v Stevenson* did not apply to realty, there is no doubt under modern authority that a builder of defective premises may be liable in negligence to persons who thereby suffer injury.

Nature of the damages recoverable and arising of the cause of action. There are many questions here which do not directly arise at this stage and which may never arise if the actions are tried. But some conclusions are necessary if we are to deal with the issue as to limitation. The damages recoverable include all those which foreseeably arise from the breach of the duty of care which, as regards the council, I have held to be a duty to take reasonable care to secure compliance with the byelaws. Subject always to adequate proof of causation, these damages may include damages for personal injury and damage to property. In my opinion they may also include damage to the dwelling house itself; for the whole purpose of the byelaws in requiring foundations to be of a certain standard is to prevent damage arising from weakness of the foundations which is certain to endanger the health or safety of occupants.

To allow recovery for such damage to the house follows, in my opinion, from normal principle. If classification is required, the relevant damage is in my opinion material, physical damage, and what is recoverable is the amount of expenditure necessary to restore the dwelling to a condition in which it is no longer a danger to the health or safety of persons occupying and possibly (depending on the circumstances) expenses arising from necessary displacement.

[**Result**: The House of Lords agreed 4–1 with **Lord Wilberforce**.]

Brown v Heathcote County Council

[1986] 1 NZLR 76 (CA)

Cooke P:

... The English cases [concerning issues of council liability] proceed in a context of the functions of local authorities under Public Health Acts. In New Zealand the functions of local authorities regarding the subdivision and development of land have to be considered in the light of statutes of much wider scope.

... Local authorities, whether their functions are multiple or special, are concerned generally with matters going well beyond the range of personal health and safety; the preservation of community building and living standards, property values and amenities is part of their proper sphere ... .

The present case

...

In outline they are that the section in question lies on sloping and partly low-lying land behind the home of Mrs Brown's father. He bought the section in 1949 and a separate title was issued for it. It was used as an orchard until being bought by Mrs Brown and her husband about the time of their marriage in 1974. Palatine Terrace, then unformed, separated the section from the Heathcote River: it was formed not long after the Browns' house was built. Mr Brown, who had just finished his time as an apprentice carpenter, planned and built the house himself. He applied to the County Council for a building permit and a rear yard dispensation, the latter being required because he moved the site of the house to rather higher ground than at first planned, so as to minimise any risk of an unforeseen flood.

An officer of the Council and the [Drainage] Board's inspector (since deceased) each visited the site on separate occasions before the purchase was completed, and each indicated to Mr Brown that what he proposed as to building appeared to be in order. The building permit application, though not the rear yard dispensation order, was referred by the Council to the Board, in accordance with established practice; Mr Brown probably took the building permit application to the Board himself. On 5 July 1973 the Board sent the Council a memorandum of its approval, subject to some conditions about sewerage and drainage. The building permit was issued on 10 September 1973 and the house was ready for occupation by mid 1974. During the construction the Board's inspector returned to the site twice, once when there was a problem about whether there was sufficient fall to the sewerage intake and once when final approval for the connection with the Palatine Terrace sewer was given. At no stage did he say anything about the flood risk. On the other hand, at no stage was he expressly asked about this.

In winter storms of three successive years, 1975, 1976 and 1977, the river overflowed its banks to such a height as to enter the plaintiffs' house. The damages awarded by the Judge represented the cost of raising the house and the section.

Such strength as the Board's case has, and it was naturally urged on us by Mr Atkinson, lies in the undoubted fact that the Board was never specifically asked to advise about the extent of possible flooding. I am far from saying that the Board was under any general duty to offer unsolicited advice on such matters when consulted by the Council about building permit applications ... .

The special factors in the present case are the following. The Board was the one authority in Christchurch with comprehensive and accurate information about the flood levels of the Heathcote and Avon Rivers and the other watercourses vested in it. (All watercourses within its district are vested in it by s 36 of the Christchurch District Drainage Act 1951.) The evidence established that it was looked to by local authorities and property owners as the repository of knowledge about the rivers. The Judge found that, although the building permit application was sent to the Board primarily for consideration of matters of drainage and plumbing under the regulations, it had adopted the practice of providing, without specific request, information and advice about possible flood risks and similar matters of likely concern to the County Council and applicants for building permits. That finding was challenged on appeal by counsel for the Board, but no evidence was called for the Board at the trial and I think that evidence called by the County Council and summarised by the Judge in [1982] 2 NZLR 591–2 justified his finding.

As an example, Mr R.J. Anderson, who was the assistant county engineer at the time of the Browns' application, said in evidence-in-chief that it was his experience that, if a house was being built close to a watercourse and there was likely to be damage by water, the Board would comment. In cross-examination it was put to him that when he sent a permit application to the Board it was to enable the Board to tell the Council whether it complied with drainage and plumbing regulations and bylaws. He replied 'Among other things. I believe they would comment further if they felt they should'. In my opinion the Judge's finding that the Board acted as what he called a consultant should be accepted, at least in the sense that the Board should have drawn attention to any unusual flooding risk if it was or should have been put on notice of such a risk.

The point about notice is all-important. The section was part of an old subdivision, made well before 1961. Before the coming into force of s 23 of the Counties Amendment Act 1961 local authorities were not required by legislation, on the presentation of a subdivisional plan to consider the risk of flooding. The position, in the words of the synopsis of argument put before us by counsel for the appellant Board, was that if a section was, like the present one, subdivided before then, the only opportunity for consideration of its susceptibility to flooding would be if the matter was considered on the making of a building permit application.

Murphy v Brentwood District Council
[1991] AC 398 (HL)
[**FACTS**: The plaintiffs alleged that the Council had been negligent in inspecting a stabilising raft constructed under their house.]
Lord Keith:
My Lords, this appeal raises directly the question whether *Anns v Merton London Borough Council* was in all respects correctly decided … .

Consideration of the nature of the loss suffered in this category of cases is closely tied up with the question of when the cause of action arises. Lord Wilberforce in *Anns* regarded it as arising when the state of the building was such that there was present an imminent danger to the health or safety of persons occupying it. That state of affairs may exist when there is no actual physical damage to the building itself, though Lord Wilberforce had earlier referred to the relevant damage being material physical damage. So his meaning may have been that there must be a concurrence of material, physical damage and also present or imminent danger to the health or safety of occupants. On that view there would be no cause of action where the building had suffered no damage (or possibly, having regard to the word 'material,' only very slight damage) but a structural survey had revealed an underlying defect, presenting imminent danger. Such a discovery would inevitably cause a fall in the value of the building, resulting in economic loss to the owner. That such is the nature of the loss is made clear in cases where the owner abandons the building as incapable of being put in a safe condition or where he chooses to sell it at the lower value rather than undertake remedial works ... .

The jump which is here made from liability under the *Donoghue v Stevenson* principle for damage to person or property caused by a latent defect in a carelessly manufactured article to liability for the cost of rectifying a defect in such an article which is *ex hypothesi* no longer latent is difficult to accept ... . [T]here is no liability in tort upon a manufacturer towards the purchaser from a retailer of an article which turns out to be useless or valueless through defects due to careless manufacture. The loss is economic. It is difficult to draw a distinction in principle between an article which is useless or valueless and one which suffers from a defect which would render it dangerous in use but which is discovered by the purchaser in time to avert any possibility of injury. The purchaser may incur expense in putting right the defect, or, more probably, discard the article. In either case the loss is purely economic.

... It being recognised that the nature of the loss held to be recoverable in *Anns* was pure economic loss, the next point for examination is whether the avoidance of loss of that nature fell within the scope of any duty of care owed to the plaintiffs by the local authority. On the basis of the law as it stood at the time of the decision the answer to that question must be in the negative. The right to recover for pure economic loss, not flowing from physical injury, did not then extend beyond the situation where the loss had been sustained through reliance on negligent mis-statements, as in *Hedley Byrne* ... .

... Upon analysis, the nature of the duty held by *Anns* to be incumbent upon the local authority went very much further than a duty to take reasonable care to prevent injury to safety or health. The duty held to exist may be formulated as one to take reasonable care to avoid putting a future inhabitant owner of a house in a position in which he is threatened, by reason of a defect in the house, with avoidable physical injury to person or health and is obliged, in order to continue to occupy the house without suffering such injury, to expend money for the purpose of rectifying the defect.

The existence of a duty of that nature should not, in my opinion, be affirmed without a careful examination of the implications of such affirmation. To start with, if such a duty is incumbent upon the local authority, a similar duty must necessarily be incumbent also upon the builder of the house. If the builder of the house is to be so subject, there can be no grounds in logic or in principle for not extending liability upon like grounds to the manufacturer of a chattel. That would open up an exceedingly wide field of claims, involving the introduction of something in the nature of a transmissible warranty of quality. The purchaser of an article who discovered that it suffered from a dangerous defect before that defect had caused any damage would be entitled to recover from the manufacturer the cost of rectifying the defect, and presumably, if the article was not capable of economic repair, the amount of loss sustained through discarding it. Then it would be open to question whether there should not also be a right to recovery where the defect renders the article not dangerous but merely useless. The economic loss in either case would be the same. There would also be a problem where the defect causes the destruction of the article itself, without causing any personal injury or damage to other property. A similar problem could arise, if the *Anns* principle is to be treated as confined to real property, where a building collapses when unoccupied.

Liability under the *Anns* decision is postulated upon the existence of a present or imminent danger to health or safety. But considering that the loss involved in incurring expenditure to avert the danger is pure economic loss, there would seem to be no logic in confining the remedy to cases where such danger exists. There is likewise no logic in confining it to cases where some damage (perhaps comparatively slight) has been caused to the building, but refusing it where the existence of the danger has come to light in some other way, for example through a structural survey which happens to have been carried out, or where the danger inherent in some particular component or material has been revealed through failure in some other building. Then there is the question whether the remedy is available where the defect is rectified, not in order to avert danger to an inhabitant occupier himself, but in order to enable an occupier, who may be a corporation, to continue to occupy the building through its employees without putting those employees at risk.

In my opinion it is clear that *Anns* did not proceed upon any basis of established principle, but introduced a new species of liability governed by a principle indeterminate in character but having the potentiality of covering a wide range of situations, involving chattels as well as real property, in which it had never hitherto been thought that the law of negligence had any proper place.

My Lords, I would hold that *Anns* was wrongly decided as regards the scope of any private law duty of care resting upon local authorities in relation to their function of taking steps to secure compliance with building byelaws or regulations and should be departed from. It follows that *Dutton* should be overruled, as should all cases subsequent to *Anns* which were decided in reliance on it.

In the circumstances I do not consider it necessary to deal with the question whether, assuming that the council were under a duty of the scope contended for by the plaintiff, they discharged that duty by acting on the advice of competent consulting engineers.

[**Result**: Six other Law Lords, including **Lord McKay of Clashfern LC**, agreed.]

Invercargill City Council v Hamlin

[1994] 3 NZLR 513 (CA)

[**FACTS**: Hamlin sued the Invercargill City Council for having negligently inspected his house when it was built in 1972 and therefore having failed to notice that the house's foundations were negligently constructed.]

Cooke P:
The legal issues

On the law the main arguments for the appellant were that New Zealand common law should now be changed to conform with the decisions in *Murphy* and *Pirelli*. It was conformity rather than any other principle which Miss Bates put in the forefront of her argument. As to *Pirelli* she expressly abjured arguing for its merits and correctness. Without expressly going so far as to *Murphy*, she rested her argument on the proposition that 'There being no features to the decision which might allow it to be distinguished in a New Zealand context, the Court of Appeal in New Zealand should follow *Murphy*'.

I doubt whether the view that the contexts are materially the same can survive the analysis made by Richardson J in his judgment in this Court.

A main point is that, whatever may be the position in the United Kingdom, homeowners in New Zealand do traditionally rely on local authorities to exercise reasonable care not to allow unstable houses to be built in breach of the bylaws. Casey J illuminates this aspect in his judgment in this case. The linked concepts of reliance and control have underlain New Zealand case law in this field from *Bowen* onwards.

In *Brown v Heathcote County Council* [1987] 1 NZLR 720, 726, the Privy Council held that an assumption of a duty of care and reliance can arise from practice and indirectly (there the practice of the Drainage Board to check flood levels when building permit applications were referred to it by the Council). A case like the present is a fortiori, the reliance being direct. In *Heathcote* the Privy Council also accepted that the fact that the loss in question is merely economic is not automatically fatal to the recognition of a tort duty of care. That appears not only from the structure of Lord Templeman's judgment at 725 but also by implication from the actual decision, which was to uphold an award for remedial expenditure. On analysis *Heathcote* can be seen as an important authority in favour of the claim in the present case. More generally it has recently been reaffirmed by the House of Lords in [*Merrett Syndicate*] that a tortious duty to take reasonable care to avoid causing economic loss can arise from assumption of responsibility, whether by contract or otherwise … .

Another major United Kingdom judicial development, now enjoying little judicial support in England, was the decision of the House of Lords in *Junior Books Ltd v Veitchi Co Ltd* [1983] 1 AC 520 affirming decisions of the Scottish Courts and according to factory owners a cause of action in tort for negligence against specialist flooring sub-contractors. Estimated replacement costs and incidental damages were claimed. A majority of Their Lordships held that there was a duty to take reasonable care to avoid causing 'pure' economic loss and defects in the work itself …

Following the general New Zealand approach to duty of care questions, restated in *South Pacific Manufacturing Co Ltd v New Zealand Security Consultants & Investigations Ltd* it would be open to us to hold that in such a case of industrial construction the network of contractual relationships normally provides sufficient avenues of redress to make the imposition of supervening tort duties not demanded. It might be said, in the words of Lord Goff in [*Merrett Syndicate*], that there is 'no assumption of responsibility by the sub-contractor or supplier direct to the building owner, the parties having so structured their relationship that it is inconsistent with any assumption of responsibility'. But in Scotland, where *Junior Books* is still apparently treated as authoritative, it has been suggested that, where the pursuer and defender are connected by a series of *existing* contracts, the defender owes a duty of care to the pursuer not to perform his contract with another party in the chain in a careless way, if the defender knows the identity of the pursuer, knows that the pursuer is part of the contractual structure, and knows that as a result of the 'chain reaction' of subsequent defective performance along the line the pursuer will suffer economic loss. See a note by J.M. Thomson, 'A Prophet Not Rejected In His Own Land' in (1994) 110 LQR 361 and the cases there cited.

Whatever answer be given to the *Junior Books* situation, Lord Roskill's observations quoted above would seem to ring true. Harm to the person is one thing: harm to economic interests, whether caused by damage to property or in some less tangible way, is another. Broad distinctions, if required, can perhaps be more usefully and more realistically drawn on those lines than on the basis of sometimes metaphysical and controversial distinctions between 'pure' and 'impure' economic damage. Much tort law, possibly even most, is concerned with economic damage of some kind. In New Zealand this is the more markedly so because actions for personal injuries are largely barred by the Accident Compensation legislation.

To return to the narrative, then came in England the trilogy of House of Lords decisions, *D & F Estates Ltd v Church Commissioners for England* [1989] AC 177, *Murphy*, and *Department of the Environment v Thomas Bates and Son Ltd* [1991] 1 AC 499, re-analysing and limiting the grounds on which, in cases of defective buildings, damages in tort for negligence may be recovered against builders or local authorities. As a result there is no doubt that *Anns* and *Dutton* ... have been overruled and that *Junior Books* has been at least narrowly restricted ...

The upheavals in high level precedent in the United Kingdom which I have outlined have had no counterpart in New Zealand. The case law has been at least reasonably constant. Since *Bowen* in 1976 it has been accepted that a duty of reasonable care actionable in tort falls on house builders and controlling local authorities, and in that case one member of the Court ventured to question the value in this field of an attempted distinction between pure economic loss and damage to the building. *Bowen* has been followed in many High Court cases without as far as is known any sense that it does other than justice ... .

As Miss French argued, in a house-building case where the basic defect is in the foundations, classifying the damage as economic assists the conclusion that time runs from the date when a significant defect in the foundations is or ought to have been discovered. Until then the defect is latent and the market value of the property has not been diminished by it. Some of the decisions already cited point to a wider scope for the test of date of discovery or reasonable discoverability. An opinion on any wider question is not called for in this case. I would prefer to proceed step by step.

In the present context it is necessary to add that in ... *Norsk* ... all seven Judges of the Supreme Court of Canada were agreed that *Murphy* does not represent the law of Canada ... . The more pragmatic *Kamloops* approach was preferred. So, too, in the present case it will be found that the five Judges sitting in this Court are unanimous in their view as to *Murphy*, while four of the Judges take a similar view as to *Pirelli*. Naturally this is far from implying any disrespect for the opinions of the eminent English and

Scottish Law Lords who sat in those cases. There can be few lawyers who would not agree that the field is difficult and reasonably open to varying solutions. And national perspectives can differ. Although more extensively expounded, the general approach of the Canadian Supreme Court in this area seems, with respect, much the same as the approach followed in this Court over many years. Both emphasise that formulae and doctrine do not provide the answers to new duty of care questions. In the end it is a matter of judicial judgment, formed after looking at established signposts and analogies.

One need hardly labour that Judges in different common law countries may legitimately differ in their conclusions in such a field. So much was explicitly recognised in general terms by the Privy Council in *Australian Consolidated Press Ltd v Uren* [1969] 1 AC 590 and has been affirmed again in *Attorney-General for Hong Kong v Reid* [1994] 1 AC 324.

While the disharmony may be regrettable, it is inevitable now that the Commonwealth jurisdictions have gone on their own paths without taking English decisions as the invariable starting point. The ideal of a uniform common law has proved as unattainable as any ideal of a uniform civil law. It could not survive the independence of the United States; constitutional evolution in the Commonwealth has done the rest. What of course is both desirable and feasible, within the limits of judicial and professional time, is to take into account and learn from decisions in other jurisdictions. It behoves us in New Zealand to be assiduous in that respect.

Against the background already sketched four decisive points may be identified as standing out. First, the principles in *Bowen* and *Johnson* have not been shown to have been 'developed by processes of faulty reasoning' or 'founded upon misconceptions', within the language of *Australian Consolidated Press Ltd v Uren*. Secondly, there are the dictates of the particular New Zealand social and historical context.

Richardson J:

Legislation must be seen in its social setting and the common law of New Zealand should reflect the kind of society we are and meet the needs of our society.

It is I think important to consider the social and governmental context in which during the 1970s and 1980s the Courts of New Zealand consistently upheld duties of care on the part of local authorities towards house owners in relation to building inspections. There were six distinctive and long-standing features of the New Zealand housing scene at that time.

1 The first was the high proportion of occupier–owned housing. Home ownership by people in all walks of life was the goal and to a large extent the reality. Reference to the *New Zealand Official Year Books* confirms that over 70 per cent of permanent housing was occupier owned and that over 80 per cent of permanent housing was in detached houses on their own sections.

2 The second was that much of the housing construction, including low cost housing, was undertaken by small-scale cottage builders for individual purchasers. Reporting in 1971 the 'Commission of Inquiry into Housing in New Zealand' ([1971] 4 AJHR H-51) chaired by R.B. Cooke QC noted at p 192 that the New Zealand house was not a factory-produced article but was custom built to suit the site and the owner. Apart from comparatively few major operators most firms in the building industry were small with some 85 per cent of home builders employing fewer than six

workers (p 186). Over the last 40 years the ratio of state/private housing starts has seldom reached 10 per cent.

3 The third was the nature and extent of governmental support for private home building and home ownership. From last century the state accepted substantial responsibility for financing low cost housing. For many decades the State Advances Corporation was the vehicle through which low interest loans were made available for low cost new housing purchases and state house tenants were financed into the purchases of houses they had been renting. Amongst the innovative schemes designed to facilitate home ownership were suspensory loans, homestart and sweat equity programmes, state guarantees of mortgages and the capitalisation of the family benefit, the last of which helped nearly 100 000 families into their own homes in the 1960s (p 56)—at a time when the total population of New Zealand was only about 2.5m.

4 The fourth was the surge in house building construction in the buoyant economy of the 1950s and 1960s. In 25 years through to the mid-1970s the housing stock more than doubled.

5 The fifth was the wider central and local governmental support for private home building. The first standard model building bylaw was published in 1935 and by the 1970s almost all territorial local authorities had adopted and were working under the New Zealand Standard Model Building Bylaw NZSS1900 published by the Standards Association of New Zealand in 1964. 'The Review of Planning and Building Controls' published by the Office of the Review of Building Controls in 1983 noted in para 10.10 (p 25) that building inspectors filled a significant advisory and educative role spending 10 per cent to 60 per cent (depending on location) of their time in that way. The Review also noted (para 7.1) (p 16) that while health and safety seemed to be the prime considerations it was clear that 'health' had included comfort or convenience and 'safety' had moved into the area of good standards of workmanship or durability or sound construction. Again, the Commission of Inquiry Report noted (pp 193–4) that the Building Research Association, which was funded by the levies paid on construction work normally due when the building permit was issued, intended to provide a central source of information, advice, testing and research on housing design, cost, user, and planning requirements. The high social interest in standards and amenities was also reflected in the terms of reference of the Commission and the discussion in its report.

6 The sixth was that it has never been a common practice for new house buyers, including those contracting with builders for construction of houses, to commission engineering or architectural examinations or surveys of the building or proposed building. In the low-cost housing field the ordinarily inexperienced owner was contracting with a cottage builder on fairly standard plans amended to suit the owner's wishes and pocket. That contracting was within the framework of encouragement and often financial support from the state and of the protection provided by local body controls and adherence to the standard bylaws. It accorded with the spirit of the times for local authorities to provide a degree of expert oversight rather than expect every small owner to take full responsibility and engage an expert adviser.

To sum up at this point. The bylaws and the question of whether it was just and equitable for the local authority to be under a duty of care to the owner (and successors in title) in discharging responsibilities in relation to the inspection of houses under construction, have to be considered against that background which was special to New Zealand of the times ... .

The point of all this is that over a period of ten years building controls were the subject of detailed consideration, quite dramatic changes in approach were taken reflecting a particular economic and philosophical perspective, but without questioning the duty of care which the New Zealand Courts have required of local authorities in this field. While it may be going too far to characterise the Building Act 1991 as a ringing legislative endorsement of the approach of the New Zealand Courts over the last 20 years, there is nothing in the recent legislative history to justify reconsideration by this Court of its previous decisions in this field.

Decisions of the House of Lords although afforded great respect are not binding on this Court. Ultimately we have to follow the course which in our judgment best meets the needs of this society. Those distinctive social circumstances must be taken to have influenced the New Zealand Courts to require of local authorities a duty of care to home-owners in issuing building permits and inspecting houses under construction for compliance with the bylaws. In none of the more than 20 such decided cases has any New Zealand Judge expressed any reservations concerning the imposition of a duty of care on local authorities. After a detailed series of studies over a decade the Building Industry Commission recommended major changes in building controls but did not question the responsibility of territorial authorities to home-owners for the carelessness of their building inspectors. The Building Act 1991 contains no limitations on what has now been for over 18 years the law of New Zealand in this field embodying what is essentially a social value judgment.

Against this background I consider that any change in the law should come from the Parliament of New Zealand, not from the Courts. There are obvious difficulties in examining a 1972 case concerned with local authority negligence from a 1994 perspective. The initial cases which imposed a duty of care on local bodies inspecting building sites were necessarily influenced by the Court's assessment at the time of the particular social conditions of the late 1960s and early 1970s. Since then those cases have themselves been an important catalyst engendering public expectations regarding the role of local authorities in the building control process. Furthermore the cases have been the basis for legislative action. Law and social expectation have enjoyed a symbiotic relationship.

Apart from the special features of the New Zealand legal scene already noted there are at least three further relevant public policy considerations which Parliament would, I think, be bound to take into account. The first is that to change tort law as it has been understood in New Zealand would have significant community implications particularly affecting home-owners, the building industry, local bodies, approved certifiers and insurers. The relationships and fee structures developed under the building control regime provided for under the Building Act 1991 would have to change if it were decided that there should be no remedy in tort by house-owners against local authorities. Insurance practices would have to change. No doubt owners having a house built and purchasers of existing homes could at a price obtain engineering surveys and insurance protection against the risk of subsidence and other design or construction defects. Or they could bargain for an indemnity from the builder/vendor. But, this would call for a major attitudinal shift which Parliament would need to weigh.

... The third concerns the practical implications and limitations of following down the contractual path foreshadowed by the House of Lords in *Linden Gardens Trust Ltd v Lenesta Sludge Disposals Ltd* [1994] 1 AC 85 in relation to recovery by subsequent purchasers in respect of unknown or known building defects. That path is premised on the right to sue as assignee of the vendors'/developers' rights against a negligent builder (and architect—and local body and certifier?) and with, in what is described in that case as the radical approach, the measure of damages being the difference between what had been contracted for and what was supplied. See for recent commentaries on the House of Lords decision I.N. Duncan Wallace, 'Assignment of Rights to Sue: Half a Loaf' (1994) 110 LQR 42; and A. Tettenborn, 'Loss, Damage and the Meaning of Assignment' (1994) 53 CLJ 24. In *Lenesta*, Lord Browne-Wilkinson at p 112 noted that the radical approach might have profound effects on commercial contracts and invited academic consideration. As only one aspect of the wider question of risk allocation under building control regimes and having regard to the current position in this country, any move down that path would require a wide-ranging analysis and assessment of all the economic and social implications.

Invercargill City Council v Hamlin

[1996] 1 All ER 756; [1996] 1 NZLR 513 (PC)

Lord Lloyd of Berwick:

Duty of care

Miss Bates's argument [for the defendant] can be stated in very simple terms. The decision in *Bowen*'s case was explicitly based on the English decision in *Dutton v Bognor Regis* ... The authority of the line of cases which followed *Bowen*'s case was reinforced by the decision of the House of Lords in *Anns*. Both those English cases are now known to have been wrongly decided. If English law had not taken a wrong turning in 1972, New Zealand law would never have followed. The present appeal affords an opportunity for the Board, as the final appellate court for New Zealand, to put New Zealand law back on the correct path.

Where the New Zealand Court of Appeal is purporting to apply settled principles of English common law, then it is the function of the Board to ensure that those principles are applied correctly ... .

But in the present case the judges in the New Zealand Court of Appeal were consciously departing from English case law on the ground that conditions in New Zealand are different. Were they entitled to do so? The answer must surely be 'Yes'. The ability of the common law to adapt itself to the differing circumstances of the countries in which it has taken root, is not a weakness, but one of its great strengths. Were it not so, the common law would not have flourished as it has, with all the common law countries learning from each other.

By the same token, the Court of Appeal of New Zealand should not be deflected from developing the common law of New Zealand (nor the Board from affirming their decisions) by the consideration that the House of Lords in *D & F Estates Ltd* and *Murphy* ... have not regarded an identical development as appropriate in the English setting.

The particular branch of the law of negligence with which the present appeal is concerned is especially unsuited for the imposition of a single monolithic solution.

There are a number of reasons why this is so. The first and most obvious reason is that there is already a marked divergence of view among other common law jurisdictions.

In Canada, it is well established that a municipality may be liable for economic loss caused by the negligence of a building inspector. Thus in *City of Kamloops v Nielsen* (1984) 10 DLR (4th) 641, the facts of which were very similar to the present case, the plaintiff, a subsequent purchaser, sued the municipality for failing to prevent his house being built with defective foundations in breach of a local byelaw. He also sued the builder. He succeeded against both ...

In Australia, the High Court at first declined to hold local authorities liable for economic loss suffered by reason of houses being built with defective foundations: see *Sutherland Shire Council v Heyman* (1985) 60 ALR 1. A lengthy passage from Brennan J's judgment in that case was quoted with approval by Lord Keith of Kinkel in *Murphy*'s case. But ten years later Brennan J found himself in a minority of one when the High Court changed tack. In *Bryan v Maloney* (1995) 128 ALR 163 it was held that the negligent builder was liable for economic loss suffered by a subsequent purchaser ...

Their Lordships cite these judgments in other common law jurisdictions not to cast any doubt on *Murphy*'s case, but rather to illustrate the point that in this branch of the law more than one view is possible: there is no single correct answer. In *Bryan v Maloney* the majority decision was based on the twin concepts of assumption of responsibility and reliance by the subsequent purchaser. If that be a possible and indeed respectable view, it cannot be said that the decision of the Court of Appeal in the present case, based as it was on the same or very similar twin concepts, was reached by a process of faulty reasoning, or that the decision was based on some misconception: see *Australian Consolidated Press Ltd v Uren*.

In truth, the explanation for divergent views in different common law jurisdictions (or within different jurisdictions of the United States of America) is not far to seek. The decision whether to hold a local authority liable for the negligence of a building inspector is bound to be based at least in part on policy considerations. As Mason CJ said in *Bryan v Maloney* ... at 166: 'Inevitably, the policy considerations which are legitimately taken into account in determining whether sufficient proximity exists in a novel category will be influenced by the court's assessment of community standards and demands.'

In a succession of cases in New Zealand over the last 20 years it has been decided that community standards and expectations demand the imposition of a duty of care on local authorities and builders alike to ensure compliance with local byelaws. New Zealand judges are in a much better position to decide on such matters than the Board. Whether circumstances are in fact so very different in England and New Zealand may not matter greatly. What matters is the perception. Both Richardson J and McKay J in their judgments in the court below stress that to change New Zealand law so as to make it comply with *Murphy*'s case would have 'significant community implications' and would require a 'major attitudinal shift'. It would be rash for the Board to ignore those views.

In one important respect circumstances prevailing in England at the time of *Murphy* and those prevailing in New Zealand are indeed very different. Their Lordships have in mind the statutory background. In *Murphy* the House of Lords attached great weight to the passing of the Defective Premises Act 1972.

It is neither here nor there that the 1991 Act was not in force at the time of the inspection of the foundations in the present case. The question is whether New Zealand law should now be changed so as to bring it into line with *Murphy*'s case. If the New Zealand Parliament has not chosen to do so, as a matter of policy, it would hardly be appropriate for their Lordships to do so by judicial decision.

It follows that on the [duty] question their Lordships are content to adopt the reasoning of the unanimous judgments of the Court of Appeal.

Problems

Advise Percy Smith as to what remedies he might have in negligence. Consider what further facts you would seek and how those facts would affect your advice.

In early 1993, Percy Smith bought a section in an exclusive residential area overlooking a picturesque harbour. He planned to build a low-lying house with extensive, and expensive, picture windows on the harbour side. He was attracted to the section by the uninterrupted view he could have of the harbour. He dreamt of a quiet retirement, sunsets and a good investment. Although there was another section further down the hill, between his new section and the harbour, he understood that that land was a local council reserve and would not be built on. Before he commenced building, indeed before he signed the final purchase agreement, he asked his architect to check with the Council that there were no plans to build on or sell the reserve.

His architect, Dave Jones (who did not know anything about local planning laws), contacted a surveyor friend, Ian, and got him to ring his 'contact' at the Council, as he had done a few times in the past. Because Ian's contact was not there, Ian simply asked an unidentified clerk (as he had done many times before) in the Reserves Department to check whether there were any sale plans for reserves in Percy's area. The clerk phoned back, 'No, not as far as we are aware'. In fact, the Finance Department had just finalised a policy indicating that all public reserves in highly sought-after areas should be sold to raise money to pay for Council flats for the elderly. Dave later gave Ian $200 for his efforts and charged Percy for the $200 as an incidental expense. The local building inspector, Chris, approved the original plans and visited the site three times while the foundations were being laid. Because he was away the day when the Council's new policy was discussed in the tea room, he did not know about it until it was too late to advise Dave and Percy to change the design. So he just kept quiet.

Six months ago, the Finance Committee, in a secret session (contrary to normal practice, which involved public submissions), sold the reserve to Ike Kennedy and last month the Council approved Ike's plans to build a four-storey apartment complex. Contrary to its normal policy, the Council failed to advertise the hearing that approved the building, so Percy had no idea what was planned until the day building began. He is furious because he would have made an objection and believes that he would have had a good chance of at least forcing a design change to retain some of the view that he will lose. Percy has been told that there is no way to reverse the Council's decision and stop the building. To make matters worse, Dave has recently become bankrupt as a result of losing a large negligence claim last month.

Part 3: Limits of negligence

As we have seen, the principle behind imposing liability can be expressed in wide terms. This final section deals with how negligence interacts with other areas of the law. The first four cases, *Barrett*, *Prince*, and *B v Attorney-General* build on *Anns* by asking whether it is appropriate to find liability when a minister or local body is exercising statutory functions, an area normally regulated by administrative law. The next two cases, *South Pacific Manufacturing* and *Spring*, present contrasting views on the interaction of defamation and negligence. Finally, *McLaren Maycroft*, *South Pacific Manufacturing*, *Merrett Syndicates*, and *Turton v Kerslake* investigate the interaction of negligence with contract law. Each case asks what is important about the balances struck in other areas of the law and to what extent an expanding law of negligence should be made to respect those policies. What is the plaintiff trying to achieve by suing in negligence that cannot be achieved in administrative law, defamation, and contract? Should negligence be used to reform these other areas to aid deserving plaintiffs?

The private law/public law boundary

Public law does not usually allow the recovery of damages. As in *Takaro*, the usual remedy for an invalid administrative act is to require the decision to be retaken. Traditionally, someone suffering loss had to establish, before recovering damages, that a private right, say a property right, had been infringed or that under the tort of misfeasance in public office that the decision-maker had acted with malice or actual knowledge that a decision was invalid or an action unauthorised. There might also be liability for breach of statutory duty, but that has become an uncertain action as courts often struggle to find parliamentary intent either to create a specific class of beneficiaries or a private remedy. *Anns* opened up the possibility that, in addition to their public law duties, public authorities might owe private law duties which give rise to damages.

Will *Baigent's Case* (*Simpson v Attorney-General* [1994] 3 NZLR 667) have an impact on the way tort law and administrative law interact in the future?

Section 27 of the New Zealand Bill of Rights 1990 provides:

27. Right to Justice—
(1) Every person has the right to the observance of the principles of natural justice by any tribunal or other public authority which has the power to make a determination in respect of that person's rights, obligations, or interests protected or recognised by law ...
(3) Every person has the right to bring civil proceedings against, and to defend civil proceedings brought by the Crown, and to have those proceedings heard, according to the law, in the same way as civil proceedings between individuals.

Could the claims in *Takaro*, *Bedfordshire*, *Barett* or *Prince* have been rephrased as Bill of Rights actions?

Takaro Properties Ltd v Rowling

[1987] 2 NZLR 700 (PC)

[**FACTS**: Takaro Properties, in serious financial trouble, had obtained offers of life-saving investment from Japan. The Minister of Finance (Rowling) refused to grant the necessary regulatory approvals for such investments, seemingly motivated by a desire that the company's Fiordland assets should revert to New Zealand ownership. By the time that Takaro had successfully judicially reviewed the Minister's decision, the opportunity had collapsed and Takaro Properties was insolvent.

The New Zealand Court of Appeal held that the Minister has misinterpreted the regulations and that as a result he had breached a duty owed to Takaro Properties. The Privy Council held that this conclusion was incorrect. While not necessary, Lord Keith considered whether the Court of Appeal had been correct in holding that Rowling owed a duty of care.]

Lord Keith of Kinkel:

1 *Duty of care*

Quilliam J considered the question with particular reference to the distinction between policy (or planning) decisions and operational decisions ... .

Their Lordships feel considerable sympathy with Quilliam J's difficulty in solving the problem by simple reference to this distinction. They are well aware of the references in the literature to this distinction (which appears to have originated in the United States of America), and of the critical analysis to which it has been subjected. They incline to the opinion, expressed in the literature, that this distinction does not provide a touchstone of liability, but rather is expressive of the need to exclude altogether those cases in which the decision under attack is of such a kind that a question whether it has been made negligently is unsuitable for judicial resolution, of which notable examples are discretionary decisions on the allocation of scarce resources or the distribution of risks (see especially the discussion in Craig, *Administrative Law* (1983) at pp 534–8). If this is right, classification of the relevant decision as a policy or planning decision in this sense may exclude liability; but a conclusion that it does not fall within that category does not, in their Lordships' opinion, mean that a duty of care will necessarily exist.

It is at this stage that it is necessary, before concluding that a duty of care should be imposed, to consider all the relevant circumstances. One of the considerations underlying certain recent decisions of the House of Lords ... is the fear that a too literal application of the well-known observation of Lord Wilberforce in *Anns* may be productive of a failure to have regard to, and to analyse and weigh, all the relevant considerations in considering whether it is appropriate that a duty of care should be imposed. Their Lordships consider that question to be of an intensely pragmatic character, well suited for gradual development but requiring most careful analysis. It is one upon which all common law jurisdictions can learn much from each other; because, apart from exceptional cases, no sensible distinction can be drawn in this respect between the various countries and the social conditions existing in them. It is incumbent upon the Courts in different jurisdictions to be sensitive to each other's reactions; but what they are all searching for in others, and each of them striving to achieve, is a careful analysis and weighing of the relevant competing considerations.

It is in this spirit that a case such as the present has, in their Lordships' opinion, to be approached. They recognise that the decision of the Minister is capable of being described as having been of a policy rather than an operational character: but, if the function of the policy/operational dichotomy is as they have already described it, the allegation of negligence in the present case is not, they consider, of itself of such a character as to render the case unsuitable for judicial decision. Be that as it may, there are certain considerations which militate against imposition of liability in a case such as the present.

Their Lordships wish to refer in particular to certain matters which they consider to be of importance. The first is that the only effect of a negligent decision, such as is here alleged to have been made, is delay. This is because the processes of judicial review are available to the aggrieved party; and, assuming that the alleged error of law is so serious that it can properly be described as negligent, the decision will assuredly be quashed by a process which, in New Zealand as in the United Kingdom, will normally be carried out with promptitude. The second is that, in the nature of things, it is likely to be very rare indeed that an error of law of this kind by a Minister or other public authority can properly be categorised as negligent. As is well known, anybody, even a Judge, can be capable of misconstruing a statute; and such misconstruction, when it occurs, can be severely criticised without attracting the epithet 'negligent'. Obviously, this simple fact points rather to the extreme unlikelihood of a breach of duty being established in these cases, a point to which their Lordships will return; but it is nevertheless a relevant factor to be taken into account when considering whether liability in negligence should properly be imposed.

The third is the danger of overkill. It is to be hoped that, as a general rule, imposition of liability in negligence will lead to a higher standard of care in the performance of the relevant type of act; but sometimes not only may this not be so, but the imposition of liability may even lead to harmful consequences. In other words, the cure may be worse than the disease. There are reasons for believing that this may be so in cases where liability is imposed upon local authorities whose building inspectors have been negligent in relation to the inspection of foundations, as in the case of *Anns* itself; because there is a danger that the building inspectors of some local authorities may react to that decision by simply increasing, unnecessarily, the requisite depth of foundations, thereby imposing a very substantial and unnecessary financial burden upon members of the community. A comparable danger may exist in cases such as the present, because, once it became known that liability in negligence may be imposed on the ground that a Minister has misconstrued a statute and so acted *ultra vires*, the cautious civil servant may go to extreme lengths in ensuring that legal advice, or even the opinion of the Court, is obtained before decisions are taken, thereby leading to unnecessary delay in a considerable number of cases.

Fourth, it is very difficult to identify any particular case in which it can properly be said that a Minister is under a duty to seek legal advice. It cannot, their Lordships consider, reasonably be said that a Minister is under a duty to seek legal advice in every case in which he is called upon to exercise a discretionary power conferred upon him by legislation; and their Lordships find it difficult to see how cases in which a duty to seek legal advice should be imposed should be segregated from those in which it should not. In any event, the officers of the relevant department will be involved; the matter will be processed and presented to the Minister for decision in the usual way, and by this means his mind will be focused upon the relevant issue. Again, it is not to be forgotten that the Minister, in exercising his statutory discretion, is acting essentially as a guardian of the public interest; in the present case, for example, he was acting under legislation enacted not for the benefit of applicants for consent to share issues but for the protection of the community as a whole. Furthermore he is, so far as their Lordships are aware, normally under no duty to exercise his discretion within any particular time; and if, through a mistaken construction of the statute, he acts *ultra vires* and delay thereby occurs before he makes an *intra vires* decision, he will have in any event to exercise his discretion anew and, if his discretion is then exercised in the plaintiff's favour, the effect of the delay will only be to postpone the receipt by the plaintiff of a benefit which he had no absolute right to receive.

No doubt there may be possible answers to some of these points, taken individually. But if the matter is looked at as a whole, it cannot be said to be free from difficulty. Indeed their Lordships share the opinion expressed by Richmond P ... that the whole subject is of the greatest importance and difficulty, as is well demonstrated by the valuable, though understandably inconclusive, discussions of the problem by Woodhouse and Richardson JJ in the same case. Doubtless it was considerations such as those to which their Lordships have already referred that led Lord Diplock in *Dunlop v Woollahra Municipal Council* [1982] AC 158, 171, to express doubts whether a duty of care can exist in such circumstances. In particular, it is being suggested that liability in negligence should be imposed in cases such as the present, when the effect of any such imposition of liability will on the one hand lead to recovery only in very rare cases and then only for the consequences of delay which should not be long; and may, on the other hand, lead to considerable delay occurring in a greater number of cases, for which there can be no redress. In all the circumstances, it must be a serious question for consideration whether it would be appropriate to impose liability in negligence in these cases, or whether it would not rather be in the public interest that citizens should be confined in their remedy, as at present, in those cases where the Minister or public authority has acted in bad faith.

Their Lordships do not think it would be right for them to answer that question in the present case; indeed they must not be thought to be expressing any opinion on the point. This is partly because, as they have said, the matter was not fully exposed in argument. But in any event they are very conscious of the fact, already referred to, that, in the great majority of cases where it is alleged that there has been negligence in the construction of a statute, it is likely to prove that the error cannot be described as negligent; and they have come to the conclusion that, on the findings of fact of Quilliam J, the present is quite simply a typical example of such a case. They will therefore leave the question of the duty of care and turn to what appears to them to be the more relevant question of breach of duty, which they consider to be the central question in the case. However, consideration of that question involves in the first instance an examination of the legislation which conferred the Ministerial powers and duties ...

Barrett v Enfield London Borough Council

[1999] 3 All ER 193; [1999] 3 WLR 79 (HL)

The United Kingdom Government subsequently conceded before the European Court of Human Rights that the failure to provide a remedy in *Bedfordshire* was a breach of its obligation to provide an effective remedy under Article 15 of the European Convention on Human Rights, see *Z v United Kingdom* [2001] 2 FLR 245, page 234.

Lord Slynn:

... The negligence alleged consisted of the way in which the plaintiff was placed with the various foster parents and in the homes to which I have referred. They were unsuitable and it was wrong not to consider whether he could be placed with his half-sister on a long-term basis and wrong to fail to consider what would be the effect of separating them. The respondent and its employees failed to have regard to his health and hygiene. They failed to find a proper home for him or to direct and plan his care so that, due to their negligence, he continued to remain in foster care or children's homes without being adopted. They failed properly to arrange and conduct his meetings with his mother after eleven years of separation and they failed to obtain appropriate psychiatric treatment for him.

If these breaches of duty had not occurred, consideration would have been given to whether he really could be rehabilitated with his mother, whether any other relative could care for him, whether he could have been adopted or suitably placed with prospective adopters and he would not have suffered the damage and injury which he did suffer. If the duties which lay upon the respondents had not been breached, he would not:

> [o]n the balance of probabilities have left the care of the Local Authority as a young man of eighteen years with no family or attachments whatsoever, who had developed a psychiatric illness causing him to self-harm and who had been involved in criminal activities.

His injuries included in addition to self-harm and behavioural problems, the failure of his marriage, an inability to find work and an alcohol problem.

The proceedings

... It is therefore an important question as to whether the decision in *X v Bedfordshire County Council* [1995] 2 AC 635 concludes the present appeal. In the various cases claims were made (a) that a local authority and a psychiatrist employed by it were in breach of duty under the Child Care Act 1980 and were negligent in failing to investigate the case of a child suspected of having been sexually abused; (b) that a local authority, a social worker and a health visitor employed by it had failed to take action in respect of children living in appalling conditions and had failed to prevent ill-treatment and ill-health negligently and in breach of [their statutory obligations]; (c) that negligently and in breach of the Education Acts of 1944 and 1981, a local authority and the headmaster of a local authority school had failed to discover that children had special educational needs or to provide for those needs. The Statement of Claim was struck out by the judge in (a) and (b) and the judge's decision upheld by the Court of Appeal. In the case of (c), the Court of Appeal upheld the judge's order, striking out the claims for breach of statutory duty, but held that the claims in negligence should not be struck out, since they were not 'unarguable or incontestably bad.'

On appeal, Lord Browne-Wilkinson, with whom the other members of the House agreed, analysed the different categories of cases, where damages may be claimed for injury allegedly caused by acts or omissions arising from the existence of, or in the performance of, a statutory power or duty. As it is no longer contended that the plaintiff here can rely on a breach of statutory duty, the questions relevant for the present appeal are (a) whether … a common law duty of care arises either (i) from the existence of the statutory duty, or (ii) because in the performance of the statutory duty, the defendant assumes an obligation to exercise reasonable care towards the plaintiff, or (b) whether the defendant is liable for a breach of a duty of care owed by an employee for whose acts or omissions the defendant is vicariously liable.

Lord Browne-Wilkinson referred to the distinction between the cases where it was sought to say that a duty of care was owed in the way in which a statutory discretion was exercised and those where the duty of care was said to arise from the way in which the statutory duty had been exercised in practice. As to the former …

> Most statutes which impose a statutory duty on local authorities confer on the authority a discretion as to the extent to which, and the methods by which, such statutory duty is to be performed. It is clear both in principle and from the decided cases that the local authority cannot be liable in damages for doing that which Parliament has authorised. Therefore if the decisions complained of fall within the ambit of such statutory discretion they cannot be actionable in common law. However if the decision complained of is so unreasonable that it falls outside the ambit of the discretion conferred upon the local authority, there is no a priori reason for excluding all common law liability.

My Lords, in deciding whether the present case is concluded by what is said in '*X*', it is important to have regard to the facts in '*X*' as to the distinction drawn between what could and what could not be struck out before trial. There were two groups of cases consisting, firstly, of the abuse cases where children were alleged to have been abused either physically or sexually and where the local authority had failed to put children on the Child Protection Register or to take them in to care despite disturbing reports having been produced and, secondly, the education cases where the local authority had failed to investigate or to take steps to deal with children who have special educational needs.

As to the abuse cases, Lord Browne-Wilkinson held that where very difficult and sensitive decisions had to be taken in a statutory framework, very clear language would be needed to establish a right to damages under the Statute if an erroneous decision was taken: such a right was not to be found in the Children and Young Persons Act 1969 or the Childrens Act 1989. As to the common law claim, it was accepted that some of the allegations made did not require the investigation of policy matters outside the remit of the court. On the other hand, having referred to the question as to whether the allegations of breach of duty were all in respect of 'decisions within the ambit of the local authority's statutory discretion' he continued in '*X*' *v Bedfordshire* …

I strongly suspect that, if the case were to go to trial, it would eventually fail on this ground since, in essence, the complaint is that the local authority failed to take steps to remove the children from the care of their mother, ie negligently failed properly to exercise a discretion which Parliament has conferred on the local authority. But again, it would not be right to strike out the claim on this ground because it is possible that the plaintiffs might be able to demonstrate at trial that the decisions of the local authority were so unreasonable that no reasonable local authority could have reached them and therefore, for the reasons given by Lord Reid in the *Dorset Yacht* case ... fall outside the ambit of the discretion conferred by Parliament.

However, applying the third test in the decision in the *Caparo* case, it was not just and reasonable to impose on the local authority a common law duty of care in relation to the performance of its statutory duties to protect children, partly because such decisions require the participation of several bodies acting jointly, partly because such decisions involved a very delicate task, partly because if such liability existed authorities would be likely to be more cautious and defensive, which could be to the disadvantage of the child, and partly because other procedures were available to investigate grievances. Having stressed the need for caution, he concluded that there was no duty of care owed personally to the child by individual psychiatrists or social workers engaged to advise the local authority so as to make the local authority vicariously liable if those individuals were negligent. Accordingly the claims of the plaintiffs in the child abuse cases failed both at common law and under the statutes.

In the education cases (*Dorset, Hampshire, Bromley*) where it was alleged that the authorities had failed to investigate the need for or to provide proper schooling, the Court of Appeal had held that the claims for damages based on the Education Acts had rightly been struck out, but that the claims based on common law negligence should not have been struck out, since they were not manifestly bad.

Before the House it was contended in the *Dorset* case (a) that the authority had failed to perform carefully the duty imposed on it by the Education Act 1981; (b) that the authority was secondarily liable for the negligent advice given by the psychology service provided by the local authority. As to (a), the House accepted that it was arguable that the result depended on whether the decisions made carelessly were such that no reasonable authority could have breached them, which depended on an investigation of the facts. It held, however, that it would not be right to superimpose on the statutory machinery a duty of care to exercise the statutory discretions carefully, even limiting liability to cases where no reasonable authority could have reached the same conclusion, since the parents were involved in the process of decision making and could appeal, the number of cases which might be brought would be very great, but the success rate would be very small. In addition another remedy was available in the vicarious liability of the authority for the professional advice on which the authority's decisions were taken. On the other hand, once it actually provided a psychology service, the defendant authority might be under a statutory duty of care and:

> [O]nce the decision is taken to offer such a service, a statutory body is in general in the same position as any private individual or organisation holding itself

out as offering such a service. By opening its doors to others to take advantage of the service offered, it comes under a duty of care to those using the service to exercise care in its conduct. The position is directly analogous with a hospital conducted, formerly by a local authority now by a health authority, in exercise of statutory powers. In such a case the authority running the hospital is under a duty to those whom it admits to exercise reasonable care in the way in which it runs it.

The educational psychologist and other staff exercising skill owed a duty to use reasonable skill and care in assessing and determining the child's educational needs and the authority would be vicariously liable if they were in breach, though the test in *Bolam* ... would apply to them. These were matters which needed to be investigated ...

Thus in '*X*', your Lordships' House accepted that in considering the direct liability in common law of the local authorities, 'the public policy consideration which has first claim on the loyalty of the law is that wrongs should be remedied and that very potent counter considerations are required to overrule that policy.' Yet a number of policy considerations in those cases led to the conclusion that it would not be fair, just and reasonable (the third test in the *Caparo* case) to impose a duty of care on the local authorities. Lord Browne-Wilkinson in his speech attached importance in particular (i) to the multi-disciplinary Child Protection Conference involved in deciding whether a child should be placed on the Child Protection Register; (ii) to the balance involved in dealing with the 'extraordinarily delicate decisions' in having regard to the rights of the child, but also to the advantages of not disrupting the family environment; (iii) to the risk of the authority being over-cautious and defensive if it were subject to judicial decisions in a damages claim; (iv) to the fact that the statutory complaints procedure and the Ombudsman would allow complaints to be investigated; (v) to the fact that no analogous duty had been recognised before.

Whilst not casting doubt on the validity of these factors in the context of the investigations, or the steps which it was said should have been taken, in those cases of child abuse and neglect of educational needs, it does not seem to me that they necessarily have the same force separately or cumulatively in the present case. Thus, although once a child is in care, there may well be co-operation between different social welfare bodies, the responsibility is that of the local authority and its social and other professional staff. The decision to remove the child from its home is already taken and the authority has statutory powers in relation to the child which do not necessarily involve the exercise of the kind of discretion involved in taking a child from its family into care. As to the likelihood of an authority being over-cautious, I am of the same opinion as Evans LJ in the Court of Appeal in this case at p 380A to B:

> I would agree that what is said to be a 'policy' consideration, namely that imposing a duty of care might lead to defensive conduct on the part of the person concerned and might require him to spend time or resources on keeping full records or otherwise providing for self-justification, if called upon to do so, should normally be a factor of little, if any, weight. If the conduct in question is of a kind which can be measured against the standards of the

reasonable man, placed as the defendant was, then I do not see why the law in the public interest should not require those standards to be observed.

Nor do I think that the remedies accepted to be available in 'X' are likely to be as efficacious as the recognition by the court that a duty of care is or may be owed at common law ...

In summary 'X' establishes that decisions by local authorities whether or not to take a child into care with all the difficult aspects that involves and all the disruption which may come about are not ones which the courts will review by way of a claim for damages in negligence, though there may be other remedies by way of judicial review or through extra judicial routes such as the Ombudsman.

The question in the present case is different, since the child was taken into care; it is therefore necessary to consider whether any acts or omissions and if so what kind of acts or omissions can ground a claim in negligence. The fact that no completely analogous claim has been accepted by the courts previously points to the need for caution and the need to proceed 'incrementally' and 'by analogy with decided cases.'

... It is obvious from previous cases and indeed is self-evident that there is a real conflict between on the one hand the need to allow social welfare services exercising statutory powers to do their work in what they as experts consider is the best way in the interests first of the child, but also of the parents and of society, without an unduly inhibiting fear of litigation if something goes wrong, and on the other hand the desirability of providing a remedy in appropriate cases for harm done to a child through the acts or failure to act of such services.

It is no doubt right for the courts to restrain within reasonable bounds claims against public authorities exercising statutory powers in this social welfare context. It is equally important to set reasonable bounds to the immunity such public authorities can assert ...

The position is in some respects clear; in others it is far from clear. Thus it is clear that where a statutory scheme requires a public authority to take action in a particular area and injury is caused, the authority taking such action in accordance with the Statute will not be liable in damages unless the Statute expressly or impliedly so provides. Nor will the authority be liable in damages at common law if its acts fall squarely within the statutory duty. Where a statute *empowers* an authority to take action in its discretion, then if it remains within its powers, the authority will not normally be liable under the statute, unless the statute so provides, or at common law. This, however, is subject to the proviso that if it purports to exercise its discretion to use, or it uses, its power in a wholly unreasonable way, it may be regarded as having gone outside its discretion so that it is not properly exercising its power, when liability in damages at common law may arise. It can no longer rely on the statutory power or discretion as a defence because it has gone outside the power.

Thus in *Dorset Yacht* ... at p 1031 Lord Reid said:

Where Parliament confers a discretion the position is not the same. Then there may, and almost certainly will, be errors of judgment in exercising such a discretion and Parliament cannot have intended that members of the public should be entitled to sue in respect of such errors. But there must come a stage when the discretion is exercised so carelessly or unreasonably that there has been no real exercise of the discretion which Parliament has conferred. The person purporting to exercise his discretion has acted in abuse or excess of his power. Parliament cannot be supposed to have granted immunity to persons who do that.

Lord Diplock in *Dorset Yacht* approached the question as to how far an authority could be liable at common law for the exercise of a discretion given by statute by asking whether the act was *ultra vires* the power conferred in an administrative law sense. This on the face of it may be different from the approach of the other members of the House, but I do not consider that there is any real difference between them as to the substance of the test, since Lord Reid considers that, before the common law duty of care can arise, the authority must have acted so carelessly or unreasonably that there has been no real exercise of the discretion and the authority has 'acted in abuse or excess of its power', which is very much the administrative law test. Lord Wilberforce in *Anns* ... accepted this [policy/operation]test.

> But this duty, heavily obligational though it may be, is still a duty arising under the statute. There may be a discretionary element in its exercise—discretionary as to the time and manner of inspection, and the techniques to be used. A plaintiff complaining of negligence must prove, the burden being on him, that action taken was not within the limits of a discretion bona fide exercised before he can begin to rely upon a common law duty of care.

> On this basis, if an authority acts wholly within its discretion—ie it is doing what Parliament has said it can do, even if it has to choose between several alternatives open to it, then there can be no liability in negligence. It is only if a plaintiff can show that what has been done is outside the discretion and the power, then he can go on to show the authority was negligent. But if that stage is reached, the authority is not exercising a statutory power, but purporting to do so and the statute is no defence.

> This, however, does not in my view mean that if an element of discretion is involved in an act being done subject to the exercise of the overriding statutory power, common law negligence is necessarily ruled out. Acts may be done pursuant and subsequent to the exercise of a discretion where a duty of care may exist—as has often been said even knocking a nail into a piece of wood involves the exercise of some choice or discretion and yet there may be a duty of care in the way it is done. Whether there is an element of discretion to do the act is thus not a complete test leading to the result that, if there is, a claim against an authority for what it actually does or fails to do must necessarily be ruled out.

> Another distinction which is sometimes drawn between decisions as to 'policy' and as to 'operational acts' sounds more promising. A pure policy decision where Parliament has entrusted the decision to a public authority is not something which a court would normally be expected to review in a claim in negligence. But again this is not an absolute test. Policy and operational acts are closely linked and the decision to do an operational act may easily involve and flow from a policy decision. Conversely, the policy is affected by the result of the operational act ...

Where a statutory power is given to a local authority and damage is caused by what it does pursuant to that power, the ultimate question is whether the particular issue is justiciable or whether the court should accept that it has no role to play. The two tests (discretion and policy/operational) to which I have referred are guides in deciding that question. The greater the element of policy involved, the wider the area of discretion accorded, the more likely it is that the matter is not justiciable so that no action in negligence can be brought. It is true that Lord Reid and Lord Diplock in the *Dorset Yacht* case accepted that before a claim can be brought in negligence, the plaintiffs must show that the authority is behaving so unreasonably that it is not in truth exercising the real discretion given to it. But the passage I have cited was, as I read it, obiter, since Lord Reid made it clear that the case did not concern such a claim, but rather was a claim that Borstal officers had been negligent when they had disobeyed orders given to them. Moreover, I share Lord Browne-Wilkinson's reluctance to introduce the concepts of administrative law into the law of negligence, as Lord Diplock appears to have done. But in any case I do not read what either Lord Reid or Lord Wilberforce in the *Anns* case (and in particular Lord Reid) said as to the need to show that there has been an abuse of power before a claim can be brought in negligence in the exercise of a statutory discretion as meaning that an action can never be brought in negligence where an act has been done pursuant to the exercise of the discretion. A claim of negligence in the taking of a decision to exercise a statutory discretion is likely to be barred, unless it is wholly unreasonable so as not to be a real exercise of the discretion, or if it involves the making of a policy decision involving the balancing of different public interests; acts done pursuant to the lawful exercise of the discretion can, however, in my view be subject to a duty of care, even if some element of discretion is involved. Thus accepting that a decision to take a child into care pursuant to a statutory power is not justiciable, it does not in my view follow that, having taken a child into care, an authority cannot be liable for what it or its employees do in relation to the child without it being shown that they have acted in excess of power. It may amount to an excess of power, but that is not in my opinion the test to be adopted: the test is whether the conditions in the *Caparo* case have been satisfied.

In ... *Takaro Properties* ... Lord Keith ... said ... in relation to the policy/operational test [that it was not a touchstone of liability]:

> They incline to the opinion, expressed in the literature, that ... but rather is expressive of the need to exclude altogether those cases in which the decision under attack is of such a kind that a question whether it has been made negligently is unsuitable for judicial resolution, of which notable examples are discretionary decisions on the allocation of scarce resources or the distribution of risks ...

Both in deciding whether particular issues are justiciable and whether if a duty of care is owed, it has been broken, the court must have regard to the statutory context and to the nature of the tasks involved. The mere fact that something has gone wrong or that a mistake has been made, or that someone has been inefficient does not mean that there was a duty to be careful or that such duty has been broken. Much of what has to be done in this area involves the balancing of delicate and difficult factors and courts should not be too ready to find in these situations that there has been negligence by staff who largely are skilled and dedicated.

Yet although in my view the staff are entitled to rely *mutatis mutandis* on the principle stated in *Bolam* ... the jurisdiction to consider whether there is a duty of care in respect if their acts and whether it has been broken is there. I do not see how the interests of the child can be sufficiently protected otherwise ...

... Lord Browne-Wilkinson in '*X*', as has been shown, accepted that in respect of some matters—failing to detect or to take action when a child was clearly not doing as well as he could be doing, a psychiatrist failing to detect and report on the child's problem—the failure could be actionable.

This means I accept that each case has to be looked at on its own facts and in the light of the statutory context. But this is so in many areas of the law and it is not in itself a reason for refusing to recognise a liability in negligence.

In the present case, the allegations which I have summarised are largely directed to the way in which the powers of the local authority were *exercised*. It is arguable (and that is all we are concerned with in this case at this stage) that if some of the allegations are made out, a duty of care was owed and was broken. Others involve the exercise of a discretion which the court may consider to be not justiciable—eg whether it was right to arrange adoption at all, though the question of whether adoption was ever considered and if not, why not, may be a matter for investigation in a claim of negligence. I do not think it right in this case to go through each allegation in detail to assess the chances of it being justiciable. The claim is of an on-going failure of duty and must be seen as a whole. I do not think that it is the right approach to look only at each detailed allegation and to ask whether that in itself could have caused the injury. That must be done but it is appropriate also to consider whether the cumulative effect of the allegations, if true, could have caused the injury. Nor do I accept that because the court should be slow to hold that a child can sue its parents for negligent decisions in its upbringing that the same should apply necessarily to all acts of a local authority. The latter has to take decisions which parents never or rarely have to take (eg as to adoption or as to an appropriate foster parent or institution). In any case, in respect of some matters, parents do have an actionable duty of care.

On the basis that '*X*' does not conclude the present case in my view it is arguable that at least in respect of some matters alleged both individually and cumulatively a duty of care was owed and was broken.

Causation

... Lord Woolf MR said ... that even if there were situations where a social worker could be negligent in implementing the decisions of the Authority [the plaintiff] would be quite unable to attribute any part of his condition to that sort of incident. ...

... With great respect to the opinion of the members of the Court of Appeal, I have come to the view that this claim should not be struck out at this stage on that ground. It may well be that many of the allegations will be difficult to establish and that they will fail. In my opinion, however, the importance of seeing in each case whether what has been done is an act which is justiciable or whether it is an act done pursuant to the exercise or purported exercise of a statutory discretion which is not justiciable requires in this kind of matter, except in the clearest cases, an investigation of the facts …

[**Result**: **Lord Browne-Wilkinson** and **Lord Hutton**
also gave speeches that allowed the plaintiff's claim to go to trial.
Lords Steyn and **Nolan** agreed with them.]

Attorney General v Prince and Gardner

[1998] 1 NZLR 262 (CA)

[**FACTS**: A birth mother (Gardner) and her son, Prince, sued the Department of Social Welfare. Gardner alleged that at the time her son was adopted, social workers had assured her that if the placement was unsuitable, her son would be returned to her. Prince alleged that the Department had failed to act on reports in 1983 that he was being neglected by his adoptive parents.]

Richardson P:

Adoption: a common law duty of care?

It is common ground that the social workers and the department could foresee damage to the child (and to the natural mother) if their statutory responsibilities were carried out negligently, and that the relationship between them (and the department) and the child (and the mother) is sufficiently proximate. The question then is whether it is just and reasonable to impose a common law duty of care on the social workers for which the Crown is liable. Although the case is concerned with the rights of an adopted child and natural mother in relation to particular aspects of the adoption process, it must raise the broader question of whether the law should recognise that those responsible for carrying out functions contemplated by the Adoption Act are under a duty of care to persons who foreseeably may be caused damage by their actions. If there is no such general duty owed, there would seem not to be any particular circumstances in this case which would require the imposition of such a duty.

Persons immediately affected by the adoption process are at the three corners of the triangle: the child, the natural parents or guardians of the child, and the adoptive parents (including the spouse of an adoptive parent where the application is not joint). Those having obligations under the Act (other than the child) include the Director-General, the department, social workers, the police, solicitors and others certifying consents, and the adoptive applicants.

The implications of imposing a duty are these. First, in relation to the child there is the risk of liability for influencing the adoption court to make an adoption order in favour of unsuitable applicants; for adverse consequences of being placed in an approved home (s 6 [Adoption Act 1955]); and for bad parenting by adoptive parents. Second, in relation to natural parents (or guardians) there is the risk of liability for adverse consequences of careless advice as to the suitability and particular qualities of adoptive applicants, and as to the effects of adoption; and for mental anguish and distress of discovering the child suffered from bad parenting by adoptive parents. Third, in relation to adoptive parents, there is the risk of liability for their adopting an unsuitable child.

The essential claim by Mr Prince is that because of the negligence on the part of the social worker and the department the adoption was made and he has suffered from bad parenting by the adoptive parents. The essential claim by Ms Gardner is that her consent to the adoption was wrongfully induced by negligent misrepresentations as to the suitability of any adoptive parents and the assurance that her further consent would be required should they part or die. The misrepresentations which are pleaded are within the scope of the matters which would be, or properly could be expected to be, traversed and resolved as part of the process for obtaining the consent of the natural mother. Consequently, Ms Gardner's claim cannot be divorced from the adoption regime and is subject to essentially the same policy concerns.

Policy factors
There are we think two major policy considerations which support the imposition of a duty of care on those responsible for carrying out functions under the Act. First, as it was put in … *Bedfordshire* … the proper consideration which has first claim on the loyalty of the law is that errors should be remedied and that very potent counter considerations are required to override that policy. Second, as independent professionals social workers are expected to exercise reasonable care and skill in carrying out their statutory functions; and in the present situation the fulfilment of the duty to the child (or the mother) is consistent with the social worker's duty to the court. There is, too, an element of reliance: explicit reliance by the mother on the pleaded negligent misrepresentations and assurances; implicit reliance by the child on the exercise of reasonable care and skill by the social worker.

However, the countervailing considerations are in our view much stronger overall. First, and particularly significant, it would be inconsistent with the policy and scheme of the Act to allow individual claims in negligence in respect of particular acts or omissions in the carrying out of the statutory functions.

The legislation establishes a process leading to judicial consideration and determination on the evidence then before the adoption court of whether an adoption order should be made. The social worker has an important role. So do others in exercising their rights and discharging their obligations under the statutory process. The applicants provide relevant information concerning their family situation, their health, their financial circumstances and their reasons for wanting to adopt the child. The social worker furnishes a report and is entitled to take part at the hearing of the application. Anything known to the Police about the character of the applicants is also conveyed to the adoption court. The adoption court is required to consider any report which the social worker may furnish (s 10(1)). It is not obliged to accept the report or its recommendations. The court makes its own assessment of all the material including any oral evidence and cross-examination. It is the court which must be satisfied that the requirements of ss 4 and 11 are met and the necessary consents have been given or should be dispensed with (ss 7 and 8).

The natural parent may impose a condition with respect to the religious upbringing of the child (s 11(c)) but in a closed stranger adoption is not otherwise involved in the assessment by the adoption court under s 11 as to whether the applicants are suitable adoptive parents (s 11(a)) and whether the welfare and interests of the child will be promoted by the adoption (s 11(b)). The comprehensive consent provisions have special features designed to show on their face that informed consent has been given: the 10-day waiting period after the birth of the child before the consent document is signed; the form of consent with its explanation of the effects of an adoption order; and the certificate by an independent solicitor or statutory officer that he or she has personally explained the effect of an adoption order to the person giving consent, who appeared fully to understand the same. The social worker does not have a direct statutory role in the giving of consent and the legislation proceeds on the premise that consents completed in accordance with the statutory requirements and filed in the court are valid and effective.

There is nothing in the legislation to indicate a Parliamentary purpose to create actionable obligations. On the contrary, to impose a common law duty of care on social workers involved in that process and on the department would cut across that statutory regime. The adoption court makes the ultimate decision. Social workers see the parties and assess the prospects for successful adoption. The social worker contributes to the information before the court, but the report is not accorded any statutory primacy when the adoption court is deciding whether or not to make an interim order or adoption order.

Further, to allow a claim in negligence would undermine the intended finality of the adoption. The legislation does not contemplate any subsequent performance appraisal of the adoptive parents or of the well being of the child. Any claim in negligence would constitute an indirect attack on the adequacy of the statutory process and the integrity of the adoption order. It would be extraordinary if a claimant could allow the adoption to stand unchallenged, including in the case of the mother the validity of her consent, but still seek damages on the footing that the adoption order should not have been made and her consent was induced by material misrepresentations. And it would be inconsistent with the deliberately narrow remedies and sanctions provided in the statute (s 12 for revocation of an interim order, s 20 for variation and discharge of an adoption order, and s 27(1)(f) for making a false statement for the purpose of obtaining or opposing an interim order or adoption order). The application for the discharge of an adoption order requires the prior approval of the Attorney-General and no adoption order or adoption can be discharged unless it was 'made by mistake as to a material fact or in consequence of a material misrepresentation to the court or to any person concerned'. As the authorities under the section show, a long time lapse is not a bar, but it is only in those narrow circumstances that the integrity of the adoption can be challenged. The need to obtain the approval of the Attorney-General to make the application and the existence of an ultimate discretion in the court to refuse the application reinforce the legislative intent to circumscribe challenges to adoption. Significantly, too, the offence provisions of s 27(1)(f) provide a limited sanction (3 months imprisonment and a fine not exceeding $100) for making a false statement for the purpose of obtaining or opposing an interim order or an adoption order.

Finally, the secrecy provisions do not envisage the disclosure of what would be essential information in determining negligence suits. Section 23 provides a narrow exception to the general unavailability for production or inspection of adoption records. The exception is that the court may make an order (a) for the purposes of a prosecution for making a false statement, or (b) in the event of any question as to the validity or effect of an interim order or an adoption order, or (c) 'on any other special ground'. Statutory powers must be exercised in accordance with the policy and purpose of the legislation. Given the statutory emphasis on confidentiality and secrecy of adoptions and the special grounds designated in (a) and (b), it would seem impossible to justify making an order under (c) to support private, civil litigation, necessarily undermining the adoption.

The second set of policy considerations pointing against recognising a duty of care can be summarised very shortly. They are less significant in the overall assessment than the considerations to be drawn from the adoption legislation which we have been discussing, but they are still important in public policy terms. If a principal cause of the child's problems as they emerge over the years can be ascribed to bad parenting it is incongruous to allow a suit against a secondary party but not against the parents, whether adoptive or natural—and it was not suggested that the child could bring such a suit in negligence against parents. And if for public policy reasons a child cannot sue the social worker and the department there could be no policy justification for allowing the natural mother to sue on learning of the child's problems while leaving the adoption unchallenged. Further, the imposition of the duty of care contended for could not sensibly be confined to social workers and the department. Others involved in the adoption process (apart from the court which is the effective decision maker) could scarcely be excluded. The consequences for the public interest would in our view be unacceptably expansive.

As well, there are fair trial considerations. Disentangling factors that contributed to the decision of the adoption court, usually long after the event, and determining to what extent the adoption court was influenced by the alleged negligence of the social worker would be difficult, if not often impossible. Causation, including weighing the respective influences of nurture and nature in shaping the child and affecting his or her life prospects, and quantification of any loss are likely to be highly speculative, if indeed justiciable. Finally, there are other systems of accountability for performance by social workers of their professional responsibilities and for maladministration of the department. Standard public law remedies apply in respect of the exercise of statutory powers. Departments are subject to ministerial and parliamentary oversight. Social workers are subject to departmental disciplinary regimes. Complaints may be made to the Ombudsman.

For these reasons we would hold that the claims in negligence as pleaded by Mr Prince and Ms Gardner do not lie and should be struck out.

The Children and Young Persons Act 1974
The Department of Social Welfare Act 1971 which established the department (s 3), (by subsequent amendment) charged the department with the administration of the Children and Young Persons Act 1974 under the control of the Minister (s 4(1)(a)) and required the department to provide such social welfare services as the Minister from time to time directed (s 4(2)(b)). The Director-General had wide powers of delegation (s 12) and the Act provided for the appointment of such officers and employees as social workers as might be necessary for the effective and efficient carrying out of the functions of the department (s 8).

... The purpose of the 1974 Act, as stated in the long title, was 'to make provision for preventive and social work services for children and young persons whose needs for care, protection, or control are not being met by parental or family care and who are, or are at risk of becoming, deprived, neglected, disturbed, or ill-treated, or offenders against the law' ...

... To sum up, the 1974 Act was welfare legislation in which the interests of the child or young person were the first and paramount consideration. The statute reflected significant policy changes in the roles and responsibilities of the department and social workers when compared with the replaced legislation, the Child Welfare Act 1925 and the Infants Act 1908. The statement of objects (s 3), the focus on the interests of the child (ss 4 and 4A) and the imposition of duties on the Director-General to take preventive action and to investigate complaints of neglect were all new; and so, too, was the Children and Young Persons Court ... The Act contemplated intervention by the State, between the young person on the one hand and the parents on the other. The powers of social workers were broadly defined and their exercise and the discharge of the duties imposed on the Director-General and social workers called for sensitivity and judgment.

The 1983 complaint: a duty of care

On the argument of the appeal the appellant sought leave to adduce affidavit evidence of two departmental officers as to the resource implications and the effect on social worker practices of potential liability in negligence. Apart from the timing of the application and the inappropriateness on a striking out application of receiving factual and opinion material that the respondents would dispute, that proposed material was directed in the main to the 1989 legislation and the current position. But the focus in the present inquiry is necessarily on whether the department owed a duty of care to Mr Prince when responding or failing to respond to the complaint alleged to have been made to it in 1983.

The philosophy and thrust of the 1989 legislation are different. Significantly s 5 of the 1974 Act has been replaced by diffuse and diluted investigation provisions far different from the positive duties under s 5. As well, public sector processes have been substantially affected by legislative and organisational reforms of the last decade. The detailed guidelines introduced by the Children and Young Persons and Their Families Service during the last year for responses to situations of alleged abuse or negligence obviously cannot simply be transposed back to 1983. And, unlike the statute in the *Bedfordshire* case, the 1974 Act did not provide for social service functions to be exercised in accordance with such directions as might be given by the Secretary of State. And so any (as yet undisclosed) guidelines existing in 1983 lacked statutory force.

[**Note**: While s 5 of the 1989 Act requires the Director General to take account of cultural factors and the importance of maintaining family groups, s 6 reasserts the paramountcy of the child's welfare, and s 7 imposes obligations that are similar to s 5 of the 1974 Act.]

It may be accepted that in 1983 social workers could be expected to exercise judgment when considering complaints received, assessing the situation of the young person, and determining the urgency of any response. It may be accepted that acting in the best interests of the young person the department would also seek to avoid unnecessary intrusion on the family. But the first difficulty in the present striking out is that in terms of the pleadings the case cannot be characterised as one of total failure to consider the alleged complaint—the allegation is of failure to investigate the complaint 'adequately or at all'. There is no basis for determining striking out on the footing that it is necessarily a pure omission case, or that the Director-General or a social worker exercised any particular judgment. It cannot be predicated that the department made any particular decision in relation to the complaint, let alone that the decision was not outside the ambit of discretion granted to the department and social workers by the legislation. The pleadings are wide enough to cover simple administrative carelessness or an absence of any real exercise of any professional discretion. These considerations suggest that a sharp focus on the facts proved at trial is a more appropriate means of determining whether there is a duty of care than considering every factual possibility across the wide spectrum of these pleadings.

Proximity

The two broad fields of inquiry in determining whether it is just and reasonable to recognise a duty of care in new situations are the degree of proximity or relationship between the alleged wrong-doer and the person who has suffered damage, and the assessment of other policy considerations bearing on the existence of a duty of care in that class of case.

Proximity was, it seems, accepted by the Crown in the High Court. However on the argument of the appeal it was submitted that the degree of proximity was insufficient considered on the basis of analogy with decided cases, competing moral claims and an absence of assumed responsibility towards Mr Prince as a 14-year-old young person.

The substantial argument to the contrary which we prefer may be put very shortly. Governmental agencies discharging statutory functions are often performing professional tasks. The Department of Social Welfare Act 1971 provides for the appointment of such social workers as necessary for the effective and efficient carrying out of the functions of the department. The 1974 Act is directed to the care and protection of children and young persons. The class of persons for whom the statutory protection was enacted is clear. The discharge of the particular function calls for the exercise of special social work skills and responsibilities. There is a professional relationship between social worker and client child or young person. Children and young persons are seen as vulnerable. Because of their youth and immaturity they cannot assert their own rights and needs. Others must do it for them. Just as it is right that the department and its professionals have a generalised duty under the statute to promote the well-being of children and young persons (s 3), so, too, when exercising their statutory powers in respect of a particular child or young person they assume a responsibility to that child or young person (s 4). And the duty to consider a complaint of neglect is specific to the particular child or young person, the subject of the complaint (s 5). While a deprived child or young person may have no particular expectation that the department will seek to assist him or her, given general community expectations reflected in the statute it is not unreasonable to conclude that a child or young person is to be regarded as implicitly relying on the department and its officers to consider complaints that they are in need. Finally, it is readily foreseeable that inadequate consideration of complaints that a young person is neglected might cause harm. A young person who is the subject of the complaint is directly within the contemplation of the departmental officer receiving the complaint. The complaint here was that this 14-year-old was neglected or likely to be neglected by his parents. In such a case the officer must have known that failure to give adequate consideration to the complaint and take any appropriate action might increase the risk of harm. For its part the department is not in a position to say that the imposition of a duty of care would expose the officer and the department to a burden out of proportion to their moral culpability.

Wider policy considerations

The 1974 Act is the starting point. It sets the framework within which the department carries out its functions and the department and social workers discharge their duties and exercise their powers. The positive duties imposed by s 5 are of central importance. It is the duty of the Director-General 'to take positive action and such steps under this Act as in his opinion may assist in preventing children or young persons from being exposed to unnecessary suffering or deprivation'. The Director-General is required to be pro-active in preventing children and young persons from suffering harm. He or she is also required to take appropriate steps under the Act to attain that end with the decision as to which of those steps to take being a matter for the Director-General's judgment. In pursuance of that duty s 5(2) requires the Director-General to 'arrange ... for prompt inquiry where he knows or has reason to suspect that any child or young person is ... suffering or likely to suffer from ... inadequate care or control' (para (a)). The subsection also requires the Director-General to inquire into any allegation that a young person who is being cared for away from his or her parents or guardian is not being properly cared for (para (c)). Those specific duties cannot be put aside or excused as if they were generalised duties to the community at large. The duty contended for here arises only when a specific complaint is made to the department in relation to a particular young person. They are matters of obligation, not the exercise of discretionary power.

The stated purpose of the Act is to provide for the care and protection of children at risk. The department is charged with the administration of the Act and by necessary implication is responsible for establishing and maintaining systems and processes to enable it to perform its statutory functions and duties and exercise its statutory powers and within that framework facilitate the exercise by its social workers of their statutory responsibilities and powers. That being so it is also arguable that the department was required to develop processes to allow for the proper and timely consideration of allegations that children or young persons were being neglected or at risk in order to respond to any allegations under s 5(2)(c) and to determine whether the threshold requirement of s 5(2)(a) was met, namely that the Director-General or a social worker carrying a delegated responsibility 'knows or has reason to suspect' that the young person concerned has suffered from or was likely to suffer from inadequate care or control. If that threshold is met the Director-General is required to arrange for prompt inquiry. If the result of that inquiry, supported as it is by the power to seek warrants under s 7 (or of the inquiry under para (c)), is that a social worker 'reasonably believes' that the young person is 'in need of care' as that expression is relevantly defined in s 27(2), the social worker may make a complaint under the section requiring the young person to be brought before a Children and Young Persons Court. Other steps may be taken to deal with the situation where it is reasonably believed that a young person is in need of care, eg providing financial or other assistance to a care giver to assist in overcoming deficiencies in the care (s 5(2)(b)), and seeking a warrant to remove the young person from his or her surroundings (s 28(1)) and thereafter following the statutory steps. But the statute does not contemplate that nothing at all need be done by the department where its responsible officer reasonably believes that the young person is in need of care. The complaint proceedings could result in the young person being placed under the guardianship of the Director-General or under the supervision of a social worker and the statute also contemplates earlier removal of a young person from an unsatisfactory environment. It follows that the responsiveness of the department and its systems to an allegation of neglect is a crucial step in the statutory process.

That statutory scheme does not lead inevitably to a conclusion that there was a common law duty of care to take proper steps to investigate allegations of neglect and thereafter to take such further and successive steps as the circumstances required. The question is whether it is just and reasonable to superimpose a common law duty of care on the department in relation to the performance of its statutory responsibilities for the protection and care of children and young persons. But, given the conclusion that proximity is satisfied, the statutory framework within which the department and its social workers act is consistent with the imposition of a common law duty of care. The narrow argument is that liability may arise where the person charged with the responsibility either unreasonably fails to carry out the duty to consider the matter or reaches a conclusion so unreasonable as to show failure to do its duty.

Given the important features of the 1974 Act which we have been emphasising, it cannot be said that a common law duty of care in these terms would cut across the whole statutory scheme. At that early triggering step a specific positive duty rests on the Director-General. At that step it does not require participation with other agencies. The duty suggested does not conflict with any other duty by the department and its officers. On the contrary it enhances it.

In the *Bedfordshire* case Lord Browne-Wilkinson ... emphasised that the question whether there is a common law duty, and if so its ambit, must be profoundly influenced by the statutory framework within which the acts complained of were done. In the various respects we have been discussing the Children and Young Persons Act 1974 is clearly distinguishable from the statutes before the House of Lords in the *Bedfordshire* case and the statutes under consideration in the large number of cases (but few in the child protection field) canvassed in argument. Little is to be gained from a point by point comparison. Also, the rescue cases are not comparable because in those cases any statutory framework was very different from the 1974 Act.

There are other policy considerations to be considered although we would not weigh them as heavily in this case as the scheme and policy of the 1974 Act. First, the difficulty and delicacy of the social worker's task and its judgmental nature are relevant. Intrusion into the family has to be handled with tact in the interests of the child or young person. The social worker must also have regard to the advantages of not disrupting the family environment and to the advantages and disadvantages of other options for the care of the young person. Clearly a plaintiff would have difficulty in establishing that an assessment made by a social worker fell outside the bounds sanctioned by professional opinion. Nevertheless considerations of that kind cannot absolve the department and social workers from the responsibility of considering and responding to specific complaints with professional skill and care.

Next, the Solicitor-General submitted that the imposition of a duty would or could cause the department and social workers to adopt a more cautious and defensive approach to their duties. He drew our attention to a considerable body of professional literature on that point ... But like lawyers and doctors, social workers are professionals. At that triggering step (and at other steps) they should be expected to have shouldered willingly a standard of reasonable skill and care that their private sector counterparts were expected to discharge. And in the absence of any data as to potential claims based on the roles and responsibilities of the department and social workers under the 1974 Act, which was replaced eight years ago by a very different legislative scheme, it would be unwise to give any particular weight to the resource implications of allowing for a common law duty of care.

Finally, and as pointing against the imposition of a duty, there are the obvious difficulties of reaching conclusions as to causation and damages. Clearly any such claims would be very difficult to establish. That in itself cannot, we think, be adequate justification for ruling out the possibility of any claim for negligence whatever the circumstances ...

Tipping J:

... Similarly, Ms Gardner has no cause of action for the harm she claims to have suffered because she was given what she says was erroneous information about the parents who would adopt her baby son. While at first glance her claim for negligent misstatement might be thought to fall within conventional *Hedley-Byrne* principles, the case is novel in relation to the nature of the damage she claims to have suffered; and in any event the identified policy consideration of finality overwhelms whatever prima facie entitlement to relief she may be thought to have. The claims for breach of fiduciary duty must fall with the claim in negligence. As pleaded, they add nothing more to the negligence claims. The asserted characterisation of the duty as fiduciary cannot convert an unsustainable claim at common law into a sustainable claim in equity.

> [**Result**: **Tipping J** concurred, while **Henry J** dissented in the care and protection action, arguing that it would have been more consistent to strike out that claim as well.]

B v Attorney-General
[1999] 2 NZLR 296 (CA)

[**FACTS**: Two daughters were removed from their father's care after one daughter made a number of comments at school that were taken to indicate that she was being abused. The father and the daughters sued, alleging that the failure to properly investigate the allegations meant that the children were kept unnecessarily from their father.]

Keith J: (Writing for himself and **Blanchard J**)
The allegations of negligence
[9] ... In brief [the father and daughters] allege the department inadequately oversaw and controlled the investigation by the clinical psychologist and the social worker; failed to record and evaluate the information provided by the family friend; and allowed the proceedings in the District Court to proceed on an improperly considered and investigated premise, given the denials of sexual abuse by the father. The clinical psychologist failed in her interviewing technique in part because of an associated mindset that the reported abuse was or must be true; failed to take notice of and evaluate certain known factual errors; and failed to consider, evaluate or investigate adequately what was said by the doctor and by the family friend. The social worker failed to initiate or play any part in any further evaluation or investigation of the information from the doctor and the family friend ...

A duty of care?
... [14] The [proximity] question received relatively limited attention in the course of argument before us and because of the conclusion we reach on the second we can treat it briefly. Ms McDonald was at first inclined to argue that her client, the registered clinical psychologist, as a professional, in an independent contractual relationship with the department and not as an employee, did not have a sufficient degree of proximity. When pressed she did not, however, pursue that contention—and rightly since we can see no reason in principle or on the facts to distinguish between the different individuals involved in the sexual abuse team in this case. Rather, she relied ... on the proposition that the policy of the statute excluded any liability ...

The temporal scope of the duty of care
[24] That temporal issue is critical in the circumstances of this case. By contrast to the facts alleged in *Prince*, the facts complained of here occurred after the immediate triggering step. That step was the response by the department to the information provided by the mother of the friend of H including the decision to arrange for the prompt inquiry. By contrast, the criticised actions were various actions and failures occurring in the course of the investigation which followed and which continued beyond the initiation of the Court process.

[25] A second possible distinction between *Prince* and this case is between the failure to take action (that case) and the taking of action (this), including, to refer to a third possible distinction, the bringing of proceedings before the Court. While we do not have to rule on these matters, we do not see either distinction as significant. The obligation to 'arrange for prompt inquiry' in the defined circumstances could be breached for instance not just by taking no action, but also by having a system which, without any real consideration of the information received, automatically initiates an inquiry or by 'reach[ing] a conclusion [whether it is to carry on an inquiry or not] so unreasonable as to show failure to do its duty' ... The third distinction, immunising acts when Court proceedings are brought, might create an inappropriate incentive to commence proceedings for the protection from liability in negligence which that might afford. As well, in principle, the existence of a duty of care at a particular stage should not

depend on whether a decision is later taken to bring or not bring proceedings. That later stage of the process for the care, protection and control of children under the 1974 Act is however significant for the temporal element which we see as critical in this case and to which we now turn.

[26] The duty of care, enforceable through negligence proceedings, recognised in *Prince* is limited in time to the triggering and closely-related steps. It is to be tied to the 'positive duty' stated by Parliament relating to that initial stage of deciding whether to arrange a 'prompt inquiry' and when appropriate arranging it. In terms of its temporal scope it is to be contrasted with the obligation to provide financial and other assistance created by para (b) of s 5(2): that obligation has none of the temporal limit indicated by the word 'prompt'. Such a temporal limit also arises directly from the scheme and system of the legislation. The 'prompt inquiry' in some situations would later lead, through the exercise of the operational discretions of the department, to assessments that the children were (to relate the process to the facts in this case) suffering or likely to suffer from ill-treatment. At that later stage the departmental officers would have to decide whether to exercise their powers to file a complaint for care and protection, and to seek warrants in support. The Children and Young Persons Court and its officials and other public agencies (including the police) then had related powers. At those later stages, to use the wording of *Prince*, a common law duty of care would cut across the statutory scheme; as well, other bodies would be participating. By that time there was in addition the prospect of the Court assessing the validity of the allegations and the evidence given in support of them—as happened at length in this case, as we have noted. The Court, with the assistance of those most directly involved, their counsel and their witnesses, would have been in a much better position to make those assessments than were the departmental officers and others involved at the preceding stage. There is also the distinction that at that stage only preliminary assessments were required (involving reasonable belief or reasonable grounds for suspicion). By contrast orders could be made at the end of the hearing only if the s 27 ground is 'proved' (s 31). Findings and orders were also subject to appeal and review (Part VI).

[27] ... [Counsel for the plaintiffs] frankly acknowledged that the statement of claim made no attack on the obtaining of the warrants or the filing of the complaints. There was no allegation of negligence in what the departmental officer put to the Court. Nor was there any question of suing the judicial officer or challenging the warrant. We are not saying that the bringing of those legal processes prevents all possibility of action by, in effect, regularising any earlier failings, although such processes would raise major problems about causation. There would remain for instance the possibility of actions for malicious prosecution or of professional disciplinary proceedings ... Rather, to repeat, the statutory scheme cuts across a common law duty of care once the triggering step to the 'prompt inquiry' is completed and the officials are moving beyond that initial obligation and are assembling relevant information before considering whether to exercise their statutory powers.

[28] We have no doubt that the breaches of duty alleged in this case fall outside that initial period of positive statutory obligations during which, in accordance with *Prince*, a common law duty of care may also arise. In this case the process moved rapidly from the initial stage, involving a duty, to the operational stage of information-gathering and considering the exercise of statutory powers and then to the exercise of those

powers. At this stage the department is exercising a discretion. No doubt the line between the stages will be difficult to draw in some cases, although we recall Lord Reid's quick dismissal, when talking of natural justice, of 'the perennial fallacy that because something cannot be cut and dried or nicely weighed and measured therefore it does not exist', *Ridge v Baldwin* [1964] AC 40[,] 64–5. The difficulties may be greater when a decision is made not to launch Court proceedings. In some cases that decision may be so unreasonable as to amount to a failure of the department to do its duty. But we do not in this case have to give precise definition to the line. The facts here lie clearly beyond it.

[29] It follows that no tenable case can be made to establish liability in negligence in the present circumstances. The legislative judgment, as we read it, is that the greater public good in ensuring so far as possible that children who may be at risk are cared for is to prevail over possible instances of individual injustice; the harm which is claimed is contemplated by the Act. The law not uncommonly strikes such a balance ... In the present situation the 1974 Act attempts to prevent or mitigate that possibility by establishing careful Court processes designed to protect the rights when proceedings are brought, or, if they are not, by not standing in the way of a new inquiry. At the relevant time other review and inquiry processes, for instance through the Ombudsman, were available. The temporal limit on and general denial of liability in negligence are also supported by the disadvantages of the imposition of a duty of care to the prejudice of the prompt and efficient exercise of the operational powers and discretions in issue in this case ...

Tipping J:

...

[48] It is inherently necessary to draw a line between the so-called triggering step(s) and follow-up action. Events which occur prior to that line being crossed are distinguishable, on account of the positive statutory obligation, from the general investigative roles performed by the police as in *Hill* ... and by the fraud investigators in *Taylor v Director of the Serious Fraud Office* [1998] 3 WLR 1040.

[49] The positive duty created by s 5(1) is amplified by s 5(2) into a duty, in the stipulated circumstances, to arrange for prompt inquiry. While there must be an expectation that the Director-General will follow up that inquiry with appropriate action when it is called for, the only logical duty of care watershed on the continuum is that between inquiry and follow-up. It is there that obligation becomes discretion in statutory terms. If, on this basis, it is said that there will often be a duty to exercise the discretionary follow-up powers, I would reply that, whereas for policy reasons the inquiry duty gives rise to a common law duty of care, the follow-up duty, if so classified, does not.

[50] I accept it might be thought inconsistent to have a duty of care at the inquiry stage and none at the follow-up stage; for it is at the second stage that concrete steps are expected to be taken to protect the child or young person. A duty at the first stage might be thought rather hollow without a corresponding duty at the second stage. This distinction is, however, the product of trying to harmonise considerations of public policy with the express duty to take positive action cast on the Director-General. It could also be said that the duty at stage one is not hollow because, if breached, the plaintiff may seek to show that, had proper care been taken at stage one,

different and more appropriate follow-up action would probably have ensued, despite there being no duty of care at that stage. Such an assertion is not made in the present case. The difficulties inherent in establishing such a proposition, as mentioned in *Prince*, are immediately apparent; particularly as this is a case of an allegation that those involved went too far in applying for the warrant, rather than an allegation they did nothing or did not go far enough.

Problems

1   Charles and Di are parents of William. They are divorced but live within a street of each other in Khandallah. William is now aged nine. They share custody of him so that he spends about the same time at each household every week. William has been a 'problem child' since birth and has a propensity to light fires. Di was due to go on a business trip to Auckland when Charles was called away to his ailing mother in Dunedin. After consulting Charles, Di decided to leave William in the care of Margaret, an acquaintance who also lives in Khandallah. Di did not tell Margaret about William's problem with fires. Three days into the stay with Margaret, William found some matches and burnt Margaret's house plus the house next door belonging to Andrew and Fergie.

Discuss whether Margaret, and Andrew and Fergie, can sue anyone in negligence.

2   Section 334A of the Local Government Act 1974 reads as follows:

(1) A council may do all things necessary to light, with any form of energy, roads, private roads, public places, and (with the consent of the owner) private ways in the district.

In the exercise of the powers conferred by subsection (1) of this section, the council may—

...

(f) Do all things necessary to keep roads and everything appertaining to the lighting of roads, private roads, public places, and (with the consent of the owner) private ways in the district in good repair.

(3) A council may—

(a) Contract with any other body or person to light the roads, private roads, public places, and (with the consent of the owner) private ways within the district with any form of energy.

Consider whether there can be liability in negligence in the following situations:

a   The Wellington City Council decides to modernise lighting in Karori and Khandallah, but not in Island Bay. Rambo's expensive car was converted in an ill-lit street in Island Bay. Rambo normally used his car as a taxi, but was unable to do so for a month until his car was recovered.

b   The Council's plans to modernise street lighting throughout the city have been put into effect very slowly, basically because the staff concerned are lazy. As above, Rambo's car was converted.

c   The Council has contracted the city lighting project to Highlighting Co Ltd. Highlighting has overstretched its budget and has failed to carry out what it was contracted to do. Same result for Rambo.

3 Monica was told by Work and Income New Zealand (WINZ) that she was not entitled to a domestic purposes benefit because of her relationship with Bill. She challenged this decision through the Social Security Appeal Authority, the High Court, and eventually succeeded in the Court of Appeal. Under the Social Security Act, WINZ has a discretion to regard as husband and wife any man and woman who, not being legally married, have entered into a relationship in the nature of marriage and may adjust benefits accordingly (section 63). Can Monica sue WINZ in negligence for legal costs incurred?

Negligence and defamation—exclusive or complementary?

South Pacific Manufacturing Co Ltd v New Zealand Security
Consultants and Investigations Ltd
Mortensen v Laing
[1992] 2 NZLR 282 (CA)
[**FACTS**: *South Pacific* and *Laing* the plaintiffs, having lost their businesses to fire, alleged that investigators employed by their insurance companies had been negligent in concluding that the fires had been started by the plaintiffs.]
Cooke P:
[**Note**: His Honour traversed the general consideration at p 309 and continued.]
...

(xiv) The acceptance by the New Zealand Parliament in 1974 that third parties affected by the activities of licensed private investigators should have the right to file a disciplinary complaint based on negligence is, in my opinion, one of the strongest points in favour of recognising in this country a corresponding common law duty of care. The statute is hardly a controversial or party-political one. Rather it aims at regulating in the public interest the activities of a type of business closely affecting members of the public. To be investigated is an intrusion into one's life, in return for submitting to which it is not unreasonable to ask for reasonable care.

(xv) Conversely, a point telling against recognising a new common law duty of care arises when such a duty would cut across established patterns of law in special fields wherein experience has shown that certain defences, not dependent on absence of negligence, are needed; or wherein an adequate remedy is already available to a party who takes the necessary steps. A leading instance of the latter situation is to be found in the speech of Lord Brandon of Oakbrook in *Leigh and Sillavan Ltd v Aliakmon Shipping Co Ltd* [1986] AC 785, 819: his Lordship indicated that the ordinary law of contract and assignability of rights, in an intricate area of commercial law, would have sufficiently protected the buyers if they had been properly advised. As to the former situation, in *Bell-Booth Group Ltd v Attorney-General* [1989] 3 NZLR 148 this Court declined to extend negligence law to a claim that the reputation of the plaintiffs had been damaged by a television broadcast. In the field of injury to reputation the defences of justification, privilege and fair comment, and the balance of competing interests represented thereby, would have been undermined by superimposing a right to sue in negligence. The approach was taken a degree further in this Court in *Balfour v Attorney-General* [1991] 1 NZLR 519, 529, where it was said that the cause of action unsuccessfully alleged came 'perilously close to defamation' and that any attempt to merge defamation and negligence is to be resisted.

Applying the principles

The present cases are among the first in which this Court has had to consider the principles of the law of negligence since the decision of the House of Lords in *Murphy* ... That case was a major one in the history of English law, so I make no apology for the length of the preceding discussion of principle. Next it is necessary to turn more directly to the application of the relevant principles or considerations to the particular facts of these cases.

To dispose of what is probably the easiest question first, I think that the claims in the *South Pacific* case, being claims made by a creditor and a shareholder of the insured, fail because, even if the investigators owed a duty of care to the insured, such a duty would not extend to persons financially interested in the insured ... .

The more difficult question, whether fire investigators appointed by an insurer owe a duty of care to the insured, strictly requires decision in the *Laing* case only. It is capable of decision, however, without founding any reasoning on the particular facts and allegations in that case ... .

In undertaking it, what is plainly at the forefront of the factors telling in favour of a duty is the close proximity between the investigators and the insured. True the contract of the investigators is only with the insurer, but by entering into the contract of insurance the insured has placed himself in a position where he must submit to investigation by the insurer's representatives in the event of a claim. Inevitably an honest insured has to rely to a considerable extent on the probity and carefulness of the insurer's investigators. The element of reliance is thus present. In turn those representatives must be well aware that a report by them adverse to the insured is likely to be seriously damaging to the interests of the insured. Certainly the insurer will not necessarily decline liability if there is an adverse report, but the risk for the insured is high. In agreement with the Master I regard the risk as so obvious and so serious as to point unmistakably towards a duty. The affidavits and arguments presented on behalf of the investigators are unpersuasive in their attempts to insulate them from the decision of the insurer.

That close proximity is underlined by the acceptance by Parliament in the Private Investigators and Security Guards Act that persons investigated have a legitimate interest in the carefulness or otherwise of those carrying on the business of investigation. It is further underlined by the weight given to it in the handful of American state decisions previously cited.

Further, that close proximity means that neither the fact that the alleged loss is economic nor the preference of Judges for proceeding step by step or 'incrementally' creates any obstacle to a decision in favour of a duty of care. If the research reflected in the arguments of counsel in the present cases is sufficient, there have been no relevant reported cases quite like these except in the United States. Still, by accepting by their contract with the insurer the responsibility of investigation, the investigators have brought themselves into immediate proximity to the insured whose actions they have agreed to investigate. However limited their instructions, it would be unreal to suppose that the insurer did not reasonably expect them to report any facts apparently suggestive of arson. The relationship between the persons investigated and the investigators is at least as close as, if not closer than, the various relationships hitherto held to give rise to a duty of reasonable care to avoid economic loss which are mentioned in para (vii) above.

Two other examples may be added here. First, it could hardly be plausibly suggested that the relationship now under consideration is less close than that of prospective mortgagor and mortgagee's valuer (paid for directly or indirectly by the mortgagor) upon which the House of Lords ruled in favour of a duty of care in *Smith v Eric S Bush* ... There is the difference that the insured would not be expending money in reliance on the report of the investigators; but that is fairly superficial, as the report could cause the insured to lose money. In one way the *Smith v Bush* relationship is indeed less close, in that the valuers had purported to disclaim liability (though in the exercise of a statutory jurisdiction the House of Lords held the disclaimer ineffective for unreasonableness). As to payment, the cost of investigations will be reflected in the insurer's premium rates, so indirectly all insured persons contribute to it ... .

So far then there are weighty considerations in favour of a duty in the kind of situation with which we are now dealing. But in the other scale there have to be put a series of formidable objections arising because the duty asserted would cut across established principles of law in fields other than negligence.

The first is the one that weighed most with this Court in *Bell-Booth*, namely the defences available in a defamation action. Any shortcomings in the investigation of a fire insurance claim are unlikely in themselves to harm the insured. If there is real harm it will probably arise from the report by the investigators to the insurer. To the extent that the report reflects adversely on the insured by suggesting that he may have been guilty of arson the insured will *prima facie* have a cause of action in defamation. Initially at least, the publication may be very limited; yet it could have most serious consequences for the insured and warrant substantial general or special damages ... . It will be a defence, however, if the investigators can prove the truth of the imputation. And more importantly in the present context, the report of the investigators made pursuant to their contractual duty to the insurer will be the subject of qualified privilege.

Qualified privilege can be defeated by proof of malice, but not by proof of mere negligence. The suggested cause of action in negligence would therefore impose a greater restriction on freedom of speech than exists under the law worked out over many years to cover freedom of speech and its limitations. By a side wind the law of defamation would be overthrown. That this is reality, not mere theory, is apparent from the various causes of action in defamation pleaded in the *South Pacific* case and from the plea in *Laing v Mortensen* that the plaintiffs have suffered loss of reputation. Qualified privilege is conferred because of reciprocal duty and interest between a writer or speaker and those with whom he communicates. To cut down the practical scope of the protection would run counter to public policy in this field.

The pleadings in *Laing v Mortensen*, in so far as they refer to complaint to the police and subsequent prosecution, likewise bring out that to impose a duty of care would tend to cut across the law of malicious prosecution. The necessary ingredients of that tort include malice, want of reasonable and probable cause, and the setting of the law in motion by the defendant.

The law is quite complicated as to the respective functions of Judge and jury ... and as to when the defendant can properly be found to have set the law in motion, which was the aspect considered in this Court in *Commercial Union Assurance Co of NZ Ltd v Lamont* [1989] 3 NZLR 187, and also by Drake J in another part of his judgment in the *London Hospital Medical College* case. As pointed out in *Lamont* the law in this field represents a balancing of competing public interest factors—just as defamation law does. It is settled that a person who goes as far as to set the law in motion cannot be liable to the plaintiff without proof of malice and want of reasonable and probable cause. That being so, it would be very odd if a person whose involvement falls short of setting the law in motion were liable for mere negligence ... .

Last it is most important to bear in mind that the insured has his ordinary remedy against the insurer if liability is wrongly declined as a result of a report by investigators. Possibly negligence on the part of investigators could give rise to certain heads of damage not recoverable from the insurer, such as damages for delay and vexation. I will assume, without deciding, that such is the position. Nevertheless the basic remedy against the insurer remains. The history of *Laing v Mortensen* suggests that a negligence action against the investigators could be used as a means of attempting to avoid determination between the insured and the insurer of the central issue: whether the insured was privy to the lighting of the fire and has made a fraudulent claim. That indirectness should be discouraged by the Court. The proper vehicle for determining responsibility for the fire is a proceeding between insured and insurer. Such a proceeding provides the insured with a reasonable, even if not entirely comprehensive, remedy.

In the end I do not think that there can be much doubt about the result of the weighing exercise. Although between the insured and the insurer's investigators there is a high degree of proximity, and although in effect it has been legislatively recognised, the factors telling against a duty of care are cumulatively almost overwhelmingly strong. The balance of public interest embodied in the detailed rules of law as to defamation, malicious prosecution, witness immunity and evidential privilege would be unjustifiably disturbed by superimposing the claimed duty of care.

For these reasons I would dismiss the appeal in the *South Pacific* case but set aside the decisions in question in the *Laing* case, with the result that the pleaded cause of action against the defendant, Mortensen, in that case (at paras 1 to 18 of the statement of claim) would be struck out and that defendant be dismissed from the suit.

Spring v Guardian Assurance
[1995] 2 AC 296 (HL)
[**FACTS**: An insurance company, prospective employers of Spring, requested a reference from his previous employers, Guardian Assurance. This was required under the rules of the insurance industry. The reference suggested that Spring was not a good team worker and had been dishonest with clients. Spring was not employed and he sued.]
Lord Goff:

The central issue in this appeal is whether a person who provides a reference in respect of another who was formerly engaged by him as a member of his staff (at this point I use a deliberately neutral term) may be liable in damages to that other in respect of economic loss suffered by him by reason of negligence in the preparation of the reference. That issue can, for the sake of convenience, be subdivided into two questions. (1) Whether the person who provided the reference prima facie owes a duty of care, in contract or tort, to the other in relation to the preparation of the reference. (2) If so, whether the existence of such a duty of care will nevertheless be negatived because it would, if recognised, pro tanto undermine the policy underlying the defence of qualified privilege in the law of defamation … .

Whether prima facie such a duty of care is owed, in contract or in tort

In a series of well-known cases, your Lordships' House has commended a gradual case-by-case approach to the development of the law of negligence, particularly in cases concerned with claims in respect of pure economic loss. Even so, one broad category of cases has been recognised in which there may be liability in negligence for loss of this kind. These are the cases which spring from, or have been gathered under the umbrella of the landmark decision of your Lordships' House in the *Hedley Byrne* case … .

The wide scope of the principle recognised in *Hedley Byrne* is reflected in the broad statements of principle which I have quoted. All the members of the Appellate Committee in this case spoke in terms of the principle resting upon an assumption or undertaking of responsibility by the defendant towards the plaintiff, coupled with reliance by the plaintiff on the exercise by the defendant of due care and skill. Lord Devlin, in particular, stressed that the principle rested upon an assumption of responsibility when he said, at p 531, that 'the essence of the matter in the present case and in others of the same type is the acceptance of responsibility.' For the purpose of the case now before your Lordships it is, I consider, legitimate to proceed on the same basis. Furthermore, although *Hedley Byrne* itself was concerned with the provision of information and advice, it is clear that the principle in the case is not so limited and extends to include the performance of other services, as for example the professional services rendered by a solicitor to his client. Accordingly where the plaintiff entrusts the defendant with the conduct of his affairs, in general or in particular, the defendant may be held to have assumed responsibility to the plaintiff, and the plaintiff to have relied on the defendant to exercise due skill and care, in respect of such conduct.

The fact that the inquiry in *Hedley Byrne* itself was directed, in a case concerned with liability in respect of a negligent misstatement (in fact a reference), to whether the maker of the statement was liable to a recipient of it who had acted in reliance upon it, may have given the impression that this is the only way in which liability can arise under the principle in respect of a misstatement. But, having regard to the breadth of the principle as stated in *Hedley Byrne* itself, I cannot see why this should be so. Take the case of the relationship between a solicitor and his client treated implicitly by Lord Morris and expressly by Lord Devlin as an example of a relationship to which the principle may apply. I can see no reason why a solicitor should not be under a duty to his client to exercise due care and skill when making statements to third parties, so that if he fails in that duty and his client suffers damage in consequence, he may be liable to his client in damages. The question whether a person who gives a reference to a third party may, if the reference is negligently prepared, be liable in damages not to the recipient but to the subject of the reference did not arise in *Hedley Byrne* and so was not addressed in that case. That is the central question with which we are concerned in the present case, and I propose first to consider it in the context of an ordinary relationship between employer and employee, and then to turn to apply the relevant principles to the more complex relationships which existed in the present case.

Prima facie (ie, subject to the point on defamation, which I will have to consider later), it is my opinion that an employer who provides a reference in respect of one of his employees to a prospective future employer will ordinarily owe a duty of care to his employee in respect of the preparation of the reference. The employer is possessed of special knowledge, derived from his experience of the employee's character, skill and diligence in the performance of his duties while working for the employer. Moreover, when the employer provides a reference to the third party in respect of his employee, he does so not only for the assistance of the third party, but also, for what it is worth, for the assistance of the employee. Indeed, nowadays it must often be very difficult for an employee to obtain fresh employment without the benefit of a reference from his present or a previous employer. It is for this reason that, in ordinary life, it may be the employee, rather than a prospective future employer, who asks the employer to provide the reference; and even where the approach comes from the prospective future employer, it will (apart from special circumstances) be made with either the express or the tacit authority of the employee. The provision of such references is a service regularly provided by employers to their employees; indeed, references are part of the currency of the modern employment market. Furthermore, when such a reference is provided by an employer, it is plain that the employee relies upon him to exercise due skill and care in the preparation of the reference before making it available to the third party. In these circumstances, it seems to me that all the elements requisite for the application of the *Hedley Byrne* principle are present. I need only add that, in the context under consideration, there is no question of the circumstances in which the reference is provided being, for example, so informal as to negative an assumption of responsibility by the employer … .

(2) *If so, whether such a duty will nevertheless be negatived because it would, if recognised, pro tanto undermine the policy underlying the defence of qualified privilege in the law of defamation*

I think it desirable that I should first of all identify the nature of this policy objection. As I understand it, the objection is as follows. First of all, reference is made to the description of the policy underlying the defence of qualified privilege given by Lord Diplock in *Horrocks v Lowe* [1975] AC 135, 149, in the course of which he said:

> The public interest that the law should provide an effective means whereby a man can vindicate his reputation against calumny has nevertheless to be accommodated to the competing public interest in permitting men to communicate frankly and freely with one another about matters in respect of which the law recognises that they have a duty to perform or an interest to protect in doing so. What is published in good faith on matters of these kinds is published on a privileged occasion. It is not actionable even though it be defamatory and turns out to be untrue.

Second, it is suggested that the policy which underlies the defence of qualified privilege, viz that in the relevant circumstances men should be permitted to communicate frankly and freely with one another about all relevant matters, prevents the recognition of a duty of care owed by the giver of the reference to the subject of the reference. In this connection, reliance is placed in particular upon decisions of the Court of Appeal of New Zealand in *Bell-Booth Group Ltd v Attorney-General* [1989] 3 NZLR 148 and *South Pacific Manufacturing Co Ltd* ...

In these circumstances it is, I consider, necessary to approach the question as a matter of principle. Since, for the reasons I have given, it is my opinion that in cases such as the present the duty of care arises by reason of an assumption of responsibility by the employer to the employee in respect of the relevant reference, I can see no good reason why the duty to exercise due skill and care which rests upon the employer should be negatived because, if the plaintiff were instead to bring an action for damage to his reputation, he would be met by the defence of qualified privilege which could only be defeated by proof of malice. It is not to be forgotten that the *Hedley Byrne* duty arises where there is a relationship which is, broadly speaking, either contractual or equivalent to contract. In these circumstances, I cannot see that principles of the law of defamation are of any relevance.

It is true that recognition of a duty of care to an employee in cases such as the present, based on the *Hedley Byrne* principle, may have some inhibiting effect on the manner in which references are expressed, in the sense that it may discourage employers from expressing views ... . For my part, however, I suspect that such an inhibition exists in any event. Employers may well, like many people, be unwilling to indulge in unnecessary criticism of their employees. In all the circumstances, I do not think that we may fear too many ill effects from the recognition of the duty. The vast majority of employers will continue, as before, to provide careful references. But those who, as in the present case, fail to achieve that standard, will have to compensate their employees or former employees who suffer damage in consequence. Justice, in my opinion, requires that this should be done and I, for my part, cannot see any reason in policy why that justice should be denied.

For these reasons I would allow the appeal; but I would nevertheless remit the matter to the Court of Appeal to consider the issue of the extent to which the damage suffered by the plaintiff was caused by the breach of duty of the defendants.

[**Result**: **Lord Keith** dissented; the majority, however, agreed with **Lord Goff**.]

Tort and contract—which rules?

While tort and contract are the heart of the common law of obligations, they are also fundamentally different. In tort, judges impose obligations; in contract, the parties agree to their own obligations. What effect does the existence of a contract have on tort liability? Often a tort duty will look very similar to a contract duty—the agents in *Merrett* had an implied duty of care in contract as well as a duty of care in tort. However, as Lord Goff explains, there are advantages sometimes in being able to sue in tort, especially with respect to the potentially longer limitation period. Should the existence of a contract exclude a plaintiff from seeking those tort advantages? Compare Lord Goff's approach to this question to Richardson J's approach in *South Pacific Manufacturing* where he considers, as La Forest J did in *Norsk*, whether tort law should be used to achieve a result that the parties could have achieved in their contractual relationship but did not.

McLaren Maycroft & Co v Fletcher Development Co Ltd
[1973] 2 NZLR 100 (CA)
[**FACTS**: F engaged M, consulting engineers, to supervise a subdivision scheme. F was sued by a purchaser of a section whose house subsided. F sought to recover contribution, under the Law Reform Act 1936, from M as a joint tortfeasor.]
Richmond J:
... In my opinion ... the only right of action ... was an action for breach of contract. There are numerous authorities which deal with the true nature of an action brought against a professional man for damage caused by lack of proper professional skill and care ... . Diplock LJ ... in *Bagot v Stevens Scanlon & Co* ... said:

> It seems to me that, in this case, the relationship which created the duty of exercising reasonable skill and care by the architects to their clients arose out of the contract and not otherwise. The complaint that is made against them is of a failure to do the very thing which they contracted to do. That was the relationship which gave rise to the duty which was broken. It was a contractual relationship, a contractual duty, and any action brought for failure to comply with that duty is, in my view, an action founded on contract. It is also, in my view, an action founded upon contract alone. ([1966] 1 QB 197, 204)

South Pacific Manufacturing Co Ltd v New Zealand Security Consultants and Investigations
Mortensen v Laing
[1992] 2 NZLR 282 (CA)
Richardson J:
... [P]roximity reflects a balancing of the plaintiff's moral claim to compensation for avoidable harm and the defendant's moral claim to be protected from an undue burden of legal responsibility.

There are four features of the case under this head which together satisfy me that the relationship between the parties was sufficiently proximate to raise a prima facie duty of care. The first is the direct and close nexus between the defendant's negligence as alleged and the plaintiff's loss ... .

The second is that the defendant is not in a position to say that the imposition of a duty of care would expose him to a burden out of proportion to his moral culpability. It is not suggested that there is any significant conflict between his obligations to the insurer under the contractual duty of care and any obligations to the plaintiffs under the common law duty of care. It is not suggested that the cost of being careful, of carrying out the investigation and making his report with due care, would have been unfairly onerous.

The third is that the statute under which the defendant's company was in due course licensed to carry out such investigations reflects a public interest in the competency of investigators. The statute is the Private Investigators and Security Guards Act 1974. In terms of the long title and as it applies to private investigators its object is to:

> ... provide for the licensing of private investigators as a means of affording greater protection to the individual's right to privacy against possible invasion by private investigators ... and to regulate the conduct of business by private investigators ... .

An investigator such as the defendant, who in the course of his business is seeking information for the insurer relating to the actions and behaviour of an insured, is a private investigator within the meaning of s 3 and is required to hold a licence under the Act. While there is particular emphasis on the personal character and fitness of a licensed investigator and the statute provides its own sanctions under the disciplinary and offence provisions, one specific ground of complaint to the Registrar is that the licensee has been guilty of negligence in the course of the business to which the licence relates (s 53(4)(d)), and civil remedies that any person may have against a licensee are not affected by the Act (s 73). The important point is that the relationship between investigator and the subject of the investigation is recognised as sufficiently proximate in its likely effects on those investigated to call for legislative oversight.

Finally, viewed simply in terms of proximity there is a clear parallel with two categories of cases where a duty of care has been recognised. One is the duty owed by a solicitor to a designated beneficiary under a will where the solicitor has accepted instructions to prepare the will for execution but has failed to do so before the testatrix died (*Gartside v Sheffield, Young & Ellis* [1983] NZLR 37). The other is the duty owed by a receiver appointed by a debenture holder to the holder of a subordinate security, the value of which is adversely affected by the conduct of the receiver (*First City Corporation Ltd v Downsview Nominees Ltd* [1990] 3 NZLR 265). In those two cases, as here, the defendant assumes a responsibility to act carefully in undertaking an activity; in each there is a similar dependence and power relation between the plaintiff and the defendant; in each there is a high degree of likelihood that careless performance of that responsibility will cause harm to the plaintiff.

Wider policy concerns

While the proximity of the relationship may be said to raise a prima facie duty of care there are in my view overwhelming policy reasons for denying such a duty in this case.

First, there are various public policy considerations arising from any superimposing of a direct duty of care in tort owed by the investigator to the insured on top of the immediate contractual relationship between insured and insurer on the one hand and insurer and investigator on the other. Under the insurance contract each party has duties of good faith and fair dealing to the other. The common law also imposes on a person who contracts to carry out an operation an obligation to exercise reasonable care and skill (*Smith v Eric S Bush* ...), although that implied obligation may be excluded in the particular contract. The insurance policy in this case is not in evidence. It would be surprising, however, if the insured did not have a remedy against the insurer for failure to take reasonable care in investigating and determining the insured's claim under the policy.

These were commercial premises and commercial insurance contracts are frequently negotiated through brokers. The amount of the premium is the price for the particular cover agreed. If the insured have a remedy in contract against the insurer they should exercise that remedy. If they do not have an adequate remedy that is because they only paid a premium which gave them that lesser protection. In that situation I cannot see any justification for allowing them a greater recovery through tort than they were prepared to pay for in contract.

The second contract is between insurer and investigator. There, too, the parties have their expressly or impliedly agreed remedies for any negligence in the performance of the contract (*Gold Star Insurance Co Ltd v Dominion Adjusters Ltd* [1982] 2 NZLR 38); and in the absence of an exclusion of liability the duty of care applies both to the work of the investigator which results in the report and to the report itself.

It is in relation to remedies that the present case differs markedly from *Gartside* and *Downsview*. Here contractual remedies are an appropriate sanction against want of care in performance of the activity. No claim under the contract was available in those cases in respect of that kind of negligent performance for the simple reason that the other party (the testatrix and her estate in *Gartside* and the first debenture holder in *Downsview*) suffered no loss.

Those were the respective bargains the present parties made. Tort theory should remain consistent with contract policies. In public policy terms I consider that where, as here, contracts cover the two relationships, those contracts should ordinarily control the allocation of risk unless special reasons are established to warrant a direct suit in tort. That accords, too, with *Simaan General Contracting Co v Pilkington Glass Ltd* (*No 2*) [1988] QB 758 where for policy reasons the English Court of Appeal concluded that any claims by A (Simaan) against B (Feal) and by B against C (Pilkington) could and should be pursued down the contractual chain and that there was no warrant for extending the law of negligence to impose direct liability in tort on C in favour of A.

No special factors such as those in *Smith v Bush* have been advanced in this case. In particular, it was not suggested that through oligopolistic

> trade practices or other market failure the parties to such commercial insurance arrangements could not be expected to arrive at commercially acceptable bargains and that state intervention through the imposition of legal obligations in tort was required in the public interest to redress that kind of imbalance. That was not contended for.

Here the plaintiffs seek relief in tort for what are essentially contract-based losses in circumstances where there are no discernible public interest considerations warranting departure from the allocation of risks as agreed contractually. And it is not as if the case involves a choice between letting the loss remain with the injured party and transferring it to another through a tort action. Where those are the stark alternatives it may be reasonable to focus particularly on the respective moral claims of one as against the other. But a plaintiff who has had the opportunity under her or his primary contract to obtain full contractual protection against that kind of loss cannot expect society to provide further protection through tort law.

Henderson v Merrett Syndicates Ltd
[1995] 2 AC 145 (HL)
Lord Goff:
Introduction
The appeals now before your Lordships' House arise out of a number of actions brought by underwriting members (known as Names) of Lloyd's against their underwriting agents, in an attempt to recoup at least part of the great losses which they have suffered following upon recent catastrophic events, mainly in the United States of America, which have led to unprecedented claims being made upon Lloyd's underwriters ...

I *Merrett and Feltrim appeals*
A Duty of care—Liability of managing agents to Names (both direct and indirect Names) in tort

1 Introduction
I turn now to the tortious issues which arise in the Merrett and Feltrim appeals. The first issue, in the order in which they are stated, is concerned with the question whether managing agents, which were not also members' agents, owed to indirect Names a duty of care in tort to carry out their underwriting functions with reasonable care and skill. The second issue is concerned with the question whether managing agents, which were also members' agents, owed such a duty to direct Names ...
[**FACTS**: Member agents placed Names in syndicates, managing agents managed syndicates, whereas combined agents performed both functions. Direct Names were those whose member agent acted also as a managing agent of a syndicate they were in, while indirect Names were in syndicates managed by a separate managing agent.]
... It is desirable that I should at once identify the reasons why Names in the Merrett and Feltrim actions are seeking to establish that there is a duty of care owed to them by managing agents in tort. First, the direct Names in the Merrett actions seek to hold the managing agents concurrently liable in contract and in tort. Where, as in the case of direct Names, the agents are combined agents, there can be no doubt that there is a contract between the Names and the agents, acting as managing agents, in respect of the underwriting carried out by the managing agents on behalf of the Names as members of the syndicate or syndicates under their management, the only question being as to the scope of the managing agents' contractual responsibility in this respect. Even so, in the Merrett actions, Names are concerned to establish the existence of a concurrent duty of care in tort, if only because there is a limitation issue in one of the actions, in which Names wish therefore to be able to take advantage of the more favourable date for the accrual of the cause of action in tort, as opposed to that in contract. Second, the indirect Names in both the Merrett and the Feltrim actions are seeking to establish the existence of a duty of care on the part of the managing agents in tort, no doubt primarily to establish a direct liability to them by the managing agents, but also, in the case of the Merrett actions, to take advantage of the more advantageous position on

limitation. Your Lordships were informed that there is no limitation issue in the Feltrim actions.

2 The argument of the managing agents

The main argument advanced by the managing agents against the existence of a duty of care in tort was that the imposition of such a duty upon them was inconsistent with the contractual relationship between the parties. In the case of direct Names, where there was a direct contract between the Names and the managing agents, the argument was that the contract legislated exclusively for the relationship between the parties, and that a parallel duty of care in tort was therefore excluded by the contract. In the case of indirect Names, reliance was placed on the fact that there had been brought into existence a contractual chain, between Name and members' agent, and between members' agent and managing agent; and it was said that, by structuring their contractual relationship in this way, the indirect Names and the managing agents had deliberately excluded any direct responsibility, including any tortious duty of care, to the indirect Names by the managing agents … .

3 The governing principle

… I turn immediately to the decision of this House in *Hedley Byrne* …

The case has always been regarded as important in that it established that, in certain circumstances, a duty of care may exist in respect of words as well as deeds, and further that liability may arise in negligence in respect of pure economic loss which is not parasitic upon physical damage. But, perhaps more important for the future development of the law, and certainly more relevant for the purposes of the present case, is the principle upon which the decision was founded … .

We can see that it rests upon a relationship between the parties, which may be general or specific to the particular transaction, and which may or may not be contractual in nature. All of their Lordships spoke in terms of one party having assumed or undertaken a responsibility towards the other. On this point, Lord Devlin spoke in particularly clear terms … . Further, Lord Morris spoke of that party being possessed of a 'special skill' which he undertakes to 'apply for the assistance of another who relies upon such skill.' But the facts of *Hedley Byrne* itself, which was concerned with the liability of a banker to the recipient for negligence in the provision of a reference gratuitously supplied, show that the concept of a 'special skill' must be understood broadly, certainly broadly enough to include special knowledge. Again, though *Hedley Byrne* was concerned with the provision of information and advice, the example given by Lord Devlin of the relationship between solicitor and client, and his and Lord Morris's statements of principle, show that the principle extends beyond the provision of information and advice to include the performance of other services. It follows, of course, that although, in the case of the provision of information and advice, reliance upon it by the other party will be necessary to establish a cause of action (because otherwise the negligence will have no causative effect), nevertheless there may be other circumstances in which there will be the necessary reliance to give rise to the application of the principle. In particular, as cases concerned with solicitor and client demonstrate, where the plaintiff entrusts the defendant with the conduct of his affairs, in general or in particular, he may be held to have relied on the defendant to exercise due skill and care in such conduct.

In subsequent cases concerned with liability under the *Hedley Byrne* principle in respect of negligent misstatements, the question has frequently arisen whether the plaintiff falls within the category of persons to whom the maker of the statement owes a duty of care. In seeking to contain that category of persons within reasonable bounds, there has been some tendency on the part of the courts to criticise the concept of 'assumption of responsibility' as being 'unlikely to be a helpful or realistic test in most cases' (see *Smith v Eric S Bush* ... 864–5, *per* Lord Griffiths) ... However, at least in cases such as the present, in which the same problem does not arise, there seems to be no reason why recourse should not be had to the concept, which appears after all to have been adopted, in one form or another, by all of their Lordships in *Hedley Byrne*. Furthermore, especially in a context concerned with a liability which may arise under a contract or in a situation 'equivalent to contract,' it must be expected that an objective test will be applied when asking the question whether, in a particular case, responsibility should be held to have been assumed by the defendant to the plaintiff: see *Caparo* ... *per* Lord Oliver. In addition, the concept provides its own explanation why there is no problem in cases of this kind about liability for pure economic loss; for if a person assumes responsibility to another in respect of certain services, there is no reason why he should not be liable in damages for that other in respect of economic loss which flows from the negligent performance of those services. It follows that, once the case is identified as falling within the *Hedley Byrne* principle, there should be no need to embark upon any further enquiry whether it is 'fair, just and reasonable' to impose liability for economic loss—a point which is, I consider, of some importance in the present case. The concept indicates too that in some circumstances, for example where the undertaking to furnish the relevant service is given on an informal occasion, there may be no assumption of responsibility: and likewise that an assumption of responsibility may be negatived by an appropriate disclaimer. I wish to add in parenthesis that, as Oliver J recognised in *Midland Bank Trust Co Ltd v Hett, Stubbs & Kemp* [1979] Ch 384, 416F–G, (a case concerned with concurrent liability of solicitors in tort and contract, to which I will have to refer in a moment) an assumption of responsibility by, for example, a professional man may give rise to liability in respect of negligent omissions as much as negligent acts of commission, as for example when a solicitor assumes responsibility for business on behalf of his client and omits to take a certain step, such as the service of a document, which falls within the responsibility so assumed by him.

4 The application of the principle to managing agents at Lloyd's
Since it has been submitted on behalf of the managing agents that no liability should attach to them in negligence in the present case because the only damage suffered by the Names consists of pure economic loss, the question arises whether the principle in *Hedley Byrne* is capable of applying in the case of underwriting agents at Lloyd's who are managing agents. Like Saville J and the Court of Appeal, I have no difficulty in concluding that the principle is indeed capable of such application. The principle has been expressly applied to a number of different categories of person who perform services of a professional or quasi-professional nature, such as bankers (in *Hedley Byrne* itself); solicitors (as

foreshadowed by Lord Devlin in *Hedley Byrne*, and as held in the leading case of *Midland Bank Trust Co Ltd v Hett, Stubbs & Kemp* ... and other cases in which that authority had been followed); surveyors and valuers (as in *Smith v Eric S Bush* ...); and accountants (as in *Caparo* ...). Another category of persons to whom the principle has been applied, and on which particular reliance was placed by the Names in the courts below and in argument before your Lordships, is insurance brokers ... .

For my part I can see no reason why a duty of care should not likewise be owed by managing agents at Lloyd's to a Name who is a member of a syndicate under the management of the agents. Indeed, as Saville J and the Court of Appeal both thought, the relationship between Name and managing agent appears to provide a classic example of the type of relationship to which the principle in *Hedley Byrne* applies. In so saying, I put on one side the question of the impact, if any, upon the relationship of the contractual context in which it is set. But, that apart, there is in my opinion plainly an assumption of responsibility in the relevant sense by the managing agents towards the Names in their syndicates. The managing agents have accepted the Names as members of a syndicate under their management. They obviously hold themselves out as possessing a special expertise to advise the Names on the suitability of risks to be underwritten; and on the circumstances in which, and the extent to which, reinsurance should be taken out and claims should be settled. The Names, as the managing agents well knew, placed implicit reliance on that expertise, in that they gave authority to the managing agents to bind them to contracts of insurance and reinsurance and to the settlement of claims. I can see no escape from the conclusion that, in these circumstances, prima facie a duty of care is owed in tort by the managing agents to such Names. To me, it does not matter if one proceeds by way of analogy from the categories of relationship already recognised as falling within the principle in *Hedley Byrne* or by a straight application of the principle stated in the *Hedley Byrne* case itself. On either basis the conclusion is, in my opinion, clear. Furthermore, since the duty rests on the principle in *Hedley Byrne*, no problem arises from the fact that the loss suffered by the Names is pure economic loss.

5 Absolute discretion

I can deal with this point briefly because, like the Court of Appeal, I agree with Saville J that there is no substance in it. It was the submission of the managing agents in the Merrett appeals before your Lordships, as it had been before Saville J, that there was an unbroken line of authority supporting the proposition that the expression 'absolute discretion' in the context of a private law agreement meant that the exercise of the power given by the agreement to the recipient of the power cannot be challenged by the donor or beneficiary of the power unless (a) the exercise of the power is in bad faith, or (b) (arguably) the exercise of the power is totally unreasonable. It followed, so the argument ran, that a duty to exercise due skill or care, whether contractual or extra-contractual, was inconsistent with the bargain and so must be excluded. However, it appears to me, as it did the judge, that in the present context the words used cannot have the effect of excluding a duty of care, contractual or otherwise. Clear words are required to exclude liability in negligence; and in the present case the words can, and in my opinion should, be directed towards the scope of the agents' authority.

No doubt the result is that very wide authority has been vested in the agents; but the suggestion that the agent should as a result be under no duty to exercise due skill and care in the exercise of his function under the agreement is, in the present context, most surprising … .

6 The impact of the contractual context

All systems of law which recognise a law of contract and a law of tort (or delict) have to solve the problem of the possibility of concurrent claims arising from breach of duty under the two rubrics of the law. Although there are variants, broadly speaking two possible solutions present themselves: either to insist that the claimant should pursue his remedy in contract alone, or to allow him to choose which remedy he prefers … . France has adopted the former solution in its doctrine of *non cumul*, under which the concurrence of claims in contract and tort is outlawed (see Tony Weir in XI *Int Encycl Comp L*, Ch 12, paras 47–72, at para 52). The reasons given for this conclusion are (1) respect for the will of the legislator, and (2) respect for the will of the parties to the contract (see para 53). The former does not concern us: but the latter is of vital importance. It is however open to various interpretations. For such a policy does not necessarily require the total rejection of concurrence, but only so far as a concurrent remedy in tort is inconsistent with the terms of the contract. It comes therefore as no surprise to learn that the French doctrine is not followed in all civil law jurisdictions, and that concurrent remedies in tort and contract are permitted in other civil law countries, notably Germany (see para 58). I only pause to observe that it appears to be accepted that no perceptible harm has come to the German system from admitting concurrent claims … .

The situation in common law countries, including of course England, is exceptional, in that the common law grew up within a procedural framework uninfluenced by Roman law. The law was categorised by reference to the forms of action, and it was not until the abolition of the forms of action by the Common Law Procedure Act 1852 (15 & 16 Vict c 76) that it became necessary to reclassify the law in substantive terms. The result was that common lawyers did at last segregate our law of obligations into contract and tort, though in so doing they relegated quasi-contractual claims to the status of an appendix to the law of contract, thereby postponing by a century or so the development of a law of restitution. Even then, there was no systematic reconsideration of the problem of concurrent claims in contract and tort. We can see the courts rather grappling with unpromising material drawn from the old cases in which liability in negligence derived largely from categories based upon the status of the defendant. In a sense, we must not be surprised; for no significant law faculties were established at our universities until the late nineteenth century, and so until then there was no academic opinion available to guide or stimulate the judges. Even so, it is a remarkable fact that there was little consideration of the problem of concurrent remedies in our academic literature until the second half of the twentieth century, though in recent years the subject has attracted considerable attention.

In the result, the courts in this country have until recently grappled with the problem very largely without the assistance of systematic academic study. At first, as is shown in particular by cases concerned with liability for solicitors' negligence, the courts adopted something very like the French solution, holding that a claim against a solicitor for negligence must be pursued in contract, and not in tort ... .

It has to be said, however, that decisions such as these [establishing the rule against concurrent liability], though based on prior authority, were supported by only a slender citation of cases, none of great weight; and the jurisprudential basis of the doctrine so adopted cannot be said to have been explored in any depth. Furthermore when, in *Bagot v Stevens Scanlan & Co Ltd* [1966] 1 QB 197, Diplock LJ adopted a similar approach in the case of a claim against a firm of architects, he felt compelled to recognise (pp 204–5) that a different conclusion might be reached in cases 'where the law in the old days recognised either something in the nature of a status like a public calling (such as common carrier, common innkeeper, or a bailor and bailee) or the status of master and servant.' To this list must be added cases concerned with claims against doctors and dentists. I must confess to finding it startling that, in the second half of the twentieth century, a problem of considerable practical importance should fall to be solved by reference to such an outmoded form of categorisation as this.

I think it is desirable to stress at this stage that the question of concurrent liability is by no means only of academic significance. Practical issues, which can be of great importance to the parties, are at stake. Foremost among these is perhaps the question of limitation of actions. If concurrent liability in tort is not recognised, a claimant may find his claim barred at a time when he is unaware of its existence. This must moreover be a real possibility in the case of claims against professional men, such as solicitors or architects, since the consequences of their negligence may well not come to light until long after the lapse of six years from the date when the relevant breach of contract occurred ... .

This leads to the startling possibility that a client who has had the benefit of gratuitous advice from his solicitor may in this respect be better off than a client who has paid a fee. Other practical problems arise, for example, from the absence of a right to contribution between negligent contract-breakers; from the rules as to remoteness of damage, which are less restricted in tort than they are in contract; and from the availability of the opportunity to obtain leave to serve proceedings out of the jurisdiction. It can of course be argued that the principle established in respect of concurrent liability in contract and tort should not be tailored to mitigate the adventitious effects of rules of law such as these, and that one way of solving such problems would no doubt be to rephrase such incidental rules as have to remain in terms of the nature of the harm suffered rather than the nature of the liability asserted (see Tony Weir, XI *Int Encycl Comp L*, ch 12, para 72). But this is perhaps crying for the moon; and with the law in its present form, practical considerations of this kind cannot sensibly be ignored.

Moreover I myself perceive at work in these decisions not only the influence of the dead hand of history, but also what I have elsewhere called the temptation of elegance. Mr Tony Weir (XI *Int Encycl Comp L*, Ch 12, para 55) has extolled the French solution for its elegance; and we can discern the same impulse behind the much-quoted observation of Lord Scarman when delivering the judgment of the Judicial Committee of the Privy Council in *Tai Hing Cotton Mill Ltd v Liu Chong Hing Bank Ltd*.

[**Note**: His Lordship went on to consider cases supporting concurred liabilities.]

First, and most important, in 1963 came the decision of your Lordships' House in *Hedley Byrne* ... I have already expressed the opinion that the fundamental importance of this case rests in the establishment of the principle upon which liability may arise in tortious negligence in respect of services (including advice) which are rendered for another, gratuitously or otherwise, but are negligently performed—viz, an assumption of responsibility coupled with reliance by the plaintiff which, in all the circumstances, makes it appropriate that a remedy in law should be available for such negligence. For immediate purposes, the relevance of the principle lies in the fact that, as a matter of logic, it is capable of application not only where the services are rendered gratuitously, but also where they are rendered under a contract ... .

Meanwhile in New Zealand the Court of Appeal had appeared at first, in *McLaren Maycroft & Co v Fletcher Development Co Ltd* to require that, in cases where there are concurrent duties in contract and tort, the claimant must pursue his remedy in contract alone. There followed a period of some uncertainty, in which differing approaches were adopted by courts of first instance. In 1983 Miss Christine French published her article on 'The Contract/Tort Dilemma' in (1981–84) 5 Otago LR 236, in which she examined the whole problem in great depth, with special reference to the situation in New Zealand, having regard to the 'rule' in *McLaren Maycroft*. Her article, to which I wish to pay tribute, was of course published before the decision of the Supreme Court of Canada in the *Central Trust* case (1986) 31 DLR (4th) 481. Even so, she reached a conclusion which, on balance, favoured a freedom for the claimant to choose between concurrent remedies in contract and tort. Thereafter in *Rowlands v Collow* [1992] 1 NZLR 178 Thomas J, founding himself principally on the *Central Trust* case and on Miss French's article, concluded that he was free to depart from the decision of the New Zealand Court of Appeal in the *McLaren Maycroft* case and to hold that a person performing professional services (in the case before him an engineer) may be sued for negligence by his client either in contract or in tort. He said, at p 190:

> The issue is now virtually incontestable; a person who has performed profes-
> sional services may be held liable concurrently in contract and in negligence
> unless the terms of the contract preclude the tortious liability.

... It is however my understanding that by the law in this country contracts for services do contain an implied promise to exercise reasonable care (and skill) in the performance of the relevant services; indeed, as Mr Tony Weir has pointed out (IX *Int Encycl Comp L*, ch 12, para 67), in the nineteenth century the field of concurrent liabilities was expanded 'since it was impossible for the judges to deny that contracts contained an implied promise to take reasonable care, at the least, not to injure the other part.' My own belief is that, in the present context, the common law is not antipathetic to concurrent liability, and that there is no sound basis for a rule which automatically restricts the claimant to either a tortious or a contractual remedy. The result may be untidy; but, given that the tortious duty is imposed by the general law, and the contractual duty is attributable to the will of the parties, I do not find it objectionable that the claimant may be entitled to take advantage of the remedy which is most advantageous to him, subject only to ascertaining whether the tortious duty is so inconsistent with the applicable contract that, in accordance with ordinary principle, the parties must be taken to have agreed that the tortious remedy is to be limited or excluded.

7 Application of the above principles in the present case
... It is however submitted on behalf of the managing agents that the indirect Names and the managing agents, as parties to the chain of contracts contained in the relevant

agency and sub-agency agreements, must be taken to have thereby structured their relationship so as to exclude any duty of care owed directly by the managing agents to the indirect Names in tort.

In essence the argument must be that, because the managing agents have, with the consent of the indirect Names, assumed responsibility in respect of the relevant activities to another party, ie the members' agents, under a sub-agency agreement, it would be inconsistent to hold that they have also assumed responsibility in respect of the same activities to the indirect Names. I for my part cannot see why in principle a party should not assume responsibility to more than one person in respect of the same activity. Let it be assumed (unlikely though it may be) that, in the present case, the managing agents were in a contractual relationship not only with the members' agents under a sub-agency agreement but also directly with the relevant Names, under both of which they assumed responsibility for the same activities. I can see no reason in principle why the two duties of care so arising should not be capable of co-existing.

Turton v Kerslake
[2000] 2 NZLR 406 (CA)
Henry and Keith JJ:
[1] The issue raised in this appeal … is whether an engineer who has prepared the mechanical services specification for incorporation into a contract to construct a building owes a duty of care to a contractor who has undertaken those mechanical services as part of the overall construction. In the District Court Moran DCJ held that no duty arose in the particular circumstances, and that decision was upheld by Panckhurst J on appeal to the High Court.

[2] In 1987 the Southland Area Health Board decided to build a new hospital near Queenstown. For that purpose it employed the architect firm of Gray Hesslan and Baxter to design the building, oversee the tendering process, and supervise construction. For the purposes of its functions, the architect engaged an engineering firm (the respondent) to advise on engineering aspects of the project, including preparing the mechanical services specification and the corresponding subcontract, and supervising the engineering side of the construction. The specification for mechanical services included … [specifications for a heat pump] …

[3] The appellant (Turton), now in liquidation, received the tender documents from the architects … Turton won the head contract. The tender which was accepted included the tender for the mechanical services subcontract submitted by George Mechanical Limited, now in receivership. George Mechanical had been the alternative subcontractor nominated in Turton's tender documents. Turton's preferred subcontractor, NZ Mechanical, had tendered a cheaper price based on substituting a different heat pump for that required by the mechanical services specification. George Mechanical had also submitted an alternative price based on a different heat pump; however, the accepted tender was that of George Mechanical based on the heat pumps to be provided as specified. The contract price for construction of the hospital was $5 934 680.18. The subcontract price for the mechanical services section was $1 458 216.00.

[4] A problem arose with the heating system. Following installation it was found that it would not perform to the specified standard …

[5] Turton commenced proceedings in the District Court, raising in issue a number of matters, most of which are not presently relevant and can be ignored. But included and directly in issue was a claim against the Health Board for $73 542.03 being the cost to Turton of remedial work to the heating system. Claims for that based on variation of the head contract and on *quantum meruit* were rejected. However Turton also claimed the same amount from the engineer pleading the tort of negligence. It too failed, on the basis that the engineer owed no relevant duty of care to Turton. It is that last finding, upheld in the High Court, which is now under challenge.

[6] It is common ground that Turton undertook responsibility to carry out the work in accordance with the terms of the contract, including the mechanical services specification. It must also now be accepted that the remedial work in question carried out on the heat pumps was required in order for Turton to fulfil its own contractual obligations. The question is whether Turton has a right of action against the engineer founded on the tort of negligence entitling it to recover the cost of the remedial work. The first step in the enquiry, and for the purposes of this appeal the only element of the cause of action which falls for determination, is whether a common law duty of care is imposed on the engineer.

Duty of care

[7] The basis of the claim in tort is negligent misstatement. In short, did the engineer owe a duty to Turton to take reasonable care in drawing up the specification? The foundation of such a duty lies in the House of Lords decision in *Hedley Byrne*. As succeeding cases have demonstrated, the search for any single formula which will serve as a general test of liability in this area inevitably causes difficulties. Lord Oliver in *Caparo* ... likened it to pursuing a will-o'-the wisp. The existence, or non-existence, of a duty will always be fact dependent, and although general criteria which have emerged are to be applied, they are not absolutes—they are neither conclusive nor exclusive. What is now well established is that if the statement in question is made in a contractual setting, that setting will be relevant in determining whether a duty in tort is to be imposed.

[8] The modern doctrine of concurrent liability in tort and contract establishes that the mere fact that a defendant's alleged tortious liability arises from actions taken in respect of a contract, whether with the plaintiff or another, does not of itself negate a common law duty of care. That is now well-established law, and Mr Macdonald, for the engineering firm, did not contend otherwise. The authorities, however do show that the existence and terms of contracts under which work is carried out may militate against the existence of a separate duty of care ...

[9] Acceptance of the doctrine of concurrency of duties does not conflict with the principle that regard must be had to the existence of any contracts, or indeed a contractual matrix, in the decision to impose a duty in tort or not. Concurrency is concerned with remedies, specifically that one remedy is not to be preferred over another. While theories of the primacy of contractual remedies over tortious ones found support in some of the early decisions, the main and now accepted rationale behind the contractual matrix principle is concerned not with the existence of a contractual remedy, but with the way in which the contractual intention can help to enlighten the

often difficult question of when the relationship between two parties is such as to warrant the intervention of the general law of tort ...

[10] In a case such as this, while the terms of the contracts may inform the various allocations of risk, the manner in which the contracts are structured amongst the variously connected parties will also be important in assessing the relationships ...

The contractual relationship between the parties

[16] Critical in this appeal is the contractual setting against which the duty of care issue falls to be determined ... The architect contracted with the Area Health Board to design the building and prepare the necessary contract documents for that purpose. The engineer contracted with the architect to prepare the mechanical services section. Turton contracted with the Area Health Board to construct the building in accordance with, inter alia, the mechanical services specifications. And George Mechanical subcontracted with Turton to carry out the mechanical services section. It would also appear to be the position that in turn Wildridge and Sinclair contracted with George Mechanical for supply of the heat pump packages as specified in cl 19.6.02 of the subcontract.

[17] It is therefore essential to consider the various contractual provisions between the various parties in the particular circumstances of this case. First, as already mentioned, Turton undertook to carry out the whole of the contract works. The documents make it clear that the mechanical services section of the works was to be carried out under subcontract by an approved subcontractor, but without affecting the primary liability of Turton to the Area Health Board for completion of that section in accordance with the specifications ...

The other *Hedley Byrne* factors, especially of reliance

...

[27] To repeat, this is a case of alleged negligent misstatement. In terms of *Hedley Byrne* and later cases we are to consider questions such as the following: was the defendant possessed of special skills, did it undertake to apply that skill for the assistance of another person, and did that person rely on it and suffer loss as a result of the defendant's breach of its duty of care in applying that skill? ... We have already referred to the critical relevant elements of the contractual relationships between the various parties involved in the construction of the hospital.

[28] We doubt that Kerslake, the engineers, possessed any special skill as against Turton. So far as Kerslake's special skill is concerned, the particular terms of the specifications must be critical and be able to be balanced against its expertise in mechanical engineering. [The District court had so held] ...

[30] The argument that Kerslake undertook responsibility and that Turton relied on that undertaking must also meet in some way the District Court finding that Turton did not approach Kerslake seeking information and the related absence of any clear indication that Turton would be relying on information given by Kerslake. That finding is well supported by the evidence. Mr R.M. Turton, the director of Turton, after mentioning the choice that had been made between subcontractors ... said that

with a job of that size and nature you have to look at [the tender documents] carefully.

He accepted that by the time he tendered for the project he was an experienced tenderer ...

Q I take it that doesn't include sitting down personally and going through the mechanical services specification.

A Generally with a nominated specific subcontractor package like mechanical we flick through the document to see if there is anything relevant to us and pass it on to the mechanical services guy.

Q You are really relying upon skill and expertise of your subcontractor for that part of the contract?

A We are relying on them to put a tender together that relies on documents.

[31] Later, he agreed that Turton had a fair amount of confidence in the two proposed subcontractors, George Mechanical and New Zealand Mechanical. Neither had warned Mr Turton that the specification as written was not capable of producing the energy required but, he added, it was not their responsibility to check the engineer design, especially in the tender period. He agreed that George Mechanical would have contacted Wildridge and Sinclair and APV Baker. He assumed that Kerslake would have obtained its information from Wildridge and Sinclair. He accepted that there was a circle with Kerslake getting the information (originally) from Wildridge and Sinclair, and George Mechanical, when putting the subcontract together, going back to Wildridge and Sinclair.

[32] We return to the contracts. In our view the duty contended for in respect of the alleged representation that the componentry would achieve the required output would cut across and be inconsistent with the overall contractual structure which defines the relationships of the various parties to this work, and in the circumstances of this case it would not be fair, just or reasonable to impose the claimed duty of care. The factors which demonstrate that conclusion can be drawn from the preceding discussion and summarised. First, the relationships as between all the relevant parties—the Area Health Board, the architect, the engineer, the contractor and the subcontractor—are carefully spelt out in the separate contracts. All were aware of the existence of the contractual chain. Second, those contracts define the rights and obligations of the respective parties to them. If the loss in question is the cost of work necessary to remedy a defect in the specifications, as between the owner and the engineer, the risk rested with the engineer (subject to the exclusion and limitation provisions). As between the owner and the contractor, it rested with the contractor. As between the contractor and the subcontractor, it rested in the subcontractor. And as between the subcontractor and the supplier, it rested (probably) in the supplier. In that overall situation, and taking into account the reliance that Turton placed on the expertise of its subcontractor, we do not see any justification for holding that in addition the engineer should be regarded as having voluntarily assumed a responsibility to contractors and subcontractors. Third, the engineer has carefully defined and confined its potential liability for negligence. Fourth, the engineer has the right to have any dispute as to its liability resolved by arbitration.

Fifth is the extent of any potential liability which would arise from the imposition of the separate duty of care. Logically the duty must extend to all potential tenderers for the head contract, and to all potential tenderers for the mechanical services sub-contract. Sixth, it would seem that the Area Health Board, which invited tenders on the basis of the specifications would not itself be under any such duty of care to a contractor, notwithstanding the representation.

The Edgeworth Case *and related policy matters*

[33] Mr Kirkland, for Turton, placed substantial reliance on the decision of the Supreme Court of Canada in *Edgeworth Construction Ltd v N D Lea & Associates Ltd* (1994) 107 DLR (4th) 169 …

[**Note**: This case was described in *Natural Health Foods* at page 340.]

[34] Like Panckhurst J, we do not see *Edgeworth* of much present assistance. The contractual setting was quite different, and the one contract at issue and relied upon by the engineer was one to which it was not a party and one which did not in its terms impinge on the engineer's own position and its general legal liabilities. Although McLachlin J referred to reasons of policy which, in the absence of any relevant contractual background may arguably have some significance, we do not think they support the existence of a duty in a case such as the present where an expert subcontractor is to be retained. As was stressed in *British Telecommunications* each case must be considered in the light of its own environment. In submitting its tender Turton was required to include the tender of its nominated subcontractor. The engineer here did not hold itself out as giving advice to either the contractor or the subcontractor.

[35] It is necessary to make a further observation. There are, here, no broad policy issues to be considered. In a case such as this, therefore, we would not endorse the concept of a two-stage inquiry, which somehow first considers the general criteria (possession of skill, foreseeability, reasonable reliance) as establishing a prima facie duty of care, and then goes on to consider whether the contractual matrix negates the prima facie duty. There is no prima facie duty in that sense. The imposition of the duty will depend upon a consideration of all the circumstances, which must include the contractual matrix. The criteria cannot properly be considered in its absence.

[36] The test is based on broad formulations including fairness, reasonableness and justice. In considering those concepts the Court must examine the whole of the circumstances and the relationship between the parties. This examination is usefully focussed on the relevant matters by inquiring into factors such as those mentioned in the preceding paragraph, but in the end the Court must be satisfied that the relationship is such that there has been an undertaking of responsibility to the particular plaintiff and the imposition of a duty of care is justified. In a case such as the present this cannot be done without considering the various contractual rights and obligations. In a comprehensive contractual situation such as existed here, the Court should be hesitant to go beyond that relationship. A tortious duty of care outside that framework, but affecting the rights and liabilities of the various separate parties coming within the very contractual setting, should not lightly be imposed.

We see no relevance in the fact that there has been an insolvency, and little in the argument that insolvency was a known risk at the time of contracting so therefore it is appropriate to look beyond the insolvent contractor for possible relief. In the absence of evidence which could somehow show the possibility of George Mechanical's future insolvency affecting the establishment of the relationship between Turton and the engineer which was created as part of the contractual matrix, we do not consider this factor of any assistance to Turton. One of the known risks in this kind of situation is the insolvency of a party who is contractually responsible for a loss suffered. Here that risk was accepted by Turton when it contracted with George Mechanical.

We also find little attraction to a general statement of principle which would impose a duty of care in this kind of situation simply because otherwise a contractor may be required to review the professional accuracy of plans and specifications. The economic impact is but one factor, and must be put into the context of the particular case. Here, as we have already emphasised, the contract documents required Turton to employ a specialist subcontractor to carry out this work. The componentry was a shelf item which the supplier apparently claimed would achieve the required output. The defect in question is said on behalf of Turton to be one readily ascertainable by a competent engineer. George Mechanical described itself as a design and contract engineer, specialising in heating and ventilation. It was held out by Turton as such in submitting its own tender. In our view these facts militate against, rather than support, the imposition of the claimed duty. We also have a measure of real concern in endorsing what could be construed as a general principle, namely that in a building contract situation, an architect or engineer will be liable in tort to contractors and subcontractors for negligence in design or specification.

Thomas J (dissenting):
The question in issue
Hedley Byrne

...

(1) Negligent misstatement
[78] Kerslake disputes the claim that it made any representation as to the capacity of the Wildridge and Sinclair Heat Pumps at all. It argued that the specification set the performance level which Turton was required to meet. A close examination of the specification is therefore required to determine whether it is a representation that the Wildridge and Sinclair Heat Pumps would produce a minimum capacity of 185 kw output. It is common ground that the pumps did not have that capacity.

[79] In my view, the plain wording of the specification indicates that the reference to the output of 185 kw is a statement of the specified heat pumps' capacity when installed with the specified componentry. The reference to the pumps in the first sentence could possibly be construed as being either descriptive or prescriptive, or even both. But the next sentence opens with the words: 'This output shall be achieved ...'. ... The concrete details by which the output will be achieved are then specified in some detail. Each of the componentry are made mandatory by the use of the word 'shall'. As a matter of contract, and common-sense, all Turton was required to do was to provide and install three Wildridge and Sinclair Heat Pumps with the specified componentry.

[80] Thus, Turton had to provide and install the heat pumps complete with 'compression, refrigerant cooled oil cooler, evaporator, condenser and complete control systems'. The compressor had to be a R53E-40 STAL Miniscrew compressor 'with direct

drive from flanged mounted 50 Hz motor'. The oil cooler had to be supplied with an economiser and interconnecting pipework. The evaporator had to be a correctly sized SBE10/800 DX model with flanged connections. The condenser was required to be a CR 105-76 unit of specified dimensions with connections. Finally, the heat pumps had to be controlled by a Stalectronic 400 operating system with a side-mounted control panel, alarm unit and 'all interlocks, inputs and outputs necessary'.

[81] I am not suggesting that every statement in a specification would amount to a representation for the purposes of *Hedley Byrne*. Far from it. A quick perusal of the specification as a whole in this case reveals that clause 19.6.02 is singularly obligatory in its terms. It contains a firm and detailed statement that the specified pumps, when installed with the componentry as directed and required, will achieve an output of 185 kw. This case begins with that positive representation ...

(2) Special skills ...

[83] It cannot be seriously disputed that Kerslake had the necessary special skills. The company's expertise in mechanical engineering is the very reason why the Hospital Board employed it. The assumption that the company would—or should—know what it was talking about in this area is secure. Kerslake was a qualified mechanical engineering firm. It will have spent many months preparing the mechanical engineering specifications. It was either responsible for the idea that the temperature of the lake water should be utilised in obtaining the necessary energy to be generated by the heat pumps or had been closely associated with the development of that idea. It carried out all the enquiries and research which were required and finally stipulated the kind of heat pumps to be used. When the problem with the capacity in the pumps emerged, Kerslake played a dominant role in determining what should be done to remedy the inadequacy. Its skill and expertise cannot be denied.

[84] Nor can it be seriously contended that Kerslake did not assume responsibility for the accuracy of its representation or that it was not foreseeable that tenderers would rely upon it. As the Hospital Board's consulting mechanical engineer, employed by the Board's architects, Kerslake clearly owed a duty to its employer to produce an accurate specification. It did so in the knowledge that the specification it prepared would be advertised by the Hospital Board for the purpose of inviting tenders. It was fully aware that its specification would be used by tenderers as the basis of their tender, including the pricing of the work. Indeed, this use was the function of the specification—it defined the Hospital Board's work for which tenders were being called. Kerslake also knew that the tenderers had a limited time within which to prepare a tender, and it was well aware that the tender accepted in accordance with its specification would become part of the final contract. The successful tenderer would be contractually bound to complete the work in accordance with the contract. As the consulting engineer responsible for the specification, the company clearly accepted responsibility for its statement in clause 19.6.02 as to the capacity of the Wildridge and Sinclair Heat Pumps when installed with the specified componentry.

[85] The more difficult question, perhaps, is whether Turton actually relied upon the statement.

(3) Reliance

[86] In my opinion it was reasonable for Turton, as well as other tenderers and sub-contractors, to rely upon the specification and, in preparing and making a bid for the contract, Turton and its subcontractors did in fact rely upon it. A number of factors support this conclusion.

[87] First, the wording of the specification itself invites reliance. The contractor is required to install three Wildridge and Sinclair Heat Pumps, each with a minimum capacity of 185 kw output, with specified componentry. This requirement was specified after many months of investigation by Kerslake and ultimately included in the specification. Clause 19.6.02 is a firm and detailed statement. It is difficult to see why any tenderer or subcontractor would not rely on this firm and detailed statement and tender in accordance with it, as they were invited to do ...

[88] Secondly, Turton tendered for the contract on the basis of the specification. It expressly submitted George Mechanical's tender 'as specification', thus indicating reliance on the specification.

[89] Thirdly, the guarantee given by Turton provides some support for the notion that the company must have relied on the statement in the specification. There is no other plausible basis for giving the guarantee than that the statements in the specification have been taken to be correct.

[90] Fourthly, although there is a dispute as to the significance of the evidence, Kerslake's preference for the specified Wildridge and Sinclair Heat Pumps tends to confirm that they were regarded as obligatory. A less expensive heat pump offered by George Mechanical as an alternative was declined. An even lower bid by New Zealand Mechanical offering different pumps to those specified in the specification was also rejected. The impression which is created is that Wildridge and Sinclair Heat Pumps were required to be installed. It would follow that the pumps could be taken to have the capacity attributed to them. I acknowledge that the fact two subcontractors submitted tenders including different kinds of heat pumps might suggest that tenderers did not consider themselves bound by the specification to provide Wildridge and Sinclair Heat Pumps. But it is to be borne in mind that, in George Mechanical's case, the other heat pumps were put forward as an 'alternative' to what was stated in the specification and that, in both cases, the alternative pumps were less expensive. Safeguarding a bid by submitting the lowest possible price, although not necessarily in the terms of the specification, is an understandable response from tenderers who wish to avoid the risk of being undercut by a more competitive price.

[91] Fifthly, Turton had little time within which to put the tender together. It received the tender in late July 1997. In accordance with the Hospital Board's requirements, it submitted its tender on 10 September 1987, some one-and-a-half months later. Realistically, Turton did not have time to do other than rely on what was stated in the specification.

[92] Turton's subcontractors faced the same or even more severe time limitation. Any impression that all that was required of them to investigate the accuracy of the specification was to communicate with the supplier and confirm the output of the nominated pumps should be laid to rest. Certainly, it is all that George Mechanical, or any other

subcontractor, could realistically have done. But Kerslake's position as the consulting engineer was quite different. In the first place, it is not known whether the supplier in fact made any claim relating to the output of the Wildridge and Sinclair heat pumps. As the stipulated output is intrinsically related to the installation of the specified componentry, it is probably unsafe to think of the heat pumps as a 'shelf item' having that output. Secondly, it was Kerslake, and not the subcontractors, who had the time and opportunity to investigate the accuracy of any claims made for the heat pumps by the supplier. Kerslake was responsible for the system utilising the temperature of the adjacent lake water and would obviously need to ensure that the specified heat pumps installed with the componentry which it had decided upon would perform as required. Its novel system was at stake. In the course of preparing the specification it would need to check the accuracy of any claims made by the supplier and confirm that the heat pumps with the specified componentry would meet the requisite output.

[93] Finally, the evidence at trial confirmed the fact that Turton relied on the specification and that it was reasonable for it to do so. Mr Turton's evidence is the only direct evidence on the point. He explained how the tender relating to the mechanical services was assembled. He described the specification for the heat pumps as a 'nominated specific subcontractor package'. In such cases, he said, he or his company would 'flick' through the specifications to see if there was anything relevant to pass on to the prospective mechanical services subcontractors. When specifically asked whether he would rely upon the skill and expertise of the subcontractors for that part of the contract, he said that his company relied on them to put a tender together but that they in turn relied upon the specification.

[94] Mr Turton was also asked to confirm that his company had not supplied heat pumps in terms of the level of performance specified in the specification. He agreed that it had not, but at once added that his company could not be held responsible for the mistake made by the consulting engineers in the design part of the contract. Mr Turton testified that Kerslake had the responsibility of ensuring that its design would produce what was required. It was not his company's responsibility to assume the risk of performance. In fact, neither of Turton's mechanical engineering subcontractors made any inquiry as to the performance level tending to confirm that they too relied upon Kerslake's specification.

[95] Twice Mr Turton affirmed that his company had limited freedom in supplying, installing and commissioning the various parts of the specification plant as the specification had been written in such a manner as to specify major parts and parameters. There was some freedom in determining how to put the componentry together but not enough to affect the overall performance of the pumps ...

The contractual matrix

[102] The substantial reason given in the Court below for rejecting Turton's claim was that the contractual structure or matrix made the imposition of a duty of care between the consulting engineers and the contractor inappropriate. The Judge considered that the significant feature of the case was the 'contractual nexus' between the various parties. Turton's contract was with the Hospital Board, the Hospital Board had a contract with the architects, and the architects had a subcontract with Kerslake to prepare the

mechanical engineering specification for the mechanical engineering work. Turton had a subcontract with George Mechanical, who in turn had a subcontract with Wildridge and Sinclair Ltd, who in turn had a subcontract with the supplier of some of the component parts. The various parties had chosen to regulate their relationship through this quite intricate contractual arrangement.

[103] I cannot accept this argument for a number of reasons.

[104] First, the principle of concurrent liability in contract and tort must be applied. Unless it is negated by the contract, the tortious duty remains intact and may be sued upon. The notion that once a contract or a contractual structure is in place the contract or structure must prevail is essentially contrary to the principle of concurrent liability. As was observed in *Rowlands v Collow* [1992] 1 NZLR 178, at 190, the main impediment to the acceptance of concurrent liability has been the lawyer's deep-rooted but misplaced deference to the primacy of contract. This deference expanded in the mid-nineteenth century when the classical theory of contract took hold. Yet, the common law had thrived for several centuries without the courts realising that there was such a thing as the law of contract at all and then, when its existence became clear, without being self-conscious about divisions and categories in the field of civil liability. Rigidity in classification came later as the concept of freedom of contract developed and the dominance of the parties' intention was accepted. The introduction of formalistic requirements which were intended to narrow the scope of contractual liability assisted this development. In a sense, contract had appropriated an enclave of civil liability within the general domain of tort, but within its bounds it was an enclave which was presumed by generations of judges, lawyers and academics as being dominant and exclusive. Just as this deference eventually had to yield to the notion that the existence of a contract did not exclude tortious liability in the absence of a negation of such liability, so too, any lingering deference must yield to the logical corollary that the existence of a contractual structure or matrix does not exclude tortious liability.

[105] This logical corollary was accepted by this Court in *Price Waterhouse v Kwan* (2000) 6 NZBLC 102,945. Counsel's argument that the chain of contracts between client and solicitor, and then between solicitor and auditor, precluded the client from suing the auditor in tort was rejected. Tipping J had this to say (at para 17):

> It is desirable to address first Mr Camp's contention that the parties should be left to their claims in contract. This would mean that the clients could not sue *Price Waterhouse* because it is common ground there was no contract between them. The chain of contract was between client and solicitor, and then between solicitor and auditor. The proposition that only contractual relationships should be recognised in present circumstances seems to us to hark back to the days when it was thought that when there was a contract there could be no concurrent liability in tort. That stance has been firmly rejected in England and elsewhere: see the decision of the House of Lords in ... *Merrett Syndicates* ... The decision of this Court in *McLaren Maycroft* ... might be thought to have some lingering effect precluding concurrent liability in tort and contract in New Zealand. That decision can now, however, safely be regarded as having been overtaken by later developments. It can no

longer be taken as representing the law in New Zealand. The consequence is that a solicitor's client can sue the solicitor in both contract and tort, the latter subject to any relevant contractual restraints or limitations. The client is not confined to suing the solicitor in contract when a concurrent cause of action is available in tort. Thus the exclusively contractual chain for which Mr Camp contended breaks down at the outset.

...

[106] Secondly, the argument that the contractual arrangement 'regulates' the rights and obligations of the parties cannot apply in this case. While the Hospital Board and Turton have sought to regulate their relationship, they have not sought to regulate the relationship of the tenderers to the architects and mechanical engineers. The notion that all parties will go either up or down each leg of the contractual chain until combat is joined between the Hospital Board and the contractor can only achieve acceptance by way of an arbitrary implication of law. But, in effect, the argument that the parties have regulated the position by contract beggars the question. It is not until the Court has decided that, because of the contractual matrix, at least one of the elements of *Hedley Byrne* has not been made out thereby precluding any liability in tort, that the contract can be said to be the sole means of regulating their relationship.

[107] Thirdly, a person who is outside the contractual structure or matrix may suffer loss from a negligent misstatement in the specification. An unsuccessful tenderer, for example, may tender a bid in reliance on the specification provided by the owner and suffer damage as a result. In such circumstances, there can be no logical reason why the unsuccessful tenderer could not sue in tort providing he or she can make out the elements of assumption of responsibility and reliance. The contractual matrix cannot then avail the engineer responsible for the specification. It is anomalous that a person outside the contractual structure, such as an unsuccessful tenderer, would have a cause of action in tort but not the tenderer who was successful. Indeed, it is worse than anomalous, it is illogical, and as Lord Devlin said: 'The common law is tolerant of much illogicality, especially on the surface; but no system of law can be workable if it has not got logic at the root of it' (*Hedley Byrne*, supra, at 516).

[108] Fourthly, the contractual matrix argument ignores the ever-present possibility of insolvencies. It presumes that if A has contracted with B, and B becomes insolvent, that is A's bad luck—even though in entering into the contract A may have relied on the negligent misstatement of C with whom he or she has no contract. Thus, if A contracts with B, and B contracts with C, and C contracts with D, and D contracts with E—as is very much the case here—and D becomes insolvent, A may recover in contract against B, and B can then recover in contract against C, but C cannot then recover in contract against D who is insolvent. E, who may still be solvent and ultimately responsible, will remain untouched. The parties cannot be thought to have ignored the random consequences of insolvency and implicitly accepted that their rights are prescribed by the contractual matrix. Insolvency is a fact of life. It is highly probable that someone in a contractual chain involving multiple parties will founder. Indeed, in this case, a number of companies involved in the construction of the hospital went into liquidation. As a means of allocating risk (other than for the purpose of

excluding liability where there is a direct contract) and determining where any loss incurred in the course of construction will fall, the contractual matrix concept comes close to being a fiction. Losses may be borne by parties to whom the risk has not been allocated under the contractual matrix simply because a party in the contractual chain has gone into liquidation. If that party would otherwise have a good cause of action in tort there is no sound reason why that party should not be able to pursue it simply because contractual recourse is improvident.

[109] For the above reasons I am not prepared to accept that the contractual structure or matrix precludes Kerslake being liable to Turton on the basis of the cause of action founded in *Hedley Byrne*.

Policy considerations

[**Note**: His Honour then reviewed the policy argument that contract ought to prevail over tort and then continued.]

...

[124] In the first place, as is to be expected, this point of view gained prevalence long before concurrent liability in contract and tort became the law of the land ...

[125] In the second place, the above argument is directed at the 'imposition of tort duties that cut across ... contractual lines'. Worded generally in this manner it may be easier to reach the conclusion that the terms of a contract or the effect of a contractual matrix negate a duty of care. The opposite conclusion, however, may also be reached by reference to the contract or contractual matrix. When the inquiry is focused on the criteria in *Hedley Byrne* the contractual matrix may more readily be perceived as, in fact, giving rise to the circumstances which create the special relationship as the basis of liability.

[126] In the third place, any express negation of liability as between the owner and the contractor cannot assist the owner's engineer. By virtue of the terms of the contract the owner may have effectively distanced itself from the contractor. It may even have excluded tortious liability. But this express contractual negation of liability cannot operate to distance the engineer from the contractor. Their relationship remains direct in that the contractor looks to the plans and specifications prepared by the engineer specifically for the purpose of defining the work which is to be carried out ...

[127] Finally, and fundamentally, the argument ignores the commercial realities of the tendering process. It is in this respect that Canadian jurisprudence has made a major contribution. The old attitude which prevailed in England is illustrated by Lord Chelmsford's opinion in *Thorn*'s case in 1876, supra, that it is only reasonable to expect proper investigation of the plans and specifications by the contractor. The Law Lord said (at 133):

> If the plaintiff had considered, as he was bound to do, the terms of the specification, he would either have abstained from tendering for the work, or he would have asked the Defendants to protect him from the loss he was likely to sustain if the plan of working described in the specification should turn out to be an improper one.

[128] It is entirely unrealistic today to suggest that a tenderer should either not tender or ask the owner to protect him or her from possible loss. To hold that a building

contractor should decide not to put in a tender because of one specification (or one clause in one specification) in one subcontract in a multi-million dollar construction deal is patently unreal. If, instead, the contractor tendered on the basis that the owner would indemnify him or her against possible loss or sought an assurance to that effect, they would be quickly dismissed. At most, the tenderer (if required to check the specification) would draw attention to the discrepancy. But even this precaution could lose the tenderer the chance of being accepted as the successful contractor, at least if it were not accompanied by a tender in accordance with the consulting engineer's terms.

[129] The limitation of time inherent in the tendering process must also be acknowledged. Such is the short time between calling for tenders and the receipt of tenders that it is impractical for tenderers and their subcontractors to carry out a full analysis and investigation. Of necessity they often have no option but to rely upon the specifications. The owner's engineers will have had considerable time to carry out their own investigation and prepare the plans and specifications. They are also likely to be in possession of data and information which the tenderers will have neither the time nor the opportunity to process. Of necessity, they are not in as good a position as the engineers to carry out the extensive research which is required.

[130] Nor, having regard to the fiercely competitive nature of tendering, is it likely that the tenderer will be able to allow for possible defects in the plans or specifications in pricing the work. Then, even if, in the limited time available, it is possible for the tenderer to reinvestigate or rework the engineer's specification, it is possible that the defect will not be detected. The tenderer or its subcontractors are qualified, but their qualifications will be utilised to progress the task of carrying out the work as specified
...

[133] ... What is undeniable is that in many cases it will be unrealistic to expect a tenderer not to tender if he or she is of the view that a representation in a specification is suspect. It is also undeniable that in many cases it will be impractical for the tenderer to carry out the requisite investigation to fault a specification which it has taken the consulting engineer many months to prepare and complete. So it is in this case. It would be unrealistic to have expected Turton not to have submitted a tender for the building contract worth $5.9 million because of one item in one subcontract. It would also have been impractical for Turton, in the time available, to have reinvestigated all the engineer's specifications in all the engineering subcontracts which form part of the building contract. Kerslake's expertise was the very reason it was engaged and, if it has been negligent, it would seem both sensible and just that it should accept financial responsibility for its defective specification.

A matter of approach

[134] Since writing the above judgment I have received and perused the outstanding judgment in draft of Henry and Keith JJ. The difference between us is essentially one of approach. I have asked whether, the elements of liability under *Hedley Byrne* having been made out, the contractual matrix precludes a consultant engineer being liable to a contractor for negligent misstatement. Henry and Keith JJ have asked whether, having regard to that matrix, the consulting engineer owes a duty of care to the contractor. In my view, both approaches should result in the same answer.

[135] Henry and Keith JJ and myself accept that a contract or contractual matrix may militate against a duty of care. There is no question but that a contract may negate liability in tort. But the inquiry whether the consulting engineer has assumed responsibility to the contractor for a statement which the contractor then relied upon for the purposes of *Hedley Byrne* is effectively the question whether the parties are in sufficient proximity to each other for a duty of care to arise. As I said above … questions of proximity and foreseeability are subsumed in the questions posed by *Hedley Byrne*: whether a person possessed of special skills has assumed responsibility for his or her statement and is able to perceive that the recipient may reasonably rely upon it. If the answer to that question is in the affirmative, the question is then whether there is anything in the contract or contractual matrix which negates or is inconsistent with that liability. It is not good enough to say that, because of the contractual matrix, no duty of care arises but fail to reconcile this conclusion with the fact that the consulting engineer has assumed responsibility to the contractor for his statement and that the contractor has relied upon it …

Chapter 5
Land-based Torts

Trespass to land

Introduction

English law provides very strong protection against intentional incursions onto a person's land. Traditionally, this was to ensure that a person who had possessory rights in land did not have them eroded or removed by someone who simply assumed occupation. The person with stronger possessory interests could have the other ejected with reasonable ease by a writ of disseisin. Any incursion onto land was a potential threat to possessory interests and could be protected by an action in trespass to land. It acted therefore as a protection for the financial and other benefits that land ownership or tenancy could offer.

The strength of this protection continues today. Trespass is still actionable per se: no damage needs to be proved. However, its most interesting developments arguably focus more on protecting a person's ability to be left alone in a zone which can be called his or her own than on protection of possession as such. That is, trespass has come to be used as a way of protecting a person's privacy. That was always one aspect of the action, as *Entick v Carrington* illustrates. However, recent developments in the field of implied licence have been particularly interesting on this point. The law has always accepted that there will be instances where an incursion onto someone's land is properly authorised or acceptable in the circumstances. And unintentional entries onto land do not attract liability, originally at least, because they are often indirect and would therefore traditionally raise an action on the case rather than attract a writ of trespass. But the area of implied authorisation is open to much more varied argument than whether a warrant was properly issued or not. When is it acceptable, within the bounds of social convention, to enter a person's property? When is a licence revoked? When reading these cases, consider what the law is attempting to do here. Protect the plaintiff's property? His or her privacy? Punish the defendant for high-handed behaviour?

Entick v Carrington

(1765) 19 ST TR 1030; 95 ER 807 (CP)

[**FACTS**: This was an action of trespass for breaking and entering the plaintiff's house and seizing his papers. The defendants, who were King's Messengers, pleaded that they had a warrant from the Secretary of State that ordered them to search for the plaintiff and bring him, together with his books and papers, to safe custody. The jury found a special verdict and assessed the damages (if any) at £300.]

Lord Camden CJ:

... I come in my last place to the point, which is made by the justification; for the defendants ... are under a necessity to maintain the legality of the warrants, under which they have acted, and to shew that the Secretary of State, in the instance now before us, had a jurisdiction to seize the defendants' papers. If he had no such jurisdiction, the law is clear, that the officers are as much responsible for the trespass as their superior ...

This power, so claimed by the Secretary of State, is not supported by one single citation from any law book extant. It is claimed by no other magistrate in the kingdom but himself ...

The arguments, which the defendants' counsel have thought fit to urge in support of this practice are of this kind.

That such warrants have issued frequently since the Revolution ...

They say too, that they have been executed without resistance upon many printers, booksellers, and authors, who have quietly submitted to the authority; that no action hath hitherto been brought to try the right; and ... no court of justice has ever declared them illegal.

And it is further insisted, that this power is essential to government, and the only means of quieting clamours and sedition ...

Before I state the question, it will be necessary to describe the power claimed by this warrant in its full extent. If honestly exerted, it is a power to seize that man's papers, who is charged upon oath to be the author or publisher of a seditious libel; if oppressively, it acts against every man, who is so described in the warrant, though he be innocent. It is executed against the party, before he is heard or even summoned; and the information, as well as the informers, is unknown ... If this injury falls upon an innocent person, he is as destitute of remedy as the guilty: and the whole transaction is so guarded against discovery, that if the officer should be disposed to carry off a bank-bill, he may do it with impunity, since there is no man capable of proving either the taker or the thing taken ...

Nor is there pretence to say, that the word 'papers' here mentioned ought in point of law to be restrained to the libellous papers only. The word is general, and there is nothing in the warrant to confine it; nay, I am able to affirm, that it has been upon a late occasion executed in its utmost latitude: for in the case of *Wilkes v Wood*, when the messengers hesitated about taking all the manuscripts, and sent to the Secretary of State for more express orders for that purpose, the answer was, 'that all must be taken, manuscripts and all'. Accordingly, all was taken, and Mr Wilkes' private pocket-book filled up the mouth of the sack ...

Such is the power, and therefore one should naturally expect that the law to warrant it should be clear in proportion as the power is exorbitant.

If it is law, it will be found in our books. If it is not to be found there, it is not law.

The great end, for which men entered into society, was to secure their property. That right is preserved sacred and incommunicable in all instances, where it has not been taken away or abridged by some public law for the good of the whole. The cases where this right of property is set aside by positive law, are various. Distresses, executions, forfeitures, taxes, etc are all of this description; wherein every man by common consent gives up that right for the sake of justice and the general good.

By the laws of England, every invasion of private property, be it ever so minute, is a trespass. No man can set his foot upon my ground without my licence, but he is liable to an action, though the damage be nothing; which is proved by every declaration in trespass, where the defendant is called upon to answer for bruising the grass and even treading upon the soil. If he admits to the fact, he is bound to shew by way of justification, that some positive law has empowered or excused him. The justification is submitted to the judges, who are to look into the books; and see if such justification can be maintained by the text of the statute law, or by the principles of common law. If no such excuse can be found or produced, the silence of the books is an authority against the defendant, and the plaintiff must have judgment.

According to this reasoning, it is now incumbent upon the defendants to shew the law, by which this seizure is warranted. If that cannot be done, it is a trespass.

Papers are the owner's goods and chattels: they are his dearest property and are so far from enduring a seizure, that they will hardly bear an inspection and though the eye cannot by the laws of England be guilty of a trespass, where private papers are removed and carried away, the secret nature of those goods will be an aggravation of the trespass, and demand more considerable damages in that respect. Where is the written law that gives any magistrate such a power? I can safely answer, there is none; and therefore it is too much for us without such authority to pronounce a practice legal, which would be subversive of all the comforts of society.

... What would the Parliament say, if the judges should take it upon themselves to mould an unlawful power into a convenient authority, by new restrictions? That would be, not judgment, but legislation.

I come now to the practice since the Revolution, which has been strongly urged, with this emphatical addition, that an usage tolerated from the aera of liberty, and continued downwards to this time through the best ages of the constitution, must necessarily have a legal commencement ...

If the practice began then, it began too late to be law now. If it was more ancient, the Revolution is not to answer for it; and I could have wished, that upon this occasion the Revolution had not been considered as the only basis of our liberty.

With respect to the practice itself, if it goes no higher, every lawyer will tell you, it is much too modern to be evidence of the common law; and if it should be added, that these warrants ought to acquire some strength by the silence of those Courts, which have heard them read so often upon returns without censure or animadversion, I am able to borrow my answer to that pretence from the Court of King's Bench, which lately declared with great unanimity in the *Case of General Warrants*, that as no objection was taken to them upon the returns, and the matter passed *sub silentio*, the precedents were of no weight. I most heartily concur in that opinion …

To search, seize, and carry away all the papers of the subject upon the first warrant: that such a right should have existed from the time whereof the memory of man runneth not to the contrary, and never yet have found a place in any book of law; is incredible. But if so strange a thing could be supposed, I do not see how we could declare the law upon such evidence.

But still it is insisted, that there has been a general submission, and no action brought to try the right. I answer, there has been a submission of guilt and poverty to power and the terror of punishment. But it would be strange doctrine to assert that all the people of this land are bound to acknowledge that to be universal law, which a few criminal booksellers have been afraid to dispute.

… As therefore no authority in our books can be produced to support such a doctrine … I cannot be persuaded, that such a power can be justified by the common law.

I have now done with the argument, which has endeavoured to support this warrant by the practice since the Revolution. It is then said, that it is necessary for the ends of government to lodge such a power with a state officer; and that it is better to prevent the publication before than to punish the offender afterwards. I answer, if the legislature be of that opinion, they will revive the Licensing Act. But if they have not done that, I conceive they are not of that opinion. And with respect to the argument of state necessity, or a distinction that has been aimed at between State officers and others, the common law does not understand that kind of reasoning, nor do our books take notice of any such distinctions.

Serjeant Ashley was committed to the Tower in the 3rd [year] of Charles 1st, by the House of Lords only for asserting in argument, that there was a 'law of State' different from the common law; and the Ship-Money judges were impeached for holding, first, that State-necessity would justify the raising of money without consent of parliament; and secondly, that the king was judge of that necessity.

If the king himself has no power to declare when the law ought to be violated for reason of State, I am sure we his judges have no such prerogative.

Lastly, it is urged as an argument of utility, that such a search is a means of detecting offenders by discovering evidence …

In the criminal law such a proceeding was never heard of; and yet there are some crimes, such for instance as murder, rape, robbery, and house-breaking, to say nothing of forgery and perjury, that are more atrocious than libelling. But our law has provided no paper-search in these cases to help forward the conviction …

If, however, a right of search for the sake of discovering evidence ought in any case to be allowed, this crime above all others ought to be excepted, as wanting such a discovery less than any other. It is committed in open daylight, and in the face of the world; every act of publication makes new proof; and the solicitor of the treasury, if he pleases, may be the witness himself …

I have now taken notice of everything that has been urged upon the present point; and upon the whole we are all of opinion, that the warrant to seize and carry away the party's papers in the case of a seditious libel, is illegal and void.

The New Zealand Bill of Rights Act recognises the constitutional importance of freedom from unreasonable search and seizure.

21. Unreasonable search and seizure—

Everyone has the right to be secure against unreasonable search or seizure, whether of the person, property, or correspondence or otherwise.

Davies v Bennison

(1927) 22 Tasmania LR 52 (SC of Tas)

Nicholls CJ:

The relevant facts in this case are that the defendant, while in his own yard, fired a bullet from a small-bore rifle at, and killed, the plaintiff's cat, which was upon the roof of a shed in her yard.

The plaintiff claimed to be entitled to damages:

1 For illness caused by fright and shock, resulting from the firing of the bullet close to her.

2 For the value of the cat and for illness resulting from the fright and shock of seeing it killed before her eyes.

3 For trespass by firing the bullet into her land.

The defendant paid £2 into Court, as covering the value of the cat, but contended that he had committed no trespass to plaintiff's land and that the damage from the shock, etc, was too remote to be recoverable, even if proved.

The case was left by me to the jury to say:

1 Whether the amount paid in was sufficient as damages for the killing of the cat.

2 Whether they found that plaintiff's illness was the result of the firing of the bullet, and, if it was, then to assess damages subject to a reserved non-suit point.

3 To assess damages for the trespass to land.

The jury found for the defendant on all the issues, evidently not realising that they had been directed to assess damages for the trespass to the land.

This is an application for a new trial as to:

1 The issue of trespass to land, upon the ground that the jury ignored the direction given from the bench.

2 As to damages for shock, etc, upon the ground that the verdict was against the weight of evidence.

I left the whole of this latter matter to the jury, reserving defendant's application for a non-suit. The burden of proof was upon the plaintiff. There seemed to me to be little doubt that the illness of the plaintiff was caused by anger and agitation (at seeing her cat killed in her own yard) increasing an already disturbed condition of health, consisting of neurasthenia and long-standing gastric trouble. Shock caused by seeing an injury occur to another human being is in law considered too remote from the original wrongful act of the defendant causing the injury to be a ground for damages, and it seems to me to be quite clear that a pet animal, however cherished, cannot be regarded as nearer and dearer than a child or other loved relative.

I do not think that there are grounds for a new trial on this issue.

The question of trespass to land is much more difficult. If it was a trespass, then it was committed in circumstances and in a manner which aggravated it. It is curious that the law as to trespass by missiles which do not touch the ground never has been authoritatively laid down in England nor (as far as I can discover) in the United States of America.

I have to make an original decision.

Trespass is actionable without pecuniary damage being proved, so that if this is a trespass it could be the subject of substantial damages if a jury were to take a serious view of the circumstances of aggravation.

Trespass is a breach of the negative duty, incumbent upon all, not to interfere directly and illegally with ownership.

Ownership, whether permanent or temporary, is a right *in rem*, a right to use, deal with and enjoy the thing owned to an indefinite and almost unlimited extent.

The ownership of land, part of the earth's surface, is necessarily different from that of moveables, and is generally described by the application of the maxim *Cujus est solum ejus est usque ad coelum.*

A man who walks from his roof on to that of his neighbour is clearly guilty of trespass. The neighbour's house is part of his freehold. But when the intrusion consists of sending something such as a balloon, a bird, a kite, or a missile over another's land without touching it or anything built or growing upon it important fundamental and subtle questions arise. The only direct dictum upon the point is that of Lord Ellenborough in *Pickering v Rudd*, 4 Campbell 219. Lord Ellenborough says: 'I do not think it is a trespass to interfere with the column of air superincumbent on the close. I once had occasion to rule upon the circuit, that a man who, from the outside of a field, discharged a gun into it, so as that the shot must have struck the soil, was guilty of breaking and entering it. A very learned judge, who went the circuit with me, at first doubted the decision, but I believe he afterwards approved of it, and that it met with the general concurrence of those to whom it was mentioned. But I am by no means prepared to say, that firing across a field *in vacuo*, no part of the contents touching it, amounts to a *clausum fregit*. Nay, if this board overhanging the plaintiff's garden be a trespass, it would follow that an aeronaut is liable to an action of trespass *quare clausum fregit*, at the suit of the occupier of every field over which his balloon passes in the course of his voyage. Whether the action can be maintained cannot depend upon the length of time for which the superincumbent air is invaded'.

Of this dictum, that great lawyer Lord Blackburn said, in *Kenyon v Hart*, [6 B & S 249]: 'I understand the good sense of that doubt, though not the legal reason of it', and Sir Frederick Pollock, whose every word on the law of Torts is valuable, says (8th edn, p 347):

> It has been doubted whether it is a trespass to pass over land without touching the soil, as one may in a balloon, or to cause a material object, as shot fired from a gun, to pass over it. Lord Ellenborough thought it was not in itself a trespass 'to interfere with the column of air superincumbent on the close', and that the remedy would be by action on the case for any actual damage: though he had no difficulty in holding that a man is a trespasser who fires a gun on his own land so that the shot fall on his neighbour's land. Fifty years later Lord Blackburn inclined to think differently, and his opinion seems the better.

Clearly there can be wrongful entry on land below the surface, as by mining, and in fact this kind of trespass is rather prominent in our modern books. It does not seem possible on the principles of the common law to assign any reason why any entry above the surface should not also be a trespass, unless indeed it can be said that the scope of possible trespass is limited by that of effective possession, which might be the most reasonable rule. Clearly, it would be a trespass to sail over another man's land in a balloon (much more in a controllable airship) at a level within the height of ordinary buildings, and it might be a nuisance to keep a balloon hovering over the land even at a greater height. As regards shooting, it would be strange if we could object to shots being fired point blank across our land only in the event of actual injury being caused, the passage of the foreign body in the air above our soil being thus a mere incident in a distinct trespass to person or property. But the projectiles of modern artillery, when fired from extreme range, have attained in the course of their trajectory, as is computed, an altitude exceeding that of Mont Blanc or even Elbruz. It may remain in doubt whether the passage of a projectile at such a height could in itself be a trespass.

It seems an absurdity to say that if I fire at another's animal on his land, hit it, kill it, and so leave the bullet in it, I have committed no trespass, and yet, if I miss the animal and so let the bullet fall into the ground, have committed a trespass. Such distinctions have no place in the science of the Common Law.

If the hovering aeroplane is perfected the logical outcome of Lord Ellenborough's dictum would be that a man might hover as long as he pleased at a yard, or a foot, or an inch, above his neighbour's soil, and not be a trespasser, yet if he should touch it for one second he would be.

A man has the undoubted right to build a high tower on his land, and the space above the land is exclusively his for that purpose. Then why not for any other legal purpose? It seems to me that the only real difficulty is in saying (what I need not say here), viz, how far the rights of a landowner *ad coelum* will have to be reduced to permit the free use of beneficial inventions, such as flying machines, etc.

So far as the ability to use land, and the air above it, exists, mechanically speaking, to my mind any intrusion above land is a direct physical breach of the negative duty not to interfere with the owner's use of his land, and is in principle a trespass. At any rate, I can see no doubt whatever that an owner's rights extend to a height sufficient to cover the facts of this case. In my opinion the direction was right and damages for the trespass should have been and must be assessed. There will have to be a new trial on this issue.

Bernstein of Leigh (Baron) v Skyviews & General Ltd
[1985] 1 QB 479 (HC)

[**FACTS**: The defendant company took aerial photographs of property in order to offer them for sale to the property owners. Lord Bernstein's property was photographed on 3 August 1974. When he received a letter inviting him to buy the photograph, he took serious offence and said so in a letter. Unfortunately, the company's managing director was away. The staff member who dealt with the matter answered Lord Bernstein's letter by offering to sell him the negative. This made matters considerably worse. Lord Bernstein sued the company for trespass to land, citing the defendant's actions as an invasion of his privacy.

Griffiths J found that it was highly likely that at some stage the defendant's aircraft had flown over the boundary of Lord Bernstein's property, and so had passed above his land, albeit several hundred feet up.]

Griffiths J:

... I turn now to the law. The plaintiff claims that as owner of the land he is also owner of the air space above the land, or at least has the right to exclude any entry into the air space above his land. He relies upon the old Latin maxim, *cujus est solum ejus est usque ad coelum et ad inferos*, a colourful phrase often upon the lips of lawyers since it was first coined by Accursius in Bologna in the thirteenth century. There are a number of cases in which the maxim has been used by English judges, but an examination of those cases shows that they have all been concerned with structures attached to the adjoining land, such as overhanging buildings, signs or telegraph wires, and for their solution it has not been necessary for the judge to cast his eyes towards the heavens; he has been concerned with the rights of the owner in the air space immediately adjacent to the surface of the land.

That an owner has certain rights in the air space above his land is well established by authority. He has the right to lop the branches of trees that may overhang his boundary, although this right seems to be founded in nuisance rather than trespass: see *Lemmon v Webb* [1894] 3 Ch 1. In *Wandsworth Board of Works v United Telephone Co Ltd* (1884) 13 QBD 904, the Court of Appeal did not doubt that the owner of land would have the right to cut a wire placed over his land. Fry LJ said, at p 927:

> As at present advised, I entertain no doubt that an ordinary proprietor of land can cut and remove a wire placed at any height above his freehold ...

Fry LJ added that the point was not necessary for his decision (it is therefore obiter), and I hasten to add that it would be subject to any statutory rights given to the post office and other undertakers to erect telegraph lines or other installations.

In *Gifford v Dent* [1926] WN 336, Romer J held that it was a trespass to erect a sign that projected 4 ft 8 ins over the plaintiff's forecourt and ordered it to be removed. He invoked the old maxim in his judgment; the report reads:

> ... the plaintiffs were tenants of the forecourt and were accordingly tenants of the space above the forecourt *usque ad coelum*, it seemed to him that the projection was clearly a trespass upon the property of the plaintiffs.

That decision was followed by McNair J in *Kelsen v Imperial Tobacco Co (of Great Britain and Ireland) Ltd* [1957] 2 QB 334, in which he granted a mandatory injunction ordering the defendants to remove a sign which projected only 8 ins over the plaintiff's property. The plaintiff relies strongly upon this case ...

... I very much doubt ... McNair J was intending to hold that the plaintiff's rights in the air space continued to an unlimited height or 'ad coelum' as Mr Gray submits. The point that the judge was considering was whether the sign was a trespass or a nuisance at the very low level at which it projected. This to my mind is clearly indicated by his reference to *Winfield on Tort*, 6th edn (1954) in which the text reads, at p 380: 'it is submitted that trespass will be committed by [aircraft] to the air space if they fly so low as to come within the area of ordinary use'. The author in that passage is careful to limit the trespass to the height at which it is contemplated an owner might be expected to make use of the air space as a natural incident of the user of his land. If, however, the judge was by his reference to the Civil Aviation Act 1949 and his disapproval of the views of Lord Ellenborough in *Pickering v Rudd* (1815) 4 Camp 219, indicating the opinion that the flight of an aircraft at whatever height constituted a trespass at common law, I must respectfully disagree.

I do not wish to cast any doubts upon the correctness of the decision upon its own particular facts. It may be a sound and practical rule to regard any incursion into the air space at a height which may interfere with the ordinary user of the land as a trespass rather than a nuisance. Adjoining owners then know where they stand; they have no right to erect structures overhanging or passing over their neighbours' land and there is no room for argument whether they are thereby causing damage or annoyance to their neighbours about which there may be much room for argument and uncertainty. But wholly different considerations arise when considering the passage of aircraft at a height which in no way affects the user of the land.

There is no direct authority on this question, but as long ago as 1815 Lord Ellenborough in *Pickering v Rudd* expressed the view that it would not be a trespass to pass over a man's land in a balloon; and in *Saunders v Smith* (1838) 2 Jur 491, Shadwell VC said, at p 492:

> Thus, upon the maxim of law, *Cujus est solum ejus est usque ad coelum*, an injunction might be granted for cutting timber and severing crops; but, suppose a person should apply to restrain an aerial wrong, as by sailing over a person's freehold in a balloon; this surely would be too contemptible to be taken notice of.

...

I can find no support in authority for the view that a landowner's rights in the air space above his property extend to an unlimited height. In *Wandsworth Board of Works v United Telephone Co Ltd*, 13 QBD 904 Bowen LJ described the maxim, *usque ad coelum*, as a fanciful phrase, to which I would add that if applied literally it is a fanciful notion leading to the absurdity of a trespass at common law being committed by a satellite every time it passes over a suburban garden. The academic writers speak with one voice in rejecting the uncritical and literal application of the maxim ... I accept their collective approach as correct. The problem is to balance the rights of an owner to enjoy the use of his land against the rights of the general public to take advantage of all that science now offers in the use of air space. This balance is in my judgment best struck in our present society by restricting the rights of an owner in the air space above his land to such height as is necessary for the ordinary use and enjoyment of his land and the structures upon it, and declaring that above that height he has no greater rights in the air space than any other member of the public.

Applying this test to the facts of this case, I find that the defendants' aircraft did not infringe any rights in the plaintiff's air space, and thus no trespass was committed. It was on any view of the evidence flying many hundreds of feet above the ground and it is not suggested that by its mere presence in the air space it caused any interference with the use of his land but that a photograph was taken from it. There is, however, no law against taking a photograph, and the mere taking of a photograph cannot turn an act which is not a trespass into the plaintiff's air space into one that is a trespass.

[**Note**: The Judge then commented that had it been a trespass, Lord Bernstein's remedy would have been sterile; he could injunct the defendants against flying over the boundary, but could not prevent them from taking a virtually identical photograph without flying over the boundary. He then considered section 40 of the Civil Aviation Act 1949, and decided that it gave the plaintiff no further protection.]

...

For example, the section would give no protection against the deliberate emission of vast quantities of smoke that polluted the atmosphere and seriously interfered with the plaintiff's use and enjoyment of his property; such behaviour remains an actionable nuisance. Nor would I wish this judgment to be understood as deciding that in no circumstances could a successful action be brought against an aerial photographer to restrain his activities. The present action is not founded in nuisance for no court would regard the taking of a single photograph as an actionable nuisance. But if the circumstances were such that a plaintiff was subjected to the harassment of constant surveillance of his house from the air, accompanied by the photographing of his every activity, I am far from saying that the court would not regard such a monstrous invasion of his privacy as an actionable nuisance for which they would give relief ...

In New Zealand, the Civil Aviation Act 1990 (NZ) provides for nuisance, trespass, and responsibility for damage.

97. Nuisance, trespass, and responsibility for damage—

...

(2) No action shall lie in respect of trespass, or in respect of nuisance, by reason only of the flight of aircraft over any property at a height above the ground which having regard to wind, weather, and all the circumstances of the case is reasonable, so long as the provisions of this Act and of any rules made under this Act are duly complied with.

(3) Where material damage or loss is caused to property on land or water by an aircraft in flight, taking off, landing, or alighting, or by any person or article in or falling from any such aircraft, damages shall be recoverable from the owner of the aircraft, without proof of negligence or intention or other cause of action, as if the damage or loss was caused by his or her fault, except where the damage or loss was caused by or contributed to by the fault of the person by whom the same was suffered.

Robson v Hallett
[1967] 2 All ER 407 (CA)

[**FACTS**: Three police officers on duty received a call-out to Mr Robson's council house, where a misdemeanour had been reported. They did not expect to make an arrest at this time and were simply making enquiries. They had no warrant of any kind.

The officers walked through the garden gate and up the steps to the front door. They knocked. Thomas Robson, one of the tenant's sons, opened the door. He invited the Sergeant McCaffrey inside and took him into the living room, but told the two constables to stay in the garden, which they did. Mr Robson senior, the tenant, came into the living room and told the sergeant to leave, which he immediately tried to do. However, when he got to the front door, Thomas Robson jumped on his back and began punching him. The sergeant fell through the open doorway. The other officers came to his aid, whereupon they were pulled at by Mr Robson senior and then attacked by his other son, Dennis.

Dennis and Thomas Robson were convicted of several counts of assault on a police officer. The material convictions were upheld on appeal. This is the further appeal against those convictions. The principal ground of appeal was that the police officers were trespassing, and that the occupants of the house were entitled to use reasonable force to eject them from the premises. If the police officers were trespassing, they were not acting in the course of their duties.]

Lord Parker CJ:

What is said in this case, and this is really the foundation of counsel for the appellants' argument, is that all three police officers were trespassers *ab initio*; having arrived at the garden gate, although up till then they were acting in the execution of their duty, making inquiries into an offence committed that night, yet the moment when they set foot onto the steps leading up to the front door they were all three trespassers. For my part, it is no doubt true that the law is sometimes said to be an ass, but I am happy to think that it is not an ass in this respect, because I am quite satisfied that these three police officers, like any other members of the public, had implied leave and licence to walk through that gate up those steps and to knock on the door of the house. We are not considering for this purpose the entering of private premises in the form of a dwelling-house, but of the position between the gate and the front door. There, as it seems to me, the occupier of any dwelling-house gives implied licence to any member of the public coming on his lawful business to come through the gate, up the steps, and knock on the door of the house.

… Accordingly, in my judgment, all three police officers were lawfully on those premises while they were outside the house.

What happened then was … that Sgt McCaffrey was to enter the house by the permission of the occupier's son. It was not suggested that the occupier's son had no authority so to do, and, accordingly, when Sgt McCaffrey was in the house he was lawfully in the house and was still acting in the execution of his duty. What counsel for the appellants says in regard to Sgt McCaffrey is this, that the moment Mr Robson senior said, 'Get out' he at once became a trespasser and at once, *instanter*, ceased to be acting in the execution of his duty. That proposition, which I confess sounds remarkable, is based as I understand it on the last sentence in the judgment of Goddard J in *Davis v Lisle* [1936] 2 KB 434, 441], where he said: 'He had no right to be on the premises once he had been asked to leave'. In my judgment, it is quite wrong to read those words as words of a statute; they were in relation to a case where the police officer having been plainly told to leave, was remonstrating and asserting his right to stay. In the present case, Sgt McCaffrey was doing all he could to leave, and was not asserting any right to stay. It seems to me that, when a licence is revoked as a result of which something has to be done by the licensee, a reasonable time must be implied in which he can do so, in this case to get off the premises; no doubt it will be a very short time, but he was doing here his best to leave the premises. Looked at in a slightly different way, it is argued that he was acting in the execution of his duty up to the very moment when he was told to get out, and one asks oneself what he was doing when he was assaulted. He was surely carrying on his duty, which was a duty to get out.

... In regard to the two remaining assaults, those by the appellants Dennis and Thomas Robson on PC Paxton, counsel for the appellants' case is really based on the submission that the officers were throughout and remained trespassers. As I have already said, I think that they were lawfully on those premises when they entered them; they, as opposed to Sgt McCaffrey, had never been told to get out, their implied licence to be there had never been revoked, and, accordingly, there they were in this little garden seeing Sgt McCaffrey set on by the appellant Thomas Robson and a general melee developing. It seems to me quite impossible in those circumstances to say that they were not acting in the execution of their duty in coming to the assistance of Sgt McCaffrey, and also avoiding any further breach of the peace. It is really unnecessary to go further, but, even if they had been outside the gate, it seems to me that they would have had abundant right to come on to private property in those circumstances ...

Diplock LJ:

I agree. These appeals raise three simple points on the law of trespass on land which affect all members of the public as well as the police officers with whom this appeal is concerned. The points are so simple that the combined researches of counsel have not revealed any authority on them. There is no authority because no one has thought it plausible up till now to question them. The first is this, that when a householder lives in a dwelling-house to which there is a garden in front and does not lock the gate of the garden, it gives an implied licence to any member of the public who has lawful reason for doing so to proceed from the gate to the front door or back door, and to inquire whether he may be admitted and to conduct his lawful business. Such implied licence can be rebutted by express refusal of it, as in this case the Robsons could no doubt have rebutted the implied licence to the police officers by putting up a notice on their front gate 'No admittance to police officers'; but that was not done in this case. The second proposition is this, that when, having knocked at the front door of the dwelling-house, someone who is inside the dwelling-house invites the person who has knocked to come in, there is an implied authority in that person, which can be rebutted on behalf of the occupier of the dwelling-house, to invite him to come in and so licence [sic] him to come into the dwelling-house itself. In the present case, it was the son, the appellant, Thomas Robson, and not the father who was the occupier who invited Sgt McCaffrey to come in. In those circumstances, Sgt McCaffrey, whilst in the dwelling-house on the invitation of the son, was no trespasser. The licence, however, could be withdrawn by the father who was the person entitled to give it. He withdrew it and, on its being withdrawn, the sergeant had a reasonable time to leave the premises by the most appropriate route for doing so, namely, out of the front door, down the steps and out of the gate, and provided that he did so with reasonable expedition, he would not be a trespasser while he was so doing ...

As regards PC Paxton and PC Jobson, it does not seem to me to matter whether, when they were denied entrance at the front door, they were trespassers in remaining in the garden if they did remain in the garden after that, because there are two ways in which a person who enters land of another person may fail to be a trespasser. One is leave, and licence of the person entitled to possession, to which I have already referred; the other is in the exercise of an independent right to proceed on the land. In the case of PC Paxton and PC Jobson, once a breach of the peace was taking place under their eyes, they had not only an independent right but a duty to go and stop it, and it matters not from that moment onwards whether they started off on their journey to stop it from outside the premises or from inside the premises. They were entitled, once the breach of the peace occurred, to be on the premises for the purpose of preventing it or stopping it ...

Davidson v Toronto Blue Jays Baseball Ltd
(1999) 170 DLR 4th 559 (Ont Gen Div)
[**FACTS**: The plaintiff was a season ticket holder for two pairs of SkyClub seats in the 200 level. The SkyClub is, as its name suggests, a club available only to the premium SkyClub ticket holders in the SkyDome. An annual payment is made for the privilege of being a SkyClub member. For the 1995 season the annual fees were just over $800.00. Being a SkyClub member allows members access to three bars within the parameters of the SkyClub seats. A feature of membership is that SkyClub ticket holders have the right of first refusal for their SkyClub seats for all other SkyDome functions. Until 1995, access to the three SkyClub bars was limited to the SkyClub members. The plaintiff is also a member of the Founders Club. It too is a club used exclusively by its members. There are annual dues, and quarterly minimum food purchases. The membership of the SkyClub is distinct from that of the Founders Club.

On 28 April 1995, the plaintiff with a business associate and friend took the elevator to the Founders Club and had dinner. On the elevator the attendant did not ask for the plaintiff's ticket. Founders Club members may or may not have tickets to the ball game on a given evening. The baseball game started that evening at 7.35 pm. The plaintiff and his friend finished their dinner and watched the beginning of the ball game on the screen at the Founders Club.

To get to the 200 level where the plaintiff's seats were located, it is possible to take the stairs, or elevator. They chose to take the stairs. There is a turnstile, at the entrance to the SkyClub. It was the plaintiff's evidence, and it was not disputed, that approximately half of the time there would be a member of the Blue Jays personnel present to check tickets. On April 28, 1995 there were no Blue Jays personnel checking for tickets. The plaintiff and his friend therefore went to aisle 224 and proceeded to his seats without showing the tickets. The usherette did not ask to see the plaintiff's tickets while he was being seated.

At the 6th or 7th innings, the plaintiff and his friend went to the Home Plate Bar to have a cigarette. All of the SkyClub facilities, including the three bars, are serviced by MacDonald's [sic]. Upon exiting the Home Plate Bar, the plaintiff refused to show his ticket when requested to do so by a MacDonald's employee. This refusal gave rise to subsequent events terminating in the arrest of the plaintiff and his violent ejection from the premises.

The plaintiff was asked to leave the premises. He refused. Police were called. They pinned the plaintiff to the ground and pulled his hair in the course of escorting him off the premises.]

Wilson J:

The jury has answered questions and rendered a verdict in this matter in favour of the plaintiff, Michael Davidson. Based upon the answers to the questions asked, counsel concede that there were no reasonable and probable grounds for the plaintiff's arrest, which was made pursuant to Trespass to Property Act, RSO 1990, c T 21 (the 'Act'). This case raises a novel issue and a more fundamental question, however. Do the arrest provisions of the Act apply in the context of ticket holders with a licence to attend the premises? As this question has not been considered before, counsel asked me to provide reasons to clarify this question. In light of the jury's answers to the questions asked, however, these comments are obiter.

The plaintiff was arrested by three off-duty Metropolitan Toronto police officers while attending a Blue Jays game at the SkyDome on April 28, 1995. At the time of the arrest the plaintiff was told that he was arrested pursuant to the Act. The plaintiff alleges that the arrest was unlawful, and that the Blue Jays and the Metropolitan Toronto Police Board and the three named police officers involved (the Police) are liable for general, special, aggravated and punitive damages.

It was the plaintiff's alternative position that even if the arrest was lawful, the Police and the Blue Jays were liable for the excessive use of force in carrying out the arrest, and that the plaintiff was entitled to general, special, aggravated and punitive damages for the excessive force used.

…

The defendants rely upon sections 2 and 9 of the Act. If the plaintiff refused to show his ticket to any of the Blue Jay personnel, or to any of the Police, then it is the position of the Police that they had reasonable and probable grounds to believe that the plaintiff was a trespasser on the premises contrary to section 2(1)(b). Sections 2 and 9 provide:

> 2(1) Every person who is not acting under a right or authority conferred by law and who,
>> (a) without the express permission of the occupier, the proof of which rests on the defendant,
>>> (i) enters on premises when entry is prohibited under this Act; or
>>> (ii) engages in an activity on premises when the activity is prohibited under this Act; or
>> (b) does not leave the premises immediately after he or she is directed to do so by the occupier of the premises or a person authorised by the occupier,
>>> is guilty of an offence and on conviction is liable to a fine of not more than $2000.
>
> 9(1) A police officer, or the occupier of premises, or a person authorised by the occupier may arrest without warrant any person he or she believes on reasonable and probable grounds to be on the premises in contravention of section 2.

2) *Whether section 2 of the Act applies in this case given the contractual terms stipulated on the reverse side of the ticket and the relevant case law*

I raised the issue with counsel well into the trial whether section 2(1) of the Act, which defines the offence of trespass, applies to ticket cases, given the exclusionary language of the offence of trespass that it applies only to '[e]very person who is not acting under a right or authority conferred by law …'.

What is a ticket, and is it a right or authority conferred by law thereby excluding the applicability of the Act?

I turn to consider first the fine print of the contractual provisions on the reverse of the Blue Jays ticket. It provides:

> Notice and Agreement—This ticket is a personal, revocable licence, which cannot be replaced if destroyed, lost or stolen, and the holder agrees that the management may refuse admission or remove from the premises any person who has obtained admission by this ticket by refunding purchase price. Holder further agrees to observe all municipal, provincial and federal regulations and by-laws, and may be refused admission, or may be removed from the premises for failure to do so without compensation.

It is not disputed that the plaintiff was never offered, nor did he receive, a refund for the purchase price of his tickets. Further it is agreed that the plaintiff was not in breach of any municipal, provincial or federal regulation or by-law prior to his arrest. By the terms of the ticket itself, the plaintiff was at the baseball game with a personal, revocable licence to be present. In accordance with the contractual terms of the ticket there were no grounds to validly revoke the plaintiff's licence to attend the baseball game to its conclusion. It is the plaintiff's position that the contractual terms should be strictly construed against the Blue Jays whose counsel drafted the terms of the ticket.

The decision of *Hurst v Picture Theatres Ltd* [1915] 1 KB 1 (CA), confirms that the purchaser of a ticket for a seat at the theatre has the right to remain and attend the entire performance. The licence granted by the ticket includes a contract not to arbitrarily revoke the licence during a performance. The right to remain is subject to the implied contractual condition that the patron behaves properly, and complies with the rules of management. It appears clear that a ticket holder for a performance is 'acting under a right or authority conferred by law', and therefore *prima facie* the trespass provisions of the Act do not apply.

The *Hurst* decision has been adopted in Canada. In *Hurst* the plaintiff had purchased a ticket for the cinema, but was forcibly ejected by the manger, who erroneously believed that the plaintiff had not paid for his ticket. The jury awarded substantial damages for assault and false imprisonment. The jury award was upheld on appeal. The facts of *Hurst* are outlined at page 2 of the decision:

> [H]e went to that theatre on March 17, 1913, for the purpose of seeing it. At the pay office he tendered a florin and asked for a sixpenny seat, and was given a metal check and the change; the check entitled him to an unreserved seat. He gave up his check at the door leading into the theatre, and was shown into a seat by a young woman with an electric torch. After the performance had

proceeded for some little time, a girl came up and asked plaintiff if he had come in with a ticket, and, on his replying that he had, the girl went away. Shortly afterwards another girl came up and asked him to come out and see the manager, but he refused. Then a man in evening dress came up and asked him to come and see the manager, but he again refused. Then the manager himself came up and asked the plaintiff to go out, which he refused to do. The porter went out and returned with a policeman, whom he asked to put the plaintiff out. This the policeman refused to do, suggesting that the porter should do it himself. The porter then made his way into the row of seats and, taking hold of the plaintiff under the arms, lifted him out of his seat. The plaintiff then walked quietly out. No unnecessary violence was used in thus ejecting the plaintiff.

...

In the case at bar, there were no posted rules by the SkyDome or by the Blue Jays management. The programme, which may be purchased by those attending each game, contains the rules of fan conduct. The rules of fan conduct are common-sense courtesies to ensure the safety of the players and the fans alike. If these rules are intended to be enforceable with respect to all ticket holders, it would be appropriate to bring them to the attention of all the fans by making them clearly visible to all. In any event, there is nothing in the rules of fan conduct stipulating that fans must present their tickets upon demand once on the premises.

Prior to this incident there is no allegation that the plaintiff was misbehaving or not in compliance with the rules of management. He was simply enjoying the ball game with his friend. It is clear that the plaintiff was vocal and rude when he was requested to accompany the Blue Jays personnel and the police to discuss this incident. The plaintiff refused to leave his seat. The issue is who was responsible for escalating the situation—the plaintiff or the Blue Jays' personnel. I concur with the findings of the jury that it was unfortunate that the Blue Jays personnel escalated the situation to the point of unnecessary conflict culminating in the plaintiff's arrest.

I conclude after review of the terms of the ticket, and the relevant case law that the defendants are not entitled to revoke at will the licence granted to the plaintiff, and to treat the plaintiff as a trespasser after he refused to voluntarily leave the SkyDome. ...

Conclusions

1) Application of the Act to ticket holders

The Act does not apply in the context of ticket holders. Any arrest pursuant to the Act is therefore unlawful. The ticket is a personal revocable licence, and provides the holder a right or authority conferred by law to be present in the premises of the Sky-Dome. The licence may be revoked by management in accordance with the terms and conditions stipulated on the reverse side of each ticket. If the holder is in breach of any municipal, provincial or federal by-law or regulation he or she may be removed without compensation. In accordance with the common law, the ticket holder has a licence for value that is an enforceable right to attend the event in question until its conclusion, provided the ticket holder behaves properly and complies with the rules of management.

2) *Validity of the licence*

The defence argues that as the plaintiff had never presented his ticket, he was a trespasser, and the Act therefore applies. I do not accept this argument. I conclude that the plaintiff's licence was engaged, even though his ticket had not been inspected by Blue Jays personnel when he first entered the premises.

In the ordinary course all ticket holders for general admission tickets have their tickets inspected upon admission to the SkyDome. For those attending the Founders Club and the SkyClub seats, it appears that Blue Jays personnel are present to check tickets in approximately half of the time. If an usher or usherette does not check a holder's ticket upon admission to the section, there is no obligation of the holder to seek out the usher. The ticket holder may simply proceed to his assigned seat. It is the decision of the Blue Jays whether they post personnel to check ticket holders coming into the SkyClub from the Founders Club. Whether a holder's ticket has been inspected or not, it is still a valid personal revocable licence enforceable in accordance with its terms.

3) *Reasonable implied terms*

The final argument of the defence is that it is an implied contractual term of the ticket, that it must be presented on demand at any time during the game to a Blue Jays representative or its delegate (in this case an employee of MacDonald's). Failure to present the ticket on demand constitutes breach of the implied contractual term of the ticket, allowing management to revoke the licence, thereby rendering the ticket holder a trespasser.

I conclude that it is reasonable to imply the contractual term that the holder must present his ticket upon admission to the premises, and when he or she is being initially seated in a section. However, once the game begins, it is not reasonable to demand that tickets be shown at any time, unless there is evidence that the person had just arrived at the seat in question, or if there is a specific dispute about entitlement to a seat, where two patrons assert a right to the same seat.

Further, in the context of the SkyClub, it was an implied term in April 1995 that the holder be required to show his ticket to a MacDonald's employee upon exiting the Home Plate Bar. Since 1989, SkyClub members had enjoyed free movement within the SkyClub facilities without inspection of tickets. After 1995, the practice of inspecting tickets ceased. In the result, it was not an implied contractual term to inspect the ticket after exiting the Home Plate Bar. Nor was it an implied term for the Blue Jays personnel to request to see the plaintiff's ticket when he returned to his seat, without some reliable evidence that he was an interloper who had just arrived from another seating area.

[**Result**: The jury assessed damages for false arrest and imprisonment at:

a) General damages $35 000.00

b) Special damages $54.00

c) Aggravated damages $50 000.00

d) Punitive damages $125 000.00.]

Trespass Act 1980 (NZ)

3. Trespass after warning to leave—

(1) Every person commits an offence against the Act who trespasses on any place and, after being warned to leave that place by an occupier of that place, neglects or refuses to do so.

(2) It shall be a defence to a charge under subsection (1) of this section if the defendant proves that it was necessary for him to remain in or on the place concerned for his own protection or the protection of some other person, or because of some emergency involving his property or the property of some other person.

4. Trespass after warning to stay off—

(1) Where any person is trespassing or has trespassed on any place, an occupier of that place may, at the time of the trespass or within a reasonable time thereafter, warn him to stay off that place.

(2) Where an occupier of any place has reasonable cause to suspect that any person is likely to trespass on that place, he may warn that person to stay off that place.

(4) Subject to subsection (5) of this section, every person commits an offence against this Act who, being a person who has been warned under this section to stay off any place, wilfully trespasses on that place within 2 years after the giving of the warning.

(5) It shall be a defence to a charge under subsection (4) of this section if the defendant proves that—

    (a) The person by whom or on whose behalf the warning concerned was given is no longer an occupier of the place concerned; or

    (b) It was necessary for the defendant to commit the trespass for his own protection or for the protection of some other person, or because of some emergency involving his property or the property of some other person.

Lincoln Hunt Australia Pty Ltd v Willesee

(1986) 4 NSWLR 457 (NSW SC)

Young J:

At the end of the hearing yesterday I said that I was of the view that by entering the premises of the plaintiff with TV cameras the defendants, prima facie, committed a trespass, but that I was also of the view that damages were an adequate remedy and accordingly declined to grant an injunction and stood the matter over until this morning to give my reasons.

In many ways this is a most important piece of litigation to citizens at large and thus in many respects it is a pity that it is being dealt with very summarily on an application for interlocutory injunction, which had to be concluded within a limited time.

The factual material is relatively brief. For some time the plaintiff has been carrying on an investment scheme which would appear has attracted some dissatisfied customers. One of these customers had been in contact with the plaintiff and arrangements had been made for her to pick up a cheque at about 2.15 on the afternoon of 11 February. At 3 pm this lady called, together with other persons, some of whom were holding television equipment and one, a female, appeared to be a reporter. According to the evidence, which is not contradicted, the reporter continually harassed the persons who were on the premises and the cameramen not only took video tape of the lobby of the plaintiff's office, but also opened interior doors. The plaintiff says that it fears that if this video tape is shown on television it will be severely prejudiced in the goodwill of its business. The plaintiff has asked the defendants not to show the tape. The defendants have refused to undertake not to show it, hence this application for injunction.

...

The plaintiff seeks to restrain the publication of the tape on four bases. One, that the tape was taken whilst the defendant was trespassing ... It is a case of trespass because even though the defendants have acted by agents the evidence at this stage shows that the defendants commanded their agents to act in the way they did so that the matter is one of trespass and not just an action on the case: see *McCorquodale v Shell Oil of Australia Ltd* (1932) 33 SR (NSW) 151; 50 WN 77.

Trespass to land is committed whenever a person without excuse and without consent or invitation of a land holder enters that holder's property. In the instant case entry is not denied, at least at this stage, but it is said that such entry was by licence. The licence is said to have arisen because the plaintiff is a person carrying on a business in the city seeking customers, who is quite content for any member of the public to call on it during business hours to discuss business. It is said that the plaintiff would have welcomed the defendant's reporter or cameramen had they come in and asked to speak to one of its representatives about investment and it is asked why are things any different if those persons come with TV cameras and lights and a vocally dissatisfied customer.

The answer to this is found in recent decisions of the High Court of Australia as well as other cases of respectable pedigree. The High Court reviewed the authorities in *Halliday v Nevill* (1984) 155 CLR 1 at 7–8 and indicated that in this law of licence the law must not be seen to be an ass so as to make people first go to a householder to ask for permission to enter his or her land to retrieve a hat which had blown over a fence from a public street. Thus a commonsense attitude to entry onto private premises without explicit permission was adopted by the Court. However, it must also be remembered that the previous year in *Barker v The Queen* (1983) 153 CLR 338 at 344 the High Court made it quite clear, if it were not clear before that, that one must analyse the invitation, express or implied, given by the occupier in each case. It may be that circumstances show that there is an implied general invitation, in which case anybody may enter ... and if it is, then the motives of the defendants in entering are irrelevant. However, most implied invitations will be held to be for limited purposes and in such cases an entry unrelated to those purposes will be a trespass right from the moment of entry ...

The evidence before me suggests that the implied invitation by the plaintiff for the public to visit its premises was limited to members of the public bona fide seeking information or business with it or to clients of the firm, but not to people, for instance, who wished to enter to hold up the premises and rob them or even to people whose motives were to go onto the premises with video cameras and associated equipment or a reporter to harass the inhabitants by asking questions which would be televised throughout the State.

It is important to decide whether the defendants' agents trespassed from the moment of entry or only from a reasonable time after being asked to leave. This is because, for reasons which I will go into shortly, there would be no rights to have an injunction granted to restrain publication of a film taken when the maker was not a trespasser. The mere fact that a licence was revoked later would not operate respectively ...

There was a faint attempt to justify the entry in the public interest in highlighting a matter of public importance. Accepting for present purposes that the matter which the defendants were seeking to televise was one of great public interest, this would not, in my view, justify their entry. The reference in Hunt J's decision previously noted as to the great importance of freedom of the press and freedom of speech must not be read too widely. In none of those cases was there a rude intrusion onto private property and harassment of citizens going quietly about their own business on their own property ...

[**Note**: The Judge reviewed the authority of *Entick v Carrington*, and also noted that even in the United States, with its constitutional guarantee of freedom of speech, news gatherers did not have a licence to trespass.]

The defendant then says that even if it is a trespass to enter private property, for which damages may be awarded, the court has no power or alternatively it is inappropriate for the court to grant an injunction to prevent publication of photographs taken while the photographer was trespassing.

This submission goes into very deep waters. First, it is clear that one does not commit a tort merely by looking. The *Entick* case referred to above provided the dictum from Lord Camden (at 1066): ' ... the eye cannot by the laws of England be guilty of a trespass'.

Just as it is not a trespass just to look, so it is not a trespass to sketch what one sees: *Hickman v Maisey* [1900] 1 QB 752 at 756, or to broadcast what one sees: *Victoria Park Racing and Recreation Grounds Co Ltd v Taylor* (1937) 58 CLR 479 or to photograph it: *Sports and General Press Agency Ltd v 'Our Dogs' Publishing Co Ltd* [1916] 2 KB 880; affirmed [1917] 2 KB 125 ...

If a trespass to land is threatened it can be enjoined if it appears that the defendant is likely to carry out his threat and that the plaintiff will suffer irreparable damage if he does. If a defendant has once trespassed and appears likely to repeat his trespass then an injunction can be granted either at common law or in equity. Neither of these situations occurred in the instant case. The defendants make no threat to trespass again, they merely wish to make use of the tape they have already obtained ...

The court can clearly grant an injunction to restrain further trespasses and if a breach of contract has occurred it can, in appropriate cases, trace the money paid and in the case of unconscionable commercial dealings even impose a resulting trust in cases outside the contract. Further, it has wide powers to restrain material obtained in breach of confidence. It has wide powers to stop damage to children who are wards of courts and indeed, if one considers the matter, the court has power to restrain almost all sorts of unconscionable conduct, except in this very narrow class of case, according to the defendants' submission that someone has obtained the fruits of his tort without holding money or property of the plaintiff and without a breach of confidentiality. In that case it is said the court is powerless.

From early times, however, the jurisdiction of this Court has not been compartmentalised, but has been a general one based on the need to restrain unconscionable conduct. This jurisdiction has been exercised in many different forms over the centuries ... This Court still continues both in private and commercial disputes to function as a court of conscience. What is unconscionable will depend to a great degree on the court's view as to what is acceptable to the community as decent and fair at the time and in the place where the decision is made ...

Thus I am of the view that the Court has power to grant an injunction in the appropriate case to prevent publication of a videotape or photograph taken by a trespasser even though no confidentiality is involved. However, the Court will only intervene if the circumstances are such to make publication unconscionable. Some American cases highlight where the dividing line lies. In the *Pentagon Papers* case, *New York Times Co v United States* (1971) 403 US 713, the United States Supreme Court declined to restrain the *New York Times* and *Washington Post* from publishing classified material which was obtained as a result of trespass. The Court clearly acknowledged that there was power to grant an injunction, but considered that the United States Government, as plaintiff, had not met the heavy burden of showing that in the light of the circumstances by which the information was obtained that such a restraint on the freedom of publication was warranted. On a lesser level a New York court held that a TV film of conditions in a children's home taken whilst trespassing should not be restrained: *Quinn v Johnson* (1976) 381 NYS 2d 875. However, a different result was obtained where photographs were taken of a home for mentally ill people in *Commonwealth v Wiseman* (1969) 249 NE 2d 610.

In the instant case, on a prima facie basis, I would have thought that there is a lot to be said in the Australian community where a film is taken by a trespasser, made in circumstances as the present, upon private premises in respect of which there is some evidence that publication of the film would affect goodwill, that the case is one where an injunction should seriously be considered. However, there is a long way to go from that point to the point where the court actually grants an injunction. The court will only grant an injunction if it can be seen that irreparable damage will be suffered by the plaintiff if such an injunction is not given. Such may occur where the damages are virtually impossible of quantification. It is not only that the plaintiff merely show that there is a strong prima facie case that the trespass is committed and that it is the sort of case where the court may grant an injunction ...

Were the trespass proved at the final hearing it would be open for the court to award exemplary damages (see eg *Carmyllie Pty Ltd v Mudgee Shire Council* (Lusher J, 15 November 1984, unreported)); such damages could conceivably be of immense proportions. It is interesting, but, of course, legally irrelevant, to note that in the *Le Mistral* case a New York jury gave a quarter of a million dollars for just such a trespass. The availability of exemplary damages takes away any problems there may be for the plaintiff in quantifying damages because even after the telecast it may be that the plaintiff's goodwill may not have been affected at all or it can demonstrate a fall-off of business. In either case the jury may award, if it considers it appropriate to do so, large exemplary damages. There is no dispute that the defendants are able to meet such demands, if awarded, and in such circumstances it seems to me hard to show that irreparable damage would be suffered by the plaintiff if an injunction were not granted ...

It is also unnecessary, in view of the opinion that I have formed as to damages, to go into the question of the balance of convenience ... Thus I do not have to decide between the public interest in having full dissemination of news of matters of general importance, on the one hand, and the Court's duty to prevent persons in positions of power riding roughshod over the personal and proprietary rights of other citizens, on the other hand, and nor do I have to weigh the prejudice suffered by the defendants if the story, on which is doubtless invested considerable sums of money, might go stale as against the possible prejudice to the plaintiff's business if it were telecast. All these questions would have required very serious consideration of public policy and balance of justice issues.

[**Note**: The High Court of Australia more recently considered *Willesee* and agreed that courts can issue an injunction in appropriate circumstances if the information results from trespass. On the facts of *ABC v Lenah Game Meats Pty Ltd* [2001] HCA 63 the Court decided that an injunction was inappropriate.]

TV3 Network Services Ltd v Broadcasting Standards Authority
[1995] 2 NZLR 721 (HC)

[**FACTS**: On 11 July 1993, TV3 screened a '20/20' programme on the subject of incest. In particular, it focused on the case of one man who had recently been convicted of offences committed against his five daughters. This had been the subject of considerable publicity. The programme contained interviews with three of the daughters whose identities were disguised. It also contained an interview with their mother, Mrs S, which had been surreptitiously filmed. A reporter had come onto Mrs S's land to talk with her. A film crew stationed on neighbouring public land filmed the encounter without her knowledge. Mrs S's identity was disguised. It was found that she would not have consented to an interview being filmed and that the reporter and film crew knew this.

Mrs S complained to the Broadcasting Standards Authority that TV3 had breached her privacy. The Authority upheld her complaint as a breach of its privacy principles, established to give effect to section 4(1)(c) of the Broadcasting Act 1989, which requires broadcasters to maintain standards consistent with the privacy of the individual. TV3 appealed to the High Court against the decision.

Eichelbaum CJ considered the situation in light of the privacy principles first. He concluded both that the Authority was justified in specifying those principles, and in coming to its conclusion that they had been breached. In discussing whether the surreptitious acquisition of the information was justified, he referred for assistance to the way in which trespass law protects the privacy of the individual.]

Eichelbaum CJ:

… Turning to the finding relating to the surreptitious filming, on the authorities it is clear that no tort is committed by photographing another person's private property without consent. There is a range of authorities but I cite only *Bathurst City Council v Saban* (1985) 2 NSWLR 704 and *Victoria Park Racing and Recreation Grounds Co Ltd v Taylor* (1937) 58 CLR 479. In the latter Latham CJ said at p 494:

> Any person is entitled to look over the plaintiff's fences and to see what goes on in the plaintiff's land. If the plaintiff desires to prevent this, the plaintiff can erect a higher fence … The defendant does no wrong to the plaintiff by looking at what takes place on the plaintiff's land. Further, he does no wrong to the

plaintiff by describing to other persons, to as wide an audience as he can obtain, what takes place on the plaintiff's ground. The court has not been referred to any principle of law which prevents any man from describing anything which he saw anywhere if he does not make defamatory statements, infringe the law as to offensive language, &c, break a contract, or wrongfully reveal confidential information.

In *Bathurst City Council v Saban* Young J relied on this authority, among others, to reach the conclusion that no tortious conduct was involved in taking a photograph of another's private property without consent.

Regarding the TV3 reporter, Mr Allan submitted that in accordance with the principles in *Robson v Hallett* [1967] 2 QB 939 (a precedent followed in a series of New Zealand cases) she was not a trespasser. The reporter was entitled, he said, to go on to the complainant's property to ascertain if she was prepared to be interviewed. The authority's findings of fact were that Mrs S knew she was a reporter, but did not know the conversation was being recorded and filmed from a secret location.

My view is that the reporter's position did not fall within the principles in *Robson v Hallett*. In that case it was held that in general the occupier of a dwelling gave an implied licence to any member of the public on lawful business to come through the gate and knock on the door of the house. While media reporters have no greater rights than the general public they do not have any less and usually a reporter would be entitled to go to the door to ascertain whether the occupier was willing to be interviewed. Reference may be made to *Marris v TV3 Network Ltd* (High Court, Wellington, CP 754/91, 14 October 1991); Neazor J at p 14. However, the concept of an implied licence raises the question of the purposes for which a licence may be implied. See, for example, *Lincoln Hunt Australia Pty Ltd v Willesee* (1986) 4 NSWLR 457, 460. Such a licence has been expressed as limited to lawful purposes, but it does not follow that only an entry for unlawful purposes will be outside the terms of the licence. Purposes for which it is known or understood that the occupier would not give consent will be outside the ambit of implication.

Here, no doubt the purpose of the visit was to obtain an interview if that could be achieved; but if it could not TV3 was ready to film whatever encounter ensued and record such statements as the occupier might make, without her being aware of it. The occupier would not have agreed to the reporter coming onto the premises for that purpose, and the inference is open that TV3 was aware of that. In the circumstances the reporter's entry did not fall within the terms of the normal implied licence, and for purposes of action in tort was a trespass from the outset.

In summary, for the reasons stated I consider that while the conduct of the camera crew was not unlawful, the reporter was a trespasser ...

TV3 Network Services Ltd v Fahey
[1999] 2 NZLR 129 (CA)
Richardson P:

On 5 October 1998 TV3 screened a '20/20' programme focusing on alleged sexual improprieties and professional misconduct on the part of Dr Morgan Fahey. He is well known in Christchurch as a public figure and medical professional and the programme was screened shortly before the local body elections where he was standing for the mayoralty. The programme featured allegations by three former female patients of Dr Fahey.

The following day Dr Fahey issued defamation proceedings against TV3. TV3's statement of defence pleads that the statements of fact in the transcript of the programme are true. It also pleads the defences of honest opinion and qualified privilege.

Another former patient, X, made contact with TV3 and on 19 October made an appointment with Dr Fahey in the guise of a patient seeking a consultation. She confronted Dr Fahey about his alleged sexual misconduct with her as a patient 28 years previously, employing a concealed camera to make a video recording of the interview. On 21 October TV3 advised Dr Fahey's solicitors of its intention to show the video in its '20/20' programme on 25 October and gave them an opportunity to respond.

On 22 October Dr Fahey obtained an ex parte interim injunction restraining TV3 from screening a '20/20' programme concerning Dr Fahey. TV3 applied to have it set aside. The affidavit in support states that following the broadcast of 5 October 1998 TV3 had received approaches from a number of other women who had made complaints against Dr Fahey's conduct, including a number of former and current staff members of a commercial organization; that X said she intended to confront Dr Fahey with her allegations and wished either to have a witness present or to make a tape recording of the conversation; and that TV3 had provided X with a camera with which to video-record the interview with Dr Fahey.

In an oral judgment of 4 November Chisholm J dismissed TV3's application to set aside the interim injunction. Three grounds for sustaining the injunction had been advanced on behalf of Dr Fahey:

1 that TV3's letter of 21 October forwarding the transcript of X's interview with Dr Fahey evidenced a threat to Dr Fahey to disclose sexual misconduct on his part in breach of s 238 of the Crimes Act 1961;
2 that TV3's action constituted civil contempt affecting Dr Fahey's pending defamation claim arising from the first programme; and
3 that the confrontation in Dr Fahey's surgery and the taping of the interview by X amounted to trespass or unlawful invasion of Dr Fahey's privacy.

Applying, it seems, a standard *American Cyanamid* approach to interim injunctions [see *American Cyanamid Co v Ethicon Ltd* [1975] AC 396], and doing so in the judgment under the heads 'Whether there is a serious issue to be tried' and 'Balance of convenience', Chisholm J concluded that overall justice favoured the continuation of injunction protection.

He said that if considered in isolation he would be hesitant about finding an arguable case on the first ground. Turning to the second ground, he concluded that there was an arguable case that the screening of the proposed programme would constitute civil contempt of Court. In his judgment the proposed programme is capable of striking at the very heart of the issues likely to be involved in the defamation proceeding. It would be perfectly capable of influencing potential jurors against Dr Fahey. The Judge went on to consider trespass and invasion of privacy. He concluded that there must be a relatively strong case that the entry of Dr Fahey's former patient into his surgery on 19 October amounted to trespass. Although the implied licence was for the former patient to consult the plaintiff in his capacity as a medical practitioner, that was not the purpose of the visit. Instead the underlying purpose of the visit was to enable the former patient to confront Dr Fahey and to record the exchanges for a television programme. It followed, he said, that there must also be an arguable case that the television footage now intended for broadcast as part of the '20/20' programme was obtained illegally.

On the balance of convenience the Judge noted that freedom of expression and comment are weighty factors but considered that this was a relatively exceptional case. First, there was the combination of factors already noted counting against TV3. Second, if the programme is screened the prospect of a fair trial could be seriously compromised by the reference to alleged criminal conduct by Dr Fahey. Third, that the programme had the potential to prejudice a fair trial in the existing defamation proceedings which could not be compensated in damages. Fourth, it was not for the Court to say whether Dr Fahey had made admissible admissions during the 19 October interview. Fifth, it was difficult to see how the screening of the programme could serve any public interest that would not be served by TV3 passing on the information it has gathered to the police, medical authorities and commercial organization. Moreover, the public interest argument that might have been available prior to the local body elections no longer existed.

We are satisfied that Chisholm J erred in his approach and therefore in his conclusion. Any prior restraint of free expression requires passing a much higher threshold than the arguable case standard. In *Attorney-General v British Broadcasting Corporation* [1981] AC 303 at p 362 Lord Scarman said:

> [T]he prior restraint of publication, though occasionally necessary in serious cases, is a drastic interference with freedom of speech and should only be ordered where there is a substantial risk of grave injustice.

Over a century ago the Court of Appeal in *Bonnard v Perryman* [1891] 2 Ch 269 said at p 284:

> ... the subject-matter of an action for defamation is so special as to require exceptional caution in exercising the jurisdiction to interfere by injunction before the trial of an action to prevent an anticipated wrong ... Until it is clear that an alleged libel is untrue, it is not clear that any right at all has been infringed; and the importance of leaving free speech unfettered is a strong reason in cases of libel for dealing most cautiously and warily with the granting of interim injunctions.

[**Note**: Richardson P canvassed the New Zealand authorities on interim injunctions in defamation actions and concluded that the Court 'has jurisdiction to restrain the publication of defamatory matter but it is exercisable only for clear and compelling reasons'. These authorities include *New Zealand Mortgage Guarantee Co Ltd v Wellington Newspapers Ltd* [1989] 1 NZLR 4, and *Auckland Area Health Board v Television New Zealand Ltd* [1992] 3 NZLR 406.]

...

In the present case, the injunction application was made in the existing defamation proceedings and in the context of defamation proceedings. The three grounds relied on by Dr Fahey all relate to interfering with the administration of justice in the existing proceedings or in proceedings which may follow the screening of the second programme ...

[W]here both free expression and other rights and values are raised the Court must seek to accommodate and balance both sets of values. In that situation, too, the same general principle should apply, namely that the jurisdiction to restrain the proposed publication is exercisable only for clear and compelling reasons ...

[**Note**: His Honour considered the grounds pleaded under civil contempt and threatening to accuse Dr Fahey of a crime if he did not discontinue the defamation proceedings. Both were rejected on the facts.]

This brings us to the third ground, trespass and invasion of privacy. Trespass is a civil wrong and entering and remaining on Dr Fahey's premises for the purpose of confronting him with allegations of sexual and professional misconduct and surreptitiously recording the conversation could scarcely come within the terms of the normal implied licence to attend at a doctor's surgery. Clearly TV3 encouraged and facilitated X's action. As to the privacy implications discussed in Todd, *The Law of Torts in New Zealand* (2nd edn, 1997) at p 951, in terms of the Broadcasting Act 1989 TV3 was and is responsible for maintaining in its programmes and their presentation standards which are consistent with the privacy of the individual (s 4(1)(c)) but is not under a civil liability in respect of any failure to comply with any provisions of the section (s 4(3)).

In circumstances where the programme proposed to be broadcast may have been obtained in breach of the plaintiff's rights, the Court, when considering the grant of an injunction, is required to weigh and balance the competing rights and values at stake. In that assessment the context and circumstances in which the impugned methods were employed, any special public interest considerations for broadcasting the programme, and the adequacy of damages as an available remedy for any wrong proved at trial, are amongst the considerations which must ordinarily be weighed. We shall refer briefly to those three matters as on the material before the Court they affect the present case.

Following the screening of the first programme Dr Fahey immediately denied the allegations of sexual and professional impropriety made against him by the former patients and issued defamation proceedings against TV3 claiming general and exemplary damages At the very least TV3's credibility was put on the line and it must have known that any further programme implicating Dr Fahey would be likely to give rise to a credibility challenge. TV3 may well have had mixed motives in encouraging and assisting X: to obtain evidence which could support its defence of the existing proceedings; to add to the drama of any screening of the interview; to protect the credibility of the account of X's intended conversation with Dr Fahey; and to assist X to protect her credibility against any attacks on her by providing the means of accurately recording the confrontation. Clearly, then, TV3's conduct could not be condemned out of hand. There is the additional dimension that Dr Fahey has said on oath that he thought X was mentally disordered and deluded. That possible line of defence could reasonably have been anticipated by X and TV3. Obtaining a surreptitious film was, in those circumstances, an understandable preemptive course of action, and its screening can be said to be in the public interest in the light of Dr Fahey's probable reaction to a programme without the support of the film.

This leads on to the second special factor to be weighed in the balancing exercise, the public interest in the imparting and receiving of that information. There may in particular circumstances be a legitimate public interest in the exposure of misconduct. Here the person concerned is a professional man and public figure and the proposed programme including the recording of X's exchanges with him raised further allegations of sexual improprieties with patients and considerations affecting his reputation in public affairs and continuing medical practice. It is not in dispute that in principle the law of New Zealand recognises that a public interest (in some cases properly described as 'iniquity') defence or justification is available in appropriate cases where the information has been obtained unlawfully or tortiously (*Attorney-General for United Kingdom v Wellington Newspapers Ltd (No 2)* [1988] 1 NZLR 180 at p 182). A major factor in this aspect of the balancing exercise is whether on the evidence before the Court TV3 has a seriously arguable case for the allegations (*European Pacific Banking Corporation Ltd v Television New Zealand Ltd* [1994] 3 NZLR 43 at p 47). In the original *Spycatcher* case in this Court, *Attorney-General for the United Kingdom v Wellington Newspapers Ltd* [1988] 1 NZLR 129, Cooke P at p 170 cited Bingham LJ's observation in the English *Spycatcher* case [see [1990] 1 AC 109], that the prospective publisher should attempt to verify the truth as far as it reasonably could and that there should be 'such appearance of truth as it would be reasonable in all the circumstances to expect'. And McMullin J at p 179 noted that 'The more credence the material receives the more powerful the considerations of public interest that tell in favour of its publication'. In this regard it is clearly arguable that in the conversation with X Dr Fahey went some distance to acknowledging and expressing regret for any misconduct he may have committed.

The third aspect is the adequacy of damages as a remedy for any trespass associated with the obtaining of the recording. An applicant for an injunction must show that harm not reparable by an award of damages is likely to be suffered if an injunction is not granted (*Lincoln Hunt Australia Pty Ltd v Willesee* (1986) 4 NSWLR 457 at p 464). Mr Hodson QC for Dr Fahey accepted that TV3 could not be restrained on this ground from screening a programme in which X described to the best of her recollection the conversation which took place in his surgery in which he participated without apparent demur. The only aspect which could be the subject of objection is the surreptitious recording on film of the conversation and screening of that film, but the substance of the conversation could be published in any event. TV3 has indicated it will seek to prove the truth of what is to be published in the disputed second programme. That engages the well-established rule that prior restraint should only be entertained in clear and compelling circumstances. While the question of trespass or invasion of privacy is analytically a separate issue it is, in substance, very much bound up with the question of truth. If TV3 establishes the truth of what is to be published, there could be little room for a significant award of damages for any trespass as such. What is more, in such circumstances, damages would clearly be an adequate remedy. If TV3 fails to prove truth, the circumstances in which the defamatory material, or part of it, was obtained would be relevant to the amount of damages, both compensatory and potentially of an exemplary nature.

Our decision in this case should not be seen as supporting any general proposition that the ends of news–gathering justify the means. If information has been obtained in circumstances which are at least arguably unlawful, that will be an important factor to weigh in the balancing exercise involved. Such unlawfulness may amount to an offence, or it may constitute a civil wrong. The more serious the breach, the stronger will be the case for restraining use of any material obtained as a result. The Courts will be careful to ensure that the rights of others are properly weighed and that the media is not simply provided with an incentive to engage in and benefit from unlawful conduct whenever it claims it is acting in the exercise of freedom of expression.

The appeal is allowed and the interim injunction is set aside.

Private nuisance

Introduction

Private nuisance tries to define the limits of a person's ability to use land in his or her possession when that adversely affects another landholder. It draws a broad distinction between behaviour causing physical damage to another's land or materially devaluing it, and behaviour interfering with comfort or convenience. In the latter instance, the law has to decide whether the defendant's activities are reasonable or not. This will require in-depth consideration of the facts and the context of the case, more than legal principle, as *Halsey v Esso Petroleum* illustrates perfectly.

Recently in particular, however, there have been some interesting legal developments in the field of private nuisance. Perhaps the most famous (or infamous, depending on one's viewpoint) is the decision of the House of Lords in *Hunter v Canary Wharf* regarding who has standing to sue in private nuisance. The position is still unsettled in New Zealand law. Will our courts follow the majority decision, represented here by Lord Goff's speech, or will we embrace the broader points made by our own Lord Cooke of Thorndon in his dissenting speech? It is also unclear what implications the decision will have for defendants. Will those with non-recognised connections to land be insulated from liability in private nuisance?

Another important trend is analysing the links between negligence and nuisance, particularly as regards the issue of whether foreseeability of damage is required for private nuisance and exactly what that means. While most major statements on this point have probably been made in the context of *Rylands v Fletcher* cases (see the section 'The rule in *Rylands v Fletcher*' below), this is something to consider while reading these next cases, and to return to when thinking about public nuisance. Related to this, there is an interesting split on whether nuisance needs to be a continuing action or whether it can be an isolated event. Predominantly, the answer to that question seems to favour the former position, though, as *Sedleigh-Denfield* illustrates, it may depend most logically on the type of damage caused. Another split in authority discusses whether activities that take place on the plaintiff's own land can lead to liability in private nuisance. It is suggested with respect that the answer in *Clearlite Holdings* is anomalous. The case seems out of line with the philosophy of nuisance as representing a competition between neighbouring landowners' use of their property. Consider alternative approaches. For example, given the discussions above in the section 'Trespass to land' as to the ambit of a licence to enter land, could this have provided a sounder reason for finding for the successful party in the case?

Other important aspects to consider are whether the public or social utility of the defendant's activity should have any bearing on liability, and how the courts come to decisions about appropriate remedy. The most notorious example of both is *Miller v Jackson*, with Lord Denning's delightfully wrong judgment and the agonies experienced by his fellow cricket fans on the bench (see Hardie Boys J's criticisms of the case in *BNZ v Greenwood*). There is little doubt, though, about the harshness of rules disallowing a defence of 'coming to the nuisance' or disallowing mitigation as a result of the beneficial effects of an activity. Consider, for example, the impact of the growing number of inner-city apartment dwellers in Wellington on the businesses that operate near them. Readers may well have considerable sympathy with the defendants in *Miller* and in *Sturges v Bridgman*. However, this is where the 'reasonableness' of the activity in the context of the neighbourhood and the pragmatism of considerations as to remedy can really come to the fore.

St Helen's Smelting Co v Tipping
(1865) HLR 642; 11 ER 1483 (HL)
[**FACTS**: The plaintiff bought a manor house and a large area of valuable land in June 1860. Close to this property, the defendants owned land on which were copper-smelting works. In September 1860, the defendants began very extensive smelting operations on this site. These activities produced noxious fumes, which caused considerable damage to trees and fruit, and other plants on the plaintiff's property. His cattle also became unhealthy as a result of the pollution.]

The Lord Chancellor:

… My Lords, in matters of this description it appears to me that it is a very desirable thing to mark the difference between an action brought for a nuisance upon the ground that the alleged nuisance produces material injury to the property, and an action brought for a nuisance on the ground that the thing alleged to be a nuisance is productive of sensible personal discomfort. With regard to the latter, namely, the personal freedom, anything that discomposes or injuriously affects the senses or the nerves, whether that may or may not be denominated a nuisance, must undoubtedly depend greatly on the circumstances of the place where the thing complained of actually occurs. If a man lives in a town, it is necessary that he should subject himself to the consequences of those operations of trade which may be carried on in his immediate locality, which are actually necessary for trade and commerce, and also for the enjoyment of property, and for the benefit of the inhabitants of the town and of the public at large. If a man lives in a street where there are numerous shops, and a shop is opened next door to him, which is carried on in a fair and reasonable way, he has no ground for complaint, because to himself individually there may arise much discomfort from the trade carried on in that shop. But when an occupation is carried on by one person in the neighbourhood of another, and the result of that trade, or occupation, or business, is a material injury to property, then there unquestionably arises a very different consideration. I think, my Lords, that in a case of that description, the submission which is required from persons living in society to that amount of discomfort which may be necessary for the legitimate and free exercise of the trade of their neighbours, would not apply to circumstances the immediate result of which is sensible injury to the value of the property.

... Of the effect of the vapours exhaling from those works upon the plaintiff's property, and the injury done to his trees and shrubs, there is abundance of evidence in the case.

My Lords, the action has been brought upon that, and the jurors have found the existence of the injury; and the only ground upon which your Lordships are asked to set aside that verdict, and to direct a new trial, is this, that the whole neighbourhood where these copper smelting works were carried on, is a neighbourhood more or less devoted to manufacturing purposes of a similar kind, and therefore it is said, that inas-much as this copper smelting is carried on in what the Appellant contends is a fit place, it may be carried on with impunity, although the result may be the utter destruction, or the very considerable diminution, of the value of the plaintiff's property. My Lords, I apprehend that that is not the meaning of the word 'suitable', or the meaning of the word 'convenient', which has been used as applicable to the subject. The word 'suita-ble' unquestionably cannot carry with it this consequence, that a trade may be carried on in a particular locality, the consequence of which may be injury and destruction to the neighbouring property ...

On these grounds, therefore ... I advise your Lordships to affirm the decision of the Court below, and to refuse the new trial and to dismiss the appeal with costs.

Lord Cranworth:

... I perfectly well remember, when I had the honour of being one of the Barons of the Court of Exchequer, trying a case in the county of Durham, where there was an action for injury arising from smoke, in the town of Shields. It was proved incontesta-bly that smoke did come and in some degree interfere with a certain person; but I said, 'You must look at it not with a view to the question whether, abstractedly, that quan-tity of smoke was a nuisance, but whether it was a nuisance to a person living in the town of Shields'; because, if it only added in an infinitesimal degree to the quantity of smoke, I held that the state of the town rendered it altogether impossible to call that an actionable nuisance.

There is nothing of that sort, however, in the present case.

Halsey v Esso Petroleum Co Ltd

[1961] 1 WLR 683 (HC)

Veale J:

... This is a case, if ever there was one, of the little man asking for the protection of the law against the activities of a large and powerful neighbour. I hasten to say that there is not, and never has been, and could not be, any suggestion of deliberate annoy-ance. Indeed, the defendants have gone to great lengths in some directions to do what they can to minimise causes of annoyance. On the other hand, the plaintiff alleges that the conduct of the defendants in other directions entitles him to exemplary damages.

The claim is broadly put on two bases: pollution of the atmosphere and noise; but that is perhaps an over-simplification. The alleged pollution takes the form of smells (which do not cause any real injury to health unless one is allergic to such smells) and also of deposits consisting of acid smuts and oily drops which fall on washing put out to dry, on fabrics inside the house such as curtains, and on paintwork, including the paintwork of a motor-car. The alleged noise comprises noise from boilers, pumps and vehicles, the latter category embracing not only the noise of the vehicle itself in motion, but noises caused by the driver and workmen such as shouting, slamming doors and banging pipes.

It is important that the nature of the district should be borne in mind. I have seen a map of the district and also certain photographs. These are helpful, but not as helpful as an actual view. There is an undoubted strip on the river bank of industrial development. This strip is zoned for industrial purposes. There are various kinds of industrial activity carried on, and the defendants' premises are not the only place where oil is dealt with. On the other hand, the houses in Rainville Road and in the streets adjacent to Rainville Road are in a residential area. They are not affected by traffic in Fulham Palace Road. They are what might be described as nice small terrace houses. This area is zoned for residential purposes.

… In this case smell and noise come into one category; actual deposits in the way of harmful smuts and oil drops come into the other. I bear in mind the observations of Lord Loreburn LC in *Polsue and Alfieri Ltd v Rushmer* [[1907] AC 121]. Lord Loreburn said [at 123]: 'The law of nuisance undoubtedly is elastic, as was stated by Lord Halsbury in the case of *Colls v Home and Colonial Stores* [[1904] AC 179, 185]. He said: "What may be called the uncertainty of the test may also be described as its elasticity. A dweller in towns cannot expect to have as pure air, as free from smoke, smell, and noise as if he lived in the country, and distant from other dwellings, and yet an excess of smoke, smell and noise may give a cause of action, but in each of such cases it becomes a question of degree, and the question is in each case whether it amounts to a nuisance which will give a right of action". This is a question of fact'.

Later in his speech, Lord Loreburn said: 'I agree with Cozens-Hardy LJ when he says: "It does not follow that because I live, say, in the manufacturing part of Sheffield I cannot complain if a steam-hammer is introduced next door, and so worked as to render sleep at night almost impossible, although previously to its introduction my house was a reasonably comfortable abode, having regard to the local standard; and it would be no answer to say that the steam-hammer is of the most modern approved pattern and is reasonably worked"'.

… So far as the present case is concerned, liability for nuisance by harmful deposits could be established by proving damage by the deposits to the property in question, provided of course that the injury was not merely trivial. Negligence is not an ingredient of the cause of action, and the character of the neighbourhood is not a matter to be taken into consideration. On the other hand, nuisance by smell or noise is something to which no absolute standard can be applied. It is always a question of degree whether the interference with comfort or convenience is sufficiently serious to constitute a nuisance. The character of the neighbourhood is very relevant and all the relevant circumstances have to be taken into account. What might be a nuisance in one area is by no means necessarily so in another. In an urban area, everyone must put up with a certain amount of discomfort and annoyance from the activities of neighbours, and the law must strike a fair and reasonable balance between the right of the plaintiff on the one hand to the undisturbed enjoyment of his property, and the right of the defendant on the other hand to use his property for his own lawful enjoyment. That is how I approach this case.

It may be possible in some cases to prove that noise or smell have in fact diminished the value of the plaintiff's property in the market. That consideration does not arise in this case, and no evidence has been called in regard to it. The standard in respect of discomfort and inconvenience from noise and smell which I have to apply is that of the ordinary reasonable and responsible person who lives in this particular area of Fulham. This is not necessarily the same as the standard which the plaintiff chooses to set up for himself. It is the standard of the ordinary man, and the ordinary man, who may well like peace and quiet, will not complain, for instance, of the noise of traffic if he chooses to live on a main street in an urban centre, nor of the reasonable noises of industry, if he chooses to live alongside a factory.

[**Note**: His Lordship considered the evidence, found the facts summarised above, and continued.]

I have no doubt at all that the defendants have been the cause of the emission into the atmosphere of noxious smuts which have caused damage to the plaintiff's washing and to his motor-car. The smuts are noxious acid smuts, and it does not matter whether they contain sulphate or sulphuric acid. For this damage the defendants in my judgment are liable, both as for a nuisance and under *Rylands v Fletcher*. It is necessary for the plaintiff to prove the fact of it happening, and this I am satisfied he has done.

… I am not impressed by any argument based on the fact that noxious smuts are to be found elsewhere and on many urban buildings. In the vast majority of such places, although they may be unsightly, they do no damage or no appreciable damage, and their origin cannot be traced. In the present case, acid smuts have done damage and their origin has been traced. There is not and cannot be any doubt that the emission of acid smuts is a well-known problem.

[**Note**: The Court held that there was no defence to this action so far as noxious smuts were concerned.]

… I turn now to the question of smell. At the time of my official view of the locality yesterday, on February 22, there was no appreciable smell at all, either inside or outside the defendants' depot. But a large body of witnesses have given evidence of smell, and I have no doubt but that smells escape from the defendants' depot. That is not surprising of itself, because the depot is, after all, an oil depot. The defendants contend first that there is no smell escaping; alternatively, that if any smell escapes, it does not amount to a nuisance; alternatively, that if there is any smell, there is a prescriptive right to cause it.

Over a period of much more than 20 years, the defendants have dealt with different kinds of oil at the depot. I think from time to time, over the years, smells of oil have escaped. No doubt the frequency and intensity of these smells has varied, but more than one witness has told me that there has always been some sort of smell. What I might call the general background of occasional oily smells is something in respect of which, in my judgment, the plaintiff is not entitled to complain. It is not, however, of this type of smell that the plaintiff does complain in the action. On occasions, he says, the smell is much worse. 'You have to be there to realise it,' he said, 'it really makes you feel sick'. The further and better particulars to the statement of claim refer to the smell which arises from heating oil and also use the words, 'a pungent rather nauseating smell of an oily character'. It is of this that the plaintiff complains in this action.

It is often very difficult to put into words the nature of a smell. I have had various descriptions given to me. The plaintiff ascribed it to hot oil. His wife said it was an awful smell of burning oil, a sickly smell which made her feel sick in the stomach. 'Absolutely horrible', 'absolutely shocking', 'nauseating', 'definitely vile', are only some of the epithets which have been used by the witnesses. 'Nauseating' was a word used by others.

I have carefully considered the evidence of the different witnesses on this point. I find as a fact that over and above the occasional smell of oil which has been present from time to time for many years, during recent years and growing over the years in frequency and intensity there has been emitted from the defendants' depot a particularly pungent smell, which goes far beyond any triviality, far beyond any background smell of oil, and it is a serious nuisance to local residents, including the plaintiff. I have no doubt whatever but that this smell comes from the defendants' depot. This smell is not only strictly local to the defendants' depot, but I accept the evidence of the witnesses who have tracked it down to the depot … It may be that those who work at the depot or for the defendants' company are used to oily smells and do not notice anything. The plaintiff does not work in the depot, and I am quite satisfied that there is on occasion a smell escaping from the depot which is far more than what would affect a sensitive person. There is something which is a nauseating smell, and this is so frequent as to be an actionable nuisance.

… Whether or not this smell amounts to a nuisance depends of course upon the whole of the circumstances, including the character of the neighbourhood and the nature, intensity and frequency of the smell. I hold that this smell, of which the witnesses have given evidence, and which may or may not be due to heated oil, does amount to a nuisance …

I approach this question with caution, as Mr Gardiner asked me to do, since there has been no injury to health, but injury to health is not a necessary ingredient in the cause of action for nuisance by smell … I reject the contention that the evidence for the plaintiff has been exaggerated by people who feel strongly against the defendants on other grounds. I accept the evidence for the plaintiff, and it is right to add that the description by the witnesses of the nature of the smell was confirmed by my own experience on the night of February 10. On that night, at half past eleven, there was in Rainville Road and Wingrave Road clearly emanating from the defendants' depot, a nasty smell which could properly be described, as the plaintiff has described it in his further and better particulars, namely, 'a pungent, rather nauseating smell of an oily character'. The defendants in my judgment are liable for nuisance by smell.

I turn now to the question of nuisance by noise. This question relates to two distinct matters: the noise of the plant and the noise of the vehicles, the latter complaint including the noise of the vehicles themselves and the attendant noises made by drivers shouting and slamming doors and banging pipes. It is in connection with noise that, in my judgment, the operations of the defendants at night are particularly important. After all, one of the main objects of living in a house or flat is to have a room with a bed in it where one can sleep at night. Night is the time when the ordinary man takes his rest. No real complaint is made by the plaintiff so far as the daytime is concerned; but he complains bitterly of the noise at night.

… I accept the evidence of the plaintiff as to noise and I hold it is a serious nuisance, going far beyond a triviality, and one in respect of which the plaintiff is entitled to complain. Because of the noise made by the boilers, I think that the plaintiff is not so much, certainly since the throbbing of the steam pumps ceased, troubled by the noise of the electric pumps. But that is because the noise of the pumps is largely drowned by the noise of the boilers, and even if the noise of the boilers stopped, it might be that the plaintiff could justifiably complain of the noise of the pumps.

I have been assisted on this aspect of the case by the scientific evidence. Scientific evidence is helpful in that it may tend to confirm or disprove the evidence of other witnesses. The scale of decibels from nought to 120 can be divided into colloquial descriptions of noise by the use of words: faint, moderate, loud, and so on. Between 40 and 60 decibels the noise is moderate, and between 60 and 80 it is loud. Between 80 and 100 it is very loud, and from 100 to 120 it is deafening. On November 29, 1960, readings were taken on a Dawmeter outside the plaintiff's house. Six tests between 9 and 11 o'clock in the evening showed readings of 64 to 68 decibels, all rising to about 68 as a peak. There was, therefore, a constant 'loud' noise outside the plaintiff's house. When a tanker passed the reading was 83 decibels, though at the moment I am concerned with the plant and in particular the boilers.

On January 25, 1961, between 6 and 8 o'clock in the evening inside the house, with the window open three inches, further tests showed that the noise inside the house was substantially above the maximum permissible intrusive noise, which is the level at which a noise would interfere with ordinary conversation. The noise outside the house was again found to be 68 decibels. This is something which happens, no doubt with variations in intensity, not just now and again, but every night and all night, and I have no doubt at all but that it is an actionable nuisance. I think it would disturb an ordinary man.

[**Note**: His Lordship considered the evidence, found that the noise of the boilers was not the same at all times, accepted the peak figure of 68 decibels, and continued.]

But bearing in mind, I hope, all the relevant considerations, in my judgment the defendants are liable in nuisance for the noise of their plant, though only at night. Applying and adapting the well-known words of Knight-Bruce V-C in *Walter v Selfe*, this inconvenience is, as I find to be the fact, more than fanciful, more than one of mere delicacy or fastidiousness. It is an inconvenience materially interfering with the ordinary comfort physically of human existence, not merely according to elegant or dainty modes of living, but according to plain and sober and simple notions among ordinary people living in this part of Fulham.

[**Note**: The Court then considered the noise made by the tanker trucks—in the 'very loud' category—and found that to be a nuisance as well.]

Matheson v Northcote College
[1975] 2 NZLR 106 (HC)

[**FACTS**: The plaintiffs' house stood on land adjoining Northcote College. On numerous occasions, over eight years, the students at the College created problems for the Mathesons. They threw firecrackers and other objects onto the property, hit golf balls onto it, and trespassed onto it, stealing fruit and generally being annoying, and sometimes causing damage.]

McMullin J:

The first question of law is whether the facts and matters alleged in the statement of claim constitute an actionable nuisance. Mr Sheppard submitted that the acts complained of by the plaintiffs were acts of physical intrusion into the plaintiffs' land by persons or things. These he said were acts of trespass and not nuisance. He contended that no cause of action in nuisance lay against the defendant and none had been pleaded in trespass ... The distinction between the two torts is also made in *Fleming's Law of Torts* (4th edn) 344, where the learned author says:

> The gist of private nuisance is interference with an occupier's interest in the beneficial use of his land. The action is thus complementary to trespass which protects his related interest in exclusive possession. The distinction is that between the old actions of trespass and case, traditionally illustrated by contrasting the pointing of a waterhose unto neighbouring land and constructing a rainspout from which the water eventually flows upon it. The former invasion is trespass, being a 'direct' infringement of the plaintiff's possession; the latter is a nuisance, because the injury is treated as merely 'consequential'. The harms against which protection is afforded by either action usually differ somewhat in character, in that trespass applies only to physical intrusions by tangible objects, be they persons or things, whereas nuisance extends also to invasions by noise, smell, vibrations, and even high frequency interference with television screens. *Again, trespass postulates that the defendant's conduct consist in a physical act done directly unto the plaintiff's land; whereas a nuisance may (and according to the older view must) be caused by something taking place outside the land affected.* The distinction, however elusive and unattractive to the modern mind, is still attended with practical significance: for the one, there is liability without actual harm, *for the other, damage is essential; every trespassory intrusion is tortious unless privileged, while a nuisance is never actionable unless it is unreasonable* [emphasis added].

Mr Sheppard submitted that the acts complained of, while possibly amounting to trespass by the individual pupils of the school, did not constitute a nuisance on the part of the defendant and that the plaintiffs' first cause of action could not, therefore, survive. I think it follows from Mr Sheppard's submission, and I did not understand Mr Littlewood to disagree with it, that, because pupils of the school could not be said to be in any way agents of the defendant, the defendant would not be liable for any trespass committed by them, although the pupils themselves might be individually liable to plaintiffs.

Mr Littlewood, while accepting the differentiation made between the torts of nuisance and trespass on an historical basis, contended that this differentiation was not decisive of the question in this case in that, although the defendant might not be liable in tort for the trespass of its pupils, it could be liable in tort for the nuisance which it had itself permitted in that it so conducted the college that it allowed the pupils to commit trespass. What then constitutes the tort of nuisance? 'Nuisance' is defined in *Salmond on Torts* (16th edn) 53–4 as follows:

> Nuisance is commonly a continuing wrong—that is to say, it consists in the establishment or maintenance of some state of affairs which continuously or repeatedly causes the escape of noxious things onto the plaintiff's land (eg a stream of foul water, or the constant noise or smell of a factory). An escape of something on a single occasion would

not ordinarily be termed a nuisance. Thus in *Stone v Bolton* the plaintiff, while standing on the highway, was injured by a cricket ball struck from the defendant's field. It was held that an isolated act of hitting a cricket ball into a road cannot amount to a nuisance. The very word connotes some continuity. But it seems better to say that in such a case the gist of the claim of nuisance is not the isolated act of hitting a ball into the highway but the organising or carrying on of a game on property adjacent to the highway whereby the public right of passage is rendered dangerous, and the fact that balls reach the highway only very occasionally is evidence that no dangerous state of affairs exists in the adjoining field. A similar principle governs cases of private, as distinct from public, nuisance. This approach would enable us to explain cases of good authority in which the plaintiff has recovered for damage caused by a single escape of a dangerous thing— water, gas, metal foil or fire. So it has been rightly pointed out that 'an intermittent noise, particularly when it does not come at stated intervals, is likely to be more disagreeable than if it were constant'. It has never been seriously suggested that the plaintiff whose house has been flooded or blown up as a result of the defendant's activities can recover only for the second or subsequent but not the first of such incidents. The truth is that all wrongful escapes of deleterious things, whether continuous, intermittent, or isolated, are equally capable of being classed as nuisances; the type of harm caused by the escape, the gravity of that harm, and the frequency of its occurrence are each relevant (but not conclusive) factors in determining whether the defendant has maintained on his premises a state of affairs which is a potential nuisance [emphasis added].

The importance of the existence of a 'state of affairs' is also stressed in *Street on Torts* (5th edn) 219 under the heading 'State of Affairs'. A consideration of the cases demonstrates that in considering whether or not an actionable nuisance has been established the courts have been concerned with a state of affairs, whether it be a state of affairs which continues without intermission or whether it be a state of affairs constituted by intermittent but repetitive acts which collectively, though not individually, amount to a nuisance.

On the present motion it must be accepted that the plaintiffs are in the position where they can prove all the acts alleged in the particulars in the statement of claim. Accepting that situation, Mr Sheppard submitted that only the actual trespassers were liable to the plaintiffs, whether in trespass or nuisance, because the defendant had not committed the acts complained of and the pupils were not their servants or agents. To this submission Mr Littlewood replied by saying that the defendant had so badly supervised and controlled the school that pupils were not prevented from committing acts of trespass and that the board had not taken steps in the way of erecting fences to prevent the acts complained of. He said that the damage to the plaintiffs' property was a consequence of the state of affairs for which the board was responsible and therefore amounted to a private nuisance.

I am of the opinion that Mr Littlewood's submission is sound. There are a number of cases where people or organisations who have attracted crowds, the individual members of which commit acts of trespass, have been held liable in nuisance for those acts of trespass committed by the individual, even though there has never been a suggestion of a master–servant relationship or principal–agent relationship existing between the organisers and individuals. In some cases organisers have been held liable for the acts of total strangers whom they have induced to come onto their property. The true test to determine whether a defendant is under any liability in nuisance lies in whether what the plaintiffs complain of was a natural and probable consequence of letting pupils play unsupervised …

It is not hard to see why the law has afforded a remedy in nuisance to persons aggrieved by the acts of individual trespassers against the 'controller'. Such individuals may differ from time to time and be difficult to identify. If the aggrieved party were allowed a remedy against them only, the difficulties of proof and enforcement might be such as to make the remedy of little value …

… But a further question [is] required to be considered in relation to nuisance. It is whether the present action alleges a public or a private nuisance. Whether an action is brought in public or private nuisance may be important because different considerations arise according to the type of nuisance alleged. The difference between the two kinds of nuisance is set out in *Fleming's Law of Torts* (4th edn) 340. It is:

> *Private* nuisance traditionally was, and still is, confined to invasions of the interest in the use and enjoyment of land, although occasionally an occupier may recover for incidental injury sistained [*sic*] by him in the exercise of an interest in land, such as for illness caused by noxious gases from an adjoining factory. A *public* nuisance, in contrast, confers a cause of action for damages on anyone sustaining personal injury or other loss, although no rights or privileges in land of his have been invaded at all.

Halsbury's Laws of England (3rd edn), vol 28, 128, expresses the difference as follows:

> A *public* nuisance is one which inflicts damage, injury, or inconvenience upon all the Queen's subjects, or upon all of a class who come within the sphere or neighbourhood of its operation …
>
> A *private* nuisance is one which does not cause damage or inconvenience to the public at large, but which does interfere with a person's use or enjoyment of land or of some right connected with land.

On the application of this distinction to the present case, the nuisance for which the defendant is said to be liable would be a private nuisance. That being the case, the plaintiffs must show that the enjoyment of their land has in some way been affected (this consideration is not important where the allegation is one of public nuisance), but they need not show that they have suffered particular damage beyond that suffered by the rest of the community, as would be the case in an action in public nuisance …

In the result I am of the view that what the plaintiffs allege in the relevant paragraphs of the statement of claim may constitute an actionable nuisance.

Sedleigh-Denfield v O'Callaghan
[1940] AC 880 (HL)
[**FACTS**: The defendants, the St Joseph's Society for Foreign Missions, owned a property that was on sloping ground above property owned by the plaintiff. At the upper end

of the plaintiff's property, on the boundary of the St Joseph's estate, there was a ditch and a bank with trees. Before 1934, the ditch was an open course carrying storm water safely away, but in that year the Middlesex County Council put a culvert, a 15-inch pipe, in the ditch and covered it with earth, connecting the lower end of the culvert with the local storm water drains. Apparently, the Council made these improvements without authority from St Joseph's. The Council negligently failed to secure a proper grating at the proper place at the mouth of the culvert, and the pipe became clogged with sticks and leaves, which fell from the trees above. In 1937 there was a very heavy rain, and the blocked culvert led to flooding of the plaintiff's premises. There was evidence that the defendants' servants had periodically cleaned out the ditch and the mouth of the culvert. The plaintiff lost in the court below on the ground that the defendants had no duty with respect to a nuisance that had been put in place without authority by a third party.]

Lord Atkin:

My Lords, I do not propose to recapitulate the facts in this case which have been sufficiently stated in the opinion just delivered by the noble Lord on the woolsack. I treat it as established that the entrance to the offending pipe when laid was on the defendants' land abutting on the premises occupied by the plaintiff. I agree with the finding of the learned judge, accepted by the Court of Appeal, that the laying of a 15-inch pipe with an unprotected orifice was in the circumstances the creation of a nuisance or of that which would be likely to result in a nuisance. It created a state of things from which when the ditch was flowing in full stream an obstruction might reasonably be expected in the pipe, from which obstruction flooding of the plaintiff's ground might reasonably be expected to result … Now, if the defendants had themselves laid the pipe in the manner described, I have no hesitation in saying that the plaintiff once he had suffered damage from flooding so caused, would have had a good cause of action against them for nuisance. It is probably strictly correct to say that as long as the offending condition is confined to the defendant's own land without causing damage it is not a nuisance, though it may threaten to become a nuisance. But where damage has accrued the nuisance has been caused. I should regard the case on this hypothesis as having the same legal consequences as if the defendants, instead of laying a pipe, had placed an obvious obstruction in the course of the ditch. The question here is what is the legal position if such an obstruction is placed by a trespasser. In the present case I consider it established that the defendants by their responsible agents had knowledge both of the erection of the pipe, of the reasonable expectation that it might be obstructed and of the result of such obstruction, and of its continued existence in the condition complained of, since it was first placed in position …

In this state of the facts the legal position is not I think difficult to discover. For the purpose of ascertaining whether as here the plaintiff can establish a private nuisance I think that nuisance is sufficiently defined as a wrongful interference with another's enjoyment of his land or premises by the use of land or premises either occupied or in some cases owned by oneself. The occupier or owner is not an insurer; there must be something more than the mere harm done to the neighbour's property to make the party responsible. Deliberate act or negligence is not an essential ingredient but some degree of personal responsibility is required, which is connoted in my definition by the word 'use'. This conception is implicit in all the decisions which impose liability only where the defendant has 'caused or continued' the nuisance. We may eliminate in this case 'caused'. What is the meaning of 'continued'? In the context in which it is used 'continued' must indicate mere passive continuance. If a man uses on premises something which he found there, and which itself causes a nuisance by noise, vibration, smell or fumes, he is himself in continuing to bring into existence the noise, vibration, etc, causing a nuisance. Continuing in this sense and causing are the same thing. It seems to me clear that if a man permits an offensive thing on his premises to continue to offend, that is, if he knows that it is operating offensively, is able to prevent it, and omits to prevent it, he is permitting the nuisance to continue; in other words he is continuing it.

Clearlite Holdings Ltd v Auckland City Corporation
[1976] 2 NZLR 729 (HC)
[**FACTS**: Auckland City Corporation engaged a contractor to lay new drainage pipes. In order to do this, the contractor had to drive a tunnel from one street to another. This tunnel passed under the plaintiff's factory. As a result of the tunnelling, the concrete floor of the factory cracked and subsided by two inches. The plaintiff was able to move the machinery and so was able to continue production. However, it was negotiating to move into new premises and stood to lose financially as a result of the damage to its current premises. Consequently, it sued Auckland City Corporation and the contractor in negligence and nuisance. It was found, however, that there was no negligence on the part of either defendant.]
Mahon J:
… *Salmond on Torts* (16th edn) 52 [states that]:

> As nuisance is a tort arising out of the duties owed by neighbouring occupiers, the plaintiff cannot succeed if the act or omission complained of is on premises in his occupation. The nuisance must have arisen elsewhere than in or on the plaintiff's premises.

… If that statement of the law is correct, then the claim of nuisance in the present case necessarily fails. Although the tunnelling commenced on a public street and was extended therefrom under the plaintiff's premises, the suggested actionable conduct did not emanate from the public street in the occupation of the Corporation so as to cause harm to the plaintiff's land based upon the use by the Corporation of the street. The actionable conduct was the act of the contractor in tunnelling under the plaintiff's building so as to cause damage to that building and so the supposedly tortious act certainly took place upon the plaintiff's own premises. So far as I can ascertain, the quoted statement in *Salmond* does not appear in the other textbooks on the law of tort. As it stands, it is fatal to the plaintiff's claim, but the statement is, in my view, not correct and I must now give my reasons for holding that opinion.

The tort of nuisance is not capable of one comprehensive definition. The right of action which it creates has been applied to such a diversity of situations as to make a generic classification impracticable. But in essence it consists in unlawful damage either to the land of another or to the proper use and enjoyment of that land. Historically there were three ways in which unlawful interference might occur to the rights of an occupier in respect of his land. He might be dispossessed of his land, he might suffer trespass of his land, and he might be the victim of nuisance. The act of dispossessing the plaintiff or some act achieving equivalent effect, gave the plaintiff a right of action at the assize of novel disseisin. To go on to the plaintiff's land without authority was to trespass, for which the writ of trespass was the appropriate remedy, and to damage the plaintiff in the enjoyment of his land by an act committed elsewhere was a nuisance for which the assize of nuisance provided the approved relief. It therefore followed from this that a nuisance could never be committed on the plaintiff's land. Any act done on the plaintiff's land would be either disseisin or trespass according to the circumstances. There are two cases in the Year Books cited by Professor Newark, 'The Boundaries of Nuisance' (1949) 65 LQR 480, 482, note 18, in which it was held that an action for nuisance failed because the tortious act had been committed upon the plaintiff's land. Leaving disseisin or dispossession on one side, the later development of the forms of action became settled so as to provide an action for trespass as a remedy against the commission of that tort, and the action on the case as a remedy for the tort of nuisance. Those two forms of action were intractably distinct and this appears to be the original foundation for the view, if it is still valid, that because the action on the case for injury to land postulated conduct stopping short of entry on to the plaintiff's land, therefore the tort of nuisance could never be committed on the plaintiff's land, although eventually, as negligence developed as a separate tort, damage to the land of a plaintiff occasioned by negligent conduct was actionable in proceedings based on negligence wherever the tortious conduct took place ...

... I can see no objection to the plaintiff in a case like the present succeeding in an action for nuisance where the person causing the damage has been at the relevant time a licensee of the land occupied by the plaintiff. If I am not correct in that view then various anomalous results would certainly follow. If in the present case the contractors had been driving the same type of tunnel under the public street and parallel to the boundary of the plaintiff's premises, then the loss caused by any subsidence to the plaintiff's land and consequent damage to structures thereon would be recoverable from the contractor on the ground of private nuisance, and the same results would follow if similar damage occurred through the contractor mistakenly crossing the boundary into the plaintiff's land in the course of the tunnelling operations. In the latter case the loss of which I have spoken would be recoverable in an action for trespass. It seems in the highest degree illogical that the same damage could not be recovered from the same act merely because at the time of commission of that act the tortfeasor is on the plaintiff's land pursuant to a licence granted to him by the plaintiff. Another example demonstrating an anomaly arising from the adoption of the rule noted in *Salmond* can be related to a commonplace liability for nuisance. In the case of a continually barking dog, so long as the dog remains within his owner's territorial boundary, a neighbour suffering substantial annoyance would have a right of action for private nuisance. But as from the moment when the barking dog crossed the boundary into the plaintiff's property all rights of action would be extinguished. No action for trespass would lie because at common law the owner of a dog is not liable for the trespass of the animal: *Lee v Riley* (1865) 18 CBNS 722; 144 ER 629.

In any common law system certain anomalies will inevitably occur and their existence will not necessarily justify the conclusion that some settled rule is wrong. But on this particular branch of the law of nuisance the supposed inability of the plaintiff to recover for a nuisance committed on his own land seems to me to be nothing more than a medieval relic having its origin in those distant days when recovery for injury to proprietary rights in real property could only be obtained, apart from cases of disseisin, by writ of trespass or by action on the case limited to tortious conduct on the part of a neighbouring occupier. The gist of a claim for private nuisance lies in the damage which has been caused. The nature of the conduct causing that damage is subsidiary to the major concept. I agree with the view expressed in *Prosser's Law of Torts* (3rd edn) 593 that undue emphasis has been placed in many of the reported cases upon the type of conduct which may give rise to the tort. A private nuisance is a civil wrong based on a disturbance by the defendant of rights in land. It seems to me immaterial, in a case of actual damage to the land itself, to base any distinction upon the locality of the conduct complained of. All that is required in a case of this kind is a positive act creating the damage. In contrast with cases of public nuisance, absence of negligence is no defence. In contrast also with actions for nuisance based upon interference with the enjoyment of rights in property, the utility or reasonableness of a defendant's conduct is irrelevant. As Lord Westbury LC pointed out in *St Helen's Smelting Co v Tipping* (1865) 11 HL Cas 642, 650; 11 ER 1483, 1486, there is an essential distinction between material injury to property, on the one hand, and those other indirect interferences which produce sensible personal discomfort, on the other.

I therefore arrive at the conclusion that in the present case the damage caused to the factory of the plaintiff by the excavations made under the factory by the tunnelling contractors is actionable as a private nuisance at the suit of the plaintiff against both the contractor and its employer, the Auckland City Corporation, whose statutory powers do not include the right to commit a nuisance: Municipal Corporations Act 1954, s 168 ...

In litigation involving private nuisance the test of liability is not whether the tortious interference reflects negligent conduct, but whether it is unreasonable having regard to the legitimate interests of the plaintiff, and where direct physical damage to property results then, in my opinion, the invasion of the plaintiff's rights is actionable without fault so long as the damage represents the consummation of a risk, no matter how remote, factually inherent in the conduct of the defendant. In the present case, as in all cases which contemplate the driving of a tunnel only a few feet below the surface of the ground, the possibility of some degree of subsidence of the land above must have been within reasonable contemplation as a possible though remote contingency. In most cases such a result of the tunnelling operations would be of no consequence, but when tunnelling at a shallow depth under an existing building it might be of some consequence. I think that in such circumstances the operations of a contractor in a case like the present require, in accordance with settled policy on this branch of the law, the application of strict liability ...

Sturges v Bridgman
(1879) 11 Ch D 852 (CA)

[**FACTS**: The plaintiff was a doctor, who lived in London. In 1873, he built a consulting room at the end of his garden. It shared a wall with the defendant's confectionery kitchen. The defendant had two large marble mortars built in against the party wall, which were used for pounding sugar loaf and other hard substances, and for pounding meat. This equipment was used at various times, depending upon the defendant's business, but they were generally in use between 10 am and 1 pm. Unfortunately, this coincided with the plaintiff's consulting times. The noise and vibration caused by the machinery was considerable, and it materially interfered with the plaintiff's ability to work in his consulting room. The defendant's business had been there a long time; one of the mortars and pestles had been operating in this way for more than sixty years, and the second for more than twenty-six years, without being a nuisance to anyone. The defendant also pointed out that if the plaintiff had built his consulting room with a separate wall, he would not have suffered from the noise or vibration at all.]

Jessel MR:

I think this is a clear case for the plaintiff. There is really no dispute as to this being a nuisance; in fact, the evidence is all one way, and, as has been often said in these cases, the plaintiff is not bound to go on bringing actions for damages every day, when he is entitled to an injunction.

... Now the facts seem to be that until a very recent period it was not a nuisance at all. There was an open garden at the back of and attached to the plaintiff's house, and the noise, it seems, if it went anywhere, went over the garden, and, of course, was rapidly dispersed; as far as I can see upon the evidence before me, there was until a recent period no nuisance to anybody—no actionable nuisance at all. The actionable nuisance began when the plaintiff did what he had a right to do, namely, built a consulting-room in his garden, and when, on attempting to use the consulting-room for a proper purpose, he found this noise too great for anything like comfort. That was the time to bring an action for nuisance.

... If a man has a noisy business in the middle of a barren moor which belongs to somebody else to whom the business carried on does no injury, the owner of the moor cannot bring an action and he cannot interrupt. Take the case of putting a blacksmith's forge in the middle of a moor: you cannot enter the blacksmith's forge, inasmuch as that belongs either to him or to his landlord, and the owner of a moor which has no game upon it has nothing which can be injured by the noise. There is no remedy whatever, because it is a barren moor. Presently, this which is useless as a barren moor becomes available for building land by reason of the growth of a neighbouring town: is it to be said that the owner has lost the right to this barren moor, which has now become worth perhaps hundreds of thousands of pounds, by being unable to build upon it by reason of this noisy business? The answer would be simply, 'I could not stop you: I could not interrupt. It is physically impossible, because it would be a trespass; legally impossible, because I had suffered no damage and could not maintain an action. How could you therefore acquire a right to deprive me of the fair and ordinary use of my property?' That seems to me to be an answer to all the cases put. You must have regard to the position of the property and all the surrounding circumstances ... The fact that the man has made a noise which has not injured me or interfered with my comfort or enjoyment in any way, cannot deprive me of my right to the land, or interfere with my right to come to the Court when it does seriously interfere with my comfortable enjoyment.

Miller v Jackson
[1977] 3 All ER 338 (CA)
Lord Denning MR:

In summer time village cricket is the delight of everyone. Nearly every village has its own cricket field where the young men play and the old men watch. In the village of

Lintz in County Durham they have their own ground where they have played these last 70 years. They tend it well. The wicket area is well rolled and mown. The outfield is kept short. It has a good club-house for the players and seats for the onlookers. The village team play there on Saturdays and Sundays. They belong to a league, competing with the neighbouring villages. On other evenings after work they practise while the light lasts. Yet now after these 70 years a judge of the High Court has ordered that they must not play there any more. He has issued an injunction to stop them. He has done it at the instance of a newcomer who is no lover of cricket. This newcomer has built, or has had built for him, a house on the edge of the cricket ground which four years ago was a field where cattle grazed. The animals did not mind the cricket. But now this adjoining field has been turned into a housing estate. The newcomer bought one of the houses on the edge of the cricket ground. No doubt the open space was a selling point. Now he complains that, when a batsman hits a six, the ball has been known to land in his garden or on or near his house. His wife has got so upset about it that they always go out at weekends. They do not go into the garden when cricket is being played. They say that this is intolerable. So they asked the judge to stop the cricket being played. And the judge, much against his will, has felt that he must order the cricket to be stopped; with the consequences, I suppose, that the Lintz Cricket Club will disappear. The cricket ground will be turned to some other use. I expect for more houses or a factory. The young men will turn to other things instead of cricket. The whole village will be much the poorer. And all this because of a newcomer who has just bought a house there next to the cricket ground.

I must say that I am surprised that the developers of the housing estate were allowed to build the houses so close to the cricket ground. No doubt they wanted to make the most of their site and put up as many houses as they could for their own profit. The planning authorities ought not to have allowed it. The houses ought to have been so sited as not to interfere with the cricket. But the houses have been built and we have to reckon with the consequences.

At the time when the houses were built it was obvious to the people of Lintz that these new houses were built too close to the cricket ground. It was a small ground, and there might be trouble when a batsman hit a ball out of the ground. But there was no trouble in finding purchasers. Some of them may have been cricket enthusiasts. But others were not. In the first three years, 1972, 1973 and 1974, quite a number of balls came over or under the boundary fence and went into the gardens of the houses, and the cricketers went round to get them. Mrs Miller [the second plaintiff] was very annoyed about this. To use her own words:

> When the balls come over, they, the cricketers, either ring or come round in twos and threes and ask if they can have the ball back, and they never ask properly. They just ask if they can have the ball back, and that's it. They have been very rude, very arrogant and very ignorant, and very deceitful ... to get away from any problems we make a point of going out on Wednesdays, Fridays and the weekends.

Having read the evidence, I am sure that that was a most unfair complaint to make of the cricketers. They have done their very best to be polite. It must be admitted, however, that on a few occasions before 1974 a tile was broken or a window smashed. The householders made the most of this and got their rates reduced. The cricket club then did everything possible to see that no balls went over. In 1975, before the cricket season opened, they put up a very high protective fence. The existing concrete fence was only six feet high. They raised it to nearly 15 feet high by a galvanised chain-link fence. It cost £700. They could not raise it any higher because of the wind. The cricket ground is 570 feet above sea level. During the winter even this high fence was blown down on one occasion and had to be repaired at a cost of £400. Not only did the club put up this high protective fence. They told the batsmen to try to drive the balls low for four and not hit them up for six. This greatly reduced the number of balls that got into the gardens. So much so that the rating authority no longer allowed any reduction in rates.

Despite these measures, a few balls did get over. The club made a tally of all the sixes hit during the seasons of 1975 and 1976. In 1975 there were 2221 overs, that is, 13 326 balls bowled. Of them there were 120 six hits on all sides of the ground. Of these only six went over the high protective fence and into this housing estate. In 1976 there were 2616 overs, that is 15 696 balls. Of them there were 160 six hits. Of these only nine went over the high protective fence and into this housing estate.

No one has been hurt at all by any of these balls, either before or after the high fence was erected. There has, however, been some damage to property, even since the high fence was erected. The cricket club have offered to remedy all the damage and pay all expenses. They have offered to supply and fit unbreakable glass in the windows, and shutters or safeguards for them. They have offered to supply and fit a safety net over the garden whenever cricket is being played. In short, they have done everything possible short of stopping playing cricket on the ground at all. But Mrs Miller and her husband have remained unmoved. Every offer by the club has been rejected. They demand the closing down of the cricket club. Nothing else will satisfy them. They have obtained legal aid to sue the cricket club.

In support of the case, the plaintiff relies on the dictum of Lord Reid in *Bolton v Stone*. 'If cricket cannot be played on a ground without creating a substantial risk, then it should not be played there at all.' I would agree with that, saying if the houses or road were there first, and the cricket ground came there second. We would not allow the garden of Lincoln's Inn to be turned into a cricket ground. It would be too dangerous for windows and people. But I do not agree with Lord Reid's dictum when the cricket ground has been there for 70 years and the houses are newly built at the very edge of it. I recognise that the cricket club are under a duty to use all reasonable care consistently with the playing of the game of cricket, but I do not think the cricket club can be expected to give up the game of cricket altogether. After all they have their rights in their cricket ground. They have spent money, labour and love in the making of it; and they have the right to play on it as they have done for 70 years. Is this all to be rendered useless to them by the thoughtless and selfish act of an estate developer in building right up to the edge of it? Can the developer or purchaser of a house say to the cricket club: 'Stop playing. Clear out'. I do not think so. And I will give my reasons.

The law in the 19th century

If we were to approach this case with the eyes of the judges of the 19th century they would, I believe, have seen it in this way. Every time that a batsman hit a ball over the fence so that it landed in the garden, he would be guilty of a trespass. If he hit it so that it went under the fence and down the bank, he would be guilty of a trespass. So would the committee of the cricket club, because they would have impliedly authorised it. They cheered the batsman on. If one or two of the players went round and asked the house-holder if they could go into the garden to find it, the householder could deny them access; he could say: 'You are not to come in here to get your ball. I am not going to get it for you. Nor will I let you. It is going to stay there'. If the cricketers said: 'It's a new ball. It cost us over £6', the householder could say: 'That is your look-out. You ought not to have put it there'. Of course, if the householder picked up the ball himself and gave it to his son to play with, he would be liable in conversion. But otherwise he would not be liable at all. He could say: 'An Englishman's house is his castle. You are not coming in. Nor are you to hit your cricket ball in here. If you go on doing it, I am going to get an injunction to stop you. Once I prove the violation of a legal right, the Court of Chancery will grant me an injunction to prevent the recurrence of that violation': see *Imperial Gas Light & Coke Co v Broadbent*. Even if there was any doubt about the plaintiff's right to sue in trespass, he would have a claim in nuisance, once he proved that the balls were repeatedly coming over or under the fence and making things uncomfortable for him. To those claims, in the 19th century, either in trespass or in nui-sance, the committee of the cricket club would have no answer. They could not claim an easement because there is no such easement known to the law as a right to hit cricket balls into your neighbour's land. It would be no good for them to say that the cricket ground was there before the house was built. The householder could rely on the case a hundred years ago of the physician who built his new consulting-room next to the old established kitchen of his neighbour. The physician was held entitled to stop the work-ing of the kitchen on the ground that the noise was a nuisance to him in his consulting-room: see *Sturges v Bridgman*.

The only way in which the cricket club could have succeeded in the 19th century would have been by involving the doctrine of 'derogation from grant'. We were told that until recently the cricket ground and the neighbouring fields were all owned by the National Coal Board. The coal board let the cricket ground to the cricket club on a long lease for years knowing that the very purpose of the lease was that the club should play cricket on it for the term of the lease. So long as the National Coal Board owned the neighbouring field, they could not complain of the occasional ball being hit out of the ground onto the field; nor could they have got an injunction to restrain the playing of cricket on the ground, seeing that they had leased it to the club for that very purpose. The reason being simply that it would be a derogation from the grant of the lease for them to do so. And if the National Coal Board sold the land to a purchaser (as they did), the purchaser and subsequent successors in title also could not complain of the occasional ball; nor could they have got an injunction, for the obligation imported by the doctrine of 'derogation from grant' runs with the land just as do obligations which arise from a restrictive covenant: see *Browne v Flower*, by Parker J. '[They] bind not only the grantor but also all who claim through him ... .' It is in this that the importance of the doctrine lies: see *Wade and Megarry's Law of Real Property*.

The law in the 20th century

The case here was not pleaded by either side in the formulae of the 19th century. The plaintiffs did not allege trespass. The defendants did not raise the doctrine of derogation from grant. The case was pleaded in negligence or alternatively nuisance. That was, I think, quite right, having regard to the decision of the House of Lords in *Bolton v Stone*. Miss Stone had just stepped out of her garden gate on to the pavement when she was hit by a cricket ball. She did not sue in trespass to the person. That would be quite out of date. As I said in *Letang v Cooper*:

> If [the defendant] does not inflict injury intentionally, but only unintentionally, the plaintiff has no cause of action today in trespass. His only cause of action is in negligence, and then only on proof of want of reasonable care.

Miss Stone did seek to put her case on the doctrine of *Rylands v Fletcher*. She suggested that a cricket ball was a dangerous thing which the defendants had brought on to the cricket ground and it had escaped. That suggestion was dismissed by the House of Lords out of hand. Lord Reid said: '... there is no substance in that argument'. She also suggested that the club were liable in nuisance, but this was not pressed in the House of Lords, because nuisance was not distinguishable from negligence. Lord Porter remarked that 'in the circumstances of this case nuisance cannot be established unless negligence is proved'.

In our present case, too, nuisance was pleaded as an alternative to negligence. The tort of nuisance in many cases overlaps the tort of negligence. The boundary lines were discussed in two adjoining cases in the Privy Council: *The Wagon Mound (No 2)* and *Goldman v Hargrave*. But there is at any rate one important distinction between them. It lies in the nature of the remedy sought. Is it damages? Or an injunction? If the plaintiff seeks a remedy in damages for injury done to him or his property, he can lay his claim either in negligence or in nuisance. But, if he seeks an injunction to stop the playing of cricket altogether, I think he must make his claim in nuisance. The books are full of cases where an injunction has been granted to restrain the continuance of a nuisance. But there is no case, so far as I know, where it has been granted so as to stop a man being negligent. At any rate in a case of this kind, where an occupier of a house or land seeks to restrain his neighbour from doing something on his own land, the only appropriate cause of action, on which to base the remedy of an injunction, is nuisance: see the report of the Law Commission. It is the very essence of a private nuisance that it is the unreasonable use by a man of his land to the detriment of his neighbour. He must have been guilty of the fault, not necessarily of negligence, but of the unreasonable use of the land: see *The Wagon Mound (No 2)*, by Lord Reid.

It has been often said in nuisance cases that the rule is *sic utere tuo ut alienum non laedas*. But that is a most misleading maxim. Lord Wright put it in its proper place in *Sedleigh-Denfield v O'Callaghan*:

> [It] is not only lacking in definiteness but is also inaccurate. An occupier may make in many ways a use of his land which causes damage to the neighbouring landowners, and yet be free from liability ... a useful test is perhaps what is reasonable according to the ordinary usages of mankind living in society, or, more correctly, in a particular society.

I would, therefore, adopt this test: is the use by the cricket club of this ground for play-ing cricket a reasonable use of it? To my mind it is a most reasonable use. Just consider the circumstances. For over 70 years the game of cricket has been played on this ground to the great benefit of the community as a whole, and to the injury of none. No one could suggest that it was a nuisance to the neighbouring owners simply because an enthusiastic batsman occasionally hit a ball out of the ground for six to the approval of the admiring onlookers. Then I would ask: does it suddenly become a nuisance because one of the neighbours chooses to build a house on the very edge of the ground, in such a position that it may well be struck by the ball on the rare occasion when there is a hit for six? To my mind the answer is plainly No. The building of the house does not con-vert the playing of cricket into a nuisance when it was not so before. If and insofar as any damage is caused to the house or anyone in it, it is because of the position in which it was built. Suppose that the house had not been built by a developer, but by a private owner. He would be in much the same position as the farmer who previously put his cows in the field. He could not complain if a batsman hit a six out of the ground and, by a million to one chance, it struck a cow or even the farmer himself. He would be in no better position than a spectator at Lord's or the Oval or at a motor rally. At any rate, even if he could claim damages for the loss of the cow or the injury, he could not get an injunction to stop the cricket. If the private owner could not get an injunction, neither should a developer or a purchaser from him.

It was said, however, that the case of the physician's consulting-room was to the contrary. But that turned on the old law about easements and prescriptions, and so forth. It was in the days when rights of property were in the ascendant and not subject to any limitations except those provided by the law of easements. But nowadays it is a matter of balancing the conflicting interests of the two neighbours. That was made clear by Lord Wright in *Sedleigh-Denfield v O'Callaghan*, when he said: 'A balance has to be maintained between the right of the occupier to do what he likes with his own and the right of his neighbour not to be interfered with'.

In this case it is our task to balance the right of the cricket club to continue playing cricket on their cricket ground, as against the right of the householder not to be inter-fered with. On taking the balance, I would give priority to the right of the cricket club to continue playing cricket on the ground, as they have done for the last 70 years. It takes precedence over the right of the newcomer to sit in his garden undisturbed. After all he bought the house four years ago in mid-summer when the cricket season was at its height. He might have guessed that there was a risk that a hit for six might possibly land on his property. If he finds that he does not like it, he ought, when cricket is played, to sit in the other side of the house or in the front garden, or go out; or take advantage of the offers the club have made to him of fitting unbreakable glass, and so forth. Or, if he does not like that, he ought to sell his house and move else-where. I expect there are many who would gladly buy it in order to be near the cricket field and open space. At any rate he ought not to be allowed to stop cricket being played on this ground.

This case is new. It should be approached on principles applicable to modern condi-tions. There is a contest here between the interest of the public at large and the interest of a private individual. The public interest lies in protecting the environment by preserving our playing fields in the face of mounting development, and by enabling our youth to enjoy all the benefits of outdoor games, such as cricket and football. The private interest lies in securing the privacy of his home and garden without intrusion or interference by anyone. In deciding between these two conflicting interests, it must be remembered that it is not a question of damages. If by a million-to-one chance a cricket ball does go out of the ground and cause damage, the cricket club will pay. There is no difficulty on that score. No, it is a question of an injunction. And in our law you will find it repeatedly affirmed that an injunction is a discretionary remedy. In a new situation like this, we have to think afresh as to how discretion should be exercised. On the one hand, Mrs Miller is a very sensitive lady who has worked herself up into such a state that she exclaimed to the judge: 'I just want to be allowed to live in peace. Have we got to wait until someone is killed before anything can be done?' If she feels like that about it, it is quite plain that, for peace in the future, one or other has to move. Either the cricket club have to move, but goodness knows where. I do not suppose for a moment there is any field in Lintz to which they could move. Or Mrs Miller must move elsewhere. As between their conflicting interests, I am of opinion that the public interest should prevail over the private interest. The cricket club should not be driven out. In my opinion the right exercise of discretion is to refuse an injunction; and, of course, to refuse damages in lieu of an injunction. Likewise as to the claim for past damages. The club were entitled to use this ground for cricket in the accustomed way. It was not a nuisance, nor was it negligence of them so to run it. Nor was the batsman negligent when he hit the ball for six. All were doing simply what they were entitled to do. So if the club had put it to the test, I would have dismissed the claim for damages also. But as the club very fairly say that they are willing to pay for any damage, I am content that there should be an award of £400 to cover any past or future damage.

I would allow the appeal, accordingly.

Geoffrey Lane LJ:

...

Nuisance

In circumstances such as these it is very difficult and probably unnecessary, except as an interesting intellectual exercise, to define the frontiers between negligence and nuisance: see Lord Wilberforce in *Goldman v Hargrave*. Was there here a use by the defendants of their land involving an unreasonable interference with the plaintiffs' enjoyment of their land? There is here in effect no dispute that there has been and is likely to be in the future an interference with the plaintiffs' enjoyment of no. 20, Brackenridge. The only question is whether it is unreasonable. It is a truism to say that this is a matter of degree. What that means is this. A balance has to be maintained between on the one hand the rights of the individual to enjoy his house and garden without the threat of damage and on the other hand the rights of the public in general or a neighbour to engage in lawful pastimes. Difficult questions may sometimes arise when the defendants' activities are offensive to the senses, for example by way of noise. Where, as here, the damage or potential damage is physical the answer is more simple. There is, subject to what appears hereafter, no excuse I can see which exonerates the defendants from liability in nuisance for what they have done or from what they threaten to do. It is true no one has yet been physically injured. That is probably due to a great extent to the fact that the householders in Brackenridge desert their gardens whilst cricket is in progress. The danger of injury is obvious and is not slight enough to be disregarded. There is here a real risk of serious injury.

There is, however, one obviously strong point in the defendants' favour. They or their predecessors have been playing cricket on this ground (and no doubt hitting sixes out of it) for 70 years or so. Can someone by building a house on the edge of the field in circumstances where it must have been obvious that balls might be hit over the fence, effectively stop cricket being played? Precedent apart, justice would seem to demand that the plaintiffs should be left to make the most of the site they have elected to occupy with all its obvious advantages and all its equally obvious disadvantages. It is pleasant to have an open space over which to look from your bedroom and sitting-room windows, so far as it is possible to see over the concrete wall. Why should you complain of the obvious disadvantages which arise from the particular purpose to which the open space is being put? Put briefly, can the defendants take advantage of the fact that the plaintiffs have put themselves in such a position by coming to occupy a house on the edge of a small cricket field, with the result that what was not a nuisance in the past now becomes a nuisance? If the matter were *res integra*, I confess I should be inclined to find for the defendants. It does not seem just that a long-established activity, in itself innocuous, should be brought to an end because someone chooses to build a house nearby and so turn an innocent pastime into an actionable nuisance. Unfortunately, however, the question is not open. In *Sturges v Bridgman* this very problem arose. The defendant had carried on a confectionery shop with a noisy pestle and mortar for more than 20 years. Although it was noisy, it was far enough away from neighbouring premises not to cause trouble to anyone, until the plaintiff, who was a physician, built a consulting-room on his own land but immediately adjoining the confectionery shop. The noise and vibrations seriously interfered with the consulting-room and became a nuisance to the physician. The defendant contended that he had acquired the right either at common law or under the Prescription Act 1832 by uninterrupted use for more than 20 years to impose the inconvenience. It was held by the Court of Appeal, affirming the judgment of Jessel MR, that use such as this which was, prior to the construction of the consulting-room, neither preventable nor actionable, could not found a prescriptive right. That decision involved the assumption, which so far as one can discover has never been questioned, that it is no answer to a claim in nuisance for the defendant to show that the plaintiff brought the trouble on his own head by building or coming to live in a house so close to the defendant's premises that he would inevitably be affected by the defendant's activities, where no one had been affected previously. See also *Bliss v Hall*. It may be that this rule works injustice; it may be that one would decide the matter differently in the absence of authority. But we are bound by the decision in *Sturges v Bridgman* and it is not for this court as I see it to alter a rule which has stood for so long.

Injunction

Given that the defendants are guilty of both negligence and nuisance, is it a case where the court should in its discretion give relief, or should the plaintiffs be left to their remedy in damages? There is no doubt that if cricket is played damage will be done to the plaintiffs' tiles or windows or both. There is a not inconsiderable danger that if they or their son or their guests spend any time in the garden during the weekend afternoons in the summer they may be hit by a cricket ball. So long as this situation exists it seems to me that damages cannot be said to provide an adequate form of relief. Indeed, quite apart from the risk of physical injury, I can see no valid reason why the plaintiffs should have to submit to the inevitable breakage of tiles and/or windows, even though the defendants have expressed their willingness to carry out any repairs at no cost to the plaintiffs. I would accordingly uphold the grant of the injunction to restrain the defendants from committing nuisance. However, I would postpone the operation of the injunction for 12 months to enable the defendants to look elsewhere for an alternative pitch.

So far as the plaintiffs are concerned, the effect of such postponement will be that they will have to stay out of their garden until the end of the cricket season but thereafter will be free to use it as they wish.

I have not thought it necessary to embark on any discussion of the possible rights of the defendants arising from matters which were neither pleaded nor argued.

Cumming-Bruce LJ:

I agree with all that Geoffrey Lane LJ has said in his recital of the relevant facts and his reasoning and conclusion on the liability of the defendants in negligence and nuisance, including his observation about the decision in *Sturges v Bridgman* ...

The only problem that arises is whether the learned judge is shown to be wrong in deciding to grant the equitable remedy of an injunction which will necessarily have the effect that the ground which the defendants have used as a cricket ground for 70 years can no longer be used for that purpose ... There is authority that in considering whether to exercise a judicial discretion to grant an injunction the court is under a duty to consider the interests of the public. So said Lord Romilly MR over a hundred years ago in *Raphael v Thames Valley Railway Co*, but the conflict of interest there was between proprietary private rights and the inconvenience to be suffered by users of a railway: see also *Wood v Sutcliffe*. Courts of equity will not ordinarily and without special necessity interfere by injunction where the injunction will have the effect of very materially injuring the rights of third persons not before the court ...

So on the facts of this case a court of equity must seek to strike a fair balance between the right of the plaintiffs to have quiet enjoyment of their house and garden without exposure to cricket balls occasionally falling like thunderbolts from the heavens, and the opportunity of the inhabitants of the village in which they live to continue to enjoy the manly sport which constitutes a summer recreation for adults and young persons, including one would hope and expect the plaintiffs' son. It is a relevant circumstance which a court of equity should take into account that the plaintiffs decided to buy a house which in June 1972 when completion took place was obviously on the boundary of a quite small cricket ground where cricket was played at weekends and sometimes on evenings during the working week. They selected a house with the benefit of the open space beside it. In February, when they first saw it, they did not think about the use of this open space. But before completion they must have realised that it was the village cricket ground, and that balls would sometimes be knocked from the wicket into their garden, or even against the fabric of the house. If they did not realise it, they should have done. As it turns out, the female plaintiff has developed a somewhat obsessive attitude to the proximity of the cricket field and the cricketers who visit her to seek to recover their cricket balls. The evidence discloses a hostility which goes beyond what is reasonable, although as the learned judge found she is reasonable in her fear that if the family use the garden while a match is in progress they will run risk of serious injury if a great hit happens to drive a ball up to the skies and down into their garden. It is reasonable to decide that during matches the family must keep out of the garden. The risk of damage to the house can be dealt with in other ways, and is not such as to fortify significantly the case for an injunction stopping play on this ground.

With all respect, in my view the learned judge did not have regard sufficiently to these considerations. He does not appear to have had regard to the interest of the inhabitants of the village as a whole. Had he done so he would in my view have been led to the conclusion that the plaintiffs having accepted the benefit of the open space marching with their land should accept the restrictions on enjoyment of their garden which they may reasonably think necessary. That is the burden which they have to bear in order that the inhabitants of the village may not be deprived of their facilities for an innocent recreation which they have so long enjoyed on this ground. There are here special circumstances which should inhibit a court of equity from granting the injunction claimed. If I am wrong in that conclusion, I agree with Geoffrey Lane LJ that the injunction should be suspended for one year to enable the defendants to see if they can find another ground.

Appeal allowed. Past and future damages at £400.

Kennaway v Thompson

[1981] 1 QB 88 (CA)

Lawton LJ read the following judgment of the court:

This appeal, which is from a judgment of Mais J delivered at Reading on May 24, 1979, is concerned with remedies, not liability. The defendants, who are sued are representatives of the Cotswold Motor Boat Racing Club, have accepted that in this court they have no grounds for challenging the judge's finding that some of the club's activities caused a nuisance to the plaintiff's house, Mallam Waters, near Fairford in Gloucestershire. The judge awarded her £1000 damages for the damage she had suffered up to the date of the trial and £15000 damages under Lord Cairns's Act 1858 for the damage which she is likely to suffer in the future. He refused an injunction. The plaintiff does not want damages. She wants to live in her house without having to put up with a great deal of noise each year from the end of March to the beginning of November, the period during which the club carries on its racing activities on a nearby man-made lake which the judge referred to as the club's water. It was a gravel pit, as was the lake alongside which stands the plaintiff's house.

Both the club's water and Mallam Water are situated about a mile to the east of Fairford. They are separated from one another by a minor public highway. The club's water covers an area of 38.31 acres, Mallam Water 12.18 acres. The plaintiff's house stands on a spit of land about half-way along Mallam Water. Bordering the road, there is a belt of trees on the west side of Mallam Water. The distance from the plaintiff's house to the starting line for the races organised by the club is 390 yards.

In the early 1960s the club's water began to be used for motor-boat racing; but at that time only small boats were used. The plaintiff knew what was going on as she had been brought up in the area and her father owned land to the east of the road including Mallam Water.

In 1969 the plaintiff, who by this time had become the owner of Mallam Water, her father having died in 1966, applied for planning permission to build a house alongside it. She was granted permission and in May 1972 the house was ready for occupation. When she applied for planning permission the racing activities on the club's water were not such as to make her think that the noise could interfere with her comfort when she came to live in her house: but between 1969 and 1972 there was a considerable increase in the amount of racing activity on the club's water. This was organised by the club. The boats used for racing were bigger than they had been in the 1960s and were making more noise. This tendency continued after 1972 and by the time proceedings were started in 1977 the club's water had become a well-known centre for motor-boat racing at club, national and international levels. In 1977, for example, there were races most weekends between April 3 and October 30. There were national meetings on the club's water on five occasions and an international meeting on one. Some of these meetings lasted two days. Before each meeting there would be hours and days of practising. The boats used for the national and international meetings were large. The largest class of boats were supposed to have a noise limit of 85 decibels, with an upward tolerance of a further 10 decibels. Experiments carried out showed that nearly all the large boats took advantage of this tolerance and the noise made by a number exceeded 100 decibels. We do not consider it necessary to go into the details of the evidence about noise level as there was no issue before us about liability. It suffices to record that we heard tape recordings taken in the plaintiff's house whilst racing, probably with the largest boats, was going on and we saw and heard a sound film taken and recorded during racing at a distance of 25 feet from the club's water's edge. We were all of the opinion that noise caused by the club's activities, which include practising, racing, and water skiing, has interfered to a considerable extent with the plaintiff's use and enjoyment of her house. To have to live each year, from about 9 am until dusk each day from the end of March to the beginning of November in the expectation that at any moment, particularly at weekends, she would be subjected to unpleasant noises was a burden which prima facie she ought not to have to bear. The law provides the remedy of injunction for anyone subjected, as the plaintiff has been, and expects to be unless the court intervenes, to such a nuisance.

The judge, however, refused an injunction and made an award of damages under Lord Cairns's Act 1858, to compensate her for future nuisance. In his judgment he said that the form of injunction asked for by the plaintiff's counsel was too wide, but he went on as follows:

> As I said, the noise I consider at times is quite intolerable and wholly unreasonable and I would be prepared to grant an injunction in terms that the defendants be restrained from using or permitting the use of the waters in such a way as to be a nuisance or cause a nuisance to the plaintiff or to pursue their activities in such a way as to interfere with the plaintiff's reasonable enjoyment and occupation of her premises. But as I indicated ... if I were to grant such an

injunction this would only lead to further litigation almost certainly, and it does not appear to me to be the right approach.

He went on to consider a form of injunction which had been requested at a late stage of the case on behalf of the plaintiff. This would have had the effect of limiting racing to ten days a year, during one bank holiday and two periods of continuous days. He thought this would be unreasonable having regard to the history of the club. He continued as follows:

> The question remains as to whether I should grant an injunction. I have considered the question most carefully and as to whether damages in this case would meet the position—and substantial damages. I have come to the conclusion from what I have heard there is considerable public interest in this club, that the public do attend in large numbers and that it would be oppressive in all the circumstances to grant an injunction, other than the injunction I have indicated, which would merely cause further litigation.

He then made the awards of damages to which we have referred.

The plaintiff, through Mr Kempster, has submitted that the judge misdirected himself. What he did, it was said, was to allow the club to buy itself the right to cause a substantial and intolerable nuisance. It was no justification to say that this was for the benefit of that section of the public which was interested in motor-boat racing. Once the plaintiff had proved that the club had caused a nuisance which interfered in a substantial and intolerable way with the use and enjoyment of her house she was entitled to have it stopped by injunction.

Mr Gorman submitted that this court should not interfere with the exercise of the judge's discretion. He was entitled to take into account the effect which an injunction would have on the club and upon those members of the public who enjoyed watching or taking part in motor-boat racing.

Mr Kempster based his submissions primarily on the decision of this court in *Shelfer v City of London Electric Lighting Co* [1895] 1 Ch 287. The opening paragraph of the headnote, which correctly summarises the judgment, is as follows:

> Lord Cairns's Act 1858, in conferring upon courts of equity a jurisdiction to award damages instead of an injunction, has not altered the settled principles upon which those courts interfered by way of injunction; and in cases of continuing actionable nuisance the jurisdiction so conferred ought only to be exercised under very exceptional circumstances.

In a much quoted passage, Lindley LJ said, at pp 315–16:

> ... ever since Lord Cairns's Act was passed the Court of Chancery has repudiated the notion that the legislature intended to turn that court into a tribunal for legalising wrongful acts; or in other words, the court has always protested against the notion that it ought to allow a wrong to continue simply because the wrongdoer is able and willing to pay for the injury he may inflict. Neither has the circumstance that the wrongdoer is in some sense a public benefactor (eg a gas or water company or a sewer authority) ever been considered a

sufficient reason for refusing to protect by injunction an individual whose rights are being persistently infringed.

AL Smith LJ, in his judgment, set out what he called a good working rule for the award of damages in substitution for an injunction. His working rule does not apply in this case. The injury to the plaintiff's legal rights is not small; it is not capable of being estimated in terms of money save in the way the judge tried to make an estimate, namely by fixing a figure for the diminution of the value of the plaintiff's house because of the prospect of a continuing nuisance—and the figure he fixed could not be described as small. The principles enunciated in *Shelfer's* case, which is binding on us, have been applied time and time again during the past 85 years. The only case which raises a doubt about the application of the Shelfer principles to all cases is *Miller v Jackson* [1977] QB 966, a decision of this court. The majority (Geoffrey Lane and Cumming-Bruce LJJ, Lord Denning MR dissenting) adjudged that the activities of an old-established cricket club which had been going for over 70 years, had been a nuisance to the plaintiffs by reason of cricket balls landing in their garden. The question then was whether the plaintiffs should be granted an injunction. Geoffrey Lane LJ was of the opinion that one should be granted. Lord Denning MR and Cumming-Bruce LJ thought otherwise. Lord Denning MR said that the public interest should prevail over the private interest. Cumming-Bruce LJ stated that a factor to be taken into account when exercising the judicial discretion whether to grant an injunction was that the plaintiffs had bought their house knowing that it was next to the cricket ground. He thought that there were special circumstances which should inhibit a court of equity from granting the injunction claimed. Lord Denning MR's statement that the public interest should prevail over the private interest runs counter to the principles enunciated in *Shelfer's* case and does not accord with Cumming-Bruce LJ's reason for refusing an injunction. We are of the opinion that there is nothing in *Miller v Jackson* [1977] QB 966 binding on us, which qualifies what was decided in *Shelfer's* case. Any decisions before *Shelfer's* case (and there were some at first instance, as Mr Gorman pointed out) which give support for the proposition that the public interest should prevail over the private interest must be read subject to the decision in *Shelfer's* case.

It follows that the plaintiff was entitled to an injunction and that the judge misdirected himself in law in adjudging that the appropriate remedy for her was an award of damages under Lord Cairns's Act. But she was only entitled to an injunction restraining the club from activities which caused a nuisance, and not all of their activities did. As the judge pointed out, and the plaintiff, by her counsel, accepted in this court, an injunction in general terms would be unworkable.

Our task has been to decide on a form of order which will protect the plaintiff from the noise which the judge found to be intolerable but which will not stop the club from organising activities about which she cannot reasonably complain.

When she decided to build a house alongside Mallam Water she knew that some motor-boat racing and water skiing was done on the club's water and she thought that the noise which such activities created was tolerable. She cannot now complain about that kind of noise provided it does not increase in volume by reason of any increase in activities. The intolerable noise is mostly caused by the large boats: it is these which attract the public interest.

Now nearly all of us living in these islands have to put up with a certain amount of annoyance from our neighbours. Those living in towns may be irritated by their neighbours' noisy radios or incompetent playing of musical instruments; and they in turn may be inconvenienced by the noise caused by our guests slamming car doors and chattering after a late party. Even in the country the lowing of a sick cow or the early morning crowing of a farmyard cock may interfere with sleep and comfort. Intervention by injunction is only justified when the irritating noise causes inconvenience beyond what other occupiers in the neighbourhood can be expected to bear. The question is whether the neighbour is using his property reasonably, having regard to the fact that he has a neighbour. The neighbour who is complaining must remember, too, that the other man can use his property in a reasonable way and there must be a measure of give and take, live and let live.

Understandably the plaintiff finds intolerable the kind of noise which she has had to suffer for such long periods in the past; but if she knew that she would only have to put up with such noise on a few occasions between the end of March and the beginning of November each year, and she also knew when those occasions were likely to occur, she could make arrangements to be out of her house at the material times. We can see no reason, however, why she should have to absent herself from her house for many days so as to enable the club members and others to make noises which are a nuisance. We consider it probable that those who are interested in motor-boat racing are attracted by the international and national events, which tend to have the larger and noisier boats. Justice will be done, we think, if the club is allowed to have, each racing season, one international event extending over three days, the first day being given over to practice and the second and third to racing. In addition there can be two national events, each of two days but separated from the international event and from each other by at least four weeks. Finally there can be three club events, each of one day, separated from the international and national events and each other by three weeks. Any international or national event not held can be replaced by a club event of one day. No boats creating a noise of more than 75 decibels are to be used on the club's water at any time other than when there are events as specified in this judgment. If events are held at weekends, as they probably will be, six weekends, covering a total of ten days, will be available for motor-boat racing on the club's water. Water skiing, if too many boats are used, can cause a nuisance by noise. The club is not to allow more than six motor-boats to be used for water skiing at any one time. An injunction will be granted to restrain motor-boat racing, water skiing and the use of boats creating a noise of more than 75 decibels on the club's water save to the extent and in the circumstances indicated.

Bank of New Zealand v Greenwood
[1984] 1 NZLR 525 (HC)
Hardie Boys J:
This is an action in nuisance. The plaintiffs seek an injunction to prevent the reflection of sunlight into their south-facing windows from glass roofing panels forming the verandah of the defendants' building across the road. The case raises in an interesting way the difficult and important problem of reconciling conflicting rights and interests in modern urban society.

The defendants' building is the High Street Arcade, which is situated in the midst of Christchurch's central commercial and shopping area, with frontages on High Street and Hereford Street, close to Colombo Street. It is of two storeys and was built in 1977–78. The design enables shoppers to walk through from one street to the other, and to look upwards to a gallery around which the first floor shops are set. This visual cohesion of the two floors is an essential part of the design. It is carried through to the exterior by extending the shop windows on the street frontages almost to the top of the building and then by carrying the verandah, constructed predominantly of glass, on a slope of approximately 60 degrees from the regulation height above the kerb to the level of the first-floor ceiling. Thus the first-floor shops can be seen from the footpath opposite, people in the first floor can look out as well as down, and brightness falls onto the footpath below, enhancing the aspect of the building and the impact of the design.

Mr Miles Warren, the architect who designed the Arcade, said that the use of glass to replace the traditional flat opaque verandah, particularly in conjunction with two-storey buildings, is one of the most distinctive architectural forms developed in New Zealand in recent years. This building is one of the first examples, and many others have followed, most particularly in Wellington. They show a variety of form and shape, although for safety reasons they are not permitted to be flat. This is the only one in Christchurch to be set at a constant slope, the others being set on more than one plane, or rounded, but there are a number such as this elsewhere. Mr Warren said this is the first occasion on which he has heard of any complaint in New Zealand about reflection from glass in buildings, but even when he designed the building he was aware of instances overseas, and so had selected the least reflective of the many kinds of glass now on the market. Its reflectance is only 5 per cent (ie it reflects only 5 per cent of the light of the sun), as compared with 7 per cent for standard clear float glass, and up to 59 per cent for silver mirror glass. The much more highly reflective glasses have for some years been used for cladding large city buildings overseas, and are now being similarly used in New Zealand. But as reflections from them are cast horizontally or downwards, they do not give rise to quite the same problem as is encountered in this case.

The problem is this, that the verandah on Hereford Street reflects the sunlight across the road and into the windows of the two buildings opposite, BNZ House and Challenge House (which adjoins it to the east), causing considerable discomfort and inconvenience to those within. I heard evidence from 13 of these people, who gave, conscientiously I am sure, their account of the way in which they, and others they had observed, are being affected. This was very much evidence of impressions, as such susceptible no doubt to some overstatement, but nonetheless I find it clearly established that on a sunny day the verandah throws off a dazzling glare that is too intense for the naked eye to bear; and that those subjected to it cannot reasonably be expected to tolerate. People are momentarily blinded by it, have to shield their eyes from it, cannot look out the windows at it, need to sit with their backs to it. Sometimes they get headaches. It is a continuing cause of irritation and complaint, not only to those working there but also to the plaintiffs' customers and clients ...

Since life began, most of its forms have had to take some protective measures against the heat and glare of the sun. Those whose evolutionary development enables them to erect buildings in this hemisphere, as a matter of course equip them when they face north with appropriate screening glass, awnings, blinds, curtains. Ought they to be required to do the same on buildings facing south, to avoid reflected glare? Or is it an actionable nuisance for a north-facing building to be so constructed that it reflects the glare onto its neighbours? Those are the questions raised in this action, although no sooner is the second stated than it becomes obvious that its scope must be reduced. Because it is not reflection as such that is in issue, or even merely reflection onto a south-facing wall, but reflection from a relatively large surface and on an unaccustomed angle. For I think that much of the distinction drawn in this case by witnesses working on the higher floors between direct sunlight and the reflected sunlight is due first to the fact that the latter is cast upward and secondly to the fact that as a result of diffusion the glare is reflected off a much larger area than if the surface were a pure mirror reflecting the sun itself.

The tort of nuisance is not capable of a single comprehensive definition, and it is sufficient for present purposes to state that we are concerned with that part of it which gives a remedy for certain interferences with the occupier's use or enjoyment of his land. It may on an appropriate occasion be necessary to emphasise the distinction between this kind of case and those where the complaint is of physical damage to the land or something upon it. For in the latter, liability is probably strict, whilst in the former, it is certainly arguable that fault must be established. (See, for example, *Winfield and Jolowicz on Tort* (11th edn, 1979) pp 357 and 362, and the article 'The Essentials of Nuisance' by Mrs Margaret Vennell in 4 *Otago Law Review* 56; and also *Clearlight Holdings Ltd v Auckland City Council* [1976] 2 NZLR 729.) This case does not require participation in the controversy, for the plaintiffs seek only an injunction and not damages, and thus the Court's inquiry is limited to whether there is a continuing interference with their rights, which they are entitled to have stopped.

... [T]he test is simply whether a reasonable person, living or working in the particular area, would regard the interference as unacceptable. The reasonable person, much loved of lawyers, is as was pointed out in the 17th edition of *Salmond on the Law of Torts* (1977) at p 56, not necessarily the same as the average person. The expression 'connotes a person whose notions and standards of behaviour and responsibility correspond with those generally obtained among ordinary people in our society at the present time, who seldom allows his emotions to overbear his reason and whose habits are moderate and whose disposition is equable': probably not an accurate description of the average citizen.

The balancing of conflicting interests is accomplished by according to this reasonable person the attribute of acknowledging the reasonable exercise of rights by his neighbours. Over a hundred years ago, Bramwell B said that the law must allow 'those acts necessary for the common and ordinary use and occupation of land and houses' to be done, 'if conveniently done', without subjecting those who do them to an action:

> There is an obvious necessity for such a principle as I have mentioned. It is as much for the advantage of one owner as of another; for the very nuisance the one complains of, as the result of the ordinary use of his neighbour's land, he himself will create in the ordinary use of his own, and the reciprocal nuisances are of a comparatively trifling character. The convenience of such a rule may

be indicated by calling it a rule of give and take, live and let live (*Bamford v Turnley* (1862) 3 B & S 66, 83–4).

I emphasise the words 'if conveniently done' for they bring us back to the balance that must be maintained, in a way that *Salmond* put thus at p 61:

> He who causes a nuisance cannot avail himself of the defence that he is merely making a reasonable use of his own property. No use of property is reasonable which causes substantial discomfort to other persons, or is a source of damage to their property.

In striking the balance, the Court must have regard to all the relevant circumstances:

> ... including, for example, the time of commission of the act complained of, the place of its commission, the manner of committing it, that is, whether it is done wantonly or in the reasonable exercise of rights, and the effects of its commission, that is, whether those effects are transitory or permanent, occasional or continuous ... (34 *Halsbury's Laws of England* (4th edn) para 310).

... [I]t is not essential that there be an activity for there to be a nuisance. Rather, it arises from a state of affairs, which may indeed be no more than an activity, such as drilling, ringing Church bells, or even playing tennis (*Abbot v Arcus* (1948) 50 WALR 41) which the defendant allows to occur or continue on his land. (That is the real basis of the village cricket club case, *Miller v Jackson* [1977] 1 QB 966 (CA); and see *Salmond* 18th edn, p 49). The state of affairs need not have been brought about by the defendant. A recent example of such a nuisance, indeed of one arising merely from the natural state of the land, is *Leakey v National Trust* [1980] 2 WLR 65 (CA), where a landslip brought about by natural causes was held to be a nuisance. In the present case, the problem is really not due to natural causes, but to the deflection of the sunlight from its natural course by an artificial structure. Perhaps the closest well-known parallel is the diversion of surface water, which is clearly a nuisance.

A plaintiff's ability to shut out the nuisance cannot be more than a factor to be taken into account in considering whether the interference is at an unacceptable level. If only because a line would somewhere have to be drawn between what could and could not properly be expected of him, it cannot be determinative of liability. It was not suggested that the plaintiffs ought to have failed in *Miller v Jackson* because they could have built a higher fence than the cricket club had, or in *Leakey v National Trust* because they could have erected a barrier against the slip. To hold otherwise could be to require the plaintiff to remedy the defendant's wrong, and the law would not countenance such an absurdity.

The plaintiffs' case is simply that there is a substantial and unacceptable interference with the enjoyment of their premises; that the existing blinds and curtains are inadequate to counter it; and that it is not reasonable to expect them to install, and then operate and maintain, adequate blinds or curtains, which were not needed before the verandah was built. The defendants joined issue on both propositions.

On the first, Mr Sissons pointed to the intermittent nature of the problem, and to the small proportion of the total time during which the premises are used, in which it occurs. Mr Warren acknowledged that he would not regard it as lightly as that; nor would I. The number of hours in a given period over which the glare is experienced in any one plaintiff's premises, or even in any one room, cannot be calculated from the evidence, but some indication may be obtained from records produced by one of the Bank's witnesses which showed that over a period of 33 business days between mid-December 1978 and mid-January 1979 the glare was troublesome on the first floor for approximately 30 per cent of the time the Bank was open to the public; and for approximately 20 per cent of the time over a shorter period within the same time span on the ground floor. (It should be added that although there was ample evidence of customers being incommoded, there was no suggestion that the Bank had lost business as a result.) These are not insubstantial periods for business premises during business hours. Moreover, the level of the inconvenience is not to be measured solely to the length of time over which it is experienced. It is not time that is important so much as effect. Other relevant factors in that respect are the intensity of the glare; the direction from which it comes; and the fact that there is no escape from it, for the plaintiffs cannot simply close down when the problem arises, or even alleviate its effects by closing down sometimes (cf the Court's solution in *Kennaway v Thompson* which I discuss below). Another most significant feature, which I consider increases rather than diminishes the inconvenience, is the intermittent nature of the problem, not only its arrival and departure as the direction of the reflection changes, but also as the sun is obscured by cloud and then clears. This must all be very trying to those concerned, and is awkward for them to deal with, without proper curtains or blinds, drawn for considerably longer than may actually be necessary. For these reasons I conclude that despite the relatively short time overall in which the problem occurs, it amounts to a substantial and unacceptable imposition.

However, I limit that conclusion to the Bank and Challenge Properties Ltd. I consider that Duncan Cotterill & Co are in a different position, which is shared, although it makes no difference to the Bank's case, by the second floor of the Bank building. Whilst it may be awkward, I do not think it unreasonable for persons in offices fitted with venetian blinds to have to close these when necessary to keep out the glare, or even to keep them closed while the likelihood of glare persists. It is a perfectly normal thing for people to have to do. It is part of what venetian blinds are designed for. And Duncan Cotterill's own principals and staff do it on the north side of their premises. No doubt when the blinds are closed completely the rooms are darkened, but the interior lights are on all day, and I do not see that as a serious imposition in all the circumstances. I was told that even when the blinds are closed completely the glare may penetrate at the edges, but that seems to me a relatively minor matter. I exclude from consideration the one room in which there are no blinds, for that is the result of deliberate choice. I accordingly agree with Mr Sissons in relation to Duncan Cotterill & Co, and hold that it has not established the basic premise on which its action depends.

The situation is obviously different with those windows which are not presently fitted with blinds or curtains. With respect to these the defendants' argument is simply that on those windows the plaintiffs concerned should provide whatever is suitable to their needs and will be an effective barrier. But as there would be no reason for either plaintiff to do anything were it not for the glare from the defendants' verandah, the argument does not impress me. It may well be the case that many buildings do have heavy curtains on their south-facing windows, but I am sure that the purpose of that is not to keep out sunlight. It is one thing to take measures against it to the north, quite another to the south. To expect these plaintiffs to provide sun barriers on their south-facing windows as part of the give and take of business in the central city would in reality be to require them to accept total responsibility for eliminating the defendants' nuisance. As I have stated, the law will not require that.

As against these factors weighing in the plaintiffs' favour, counsel for the defendants principally relied on three arguments as tilting the balance the other way. This is not quite how he put his case, but I take the liberty of putting it so because of my view that this kind of claim requires the Court to undertake such a balancing of competing considerations.

The first argument to which I refer raised the question of relative costs: the cost to the plaintiffs of fitting curtains or blinds as compared with the cost to the defendants of altering or replacing the verandah. I do not think this is a relevant consideration. If one creates an actionable nuisance, he must eliminate it, whatever the cost. The fact that it will be expensive does not affect his liability. Nor does the fact that his innocent neighbour could eliminate its effects more cheaply, unless of course the cost of eliminating them were so disproportionately small as to lead the Court to the conclusion that there had not been a substantial invasion of his rights—and hence no actionable nuisance—at all. That is not the case here. Where the nuisance complained of derives from a hazard accidentally arising on the defendant's land, questions of cost are relevant in considering whether he acted reasonably in not removing it (*Goldman v Hargrave* [1967] 1 AC 645, *Leakey v National Trust* [1980] 2 WLR 65). But that is quite a different matter from this, and even there it is not a question of weighing relative costs. To take account of relative costs where an actionable nuisance has been prima facie established would in my view again be to impose the impermissible requirement that the plaintiffs carry the burden of the defendants' tort.

Mr Sissons next argued, and on this I think he placed his greatest reliance, and in my mind it raises the greatest difficulty in the case, that the defendants were doing no more than making ordinary and reasonable use of their land. The verandah was not in breach of any relevant statutory prohibition (such as s 77 of the Town and Country Planning Act 1977) and complied with local authority requirements—neither of these of course being in any way conclusive—and indeed discharged an obligation imposed by the local authority on all building owners to provide verandahs over central city footpaths. It was a normal structure, built of standard materials. All that there was different about it was the slope of the glass, which itself would have caused no difficulty had it faced in another direction or not faced another building.

In my opinion there is implicit in the 'mutual sufferance' notion that a reasonable person will tolerate the reasonable activities of his neighbour, the condition that only the normal and reasonable consequences of those activities will be encountered. If that condition is not satisfied, then the balance is upset and it may then be necessary to apply the dictum of Kekewich J in *Attorney-General v Cole & Son* [1901] 1 Ch 205, 207 that 'If [a man] creates a nuisance, he cannot say that he is acting reasonably. The two things are self-contradictory'. It is not a normal or a reasonable consequence of the construction of a verandah for a dazzling glare to be reflected into premises opposite, and so create a nuisance there.

Further, whilst the construction of a glass verandah may be regarded in isolation as an ordinary and reasonable use of land, that use must be considered, as Lawton LJ said in *Kennaway v Thompson*, having regard to the fact that there are neighbours; here, neighbours upon whose southern windows the verandah, located and set as it is, directs the glare of the sun.

It is therefore not enough for the defendants to say that it is a normal and reasonable thing to build a glass verandah. For that is not the point. The point is that the glass verandah was so built as to reflect the sun's diffused light across the street into the south-facing windows opposite. To build it in that way, so as to produce, albeit unwittingly, that result, is not in my opinion the kind of activity which the reasonable man should be expected to accept as part of the reciprocity of urban neighbourliness.

Mr Sisson's third point is perhaps best expressed in the words of Mr Warren, who said that because of the extensive use of glass verandahs in building design in recent times, 'it would have a resounding effect throughout the country if this verandah had to be modified'.

To the extent that this is an appeal to set the public interest ahead of the private interests of the plaintiffs, then I regret that authority requires me to close my ears to it. Despite the valiant efforts of the cricket-loving members of the Court in *Miller v Jackson*, it has been made clear in *Kennaway v Thompson* that a long line of authority going back to *Shelfer v City of London Electric Lighting Company* [1895] 1 Ch 287 has maintained inviolate the principle that, in the words of Lindley LJ in the latter case (p 316): '... the circumstances that the wrong-doer is in some sense a public benefactor ... [has not] ever been considered a sufficient reason for refusing to protect by injunction an individual whose rights are being persistently infringed'.

The only consolation I can offer is that every case in nuisance is a decision on its own particular facts ...

For these various reasons, I hold that the Bank and Challenge Properties Ltd have made out their case that the defendants are maintaining an actionable nuisance.

The plaintiffs seek an injunction and not damages, although Mr Forbes intimated that they would reluctantly accept the latter if they could not obtain the former. Again despite the majority view in *Miller v Jackson*—which I hope it may not be impertinent to suggest may have been different if the defendant had been for instance a baseball club—it is clear that if an actionable nuisance of a continuing nature is established, the plaintiff is entitled to have the nuisance stopped, and not to be paid off in damages, for that would result in the Court licensing his wrongdoing: *Shelfer v City of London Electric Lighting Company*, *Kennaway v Thompson*. On this basis, Mr Sissons acknowledged that he could not press for damages in lieu of an injunction.

The purpose of an injunction is to prevent the nuisance and not necessarily to eliminate the state of affairs which gives rise to it. For the basic principle of neighbourly reciprocity comes into play here too. The Court will intervene only to the extent of reducing the interference to a reasonably tolerable level. The plaintiff cannot achieve a more favourable state of affairs than he would have had to accept had the level of interference not become unreasonable ...

It seems to me that to require the defendants to take steps to eliminate the glare altogether would be to give the Bank and Challenge Properties Ltd more extensive relief than they are entitled to have. For as will be clear from the conclusion I have reached upon Duncan Cotterill & Co's claim, I consider that the glare is not an actionable nuisance where it can reasonably be excluded by drawing venetian blinds. The provision of blinds (I accept that curtains will not do but vertical venetians seem entirely suitable) at the defendants' expense would thus satisfy the plaintiffs' rights and discharge the defendants' obligations. It would achieve these results at what is likely to be a much lower cost to the defendants, both in terms of money and detrimental effect. And it would avoid the possibility which might occur if the verandah had to be replaced, of the defendants being imposed with a burden quite out of proportion to the injury being done to the plaintiffs.

To solve the matter in this way is not of course to decide the case on the basis of relative costs to the parties, for clearly the plaintiffs should not have to pay anything. Nor is it an award of damages in lieu of an injunction. It is in reality allowing the defendants to choose the means by which they will eliminate the nuisance. They may indeed prefer to eliminate it at its source, but I consider that they are entitled to deal with it if they prefer by reducing its effects to reasonable limits.

Clearly, having expressed that conclusion, I cannot take the matter further at this stage. The defendants will no doubt wish to consider their position. If they choose to pay for the installation of blinds, the plaintiffs will have to be consulted and their approval obtained to what may be proposed. It may be necessary to obtain further directions from the Court. The plaintiffs may not wish to have blinds. In that event, they will not be entitled to an injunction, but their right to damages will have to be considered. The action is therefore adjourned *sine die* to be brought on by any of the parties on seven days' notice.

Hunter v Canary Wharf Ltd

[1997] AC 655 (HL)

[**FACTS**: The plaintiffs were 690 residents of the Isle of Dogs in London. In 1989, construction began on the Canary Wharf Tower, on land developed by the defendants. A special government scheme was in place to encourage development of the area, which fast-tracked planning permission. Residents therefore did not get the usual opportunities to object to building work.

For two years or so after the tower was built, the plaintiffs apparently suffered loss of or interference with television reception as a result of the tower's presence. This lasted until a relay transmitter was built and the plaintiffs' aerials were adjusted or replaced. The plaintiffs sued for damages in nuisance and negligence, though the negligence action was later abandoned.

There was also a second nuisance action regarding the dust created when the defendants were building a link road. There were 513 plaintiffs in this action.

Some of the plaintiffs were owners or tenants of the property in which they lived, but some were spouses, family members or other people living in the property. The issues before their Lordships were therefore (1) whether interference with television reception is capable of being an actionable nuisance and (2) whether it is necessary to have an interest in property to be able to claim in private nuisance (and, if so, what type of interest is needed).

The trial judge answered both questions in the affirmative. The Court of Appeal reversed his decision on both counts, however, for reasons stated more fully in **Lord Goff**'s speech below.

Note that some points in this decision may help to distinguish more clearly between negligence and nuisance, addressing some of the confusions experienced by the Court in *Wagon Mound* (*No 2*) (the case is discussed in Chapter 4). The views of the House of Lords here can be discussed further in light of later pronouncements under the *Rylands* doctrine (see below).]

Lord Goff:

…

Interference with television signals

I turn first to consider the question whether interference with television signals may give rise to an action in private nuisance. This question was first considered over thirty years ago by Buckley J in *Bridlington Relay Ltd v Yorkshire Electricity Board* [1965] Ch. 436. That case was concerned not with interference caused by the presence of a building, but with electrical interference caused by the activities of the defendant electricity board. Buckley J held that such interference did not constitute a legal nuisance, because it was interference with a purely recreational facility, as opposed to interference with the health or physical comfort or well-being of the plaintiffs. He did not however rule out the possibility that ability to receive television signals free from interference might one day be recognised as 'so important a part of an ordinary householder's enjoyment of his property that such interference should be regarded as a legal nuisance': p 447. Certainly the average weekly hours for television viewing in this country, which your Lordships were told were twenty-four hours per week, show that many people devote much of their leisure time to watching television, even allowing for the fact that it is not clear whether the relevant statistic is based more on the time when television sets are turned on, rather than being actually watched. Certainly it can be asserted with force that for many people television transcends the function of mere entertainment, and in particular that for the aged, the lonely and the bedridden it must provide a great distraction and relief from the circumscribed nature of their lives. That interference with such an amenity might in appropriate circumstances be protected by the law of nuisance has been recognised in Canada, in *Nor-Video Services Ltd v Ontario Hydro* (1978) 84 DLR (3d) 221, 231.

However, as I see the present case, there is a more formidable obstacle to this claim. This is that the complaint rests simply upon the presence of the defendant's building on land in the neighbourhood as causing the relevant interference. The gravamen of the plaintiffs' case is that the defendants, by building the Canary Wharf Tower, interfered with the television signals and so caused interference with the reception on the plaintiffs' television sets; though it should not be overlooked that such interference might be caused by a smaller building and moreover that, since it is no defence that the plaintiff came to the nuisance, the same complaint could result from the simple fact of the presence of the building which caused the interference. In this respect the present case is to be distinguished from the *Bridlington Relay* case, in which the problem was caused not just by the presence of a neighbouring building but by electrical interference resulting from the defendant electricity board's activities.

As a general rule, a man is entitled to build on his own land, though nowadays this right is inevitably subject to our system of planning controls. Moreover, as a general rule, a man's right to build on his land is not restricted by the fact that the presence of the building may of itself interfere with his neighbour's enjoyment of his land. The building may spoil his neighbour's view ... ; in the absence of an easement, it may restrict the flow of air on to his neighbour's land ... ; and, again in the absence of an easement, it may take away light from his neighbour's windows ... : nevertheless his neighbour generally cannot complain of the presence of the building, though this may seriously detract from the enjoyment of his land ...

From this it follows that, in the absence of an easement, more is required than the mere presence of a neighbouring building to give rise to an actionable private nuisance. Indeed, for an action in private nuisance to lie in respect of interference with the plaintiff's enjoyment of his land, it will generally arise from something emanating from the defendant's land. Such an emanation may take many forms—noise, dirt, fumes, a noxious smell, vibrations, and suchlike. Occasionally activities on the defendant's land are in themselves so offensive to neighbours as to constitute an actionable nuisance, as in *Thompson-Schwab v Costaki* [1956] 1 WLR 335, where the sight of prostitutes and their clients entering and leaving neighbouring premises were held to fall into that category. Such cases must however be relatively rare. In one New Zealand case, *Bank of New Zealand v Greenwood* [1984] 1 NZLR 525, the glass roof of a verandah which deflected the sun's rays so that a dazzling glare was thrown on to neighbouring buildings was held, prima facie, to create a nuisance; but it seems that the effect was not merely to reflect the sunlight but to deflect it at such an angle and in such a manner as to cause the dazzling glare, too bright for the human eye to bear, to shine straight into the neighbouring building ... On that basis, such a case can be distinguished from one concerned with the mere presence of a building on neighbouring land. At all events the mere fact that a building on the defendant's land gets in the way and so prevents something from reaching the plaintiff's land is generally speaking not enough for this purpose ...

[**Note**: His Lordship noted that the same conclusion is reached in German law under the German Civil Code; the claim in *G v City of Hamburg*, which involved interference with television reception, failed because there were no emissions from the defendant's land.]

In the result I find myself to be in agreement on this point with Pill LJ, who delivered the judgment of the Court of Appeal ... when he expressed the opinion that no action lay in private nuisance for interference with television caused by the mere presence of a building. That a building may have such an effect has to be accepted. If a large building is proposed in a neighbouring area, it will usually be open to local people to raise the possibility of television interference with the local planning authority at the stage of the application for planning permission. It has, however, to be recognised that the problem may well not be appreciated until after the building is built, when it will be too late for any such representations to be made. Moreover in the present case, in which the Secretary of State had designated the relevant area as an enterprise zone with the effect that planning permission was deemed to have been granted for any form of development, no application for permission had to be made. But in any event, with the rapid spread of the availability of cable television in urban areas, interference of this kind is likely to become less and less important; and it should not be forgotten that satellite television is also available. In the present case, the problem was solved in the end by the introduction by the BBC of a new relay station, though not until after a substantial lapse of time ...

Right to sue in private nuisance

I turn next to the question of the right to sue in private nuisance. In the two cases now under appeal before your Lordships' House, one of which relates to interference with television signals and the other to the generation of dust from the construction of a road, the plaintiffs consist in each case of a substantial group of local people. Moreover they are not restricted to householders who have the exclusive right to possess the places where they live. They include people with whom householders share their homes, for example as wives or husbands or partners, or as children or other relatives. All of these people are claiming damages in private nuisance, by reason of interference with their television viewing or by reason of excessive dust.

Judge Havery held that the right to sue in private nuisance did not extend to include so wide a class of plaintiffs, but was limited to those with a right to exclusive possession of the relevant property. His decision on this point was however reversed by the Court of Appeal who, in the judgment delivered by Pill LJ, held ... :

> A substantial link between the person enjoying the use and the land on which he or she is enjoying it is essential but, in my judgment, occupation of property, as a home, does confer upon the occupant a capacity to sue in private nuisance.

Against that decision, the defendants in both actions now appeal to your Lordships' House.

The basic position is, in my opinion, most clearly expressed in Professor Newark's classic article on 'The Boundaries of Nuisance' (1949) 65 LQR 480 when he stated, at p 482, that the essence of nuisance was that 'it was a tort to land. Or to be more accurate it was a tort directed against the plaintiff's enjoyment of rights over land ...' ... [W]hen distinguishing cases of personal injury, he stated, at pp 488–9:

> In true cases of nuisance the interest of the plaintiff which is invaded is not the interest of bodily security but the interest of liberty to exercise rights over land in the amplest manner. A sulphurous chimney in a residential area is not a nuisance because it makes householders cough and splutter but because it prevents them taking their ease in their gardens. It is for this reason that the plaintiff in an action for nuisance must show some title to realty.

... There are many authoritative statements which bear out this thesis of Professor Newark. I refer in particular to *Sedleigh-Denfield v O'Callaghan* [1940] AC 880, 902–3 per Lord Wright; *Read v J Lyons & Co Ltd* [1947] AC 156, 183 per Lord Simonds; *Tate & Lyle Food and Distribution Ltd v Greater London Council* [1983] 2 AC 509, 536–7 per Lord Templeman; Fleming *The Law of Torts*, 8th edn, (1992), p 416.

Since the tort of nuisance is a tort directed against the plaintiff's enjoyment of his rights over land, an action of private nuisance will usually be brought by the person in actual possession of the land affected, either as the freeholder or tenant of the land in question, or even as a licensee with exclusive possession of the land ... though a reversioner may sue in respect of a nuisance of a sufficiently permanent character to damage his reversion. It was however established in *Foster v Warblington Urban District Council* [1906] 1 KB 648, that ... a person who is in exclusive possession of land may sue even though he cannot prove title to it. That case was concerned with a nuisance caused by the discharge of sewage by the defendant council into certain oyster beds. The plaintiff was an oyster merchant who had for many years been in occupation of the oyster beds which had been artificially constructed on the foreshore, which belonged to the lord of the manor. The plaintiff excluded everybody from the oyster beds, and nobody interfered with his occupation of the oyster beds or his removal and sale of oysters from them. It was held by the Court of Appeal that he could sue the defendant council in nuisance, notwithstanding that he could not prove his title ...

This decision was followed and applied by Mahon J in *Paxhaven Holdings Ltd v Attorney-General* [1974] 2 NZLR 185. He said, at p 189:

> In my opinion, however, the matter is clear in principle. In an action for nuisance the defence of jus tertii is excluded, and it is no answer for the respondent to contend in the present case that the nuisance was committed on an area of land mistakenly included in the grant of lease to the appellant from its landlord. De facto possession is sufficient to give the appellant his remedy ...

I have referred to this point at some length because I will have to return to it at a later stage.

Subject to this exception, however, it has for many years been regarded as settled law that a person who has no right in the land cannot sue in private nuisance. For this proposition, it is usual to cite the decision of the Court of Appeal in *Malone v Laskey* [1907] 2 KB 141. In that case, the manager of a company resided in a house as a licensee of the company which employed him. The plaintiff was the manager's wife who lived with her husband in the house. She was injured when a bracket fell from a wall in the house. She claimed damages from the defendants in nuisance and negligence, her claim in nuisance being founded upon an allegation, accepted by the jury, that the fall of the bracket had been caused by vibrations from an engine operating on the defendants' adjoining premises. The Court of Appeal held that she was unable to succeed in her claim in nuisance ...

Fletcher Moulton LJ said, at pp 153–4:

> So far as the plaintiff's case is based on nuisance, the contention on her behalf appears to me to be supported by no authority. Witherby & Co were the tenants and occupiers of these premises, and if the premises had been injured or

the enjoyment of them interfered with by the vibration it was open to them to take any one of three courses—they might come to the courts for an injunction to stop the vibration, or they might simply have tolerated it, or they might have authorised its continuance either gratuitously or for a valuable consideration. A person in the position of the plaintiff, who was in the premises as a mere licensee, had no right to dictate to Witherby & Co which course they should take … a person who is merely present in the house cannot complain of a nuisance which has in it no element of a public nuisance.

… The decision in *Malone v Laskey* on nuisance has since been followed in many cases, of which notable examples are *Cunard v Antifyre Ltd* [1933] 1 KB 551 and *Oldham v Lawson (No 1)* [1976] VR 654. Recently, however, the Court of Appeal departed from this line of authority in *Khorasandjian v Bush* [1993] QB 727, a case which I must examine with some care.

The plaintiff, a young girl who at the time of the appeal was 18, had formed a friendship with the defendant, then a man of 28. After a time, the friendship broke down and the plaintiff decided that she would have no more to do with the defendant, but the defendant found this impossible to accept. There followed a catalogue of complaints against the defendant, including assaults, threats of violence, and pestering the plaintiff at her parents' home where she lived … The home was the property of the plaintiff's mother, and it was recognised that her mother could complain of persistent and unwanted telephone calls made to her; but it was submitted that the plaintiff, as a mere licensee in her mother's house, could not invoke the tort of private nuisance to complain of unwanted and harassing telephone calls made to her in her mother's home. The majority of the Court of Appeal (Peter Gibson LJ dissenting) rejected this submission, relying on the decision of the Appellate Division of the Alberta Supreme Court in *Motherwell v Motherwell* (1976) 73 DLR (3d) 62. In that case, the Appellate Division not only recognised that the legal owner of property could obtain an injunction, on the ground of private nuisance, to restrain persistent harassment by unwanted telephone calls to his home [by his sister, who suffered from a paranoid condition], but also that the same remedy was open to his wife who had no interest in the property. In the Court of Appeal Peter Gibson LJ dissented on the ground that it was wrong in principle that a mere licensee or someone without any interest in, or right to occupy, the relevant land should be able to sue in private nuisance.

It is necessary therefore to consider the basis of the decision in *Motherwell v Motherwell* … Clement JA said, at p 78:

Here we have a wife harassed in the matrimonial home. She has a status, a right to live there with her husband and children. I find it absurd to say that her occupancy of the matrimonial home is insufficient to found an action in nuisance. In my opinion, she is entitled to the same relief as is her husband, the brother.

This conclusion was very largely based on the decision of the Court of Appeal in *Foster v Warblington Urban District Council* [1906] 1 KB 648, which Clement JA understood to establish a distinction between 'one who is "merely present"' and 'occupancy of a substantial nature', and that in the latter case the occupier was entitled to sue in private nuisance. However *Foster v Warblington Urban District Council* does not in my opinion provide authority for the proposition that a person in the position of a mere licensee, such as a wife or husband in her or his spouse's house, is entitled to sue in that action. This misunderstanding must, I fear, undermine the authority of *Motherwell v Motherwell* on this point; and so far as the decision in the Court of Appeal in *Khorasandjian v Bush* is founded upon *Motherwell v Motherwell* it is likewise undermined.

But I must go further. If a plaintiff, such as the daughter of the householder in *Khorasandjian v Bush*, is harassed by abusive telephone calls, the gravamen of the complaint lies in the harassment which is just as much an abuse, or indeed an invasion of her privacy, whether she is pestered in this way in her mother's or her husband's house, or she is staying with a friend, or is at her place of work, or even in her car with a mobile phone. In truth, what the Court of Appeal appears to have been doing was to exploit the law of private nuisance in order to create by the back door a tort of harassment which was only partially effective in that it was artificially limited to harassment which takes place in her home. I myself do not consider that this is a satisfactory manner in which to develop the law, especially when, as is the case in question, the step so taken was inconsistent with another decision of the Court of Appeal, viz *Malone v Laskey* ... by which the court was bound. In any event, a tort of harassment has now received statutory recognition: see the Protection from Harassment Act 1997. We are therefore no longer troubled with the question whether the common law should be developed to provide such a remedy. For these reasons, I do not consider that any assistance can be derived from *Khorasandjian v Bush* by the plaintiffs in the present appeals.

It follows that, on the authorities as they stand, an action in private nuisance will only lie at the suit of a person who has a right to the land affected. Ordinarily, such a person can only sue if he has the right to exclusive possession of the land, such as a freeholder or tenant in possession, or even a licensee with exclusive possession. Exceptionally, however, as *Foster v Warblington Urban District Council* shows, this category may include a person in actual possession who has no right to be there; and in any event a reversioner can sue in so far as his reversionary interest is affected. But a mere licensee on the land has no right to sue.

The question therefore arises whether your Lordships should be persuaded to depart from established principle, and recognise such a right in others who are no more than mere licensees on the land. At the heart of this question lies a more fundamental question, which relates to the scope of the law of private nuisance. Here I wish to draw attention to the fact that although, in the past, damages for personal injury have been recovered at least in actions of public nuisance, there is now developing a school of thought that the appropriate remedy for such claims as these should lie in our now fully developed law of negligence, and that personal injury claims should be altogether excluded from the domain of nuisance. The most forthright proponent of this approach has been Professor Newark, in his article 'The Boundaries of Nuisance' ... from which I have already quoted. Furthermore, it is now being suggested that claims in respect of physical damage to the land should also be excluded from private nuisance: see, eg, the article by Mr Conor Gearty on 'The Place of Private Nuisance in a Modern Law of Torts' [1989] CLJ 214. In any event, it is right for present purposes to regard the typical cases of private nuisance as being those concerned with interference with the enjoyment of land and, as such, generally actionable only by a person with a right in the land. Characteristic examples of cases of this kind are those concerned with noise, vibrations, noxious smells and the like. The two appeals with which your Lordships are here concerned arise from actions of this character.

For private nuisances of this kind, the primary remedy is in most cases an injunction, which is sought to bring the nuisance to an end, and in most cases should swiftly achieve that objective. The right to bring such proceedings is, as the law stands, ordinarily vested in the person who has exclusive possession of the land. He or she is the person who will sue, if it is necessary to do so. Moreover he or she can, if thought appropriate, reach an agreement with the person creating the nuisance ... [as] expressly contemplated by Fletcher Moulton LJ in his judgment in *Malone v Laskey* ... But the efficacy of arrangements such as these depends upon the existence of an identifiable person with whom the creator of the nuisance can deal for this purpose. If anybody who lived in the relevant property as a home had the right to sue, sensible arrangements such as these might in some cases no longer be practicable.

Moreover, any such departure from the established law on this subject, such as that adopted by the Court of Appeal in the present case, faces the problem of defining the category of persons who would have the right to sue. The Court of Appeal adopted the not easily identifiable category of those who have a 'substantial link' with the land, regarding a person who occupied the premises 'as a home' as having a sufficient link for this purpose. But who is to be included in this category? It was plainly intended to include husbands and wives, or partners, and their children and even other relatives living with them. But is the category also to include the lodger upstairs, or the au pair girl or resident nurse caring for an invalid who makes her home in the house while she works there? If the latter, it seems strange that the category should not extend to include places where people work as well as places where they live, where nuisances such as noise can be just as unpleasant or distracting. In any event, the extension of the tort in this way would transform it from a tort to land into a tort to the person, in which damages could be recovered in respect of something less serious than personal injury and the criteria for liability were founded not upon negligence but upon striking a balance between the interests of neighbours in the use of their land. This is, in my opinion, not an acceptable way in which to develop the law.

It was suggested in the course of argument that at least the spouse of a husband or wife who, for example as freeholder or tenant, had exclusive possession of the matrimonial home should be entitled to sue in private nuisance. For the purposes of this submission, your Lordships were referred to the relevant legislation, notably the Matrimonial Homes Act 1983 and the Family Law Act 1996. I do not however consider it necessary to go through the statutory provisions. As I understand the position, it is as follows. If under the relevant legislation a spouse becomes entitled to possession of the matrimonial home or part of it, there is no reason why he or she should not be able to sue in private nuisance in the ordinary way. But I do not see how a spouse who has no interest in the matrimonial home has, simply by virtue of his or her cohabiting in the matrimonial home ... a right to sue. No distinction can sensibly be drawn between such spouses and other cohabitees in the home, such as children, or grandparents. Nor do I see any great disadvantage flowing from this state of affairs. If a nuisance should occur then the spouse who has an interest in the property can bring the necessary proceedings to bring the nuisance to an end, and can recover any damages in respect of the discomfort or inconvenience caused by the nuisance. Even if he or she is away from home, nowadays the necessary authority to commence proceedings for an injunction can usually be obtained by telephone. Moreover, if the other spouse suffers personal injury, including injury to health, he or she may, like anybody else, be able to recover damages in negligence ...

Since preparing this opinion, I have had the opportunity of reading in draft the speech of my noble and learned friend, Lord Cooke of Thorndon, and I have noticed his citation of academic authority which supports the view that the right to sue in private nuisance in respect of interference with amenities should no longer be restricted to those who have an interest in the affected land ... I have to say (though I say it in no spirit of criticism, because I know full well the limits within which writers of textbooks on major subjects must work) that I have found no analysis of the problem; and in circumstances such as this, a crumb of analysis is worth a loaf of opinion ...

For all these reasons, I can see no good reason to depart from the law on this topic as established in the authorities. I would therefore hold that *Khorasandjian v Bush* must be overruled in so far as it holds that a mere licensee can sue in private nuisance, and I would allow the appeal or cross-appeal of the defendants in both actions and restore the order of Judge Havery on this issue.

[**Note: Lord Goff** was joined by **Lords Lloyd, Hoffmann** and **Hope**.]

Lord Cooke of Thorndon: (dissenting on the issue of standing to sue)

My Lords, having had the privilege of reading in draft the opinions of the other four members of your Lordships' Committee in these cases, I begin my own contribution by respectfully acknowledging that they achieve a major advance in the symmetry of the law of nuisance. Being less persuaded that they strengthen the utility or the justice of this branch of the common law, I am constrained to offer an approach which, although derived from concepts to be found in those opinions, would lead to principles different in some respects. Naturally I am diffident about disagreeing in any respect with the majority of your Lordships, but such assistance as I may be able to give in your deliberations could not consist in mere conformity and deference; and, if the common law of England is to be directed into the restricted path which in this instance the majority prefer, there may be some advantage in bringing out that the choice is in the end a policy one between competing principles.

My Lords, the lineaments of the law of nuisance were established before the age of television and radio, motor transport and aviation, town and country planning, a 'crowded island', and a heightened public consciousness of the need to protect the environment. All these are now among the factors falling to be taken into account in evolving the law. It is possible for the courts to cater for such developments because the forms which nuisance may take are protean ... and nuisance is a term used to cover a wide variety of tortious acts or omissions, and in many negligence in the narrow sense is not essential ...

Further, as to impairment of the enjoyment of land, the governing principle is that of reasonable user—'the principle of give and take as between neighbouring occupiers of land': *Cambridge Water Co v Eastern Counties Leather Plc* [1994] 2 AC 264, 299 per Lord Goff of Chieveley. The principle may not always conduce to tidiness, but tidiness has not had a high priority in the history of the common law. What has made the law of nuisance a potent instrument of justice throughout the common law world has been largely its flexibility and versatility. The judgment of Hardie Boys J in the glare case, *Bank of New Zealand v Greenwood* [1984] 1 NZLR 525 appeals to me as an admirable example and I do not share the view that it may overlook that nuisance and negligence are different torts ...

Private nuisance is commonly said to be an interference with the enjoyment of land and to be actionable by an occupier. But 'occupier' is an expression of varying meanings, as a perusal of legal dictionaries shows. Compare, for instance, *Paterson v Gas Light and Coke Co* [1896] 2 Ch 476,482; *Reg v Tao* [1977] QB 141; *Street v Mountford* [1985] AC 809. In the latter case the expression was used as a neutral one covering either a tenancy or a licence but it was held that, generally speaking, exclusive possession for a fixed or periodic term at a stated rent carries a tenancy. Your Lordships' House does not appear to have been called on hitherto to lay down precisely the meaning to be given to the expression in relation to interference with the amenities of land. There is a dictum by Lord Simonds in *Read v J Lyons & Co Ltd* [1947] AC 156, 183 restricting a lawful claim in nuisance to one who has suffered an invasion of some proprietary or other interest in land; but it was obiter and not focused on interference with amenities. Where interference with an amenity of a home is in issue there is no a priori reason why the expression should not include, and it appears natural that it should include, anyone living there who has been exercising a continuing right to enjoyment of that amenity ... A temporary visitor, however, someone who is 'merely present in the house' (a phrase used by Fletcher Moulton LJ in *Malone v Laskey* [1907] 2 KB 141, 154), would not enjoy occupancy of sufficiently substantial nature.

I cannot avoid adding that it seems to me less than probable that Clement JA misunderstood the plain meaning of the passage which he quoted from *Foster*. As I read his judgment, he mentioned *Foster* only as authority for the proposition that substantial de facto occupation may be enough—and the case is indeed authority for that—but his reason for holding that a resident wife had standing was not based on *Foster* but on altogether different and wider considerations relating to the family home.

Malone v Laskey, a case of personal injury from a falling bracket rather than an interference with amenities, is not directly in point, but it is to be noted that the wife of the subtenant's manager, who had been permitted by the subtenant to live on the premises with her husband, was dismissed by Sir Gorell Barnes P, at p 151, as a person who had 'no right of occupation in the proper sense of the term' and by Fletcher Moulton LJ as being 'merely present'. My Lords, whatever the acceptability of those descriptions 90 years ago, I can only agree with the Appellate Division of the Alberta Supreme Court in *Motherwell v Motherwell*, at p 77, that they are 'rather light treatment of a wife, at least in today's society where she is no longer considered subservient to her husband'. Current statutes give effect to current perceptions by according spouses a special status in respect of the matrimonial home, as by enabling the court to make orders regarding occupation ... Although such provisions and orders thereunder do not of themselves confer proprietary rights, they support in relation to amenities the force and common sense of the words of Clement JA in *Motherwell v Motherwell*, at p 78:

> Here we have a wife harassed in the matrimonial home. She has a status, a right to live there with her husband and children. I find it absurd to say that her occupancy of the matrimonial home is insufficient to found an action in nuisance.

As between spouses and de facto partners the question whether contributions in money or service give a proprietary equitable interest in a matrimonial home is a notoriously difficult one today, wrestled with throughout the common law world. Nuisance actions would seem better left free of the complication of this side issue.

The status of children living at home is different and perhaps more problematical but, on consideration, I am persuaded by the majority of the Court of Appeal in *Khorasandjian v Bush* [1993] QB 727 and the weight of North American jurisprudence to the view that they, too, should be entitled to relief for substantial and unlawful interference with the amenities of their home. Internationally the distinct interests of children are increasingly recognised. The United Nations Convention on the Rights of the Child, ratified by the United Kingdom in 1991 and the most widely ratified human rights treaty in history, acknowledges children as fully fledged beneficiaries of human rights. Article 16 declares, inter alia, that no child shall be subjected to unlawful interference with his or her home and that the child has the right to the protection of law against such interference. International standards such as this may be taken into account in shaping the common law.

The point just mentioned can be taken further. Article 16 of the Convention on the Rights of the Child adopts some of the language of article 12 of the Universal Declaration of Human Rights and article 8 of the European Convention for the Protection of Human Rights and Fundamental Freedoms (1953) (Cmd 8969). These provisions are aimed, in part, at protecting the home and are construed to give protection against nuisances: see *Arrondelle v United Kingdom*, Application No 7889/77 (1982) 26 D & R 5 (aircraft noise) and *Lopez Ostra v Spain* (1994) 20 EHRR 277 (fumes and smells from a waste treatment plant). The protection is regarded as going beyond possession or property rights: see Harris, O'Boyle and Warbrick, *Law of the European Convention on Human Rights* (1995) p 319. Again, I think that this is a legitimate consideration in support of treating residence as an acceptable basis of standing at common law in the present class of case ...

As is only to be expected in the light of the practical importance of nuisance liability in developed society, there is a vast sea of United States case law into which a judgment cannot conveniently do more than dip. It will have to be enough to rely on the summary in the American Law Institute's Restatement which echoes *Prosser and Keeton on Torts*, 5th edn, pp 621–2 ... The American Law Institute, *Restatement of the Law, Torts*, 2d (1979), section 821E, includes:

> d *Members of the family*. 'Possession' is not limited to occupancy under a claim of some other interest in the land, but occupancy is a sufficient interest in itself to permit recovery for invasions of the interest in the use and enjoyment of the

land. Thus members of the family of the possessor of a dwelling who occupy it along with him may properly be regarded as sharing occupancy with intent to control the land and hence as possessors, as defined in section 328E. When there is interference with their use and enjoyment of the dwelling they can therefore maintain an action for private nuisance. Although there are decisions to the contrary, the considerable majority of the cases dealing with the question have so held.

...

The preponderance of academic opinion seems also to be against confining the right to sue in nuisance for interference with amenities to plaintiffs with proprietary interests in land. Professor John G Fleming's condemnation of a 'senseless discrimination'—see now his 8th edn, p 426—has already been mentioned. His view is that the wife and family residing with a tenant should be protected by the law of nuisance against forms of discomfort and also personal injuries, 'by recognising that they have a "right of occupation" just like the official tenant'. *Clerk & Lindsell on Torts*, 17th edn, pp 910–11, para 18-39, is to the same effect, as is Linden, *Canadian Tort Law*, 5th edn (1993), pp 521–2; while *Winfield & Jolowicz on Tort*, 14th edn (1994), pp 419–20 and Markesinis & Deakin, *Tort Law*, 3rd edn (1994), pp 434–5 would extend the right to long-term lodgers. *Salmond & Heuston on the Law of Torts*, 21st edn (1996), p 63, n 96 and the New Zealand work Todd, *The Law of Torts in New Zealand*, 2nd edn (1997), p 537 suggest that the status of spouses under modern legislation should at least be enough ...

My Lords, there is a maxim *communis error facit jus*. I have collected the foregoing references not to invoke it, however, but to suggest respectfully that on this hitherto unsettled issue the general trend of leading scholarly opinion need not be condemned as erroneous. Although hitherto the law of England on the point has not been settled by your Lordships' House, it is agreed on all hands that some link with the land is necessary for standing to sue in private nuisance. The precise nature of that link remains to be defined, partly because of the ambiguity of 'occupy' and its derivatives. In ordinary usage the verb can certainly include 'reside in', which is indeed the first meaning given in the *Concise Oxford Dictionary*.

In logic more than one answer can be given. Logically it is possible to say that the right to sue for interference with the amenities of a home should be confined to those with proprietary interests and licensees with exclusive possession. No less logically the right can be accorded to all who live in the home. Which test should be adopted, that is to say which should be the governing principle, is a question of the policy of the law. It is a question not capable of being answered by analysis alone. All that analysis can do is expose the alternatives. Decisions such as *Malone v Laskey* ... do not attempt that kind of analysis, and in refraining from recognising that value judgments are involved they compare less favourably with the approach of the present-day Court of Appeal in *Khorasandjian* and this case. The reason why I prefer the alternative advocated with unwonted vigour of expression by the doyen of living tort writers is that it gives better effect to widespread conceptions concerning the home and family.

Of course in this field as in most others there will be borderline cases and anomalies wherever the lines are drawn. Thus there are, for instance, the lodger and, as some of your Lordships note, the au pair girl (although she may not figure among the present plaintiffs). It would seem weak, though, to refrain from laying down a just rule for spouses and children on the ground that it is not easy to know where to draw the lines regarding other persons. Without being wedded to this solution, I am not persuaded that there is sufficient justification for disturbing the conclusion adopted by Pill LJ with the concurrence of Neill and Waite LJJ. Occupation of the property as a home is, to me, an acceptable criterion, consistent with the traditional concern for the sanctity of family life and the Englishman's home—which need not in this context include his workplace. As already mentioned, it is consistent also with international standards.

Other resident members of the family, including such de facto partners and lodgers as may on the particular facts fairly be considered as having a home in the premises, could therefore be allowed standing to complain of truly serious interference with the domestic amenities lawfully enjoyed by them. By contrast, the policy of the law need not extend to giving a remedy in nuisance to non-resident employees in commercial premises. The employer is responsible for their welfare. On this part of the case, I have only to add that normally there should not be any difficulty about sensible compromises with the author of the nuisance. Members of a household impliedly authorise the householder to represent them in such matters.

As interferences with the amenities of land and personal injuries arising during the use of land are cognate subjects, it may be appropriate to add a few words about personal injuries from private nuisance. *Malone v Laskey* ... appears to assume that these will be actionable at the suit of a qualified plaintiff. A recent writer has concluded after a survey of the field that, although there is not much authority on the point, an occupant of property affected there by a nuisance can probably recover for personal injuries (Martin Davies, 'Private Nuisance, Fault and Personal Injuries' (1990) 20 UWALR 129). In his 1949 article, 'The Boundaries of Nuisance', 65 LQR 480, Professor Newark partly denied this, but made a major qualification of his thesis by conceding (n 55, p 490) that:

It may well be that where an actionable nuisance is committed which in addition to interfering with the plaintiff's enjoyment of rights in land also damages his person or chattels, he can recover in respect of the damage to his person or chattels as consequential damages.

... In truth, it has become solidly established that an action lies for personal injuries from a public nuisance ... and so much was implicitly accepted by this House in *Jacobs v London County Council* [1950] AC 361, 374, 377, where Lord Simonds said that the law of nuisance had travelled far beyond its original limits.

My Lords, as to the kind of harm actionable it would be hard to see any sensible difference between public and private nuisance. So, too, between nuisance and *Rylands v Fletcher* ... liability, at least since the identification in *Cambridge Water Co v Eastern Counties Leather Plc* [1994] 2 AC 264 of reasonable foresight of damage as an essential ingredient of liability under either head ...

Similarly, a plaintiff with standing to sue, including on my approach a member of the household, should be entitled to recover in nuisance for damage to chattels ... If a husband's car and his wife's are both damaged by spray from an adjacent property, they should alike be entitled to sue in nuisance even if he alone has a proprietary interest in the land ...

If the adoption of such principles might add marginally to building or operating costs in some cases, that could hardly be a more significant argument against them than is the cost of reasonable safeguards in any other field of the law.

Turning to the television action, I am in the happier position of being able to agree with all your Lordships and the Court of Appeal that this cannot succeed. Television has become a significant, and, to many, almost an indispensable amenity of domestic life ... I agree that, in appropriate cases, television and radio reception can and should be protected by the law of nuisance, although no doubt rights to reception cannot be acquired by prescription. Inhabitants of the Isle of Dogs and many another concentrated urban area might react with incredulity, and justifiably so, to the suggestion that the amenity of television and radio reception is fairly comparable to a view of the surroundings of their homes. Neither in nature nor in value is that so. It may be suspected that only a lawyer would think of such a suggestion.

What in my opinion must defeat an action for interference with television reception by the construction of a building, not only in this but in most cases, is the principle of reasonable user, of give and take ...

Control of building height is such a common feature of modern town planning regimes that it would be inadequate to say that at the present day owners of the soil generally enjoy their rights *usque ad coelum et ad inferos*. Although the primary responsibility for enforcement falls on the administering authorities, I see no reason why neighbours prejudicially affected should not be able to sue in nuisance if a building does exceed height, bulk or location restrictions. For then the developer is not making either a lawful or a reasonable use of landowning rights. This is to treat planning measures not as creating rights of action for breach of statutory duty but as denoting a standard of what is acceptable in the community.

In the light of the versatility of human malevolence and ingenuity, it is as well to add a second qualification. The malicious erection of a structure for the purpose of interfering with television reception should be actionable in nuisance on the principle of such well-known cases as *Christie v Davey* [1893] 1 Ch 316 and *Hollywood Silver Fox Farm Ltd v Emmett* [1936] 2 KB 468. Obviously this has no bearing on the present case or on the vast majority of cases. All the same it is not inconceivable. In his book *Canadian Tort Law*, Allen Linden cites *Attorney-General of Manitoba v Campbell* (1983) 26 CCLT 168 where a farmer was found to have put up a 74-foot steel tower of no practical use in his farming, directly in line with the runway of an adjoining airport, with no purpose other than as part of a maliciously conceived plan to prevent the upgrading of the airport. This he did just before the effective date of a planning order covering the height and locality of adjacent structures. A mandatory injunction to dismantle the tower was granted and obeyed ... I do not think ... that the view that malice is irrelevant in nuisance would have wide acceptance today.

Even putting malice aside, compliance with planning controls is not itself a defence to a nuisance action, as is brought out by the pig-house case *Wheeler v JJ Saunders Ltd* [1996] Ch 19, an instance of an injudicious grant of planning consent, procured apparently by the supply of inaccurate and incomplete information. But it must be of major importance that the Canary Wharf Tower, although said to be the highest building in Great Britain and certainly an exceptional feature of the London skyline, was built in an enterprise zone in an urban development area and authorised under the special procedure designed to encourage regeneration …

For these reasons, while not satisfied that a categorical universally applicable answer can be given to the issue about television reception, I agree that in this case the claim of nuisance consisting of interference with such reception cannot succeed …

The rule in *Rylands v Fletcher*

The 1868 decision in the case of *Rylands v Fletcher* was seen over time as establishing a separate tort of strict liability. It was consistently pleaded as a separate cause of action along with private or public nuisance or negligence. It is rather unlikely, however, that the judges in *Rylands* itself perceived the rule they established as anything other than an extension of private nuisance to cover the increasing number of disastrous incidents involving flooding from private dams.

Recently, the separate status of *Rylands* has come under attack. Most modern writing focuses on *Rylands'* links with other causes of action. There is a fascinating split in judicial authority on where such instances fit, however. In the United Kingdom, the House of Lords in *Cambridge Water v Eastern Leather Co* has aligned *Rylands* with private nuisance but the High Court of Australia in *Burnie Port Authority v General Jones* viewed it as subsumed by the expanding law of negligence. New Zealand's Court of Appeal in *Hamilton v Papakura DC* has chosen to follow the House of Lords approach, probably for reasons similar to those given by the minority in the earlier judgment of *Autex Industries v Auckland CC*. But there was no direct discussion in *Hamilton* of the exact reasons for choosing one approach over the other: the Court did not discuss *Burnie Port Authority* at all. It is therefore perhaps still open to debate which approach is preferable. Also, the scope of *Rylands* coverage in New Zealand is still questionable, particularly as regards the definition of a non-natural use of land, and the exact scope of the foreseeability requirement, which the House of Lords introduced in *Cambridge Water* to modify the strictness of the liability in *Rylands*—and, importantly, other private nuisance—situations. Bringing these activities within private nuisance also raises the question of the impact of *Hunter v Canary Wharf* (above) on *Rylands* situations.

It is worth noting briefly that the situation in the United States is different again. It is represented here by the case of *Siegler v Kuhlman*. There, the rule is one imposing strict liability for ultra-hazardous activities. This goes further than *Rylands*, and also raises important policy considerations that are worth exploring as they have been influential in the New Zealand context.

Rylands v Fletcher
(1868) LR 3 HL 330
[**FACTS**. Fletcher, the plaintiff, had a coal mine. Rylands and Horrocks were mill-owners in the neighbourhood, who built a reservoir to support their mill activities. Unknown to them, there were some disused mine shafts under the land where the reservoir was built. When the reservoir was filled, the ground above these workings gave way under the weight. Unfortunately for the plaintiff, his mine workings connected

with those under Rylands' land, so the water from the reservoir also flooded his mine. It seemed that the contractors building the reservoir did not exercise all due care, but they were not sued by the plaintiff nor joined by the defendants. The case therefore revolves simply around whether Rylands was liable to Fletcher for the damage caused by the escaping water.

Fletcher lost at first instance. He appealed to the Court of Exchequer Chamber where he succeeded (see Blackburn J's judgment). Rylands' appeal to the House of Lords failed (see Lord Cairns's judgment) and he was held liable for the damage.]

Blackburn J: [delivering the judgment of the Exchequer Chamber in *Fletcher v Rylands* (1866) LR 1 Ex 265 (Exchequer Chamber)]

The plaintiff, though free from all blame on his part, must bear the loss, unless he can establish that it was the consequence of some default for which the defendants are responsible. The question of law therefore arises, what is the obligation which the law casts on a person who, like the defendants, lawfully brings on his land something which, though harmless whilst it remains there, will naturally do mischief if it escapes out of his land. It is agreed on all hands that he must take care to keep in that which he has brought on the land and keeps there, in order that it may not escape and damage his neighbours, but the question arises whether the duty which the law casts upon him, under such circumstances, is an absolute duty to keep it in at his peril, or is, as the majority of the Court of Exchequer have thought, merely a duty to take all reasonable and prudent precautions, in order to keep it in, but no more. If the first be the law, the person who has brought on his land and kept there something dangerous, and failed to keep it in, is responsible for all the natural consequences of its escape. If the second be the limit of his duty, he would not be answerable except on proof of negligence, and consequently would not be answerable for escape arising from any latent defect which ordinary prudence and skill could not detect ... We think that the true rule of law is, that the person who for his own purposes brings on his lands and collects and keeps there anything likely to do mischief if it escapes, must keep it in at his peril, and, if he does not do so, is *prima facie* answerable for all the damage which is the natural consequence of its escape. He can excuse himself by shewing that the escape was owing to the plaintiff's default; or perhaps that the escape was the consequence of *vis major*, or the act of God; but as nothing of this sort exists here, it is unnecessary to inquire what excuse would be sufficient. The general rule, as above stated, seems on principle just. The person whose grass or corn is eaten down by the escaping cattle of his neighbour, or whose mine is flooded by the water from his neighbour's reservoir, or whose cellar is invaded by the filth of his neighbour's privy, or whose habitation is made unhealthy by the fumes and noisome vapours of his neighbour's alkali works, is damnified without any fault of his own; and it seems but reasonable and just that the neighbour, who has brought something on his own property which was not naturally there, harmless to others so long as it is confined to his own property, but which he knows to be mischievous if it gets on his neighbour's, should be obliged to make good the damage which ensues if he does not succeed in confining it to his own property. But for his act in bringing it there no mischief could have accrued, and it seems but just that he should at his peril keep it there so that no mischief may accrue, or answer for the natural and anticipated consequences. And upon authority, this we think is established to be the law whether the things so brought be beasts, or water, or filth, or stenches.

The case that has most commonly occurred, and which is most frequently to be found in the books, is as to the obligation of the owner of cattle which he has brought on his land, to prevent their escaping and doing mischief. The law as to them seems to be perfectly settled from early times; the owner must keep them in at his peril ... In the recent case of *Cox v Burbidge* [(1863)13 CB (NS) 430; 143 ER 171], Williams, J says, 'I apprehend the general rule of law to be perfectly plain. If I am the owner of an animal in which by law the right of property can exist, I am bound to take care that it does not stray into the land of my neighbour, and I am liable for any trespass it may commit, and for the ordinary consequences of that trespass. Whether or not the escape of the animal is due to my negligence is altogether immaterial'. So in *May v Burdett*, [(1846) 9 QB 101; 115 ER 1213], the Court, after an elaborate examination of the old precedents and authorities, came to the conclusion that, 'a person keeping a mischievous animal, with knowledge of its propensities, is bound to keep it secure at his peril' ... These authorities, and the absence of any authority to the contrary, justify Williams, J, in saying, as he does in *Cox v Burbidge* [*supra*], that the law is clear that in actions for damage occasioned by animals that have not been kept in by their owners, it is quite immaterial whether the escape is by negligence or not.

As has been already said, there does not appear to be any difference in principle, between the extent of the duty cast on him who brings cattle on his land to keep them in, and the extent of the duty imposed on him who brings on his land, water, filth, or stenches, or any other thing which will, if it escape, naturally do damage, to prevent their escaping and injuring his neighbour ...

... [E]very one must so use his own as not to do damage to another; and as every man is bound so to look to his cattle as to keep them out of his neighbour's ground, that so he may receive no damage; so he must keep in the filth of his house or office that it may not flow in upon and damnify his neighbour ... So a man shall not lay his dung so high as to damage his neighbour ... No case has been found in which the question as to the liability for noxious vapours escaping from a man's works by inevitable accident has been discussed, but the following case will illustrate it. Some years ago several actions were brought against the occupiers of some alkali works at Liverpool for the damage alleged to be caused by the chlorine of their works. The defendants proved that they at great expense erected contrivances by which the fumes of chlorine were condensed, and sold as muriatic acid, and they called a great body of scientific evidence to prove that this apparatus was so perfect that no fumes possibly could escape from the defendants' chimneys. On this evidence it was pressed upon the jury that the plaintiff's damage must have been due to some of the numerous other chimneys in the neighbourhood; the jury, however, being satisfied that the mischief was occasioned by chlorine, drew the conclusion that it had escaped from the defendants' works somehow, and in each case found for the plaintiff. No attempt was made to disturb these verdicts on the ground that the defendants had taken every precaution which prudence or skill could suggest to keep those fumes in, and that they could not be responsible unless negligence were shewn; yet, if the law be as laid down by the majority of the Court of Exchequer, it would have been a very obvious defence ... There is no difference in this respect between chlorine and water; both will, if they escape, do damage, the one by scorching, and the other by drowning, and he who brings them there must at his peril see that they do not escape and do that mischief ...

Lord Cairns [in the House of Lords]:

My Lords, the principles on which this case must be determined appear to me to be extremely simple. The Defendants, treating them as the owners or occupiers of the close on which the reservoir was constructed, might lawfully have used that close for any purpose for which it might in the ordinary course of the enjoyment of land be used; and if, in what I may term the natural user of that land, there had been any accumulation of water, either on the surface or underground, and if, by the operation of the laws of nature, that accumulation of water had passed off into the close occupied by the Plaintiff, the Plaintiff could not have complained that that result had taken place. If he had desired to guard himself against it, it would have lain upon him to have done so, by leaving, or by interposing, some barrier between his close and the close of the Defendants in order to have prevented that operation of the laws of nature.

... On the other hand if the Defendants, not stopping at the natural use of their close, had desired to use it for any purpose which I may term a non-natural use, for the purpose of introducing into the close that which in its natural condition was not in or upon it, for the purpose of introducing water either above or below ground in quantities and in a manner not the result of any work or operation on or under the land, and if in consequence of their doing so, or in consequence of any imperfection in the mode of their doing so, the water came to escape and to pass off into the close of the Plaintiff, then it appears to me that that which the Defendants were doing they were doing at their own peril; and, if in the course of their doing it, the evil arose to which I have referred, the evil, namely, of the escape of the water and its passing away to the close of the Plaintiff and injuring the Plaintiff, then for the consequence of that, in my opinion, the Defendants would be liable.

Rickards v Lothian

[1913] AC 263 (PC)

[**FACTS**: The defendant was the lessee of a building in Melbourne. The plaintiff subtenant occupied part of the second floor. There was a men's lavatory on the fourth floor of the building, which was checked and maintained by the defendant's caretaker. On the evening of 18 August 1909, the caretaker checked the lavatory as usual and found nothing amiss. The following morning, however, the plaintiff arrived to find his premises flooded and his stock badly damaged by water coming from above. It transpired that an unknown person had deliberately blocked the overflow from the basin in the lavatory room and had turned the water tap full on. The plaintiff's claim in negligence failed.]

Lord Moulton:

[**Note**: Under the *Rylands v Fletcher* claim, the Privy Council held that the malicious act of a third person is a good defence, or 'excuse' in terms of Lord Cairns's judgment in the *Rylands* case.]

But there is another ground upon which their Lordships are of opinion that the present case does not come within the principle laid down in *Fletcher v Rylands* ... It is not every use to which land is put that brings into play that principle. It must be some special use bringing with it increased danger to others, and must not merely be the ordinary use of the land or such a use as is proper for the general benefit of the community ... In giving judgment for the defendant [in *Blake v Woolf* [1878] 2 QB 426] Wright J says: 'The general rule as laid down in *Rylands v Fletcher* is that *prima facie* a person occupying land has an absolute right not to have his premises invaded by injurious matter, such as large quantities of water which his neighbour keeps upon his land. That general rule is, however, qualified by some exceptions, one of which is that, where a person is using his land in the ordinary way and damage happens to the adjoining property without any default or negligence on his part, no liability attaches to him. The bringing of water on to such premises as these and the maintaining of a cistern in the usual way seems to me to be an ordinary and reasonable use of such premises as these were; and, therefore, if the water escapes without any negligence or default on the part of the person bringing the water in and owning the cistern, I do not think that he is liable for any damage that may ensue'.

This is entirely in agreement with the judgment of Blackburn J in *Ross v Fedden* [(1872) LR 7 QB 661]. In that case the defendants were the occupiers of the upper floor of a house of which the plaintiff occupied the lower floor. The supply and overflow pipes of a water-closet, which was situated in the defendants' premises and was for their use and convenience, got out of order and caused the plaintiff's premises to be flooded. Negligence was negatived. In giving judgment in favour of the defendants Blackburn J says: 'I think it is impossible to say that defendants as occupiers of the upper storey of a house were liable to the plaintiff under the circumstances found in the case. The water-closet and the supply pipe are for their convenience and use, but I cannot think there is any obligation on them at all hazards to keep the pipe from bursting or otherwise getting out of order. The cause of the overflow was the valve of the supply pipe getting out of order and the escape pipe being choked with paper, and the judge has expressly found that there was no negligence ... Negligence is negatived; and probably, if the defendants had got notice of the state of the pipe and valve and had done nothing, there might have been ground for the argument that they were liable for the consequences; but I do not think the law casts on the defendants any such obligation as the plaintiff contends for'.

Their Lordships are in entire sympathy with these views. The provision of a proper supply of water to the various parts of a house is not only reasonable, but has become, in accordance with modern sanitary views, an almost necessary feature of town life. It is recognized as being so desirable in the interests of the community that in some form or other it is usually made obligatory in civilized countries. Such a supply cannot be installed without causing some concurrent danger of leakage or overflow. It would be unreasonable for the law to regard those who install or maintain such a system of supply as doing so at their own peril, with an absolute liability for any damage resulting from its presence even when there has been no negligence. It would be still more unreasonable if, as the respondent contends, such liability were to be held to extend to the consequences of malicious acts on the part of third persons. In such matters as the domestic supply of water or gas it is essential that the mode of supply should be such as to permit ready access for the purpose of use, and hence it is impossible to guard against wilful mischief. Taps may be turned on, ball-cocks fastened open, supply pipes cut, and waste-pipes blocked. Against such acts no precaution can prevail. It would be wholly unreasonable to hold an occupier responsible for the consequences of such acts which he is powerless to prevent, when the provision of the supply is not only a reasonable act on his part but probably a duty. Such a doctrine would, for example, make a householder liable for the consequences of an explosion caused by a burglar breaking into his house during the night and leaving a gas tap open. There is, in their Lordships' opinion, no support either in reason or authority for any such view of the liability of a landlord or occupier. In having on his premises such means of supply he is only using those premises in an ordinary and proper manner, and, although he is bound to exercise all reasonable care, he is not responsible for damage not due to his own default, whether that damage be caused by inevitable accident or the wrongful acts of third persons.

On the above grounds their Lordships are of opinion that the direction of the learned judge at the trial to the effect that 'if the plugging up were a deliberately mischievous act by some outsider unless it were instigated by the defendant himself, the defendant would not be responsible', was correct in law, and that upon the finding of the jury that the plugging up was the malicious act of some person the judge ought have directed the judgment to be entered for the defendant.

Read v J Lyons & Co
[1947] AC 156; [1945] KB 216 (HL)
[**FACTS**: On 31 August 1942, Norah Read was working as an inspector in the shell-filling shop of a factory in Bedfordshire which manufactured high explosive shells for the government. An explosion occurred, which killed one man and injured her and others. She was working there against her wishes, having been given no choice in her place of service under the National Service Act. She sued (among other causes of action) under *Rylands v Fletcher* for her injuries.]

Viscount Simon:

My Lords, no negligence was averred or proved against the respondents ... [T]he simple question for decision is whether in these circumstances the respondents are liable, without any proof or inference that they were negligent, to the appellant in damages, which have been assessed at £575 2s 8d for her injuries. Cassels J who tried the case, considered that it was governed by *Rylands v Fletcher*, and held that the respondents were liable, on the ground that they were carrying on an ultra-hazardous activity and so were under what is called a 'strict liability' to take successful care to avoid causing harm to persons whether on or off the premises. The Court of Appeal (Scott, MacKinnon, and du Parcq LJJ) reversed this decision, Scott LJ in an elaborately reasoned judgment holding that a person on the premises had, in the absence of any proof of negligence, no cause of action, and that there must be an escape of the damage-causing thing from the premises and damage caused outside before the doctrine customarily associated with the case of *Rylands v Fletcher* can apply. I agree that the action fails. The appellant was a person present in the factory in pursuance of a public duty (like an ordinary factory inspector) and was consequently in the same position as an invitee. The respondents were managers of the factory as agents for the Ministry of Supply and had the same responsibility to an invitee as an ordinary occupier in control of the premises. The duties of an occupier of premises to an invitee have been analysed in many reported cases, but in none of them, I think, is there any hint of the proposition necessary to support the claim of the appellant in this case. The fact that the work that was being carried on was of a kind which requires special care is a reason why the standard of care should be high, but it is no reason for saying that the occupier is liable for resulting damage to an invitee without any proof of negligence at all.

Blackburn J, in delivering the judgment of the Court of Exchequer Chamber in *Fletcher v Rylands* laid down the proposition that 'the person who for his own purposes brings on his lands and collects and keeps there anything likely to do mischief if it escapes, must keep it in at his peril, and, if he does not do so, is *prima facie* answerable for all the damage which is the natural consequence of its escape'.

It has not always been sufficiently observed that in the House of Lords, when the appeal from *Fletcher v Rylands* was dismissed and Blackburn J's pronouncement was expressly approved, Lord Cairns LC emphasized another condition which must be satisfied before liability attaches without proof of negligence. This is that the use to which the defendant is putting his land is 'a non-natural use'. Blackburn J had made a parenthetic reference to this sort of test when he said [LR 1 Ex 265, 280]: 'it seems but reasonable and just that the neighbour, who has brought something on his own property, *which was not naturally there*, harmless to others so long as it is confined to his own property, but which he knows to be mischievous if it gets on his neighbour's, should be obliged to make good the damage which ensues if he does not succeed in confining it to his own property'. I confess to finding this test of 'non-natural' user (or of bringing on the land 'what was not naturally there', which is not the same test) difficult to apply. Blackburn J, in the sentence immediately following that which I have last quoted, treats cattle-trespass as an example of his generalization. The pasturing of cattle must be one of the most ordinary uses of land, and strict liability for damage done by cattle enclosed on one man's land if they escape thence into the land of another, is one of the most ancient propositions of our law. It is in fact a case of pure trespass to property, and thus constitutes a wrong without any question of negligence ... The circumstances in *Fletcher v Rylands* did not constitute a case of trespass because the damage was consequential, not direct. It is to be noted that all the counts in the declaration in that case set out allegations of negligence but in the House of Lords Lord Cairns begins his opinion by explaining that ultimately the case was treated as determining the rights of the parties independently of any question of negligence. The classic judgment of Blackburn J, besides deciding the issue before the court and laying down the principle of duty between neighbouring occupiers of land on which the decision was based, sought to group under a single and wider proposition other instances in which liability is independent of negligence, such for example as liability for the bite of a defendant's monkey, *May v Burdett* [(1846) 9 QB 101; 115 ER 1213]; see also the case of a bear on a chain on the defendant's premises, *Besozzi v Harris* [(1858) 1 F & F 92; 175 ER 640]. There are instances, no doubt, in our law in which liability for damage may be established apart from proof of negligence, but it appears to me logically unnecessary and historically incorrect to refer to all these instances as deduced from one common principle ... It seems better, therefore, when a plaintiff relies on *Rylands v Fletcher*, to take the conditions declared by this House to be essential for liability in that case and to ascertain whether these conditions exist in the actual case.

Now, the strict liability recognized by this House to exist in *Rylands v Fletcher* is conditioned by two elements which I may call the condition of 'escape' from the land of something likely to do mischief if it escapes, and the condition of 'non-natural use' of the land. This second condition has in some later cases, which did not reach this House, been otherwise expressed, for example as 'exceptional' user, when such user is not regarded as 'natural' and at the same time is likely to produce mischief if there is an 'escape'. Dr Stallybrass, in a learned article on 'Dangerous Things and Non-Natural User of Land' in 3 *Cambridge Law Journal*, p 376, has collected the large variety of epithets that have been judicially employed in this connexion. The *American Restatement of the Law of Torts*, vol 3, s 519, speaks of 'ultra-hazardous activity' ... It is not necessary to analyse this second condition on the present occasion, for in the case now before us the first essential condition of 'escape' does not seem to me to be present at all ... In these circumstances it becomes unnecessary to consider other objections that have been raised, such as the question whether the doctrine of *Rylands v Fletcher* applies where the claim is for damages for personal injury as distinguished from damages to property ...

Lord Macmillan:

My Lords, nothing could be simpler than the facts in this appeal; nothing more far-reaching than the discussion of fundamental legal principles to which it has given rise ...

In my opinion the appellant's statement of claim discloses no ground of action against the respondents. The action is one of damages for personal injuries. Whatever may have been the law of England in early times I am of opinion that as the law now stands an allegation of negligence is in general essential to the relevancy of an action of reparation for personal injuries ... Suffice it to say that the process of evolution has been from the principle that every man acts at his peril and is liable for all the consequences of his acts to the principle that a man's freedom of action is subject only to the obligation not to infringe any duty of care which he owes to others. The emphasis formerly was on the injury sustained and the question was whether the case fell within one of the accepted classes of common law actions; the emphasis now is on the conduct of the person whose act has occasioned the injury and the question is whether it can be characterized as negligent.

[**Result**: Appeal dismissed.]

Different modern directions on *Rylands* situations

UNITED STATES

Siegler v Kuhlman

(1973) 502 P 2d 1181 (Wash)

[**FACTS**: Mr Kuhlman was an experienced truck driver. On 22 November 1967, he was driving a petrol truck and trailer unit, with a full load, along a highway. The trailer broke free and crashed through a fence, coming to rest upside down on the road below. Petrol spilled everywhere. Tragically, at the same time, 17-year-old Carol House was driving home along the road where the trailer had landed. There was an explosion, possibly caused by the headlights of her car when it came into contact with the spilled petrol. The car was engulfed in flames, and Ms House died at the scene.

The jury found that the defendant truck company was not negligent. The truck had been properly constructed. Mr Kuhlman was also not negligent. He had done a routine check of the unit before driving it, and even a careful inspection could apparently not have revealed the metal fatigue which caused the trailer to break loose. He also did not drive negligently. All the indications were that this was a tragic freak accident.]

Hale AJ:

… Strict liability is not a novel concept; it is at least as old as *Fletcher v Rylands*, LR 1 Ex 265, 278 (1866), affirmed, House of Lords, 3 HL 330 (1868). In that famous case, where water impounded in a reservoir on defendant's property escaped and damaged neighboring coal mines, the landowner who had impounded the water was held liable without proof of fault or negligence. Acknowledging a distinction between the natural and non-natural use of land, and holding the maintenance of a reservoir to be a non-natural use, the Court of Exchequer Chamber imposed a rule of strict liability on the landowner. The *ratio decidendi* included adoption of what is now called strict liability, and at page 278 announced, we think, principles which should be applied in the instant case:

> [T]he person who for his own purposes brings on his lands and collects and keeps there anything likely to do mischief if it escapes, must keep it in at his peril, and, if he does not do so, is prima facie answerable for all the damage which is the natural consequence of its escape.

All of the Justices in *Fletcher v Rylands* did not draw a distinction between the natural and non-natural use of land, but such a distinction would, we think, be irrelevant to the transportation of gasoline. The basic principles supporting the Fletcher doctrine, we think, control the transportation of gasoline as freight along the public highways the same as it does the impounding of waters and for largely the same reasons. *See* Prosser, *Torts*, § 78 (4th edn, 1971).

In many respects, hauling gasoline as freight is no more unusual, but more dangerous, than collecting water. When gasoline is carried as cargo—as distinguished from fuel for the carrier vehicle—it takes on uniquely hazardous characteristics, as does water impounded in large quantities. Dangerous in itself, gasoline develops even greater potential for harm when carried as freight—extraordinary dangers deriving from sheer quantity, bulk and weight, which enormously multiply its hazardous properties. And the very hazards inhering from the size of the load, its bulk or quantity and its movement along the highways presents another reason for application of the *Fletcher v Rylands* rule not present in the impounding of large quantities of water—the likely destruction of cogent evidence from which negligence or want of it may be proved or disproved. It is quite probable that the most important ingredients of proof will be lost in a gasoline explosion and fire. Gasoline is always dangerous whether kept in large or small quantities because of its volatility, inflammability and explosiveness. But when several thousand gallons of it are allowed to spill across a public highway—that is, if, while in transit as freight, it is not kept impounded—the hazards to third persons are so great as to be almost beyond calculation. As a consequence of its escape from impoundment and subsequent explosion and ignition, the evidence in a very high percentage of instances will be destroyed, and the reasons for and causes contributing to its escape will quite likely be lost in the searing flames and explosions ...

The rule of strict liability rests not only upon the ultimate idea of rectifying a wrong and putting the burden where it should belong as a matter of abstract justice, that is, upon the one of the two innocent parties whose acts instigated or made the harm possible, but it also rests on problems of proof:

> One of these common features is that the person harmed would encounter a difficult problem of proof if some other standard of liability were applied. For example, the disasters caused by those who engage in abnormally dangerous or extra-hazardous activities frequently destroy all evidence of what in fact occurred, other than that the activity was being carried on. Certainly this is true with explosions of dynamite, large quantities of gasoline, or other explosives. It frequently is the case with falling aircraft. Tracing the course followed by gases or other poisons used by exterminators may be difficult if not impossible. The explosion of an atomic reactor may leave little evidence of the circumstances which caused it. Moreover, application of such a standard of liability to activities which are not matters of common experience is well-adapted to a jury's limited ability to judge whether proper precautions were observed with such activities.
>
> Problems of proof which might otherwise have been faced by shippers, bailors, or guests at hotels and inns certainly played a significant role in shaping the strict liabilities of carriers, bailees, and innkeepers. Problems of proof in suits against manufacturers for harm done by defective products became more severe as the composition and design of products and the techniques of manufacture became less and less matters of common experience; this was certainly a factor bringing about adoption of a strict liability standard. (Footnote omitted. C. Peck "Negligence and Liability Without Fault in Tort Law" 46 Wash L Rev 225.240 (1971).)

Thus, the reasons for applying a rule of strict liability obtain in this case. We have a situation where a highly flammable, volatile and explosive substance is being carried at a comparatively high rate of speed, in great and dangerous quantities as cargo upon the public highways, subject to all of the hazards of high-speed traffic, multiplied by the great dangers inherent in the volatile and explosive nature of the substance, and multiplied again by the quantity and size of the load. Then we have the added dangers of ignition and explosion generated when a load of this size, that is, about 5000 gallons of gasoline, breaks its container and, cascading from it, spreads over the highway so as to release an invisible but highly volatile and explosive vapor above it.

Danger from great quantities of gasoline spilled upon the public highway is extreme and extraordinary, for any spark, flame or appreciable heat is likely to ignite it. The incandescent filaments from a broken automobile headlight, a spark from the heat of a tailpipe, a lighted cigarette in the hands of a driver or passenger, the hot coals from a smoker's pipe or cigar, and the many hot and sparking spots and units of an automobile motor from exhaust to generator could readily ignite the vapor cloud gathered above a highway from 5000 gallons of spilled gasoline. Any automobile passing through the vapors could readily have produced the flames and explosions which killed the young woman in this case and without the provable intervening negligence of those who loaded and serviced the carrier and the driver who operated it. Even the most prudent and careful motorists, coming unexpectedly and without warning upon this gasoline pool and vapor, could have driven into it and ignited a holocaust without knowledge of the danger and without leaving a trace of what happened to set off the explosion and light the searing flames.

Stored in commercial quantities, gasoline has been recognized to be a substance of such dangerous characteristics that it invites a rule of strict liability—even where the hazard is contamination to underground water supply and not its more dangerous properties such as its explosiveness and flammability. See *Yommer v McKenzie* (1969) 255 Md 220, 257 A 2d 138. It is even more appropriate, therefore, to apply this principle to the more highly hazardous act of transporting it as freight upon the freeways and public thoroughfares.

The rule of strict liability, when applied to an abnormally dangerous activity, as stated in the *Restatement (Second) of Torts* § 519 (Tenth Draft No 10, 1964), was adopted as the rule of decision in this state in *Pacific Northwest Bell Tel Co v Port of Seattle*, at 64, 491 P 2d, at 1039, 1040, as follows:

> (1) One who carries on an abnormally dangerous activity is subject to liability for harm to the person, land or chattels of another resulting from the activity, although he has exercised the utmost care to prevent such harm.
>
> (2) Such strict liability is limited to the kind of harm, the risk of which makes the activity abnormally dangerous.

As to what constitutes an abnormal activity, § 520 states:

> In determining whether an activity is abnormally dangerous, the following factors are to be considered:
>
> (a) Whether the activity involves a high degree of risk of some harm to the person, land or chattels of others;
>
> (b) Whether the gravity of the harm which may result from it is likely to be great;
>
> (c) Whether the risk cannot be eliminated by the exercise of reasonable care;
>
> (d) Whether the activity is not a matter of common usage;
>
> (e) Whether the activity is inappropriate to the place where it is carried on; and
>
> (f) The value of the activity to the community.

Transporting gasoline as freight by truck along the public highways and streets is obviously an activity involving a high degree of risk; it is a risk of great harm and injury; it creates dangers that cannot be eliminated by the exercise of reasonable care. That gasoline cannot be practicably transported except upon the public highways does not decrease the abnormally high risk arising from its transportation. Nor will the exercise of due and reasonable care assure protection to the public from the disastrous consequences of concealed or latent mechanical or metallurgical defects in the carrier's equipment, from the negligence of third parties, from latent defects in the highways and streets, and from all of the other hazards not generally disclosed or guarded against by reasonable care, prudence and foresight. Hauling gasoline in great quantities as freight, we think, is an activity that calls for the application of principles of strict liability.

The case is therefore reversed and remanded to the trial court for trial to the jury on the sole issue of damages.

UNITED KINGDOM

Cambridge Water Co v Eastern Counties Leather Plc
[1994] 2 AC 264 (HL)

[**FACTS**: For about thirty years, from the 1960s to 1991, Eastern Leather used a solvent called perchloroethene (PCE) as a degreasing agent in its tanning process. This was standard industry practice. During the time it was in use, small quantities of PCE were regularly spilt onto the floor of Eastern Leather's premises. PCE is highly volatile, and all available scientific information indicated that small spillages would simply evaporate. This was not the case, however. Instead, the PCE seeped through the ground into the subsoil, where pockets of it accumulated in the chalk and then leached into the water supply. The court found that it was not foreseeable by a reasonable supervisor that this would occur.

Cambridge Water Co (CWC) was the licensed water supplier for the area. It purchased the affected borehole in 1976. New scientific tests in the later 1970s allowed detection of PCE in the quantities available. While the water was not dangerous to drink, it was not 'wholesome' in terms of the European Community Directive, and so could not lawfully be supplied as drinking water. Cambridge Water sued for the damage sustained by the inability to use the borehole.]

Lord Goff:

… In order to consider the question in the present case in its proper legal context, it is desirable to look at the nature of liability in a case such as the present in relation both to the law of nuisance and the rule in *Rylands v Fletcher*, and for that purpose to consider the relationship between the two heads of liability.

I begin with the law of nuisance. Our modern understanding of the nature and scope of the law of nuisance was much enhanced by Professor Newark's seminal article on 'The Boundaries of Nuisance' (1949) 65 LQR 480. The article is avowedly a historical analysis, in that it traces the nature of the tort of nuisance to its origins, and demonstrates how the original view of nuisance as a tort to land (or more accurately, to accommodate interference with servitudes, a tort directed against the plaintiff's enjoyment of rights over land) became distorted as the tort was extended to embrace claims for personal injuries, even where the plaintiff's injury did not occur while using land in his occupation. In Professor Newark's opinion (p 487), this development produced adverse effects, viz, that liability which should have arisen only under the law of negligence was allowed under the law of nuisance which historically was a tort of strict liability; and that there was a tendency for 'cross-infection to take place, and notions of negligence began to make an appearance in the realm of nuisance proper'. But in

addition, Professor Newark considered, at pp 487–8, it contributed to a misapprecia-
tion of the decision in *Rylands v Fletcher.*

> This case is generally regarded as an important landmark—indeed, a turning
> point—in the law of tort; but an examination of the judgments shows that
> those who decided it were quite unconscious of any revolutionary or reaction-
> ary principles implicit in the decision. They thought of it as calling for no
> more than a restatement of settled principles, and Lord Cairns went so far as to
> describe those principles as 'extremely simple'. And in fact the main principle
> involved was extremely simple, being no more than the principle that negli-
> gence is not an element in the tort of nuisance. It is true that Blackburn J in his
> great judgment in the Exchequer Chamber never once used the word 'nui-
> sance,' but three times he cited the case of fumes escaping from an alkali
> works—a clear case of nuisance—as an instance of liability under the rule
> which he was laying down. Equally it is true that in 1866 there were a number
> of cases in the reports suggesting that persons who controlled dangerous things
> were under a strict duty to take care, but as none of these cases had anything to
> do with nuisance Blackburn J did not refer to them.
>
> But the profession as a whole, whose conceptions of the boundaries of nui-
> sance were now becoming fogged, failed to see in *Rylands v Fletcher* a simple
> case of nuisance. They regarded it as an exceptional case—and the Rule in
> *Rylands v Fletcher* as a generalisation of exceptional cases, where liability was to
> be strict on account of 'the magnitude of danger, coupled with the difficulty of
> proving negligence' [Pollock, *Law of Torts*, 14th edn (1939), p 386], rather than
> on account of the nature of the plaintiff's interest which was invaded. They
> therefore jumped rashly to two conclusions: firstly, that the Rule in *Rylands v
> Fletcher* could be extended beyond the case of neighbouring occupiers; and sec-
> ondly, that the Rule could be used to afford a remedy in cases of personal
> injury. Both these conclusions were stoutly denied by Lord Macmillan in *Read
> v Lyons* [1947] AC 156, but it remains to be seen whether the House of Lords
> will support his opinion when the precise point comes up for decision.

We are not concerned in the present case with the problem of personal injuries, but
we are concerned with the scope of liability in nuisance and in *Rylands v Fletcher*. In
my opinion it is right to take as our starting point the fact that, as Professor Newark
considered, *Rylands v Fletcher* was indeed not regarded by Blackburn J as a revolutionary decision: see, eg, his observations in *Ross v Fedden* (1872) 26 LT 966, 968. He
believed himself not to be creating new law, but to be stating existing law, on the basis
of existing authority; and, as is apparent from his judgment, he was concerned in particular with the situation where the defendant collects things upon his land which are
likely to do mischief if they escape, in which event the defendant will be strictly liable
for damage resulting from any such escape. It follows that the essential basis of liability
was the collection by the defendant of such things upon his land; and the consequence
was a strict liability in the event of damage caused by their escape, even if the escape
was an isolated event. Seen in its context, there is no reason to suppose that Blackburn
J intended to create a liability any more strict than that created by the law of nuisance;

but even so he must have intended that, in the circumstances specified by him, there should be liability for damage resulting from an isolated escape.

Of course, although liability for nuisance has generally been regarded as strict, at least in the case of a defendant who has been responsible for the creation of a nuisance, even so that liability has been kept under control by the principle of reasonable user— the principle of give and take as between neighbouring occupiers of land, under which 'those acts necessary for the common and ordinary use and occupation of land and houses may be done, if conveniently done, without subjecting those who do them to an action': see *Bamford v Turnley* (1862) 3 B & S 66, 83, per Bramwell B. The effect is that, if the user is reasonable, the defendant will not be liable for consequent harm to his neighbour's enjoyment of his land; but if the user is not reasonable, the defendant will be liable, even though he may have exercised reasonable care and skill to avoid it. Strikingly, a comparable principle has developed which limits liability under the rule in *Rylands v Fletcher*. This is the principle of natural use of the land. I shall have to consider the principle at a later stage in this judgment. The most authoritative statement of the principle is now to be found in the advice of the Privy Council delivered by Lord Moulton in *Rickards v Lothian* [1913] AC 263, 280, when he said of the rule in *Rylands v Fletcher* :

> It is not every use to which land is put that brings into play that principle. It must be some special use bringing with it increased danger to others, and must not merely be the ordinary use of the land or such a use as is proper for the general benefit of the community.

It is not necessary for me to identify precise differences which may be drawn between this principle, and the principle of reasonable user as applied in the law of nuisance. It is enough for present purposes that I should draw attention to a similarity of function. The effect of this principle is that, where it applies, there will be no liability under the rule in *Rylands v Fletcher*; but that where it does not apply, ie where there is a non-natural use, the defendant will be liable for harm caused to the plaintiff by the escape, notwithstanding that he has exercised all reasonable care and skill to prevent the escape from occurring.

Foreseeability of damage in nuisance

It is against this background that it is necessary to consider the question whether foreseeability of harm of the relevant type is an essential element of liability either in nuisance or under the rule in *Rylands v Fletcher*. I shall take first the case of nuisance. In the present case, as I have said, this is not strictly speaking a live issue. Even so, I propose briefly to address it, as part of the analysis of the background to the present case.

It is, of course, axiomatic that in this field we must be on our guard, when considering liability for damages in nuisance, not to draw inapposite conclusions from cases concerned only with a claim for an injunction. This is because, where an injunction is claimed, its purpose is to restrain further action by the defendant which may interfere with the plaintiff's enjoyment of his land, and *ex hypothesi* the defendant must be aware, if and when an injunction is granted, that such interference may be caused by the act which he is restrained from committing. It follows that these cases provide no guidance on the question whether foreseeability of harm of the relevant type is a pre-requisite of the recovery of damages for causing such harm to the plaintiff. In the present case, we are not concerned with liability in damages in respect of a nuisance which has arisen through natural causes, or by the act of a person for whose actions the defendant is not responsible, in which cases the applicable principles in nuisance have become closely associated with those applicable in negligence: see *Sedleigh-Denfield v O'Callaghan* [1940] AC 880 and *Goldman v Hargrave* [1967] 1 AC 645. We are concerned with the liability of a person where a nuisance has been created by one for whose actions he is responsible. Here, as I have said, it is still the law that the fact that the defendant has taken all reasonable care will not of itself exonerate him from liability, the relevant control mechanism being found within the principle of reasonable user. But it by no means follows that the defendant should be held liable for damage of a type which he could not reasonably foresee; and the development of the law of negligence in the past 60 years points strongly towards a requirement that such foreseeability should be a prerequisite of liability in damages for nuisance, as it is of liability in negligence. For if a plaintiff is in ordinary circumstances only able to claim damages in respect of personal injuries where he can prove such foreseeability on the part of the defendant, it is difficult to see why, in common justice, he should be in a stronger position to claim damages for interference with the enjoyment of his land where the defendant was unable to foresee such damage. Moreover, this appears to have been the conclusion of the Privy Council in *Overseas Tankship (UK) Ltd v Miller Steamship Co Pty (The Wagon Mound (No 2))* [1967] 1 AC 617. The facts of the case are too well known to require repetition, but they gave rise to a claim for damages arising from a public nuisance caused by a spillage of oil in Sydney Harbour. Lord Reid, who delivered the advice of the Privy Council, considered that, in the class of nuisance which included the case before the Board, foreseeability is an essential element in determining liability. He then continued, at p 640:

> It could not be right to discriminate between different cases of nuisance so as to make foreseeability a necessary element in determining damages in those cases where it is a necessary element in determining liability, but not in others. So the choice is between it being a necessary element in all cases of nuisance or in none. In their Lordships' judgment the similarities between nuisance and other forms of tort to which *The Wagon Mound (No 1)* applies far outweigh any differences, and they must therefore hold that the judgment appealed from is wrong on this branch of the case. It is not sufficient that the injury suffered by the respondents' vessels was the direct result of the nuisance if that injury was in the relevant sense unforeseeable.

It is widely accepted that this conclusion, although not essential to the decision of the particular case, has nevertheless settled the law to the effect that foreseeability of harm is indeed a prerequisite of the recovery of damages in private nuisance, as in the case of public nuisance. I refer in particular to the opinion expressed by Professor Fleming in *Fleming on the Law of Torts*, 8th edn (1992), pp 443–4. It is unnecessary in the present case to consider the precise nature of this principle; but it appears from Lord Reid's statement of the law that he regarded it essentially as one relating to remoteness of damage.

Foreseeability of damage under the rule in *Rylands v Fletcher*

It is against this background that I turn to the submission advanced by ECL before your Lordships that there is a similar prerequisite of recovery of damages under the rule in *Rylands v Fletcher*.

[**Note**: His Lordship quoted from Blackburn J's judgment.]

In that passage, Blackburn J spoke of 'anything *likely* to do mischief if it escapes'; and later he spoke of something 'which he *knows* to be mischievous if it gets on his neighbour's [property]', and the liability to 'answer for the natural and anticipated consequences'. Furthermore, time and again he spoke of the strict liability imposed upon the defendant as being that he must keep the thing in at his peril; and, when referring to liability in actions for damage occasioned by animals, he referred, at p 282, to the established principle that 'it is quite immaterial whether the escape is by negligence or not'. The general tenor of his statement of principle is therefore that knowledge, or at least foreseeability of the risk, is a prerequisite of the recovery of damages under the principle; but that the principle is one of strict liability in the sense that the defendant may be held liable notwithstanding that he has exercised all due care to prevent the escape from occurring ...

... The point is one on which academic opinion appears to be divided: cf *Salmond & Heuston on the Law of Torts*, 20th edn (1992), pp 324–5, which favours the prerequisite of foreseeability, and *Clerk & Lindsell on Torts*, 16th edn (1989), p 1429, para 25.09, which takes a different view. However, quite apart from the indications to be derived from the judgment of Blackburn J in *Fletcher v Rylands*, LR 1 Ex 265 itself, to which I have already referred, the historical connection with the law of nuisance must now be regarded as pointing towards the conclusion that foreseeability of damage is a prerequisite of the recovery of damages under the rule. I have already referred to the fact that Blackburn J himself did not regard his statement of principle as having broken new ground; furthermore, Professor Newark has convincingly shown that the rule in *Rylands v Fletcher* was essentially concerned with an extension of the law of nuisance to cases of isolated escape. Accordingly since, following the observations of Lord Reid when delivering the advice of the Privy Council in *The Wagon Mound (No 2)* [1967] 1 AC 617, 640, the recovery of damages in private nuisance depends on foreseeability by the defendant of the relevant type of damage, it would appear logical to extend the same requirement to liability under the rule in *Rylands v Fletcher*.

Even so, the question cannot be considered solely as a matter of history. It can be argued that the rule in *Rylands v Fletcher* should not be regarded simply as an extension of the law of nuisance, but should rather be treated as a developing principle of strict liability from which can be derived a general rule of strict liability for damage caused by ultra-hazardous operations, on the basis of which persons conducting such operations may properly be held strictly liable for the extraordinary risk to others involved in such operations. As is pointed out in *Fleming on the Law of Torts*, pp 327–8, this would lead to the practical result that the cost of damage resulting from such operations would have to be absorbed as part of the overheads of the relevant business rather than be borne (where there is no negligence) by the injured person or his insurers, or even by the community at large. Such a development appears to have been taking place in the United States, as can be seen from paragraph 519 of the *Restatement of Torts* (2d) vol 3 (1977). The extent to which it has done so is not altogether clear; and I infer from paragraph 519, and the Comment on that paragraph, that the abnormally dangerous activities there referred to are such that their ability to cause harm would be obvious to any reasonable person who carried them on.

I have to say, however, that there are serious obstacles in the way of the development of the rule in *Rylands v Fletcher* in this way. First of all, if it was so to develop, it should logically apply to liability to all persons suffering injury by reason of the ultra-hazardous operations; but the decision of this House in *Read v J Lyons & Co Ltd* [1947] AC 156, which establishes that there can be no liability under the rule except in circumstances where the injury has been caused by an escape from land under the control of the defendant, has effectively precluded any such development. Professor Fleming has observed that 'the most damaging effect of the decision in *Read v J Lyons Co Ltd* is that it prematurely stunted the development of a general theory of strict liability for ultra-hazardous activities' (see *Fleming on Torts*, p 341). Even so, there is much to be said for the view that the courts should not be proceeding down the path of developing such a general theory. In this connection, I refer in particular to the *Report of the Law Commission on Civil Liability for Dangerous Things and Activities* (1970) (Law Com No 32). In paragraphs 14–16 of the Report, the Law Commission expressed serious misgivings about the adoption of any test for the application of strict liability involving a general concept of 'especially dangerous' or 'ultra-hazardous' activity, having regard to the uncertainties and practical difficulties of its application. If the Law Commission is unwilling to consider statutory reform on this basis, it must follow that judges should if anything be even more reluctant to proceed down that path.

Like the judge in the present case, I incline to the opinion that, as a general rule, it is more appropriate for strict liability in respect of operations of high risk to be imposed by Parliament, than by the courts. If such liability is imposed by statute, the relevant activities can be identified, and those concerned can know where they stand. Furthermore, statute can where appropriate lay down precise criteria establishing the incidence and scope of such liability.

It is of particular relevance that the present case is concerned with environmental pollution. The protection and preservation of the environment is now perceived as being of crucial importance to the future of mankind; and public bodies, both national and international, are taking significant steps towards the establishment of legislation which will promote the protection of the environment, and make the polluter pay for damage to the environment for which he is responsible—as can be seen from the WHO, EEC and national regulations to which I have previously referred. But it does not follow from these developments that a common law principle, such as the rule in *Rylands v Fletcher*, should be developed or rendered more strict to provide for liability in respect of such pollution. On the contrary, given that so much well-informed and carefully structured legislation is now being put in place for this purpose, there is less need for the courts to develop a common law principle to achieve the same end, and indeed it may well be undesirable that they should do so.

Having regard to these considerations, and in particular to the step which this House has already taken in *Read v J Lyons & Co Ltd* [1947] AC 156 to contain the scope of liability under the rule in *Rylands v Fletcher*, it appears to me to be appropriate now to take the view that foreseeability of damage of the relevant type should be regarded as a prerequisite of liability in damages under the rule. Such a conclusion can, as I have already stated, be derived from Blackburn J's original statement of the law; and I can see no good reason why this prerequisite should not be recognised under the rule, as it has been in the case of private nuisance ... It would moreover lead to a more coherent body of common law principles if the rule were to be regarded essentially as an extension of the law of nuisance to cases of isolated escapes from land, even though the rule as established is not limited to escapes which are in fact isolated. I wish to point out, however, that in truth the escape of the PCE from ECL's land, in the form of trace elements carried in percolating water, has not been an isolated escape, but a continuing escape resulting from a state of affairs which has come into existence at the base of the chalk aquifer underneath ECL's premises. Classically, this would have been regarded as a case of nuisance; and it would seem strange if, by characterising the case as one falling under the rule in *Rylands v Fletcher*, the liability should thereby be rendered more strict in the circumstances of the present case.

The facts of the present case

Turning to the facts of the present case, it is plain that, at the time when the PCE was brought onto ECL's land, and indeed when it was used in the tanning process there, nobody at ECL could reasonably have foreseen the resultant damage which occurred at CWC's borehole at Sawston.

However there remains for consideration a point adumbrated in the course of argument, which is relevant to liability in nuisance as well as under the rule in *Rylands v Fletcher*. It appears that, in the present case, pools of neat PCE are still in existence at the base of the chalk aquifer beneath ECL's premises, and the escape of dissolved phase PCE from ECL's land is continuing to the present day. On this basis it can be argued that, since it has become known that PCE, if it escapes, is capable of causing damage by rendering water available at boreholes unsaleable for domestic purposes, ECL could be held liable, in nuisance or under the rule in *Rylands v Fletcher*, in respect of damage caused by the continuing escape of PCE from its land occurring at any time after such damage had become foreseeable by ECL.

For my part, I do not consider that such an argument is well founded. Here we are faced with a situation where the substance in question, PCE, has so travelled down through the drift and the chalk aquifer beneath ECL's premises that it has passed beyond the control of ECL. To impose strict liability on ECL in these circumstances, either as the creator of a nuisance or under the rule in *Rylands v Fletcher*, on the ground that it has subsequently become reasonably foreseeable that the PCE may, if it escapes, cause damage, appears to me to go beyond the scope of the regimes imposed under either of these two related heads of liability. This is because when ECL created the conditions which have ultimately led to the present state of affairs—whether by bringing the PCE in question onto its land, or by retaining it there, or by using it in its tanning process—it could not possibly have foreseen that damage of the type now complained of might be caused thereby. Indeed, long before the relevant legislation came into force, the PCE had become irretrievably lost in the ground below. In such circumstances, I do not consider that ECL should be under any greater liability than that imposed for negligence. At best, if the case is regarded as one of nuisance, it should be treated no differently from, for example, the case of the landslip in *Leakey v National Trust for Places of Historic Interest or National Beauty* [1980] QB 485.

I wish to add that the present case may be regarded as one of what is nowadays called historic pollution, in the sense that the relevant occurrence (the seepage of PCE through the floor of ECL's premises) took place before the relevant legislation came into force; and it appears that, under the current philosophy, it is not envisaged that statutory liability should be imposed for historic pollution (see, for example, the Council of Europe's Draft Convention on Civil Liability for Damage Resulting from Activities Dangerous to the Environment (Strasbourg 26 January 1993) article 5.1, and paragraph 48 of the Explanatory Report). If so, it would be strange if liability for such pollution were to arise under a principle of common law.

In the result, since those responsible at ECL could not at the relevant time reasonably have foreseen that the damage in question might occur, the claim of CWC for damages under the rule in *Rylands v Fletcher* must fail.

Natural use of land

I turn to the question whether the use by ECL of its land in the present case constituted a natural use, with the result that ECL cannot be held liable under the rule in *Rylands v Fletcher*. In view of my conclusion on the issue of foreseeability, I can deal with this point shortly.

The judge held that it was a natural use. He said:

In my judgment, in considering whether the storage of organochlorines as an adjunct to a manufacturing process is a non-natural use of land, I must consider whether that storage created special risks for adjacent occupiers and whether the activity was for the general benefit of the community. It seems to me inevitable that I must consider the magnitude of the storage and the geographical area in which it takes place in answering the question. Sawston is properly described as an industrial village, and the creation of employment is clearly for the benefit of that community. I do not believe that I can enter upon an assessment of the point on a scale of desirability that the manufacture of wash leathers comes, and I content myself with holding that this storage in this place is a natural use of land.

It is a commonplace that this particular exception to liability under the rule has developed and changed over the years. It seems clear that, in *Fletcher v Rylands* LR 1 Ex 265 itself, Blackburn J's statement of the law was limited to things which are brought by the defendant onto his land, and so did not apply to things that were naturally upon the land. Furthermore, it is doubtful whether in the House of Lords in the same case Lord Cairns, to whom we owe the expression 'non-natural use' of the land, was intending to expand the concept of natural use beyond that envisaged by Blackburn J. Even so, the law has long since departed from any such simple idea, redolent of a different age; and, at least since the advice of the Privy Council delivered by Lord Moulton in *Rickards v Lothian* [1913] AC 263, 280, natural use has been extended to embrace the ordinary use of land. I ask to be forgiven if I again quote Lord Moulton's statement of the law, which has lain at the heart of the subsequent development of this exception:

> It is not every use to which land is put that brings into play that principle. It must be some special use bringing with it increased danger to others, and must not merely be the ordinary use of the land or such a use as is proper for the general benefit of the community.

Rickards v Lothian itself was concerned with a use of a domestic kind, viz the overflow of water from a basin whose runaway had become blocked. But over the years the concept of natural use, in the sense of ordinary use, has been extended to embrace a wide variety of uses, including not only domestic uses but also recreational uses and even some industrial uses.

It is obvious that the expression 'ordinary use of the land' in Lord Moulton's statement of the law is one which is lacking in precision. There are some writers who welcome the flexibility which has thus been introduced into this branch of the law, on the ground that it enables judges to mould and adapt the principle of strict liability to the changing needs of society; whereas others regret the perceived absence of principle in so vague a concept, and fear that the whole idea of strict liability may as a result be undermined. A particular doubt is introduced by Lord Moulton's alternative criterion: 'or such a use as is proper for the general benefit of the community'. If these words are understood to refer to a local community, they can be given some content as intended to refer to such matters as, for example, the provision of services; indeed the same idea can, without too much difficulty, be extended to, for example, the provision of services to industrial premises, as in a business park or an industrial estate. But if the words are extended to embrace the wider interests of the local community or the general benefit of the community at large, it is difficult to see how the exception can be kept within reasonable bounds. A notable extension was considered in your Lordships' House in *Read v J Lyons & Co Ltd* [1947] AC 156, 169–70, per Viscount Simon, and p 174, per Lord Macmillan, where it was suggested that, in time of war, the manufacture of explosives might be held to constitute a natural use of land, apparently on the basis that, in a country in which the greater part of the population was involved in the war effort, many otherwise exceptional uses might become 'ordinary' for the duration of the war. It is however unnecessary to consider so wide an extension as that in a case such as the present. Even so, we can see the introduction of another extension in the present case, when the judge invoked the creation of employment as clearly for the benefit of the local community, viz 'the industrial village' at Sawston. I myself, however, do not feel able to accept that the creation of employment as such, even in a small industrial complex, is sufficient of itself to establish a particular use as constituting a natural or ordinary use of land.

Fortunately, I do not think it is necessary for the purposes of the present case to attempt any redefinition of the concept of natural or ordinary use. This is because I am satisfied that the storage of chemicals in substantial quantities, and their use in the manner employed at ECL's premises, cannot fall within the exception. For the purpose of testing the point, let it be assumed that ECL was well aware of the possibility that PCE, if it escaped, could indeed cause damage, for example by contaminating any water with which it became mixed so as to render that water undrinkable by human beings. I cannot think that it would be right in such circumstances to exempt ECL from liability under the rule in *Rylands v Fletcher* on the ground that the use was natural or ordinary. The mere fact that the use is common in the tanning industry cannot, in my opinion, be enough to bring the use within the exception, nor the fact that Sawston contains a small industrial community which is worthy of encouragement or support. Indeed I feel bound to say that the storage of substantial quantities of chemicals on industrial premises should be regarded as an almost classic case of non-natural use; and I find it very difficult to think that it should be thought objectionable to impose strict liability for damage caused in the event of their escape. It may well be that, now that it is recognised that foreseeability of harm of the relevant type is a prerequisite of liability in damages under the rule, the courts may feel less pressure to extend the concept of natural use to circumstances such as those in the present case; and in due course it may become easier to control this exception, and to ensure that it has a more recognisable basis of principle. For these reasons, I would not hold that ECL should be exempt from liability on the basis of the exception of natural use.

However, for the reasons I have already given, I would allow ECL's appeal with costs before your Lordships' House and in the courts below ...

AUSTRALIA
Burnie Port Authority v General Jones Pty Ltd
(1994) 179 CLR 520 (HCA)

[**FACTS**: Burnie Port Authority was extending its cold storage facilities in Tasmania. General Jones Pty Ltd was one of the tenants in the cold storage building, where it kept very large quantities of frozen vegetables. The Authority's contractor, Wildridge & Sinclair (W & S), was welding in part of the building. Sparks of molten metal from the apparently negligent unguarded welding fell on nearby cardboard cartons of Isolite, an expanded polystyrene material, which was required for the construction work. Although generally ignition-resistant, it was well known that Isolite could be set alight if it came into sustained contact with a burning substance. The cartons and then the Isolite did ignite, spectacularly, and the resultant fire destroyed the entire complex, including General Jones' stock and premises, in a matter of minutes. It was found that the Authority took no steps to avoid the risk of fire from unguarded welding near the stacked cartons.]

Mason CJ, Deane, Dawson, Toohey and **Gaudron JJ**:

... The learned trial judge (Neasey J) found that General was entitled to judgment against the Authority and W & S for the damage (to be assessed) which it had sustained by reason of the loss of its frozen vegetables. His Honour held that W & S's liability resulted from the application of the ordinary principles of the law of negligence ('ordinary negligence') and from the application of a special rule relating to an occupier's liability for damage caused by the escape of fire from his or her premises (the ignis suus rule). His Honour held that the Authority's liability resulted from the application of the ignis suus rule. As between the Authority and W & S, his Honour found that the Authority was, by reason of W & S's negligence, entitled to be indemnified by W & S in respect of any damages which it paid to General. The Authority's and W & S's third party claims against Olympic were dismissed.

The Authority appealed to the Full Court from the trial judge's order that judgment be entered in General's favour against it. The Full Court (Cox, Crawford and Zeeman JJ) affirmed the Authority's liability to General and ordered that the appeal be dismissed. However, the members of the Full Court concluded that the basis of the Authority's liability to General lay not in any special rule relating only to the escape of fire but in a more general common law rule, the rule in *Rylands v Fletcher*, relating to the liability of an occupier for damage caused by the escape of dangerous substances introduced to his or her premises. The present appeal is by the Authority from the judgment and order of the Full Court ...

The 'true rule' in Rylands v Fletcher

In *Fletcher v Rylands*, a strong Court of Exchequer Chamber, in a judgment delivered by Blackburn J, identified what was described as 'the true rule of law':

> ... the person who for his own purposes brings on his lands and collects and keeps there anything likely to do mischief if it escapes, must keep it in at his peril, and, if he does not do so, is prima facie answerable for all the damage which is the natural consequence of its escape. He can excuse himself by shewing that the escape was owing to the plaintiff's default; or perhaps that the escape was the consequence of vis major, or the act of God; but as nothing of this sort exists here, it is unnecessary to inquire what excuse would be sufficient.

Notwithstanding the many accolades which have been, and continue to be, lavished on Blackburn J's judgment, that brief exposition of 'the true rule of law' is largely bereft of current authority or validity if it be viewed, as it ordinarily is, as a statement of a comprehensive rule. Indeed, it has been all but obliterated by subsequent judicial explanations and qualifications. Thus, the phrase 'for his own purposes' has been largely discarded as a general qualification. While it occasionally re-emerges in general statements of the rule, its current role would seem to be confined to that of a bolster of the requirement of 'natural use' in cases involving the use of premises for public or patriotic purposes. The possessive 'his' before 'lands', apparently used to denote ownership, must be expanded to include the non-owning occupier. Arguably, it should be further expanded to the stage where it would include any person in control. On the other hand, it is arguable that it should be confined to exclude the non-occupying owner. The word 'lands', used in conjunction with 'escapes', is too narrow. The precise extent to which it should be extended is, however, a matter of complete uncertainty. The conjunctive 'and' before 'collects' and 'keeps' should be read as the disjunctive 'or'. The phrase 'anything likely to do mischief if it escapes' has, in a process commenced by Blackburn J himself, largely been supplanted by the word 'dangerous'. The reference to 'all the damage which is the natural consequence of its escape' is too wide. The statement that it was 'unnecessary to inquire what excuse would be sufficient' has inevitably been overlaid by decisions identifying such excuses. It does, however, serve the continued purpose of highlighting the fact that the rule enunciated by Blackburn J was, as his Lordship made clear, one of prima facie liability.

The Court of Exchequer Chamber in *Fletcher v Rylands* itself recognized that the above statement of the 'true rule of law' is too wide, even as an exposition of a prima facie rule, unless it is accompanied by some overriding qualifications. Thus, Blackburn J commented that:

> … it seems but reasonable and just that the neighbour, who has brought something on his own property *which was not naturally there*, harmless to others so long as it is confined to his own property, but *which he knows to be mischievous if it gets on his neighbour's*, should be obliged to make good the damage which ensues if he does not succeed in confining it to his own property. (Emphasis added.)

Again, however, Blackburn J's statement of those qualifications has long been overlaid and effectively displaced. The qualification 'which was not naturally there' was adverted to with apparent approval by Lord Cairns LC in the House of Lords in *Rylands v Fletcher* but converted, without explanation and perhaps inadvertently, into a quite different requirement of 'non-natural use'. The qualification 'which he knows to be mischievous' has been, in the context of private nuisance and the development of the modern law of negligence, transformed from an apparent requirement of actual knowledge into a requirement closely resembling, or perhaps even amounting to, a requirement of foreseeability of relevant damage in the event of the escape of the dangerous substance.

Unfortunately, the subsequent judicial alterations and qualifications of Blackburn J's statement of the 'true rule' have introduced and exacerbated uncertainties about its content and application. Thus, while it is clear that the requirements of 'for his own purposes', 'brings on', 'his' (in the sense of ownership) and 'lands' are all too narrowly identified, there remains room for legitimate dispute about precisely what, if anything, should be substituted for each of them. In addition, it is unclear whether another requirement, that of 'escape', refers to escape from the defendant's 'land' or other 'premises' or merely escape from control. The critical obscurity resides, however, in the twin requirements of 'dangerous substance' and 'non-natural use'. If, as *Rylands v Fletcher* itself decided, water can be a dangerous substance for the purposes of the rule, it is difficult to identify anything which, accumulated either in sufficient quantity or under sufficient pressure, might not be a dangerous substance. In that regard, it would seem that Blackburn J's own exclusion of things 'naturally there' was intended to be understood as referring to things 'naturally there' in their 'mischievous' state since the report of proceedings in the Court of Exchequer discloses that, notwithstanding Blackburn J's repeated use of the words 'brings on' and 'brought on', the water in the defendants' reservoir in *Fletcher v Rylands* had come 'to their land naturally'.

Lord Cairns LC's requirement of 'non-natural use' may have originally been intended to echo Blackburn J's 'not naturally there' and to refer to a use of land other than in its natural state. If so, that narrow interpretation of the requirement did not survive. The most influential of the subsequent explanations of the requirement of 'non-natural use' has proved to be that formulated by the Privy Council, in a judgment delivered by Lord Moulton on an appeal from this Court, in *Rickards v Lothian*:

> … It is not every use to which land is put that brings into play [the principle in *Rylands v Fletcher*]. It must be some special use bringing with it increased

danger to others, and must not merely be the ordinary use of the land or such a use as is proper for the general benefit of the community.

That formulation, which was to some extent based on the judgment of Wright J in *Blake v Woolf*, has been adopted both in this Court and in the House of Lords. The descriptions which it uses—'special' and 'not ... ordinary'—seem to focus, like Lord Cairns LC's 'non-natural', on the nature of the use.

However, other cases have made clear that, in determining whether a use satisfies the 'non-natural', 'special' or 'not ordinary' description, regard may be had to the manner as well as to the nature of the use. Increasingly, *Rylands v Fletcher* liability has come to depend on all the circumstances surrounding the introduction, production, retention or accumulation of the relevant substance. That being so, the presence of reasonable care or the absence of negligence in the manner of dealing with a substance or carrying out an activity may intrude as a relevant factor in determining whether the use of land is a 'special' and 'not ordinary' one. Certainly, the factors which are relevant in determining whether a defendant has been guilty of negligence in a case involving damage caused by the escape from premises of a dangerous substance will almost inevitably also be relevant on the question whether the defendant's use of those premises was a 'natural' one. As Lord Porter said in *Read v J Lyons & Co Ltd*:

> [the questions whether something 'is dangerous' and whether a 'use' is a 'non-natural' one seem to be questions] of fact subject to a ruling of the judge as to whether the particular object can be dangerous or the particular use can be non-natural, and in deciding this question I think that all the circumstances of the time and place and practice of mankind must be taken into consideration so that what might be regarded as dangerous or non-natural may vary according to those circumstances.

Those comments are not inconsistent with the statement of Gavan Duffy CJ, Rich, Dixon and McTiernan JJ in *Hazelwood v Webber* that the question of non-natural use 'is not one to be decided by a jury on each occasion as a question of fact'. Indeed, the sentences in their Honours' judgment which immediately precede that statement, tend to emphasize the importance of the particular factual circumstances:

> Now in applying this doctrine to the use of fire in the course of agriculture, the benefit obtained by the farmer who succeeds in using it with safety to himself and the frequency of its use by other farmers are not the only considerations. The degree of hazard to others involved in its use, the extensiveness of the damage it is likely to do and the difficulty of actually controlling it are even more important factors. These depend upon climate, the character of the country and the natural conditions.

Obviously, the question whether there has been a non-natural use in a particular case is a mixed question of fact and law which involves both ascertainment and assessment of relevant facts and identification of the content of the legal concept of a 'non-natural' use.

Indeed, it is one of those questions which may be misleadingly converted into a pure question of fact or a pure question of law by an unexpressed assumption that either the precise content of applicable legal concepts or the relevant facts and factual conclusions are manifest and certain. Be that as it may, and regardless of whether one emphasizes the legal or factual aspect of the question of non-natural use, the introduction of the descriptions 'special' and 'not ordinary' as alternatives to 'non-natural', without any identification of a standard or norm, goes a long way towards depriving the requirement of 'non-natural use' of objective content.

In *Read v J Lyons & Co Ltd*, Lord Porter referred to a possible future need 'to lay down principles' for determining whether the twin requirement of 'something which is dangerous' and 'non-natural use' have been satisfied. We are unable to extract any such principles from the decided cases. Indeed, if the rule in *Rylands v Fletcher* is regarded as constituting a discrete area of the law of torts, it seems to us that the effect of past cases is that no such principles exist. In the absence of such principles, those twin requirements compound the other difficulties about the content of the 'rule' to such an extent that there is quite unacceptable uncertainty about the circumstances which give rise to its so-called 'strict liability'. The result is that the practical application of the rule in a case involving damage caused by the escape of a substance is likely to degenerate into an essentially unprincipled and ad hoc subjective determination of whether the particular facts of the case fall within undefined notions of what is 'special' or 'not ordinary'.

If the problems of the rule in *Rylands v Fletcher* were confined to the uncertainties of its content and application, it would be necessary for the courts to continue their so far spectacularly unsatisfactory efforts to resolve them. The problems are not, however, so confined. In the more than a century and a quarter that has passed since its formulation by Blackburn J, the rule has been progressively weakened and confined from within and the area of its effective operation, in the sense of the area in which it applies to impose liability where it would not otherwise exist, has been progressively diminished by increasing assault from without. From within, the broadening of Blackburn J's exception of things 'naturally there', which would seem to have been used in the sense of without human intervention, into an exception of 'natural', 'ordinary' or not 'special' use has reduced the scope of the rule to the stage where a majority of the House of Lords in *Read v J Lyons & Co Ltd* could indicate a view that, in the circumstances of that case, the use of land for the obviously dangerous activity of manufacturing high-explosive shells may have been outside the scope of the rule. From without, ordinary negligence has progressively assumed dominion in the general territory of tortious liability for unintended physical damage, including the area in which the rule in *Rylands v Fletcher* once held sway. Ultimately, as will be seen, the resolution of this case largely turns upon a consideration of the present relationship between ordinary negligence and the rule in *Rylands v Fletcher*. A starting point of that consideration is an understanding of the role played by the conception of proximity in the development of the unified modern law of negligence.

Negligence

Fletcher v Rylands was decided by the Court of Exchequer Chamber some seventeen years before Lord Esher (then Brett MR), in *Heaven v Pender*, formulated the general, or 'larger', proposition which constituted the first step in the perception of a coherent jurisprudence of common law negligence. Almost half a century later, the House of Lords in *Donoghue v Stevenson* effectively completed the process. The judgment of Brett MR in *Heaven v Pender* and the speech of Lord Atkin in *Donoghue v Stevenson* were both concerned with identifying a general unifying proposition which explained why a duty to take care to avoid injury to another had been recognized in past cases in the courts. Essentially, the methodology of both was identical: the identification of a general proposition which selected 'recognized cases suggest, and which is, therefore, to be deduced from them' and the confirmation of the validity of the proposition by ascertaining that no 'obvious case can be stated in which the liability must be admitted to exist, and which yet is not within this proposition'.

The 'larger proposition' formulated by Brett MR in *Heaven v Pender* was one of foreseeability:

> ... whenever one person is by circumstances placed in such a position with regard to another that every one of ordinary sense who did think would at once recognize that if he did not use ordinary care and skill in his own conduct with regard to those circumstances he would cause danger of injury to the person or property of the other, a duty arises to use ordinary care and skill to avoid such danger.

It was, however, expressly rejected by the majority of the English Court of Appeal (Cotton and Bowen LJJ) in that case for the reason that 'there are many cases in which the principle was impliedly negatived'. In *Donoghue v Stevenson*, Lord Atkin emphatically endorsed that rejection of it as an unqualified proposition. On the other hand, he concluded that 'the judgment of Lord Esher [in *Heaven v Pender*] expresses the law of England' if the requirement of a relationship of proximity, partly derived from the judgments of Lord Esher MR himself and AL Smith LJ in *Le Lievre v Gould*, were recognized as a general overriding control—'this necessary qualification'—of the test of foreseeability.

The 'general conception' of a relationship of proximity was identified by Lord Atkin as the 'element common to the cases where [liability in negligence] is found to exist' and as the basis of the duty of care which is common to all such cases. It has been stressed and developed in judgments in recent cases in the Court. As Deane J pointed out in *Stevens v Brodribb Sawmilling Co Pty Ltd*, that common element of a relationship of proximity 'remains the general conceptual determinant and the unifying theme of the categories of case in which the common law of negligence recognizes the existence of a duty to take reasonable care to avoid a reasonably foreseeable risk of injury to another'. Without it, the tort of negligence would be reduced to a miscellany of disparate categories among which reasoning by the legal processes of induction and deduction would rest on questionable foundations since the validity of such reasoning essentially depends upon the assumption of underlying unity or consistency.

Ordinary negligence and the rule in **Rylands v Fletcher**

Much has been written in the past about precisely where, among the old forms of action, one should locate the source or sources of the rule in *Rylands v Fletcher*.

However, the subsequent emergence of a coherent law of negligence to dominate the territory of tortious liability for unintentional injury to the person or property of another has deprived the question of much of its practical significance. Regardless of the parental claims of nuisance or even trespass, the rule has been increasingly qualified and adjusted to reflect basic aspects of the law of ordinary negligence. As has been said, Blackburn J's qualification: 'which he knows to be mischievous', has been refined into an objective test which is (at the least) a close equivalent of foreseeability of damage of the relevant kind. As has been seen, the absence of reasonable care or the presence of 'negligence' has itself intruded as a factor in determining whether, for the purposes of the rule, the use of land is 'non-natural', 'special' or 'not ordinary'. Moreover, the various defences of an occupier of premises against *Rylands v Fletcher* 'strict liability' closely correspond with grounds of denial of fault liability under the law of negligence. Thus, 'consent' and 'default of the plaintiff' are analogous to voluntary assumption of risk and contributory negligence. Again, while Blackburn J recognized them as possible excuses, defences of 'consequence of vis major, or the act of God', in the context of damage caused by the 'escape' of the dangerous substance, are more attuned to the notion of fault liability than that of strict liability. Where the defence of statutory authority is available, the issue will commonly become one of negligence simpliciter. Clearly, there is validity in Professor Fleming's comment that '[t]he aggregate effect of these exceptions makes it doubtful whether there is much left of the rationale of strict liability as originally contemplated in 1866'.

Similarly, former restrictions upon the damages recoverable under the rule in *Rylands v Fletcher* have, at least in this country, been relaxed towards correspondence with the rules controlling recoverable damages in an action in ordinary negligence. In *Benning v Wong*, Windeyer J correctly saw that relaxation as part of a wider movement in the law of torts:

> … Developments in the law of tort are towards a liability for personal harm done to persons who are neighbours in Lord Atkin's sense. They need not be persons having an interest in land in the neighbourhood. The movement of the common law is away from any preoccupation it may once have had with the protection of rights in land … I think this Court should … treat the doctrine of *Rylands v Fletcher* as having become in this matter emancipated from restrictions its origin in or relationship with nuisance might impose.

It would seem that, in England, recoverable damages under the rule in *Rylands v Fletcher* may still be confined to compensation for damage to property sustained by the owner or occupier of neighbouring land 'on to' which the dangerous thing 'passes' and 'does damage'. In this country, such damages are not so confined but extend to personal injury or damage to property sustained outside the relevant premises by persons having no relationship to neighbouring land apart from being on it. As Windeyer J said in *Benning v Wong*:

> A plaintiff can I think recover under it for personal injuries, or harm to his personal effects if, at the time when the escaping thing came upon him, he was in a place where he was lawfully entitled to be as a licensee, or as a member of the public, such as on a highway or in a public park.

Inevitably, the past adjustments and qualifications of the rule in *Rylands v Fletcher* to reflect aspects of the law of ordinary negligence have greatly reduced the likelihood that *Rylands v Fletcher* liability will exist in a case where liability would not exist under the principles of negligence. Thus, the editors of the last five editions of *Winfield and Jolowicz on Tort* have expressed the view that, putting to one side the factual situations in which a plaintiff will succeed equally well either under the rule or in nuisance, '[w]e have virtually reached the position where a defendant will not be considered liable when he would not be liable according to the ordinary principles of negligence'. A similar view has been expressed by other distinguished academic writers. Nonetheless, there remains the perception of an underlying antithesis between the rule in *Rylands v Fletcher* and the principles of negligence. Liability under the rule is still theoretically seen as 'strict liability' in the sense that it can arise without personal fault whereas liability in negligence is fault liability, that is to say, liability flowing from breach of a duty owed by the defendant to the plaintiff. The judicial transformation of Blackburn J's requirement of 'not naturally there' into a test of 'special' and 'not ordinary' use and the expanded defences to a *Rylands v Fletcher* claim have, as has been seen, deprived that perception of underlying antithesis of some of its theoretical validity and most of its practical significance. However, as Professor Thayer indicated in a posthumous article published in the *Harvard Law Review* in 1916, the final answer to any argument based on that perceived theoretical contrast lies in ordinary negligence's concept of a 'non-delegable' duty and a variable standard of care.

The present case
The difference of opinion between the learned trial judge and the members of the Full Court about whether the circumstances of the present case attracted the rule in *Rylands v Fletcher* resulted from the fact that the trial judge considered that the rule's requirement of 'non-natural use' was not satisfied while the Full Court concluded that it was. That disagreement between the trial judge and the members of the Full Court is not surprising in the context of the 'rough sea of contradictory authority' in which one can find powerful support for both the proposition that the escape of the contents of an ordinary privy satisfies the requirements of the rule and the proposition that the manufacture of high-explosives does not necessarily satisfy the requirement of 'non-natural' use. Fortunately, our conclusion that the rule in *Rylands v Fletcher* has been absorbed by the principles of ordinary negligence makes it unnecessary to attempt to derive from the decided cases some basis in principle for answering the question whether the welding activities in the circumstances of the present case were or were not a 'non-natural' or 'special' use of the Authority's premises. The critical question for the purposes of applying the principles of ordinary negligence to the circumstances of the present case is whether the Authority took advantage of its occupation and control of the premises to allow its independent contractor to introduce or retain a dangerous substance or to engage in a dangerous activity on the premises. The starting point for answering that question must be a consideration of what relevantly constitutes a dangerous substance or activity.

In the context of the ordinary law of negligence, the character of 'dangerous' is not confined to those classes of things, such as poison, a loaded gun or explosives, which are 'inherently dangerous' or 'dangerous in themselves'.

... The fact that a particular substance or a particular activity can be seen to be 'inherently' or 'of itself' likely to do serious injury or cause serious damage will, of course, ordinarily make characterization as 'dangerous' more readily apparent. That fact does not, however, provide a criterion of what is and what is not dangerous for the purpose of determining whether the duty of a person in occupation or control of premises to take care to avoid injury or damage outside the premises is or is not a delegable one. It suffices for that purpose that the combined effect of the magnitude of the foreseeable risk of an accident happening and the magnitude of the foreseeable potential injury or damage if an accident does occur is such that an ordinary person acting reasonably would consider it necessary to exercise special care or to take special precautions in relation to it.

Similarly, a substance or activity entrusted to an independent contractor or other agent may be relevantly dangerous notwithstanding that foreseeable injury or danger will arise only in the event of what is commonly described as 'collateral' negligence. If X engages an independent contractor to separately move two chemicals, which will cause a major explosion if they come into contact with one another, into separate storage areas, there may be no real risk of injury or damage at all if the independent contractor does what he or she is engaged to do. The activity is, however, obviously fraught with danger unless special precautions are taken to ensure that the independent contractor does not, through 'collateral' negligence, transport the two chemicals together and in a way which causes contact between them. As Professor Thayer correctly pointed out, 'collateral' is used in this context as a 'most conveniently question-begging adjective' which, so far as it points to a definite conception, does no more than 'indicate a distinction according to the definiteness of the danger inherent and visible in the nature of the undertaking'.

In the present case, the particular qualities of EPS made the stacked cardboard containers of Isolite in the roof area of the Authority's premises a dangerous substance in the sense that, if one of the cardboard containers were accidently set alight, an uncontrollable conflagration would almost inevitably result. Clearly, the introduction of more than twenty of those cardboard containers called for special precautions to be taken to avoid any risk of that happening. A fortiori, the carrying out of welding activities in the premises within which the cardboard containers of Isolite were stacked was itself a dangerous activity in that it was reasonably foreseeable that, unless special precautions were taken, sparks or molten metal might fall upon one of the containers and set the cardboard alight.

As has been seen, the evidence established that the Authority (through one of its employees) was aware that the cardboard containers of Isolite were being stored in the roof area near where welding work was to be carried out by W & S. It is, however, unnecessary that that was so. It suffices for present purposes that the Authority engaged and authorized its independent contractor to carry out work within its premises which required both the introduction of such large quantities of EPS to the premises and the carrying out of extensive welding work within the premises. It has not been suggested that it was not reasonably foreseeable that the large quantities of EPS which W & S was authorized and required by the Authority to use would be contained in a combustible container such as cardboard. To the contrary, the evidence established that the Isolite had been used in Stage 1 of the building and, as has been said, that an employee of the Authority actually saw the cardboard containers being raised into the roof of the premises. In these circumstances, the overall work which the independent contractor was engaged to carry out on the premises was a dangerous activity in that it involved a real and foreseeable risk of a serious conflagration unless special precautions were taken to avoid the risk of serious fire. It was obvious that, in the event of any serious fire on the premises, General's frozen vegetables would almost certainly be damaged or destroyed. In these circumstances, the Authority, as occupier of those parts of the premises into which it required and allowed the Isolite to be introduced and the welding work to be carried out, owed to General a duty of care which was non-delegable in the sense we have explained, that is to say, which extended to ensuring that its independent contractor took reasonable care to prevent the Isolite being set alight as a result of the welding activities. It is now common ground that W & S did not take such reasonable care.

It follows that the Authority was liable to General pursuant to the ordinary principles of negligence for the damage which General sustained. The appeal must be dismissed.

NEW ZEALAND

Autex Industries Ltd v Auckland City Council
[2000] NZAR 324 (CA)
[**FACTS**: On 3 August 1996 an Auckland City Council water main running under a road burst at a point about 8 metres from premises owned by Autex Industries. Water from the burst pipe damaged Autex's premises, plant, equipment and stock. Autex sued the Council in the High Court for $206 780.17. It applied for summary judgment for that sum on the ground that the Council had no defence to the claim. The material action was framed in terms of strict liability—that is, a *Rylands v Fletcher* type of claim. The High Court was bound by the 1939 case of *Irvine and Co Ltd v Dunedin City Corporation* [1939] NZLR 741, which was on all fours with the application in this case and would have found the defendant liable. Given the considerable developments in other jurisdictions in this area of the law, however, Master Kennedy-Grant removed the application to the Court of Appeal for consideration of what the current law on *Rylands* is in New Zealand.

The judgment of the majority (Richardson P, Gault and Henry JJ) dismissed the application for summary judgment with costs to Autex of $10 000. The reason for this was that, despite there being no apparent defence available to the claim, further evidence was possibly available, which could come out at a full hearing. This evidence might deal with changes in the provision of water to public and private premises, which could affect the risk of escape. Such evidence could help to determine whether the Council was seen to be a reasonable or natural user of the land. The majority also stated that expert evidence as to the likely economic and social implications of alternative legal rules could also be of assistance to the Court.

However, Keith and Blanchard JJ delivered a minority judgment dealing more specifically with the categorisation of *Rylands* in modern tort law.]
Blanchard J: (Delivering on behalf of **Keith J**)
… Having obtained an order moving the application into this Court the council belatedly asks for the opportunity to call evidence to show that its water main, which burst

only a few feet away from the plaintiff's property causing considerable damage, was constructed, maintained and monitored in accordance with usual and proper practices. The evidence would also confirm, it is said, that there was no negligence on the part of the council giving rise to the escape of the water. Under the head of claim in respect of which summary judgment is sought, negligence is not alleged or admitted. It is, however, conceded by the council that damage to the plaintiff's property from flooding was foreseeable if the main burst.

The council argues that this Court should follow the decision of the majority of the High Court of Australia in *Burnie Port Authority v General Jones Pty Ltd* ... who said that the rule in *Rylands v Fletcher* has been absorbed by the tort of negligence. But, in a cryptic passage, a qualification was added, namely that

> There may remain cases in which it is preferable to see a defendant's liability in a *Rylands v Fletcher* situation as lying in nuisance (or even trespass) and not in negligence. (p 556)

...

The council, in the alternative, argues that if *Rylands v Fletcher* remains part of the law of New Zealand, either as a separate tort or as a branch of the law of nuisance, its use of the sub-soil of the roadway for the conveyance of water was a natural and reasonable use and accordingly it has a defence to the claim. It is convenient to deal first with this defence.

Rylands v Fletcher was the law's response to some catastrophic dam or reservoir collapses ... The rule began its life, then, with a concern about the drastic effects on neighbouring landowners or occupiers of the release upon their properties of large quantities of water ...

Lord Cairns thought the principles to be 'extremely simple'. The plaintiff could not complain of the consequences of natural accumulation of water passing off the defendants' land but, if the defendants' land were used for a non-natural use, ie 'for the purpose of introducing into the close that which, in its natural condition, was not in or upon it', then the defendants acted at their own peril. It does not appear that the Judges in *Rylands v Fletcher* thought that they were dealing with anything more than a particular kind of legal nuisance.

If the interference with the use and enjoyment of the plaintiff's land or the plaintiff's proprietary rights over land resulted from the escape of a hazardous substance or thing, the plaintiff suing in nuisance did not need to prove negligence on the part of the defendant landowner. That remains so today: *Cambridge Water Co v Eastern Counties Leather plc* and *Hunter v Canary Wharf Ltd* ... The former case also confirms that under the law of England *Rylands v Fletcher* is concerned with an extension of the law of nuisance to cases of isolated escape (as compared with continuing or intermittent events) and holds that foreseeability of damage of the relevant type is to be regarded as a prerequuisite of liability in damages under the rule, as it is in nuisance generally.

No artificial damming and piping of water is a natural occurrence; nor is the conveyance of electricity or gas in cables or pipes. But, as a matter of policy, there is no good reason to apply *Rylands v Fletcher* to smaller pipes and wires by means of which utility services are transmitted to the property of individual users; for there is not the same level of risk to adjoining properties as attends the use of mains and cables ... [:] *Rickards v Lothian ...*

[B]y the time *Irvine & Co Ltd v Dunedin City Corporation* [1939] NZLR 741 came before five Judges of this Court it was well established that bulk conveyance of water, gas and electricity, however common, was a 'non-natural user'. So much was this accepted that it apparently did not require argument, the issue in *Irvine* revolving around sections 171 and 173 of the Municipal Corporations Act 1933 (provisions very like sections 347G and 347H of the Local Government Act 1979, which were enacted by Parliament in full knowledge, it is to be assumed, of the decision in *Irvine*). Section 173 was in the following terms:

> Nothing in this Act shall entitle the Council to create a nuisance, or shall deprive any person of any right or remedy he would otherwise have against the Corporation or any other person in respect of any such nuisance.

... Smith J commented that

> the very presence of the nuisance clause [s 173] seems to imply that the Legislature regards a municipal Corporation as a fit subject for the application of the doctrine of *Rylands v Fletcher*. (p 177)

He also said at p 775 that

> Nothing could be more usual in New Zealand tha[n] the use of streets or the land underneath them for the laying of water-mains. Yet I do not think that makes the use a natural one. Water is not always dangerous, and is sometimes regarded as falling within the rule and sometimes not. In this case, the water was carried in bulk in mains. That renders its use dangerous ... In my opinion, that is sufficient to prevent the use of the streets for that purpose from being a natural or ordinary use.

... [T]here remains an inherent residual danger in the bulk carriage of water under roadways, although it may well be that the risk has been reduced. This case demonstrates that there is still an occasional escape which is not the result of negligence (here denied) or the act of the plaintiff or a third party (which is not suggested). As to the so-called vis major or Act of God exception about which Blackburn J was equivocal, the burden of proof lies on the defendant ... and no such argument is being raised on behalf of the council. We add that the view may be taken that there is no room for such a defence once the plaintiff has shown that damage from an escape of a potentially dangerous substance was foreseeable.

[**Note:** Blanchard J then discussed *Cambridge Water*, noting that it did not express a concern about the assumptions made by the bulk carriage cases, that is, that the use of the land was non-natural. He also discussed, but was not persuaded by, submissions made on the Canadian position in *Rylands* situations, including *Tock v St John's Metropolitan Area Board* (1989) 64 DLR (4th) 620 which found a sewage system was so indispensable that it had become a natural use, but nonetheless found the defendant liable in nuisance.]

... [W]e do not consider that there is a tenable argument that in New Zealand *Rylands v Fletcher* has been absorbed by the law of negligence. It is scarcely likely that the Privy

Council would now depart from the view unanimously expressed by the House of Lords in 1993 [in *Cambridge Water*]. Moreover, the High Court of Australia in *Burnie*, a case concerned with fire caused by welding activities, left the door open for the continued application of the law of nuisance in appropriate cases. Whatever conclusion may ultimately be reached about damage resulting from the spread of fire, in our view cases about bulk storage or conveyance of things which are likely [to] cause damage if they escape—the actual concern in *Rylands v Fletcher*—are most appropriately the subject of the law of nuisance.

[There is] a sound policy reason why that should be so. The payment of damages to those injured by non-negligent failure of a public water system ought to be a cost of running the system. The local authority can determine the relative economics of expenditure on preventing escapes, meeting insurance costs or paying compensation. Reference can be made to the remarks of La Forest J in *Tock* at p 646 concerning the need for a cost–benefit analysis in determining the level of preventative expenditure. The risk of calamitous loss to a neighbour, who is necessarily unable to forestall an escape occurring on adjacent property, ie is unable to manage the risk, is spread amongst all ratepayers or borne by the local authority's public liability underwriter. Such a rule of strict liability protects those who may not be able to obtain insurance (eg owners of undeveloped land) or who have misunderstood the need for it, perhaps because they are unaware of the presence of underground mains. It also minimises any doubling up of insurance premiums. (Those able to obtain insurance still need it lest the escape of the dangerous substance results from the act of an unknown or impecunious third party unaccompanied by negligence on the part of the council, but the slightness of that possibility will be reflected in minimal premiums.)

The High Court of Australia criticised the rule in *Rylands v Fletcher* for its 'difficulties, uncertainties, qualifications and exceptions' (which largely do not apply in the current context) but has put in its place the practical uncertainties and the transaction costs of the law of negligence, a substitution for which it provided a justification by requiring a heightened degree of care for the handling of dangerous things and by pointing to the tactical advantage for a plaintiff of the doctrine of *res ipsa loquitur*. But that can provide no guarantee of recovery for someone in the position of the present plaintiff. How could it or its insurer have achieved protection against the risk of damage from the bursting main?

We find persuasive Professor Fleming's negative commentary on *Burnie* in (1995) *Tort Law Review* 56 in which he describes *Rylands v Fletcher* as a vital component of tort theory and points out that the theories underlying strict liability and negligence are quite different:

> Negligence deals with activities that present no undue risk to others if reasonable care is observed by the actor. But failure to do so makes his or her conduct unlawful so that continuance of the negligent activity can be enjoined. By contrast, strict liability is appropriate for activities which present an abnormal risk, even if all due care is observed. Such activities are nonetheless tolerated, because of their preponderant social utility (but for which they would be prohibited). Putting it a different way: negligence deals with the wrong way of

carrying on an activity, the residuary risk of which it is not unfair for victims to shoulder themselves. Strict liability deals with activities which even when carried out with due care retain an abnormal risk and could be deemed negligent as such but for their countervailing utility. (p 60)

He adds that the protective effect of strict liability is increasing proportionately to the progress of the technological complexity of society ...

We would enter summary judgment in favour of the plaintiff for the amount of its claim, quantum of loss not being in dispute.

Hamilton v Papakura District Council
[2000] 1 NZLR 265 (CA)

[**FACTS**: The Hamiltons grew hydroponic cherry tomatoes. One year, they found their plants were suffering from severe damage. There were also some similar problems with neighbours' tomatoes. Expert evidence indicated that the most likely source of the damage was contamination of the water supply by the herbicide triclopyr, following weed spraying near the water source. There had at one stage been a fairly large spillage of the herbicide through a hose break. Chemical testing of the plants did not show up any unusual contaminant levels, however. The experts were puzzled. Also, the levels of herbicide in the water were approximately one-tenth of what is allowed in drinking water. Papakura District Council was the provider of the town water supply, and Watercare Services, the second defendant, was the bulk water supplier.

Williams J in the High Court denied the Hamiltons' claim, predominantly because they could not prove on the balance of probabilities that there were sufficient herbicide residues in the water to cause the plants damage. He also found that, even if that proof had been available, the Hamiltons could not succeed under negligence, *Rylands v Fletcher* or the other causes of action they had advanced. However, he described the circumstantial evidence of damage from water contamination as being quite high.

The Court of Appeal agreed. It suggested that the particular types of plants in those growing conditions may have been sensitive to very low levels of chemicals. While reluctant to disturb the Judge's findings of fact, the Court proceeded on the basis that it was probable that the damage was caused by herbicide contamination.]

Gault J:

[**Note**: The Court first concluded that neither Watercare Services nor the Council were liable to the Hamiltons in negligence.]

...

Nuisance: **Rylands v Fletcher**

... This was pleaded against Watercare and rests on the spraying in the catchment area. It was said this was done in such manner that overspray and run-off entered the lake and was transported to the tomato crops. Williams J decided against Mr and Mrs Hamilton on the ground that Watercare had no reason to foresee harm to the tomato crops from the spraying that was carried out. Mr Casey challenged that conclusion, although he did not entirely abandon, on the ground that it is unsettled, that foreseeability is not an element of liability under *Rylands v Fletcher*.

The similarities between the *Rylands v Fletcher* cause of action and the cause of action in nuisance are clear. *Rylands v Fletcher* deals with an isolated instance of escape while nuisance is concerned with a continuing wrong. The true nuisance should normally have some degree of continuance about it because the plaintiff must show some act of the defendant on his land that disturbs the actual or prospective enjoyment of the plaintiffs' rights over land. However, an isolated escape can give rise to an action in nuisance. Examples include a water main bursting … , a blocked drain causing a flood … , and a gas explosion … This illustrates the close relationship between the law of nuisance and the rule in *Rylands v Fletcher* … but the former usually focuses on the acts of the defendant, while the latter always focuses on the event of an escape of some mischievous thing which the defendant brought onto his land.

… This Court accepted that *Rylands v Fletcher* was a form of nuisance in *Irvine & Co Ltd v Dunedin City Corp* [1939] NZLR 741 … The principle that the *Rylands v Fletcher* action is a subset of the nuisance action was recognised by the House of Lords in *Cambridge Water Co v Eastern Counties Leather plc* [1994] 2 AC 264, and has been affirmed more recently by two Judges of this Court in *Autex Industries Ltd v Auckland CC* [[2000] NZAR 324], where they also accepted that foreseeability was a prerequisite to both forms of action.

It has long been considered that liability in nuisance is strict; once the plaintiff has proven damage to his property or loss of enjoyment of one of the naturally occurring rights in his property, the plaintiff has established a prima facie case of nuisance. It is then incumbent on the defendant to raise a defence, such as that he was exercising reasonable skill and care in the ordinary and natural use of land. As recognised in *Cambridge Water* this defence moderates the application of the principle of strict liability. The scope of the cause of action in nuisance was further narrowed, and the doctrine of strict liability eroded further, by the House of Lords when they included foreseeability of damage on the part of the defendant as a prerequisite to establishing liability …

This conclusion accords with the judgment of the Privy Council on appeal from the High Court of Australia in *The Wagon Mound (No 2)* … That decision settled the law to the effect that foreseeability of harm is a prerequisite to the recovery of damages in private nuisance. For the reasons advanced by the House of Lords, this principle was accepted by the minority Judges of this Court, who addressed the issue in *Autex Industries* … The majority found it unnecessary to decide this point for the purposes of the appeal. We consider it must now be taken as clear that foreseeability is an element necessary to establish liability under *Rylands v Fletcher*. Of course, once it has been shown that the damage was foreseeable, it is irrelevant that the actual act causing the damage was not the fault of the defendant, or that the defendant acted with reasonable skill and care. This applies equally to the law of nuisance as to the rule in *Rylands v Fletcher*.

We have expressed the view that Williams J was correct in his conclusion that the damage complained of was not reasonably foreseeable by Watercare as would be required to establish liability in negligence. Mr Casey argued that any requirement of foreseeability in nuisance or under *Rylands v Fletcher* is different. He argued that in nuisance foreseeability 'need only relate to the type of damage' which draws upon the speech of Lord Goff in the *Cambridge Water* case. But we do not understand the foreseeability requirement in negligence to be any different. The distinction between strict liability in nuisance and liability that depends on failure to take reasonable care in negligence does not carry over so as to dictate different levels of foreseeability. The test is whether, when it carried out the weed spraying on its catchment land in the manner it did, Watercare could have foreseen that run-off into the water storage reservoir with its consequent dilution of the town water would have proved toxic to plants sensitive to contamination levels at or below 10 ppb [parts per billion]. That is the 'type of damage' to which Lord Goff was referring. We do not accept it could be sufficient to show, as Mr Casey contended, that Watercare would have foreseen no more than that the escape of herbicides could harm plants ... Accordingly, no different conclusion on foreseeability is justified under this head of claim.

Public nuisance

[As these cases illustrate, public nuisance is conceptually rather different from private nuisance, though there are facts in which the actions can co-exist. Broadly speaking, public nuisance is an action taken to deal with activities affecting a section of the public as a whole, such as blocking of a highway, general air pollution and so on. The action therefore tends to be taken by the Attorney-General, or by a local authority, on behalf of the public rather than relying on individuals to sue to protect their individual private interests. This has been carried further: if the nuisance is categorised as a public nuisance rather than a more straightforward dispute between users of land, an affected person cannot sue individually unless he or she has suffered damage over and above what others affected have suffered (see especially *Ball v Consolidated Rutile*, below). The origins of the tort, which developed from a collection of common law crimes, may have much to do with this. The ability to get something done about interferences therefore relies on strong lobbying of local bodies or central government, and on the political willingness of those bodies to act.]

Attorney-General v PYA Quarries Ltd
[1957] 2 QB 169 (CA)
[**FACTS**: The defendants conducted blasting operations at their Glamorgan quarry which had a serious effect on the residents of the area. The blasting created severe vibrations, and flung stones and splinters over a wide area. This caused damage to nearby houses, created a danger on the highway and upset the residents. The quarrying operations also produced considerable quantities of dust. The residents complained at length to the Council, which at first prevaricated. The defendant was notified of the problems but did nothing. Eventually, the Council decided to proceed against the defendant, though it was some time before proceedings were actually filed.]
Romer LJ:
... The action came on for hearing before Oliver J on April 11, 1956, and the trial occupied nine or ten days. In addition, the judge devoted a day to a view of the premises, and blasting operations were carried out in his presence. In the course of his judgment he arrived (in brief) at the following findings. So far as the flying stones were concerned, he said that there was really no defence at all; that the case was 'absolutely proved at the time the writ was issued'; and that, notwithstanding the installation of the wagon drill, he was quite satisfied that the nuisance had not been wholly abated

and that he should grant an injunction. As to vibration, he came to the conclusion 'that for some reason—I cannot tell what it is—there is on occasion such vibration as to frighten people, to shake their houses and to make them thoroughly uncomfortable, and that such vibration as that, when it is caused, is a nuisance and must cease'. With regard to dust, he said that it would not be right to base an injunction on the explosions, having regard to their comparative rarity since the end of 1953, but that excessive dust emanated from the secondary crusher when the door leading into it was left open, as was frequently the case. Finally he said: 'I have no doubt that there is dust nuisance from this place—of course, only in dry weather. I have no doubt that they have not done anything to cope with it and I am going to order them to do so by injunction ...'.

... The following definition of nuisance appears in *Blackstone's Commentaries* (Vol III, Chapter 13, page 216): 'Nuisance, *nocumentum*, or annoyance, signifies anything that worketh hurt, inconvenience, or damage. And nuisances are of two kinds; *public* or common nuisances, which affect the public, and are an annoyance to *all* the King's subjects; for which reason we must refer them to the class of public wrongs, or crimes and misdemeanors: and private nuisances; which are the objects of our present consideration, and may be defined, anything done to the hurt or annoyance of the lands, tenements or hereditaments of another'. This passage from *Blackstone* is cited in *Pearce & Meston's Law of Nuisances*, page 1, and the learned authors point out that 'anything that worketh hurt, inconvenience or damage' is too broad as including many things which are not nuisances, being *damna sine injuria* ...

... It is difficult to ascertain with any precision from these citations how widely spread the effect of a nuisance must be for it to qualify as a public nuisance and to become the subject of a criminal prosecution or of a relator action by the Attorney-General. It is obvious, notwithstanding *Blackstone's* definition, that it is not a prerequisite of a public nuisance that all of Her Majesty's subjects should be affected by it; for otherwise no public nuisance could ever be established at all.

In *Soltau v De Held* Kindersley VC said: 'I conceive that, to constitute a public nuisance, the thing must be such as, in its nature or its consequences, is a nuisance—an injury or a damage, to all persons who come within the sphere of its operation, though it may be so in a greater degree to some than it is to others' ...

... I do not propose to attempt a more precise definition of a public nuisance than those which emerge from the textbooks and authorities to which I have referred. It is, however, clear, in my opinion, that any nuisance is 'public' which materially affects the reasonable comfort and convenience of life of a class of Her Majesty's subjects. The sphere of the nuisance may be described generally as 'the neighbourhood'; but the question whether the local community within that sphere comprises a sufficient number of persons to constitute a class of the public is a question of fact in every case. It is not necessary, in my judgment, to prove that every member of the class has been injuriously affected; it is sufficient to show that a representative cross-section of the class has been so affected for an injunction to issue ...

... Mr Beney's main submission with regard to vibration was that, even on the assumption (which he did not admit) that one or more individuals might have successfully instituted proceedings for private nuisance in 1952, the evidence does not show that a sufficient number of persons were affected by vibration to justify the nuisance (if any) being regarded as a public nuisance. He said that vibration differs fundamentally from such things as noise or the pollution of the atmosphere. In nuisances such as those, he said, the court might well infer from the evidence of some of the affected class an injury to the class as a whole; but that no such inference can fairly be drawn in the case of vibration, which is largely a matter of individual susceptibility. I agree with Mr Beney that vibration is in some respects to be approached on a different footing from noise and smell; and the fact that one person reasonably suffers discomfort from vibration does not necessarily establish that his neighbour has been similarly affected. I am in the present case satisfied, however, that a nuisance from vibration existed in 1952 and that it was sufficiently widespread to amount to a common, or public, nuisance.

As I have earlier indicated, this question is one of fact, and the judge decided it adversely to the defendants, and it appears to me to be impossible to say that in view of the 1949 petition, the letters of complaint and the oral evidence, the judge arrived at a wrong decision. It is true that the complaints as to vibration (and indeed as to dust) were fewer and less emphatic than the complaints as to flying stones; they came, however, from a number of persons living to the east and south of the quarry; and the judge, who saw the witnesses, was satisfied that the complaints were genuine. Mr Beney's complaint that the judge paid no or insufficient attention to the vibration tests and to the evidence of Stenhouse (an expert on vibration on the staff of ICI) is, in my opinion, ill-founded. It seems clear to me that he had these matters in mind when he considered in the course of his judgment whether the plaintiffs had established that the vibration had caused structural damage to houses and came to the conclusion that they had not …

… Finally, then comes the question already mentioned: is the Attorney-General entitled to an injunction or ought some more limited form of relief to be granted in view of the various steps which the defendants have taken since 1952? The defendants contend that these measures have been so effectual that the proper order is to give the plaintiffs liberty to apply for injunctions with regard to vibration and dust; and that the injunctions granted by the judge should accordingly be discharged. *Prima facie*, if a nuisance, whether public or private, is shown to have existed at the time the writ was issued the plaintiff is entitled to an injunction. If, however, between the writ and the trial the nuisance has been abated the court will usually stay its hand and merely give the plaintiff leave to apply in the action for an injunction if the trouble should recur. It seems to me, however, that it is quite impossible to say that the nuisance from vibration or dust had been wholly abated at the time when this action came to trial. As a result of installing the wagon drill towards the end of 1953, blasting had undoubtedly become far less frequent; on the other hand, its effects had become far more violent.

Dealing with this aspect of the matter the judge said: 'There are three main dates complained of, but there are a number of other occasions when tremendous vibration is complained of. The three main dates, as I call them, are July 1, 1955, August 20, 1955, and January 3, 1956, and there is a mass of evidence to the effect that, whilst in recent times the explosions have been far fewer, and therefore the incidents far fewer … they have been far more violent, at least on occasions, and those three dates I have given are three occasions. Each of them resulted in a petition signed by many people in the neighbourhood and presented to the local authority, complaining of this frightful shattering vibration'. The judge then referred to some of the evidence which had been called before him as to these recent explosions and which left him in no doubt as to their violence. There is obviously, therefore, still ground for serious complaint of vibration, and in my judgment the judge was quite right in granting an injunction.

With regard to dust, the judge relied to some extent on what he saw when he visited the quarry premises towards the end of the trial. The main thing which impressed him was the amount of dust which resulted from the crushing operations. He said that he saw the door into the secondary crusher both open and shut, 'and no one who saw it open could avoid seeing the cloud of stuff that came pouring out from inside into the air'. Apart altogether, however, from the judge's own observations there was ample evidence from local residents to show that they were still being troubled at the time of the trial by dust from the quarry during dry weather. There is no ground, therefore, in my opinion, upon which this court should interfere with regard to the injunction which the judge granted to restrain this nuisance.

Apart from the fact that the defendants had not abated (or, at all events, had not wholly abated) the nuisances by vibration and dust when the action came on for hearing, there are certain additional considerations which support the granting of the injunctions. In the first place, there is expert evidence to show that these nuisances are not inevitable; they can be avoided by the exercise of proper care. The second consideration arises from the past conduct of the defendants and their attitude from the outset to the very reasonable complaints which were brought to their attention. This element affords no ground in itself, of course, for any penal order being made; but it seems to me that an attitude of indifference to complaints tends to show irresponsibility and that, I think, is not an irrelevant consideration where the granting of an injunction is concerned. The judge expressed strongly his view that the defendants in the present case paid scant attention to the complaints of the residents or to the representations of the local authorities before (somewhat belatedly) the writ was issued; that they were dilatory in adopting an expert's suggestion as to the wagon drill; and that they never really exerted themselves to ensuring that the door to the crusher was kept shut as they were constantly being pressed to do, or to take other steps by the use of water or otherwise to prevent the escape of dust from the crushing plant. I do not propose to add to this already lengthy judgment by referring further than I have already done to the material upon which the judge based his view as to the defendants' conduct in the past, but it is obvious to me that the view was amply justified.

In my judgment, accordingly, the injunctions against which this appeal has been brought were rightly granted and the appeal fails. Mr Beney, on behalf of the appellants, expressed some concern as to the future if the injunctions were not discharged. He said that, even though the expert witnesses had expressed views (as to vibration and dust respectively) that the quarry could be operated without occasioning a nuisance, an occasional incident might from time to time arise, unpredictable and unavoidable, which would or might lead to applications based upon contempt of court. Mr Beney had especially in mind the fact that for no apparent reason some particular explosion was far more violent than those which normally occurred. Such an explosion had in fact occurred, for example, on January 3, 1956. Wyndham Thomas (a director of the company), amongst other witnesses, gave evidence as to these particularly heavy explosions and said they may occur when blasting for what he described as a 'tight corner'. He said: 'It is a very unusual shot, a freak blast which you get sometimes, that might not happen in another ten years'. The defendants fear that this kind of thing, if and when it happens again, may be regarded by the inhabitants as a breach of the injunction as to vibration and be followed by an application for sequestration or attachment. I would point out, however, that none of the inhabitants could make such an application. The Attorney-General alone could make it, and presumably he would not apply unless, in his view, the circumstances warranted it. It may well be that he would not found an application upon some isolated incident if he were satisfied that no reasonable care on the part of the defendants could have avoided it. The defendants will doubtless adopt such expert advice as may be given to them with somewhat greater energy than they have shown at times in the past.

I would dismiss the appeal.

Denning LJ:

I entirely agree with the judgment of Romer LJ and have little to add. Mr Beney raised at the outset this question: what is the difference between a public nuisance and a private nuisance? He is right to raise it because it affects his clients greatly. The order against them restrains them from committing a public nuisance, not a private one. The classic statement of the difference is that a public nuisance affects Her Majesty's subjects generally, whereas a private nuisance only affects particular individuals. But this does not help much. The question 'When do a number of individuals become Her Majesty's subjects generally?' is as difficult to answer as the question 'When does a group of people become a crowd?' Everyone has his own views. Even the answer 'Two's company, three's a crowd' will not command the assent of those present unless they first agree on 'which two'. So here I decline to answer the question how many people are necessary to make up Her Majesty's subjects generally. I prefer to look to the reason of the thing and to say that a public nuisance is a nuisance which is so widespread in its range or so indiscriminate in its effect that it would not be reasonable to expect one person to take proceedings on his own responsibility to put a stop to it, but that it should be taken on the responsibility of the community at large.

Take the blocking up of a public highway or the non-repair of it. It may be a footpath very little used except by one or two householders. Nevertheless, the obstruction affects everyone indiscriminately who may wish to walk along it. Take next a landowner who collects pestilential rubbish near a village or permits gypsies with filthy habits to encamp on the edge of a residential neighbourhood. The householders nearest to it suffer the most, but everyone in the neighbourhood suffers too. In such cases the Attorney-General can take proceedings for an injunction to restrain the nuisance: and when he does so he acts in defence of the public right, not for any sectional interest: see *Attorney-General v Bastow*. But when the nuisance is so concentrated that only two or three property owners are affected by it, such as the three attorneys in Clifford's Inn, then they ought to take proceedings on their own account to stop it and not expect the community to do it for them: see *Rex v Lloyd*, and the precedent in *Chitty's Criminal Law* (1826), vol III, pp 664–5.

Applying this test, I am clearly of opinion that the nuisance by stones, vibration and dust in this case was at the date of the writ so widespread in its range and so indiscriminate in its effect that it was a public nuisance.

But the defendants have now taken such good remedial measures that objectionable incidents take place only rarely and then by accident. So far as stones are concerned, the injunction is absolute: but so far as dust and vibration are concerned it is dependent on it being a nuisance 'to Her Majesty's subjects', that is, a public nuisance.

The question then arises whether every rare incident is a public nuisance. Suppose six months went by without any excessive vibration and then there was by some mischance a violent explosion on an isolated occasion terrifying many people. Would that be a public nuisance? Would it subject the defendants to proceedings for contempt? I should have thought that it might, but the punishment would be measured according to the degree to which the defendants were at fault.

I quite agree that a private nuisance always involves some degree of repetition or continuance. An isolated act which is over and done with, once and for all, may give rise to an action for negligence or an action under the rule in *Rylands v Fletcher*, but not an action for nuisance. A good example is an explosion in a factory which breaks windows for miles around. It gives rise to an action under *Rylands v Fletcher*, but no other action if there was no negligence: see *Read v J Lyons & Co*. But an isolated act may amount to a public nuisance if it is done under such circumstances that the public right to condemn it should be vindicated. I referred to some authorities on this point in *Southport Corporation v Esso Petroleum Co*. In the present case, in view of the long history of stones, vibrations and dust, I should think it incumbent on the defendants to see that nothing of the kind happens again such as to be injurious to the neighbourhood at large, even on an isolated occasion.

I, too, would dismiss the appeal.

[**Result**: Appeal dismissed.]

Ball v Consolidated Rutile Ltd

[1991] 1 Qd R 524 (SC of QLD)

Ambrose J:

This is an application for disposal of points of law raised upon the pleadings pursuant to RSC O 22 rr 27 and 28.

It is conceded that for the purpose of this application I should assume the existence of the facts pleaded and particularized in the plaintiffs' pleadings.

I shall state briefly what appear to be those facts:

1   At material times the plaintiffs all carried on business as professional fishermen and conducted at least some of their fishing activities in Moreton Bay in the vicinity of North Stradbroke Island. They held licences the effect of which was to permit them to take prawns for a commercial purpose by the use of nets operated from their licensed fishing vessels in waters in various parts of Queensland including Moreton Bay. It was not lawful for persons who did not have licences of the sort held by the plaintiffs to take prawns with such nets in those waters.

2   The defendant conducted sand mining operations on the west coast of North Stradbroke Island and in the course of those operations formed a sand dune on the island abutting the waters of Moreton Bay. On about 22 March 1982 the sand dune or at least part of it slipped into the waters of Moreton Bay along with 400 metres of its shoreline, carrying with it about 570 trees of an average height of five metres together with approximately 114 000 cubic metres of root masses and other types of vegetation.

3   After slippage of the sand dune, tidal currents carried the trees, root masses and vegetation into southern parts of Moreton Bay which included waters in which prawn trawling by the plaintiffs was permitted. When the plaintiffs attempted to

fish in those waters they suffered damage to their fishing gear due to the trees, roots, vegetation etc coming into contact with it. All told about $19 880 worth of fishing gear was destroyed and other gear was damaged to such an extent that its repair cost $20 000. The gear was damaged when it became snagged on the material carried by the slippage of the sand dune into Moreton Bay and also because trawl nets became so filled with vegetation and debris generally and so entangled with such floating material that they could not withstand the weight and failed.

Because some of the material on the bed of parts of the bay caused the trawl nets to become snagged and/or fail resulting in unacceptable loss of and damage to fishing gear, it became uneconomical to fish in those parts.

4   As the result of the deposit of material in those prawning grounds in Moreton Bay affected by the slippage the plaintiffs were unable to fish there economically with their trawl nets and lost catches of prawns from them to the extent of:

40 000 kgs in the 1981–82 season, which was valued at $264 000;

80 000 kgs in the 1982–83 season, which was valued at $528 000;

40 000 kgs in the 1983–84 season, which was valued at $334 000; and

10 000 kgs in the 1984–85 season, which was valued at $94 000.

The value of the 'catch of prawns foregone' over the four fishing seasons to which I have referred was $1 220 000.

At all material times the defendant knew or ought to have known that there were professional fishermen who regularly carried on the business of prawn trawling in the grounds to which I have referred and that those fishermen would be likely to be detrimentally affected by slippage of the sand dune.

A cause of the slippage of the sand dune was the defendant's acts in:

(i)   causing or permitting the sand dune to be formed in an area where the defendant knew or ought to have known that it would be affected by fresh water springs and seepage from lakes in the area adjacent to it;

(ii) causing or permitting the dune to be formed with a slope angle which was too steep in the circumstances;

(iii) causing or permitting the dune to be formed in a position closer to the western shoreline of Moreton Island than that occupied by the natural dune which it replaced, and with its toe extending over tidal flats.

On and after 22 March 1982 the defendant knew that the slippage had occurred but did nothing at any time to prevent or minimise the detrimental effects which had been caused to the plaintiffs as professional fishermen as a result. In particular the defendant failed to take any reasonable steps to remove the tidal vegetation and other debris from the fishing grounds used by the plaintiffs and failed to take any reasonable steps to cover with sand certain of the vegetation, trees, roots, etc which had sunk to parts of the bottom of Moreton Bay which constituted fishing grounds.

As a consequence of the deposit of the trees, roots, vegetation, etc within the fishing grounds used by the plaintiffs they had to travel further distances than they would otherwise have had to travel so that they might fish in fishing grounds unaffected by the slippage.

It is pleaded that the defendant's acts with respect to the slippage of the sand dune and also with respect to its failure to remove the vegetable material washed into Moreton Bay and carried by tidal currents into fishing grounds used by the plaintiffs were negligent. It is also pleaded that the defendant's acts resulting in the slippage amounted to causing a public nuisance and an unlawful interference with a public right and that the plaintiffs' loss and damage were caused also by the failure of the defendant to abate that nuisance and to terminate that interference.

... [T]he points of law for determination here are whether the slippage of the sand dune into Moreton Bay as the consequence of acts or omissions on the part of the defendant amounted to a public nuisance and if it did whether the plaintiffs may recover their economic loss resulting from their inability to fish for prawns for four seasons as particular damage. It seems to me that [the question] relates not merely to the economic loss suffered by the plaintiffs but also to the destruction of and damage to fishing gear to the extent of nearly $40 000.

In *Attorney-General v PYA Quarries Ltd* [1957] 2 QB 169 at 191 Denning LJ defined public nuisance in the following terms:

> A public nuisance is a nuisance so widespread in its range or so indiscriminate in its effect that it would not be reasonable to expect one person to take proceedings on his own responsibility to put a stop to it but that it should be taken on the responsibility of the community at large.

For interesting historical analyses of the development of the law relating to public nuisance I refer to 'The Boundaries of Nuisance' by FH Newark 65 LQR (1949) 480, and to 'Public Nuisance—A Critical Examination' by JR Spencer (1989) 48 *Cambridge Law Journal* 55.

I refer also to *Halsbury* 4th edn, vol 34, paras 305–6, at p 102 where it is stated:

> A public nuisance is one which inflicts damage, injury or inconvenience on all the Queen's subjects or on all members of a class who come within the sphere or neighbourhood of its operation. However, it may affect some to a greater extent than others. The question whether the number of persons affected is sufficient to constitute a class is one of fact ...
>
> There are many statutory provisions which impose penalties for nuisances affecting public health, morals and comfort. However, the common law liability remains, and any person who by any act unwarranted by law or by any omission to carry out a legal duty endangers the life, health, property, morals or comfort of the public commits an offence known as public nuisance.

It is clear that to be indictable under s 230 of *The Criminal Code* an act or omission with respect to property under a person's control must:

(a) cause danger to the lives, safety and health of the public; or
(b) cause danger to the property or comfort of the public or obstruct the public in the exercise or enjoyment of a right common to all members of the public and thereby cause personal injury to some person.

In *McKell v Rider* (1908) 5 CLR 480 at 485 Griffith CJ expressed the view that at common law a public nuisance was 'an indictable nuisance'.

I was referred to no statutory enactment making the acts or omissions of the defendant, which had the effect of preventing prawn trawling with nets an offence whether indictable or otherwise. Section 230 of *The Criminal Code* clearly has no application.

For the plaintiffs to have a right to sue in public nuisance they must show that:

(1) The defendant was responsible for the slippage of the sand dune into Moreton Bay;

(2) That that slippage interfered with the public right to catch prawns in that part of Moreton Bay so effected;

(3) That that interference constituted a public nuisance; and

(4) That the plaintiffs suffered some special damage peculiar to themselves by reason of the interference with that public right.

I refer to *Boyce v Paddington Borough Council* [1903] 1 Ch 109 per Buckley J at 114. My research has revealed only two cases where an act although not impeding access to fishing grounds in public waters, made it more difficult to catch fish in those grounds and for this reason was assumed or held to constitute a public nuisance. In *Fillion v New Brunswick International Paper Co* (1934) 3 DLR 22, the Appeals Division of the New Brunswick Supreme Court held that the pollution of sea water near the plaintiff's fishing grounds with wood particles which had the result of his nets being fouled and damaged by masses of ice resulting from that pollution and of inhibiting the freezing of river water thus delaying his setting of nets with consequent financial loss of income, if it did constitute a public nuisance did not cause the plaintiff a sufficiently special or particular damage to allow him to recover damages in public nuisance. Baxter J in delivering the judgment of the court said at 26:

> Assuming then that the defendant's act constituted a public nuisance and if it is wrongful I do not see how it can be anything else, the plaintiff has suffered differently from the rest of the public only in degree … [N]early all of the cases in which this principle has been invoked concern the obstruction of a highway … Lord Haldane in *A-G BC v A-G Can* 15 DLR at p 315 assimilates the right of public fishing to that of navigation or 'the right to use a navigable river as a highway'.

In *McRae v British Norwegian Whaling Co Ltd* [1927–31] Nfld LR 274 there was pollution of sea waters from waste materials discharged by a whaling factory which greatly hampered local fishermen. Kent J at 282 observed:

> It is an established principle that the right to fish in the sea and public navigable waters is free and open to all. It is a public right that may be exercised by any of the King's subjects and for any interference with it the usual remedies to vindicate a public right must be employed.

His Honour then referred to *Benjamin v Storr* (1874) 43 LJCP 162 (a highway case) at 166 per Brett J and treating the pollution of the sea as a public nuisance went on to hold that the plaintiff's damage was not sufficiently particular to permit recovery of damages by the plaintiff in public nuisance.

In *Hickey et al v Electric Reduction Co of Canada Ltd* (1970) 21 DLR (3d) 371 the defendant discharged poisonous substances into the waters of a bay causing the death of fish life in it. The plaintiffs were fishermen whose livelihood was impaired by the destruction of those fish. It was held that the pollution of the bay waters amounted to a public nuisance. Furlong CJ referred to *McRae* and *Fillion* to support this conclusion.

His Honour however came to the conclusion that the damage suffered by those fishermen was not sufficiently special or particular to them to permit them to sue for the loss which they had suffered. At 371–2 his Honour said:

> Counsel for the plaintiffs ... argued that when a public nuisance has been created anyone who suffers special damage, that is, direct damage has a right of action. I am unable to agree to this rather wide application of *Salmond*'s view that a public nuisance may become a tortious act. I think the right view is that any person who suffers peculiar damage has a right of action but where the damage is common to all persons of the same class then a personal right of action is not maintainable. Mr Wells suggests that the plaintiffs' right to outfit for the fishery and their right to fish is a particular right and this right having been interfered with they have a cause of action. This right which they enjoy is a right in common with all Her Majesty's subjects an interference with which is the whole test of the public nuisance; a right which can only be vindicated by the appropriate means which is an action by the Attorney-General either with or without a relator in the common interest of the public.

While *Hickey et al v Electrical Reduction Co of Canada Ltd* is authority for the proposition that the discharge of poisonous materials into a bay containing fish from time to time caught by professional fishermen for human consumption constitutes a nuisance if it causes the death of those fish, it is not in my view authority for the proposition that the causing of trees, roots and vegetation to fall into a bay making it uneconomic to use nets to catch prawns constitutes that event a public nuisance. As I have already indicated there is nothing to suggest that the deposition of that material in Moreton Bay in this case would have been in any way harmful to marine life. It must be kept in mind that in times of flood, trees, roots, vegetation, etc are frequently carried from rivers and waterways into bays. With the exception of *Fillion* and *McRae* I have discovered no authority supporting the proposition that deposition of such material by man in a bay in such a way that it does not adversely interfere with marine life and is not demonstrated to impede the navigation of the bay by boats amounts to a public nuisance.

In my view the fishing licences which permitted the holders thereof lawfully to catch prawns with nets cannot be said to give those holders any right whether public or private to have the fishing grounds where they fish pursuant to such licences kept free of material of the sort deposited in Moreton Bay by the slippage in issue. It cannot be said therefore that in any relevant sense the right of the plaintiffs to take prawns by commercial nets of designated size and design is any different from the right of any other members of the public to take prawns or fish without using such nets.

I am unpersuaded upon the authorities that the depositing of material in fishing grounds which makes it more difficult to catch fish by using certain types of fishing gear so interferes with 'a right' of a public nature as to constitute it a public nuisance. I am aware of no authority which supports such a contention apart from two of the Canadian cases to which I have referred and such an interference seems to have no analogy with an interference with a public right of way upon land or a public right to navigate upon Moreton Bay.

However let it be assumed that the slippage of the sand dune into Moreton Bay, for practical purposes making it impossible economically to fish for prawns in those parts of the bay affected, was sufficient to constitute a public nuisance; the next point for determination is whether the plaintiffs were so specially or particularly damaged as to permit them to sue for damages in this case.

I have discovered no authority for the proposition that there is any constraint on the limits of foreseeability as a determinant of liability for damage for public nuisance similar to the constraint of proximity upon the existence of a duty of care to avoid foreseeable damage of certain sorts in the tort of negligence.

I have already indicated that it is my view that in the present case there is not sufficient proximity between the plaintiffs and the defendant with respect to the foreseeable economic loss which would accrue to the plaintiffs should the sand dune under the control of the defendant slip into Moreton Bay to impose upon the defendant a duty in negligence to take reasonable steps to avoid causing such economic loss to the plaintiffs. It would be a quite unsatisfactory state of affairs if upon the same facts by pursuing an action for damages for public nuisance the plaintiffs were able to avoid satisfying the test of proximity and recover in nuisance damages for economic loss caused to them in their prawn fishing endeavours which would not be recoverable in negligence. I would adopt the approach of Lord Radcliffe in *Esso Petroleum Co Ltd v Southport Corporation* [1956] AC 218 at 242, and conclude that an essential issue in the plaintiff's cause of action in public nuisance on the facts in this case is the negligence of the defendant in the construction of the sand dune which caused its slippage into Moreton Bay.

Newark in his consideration of the 'Boundaries of Nuisance' 65 LQR at pp 483 and 485 draws attention to aspects of the development of the law governing the right of a person to recover damages for public nuisance which suggest that for practical purposes that right was similar to that in negligence to recover damages. I refer also to Spencer's conclusions in (1989) 48 *Cambridge Law Journal* at pp 81–3.

In *An Introduction to English Legal History* (2nd edn, 1979) at 362 J.H. Baker observes with respect to the development of the right of persons who can show 'particular damage' to recover in public nuisance:

> Some conceptual confusion has arisen from calling these private actions 'nuisance'. They have little, if any, affinity with private nuisance and were in fact innominate actions to recover compensation for the special loss. If they belong to any particular genus it is the tort of negligence. The significance of common or public nuisance in the realms of tort is not that it furnishes a distinct cause of action which would not otherwise exist, but that it takes away existing causes of action in order to prevent a multiplicity of lawsuits.

It is unnecessary for me however to give further consideration to this matter and in particular upon the assumed facts in this case to answer the defendant's question whether the 'controls' applied in negligence to recovery of a loss are applicable to a claim for that loss in nuisance. In nuisance one 'control' is the necessity for the plaintiff to show particular damage. However to the extent that fault must be shown to establish public nuisance, *The Wagon Mound (No 2)* is authority for the proposition that foreseeability of injury or damage is relevant. One control in negligence, that of proximity, is expressed to go to the extent of the duty while in public nuisance, the control of particularity, is expressed to go to the nature of the damage recoverable. Foreseeability would seem to be a constraint in both negligence and public nuisance. While no doubt it is desirable that the plaintiffs' rights to recover their economic loss against the defendant be equally constrained in negligence and public nuisance having regard to the views I have already expressed, it is unnecessary and unhelpful to embark upon any consideration of the extent to which the 'controls' for recovery of economic loss in negligence and public nuisance upon the facts of this case may in theory or in effect coincide or overlap.

It is my view that in permitting or causing the sand dune to slip into Moreton Bay so as to interfere with the capacity of persons to net prawns in parts of that bay for a number of years there was not an interference with a public right of such a nature as to constitute the slippage a public nuisance for which the defendant is responsible.

I would answer Question 3 posed by the parties to this application in the negative.

I am also of the view that even if the slippage resulting from the defendant's failure to take reasonable care did amount to a public nuisance the economic loss suffered by the plaintiffs was not particular damage for which they could recover in an action in public nuisance. I have already dealt with authorities that support this view and in particular the Canadian cases to which I have referred.

The damage to the plaintiffs' fishing gear amounting to nearly $40 000 would be sufficiently particular to enable them to recover that damage if the deposition of the material in Moreton Bay as a result of the slippage of the dune constituted a public nuisance.

However the economic loss which the plaintiffs suffered is not in any way consequential upon the damage to the fishing gear which would be particular damage. The economic loss flowed not from any particular damage but from the inability of the plaintiffs to trawl for prawns with their prawning nets for four seasons in that part of Moreton Bay affected by the slippage. This loss flowed from an impediment upon fishing which existed for all licensed fishermen who might wish to trawl their nets for prawns in this part of Moreton Bay.

Had the deposition of material in the Bay had the effect of so confining the plaintiffs' vessels in a part of the bay that they were unable to work anywhere so that they were obliged to expend money to free their boats from such confinement such economic loss in my view may have been sufficiently particular to be recoverable. *Tate & Lyle v GLC* is clear authority for the proposition that provided it is sufficiently particular, loss which is merely economic is recoverable in public nuisance.

However those are not the facts of the present case. The economic loss which the plaintiffs suffered in the present case flowed simply from the fact that they were unable to trawl for prawns for four seasons in certain parts of Moreton Bay because to do so would cause too much damage to their nets. This in my view is not sufficiently particular to give them a cause of action even if the slippage did constitute a public nuisance.

Railtrack Plc v Mayor & Burgesses of London Borough of Wandsworth

[2001] EWCA 1236 (30 July 2001)

Kennedy LJ:

This is a defendant's appeal from a decision of Gibbs J reported at [2001] 1 WLR 368. It concerns the problem caused by pigeons roosting on the underside of the railway bridge which crosses Balham High Street in south London. Their droppings foul the pavement, and at times the pedestrians as well, and in this action the local authority has brought proceedings alleging public nuisance, private nuisance and negligence. They have sought a declaration that the defendants were liable to abate the nuisance and an injunction requiring the defendants to abate it by clearing the bridge of pigeons and nests, cleansing it, and thereafter placing netting to prevent their return. The local authority has also claimed damages limited to £10 000.

Facts

At the trial there was evidence about pigeon behaviour which I need not rehearse for the purposes of this appeal. Suffice to say that wild pigeons are attracted to urban areas where there is food, and there were at the material time 89 food outlets within 500 metres of the bridge in addition to those that members of the population who deliberately feed pigeons [*sic*]. They also make pavements slippery, and can cause disease. On behalf of the local authority it was accepted by Mr Porten QC that the risk of injury to health presented by the Balham pigeons was not in itself sufficient to constitute an actionable nuisance, but it was and is a facet of the problem.

Although the present substantial bridge has been in position since 1929, when it replaced an earlier bridge so the road could be widened, complaints about pigeon droppings did not begin to be expressed and recorded until about twenty years ago. Whether that is because previously people were less inclined to register complaints, or because with the increasing number of food outlets the problem has worsened is not clear, and for present purposes it does not matter.

In April 1990 the local authority, with the permission of British Rail, the predecessor of Railtrack as bridge owners, installed netting and panels to prevent pigeons from getting into the structure from above. That was quite successful, but some pigeons did get in, got trapped and died, and that led to the removal of the netting in March 1995. That resulted in a renewal of complaints about fouling, and a petition. The local authority's stance was that it was for Railtrack to prevent the pigeons from roosting. Meanwhile the local authority arranged for the pavements to be cleaned every day. Railtrack offered to let the local authority re-pigeon-proof the bridge, but only at the local authority's own expense. By the time of trial that would have cost £9000, but the cleaning cost was £12 000 a year. As the judge found, the roosting places beneath the bridge can be effectively sealed off by fixing permanent netting or mesh across them, and that finding has not been challenged before us. The pigeons will move on, but they are unlikely to be such a problem for pedestrians.

Litigation

These proceedings began in 1998, and the emphasis of the local authority as claimants has throughout been on public nuisance. When there is such a nuisance which affects the public right to use and enjoy the highway, the highway authority is empowered by section 130 of the Highways Act 1980 to bring legal proceedings to protect the public's rights. Similarly section 222(1) of the Local Government Act 1972 enables a local authority to institute civil legal proceedings in its own name where it considers it expedient to do so for the promotion or protection of the interests of the inhabitants of its area, and it was those two statutory provisions upon which the local authority relied in this case.

Public nuisance is also a crime, and a person is said to be guilty if he does an act not warranted by law or omits to discharge a legal duty if the effect of the act is to endanger the life, health, property, morals or comfort of the public, or to obstruct the public in the exercise or enjoyment of rights common to all (see Archbold *Criminal Pleadings, Evidence and Practice* 2001 at paragraph[s] 31–40). Private nuisance is different. It is the wrongful interference with another's use [or] enjoyment of land, or of some right over or in connection therewith, and negligence arises where the relationship between the parties is such as to give rise to a duty of care. Having found in favour of the claimant on the basis of public nuisance the judge did not find it necessary to reach a final conclusion in relation to private nuisance or negligence, and in my judgment he was right to take that stance.

Authorities

In skeleton arguments and in submissions our attention has been invited to a large number of decided cases, but I need only refer to some of them, and I can begin, as Mr Porten did with *Attorney General v Tod Heatley* [1897] 1 Ch 560. In that case the defendant was the owner and occupier of a vacant piece of land in London. He surrounded it with a hoarding, but people threw filth and refuse over the hoarding and broke it down, so that the condition of the land and the use to which it was put constituted a public nuisance. The Attorney General, representing the public, brought proceedings, and at 566 Lindley LJ said:

> It is no defence to say 'I did not put the filth on but somebody else did'. He must provide against this if he can. His business is to prevent his land from being a public nuisance.

At 567 he continued:

> The mere fact that it puts the wrongdoer to expense, or that it is difficult for him to get rid of it, is no defence in point of law, or any reason at all why the rights of the public should not be enforced.

Lindley LJ accepted that by statute the vestry could have cleaned the land at the expense of the rate payers, and at 568 he said:

> But upon what principle of justice can the expense of keeping this place clean be thrown upon the rate payers? It is the common law duty of the owner to prevent this piece of land from being a nuisance. Why should the ratepayers pay for it?

Mr Porten submits that whatever may have been the nineteenth century position in relation to private nuisance and negligence, so far as public nuisance was concerned the law was as stated in *Tod Heatley* and it has not changed.

In an important article in 4 *Cambridge Law Journal* in 1930 Professor AL Goodhart considered liability for things naturally on the land. He therefore looked at both public and private nuisance, and at page 30 he said:

The correct principle seems to be that an occupier of land is liable for a nuisance of which he knows, or ought to know, whether that nuisance is caused by himself, his predecessor in title, a third person or by nature. Whether a natural condition is or is not a nuisance is, of course, a question of fact. Is the injury caused by the natural condition more than a reasonable neighbour can be asked to bear under the rule of 'live and let live'? In other words, the ordinary rules of nuisance apply in the case of natural conditions. As we must all bear with our neighbour's piano-playing so we must also submit to his thistle down. This does not mean that we have no remedy if he introduces a large orchestra, or if he allows his tree, even of natural growth, to remain in a dangerous condition along the highway.

That approach was applied by the House of Lords in *Sedleigh-Denfield v O'Callaghan* [1940] AC 880 where a pipe laid by a trespasser on the respondent's land, but of which the respondent was aware, became clogged with leaves so that water overflowed on to the appellant's premises and caused damage. The claim was won in private nuisance, but *Tod-Heatley* was referred to with approval as representing the law in relation to public nuisance, and at 894 Viscount Maugham said:

In my opinion an occupier of land 'continues' a nuisance if with knowledge or presumed knowledge of its existence he fails to take any reasonable means to bring it to an end though with ample time to do so. He 'adopts' it if he makes any use of the erection, building, bank or artificial contrivance which constitutes the nuisance.

He went on to hold that the respondents had both continued and adopted the nuisance. Similarly, at 899, Lord Atkin said:

In my opinion the defendants clearly continued the nuisance for they come clearly within the terms I have mentioned above, they knew the danger, they were able to prevent it and they omitted to prevent it. In this respect at least there seems to me to be no difference between the case of a public nuisance and a private nuisance, and the case of *Attorney General v Tod-Heatley* is conclusive to show that where the occupier has knowledge of a public nuisance, has the means of remedying it and fails to do so he may be enjoined from allowing it to continue. I cannot think that the obligation not to 'continue' can have a different meaning in 'public' and in 'private' nuisances.

Slater v Worthington's Cash Stores (1930) Ltd [1941] 1 KB 488 was another decision of the Court of Appeal in relation to public nuisance. The plaintiff was on the pavement looking in the window of the defendant's shop when she was injured by a mass of snow which fell on her from the roof. The defendants were aware of its existence and could have removed it over the preceding four days, but they did not do so, nor did they give any warning of the danger. Oliver J found that the overhanging snow was a public nuisance and that because the defendants knew of it and did nothing to abate it they were liable in damages to the plaintiff. That conclusion was upheld by the Court of Appeal.

Goldman v Hargrave [1967] AC 645 was an appeal to the Privy Council from the High Court of Australia. A fire in a red gum tree, which the appellant had left to burn out, spread across his paddock to the respondent's property. At 657 Lord Wilberforce said:

> the tort of nuisance, uncertain in its boundary, may comprise a wide variety of situations, in some of which negligence plays no part, in others of which it is decisive. The present case is one where liability, if it exists, rests upon negligence and nothing else; whether it falls within or overlaps the boundaries of nuisance is a question of classification which need not here be resolved.

Having looked at the authorities Lord Wilberforce continued at 663:

> One may say in general terms that the existence of a duty must be based upon knowledge of the hazard, ability to foresee the consequences of not checking or removing it, and the ability to abate it. And in many cases, as for example, Scrutton LJ's hypothetical case of stamping out a fire, or the present case, where the hazard could have been removed with little effort and no expenditure, no problem arises. But other cases may not be so simple. In such situations the standard ought to be to require of the occupier what is reasonable to expect of him in his individual circumstances.

In *Leakey v National Trust* [1980] 1 QB 485 the plaintiff owned land adjacent to that owned by the Trust on which there was, as the Trust knew, an unstable mound, which eventually fell and caused damage to the plaintiff's property. As Megaw LJ pointed out at 523, even before the fall the plaintiff could arguably have entered the Trust's land to abate the nuisance, and if that right of abatement existed it could only do so because the Trust owed to the plaintiff a duty. Having referred to *Tod-Heatley*, *Sedleigh-Denfield* and *Goldman* he continued at 524:

> The duty is a duty to do that which is reasonable in all the circumstances, and no more than what, if anything, is reasonable, to prevent or minimise the known risk of damage or injury to one's neighbour or to his property. The considerations with which the law is familiar are all to be taken into account when deciding if there has been a breach of duty, and, if so, what that breach is, and whether it is causative of the damage in respect of which the claim is made. Thus, there will fall to be considered the extent of the risk; what, so far as reasonably can be foreseen, are the chances that anything untoward will happen or that any damage will be caused? What is to be foreseen as to the possible extent of the damage if the risk becomes a reality? Is it practicable to prevent, or to minimise, the happening of any damage? If it is practicable, how simple or how difficult are the measures which could be taken, how much and how lengthy work do they involve, and what is the probable cost of such work? Was there sufficient time for preventative action to have been taken, by persons acting reasonably in relation to the known risk, between the time when it became known to, or should have been realised by, the defendant, and the time when the damage occurred? Factors such as these, so far as they apply

in a particular case, fall to be weighed in deciding whether the defendant's duty of care requires, or required, him to do anything, and if so, what.

All of that, it must be remembered, was said in the context of a claim in private nuisance, and in similar vein Megaw LJ said at 526 E:

> The defendant's duty is to do that which is reasonable for him to do. The criteria of reasonableness include, in respect of a duty of this nature, the factor of what the particular man—not the average man [—] can be expected to do, having regard, amongst other things, where a serious expenditure of money is required to eliminate or reduce the danger, to his means. Just as, where physical effort is required to avert an immediate danger, the defendant's age and physical condition may be relevant in deciding what is reasonable, so also logic and good sense require that, where the expenditure of money is required, the defendant's capacity to find the money is relevant. But this can only be in the way of a broad and not a detailed assessment; and in arriving at a judgment on reasonableness a similar broad assessment may be relevant in some cases as to the neighbour's capacity to protect himself from damage, whether by way of some form of barrier on his own land or by way of providing funds for expenditure on agreed works on the land of the defendant.

Cumming-Bruce LJ agreed with Megaw LJ and so did Shaw LJ but, as Mr Dutton QC for Railtrack points out, Shaw LJ had misgivings 'as to the course which the law of England has taken (note the past tense) in regard to the liability of a land owner for a nuisance arising upon his land independently of the intervention of any human agency'. He suggested at 529 E that:

> The judgment in *Goldman v Hargrave* may represent the climax to the movement in the law of England expanding that part of the law which relates to the liability for nuisance.

The last authority to which I need refer at this stage is *Holbeck Hall Hotel Ltd v Scarborough BC* [2000] 2 WLR 1396. The hotel was on a cliff and the local authority owned the land forming the under cliff between the hotel grounds and the sea. Landslips were not uncommon, and in 1993 a massive landslip caused loss of support for the hotel grounds and part of the hotel, so here again there was no allegation of public nuisance. It was argued that the principle in *Sedleigh-Denfield*, *Goldman* and *Leakey* should be confined to cases where there was an escape of some noxious thing from the defendant's land to that of the claimant, but that was rejected, and at 1411 Stuart-Smith LJ said:

> There seems no reason why, where the defendant does not create the nuisance, but the question is whether he had adopted or continued it, different principles should apply to one kind of nuisance rather than another. In each case liability only arises if there is negligence; the duty to abate the nuisance arises from the defendant's knowledge of the hazard that will affect his neighbour.

At 1415 it was pointed out that the case was one of non-feasance, so the scope of the duty was more restricted. After referring to the three-stage test for the existence of a duty of care set out in *Caparo Industries plc v Dickman* [1990] 2 AC 605 and adopted in *Marc Rich & Co AG v Bishop Rock Marine Company Ltd* [1996] AC 211 in relation to all types of damage, Stuart-Smith LJ said at 1417 F:

> the requirement that it must be fair, just and reasonable is a limiting condition where foreseeability and proximity are established. In my judgment very similar considerations arise whether the court is determining the scope of the measured duty of care or whether it is fair, just and reasonable to impose a duty or the extent of that duty. And for my part I do not think it is just and reasonable in a case like the present to impose liability for damage which is greater in extent than anything that was foreseen or foreseeable (without further geological investigation), especially where the defect and danger existed as much on the plaintiff's land as Scarborough's.

The judge's conclusions

Having set out the authorities I turn now to the findings of the judge, and the submissions made on behalf of the appellants. The judge found, as a matter of fact and degree, that the pigeon infestation and the fouling caused by it amounted to a nuisance, in that they interfered substantially with the comfort and convenience of the public, or a significant class of the public who use the pavements. In this court there has been no direct challenge to that finding.

The judge went on to accept that Railtrack had made no unnatural or unreasonable use of its land, and that the local authority had done nothing which caused or contributed to the infestation. The local authority had done all that it reasonably could do to restrict the sources of food available to pigeons in the area. That too is accepted for the purposes of this appeal.

The judge then held that although the bridge had become infested with pigeons to such an extent as to cause or amount to a nuisance without any act or default on the part of Railtrack or its predecessors, Railtrack had omitted to remedy the situation within a reasonable time or at all although it could have done so. It was, the judge said, no excuse to say that the pigeons were wild, or that the nuisance did not involve physical injury or damage to property. The judge accepted that Railtrack might be found liable in respect of other bridges, but it was not shown that the financial burden would be enormous, and it was no defence for Railtrack to say that the local authority had its own statutory powers to maintain roads and deal with pigeons, or that keeping the pigeons out of the bridge would only cause them to move elsewhere.

Submissions

I turn now to Railtrack's grounds of appeal. The first ground of appeal is that the judge failed properly to apply the decision of the Court of Appeal in *Leakey* in that he distinguished between liability in nuisance and negligence when there is no proper distinction between the two torts in these circumstances. Mr Dutton submits that the distinction between the two torts cannot properly be made in cases concerning liability for nuisances which were not created by the tortfeasor. In my judgment it has been clear, at least since *Tod Heatley* was decided in 1897, that where there is a public nuisance on the defendant's land it does not matter whether it was created by the defendant or some third party, or by natural causes (see *Slater*). If the defendant is aware of it, has had a reasonable opportunity to abate it, has the means to abate it, and has chosen not to do so, then he is liable, and there is no reason to approach the matter as though it were a claim in negligence or private nuisance.

In the second ground of appeal it is asserted that the judge was wrong to extend the principle set out in *Leakey* to a case which did not involve a nuisance causing physical damage to neighbouring land, but only an interference with the enjoyment of that land, and which arose out of the activities of wild birds and not out of the state of Railtrack's land. In my judgment this ground of appeal elides two separate issues, the first issue being whether a nuisance does in fact exist, and the second being concerned once again with the cause of the problem. I accept that where there is physical damage to land (as in *Leakey* and *Holbeck Hall Hotel*) or injury to a claimant (as in *Slater*) it may be easier for the claimant to prove that the antecedent threat amounted to a nuisance. For example, it is well established that where a complaint relates only to foul smells in an industrial area (see *St Helen's Smelting Company v Tipping* [1865] 11 HLC 642), that cannot amount to actionable nuisance, but it is clear beyond argument that interference with the right of the public to enjoy the highway in reasonable comfort and convenience can amount to a public nuisance (see the definition of public nuisance referred to earlier in this judgment, and *Tod Heatley*, albeit the state of the land in that case was said to be injurious to public health). So, in my judgment, the judge was entitled to find as a fact, as he did, that in this case there was a public nuisance, and to some extent the second ground of appeal is an attempt to outflank that finding, which, as I have said, Railtrack have indicated that they accept. The acceptance is not surprising, because the evidence to support the finding was overwhelming.

The second issue raised by the second ground of appeal, namely that the problem arose out of the activities of wild birds is an issue which I have considered when dealing with the first ground of appeal. Whether the cause of the nuisance on a defendant's land was a fall of snow or the arrival of wild birds is immaterial if the defendant had the necessary knowledge, opportunity and means to abate the nuisance. It is submitted by Mr Dutton that the pigeons proliferate because the community provides food, so the local authority, representing the community, should solve the problem by the exercise of statutory powers given to it in section 74 of the Public Health Act 1961 to abate any nuisance, annoyance or damage caused by the congregation of pigeons in any built-up area, and by the exercise of its contractual and statutory street-cleaning obligations. But this case is not concerned with the problem of pigeons in general. It is concerned with the nuisance caused by the pigeons which roost under the railway bridge which crosses Balham High Street, and that is a nuisance which, as it seems to me, Railtrack had a clear legal duty to address. If that is right then, as Lindley LJ pointed out in *Tod Heatley*, there would seem to be no reason why the burden should be passed to the council tax payers ...

In the third ground of appeal it is said that the judge failed properly to consider whether Railtrack owed any duty of care to the local authority, and if there was a duty of care the scope of that duty, and in the fourth ground of appeal it is said that the judge failed properly to consider what was required of Railtrack to discharge the duty, the submission being that it was sufficient for Railtrack to invite the local authority to pigeon-proof the bridge at its own expense. In my judgment those two grounds of appeal are misconceived because this was primarily a claim in public nuisance, and the judge rightly so regarded it. As Mr Porten submitted, that meant that in reality there were three questions to be addressed, namely:

(1) Do the matters complained of constitute a hazard, ie being dangerous or materially affecting the comfort and convenience of the public on the highway;

(2) Does Railtrack, as landowner, have knowledge of the hazard;

(3) Has Railtrack taken reasonable steps to prevent the foreseeable effects of the hazard?

Mr Dutton contends that such a simple approach, founded on *Tod Heatley*, cannot be sustained in the light of later authorities, which require a claimant to identify a duty of care, an unreasonable use of the land by a defendant, and a failure by the defendant to take reasonable steps to safeguard the claimant before the claimant can hope to obtain redress. In my judgment where the cause of action is public nuisance *Tod Heatley* still represents the law, and nothing in the later authorities suggests otherwise.

The final two grounds of appeal relate to damages. It is submitted that the judge was wrong to hold that the local authority was entitled to damages in addition to the declaration that he granted. He entered judgment for damages to be assessed. It is further submitted that if Railtrack is to be required to abate the nuisance the local authority should have been required to contribute to the cost. In my judgment there is no reason why the capital cost of pigeon-proofing the bridge should not fall wholly upon Railtrack. As to damages it seems to me that the local authority is entitled to the extra costs of pavement cleaning which it incurred up to 1996 when Railtrack gave the local authority permission to abate the nuisance at its own expense. 'Thereafter' as the judge said, 'damages should be assessed bearing in mind the offer to permit abatement'.

[**Result**: **Chadwick LJ** and **Rougier J** agreed. The appeal was dismissed with costs to be assessed, but an interim payment of £15 000 to be paid on account.]

Chapter 6
Defamation

Introduction

One of Shakespeare's consummate villains, Iago, contrived to contrast the petty insignificance of conversion of chattel with the all-consuming tort of defamation (*Othello*, act 3, scene 3, lines 157–61):

> Who steals my purse steals trash; 'tis something, nothing; …
>> But he that filches from me my good name
>> Robs me of that which not enriches him,
>> And makes me poor indeed.

The unfortunate Cassio had earlier cried (in act 2, scene 3, lines 264–7):

> Reputation, reputation, reputation! O! I have lost my reputation. I have lost the immortal part of myself, and what remains is bestial. My reputation, Iago, my reputation!

Contrast these sentiments with s 14 of the New Zealand Bill of Rights Act 1990:

> **Freedom of expression**—Everyone has the right to freedom of expression, including the freedom to seek, receive, and impart information and opinions of any kind in any form.

The impact of this provision on the law of defamation is slowly being felt. It received a boost in much publicised litigation brought by David Lange, former Prime Minister. The various judgments are tracked later in this chapter under the heading 'Qualified privilege'. The extent to which the law has been reshaped is a matter of debate but the balance has certainly been tipped in favour of freedom of expression.

Earlier, the Court of Appeal had noted that s 28 of the New Zealand Bill of Rights Act preserves other existing rights and freedoms, one such being a 'right to integrity of reputation' (*Television New Zealand v Quinn* [1996] 3 NZLR 24, 56). This right must be reconciled with freedom of expression. A conservative judicial line is apparent in the words of McKay J in the same case: 'I am not persuaded that the Bill of Rights has the result of putting the media freedoms above the right to one's reputation, nor that this case has anything to do with the proper freedom of the media, as distinct from a licence to be irresponsible'. McKay J nearly twenty years earlier had chaired a committee which had recommended a special defence for the media (*The Report of the Committee on Defamation*, paras 230–68). Now in *Quinn*, a case that involved allegations of horse doping and corruption in the trotting industry, the judge found 'defamation of the worst kind' (p 45). The two television programmes in that case showed 'no evidence that previous damages awards had had any chilling effect on TVNZ's investigative reporting' (pp 43–4). The jury had awarded the plaintiff $400 000 and $1.1 million in damages. The Court of Appeal preserved the first award but upheld the trial court judge in setting aside the second, ordering a new trial on damages.

Damages in defamation cases are often very elusive. In *Quinn*, there was no evidence of financial loss, yet the Court of Appeal thought that there was 'room for substantial added punitive ingredients in each award' (p 38, Cooke P). A jury in an earlier case thought that it would be a good idea to calculate the damages according to 'all legal fees' incurred by the plaintiff. The Court of Appeal ordered a new trial limited to damages, as the jury's understandable approach nevertheless confused damages with costs (*Television New Zealand v Keith* [1994] 2 NZLR 84).

In 1992, Parliament passed a revised Defamation Act. Many of the recommendations of the Committee on Defamation were incorporated but any radical shifting of the balance away from reputation and towards free speech was resolutely eschewed by MPs. The defences of justification and fair comment have been renamed truth and honest opinion and new rules for both defences must be carefully studied. The Act contains a reformulated statutory version of the defence of qualified privilege. Among the rules on remedies and procedure is a new power given to the Court to recommend that the defendant, instead of paying damages, publish a correction and pay at the higher rate of solicitor and client costs. Often, what a plaintiff wants is to stop publication of the offending story. But the courts have set a high threshold for the award of an interim injunction, especially where the defendant pleads truth (see *TV3 Network Services Ltd v Fahey* [1999] 2 NZLR 129).

Section 4 of the Defamation Act 1992 states that in defamation 'it is not necessary to allege or prove special damage'. The significance of this is lost without some reference to the common law. 'Libel' referred to defamations in some permanent form, usually in writing. Damages for libel were at large. 'Slander' on the other hand referred typically to spoken defamations and could be sued on only if the plaintiff could show some material or pecuniary loss, not mere damage to reputation. In New Zealand as a result of s 4, the distinction between libel and slander is effectively removed.

For a summary of New Zealand law, see 'Defamation', *The Laws of New Zealand* (written by Justice McKay).

Part 1: The plaintiff's case

Defamatory meaning

[One of the early classic definitions of a defamatory publication is found in Baron Parke's judgment in *Parmiter v Coupland* (1840) 6 M & W 105, 108, 151 ER 340, 342: 'A publication, without justification or lawful excuse, which is calculated to injure the reputation of another by exposing him to hatred, contempt, or ridicule, is a libel'. Baron Parke's definition was apparently not meant to be exhaustive; how much broader should the definition be?]

Sim v Stretch
[1936] 2 All ER 1237 (HL)
[**FACTS**: Both parties were landed gentry. A third person, Ms Edith Saville, had been employed by both parties as a housemaid at their respective estates. A telegram was sent by the defendants (from Maidenhead) to the plaintiffs (whose estate was at Cookham Dean) informing them that 'Edith has resumed her service with us today. Please send her possessions and the money you borrowed also her wages to Old Barton'. The plaintiffs allege that the suggestion that they borrowed money from a housemaid is defamatory.]
Lord Atkin:
… The question, then, is whether the words in their ordinary signification are capable of being defamatory. Judges and textbook writers alike have found difficulty in defining with precision the word 'defamatory'. The conventional phrase, 'exposing the plaintiff to hatred, ridicule and contempt', is probably too narrow. The question is complicated by having to consider the person or class of persons whose reaction to the publication is the test of the wrongful character of the words used. I do not intend to ask your Lordships to lay down a formal definition, but after collating the opinions of many authorities I propose in the present case the test: would the words tend to lower the plaintiff in the estimation of right-thinking members of society generally? … Now, in the present case it is material to notice that there is no evidence that the words were published to anyone who had any knowledge at all of any of the facts that I have narrated above. There is no direct evidence that they were published to anyone who had ever heard of the plaintiff. The post office officials at Maidenhead would not be presumed to know him, and we are left without any information as to the officials at Cookham Dean. The plaintiff and his wife dealt at the shop at which was the sub-post office, but there is no evidence that the shopkeeper was the telegraph clerk; the probability is that he was not. It might, however, be inferred that the publication of the telegram at Cookham Dean was to someone who knew the plaintiff. What would he or she learn by reading the telegram? That Edith Saville had been in the plaintiff's employment; that she had that day entered the defendant's employment; and that the former employer was requested to send on to the new place of employment the servant's possessions together with the money due to her for money borrowed and for wages. How could perusal of that communication tend to lower the plaintiff in the estimation of the right-thinking peruser who knows nothing of the circumstances but what he or she derives from the telegram itself? The defamatory imputation is said to be in the words 'the money you borrowed,' coupled with the request for the return of it sent in a telegram. It was said by the learned judge at the trial and accepted by the two members of the Court of Appeal who affirmed the judgment that the words were capable of conveying to anybody that the plaintiff had acted in a mean way borrowing money from his own maid and not paying her as he was required to and required to by telegram and also withholding her wages. With the greatest respect, that is imput-

ing to the words a suggestion of meanness both in borrowing and in not repaying which I find it impossible to extract from their ordinary meaning. The sting is said to be in the borrowing. It happens that the phrase is substantially true. I myself have no doubt that if we were merely regarding legal technicalities the transaction which I have described as to the 14s which was still unpaid could be covered by an indebitatus count for money lent as well for money paid. In substance and in fact a justification of money borrowed would have been made out. But I am at a loss to understand why a person's character should be lowered in anyone's estimation if he or she has borrowed from a domestic servant. I should have thought it such a usual domestic occurrence for small sums to be advanced in such circumstances as the present and with the assent of everyone concerned to be left outstanding for some days that the mere fact of borrowing from a servant bears not the slightest tinge of 'meanness'.

Notes

1 The 14s referred to by Lord Atkin was a sum paid by Ms Saville to a victualler who supplied the household. The Simses had been away for a few days and had left Ms Saville money to pay the accounts. It was agreed, having been suggested by Ms Saville, that Ms Saville would pay any shortfall out of her own pocket.

2 Lord Atkin has expanded the definition from the 'hatred, ridicule and contempt' test to a 'right-thinking member of society' test. The problem now is whether that definition is itself too restrictive.

3 'Right-thinking' persons would surely not lower their estimation of a woman who has allegedly been raped, would they? In *Youssoupoff v MGM* (1934) 50 TLR 581, a princess of the Russian ruling Romanov family sued film-makers for their production *Rasputin, the Mad Monk*. The defendants claimed that their portrayal of Rasputin's rape of the princess was not defamatory. Scrutton LJ characterised the defendants' argument in the following terms, '[the defendants' claim is this] which was solemnly put forward, that to say of a woman of good character that she has been ravished by a man of the worst possible character is not defamatory'.

   The Court of Appeal upheld a jury verdict in the plaintiff's favour of £25 000. A note on this aspect of the case can be found at (1931) 51 LQR 281.

4 You would not hate or ridicule a person who was mentally ill, would you? In *Morgan v Lingem* (1863) 8 LT 800, a surgeon described a woman as being 'fairly off her head', possessed of paranoid 'delusions'. The appellate tribunal held that (at 801) 'a statement in writing that a lady's mind is affected, and that seriously, is ... *prima facie* a libel'.

   What about a statement that P has attempted suicide? See *Wanst v Hearst's Chicago American* (1900) 129 Wis 419, 109 NW 70.

   A newspaper publishes a letter, which includes a reference to the plaintiff, as follows: 'At times, Mr Symes is not quite responsible for what he does'. The defendant's explanation is that Mr Symes is excitable and 'lacking in self-control'. Does Mr Symes have a good case? See *Pearce v Symes* (1909) 28 NZLR 562.

5 Assuming that adult male homosexual relations are not illegal at the relevant time, is it defamatory to call a man a homosexual? Is it defamatory to call a woman a lesbian? (See *New Zealand Magazines Ltd v Hadlee* (unreported, CA 74/96, 24 October 1996)). If your answer is yes, why is it? It has been held defamatory to call a man a 'pansy'

(*Thaarup v Hulton Press Ltd* (1943) 169 LT 309) or a 'queer' (*Buck v Savage* (1959) 323 SW 2d 363, Texas), and in *R v Bishop* [1975] QB 274, 281, Stephenson LJ said 'We are not behind the times in holding that Mr Price's character was clearly impugned by the allegation of homosexual conduct made against him by the defendant'. In the *Thaarup* appeal, on the meaning of the word 'pansy', Scott LJ noted at 169 LT 309, 310 that 'I personally was not alive to the slang meaning of the word, nor I think was my brother MacKinnon, but my brother Goddard fortunately was quite alive to it, having had judicial experience as a result of which he had come to know about it'.

The piano artiste Liberace prevailed in a case against a London daily newspaper, wherein the plaintiff was described as 'the summit of sex—the pinnacle of masculine, feminine, and neuter. Everything that he, she or it can ever want to be ... [a] deadly, winking, sniggering, snuggling, chromium-plated, scent-impregnated, luminous, quivering, giggling, fruit-flavoured, ice-covered heap of motherly love': *Liberace v Daily Mirror Newspaper* [1959], *The Times*, 17 and 18 June. The case held that the words taken together, in their 'ordinary' meaning, meant that Liberace was a homosexual, and that was defamatory.

6 Lord Atkin deliberately chose the term 'right-thinking' instead of the more familiar 'reasonable'. There may be a difficulty in situations where the plaintiff's friends and associates take a view of the plaintiff's alleged behaviour which is at variance from the view that would be taken by a more distant right-thinking citizen. If a newspaper falsely reports that a named member of the Mongrel Mob is helping the police with their enquiries by identifying other members of the Mob responsible for a serious crime, that person may well be held in contempt, or worse, by his associates, but a 'right-thinking' person will applaud those who give assistance to the forces of law and order. As the Court of Appeal said in *Byrne v Deane* [1937] 1 KB 818, 'to allege of a man ... that he has reported certain acts, wrongful in law, to the police, cannot possibly be said to be defamatory'. (In that case, Byrne was wrongly said to have 'grassed' to the police about a gambling machine illegally operated in Byrne's golf club.) Slesser LJ at 833 described it this way: 'What [would] a good and worthy subject of the King ... think of some person of whom it had been said that he had put the law into motion against wrong doers?' He then cited two other cases, which note that an 'informer' would be exposed to great odium among the criminal classes, but 'the very circumstances which will make a person be regarded with disfavour by the criminal classes will raise his character in the estimation of right-thinking men'. See also the dissenting judgment of Green LJ (at 831), which interprets the published remark as meaning that Byrne is 'guilty of underhand disloyalty to his fellow members of the club'.

Compare *Prinsloo v SA Associated Newspapers Ltd* [1959] 2 SA 693, where a student was wrongly accused of being an agent for the police. De Wet J cited *Byrne v Deane* (above) at 695: 'And I ask myself, applying the well-established test, will any right-thinking person think that a person is of bad character or is not an ordinary nice member of society if that person is a university student and is prepared to report to the police about criminal activities which are going on at the University?' Would it be defamatory in New Zealand today for a student newspaper mistakenly to identify and name a student politician as a paid agent of the New Zealand Security Intelligence Service?

7 Is it defamatory to say that a person is a communist? It has been held so in three leading jurisdictions: *Braddock v Bevins* [1948] 1 All ER 450; *Brannigan v Seafarers' Union* (1963) 42 DLR 2d 249; *Cross v Denley* (1952) 52 SR (NSW) 112.

In New Zealand it was held that 'way-out militant' and 'way-out left-winger' are defamatory: *Brooks v Muldoon* [1973] 1 NZLR 1.

On the other side of the political spectrum, it has also been held in New Zealand that it is defamatory of trade union leaders to associate them with 'Hitler fascist people' and 'Hitler's puppets': see *Gwynne and Small v Wairarapa Times Age Co Ltd* [1972] NZLR 586.

8 P has a cheque account with a bank, with an agreed overdraft facility. While still under that agreed level, the bank rejects cheques made out by P, marking them 'R/D' (which means 'Return to Drawer'). Has the bank made a defamatory statement? See *Hill v National Bank of New Zealand* [1985] 1 NZLR 736, 747. What about the words 'Present Again'?

9 Jimminy Cricket is a well-known MP who espouses right-wing causes. The following is part of an article published in *Private Ear*.

> The sincerity of Cricket's stand on many issues must be questioned. After all, he is often associated with Danny la Disney. Danny is a strong force in Gay Liberation and has been influenced by socialist ideology.

What, if anything, is defamatory about this statement? Would it make any difference if Cricket and la Disney were women?

10 Lucy is a member of the local French Club. At a luncheon sponsored by the Club and attended by persons with a good knowledge of the French language, Bill called Lucy a 'cocotte'. Lucy sues and at trial an expert on the French language testifies that 'cocotte' can mean a 'prostitute' or it can mean a 'poached egg'. Should the judge allow the case to go to the jury?

Charleston v News Group Newspapers Ltd
[1995] 2 AC 65; [1995] 2 WLR 450 (HL)

[**FACTS**: The defendant tabloid newspaper ran a story about a pornographic computer game, which used the faces of actors from the television programme *Neighbours*, superimposed on naked or semi-naked bodies engaging in sexual acts. The actors had not consented to the use of their faces in this way. While the main text of the story was critical of the game, the prominent headlines and accompanying photographs conveyed the suggestion that the plaintiffs had willingly taken part in the production of the game. The lower courts had held that the publication was not capable of being defamatory either in its natural and ordinary meaning or by innuendo.]

Lord Bridge of Harwich:

... The plaintiffs must have found this publication deeply offensive and insulting. Many people will not only deplore this kind of gutter journalism but will think that the law ought to give some redress to the plaintiffs against the publication of such degrading faked photographs, irrespective of what the accompanying text may have said. I have considerable sympathy with this point of view.

However, your Lordships are not concerned to pronounce on any question of journalistic ethics nor to consider whether the publication of the photographs by itself constituted some novel tort. The single question of law to which the appeal gives rise is whether the plaintiffs have any remedy in the tort of defamation on the basis of their pleaded claim, and this in turn narrows down to the question whether a claim in defamation in respect of a publication which, it is conceded, is not defamatory if considered as a whole, may nevertheless succeed on the ground that some readers will have read part only of the published matter and that this part, considered in isolation, is capable of bearing a defamatory meaning.

The plaintiffs' statement of claim alleges that the publication conveyed to the reader a number of defamatory meanings. The basis on which all these alleged meanings rest is that the reader would have drawn the inference that the plaintiffs had been willing participants in the production of the photographs, either by posing for them personally or by agreeing that their faces should be superimposed on the bodies of others. But it is conceded on the plaintiffs' behalf, and is indeed obvious, that no reader could possibly have drawn any such inference if he had read beyond the first paragraph of the text.

Thus the essential basis on which Mr Craig's argument in support of the appeal rests is that, in appropriate circumstances, it is possible and legitimate to identify a particular group of readers who read only part of a publication which conveys to them a meaning injurious to the reputation of a plaintiff and that in principle the plaintiff should be entitled to damages for the consequent injury he suffers in the estimation of this group ... .

The first formidable obstacle which Mr Craig's argument encounters is a long and unbroken line of authority, the effect of which is accurately summarised in *Duncan and Neill on Defamation*, 2nd edn (1983), p 13, para 4.11, as follows:

> In order to determine the natural and ordinary meaning of the words of which the plaintiff complains it is necessary to take into account the context in which the words were used and the mode of publication. Thus a plaintiff cannot select an isolated passage in an article and complain of that alone if other parts of the article throw a different light on that passage.

The *locus classicus* is a passage from the judgment of Alderson B in *Chalmers v Payne* (1835) 2 CM & R 156, 159, who said:

> But the question here is, whether the matter be slanderous or not, which is a question for the jury; who are to take the whole together, and say whether the result of the whole is calculated to injure the plaintiff's character. In one part of this publication, something disreputable to the plaintiff is stated, but that is removed by the conclusion; the bane and antidote must be taken together.

This passage has been so often quoted that it has become almost conventional jargon among libel lawyers to speak of the bane and the antidote. It is often a debatable question which the jury must resolve, whether the antidote is effective to neutralise the bane, and in determining this question the jury may certainly consider the mode of publication and the relative prominence given to different parts of it. I can well envisage also that questions might arise in some circumstances as to whether different items of published material relating to the same subject matter were sufficiently closely connected as to be regarded as a single publication. But no such questions arise in the instant case. There is no dispute that the headlines, photographs and article relating to these plaintiffs constituted a single publication nor that the antidote in the article was sufficient to neutralise any bane in the headlines and photographs. Thus it is essential to the success of Mr Craig's argument that he establish the legitimacy in the law of libel of severance to permit a plaintiff to rely on a defamatory meaning conveyed only to the category of limited readers ... .

The theme of Mr Craig's argument runs on the following lines. All the earlier authorities, he submits, are explicable on the basis that the allegedly defamatory matter with which they were concerned was located somewhere in a document in which there was no likelihood that it would be read in isolation. In such a situation it is natural and proper to look for the meaning conveyed to the reader by considering the publication as a whole. The techniques of modern tabloid journalism, however, confront the courts with a novel situation with which the law has not hitherto had to grapple. It is plain that the eye-catching headline and the eye-catching photograph will first attract the reader's attention, precisely as they were intended to do, and equally plain that a significant number of readers will not trouble to read any further. This phenomenon must be well known to newspaper editors and publishers, who cannot, therefore, complain if they are held liable in damages for any libel thus published to the category of limited readers.

At first blush this argument has considerable attractions, but I believe that it falls foul of two principles which are basic to the law of libel. The first is that, where no legal innuendo is alleged to arise from extrinsic circumstances known to some readers, the 'natural and ordinary meaning' to be ascribed to the words of an allegedly defamatory publication is the meaning, including any inferential meaning, which the words would convey to the mind of the ordinary, reasonable, fair-minded reader. This proposition is too well established to require citation of authority. The second principle, which is perhaps a corollary of the first, is that, although a combination of words may in fact convey different [sense] to the minds of different readers, the jury in a libel action, applying the criterion which the first principle dictates, is required to determine the single meaning which the publication conveyed to the notional reasonable reader and to base its verdict and any award of damages on the assumption that this was the one sense in which all readers would have understood it.

[**Result**: The House of Lords dismissed the appeal.]

Notes

I   Suppose that there was a fraud trial involving Joe Walters, which received a considerable amount of publicity in the media. After lengthy hearings, which were fully reported in the press, the jury returned verdicts of not guilty on the ten charges that Joe Walters faced. This came as something of a surprise to sections of the public. The *Internet News*, a news medium that uses the Internet as a mode of dissemination, ran an article about the trial, of which the following is an extract from an early part of the article:

> The verdict of the jury is surely astonishing. We are amazed that twelve people could have so easily abandoned their oaths to find the truth. The incentive to do so must have been too great a temptation to resist. Worth it for Joe Walters, however.

The article proceeded to explore at length the virtues of juries and floated the idea that human juries could be replaced by computerised ones. At the very end of the lengthy article, the following appeared:

> Whether a computer would have reached a different decision in the Joe Walters case is pure speculation. And by the way, we did not mean what we said about the Joe jury. We actually think they got it right!

The members of the jury learnt about this article and met to discuss it. They decided that they needed some legal advice. One of them, Jane Simpson, has approached you. She would like to know whether she can sue *Internet News* in defamation, and whether the foreman of the jury, Clarence Matthewson, has a better chance of success than the rest. Matthewson's wife, Beryl, has received unfavourable remarks at her local tennis club. 'Can she sue as well?' asks Jane.

2   In *New Zealand Magazines Ltd v Hadlee* (unreported, CA 74/96, 24 October 1996), the *New Zealand Women's Weekly* published a story 'to set the record straight', quoting a television presenter, Anita McNaught, as not having had an affair with Lady Hadlee, wife of a famous New Zealand cricketer. The Court of Appeal held that the antidote was incomplete. While the article dispelled any suggestion of a relationship between the two women, it did not expressly deny the notion that Lady Hadlee was a lesbian or bisexual.

True or legal innuendo

[In the law of defamation, innuendo is 'a defamatory imputation which extrinsic facts known to the reader import into the words as an addition or alteration of their ordinary meaning' (Holroyd Pearce LJ in the Court of Appeal decision of *Lewis v Daily Telegraph* [1963] 1 QB 340, 364). A good example of a defamatory innuendo lurking behind an innocent statement is *Tolley v Fry* [1931] AC 333 where the defendant chocolate manufacturer advertised its product in a cartoon featuring the plaintiff, a noted amateur golfer. The plaintiff's caddy was pictured as saying in doggerel verse that the defendant's chocolate is as good as the plaintiff's golf game. The plain or ordinary meaning may be that Tolley consumes and endorses Fry's chocolate. While there is nothing defamatory about an association with chocolate, the innuendo was that Tolley, as an amateur, had improperly entered into a commercial agreement, and thus compromised his status. Tolley prevailed on that innuendo.]

Lewis v Daily Telegraph Ltd
[1964] AC 234 (HL)
[**FACTS**: These facts are largely taken from the speech delivered by **Lord Hodson**:
My Lords, in these actions large damages were awarded to the plaintiff, Mr Lewis, and to the company, Rubber Improvement Ltd, of which the first plaintiff is the managing director. In the first pair of actions, which were consolidated with one another, the *Daily Telegraph* was the defendant, in the second pair, likewise consolidated, Associated Newspapers Ltd, proprietors of the *Daily Mail* were defendants ...
The words complained of in the first actions are as follows:

INQUIRY ON FIRM BY CITY POLICE

Daily Telegraph Reporter.

Officers of the City of London Fraud Squad are inquiring into the affairs of Rubber Improvement Ltd and its subsidiary companies. The investigation was requested after criticisms of the chairman's statement and the accounts by a shareholder at the recent company meeting.

The Chairman of the company, which has an authorised capital of £1 million, is Mr John Lewis, former Socialist MP for Bolton.

In the second action the words were:

FRAUD SQUAD PROBE FIRM

The City Fraud Squad, under Superintendent Francis Lea, are inquiring into the affairs of Rubber Improvement Ltd. Chairman of the £4 000 000 group, whose shares have dropped from 22s last year to 7s 4d yesterday, is Mr John Lewis, former Socialist.

The Company specialises in flexible rubber conveyor belting designed for the National Coal Board.

Both articles appeared on the front page of the respective newspapers on December 23, 1958.

The facts leading up to and surrounding the publication differed to some extent in respect of the two publications, but the general effect was the same. In the *Daily Telegraph* actions the plaintiff, Lewis, obtained £25 000 damages and the plaintiff company £75 000, and in the *Daily Mail* actions he obtained £17 000 and the company £100 000.

The Court of Appeal ordered a new trial, holding that in any event the damages were so excessive that no reasonable jury could have awarded so large a figure, and that there was a misdirection on the part of the trial judge in respect of the meaning of the libels …

The appellants recognise that in awarding such large damages on each trial the juries must have taken the view that the words of which they complain meant that they had been actually guilty of fraud, a meaning which the defendants have throughout disclaimed.]

Lord Devlin:

My Lords, the natural and ordinary meaning of words ought in theory to be the same for the lawyer as for the layman, because the lawyer's first rule of construction is that words are to be given their natural and ordinary meaning as popularly understood. The proposition that ordinary words are the same for the lawyer as for the layman is as a matter of pure construction undoubtedly true. But it is very difficult to draw the line between pure construction and implication, and the layman's capacity for implication is much greater than the lawyer's. The lawyer's rule is that the implication must be necessary as well as reasonable. The layman reads in an implication much more freely; and unfortunately, as the law of defamation has to take into account, is especially prone to do so when it is derogatory.

In the law of defamation these wider sorts of implication are called innuendoes. The word explains itself and is very apt for the purpose. In *Rex v Horne* [2 Cowp 672, 684] De Grey CJ said: 'In the case of a libel which does not in itself contain the crime, without some extrinsic aid, it is necessary that it should be put upon the record, by way of introduction, if it is new matter; or by way of innuendo, if it is only matter of explanation. For an innuendo means nothing more than the words, "id est," "scilicet," or "meaning," or "aforesaid," as, explanatory of a subject-matter sufficiently expressed before'.

... To be on the safe side, a pleader used an innuendo whenever the defamation was not absolutely explicit. That was very frequent, since scandalmongers are induced by the penalties for defamation to veil their meaning to some extent. Moreover, there were some pleaders who got to think that a statement of claim was somehow made more forceful by an innuendo, however plain the words. So rhetorical innuendoes were pleaded, such as to say of a man that he was a fornicator meant and was under-stood to mean that he was not fit to associate with his wife and family and was a man who ought to be shunned by all decent persons and so forth. Your Lordships were told, and I have no doubt it is true, that before 1949 it was very rare indeed to find a statement of claim in defamation without an innuendo paragraph.

[**Note**: Lord Devlin then discussed the new High Court Rule, Ord 19, r 6(2), which took effect in 1949: 'In an action for libel or slander if the plaintiff alleges that the words or matter complained of were used in a defamatory sense other than their ordinary meaning, he shall give particulars of the facts and matters on which he relies in support of such sense'.]

... The word 'innuendo' is not used. But the effect of the language is that any meaning that does not require the support of extrinsic fact is assumed to be part of the ordinary meaning of the words. Accordingly, an innuendo, however well concealed, that is capable of being detected in the language used is deemed to be part of the ordinary meaning.

This might be an academic matter if it were not for the principle that the ordinary meaning of words and the meaning enlarged by innuendo give rise to separate causes of action ... . How is this principle affected by the new rule? Are there now three causes of action? If there are only two, to which of them does the innuendo that is inherent in the words belong? In *Grubb v Bristol United Press Ltd* [1963] 1 QB 309] the Court of Appeal ... decided in effect that there were only two causes of action and that the innuendo cause of action comprised only the innuendo that was supported by extrinsic facts.

My Lords, I think, on the whole, that this is the better solution, though it brings with it a consequence that I dislike, namely, that at two points there is a divergence between the popular and the legal meaning of words. Just as the popular and legal meanings of 'malice' have drifted apart, so the popular and legal meanings of 'innuendo' must now be separated. I shall in the rest of my speech describe as a legal innuendo the innuendo that is the subject matter of a separate cause of action. I sup-pose that it does not matter what terminology is used so long as it is agreed. But I do not care for the description of the popular innuendo as a false innuendo; it is the law and not popular usage that gives a false and restricted meaning to the word. The other respect is that the natural and ordinary meaning of words for the purposes of defamation is not their natural and ordinary meaning for other purposes of the law. There must be added to the implications which a court is prepared to make as a matter of construction all such insinuations and innuendoes as could reasonably be read into them by the ordinary man.

The consequence of all this is, I think, that there will have to be three paragraphs in a statement of claim where previously two have served. In the first paragraph the defamatory words will be set out as hitherto. It may be that they will speak for themselves. If not, a second paragraph will set out those innuendoes or indirect meanings which go beyond the literal meaning of the words but which the pleader claims to be inherent in them. Thirdly, if the pleader has the necessary material, he can plead a secondary meaning or legal innuendo supported by particulars under Ord 19, r 6(2). Hitherto it has been customary to put the whole innuendo into one paragraph, but now this may easily result in the confusion of two causes of action and in consequent embarrassment. The essential distinction between the second and third paragraph will lie in the fact that particulars under the rule must be appended to the third. That is, so to speak, the hallmark of the legal innuendo ... .

... But the essential thing is that if a paragraph is unaccompanied by particulars it cannot be a legal innuendo since for a legal innuendo particulars are mandatory and the innuendo cannot be proved without them.

... My Lords, I have made a very long preliminary to the consideration of the pleading point in this case. Your Lordships were invited from the Bar to deal in detail with all the difficulties of pleading involved in that point and that have recently come to the fore in other cases, and I have thought it right to do so. I must now state how in the light of what I have said generally I should decide the point at issue. Paragraph 4 of the statement of claim is as follows: 'By the said words the defendants meant and were understood to mean that the affairs of the plaintiffs and/or its subsidiaries were conducted fraudulently or dishonestly or in such a way that the police suspected that their affairs were so conducted'.

The Court of Appeal considered this paragraph to be defective, and I agree with them. This does not involve any sort of criticism of the learned pleader, who drafted his statement of claim at a time when it was possible to take almost any view of the points I have been canvassing. It is plain now that paragraph 4 must be treated as in form a plea of a legal innuendo. But in substance it is not a legal innuendo because no extrinsic facts are pleaded: general knowledge is, as I have indicated already, not an extrinsic fact for the purpose of rule 6(2), but is matter, not requiring to be proved, in the light of which the jury can interpret the publication. In substance the paragraph is a plea of popular innuendo and the confusion between substance and form makes it embarrassing.

... I turn now to the main ground for ordering a new trial. This was that the judge misdirected the jury by failing to tell them that the words were not capable of bearing one or more of the defamatory meanings alleged in paragraph 4 of the statement of claim. It is admitted that the words are capable of some defamatory meaning, and I think it is undoubtedly defamatory of a company to say that its affairs are being inquired into by the police. But paragraph 4 alleges that the words meant 'that the affairs of the plaintiffs and/or its subsidiaries were conducted fraudulently or dishonestly or in such a way that the police suspected that their affairs were so conducted'. This is saying that the words mean either that the plaintiffs were guilty of fraud or that they were suspected of fraud. If it is permissible to distinguish between these two meanings, then for reasons which I shall give as I proceed I should hold that the words are capable of the latter meaning but not of the former, and I should on this basis agree with the Court of Appeal that the jury should have been so directed and that, since they were not, there should be a new trial … .

It is not … correct to say as a matter of law that a statement of suspicion imputes guilt. It can be said as a matter of practice that it very often does so, because although suspicion of guilt is something different from proof of guilt, it is the broad impression conveyed by the libel that has to be considered and not the meaning of each word under analysis. A man who wants to talk at large about smoke may have to pick his words very carefully if he wants to exclude the suggestion that there is also a fire; but it can be done … .

In the libel that the House has to consider there is … no mention of suspicion at all. What is said is simply that the plaintiffs' affairs are being inquired into. That is defamatory, as is admitted, because a man's reputation may in fact be injured by such a statement even though it is quite consistent with innocence. I dare say that it would not be injured if everybody bore in mind, as they ought to, that no man is guilty until he is proved so, but unfortunately they do not … . Let it be supposed, first, that a statement that there is an inquiry conveys an impression of suspicion; and, secondly, that a statement of suspicion conveys an impression of guilt. It does not follow from these two suppositions that a statement that there is an inquiry conveys an impression of guilt. For that, two fences have to be taken instead of one. While, as I have said, I am prepared to accept that the jury could take the first, I do not think that in a case like the present, where there is only the bare statement that a police inquiry is being made, it could take the second in the same stride. If the ordinary sensible man was capable of thinking that wherever there was a police inquiry there was guilt, it would be almost impossible to give accurate information about anything: but in my opinion he is not. I agree with the view of the Court of Appeal.

Notes

1   The House of Lords referred to 'true', 'false', 'legal', and 'popular' innuendo—what does each mean? Lord Devlin said he 'did not care for the description of the popular innuendo as a false innuendo'. Why not?

2   Note the pleading requirements for a legal innuendo in s 37(3) of the Defamation Act 1992:

> Where the plaintiff alleges that the matter that is the subject of the proceedings was used in a defamatory sense other than its natural and ordinary meaning, the plaintiff shall give particulars specifying:
> (a)   The persons or class of persons to whom the defamatory meaning is alleged to be known; and
> (b)   The other facts and circumstances on which the plaintiff relies in support of the plaintiff's allegations.

3   A newspaper refers to a broadcaster as 'bent'. What is the innuendo? A spinal deformity? What type of innuendo is this? See *Allsop v Church of England Newspaper Ltd* [1972] 2 QB 161.

4 Explain what Lord Devlin is alluding to when he says that a man talking about smoke needs to be careful to exclude the suggestion of fire.

5 The defendant exhibited a wax effigy of the plaintiff. Other characters exhibited in the same room had either been convicted of or charged with murder and not yet been brought to trial. The defendant had been tried for murder, and the Scottish jury had returned a verdict of 'not proven'. Does the plaintiff need to plead innuendo in the defamation action? See *Monson v Tussaud's Ltd* [1894] 1 QB 671.

6 Noddy, the Prime Minister of Toyland, recently held a news conference in which the question of the government's anti-nuclear policy was raised. Particular attention was given to remarks made the day before by Sir Biggy Ears, who had challenged the desirability of the government's policy. Sir Biggy Ears used to be Director of Spies, or head of the Security Intelligence Service, and is a high-profile figure in Toyland. In response to a journalist's question, Noddy said: 'He has done nothing for twenty years except be blind to everything except the American perspective. My view of Sir Biggy Ears has not changed in twenty years. He would be well advised now to keep quiet'.

This answer was reported in the local newspaper (the *Toyland Times*) the next day. The key part of the story read as follows:

> The Prime Minister has counter-attacked Sir Biggy Ears and questioned his credibility. At yesterday's news conference, Sir Biggy was described as being blind to the Toyland government's position and always following the American position. According to the Prime Minister, he had done this for twenty years and would be well advised to keep quiet.

Sir Biggy Ears has always detested Noddy and took instant offence to his remarks at the news conference. He has sued both Noddy and the *Toyland Times* in defamation. The statement of claim in the action brought against Noddy reads as follows:

> The said words in their natural and ordinary meaning or alternatively by reason of the facts and matters hereinafter set out meant and were understood to mean that:
>
> (i) As Director of Spies the plaintiff did not act in the best interests of Toyland and instead was blind to everything except the American perspective, and/or
>
> (ii) The plaintiff failed to carry out his duties, functions, and responsibilities as Director of Spies in an objective and professional manner, and/or
>
> (iii) If the plaintiff did not keep quiet there were other matters to his discredit which the defendant could reveal, and/or
>
> (iv) The plaintiff was a person of low moral character.
>
> *Particulars*
> The plaintiff was, and it was widely known that he was, Director of Spies in control of the Toyland Security Intelligence Service for almost twenty years.

Noddy has now consulted you and asks you to explain what this part of the statement of claim is all about. He suggests that the statement of claim (or at least parts of it) should be struck out. He wonders how anyone can take what he said to be libellous.

Outline your advice to Noddy. It is a fortunate coincidence that the law of Toyland is precisely the same as that of New Zealand.

Comment also on whether the item in the *Toyland Times* is defamatory.

Intention

Hulton v Jones
[1910] AC 20 (HL)

[**FACTS**: The defendant newspaper published a story that purported to be about one Artemus Jones, a churchwarden from Peckham, London. The story described Mr Jones engaging in salacious activities in France, which were clearly defamatory, but the author had intended that the story be fictitious. There happened, however, to be a real person by the name of Artemus Jones, who worked as a barrister in Wales and who had written occasional articles for the newspaper. He sued.]

Lord Loreburn LC:

… My Lords, I think this appeal must be dismissed. A question in regard to the law of libel has been raised which does not seem to me to be entitled to the support of our Lordships. Libel is a tortious act. What does the tort consist in? It consists in using language which others knowing the circumstances could reasonably think to be defamatory of the person complaining of and injured by it. A person charged with libel cannot defend himself by shewing that he intended in his own breast not to defame, or that he intended not to defame the plaintiff if in fact he did both. He has none the less imputed something disgraceful and has none the less injured the plaintiff. A man in good faith may publish a libel believing it to be true, and it may be found by the jury that he acted in good faith believing it to be true, and reasonably believing it to be true, but that in fact the statement was false. Under those circumstances he has no defence to the action, however excellent his intention. If the intention of the writer be immaterial in considering whether the matter written is defamatory, I do not see why it need be relevant in considering whether it is defamatory of the plaintiff. The writing, according to the old form, must be malicious, and it must be of and concerning the plaintiff. Just as the defendant could not excuse himself from malice by proving that he wrote it in the most benevolent spirit, so he cannot shew that the libel was not of and concerning the plaintiff by proving that he never heard of the plaintiff. His intention in both respects equally is inferred from what he did. His remedy is to abstain from defamatory words. It is suggested that there was a misdirection by the learned judge in this case. I see none. He lays down in his summing up the law as follows: 'The real point upon which your verdict must turn is, ought or ought not sensible and reasonable people reading this article to think that it was a mere imaginary person such as I have said—Tom Jones, Mr Pecksniff as a humbug, Mr Stiggins, or any of that sort of names that one reads of in literature used as types? If you think any reasonable person would think that, it is not actionable at all. If, on the other hand, you do not think that, but think that people would suppose it to mean some real person—those who did not know the plaintiff of course would not know who the real person was, but those who did know of the existence of the plaintiff would think that it was the plaintiff—then the action is maintainable, subject to such damages as you think under all the circumstances are fair and right to give to the plaintiff'.

I see no objection in law to that passage. The damages are certainly heavy, but I think your Lordships ought to remember two things. The first is that the jury were entitled to think, in the absence of proof satisfactory to them (and they were the judges of it), that some ingredient of recklessness, or more than recklessness, entered into the writing and the publication of this article, especially as Mr Jones, the plaintiff, had been employed on this very newspaper, and his name was well known in the paper and also well known in the district in which the paper circulated. In the second place the jury were entitled to say this kind of article is to be condemned. There is no tribunal more fitted to decide in regard to publications, especially publications in the newspaper Press, whether they bear a stamp and character which ought to enlist sympathy and to secure protection. If they think that the licence is not fairly used and that the tone and style of the libel is reprehensible and ought to be checked, it is for the jury to say so; and for my part, although I think the damages are certainly high, I am not prepared to advise your Lordships to interfere, especially as the Court of Appeal have not thought it right to interfere, with the verdict.

Notes

1   What is the result if, in all innocence, a newspaper publishes a photograph of a man and a woman with the caption 'Mr Corrigan, the racehorse owner, and Miss "X" whose engagement has been announced'? If Mr Corrigan were already married, can Mrs Corrigan sue? Would a legal innuendo be necessary? See *Cassidy v Daily Mirror* [1929] 2 KB 331. See also *Newstead v London Express Newspaper Ltd* [1940] 1 KB 377, where the *London Express* published a true story about a bigamist named Harold Newstead of Camberwell. The other Harold Newstead of Camberwell sued.

2   Section 6 of the Defamation Act 1954 set out a special defence of unintentional defamation, which applied if, *inter alia*, the author had exercised all reasonable care. This defence has not resurfaced in the 1992 Act. However, some people involved downstream in the publishing process may be able to take advantage of s 21:

> **Innocent dissemination**—In any proceedings for defamation against any person who has published the matter that is the subject of the proceedings solely in the capacity of, or as the employee or agent of, a processor or a distributor, it is a defence if that person alleges and proves:
>
> (a)   That that person did not know that the matter contained the material that is alleged to be defamatory; and
>
> (b)   That that person did not know that the matter was of a character likely to contain material of a defamatory nature; and
>
> (c)   That that person's lack of knowledge was not due to any negligence on that person's part.

> This section is largely a codification of a common law defence found in *Vizetelly v Mudie's Select Library Ltd* [1900] 2 QB 170. The library in that case was nevertheless held liable for distributing copies of a book containing defamatory matter because the library had ignored a publisher's circular requesting return of the book for alteration. In

Jensen v Clark [1982] 2 NZLR 268, the printers of a student newspaper failed in their defence because they were on notice that the copy contained a potentially defamatory attack by students on one of their professors. Would s 21 alter this result?

3   Suppose that a newspaper, the *Sunday Special*, has a reputation for running controversial stories. It recently ran an article on what it called the immorality of Anglican clergy. In the course of the article, it stated this:

> Few appear to be untainted. There might be a Rev John Smith in one of our cities who is virtuous. On the other hand, if we heard a rumour that Rev John Smith was involved in vice, we would reply, 'Now, we would not believe it but you can believe what you like'. The time has come for the church authorities to have a good clean-up.

> There is a Reverend John Smith who is the Presbyterian Minister in the town of Te Kuiti. He is taken aback to discover that his name has been associated with immoral or illegal activities. Can he sue in defamation?

Identification of the plaintiff

[An essential element in the tort of defamation is that the offending matter refer to the plaintiff. The obvious way in which this will be done is by naming the plaintiff—see *Hulton v Jones*, above—but remember that, even where a name is used, it does not automatically follow that the plaintiff has been identified if the context points elsewhere. A reference to 'Dr Warner of *Shortland Street*' (the television programme) does not necessarily entitle a real Dr Warner to sue if it is clear from the publication that a character from the soap opera is being referred to.

Most problems associated with identification arise where the plaintiff is not named but is referred to by implication.]

Morgan v Odhams Press Ltd
[1971] 1 WLR 1239; [1971] 2 All ER 1156 (HL)
[**FACTS**: The defendant owned both *The Sun* and *The People*, which are London newspapers. The plaintiff complained of a libel published in *The Sun* of 8 November 1965, which incorporated material from *The People* of 7 November. The relevant articles are, in part, taken from the judgment of Lord Guest (p 1256).

DOG-DOPING GIRL GOES INTO HIDING
By Peter Campling

A girl who is likely to be a key witness in a dog-doping scandal went into hiding yesterday after threats were made on her life.

Margo Murray left her lodgings in Elsham Road, Shepherds Bush, accompanied by two men.

It is estimated that the doping gangs have made more than £250 000 in the last few months with coups all over the country. They are known to have operated at tracks in Ramsgate, Slough, Reading and the Midlands. Many arrests are expected in the next few weeks.

Miss Murray, a 25-year-old Canadian, was kidnapped last week by members of the gang when they heard she had made a statement to police.

She was kept in a house in Finchley, but was eventually allowed to leave when she promised that she would return to Canada.

Flying Squad

Before she went into hiding following an exposure of the doping gangs in *The People* yesterday, Miss Murray said: 'I told the police everything. The gang got me to dope more than 20 dogs at Walthamstow one night'. Scotland Yard's Flying Squad yesterday went to several houses, in the Hammersmith, Kilburn and Finchley areas.

A man known as 'The Paymaster,' who is believed to have financed the dog dopers, has left the country after hearing that police had interviewed a kennel girl.

The Scotland Yard investigations are headed by Chief Superintendent Tom Butler, who led the hunt for the Great Train Robbery gang.

The name 'Johnny Morgan' did not appear in the article and the appellant therefore relied on certain extrinsic evidence which, he said, would entitle an ordinary reader to understand that the article referred to him.

Previously on November 7 there had appeared in *The People* newspaper an article headed:

DOG RACING SENSATION
We name the dopers. These men boss the gang.
By Michael Gabbert

Today we are able to unmask the most highly-organised gang of dog dopers in the history of British Greyhound Racing ... . Once I did twenty dogs in one day! ... Margo Murray: she was worked into the Walthamstow kennels via the Labour Exchange.

In fact Margo Murray had not been kidnapped by anyone. She had decided quite voluntarily to 'go to ground' at the plaintiff's flat. She did in fact give evidence at the criminal trial, and some of 'the gang' were convicted. The plaintiff's case against Odham's Press had a complicated procedural course, with pre-verdict motions heard in the Court of Appeal. After a jury verdict in the plaintiff's favour for £4750, the Court of Appeal overturned that verdict, on the grounds that there was 'no key or pointer' in the article identifying Morgan. Morgan appealed to the House of Lords.]
Lord Morris of Borth-y-gest:

... The action related to an article which was published in *The Sun* newspaper on November 8, 1965. On the following day the plaintiff consulted his solicitors and they wrote in complaint on his behalf on November 12. The plaintiff was not mentioned by name. But it is manifest that someone may be referred to in an article without being named. In some circumstances nearly every reader of an article will at once understand that a reference is to a particular person even though he is not named. In other circumstances such understanding will only be by limited groups of people.

There is here no mysterious principle of law. It is ordinary plain commonsense that a hurtful statement may be made concerning a person though his name is not given. In the language of the law a plaintiff will have a cause of action if he proves that there has been publication of and concerning him of words which are defamatory of him. The simple issue in this case was whether there was such a publication.

The article which was published clearly states that there had been dog doping on a vast scale: that those responsible had reaped great financial gain: that their arrest was likely and imminent: and that a girl named Margo Murray, who, at their instigation had done much of the doping, had made a full statement to the police and was likely to be a key witness in the expected criminal proceedings. The article then proceeds to state that the girl had gone into hiding (following threats on her life) after leaving her lodgings accompanied by two men and that in the previous week she had been kidnapped by members of the gang and kept in a house in Finchley until she was allowed to leave on promising to return to Canada.

In fact the girl had been in the plaintiff's house for some days and nights. She had been seen by many people to be in his company. They knew that she was Margo Murray. Witnesses came forward and gave evidence to the effect that they had read the article and concluded that it referred to the plaintiff. While all agreeing that it referred to the plaintiff they differed as to which part of the article contained the more grave allegation against him.

In my view, the article sets out as clearly as possible that the person or persons who had kept Margo Murray in a house in Finchley had kidnapped her and had done so by reason of membership of or association with the dog doping gang. If witnesses who knew that Margo Murray had been in the company of and in the house of the plaintiff said that on reading the article they concluded that the article referred to the plaintiff were they telling the truth? That was essentially a matter for the jury. Had they been reasonable in so concluding that the article referred to the plaintiff? That was also essentially a matter for the jury. If the jury accepted the evidence of the witnesses as being truthful and reasonable it would be for the jury further to decide whether the words were defamatory. They would have little difficulty in so deciding. If the jury thought that the words of the article recorded that whoever had kept Margo Murray in a house in Finchley had done so in the interests of or as a member of the dog doping gang and after she had been kidnapped by members of the gang and if the jury accepted that the witnesses had reasonably identified the plaintiff as being referred to they could hardly fail to conclude that the plaintiff was most gravely defamed. The jury by their verdict must have accepted that it was reasonable for those who knew certain facts to conclude, as they did, that the plaintiff was designated.

... Certain facts were not in dispute. In 1965 the plaintiff got to know a journalist, Mr Gabbert. Mr Gabbert became interested to investigate, to enquire into and to collect information in regard to dog doping. When he had collected his material he would be able to write an article in which there would be an exposure of a startling and sensational nature. He got to know a girl, Margo Murray, who, at the instigation and for the advantage of others, had actually carried out dog doping. She made a statement to the police. A prosecution was likely and in spite of her personal involvement she was to be a witness for the prosecution. It became obvious, therefore, that she should be looked after and that she should be protected. It is easy to imagine the steps that those in peril of prosecution might be tempted to take if they had knowledge of an impending prosecution and of her likely role. With the knowledge and concurrence of the police Mr Gabbert found accommodation for her and provided finance for her.

The plaintiff and Mr Gabbert were in touch with each other because the plaintiff had some journalistic projects in view. On one occasion Mr Gabbert introduced the girl Margo Murray to the plaintiff. The three met on a later occasion. Subsequently the plaintiff entertained Margo Murray to an evening meal at a restaurant in the Finchley Road. The hour got very late and the weather very foggy and in the result Margo Murray accepted his suggestion that she could have accommodation in his flat. In fact she stayed there in the period from October 26 to November 1.

... There was evidence before the jury as to what various people understood when they read the article. There was a Mr Wood who was a detective constable. He came to know the plaintiff and said that the plaintiff (who had retired from being a professional wrestler and had become a writer) was very well known in the Willesden and Kilburn area. Mr Wood saw the plaintiff in a restaurant on Thursday October 28 and the plaintiff introduced Margo Murray to him. She told her story about dog doping. She was distressed. Much detailed evidence was given as to that occasion and as to subsequent meetings and movements. On reading the article in *The Sun* Mr Wood's immediate conclusion was that the plaintiff was one of the 'two men' mentioned: he thought that the plaintiff 'was involved in the dog doping business' though he thought that 'the kidnapping part' was 'just paper talk'. There was a police detective sergeant. He knew the plaintiff well. He described a meeting with the plaintiff and Margo Murray on October 28: he saw no reason why the girl should not continue, if she so wished, to stay in the plaintiff's flat. He advised that it was a sensible course. He gave evidence as to various occasions and interviews in the days following. He saw the article in *The Sun*. 'I was convinced that this article in substance referred to Mr Morgan.' He knew, however, that the whole matter was in police hands and he considered that the suggestion that the plaintiff had kidnapped Margo Murray was rubbish. Though he did not believe the story and though there had been a lapse of a week between the time when the girl was with the plaintiff and the publication of the article he 'could put no construction other than this article or part of it referred to him'. The part was that which mentioned kidnapping.

... It was not suggested, and could not have been, that the words which were published were not capable of bearing defamatory meanings. They were clearly very defamatory of someone. The real issue was whether the words were published of and concerning the plaintiff. It mattered not what was the intention of the writer. In any event the jury had no means of knowing it. As the defendant did not give evidence the jury could not know whether the defendant had in some unfortunate way been misled or had based himself on some idle gossip: they would perhaps be disposed to give him the credit for not having merely invented a sensational story. But the question was 'who was hit' by the words which were published. The issue was—was the plaintiff hit? If the words referred to the plaintiff there was no suggestion that the words were true. The question for the judge at the end of the plaintiff's case was whether there was evidence upon which the jury could (not would) decide in favour of the plaintiff. That in turn raised the question whether the jury could decide that some readers (having knowledge of certain circumstances) would reasonably understand the words as referring to the plaintiff. If no reasonable reader could have understood the words as referring to the plaintiff, then there would be nothing to be left to the jury.

... Here I must refer to a contention which was raised in argument. It was submitted that if defamatory words concerning A are published to B who refuses to believe that the words are true, then A would have no cause of action. I consider that such a contention is completely fallacious. Apart from any question affecting the measure of damages, A's rights would be unaffected by the circumstance that B in fact disbelieved the words. I agree with what Goddard LJ said in *Hough v London Express Newspaper Ltd* [1940] 2 KB 507, 515:

> If words are used which impute discreditable conduct to my friend, he has been defamed to me, although I do not believe the imputation, and may even know that it is untrue.

It is necessary to consider what was the submission that was made to the learned judge at the close of the plaintiff's case. It was contended that 'the article in question identifies nobody nor does it permit the identification of anybody except those who are named': accordingly it was contended as a matter of law that 'when there is nothing in the article itself to identify or point to the identification of a particular plaintiff it is not open to him, by calling evidence supposedly of people with special knowledge to prove or attempt to prove that they thought that he was implicated in some way': so it was said that 'one must have something in the words complained of themselves which points to a particular individual as having done something wrong'. The proposition of law was advanced that the evidence which had been given in the case 'is only of weight if there be a hook upon which it can be hung, and there is no identification of any individual sufficient to constitute a hook or peg for that purpose in this case'.

... The question for decision was whether a jury could come to the conclusion that the words referred to the plaintiff. As Lord Alverstone CJ said in *Jones v E Hulton & Co* [1909] 2 KB 444, 454:

> ... if, in the opinion of a jury, a substantial number of persons who knew the plaintiff, reading the article, would believe that it refers to him, in my opinion an action, assuming the language to be defamatory, can be maintained. [So also:] If upon the evidence the jury are of opinion that ordinary sensible readers, knowing the plaintiff, would be of opinion that the article referred to him, the plaintiff's case is made out.

The principle was succinctly expressed by Viscount Simon LC in his speech in *Knupffer v London Express Newspaper Ltd* [1944] AC 116 when he said, at p 119: 'Where the plaintiff is not named, the test which decides whether the words used refer to him is the question whether the words are such as would reasonably lead persons acquainted with the plaintiff to believe that he was the person referred to'.

To the same effect were the words of Lord Loreburn LC in describing (in *E Hulton & Co v Jones* [1910] AC 20, 23) the tort of libel—'It consists in using language which others knowing the circumstances would reasonably think to be defamatory of the person complaining of and injured by it'.

Having regard to the evidence that was given it would, in my view, have been quite wrong for the judge to have withdrawn the case from the jury, once he was of the opinion that a jury could come to the conclusion that reasonable readers would understand the words as referring to the plaintiff. It then became a matter of fact for the jury to decide whether some readers (knowing certain circumstances) would reasonably understand that the article referred to the plaintiff. It was for the jury to assess the witnesses and their reasonableness and to decide whether reasonable people would reasonably understand that the plaintiff was referred to. It could not possibly have been said in this case that all the evidence was so irrational that it could not be accepted by anyone and accordingly did not merit consideration by the jury.

The argument which was addressed to the learned judge and to which I have referred, foreshadowed the argument which later found favour with the Court of Appeal. It was held that there was no 'key or pointer' in the article itself which indicated that it referred to the plaintiff and it was held that in order to be actionable an article must contain some words which could be pointed to by a pleader as 'meaning thereby the plaintiff'. With respect I do not agree ... . Further, it was said that what must be contemplated is that a person would read an article with care. With respect I do not agree. What must be contemplated is a reading of a newspaper in what a jury would consider to be the ordinary way in which a newspaper article would be read. The average reader does not read a sensational article with cautious and critical analytical care. The plaintiff who successfully complained of an article which described someone as a churchwarden at Peckham was neither a churchwarden nor did he reside at Peckham (*Jones v E Hulton & Co* [1909] 2 KB 444; [1910] AC 20). Three points influenced the Court of Appeal. First, it was said that if the witnesses had reflected they would have decided that Margo Murray was under no restraint when with the plaintiff and could not have been kidnapped by him and so the reference must have been to someone else. Any such process of reflection might, however, have led them after reading the article to ascribe kidnapping as the reason for the state of distress that they had witnessed. It is also to be remembered throughout that the issue was not whether the witnesses believed the words to be true but whether the words were reasonably understood to refer to the plaintiff. Secondly, it was said that if the witnesses had reflected they would have said that the plaintiff's house was not in Finchley and so the reference must have been to someone else. Some of the witnesses were asked about this. Though Finchley was in fact three miles from the plaintiff's flat readers are often not very precise in their knowledge of districts which broadly speaking are within the same area. One witness said that he did not attach much importance to newspaper references to districts as they were never very accurate: he lived just off the Finchley Road and people thought that he lived in Finchley though the Borough of Finchley was three miles away. Thirdly, it was said that the article said 'last week' and if the witnesses had reflected they would have remembered that some incidents they had seen had taken place more than a week earlier and so they ought to have concluded that the reference was not to the plaintiff. Some of the witnesses, however, did not know when it was that the girl had left the plaintiff's flat.

My Lords, these were all points for the consideration of the jury. It was for them to say whether any of these points negatived the view that readers with knowledge of the plaintiff would reasonably have understood that the words referred to him. It would not have been right for the learned judge on any of these grounds to withdraw the case from the jury.

Notes

1   A new trial was awarded on the quantum of damage. It was a near thing for Morgan, as the House of Lords was split three to two in his favour. The Court of Appeal was three to zero against him; counting the trial judge, the weight of judicial opinion was against him, five to four.

2   An older case much relied upon is *Le Fanu v Malcolmson* (1848) 1 HLC 637, 9 ER 910, where D published a letter that said 'the cruelties of the slave trade or the Bastille are not equal to those practised in some of the Irish factories'. The plaintiffs, who were factory owners in Waterford, Ireland, prevailed. Why did they succeed? In *Foxcroft v Lacy* (1613) Hob 89, 80 ER 239, P was one of a group of 17 defamed by a group libel and succeeded. The result was the same when seven bishops sued under the identity of 'Roman Catholic religious authorities in the town of Queenstown': *Browne v Thomson* [1912] SC 359. In the leading American case, *Fawcett Publication Inc v Morris* (1962) 377 P 2d 42 (Okla), *True* magazine associated the entire University gridiron football team with amphetamines and other illicit drugs as a means of enhancing performance. P was a reserve fullback in a squad that numbered some sixty or seventy players. Damages of $75 000 were upheld on appeal.

3   In *Clarke v Vare* [1930] NZLR 430, C and V were rival neighbouring shopkeepers in a small community. Their rivalry was well known in the community. C's business was devoted to draperies but he also carried a line of boots. V's shop was devoted solely to footwear. C was living apart from his wife and employed a live-in housekeeper. V displayed a placard in his shop window, a form of advertising common to both parties, which read 'One man, one wife, one trade'. C sued and lost in the lower court. In the Supreme Court, V's counsel argued that there was no reference to the plaintiff. How would the case be decided in the light of *Morgan*?

4   Hulk Hogan and his wife Juliana have for many years been engaged by the Department of Social Welfare in Wellington to foster children taken into care. However, recent allegations of sexual misconduct by Hulk led to criminal charges being laid against him. After a three-day trial, Hulk was acquitted of all charges. The Department sends round a regular newsletter to social workers and other departmental officers throughout the country, informing them of the latest developments affecting their work. Included in one such newsletter was the following:

> Despite the recent acquittal, it should be noted that under no circumstances are Mr and Mrs M. Hogan to be given care of any children under the Department's control.

Hulk and Juliana learnt about the newsletter. They have approached you for advice. They say that it must refer to them and that the 'M' preceding 'Hogan' is just a typographical error. They would like to know whether they can sue the Department in defamation. Advise them on the essential elements of the tort.

Knupffer v London Express Newspaper Ltd
[1944] AC 116 (HL)
[**FACTS**: The plaintiff was a member of an émigré political group called the Young Russia Party, and the entire party was libelled by the defendant newspaper. The plaintiff sued in his own name as one of 24 party members in Great Britain, there being some 200 members in total. The defamation was that Hitler would pick one of the party to be a puppet Führer of conquered Russia.]
Lord Atkin:
... I venture to think that it is a mistake to lay down a rule as to libel on a class, and then qualify it with exceptions. The only relevant rule is that in order to be actionable the defamatory words must be understood to be published of and concerning the plaintiff. It is irrelevant that the words are published of two or more persons if they are proved to be published of him, and it is irrelevant that the two or more persons are called by some generic class name. There can be no law that a defamatory statement made of a firm, or trustees, or the tenants of a particular building is not actionable, if the words would reasonably be understood as published of each member of the firm or each trustee or each tenant. The reason why a libel published of a large or indeterminate number of persons described by some general name generally fails to be actionable is the difficulty of establishing that the plaintiff was, in fact, included in the defamatory statement, for the habit of making unfounded generalizations is ingrained in ill-educated or vulgar minds, or the words are occasionally intended to be a facetious exaggeration. Even in such cases words may be used which enable the plaintiff to prove that the words complained of were intended to be published of each member of the group, or, at any rate, of himself. Too much attention has been paid, I venture to think, in the textbooks and elsewhere to the ruling of Willes J in 1858 in *Eastwood v Holmes* [1 F & F 347, 175 ER 758], a case at *nisi prius* in which the judge non-suited the plaintiff both because he thought there was no evidence that the words were published of the plaintiff and for other reasons, and, so far as the first ground is concerned, it appears to me on the facts to be of doubtful correctness. His words: 'it only reflects on a class of persons' are irrelevant unless they mean 'it does not reflect on the plaintiff', and his instance 'All lawyers were thieves' is an excellent instance of the vulgar generalizations to which I have referred. It will be as well for the future for lawyers to concentrate on the question whether the words were published of the plaintiff rather than on the question whether they were spoken of a class. I agree that in the present case the words convey imputations of disgraceful conduct, but not such as could reasonably be understood to be spoken of the appellant. It becomes unnecessary to deal with the question of excessive damages. I content myself by saying that, if the libel had been published of the appellant, while the damages awarded are possibly too high, I do not find myself in any degree in accord with the estimate of the damages suggested by the Court of Appeal.

Notes

1 Could the Young Russia Party as a whole have sued in *Knupffer?*

2 Where a group is an incorporated body, the rules change. Section 6 of the Defamation Act 1992 states:

> Proceedings for defamation brought by a body corporate shall fail unless the body corporate alleges and proves that the publication of the matter that is the subject of the proceedings—
>
> (a) Has caused pecuniary loss; or
>
> (b) Is likely to cause pecuniary loss—
>
> to that body corporate.

The facts of *Mount Cook Group Ltd v Johnstone Motors Ltd* [1990] 2 NZLR 488 were as follows. A poster depicted a bride and groom in lewd pose. The caption read 'PLEASE DARLING NO CHILDREN YET—FUN FIRST LET'S SKI CORONET PEAK QUEENSTOWN'. The poster was sold through the defendant's shop. The plaintiffs were the owners of the ski fields at Coronet Peak and also ran coach and airline services. They had not promoted the poster in any way and, after receiving complaints from the public, asked that the defendants withdraw the poster from display and sale. When this did not happen, defamation proceedings were commenced. The only other nearby ski field to Coronet Peak was also owned by Mt Cook. Although there does not appear to have been any evidence of a general loss of profits to Mt Cook's activities, at least one member of the public indicated that she had flown to Auckland on a different airline from Mt Cook because of her objections to the poster. What is defamatory about the poster in this case? Can Mt Cook be identified in these circumstances? Does Mt Cook satisfy the test in s 6?

3 In *Derbyshire County Council v Times Newspapers Ltd* [1993] AC 534, the House of Lords was asked to consider whether a local authority can sue in defamation for words that reflect on its administrative and governmental functions. The articles there questioned the propriety of certain investments made by the council of moneys in its superannuation fund. After referring to the law on trading corporations, trade unions and charities, Lord Keith said (pp 547 and 549):

> There are, however, features of a local authority which may be regarded as distinguishing it from other types of corporation, whether trading or non-trading. The most important of these features is that it is a governmental body. Further, it is a democratically elected body, the electoral process nowadays being conducted almost exclusively on party political lines. It is of the highest public importance that a democratically elected governmental body, or indeed any governmental body, should be open to uninhibited public criticism. The threat of civil action for defamation must inevitably have an inhibiting effect on freedom of speech … . I regard it as right for this House to lay down that not only is there no public interest favouring the right of organs of government, whether central or local, to sue for libel, but that it is contrary to the public interest because to admit such actions would place an undesirable fetter on freedom of speech.

Does this decision apply in New Zealand? Does it apply to all local body activities, including those, such as running buses, which might have a trading aspect? The House of Lords envisaged the same rule applying to departments of state. Would it apply to regional health boards, state-owned enterprises, or universities? Are there any circumstances in which individual local-body councillors could sue? If there were evidence that the defendant deliberately set out to make a false statement with intent to cause harm, the local authority might be able to sue in malicious falsehood. The plaintiff must prove that the statement was false and was made with the necessary intent to injure. Under s 5 of the Defamation Act 1992, it is sufficient if the publication of the matter 'is likely to cause pecuniary loss to the plaintiff' and it is thus not necessary to prove special damage. For further discussion of the *Derbyshire* case, see E. Barendt 'Libel and Freedom of Speech in English Law' [1993] *Public Law* 449.

Publication to third party

[The tort of defamation is not complete when the defendant composes the defamatory remarks. Nor is it complete when the defendant publishes the remarks to the plaintiff (although such publication could be intentional infliction of emotional distress). As the tort of defamation is not a remedy for wounded feelings, the tort is only complete when the defendant publishes the remarks to a third party. The plaintiff's injury, therefore, is the damage to the plaintiff's reputation, the estimation held of the plaintiff by others.

Has the defendant published a defamation in the following cases?
- D sends P a defamatory telegram. Has the Post Office published the defamation?
- D sends P defamatory remarks on the back of a postcard. What if the message, mailed in New Zealand, is written in Serbo-Croatian?
- A store detective asserts wrongly that a shopper is a thief. The conversation takes place privately in the manager's office, with no one else present, but D negligently leaves on the store's public address system.
- D intentionally publishes the defamatory remarks to a third party, but D does not know that the third party is a journalist, who prepares a story for a major newspaper.
- D publishes the defamatory remarks to a third party, but prefaces the remarks with, 'I heard this about P from X, but I don't believe it, and I suggest that you not take it seriously'.]

Pullman v Hill
[1891] 1 QB 524 (CA)
[**FACTS**: The defendant Hill had a civil dispute with P over an advertising contract. Hill prepared a letter (by means of 'a clerk and a copy-boy') and sent it to P's partnership. The letter accused P of the serious crime of obtaining money by a false pretence.]
Lord Esher MR:
... The first question is, whether, assuming the letter to contain defamatory matter, there has been a publication of it. What is the meaning of 'publication'? The making known the defamatory matter after it has been written to some person other than the person of whom it is written. If the statement is sent straight to the person of whom it is written, there is no publication of it; for you cannot publish a libel of a man to

himself. If there was no publication, the question whether the occasion was privileged does not arise. If a letter is not communicated to any one but the person to whom it is written, there is no publication of it. And, if the writer of a letter locks it up in his own desk, and a thief comes and breaks open the desk and takes away the letter and makes its contents known, I should say that would not be a publication. If the writer of a letter shews it to his own clerk in order that the clerk may copy it for him, is that a publication of the letter? Certainly it is shewing it to a third person; the writer cannot say to the person to whom the letter is addressed, 'I have shewn it to you and to no one else'. I cannot, therefore, feel any doubt that, if the writer of a letter shews it to any person other than the person to whom it is written, he publishes it. If he wishes not to publish it, he must, so far as he possibly can, keep it to himself, or he must send it himself straight to the person to whom it is written. There was, therefore, in this case a publication to the type-writer.

... Then again, as to the publication at the other end—I mean when the letter was delivered. The letter was not directed to the plaintiffs in their individual capacity; it was directed to a firm of which they were members. The senders of the letter no doubt believed that it would go to the plaintiffs; but it was directed to a firm. When the letter arrived it was opened by a clerk in the employment of the plaintiff's firm, and was seen by three of the clerks in their office. If the letter had been directed to the plaintiffs in their private capacity, in all probability it would not have been opened by a clerk. But mercantile firms and large tradesmen generally depute some clerk to open business letters addressed to them. The sender of the letter had put it out of his own control, and he had directed it in such a manner that it might possibly be opened by a clerk of the firm to which it was addressed. I agree that under such circumstances there was a publication of the letter by the sender of it, and in this case also the occasion was not privileged for the same reasons as in the former case. There were therefore, two publications of the letter, and neither of them was privileged ... . I do not think that the necessities or the luxuries of business can alter the law of England. If a merchant wishes to write a letter containing defamatory matter, and to keep a copy of the letter, he had better make the copy himself. If a company have deputed a person to write a letter containing libellous matter on their behalf, they will be liable for his acts. He ought to write such a letter himself, and to copy it himself, and, if he copies it into a book, he ought to keep the book in his own custody.

Notes

1   The principal case is presumably responsible for the business practice of marking sensitive letters 'Personal' or 'Private'. What about 'To be opened by addressee only: defamatory matter contained herein'? Is it sufficient to mark a letter 'Private' when it is sent to a very busy public figure such as a Prime Minister? (See M Brazier *Street on Torts* (8th edn, 1988) 400.)

2   A private letter sent to a private address is not published when the addressee's butler opens it: *Huth v Huth* [1915] 3 KB 32. What about a husband who opens an unstamped manila envelope addressed to his wife? (See *Theaker v Richardson* [1962] 1 All ER 229.)

3   Another leading case on this point is *Weld Blundell v Stephens* [1920] AC 956, where the defendant negligently left, or dropped, a letter containing defamatory comments on

the floor of an office, from where it came to be read by several persons. Is the defendant liable? Viscount Finlay noted that the person who found it (and who copied it) was no gentleman, but was 'someone who is not sensible of the obligations of honour' (p 972).

4   Modern communication developments including telephone, facsimile, e-mail and the Internet present similar issues to the letter. A recent case concerns an Internet service provider (*Godfrey v Demon Internet Ltd* [2000] 3 WLR 1020). The judgment found that a posting on a website by a third party, containing defamatory remarks concerning the plaintiff, made available by the company, constituted a publication, and was analogous to a library circulating a defamatory book.

5   Does an owner/occupier of premises become a publisher, and thus responsible, if he or she fails to remove unsigned defamatory material from their bulletin board? Is a university liable when an anonymous group of feminist students posts a defamatory attack on a lecturer on a hundred walls and notice boards around the university? See *Hellar v Bianco* (1952) 244 P 2d 757. See also the lampoon on the wall of the golf club in *Byrne v Deane* [1937] 1 KB 818.

Part 2: The defendant's case

If publication of a defamatory remark of and concerning the plaintiff has been proven, then the plaintiff's burden has been met. The elements of the tort have been met and the plaintiff will win unless the defendant successfully raises a defence. The principal defences are truth, privilege (absolute privilege, common law qualified privilege, and statutory qualified privilege), and honest opinion.

Truth

The plaintiff is not obliged to call evidence to prove the falsity of the defendant's remarks. The defendant has the burden of proving their truthfulness. While the notion seems inviting, it is not, however, very easy to prove the truth of what was said. In fact, a failure to prove the truth can compound the damage caused to the plaintiff's reputation. The basic premise of the defence is to stand by the defamatory imputations while attempting to provide sufficient justification or proof of the remarks. A failed truth defence may result in increased damages, so defendants are often advised to not rely on the defence.

At common law, the defence was known as 'justification'. By virtue of s 8(1) of the Defamation Act 1992, the defence is now called 'truth' in New Zealand. The traditional method of proving truth was to show that each of the defamatory charges were, in fact, true. The case of *Templeton v Jones* (below) illustrates this process. However, several judgments following this case considered the case incorrectly decided and a more holistic approach to truth was championed. The courts have more recently focused on the severability of certain statements from the whole of the charge.

New Zealand, similarly, changed the general formation of the truth defence by incorporating s 8 of the Defamation Act 1992. It contains the following provisions:

(2) In proceedings for defamation based on only some of the matter contained in a publication, the defendant may allege and prove any facts contained in the whole of the publication.

(3) In proceedings for defamation, a defence of truth shall succeed if—

    (a) The defendant proves that the imputations contained in the matter that is the subject of the proceedings were true, or not materially different from the truth; or

    (b) Where the proceedings are based on all or any of the matter contained in a publication, the defendant proves that the publication taken as a whole was in substance true, or was in substance not materially different from the truth.

Thus, the interesting question to consider is whether this particular provision would change the outcome of *Templeton*. Certainly, it accords the defendant the opportunity to prove that all the published allegations taken as a whole were in substance true or not materially different from the truth. As discussed by the English Court of Appeal in *Polly Peck Plc v Trelford* [1986] 1 QB 1000, 1031 when considering *Templeton*, the defendant may well be able to prove the sting of the passage as a whole, that is, the so-called 'politics of hatred'. In considering the implications arising from s 8, what if the defendant accused the plaintiff of being a murderer, a rapist, and a petty thief? Can the defendant succeed simply by proving that the plaintiff was a petty thief? While the actual decision in *Templeton* may be called into question, it still provides a useful illustration of the difficulties of proving truth. Similarly, if particular fragments of defamatory imputations are genuinely severable, then a s 8 defence based upon the whole of the publication may fail.

Templeton v Jones
[1984] 1 NZLR 448 (CA)
[**FACTS**: The plaintiff, Mr Bob Jones, was a well-known businessman and founder of the short-lived New Zealand Party. The defendant, the Hon Hugh Templeton, was the sitting MP for the Wellington seat of Ohariu and a Cabinet Minister in the National Government. Bob Jones stood against Mr Templeton in the 1984 election and the case arose out of the campaign, which began in 1983. Templeton had written a speech for the annual general meeting of the Ohariu Branch of the National Party and distributed copies to the parliamentary press gallery. The speech was reported on television news. The report said: 'Among other things, Mr Templeton described Mr Jones as a man who despised bureaucrats, politicians, women, Jews and professionals … . Mr Jones is a man who seems to hate. Mr Jones is a man who despises many people … bureaucrats, civil servants, politicians, women, Jews and professionals. Doesn't it sound familiar? The politics of hatred'. Jones relied in his statement of claim upon the allegation that he despised Jews.]
Cooke J:
… The defence of justification is pleaded in the amended statement of defence as follows:

B *As a second and alternative defence*

7 The extracts referred to in paragraph 5 of the Statement of Claim taken in the context of the speech notes referred to in paragraph 3 herein were true in substance and in fact.

Particulars

(a) Some years ago, the Plaintiff made a statement at The Settlement [restaurant] in Wellington to the following effect to two people (husband and wife) known to the Defendant to be of good repute, and one of whom was Jewish:

The only mistake Hitler made was not to get all the Jews.

(b) One of the two people advised the Defendant that the Plaintiff had made such a statement prior to his preparing his speech notes.

(c) The Plaintiff made a statement to the following effect in the course of being interviewed by a representative of the student newspaper, *Salient*, which statement was published in *Salient* on 5 July 1973:

I admire people who are moral people and a moral person in my view is someone who acts according to his conscience. It's conceivable that Hitler was a man to be highly admired in terms of killing six million Jews, because he had the courage to do so. A lot of people don't like Jews, they've been a popular target for many centuries, but Hitler had the courage to carry out his convictions.

(d) On the dust jacket of a book written by the Plaintiff and entitled *Jones on Property* it is stated that the Plaintiff:

Loathes socialists, public servants.

(e) In an article in the *Auckland Star* dated 23 March 1983 a comment is attributed to the Plaintiff in 1977 that staff of the Ministry of Transport were:

Mediocre little bureaucrats, ranking slightly below shoplifters on the social scale.

(f) On the dust jacket of a book written by the Plaintiff and entitled *New Zealand The Way I Want It* the following comment is attributed to the Plaintiff:

The proper treatment of women for maximum benefit to their owners is identical with the proper treatment of dogs.

(g) In an article written by the Plaintiff and published in *Salient* on 26 September 1973 the Plaintiff stated (in connection with a suggestion that President Allende be nominated for the Nobel Peace Prize):

The fact that [the suggestion] came from a female Labour MP (Ms Liv Aasen—a Norwegian parliamentarian) are three counts against it being taken seriously …

(h) The Plaintiff has from time to time criticised in similarly outrageous and hurtful language the same groups, and other groups and people in the community such as Brownies, Girl Guides, Boy Scouts, youth groups based on religion like the Girls and Boys Brigades and those associated with them, referring for example to the Boy Scouts as 'obviously a homosexual's paradise'.

(i) The public statements of the Plaintiff indicate that he despises various groups and people within the community and have created the impression of a person who appears to hate the same.

Ongley J struck out paras (d) to (i) inclusive, on the ground that the plaintiff has chosen to limit his complaint to the allegation that he despises Jews, and that the particulars pleaded in paras (d) to (i) are irrelevant to the truth or otherwise of that allegation.

The Judge's ruling is a straightforward application of a long-recognised principle of defamation law. It is elementary that a defendant may not justify—that is to say, prove the truth of—that of which the plaintiff does not complain. If an article or speech or a broadcast makes several charges against the plaintiff, he is entitled to sue on one charge only. The defendant may then justify that charge if he can, but he is not allowed to confuse the issue by bringing evidence that the other charges are true. He is fully entitled to point out to the tribunal of fact, usually a jury in defamation cases, that the plaintiff has not complained of the other charges made at the same time. But that goes only to damages. For instance, the defendant can urge on the jury that the one charge of which the plaintiff has chosen to complain has had a negligible effect on his reputation by comparison with the others. If the jury take that view, they can give only nominal or small damages, even if they find that the defendant has not proved the truth of the charge sued on.

The principle that the defendant cannot go into evidence bearing on charges of which the plaintiff does not complain has been established for more than a century. And by Judges of the authority of Willes J and Blackburn J. See *Bremridge v Latimer* (1864) 12 WR 878; 10 LT 816; *Watkin v Hall* (1868) LR 3 QB 396, 402. The basic reason for the principle is simple. It is no excuse for making discreditable statements about a person which are false that one has also made other discreditable statements about him which may be true. A further reason is that to allow the defendant to call such evidence could greatly lengthen and complicate the trial. That would add unnecessarily to the difficulties for the jury, formidable enough already in defamation cases.

The principle does not apply if the words are not severable in that there are not distinct charges but in substance only one. The example given in *Bremridge* by Willes J of such a case is *Morrison v Harmer* (1837) 3 Bing NC 759. There an article accused the plaintiffs of wholesale poisoning by quack medicines and referred to them as 'scamps and rascals'. It was held that the latter words did not have to be separately justified by the defence: they were not a different and distinct charge. That was not a case where in fact the plaintiffs had tried to single out a few inseverable words to sue on, but Willes J implies that they could not have done so.

In the present case, however, the allegation that the plaintiff despises Jews is not reasonably capable of being treated as other than a distinct charge. It is obviously different, for instance, from the allegation that he despises women. It is true that many of the allegations in the passage quoted in para 5 of the statement of claim are variations on or illustrations of a theme: namely that the plaintiff indulges in the politics of hatred. They are specific and severable allegations nonetheless.

[**Note**: The Court then discussed, at some length, two English cases, the decision of the House of Lords in *Speidel v Plato Films Ltd* [1961] AC 1090 and that of the Court of Appeal in *S and K Holdings Ltd v Throgmorton Publications Ltd* [1972] 3 All ER 497. The latter case was distinguished on its facts, and, in any event, was thought to be 'rather dubious authority'.

The former case was brought by General Hans Speidel, then a high-ranking officer with NATO troops in Europe. During World War II, General Speidel had served in occupied France from 1940 to 1942 and subsequently was Chief of General Staff to German army groups on the eastern front. Defendants produced a film in 1958, called *Operation Teutonic Sword*. The film depicted General Speidel as privy to two murders in 1934 and as having been responsible for the betrayal of Field-Marshal Rommel in 1944. It was suggested that the film also portrayed Speidel as a war criminal, as author of atrocities both in France and the Soviet Union. Speidel sued on the former specific charges, but not the latter, more general, allegations. Defendants accepted that they could not plead justification to the charges not complained of; nor could they refer in their pleadings to war crimes and atrocities, 'the truth of which the plaintiff in his amended statement of claim does not deny'. See [1961] AC 1090 at 1125, 1127, and 1142–3.]

… The Faulks Committee on Defamation in the United Kingdom recommended (Cmnd 5909,1975, para 134) that a defendant should be entitled to rely on the whole publication in answer to a claim by a plaintiff complaining only of part of it. The Committee's discussion of the present law shows that they regarded the concession underlying *Speidel*'s case as correct. They do not mention the *S and K* case in this part of their report. Their recommendation has not been enacted by the United Kingdom Parliament. As we have already mentioned, if other allegations were made at the same time as the alleged defamation but have not been challenged in the action, the defendant is entitled to point to this at the trial in mitigation of damages. Having regard to that, there does not seem to be strong enough reason for introducing the change recommended by the Committee by judicial legislation in New Zealand.

Ongley J's striking out of the particulars in question was in accordance with the existing law. In our opinion it should be upheld.

Note

As mentioned earlier, the English Court of Appeal doubted the approach of the New Zealand Court of Appeal. O'Connor LJ, in *Polly Peck Plc v Trelford*, queried the severability of the anti-Semitism from the whole speech. He stated, 'I would have thought that the words in their context were at least capable of meaning that the plaintiff was an intolerant bigot, preaching politics of hatred in the hope of political advantage and that, if that was the sting of the passage as a whole, the defendant was entitled to introduce the particulars which were rejected' (1031).

Honest opinion

[At common law, the defendant could raise the defence of fair comment. In New Zealand, by virtue of s 9 of the Defamation Act 1992, the defence is now known as 'honest opinion'. The 1992 Act contains several other provisions relating to the defence of honest opinion. Fair comment was a defence that lacked precision. Apart from determining that a statement was a comment rather than a statement of purported fact, two particular difficulties were the requisite standard of fairness: whether it was a reasonableness test, or an honesty test, or a hybrid; and the relationship of the comment or opinion to the underlying facts. The 1992 Act does little to clarify these problems and may indeed add new difficulties of its own. In order to understand the present New Zealand law, it is necessary to understand the common law rules and ask whether they have been modified by the 1992 statute.]

Eyes v Henderson
[1873] 1 NZ Jur 34 (SC)
[**FACTS**: The plaintiff (Eyes) was a JP, a sheriff, and a Commissioner of Crown Land for the Province of Marlborough. The defendant (Henderson) was the Mayor of Blenheim, who presided over a public meeting that was called to discuss the affairs of Eyes. Henderson published a resolution that said of Eyes that he was 'leading a life of open and flagrant immorality, thus bringing a scandal on the district'. (The details of this concern are never set out.) Henderson defended the action on grounds of privilege, which was rejected, and fair comment.]
Richmond J:
The third plea to the first count alleges that the resolution is a 'fair comment' upon the matters therein referred to, and upon the conduct of the plaintiff as a public officer. This plea is demurred to on the ground that the resolution, on the face of it, goes beyond comment, and contains substantive defamatory averments. What the resolution asserts is this, that there exists good reason to believe that the plaintiff is leading a life of open and flagrant immorality. Now the plaintiff may be leading either such a life as is described, or a decent and reputable life. In the latter case the resolution cannot be a fair comment upon facts. In the former case the resolution is justified, not as fair comment, but as the absolute truth. In neither case is there really any room for what is termed 'comment'; which means, in this connection, the expression of opinion concerning that which is in its nature doubtful, and a matter of opinion.

... The right of free comment upon the actions of public men—understanding thereby the right of saying what people honestly think on the subject, however unjust, unwise, or improbable their thoughts may be—is confined, as I understand the matter, not merely to such actions as directly concern the public, but also to such subjects as are allowed to be matters of opinion as distinguished from ascertainable matters of fact. Thus it may be allowable to question, in a general way, the patriotism or political purity of a member of Parliament, but falsely to publish of him that he had taken a bribe for his vote, would of course be libellous; or the military capacity and conduct of a general officer may be severely criticised, but it would not be permitted to write of him falsely, that he ran away from the enemy on a particular occasion.

Notes

1   The defendant also pleaded 'justification' (truth); having lost on his other pleas, the defendant's case returned to trial for him to call factual evidence of 'flagrant immorality'. There is no reported record of whether the defendant succeeded, or what proof the defendant offered.

2   Was the resolution 'unfair', or was it fact, instead of 'opinion'?

3   The common law maintains a distinction between the public duties and the private life of public officers. The former is a legitimate target for rumbustious and wrong-headed opinion. The latter is not. Is it possible for a politician's family life and extra-marital adventures to be the subject of fair comment? Can a political candidate make his private moral rectitude into a public issue?

4   Some thirteen years later, the Mayor of Blenheim wrote a letter to the *Marlborough Times*, accusing a Mr Sinclair of 'underhand work', 'sharp practices', and fraudulent concealment in a land deal with the Council. Sinclair sued the proprietor of the newspaper, rather than the Mayor (Henderson) and the defence of fair comment was again relied upon. The Court noted the distinction between 'the right to criticize, even with severity, the acknowledged or proven acts of a public man, and the assertion that he has been guilty of particular acts of misconduct'. See *Sinclair v Hornby* (1887) 5 NZLR 113 (SC).

5   What if a Member of Parliament is called a 'brutal wife-basher'? Is it honest opinion if he is chairing a select Committee to reform the law of divorce and separation? See *Mutch v Sleeman* (1928) 29 SR (NSW) 125, 137 and compare with *Gardiner v Fairfax* (1942) 42 SR (NSW) 171, 174. What if the factual foundation for the wife-beating charge is that, several years before, in a divorce proceeding, the plaintiff's former wife testified that he once struck her? (Mutch won £3500 at trial.)

6   Does the common law rule that the opinion must be on a matter of public interest survive the passage of the Defamation Act 1992? While the point is not mentioned in the Act, s 9 appears on the surface to simply be a name change and the common law, except as expressly altered by the following sections in the Act, would therefore be incorporated in the defence of honest opinion. However, the continued relevance of the public interest rule is doubted by Justice McKay writing ex-judicially: 'Defamation', *The Laws of New Zealand*, para 133. This is supported by Tompkins J in *Shadbolt v Independent News Media (Auckland) Ltd* (7 February 1997) unreported, Auckland, High Court, CP 207/95. For a compelling critique of this view, see J Ferguson 'Honest Opinion and Public Interest' [1998] NZLJ 14.

7   Section 9 of the Defamation Act 1992 labels the defence as 'honest opinion'. But what exactly does that require the defendant to prove? For this we must turn, at least initially, to s 10.

10. Opinion must be genuine—

(1) In any proceedings for defamation in respect of matter that includes or consists of an expression of opinion, a defence of honest opinion by a defendant who is the author of the matter containing the opinion shall fail unless the defendant proves that the opinion expressed was the defendant's genuine opinion.

(2) In any proceedings for defamation in respect of matter that includes or consists of an expression of opinion, a defence of honest opinion by a defendant who is not the author of the matter containing the opinion shall fail unless—

(a) Where the author of the matter containing the opinion was, at the time of the publication of that matter, an employee or agent of the defendant, the defendant proves that—

    (i) The opinion, in its context and in the circumstances of the publication of the matter that is the subject of the proceedings, did not purport to be the opinion of the defendant; and

    (ii) The defendant believed that the opinion was the genuine opinion of the author of the matter containing the opinion:

(b) Where the author of the matter containing the opinion was not an employee or agent of the defendant at the time of the publication of that matter, the defendant proves that—

    (i) The opinion, in its context and in the circumstances of the publication of the matter that is the subject of the proceedings, did not purport to be the opinion of the defendant or of any employee or agent of the defendant.

    (ii) The defendant had no reasonable cause to believe that the opinion was not the genuine opinion of the author of the matter containing the opinion.

(3) A defence of honest opinion shall not fail because the defendant was motivated by malice.

It appears that s 10 requires that the defendant's opinion must be 'genuine'. This raises an interesting dichotomy as to whether 'genuine' equates with 'honest'. What is 'genuine'? Is the test purely subjective? If this is the correct approach, then the honest opinion defence is potentially much easier for defendants to satisfy. Is a 'genuine' opinion, however, something more than an honest opinion? No definitive judicial statement exists to clarify these concerns.

8 *Campbell v Spottiswoode* (1863) 3 F & F 421; 176 ER 188; (1863) 3 B & S 769; 122 ER 288 concerned defamatory remarks criticising Dr Campbell, an evangelical Protestant minister, and his campaign for Christian missionaries to China. Cockburn CJ made some interesting insights into the concept underpinning honest opinion (or fair comment). He stated:

> I think the fair position in which the law may be settled is this: that where the public conduct of a public man is open to animadversion, and the writer who is commenting upon it makes imputations on his motives which arise fairly and legitimately out of his conduct so that a jury shall

say that the criticism was not only honest, but also well founded, an action is not maintainable.

This case raises another familiar question, in that is an opinion 'genuine' only if it is warranted by the facts? This introduces elements of objectivity to the test if it is correct.

9   In *News Media Ownership v Finlay* [1970] NZLR 1089, the Court of Appeal was invited to ignore the rule in *Campbell v Spottiswoode*. However, the Court said 'we are not dealing with a case of honest criticism but with a case where the appellant has attributed disgraceful motives to the respondent ... Comment must not convey imputations of an evil sort except in so far as the facts truly stated warrant the imputation' (p 1098). Dr Finlay, then an Opposition MP, had been accused by the weekly newspaper *Truth* of being more interested in personal profit than in protecting the public from 'bashers'. The newspaper had been waging a campaign to 'birch the bashers' and Dr Finlay had taken exception to this in Parliament.

10   The leading article on fair comment is ID Johnston's 'Uncertainties in the Defence of Fair Comment' (1979) 8 NZULR 359. See also J Burrows and U Cheer *Media Law in New Zealand* (4th edn, OUP, Auckland, 1999) pp 86–99.

McQuire v Western Morning News Co Ltd
[1903] 2 KB 100 (CA)

[**FACTS**: The plaintiff was a dramatist, an actor, and a theatrical manager. His musical production, *The Major*, was staged in Plymouth on 24 June 1901. On 25 June the defendants published the following review:

A three-act musical absurdity entitled *The Major*, written and composed by Mr T.C. McQuire, was presented last evening before a full house by the author's company. It cannot be said that many left the building with the satisfaction of having seen anything like the standard of play which is generally to be witnessed at the Theatre Royal. Although it may be described as a play, *The Major* is composed of nothing but nonsense of a not very humorous character, whilst the music is far from attractive. This comedy would be very much improved had it a substantial plot, and were a good deal of the sorry stuff taken out of it which lowers both the players and the play. No doubt the actors and actresses are well suited to the piece, which gives excellent scope for music-hall artistes to display their talent. Among Mr McQuire's company there is not one good actor or actress, and, with the exception of Mr Ernest Braime, not one of them can be said to have a voice for singing. The introduction of common, not to say vulgar, songs does not tend to improve the character of the performance, and the dancing, which forms a prominent feature, is carried out with very little gracefulness.

The author–actor–producer sued the publisher, and was successful at trial to the extent of £100. The defendants appealed on grounds of fair comment.]

Collins MR:

... The plaintiff is an author and actor, and the action is founded upon a notice which appeared in the defendants' newspaper of a musical play written and composed by the plaintiff and produced by a company under his management at the principal theatre in

Plymouth. The plaintiff himself acted a part in the play. The notice complained of was as follows:

[**Note**: The learned judge read the alleged libel as set out above.]

It appears on the face of the statement of claim that the notice complained of was a dramatic criticism of a play publicly acted; and therefore it could not be, and was not, contended for the plaintiff that there was any libel unless the criticism exceeded the bounds of 'fair comment'. It was not suggested that there was any evidence of actual malice, there were no personal imputations, nor could any statement of fact be impugned. The innuendo set out in the claim does not charge any misstatement of fact, but confines itself to matters of opinion only. It is as follows: 'By the said words the defendants meant, and were understood to mean, and the meaning of the said words is that the said play was dull, vulgar, and degrading, that the members of the plaintiff's company were incompetent as actors, singers, and dancers, that they were music-hall artistes, and that the plaintiff was himself incompetent both as an actor and composer as aforesaid'. The plaintiff, however, contended that the notice, though comment, was not 'fair comment'; and the jury apparently adopted this view, and found for the plaintiff, with £100 damages. The defendants challenge the verdict ... .

This raises a very important question as to what are the limits of 'fair comment' on a literary work ... . One thing, however, is perfectly clear, and that is that the jury have no right to substitute their own opinion of the literary merits of the work for that of the critic, or to try the 'fairness' of the criticism by any such standard. 'Fair', therefore, in this collocation certainly does not mean that which the ordinary reasonable man, 'the man on the Clapham omnibus', as Lord Bowen phrased it, the juryman common or special, would think a correct appreciation of the work; and it is of the highest importance to the community that the critic should be saved from any such possibility. In principle, therefore, there would be nothing to leave to the jury unless there was some element in the criticism which might support an inference of unfairness in some other sense. No doubt this element might be, and has been, described in various ways and different instances of it given; but, broadly, I think Mr Duke is right in contending that, in the case of a literary work at all events, it is something that passes out of the domain of criticism itself. Criticism cannot be used as a cloak for mere invective, nor for personal imputations not arising out of the subject-matter or not based on fact. 'If', says Lord Ellenborough in *Carr v Hood*, reported in a note to *Tabart v Tipper* ... 'the commentator does not step aside from the work or introduce fiction for the purpose of condemnation he exercises a fair and legitimate right ... . Had the party writing the criticism followed the plaintiff into domestic life for the purposes of slander that would have been libellous'; and, in another passage: 'Shew me an attack on the moral character of this plaintiff, or any attack upon his character unconnected with his authorship, and I shall be as ready as any judge who ever sate here to protect him'. In *Merivale v Carson* Bowen LJ says: 'In the case of literary criticism it is not easy to conceive what would be outside that region'—ie, of fair comment— 'unless the writer went out of his way to make a personal attack on the character of the author of the work which he was criticizing. In such a case the writer would be going beyond the limits of criticism altogether, and therefore beyond the limits of fair criticism ... . Still, there is another class of cases in which, as it seems to me, the writer would be travelling out of the region of fair criticism—I mean if he imputes to the author that he has written something which in fact he has not written ...' . I think 'fair' embraces the meaning of honest and also of relevancy. The view expressed must be honest and must be such as can fairly be called criticism. I am aware that the word 'moderate' has been used in this connection—*Wason v Walter*—with reference to comment on the conduct of a public man; but I think it is only used to express the idea that invective is not criticism. It certainly cannot mean moderate in the sense that that which is deemed by a jury, in the case of a literary criticism, extravagant and the outcome of prejudice on the part of an honest writer is necessarily beyond the limit of fair comment.

Notes

1   Collins MR has substituted the concept of 'relevancy' for the 'not without foundation' test. What does 'relevancy' mean here? Relevant to what? What is the blend of subjective (honest) and objective (relevant)?

2   A classic statement of the test was made by Diplock J in his instructions to the jury in *Silkin v Beaverbrook Newspapers Ltd* [1958] 1 WLR 743, 749:

> The matter which you have to decide, and I emphasize this again, because it is so important, is not whether you, any of you, agree with that comment. You may all of you disagree with it, feel that it is comment that is not correct. But that is not the test. I will remind you of the test once more. Could a fair-minded man, holding a strong view, holding perhaps an obstinate view, holding perhaps a prejudiced view—could a fair-minded man have been capable of writing this? That is a totally different question from the question: Do you agree with what he said?
>
> So in considering this case, members of the jury, do not apply the test of whether you agree with it. If juries did that, freedom of speech, the right of the crank to say what he likes, would go. Would a fair-minded man holding strong views, obstinate views, prejudiced views, have been capable of making this comment? If the answer to that is yes, then your verdict in this case should be a verdict for the defendants.

3   Section 12 of the Defamation Act 1992 states:

> In any proceedings for defamation in which the defendant relies on a defence of honest opinion, the fact that the matter that is the subject of the proceedings attributes a dishonourable, corrupt, or base motive to the plaintiff does not require the defendant to prove anything that the defendant would not be required to prove if the matter did not attribute any such motive.

The intention of this somewhat obscurely drafted provision is to remove the distinction between honest criticism and the attribution of base motives. Section 12 leaves unanswered, however, what it is necessary for the defendant to prove.

4   At common law, there was conflicting authority on the question whether the defendant had to prove that a comment was objectively fair and subjectively honest, or whether it

was for the plaintiff to prove that the defendant was dishonest (for example, *Telnikoff v Matusevitch* [1990] 3 All ER 865—the plaintiff has the burden of proving that the defendant was dishonest; contra, *Cherneskey v Armadale Publishers Ltd* [1979] 1 SCR 1067). The Defamation Act 1992 removes any doubt in New Zealand: the defendant must prove that the opinion was genuine, and malice (where the onus rests on the plaintiff) does not defeat the defence.

Kemsley v Foot

[1952] AC 345 (HL)

[**FACTS**: An alleged libel was contained in an issue of the *Tribune* dated 10 March 1950. It began as follows:

LOWER THAN KEMSLEY
by Michael Foot

The prize for the foulest piece of journalism perpetrated in this country for many a long year, and that is certainly saying something, must go to Mr Herbert Gunn, editor of the *Evening Standard*, and all those who assisted him in the publication of an attack on John Strachey last week.

The article went on to make a somewhat violent attack on the conduct of the *Evening Standard*, a newspaper controlled by Lord Beaverbrook. Lord Kemsley was the active proprietor of the Kemsley Press, which published several well-known newspapers.]

Lord Porter:

... The comment upon these matters is said to be criticism of the way in which the plaintiff's newspapers are conducted and to assert that that conduct is of a low character, that the defendants are entitled to criticize that conduct, and, as it is a matter of public interest, to comment fairly upon it. The plaintiff, on his part, maintains that the right of comment is dependent upon the existence in the words alleged to be libellous of a statement of some fact or facts upon which comment is made so that those reading the comment may be able to judge for themselves whether it is justified or not ... .

It is not, as I understand, contended that the words contained in that article are fact and not comment: rather it is alleged that they are comment with no facts to support it. The question for your Lordships' decision is, therefore, whether a plea of fair comment is only permissible where the comment is accompanied by a statement of facts upon which the comment is made and to determine the particularity with which the facts must be stated ... .

If an author writes a play or a book or a composer composes a musical work, he is submitting that work to the public and thereby inviting comment. Not all the public will see or read or hear it but the work is public in the same sense as a case in the Law Courts is said to be heard in public. In many cases it is not possible for everyone who is interested, to attend a trial, but in so far as there is room for them in the court all are entitled to do so, and the subject-matter upon which comment can be made is indicated to the world at large.

The same observation is true of a newspaper. Whether the criticism is confined to a particular issue or deals with the way in which it is in general conducted, the subject-matter upon which criticism is made has been submitted to the public, though by no means all those to whom the alleged libel has been published will have seen or are likely to see the various issues. Accordingly, its contents and conduct are open to comment on the ground that the public have at least the opportunity of ascertaining for themselves the subject-matter upon which the comment is founded. I am assuming that the reference is to a known journal: for the present purpose it is not necessary to consider how far criticism without facts upon which to base it is subject to the same observation in the case of an obscure publication ... .

But the question whether an inference is a bare inference in this sense must depend upon all the circumstances. Indeed, it was ultimately admitted on behalf of the appellant that the facts necessary to justify comment might be implied from the terms of the impugned article and therefore the inquiry ceases to be—Can the defendant point to definite assertions of fact in the alleged libel upon which the comment is made? and becomes—Is there subject-matter indicated with sufficient clarity to justify comment being made? and was the comment actually made such as an honest, though prejudiced, man might make?

Is there, then, in this case sufficient subject-matter upon which to make comment? In an article which is concerned with what has been described as 'the Beaverbrook Press' and which is violently critical of Lord Beaverbrook's newspapers, it is, I think, a reasonable construction of the words 'Lower than Kemsley' that the allegation which is made is that the conduct of the Kemsley Press was similar to but not quite so bad as that of the press controlled by Lord Beaverbrook, ie, it is possibly dishonest, but in any case low. The exact meaning, however, is not, in my opinion, for your Lordships but for the jury. All I desire to say is that there is subject-matter and it is at least arguable that the words directly complained of imply as fact that Lord Kemsley is in control of a number of known newspapers and that the conduct of those newspapers is in question. Had the contention that all the facts justifying the comment must appear in the article been maintainable, the appeal would succeed, but the appellant's representatives did not feel able to and, I think, could not support so wide a contention. The facts, they admitted, might be implied, and the respondents' answer to their contention is: 'We have pointed to your press. It is widely read. Your readers will and the public generally can know at what our criticism is directed. It is not bare comment; it is comment on a well-known matter, much better known, indeed, than a newly printed book or a once-performed play'.

Notes

I   In considering whether the basis for an opinion must be ascertainable from the facts presented, the case of *Weir v Karam* (20 September 2000), unreported, High Court, CP 139/98 provides some notable points. Anderson J, in determining whether an honest opinion defence was available commented (at 7–8):

> Whether a statement is or is not an opinion for the purposes of the defence of honest opinion is not a semantic question. It requires an assessment which has regard to the rationale of the defence. That is founded on freedom of speech which it protects by permitting honest

statements which are presented as factually based deductions or conclusions or remarks, the worth of which can be assessed by those to whom
it is published.

It is not helpful to examine the applicability of the defence in terms
of a fact/opinion dichotomy. The correct question to ask is whether the
defence of honest opinion applies. It will apply when the words complained of appear conclusionary, the conclusion is based on apparent
facts which are true or not materially different from the truth, and the
conclusion is honestly believed by the maker of the comment ...

While this may raise concerns and questions of its own, it appears to clarify that the
facts must either be there in plain black and white or at least be apparent. The Defamation Act does not expressly require an opinion to be based on facts, but it may be
implied by s 11.

2   Can the defence of honest opinion be invoked where the opinions are based on incorrect but privileged information? See *Mangena v Wright* [1909] 2 KB 958.

3   In *Templeton v Jones* (above), could the defendant have relied on the rule in *Kemsley v
Foot* and argued that the statement that Jones despised Jews was honest opinion?

4   A rather sad case concerning honest opinion involved the greatly loved Maori
comedian Billy T James. In *Awa v Independent News Auckland Ltd* [1997] 3 NZLR 590,
the Court of Appeal considered whether fair comment could be invoked with regard
to a 'body snatching' comment. Mr Awa maintained that in removing Billy T's body to a
Marae he was acting in accordance with Maori custom. Nevertheless, the body
snatching comment was defended as referring to the manner of removal of the body,
and not the custom. The key phrase delivered by Blanchard J was (at 595):

However, provided that comment is factually based and expresses a genuinely held opinion rather that being mere invective, it will be protected
in a defamation action by the fair comment or honest opinion defence.
The insensitivity of the comment does not deprive it of that protection if
it is made honestly.

Parliamentary privilege

[A defendant who makes untrue defamatory statements may nevertheless escape liability if
the occasion on which the statement was made was privileged. At common law, qualified
privilege was lost if the plaintiff could prove malice—hence the epithet 'qualified'. By contrast, absolute privilege remains a good defence even if the defendant was motivated by
malice. The principal examples of absolute privilege are statements made in Parliament and
those made in judicial proceedings: see ss 13 and 14 of the Defamation Act 1992. By s 15,
other common law categories of absolute privilege are retained. An example of judicial privilege is *Rawlinson v Oliver* [1995] 3 NZLR 62, [1995] NZFLR 481. The Court of Appeal held
that absolute privilege applied even though the relevant proceeding was one where the
court had no jurisdiction.

The typical situation where parliamentary privilege is invoked is where a plaintiff contemplates basing a claim on something an MP has said in Parliament. The defendant MP will say

that evidence of what was said in Parliament is inadmissible. What is the position, on the other hand, where the plaintiff is an MP and the defendant wishes to admit statements made by an MP in Parliament in order to establish a defence?]

Prebble v Television New Zealand Ltd
[1994] 3 NZLR 1 (PC)
[**FACTS**: The plaintiff was a Cabinet Minister who was the subject of a television documentary, which, according to the plaintiff, alleged that he had conspired with business people and public officials to sell public assets cheaply in return for donations to the Labour Party. TVNZ invoked several defences and among the particulars pleaded were speeches in Parliament. The Court of Appeal upheld the High Court's decision to strike out these particulars because they were absolutely privileged. However, because of the prejudice to the defendant's case, the Court (McKay J dissenting) held that the proceedings should be stayed. The plaintiff appealed to the Privy Council.]
Lord Browne-Wilkinson:

...

Article 9
Article 9 of the Bill of Rights 1688 provides as follows:

> **Freedome of Speech**—That the freedome of speech and debates or proceedings in Parlyament ought not be impeached or questioned in any court or place out of Parlyament.

It is common ground that art 9 is in force in New Zealand by virtue of s 242 of the Legislature Act 1908 and the Imperial Laws Application Act 1988.

If art 9 is looked at alone, the question is whether it would infringe the article to suggest that the statements made in the House were improper or the legislation procured in pursuance of the alleged conspiracy, as constituting impeachment or questioning of the freedom of speech of Parliament.

In addition to art 9 itself, there is a long line of authority which supports a wider principle, of which art 9 is merely one manifestation, viz, that the Courts and Parliament are both astute to recognise their respective constitutional roles. So far as the Courts are concerned they will not allow any challenge to be made to what is said or done within the walls of Parliament in performance of its legislative functions and protection of its established privileges ... .

... Their Lordships are acutely conscious (as were the Courts below) that to preclude reliance on things said and done in the House in defence of libel proceedings brought by a member of the House could have a serious impact on a most important aspect of freedom of speech, viz the right of the public to comment on and criticise the actions of those elected to power in a democratic society: see *Derbyshire County Council v Times Newspapers Ltd* [1993] AC 534. If the media and others are unable to establish the truth of fair criticisms of the conduct of their elected members in the very performance of their legislative duties in the House, the results could indeed be chilling to the proper monitoring of members' behaviour. But the present case [illustrates] how public policy, or human rights, issues can conflict. There are three such issues in play in these cases: first, the need to ensure that the legislature can exercise its powers freely on behalf of its electors, with access to all relevant information; second, the need to protect freedom of speech generally; third, the interests of justice in ensuring that all relevant evidence is available to the Courts. Their Lordships are of the view that the law has been long settled that, of these three public interests, the first must prevail. But the other two public interests cannot be ignored and Their Lordships will revert to them in considering the question of a stay of proceedings.

For these reasons (which are in substance those of the Courts below) Their Lordships are of the view that parties to litigation, by whomsoever commenced, cannot bring into question anything said or done in the House by suggesting (whether by direct evidence, cross-examination, inference or submission) that the actions or words were inspired by improper motives or were untrue or misleading. Such matters lie entirely within the jurisdiction of the House, subject to any statutory exception such as exists in New Zealand in relation to perjury under s 108 of the Crimes Act 1961. However, Their Lordships wish to make it clear that this principle does not exclude all references in Court proceedings to what has taken place in the House ... .

Since there can no longer be any objection to the production of *Hansard*, the Attorney-General accepted (in Their Lordship's view rightly) that there could be no objection to the use of *Hansard* to prove what was done and said in Parliament as a matter of history. Similarly, he accepted that the fact that a statute had been passed is admissible in Court proceedings. Thus, in the present action, there cannot be any objection to it being proved what the plaintiff or the Prime Minister said in the House ... or that the State-Owned Enterprises Act 1986 was passed ... . It will be for the trial Judge to ensure that the proof of these historical facts is not used to suggest that the words were improperly spoken or the statute passed to achieve an improper purpose.

It is clear that, on the pleadings as they presently stand, the defendants intend to rely on these matters not purely as a matter of history but as part of the alleged conspiracy or its implementation. Therefore, in Their Lordships' view, Smellie J was right to strike them out. But Their Lordships wish to make it clear that if the defendants wish at the trial to allege the occurrence of events or the saying of certain words in Parliament without any accompanying allegation of impropriety or any other questioning there is no objection to that course.

Stay of proceedings

... Their Lordships are of the opinion that there may be cases in which the exclusion of material on the grounds of parliamentary privilege makes it quite impossible fairly to determine the issue between the parties. In such a case the interests of justice may demand a stay of proceedings. But such a stay should only be granted in the most extreme circumstances. The effect of a stay is to deny justice to the plaintiff by preventing him from establishing his good name in the Courts. There may be cases ... where the whole subject-matter of the alleged libel relates to the plaintiff's conduct in the House so that the effect of parliamentary privilege is to exclude virtually all the evidence necessary to justify the libel. If such an action were to be allowed to proceed, not only would there be an injustice to the defendant but also there would be a real danger that the media would be forced to abstain from the truthful disclosure of a member's misbehaviour in Parliament, since justification would be impossible. That would constitute a most serious inroad into freedom of speech.

But Their Lordships do not agree that the present case falls into that extreme category. Mr Galbraith, for the plaintiff, submitted, and Mr Tizard, for the defendants, had difficulty in denying, that the allegations struck out were comparatively marginal. The burden of the libel relates to acts done by members of the government out of the House to which questions of parliamentary privilege have no application.

Notes

1   The Privileges Committee of Parliament considered whether it could waive the privilege but determined that it had no power to do so. The Privy Council did not directly address this point but took the view that the individual MP cannot override the collective privilege of the House (p 9). It does not therefore matter whether defamation proceedings have been initiated by an MP or by an outsider.

2   In *Cushing v Peters (No 3)* [1996] DCR 322, the plaintiff sued an MP for comments made in two interviews on the Australian television programme *Four Corners*. Mr Peters MP stated that the plaintiff was offered a bribe to support recent economic reforms. However he mentioned no names at this stage and named Mr Cushing as the briber only later in Parliament. Mr Peters unsuccessfully asked Parliament's Privileges Committee to intervene to prevent the plaintiff from using the parliamentary record. The Committee refused to intervene for several reasons: (i) the case was not a test case, as *Prebble v TVNZ* had settled the law in the area; (ii) while in *Prebble* the motives behind an MP's words in the House were questioned, there was no evidence that there would be such questioning in *Cushing v Peters*; (iii) the case was similar to an earlier Court of Appeal decision, *Hyams v Peterson* [1991] 3 NZLR 648, which would allow Mr Peters' statement in the House to be admitted as evidence. Any attempt to distinguish *Hyams* could be left to the courts; (iv) Peters' delay in bringing the matter before the Privileges Committee was excessive. See Report of the Privileges Committee on the Question of Privilege Referred on 11 June 1996 Concerning the Action *Cushing v Peters* in the District Court at Wellington (1996, 1.15A). In a judgment in 1994 in an interlocutory proceeding, Judge Willy had ruled that the statement in Parliament could be admitted ([1994] DCR 803). This approach was reflected in the decision of the trial judge, Judge Dalmer, to allow reference to what was said in Parliament. Mr Peters decided then to offer no evidence at the trial and he was subsequently found liable to pay $50 000 damages.

Given that identification is a vital element in any defamation case, is it so clear that parliamentary privilege has not been breached in *Cushing v Peters*? Mr Peters MP appealed to the High Court with *Peters v Cushing* (14 November 1997) unreported, High Court, AP 183/96 resulting. Ellis and Greig JJ held that the District Court Judge was wrong to admit comments made in Parliament to prove what was said in the first interview. This restored absolute privilege to its previously understood position. Nevertheless, in the judges' view ample evidence existed outside the comments in Parliament to connect Mr Peters MP's statements in the second interview to Mr Cushing. They upheld the damages award of $50 000 and $75 000 for costs.

Qualified privilege

Qualified privilege recognises that a vast range of circumstances may give rise to an occasion of privilege, but they are not absolute in nature when compared to judicial or parliamentary proceedings. The key distinguishing feature between absolute and qualified privilege is that a qualified privilege can be defeated.

Qualified privilege arose within the bounds of common law. Two questions constituted the basic inquiry: (a) Was it an occasion of privilege? (b) Was there a misuse or abuse of that occasion? The classic case of *Watt v Longsdon* (below) includes the common law discussion of a duty/interest test. This common law qualified privilege still operates and exists in New Zealand.

The Defamation Act 1992 modified the law relating to qualified privilege. Section 16 details that the publication of those things listed in the First Schedule to the Act are protected by an additional statutory form of qualified privilege. Similar to common law malice, s 19 can be invoked by the plaintiff to defeat the occasion of privilege.

However, the biggest developments within qualified privilege have occurred recently through important decisions including New Zealand's *Lange* and the English case of *Reynolds*. Both cases concern political stories, and the extent to which they are privileged. Arguably, irrespective of the different judicial cultures, the separate and distinct tests, and the different modes of political reporting within the two countries, the two cases present similar results.

Despite this, other jurisdictions have determined the issue differently. A conservative line in respect of freedom of expression emerged from the Supreme Court of Canada in *Manning v Hill* (1995) 126 DLR (4th) 129 (also reported as *Hill v Church of Scientology* [1995] 2 SCR 1130), which considered the Canadian Charter of Rights and Freedoms. While the Charter did not apply directly, for it did not involve government action, Cory J said at p 157:

> ... in the context of civil litigation involving only private parties, the Charter will 'apply' to common law only to the extent that the common law is found to be inconsistent with Charter values. Courts have traditionally been cautious regarding the extent to which they will amend the common law. Similarly, they must not go further than is necessary when taking Charter values into account. Far-reaching changes to the common law must be left to the legislature.

Cory J continued the Charter discussion at p 170, commenting that:

> in its application to the parties to this action, the common law of defamation complies with the underlying values of the Charter and there is no need to amend or alter it.

Canada refused to incorporate into its law the American *New York Times v Sullivan* (1964) 376 US 254 rule, viz, that public officials (later extended to 'public figures') cannot succeed in defamation unless they can show that the statement was made 'with knowledge that it was false or with reckless disregard of whether it was false or not'.

It is important to note that earlier in New Zealand, the *Report of the Committee on Defamation* recommended against the public figure rule: para 16. The House of Lords was attracted to the sentiments expressed in *Sullivan* by the American Supreme Court: see *Derbyshire County Council v Times Newspapers Ltd* [1993] AC 534, but there has been some modification to this direction when considering *Reynolds*. The High Court of Australia by a majority has taken a dramatic step, drawing on an implied freedom of communication, which the Court found in the Commonwealth of Australia Constitution and echoing but not copying the rule in *Sullivan*: *Theophanous v Herald & Weekly Times* (1994) 182 CLR 104 and

Stephens v West Australian Newspapers Ltd (1994) 182 CLR 211. In *Theophanous*, the Court said (p 130):

> To our minds, it is incontrovertible that an implication of freedom of communication, the purpose of which is to ensure the efficacy of representative democracy, must extend to protect political discussion from exposure to onerous criminal and civil liability if the implication is to be effective in achieving its purpose.

They explained further, that (respectively at p 137 and pp 140–1):

> The publisher should be required to show that, in the circumstances which prevailed, it acted reasonably, either by taking some steps to check the accuracy of the impugned material or by establishing that it was otherwise justified in publishing without taking such step or steps which were adequate.

> ... the publication will not be actionable under the law relating to defamation if the defendant establishes that: (a) it was unaware of the falsity of the material published; (b) it did not publish the material recklessly, that is, not caring whether the material was true or false; and (c) the publication was reasonable in the circumstances.

The Australian courts solidified their position with the High Court judgment in *Lange v Australian Broadcasting Corporation* (1997) 189 CLR 520, highlighting that the test for political discussion would be adjudicated upon by a reasonableness test.

Thus, it is essential to realise that a diverse range of approaches exists between New Zealand, Australia, Canada, the United States, and the United Kingdom. In order to comprehend New Zealand's 'unique' method, it is important to have an understanding of those other various judicial approaches.

Irrespective of the jurisdiction, there is a further important consideration. The predominant focus of the approaches discussed above has been in determining if an occasion of privilege exists. However, qualified privilege is limited in that an abuse or misuse of the occasion of privilege will cause the occasion to be outside what is acceptable, and the defence will fail. The classic common law approach was 'malice', but New Zealand's Defamation Act 1992 effected some interesting changes to this through s 19. Section 19, which was discussed in some detail in *Lange*, reads:

> Rebuttal of qualified privilege—
> (1) In any proceedings for defamation, a defence of qualified privilege shall fail if the plaintiff proves that, in publishing the matter that is the subject of the proceedings, the defendant was predominantly motivated by ill will towards the plaintiff, or otherwise took improper advantage of the occasion of publication.
> (2) Subject to subsection (1) of this section, a defence of qualified privilege shall not fail because the defendant was motivated by malice.

Watt v Longsdon
[1930] 1 KB 130 (CA)
Scrutton LJ:
This case raises, amongst other matters, the extremely difficult question, equally important in its legal and social aspect, as to the circumstances, if any, in which a

person will be justified in giving to one partner to a marriage information which that person honestly believes to be correct, but which is in fact untrue, about the matrimonial delinquencies of the other party to the marriage. The question becomes more difficult if the answer in law turns on the existence or non-existence of a social or moral duty, a question which the judge is to determine, without any evidence, by the light of his own knowledge of the world, and his own views on social morality, a subject matter on which views vary in different ages, in different countries, and even as between man and man.

The Scottish Petroleum Company, which carried on business, amongst other places, in Morocco, had in Casa Blanca, a port in Morocco, a manager named Browne, and a managing director named Watt. The company had in England a chairman named Singer, who held a very large proportion of shares in the company, and also another director, Longsdon, a young man under thirty years of age. The latter had been in Morocco in business and friendly relations with Watt and Browne, and was a friend of Mrs Watt, who had nursed him in an illness. The company went into voluntary liquidation in November, 1927, and Longsdon was appointed liquidator. In April, 1928, Mrs Watt was in England, and her husband in Casa Blanca. It is not clear, and there is no evidence, what the effect of the liquidation had been on the actual employment of Watt and Browne, that is, whether they, or either of them, still received a salary. Watt's directorship was, under the Companies Act, in a state of suspended animation. Under these circumstances Longsdon in England received at the beginning of May from Browne in Casa Blanca a letter stating that Watt had left for Lisbon to look for a job, that he had left a bill for £88 for whiskey unpaid and that he had been for two months in immoral relations with his housemaid, who was now publicly raising claims against him for money matters. The woman was described as an old woman, stone deaf, almost blind, and with dyed hair. A number of details were given which Browne said Watt's cook had corroborated. The information was mixed up with an allegation that Watt had been scheming to compromise or seduce Mrs Browne. The letter concluded, 'From a letter shown to me by Mr Watt I now know how bitterly disappointed Mrs Watt is, and how very much troubled she is. It would therefore perhaps be better not to show her this letter as it could only increase most terribly her own feelings in regard to her husband. These awful facts might be the cause of a breakdown to her, and I think she has enough to cope with at the present. Mr Singer, however, should perhaps know'. On May 5, Longsdon, without making inquiries, sent Browne's letter on to Singer, the chairman of the board of directors. At the trial Watt's counsel put in Longsdon's answer into interrogatory 5 that he believed the statements in the letter to be true. On May 5 Longsdon wrote a long letter to Browne, in which he said that he had long suspected Watt's immorality but had not proof; that he thought it wicked and cruel that Mrs Watt, a very old friend of the writer's, should be in the dark when Watt might return to her—did not Browne agree?—that he Longsdon would not speak until he had a sworn statement in his possession, 'and only with such proof would I speak, for an interferer between husband and wife nearly always comes off the worst'. Could Browne get a written statement? 'It may even be necessary for you to bribe to do such, and if only a matter of a few hundred francs I will pay and of course the legal expenses'. Longsdon's letter described one of the women who was to make this sworn statement as 'a prostitute all her life,' a description not contained in Browne's letter. Watt returned to England in May.

Without waiting for the sworn statement, on May 12, Longsdon sent the letter to Mrs Watt. Mr and Mrs Watt separated, and Mrs Watt instituted proceedings for divorce, which apparently are still pending.

Mr Watt then instituted proceedings against Longsdon for libel—namely (1) the publication of Browne's letter to Singer; (2) the publication of the same letter to Mrs Watt; (3) Longsdon's letter of May 5 to Browne ... The defendant did not justify, but pleaded privilege. The case was tried before Horridge J and a jury. The learned judge held that all three publications were privileged, and that there was no evidence of malice fit to be left to the jury. He therefore entered judgment for the defendant. The plaintiff appeals.

... By the law of England there are occasions on which a person may make defamatory statements about another which are untrue without incurring any legal liability for his statements. These occasions are called privileged occasions. A reason frequently given for this privilege is that the allegation that the speaker has 'unlawfully and maliciously published', is displaced by proof that the speaker had either a duty or an interest to publish, and that this duty or interest confers the privilege. But communications made on these occasions may lose their privilege: (1) they may exceed the privilege of the occasion by going beyond the limits of the duty or interest, or (2) they may be published with express malice, so that the occasion is not being legitimately used, but abused ... . The classical definition of 'privileged occasions' is that of Parke B in *Toogood v Spyring* [(1834) 1 CM & R 181; 149 ER 1044], a case where the tenant of a farm complained to the agent of the landlord, who had sent a workman to do repairs, that the workman had broken into the tenant's cellar, got drunk on the tenant's cider, and spoilt the work he was sent to do. The workman sued the tenant. Parke B gave the explanation of privileged occasions in these words:

> In general, an action lies for the malicious publication of statements which are false in fact, and injurious to the character of another (within the well-known limits as to verbal slander), and the law considers such publication as malicious, unless it is fairly made by a person in the discharge of some public or private duty, whether legal or moral, or in the conduct of his own affairs, in matters where his interest is concerned. In such cases, the occasion prevents the inference of malice, which the law draws from unauthorized communications, and affords a qualified defence depending upon the absence of actual malice. If fairly warranted by any reasonable occasion or exigency, and honestly made, such communications are protected for the common convenience and welfare of society; and the law has not restricted the right to make them within any narrow limits.

It will be seen that the learned judge requires: (1) a public or private duty to communicate, whether legal or moral; (2) that the communication should be 'fairly warranted by any reasonable occasion or exigency'; (3) or a statement in the conduct of his own affairs where his interest is concerned ... . This, I think, involves that his 'situation' imposes on him a legal or moral duty. The question whether the occasion was privileged is for the judge, and so far as 'duty' is concerned, the question is: Was there a duty, legal, moral, or social, to communicate? As to legal duty, the judge should have no difficulty; the judge should know the law; but as to moral or social duties of imperfect obligation, the task is far more troublesome. The judge has no evidence as to the view the community takes of moral or social duties. All the help the Court of Appeal can give him is contained in the judgment of Lindley LJ in *Stuart v Bell* [[1891] 2 QB 341, 350]: 'The question of moral or social duty being for the judge, each judge must decide it as best he can for himself. I take moral or social duty to mean a duty recognized by English people of ordinary intelligence and moral principle, but at the same time not a duty enforceable by legal proceedings, whether civil or criminal. My own conviction is that all or, at all events, the great mass of right-minded men in the position of the defendant would have considered it their duty, under the circumstances, to inform Stanley of the suspicion which had fallen on the plaintiff'. Is the judge merely to give his own view of moral and social duty, though he thinks a considerable portion of the community hold a different opinion? Or is he to endeavour to ascertain what view 'the great mass of right-minded men' would take? It is not surprising that with such a standard both judges and text-writers treat the matter as one of great difficulty in which no definite line can be drawn.

... In 1855, in *Harrison v Bush* [(1855) 5 E & B 344, 348; 119 ER 509, 512], Lord Campbell CJ giving the judgment of the Court of Queen's Bench accepted a principle stated thus: 'A communication made bona fide upon any subject matter in which the party communicating has an interest, or in reference to which he has a duty, is privileged, if made to a person having a corresponding interest or duty, although it contain criminatory matter which, without this privilege, would be slanderous and actionable'. This is the first of a series of statements that both parties, the writer and the recipient, must have a corresponding interest or duty. Lord Esher MR says in *Pullman v Hill & Co* [[1891] 1 QB 524, 528]: 'An occasion is privileged when the person who makes the communication has a moral duty to make it to the person to whom he does make it, and the person who receives it has an interest in hearing it. Both these conditions must exist in order that the occasion may be privileged'. Lord Atkinson in *Adam v Ward* [[1917] AC 309, 334] expresses it thus: 'It was not disputed, in this case on either side, that a privileged occasion is, in reference to qualified privilege, an occasion where the person who makes a communication has an interest or a duty, legal, social, or moral, to make it to the person to whom it is made, and the person to whom it is so made has a corresponding interest or duty to receive it. This reciprocity is essential'. With slight modifications in particular circumstances, this appears to me to be well established law, but, except in the case of communications based on common interest, the principle is that either there must be interest in the recipient and a duty to communicate in the speaker, or an interest to be protected in the speaker and a duty to protect it in the recipient. Except in the case of common interest justifying intercommunication, the correspondence must be between duty and interest. There may, in the common interest cases, be also a common or reciprocal duty. It is not every interest which will create a duty in a stranger or volunteer.

[**Note**: Scrutton LJ summarized the situations where privilege arises:]
... either (1) a duty to communicate information believed to be true to a person who has a material interest in receiving the information, or (2) an interest in the speaker to be protected by communicating information, if true, relevant to that interest, to a person honestly believed to have a duty to protect that interest, and (3) a common interest in and reciprocal duty in respect of the subject matter of the communication between speaker and recipient ... . In my opinion Horridge J went too far in holding that there could be a privileged occasion on the ground of interest in the recipient

without any duty to communicate on the part of the person making the communication. But that does not settle the question, for it is necessary to consider, in the present case, whether there was, as to each communication, a duty to communicate, and an interest in the recipient.

First as to the communication between Longsdon and Singer, I think the case must proceed on the admission that at all material times Watt, Longsdon and Browne were in the employment of the same company, and the evidence afforded by the answer to the interrogatory put in by the plaintiff that Longsdon believed the statements in Browne's letter. In my view on these facts there was a duty, both from a moral and a material point of view, on Longsdon to communicate the letter to Singer, the chairman of his company, who, apart from questions of present employment, might be asked by Watt for a testimonial to a future employer. Equally, I think Longsdon receiving the letter from Browne, might discuss the matter with him, and ask for further information, on the ground of a common interest in the affairs of the company, and to obtain further information for the chairman. I should therefore agree with the view of Horridge J that these two occasions were privileged, though for different reasons ... .

The communication to Mrs Watt stands on a different footing. I have no intention of writing an exhaustive treatise on the circumstances when a stranger or a friend should communicate to husband or wife information he receives as to the conduct of the other party to the marriage. I am clear that it is impossible to say he is always under a moral or social duty to do so; it is equally impossible to say he is never under such a duty. It must depend on the circumstances of each case, the nature of the information, and the relation of speaker and recipient. It cannot, on the one hand, be the duty even of a friend to communicate all the gossip the friend hears at men's clubs or women's bridge parties to one of the spouses affected. On the other hand, most men would hold that it was the moral duty of a doctor who attended his sister in law, and believed her to be suffering from a miscarriage, for which an absent husband could not be responsible, to communicate that fact to his wife and the husband ... . If this is so, the decision must turn on the circumstances of each case, the judge being much influenced by the consideration that as a general rule it is not desirable for any one, even a mother in law, to interfere in the affairs of man and wife. Using the best judgment I can in this difficult matter, I have come to the conclusion that there was not a moral or social duty in Longsdon to make this communication to Mrs Watt such as to make the occasion privileged, and that there must be a new trial so far as it relates to the claim for publication of a libel to Mrs Watt.

Notes

1 Although the communications with Singer and Browne were privileged, the other judges in the Court of Appeal thought that there was evidence of malice and thus a new trial was ordered.

2 The case in no way discloses how the Moroccan correspondent, Browne, came to write his letter to Longsdon. Browne could have been honestly mistaken, he could have been bent on malevolent destruction of Watt, or perhaps his communication was accurate, but the defendant was unable to procure proof from Morocco.

3 What could Longsdon have done, instead of showing the letter to Mrs Watt, to fulfil what he perceived to be a moral duty to her? Would it make any difference if Mrs Watt had come to Longsdon asking if he had heard any rumours about her husband?

4   The leading case in this area, much discussed in the principal case, is *Adam v Ward* [1917] AC 309. In that case, a former army officer turned MP (Adam) made a speech in Parliament attacking, in a defamatory way, his former superior officer. Adam, at the time, was, of course, protected by parliamentary privilege. The Army investigated Adam's charges, refuted them, and then published their findings, obliquely defaming Adam in the process. In his appeal to the House of Lords, Adam argued that although the findings of the Army investigation might be privileged, that privilege was lost when the Army issued them to the press. The House of Lords was alive to the point of excessive distribution, but denied the appeal, on the grounds, first that Adam's original attack had the widest possible publication, and it was only fair to communicate in kind, and second, that those who are attacked can sometimes best defend their own character by attacking the character of the original attackers.

5   Suppose a ship's officer writes to a friend about the drunken, dangerous habits of the ship's captain. The friend gives the letter to the owner of the ship, who fires the captain. The captain sues the friend, who is unable to justify the allegations of drunkenness and poor seamanship, but who claims qualified privilege. What would the result be? See *Coxhead v Richards* (1846) 2 CB 569; 135 ER 1069.

6   The police in Edinburgh, after investigating some thefts in a local hotel, write to their counterparts in Newcastle, where Stanley, an explorer-writer on a lecture tour, had gone after leaving Edinburgh. They suspect Stanley's servant, Stuart. The Newcastle police show the letter to the mayor (Bell), who makes the decision to show the letter to Stanley, who fires Stuart. Stuart sues the mayor. What was the result? See *Stuart v Bell* [1891] 2 QB 341. Does it make a difference that Stanley and Stuart were guests in Bell's house?

7   Longsdon was privileged to communicate Browne's letter to Mr Singer, but not to Mrs Watt. Why does Singer, as chairman of the company, have a greater interest in an employee's off-the-job behaviour than the employee's wife? Does Singer have a legitimate interest in his employees' private lives? Could Singer dismiss an employee, otherwise competent, because of a sinful private life?

8   The case of *Templeton v Jones* [1984] 1 NZLR 448 (CA), discussed earlier in the context of truth, also includes a determination concerning qualified privilege. Cooke J, in the Court of Appeal, agreed with the lower courts in striking out the defence of qualified privilege. As already discussed, Mr Templeton made numerous attacks upon Mr Jones's personality under the coined phrase of 'politics of hatred'. Nevertheless, qualified privilege failed as a defence. Cooke J concluded his judgment by stating (at pp 459–60):

> As the common law of New Zealand stands it is plain enough that the mere fact that the plaintiff was a declared parliamentary candidate cannot be treated as imposing on the defendant a social or moral duty to make a defamatory statement about him to the general public. And, for the reasons already explained, we do not think that it would be right to enlarge the common law of New Zealand so as to create a new privilege ...

9   The decision that the occasion Templeton used was not privileged is consistent with an earlier leading decision, *Truth v Holloway* [1960] NZLR 69 (CA). A newspaper had run a story accusing a Cabinet Minister, Phil Holloway, of manipulating the import licensing system. The story quoted one Judd as saying 'see Phil and Phil would fix it'. The Court of Appeal said 'there is no principle of law, and certainly no case that we know of, which may be invoked in support of the contention that a newspaper can claim privilege if it publishes a defamatory statement of fact about an individual merely because the general topic developed in the article is a matter of public interest'. The Privy Council decision at [1961] NZLR 22, while not dealing directly with privilege, commented on the fact that the offensive words were a report of what someone else had said (p 26):

> If Judd did use the words attributed to him, it might be a slander by Judd of Mr Holloway in the way of his office as a Minister of the Crown. But if the words had not been repeated by the newspaper, the damage done by Judd would be as nothing compared to the damage done by the newspaper when it repeated it. It broadcast the statement to the people at large: and it made it worse by making it one of the grounds on which it called for an inquiry, for thereby it suggested that some credence was to be given to it.

Malice

[At common law, the defence of privilege and probably the defence of fair comment were defeated if the plaintiff could prove that the defendant was motivated by 'malice'. Malice is now irrelevant in New Zealand to the defence of honest opinion: s 10(3), Defamation Act 1992. A statutory version of malice is, however, preserved for qualified privilege: see s 19 set out above.

In order to understand the possible effect of s 19, it is useful to understand what malice meant at common law. *Horrocks v Lowe* provides a good commentary on common law malice considerations.]

Horrocks v Lowe
[1975] AC 135 (HL)
[**FACTS**: This case involved a dispute between Horrocks, a Conservative borough councillor, and Lowe, a Labour councillor. Horrocks's company had sold the Council some land subject to a restrictive covenant against building on it. The Council later leased the land to the Conservative Club which proceeded to erect a club house. After the existence of the covenant had been brought to everyone's attention, the Council accepted liability for finding an alternative site for the club. Horrocks had been a member of the relevant Council committee which had handled the matter but had absented himself when the matter was discussed. Lowe later made a speech at a meeting of the Council in which he accused Horrocks of brinkmanship, megalomania, and childish petulance, and of misleading the committee, his party leader, and his political and club colleagues.

The trial judge found that Lowe was not actuated by personal spite towards Horrocks, but had not fairly and objectively considered whether the evidence justified the comments.]
Lord Diplock:
... So, the motive with which the defendant on a privileged occasion made a statement defamatory of the plaintiff becomes crucial. The protection might, however, be illusory if the onus lay on him to prove that he was actuated solely by a sense of the

relevant duty or a desire to protect the relevant interest. So he is entitled to be protected by the privilege unless some other dominant and improper motive on his part is proved. 'Express malice' is the term of art descriptive of such a motive. Broadly speaking, it means malice in the popular sense of a desire to injure the person who is defamed and this is generally the motive which the plaintiff sets out to prove. But to destroy the privilege the desire to injure must be the dominant motive for the defamatory publication's knowledge that it will have that effect is not enough if the defendant is nevertheless acting in accordance with a sense of duty or in bona fide protection of his own legitimate interests.

The motive with which a person published defamatory matter can only be inferred from what he did or said or knew. If it be proved that he did not believe that what he published was true this is generally conclusive evidence of express malice, for no sense of duty or desire to protect his own legitimate interests can justify a man in telling deliberate and injurious falsehoods about another, save in the exceptional case where a person may be under a duty to pass on, without endorsing, defamatory reports made by some other person.

Apart from those exceptional cases, what is required on the part of the defamer to entitle him to the protection of the privilege is positive belief in the truth of what he published or, as it is generally though tautologously termed, 'honest belief'. If he publishes untrue defamatory matter recklessly, without considering or caring whether it be true or not, he is still in this, as in other branches of the law, treated as if he knew it to be false. But indifference to the truth of what he publishes is not to be equated with carelessness, impulsiveness or irrationality in arriving at a positive belief that it is true. The freedom of speech protected by the law of qualified privilege may be availed of by all sorts and conditions of men. In affording to them immunity from suit if they have acted in good faith in compliance with a legal or moral duty or in protection of a legitimate interest the law must take them as it finds them. In ordinary life it is rare indeed for people to form their beliefs by a process of logical deduction from facts ascertained by a rigorous search for all available evidence and a judicious assessment of its probative value. In greater or in less degree according to their temperaments, their training, their intelligence, they are swayed by prejudice, rely on intuition instead of reasoning, leap to conclusions on inadequate evidence and fail to recognise the cogency of material which might cast doubt on the validity of the conclusions they reach. But despite the imperfection of the mental process by which the belief is arrived at it may still be 'honest', that is, a positive belief that the conclusions they have reached are true. The law demands no more.

Even a positive belief in the truth of what is published on a privileged occasion—which is presumed unless the contrary is proved—may not be sufficient to negative express malice if it can be proved that the defendant misused the occasion for some purpose other than that for which the privilege is accorded by the law. The commonest case is where the dominant motive which actuates the defendant is not a desire to perform the relevant duty or to protect the relevant interest, but to give vent to his personal spite or ill-will towards the person he defames. If this be proved, then even positive belief in the truth of what is published will not enable the defamer to avail himself of the protection of the privilege to which he would otherwise have been entitled. There may be instances of improper motives which destroy the privilege apart from personal spite. A defendant's dominant motive may have been to obtain some private advantage unconnected with the duty or the interest which constitutes the reason for the privilege. If so, he loses the benefit of the privilege despite his positive belief that what he said or wrote was true.

Judges and juries should, however, be very slow to draw the inference that a defendant was so far actuated by improper motives as to deprive him of the protection of the privilege unless they are satisfied that he did not believe that what he said or wrote was true or that he was indifferent to its truth or falsity. The motives with which human beings act are mixed. They find it difficult to hate the sin but love the sinner. Qualified privilege would be illusory, and the public interest that it is meant to serve defeated, if the protection which it affords were lost merely because a person, although acting in compliance with a duty or in protection of a legitimate interest, disliked the person whom he defamed or was indignant at what he believed to be that person's conduct and welcomed the opportunity of exposing it. It is only where his desire to comply with the relevant duty or to protect the relevant interest plays no significant part in his motives for publishing what he believes to be true that 'express malice' can properly be found.

There may be evidence of the defendant's conduct upon occasions other than that protected by the privilege which justify the inference that upon the privileged occasion too his dominant motive in publishing what he did was personal spite or some other improper motive, even although he believed it to be true. But where, as in the instant case, conduct extraneous to the privileged occasion itself is not relied on, and the only evidence of improper motive is the content of the defamatory matter itself or the steps taken by the defendant to verify its accuracy, there is only one exception to the rule that in order to succeed the plaintiff must show affirmatively that the defendant did not believe it to be true or was indifferent to its truth or falsity. Juries should be instructed and judges should remind themselves that this burden of affirmative proof is not one that is lightly satisfied.

The exception is where what is published incorporates defamatory matter that is not really necessary to the fulfilment of the particular duty or the protection of the particular interest upon which the privilege is founded ... .

My Lords, what is said by members of a local council at meetings of the council or of any of its committees is spoken on a privileged occasion. The reason for the privilege is that those who represent the local government electors should be able to speak freely and frankly, boldly and bluntly, on any matter which they believe affects the interests or welfare of the inhabitants. They may be swayed by strong political prejudice, they may be obstinate and pig-headed, stupid and obtuse; but they were chosen by the electors to speak their minds on matters of local concern and so long as they do so honestly they run no risk of liability for defamation of those who are the subjects of their criticism.

In the instant case Mr Lowe's speech at the meeting of the Bolton Borough Council was upon matters which were undoubtedly of local concern. With one minor exception, the only facts relied upon as evidence from which express malice was to be inferred had reference to the contents of the speech itself, the circumstances in which the meeting of the council was held and the material relating to the subject matter of Mr Lowe's speech which was within his actual knowledge or available to him on inquiry. The one exception was his failure to apologise to Mr Horrocks when asked to do so two days later. A refusal to apologise is at best but tenuous evidence of malice, for it is consistent with a continuing belief in the truth of what one has said ... .

However prejudiced the judge thought Mr Lowe to be, however irrational in leaping to conclusions unfavourable to Mr Horrocks, this crucial finding of Mr Lowe's belief in the truth of what he said upon that privileged occasion entitles him to succeed in his defence of privilege.

Notes

1　How would this case be decided under the Defamation Act 1992? Could it be argued that Lowe was motivated by political gain and opportunism and therefore took improper advantage of the occasion? Does the improper advantage have to be the predominant motivation? What if Lowe had been partly motivated by personal antipathy towards Horrocks but at the same time had been (misguidedly) driven to expose a public scandal?

2　In *Brooks v Muldoon* [1973] 1 NZLR 1, the defendant, among other things, quoted the plaintiff as saying, 'it is not irresponsible for teachers to take direct action, it's their duty', when in fact the plaintiff had said, 'it is not irresponsible for teachers to take direct action. It's their duty to draw parents' attention to the poor deal children are getting'. The defendant explained the misquotation as a pure oversight. The Court held that there was therefore no evidence of malice. Could it be argued that Muldoon's carelessness amounts to otherwise taking improper advantage of the occasion under s 19?

3　Section 19 does not expressly refer to dishonesty. Does the defendant who knew that what was said was false fall within s 19?

Reynolds v Times Newspapers Ltd

[1999] 3 WLR 1010; [1999] 4 All ER 609 (HL)

[**FACTS**: Mr Reynolds announced to the Dáil, the Irish Parliament, on Thursday, 17 November 1994, that he was to resign as Taoiseach (prime minister) of Ireland and leader of the Fianna Fáil party. Mr Reynolds was closely associated and identified with the Northern Ireland peace process and his resignation was of immense public interest and significance. On Sunday, 20 November, the *Sunday Times* published the article entitled 'Goodbye gombeen man' in its British mainland edition (an Irish edition, published after this differed significantly from the British version). The article was subheaded 'Why a fib too far proved fatal for the political career of Ireland's peacemaker and Mr Fixit'.

In response, Mr Reynolds issued libel proceedings. Mr Reynolds pleaded that the sting of the article was that:

(a) He had deliberately and dishonestly misled the Dáil by deliberately suppressing vital information.

(b) He had deliberately and dishonestly misled his coalition cabinet colleagues by withholding this information and had lied to them about when the information had come into his possession.

At trial, Mr Reynolds received judgment for one penny. Justification and qualified privilege both failed as defences. Both parties appealed, with the Court of Appeal holding that the cumulative effects of the misdirections identified were such as to deny Mr Reynolds a fair trial. The order was set aside, and a new trial ordered. A further issue was whether the defendants would be able to rely on qualified privilege at the retrial. They held that the defendants could not. The defendants then appealed to the House of Lords for determination upon the qualified privilege issue alone.]

Lord Nicholls of Birkenhead:

… My starting point is freedom of expression. The high importance of freedom to impart and receive information and ideas has been stated so often and so eloquently that this point calls for no elaboration in this case. At a pragmatic level, freedom to disseminate and receive information on political matters is essential to the proper functioning of the system of parliamentary democracy cherished in this country. This freedom enables those who elect representatives to Parliament to make informed decisions. Freedom of expression will shortly be buttressed by statutory requirements. Under section 12 of the Human Rights Act 1998, expected to come into force in October 2000, the court is required, in relevant cases, to have particular regard to the importance of the right to freedom of expression. The common law is to be developed and applied in a manner consistent with article 10 of the European Convention for the Protection of Human Rights (sections 6 and 2). To be justified, any curtailment of freedom of expression must be convincingly established by a compelling countervailing consideration, and the means employed must be proportionate to the end sought to be achieved.

Likewise, there is no need to elaborate on the importance of the role discharged by the media in the expression and communication of information and comment on political matters. It is through the mass media that most people today obtain their information on political matters. Without freedom of expression by the media, freedom of expression would be a hollow concept. The interest of a democratic society in ensuring a free press weighs heavily in the balance in deciding whether any curtailment of this freedom bears a reasonable relationship to the purpose of the curtailment. In this regard it should be kept in mind that one of the contemporary functions of the media is investigative journalism. This activity, as much as the traditional activities of reporting and commenting, is part of the vital role of the press and the media generally.

Reputation is an integral and important part of the dignity of the individual. It also forms the basis of many decisions in a democratic society which are fundamental to its well-being: whom to employ or work for, whom to promote, whom to do business with or to vote for. Once besmirched by an unfounded allegation in a national newspaper, a reputation can be damaged forever, especially if there is no opportunity to vindicate one's reputation. When this happens, society as well as the individual is the loser. For it should not be supposed that protection of reputation is a matter of importance only to the affected individual and his family. Protection of reputation is conducive to the public good. It is in the public interest that the reputation of public figures should not be debased falsely. In the political field, in order to make an informed choice, the electorate needs to be able to identify the good as well as the bad. Consistently with these considerations, human rights conventions recognise that freedom of expression is not an absolute right. Its exercise may be subject to such restrictions as are prescribed by law and are necessary in a democratic society for the protection of the reputations of others.

The crux of this appeal, therefore, lies in identifying the restrictions which are fairly and reasonably necessary for the protection of reputation. Leaving aside the exceptional cases which attract absolute privilege, the common law denies protection to defamatory statements, whether of comment or fact, proved to be actuated by malice, in the *Horrocks v Lowe* [1975] AC 135 sense. This common law limitation on freedom of speech passes the 'necessary' test with flying colours. This is an acceptable limitation. Freedom of speech does not embrace freedom to make defamatory statements out of personal spite or without having a positive belief in their truth ...

Conclusion

My conclusion is that the established common law approach to misstatements of fact remains essentially sound. The common law should not develop 'political information' as a new 'subject matter' category of qualified privilege, whereby the publication of all such information would attract qualified privilege, whatever the circumstances. That would not provide adequate protection for reputation. Moreover, it would be unsound in principle to distinguish political discussion from discussion of other matters of serious public concern. The elasticity of the common law principle enables interference with freedom of speech to be confined to what is necessary in the circumstances of the case. This elasticity enables the court to give appropriate weight, in today's conditions, to the importance of freedom of expression by the media on all matters of public concern.

Depending on the circumstances, the matters to be taken into account include the following. The comments are illustrative only. 1. The seriousness of the allegation. The more serious the charge, the more the public is misinformed and the individual harmed, if the allegation is not true. 2. The nature of the information, and the extent to which the subject matter is a matter of public concern. 3. The source of the information. Some informants have no direct knowledge of the events. Some have their own axes to grind, or are being paid for their stories. 4. The steps taken to verify the information. 5. The status of the information. The allegation may have already been the subject of an investigation which commands respect. 6. The urgency of the matter. News is often a perishable commodity. 7. Whether comment was sought from the plaintiff. He may have information others do not possess or have not disclosed. An approach to the plaintiff will not always be necessary. 8. Whether the article contained the gist of the plaintiff's side of the story. 9. The tone of the article. A newspaper can raise queries or call for an investigation. It need not adopt allegations as statements of fact. 10. The circumstances of the publication, including the timing.

The list is not exhaustive. The weight to be given to these and any other relevant factors will vary from case to case. Any disputes of primary fact will be a matter for the jury, if there is one. The decision on whether, having regard to the admitted or proved facts, the publication was subject to qualified privilege is a matter for the judge. This is the established practice and seems sound. A balancing operation is better carried out by a judge in a reasoned argument than by a jury. Over time, a valuable corpus of case law will be built up.

In general, a newspaper's unwillingness to disclose the identity of its sources should not weigh against it. Further, it should always be remembered that journalists act without the benefit of the clear light of hindsight. Matters which are obvious in retrospect may have been far from clear in the heat of the moment. Above all, the court should have particular regard to the importance of the freedom of expression. The press discharges vital functions as a bloodhound as well as a watchdog. The court should be slow to conclude that a publication was not in the public interest and, therefore, the public had no right to know, especially when the information is in the field of political discussion. Any lingering doubts should be resolved in favour of the publication ... .

I would dismiss this appeal.

Notes

A key finding was that no generic privilege existed for political commentary. The House of Lords concluded, by a slim majority of three to two, that, on the facts, Times Newspapers Ltd was not entitled to a qualified privilege defence. Lord Nicholls of Birkenhead carefully laid down his ten-point qualified privilege test. He then applied the test to the particular situation at hand, citing numerous factual errors. These included a failure to provide Reynolds' explanation in the newspaper report, the unreliability of the sources, and a failure to include a balanced report. One of the majority judges was Lord Cooke, the New Zealand judge in *Templeton v Jones.*

The **Lange** *saga—timeline of events*

→ October 1995—Column published in *North and South* magazine, which is owned by Australian Consolidated Press. The author of the column was Joe Atkinson. It was highly critical of David Lange's performance as Prime Minister. Proceedings were issued soon after the article was published.

→ 24 February 1997—Elias J delivered judgment in the High Court. Judgment highlighted the importance of s 14 of the New Zealand Bill of Rights Act 1990—*Lange v Atkinson* [1997] 2 NZLR 22. Judgment appealed. Preliminary points only.

→ 25 May 1998—Court of Appeal delivered its first judgment in the *Lange* case. The judges set down a five-point analysis for determining an occasion of privilege—*Lange v Atkinson* [1998] 3 NZLR 424. Appealed to Privy Council.

→ 28 October 1999—House of Lords delivered judgment in *Reynolds v Times Newspapers Ltd* [1999] 3 WLR 1010. Lord Nicholls established a ten-point list of factors to illustrate whether qualified privilege will exist. The same day, the Privy Council sent *Lange* back to the New Zealand Court of Appeal for reconsideration in light of *Reynolds*. Their Lordships were careful to say that the decision in the New Zealand context was for the Court of Appeal—*Lange v Atkinson* [2000] 1 NZLR 257.

→ 21 June 2000—Court of Appeal delivered its second judgment, considering the decision of *Reynolds* in light of the New Zealand context. It chose to reaffirm its earlier analysis, with the addition of a sentence to create a six-step test—*Lange v Atkinson* [2000] 3 NZLR 385.

→ 13 December 2000—David Lange withdrew the defamation suit.

Lange v Atkinson
[2000] 3 NZLR 385 (CA)
Judgment of the Court:
Introduction

[1] In its judgment delivered on 28 October 1999 ([2000] 1 NZLR 257), the Privy Council set aside the decision of this Court reported at [1998] 3 NZLR 424 and remitted the appeal from the judgment of Elias J [1997] 2 NZLR 22 for rehearing. In so doing their Lordships observed that they considered this Court would wish to take into account the decision of the House of Lords in *Reynolds v Times Newspapers Ltd* [1999] 3 WLR 1010 delivered on the same day and by the same Judges as those who sat in the Privy Council in the present case. Their Lordships amplified this remission by saying:

> Their Lordships emphasise that they do not suggest that at the further hearing the New Zealand courts are bound to adopt either the English or the Australian solutions. Nor do they seek to influence the New Zealand courts towards either of these solutions. If satisfied that the privilege favoured in the judgment now under appeal is right for New Zealand, although wider than has been held acceptable in either England or Australia, the New Zealand Court of Appeal is entitled to maintain that position. Nevertheless, in the light of the comparative case law which has now emerged, including the clarification of the English common law in *Reynolds*, their Lordships think it appropriate to give the New Zealand Court of Appeal the opportunity to reconsider the issue. After all, the three countries are all parliamentary democracies with a common origin. Whether the differences in details of their constitutional structure and relevant statute law have any truly significant bearing on the scope of qualified privilege for political discussion is among the aspects calling for consideration.

[2] Earlier in the judgment, following a review of recent judgments, their Lordships had said this:

> Against this somewhat kaleidoscopic background, one feature of all the judgments, New Zealand, Australian and English, stands out with conspicuous clarity: the recognition that striking a balance between freedom of expression and protection of reputation calls for a value judgment which depends upon local political and social conditions. These conditions include matters such as the responsibility and vulnerability of the press. In their Lordships' view, subject to one point mentioned later, this feature is determinative of the present appeal. For some years their Lordships' Board has recognised the limitations on its role as an appellate tribunal in cases where the decision depends upon considerations of local public policy. The present case is a prime instance of such a case. As noted by Elias J and the Court of Appeal, different countries have reached different conclusions on the issue arising on this appeal. The Courts of New Zealand are much better placed to assess the requirements of the public interest in New Zealand than their Lordships' Board. Accordingly, on this issue the Board does not substitute its own views, if different, for those of the New Zealand Court of Appeal. ([2000] 1 NZLR 257, 261–2)

...

[4] The 'one point' referred to in the passage quoted in para [2] above which the Privy Council identified as standing in the way of deference to this Court's assessment of local public policy arose from the later decisions of the English Court of Appeal and the House of Lords in the *Reynolds* case. The New Zealand courts which had undertaken an analysis of the English law had not had the advantage of those decisions. While English case law is by no means determinative, an appraisal of that law is

> an important part of the background against which the Courts in New Zealand are assessing the best way forward on this important and difficult point of the common law. This is not surprising. Even on issues of local public policy, every jurisdiction can benefit from examinations of an issue undertaken by others. Interaction between the jurisdictions can help to clarify and refine the issues and the available options, without prejudicing national autonomy. ([2000] 1 NZLR 257, 263)

...

[8] Three matters arise at the outset. First, as earlier noted in its 1998 decision this Court was primarily concerned with the issue of whether it was appropriate to recognise that an extension should be made to the common law defence of qualified privilege to cover political discussion to a wide, possibly nationwide, audience. It decided that it was appropriate, a course which had already been accepted in Australia, and has now also been accepted in England. In the last few years the High Court of Australia was the first to address the issue of political discussion in *Lange v Australian Broadcasting Corporation*. Next came this Court in the present case, and then the House of Lords in *Reynolds*. Each country has recognised a new occasion or the potential for a new occasion of qualified privilege for communications made in the course of political discussion. In each case it is envisaged that the occasion may be one in which the communication is made to the public at large, thereby removing any capacity for the defence to be defeated by excess of publication. The compass of the subject matter seen as giving rise or capable of giving rise to the privilege is not the same in the three countries. In the United Kingdom the subject matter is widely defined, but the focus is directed particularly to the position of a national newspaper. In Australia the subject matter relates essentially to the conduct of politicians, both in that country and elsewhere. In New Zealand the subject matter is tightly defined, but its application is to all manner of publications. It is primarily the definition of the controls governing the extension which has given rise to differences of approach.

[9] In our 1998 decision we reviewed decisions about publications on political matters given by courts in Canada, the United States and Europe, as well as those of Australia and the United Kingdom. To this can be added decisions from South Africa (such as *National Media Ltd v Bogoshi* 1998 (4) SA 1196), India (such as *Raja Gopal v State of Tamil Nadu AIR* 1995 SC 264) and Pakistan (such as *Majid Nazami v Muhammad Rashid PLD* 1996 Lahore 410). Those cases demonstrate two things among others. The first is the critical importance accorded to freedom of speech in respect of political matters in many countries and the second the different balances which are struck in different countries according to different assessments of the competing principles, rights and interests.

[10] Secondly, it is necessary to re-state what this Court did decide in 1998. Following a lengthy survey of the development and characteristics of qualified privilege, the comparative experience (including the relevant international human rights law), freedom of expression in its wider context, the choice between court decision and legislation, the New Zealand constitutional context and the freedom of expression provision of the New Zealand Bill of Rights, the Court came to this conclusion:

(a) *Political statements may be protected by qualified privilege*

Our consideration of the development of the law leads us to the following conclusions about the defence of qualified privilege as it applies to political statements which are published generally:

(1) The defence of qualified privilege may be available in respect of a statement which is published generally.

(2) The nature of New Zealand's democracy means that the wider public may have a proper interest in respect of generally published statements which directly concern the functioning of representative and responsible government, including statements about the performance or possible future performance of specific individuals in elected public office.

(3) In particular, a proper interest does exist in respect of statements made about the actions and qualities of those currently or formerly elected to Parliament and those with immediate aspirations to such office, so far as those actions and qualities directly affect or affected their capacity (including their personal ability and willingness) to meet their public responsibilities.

(4) The determination of the matters which bear on that capacity will depend on a consideration of what is properly a matter of public concern rather than of private concern.

(5) The width of the identified public concern justifies the extent of the publication.

...

[12] The five conclusions stated in the 1998 judgment are to be read as a whole. They proceed from the first conclusion that the general publication of a statement does not of itself defeat the defence (as a survey of judgments and legislation at 442–50 had already shown). The second, based on the discussion of the New Zealand constitutional system, along with the discussion of freedom of expression in its wider context (462–5 and 460–2), is more focussed: the wider public may have a proper interest, supporting the defence, in respect of generally published statements which directly concern the functioning of representative and responsible government. The final phrase of that conclusion—'the performance or possible future performance of specific individuals in elected public office'—leads directly into the third conclusion which is to be read in the context of the previous two. The proper interest does exist and the defence is accordingly capable of applying to the statements identified in that conclusion so long as those statements directly concern the functioning of representative and responsible government. The fourth conclusion is a further essential element. It is only those matters which are properly of public concern that are protected. The assessment

of the occasion to see whether it establishes the privilege must address that issue, along with the contextual elements indicated in the second conclusion.

[13] Thirdly, it should be made clear that the five-point conclusion earlier quoted was not intended to remove from the assessment whether the occasion is privileged an inquiry into the circumstances or context of the publication. Conclusion no. 3 confirmed that statements within those parameters are those in which the wider public has a legitimate interest. Ordinarily it can be expected such a statement will warrant protection, but it is still necessary to take into account the circumstances of publication. Those circumstances will include such matters as the identity of the publisher, the context in which the publication occurs, and the likely audience, as well as the actual content of the information. As an example of circumstances where the subject matter may not be determinative, it is questionable whether a one-line reference to alleged misconduct of a grave nature on the part of a parliamentary candidate reflecting on his or her suitability, appearing in an article in a motoring magazine about that person's activities in motor sport, should receive protection. By contrast, the inclusion of such material in the course of a lengthy serious article on a coming election may justifiably attract the protection ... .

The concept of an occasion of privilege

[18] All occasions of qualified privilege are derived either from statute or from the common law. The original concept was born of a recognition that it was not always right to presume malice from the publication of false and defamatory words. In some circumstances malice could not reasonably be presumed; these circumstances became known as occasions of qualified privilege. The occasion was privileged unless actual malice could be shown. As the common law developed, a unifying principle emerged by which the most commonly occurring circumstances capable of amounting to such occasions could be recognised. That principle was the familiar duty/interest test which was expressed by Lord Atkinson in *Adam v Ward* [1917] AC 309, 334 in this way:

> Such a privileged occasion is ... an occasion where the person who makes a communication has an interest or a duty, legal, social, or moral, to make it to the person to whom it is made, and the person to whom it is so made has a corresponding interest or duty to receive it.

...

[20] A privileged occasion thus had to be an occasion in which the duty/interest test was satisfied. If in the circumstances that test was satisfied, the occasion was capable of being regarded as one of qualified privilege. But despite a communication being made between persons who might in other circumstances have a shared interest in the subject matter it could happen that the maker and recipients of the statement did not in the particular circumstance of the publication have the necessary interest or duty to satisfy what we are calling the shared interest test.

[21] That is where there is a need for amplification of our earlier conclusions. A statement the subject matter of which qualifies for protection is not by dint of that fact alone always made on an occasion of privilege. Ordinarily that will be so because the shared interest test is likely to be satisfied. But there may be times when a communication within that subject matter will not be made on an occasion of qualified privilege,

because there is in the particular circumstances no shared interest in the particular communication between its maker and recipients. To revert to the example given in para [13], a statement in the form of a gratuitous slur upon a politician in a publication concerned with a quite different topic could not sensibly be regarded as having been made on an occasion of privilege. This requirement for the occasion to qualify, as well as the subject matter, may sometimes lead to difficulties at the margins, but in reality there is likely to be comparatively little uncertainty in this area. Any bona fide communication in the course of political discussion and within the defined subject matter is very likely to be made on an occasion of qualified privilege. The possibility of the occasion not attracting privilege is unlikely to cause difficulty for news media organisations, or indeed others who are engaged in genuine political discussion. Such possibility, and the small level of uncertainty it may cause, is a necessary price to pay to guard reputations against false imputations made on occasions which are outside the purpose of the privilege; albeit within its literal subject matter.

[22] This amplification of our earlier formulation is necessary because, taken in isolation, paragraph 3 of our five-point conclusion (see para [10]) could be read, and may indeed have been read, as suggesting that a communication within the qualifying subject matter will always attract qualified privilege. The surrounding points do not themselves indicate the complete picture, which involves not only qualifying subject matter but also a qualifying occasion. The fact that ordinarily a communication within the qualifying subject matter will be made on a qualifying occasion may also have masked the need for the occasion to qualify. It is to be noted however that the heading to this part of the judgment at 467 reads—'political statements *may* be protected by qualified privilege' (emphasis added). The point is, as that mode of expression implies, that whereas in terms of point 3 a shared interest 'does' exist, it does not inevitably do so on all occasions ... .

New Zealand's constitutional structure and relevant statute law
[26] In 1998 this Court mentioned three major features of New Zealand's constitutional and political system ([1998] 3 NZLR 424, 462–5). The Privy Council asks this Court to address the differences between our system and the United Kingdom and Australian systems (para [1]). The three countries share the main relevant features of a parliamentary democracy, based on universal suffrage, with a government which is responsible to Parliament and, through it, to the electorate, and which is subject to the law. There are however major differences in the electoral systems. In particular only the New Zealand system enables each voter to vote on an equal nationwide basis for the party which the voter wishes to see in the House of Representatives and in the Government. As the Court said in 1998, the electoral system now recognises more directly than it had, the competition organised by and through political parties for the power of the state exercised through Parliament and the executive government ([1999] 3 NZLR 424, 463). By contrast, the general elections for the United Kingdom Parliament are still on a plurality, constituency by constituency basis. The limited movement towards partial proportionality as seen in the arrangements for Scotland and Wales and for European elections would not appear to be relevant to statements about candidates for and members of the United Kingdom Parliament, the equivalent situa-

tion to the present one. While the Australian electoral systems are more proportional than those of the United Kingdom, they too do not provide for voting on a national basis. In both countries of course the voting system tells only part of the story since in all three national elections are fought by parties on a country-wide basis.

[27] Freedom of information legislation was the second matter mentioned in the 1998 judgment. Here too there is a major distinction. While in New Zealand the Queen's papers have become the people's, in the United Kingdom they are still in the Queen's hands (or rather those of her Ministers and officials). United Kingdom law and practice relating to access to and release of information has yet to emphasise, in the way found here, the rights of citizens to participate in the process of policy and decision making and to call the government to account. Again, Australian state and federal legislation is closer to New Zealand's. The contrast is marked by the extensive and common release in New Zealand litigation of Cabinet and Ministerial documents.

[28] The third major matter in the 1998 judgment was the New Zealand Bill of Rights Act 1990 which as from October this year is to be matched by the United Kingdom Human Rights Act 1998. Australia, at the state and federal levels, has no comparable legislation. The New Zealand Act has a significantly narrower focus than the United Kingdom Act which gives effect to all the substantive provisions of the European Convention on Human Rights and certain of its protocols. As the Court said in 1998, the New Zealand Bill emphasises the protection of

> public processes, notably political processes, by its affirmation of the right to vote in genuine periodic elections of members of the House of Representatives by equal suffrage and to be a candidate, and the rights of freedom of expression … , freedom of assembly and freedom of association, and the right to justice. The central role of democracy is also emphasised in the recognition in s 5 that any limit on a recognised freedom has to be demonstrably justified in a free and democratic society. ([1998] 3 NZLR 424, 464).

…

[33] The Privy Council particularly mentioned differences between the responsibility and vulnerability of the media in New Zealand and in the United Kingdom (see para [2] above). On one view, this material is of limited significance since this case is less about the press and rather more about the constitutional right of all New Zealanders to participate in the discussion and evaluation of their own political leaders. That aspect of this case sharply distinguishes it from *Reynolds* and the Australian *Lange* case. The plaintiffs in those two cases were foreign politicians and accordingly would not fall within the conclusions this Court stated in 1998, as indeed the Privy Council recognised when referring to the ruling of the English Court of Appeal ([2000] 1 NZLR 257, 261).

[34] Generalisations in this area are dangerous but it is possible to say that New Zealand has not encountered the worst excesses and irresponsibilities of the English national daily tabloids. According to a New Zealand journalist in a publication issued by the Newspaper Publishers Association of New Zealand, 'some British tabloids have thrown away the rule book in their pursuit of sensational exclusives. Invasion of personal privacy, fabrication of interviews and the obtaining of information by dishonest

means have become the norm in the downmarket tabloid press'. Sir Douglas Graham, at the time the Minister of Justice, is quoted in the same publication as saying at the New Zealand Press Council's 20th anniversary that 'Compared to our British counterparts, media intrusion into our daily lives is rather tame, but I do not believe the standard of journalism is by any means inferior. If anything quite the contrary'. (Karl Du Fresne *Free Press Free Society* (1994) 26, 34.) The responsibility and vulnerability of the press are also critically dependent on the ethics and practices of the press, their ownership structures and the independence of the editorial function.

[35] The combination of the smallness of the population with the fact that the dailies are not national papers produces low circulation figures. In 1998 the largest circulation of a New Zealand daily was about 220 000 and the other 27 dailies had circulations from about 2400 to about 100 000 (*New Zealand Official Yearbook 1998* 257). Another consequence of the regional character of the dailies is that there is not the same competition that can arise, and has arisen, in the United Kingdom between national papers. The three weekly publications which contain extensive commentary on political matters have circulations of about 10 000 and 14 000 (two business weeklies) and about 90 000 (*The Listener*, which is also a television and radio guide). Two general monthly magazines which include serious political commentary have circulations of about 35 000 (*North & South*, the publication in issue in this case) and 18 000 (*Metro*). By contrast, five of the British dailies have circulations of about 1 000 000 or more with the highest being about 3 400 000. Another difference is that some of the British dailies have close associations with particular political parties; competing political positions are by contrast often expressed in the opinion pages of individual New Zealand dailies and weeklies … .

Concluding assessment

[37] The task of this Court is to consider whether the decision of the House of Lords in *Reynolds* leads us to make a different assessment of the competing considerations of the right to freedom of expression and the right to reputation from that which we made in 1998. As well, the Court has regard to the matters considered under the three preceding headings.

[38] For reasons which can be briefly restated we would not strike the balance differently from the way it was struck in 1998. First, the *Reynolds* decision appears to alter the structure of the law of qualified privilege in a way which adds to the uncertainty and chilling effect almost inevitably present in this area of law. We are not persuaded that in the New Zealand situation matters such as the steps taken to verify the information, the seeking of comment from the person defamed, and the status or source of the information, should fall within the ambit of the enquiry into whether the occasion is privileged. Traditionally such matters are not of concern to that question in the kind of setting presently under discussion. In particular, source and status may be relevant, but only in the area of reports of meetings and suchlike. For the reasons expressed in our earlier judgment, we do not consider it necessary, nor would it be in accord with principle, to import into this enquiry, for the limited purposes of the specific subject matter now under discussion but not otherwise, a specific requirement of reasonableness.

[39] The full scope of s 19 of the Defamation Act 1992 and its possible application to political discussion requires separate consideration, but as will be seen it can provide a measure of protection to or safeguard for a plaintiff which ought not to attract the restrictions sometimes applied to the common law concept of malice in this context. The idea of taking improper advantage of the occasion is important when one is considering the appropriate balance between freedom of expression and protection of reputation. Its connotations are potentially wider than the traditional concept of malice which included excess of publication and improper purpose. To that extent we are able to take a more expansive approach to defining an occasion of privilege because we have the ability in s 19 to take a correspondingly more expansive approach to what constitutes misuse of the occasion. One development is therefore capable of being matched by another so that the overall balance is kept right. The idea of taking improper advantage is appropriately applied to those who are reckless and thereby do not exhibit the necessary responsibility when purporting to act under the cloak of qualified privilege.

[40] Secondly, there are significant differences between the constitutional and political context in New Zealand and in the United Kingdom in which this body of law operates. They reflect societal differences. Thirdly, the position of the press in the two countries does appear to be significantly distinct. And, fourthly, this is an area of law in which Parliament has essentially left it to the courts to develop the governing principles and apply them to the evolving political, social and economic conditions.

[41] Our decision is to adhere to our previous conclusions and, in particular, to confirm the five-point summary (see paragraph [10] above) which we gave in our earlier judgments. A sixth point should be added to the summary to reflect what was previously implicit, but can be made explicit:

> (6) To attract privilege the statement must be published on a qualifying
> occasion.

Misuse of occasion of privilege

[42] Section 19 of the Defamation Act 1992 prevents reliance on qualified privilege if the defendant is predominantly motivated by ill will against the plaintiff or otherwise takes improper advantage of the occasion of publication. Although s 19 was designed to reflect the common law concept of malice, it has within it the same flexibility and room for development as did malice itself; particularly in its connotation of improper purpose. The purpose of the newly recognised privilege is to facilitate responsible public discussion of the matters which it covers. If the privilege is not responsibly used, its purpose is abused and improper advantage is taken of the occasion. The section is concerned with situations in which qualified privilege is lost. Occasions of privilege are both fact dependent and not limited by closed categories. Where the common law affords privilege to a particular occasion, s 19 must be applied to that occasion in an appropriate way, without any reading down of its terms.

[43] If a false and defamatory statement which qualifies for protection is made, and is disseminated to a wide audience, the motives of the publisher and whether the publisher had a genuine belief in the truth of the statement, will warrant close scrutiny. If

the publisher is unable or unwilling to disclose any responsible basis for asserting a genuine belief in truth, the jury may well be entitled to draw the inference that no such belief existed. In *Reynolds* Lord Steyn adverted to this risk at [1999] 3 WLR 1010, 1036. Furthermore, a publisher who is reckless or indifferent to the truth of what is published, cannot assert a genuine belief that it was true.

[44] At common law malice was presumed when the words published were false and defamatory. The presumption was however rebutted if the occasion was one of qualified privilege. The privilege could nevertheless be defeated if actual malice was proved by the plaintiff. What constituted malice was restated in *Horrocks v Lowe* [1975] AC 135, 149–50 by Lord Diplock, in what have since been regarded as authoritative terms. His reference in that restatement to carelessness, impulsiveness or irrationality not being equated to indifference, must be read in context. The proposition does not qualify the preceding statements which cover lack of genuine belief and recklessness. Thus while carelessness will not of itself be sufficient to negate the defence, its existence may well support an assertion by the plaintiff of a lack of belief or recklessness. In this way the concept of reasonable or responsible conduct on the part of a defendant in the particular circumstances becomes a legitimate consideration. It can also be said that in the context of political discussion an irrational belief in truth is seldom likely to feature. It is for example difficult to envisage reliance on such an argument when a newspaper is defending its publication of false and defamatory material.

[45] Recklessness as to truth has traditionally been treated as equivalent to knowledge of falsity; see for example *Fleming on Torts* (9th edn, 1998) at 639. Both deprive the defendant of qualified privilege. We note as a relevant analogy the recent approach of the House of Lords to recklessness when their Lordships were considering the tort of misfeasance in public office: see *Three Rivers District Council v Governor and Company of the Bank of England* (speeches 18 May 2000). In particular Lord Steyn, when citing from the judgment of Clarke J at first instance, approved the view that recklessness involves a lack of honesty in the exercise of the power in question. He added:

> This is an organic development, which fits into the structure of our law governing intentional torts. The policy underlying it is sound: reckless indifference to consequences is as blameworthy as deliberately seeking such consequences.

[46] By the same token, it may be said that reckless indifference to truth is almost as blameworthy as deliberately stating falsehoods. Lord Diplock gave a helpful description of recklessness in the present field when he spoke of someone who publishes defamatory material 'without considering or caring' whether it was true or false. Indifference to truth is, of course, not the same thing conceptually as failing to take reasonable care with the truth but in practical terms they tend to shade into each other. It is useful, when considering whether an occasion of qualified privilege has been misused, to ask whether the defendant has exercised the degree of responsibility which the occasion required.

[47] What constitutes recklessness is something which must take its colour from the nature of the occasion, and the nature of the publication. If it is reckless not 'to consider or care' whether a statement be true or false, as Lord Diplock indicated, it must be open to the view that a perfunctory level of consideration (against the substance,

gravity and width of the publication) can also be reckless. It is within the concept of misusing the occasion to say that the defendant may be regarded as reckless if there has been a failure to give such responsible consideration to the truth or falsity of the statement as the jury considers should have been given in all the circumstances. In essence the privilege may well be lost if the defendant takes what in all the circumstances can fairly be described as a cavalier approach to the truth of the statement.

[48] No consideration and insufficient consideration are equally capable of leading to an inference of misuse of the occasion. The rationale for loss of the privilege in such circumstances is that the privilege is granted on the basis that it will be responsibly used. There is no public interest in allowing defamatory statements to be made irresponsibly—recklessly—under the banner of freedom of expression. What amounts to a reckless statement must depend significantly on what is said and to whom and by whom. It must be accepted that to require the defendant to give such responsible consideration to the truth or falsity of the publication as is required by the nature of the allegation and the width of the intended dissemination, may in some circumstances come close to a need for the taking of reasonable care. In others a genuine belief in truth after relatively hasty and incomplete consideration may be sufficient to satisfy the dictates of the occasion and to avoid any inference of taking improper advantage of the occasion.

[49] A case at one end of the scale might be a grossly defamatory statement about a Cabinet Minister, broadcast to the world. At the other end might be an uncomplimentary observation about a politician at a private meeting held under Chatham House rules. It is not that the law values reputation more in the one case than the other. It is that in the first case the gravity of the allegation and the width of the publication are apt to cause much more harm if the allegation is false than in the second case. A greater degree of responsibility is therefore required in the first case than in the second, if recklessness is not to be inferred. Responsible journalists in whatever medium ought not to have any concerns about such an approach. It is only those who act irresponsibly in the jury's eyes by being cavalier about the truth who will lose the privilege. Such an approach reflects the fact that qualified privilege is not a licence to be irresponsible: see McKay J in *Television New Zealand Ltd v Quinn* [1996] 3 NZLR 24, 45 … .

The newspaper rule

[55] Although so described this is the rule which protects all sectors of the media from having to reveal their sources in interlocutory proceedings. The rule is designed to promote freedom of speech by allowing people to speak to the news media in confidence. It is matched by Rule 285 which prohibits interrogatories designed to elicit sources. At the trial the same subject is governed by s 35 of the Evidence Amendment Act (No. 2) 1980. The rule was affirmed by this Court in *Broadcasting Corporation of New Zealand v Alex Harvey Industries Ltd* [1980] 1 NZLR 163 on the basis that it applies unless there are special circumstances warranting a departure from it. Whether that basis for departure is too narrow (Woodhouse P saw the rule as being almost absolute) may require reconsideration on an appropriate occasion. Similarly the absoluteness of Rule 285 may require reassessment. At trial s 35 empowers the Court,

against specific statutory criteria, to balance the grounds for maintaining confidentiality against the need to do justice in the individual case. Section 35 was considered in some detail by this Court, albeit in a different contexts, in *M v L* [1999] 1 NZLR 747 and *R v H* CA38/00, judgment 28 March 2000.

[56] During the course of argument in the present case the question arose whether a news media defendant could rely on a defence of qualified privilege, while at the same time maintaining its reliance on the newspaper rule. On an occasion of qualified privilege the onus is of course on the plaintiff to demonstrate misuse of the occasion in terms of s 19 of the Defamation Act 1992. At issue may be the basis for an asserted belief in truth, or whether that belief was responsibly formed, but in any event the plaintiff is already at something of a disadvantage in having to establish the negative. We were pressed with the view that to allow a media defendant the benefit of both qualified privilege and the newspaper rule would be to place an unfair hurdle in the plaintiff's path. It is apparent that some of their Lordships in *Reynolds* were opposed to the qualified privilege sought by the newspaper in that case because of the difficulties which they considered the newspaper rule would create for plaintiffs.

[57] The whole question whether sources should be identified before trial is very much influenced by public policy as seen in the particular jurisdiction. Such policy is not immutable and both judicial and legislative reflections of it can change over time. The approach of this Court in the *Broadcasting Corporation* case and of the Rules Committee in Rule 285 should not therefore be regarded as set in stone. The relevant policy considerations must now recognise the ramifications of the extended range of qualified privilege as affirmed in this judgment ...

[58] It is neither necessary nor desirable to develop this point any further. It is not directly in issue; albeit raised as part of the argument about the existence and scope of the privilege in question. Nor did we have the benefit of any extended argument on the newspaper rule. It is sufficient to say we have kept the rule in mind, along with possible developments of it, in coming to our conclusions ...

Formal orders/costs

[60] It follows that on reconsideration this appeal cannot succeed. Amendments may be necessary to the statements of defence to reflect the law as now stated. But there is no basis upon which the defence of qualified privilege as invoked by the respondents can be wholly struck out. The appeal is accordingly dismissed.

Notes

I   Following two Court of Appeal appearances, an excursion to the Privy Council, many thousands of dollars in legal costs, and five years of legal battles, former Prime Minister David Lange withdrew his defamation case against Australian Consolidated Press and the article's author Joe Atkinson on 13 December 2000. In the report published in *The Evening Post* of 14 December 2000, Mr Lange is quoted as saying 'I've established the principle ... you can maximise your freedom of speech in New Zealand as a result of this thing as long as you do so within responsible limits'. He further commented that the case had become a 'charter for responsible freedom of expression, not for reckless freedom of expression'. Therefore, the case will remain undecided, as only preliminary issues were ever considered, and so ends the Lange defamation saga.

2   A key aspect of any qualified privilege claim, upon finding an occasion of privilege, is an enquiry into whether s 19 applies, or a consideration into whether the defendant was motivated by ill-will or took improper advantage of the occasion of privilege. As noted above, *Lange* included some detailed discussion of the possibilities of the s 19 provision.

Thus, the effect of the s 19 provision is three-fold. First, any enquiry into qualified privilege must begin with a determination as to whether the occasion of publication was privileged. Secondly, the common law malice enquiry no longer exists. Thirdly, the plaintiff may invoke a s 19 discussion to determine if the defendant was motivated with ill-will or took improper advantage of the occasion. The onus is on the plaintiff and, if successful, the defence of qualified privilege will fail. The exact requirements of this determination remain largely unresolved, although *Lange* has shed some light on the enquiry. To what extent does the *Lange* interpretation of s 19 set it apart from common law 'malice'? How would *Horrocks v Lowe* (above) be decided in New Zealand after *Lange*?

3   There has been much discussion about the *Lange* saga. For further information about the decisions and their ramifications see Bill Atkin 'Has *Lange* Tipped the Balance Too Far' [1998] NZLJ 293, Bill Atkin 'Let-Down in *Lange*?' [1999] NZLJ 442, and Bill Atkin and Steven Price '*Lange* 2000' [2000] NZLJ 236.

4   One important aspect of *Lange* was the special attention paid to the newspaper rule. This rule operates so as to protect all media sectors from revealing their sources in interlocutory proceedings. The premise of the rule is easy to express, as it seeks to promote freedom of speech by allowing people to speak to the news media in confidence. Paragraph 55 of *Lange* details the contention at issue in the said case. Simply put, could a news media defendant rely on a qualified privilege defence, while continuing to maintain reliance on the newspaper rule? The Court seemed prepared to approach these issues with a clean slate, promoting the conceptions of justice, fairness, and public policy.

Vickery v McLean

(20 November 2000) Court of Appeal, CA 125/00

[**FACTS**: The appellant, Mr Vickery, is a Papakura resident and Chairman of the local Ratepayers Association. The respondents (Messrs McLean, Smale, and Phillips) were employed officers of the Papakura District Council. They respectively held the positions of Chief Executive Officer, Director of Works, and Director of Finance. Over a series of meetings, the Council considered the contracting out of water and wastewater services within the district. One prospective franchisee was a partnership called United Water, with one of the partners being Générale Des Eaux. Mr Vickery became aware of a document suggesting Générale had been involved in corruption scandals overseas. He viewed United Water's tender as a 'jack up'. Mr Vickery sought speaking rights at subsequent Council meetings, but was denied. He approached the Ombudsman and the Auditor-General. The Ombudsman declined to intervene, but the Auditor General did investigate, producing a report in which no suggestion was made that either the Council or officers had committed any impropriety. The matter became worse. Mr Vickery and his supporters distributed a document suggesting irregularities and repeating allegations against Générale. A local newspaper published a report quoting Mr Vickery as saying that 'the Serious Fraud Office was investigating United Water over allegations of bribing city officials in three countries'. Mr Smale was named in the article. The Council's solicitors wrote to the newspaper, who retracted and apologised for the article.

Mr Vickery continued his campaign, writing to the Serious Fraud Office. On 6 June 1997, he wrote to three newspapers including the national newspaper, the *New Zealand Herald*. The sting of the letter is in the sentence 'There was serious enough circumstantial evidence to suggest that criminal irregularity may have taken place'. The Serious Fraud Office declared that the available evidence did not sustain the charges made by Mr Vickery.

The respondents commenced defamation proceedings. The primary focus was the letter of 6 June. The jury, at trial, found the words defamatory and published of and concerning the respondents. The trial judge rejected a qualified privilege defence primarily due to the width of the publication. This issue forms the basis for the appeal, with Mr Vickery seeking to extend *Lange v Atkinson* [2000] 2 NZLR 385.]

Tipping J:

...

Discussion

[15] All occasions of qualified privilege are based on an identified public interest in allowing people to speak and write freely, without fear of proceedings for defamation unless they misuse the privilege. On occasions of privilege the public interest is seen as prevailing over the protection of individual reputations. The price of the freedom is the requirement that the privilege be responsibly used. When the Courts are asked to find that a particular occasion, not directly covered by authority, is one which should attract qualified privilege, the ultimate question is whether it is in the public interest to recognize the privilege and strike the balance between freedom of expression and protection of reputation accordingly. It is unnecessary for us to decide whether *Lange No 2* should be extended to cover political discussion in the context of local government. This is because even if such extension were made, we are satisfied the present occasion should not be held to be within any such extended privilege. The rationale for the *Lange* privilege cannot be regarded as applying to the present circumstances.

[16] The essentials of the occasion at issue in the present case can be described in the following way. A disgruntled ratepayer advises the news media that he has good reason to contend that senior servants of the Council have been guilty of corruption. He has therefore asked the Serious Fraud Office to investigate. The publication is, *ex hypothesi*, defamatory of the plaintiffs otherwise the need for the asserted privilege would not exist. The context of the publication is a general complaint about the processes of the Council in tendering the franchising of its water and waste water services.

[17] It is of major moment to notice that those who have been defamed are not politicians, whether national or local. They are paid servants of a local body. They may contribute to policy making but they are not the ultimate policy makers. The subject matter of Mr Vickery's publications cannot sensibly be regarded as political discussion, much less political discussion of a kind contemplated by *Lange No 2* or any rational extension of that decision. What is more, the subject matter, even if capable of being regarded as political discussion, involves an allegation of serious criminality. The law has been clear for many years that such allegations or complaints, provided they are bona fide, may be made to the appropriate authorities under qualified privilege. But the privilege is lost if the allegations are disseminated beyond those whose proper

function it is to investigate and, if appropriate, to act upon them: see *Gatley on Libel and Slander* (9th edn, 1998) at para 14.55; *Truth (New Zealand) Ltd v Holloway* [1960] NZLR 69 (CA); and *Blackshaw v Lord* [1984] QB 1 (CA). Thus, even if this case could be brought within the first five of the six *Lange* criteria, it does not satisfy the sixth, as we will shortly indicate. This is because publications which are disseminated too widely are not made on a qualifying occasion (*Lange No 2* at paras [21] and [22]).

[18] If, as we hold, the present case cannot be brought within any appropriate development of *Lange No 2*, it is necessary for Mr Vickery to establish his asserted privilege by reference to first principles. He must show that it is in the public interest (for the common convenience and welfare of society, as Parke B classically put it in *Toogood v Spyring* (1834) 1 CM & R 181, 193; 149 ER 1044, 1050) that on an occasion such as the present, freedom of expression should prevail over protection of reputation. More specifically he must show that it is in the public interest for people to be able to make allegations of serious criminal offending, albeit in a bona fide way, to or through the news media.

[19] Even if such allegations were responsibly made, it would be contrary both to settled law and to the public interest to allow such communications to be made under qualified privilege. We do not consider that society has changed in such a way as to justify a departure from previous perceptions of the public interest in this respect. It is, in our view, demonstrably not in the public interest to have criminal allegations, even if bona fide and responsibly made, ventilated through the news media. That could only encourage trial by media and associated developments which would be inimical to the criminal justice processes. Society has mechanisms for investigating crime and determining guilt or innocence. It is not in the public interest that these mechanisms be bypassed or subverted. Parliament's view, in the context of Serious Fraud matters, and it is a view of which the common law should take notice, can be found in ss 36 and 44 of the Serious Fraud Office Act 1990. These provisions are, broadly speaking, designed to prevent or limit disclosure of matters under investigation by the Office, and specified aspects of such investigations. Parliament has thereby recognised that the very fact that a Serious Fraud Office investigation is taking place can, of itself, cause serious damage to reputations and possible subversion of criminal justice processes. Thus, freedom of expression in this area has been curtailed to reflect Parliament's assessment of how to balance the competing interests ...

[22] For the reasons given the Judge was right to hold that the occasion of publication in this case did not attract qualified privilege. The appeal is therefore dismissed.

Statutory privilege

[The Defamation Act 1992 governs statutory privilege in New Zealand. Sections 16, 17 and 18 provide the rules as to what constitutes statutory qualified privilege. Privilege based on the Defamation Act 1992 can be relied on in addition to the defence of qualified privilege at common law. Those respective sections follow.]

Defamation Act 1992
16. Qualified privilege—
(1) Subject to sections 17 and 19 of this Act, the matters specified in Part I of the First Schedule to this Act are protected by qualified privilege.

(2) Subject to sections 17 to 19 of this Act, the publication of a report or other matter specified in Part II of the First Schedule to this Act is protected by qualified privilege.

(3) Nothing in this section limits any other rule of law relating to qualified privilege.

17. Qualified privilege not to apply where publication prohibited—
Nothing in subsection (1) or subsection (2) of section 16 of this Act protects the publication of any report or other matter where the publication of that report or matter is prohibited by law, or by a lawful order, in New Zealand or in a territory in which the subject-matter of the report or matter arose.

18. Restrictions on qualified privilege in relation to Part II of First Schedule—
(1) Nothing in section 16(2) of this Act protects the publication of a report or other matter specified in Part II of the First Schedule to this Act unless, at the time of that publication the report or matter is a matter of public interest in any place in which that publication occurs.

(2) In any proceedings for defamation in respect of the publication in any newspaper or as part of a programme or service provided by a broadcaster, of a report or other matter specified in Part II of the First Schedule to this Act, a defence of qualified privilege under section 16(2) of this Act shall fail if the plaintiff alleges and proves—

(a) That the plaintiff requested the defendant to publish, in the manner in which the original publication was made, a reasonable letter or statement by way of explanation or contradiction; and

(b) That the defendant has refused or failed to comply with that request, or has complied with that request in a manner that, having regard to all the circumstances, is not adequate or not reasonable.

FIRST SCHEDULE
PUBLICATIONS PROTECTED BY QUALIFIED PRIVILEGE

PART I
Publications Not Subject to Restrictions in Section 18

1. Any delayed broadcast, by any broadcaster, of proceedings in the House of Representatives.

2. The publication of a fair and accurate report of proceedings in the House of Representatives or in any Committee of the House of Representatives.

3. The publication of a fair and accurate extract from, or summary of, any document or record to which section 13(3)(a) or (c) of this Act applies.

4. Subject to any provision to the contrary in any other enactment, the publication, in any proceedings before a tribunal or authority established by or pursuant to any enactment (other than proceedings to which section 14(1) of this Act applies), of any matter by a member of the tribunal or authority, or by a party, representative, or witness in those proceedings.

5. The publication of a fair and accurate report of the pleadings of the parties in any proceedings before any Court in New Zealand, at any time after,—

(a) In the case of proceedings before the High Court, a praecipe has been filed in those proceedings:

(b) In the case of proceedings before a District Court, the filing of an application for a fixture for the hearing of those proceedings.

6. The publication of a fair and accurate report of the proceedings of any Court in New Zealand (whether those proceedings are preliminary, interlocutory, or final, and whether in open Court or not), or of the result of those proceedings.

7. The publication of a fair and accurate translation of words from one language to another, where the publication—

    (a) Is by the person who made the translation; and

    (b) Is by that person in his or her capacity as translator of those words.

PART II

Publications Subject to Restrictions in Section 18

1. A fair and accurate report of the proceedings of a legislature of a territory outside New Zealand or of a committee of any such legislature.

2. A fair and accurate report of the proceedings of a Court outside New Zealand (whether those proceedings are preliminary, interlocutory, or final, and whether in open Court or not), or of the result of those proceedings.

3. A fair and accurate report of the proceedings in an inquiry held under the authority of—

    (a) The Government or Parliament of New Zealand; or

    (b) The Government or legislature of a territory outside New Zealand,—or a true copy of, or a fair and accurate extract from or summary of, any official report made by the person by whom the inquiry was held.

4. A fair and accurate report of the proceedings of—

    (a) An international organisation of—

        (i) Countries or representatives of countries; or

        (ii) Legislatures or representatives of legislatures; or

        (iii) Governments or representatives of governments; or

    (b) An international conference at which governments of any countries are represented.

5. A fair and accurate report of the proceedings at a meeting or sitting in any part of New Zealand of—

    (a) A local authority or committee of a local authority or local authorities; or

    (b) A person or body appointed or constituted by or under, and exercising functions under, any Act (not being a Court or a person holding an inquiry to which clause 3 of this Part of this Schedule applies),—not being proceedings from which the public or members of the news media or both were excluded.

6. A fair and accurate report of the proceedings, or of the result of the proceedings, in an inquiry held in accordance with the rules of an association formed for the purpose of—

    (a) Promoting or safeguarding the interests of any game, sport, or pastime to the playing or exercise of which members of the public are invited or admitted; or

    (b) Promoting or safeguarding the interests of any trade, business, industry, or profession, or of the persons carrying on or engaged in any trade, business, industry, or profession; or

    (c) Promoting or encouraging the exercise of, or an interest in, any art, science, religion, or learning,—being an inquiry relating to a person who is a member of the association or is subject by virtue of a contract to the control of the association.

7. A fair and accurate report of the proceedings, or of the result of the proceedings, in an inquiry held in accordance with the rules of any association formed for the purpose of promoting and safeguarding the standards of the New Zealand press.

8. A fair and accurate report of the proceedings at a meeting held in New Zealand that—

(a) Is bona fide and lawfully held for a lawful purpose and for the furtherance or discussion of any matter of public concern; and

(b) Is open to the public, whether with or without restriction.

9. (1) A fair and accurate report of—

(a) The proceedings at a general meeting of a body to which this clause applies (not being a meeting from which the public or members of the news media or both were excluded):

(b) A report or other document circulated to shareholders or members by the board of directors or other governing body of a body to which this clause applies (not being a report or document circulated on a confidential basis):

(c) A document circulated to shareholders or members by an auditor or of a body to which this clause applies (not being a document circulated on a confidential basis).

(2) This clause applies to—

(a) Any company or association constituted or registered under any Act:

(b) Any society registered under the Incorporated Societies Act 1908:

(c) Any other body corporate operating in New Zealand,—but does not apply to any private company within the meaning of the Companies Act 1955.

10. A fair and accurate report of the proceedings at a press conference given by or on behalf of any body or person (being a body or person in respect of whose proceedings the publication of any fair and accurate report is, by virtue of section 16(2) of this Act, protected by qualified privilege).

11. A fair and accurate report of a publication issued under the authority of a government or legislature of a foreign state.

12. A fair and accurate copy of or extract from a register that is kept in pursuance of any Act and that is open to inspection by the public, or of any other document that is required by the law of New Zealand to be open to inspection by the public.

13. A notice or advertisement published by or under the authority of a Court, whether within or outside New Zealand, or a Judge or officer of any Court.

14. A notice or advertisement published for the purpose of complying with a New Zealand Act; but not including a notice of an application to a Court or tribunal, or to any other statutory office or statutory body, unless the application has been filed before the publication of the notice.

15. A copy or a fair and accurate report or summary of a statement, notice, or other matter issued for the information of the public by or on behalf of the Government or any department or departmental officer, or any local authority or officer of the authority.

PART III

Interpretation

In this Schedule, unless the context otherwise requires,—

'Court' includes the International Court of Justice and any other judicial or arbitral tribunal deciding matters in dispute between states; and also includes a court martial:

'Government', in relation to a territory outside New Zealand that is subject to a central and a local government, means either of those governments:

'Legislature', in relation to a territory outside New Zealand that is subject to a central and a local legislature, means either of those legislatures:

'Local authority' means a local body or public body named or specified in the First Schedule or the Second Schedule to the Local Government Official Information and Meetings Act 1987.

Ferrymead Tavern Ltd v Christchurch Press Co Ltd
[1999] NZAR 529 (HC)

[**FACTS**: *The Christchurch Press* published an article on Monday, 27 July 1998, which referred to a 'free for all' with 'nasty racial overtones' that was broken up by Police at the Ferrymead Tavern. In fact, no such free for all had occurred, and the Police acknowledged that it was their mistake in providing the report to the *Press*. The Ferrymead Tavern was understandably unimpressed with the incorrect reporting and contacted the *Press* to set the facts straight. After consulting the Media Liaison Officer for Christchurch Police, a correction was published the day following the initial publication. The correction said:

Tavern wrongly named

The Ferrymead Tavern was incorrectly named in the *Press* yesterday as the scene of a weekend brawl. The information was wrongly supplied by police.

The plaintiff Tavern and its owners were still dissatisfied and proceedings in defamation were issued. The defendant sought summary judgment claiming that none of the causes of action alleged by the plaintiff's statement of claim could succeed. The defendant relied on statutory qualified privilege.]

Master Venning:

…

Statutory qualified privilege

…

[**Note**: the Master detailed ss 16 and 18 of the Defamation Act 1992, as well as Part II of the First Schedule, especially para 15.]

… To succeed with its defence in this case the defendant must establish that the item in the newspaper was:

1 A fair and accurate report or summary of a statement, notice, or other matter, issued for the information of the public by or on behalf of the police and;

2 That at the time of the publication the report or matter was a matter of public interest in any place in which that publication occurred.

…

Was the statement issued by or on behalf of the police?—the status requirement

The plaintiffs' challenge under this head was primarily directed at the status of the statement.

There is no challenge to the reporter's evidence that the report was a fair and accurate report of what was advised by the police ...

While the report is not verbatim of the police advice, the defendant satisfies the Court that the report that appeared in the paper was a fair and accurate report of the statement obtained from the police.

Mr Hughes-Johnson [counsel for the plaintiff] submitted that the circumstances in which the statement was obtained meant that it was not of a sufficiently official nature to qualify for privilege.

A useful starting point for consideration ... is the following statement of Jordan CJ in *Campbell v Associated Newspapers Ltd* 1948 28 NSWSR 301 (at p 303):

> The notice or report must be of a genuine official nature, and must be issued in such circumstances that it may be regarded as issued for the information of the public ...

The fact the statement was obtained in response to an inquiry from the reporter does not of itself mean that the statement was not issued by the police, see *Blackshaw v Lord* [1984] QB 1 (CA) ...

Although the information in the statement was supplied in answer to an inquiry from the reporter, it was supplied willingly by the police. Further, it was supplied from the communications room run by the police. It may be inferred the police communications room exists to provide information held by the police to the public. The information is no doubt edited and controlled by the police. One means of disseminating the information to the public is via the media.

Ms O'Hanlon [the police reporter for the *Press*] rang the police communications room specifically to obtain information about incidents the police were involved in over the weekend. The information was imparted by a person in authority, Snr Sgt Freeman. The senior sergeant was on duty at the time as the communications senior in the communications room. There is no suggestion that he was not authorized to pass on the information he did to the reporter. In those circumstances, in my view the evidence establishes that the information came from a formal source within the police. The circumstances in which the reporter obtained the information do not defeat the claim to statutory privilege ...

Mr Hughes-Johnson submitted that in the present case the statement was more in the nature of mere interesting gossip. He noted it was in direct response to the request from the journalist whether there were any 'interesting incidents over the weekend'.

However, the statement was more than gossip. It was a summary of police action taken in relation to an incident in a public place. It was not in the nature of mere interesting gossip to promote the profile of the police. The statement not only came from a police source, but more particularly from the police communications room. It is not as though it was obtained from an off-duty constable known to the reporter. It was a release of information by the police about policing matters. The statement is of a sufficiently official nature to satisfy the requirement ...

[**Note**: Master Venning similarly concluded that the information was issued for the public.]

Public interest

Mr Hughes-Johnson next submitted that the statement could not properly be said to be of public interest at the time of the publication.

He submitted it was pivotal for the plaintiffs that the term 'public interest' used in s 18 of the Act imposed a restriction on the publication of material and that in this case the statement was not of public interest.

At common law a cautionary approach has been taken to the defence of privilege on the basis that the information was of public interest. In *Truth (NZ) Ltd v Holloway* [1960] NZLR 69 the Court of Appeal noted that a newspaper had two functions. First, to publish reports of various types of proceedings; and second, to provide its readers with news and even gossip concerning current events and people. While privilege might be accorded to the first function, the Court said (at p 83):

> In this second field, ... there is no principle of law ... which may be invoked in support of the contention that a newspaper can claim privilege if it publishes a defamatory statement of fact about an individual merely because the general topic developed in the article is a matter of public interest.

... The Court effectively made a distinction between a matter of public interest and a matter in which the public is simply interested ...

[**Note**: Master Venning considered the major cases that concerned the definition of public interest, focusing predominantly on Lord Denning MR in *London Artists v Littler* [1969] 2 QB 375, and the majority and minority judgments from *Bellino v Australian Broadcasting Corp* (1996) 135 ALR 368.]

...

If the broad test of public interest favoured by Lord Denning in *London Artists v Littler* and the minority in *Bellino*'s case is adopted, then the test is satisfied. The incident in question was one that members of the public might legitimately be concerned about or interested in. However, even if the more narrow approach favoured by the majority in *Bellino*'s case is adopted, the statement in this case satisfies the requirement of public interest. If correct it was a report of criminal conduct at a public licensed premises involving racism. At the least it can be regarded as a report concerning a public entity of persons supplying services to the public ...

The publication in the present case was not directed at apprehension of the criminal, rather it was directed at publication of the incident itself. That does not make any difference. The wording of the statutory defence does not require the publication to be directed at apprehension. The police obviously consider it of sufficient importance to maintain a communications room and media tape. There is public interest in incidents which may have racial overtones in public places, particularly at taverns and hotels where alcohol is sold. A community has public interest in such matters. There is sufficient public interest in the statement's subject matter.

The locational requirement

Mr Hughes-Johnson next submitted the requirement in s 18(1) that the publication must be a matter of public interest in 'any place in which that publication occurs' was a locational requirement which mirrored the requirement at common law that to attract qualified privilege the publication must be no wider than was commensurate with the legitimate public interest.

He submitted that even if it could be said that persons in Christchurch might have a legitimate interest in the statement, it could not be said that persons on the West Coast or Nelson (being within the circulation area of the *Press*) could have such a legitimate interest. On that basis he submitted the statutory defence could not succeed because of the extent of the publication in this case.

The basis of the submission is the requirement of reciprocity in the common law defence of qualified privilege ...

To attract privilege at common law the publication must be restricted or made only to those persons who have an interest or duty to receive it. Publication to others defeats the privilege ...

The effect of Mr Hughes-Johnson's submission is to read 'any place' in s 18(1) as 'all places'. If the submission is correct it would also severely restrict the statutory defence of qualified privilege ...

With the extensive geographical distribution of newspapers in the New Zealand context, and where main suburban newspapers service a number of rural areas as well, a restriction such as argued for by Mr Hughes-Johnson would largely negate the statutory defence of qualified privilege.

It is also to be noted that in the chapter on defamation in the *Law of Torts in New Zealand* (2nd edn) Professor Burrows in his commentary on this provision states (at p 930):

> Under the new Act, the report or publication also must be of public interest at the time of publication, so that the resuscitation of matter at a later date when it has lost its topicality may cease to qualify. *However, it is enough that the matter be one of public interest in any place in which publication occurs; this could suggest that matter published in a national newspaper or on national television will be privileged if it is of public interest in any part of the country* ... [Master Venning's emphasis].

The commentator is clearly of the view that 'any' is to be read as 'any' rather than 'all'. With respect, it seems that must be the correct analysis and accords with the comments of the Court of Appeal in relation to the development of the statutory defence of qualified privilege ...

The defendant satisfies the Court that it is entitled to rely upon statutory qualified privilege in this case. It follows that the defendant is entitled to summary judgment against the plaintiffs.

Notes

I *Eyre v New Zealand Press Association Ltd* [1968] NZLR 736 concerned a particular report of a political meeting distributed by the New Zealand Press Association. Mr Eyre was a member of the House of Representatives and a cabinet minister charged with the Defence portfolio. At the meeting, the topic of North Vietnam was raised, and the subsequent news article reported Mr Eyre as saying he would 'give North Vietnam a basinful of bombs tomorrow morning if he had his way'. Mr Eyre took exception to the report, claiming numerous factual errors. The New Zealand Press Association attempted to claim qualified privilege. The Defamation Act 1954 was the appropriate statute and s 16 (now s 17 of the Defamation Act 1992) concerned statutory privilege. McGregor J held that s 17(2), now s 16(2), granted privilege only to newspapers and broadcasters and as the Press Association was neither, the privilege could not apply. This interpretation must be doubted as s 17(2), now s 16(2), contains no such restriction. Whether the report was 'fair and accurate' was a different question and, arguably, the careless editing would probably deny the existence of a statutory or common law privilege.

2   The leading case on 'public concern and benefit' may be *Boston v W S Bagshow & Sons* [1966] 1 WLR 1126. In that case, a thief made off with three little pigs at an auction. He made the successful bid, loaded up the three pigs, gave his name as 'Boston of Rugeley', and made off. A notice concerning the thief and his identity was broadcast on a 'Police 5' television programme. The real Mr Boston, of the village of Rugeley, was thereby identified and defamed. The defendants won on statutory qualified privilege, and the UK equivalent of para 13 of the first schedule (official Government announcements). Lord Denning found that apprehension of criminals, even petty pig converters, was for the public benefit.

3   Compare the more complex review of the same paragraph, in *Blackshaw v Lord* [1984] 1 QB 1. In that case, a former undersecretary of the Department of Energy sued a reporter and the *Daily Telegraph*, and prevailed. The defendants were unsuccessful in their reliance upon the 'official statement' privilege because the statement was not 'issued' but rather 'painfully extracted ... like a tooth', and the reporter's inference (naming the plaintiff) was an incorrect guess.

4   *Turkington v Times Newspapers Ltd* [2000] 3 WLR 1670, [2000] 4 All ER 913 concerned a *Times* news report criticising the performance of a firm of solicitors who had represented a Mr Clegg at trial and subsequent appeal. Mr Clegg received life imprisonment from his charges. An informal committee, called the Clegg Committee, was formed to secure the release and vindication of Mr Clegg. At one press conference, critical references were expressed regarding the solicitors. A press release accompanied the meeting. The press conference was held at a committee member's house, and invitations were sent to the press. Entry was not, however, restricted. The newspaper report followed and included aspects of the meeting and the press release. The case carefully considered the role of the Defamation Act 1955 of Northern Ireland. The House of Lords held that the press conference constituted a public meeting according to s 7 and paragraph 9 of the schedule of the Act. The trial judge and the Court of Appeal held that there was no 'public meeting' able to attract the statutory privilege. This was reversed by the House of Lords, holding that '[a] meeting is public if those who organise it or arrange it open it to the public or, by issuing a general invitation to the press, manifest an intention or desire that the proceedings of the meeting should be communicated to the wider public' (1681; 924). The press release was also held to be covered by the privilege. The Court considered that the newspaper's role as a reporter (medium of communication) was different from the role identified in *Reynolds* (above). Thus, the Court held that the statutory qualified privilege was incorrectly determined, and the case was to be remitted to trial for consideration of the fairness and accuracy of the newspaper's report and a conclusion on qualified privilege. Compare this case to clause 10 of Part II of the First Schedule of the New Zealand Defamation Act 1992.

5   On 1 June *The Evening Ghost* newspaper carried the following news item on its commercial page:

ZOOM CORPORATION FILE MYSTERY

Mystery surrounds the disappearance of part of the Zoom Corporation's file from the Companies Office in Wellington. The Registrar of Companies, Mr I. Stamp, says the Office considers the file has been stolen. He says the Office has a fair idea who took the file but lacks evidence to bring a prosecution. But the Office is expected to prosecute Zoom Corporation for not filing annual returns in accordance with the requirements of the Companies Act.

All this information was given to *The Evening Ghost* reporter by the Registrar of Companies when the reporter went to the Companies Office to search the file. The Registrar, Mr Stamp, honestly believes what he told the reporter but, unknown to him, and not ascertainable from his files, is the fact that the Zoom Corporation file was properly and legally transferred to the Dunedin Companies Office two years ago. The file left in the Wellington Office is a duplicate of the file upon which no entries have been made since the time of the transfer, thus giving an incomplete and out-of-date picture of the Corporation's affairs. The Registrar of Companies had in fact written to the Corporation and its officers asking for compliance with the provisions in the Companies Act in relation to the filing of documents. To these letters he received no reply although they were sent by registered mail. All documents required by the Act have in fact been duly filed in the Dunedin Companies Office. Advise *The Evening Ghost* in regard to an action for defamation brought by Zoom Corporation.

Select Bibliography

J.H. Baker, *An Introduction to English Legal History* (2nd edn, Butterworths, London, 1979).

R.P. Balkin and J.L.R. Davis, *Law of Torts* (Butterworths, Sydney, 1991).

M. Brazier, J. Murphy, and H. Street, *Street on Torts* (10th edn, Butterworths, London, 1999).

I. Campbell, *Compensation for Personal Injury in New Zealand: Its Rise and Fall* (Auckland University Press, Auckland, 1996).

P. Cane, *Atiyah's Accidents, Compensation and the Law* (6th edn, Butterworths, London, 1999).

J.F. Clerk, W.H.B. Lindsell, and A.M. Dugdale, *Clerk & Lindsell on Torts* (18th edn, Sweet & Maxwell, London, 2000).

D. Dewees, D. Duff, and M. Trebilcock, *Exploring the Domain of Accident Law: Taking the Facts Seriously* (Oxford University Press, New York, 1996).

C.H.S. Fifoot, *History and Sources of the Common Law: Tort and Contract* (Stevens & Sons, London, 1949).

J.G. Fleming, *The Law of Torts* (9th edn, Law Book Company, Sydney, 1998).

G.H.L. Fridman, *The Law of Torts in Canada* (2nd edn, Carswell, Toronto, 2002).

R.F.V. Heuston and R.A. Buckley, *Salmond and Heuston on the Law of Torts* (21st edn, Sweet & Maxwell, London, 1996).

P. Hogg, *Liability of the Crown* (2nd edn, Carswell, Toronto, 1989).

W.S. Holdsworth, *A History of English Law: XVI vols* (7th rev edn, Methuen, London, 1956).

O.W. Holmes, *The Common Law* (Dover Publications, New York, 1991).

T.G. Ison, *Accident Compensation: A Commentary on the New Zealand Scheme* (Croom Helm, London, 1980).

L.N. Klar, *Tort Law* (2nd edn, Carswell, Toronto, 1996).

S. Kneebone, *Tort Liability of Public Authorities* (Law Book Company, North Ryde, NSW, 1998).

A.M. Linden, *Canadian Tort Law* (6th edn, Butterworths, Toronto, 1997).

M. Lunney and K. Oliphant, *Tort Law: Text and Materials* (Oxford University Press, London, 2000).

G.P. McLay, *Butterworths Student Companion: Torts* (3rd edn, Butterworths, Wellington, 1999).

K. McLean and K. Evans, *Butterworths Questions and Answers: Torts* (Butterworths, Wellington, 2001).

B.S. Markensinis and S.F. Deakin, *Tort Law* (4th edn, Oxford University Press, Oxford, 1999).

G. Palmer, *Compensation for Incapacity: A Study of Law and Social Changes in New Zealand and Australia* (Oxford University Press, Melbourne, 1979).

T.F.T. Plucknett, *A Concise History of the Common Law* (5th edn, Butterworths, London, 1956).

W.L. Prosser and R.E. Keeton, *Prosser & Keeton on the Law of Torts* (5th edn, West Publishing Co., St Paul, 1984).

S.M.D. Todd (ed.), *The Law of Torts in New Zealand* (3rd edn, Brookers Ltd, Wellington, 2001).

W.J.V. Windeyer, *Lectures on Legal History* (2nd rev edn, Law Book Company, Sydney, 1957).

P.H. Winfield, J.A. Jolowicz, and W.V.H. Rogers, *Winfield and Jolowicz on Tort* (15th edn, Sweet & Maxwell, London, 1998).

Index